THE INTERNATIONAL BIBLIOGRAPHY OF ECONOMICS

This bibliography, with its sister publications, Sociology, Political Science, and Anthropology (known together as the *International Bibliography of the Social Sciences (IBSS))* is an essential tool for librarians, academics and researchers wishing to keep up to date with the published literature in the social sciences.

The *IBSS* offers a large scale database of journal articles and monographs from all over the world and in over 30 languages, all with English title translations where needed.

From 1991, users already familiar with the bibliography will notice major improvements in contents and currency. There is greater coverage of monographs as well as journals, with continued emphasis on international publications, especially those from the developing world and Eastern Europe. Indexing techniques have been refined: the *IBSS* now offers more specific subject and place indexes together with a name index. A subject index in French continues to be provided.

Prepared until 1989 at the *Fondation nationale des sciences politiques* in Paris, the *IBSS* is now compiled and edited by the *British Library of Political and Economic Science* at the *London School of Economics*. The UNESCO *International Committee for Social Science Information and Documentation* continues to support the publication. The new *International Bibliography* not only maintains its traditional extensive coverage of periodical literature, but considerably extends its coverage of monographic material by incorporating most of that which would previously have been included in the *London Bibliography of the Social Sciences*, publication of which has now been discontinued.

Also available from Routledge

Copies of the *International Bibliography of the Social Sciences* for previous years.

Thematic Lists of Descriptors. Four subject volumes published in 1989, following the classification and index terms of the relevant volume of the *IBSS*.

The *International Current Awareness Services (ICAS)* complement the *IBSS* with the same geographical sweep, but offering full contents information on current journals. These four new monthly services — Anthropology, Economics, Political Science and Sociology — provide coverage, with indexing by keyword, of items received during the previous month, including not only articles but also items such as book reviews, short articles, interviews, speeches, reports, editorials and letters.

Copies of the *London Bibliography of the Social Sciences* for previous years are available from Schmidt Periodicals, Dettendorf, D-8201 Bad Feilnbach 2, Germany.

INTERNATIONAL BIBLIOGRAPHY OF THE SOCIAL SCIENCES
BIBLIOGRAPHIE INTERNATIONALE DES SCIENCES SOCIALES

[published annually in four parts / paraissant chaque année en quatre parties: since 1961/ jusqu'en 1961: UNESCO, Paris]

International bibliography of sociology / Bibliographie internationale de sociologie [red cover / couverture rouge] Vol.1:1951 (publ. 1952)

International bibliography of political science/ Bibliographie internationale de science politique [grey cover / couverture grise] Vol.1: 1952 (publ. 1954)

International bibliography of economics / Bibliographie internationale de science economique [yellow cover / couverture jaune] Vol.1: 1952 (publ. 1955)

International bibliography of social and cultural anthropology / Bibliographie internationale d'anthropologie sociale et culturelle [green cover/ couverture vert] Vol.1: 1955 (publ. 1958)

Prepared by

THE BRITISH LIBRARY OF POLITICAL AND ECONOMIC SCIENCE

with the support of the International Committee for Social Science Information and Documentation with the financial assistance of UNESCO

Editor

Lynne J. Brindley
Librarian, British Library of Political and Economic Science

Editorial Manager

Christopher C.P. Doutney

Assistant Manager

Caroline S. Shaw

Consultant/Technical Manager

N.S.M. Cox

Editorial Assistants

Imogen Daulby
Louise Hilditch
Miranda Hutt
Ricarda O'Driscoll

INTERNATIONAL BIBLIOGRAPHY OF THE SOCIAL SCIENCES

1992

INTERNATIONAL BIBLIOGRAPHY OF ECONOMICS

VOLUME XLI

BIBLIOGRAPHIE INTERNATIONALE DES SCIENCES SOCIALES

BIBLIOGRAPHIE INTERNATIONALE DE LA SCIENCE ÉCONOMIQUE

Prepared with the support of the International Committee for Social Science Information and Documentation with the financial assistance of UNESCO

Établie avec le concours du Comité international pour l'information et la documentation en sciences sociales avec l'assistance financìere de l'UNESCO

London and New York

First published in 1993 by
Routledge
(on behalf of The British Library of Political and Economic Science)
UNESCO subvention 1992-1993, SHS/IST/53

11 New Fetter Lane
London EC4P 4EE
&
29 West 35th Street
New York, NY 10001

Processed and composed in Great Britain by
Information Design & Delivery Limited, Newent, Gloucestershire

Typeset in Great Britain by
W.E. Baxter Limited, Lewes, East Sussex

Printed in Great Britain by
T.J. Press (Padstow), Padstow, Cornwall

British Library Cataloguing in Publication Data

A CIP catalogue record for this book is available from the British Library.
ISBN 0–415–09212–4
ISSN 0085–204X

Editorial Correspondence should be sent to:

International Bibliography of the Social Sciences
British Library of Political and Economic Science
London School of Economics
10 Portugal Street
London WC2A 2HD
United Kingdom

Telephone: (U.K.) 071-955-7144

Fax: (U.K.) 071-242-5904

CONTENTS

PREFACE

Under the sponsorship of the International Committee for Social Science Information and Documentation, established by UNESCO in 1950, the four divisions of the *International Bibliography of the Social Sciences* (Anthropology: Economics: Political Science: Sociology) have been published from Paris since 1952. Together they form the most extensive bibliography of the social sciences in existence, with a world wide coverage achieved by no other bibliographical series. In 1990 the British Library of Political and Economic Science assumed responsibility for the compilation and editing of the *International Bibliography*.

The British Library of Political and Economic Science has published the *London Bibliography of the Social Sciences* since 1931. In 47 volumes it forms an unrivalled record of twentieth century monograph literature in social sciences. The volume covering 1989 was issued early in 1990 and it will be the last of the series. The bulk of the data which would previously have been published as the *London Bibliography* will, from 1990 onwards, appear within the structure of the *International Bibliography of the Social Sciences*.

The *International Bibliography of Economics* has been compiled from two sources: analysis of the published literature (particularly as contained in periodicals) accessible to the editors; and contributions from correspondents throughout the world, reporting publications, details of which are not easily obtainable outside their countries of origin. These dual sources of data will continue to be the basis of the *Bibliography*. The *international* emphasis will be maintained, without bias towards the publications of any one country. Some 120,000 journal articles per year are scanned for indexing in the four divisions, and a selection is made from over 20,000 monograph titles. Material in over 25 languages is included, but all titles, in addition to being cited in their original form, also appear in English. The work is produced from a computer maintained data base. The long established subject classifications continue to be the basis for indexing, governing an alphabetical arrangement by keywords.

The annual volumes of the *International Bibliography* are complemented by the *International Current Awareness Services in the Social Sciences*, issued in the same four subject divisions as the annual volumes, but on a monthly basis. The *Current Awareness Services* include full contents listings (indexed by keyword) of all relevant periodicals received at the editorial office in London during the previous month. They index not only principal articles but also more ephemeral material such as short articles and book reviews, omitted in the annual volumes. Together, the two publication series provide immediate access to new publications and form a permanent record of printed material in the social sciences.

PRÉFACE

Paris est depuis 1952 siège de la publication des quatre sections de la *Bibliographie Internationale des Sciences Sociales* (Anthropologie: Sciences Economiques: Sciences Politiques: Sociologie.) sous le patronage du Comité International pour l'Information et la Documentation des Sciences Sociales créé par l'UNESCO en 1950. Dans l'ensemble, elles constituent la bibliographie la plus étendue des sciences sociales et jouit d'une portée mondiale unique dans le domaine. En 1990, la British Library of Political and Economic Science prit responsibilité de la composition et rédaction de la *Bibliographie Internationale*.

La British Library of Political and Economic Science a publié la *London Bibliography of the Social Sciences*, depuis 1931. Ses 47 volumes présentent des archives incomparables de la littérature monographique du vingtième siècle en ce qui concerne les sciences sociales. Le volume de 1989, paru en 1990, était le dernier de la série. La plupart des données figurant auparavant dans la *London Bibliography* se trouvent maintenant dans la *Bibliographie Internationale des Sciences Sociales*.

La *Bibliographie Internationale de Sciences Économiques* recueille les informations à partir de deux sources: l'analyse par les rédacteurs de la littérature publiée (surtout des périodiques) et les contributions de correspondants dans le monde entier fournissant des comptes-rendus de publications dont on n'aurait guère connaissance hors de leurs pays d'origine. Cette dualité des sources continue à servir de base à la *Bibliographie*. Il est important de souligner la qualité véritablement internationale de cette *Bibliographie*. Chaque année une moyenne de 220,000 articles de périodiques sont analysés et indexés pour les quatre parties et les monographies sont sélectionnées parmi plus de 20,000 titres. La *Bibliographie* comprend des contributions en 25 langues: tous les titres paraissent en anglais ainsi que dans leur langue d'origine. La *Bibliographie* est produite à partir d'une base de données. Une classification établie de longue date sert de base à l'indexation et à la présentation des réferences par mots-clés.

Les volumes annuels de la *Bibliograhie Internationale* sont complétés par les *International Current Awareness Services in the Social Sciences*, publications mensuelles consacrées aux quatre mêmes disciplines des volumes annuels. Les *Current Awareness Services* comprennent les listes complètes des sujets (indexés par mots-clés) de tous les périodiques pertinents reçus à la rédaction au cours du mois précédent. Y sont indexés non seulement les articles standard, mais aussi les études plus éphémères comme de brefs articles et des comptes-rendus de livres dont les volumes annuels ne font pas mention. Ensemble, ces deux séries de publications offrent un accès immédiat aux nouvelles publications et constituent les archives permanentes des travaux publiés en sciences sociales.

PREFACIO

Las cuatro divisiones de la *Bibliografía Internacional de las Ciencias Sociales* (Antropología: Ciencias Económicas: Ciencias Políticas y Sociología) se han venido publicando en París desde el año 1952, por gentileza patrocinal del Comité Internacional de Información y Documentación de las Ciencias Sociales, establecido por UNESCO en el año 1950. En su conjunto, constituyen la bibliografía más extensa en materia de Ciencias Sociales, con alcance mundial, e inigualable en otras series bibliográficas. En 1990 la British Library of Political and Economic Science asumía la responsabilidad para la compilación y redacción de la *Bibliografía Internacional*.

La British Library of Political and Economic Science ya publicaba la *London Bibliography of the Social Sciences* a partir del año 1931. En sus 47 tomos, constituye un registro de literatura monográfica sin rival sobre temas sociocientíficos del siglo XX. El tomo que abarca el año 1989 se publicó a principios del 1990, siendo éste el último de aquella serie. La mayoría de los datos se habrían publicado en épocas anteriores bajo el título *London Bibliography*. A partir del año 1990, aparecerán dentro de la estructura de las *Bibliografía Internacional de las Ciencias Sociales*.

La *Bibliografía Internacional de Ciencias Económicas* ha sido compilada con base en dos fuentes: el análisis de la literatura publicada (en particular, tal como contenidos en los periódicos) accesible a redactores, y las contribuciones de corresponsales de todas partes del mundo, publicaciones de tipo informe, detalles de los cuales no resultan ser fácilmente obtenibles fuera de sus países de orígen. Dichas fuentes duales de información seguirán siendo la base de la Bibliografía. Se mantendrá el énfasis internacional, sin tendencias hacia las publicaciones de un sólo país dado. Se exploran al año unos 120,000 artículos para pasar a índices en las cuatro divisiones, y se efectúa una selección de más de 20,000 títulos monográficos. Se incluyen temas en más de 25 idiomas, pero todos los antedichos títulos, además de ser citados en su forma original, también aparecen traducidos al idioma inglés. Se lleva a cabo el trabajo a partir de una base de datos mantenida en ordenadores. Siguen siendo la base de la tarea de la puesta en índices, las clasificaciones por materias como se establecieron antiguamente, las cuales controlan una esquematización alfabética por palabra clave.

Los tomos anuales de la *Bibliografía Internacional* se ven complementados mediante los *International Current Awareness Services in the Social Sciences*, con acuerdo a cada una de las mismas cuatro divisiones que se emplearon para los tomos anuales, pero sobre una base mensual. The *International Current Awareness Services in the Social Sciences* comprenden relaciones completas de materias, con puesta en índice por palabra clave, en relación con citas de todos los periódicos aplicaderos recibidos en la Casa Editorial de Londres durante el mes anterior. Abarcan índices no sólo de los artículos principales, sino también más materia efémera tal como sueltos cortos y críticas literarias que fueron omitidos de los tomos anuales. En conjunto, ambas series de publicaciones facilitan un acceso inmediato a las nuevas publicaciones, y constituyen un registro permanente de materias impresas comprendidas dentro del marco de las Ciencias Sociales.

ПРЕДИСЛОВИЕ

Под покровительством Международного Комитета Социологической Информации и Документации, основанной УНЕСКО в 1950 г., четыре части Международной Библиографии Общественных Наук/Антропология: Экономика: Политические Науки: Социология/издавались из Парижа с 1952 года. Вместе они составляют наиболее обширную существующую библиографию общественных наук, с распространенным по всему свету обхватом не достигнутым никакой другой серийной библиографией. В 1990 Британская Библиотека Политических и Экономических Наук взяла на себя ответственность за составление и репактирование Международной Библиографии.

Британская Библиотека Политических и Экономических Наук издаёт Лондонскую Библиографию Общественных Наук с 1931-го года. В 47 томах это составляет непревзойдённую запись монографической литературы социологии двадцатого века. Том обхватывающий 1989-ый год был издан в начале 1990-ого года и это будет последнее издание этой серии. Большая часть данных, которая раньше должна издаваться как Лондонская Библиография с 1990-ого года будет появляться в структуре Международной Библиографии Общественных Наук.

Международная Библиография Экономный была составлена из двух источников, анализ изданной литературы/ особенно тот в периодических изданиях/ доступный для редакторов; и вклад корреспондентов со всего мира, репортажные публикации, деталь которых трудно получить, кроме в странах их происхождения. Эти двойственного характера источники данных будут являться основой Библиографии. Будет продолжаться международное значение библиографии без оказывания предпочтения изданиям каких-либо стран.

Ежегодно просматрывается некоторые 120000 журнальных статей с целью составления указателей в четырёх частях, и тогда составляется сборник из больше чем 20000 монографических титулов. Включаются материалы на больше чем 25-и языках, но все титулы, вдобавок цитируются и в оригинальной версии и по английски. Произведение издаётся с помощью компьютерской базы данных. Долгосуществующая система классификации по предметам продолжается и употребляется в качестве основы для составления указателей, которые ведут алфавитный порядок ключевых слов.

Годовые тома Международной Библиографии дополняются Международными Текущими Осведомительными Услугами в Общественных Наук, изданными в тех же самых четырёх частях по предметам что и годовые тома, но их издаются ежемесячно. Текущие Осведомительные Услуги включают указатели полных содержаний/ индексираны по ключевым словам/ всех уместных периодических журналов полученных в редакции в Лондоне в течение прошлого месяца. Они указывают не только главные статьи но тоже более эфемерные/ скоропроходящие/ материалы такие как короткие статьи и рецензии книг, пропущены в годовых томах. Вместе, эти две серии изданий предоставляют прямой доступ к новым изданиям и являются постоянной записью напечатанных материалов общественных наук.

ببليوغرافية الاقتصاد الدولية

المقدمة

قد نشرت الاجزاء الاربعة من البليوغرافية الدولية للعلوم الاجتماعية (وهي اولاً دراسة المجتمعات البشرية وثانياً علم الاقتصاد وثالثاً علم السياسة ورابعاً علم الاجتماع) من باريس منذ سنة ١٩٥٢ تحت رعاية اللجنة الدولية لمعلومات وللتدوين المستند لعلم الاجتماع والتي اسستها اليونسكو عام ١٩٥٠ وتشكل معاً هذه الاجزاء ببليوغرافية لها اوسع نطاق في الوجود ويشمل مداها انحاء العالم بكامله الى حد لم يبلغه اية سلسلة ببليوغرافية اخرى. في عام ١٩٩٠ تولت المكتبة البريطانية لعلم السياسة والاقتصاد المسؤولية لصنف البليوغرافية الدولية واعدادها للنشر.

لقد نشرت المكتبة البريطانية لعلم السياسة والاقتصاد، نشرت البليوغرافية اللندنية للعلوم الاجتماعية منذ سنة ١٩٣١ وهي تتألف من ٤٧ جزء وتكوّن سجلاً للمؤلفات التي تبحث العلوم الاجتماعية في القرن العشرين لا يضاهيه ايّ آخر وقد نشر المجلد الذي يشمل سنة ١٩٨٩ في اوائل ١٩٩٠ ويكوّن الجزء الاخير في السلسلة. ستنشر بعد سنة ١٩٩٠ في مضمون اطار البليوغرافية الدولية للعلوم الاجتماعية، ستنشر معظم تلك المعلومات التي كانت قد تكون تنشر سابقاً تحت اسم البليوغرافية اللندنية.

تم جمع وتدوين معلومات ببليوغرافية الاقتصاد الدولية من مصدرين - الاول من تحليل المؤلفات وعلى وجه خاص ما احتوته المجلات الدورية التي هي في مدى تناول المحررين وثم ما قدّمه المراسلون في جميع انحاء العالم مع مطبوعات تقريرية يصعب الحصول على تفاصيلها خارج البلاد مصدر تلك الطبوعات. هذا وان مصدري المعلومات هذين سيبقيا اساس البليوغرافية كما انه يتم الاستمرار في تولية الناحية الدولية اهمية خاصة، لكن دون اي ميول او انحياز نحو مطبوعات اي بلد. يتم تصفح حوالي ١٢٠٠٠٠ من مقالات المجلات سنوياً للادراج في قوائم الاجزاء الاربعة، كما يتم الانتقاء من بين ما يزيد عن ٢٠٠٠٠ عنوان لمؤلفات تبحث العلوم، كل موضوع منفرداً. ثم ان ضمن المحتويات هناك مواد في ما يزيد عن ٢٥ لغة

، هذا كما ان العناوين مدرجة في لغتها الاصلية بالاضافة الى تدوينها بالانجليزية ، وهذا الشغل ينتج من خلال مستودع للمعلومات والحقائق العلمية يزقّه دماغ الكتروني . هذا وستبقى تبويبات الموضوعات الجارية من مدة طويلة ، تبقى هذه التبويبات الاساس للادراج في القائمة ، تضبط وترتّب هجائياً عن طريق كلمات مفتاح معيّنة .

المجلدات السنوية من البليوغرافية الدولية ستستكملها مطبوعات خدمات الالمام الجاري الدولية للعلوم الاجتماعية وتصدر هذه المطبوعات في اجزاء الموضوعات الاربعة ذاتها ، لكنها تصدر على ترتيب شهري وتشمل مطبوعات خدمات الالمام الجاري قوائم محتويات كاملة (مدرجة عن طريق كلمات مفتاح معيّنة) لجميع المجلات الدورية التي وصلت مكتب التحرير في لندن خلال الشهر السالف ، حيث يدرجون ليس الموضوعات الرئيسية فقط ، بل كذلك مواد سريعة الزوال - كالمقالات القصيرة وعرض ونقد الكتب مثلاً وهذه مواد ليست من ضمن المجلدات السنوية - وهكذا توفر سلسلتا المؤلفات هاتان اتصالاً فورياً بالمؤلفات الجديدة وتشكلا سجلاً دائماً للمواد المطبوعة في ميادين العلوم الاجتماعية .

序文

1950年にユネスコにより設立された社会科学情報・文書取扱国際委員会後援の下に社会科学国際書誌の4部（人類学：経済学：政治学：社会学）は、1952年からパリで発行されてきております。此の4部各書誌は、現存の最も広範囲に亙る社会科学の書誌を形成し、他の書誌シリーズによっては成就されなかった世界的取材を網羅するものであります。1990年に、英国政治・経済学図書館は国際書誌の整理編集の責任を負う事になりました。

　　　　英国政治・経済学図書館は1931年より、社会科学ロンドン書誌を発行して来ております。その47巻は20世紀に於ける比類のない社会科学の各専攻文献の記録を形成するものです。1989年を網羅する版は1990年初期に発行されましたが、これは此のシリーズの最後のものとなります。ロンドン書誌として前に発行されれる筈だった膨大な資料は、1990年以降、国際社会科学書誌の構築の中に包含されることになります。

　　　　国際経済学書誌は、2つの出典から編纂されたものです。即ち、編集者が利用できる文献（特に期間誌に含まれているもの）の解析と全世界の報道員の寄稿、それは、該当各国以外では入手困難な刊行物の詳細な資料とから編纂されてきているものです。これらの資料の複式出典は継続して書誌の基礎になるものです。「国際性」の意味は、どの国の刊行物に対しても偏見無しに維持されている事を強調しています。毎年凡そ12万のジャーナル記事が図書目録のために鑑査走査され、4部門に分けられ、その上、2万以上の専攻書名から選択が行われます。25以上の各国語からの資料が包含されておりますが、すべての書名は該当国語によるものが列挙されており、それに加えて、英語でも表記されています。此の仕事はコンピュータによる維持されたデータ・ベースから作成されます。図書目録の基礎として長期に亙り定着している首題の分類法は、今迄と同様に行われ、ａｂｃ順の見出語によるように統制されています。

　　　　国際書誌年刊の各巻は、社会科学学に於ける国際現代意識サービスによって補足され、これは、各巻の年刊と同じ４部門の首題で発行されていますが、月刊を基礎にしております。現代意識サービスは、ロンドン編集事務所で受け取った前月間のすべての該当期間誌の全内容目録（見出語による目録）を含みます。これらの目録は主要記事ばかりでなく、年刊には省略される短い記事や書評などのような、その時だけの記事も含まれています。２つの刊行シリーズは共に、新刊行物への即時利用を提供し、社会科学の印刷資料の永久記録となります。

VORWORT

Die vier Teilbände der *Internationalen Bibliographie der Sozialwissenschaften* (Anthropologie: Politologie: Soziologie: Volkswirtschaft) wurden seit 1952 mit finanzieller Unterstützung des 1950 von der UNESCO eingesetzten Internationalen Komitees für Sozialwissenschaftliche Information und Dokumentation in Paris herausgegeben. Zusammen bilden sie die umfangreichste bestehende sozialwissenschaftliche Bibliographie mit einer weltweiten Reichweite in der Datenerfassung, wie sie keine andere bibliographische Reihe bietet. Im Jahr 1990 übernahm die British Library of Political and Economic Science die Verantwortung für die Erstellung und Redaktion der *Internationalen Bibliographie*.

Die British Library of Political and Economic Science veröffentlicht seit 1931 die *London Bibliography of the Social Sciences*. In 47 Bänden bildet sie ein unübertroffenes Verzeichnis der in Einzeldarstellungen erschienenen sozialwissenschaftlichen Literatur des 20. Jahrhunderts. Mit dem Band für 1989, der Anfang 1990 erschien, wurde diese Reihe eingestellt. Der Großteil der Daten, die vormals in der *London Bibliography* erschienen wären, wird von 1990 an im Rahmen der *Internationalen Bibliographie der Sozialwissenschaften* veröffentlicht werden.

Für die *Internationale Bibliographie der Volkswirtschaft* wurden zwei Arten von Quellen herangezogen: zum einen die (insbesondere in Fachzeitschriften) veröffentlichte Literatur, die der Redaktion im Original zugänglich war; zum andern Beiträge von Korrespondenten, die weltweit Publikationen erfassen, über die außerhalb ihrer Ursprungsländer nur schwer Einzelheiten in Erfahrung zu bringen sind. Diese beiden Datenquellen werden auch weiterhin die Grundlage für die *Bibliographie* bilden. Die *internationale* Ausrichtung wird erhalten bleiben, ohne Bevorzugung der Publikationen eines bestimmten Landes. Jährlich werden ca. 120.000 Zeitschriftenartikel auf eine Aufnahme in die vier Teilbände hin durchgesehen und eine Auswahl aus über 20.000 Monographien getroffen. Die *Internationale Bibliographie* enthält Material in mehr als 25 Sprachen; sämtliche Titel erscheinen außer in ihrer Originalsprache auch in englischer Übersetzung. Die vier Teilbände werden mit Hilfe einer computergestützten Datenbank erstellt. Die seit langem gebräuchliche Gliederung der Sachregister wurde beibehalten und liegt der alphabetischen Anordnung nach Schlagworten zugrunde.

Die jährlichen Bände der *Internationalen Bibliographie* werden ergänzt durch die *International Current Awareness Services in the Social Sciences*, die wie die Jahresbände in vier Teilen, jedoch monatlich erscheinen. Die *Current Awareness Services* enthalten vollständige Inhaltsverzeichnisse aller im vorausgegangenen Monat bei der Londoner Redaktion eingegangenen Zeitschriften, ergänzt um ein Schlagwortregister. Sie verzeichnen nicht nur Hauptartikel, sondern auch vergänglicheres Material wie Kurzbeiträge und Buchbesprechungen, die in den Jahresbänden unberücksichtigt bleiben. Beide Veröffentlichungen zusammen bieten direkten Zugriff auf neue Publikationen und ergeben ein dauerhaftes Verzeichnis von Druckschriften in den Sozialwissenschaften.

序文

国际社会科学书志 (International Bibliography of the Social Sciences) 的四部分 (人类学：经济学：政治学：社会学) 由联合国教育科学及文化组织 (UNESCO) 1950 年成立的社会科学情报与文书国际委员会 (International Committee for Social Science Information and Documentation) 发起，自从 1952 年由巴黎而初版。该四部分形成目前世界上最广泛的社会科学书志，具有其他书志系列未达到的世界性范围。于1990 年英国政治、经济学图书馆负起国际书志汇编和编排的责任。

自 1931 年以来，英国政治、经济学图书馆发行了社会科学的伦敦书志 (London Bibliography of the Social Sciences)。他的四十七卷形成关于社会科学二十世纪专题文献的无比记录。涉及 1989 年的卷于 1990 年初发行了，是上述系列的最后一卷。由 1990 年开始，以前所发行为伦敦书志 (London Bibliography) 的大部分资料将于国际社会科学书志的结构之内出版。

国际经济学书志由两种来源而编辑，即受编者容易会见已出版文献(特别是杂志)的解析以及来自全世界通讯员系统的贡献。他们报道在产地外不容易得到出版的详细资料。书志将继续以该资料的两种来源为基础。书志也将维持国际性的观点，不重视任何一个国家的出版物。于于上述四部分内的排列，每年发表于杂志内的约十二万论文被审视，由二万以上专题的书名做出选择。虽然资料原文的语言数二十五以上，但所有书名，除引用原文以外，又附有英文翻译。书志是采用计算机化数据库产生的。长期确定的题目分类法继续作为资料排列的基础。关键词按照字母顺序而排列。

年度出版的<u>国际书志</u>为关于社会科学国际目前认识的服务 (International Current Awareness Services in the Social Sciences) 所补充，后者采用国际书志同样四个题目分类但是每月一次发行。不但主要的论文而且缩写论和书评等，以及年度出版各卷所略去的较为朝生暮死的资料均编入索引。该两个出版系列共同提供与新出版的资料的直接接口，成为关于社会科学出版资料的永久记录。

SELECTION CRITERIA

1. Subject

Documents relevant to economics. Economic history is covered selectively, with concentration on material of the twentieth century, or the discipline of economic history itself.

2. Nature and form

Publications of known authorship and lasting significance to economics, whether in serial or monographic form, typically works with a theoretical component intending to communicate new knowledge, new ideas or making use of new materials.

Previously published materials in all formats are omitted, including most translations. Also excluded are textbooks, materials from newspapers or news magazines, popular or purely informative papers, presentations of predominantly primary data, legislative or judicial texts and items of parochial relevance only.

CORRESPONDENTS FOR ECONOMICS

This bibliography has been compiled by combining the work of the editorial office in London, which has established a large core of source publications, and the contributions of our foreign correspondents who provide first-hand knowledge of their countries' publications. We would like to to take this opportunity to thank our correspondents for their long-standing assistance and for adapting so helpfully to our new methods of working.

ARGENTINA — Fundación José María Aragón, Buenos Aires - Corina de Seoane

FRANCE — Bibliothèque de la Fondation nationale des sciences politiques, Paris - Professor Jean Meyriat

GERMANY — Akademie der Wissenschaften der DDR, Zentralinstitüt für Geschichte, Berlin - Dr. W. Wächter
— Zentralbibliothek der Wirtschaftswissenschaften, Bibliothek des Institüts für Weltwirtschaft, Kiel — Ekkehart Seusing

HUNGARY — Library of the Hungarian Parliament, Budapest — Dr. Katalin Pintér
— Municipal Library *"Szabo Ervin"*, Budapest

INDIA — National Social Science Documentation Centre, Indian Council of Social Science Research, New Delhi - Dr. K.G. Tyagi and Dr. Savitri Devi

POLAND — Polska Akademia Nauk, Ośrodek Informacji Naukowej, Warsaw - Dr. Janusz Sach

It should be noted that this list is not exhaustive, but consists only of those who contribute material in a systematic fashion on a regular basis.

LIST OF PERIODICALS CONSULTED
LISTE DES PERIODIQUES CONSULTÉS

ABA banking journal. *[ABA Bank. J.]; American Bankers Association*: 1120 Connecticut Avenue, N.W., Washington, DC. 20036, U.S.A.; **Publisher**: *Simmons-Boardman Publishing*: 345 Hudson Street, New York, NY. 10014-4502, U.S.A.

Academy of management journal. *[Acad. Manag. J.] ISSN: 0001-4273.* ; *Academy of management*: Ohio Northern University, P.O. Box 39, 300 South Union St., Ada, OH. 45810, U.S.A.

Accounting and business research. *[Acc. Bus. Res.] ISSN: 0001-4788.* ; *Institute of Chartered Accountants in England and Wales*: Chartered Accountants' Hall, Moorgate Place, London EC24 6EQ, U.K.; **Subscriptions**: *Accounting and Business Research, Subscriptions Manager*: 40 Bernard Street, London WC1N 1LD, U.K.

Accounting review. *[Acc. Review] ISSN: 0001-4826.* ; *American Accounting Association*: 5717 Bessie Drive, Sarasota, FL. 34233, U.S.A.

Accounting, business and financial history. *[Acc. Bus. Finan. Hist.] ISSN: 0958-5206.* ; *Routledge*: 11 New Fetter Lane, London EC4P 4EE, U.K.; **Subscriptions**: *Routledge*: Cheriton House, North Way, Andover, Hants SP10 5BE, U.K.

Acta oeconomica. *[Acta Oecon.] ISSN: 0001-6373.* ; *Hungarian Academy of Sciences*; **Publisher**: *Akadémiai Kiadó*: H-1363 Budapest, P.O. Box 24, Hungary

Acta politica. *[Acta Pol.] ISSN: 0001-6810.* ; *Boom*: Postbus 1058, 7940 KB Meppel, The Netherlands

Acta sociologica. *[Acta Sociol.] ISSN: 0001- 6993.* ; *Scandinavian Sociological Association*; **Publisher**: *Universitetsforlaget*: Journals Department, P.O.Box 2959 Tøyen, 0608-Oslo 6, Norway

Acta Universitatis Carolinae.:*Oeconomica [Acta Univ. Carol.] ISSN: 0563-038X.* ; *Univerzita Karlova*: Ovocný trh 5, 116 36 Prague 1, Czechoslovakia

Acta Universtatis Łódziensis.:*Folia oeconomica [Acta Univ. Łódz.] ISSN: 0208-6018.* ; *Wydawnictwo Uniwersytetu Łódzkiego*: ul. Nowotki 143, Łódz, Poland

Actualité économique. *[Act. Econ.] ISSN: 0001-771X.* ; *École des Hautes Études Commerciales/ Société canadien ne de science économique/ Association des économistes québécois*: 5255 avenue Decelles, Montréal, Québec, Canada H3T 1V6

Administration. *[Administration] ISSN: 0001-8325.* ; *Institute of Public Administration of Ireland*: 57-61 Lansdowne Road, Dublin 4, Ireland

Administration and society. *[Admin. Soc.] ISSN: 0095-3997.* ; *Sage Publications*: 2455 Teller Road, Newbury Park, CA. 91320, U.S.A.

Administration for development. *[Admin. Devel.] ISSN: 0311-4511.* ; *Administrative College of Papua New Guinea*: P.O. Box 1216, Boroko, Papua New Guinea

Administrative science quarterly. *[Adm. Sci. Qua.] ISSN: 0001-8392.* ; *Cornell University, Johnson Graduate School of Management*: Caldwell Hall, Cornell University, Ithaca, N.Y. 14853, U.S.A.

Advances in public interest accounting. *[Ad. Pub. Inter. Acc.]; JAI Press*: 55 Old Post Road, No 2., Greenwich, CN. 06836, U.S.A.

Africa. *[Africa] ISSN: 0001-9720.* ; *International African Institute*: Connaught House, Aldwych, London, WC2A 2AE, U.K.; **Publisher**: *Manchester University Press*: Oxford Road, Manchester M13 9PL, U.K.

Africa development; Afrique & developpement. *[Afr. Devel.] ISSN: 0850-3907.* ; *Council for the Development of Economic and Social Research in Africa/ Conseil pour le Développement de la Recherche Economique et Sociale en Afrique*: CODESRIA, B.P. 3304, Dakar, Senegal

Africa [Italy]. *[Africa [Italy]] ISSN: 0001-9747.* ; *Istituto Italo-Africano*: Via Ulisse Aldrovandi 16, 00197 Rome, Italy

Africa quarterly. *[Afr. Q.] ISSN: 0001-9828.* ; *Indian Council for Cultural Relations*: Azad Bhavan, Indraprastha Estate, New Delhi 110 002, India

Africa today. *[Afr. Tod.] ISSN: 0001-9887.* ; *Africa Today Associates*: c/o Graduate School of International Studies, University of Denver, Denver, CO. 80208, U.S.A.

African affairs. *[Afr. Affairs] ISSN: 0001-9909.* ; *Royal African Society*: 18 Northumberland Avenue, London WC2N 5BJ, U.K.; **Publisher**: *Oxford University Press*: Pinkhill House, Southfield Road, Eynsham, Oxford OX8 1JJ, U.K.

African development review; Revue africaine de développement. *[Af. Devel. R.]; African Development Bank*: Abidjan, Ivory Coast

African economic history. *[Afr. Econ. Hist.] ISSN: 0145-2258.* ; *Boston University, African Studies Center*: 270 Bay State Road, Boston, MA. 02215, U.S.A.

African journal of international and comparative law; Revue africaine de droit international et comparé. *[Afr. J. Int. Comp. Law] ISSN: 0954-8890.* ; *African Society of International and Comparative Law*: Aberdeen House, 22 Highbury Grove, London N5 2EA, U.K.

African notes. *[Afr. Not.] ISSN: 0002-0087.* ; *University of Ibadan, Institute of African Studies*: Ibadan, Nigeria

African review. *[Afr. R.] ISSN: 0856-0056.* ; *University of Dar es Salaam, Department of Political Science and Public Administration*: P.O. Box 35042, Dar es Salaam, Tanzania

African studies review. *[Afr. Stud. R.] ISSN: 0002-0206.* ; *African Studies Association*: Credit Union Building, Emory University, Atlanta, GA. 30322, U.S.A.

African urban quarterly. *[Afr. Urb. Q.]*; *African Urban Quarterly*: P.O. Box 74165, Nairobi, Kenya

Africana bulletin. *[Afr. Bul.] ISSN: 0002-029X.* ; *Uniwersytet Warszawski, Instytut Krajów Rozwijajacych Się*: Ul. Obozna 8, 00-032 Warsaw, Poland

Africana research bulletin. *[Afr. Res. Bul.]*; *University of Sierra Leone, Institute of African Studies*: Freetown, Sierra Leone

Afrika Spectrum. *[Af. Spec.] ISSN: 0002-0397.* ; *Institut für Afrika-Kunde*: Neuer Jungfernstieg 21, 2000 Hamburg 36, Germany

Afrique 2000. *[Afr. 2000] ISSN: 1017-0952.* ; *Institut panafricain de relations internationales*: Av. de Fré 265 - 1180, Brussels, Belgium

Afrique contemporaine. *[Afr. Cont.] ISSN: 0002-0478.* ; *Documentation française*: 29-31 Quai Voltaire, 75340 Paris Cedex 07, France

Afro-Asian solidarity. *[Af-As. Solid.]*; *Afro-Asian Peoples Solidarity Organisation (AAPSO)*: 89 Abdel Aziz Al-Seoud Street, 11451-61 Manial El-Roda, Cairo, Egypt

Ageing and society. *[Age. Soc.] ISSN: 0144-686X.* ; *Centre for Policy on Ageing/ British Society of Gerontology*; **Publisher**: *Cambridge University Press*: The Edinburgh Building, Shaftesbury Road, Cambridge CB2 2RU, U.K.

Agrekon. *[Agrekon] ISSN: 0303-1853.* ; *Landbou- Economievereniging van Suider-Afrika = Agricultural Economics Association of Southern Africa*: 210 Orion Avenue, Monument Park 0181, South Africa

Agricultura y sociedad. *[Agr. Soc.] ISSN: 0211-8394.* ; *Ministerio de Agricultura, Pesca y Alimentacion*: Centro de Publicaciones, Paseo de Infanta Isabel 1, 28071 Madrid, Spain

Agricultural history. *[Agr. Hist.] ISSN: 0002-1482.* ; *Agricultural History Society*: ERS, 1301 New York Avenue, NW., Washington DC. 20205, U.S.A.; **Publisher**: *University of California Press*: 2120 Berkeley Way, Berkeley, CA. 94720, U.S.A.

Agriculture and resources quarterly. *[Agr. Res. Q.] ISSN: 1032-9722.* ; *Australian Bureau of Agricultural and Resource Economics*: GPO Box 1563, Canberra 2601, Australia

Albania today. *[Alb. Today] ISSN: 0044-7072.* ; *Drejtoria Qendrore e Librit*: Pruga Konferenca e Pezec, Tirana, Albania

Allgemeines statistisches Archiv. *[All. Stat. A.] ISSN: 0002-6018.* ; *Deutsche Statistische Gesellschaft*; **Publisher**: *Vandenhoeck & Ruprecht*: Theaterstraße 13, 3400 Göttingen, Germany

Alternatives. *[Alternatives] ISSN: 0304-3754.* ; *Lynne Rienner Publishers*: 1800 30th Street, Boulder, CO.. 80301, U.S.A.

American economic review. *[Am. Econ. Rev.] ISSN: 0002-8282.* ; *American Economic Association*: 2014 Broadway, Suite 305, Nashville, TN. 37203, U.S.A.

American journal of agricultural economics. *[Am. J. Agr. Ec.] ISSN: 0002-9092.* ; *American Agricultural Economics Association*: 80 Heady Hall, Iowa State University, Ames, IA. 50011-1070, U.S.A.

American journal of economics and sociology. *[Am. J. Econ. S.] ISSN: 0002-9246.* ; *American Journal of Economics and Sociology*: 42 East 72 Street, New York, NY. 10021, U.S.A.

American journal of international law. *[Am. J. Int. Law] ISSN: 0002-9300.* ; *American Society of International Law*: 2223 Massachusetts Avenue, N.W., Washington DC. 20008- 2864, U.S.A.

American journal of Islamic social sciences. *[Am. J. Islam. Soc. Sci.] ISSN: 0742-6763.* ; *Association of Muslim Social Scientists/ International Institute of Islamic Thought*: P.O. Box 669, Herndon, VA 22070, U.S.A.

American journal of political science. *[Am. J. Pol. Sc.] ISSN: 0092-5853.* ; *Midwest Political Science Association*; **Publisher**: *University of Texas Press, Journals Department*: 2100 Comal, Austin TX. 78722, U.S.A.

American journal of sociology. *[A.J.S.] ISSN: 0024-9602.* ; *University of Chicago Press*: Journals Division, P.O. Box 37005, Chicago, IL. 60637, U.S.A.

American political science review. *[Am. Poli. Sci.] ISSN: 0003-0554.* ; *American Political Science Association*: 1527 New Hampshire Avenue, N.W., Washington, DC. 20036, U.S.A.

American sociological review. *[Am. Sociol. R.] ISSN: 0003-1224.* ; *American Sociological Association*: 1722 N. Street, N.W. Washington, DC. 20036, U.S.A.

Anales de estudios económicos y empresariales. *[Anal. Est. Econ. Empres.] ISSN: 0213-7569.* ; *Universidad de Valladolid, Facultad de Ciencias Económicas y Empresariales*: c/o Ramón y Cajal n° 7, 47005 Valladolid, Spain

Análise social. *[Anál. Soc.] ISSN: 0003-2573.* ; *Junta Nacional de Investigação Científica e Tecnológia/ Instituto Nacional de Investigação Científica*; **Publisher**: *Instituto de Ciências Sociais da Universidade de Lisboa*: Avenida das Forças Armadas, Edifício I.S.C.T.E., Ala Sul, 1° andar, 1600 Lisbon, Portugal

Analysis. *[Analysis] ISSN: 0003-2638.* ; *Basil Blackwell*: 108 Cowley Road, Oxford OX4 1JF, U.K.; **Subscriptions**: *Marston Book Services*: P.O. Box 87, Oxford OX2 0DT, U.K.

Annales.:*Economies, sociétés, civilisations [Annales] ISSN: 0395-2649.* ; *C.N.R.S./ Ecole des hautes études en sciences sociales*; **Publisher**: *Armand Colin*: 103 boulevard Saint-Michel, 75240 Paris Cedex 05, France; **Subscriptions**: *Armand Colin*: B.P.22, 41353 Vineuil, France

Annales de l'économie publique sociale et coopérative; Annals of public and cooperative economics. *[A. Econ. Publ. Soc. Coop.] ISSN: 0770-8548.* ; *Centre international de recherches et d'information sur l'économie publique, sociale et coopérative (CIRIEC)/ International Centre of Research and Information on the Public and Cooperative Economy (CIRIEC)*; **Publisher**: *De Boeck Université*: Avenue Louise 203, 1050 Brussels, Belgium

Annales d'économie et de statistique. *[Ann. Econ. Stat.] ISSN: 0769-489X.* ; *Association pour le Développement de la Recherche en Economie et en Statistique*; **Publisher**: *Institut National de la Statistique et des Etudes Economiques*: 18 boulevard Adolphe Pinard, 75675 Paris Cedex 14, France

Annales universitatis Mariae Curie-Skłodowska.:*Sectio H — Oeconomia [A. Univ. Mariae Curie — Oecon.] ISSN: 0459-9586.* ; *Uniwersytet Marii Curie-Skłodowskie*: Plac Marii Curie-Skłodowskiej 5, 20-031 Lublin, Poland

Annali della fondazione Luigi Einaudi. *[A. Fond. L. Einaudi]; Fondazione Luigi Einaudi*: Via P. Amedeo 34, 10123 Turin, Italy

Annali della fondazione Luigi Micheletti. *[Ann. Fond. L. Mich.]; Fondazione Luigi Micheletti, Centro de ricerca sull'età contemporanea*: Via Cairoli 9, 15122 Brescia, Italy

Annali di ca'foscari. *[A. Ca'fos.]; Università degli Studi di Venezia*: San Polo 2035, 1- 30125 Venice, Italy

Annals of regional science. *[Ann. Reg. Sci.] ISSN: 0570-1864.* ; *Western Regional Science Association*; **Publisher**: *Springer-Verlag*: Heidelberger Platz 3, W-1000 Berlin 33, Germany

Annals of the American Academy of Political and Social Science. *[Ann. Am. Poli.] ISSN: 0002-7162.* ; *American Academy of Political and Social Science*: 3937 Chestnut Street, Philadelphia, PA. 19104, U.S.A.; **Publisher**: *Sage Publications*: 2455 Teller Road, Newbury Park, CA. 91320, U.S.A.

Annals of the Association of American Geographers. *[Ann. As. Am. G.] ISBN: 0004-5608.* ; *Association of American Geographers*: 1710 Sixteenth Street, N.W., Washington, DC. 20009, U.S.A.

Annals of the Institute of Social Science. *[Ann. Inst. Soc. Sci.] ISSN: 0563-8054.* ; *University of Tokyo, Institute of Social Science*: 7-3-1 Hongo, Bunkyo-ku, Tokyo 113, Japan

Année africaine. *[Ann. Afri.] ISSN: 0570-1937.* ; *Centre d'Etude d'Afique Noire/ Centre de Recherche et d'Etude sur les Pays d'Afrique Orientale*: Institut d'Etudes Politiques de Bordeaux, Domaine University, BP 101, 33405 Talence Cedex, France; **Publisher**: *Editions A. Pedone*: Paris, France

Année sociale. *[Ann. Soc.] ISSN: 0066-2380.* ; *Univeristé libre de Bruxelles, Institut de sociologie*: Avenue Jeanne, 44-1050 Brussels, Belgium

Annuaire de l'Afrique du Nord. *[Ann. Afr. Nord] ISSN: 0242- 7540.* ; *Editions du Centre national de la recherche scientifique*: 15 quai Anatole France, 75700 Paris, France

Annual review of energy and the environment. *[Ann. R. Energy Environ.] ISSN: 0362- 1626.* ; *Annual Reviews*: P.O. Box 50139, Palo Alto, CA. 94303 0897, U.S.A.

Annual review of information science and technology. *[Ann. R. Info. Sci. Tech.] ISSN: 0066-4200.* ; *American Society for Information Science*: 8720 Georgia Avenue, Suite 501, Silver Spring, MD. 20910-3602, U.S.A.; **Publisher**: *Elsevier Science Publishers (North-Holland)*: Sara Burgerhartstraat 25, P.O. Box 211, 1000 AE Amsterdam, The Netherlands

Annual review of sociology. *[Ann. R. Soc.] ISSN: 0360-0572.* ; *Annual Reviews*: 4139 El Camino Way, P.O. Box 10139, Palo Alto, CA. 94303-0899, U.S.A.

Antipode. *[Antipode] ISSN: 0066-4812.* ; *Basil Blackwell*: 108 Cowley Road, Oxford OX4 1JF, U.K.

Anuario de estudios centroamericanos. *[An. Est. Cent.Am.] ISSN: 0377-7316.* ; *Universidad de Costa Rica, Instituto de Investigaciones Sociales*: Apartado 75, 2060 Ciudad Universitaria, Rodrigo Facio, 2050 San Pedro de Montes de Oca, San Jose, Costa Rica

Applied economics. *[Appl. Econ.] ISSN: 0003 6846.* ; *Chapman and Hall*: 2-6 Boundary Row, London SE1 8HN, U.K.; **Subscriptions**: *International Thomson Publishing Services*: North Way, Andover, Hampshire SP10 5BE, U.K.

Applied financial economics. *[Appl. Finan. Econ.] ISSN: 0960-3107.* ; *Chapman & Hall*: 2-6 Boundary Row, London SE1 8HN, U.K.; **Subscriptions**: *International Thomson Publishing Services*: North Way, Andover, Hampshire SP10 5BE, U.K.

Appropriate technology. *[Approp. Tech.] ISSN: 0305-0920.* ; *IT Publications*: 103-105 Southampton Row, London WC1B 4HH, U.K.

Apuntes. *[Apuntes] ISSN: 0252-1865.* ; *Revista Apuntes*: Apartado Postal 4683, Lima 1, Peru

Arab journal for the humanities. *[Arab J. Hum.]*; *Kuwait University*: P.O. Box 26585, Safat, 13126 Kuwait

Arab law quarterly. *[Arab Law Q.] ISSN: 0268-0556.* ; *The Society of Arab Comparative and International Law*; **Publisher**: *Graham & Trotman*: Sterling House, 66 Wilton Road, London, SW1V 1DE, U.K.

Arab studies quarterly. *[Arab St. Q.] ISSN: 0271-3519.* ; *Institute of Arab Studies/ Association of Arab-American University Graduates*: 556 Trapelo Road, Belmont, MA. 02178, U.S.A.

Archiv des öffentlichen Rechts. *[Arc. Öffen. Recht] ISSN: 0003-8911.* ; *J.C.B. Mohr (Paul Siebeck)*: Postfach 2040, Wilhelmstraße 18, 7400 Tübingen, Germany

Archiv für Kommunalwissenschaften. *[Arc. Kommunal.] ISSN: 0003- 9209.* ; *Deutsches Institut für Urbanistik*: Straße des 17. Juni 112, Postfach 12 62 24, 1000 Berlin 12, Germany; **Publisher**: *Verlag W. Kohlhammer*: Heßbrühlstraße 69, Postfach 80 04 30, 7000 Stuttgart 80 (Vaihingen), Germany

Archív orientální. *[Arch. Orient.] ISSN: 0044-8699.* ; *Czechoslovak Academy of Sciences, Oriental Institute*; **Publisher**: *Academia Publishing House*: Vodičkova 40, 112 29 Prague 1, Czechoslovakia; **Subscriptions**: *John Benjamins*: Postbus 52519, 1007 HA Amsterdam, The Netherlands

Area. *[Area] ISSN: 0004-0894.* ; *Institute of British Geographers*: 1 Kensington Gore, London SW7 2AR, U.K.

Armed forces and society. *[Arm. Forces Soc.] ISSN: 0095-327X.* ; *Inter-University Seminar on Armed Forces and Society*: Box 46, 1126 East 59th Street, Chicago, IL. 60637, U.S.A.; **Publisher**: *Transaction Periodicals Consortium*: Rutgers University, New Brunswick, NJ. 08903, U.S.A.; **Subscriptions**: *Swets Publishing Service*: Heereweg 347, 2161 CA. Lisse, The Netherlands

Artha vijñāna. *[Art. Vij.] ISSN: 0004- 3559.* ; *Gokhale Institute of Politics and Economics*: Pune 411004, India

ASEAN economic bulletin. *[ASEAN Ec. B.] ISSN: 0217-4472.* ; *Institute of Southeast Asian Studies*: Heng Mui Keng Terrace, Pasir Panjang, Singapore 0511

Asia journal of theology. *[Asia J. Theol.] ISSN: 0218-0812.* ; *Asia Journal of Theology*: 324 Onan Road, Singapore 1542

Asian and African studies. *[Asian. Afr. Stud.] ISSN: 0066-8281.* ; *University of Haifa, Gustav Heinemann Institute of Middle Eastern Studies*: Haifa 31999, Israel

Asian Economic Journal. *[Asian Econ. J.]*; *East Asian Economic Association/ Hong Kong Institute of Asia Pacific Studies/ Chinese University of Hong Kong*: Shatin, N.T., Hong Kong

Asian economic review. *[Asian Ec. Rev.] ISSN: 0004-4555.* ; *Indian Institute of Economics*: 11-6-841 Red Hills, Hyderabad-500 004, India

Asian economies. *[Asian Ec.] ISSN: 0304-260X.* ; *Research Institute of Asian Economies*: K.P.O. Box 1008, Seoul 110-610, Korea

Asian journal of public administration. *[Asian J. Pub. Admin.] ISSN: 0259-8272.* ; *University of Hong Kong, Department of Political Science*: Pokfulam Road, Hong Kong

Asian perspective [S. Korea]. *[Asian Persp. [S. Korea]]*; *Kyungnam University, Institute for Far Eastern Studies*: 28-42 Samchung-dong, Chongro-ku, Seoul 110-230, South Korea

Asian profile. *[Asian Prof.] ISSN: 0304-8675.* ; *Asian Research Service*: Rm. 704, Federal Building, 369 Lockhart Road, Hong Kong; **Subscriptions**: *idem*: G.P.O. Box 2232, Hong Kong

Asian studies review. *[Asian Stud. R.] ISSN: 0314-7533.* ; *Asian Studies Association of Australia*: c/o Social and Policy Studies in Education, University of Sydney, N.S.W. 2006, Australia

Asian survey. *[Asian Sur.] ISSN: 0004-4687.* ; *University of California Press*: Berkeley, CA. 94720, U.S.A.

Asian thought and society. *[Asian Thoug. Soc.] ISSN: 0361-3968.* ; *State University of New York-Oneonta/Boston College, Center for East Europe, Russia, and Asia/University of Hong Kong*; **Publisher**: *East-West Publishing*: 1 Bugbee Road, Oneonta, NY. 13820, U.S.A.

Asian-Pacific economic literature. *[Asian-Pacific Ec. Lit.] ISSN: 0818-9935.* ; *Australian National University, National Centre for Development Studies*: G.P.O. Box 4, Canberra, ACT 2601, Australia; **Publisher**: *Beech Tree Publishing*: 10 Watford Close, Guildford, Surrey GU1 2EP, U.K.

Asien Afrika Lateinamerika. *[Asien. Af. Lat.am.] ISSN: 0323-3790.* ; *Akademie der Wissenschaften zu Berlin*; **Publisher**: *Akademie-Verlag*: Leipziger Straße 3-4, 01086 Berlin, Germany

Aussenpolitik. *[Aussenpolitik] ISSN: 0587-3835.* ; *Interpress Verlag*: Hartwicusstraße 3-4, D-2000 Hamburg 76, Germany

Aussenwirtschaft. *[Aussenwirtschaft] ISSN: 0004-8216.* ; *Schweizerisches Institut für Aussenwirtschafts- Struktur- und Regionalforschung (SIASR)*: Dufourstrasse 48, CH-9000 St. Gallen, Switzerland; **Publisher**: *Verlag Rüegger*: Aemtlerstrasse 201, Postfach, CH-8040 Zürich, Switzerland

Australian economic history review. *[Aust. Econ. Hist. Rev.] ISSN: 0004-8992.* ; *Oxford University Press Australia*: GPO Box 2784Y, Melbourne, Vic. 3001, Australia

Australian economic papers. *[Aust. Econ. P.] ISSN: 0004-900X.* ; *Flinders University of South Australia*: G.P.O. Box 2100, Adelaide, South Australia 5042, Australia; **Subscriptions**: *University of Adelaide*: G.P.O. Box 498, Adelaide, South Australia 5001, Australia

Australian economic review. *[Aust. Ec. Rev.] ISSN: 0004-9018.* ; *University of Melbourne, Institute of Applied Economic and Social Research*: Baldwin Spencer Building, University of Melbourne, Parkville, Victoria 3052, Australia

Australian foreign affairs and trade.:*The monthly record* *[Aust. Foreign. Aff.] ISSN: 1033- 5722.* ; *Department of Foreign Affairs and Trade, Overseas Information Branch*: PO Box 12, Canberra, ACT, 2600, Australia; **Subscriptions**: *Australian Government Publishing Service*: GPO Box 84, Canberra, ACT, 2601, Australia

Australian geographer. *[Aust. Geogr.] ISSN: 0004-9182.* ; *Geographical Society of New South Wales*: P.O. Box 602, Gladesville, NSW 2111, Australia

Australian geographical studies. *[Aust. Geogr. Stud.] ISSN: 0004-9190.* ; *Institute of Australian Geographers*: Department of Geography and Oceanography, University College, University of New South Wales, Australian Defence Force Academy, Campbell, ACT 2600, Australia

Australian journal of agricultural economics. *[Aust. J. Agri. Econ.] ISSN: 0004-9395.* ; *Australian Agricultural Economics Society*: P.O. Box 330, East Melbourne, Victoria 3002, Australia

Australian journal of Chinese affairs. *[Aust. J. Chin. Aff.] ISSN: 0156-7365.* ; *Australian National University, Contemporary China Centre*: G.P.O. Box 4, Canberra ACT 2601, Australia

Australian journal of public administration. *[Aust. J. Publ.] ISSN: 0313-6647.* ; *Royal Australian Institute of Public Administration*: Box 904, GPO, Sydney, N.S.W. 2001, Australia

Australian journal of statistics. *[Aust. J. Statist.] ISSN: 0004-9581.* ; *Australian Statistical Publishing Association*: Treasurer, Statistical Society of Australia, G.P.O. Box 573, Canberra, ACT 2601, Australia

Australian quarterly. *[Aust. Q.] ISSN: 0005-0091.* ; *Australian Institute of Political Science*: P.O. Box 145, Balmain NSW 2041, Australia

Azania. *[Azania] ISSN: 0067-270X.* ; *British Institute in Eastern Africa*: P.O. Box 30710, Nairobi, Kenya/ 1 Kensington Gore, London SW7 2AR, U.K.

Banaras law journal. *[Banaras Law J.]*; *Banaras Hindu University, Law School*: Varanasi 221005, India

Banca Nazionale del Lavoro quarterly review. *[Banca Nat. Lav. Q. Rev.] ISSN: 0005-4607.* ; *Banca Nazionale del Lavoro*: Ufficio Studi 119, Via Vittorio Veneto 19, 00187 Rome, Italy

Bancaria. *[Bancaria] ISSN: 0005-4623.* ; *Associazione Bancaria Italiana*; **Publisher**: *Bancaria Editrice*: Piazza del Gesù 49, 00186 Rome, Italy

Bangladesh development studies. *[Bang. Dev. Stud.] ISSN: 0304-095X.* ; *Bangladesh Unnayan Gobeshona Protishthan = Bangladesh Institute of Development Studies*: G.P.O. Box No.3854, E-17 Agargaon, Sher-e-Bangla Nagar, Dhaka, Bangladesh

Bangladesh journal of political economy. *[Bang. J. Pol. Econ.]*; *Bangladesh Economic Association*: Department of Economics, University of Dhaka, Dhaka-1000, Bangladesh

Bangladesh journal of public administration. *[Bang. J. Pub. Admin.]*; *Bangladesh Public Administration Training Centre*: Savar, Dhaka 1343, Bangladesh

Bank of England quarterly bulletin. *[Bank of Engl. Q.] ISSN: 0005-5166.* ; *Bank of England*: Bulletin Group, Economics Division, London EC2R 8AH, U.K.

Bank-Archiv. *[Bank-Archiv] ISSN: 1015-1516.* ; *Österreichische Bankwissenschaftliche Gesellschaft*: Strauchgasse 3, A-1010 Vienna, Austria; **Publisher**: *Verlag Orac*: Graben 17, A-1010 Vienna, Austria

Banker. *[Banker] ISSN: 0005-5395.* ; *Financial Times Business Information*: Number One, Southwark Bridge, London SE1 9HL, U.K.; **Subscriptions**: *idem*: Central House, 27 Park Street, Croydon, CRO 1YD, U.K.

BC studies. *[BC. Stud.] ISSN: 0005-2949.* ; *University of British Columbia*: 2029 West Mall, University of British Columbia, Vancouver B.C. V6T 1W5, Canada

Belizean studies. *[Beliz. St.] ISSN: 0250-6831.* ; *St. John's College*: P.O. Box 548, Belize City, Belize, Central America

Benelux. *[Benelux]*; *Secretariaat-Generaal van de Benelux Economische unie = Secrétariat général de l'Union économique Benelux = Generalsekretariat der Benelux-Wirtschaftsunion*: Regentschapsstraat, 39 rue de la Régence, Brussels 1000, Belgium

Bijdragen tot de taal-, land-en volkenkunde. *[Bijdragen] ISSN: 0006- 2294.* ; *Koninklijk Instituut voor Taal-, Land-en Volkenkunde*: Reuvensplaats 2, Postbus 9515, 2300 RA Leiden, The Netherlands

Boletim informativo e bibliográfico de ciências sociais. *[Bol. Inf. Bibl. Soc.]*; *Associação Nacional de Pós-Graduação e Pesquisa em Ciências Sociais*: Editoria do BIB, Rua da Matriz 82, Botafogo 22.260. Rio de Janeiro RJ., Brazil

Boletín de fuentes para la historia económica de México. *[B. Hist. Econ. Méx.] ISSN: 0188-3259.* ; *Colegio de México, Centro de Estudios Históricos*: Camino al Ajusco 20, Pedregal de Santa Teresa, 10740 Mexico, D.F., Mexico

Boletin. Centro de estudios monetarios latinoamericanos. *[Centro Est. Monet. Latinam.] ISSN: 0186-7229.* ; *Centro de Estudios Monetarios Latinoamericanos (CEMLA)*: Departamento de Información, Durango No.54, México D.F.06700, México

Borneo review. *[Born. R.]*; *Institute for Development Studies (Sabah)*: Locked Bag 127, 88999 Kota Kinabalu, Sabah, Malaysia

Botswana notes and records. *[Bots. Not. Rec.] ISSN: 0525-5059.* ; *Botswana Society*: P.O. Box 71, Gaborone, Botswana

British journal of addiction. *[Br. J. Addict.] ISSN: 0952-0481.* ; *Society for the Study of Addiction to Alcohol and Other Drugs*: Addiction Reseach Unit, National Addiction Centre, 101 Denmark Hill, London SE5 8AF, U.K.; **Publisher**: *Carfax Publishing*: P.O. Box 25, Abingdon, Oxfordshire, OX14 3UE, U.K.

British journal of industrial relations. *[Br. J. Ind. R.] ISSN: 0007-1080.* ; *London School of Economics*: Houghton Street, London WC2A 2AE, U.K.; **Publisher**: *Basil Blackwell*: 108 Cowley Road, Oxford, OX4 1JF, U.K.; **Subscriptions**: *Journals Subscriptions, Industrial Relations Department, Marston Book Services*: P.O. Box 87, Oxford OX2 0DT, U.K.

British journal of management. *[Br. J. Manag.] ISSN: 1045-3172.* ; *British Academy of Management*; **Publisher**: *John Wiley & Sons*: Baffins Lane, Chichester, West Sussex PO19 1UD, U.K.

British journal of political science. *[Br. J. Poli. S.] ISSN: 0007-1234.* ; *Cambridge University Press*: The Pitt Building, Trumpington Street, Cambridge CB2 1RP, U.K.

British review of economic issues. *[Br. Rev. Ec. Iss.] ISSN: 0141-4739.* ; *Association of Polytechnic Teachers in Economics*: c/o Economics Department Staffordshire Polytechnic, Leek Road, Stoke-on-Trent ST4 2DE, U.K.

British tax review. *[Br. Tax Rev.] ISSN: 0007-1870.* ; *Sweet and Maxwell*: South Quay Plaza, 183 Marsh Wall, London E14 9FT, U.K.; **Subscriptions**: *Subscriptions Department*: North Way, Andover, Hampshire, SP10 5BE, U.K.

British year book of international law. *[Br. Year Int. Law.] ISSN: 0068-2691.* ; *Oxford University Press*: Walton Street, Oxford OX2 6DP, U.K.; **Subscriptions**: *Oxford University Press*: Retail Services Department, Distribution Services, Saxon Way West, Corby, Northants NN18 9ES, U.K.

Brookings papers on economic activity. *[Brookings P.] ISSN: 0007-2303.* ; *Brookings Institution*: 1775 Massachusetts Avenue, N.W., Washington DC. 20036, U.S.A.

Bulletin.:*Bank of Botswana [Bull. Bank. Bots.]*; *Bank of Botswana*: Box 712, Gaborone, Botswana

Bulletin de la Banque Nationale de Belgique. *[Ban. Natl. Belgium] ISSN: 0005-5611.* ; *Banque Nationale de Belgique*: boulevard de Berlaimont 5, 1000 Brussels, Belgium ,

Bulletin des études africaines de l'INALCO. *[B. Et. Afr. INALCO]*; *Institut national des langues et civilisations orientales*: 2 rue de Lille, 75007 Paris, France

Bulletin for international fiscal documentation. *[B. Int. Fiscal Docu.] ISSN: 0007-4624.* ; *International Fiscal Association*; **Publisher**: *International Bureau of Fiscal Documentation*: P.O. Box 20237, 1000 HE Amsterdam, The Netherlands

Bulletin of Eastern Caribbean affairs. *[B. E.Carib. Aff.] ISSN: 0254-7406.* ; *Institute of Social and Economic Research (Eastern Caribbean)*: University of the West Indies, Cave Hill, Barbados

Bulletin of economic research. *[B. Econ. Res.] ISSN: 0307-3378.* ; *Basil Blackwell*: 108 Cowley Road, Oxford OX4 1JF, U.K.

Bulletin of Indonesian economic studies. *[B. Ind. Econ. St.] ISSN: 0007-4918.* ; *Australian National University*: Department of Economics, Research School of Pacific Studies, G.P.O. Box 4, Canberra, A.C.T. 2601, Australia

Bulletin of Latin American research. *[B. Lat. Am. Res.] ISSN: 0261-3050.* ; *Society for Latin American Studies*; **Publisher**: *Pergamon Press*: Headington Hill Hall, Oxford OX3 0BW, U.K.

Bulletin of Tanzanian affairs. *[B. Tanzan. Aff.] ISSN: 0952-2948.* ; *British Tanzania Society*: 14B Westbourne Grove Terrace, London W2 5SD, U.K.

Bulletin. Bank of Finland. *[B. Bank Finland] ISSN: 0784-6509.* ; *Suomen Pankki Finlands Bank*: P.O. Box 160, SF-00101 Helsinki, Finland

Bulletin. Committee for Middle East Trade. *[B. Comm. M.East Trade]*; *Committee for Middle East Trade*: 33 Bury Street, London SW1Y 6AX, U.K.

Business economist. *[Bus. Econ.] ISSN: 0306-5049.* ; *Society of Business Economists*: Business Economist, 56 Malden Road, Watford, WD1 3EW, U.K.

Business history. *[Bus. Hist.] ISSN: 0007-6791.* ; *Frank Cass*: Gainsborough House, Gainsborough Road, London E11 1RS, U.K.

Business history review. *[Bus. Hist. Rev.] ISSN: 0007-6805.* ; *Harvard Business School*: Baker Library 5A, Harvard Business School, Boston, MA. 02163, U.S.A.

Business library review. *[Bus. Lib. Rev.] ISSN: 1045-7798.* ; *Gordon and Breach Publishers*: P.O. Box 90, Reading, Berkshire RG1 8JL, U.K.

Business quarterly. *[Bus. Q.]; University of Western Ontario, School of Business Administration*: London, Canada N6A 3KY

Cahiers africains d'administration publique; African administrative studies. *[Cah. Afr. Admin. Pub.] ISSN: 0007-9588.* ; *Centre Africain de Formation et de Recherche Administratives pour le Développement (CAFRAD)*: P.O. Box 310, Tangiers, Morocco

Cahiers des Amériques latines. *[Cah. Amer. Lat.] ISSN: 0008-0020.* ; *Université de la Sorbonne Nouvelle (Paris III), Institut des Hautes Etudes de l'Amérique latine*: 28 rue Saint-Guillaume, 75007 Paris, France

Cahiers des sciences humaines. *[Cah. Sci. Hum.] ISSN: 0768-9829.* ; *Editions de l'ORSTOM, Institut français de recherche scientifique pour le developpement en cooperation*: Commission des Sciences Sociales, 213 rue la Fayette, 75480 Paris, France; **Subscriptions**: *Editions de l'ORSTOM*: Librairie-Vente-Publicité, 70-74 Route d'Aulnay, 93143 Bondy Cedex, France

Cahiers d'études africaines. *[Cah. Et. Afr.] ISSN: 0008-0055.* ; *Editions de l'Ecole des Hautes Etudes en Sciences Sociales*: 131 boulevard Saint-Michel, 75005 Paris, France; **Subscriptions**: *Centrale des Revues*: 11 rue Gossin, 92543 Montrouge Cedex, France

Cahiers d'histoire de l'institut de recherches Marxistes. *[Cah. Inst. Rech. Marx.] ISSN: 0246-9731.* ; *Société d'Edition des Publications de l'Institut des Recherches Marxistes*: 15 rue Montmartre, 75001 Paris, France; **Subscriptions**: *Institut de Recherches Marxistes*: 64 boulevard Auguste-Blanqui, 75013 Paris, France

Cahiers du CEDAF/ ASDOC-studies. *[Cah. CEDAF] ISSN: 0250-1619.* ; *Centre d'étude et de documentation africaines = Afrika Studie-en Documentatiecentrum*: 7 Place Royale, B-1000 Brussels, Belgium

Cahiers économiques et monétaires. *[Cah. Econ. Monét.] ISSN: 0396-4701.* ; *Banque de France*: Conseil Général Bibliothèque, B.P. 140-01, 75049 Paris Cedex 01, France

California management review. *[Calif. Manag. R.] ISSN: 0008-1256.* ; *University of California, Walter A. Haas School of Business*: 350 Barrows Hall. University of California, Berkeley, CA. 94720, U.S.A.

Cambridge journal of economics. *[Camb. J. Econ.] ISSN: 0309-166X.* ; *University of Cambridge, Faculty of Economics and Politics*: Sidgwick Avenue, Cambridge CB3 9DD, U.K.; **Publisher**: *Academic Press*: 24-28 Oval Road, London NW1 7DX, U.K.; **Subscriptions**: *idem*: Foots Cray, Sidcup, Kent DA14 5HP, U.K.

Cambridge law journal. *[Camb. Law J.] ISSN: 0008-1973.* ; *University of Cambridge, Faculty of Law*; **Publisher**: *Cambridge University Press*: The Edinburgh Building, Shaftesbury Road, Cambridge CB2 2RU, U.K.

Cambridge review of international affairs. *[Cam. R. Int. Aff.] ISSN: 0955-7571.* ; *University of Cambridge, Centre for International Studies*: History Faculty Building, West Road, Cambridge CB3 9EF, U.K.

Canadian Association of African Studies newsletter; Association canadienne des études africaines bulletin. *[Can. Ass. Afr. S. News] ISSN: 0228-8397.* ; *Canadian Association of African Studies = Association canadienne des études africaines*: 308, 294 Albert Street, Ottawa, Ontario, K1P 6E6 Canada

Canadian geographer. *[Can. Geogr.] ISSN: 0008-3658.* ; *Canadian Association of Geographers*: Burnside Hall, McGill University, 805 Sherbrooke Street West, Montreal, Quebec, H3A 2KA Canada

Canadian historical review. *[Can. Hist. R.] ISSN: 0008-3755.* ; *University of Toronto Press*: 5201 Dufferin Street, Downsview, Ontario M3H 5T8, Canada

Canadian journal of African studies; Revue canadienne des études africaines. *[Can. J. Afr. St.] ISSN: 0008-3968.* ; *Canadian Association of African Studies = Association canadienne des études africaines*: Innis College, University of Toronto, 2 Sussex Avenue, Toronto, Ontario M5S IAI, Canada

Canadian journal of agricultural economics; Revue canadienne d'économie rurale. *[Can. J. Ag. Ec.] ISSN: 0008-3976.* ; *Canadian Agricultural Economics and Farm Management Society*: Suite 907, 151 Slater Street, Ottawa, Ontario, Canada K1P 5H4

Canadian journal of economics; Revue canadienne d'économique. *[Can. J. Econ.] ISSN: 0008-4085.* ; *Canadian Economics Association*; **Publisher**: *University of Toronto Press*: 5201 Dufferin Street, Downsview, Ontario M3H 5T8, Canada

Canadian journal of political science; Revue canadienne de science politique. *[Can. J. Poli.] ISSN: 0008-4239.* ; *Canadian Political Science Association = Association canadienne de science politique/ Société québécoise de science politique*: Suite 205, 1 Stewart Street, Ottawa, Ontario, Canada K1N 6H7/ Université du Québec à Montréal, Montréal, Québec, Canada H3C 3PN; **Publisher**: *Wilfrid Laurier University Press*: 75 University Avenue W., Waterloo, Ontario N2L 3C5, Canada

INTERNATIONAL BIBLIOGRAPHY OF ECONOMICS — 1992

Canadian journal of sociology; Cahiers canadiens de sociologie. *[Can. J. Soc.] ISSN: 0318-6431.* ; *University of Alberta, Department of Sociology*: Edmonton, Alberta T6G 2H4, Canada

Canadian journal of statistics; Revue canadienne de statistiques. *[Can. R. Stat.] ISSN: 0319-5724.* ; *Statistical Society of Canada – Société Statistique du Canada*: 675 Denbury Avenue, Ottawa, Ontario, Canada K2A 2P2

Canadian public administration; Administration publique du Canada. *[Can. Publ. Ad.] ISSN: 0008-4840.* ; *Institute of Public Administration of Canada*: 897 Bay Street, Toronto, Ontario M5S 1Z7, Canada

Canadian review of sociology and anthropology; Revue canadienne de sociologie et d'anthropologie. *[Can. R. Soc. A.] ISSN: 0008-4948.* ; *Canadian Sociology and Anthropology Association*: Concordia University, 1455 boulevard de Maisonneuve W., Montreal, Quebec H3G 1M8, Canada

Canadian yearbook of international law; Annuaire canadien de droit international. *[Can. Yb. Int. Law] ISSN: 0069-0058.* ; *International Law Association, Canadian Branch*; **Publisher**: *University of British Columbia Press*: 303-6344 Memorial Road, Vancouver, B.C., V16 1WS Canada

Capital and class. *[Cap. Class] ISSN: 0309-8786.* ; *Conference of Socialist Economists*: Editorial Committee, Conference of Socialist Economists, 25 Horsell Road, London N5 1XL, U.K.

Capitalism, nature, socialism. *[Cap. Nat. Social.] ISSN: 1045-5752.* ; *Guilford Publications*: 72 Spring Street, New York, NY. 10012, U.S.A.

Caribbean studies; Estudios del Caribe; Études des Caraïbes. *[Carib. Stud.] ISSN: 0008-6533.* ; *Universidad de Puerto Rico, Facultad de Ciencias Sociales, Instituto de Estudios del Caribe*: P.O. Box 23361 University Station, Pío Piedras, Puerto Rico 00931

Cato journal. *[Cato J.] ISSN: 0273-3072.* ; *The Cato Institute*: 224 Second Street SE, Washington, DC. 20003, U.S.A.

Central banking. *[Cent. Bank.] ISSN: 0960- 6319.* ; *Central Banking Publications*: 53 Clarewood Court, Crawford Street, London, W1H 5DF, U.K.

CEPAL review. *[CEPAL R.] ISSN: 0251-2920.* ; *United Nations Economic Commission for Latin America and the Caribbean*: Casilla 179-D, Santiago, Chile; **Subscriptions**: *United Nations Publications, Sales Section*: Palais des Nations, 1211 Geneva 10, Switzerland

Challenge. *[Challenge] ISSN: 0577-5132.* ; *M.E. Sharpe*: 80 Business Park Drive, Armonk, NY. 10504, U.S.A.

CHEC journal. *[CHEC J.]*; *Commonwealth Human Ecology Council*: 57/58 Stanhope Gardens, London SW7 5RF, U.K.

China business review. *[China Bus. R.] ISSN: 0163-7169.* ; *China Business Forum*: 1818 N. Street, N.W., Washington, DC. 20036-5559, U.S.A.

China newsletter. *[China News.] ISSN: 0285- 7529.* ; *Japan External Trade Organisation (JETRO)*: Publications Department, 2-5 Toranomon 2-chome, Minato-ku, Tokyo 105, Japan

China quarterly. *[China Quart.] ISSN: 0009 4439.* ; *University of London, School of Oriental and African Studies*: Thornhaugh Street, Russell Square, London WC1H 0XG, U.K.

China reform. *[China Ref.]*; *China Development Institute*: Shenzhen, China; **Publisher**: *China Reform Publishing*: P.O. Box 20013, Hennessy Road Post Office, Hong Kong

China report. *[China R.] ISSN: 0009 4455.* ; *Sage Publications India*: 32 M-Block Market, Greater Kailash I, New Delhi 110 048, India

Chinese economic studies. *[Chin. Ec. Stud.] ISSN: 0009-4552.* ; *M.E. Sharpe*: 80 Business Park Drive, Armonk, NY. 10404, U.S.A.

Cities. *[Cities] ISSN: 0264-2751.* ; *Butterworth-Heinemann*: 88 Kingsway, London WC2 6AB, U.K.; **Subscriptions**: *Turpin Transactions*: Distribution Centre, Blackhorse Road, Letchworth, Herts. SG6 1HN, U.K.

Civilisations. *[Civilisations] ISSN: 0009-8140.* ; *Université Libre de Bruxelles, Institut de Sociologie*: 44 avenue Jeanneaterloo, 1050 Brussels, Belgium

Civitas. *[Civitas] ISSN: 0009-8191.* ; *Edizioni Civitas*: Via Tirso 92, 00198 Rome, Italy

Columbia journal of transnational law. *[Columb. J. Tr.] ISSN: 0010-1931.* ; *Columbia Journal of Transnational Law Association*: Columbia University School of Law, Box D-25, New York, NY. 10027, U.S.A.

Columbia journal of world business. *[Columb. J. W. Bus.] ISSN: 0022-5428.* ; *Columbia University, Columbia Business School*: 315 Uris Hall, Columbia University, New York, NY. 10027, U.S.A.

Columbia law review. *[Columb. Law.] ISSN: 0010-1958.* ; *Columbia Law Review Association*: 435 West 116th Street, New York, NY. 10027, U.S.A.

Common market law review. *[Common Mkt. L. R.] ISSN: 0165-0750.* ; *British Institute of International and Comparative Law/ University of Leyden, Europa Instituut*; **Publisher**: *Martinus Nijhoff Publishers*: Postbus 17, 3300 AA Dordrecht, The Netherlands

Communisme. *[Communisme] ISSN: 2209-7007.* ; *Éditions L'Age d'Homme*: 5 rue Férou, 75006 Paris, France

Communist economies. *[Comm. Econ.] ISSN: 0954-0113.* ; *Centre for Research into Communist Economies*: 2 Lord North Street, London SW1P 3LB, U.K.; **Publisher**: *Carfax Publishing*: P.O. Box 25, Abingdon, Oxfordshire OX14 3UE, U.K.

Community development journal. *[Comm. Dev. J.] ISSN: 0010-3802.* ; *Oxford University Press*: Walton Street, Oxford OX2 6DP, U.K.; **Subscriptions**: *idem*: Journals Subscription Dept., Pinkhill House, Southfield Road, Eynsham, Oxon OX8 1JJ, U.K.

Comparative and international law journal of Southern Africa. *[Comp. Int. Law J. S.Afr.] ISSN: 0010-4051.* ; *University of South Africa, Institute of Foreign and Comparative Law*: P.O. Box 392, Pretoria, South Africa

Comparative economic studies. *[Comp. Econ. Stud.] ISSN: 0888-7233.* ; *Association for Comparative Economic Studies*: Department of Economics, University of Notre Dame, Notre Dame, IN. 46556, U.S.A.

Comparative political studies. *[Comp. Poli. S.] ISSN: 0010- 4140.* ; *Sage Publications*: 2455 Teller Road, Newbury Park, CA 91320, U.S.A.; **Subscriptions**: *Sage Publications*: 6 Bonhill Street, London EC2A 4PU, U.K.

Comparative politics. *[Comp. Polit.] ISSN: 0010-4159.* ; *City University of New York*: 33 West 42nd Street, New York, NY. 10036, U.S.A.

Comparative social research. *[Comp. Soc. Res.] ISSN: 0195-6310.* ; *JAI Press*: 55 Old Post Road No. 2., Greenwich, CT. 06836, U.S.A.

Comparative studies in society and history. *[Comp. Stud. S.] ISSN: 0010- 4175.* ; *Society for the Comparative Study of Society and History*; **Publisher**: *Cambridge University Press*: 40 West 20th Street, New York, NY. 10011, U.S.A.

Computational economics. *[Comput. Econ.]; Kluwer Academic Publishers Group*: P.O. Box 322, 3300 AH Dordrecht, The Netherlands

Comunità internazionale. *[Comun. Int.] ISSN: 0010-5066.* ; *Societa Italiana per l' Organizzazione Internazionale*: Via S. Marco 3, Rome, Italy; **Publisher**: *Casa Editrice Dott. Antonio Milani*: Via Japelli 5/6, Padua, Italy

Conjuntura econômica. *[Conj. Econ.] ISSN: 0010-5945.* ; *Fundação Getulio Vargas*: Praia de Botafogo 190, Caixa Postal 9.052, ZC 02 CEP 22.250, Rio de Janeiro, Brazil

Cono sur. *[Cono Sur] ISSN: 0716-8713.* ; *Faculdad Latinoamericana de Ciencias Sociales*: Casilla 3213 Correo Central, Santiago, Chile

Conservative review. *[Conserv. R.] ISSN: 1047-5990.* ; *Council for Social and Economic Studies*: 6861 Elm Street, Suite 4H, McLean, VA. 22101, U.S.A.

Constitutional political economy. *[Constit. Pol. Econ.] ISSN: 1043-4062.* ; *Center for Study of Public Choice*: George's Hall, George Mason University, Fairfax, VA 22030- 4444, U.S.A.

Contemporary accounting research. *[Cont. Account. Res.] ISSN: 0823-9150.* ; *Canadian Academic Accounting Association= Association Canadienne des Professeurs de Comptabilité*: Faculty of Management, University of Toronto, 246 Bloor Street West, Toronto, Ontario, M5S 1V4, Canada

Contemporary economic problems. *[Cont. Ec. Probl.] ISSN: 0732 4308.* ; *American Enterprise Institute for Public Policy Research*: 1150 Seventeenth Street, N.W., Washington, DC. 20036, U.S.A.

Contemporary Pacific. *[Cont. Pac.] ISSN: 1043-898X.* ; *Center for Pacific Islands Studies*: University of Hawaii at Manoa, 1890 East-West Road, 215 Moore Hall, Honolulu, Hawaii 96822, U.S.A.; **Publisher**: *University of Hawaii Press*: 2840 Kolowalu Street, Honolulu, Hawaii 96822-1888, U.S.A.

Contemporary policy issues. *[Cont. Policy] ISSN: 0735-0007.* ; *Western Economic Association International*: 7400 Center Avenue, Suite 109, Huntington Beach, CA. 92647-3039, U.S.A.

Contemporary Southeast Asia. *[Cont. S.E. Asia] ISSN: 0129-797X.* ; *Institute of Southeast Asian Studies*: Heng Mui Keng Terrace, Pasir Panjang, Singapore 0511

Continuity and change. *[Contin. Change] ISSN: 0268-4160.* ; *Cambridge University Press*: The Edinburgh Building, Shaftesbury Road, Cambridge CB2 2RU, U.K.

Contributions to political economy. *[Contrib. Pol. Econ.] ISSN: 0277-5921.* ; *Academic Press*: 24-28 Oval Road, London NW1 7DX, U.K.

Cooperation and conflict. *[Coop. Conflict] ISSN: 0010-8367.* ; *Nordic Cooperation Committee for International Politics*; **Publisher**: *Universitetsforlaget (Norwegian University Press)*: Box 2959-Tøyen, 0608 Oslo 6, Norway

Corruption and reform. *[Corr. Reform] ISSN: 0169-7528.* ; *Martinus Nijhoff Publishers*: P.O. Box 322, 3300 AH Dordrecht, The Netherlands

Coyuntura económica. *[Coy. Econ.] ISSN: 0120-3576.* ; *Fundación para la Educación Superior y el Desarrollo (FEDESARROLLO)*: Calle 78 No. 9-91, Apartado Aéreo 78504, Bogotá, Colombia

Critica marxista. *[Crit. Marx.] ISSN: 0011-152X.* ; *Editori Riuniti Riviste*: via Serchio 9, 00198 Rome, Italy

Critica sociologica. *[Crit. Sociol.] ISSN: 0011 1546.* ; *S.I.A.R.E.S.*: Corso Vittorio Emanuele 24, 00186 Rome, Italy

Critical perspectives on accounting. *[Crit. Persp. Acc.] ISSN: 1045-2354.* ; *Academic Press*: 24-28 Oval Road, London NW1 7DX, U.K.

Critical review. *[Crit. Rev.] ISSN: 0891-3811.* ; *Center for Independent Thought*: 942 Howard Street, Room 109, San Francisco, CA 94103, U.S.A.; **Publisher**: *Critical Review*: P.O. Box 14528, Chicago IL. 60614, U.S.A.

Cuadernos americanos. *[Cuad. Am.] ISSN: 0185-156X.* ; *Universidad Nacional Autónoma de México*: Ciudad Universitaria, 04510 México, D.F., Apartado Postal 965, México 1.

Cuadernos de nuestra América. *[Cuad. Nues. Am.]*; *Centro de Estudios Sobre America*: Ave. 3ra no. 1805e/ 18 y 20, Playa Zona Postal 13, Havana, Cuba

Current history. *[Curr. Hist.] ISSN: 0011-3530.* ; *Current History*: Publications Office, 4225 Main Street, Philadelphia, PA. 19127, U.S.A.

Current world leaders. *[Curr. World Lead.] ISSN: 0192-6802.* ; *International Academy*: 800 Garden Street, Suite D, Santa Barbara, CA. 93101, U.S.A.

Cyprus journal of economics. *[Cyprus J. Econ.] ISSN: 1013-3224.* ; *Cyprus Economic Society*: P.O. Box 4010, Nicosia, Cyprus

Cyprus review. *[Cyprus Rev.] ISSN: 1015-2881.* ; *Intercollege/ University of Indianapolis*: P.O. Box 4005, 17 Heroes Avenue, Ayios Andreas, Nicosia, Cyprus/ 1400 Hanna Avenue, Indianapolis, IN. 46227-3687, U.S.A.

Czechoslovak economic papers. *[Czec. Ec. Pap.] ISSN: 0590- 5001.* ; *Academia, Publishing House of the Czechoslovak Academy of Sciences*: Vodičkova 40, 112 29 Prague 1, Czechoslovakia

Debates de coyuntura económica. *[Deb. Coy. Econ.] ISSN: 0120-8969.* ; *FEDESARROLLO*: Calle 78 No. 9-91, Apartado Aéreo 75074, Bogotá, Colombia

Defence economics. *[Def. Econ.] ISSN: 1043-0717.* ; *Harwood Academic Publishers*: c/o STBS, P.O. Box 90, Reading, Berkshire RG1 8JL, U.K.

Desarrollo económico. *[Desar. Econ.] ISSN: 0046-001X.* ; *Instituto de Desarrollo Económico y Social*: Aráoz 2838, 1425 Buenos Aires, Argentina

Desarrollo y sociedad. *[Desar. Soc.] ISSN: 0120- 3584.* ; *Universidad de los Andes, Facultad de Economía, Centro de Estudios Sobre Desarrollo Económico*: Carrera 1E no. 18/A-10, Apartado Aereo 4976, Bogota D.E., Colombia

Deutschland Archiv.:*Zeitschrift für das vereinigte Deutschland [Deut. Arch.] ISSN: 0012-1428.* ; *Verlag Wissenschaft und Politik*: Salierring 14-16, 5000 Cologne, Germany

Developing economies. *[Develop. Eco.] ISSN: 0012-1533.* ; *Institute of Developing Economies*: 42 Ichigaya-Hommura-chō, Shinjuku-ku, Tokyo 162, Japan; **Subscriptions**: *Maruzen*: P.O. Box 5050, Tokyo 100-31, Japan

Development. *[Development] ISSN: 1011-6370.* ; *Society for International Development*: Palazzo della Civiltà del Lavoro, Rome 00144, Italy

Development & socio-economic progress. *[Devel. & Socio-eco. Pro.]*; *Afro-Asian Peoples' Solidarity Organisation (AAPSO)*: 89 Abdel Aziz Al-Saoud Street, 11451- 61 Manial El-Roda, Cairo, Egypt

Development and change. *[Develop. Cha.] ISSN: 0012-155X.* ; *Sage Publications*: 6 Bonhill Street, London EC2A 4PU, U.K.

Development dialogue. *[Dev. Dialog.] ISSN: 0345-2328.* ; *Dag Hammarskjöld Foundation*: Övre Slottsgatan 2, S-75220 Uppsala, Sweden

Development policy review. *[Dev. Pol. R.] ISSN: 0950-6764.* ; *Overseas Development Institute*: Regent's College, Inner Circle, Regent's Park, London NW1 4NS, U.K.; **Publisher**: *Sage Publications*: 6 Bonhill Street, London EC2A 4PU, U.K.

Development Southern Africa. *[Develop. S. Afr.] ISSN: 0376-835X.* ; *Development Bank of Southern Africa*: P.O. Box 1234, Halfway House, 1685 South Africa

Diachronica. *[Diachronica] ISSN: 0176-4225.* ; *John Benjamins Publishing*: Amsteldijk 44, P.O. Box 52519, NL-1007 HA Amsterdam, The Netherlands

Dirasat.:*Series A — the humanities [Dirasat Ser. A.] ISSN: 0255-8033.* ; *Deanship of Academic Research*: University of Jordan, Amman, Jordan

Disasters.:*Journal of disaster studies and management [Disasters] ISSN: 0361-3666.* ; *Basil Blackwell*: 108 Cowley Road, Oxford OX4 1JF, U.K.

Documents. *[Documents] ISSN: 0151- 0827.* ; *Documents*: 50 rue de Laborde, 75008 Paris, France; **Subscriptions**: *idem*: 21 rue du Faubourg-Saint-Antoine, 75011 Paris, France

Droit et pratique du commerce international. *[Dr. Prat. Commer. Int.]*; *Masson*: 120 Saint-Germain, 75006 Paris, France

Droit social. *[Droit Soc.] ISSN: 0012-6438.* ; *Éditions Techniques et Économiques*: 3, rue Soufflot, 75005 Paris, France

E & S.:*Economie et statistique [E & S] ISSN: 0336-1451.* ; *Institut national de la statistique et des études économiques*: 18 boulevard A. Pinard, 75675 Paris Cedex 14, France

East Asian review. *[E.Asian R.]*; *Institute for East Asian Studies*: 508-142 Jungnung 2-dong, Sungbuk-Ku, Seoul 136-102, Korea

East European politics and societies. *[E.Eur. Pol. Soc.] ISSN: 0888-3254.* ; *University of California*: Berkeley, CA. 94720, U.S.A.

East European quarterly. *[E. Eur. Quart.] ISSN: 0012-8449.* ; *University of Colorado*: 1200 University Avenue, Boulder, CO. 80309, U.S.A.

Eastern Africa economic review. *[E. Afr. Econ. Rev.]* *ISSN: 0012-866X.* ; *Kenyan Economic Association*: Economics Department, University of Nairobi, P.O. Box 30197, Nairobi, Kenya

Eastern Africa social science research review. *[E.Afr. Soc. Sci. Res. R.]*; *Organization for Social Science Research in Eastern Africa - OSSREA*: P.O. Box 31971, Addis Ababa, Ethiopia

Eastern Buddhist. *[East. Bud.]*; *Eastern Buddhist Society*: Otani University, Koyama, Kita-ku, Kyoto 603, Japan

Ecological economics. *[Ecol. Eco.]* *ISSN: 0921-8009.* ; *International Society for Ecological Economics*; **Publisher**: *Elsevier Science Publishers*: P.O. Box 211, 1000 AE Amsterdam, The Netherlands

Econometric reviews. *[Econom. R.]* *ISSN: 0740-4938.* ; *Marcel Dekker*: 270 Madison Avenue, New York, NY. 10016, U.S.A.

Econometric theory. *[Economet. Th.]* *ISSN: 0266-4666.* ; *Cambridge University Press*: 40 West 20th Street, New York, NY. 10011, U.S.A.

Econometrica. *[Econometrica]* *ISSN: 0012-9682.* ; *Econometric Society*: Department of Economics, Northwestern University, Evanston, IL. 60208-2400, U.S.A.; **Subscriptions**: *Basil Blackwell*: c/o Marston Book Services, P.O. Box 87, Oxford OX2 0DT, U.K.

Economia & lavoro. *[Ec. Lav.]* *ISSN: 0012-978X.* ; *Fondazione Giacomo Brodolini*: via Torino 122, 00184 Rome, Italy; **Publisher**: *Marsilio Editori*: Marittima — Fabbricato 205, 30135, Venice, Italy

Economia e banca. *[Econ. Ban.]* *ISSN: 0393-9243.* ; *Banca di Trento e Bolzano*: Via Mantova 19, 38100 Trento, Italy

Economia internazionale. *[Econ. Int.]* *ISSN: 0012-981X.* ; *Istituto di Economia Internazionale*: Via Garibaldi 4, 16124 Genoa, Italy

Economia [Lisbon]. *[Economia [Lisbon]]* *ISSN: 0870-3531.* ; *Universidade Católica Portuguesa, Faculdade de Ciências Económicas e Empresariais*: Caminho da Palma de Cima, 1600 Lisbon, Portugal

Economia [Quito]. *[Economia [Quito]]* *ISSN: 0012-9704.* ; *Universidad Central del Ecuador, Instituto de Investigaciones Economicas*: Apartado 1088, Quito, Ecuador

Economia y desarrollo. *[Econ. Desar.]* *ISSN: 0252- 8584.* ; *Universidad de la Habana, Facultad de Economia*: Calle O No.262 e/ 25 y 27, Vedado, Havana 4, Cuba

Economic affairs [Calcutta]. *[Econ. Aff. [Calcutta]]* *ISSN: 0424-2513.* ; *Himansu Roy*: BC144, Sector 1, Salt Lake City, Calcutta 700064, India

Economic affairs [London]. *[Econ. Affr.]* *ISSN: 0265-0665.* ; *Institute of Economic Affairs*: 2 Lord North Street, London, SW1P 3LB, U.K.; **Publisher**: *City Publications*: 3-4 St. Andrew's Hill, London EC4V 5BY, U.K.; **Subscriptions**: *Economic Affairs*: Magazine Subscription Department, Freepost, Luton LU1 5BR, U.K.

Economic and industrial democracy. *[Econ. Ind. Dem.]* *ISSN: 0143-831X.* ; *Arbetslivscentrum (The Swedish Center for Working Life)*: Box 5606, S-114 86 Stockholm, Sweden; **Publisher**: *Sage Publications*: 6 Bonhill Street, London EC2A 4PU, U.K.

Economic and social history in the Netherlands. *[Econ. Soc. Hist. Nether.]* *ISSN: 0925-1669.* ; *Nederlandsch Economisch-Historisch Archief = Netherlands Economic History Archive*: Cruquiusweg 31, 1019 AT Amsterdam, The Netherlands

Economic and social review. *[Econ. Soc. R.]* *ISSN: 0012-9984.* ; *Economic and Social Studies*: 4 Burlington Road, Dublin 4, Ireland

Economic bulletin. *[Econ. Bull.]* *ISSN: 0013-0036.* ; *Commerical Bank of Greece*: 11, Sophocleous Street, 102 35 Athens, Greece

Economic bulletin for Asia and the Pacific. *[Econ. B. Asia Pac.]* *ISSN: 0378-455X.* ; *Economic and Social Commission for Asia and Pacific*: Bangkok, Thailand

Economic bulletin. Banca d'italia. *[Ec. Bul. Ban. It.]*; *Banca d'Italia*: Via Nazionale 91, Rome, Italy

Economic bulletin. National Bank of Egypt. *[Econ. B. Nat. Bank of Egypt]*; *National Bank of Egypt, Research Department*: Cairo, Egypt

Economic bulletin. Norges bank. *[Econ. B. Norges Bank.]* *ISSN: 0029-1676.* ; *Norges Bank*: Information Section, P.O. Box 1179 Sentrum, N-0107 Oslo 1, Norway

Economic computation and economic cybernetics studies and research. *[Econ. Comp. Cyber. S.]* *ISSN: 0424-267X.* ; *Academy of Economic Studies*: Bucharest, Romania

Economic development and cultural change. *[Econ. Dev. Cult. Change]* *ISSN: 0013-0079.* ; *University of Chicago Press*: Journals Division, 5720 S. Woodlawn, Chicago, IL. 60637, U.S.A.

Economic development quarterly. *[Econ. Devel. Q.]* *ISSN: 0891-2424.* ; *Sage Publications*: 2455 Teller Road, Newbury Park, CA. 91320, U.S.A.

Economic eye. *[Econ. Eye]* *ISSN: 0389- 0503.* ; *Keizai Koho Center = Japan Institute for Social and Economic Affairs*: Otemachi Building 6-1, Otemache 1-chome, Chiyoda-ku, Tokyo 100, Japan

Economic geography. *[Econ. Geogr.]* *ISSN: 0013-0095.* ; *Clark University*: Worcester, MA. 01610, U.S.A.; **Publisher**: *Commonwealth Press*: 44 Portland Street, Worcester, MA., U.S.A.

Economic history review. *[Econ. Hist. R.] ISSN: 0013-0117.* ; *Economic History Society*: P.O. Box 190, 1 Greville Road, Cambridge CB1 3QG, U.K.; **Publisher**: *Basil Blackwell*: 108 Cowley Road, Oxford OX4 1JF, U.K.

Economic inquiry. *[Econ. Inq.] ISSN: 0095-2583.* ; *Western Economic Association International*: 7400 Center Avenue, Suite 109, Huntington Beach, CA. 92647-3039, U.S.A.; **Subscriptions**: *idem:* Subscription Services, P.O. Box 368, Lawrence, KS. 66044-0368, U.S.A.

Economic journal. *[Econ. J.] ISSN: 0013-0133.* ; *Royal Economic Society*: Imperial College of Science and Technology, London SW7 2AZ, U.K.; **Publisher**: *Basil Blackwell*: 108 Cowley Road, Oxford OX4 1JF, U.K.

Economic modelling. *[Econ. Model.] ISSN: 0264-9993.* ; *Butterworth-Heinemann*: P.O. Box 63, Westbury House, Bury Street, Guildford, Surrey GU25 BH, U.K.

Economic notes. *[Eco. Notes] ISSN: 0391- 5026.* ; *Monte dei Paschi di Siena*: Piazza Salimbeni 3, 53100 Siena, Italy

Economic papers [Warsaw]. *[Econ. Papers [Warsaw]] ISSN: 0324-864X.* ; *Central School of Planning and Statistics in Warsaw, Research Institute for Developing Countries*: Al. Niepodległości 167, 02-521 Warsaw, Poland

Economic papers. [Australia]. *[Ec. Pap. Aust.];* *Economic Society of Australia*: 23 Wallis Avenue, East Ivanhoe, Victoria 3079, Australia

Economic policy. *[Econ. Pol.] ISSN: 0266-4658.* ; *Centre of Economic Policy Research/ École des Hautes Études en Sciences Sociales*; **Publisher**: *Cambridge University Press/ Editions de la Maison des Sciences de l'Homme*: The Edinburgh Building, Shaftesbury Road, Cambridge CB2 2RU, U.K./ 54 boulevard Raspail, 75270 Paris, France

Economic quarterly; Wissenschaftliche beiträge. *[Econ. Q.] ISSN: 0232-4660.* ; *University of Economic Science, Institute for the Economic of Developing Countries*: Hermann-Duncker Straße 8, Berlin 1157, Germany

Economic record. *[Econ. Rec.] ISSN: 0013-0249.* ; *Economic Society of Australia*: c/o A.D. Woodland, Department of Econometrics, Sydney University, Sydney, N.S.W. 2006, Australia

Economic review. *[Econ. Rev.] ISSN: 0022-8419.* ; *Kansallis-Osake-Pankki*: Room R351, P.O. Box 4, SF-00101 Helsinki, Finland

Economic review. Bank of Israel. *[Econ. Rev. Bank Israel] ISSN: 0334-441X.* ; *Bank of Israel, Research Department*: Kiryat Ben-Gurion, P.O.B. 780, Jerusalem 91007, Israel

Economic review. Federal Reserve Bank of Cleveland. *[Ec. Rev. Fed. Res. Bank Cleveland] ISSN: 0013-0281.* ; *Federal Reserve Bank of Cleveland, Research Department*: P.O. Box 6387, Cleveland, OH. 44101, U.S.A.

Economic review. Federal Reserve Bank of Kansas City. *[Eco. R. Fed. Bank Kansas] ISSN: 0161-2387.* ; *Federal Reserve Bank of Kansas City*: 925 Grand Avenue, Kansas City, MO. 64198-0001, U.S.A.

Economic studies quarterly. *[Econ. S. Quart.] ISSN: 0557-109X.* ; *Japan Association of Economics and Econometrics*: The Institute of Statistical Research, 1-18-16 Shimbashi, Minato-ku, Tokyo, Japan 105; **Subscriptions**: *Toyo Keizai*: Books Department 1-2-1 Hongoku-cho, Nihonbashi, Chuoku, Tokyo, Japan 103

Economic systems. *[Econ. Sys.] ISSN: 0939-3625.* ; *Osteuropa-Institut München*: Scheinerstr. 11, D-8000 Munich 80, Germany; **Publisher**: *Physica-Verlag*: Tiergartenstraße 17, 6900 Heidelberg, Germany

Economic systems research. *[Econ. Sys. Res.] ISSN: 0953-5314.* ; *International Input-Output Association*: P.O. Box 40, A-3402 Klosterneuberg, Austria; **Publisher**: *Carfax Publishing*: P.O. Box 25, Abingdon, Oxfordshire OX14 3UE, U.K.

Economic theory. *[Econ. Theory] ISSN: 0938-2259.* ; *Springer-Verlag*: Heidelberger Platz 3, 1000 Berlin 33, Germany

Economica. *[Economica] ISSN: 0013-0427.* ; *London School of Economics and Political Science*: Houghton Street, London WC2A 2AE, U.K.; **Publisher**: *Basil Blackwell*: 108 Cowley Road, Oxford OX4 1JF, U.K.

Economics. *[Economics] ISSN: 0300-4287.* ; *Economics Association*: Maxwelton House, 41-3 Boltro Road, Haywards Heath, West Sussex RH16 1BJ, U.K.

Economics and philosophy. *[Econ. Philos.] ISSN: 0266-2671.* ; *Cambridge University Press*: 40 West 20th Street, New York, NY 10011, U.S.A.

Economics and politics. *[Econ. Polit.] ISSN: 0954-1985.* ; *Basil Blackwell*: 108 Cowley Road, Oxford OX4 1JF, U.K.

Economics letters. *[Econ. Lett.] ISSN: 0165-1765.* ; *Elsevier Science Publishers (North-Holland)*: P.O. Box 1991, BZ Amsterdam, The Netherlands

Economics of planning. *[Econ. Plan.] ISSN: 0013- 0451.* ; *Kluwer Academic Publishers*: P.O. Box 322, 3300 AH Dordrecht, The Netherlands

Economie & finances agricoles.*[E&FA]— [Econ. Fin. Agr.] ISSN: 0070-8798.* ; *Caisse nationale de crédit agricole*: 91-93 Boulevard Pasteur, 75015 Paris, France

Economie appliquée. *[Econ. App.] ISSN: 0013-0494.* ; *Institut de Sciences Mathematiques et Économiques Appliquées*: 11 rue Pierre et Marie Curie, 75005 Paris, France; **Publisher**: *Presses Universitaires de Grenoble*: B.P. 47 X, 38 040 Grenoble Cedex, France

Economie du centre-est. *[Econ. Cen.E.] ISSN: 0153-4459.* ; *Institut d'Économie Régionale Bourgogne-Franche-Comte*: 4 boulevard Gabriel, 21000 Dijon, France; **Publisher**: *Dijon Presses de l'Université de Bourgogne*

Économie prospective internationale. *[Ec. Pros. Int.] ISSN: 0242-7818.* ; *Centre d'Études Prospectives et d'Informations Internationales*: 9 rue Georges-Pitard, 75015 Paris, France

Economies et sociétés. *[Ec. Sociét.] ISSN: 0013-0567.* ; *I.S.M.E.A.*: 11, rue Pierre-et-Marie Curie, 75005 Paris, France; **Publisher**: *Presses Universitaires de Grenoble (PUG)*: B.P. 47 X, 38040 Grenoble Cedex, France

Economisch en sociaal tijdschrift. *[Econ. Soc. Tidj.] ISSN: 0013-0575.* ; *Universtaire Faculteiten Sint-Ignatius te Antwerpen*: Kipdorp 19, 2000 Antwerp, Belgium

Economist [Leiden]. *[Economist [Leiden]] ISSN: 0013-063X.* ; *Royal Netherlands Economic Association*; **Publisher**: *Stenfert Kroese Uitgevers*: P.O. Box 33, 2300 AA Leiden, The Netherlands

Economy and society. *[Econ. Soc.] ISSN: 0308-5147.* ; *Routledge*: 11 New Fetter Lane, London EC4P 4EE, U.K.

Ecu. *[Ecu]*; *Editions Ecu-Activities*: Clos Manuel 3, 1150 Brussels, Belgium

Einheit. *[Einheit] ISSN: 0013-2659.* ; *Sozialistische Einheitspartei Deutschlands, Zentralkomitee*; **Publisher**: *Dietz Verlag*: Postschließfach 273, Berlin 1020, Germany

Ekonomický časopis. *[Ekon. Cas.] ISSN: 0013-3035.* ; *Veda*: Klemensova 19, 814 30 Bratislava, Czechoslovakia; **Subscriptions**: *Kubon und Sagner*: Postfach 34 01 08, D- 8000 München 34, Germany

Ekonomisk debatt. *[Ekon. Deb.] ISSN: 0345-2646.* ; *Nationalekonomiska föreningen*: Box 16408, 10327 Stockholm, Sweden

Ekonomski pregled. *[Ekon. Preg.] ISSN: 0424-7558.* ; *Savez Ekonimista Hrvatske*: Berislaviceva 6, Zagreb, Yugoslavia

Employee relations. *[Employ. Relat.] ISSN: 0142-5455.* ; *MCB University Press*: 62 Toller Lane, Bradford, West Yorkshire, BD8 9BY, U.K.

Energy economics. *[Ener. Econ.] ISSN: 0140-9883.* ; *Butterworth-Heinemann*: Linacre House, Jordon Hill, Oxford OX2 8DP, U.K.

Energy policy. *[Energy Pol.] ISSN: 0301-4215.* ; *Butterworth-Heinemann*: P.O. Box 63, Westbury House, Bury Street, Guildford, Surrey GU2 5BH, U.K.; **Subscriptions**: *Turpin Transactions*: Distribution Centre, Blackhorse Road, Letchworth, Herts. SG6 1HN, U.K.

Ensayos sobre política económica. *[Ensayos Polit. Eco.] ISSN: 0120-4483.* ; *Banco de la República, Departamento de Investigaciones Económicas*: Departamento Editorial, Calle 13 No. 35-51, Bogotá, Colombia

Environment and planning A.:*International journal of urban and regional research [Envir. Plan.A.] ISSN: 0308-518X.* ; *Pion*: 207 Brondesbury Park, London NW2 5JN, U.K.

Environment and planning B.:*Planning and design [Envir. Plan. B.] ISSN: 0265-8135.* ; *Pion*: 207 Brondesbury Park, London NW2 5JN, U.K.

Environment and planning C.:*Government and policy [Envir. Plan. C.] ISSN: 0263 774X.* ; *Pion*: 207 Brondesbury Park, London NW2 5JN, U.K.

Environment and planning D.:*Society and space [Envir. Plan. D] ISSN: 0263-7758.* ; *Pion*: 207 Brondesbury Park, London, NW2 5JN, U.K

Environment and urbanization. *[Environ. Urban.] ISSN: 0956-2478.* ; *International Insitute for Environment and Development*: 3 Endsleigh Street, London, WC1H 0DD, U.K.

Environmental & resource economics. *[Environ. Resour. Econ.] ISSN: 0924- 6460.* ; *Kluwer Academic Publishers*: P.O. Box 322, 3300 AH Dordrecht, The Netherlands

Environmental law. *[Environ. Law] ISSN: 0046-2276.* ; *Northwestern School of Law of Lewis and Clark College*: 10015 S.W. Terwillige Boulevard, Portland, OR. 97219, U.S.A.

Экономист; Ekonomist. *[Ekonomist] ISSN: 0370-0356.* ; *Ministerstvo ekonomiki i prognozirovaniia SSR*; **Publisher**: *Izdatel'stvo Ekonomika*: Berezhovskaia naberezhnaia 6, 121864 Moscow, U.S.S.R.

Espace géographique. *[Espace Géogr.] ISSN: 0046- 2497.* ; *Doin editeurs*: 8 place de l'Odéon, 75006 Paris, France

Estadistica. *[Estadistica] ISSN: 0014-1135.* ; *Instituto Interamericano de Estadistica = Inter-American Statistical Institute*: Apartado 5139, Panama 5, Panama

Estrategia económica y financiera. *[Estrat. Econ. Finan.]*; *Estrategia Económica y Financiera*: Calle 18 No. 3-82, Piso 20, Bogotá, Colombia

Estudios de Asia y Africa. *[Est. Asia Afr.] ISSN: 0185-0164.* ; *El Colegio de México*: Camino al Ajusco 20, Pedregal de Santa Teresa, 10740 México D.F., México

Estudios económicos. *[Est. Econ.]*; *Colegio de México*: Departamento de Publicaciones, Camino al Ajusco 20, 10740 Mexico City, Mexico

Estudios internacionales. *[Est. Inter.] ISSN: 0716-0240.* ; *Universidad de Chile, Instituto de Estudios Internacionales*: Condell 249, Casilla 14187 Suc 21, Santiago 9, Chile

Ethics. *[Ethics] ISSN: 0014-1704.* ; *University of Chicago Press*: Journals Division, 5720 S. Woodlawn Avenue, Chicago, IL. 60637, U.S.A.

Etnografija juznih Slavena ų Madarskoj. *[Etnogr. Juz. Slav. Mad]*

Etudes internationales. *[Et. Int.] ISSN: 0014-2123.* ; *Centre québécois de relations internationales*: Faculté des sciences sociales, Université Laval, Québec, G1K 7P4 Canada

Etudes sociales. *[Etud. Soc.]; Société d'Ecomonie et de Science Sociales*: 80 rue Vaneau, 75007 Paris, France

Euromoney. *[Euromoney] ISSN: 0014-2433.* ; *Euromoney Publications*: Nestor House, Playhouse Yard, London EC4V 5EX, U.K.

Europa Archiv. *[Eur. Arch.] ISSN: 0014-2476.* ; *Deutsche Gesellschaft für Auswärtige Politik*: Adenauerallee 131, D 5300 Bonn 1, Germany; **Publisher**: *Verlag für Internationale Politik*: Bachstraße 32, Postfach 1529, 5300 Bonn 1, Germany

European accounting review. *[Eur. Account. Rev.] ISSN: 0963-8180.* ; *European Accounting Association*: C/o EIASM, rue D'Egmont-Straat 13, B-1050 Brussels, Belgium; **Publisher**: *Routledge*: 11 New Fetter Lane, London, EC4P 4EE, U.K.

European affairs. *[Eur. Aff.] ISSN: 0921-5778.* ; *Elsevier-Bonaventura*: P.O. Box 152, 1000 AD Amsterdam, The Netherlands

European business and economic development. *[Eur. Bus. Econ. Develop.] ISSN: 0966-8004.* ; *European Research Press*: Tayson House, 34-38 Chapel Street, Little Germany, Bradford BD1 5DN, U.K.

European economic review. *[Eur. Econ. R.] ISSN: 0014-2921.* ; *European Economic Association*: 34 Voie du Roman Pays, B-1348 Louvain-la-Neuve, Belgium; **Publisher**: *Elsevier Science Publishers*: P.O. Box 1991, 1000 BZ Amsterdam, The Netherlands; **Subscriptions**: *idem*: Journal Division, P.O. Box 211, 1000 AE Amsterdam, The Netherlands

European journal of operational research. *[Eur. J. Oper. Res.] ISSN: 0377-2217.* ; *Association of European Operational Research Societies*; **Publisher**: *Elsevier Science Publishers (North-Holland)*: P.O. Box 1991, 1000 BZ Amsterdam, The Netherlands

European journal of political economy. *[Eur. J. Pol. Ec.] ISSN: 0176-2680.* ; *Elsevier Science Publishers (North-Holland)*: P.O. Box 1991, 1000 BZ Amsterdam, The Netherlands

European journal of population; Revue européenne de démographie. *[Eur. J. Pop.] ISSN: 0168-6577.* ; *Elsevier Science Publishers (North Holland)*: P.O. Box 1991, 1000 BZ Amsterdam, The Netherlands

European research. *[Eur. Res.] ISSN: 0958-9082.* ; *European Research Press*: P.O. Box 75, Shipley, West Yorkshire, BD17 6EZ, U.K.

European review of agricultural economics. *[Eur. R. Agr. Eco.] ISSN: 0165-1587.* ; *Mouton de Gruyter*: Postfach 110240, D-1000 Berlin 11, Germany

European review of Latin American and Caribbean studies; Revista europea de estudios latinoamericanos y del caribe. *[R. Eur. Lat.am. Caribe] ISSN: 0924-0608.* ; *CEDLA, Interuniversitair Centrum voor Studie en Documentatie van Latijns Amerika/ RILA, Royal Institute of Linguistics and Anthropology*: Keizersgracht 395-397, 1016 Amsterdam, The Netherlands; **Publisher**: *CEDLA Edita*: Keizersgracht 395-397, 1016 Amsterdam, The Netherlands

European sociological review. *[Eur. Sociol. R.] ISSN: 0266-7215.* ; *Oxford University Press*: Pinkhill House, Southfield Road, Eynsham, Oxford OX8 1JJ, U.K.

Europe-Asia studies. *[Eur.-Asia Stud.] ISSN: 0038- 5859.* ; *Carfax Publishing*: P.O. Box 25, Abingdon, Oxfordshire OX14 3UE, U.K.

Explorations in economic history. *[Expl. Ec. His.] ISSN: 0014-4983.* ; *Academic Press*: Journal Division, 1 East First Street, Duluth, MN. 55802, U.S.A.

Federal Reserve bulletin. *[Fed. Resv. B.] ISSN: 0014-9209.* ; *Board of Governors of the Federal Reserve System*: Publications Services, Mail Stop 138, Board of Governors of the Federal Reserve System, Washington, DC. 20551, U.S.A.

Federalist. *[Federalist] ISSN: 0393-1358.* ; *Fondazione Europea Luciano Bolis*; **Publisher**: *EDIF*: Via Porta Pertusi 6, 27100 Pavia, Italy

Financial analysts journal. *[Finan. Anal. J.] ISSN: 0015-198X.* ; *Association for Investment Management and Research*: P.O. Box 3668, Charlottesville, VA. 22903, U.S.A.

Financial management. *[Finan. Manag.] ISSN: 0046-3892.* ; *Financial Management Association*: College of Business Administration, University of South Florida, Tampa, FL. 33620, U.S.A.

Financial news analysis. *[Finan. News Anal.]; Africa Centre for Monetary Studies*: B.P. 1791 Dakar, Senegal

Finanse. *[Finanse] ISSN: 0430- 4896.* ; *Państwowe Wydawnictwo Ekonomiczne*: Niecala 4a, 00-098 Warsaw, Poland

Финансы СССР; Finansy SSSR. *[Finansy] ISSN: 0130-576X.* ; *Izdatel'stvo Finansy, Statistika for Ministerstvo Finansov SSSR*: Moscow, U.S.S.R.

Finanzarchiv. *[Finanzarchiv] ISSN: 0015-2218.* ; *J.C.B. Mohr (Paul Siebeck)*: Postfach 2040, 7400 Tübingen, Germany

Fiscal studies. *[Fis. Stud.] ISSN: 0143-5671.* ; *Institute for Fiscal Studies*: 180/182 Tottenham Court Road, London W1P 9LE, U.K.

Food and foodways. *[Food Food.]* *ISSN: 0740-9710.* ; *Harwood Academic Publishers*: 270 Eighth Avenue, New York, NY.10011, U.S.A.; **Subscriptions**: *idem*: c/o STBS Limited, P.O. Box 90, Reading, Berks, RG1 8JL, U.K.

Foreign affairs. *[Foreign Aff.]* *ISSN: 0015-7120.* ; *Council on Foreign Relations*: 58 East 68th Street, New York, N.Y. 10021, U.S.A.; **Subscriptions**: *idem*: P.O. Box 53678, Boulder, CO. 80322-3678, U.S.A.

Foreign policy. *[Foreign Pol.]* *ISSN: 0015-7228.* ; *Carnegie Endowment for International Peace*: 2400 N. Street, N.W., Washington, DC. 20037-1196, U.S.A.

Foreign trade review. *[For. Tr. R.]*; *Indian Institute of Foreign Trade*: B-21 Mehrauli Institutional Area, New Delhi 110016, India

Formation emploi. *[Form. Emp.]* *ISSN: 0759-6340.* ; *Documentation Française*: 29-31 quai Voltaire, 75340 Paris Cedex 07, France; **Subscriptions**: *La Documentation Française*: 124 rue Henri Barbusse, 93308 Aubervilliers Cedex, France

Foro internacional. *[Foro Int.]* *ISSN: 0185-013X.* ; *El Colegio de México*: Departamento de Publicaciones, Camino al Ajusco 20, Pedregal de Santa Teresa, 10740 México D.F., Mexico

Free China review. *[Free China R.]* *ISSN: 0016- 030X.* ; *Kwang Hwa Publishing*: 2 Tientsin Street, Taipei, Taiwan

Games and economic behavior. *[Gam. Econ. Behav.]* *ISSN: 0899- 8256.* ; *Academic Press*: 6277 Sea Harbor Drive, Orlando, FL. 32887-4900, U.S.A.

Genèses. *[Genèses]* *ISSN: 1135-3219.* ; *Calman-Lévy*: 16, villa Saint- Jacques, 75014 Paris, France

Geneva papers on risk and insurance theory. *[Geneva Pap. Risk Insur. Theory]* *ISSN: 0926-4957.* ; *Association de Genève*: 18, chemin Rieu, 1208 Geneva, Switzerland; **Publisher**: *Kluwer Academic Publishers*: P.O. Box 322, 3300 AH Dordrecht, The Netherlands

Genève-Afrique. *[Genève-Afrique]* *ISSN: 0016-6774.* ; *Institut Universitaire d'Études du Développement (IUED)*: Case postale 136, CH-1211 Geneva 21, Switzerland

Genus. *[Genus]* *ISSN: 0016-6987.* ; *Comitato Italiano per lo Studio dei Problemi della Popolazione*: Via Nomentana 41, 00161 Rome, Italy; **Subscriptions**: *Edizioni Scientifiche Inglesi Americane*: Via Palestro 30, 00185 Rome, Italy

Geoforum. *[Geoforum]* *ISSN: 0016-7185.* ; *Pergamon Press*: Headington Hill Hall, Oxford OX3 0BW, U.K.

Geographia polonica. *[Geogr. Pol.]* *ISSN: 0016-7282.* ; *Polish Academy of Sciences, Institute of Geography and Spatial Organization*; **Publisher**: *Polish Scientific Publishers*: Krakowskie Przedmieście 7, 00-068 Warsaw, Poland

Geographical analysis. *[Geogr. Anal.]* *ISSN: 0016-7363.* ; *Ohio State University Press*: 1070 Carmack Road, Columbus, OH. 43210, U.S.A.

Geographical journal. *[Geogr. J.]* *ISSN: 0016-7398.* ; *Royal Geographical Society*: 1 Kensington Gore, London SW7 2AR, U.K.

Geographische Rundschau. *[Geogr. Rund.]* *ISSN: 0016-7460.* ; *Westermann Schulbuchverlag*: Georg-Westermann-Allee 66, 3300 Braunschweig, Germany

Geography. *[Geography]*; *Geographical Association*: 343 Fulwood Road, Sheffield S10 3PB, U.K.

George Washington journal of international law and economics. *[Geo. Wash. J. Inter. Eco.]* *ISSN: 0748-4305.* ; *George Washington University, National Law Center*: Washington, D.C. 20052, U.S.A.

German politics. *[Ger. Pol.]* *ISSN: 0964-4008.* ; *Frank Cass*: Gainsborough House, 11 Gainsborough Road, London, E11 1RS, U.K.

Gestion 2000.:*Management et prospective [Gestion]* *ISSN: 0773-0543.* ; *Université Catholique de Louvain, Institut d'administration et de gestion*: 16 avenue de l'Espinette, B-1348 Louvain-la- Neuve, Belgium

Gewerkschaftliche Monatshefte. *[Gewerk. Monat.]* *ISSN: 0016-9447.* ; *Bundesvorstand des DGB*: Hans-Böckler-Straße 39, 4000 Düsseldorf 30, Germany; **Publisher**: *Bund-Verlag*: Postfach 900840, 5000 Cologne 90, Germany

Giornale degli economisti e annali di economia. *[Gior. Econ. A.]* *ISSN: 0017-0097.* ; *Universita Commerciale Luigi Bocconi*; **Publisher**: *Istituto Editoriale Cisalpino*: Via Rezia 4, 20135 Milan, Italy

Годишник на Софийския Университет „Климент ОХридски" Катедра По Поитическа Икономия; Godishnik ha sofiiskiia universitet "Kliment Okhridski" katedra po politicheska ikonomiia. *[God. S. Uni. K. Okh. P. I.]* *ISSN: 0204-9627.* ; *Izdaelstvo na Bulgarskata Akademia na Naukite*: Bulgaria

Годишник на Висшия Финансово- Стопански Институт „Д. А. Ценов" - Свишов; Godishnik na visshiia finansovo- stopanski institut "D. A. Tsenov" - Svishtov. *[God. Vis. F. S. Inst. Tsenov - Svi.]* *ISSN: 0323-9470.* ; *Knigoizdatelstvo Georgi Bakalov*: Bulgaria

Gospodarka narodowa. *[Gosp. Nar.]* *ISSN: 0867-0005.* ; *Instytut Gospodarki Narodowej*: Plac Trzech Krzyży 5, 00-507 Warsaw, Poland

Gospodarka planowa. *[Gosp. Plan.]* *ISSN: 0017-2421.* ; *Państwowe Wydawnictwo Ekonomiczne*: ul. Niecata 4a, 00-098 Warsaw, Poland

Governance. *[Governance]* *ISSN: 0952- 1895.* ; *Basil Blackwell*: 108 Cowley Road, Oxford OX4 1JF, U.K.

Government and opposition. *[Govt. Oppos.] ISSN: 0017-257X.* ; *Government and Opposition*: Houghton Street, London WC2A 2AE, U.K.

Greek economic review. *[Gr. Econ. Rev.]*; *Society for Economic Research*: Central Post Office Box 4085, Athens 102 10, Greece

Group decision and negotiation. *[Group Decis. Negot.] ISSN: 0926-2644.* ; *Kluwer Academic Publishers*: P.O. Box 17, 3300 AA Dordrecht, The Netherlands

Hacienda pública española. *[Hac. Públ. Esp.] ISSN: 0210-1173.* ; *Instituto de Estudios Fiscales*: Ministerio de Economía y Hacienda, Plaza de Canalejas 3, 28014 Madrid, Spain

Hamburger Jahrbuch für Wirtschafts- und Gesellschaftspolitik. *[Ham. Jahrb. Wirt- Ges.pol.]*; *HWWA- Institut für Wirtschaftsforschung*; **Publisher**: *J.C.B. Mohr (Paul Siebeck)*: Postfach 2040, D-7400 Tubingen, Germany

Harvard business review. *[Harv. Bus. Re.] ISSN: 0017-8012.* ; *Harvard Business Review*: Harvard Business School, Publishing Division, Boston, MA 02163, U.S.A.; **Subscriptions**: *idem*: Subscriber Service, P.O. Box 52623, Boulder, CO 80322-2623, U.S.A.

Harvard law review. *[Harv. Law. Rev.] ISSN: 0017-811X.* ; *Harvard Law Review Association*: Gannett House, 1511 Massachusetts Avenue, Cambridge, MA. 02138, U.S.A.

Health policy and planning. *[Health Pol. Plan.] ISSN: 0268-1080.* ; *London School of Hygiene and Tropical Medicine*: Keppel (Gower) Street, London WC1E 7HT, U.K.; **Publisher**: *Oxford University Press*: Pinkhill House, Southfield Road, Eynsham, Oxford, OX8 1JJ, U.K.

Hemispheres. *[Hemispheres] ISSN: 0239-8818.* ; *Polish Academy of Sciences, Centre for Studies on non-European Countries*: Rynek 9, 50-106 Wroclaw, Poland

Heritage of Zimbabwe. *[Herit. Zimb.] ISSN: 0556-9605.* ; *History Society of Zimbabwe*: P.O. Box 8268, Causeway, Harare, Zimbabwe

High technology law journal. *[High Tech. Law J.] ISSN: 0885-2715.* ; *University of California Press*: 2120 Berkeley Way, Berkeley, CA. 94720, U.S.A.

Higher education. *[High. Educ.] ISSN: 0018-1560.* ; *Kluwer Academic Publishers*: P.O. Box 17, 3300 AA Dordrecht, The Netherlands

Himal. *[Himal] ISSN: 1012-9804.* ; *Himal Associates*: P.O. Box 42, Lalitpur, Nepal

Hispanic American historical review.*[HAHR]— [Hisp. Am. Hist. Rev.] ISSN: 0018-2168.* ; *American Historical Association, Conference on Latin American History*; **Publisher**: *Duke University Press*: Box 6697 College Station, Durham, NC. 27708, U.S.A.

Historical social research; Historische Sozialforschung. *[Hist. Soc. R.] ISSN: 0172-6404.* ; *Arbeitsgemeinschaft für Quantifizierung und Methoden in der historisch sozialwissenschaftlichen Forschung/ International Commission for the Application of Quantitative Methods in History/ Association for History and Computing*: Bachemerstr. 40, D-5000 Cologne 41, Germany/ University of London, Westfield College, Department of History, Kidderpore Avenue, London NW3 7ST, U.K.; **Publisher**: *Zentrum für Historische Sozialforschung*: Zentralarchiv für Empirische Sozialforschung, Universität zu Köln, Bachemerstr. 40, D-5000 Cologne, Germany

History of political economy. *[Hist. Polit. Ec.] ISSN: 0018-2702.* ; *Duke University Press*: Crowell Hall, East Campus, Duke University, Durham, NC. 27708, U.S.A.; **Subscriptions**: *Duke University Press*: Box 6697 College Station, Durham, NC 27708, U.S.A.

Hitotsubashi journal of commerce and management. *[Hito. J. Comm. Manag.] ISSN: 0018-2796.* ; *Hitotsubashi University, Hitotsubashi Academy*: Kunitachi, Tokyo 186, Japan; **Subscriptions**: *Japan Publications*: P.O. Box 5030 Tokyo International, Tokyo, Japan

Hitotsubashi journal of economics. *[Hito. J. Econ.] ISSN: 0018-280X.* ; *Hitotsubashi Academy Hitotsubashi University*: Kunitachi, Tokyo 186, Japan; **Subscriptions**: *Japan Publications*: P.O. Box 5030 Tokyo International, Tokyo, Japan

Homines. *[Homines] ISSN: 0252-8908.* ; *Universidad Interamericana de Puerto Rico*: Recinto Metropolitano, División de Ciencias Sociales, Apartado 1293, Hato Rey 00919, Puerto Rico

Homme et la société. *[Hom. Soc.] ISSN: 0018-4306.* ; *Centre National des Lettres/ Centre National de la Recherche Scientifique*; **Publisher**: *Editions l'Harmattan*: 5-7 rue de l'Ecole-Polytechnique, 75005 Paris, France

Hong Kong economic papers. *[Hong Kong Ec. Pap.] ISSN: 0018 4578.* ; *Hong Kong Economic Association*: P.O. Box 4004, Hong Kong; **Publisher**: *Asian Research Service*: G.P.O. Box 2232, Hong Kong

Housing policy debate. *[Hous. Pol. Deb.] ISSN: 1051-1482.* ; *Office of Housing Policy, Fannie Mae*: 3900 Wisconsin Avenue, NW Washington, DC 20016-2899, U.S.A.

Human organization. *[Human. Org.] ISSN: 0018-7259.* ; *Society for Applied Anthropology*: 5205 E.Flowler Avenue, Suite 310, Temple Terrace, FL. 33617, U.S.A.

Human relations. *[Human Relat.] ISSN: 0018-7267.* ; *Plenum Press*: 233 Spring Street, New York, N.Y. 10013, U.S.A.

IDS bulletin. *[IDS Bull.] ISSN: 0265-5012.* ; *Institute of Development Studies*: University of Sussex, Brighton BN1 9RE, U.K.

Ifo-Studien. *[Ifo-Stud.] ISSN: 0018-9731.* ; *Ifo- Institut für Wirtschaftsforschung*: Postfach 86 04 60, 8000 München 86, Germany; **Publisher**: *Duncker und Humblot*: Postfach 41 03 29, 1000 Berlin 41, Germany

Impact of science on society. *[Impact Sci.] ISSN: 0019-2872.* ; *UNESCO*: 7 place de Fontenoy, 75700 Paris, France; **Subscriptions**: *Taylor and Francis*: Rankine Road, Basingstoke, Hampshire RG24 0PR, U.K.

India quarterly. *[India Q.] ISSN: 0019-4220.* ; *Indian Council of World Affairs*: Sapru House, Barakhamba Road, New Delhi 110001, India

Indian economic and social history review. *[Indian Ec. Soc. His. R.] ISSN: 0019- 4646.* ; *Indian Economic and Social History Association*; **Publisher**: *Sage Publications*: 32 M- Block Market, Greater Kailash-I, New Delhi 110 048, India

Indian economic journal. *[Ind. Econ. J.]*; *University of Bombay*: Department of Economics, P.O. Vidyanagari, Bombay 400 098, India

Indian economic review. *[Indian Ec. Rev.] ISSN: 0019-4671.* ; *Delhi School of Economics*: University of Delhi, Delhi 110007, India

Indian geographical journal. *[Ind. Geograph. J.] ISSN: 0019-4824.* ; *Indian Geographical Society*: c/o The editor, Indian Geographical Journal, Department of Geography, University of Madras, Madras 600 005, India

Indian journal of agricultural economics. *[Ind. J. Agri. Eco.] ISSN: 0019-5014.* ; *Indian Society of Agricultural Economics*: 46-48 Esplanade Mansions, Mahatma Gandhi Road, Fort, Bombay 400 001, India

Indian journal of economics. *[Ind. J. Eco.] ISSN: 0019-5170.* ; *University of Allahabad, Departments of Economics and Commerce*: Post Box No. 2005, Allahabad 211002, India

Indian journal of industrial relations. *[Ind. J. Ind. Rel.] ISSN: 0019-5286.* ; *Shri Ram Centre for Industrial Relations and Human Resources*: 4E/16 Jhandewalan Extension, New Delhi- 110015, India

Indian journal of labour economics. *[Ind. J. Lab. Econ.]*; *Indian Society of Labour Economics*; **Publisher**: *Dr. R.C. Singh*: Department of Labour and Social Welfare, Patna University, Patna 800005, India

Indian journal of political science. *[Ind. J. Pol. Sci.] ISSN: 0019-5510.* ; *Indian Political Science Association*: Anna Centre for Public Affairs, University of Madras, Madras 600 005, India

Indian journal of public administration. *[Indian J. Publ. Admin.] ISSN: 0019-5561.* ; *Indian Institute of Public Administration*: Indraprastha Estate, Ring Road East, New Delhi 110002, India

Indian journal of regional science. *[Ind. J. Reg. Sci.] ISSN: 0046-9017.* ; *Indian Institute of Technology, Regional Science Association*: Department of Architecture and Regional Planning, Kharagpur, West Bengal, India

Indian journal of social work. *[Indian J. Soc. W.] ISSN: 0019-5634.* ; *Tata Institute of Social Sciences*: Deonar, Bombay 400 088, India

Indian labour journal. *[Indian. Lab. J.] ISSN: 0019-5723.* ; *Labour Bureau*: Cleremont Shimla - 171004, Uttar Pradesh, India; **Subscriptions**: *Controller of Publications*: Civil Lines, Delhi-110 054, India

Industria. *[Industria]*; *Società editrice il Mulino*: Strada Maggiore 37, 40125 Bologna, Italy

Industrial & environmental crisis. *[Indust. Environ. Crisis] ISSN: 0921- 8106.* ; *Bucknell University/ Industrial Crisis Institute*: Department of management, Lewisburg, PA17837, U.S.A./ New York, U.S.A.

Industrial and labor relations review. *[Ind. Lab. Rel.] ISSN: 0019-7939.* ; *Cornell University, New York State School of Industrial and Labor Relations*: 207 ILR Research Building, Cornell University, Ithaca, New York 14851-0952, U.S.A.

Industrial archaeology review. *[Ind. Arch. Rev.] ISSN: 0309- 0728.* ; *Association for Industrial Archaeology*: The Wharfage, Ironbridge, Telford, Shropshire TF8 7AW, U.K.

Industrial crisis quarterly. *[Ind. Crisis Q.] ISSN: 0921-8106.* ; *Industrial Crisis Institute*: New York, U.S.A.; **Publisher**: *Elsevier Science Publishers (North-Holland)*: P.O. Box 1991, 1000 BZ Amsterdam, The Netherlands; **Subscriptions**: *idem*: Journal Department, Postbus 211, 1000 AE Amsterdam, The Netherlands

Industrial law journal. *[Ind. Law J.] ISSN: 0395-9332.* ; *Industrial Law Society*: 28 Boundary Road, Sidcup, Kent DA15 8ST, U.K.; **Publisher**: *Oxford University Press*: Pinkhill House, Southfield Road, Eynsham, Oxford OX8 1JJ, U.K.

Industrial relations. *[Ind. Relat.] ISSN: 0019- 8676.* ; *University of California, Berkeley, Institute of Industrial Relations*: Berkeley CA. 94720, U.S.A.; **Publisher**: *Basil Blackwell*: 108 Cowley Road, Oxford OX4 1JF, U.K.

Industrial relations journal. *[Ind. Relat. J.] ISSN: 0019-8692.* ; *Basil Blackwell*: 108 Cowley Road, Oxford OX4 1JF, U.K.

Industrial relations journal of South Africa. *[Ind. Rel. J. S.Afr.] ISSN: 0258-7181.* ; *University of Stellenbosch Business School*: P.O. Box 610, Bellville 7535, South Africa

Industry of free China. *[Ind. Free China] ISSN: 0019-946X.* ; *Council for Economic Planning and Development*: 9th Floor, 87 Nanking E. Road, Sec.2, Taipei, Taiwan

Información comercial española. *[Infor. Com. Esp.] ISSN: 0019-977X.* ; *Secretaría de Estado de Comercio*: Paseo de la Castellana 162, piso 16, Madrid 28046, Spain; **Subscriptions**: *BBR/ACTION*: Príncipe de Vergara 136, 1°, 28002 Madrid, Spain

Information economics and policy. *[Inf. Econ. Pol.] ISSN: 0167-6245.* ; *International Telecommunications Society*: c/o Professor R.G. Noll, Department of Economics, Stanford University, Stanford, CA. 94305, U.S.A.; **Publisher**: *Elsevier Science Publishers*: P.O. Box 1991, 1000 BZ Amsterdam, The Netherlands

Informationen zur Raumentwicklung. *[Inf. Raum.] ISSN: 0303-2493.* ; *Bundesforschungsanstalt für Landeskunde und Raumordnung*: Am Michaelshof 8, Postfach 20 01 30, 5300 Bonn 2, Germany

Inquiry. *[Inquiry] ISSN: 0020-174X.* ; *Universitetsforlaget (Norwegian University Press)*: P.O. Box 2959 Tøyen, N-0608 Oslo 6, Norway

Insurance mathematics & economics. *[Insur. Math. Econ.] ISSN: 0167-6687.* ; *Elsevier Science Publishers*: P.O. Box 1991, 1000 BZ Amsterdam, The Netherlands

Integración latinoamericana. *[Integ. Lat.am.] ISSN: 0325- 1675.* ; *Instituto para la Integración de América Latina (INTAL)*: Esmeralda 130, 1035 Buenos Aires, Argentina

Intellectual property law. *[Intell. Prop. Law] ISSN: 0892-2365.* ; *Harwood Academic Publishers*: 270 Eighth Avenue, New York, NY.10011, U.S.A.; **Subscriptions**: *idem*: c/o STBS Limited, P.O. Box 90, Reading, Berks, RG1 8JL, U.K.

Intereconomics. *[Intereconomics] ISSN: 0020-5346.* ; *HWWA-Institut für Wirtschaftsforschung-Hamburg*: Neuer Jungfernstieg 21, 2000 Hamburg 36, Germany; **Publisher**: *Verlag Weltarchiv*: Neuer Jungfernstieg 21, 2000 Hamburg 36, Germany

Interfaces. *[Interfaces] ISSN: 0092-2102.* ; *Institute of Management Sciences and the Operations Research Society of America*: 290 Westminster Street, Providence, RI. 02903, U.S.A.

Internasjonal politikk. *[Int. Pol.] ISSN: 0020-577X.* ; *Norsk Utenrikspolitisk Institutt*: Postboks 8159 Dep., 0033 Oslo 1, Norway

International affairs [London]. *[Int. Aff. [London]] ISSN: 0020-5850.* ; *Royal Institute of International Affairs*: Chatham House, 10 St. James's Square, London SW1Y 4LE, U.K.; **Publisher**: *Cambridge University Press*: The Edinburgh Building, Shaftesbury Road, Cambridge CB2 2RU, U.K.

International affairs [Moscow]. *[Int. Aff. Mos.] ISSN: 0130-9641.* ; *Progress Publishers*: 14 Gorokhovsky Pereulok, Moscow K-16, U.S.S.R.

International and comparative law quarterly. *[Int. Comp. L.] ISSN: 0020-5893.* ; *British Institute of International and Comparative Law*: 17 Russell Square, London WC1B 5DR, U.K.

International contributions to labour studies. *[Internat. Contrib. Lab. Stud.] ISSN: 1052-9187.* ; *Academic Press*: 1250 Sixth Avenue, San Diego, CA., 92101, U.S.A.; **Subscriptions**: *Harcourt Brace Jovanovich Ltd.*: 24-28 Oval Road, London, NW1 7DX, U.K.

International currency review. *[Int. Curr. Rev.] ISSN: 0020-6490.* ; *Christopher Story*: 108 Horseferry Lane, London SW1P 2EF, U.K.

International economic journal. *[Int. Econ. J.]*; *Korea International Economic Association*: Dept. of International Economics, College of Social Sciences, Seoul University, Seoul 151-742, South Korea

International economic outlook. *[Inter. Econ. Out.]*; *Centre for Economic Forecasting*: London Business School, Sussex Place, Regent's Park, London NW1 4SA, U.K.; **Publisher**: *Basil Blackwell*: 108 Cowley Road, Oxford OX4 1JF, U.K.; **Subscriptions**: *Marston Book Services*: P.O. Box 87, Oxford OX2 0DT, U.K.

International economic review. *[Int. Econ. R.] ISSN: 0020-6598.* ; *University of Pennsylvania, Department of Economics/Osaka University, Institute of Social and Economic Research Association*: 3718 Locust Walk, University of Pennsylvania, Philadelphia, PA. 19104-6297, U.S.A./ 6-1 Mihagaoka, Ibaraki, Osaka 567, Japan

International interactions. *[Int. Inter.] ISSN: 0305-0629.* ; *Gordon and Breach Science Publishers*: P.O. Box 90, Reading, Berkshire RG1 8JL, U.K.

International journal. *[Int. J.] ISSN: 0020-7020.* ; *Canadian Institute of International Affairs*: 15 Kings College Circle, Toronto, Ontario, Canada M5S 2V9

International journal of conflict management. *[Int. J. Confl. Manag.] ISSN: 1044-4068.* ; *3-R Executive Systems*: 3109 Copperfield Court, Bowling Green, KY. 42104, U.S.A.

International journal of flexible manufacturing systems. *[Inter. J. Flex. Manufact. Syst.] ISSN: 0920-6299.* ; *Kluwer Academic Publishers*: P.O. Box 322, 3300 AH Dordrecht, The Netherlands/ P.O. Box 368, Accord Station, Hingham, MA. 02018 0358, U.S.A.

International journal of forecasting. *[Int. J. Forec.] ISSN: 0169-2070.* ; *International Institute of Forecasters*; **Publisher**: *Elsevier Science Publishers*: Box 1911, 1000 BZ Amsterdam, The Netherlands; **Subscriptions**: *idem*: P.O. Box 211, 1000 AE Amsterdam, The Netherlands

International journal of health services. *[Int. J. Health. Ser.] ISSN: 0020-7314.* ; *Baywood Publishing*: 26 Austin Avenue, P.O. Box 337, Amityville, NY. 11701, U.S.A.

International journal of human resource management. *[Int. J. Hum. Res. Man.] ISSN: 0958-5192.* ; *Routledge*: 11 New Fetter Lane, London EC4P 4EE, U.K.; **Subscriptions**: *idem*: Subscriptions Department, Cheriton House, North Way, Andover, Hants SP10 5BE, U.K.

International journal of industrial organization. *[Int. J. Ind. O.] ISSN: 0167-7187.* ; *Elsevier Science Publishers (North-Holland)*: P.O. Box 1991, 1000 BZ Amsterdam, The Netherlands; **Subscriptions**: *idem*: Journal Department, P.O. Box 211, 1000 AE Amsterdam, The Netherlands

International journal of marine and coastal law. *[Internat. J. Mar. Coast. Law] ISSN: 0927-3522.* ; *Graham & Trotman, Martinus Nijhof/ Kluwer Academic Publishers Group*: Sterling House, 66 Wilton Road, London, SW1 1DE, U.K./ 101 Philip Drive, Assinippi Park, Norwell, MA. 02061, U.S.A.

International journal of Middle East studies. *[Int. J. M.E. Stud.] ISSN: 0020-7438.* ; *Middle East Studies Association of North America*: University of Arizona, 1232 North Cherry, Tuscon, AZ. 85721, U.S.A.; **Publisher**: *Cambridge University Press*: 40 West Street 20th, New York, NY. 10011, U.S.A.

International journal of social economics. *[Int. J. Soc. E.] ISSN: 0306-8293.* ; *MCB University Press*: 62 Toller Lane, Bradford, West Yorkshire, BD8 9BY, U.K.

International journal of the sociology of law. *[Int. J. S. Law] ISSN: 0194-6595.* ; *Academic Press*: 24-28 Oval Road, London NW1 7DX, U.K.

International journal of transport economics. *[Intern. J. Trans. Econ.] ISSN: 0391-8440.* ; *S.I.E.S.*: Via G.A. Guattani, 8, Rome, Italy

International journal of urban and regional research. *[Int. J. Urban] ISSN: 0309-1317.* ; *Edward Arnold*: Mill Road, Dunton Green, Sevenoaks, Kent TN13 2YA, U.K.; **Subscriptions**: *Edward Arnold*: Subscriptions Department, 42 Bedford Square, London WC1B 3SL, U.K.

International labour review. *[Int. Lab. Rev.] ISSN: 0020-7780.* ; *International Labour Office (ILO)*: CH-1211 Geneva 22, Switzerland

International migration review. *[Int. Migr. Rev.] ISSN: 0197- 9183.* ; *Center for Migration Studies*: 209 Flagg Place, Staten Island, NY. 10304-1199, U.S.A.

International public relations review. *[Int. Pub. Relat. R.] ISSN: 0269-0357.* ; *International Public Relations Association*: Case postale 126, CH-1211 Geneva 20, Switzerland; **Publisher**: *Whiting and Birch*: 90 Dartmouth Road, Forest Hill, London SE23 3HZ, U.K.

International regional science review. *[Int. Reg. Sci. R.] ISSN: 0160-0176.* ; *Regional Research Institute*: West Virginia University, Morgantown, WV. 26506, U.S.A.

International relations. *[Int. Rel.] ISSN: 0047- 1178.* ; *David Davies Memorial Institute of International Studies*: 2 Chadwick Street, London SW1P 2EP, U.K.

International review of administrative sciences. *[Int. Rev. Admin. Sci.] ISSN: 0020-8523.* ; *International Institute of Administrative Sciences, European Group of Public Administration*: rue Defacqz 1, Box 11, B-1050 Brussels, Belgium; **Publisher**: *Sage Publications*: 6 Bonhill Street, London EC2A 4PU, U.K.

International review of applied economics. *[Int. R. Applied Ec.] ISSN: 0269-2171.* ; *Edward Arnold*: Mill Road, Dunton Green, Sevenoaks, Kent TN13 2YA, U.K.; **Subscriptions**: *Edward Arnold, Subscription Department*: 42 Bedford Square, WC11 3SL, U.K.

International review of law and economics. *[Int. R. Law Econ.] ISSN: 0144-8188.* ; *Butterworth-Heinemann*: 80 Montvale Avenue, Stoneham, MA. 02180, U.S.A.

International review of retail, distribution and consumer research. *[Int. R. Ret. Dist. Res.] ISSN: 0959-3969.* ; *Routledge*: 11 New Fetter Lane, London EC4P 4EE, U.K.

International review of strategic management. *[Inter. R. Strat. Manag.] ISSN: 1047-7918.* ; *John Wiley & Sons*: Baffins Lane, Chichester, West Sussex PO19 1UD, U.K.

International socialism. *[Int. Soc.] ISSN: 0020-8736.* ; *Socialist Workers Party*: PO Box 82, London E3, U.K.; **Subscriptions**: *Bookmarks*: 265 Seven Sisters Road, London N4 2DE, U.K.

International sociology. *[Int. Sociol.] ISSN: 0268-5809.* ; *International Sociological Association*: Consejo Superior de Investigaciones Cientificas. Pinar 25, 28006 Madrid, Spain; **Publisher**: *Sage Publications*: 6 Bonhill Street, London EC2A 4PU, U.K.

International spectator. *[Inter. Spect.] ISSN: 0393-2729.* ; *Istituto Affari Internazionali*: Via Angelo Brunetti 9, (Palazzo Rondinini), 00186 Rome, Italy; **Publisher**: *Fratelli Palombi Editori*: Via dei Gracchi 187, 00192 Rome, Italy

International studies. *[Int. Stud.] ISSN: 0020-8817.* ; *Sage Publications India*: 32 M-Block Market, Greater Kailash I, New Delhi 110 048, India

International studies quarterly. *[Int. Stud. Q.] ISSN: 0020-8833.* ; *International Studies Association*: University of South Carolina, Columbia SC. 29208, U.S.A.; **Publisher**: *Butterworth-Heinemann*: 80 Montvale Avenue, Stoneham, MA. 02180, U.S.A.

International VAT monitor. *[Inter. VAT Mon.] ISSN: 0925-0832.* ; *International Bureau of Fiscal Documentation*: P.O. Box 20237, 1000 HE Amsterdam, The Netherlands/ 600-618 Sarphatistraat, 1018 AV Amsterdam, The Netherlands

Internationales Asienforum. *[Int. Asien.] ISSN: 0020-9449.* ; *Europäisches Institut für Politische, Wirtschaftliche und Soziale Fragen*; **Publisher**: *Weltform Verlag*: Marienburger Straße 22, 5000 Cologne 51, Germany

Investigación y gerencia. *[Invest. Ger.]*; *PARAL*: Apartado 47066, Los Chaguaramos, Caracas 1041-A, Venezuela

Investigaciones economicas. *[Invest. Econ.]* *ISSN: 0210-1521*. *Fundacion Empresa Publica*: Departemento de Publicaciones, Pl. Marqués de Salamanca 8, 28006 Madrid, Spain

IPW Berichte. *[IPW Ber.]* *ISSN: 0046-970X*. *Verlag der Vertriebsgemeinschaft Dieter Joester*: Kölner Straße 66, W-6000 Frankfurt 1, Germany; **Subscriptions**: *INTERABO*: Frau Sperling, Postfach 103245, W-2000 Hamburg 20, Germany

IPW-Forschungshefte. *[IPW-Forsch.]* *ISSN: 0323-3901*. *Institut fur Internationale Politik und Wirtschaft*: Breite Straße 11, Berlin 1020, Germany; **Publisher**: *Verlag für Recht und Wirtschaft*: Otto-Grotewohl-Straße 17, Berlin 1086, Germany

Irish banking review. *[Irish Bank. Rev.]* *ISSN: 0021-1060*. *Irish Bankers' Federation*: Nassau House, Nassau Street, Dublin 2, Ireland

Israel law review. *[Isr. Law R.]* *ISSN: 0021-2237*. *Israel Law Review Association*: c/o Faculty of Law, Hebrew University, Mt. Scopus, P.O.B. 24100, Jerusalem 91240, Israel

Issues & studies. *[Iss. Stud.]* *ISSN: 1013-2511*. *National Chengchi University, Institute of International Relations*: 64 Wan Shou Road, Mucha, Taipei Taiwan, Republic of China

Известия Академии наук Республики Казохстан; Izvestiia Akademii nauk republik Kazakhstan.:*Seriia obshchectvennych nauk [Iz. Akad. Respub. Kazakh.]*

Jahrbuch der Wirtschaft osteuropas; Yearbook of East-European economics. *[Jahr. Wirt. Ost.]* *ISSN: 0449-5225*. *Osteuropa-Institut München*; **Publisher**: *Physica-Verlag*: Planung Wirtschaftswissenschaften, Postfach 105280, D-6900 Heidelberg 1, Germany

Jahrbuch für Geschichte von Staat, Wirtschaft und Gesellschaft Lateinamerikas. *[Jahrb. Ges. St. Wirt. Ges. Lat.am.]* *ISSN: 0075-2673*. *Böhlaù Verlag*: Niehler Straße 272-274, 5000 Cologne 60, Germany

Jahrbuch für Ostrecht. *[Jahrb. Ost.]* *ISSN: 0075-2746*. *Institut für Ostrecht München*: Kessenicher Straße 116, Postfach 120380, 5300 Bonn 1, Germany; **Publisher**: *Deutscher Bundes-Verlag*: 8000 München 2, Theresienstraße 40, Germany

Jahrbuch für Sozialwissenschaft. *[Jahr. Soz.schaft.]* *ISSN: 0075-2770*. *Vandenhoeck & Ruprecht*: Theaterstraße 13, P.O. Box 3753, 3400 Göttingen, Germany

Jahrbuch für Wirtschaftsgeschichte. *[Jahrb. Wirt. Gesch.]* *ISSN: 0075-2800*. *Akademie-Verlag Berlin*: Postfach 1233, Leipziger Straße 3-4 1086 Berlin, Germany

Jahrbücher für Geschichte Osteuropas. *[Jahrb. Gesch. O.eur.]* *ISSN: 0021-4019*. *Osteuropa Institut*: Scheinerstraße 11, D-8000 Munich 80, Germany; **Publisher**: *Franz Steiner Verlag*: Birkenwaldstraße 44, Postfach 10 15 26, D-7000 Stuttgart, Germany

Jahrbücher für Nationalökonomie und Statistik. *[Jahrb. N. St.]* *ISSN: 0021-4027*. *Gustav Fischer Verlag*: Wollgrasweg 49, 7000 Stuttgart 70, Germany

Japan and the world economy. *[Jpn. Wor. Econ.]* *ISSN: 0922-1425*. *New York University*: 100 Trinity Place, New York, NY. 10006, U.S.A.; **Publisher**: *Elsevier Science Publishers (North-Holland)*: P.O. Box 1991, 1000 BZ Amsterdam, The Netherlands

Japan digest. *[Jpn. Dig.]* *ISSN: 0960-1473*. *Japan Library*: Knoll House, 35 The Crescent, Sandgate, Folkestone, Kent CT20 3EE, U.K.

Japan forum. *[Jpn. Forum]* *ISSN: 0955-5803*. *British Association for Japanese Studies*; **Publisher**: *Oxford University Press*: Pinkhill House, Southfield Road, Eynsham, Oxford OX8 1JJ, U.K.

Japan review of international affairs. *[Jpn. R. Int. Aff.]* *ISSN: 0913-8773*. *Japan Institute of International Affairs*: 19th Mori Building, 1-2-20 Toranomon, Minato-Ku, Tokyo 105, Japan

Journal de la Société de Statistique de Paris. *[J. Soc. Stat. Paris]* *ISSN: 0037-914X*. *Société de Statistique de France*: B-212, INSEE, 12 rue Boulitte, 75675 Paris Cedex 14, France; **Subscriptions**: *UAP International*: 9 Place Vendôme, 75001 Paris, France

Journal du droit international. *[J. Droit Int.]* *ISSN: 0021-8170*. *Editions Techniques*: 123 rue d'Alésia, 75678 Paris Cedex 14, France

Journal for Japanese studies. *[J. Jpn. Stud.]* *ISSN: 0095-6848*. *Society for Japanese Studies*: Thomson Hall DR-05, University of Washington, Seattle, Washington 98195, U.S.A.

Journal für Entwicklungspolitik. *[J. Entwick.pol.]* *ISSN: 0258-2384*. *Mattersburger Kreis für Entwicklungspolitik an den Österreichischen Universitäten*: Weyrgasse 5, A-1030 Vienna, Austria

Journal of accounting and economics. *[J. Account. E.]* *ISSN: 0165-4101*. *Elsevier Science Publishers (North Holland)*: P.O. Box 1991, 1000 BZ Amsterdam, The Netherlands

Journal of accounting and public policy. *[J. Acc. Pub. Pol.]* *ISSN: 0278-4254*. *Elsevier Science Publishers (North-Holland)*: 655 Avenue of the Americas, New York, N.Y. 10010, U.S.A.; **Subscriptions**: *Elsevier Science Publishers*: Journals Department, P.O. Box 882, Madison Square Station, New York, NY. 10159, U.S.A.

Journal of accounting research. *[J. Account. R.] ISSN: 0021-8456. Institute of Professional Accounting*; **Publisher**: *University of Chicago, Graduate School of Business*: 1101 East 58th Street, Chicago 60637, U.S.A.

Journal of African Marxists. *[J. Afr. Marx.] ISSN: 0263-2268. Journal of African Marxists*: 23 Bevenden Street, London N1 6BH, U.K.

Journal of agricultural economics. *[J. Agr. Econ.] ISSN: 0021-857X. Agricultural Economics Society*: International Development Centre, University of Oxford, Queen Elizabeth House, 21 St. Giles, Oxford OX1 3LA, U.K.; **Subscriptions**: *idem:* Wye College, Ashford, Kent TN25 5AH, U.K.

Journal of agricultural economics research. *[J. Agr. Econ. R.]; United States Department of Agriculture, Economic Research Service*: 1301 New York Avenue, NW Washington, DC. 2005-4788

Journal of air law and commerce. *[J. Air Law Comm.] ISSN: 0021-8642. Southern Methodist University, School of Law*: Dallas, TX. 75275, U.S.A.

Journal of applied econometrics. *[J. Appl. Econ.] ISSN: 0883-7252. John Wiley and Sons*: Baffins Lane, Chichester, Sussex PO19 1UD, U.K.

Journal of applied psychology. *[J. Appl. Psychol.] ISSN: 0021-9010. American Psychological Association*: 1400 North Uhle Street, Arlington, VA. 22201, U.S.A.

Journal of architectural and planning research. *[J. Arch. Plan. Res.]; Locke Science Publishing*: P.O. Box 146413, Chicago, IL. 60614, U.S.A.

Journal of Asian and African affairs. *[J. Asian Afr. Aff.] ISSN: 1044-2979. Journal of Asian and African Affairs*: P.O. Box 23099, Washington, DC. 20026, U.S.A.

Journal of Asian and African studies [Leiden]. *[J. As. Afr. S.] ISSN: 0021 9096. E.J. Brill*: P.O. Box 9000, 2300 PA Leiden, The Netherlands

Journal of Asian studies. *[J. Asian St.] ISSN: 0021-9118. Association for Asian Studies*: 1 Lane Hall, University of Michigan, Ann Arbor, MI. 48109, U.S.A.; **Publisher**: *University of Wisconsin-Milwaukee*: Milwaukee, WI. 53201, U.S.A.

Journal of Australian political economy. *[J. Aust. Pol. Econ.] ISSN: 0156-5826. Australian Political Economy Movement*: P.O. Box 76, Wentworth Building, University of Sydney, NSW 2006, Australia

Journal of banking and finance. *[J. Bank. Fin.] ISSN: 0378-4266. Associazione Italiana Studi Finanziari (ASFI)/Association Française de Finance (AFFI)/European Finance Association (EFA)*; **Publisher**: *Elsevier Science Publishers (North-Holland)*: P.O. Box 1991, 1000 BZ Amsterdam, The Netherlands; **Subscriptions**: *Elsevier Science Publishers*: Journals Division, P.O. Box 211, 1000 AE Amsterdam, The Netherlands

Journal of BARD. *[J. BARD]; Bangladesh Academy for Rural Development*: Comilla, Bangladesh

Journal of business. *[J. Bus.] ISSN: 0021 9398. University of Chicago, Graduate School of Business*: 1101 E. 58th Street, Chicago, IL. 60637, U.S.A.; **Publisher**: *University of Chicago Press*: 5720 South Woodlawn Avenue, Chicago, IL. 60637, U.S.A.

Journal of business & economic statistics. *[J. Bus. Econ. Stat.] ISSN: 0735-0015. American Statistical Association*: 1429 Duke Street, Alexandria, VA. 22314, U.S.A.

Journal of business and society. *[J. Bus. Soc.] ISSN: 1012-2591. Cyprus College*: P.O. Box 2006, Corner Stasinos and Diogenes Streets, Nicosia, Cyprus

Journal of business ethics. *[J. Busin. Ethics] ISSN: 0167-4544. Kluwer Academic Publishers Group*: P.O. Box 322, 3300 AH Dordrecht, Holland/ P.O. Box 358, Accord Station, Hingham, MA. 02018-0358, U.S.A.

Journal of business finance and accounting. *[J. Bus. Fin. Acc.] ISSN: 0306-686X. Basil Blackwell*: 108 Cowley Road, Oxford OX4 1JF, U.K.

Journal of business law. *[J. Bus. Law] ISSN: 0021-9460. Stevens & Sons*: South Quay Plaza, 183 Marsh Wall, London E14 9FT, U.K.

Journal of Canadian studies; Revue d'études canadiennes. *[J. Can. Stud.] ISSN: 0021-9495. Trent University*: Box 4800, Peterborough, Ontario, Canada K9J 7B8

Journal of common market studies. *[J. Com. Mkt. S.] ISSN: 0021-9886. University Association for Contemporary European Studies*; **Publisher**: *Basil Blackwell*: 108 Cowley Road, Oxford, OX4 1JF, U.K.

Journal of Commonwealth & comparative politics. *[J. Comm. C. Pol.] ISSN: 03060-3631. Frank Cass*: Gainsborough House, 11 Gainsborough Road, London E11 1RS, U.K.

Journal of communist studies. *[J. Commun. S.] ISSN: 0268-4535. Frank Cass*: Gainsborough House, 11 Gainsborough Road, London W11 1RS, U.K.

Journal of comparative economics. *[J. Comp. Econ.] ISSN: 0147-5967. Association for Comparative Economic Studies*; **Publisher**: *Academic Press*: 1 East First Street, Duluth, MN. 55802, U.S.A.

Journal of conflict resolution. *[Confl. Resolut.] ISSN: 0022-0027. Peace Science Society (International)*; **Publisher**: *Sage Publications*: 2455 Teller Road, Newbury Park, CA. 91320, U.S.A.

Journal of consumer affairs. *[J. Consum. Aff.] ISSN: 0022-0078. American Council on Consumer Interests*; **Publisher**: *University of Wisconsin Press*: 114 N. Murray Street, Madison, WI. 53715, U.S.A.; **Subscriptions**: *American Council on Consumer Interests*: 240 Stanley Hall, University of Missouri, Columbia, MO. 65211, (314) 882-3817, U.S.A.

Journal of consumer policy. *[J. Consum. Pol.] ISSN: 0342-5843. Kluwer Academic Publishers*: Spuiboulevard 50, P.O. Box 17, 3300 AA Dordrecht, The Netherlands

Journal of contemporary African studies. *[J. Contemp. Afr. St.] ISSN: 0258-9001. Africa Institute of South Africa*: P.O. Box 630, Pretoria 0001, South Africa

Journal of contemporary Asia. *[J. Cont. Asia] ISSN: 0047-2336. Journal of Contemporary Asia Publishers*: P.O. Box 592, Manila, 1099 Philippines

Journal of developing areas. *[J. Dev. Areas] ISSN: 0022-037X. Western Illinois University*: 900 West Adams Street, Macomb, IL. 61455, U.S.A.

Journal of developing societies. *[J. Dev. Soc.] ISSN: 0169-796X. E.J. Brill*: P.O.B. 9000, 2300 PA Leiden, The Netherlands

Journal of development economics. *[J. Dev. Econ.] ISSN: 0304-3878. Elsevier Science Publishers (North-Holland)*: P.O. Box 1991, 1000 BZ Amsterdam, The Netherlands

Journal of development planning. *[J. Devel. Plan.] ISSN: 0085-2392. United Nations Publications*: Room DC2-853, New York, NY 10017, U.S.A.; **Subscriptions**: *Distribution and Sales Section*: Palais des Nations, CH-1211 Geneva 10, Switzerland

Journal of development studies. *[J. Dev. Stud.] ISSN: 0022-0388. Frank Cass*: Gainsborough House, 11 Gainsborough Road, London E11 1RS, U.K.

Journal of East and West studies. *[J. E. & W. Stud.]; Institute of East and West Studies*: Yonsei University, 134 Shinchondong, Seodaemoonku, Seoul 120-749, Korea

Journal of Eastern African research & development. *[J. E.Afr. Res. Devel.] ISSN: 0251-0405. Gideon S. Were*: P.O. Box 10622, Nairobi, Kenya

Journal of econometrics. *[J. Economet.] ISSN: 0304-4076. Elsevier Science Publishers (North-Holland)*: P.O. Box 1991, 1000 BZ Amsterdam, The Netherlands

Journal of economic and social measurement. *[J. Econ. Soc.] ISSN: 0747-9662. International Organisations Services*: Van Diemenstraat 94, 1013 CN Amsterdam, The Netherlands

Journal of economic behavior and organization. *[J. Econ. Beh.] ISSN: 0167-2681. Elsevier Science Publishers (North-Holland)*: Journals Division, P.O. Box 211, 1000 AE Amsterdam, The Netherlands

Journal of economic dynamics and control. *[J. Econ. Dyn. Cont.] ISSN: 0165-1889. Society of Economic Dynamics and Control*; **Publisher**: *Elsevier Science Publishers (North-Holland)*: P.O. Box 1991, 1000 BZ Amsterdam, The Netherlands; **Subscriptions**: *Elsevier Science Publishers*: Journals Division, P.O.B. 211, 1000 AE Amsterdam, The Netherlands

Journal of economic history. *[J. Econ. Hist.] ISSN: 0022-0507. Economic History Association/ University of Kansas*: Department of History, George Washington University, Washington DC. 20052, U.S.A./ 211 Watkins Home, Hall Center for the Humanities, Lawrence, KS. 66045, U.S.A.; **Publisher**: *Cambridge University Press*: 40 West 20th Street, New York, N.Y. 10011, U.S.A.

Journal of economic issues. *[J. Econ. Iss.] ISSN: 0021-3624. Association for Evolutionary Economics*: Department of Economics, University of Nebraska-Lincoln, Lincoln, NE. 68588, U.S.A.

Journal of economic literature. *[J. Econ. Lit.] ISSN: 0022-8515. American Economic Association*: 2014 Broadway, Suite 305, Nashville, TN. 37203, U.S.A.

Journal of economic perspectives. *[J. Econ. Pers.] ISSN: 0895-3309. American Economic Association*: 2014 Broadway, Suite 305, Nashville, TN. 37203, U.S.A.

Journal of economic psychology. *[J. Econ. Psyc.] ISSN: 0167-4870. International Association for Research in Economic Psychology*: Egmontstraat 13, 1050 Brussels, Belgium; **Publisher**: *Elsevier Science Publishers (North-Holland)*: P.O. Box 1991, 1000 BZ Amsterdam, The Netherlands; **Subscriptions**: *idem*: Journals Division, P.O. Box 211, 1000 AE Amsterdam, The Netherlands

Journal of economic studies. *[J. Econ. Stud.] ISSN: 0144-3585. MCB University Press*: 62 Toller Lane, Bradford, W. Yorkshire BD8 9BY, U.K.

Journal of economic surveys. *[J. Econ. Sur.] ISSN: 0950-0804. Basil Blackwell*: 108 Cowley Road, Oxford OX4 1JF, U.K.

Journal of economic theory. *[J. Econ. Theo.] ISSN: 0022-0531. Academic Press*: 41 Tempelhof, B-8000 Brugge, Belgium; **Subscriptions**: *Academic Press*: 1 East First Street, Duluth, MN. 55802, U.S.A.

Journal of economics; Zeitschrift für Nationalökonomie. *[J. Econ.] ISSN: 0931-8658. Springer-Verlag Wien*: Mölkerbastei 5, P.O. Box 367, A-1011 Vienna, Austria

Journal of economics & management strategy. *[J. Econ. Manag. Strat.] ISSN: 1058-6407. MIT Press*: Cambridge, MA. 02142, U.S.A.

Journal of environmental economics and management. *[J. Envir. Ec. Manag.] ISSN: 0095-0696. Association of Environmental and Resource Economists*: Resources for the Future, 1616 P. Street, N.W., Washington DC. 20036, U.S.A.; **Publisher**: *Academic Press*: 1 East First Street, Duluth, MN. 55802, U.S.A.

Journal of environmental law. *[J. Environ. Law.] ISSN: 0952-8873. Oxford University Press*: Pinkhill House, Southfield Road, Eynsham, OX8 1JJ, U.K.

Journal of environmental management. *[J. Environ. Manag.] ISSN: 0301-4797. Academic Press*: 24-28 Oval Road, London NW1 7DX, U.K.; **Subscriptions**: *idem*: Foots Cray, Sidcup, Kent, DA14 5HP, U.K.

Journal of environmental planning and management. *[J. Environ. Plan. Manag.] ISSN: 0964-0568. Carfax Publishing*: P.O. Box 25, Abingdon, Oxfordshire, OX14 3UE, U.K.

Journal of European economic history. *[J. Eur. Econ. His.] ISSN: 0391-5115. Banco di Roma*: Ufficio Studi, Viale Tupine 180, 00144 Rome, Italy

Journal of evolutionary economics. *[J. Evolut. Econ.] ISSN: 0936-9937. Springer-Verlag*: Heidelberger Platz 3, 1000 Berlin 33, Germany

Journal of finance. *[J. Finance] ISSN: 0022-1082. American Finance Association*: 100 Trinity Place, New York, NY 10006, U.S.A.

Journal of financial and quantative analysis. *[J. Fin. Qu. An.] ISSN: 0022-1090. University of Washington, Graduate School of Business Administration*: DJ-10 Seattle, WA. 98195, U.S.A.

Journal of financial economics. *[J. Finan. Ec.] ISSN: 0304-405X. University of Rochester, William E. Simon Graduate School of Business Administration*; **Publisher**: *Elsevier Science Publishers (North-Holland)*: P.O. Box 1991, 1000 BZ Amsterdam, The Netherlands

Journal of financial intermediation. *[J. Finan. Intermed.] ISSN: 1042-9573. Academic Press*: 6277 Sea Harbor Drive, Orlando, FL. 32887-4900, U.S.A.

Journal of financial services research. *[J. Finan. Ser. Res.] ISSN: 0920-8550. Kluwer Academic Publishers*: P.O. Box 322, 3300 AH Dordrecht, The Netherlands

Journal of forecasting. *[J. Forecast.] ISSN: 0277-6693. John Wiley & Sons*: Baffins Lane, Chichester, West Sussex PO19 1UD, U.K.

Journal of foreign exchange and international finance. *[J. For. Ex. Inter. Finan.] ISSN: 0970-3632. National Institute of Bank Management*: Kondhwe Khurd, Post Bag No. 1, Pune 411 022, India

Journal of forensic economics. *[J. Foren. Econ.] ISSN: 0898-5510. National Association of Forensic Economists*: P.O. Box 30067, Kansas City, Missouri 64112, U.S.A.

Journal of futures markets. *[J. Futur. Mark.] ISSN: 0270-7314. Center for the Study of Futures Markets, Columbia Business School*; **Publisher**: *John Wiley & Sons*: 605 Third Avenue, New York, NY. 10158, U.S.A.

Journal of health economics. *[J. Health Econ.] ISSN: 0167-6296. Elsevier Science Publishers (North-Holland)*: P.O. Box 1991, 1000 BZ Amsterdam, The Netherlands; **Subscriptions**: *idem*: P.O. Box 211, 1000 AE Amsterdam, The Netherlands

Journal of housing research. *[J. Hous. Res.] ISSN: 1052-7001. Office of Housing Policy, Fannie Mae*: 3900 Wisconsin Avenue, N.W., Washington, DC. 20016-2899, U.S.A.

Journal of human resources. *[J. Hum. Res.] ISSN: 0022-166X. University of Wisconsin Press*: 4315 Social Science Building, University of Wisconsin, 1180 Observatory Drive, Madison, WI. 53706, U.S.A.; **Subscriptions**: *University of Wisconsin Press*: 114 North Murray Street, Madison, WI. 53715, U.S.A.

Journal of industrial economics. *[J. Ind. Econ.] ISSN: 0022-1821. Basil Blackwell*: 108 Cowley Road, Oxford, OX4 1JF, U.K.

Journal of industrial relations. *[J. Ind. Relat.] ISSN: 0022-1856. Journal of Industrial Relations*: GPO Box 4479, Sydney, NSW 2001, Australia

Journal of institutional and theoretical economics; Zeitschrift für die gesamte Staatswissenschaft.*[JITE]— [J. Inst. Theo. Ec.] ISSN: 0932-4569. J.C.B.Mohr (Paul Siebeck)*: P.O. Box 2040, D-7400 Tübingen, Germany

Journal of interamerican studies and world affairs. *[J. Int. Am. St.] ISSN: 0022-1937. Institute of Interamerican Studies*; **Publisher**: *University of Miami, North-South Center*: P.O. Box 248123, Coral Gables, FL. 33124, U.S.A.

Journal of interdisciplinary economics. *[J. Interd. Ec.] ISSN: 0260-1079. A.B. Academic Publishers*: P.O. Box 42, Bicester, Oxon OX6 7NW, U.K.

Journal of interdisciplinary history. *[J. Interd. Hist.] ISSN: 0022-1953. Tufts University/ Lafayette College*: 26 Winthrop Street, Medford, MA. 02155, U.S.A.; **Publisher**: *MIT Press*: 55 Hayward Street, Cambridge, MA. 02142, U.S.A.

Journal of international business studies. *[J. Int. Bus. Stud.] ISSN: 0047-2506. Academy of International Business/ University of South Carolina, College of Business Administration*: Tulane University, A.B. Freeman School of Business, New Orleans, LA. 70118, U.S.A./ Columbia, SC. 29208, U.S.A.

Journal of international development. *[J. Int. Dev.] ISSN: 0954-1748. Institute for Development Policy and Management*: University of Manchester, Precinct Centre, Oxford Road, Manchester M13 9QS, U.K.; **Publisher**: *John Wiley & Sons*: Baffins Lane, Chichester, West Sussex PO19 1UD, U.K.

Journal of international economics. *[J. Int. Econ.] ISSN: 0022-1996. Elsevier Science Publishers (North-Holland)*: P.O. Box 1991, 1000 BZ Amsterdam. The Netherlands; **Subscriptions**: *idem*: Journal Division, P.O. Box 211, 1000 AE Amsterdam, The Netherlands

Journal of international financial management and accounting. *[J. Inter. Finan. Manag. Acc.] ISSN: 0954-1314. Basil Blackwell*: 108 Cowley Road, Oxford OX4 1JF, U.K.

Journal of international money and finance. *[J. Int. Mon. Finan.] ISSN: 0261-5606. Butterworth-Heinemann*: Westbury House, Bury Street, Guildford GU2 5BH, U.K.; **Subscriptions**: *Westbury Subscription Services*: P.O. Box 101, Sevenoaks, Kent, TN15 8PL, U.K.

Journal of Islamic economics. *[J. Islamic Ec.] ISSN: 0128-0066. International Islamic University*: P.O. Box 70, 46700 Petaling Jaya, Selangor, Malaysia

Journal of labor economics. *[J. Labor Ec.] ISSN: 0734-306X. Economics Research Center/NORC*; **Publisher**: *University of Chicago Press*: Journals Division, P.O. Box 37005, Chicago, IL 60637, U.S.A.

Journal of labor research. *[J. Labor Res.] ISSN: 0195-3613. George Mason University, Department of Economics*: Fairfax, VA. 22030, U.S.A.

Journal of Latin American studies. *[J. Lat. Am. St.] ISSN: 0022-216X. Cambridge University Press*: The Edinburgh Building, Shaftesbury Road, Cambridge CB2 2RU, U.K.

Journal of law and economics. *[J. Law Econ.] ISSN: 0022-2186. University of Chicago Press*: 5720 S. Woodlawn Avenue, Chicago IL. 60637, U.S.A.; **Subscriptions**: *University of Chicago Press, Journals Division*: P.O. Box 37005, Chicago IL. 60637, U.S.A.

Journal of law and society. *[J. Law Soc.] ISSN: 0263-323X. Basil Blackwell*: 108 Cowley Road, Oxford OX4 1JF , U.K.

Journal of law, economics, & organization. *[J. Law Ec. Organ.] ISSN: 8756-6222. Oxford University Press*: 2001 Evans Road, Cary, NC. 27513, U.S.A.

Journal of libertarian studies. *[J. Libert. Stud.] ISSN: 0363-2873. Center for Libertarian Studies*: P.O. Box 4091, Burlingame, CA. 94011, U.S.A.

Journal of macroeconomics. *[J. Macro.] ISSN: 0164-0704. Lousiana State University, College of Business Administration*; **Publisher**: *Louisiana State University Press*: Baton Rouge, LA. 70893, U.S.A.

Journal of management studies. *[J. Manag. Stu.] ISSN: 0022-2380. Basil Blackwell*: 108 Cowley Road, Oxford OX4 1JF, U.K.; **Subscriptions**: *Marston Book Services*: P.O. Box 87, Oxford OX2 0DT, U.K.

Journal of mathematical economics. *[J. Math Econ.] ISSN: 0304-4068. Elsevier Science Publishers (North-Holland)*: P.O. Box 1991, 1000 BZ Amsterdam, The Netherlands; **Subscriptions**: *Elsevier Sequoia*: P.O.B. 851, CH-1001 Lausanne 1, Switzerland

Journal of mathematical sociology. *[J. Math. Sociol.] ISSN: 0022-250X. Gordon & Breach Science Publishers*: P.O. Box 786, Cooper Station, New York, NY. 10276, U.S.A.

Journal of Mauritian studies. *[J. Maur. Stud.]; Mahatma Gandhi Institute*: Moka, Mauritius

Journal of Mediterranean studies. *[J. Mediter. St.] ISSN: 1016-3476. Mediterranean Institute*: University of Malta, Msida, Malta

Journal of modern African studies. *[J. Mod. Afr. S.] ISSN: 0022-278X. Cambridge University Press*: The Edinburgh Building, Shaftesbury Road, Cambridge CB2 2RU, U.K.

Journal of monetary economics. *[J. Monet. Ec.] ISSN: 0304-3932. University of Rochester, William E. Simon Graduate School of Business Administration and Department of Economics*: Rochester, N.Y. 14627, U.S.A.; *Elsevier Science Publishers (North-Holland)*: P.O. Box 1991, BZ Amsterdam, The Netherlands; **Subscriptions**: *Elsevier Science Publishers*: Journals Division, P.O. Box 211, 1000 AE Amsterdam, The Netherlands

Journal of money, credit and banking. *[J. Money C. B.] ISSN: 0022-2879. Ohio State University Press*: 1070 Carmack Road, Columbus, OH. 43210, U.S.A.

Journal of occupational psychology. *[J. Occup. Psychol.] ISSN: 0305-8107. British Psychological Society*: St. Andrews House, 48 Princess Road East, Leicester LE1 7DR, U.K.

Journal of Pacific studies. *[J. Pac. Stud.] ISSN: 1011-3029. University of the South Pacific, School of Social and Economic Development*: Editorial Secretariat, P.O. Box 1168, Suva, Fiji

Journal of Palestine studies. *[J. Pal. Stud.] ISSN: 0377-919X. Institute for Palestine Studies*: 3501 M Street, N.W. Washington, DC. 20007, U.S.A.; **Publisher**: *University of California Press*: 2120 Berkeley Way, Berkeley, CA. 94720, U.S.A.

Journal of peasant studies. *[J. Peasant Stud.] ISSN: 0306-6150. Frank Cass*: Gainsborough House, 11 Gainsborough Road, London E11 1RS, U.K.

Journal of philosophy. *[J. Phil.] ISSN: 0022-362X. Journal of Philosophy*: 709 Philosophy Hall, Columbia University, New York, NY. 10027, U.S.A.

Journal of planning & environment law. *[J. Plan. Environ. Law] ISSN: 0307-4870. Sweet & Maxwell*: South Quay Plaza, 183 Marsh Wall, London, E14 9FT, U.K.

Journal of planning literature. *[J. Plan. Lit.] ISSN: 0885-4122. Ohio State University Press*: 1070 Carmack Road, Columbus, OH. 43210-1002, U.S.A.

Journal of policy history. *[J. Pol. Hist.] ISSN: 0898-0306. Pennsylvania State University Press*: Suite C., Barbara Building, 820 North University Drive, University Park, PA. 16802, U.S.A.

Journal of policy modeling. *[J. Policy M.] ISSN: 0161-8938. Elsevier Science Publishing*: 655 Avenue of the Americas, New York, NY. 10010, U.S.A.; **Subscriptions**: *Journals Fullfillment Department*: P.O. Box 882, Madison Square Station, New York, NY. 10159, U.S.A.

Journal of political economy. *[J. Polit. Ec.] ISSN: 0022-3808. University of Chicago Press*: 5720 S. Woodlawn Avenue, Chicago, IL. 60637, U.S.A.

Journal of population economics. *[J. Pop. Ec.] ISSN: 0933-1433. Springer-Verlag*: Heidelberger Platz 3, D-1000 Berlin 33, Germany

Journal of post Keynesian economics. *[J. Post. Keyn. Ec.] ISSN: 0160-3477. M.E.Sharpe*: 80 Business Park Drive, Armonk N.Y. 10504, U.S.A.

Journal of productivity analysis. *[J. Prod. Anal.] ISSN: 0895-562X. Kluwer Academic Publishers*: P.O. Box 322, 3300 AH Dordrecht, The Netherlands

Journal of public economics. *[J. Publ. Ec.] ISSN: 0047-2727. Elsevier Science Publishers (North-Holland)*: P.O. Box 1991, BZ Amsterdam, The Netherlands; **Subscriptions**: *Elsevier Sequoia*: P.O. Box 564, Lausanne, Switzerland

Journal of public policy. *[J. Public Pol.] ISSN: 0143-814X. Cambridge University Press*: The Edinburgh Building, Shaftesbury Road, Cambridge CB2 2RU, U.K.

Journal of real estate finance and economics. *[J. Real Est. Finan. Econ.] ISSN: 0895-5638. Kluwer Academic Publishers*: P.O. Box 17, 3300 AA Dordrecht, The Netherlands; **Subscriptions**: *idem*: P.O. Box 322, 3300 AH Dordrecht, The Netherlands

Journal of real estate research. *[J. Real Est. Res.] ISSN: 0896-5803. American Real Estate Society*: Box B, University Station, University of North Dakota, Grand Forks, ND. 58202, U.S.A.

Journal of regional policy. *[J. Reg. Pol.]; Isveimer*: via S. Giacomo, 19 Naples, Italy

Journal of regulatory economics. *[J. Regul. Econ.] ISSN: 092-680X. Kluwer Academic Publishers*: P.O. Box 322, 3300 AH Dordrecht, The Netherlands/ 101 Philip Drive, Assinippi Park, Norwell, MA. 02061, U.S.A.

Journal of risk and uncertainty. *[J. Risk Uncert.] ISSN: 0895-5646. Kluwer Academic Publishers*: P.O. Box 322, 3300 AH Dordrecht, The Netherlands/ 101 Philip Drive, Assinippi Park, Norwell, MA. 02061, U.S.A.

Journal of rural development and administration. *[J. Rural Devel. Admin.] ISSN: 0047-2751. Academy for Rural Development*: Academy Town, Peshawar, Pakistan

Journal of rural studies. *[J. Rural St.] ISSN: 0743-0167. Pergamon Press*: Headington Hill Hall, Oxford OX3 0BW, U.K.

Journal of social development in Africa. *[J. Soc. Devel. Afr.] ISSN: 1012-1080. School of Social Work*: P/ Bag 66022 Kopje, Harare, Zimbabwe

Journal of social policy. *[J. Soc. Pol.] ISSN: 0047-2794. Social Policy Association*; **Publisher**: *Cambridge University Press*: The Edinburgh Building, Shaftesbury Road, Cambridge CB2 2RU, U.K.

Journal of social science. *[J. Soc. Sci.]; University of Malawi, Faculty of Social Science*: Chancellor College, P.O. Box 280, Zomba, Malawi

Journal of social, political and economic studies. *[J. Soc. Pol. E.] ISSN: 0193-5941. Council for Social and Economic Studies*: Suite C-2, 1133 13th St. N.W., Washington, DC. 20005-4297, U.S.A.

Journal of Southeast Asian studies. *[J. SE. As. Stud.] ISSN: 0022-4634. National University of Singapore, Department of History*: 10 Kent Ridge Crescent, Singapore 0511; **Publisher**: *Singapore University Press*: Yusof Ishak House, 10 Kent Ridge Crescent, Singapore 0511

Journal of Southern African studies. *[J. S.Afr. Stud.] ISSN: 0305-7070. Oxford University Press*: Pinkhill House, Southfield Road, Eynsham, Oxford OX8 1JJ, U.K.

Journal of the American Planning Association. *[J. Am. Plann.] ISSN: 0194-4363. American Planning Association*: 1313 East 60th Street, Chicago, IL 60637-2891, U.S.A.

Journal of the American Statistical Association. *[J. Am. Stat. Ass.] ISSN: 0162-1459. American Statistical Association*: 1429 Duke Street, Alexandria, VA. 22314, U.S.A.

Journal of the economic and social history of the orient. *[J. Ec. Soc. Hist. O.] ISSN: 0022-4995. E.J. Brill*: P.O. Box 9000, 2300 PA Leiden, The Netherlands

Journal of the Institute of Actuaries. *[J. Inst. Actuar.] ISSN: 0020-2681. Alden Press*: Osney Mead, Oxford, OX2 0EF, U.K.

Journal of the Japanese and international economies. *[J. Jap. Int. Ec.] ISSN: 0889-1583. Tokyo Center for Economic Research*; **Publisher**: *Academic Press*: 1 East First Street, Duluth, MN. 55802, U.S.A.

Journal of the Madras University.:*Section A — Humanities [J. Madras Univ. Sec. A.]; University of Madras*: Madras-600 005, India

Journal of the Maharaja Sayajirao University of Baroda. (social science number). *[J. Mahar. Saya. (Soc. Sci. No.)]; Maharaja Sayajirao University of Baroda*: Baroda-390 002, India

Journal of the Market Research Society. *[J. Market R.] ISSN: 0025-3618. Market Research Society*: 15 Northburgh Street, London EC1V 0AH, U.K.; **Subscriptions**: *NTC Publications*: P.O. Box 69, Henley-on-Thames, Oxon RG9 2BZ, U.K.

Journal of the Mysore University.:*Section A-Arts [J. Mysore Univ. Arts]; K.T. Veerappa, M.A.*: Prasaranga, Manasagangotri, Mysore-6, India

Journal of the Pacific Society. *[J. Pacific Soc.] ISSN: 0387-4745. Pacific Society*: 4-1-6 Akasaka, Minato-ku, Tokyo, Japan

Journal of the Royal Statistical Society.:*Series B (methodological) [J. Roy. Sta. B.] ISSN: 0035-9246. Royal Statistical Society*: 25 Enford Street, London W1H 2BH, U.K.

Journal of theoretical politics. *[J. Theor. Pol.] ISSN: 0951-6928. Sage Publications*: 6 Bonhill Street, London EC2A 4PU, U.K.

Journal of time series analysis. *[J. Time Ser. Anal.] ISSN: 0143-9782. Bernoulli Society for Mathematical Statistics and Probability*: c/o International Statistical Institute, 428 Prinses Beatrixlaan, 2270 AZ Voorburg, The Netherlands; **Publisher**: *Basil Blackwell*: 108 Cowley Road, Oxford, OX4 1JF, U.K.

Journal of transport economics and policy. *[J. Transp. Ec. Pol.] ISSN: 0022 5258. University of Bath/ London School of Economics and Political Science*: Claverton Down, Bath BA2 7AY, U.K./ Houghton Street, London WC2A 2AE, U.K.

Journal of urban economics. *[J. Urban Ec.] ISSN: 0094-1190. Academic Press*: 1 First East Street, Duluth, MN 55802, U.S.A.

Journal of urban history. *[J. Urban Hist.] ISSN: 0096-1442. Sage Publications*: 2455 Teller Road, Newbury Park, CA 91320, U.S.A.

Journal of world trade. *[J. World Tr.] ISSN: 1011-6702. Werner Publishing*: P.O. Box 93, 1211 Geneva 11, Switzerland

Jurnal ekonomi Malaysia. *[J. Ekon. Malay.] ISSN: 0126-1962. Universiti Kebangsaan Malaysia, Faculty of Economics*: 43600 UKM Bangi, Selangor Darul Ehsan, Malaysia

Jurnal pengurusan. *[J. Peng.] ISBN: 0127-2713. Universiti Kebangsaan Malaysia Press, Faculty of Business Management*: 43600 UKM Bangi, Selangor Darul Ehsan, Malaysia

Kansaneläkelaitoksen julkaisuja. *[Kansan. Julk.] ISSN: 0355-4821. Kansaneläkelaitoksen*: P.O. Box 78, SF-00381, Helsinki 38, Finland

Kasarinlan. *[Kasarinlan]; University of the Philippines, Third World Studies Center*: P.O. Box 210, University of the Philippines, Diliman, Quezon City, Philippines

Keio business review. *[Keio Bus. Rev.] ISSN: 0453-4557. Society of Business and Commerce*: Keio University, Mita 2, 15-45 Minato-ku, Tokyo 108, Japan

Keio economic studies. *[Keio Econ. Stud.] ISSN: 0022-9709. Keio Economic Society*: Keio University, 2-15-45 Mita, Minato-ku, Tokyo, Japan 108

Kobe economic and business review. *[Kobe Ec. Bus. Rev.] ISSN: 0075-6407. Kobe University, Research Institute for Economics and Business Administration*: Kanematsu Memorial Hall, Kobe University, Rokko, Kobe, Japan

Kölner Zeitschrift für Soziologie und Sozialpsychologie. *[Kölner Z. Soz. Soz. psy.] ISSN: 0340-0425. Westdeutscher Verlag*: Postfach 5829, D-6200 Wiesbaden 1, Germany

Коммунист; Kommunist. *[Kommunist] ISSN: 0131-1212. Kommunisticheskaya Partiia Sovetskogo Soiuza. Tsentral'nyi Komitet*; **Publisher**: *Izdatel'stvo Pravda*: Ul. Pravdy 24, 125047, Moscow, U.S.S.R.

Konjunkturpolitik. *[Konjunkturpolitik] ISSN: 0023-3498. Duncker und Humblot*: Dietrich-Schäfer-Weg 9, 1000 Berlin 41, Germany

Korea economic report. *[Korea Econ. Rep.]; Korea Economic Report*: P.O. Box 963, Seoul 150-609, Korea

Korea observer. *[Korea Obs.] ISSN: 0023-3919. Institute of Korean Studies*: C.P.O. Box 3410, Seoul 100-643, Korea

Közgazdasági szemle. *[Közg. Sz.] ISSN: 0023-4346. Magyar Tudományos Akadémiai, Committee for Economic Sciences*; **Publisher**: *Akadémiai Kiadó*: Postafiók 24, H-1363 Budapest, Hungary

Kredit und Kapital. *[Kred. Kap.] ISSN: 0023-4591. Gesellschaft zur Förderung der wissenschaftlichen Forschung über das Spar-und Girowesen*: Sigrid Wehrmeister, Adenauerallee 110, 5300 Bonn 1, Germany; **Publisher**: *Duncker & Humblot*: Postfach 410329, Dietrich-Schäfer-Weg 9, 1000 Berlin 41, Germany

Kyklos. *[Kyklos]* *ISSN: 0023-5962*. *Helbing & Lichtenhahn Verlag*: CH-4051 Basel, Switzerland

Kyoto University economic review. *[Kyoto Univ. Econ. R.]* *ISSN: 0023-6055*. *Kyoto University, Faculty of Economics*: Sakyo-Ku, Kyoto, Japan

Labor law journal. *[Lab. Law J.]* *ISSN: 0023-6586*. *Commerce Clearing House*: 4025 W. Peterson Avenue, Chicago, IL. 60646, U.S.A.

Labour [Italy]. *[Labour [Italy]]*; *Fondazione Giacomo Brodolini*: Via Torino 122, 00184 Rome, Italy; **Subscriptions**: *Libreria Commissionaria Sansoni*: Via Benedetto Fortini 120/10, Casella Postale 552, 50125 Florence, Italy

Labour, capital and society; Travail, capital et société. *[Labour Cap. Soc.]* *ISSN: 0706-1706*. *McGill University, Centre for Developing Area Studies*: 3715 rue Peel, Montréal, Québec H31 1X1, Canada

Laissez-faire. *[Laizzez-faire]* *ISSN: 0963-6633*. *International Freedom Foundation*: Suite 500, Chesham House, 150 Regent Street, London, W1R 5FA, U.K.

Land economics. *[Land Econ.]* *ISSN: 0023-7639*. *University of Wisconsin Press*: 114 North Murray Street, Madison, WI. 53715, U.S.A.

Latin American perspectives. *[Lat. Am. Pers.]* *ISSN: 0094-582X*. *Sage Publishers*: 2455 Teller Road Newbury Park, CA. 91320, U.S.A.

Latin American research review. *[Lat. Am. Res. R.]* *ISSN: 0023-8791*. *Latin American Studies Association*: Latin American Institute, 801 Yale NE, University of New Mexico, Albuquerque, NM. 87131-1016, U.S.A.

Law and contemporary problems. *[Law Cont. Pr.]* *ISSN: 0023-9186*. *Duke University, School of Law*: Room 006, Durham, NC 27706, U.S.A.

Law and policy. *[Law Policy]* *ISSN: 0265-8240*. *Basil Blackwell*: 108 Cowley Road, Oxford OX4 1JF, U.K.; **Subscriptions**: *Marston Book Services*: P.O. Box 87, Oxford OX2 0DT, U.K.

Ledelse og Erhvervsøkonomi. *[Led. Erhv.]* *ISSN: 0902-3704*. *Foreningen af Danske Civiløkonomer (FDC)*: Postboks 348, 1503 Copenhagen, Denmark

Leiden journal of international law. *[Leiden J. Int. Law]* *ISSN: 0922-1565*. *Leiden Journal of International Law Foundation*: P.O. Box 9520, 2300 RA Leiden, The Netherlands

Links. *[Links]* *ISSN: 0024-404X*. *Verlag 2000*: Bleichstraße 5/7, Postfach 10 20 62, 6050 Offenbach 1, Germany

Local economy. *[Local. Ec.]* *ISSN: 0269-0942*. *Local Economy Policy Unit*: Southbank Polytechnic, Borough Road, London SE1 0AA, U.K.; **Publisher**: *Longman Group*: 6th Floor, Westgate House, The High, Harlow, Essex CM20 1YR, U.K.

Local government studies. *[Loc. Govt. St.]* *ISSN: 0300-3930*. *Charles Knight Publishing*: Tolley House, 2 Addiscombe Road, Croydon, Surrey CR9 5AF, U.K.

Lokayan bulletin. *[Lokay. B.]* *ISSN: 0970-5406*. *Lokayan Bulletin*: 13 Alipur Road, New Delhi 110 054, India

Maandschrift economie. *[Maan. Econ.]* *ISSN: 0013-0486*. *Wolters-Noordhoff*: Postbus 58, 9700 MB Groningen, The Netherlands

Maghreb machrek monde arabe. *[Mag. Mack. Mon. Ar.]* *ISSN: 0336-6324*. *Fondation Nationale des Sciences Politiques, Centre d'Etudes et de Recherches Internationales, Section Monde arabe/ Université de Paris, Centre d'Etudes de l'Orient contemporain*; **Publisher**: *La Documentation Française*: 29-31 quai Voltaire, 75340 Paris Cedex 07, France

Management accounting research. *[Manag. Acc. Res.]*; *Chartered Institute of Management Accountants*; **Publisher**: *Academic Press*: 24-28 Oval Road, London NW1 7DX, U.K.

Management science. *[Manag. Sci.]* *ISSN: 0025-1909*. *Institute of Management Sciences*: 290 Westminster Street, Providence, RI. 02903, U.S.A.

Manchester School of economic and social studies. *[Manch. Sch. E.]* *ISSN: 0025-2034*. *Basil Blackwell*: 108 Cowley Road, Oxford, OX4 1JF, U.K.

Marine policy. *[Mar. Pol.]* *ISSN: 0308-597X*. *Butterworth-Heinemann*: P.O. Box 63, Westbury House, Bury St. Guildford, Surrey GU2 5BH, U.K.; **Subscriptions**: *Turpin Transactions*: Distribution Centre, Blackhorse Road, Letchworth, Herts SG6 1HN, U.K.

Marine resource economics. *[Marine Res. Ec.]* *ISSN: 0738-1360*. *Taylor and Francis*: 4 John Street, London WC1N 2ET, U.K.

Marketing letters. *[Market. Lett.]* *ISSN: 0923-0645*. *Kluwer Academic Publishers*: P.O. Box 322, 3300 AH Dordrecht, The Netherlands

Marxistische Blätter. *[Marx. Blät]* *ISSN: 0542-7770*. *Neue Impulse Verlag*: Hoffnungstraße 18, 4300 Essen 1, Germany

Mast.:Maritime anthropological studies *[Mast]* *ISSN: 0922-1476*. *University of Amsterdam, Department of European and Mediterranean Studies (Euromed)*: Euromed/MAST Anthropological-Sociological Center, University of Amsterdam, O.Z. Achterburgwal 185, 1012 Amsterdam, The Netherlands

Mathematical finance. *[Math. Fin.]* *ISSN: 0960-1627*. *Basil Blackwell*: 108 Cowley Road, Oxford OX4 1JF, U.K.

Mathematical social sciences. *[Math. Soc. Sc.] ISSN: 0165 4896. Elsevier Science Publishers (North-Holland)*: P.O. Box 1991, 1000 BZ Amsterdam, The Netherlands

Media culture and society. *[Media Cult. Soc.] ISSN: 0163-4437. Sage Publications*: 6 Bonhill Street, London EC2A 4PU, U.K.

Melanesian law journal. *[Melan. Law J.]*; *University of Papua New Guinea, Faculty of Law*: Box 317, University P.O., Papua New Guinea; **Subscriptions**: *W.M. Gaunt and Sons*: 3001 Gulf Drive, Holmes Beach, FL. 33510, U.S.A.

Mens en maatschappij. *[Mens Maat.] ISSN: 0025-9454. Bohn Stafleu Van Loghum*: Postbus 246, 3990 GA Houten, The Netherlands; **Subscriptions**: *Intermedia*: Postbus 4, 2400 MA Alphen aan den Rijn, The Netherlands

Metroeconomica. *[Metroeconomica] ISSN: 0026-1386. Nuova Casa Editrice L.Cappelli*: Via Farini 14, 40124 Bologna, Italy

Michigan law review. *[MI. law. R.] ISSN: 0026-2234. Michigan Law Review*: Hutchins Hall, Ann Arbor, MI. 48109-1215, U.S.A.

Middle East business and economic review. *[M.East Bus. Econ. R.]*; *International Centre for Middle East Business and Economic Research*: P.O. Box 383, Miranda, NSW 2228, Australia

Middle East journal. *[Middle E. J.] ISSN: 0026-3141. Middle East Institute*: 1761 N. Street, N.W., Washington, DC. 20036, U.S.A.; **Publisher**: *Indiana University Press*: 10th and Morton, Bloomington, IN. 47405, U.S.A.

Middle East review. *[M.East Rev.]; World of Information*: 21 Gold Street, Saffron Waldron, Essex CB10 1EJ, U.K.

Middle Eastern studies. *[Middle E. Stud.] ISSN: 0026-3206. Frank Cass*: Gainsborough House, 11 Gainsborough Road, London E11 1RS, U.K.

Milbank quarterly. *[Milbank Q.] ISSN: 0887-378X. Milbank Memorial Fund*; **Publisher**: *Cambridge University Press*: 40 West 20th Street, New York, NY. 10011, U.S.A.

Мировая Экономика имеждународные отношения Mirovaia ekonomika i mezhdunarodnye otnosheniia. *[Mir. Ek. Mez. Ot.] ISSN: 0131-2227. Izdatel' stvo Pravda*: Ul. Pravdy 24, Moscow 117418, U.S.S.R.

MIS quarterly. *[MIS Q.] ISSN: 0276-7783. MIS Research Center*: Carlson School of Management, 271 19th Avenue S., University of Minnesota, Minneapolis, MN., U.S.A.

Modern Asian studies. *[Mod. Asian S.] ISSN: 0026-749X. Cambridge University Press*: The Edinburgh Building, Shaftesbury Road, Cambridge CB2 2RU, U.K.

Modern China. *[Mod. Chi.] ISSN: 0097-7004. Sage Publications*: 2455 Teller Road, Newbury Park, CA. 91320, U.S.A.

Modern law review. *[Mod. Law R.] ISSN: 0026-7961. Basil Blackwell*: 108 Cowley Road, Oxford OX4 1JF, U.K.

Monatsberichte der Deutschen Bundesbank. *[Monatsber. Deut. Bundes.] ISSN: 0012-0006. Deutsche Bundesbank*: Wilhelm-Epstein-Straße 14, Postfach 10 06 02, 6000 Frankfurt am Main 1, Germany

Monatsberichte. Österreichisches Institut für Wirtschaftsforschung. *[Monatsberichte] ISSN: 0029-9898. Österreichisches Institut für Wirtschaftsforschung*: Postfach 91, A-1103 Vienna, Austria

Monetaria. *[Monetaria] ISSN: 0185-1136. Centro de Estudios Monetarios Latinoamericanos*: Durango 54, Col. Roma, Delegación Cuauhtemoc, 06700 México, D.F., Mexico

Monetary and economic studies. *[Mon. Econ. S.] ISSN: 0288-8432. Bank of Japan, Institute for Monetary and Economic Studies*: C.P.O. Box 203, Tokyo, 100-91 Japan

Money affairs. *[Money Aff.] ISSN: 0187-7615. Centre for Latin American Studies (CEMLA)*: Information Department, Durango 54, 06700 Mexico City, D.F. Mexico

Monthly report of the Deutsche Bundesbank. *[Mon. Rep. Deut. Bundes.] ISSN: 0418-8292. Deutsche Bundesbank*: Wilhelm-Epstein-Straße 14, Postfach 10 06 02, 6000 Frankfurt am Main 1, Germany

Monthly review.:*State Bank of India, Economic Research Department [Mon. R. S. Bank. Ind.] ISSN: 0039-0003. State Bank of India*: New Administrative Building, Backbay Reclamation, P.O. Box 12, Bombay 400 021, India

Monthly review. *[Mon. Rev.] ISSN: 0027-0520. Monthly Review Foundation*: 122 West 27th Street, New York, NY. 10001, U.S.A.

Monumenta Nipponica. *[Monu. Nippon.] ISSN: 0027-0741. Sophia University*: 7-1 Kioi-chō, Chiyoda-ku, Tokyo 102, Japan

Мост; Most.:*Economic journal on Eastern Europe and the former Soviet Union [Мост]; Nomisma S.p.A.*: Strada Maggiore, 44, 40125, Bologna, Italy

NACLA report on the Americas. *[NACLA] ISSN: 0149-1598. North American Congress on Latin America (NACLA)*: 475 Riverside Drive, Suite 454, New York, N.Y. 10115, U.S.A.

Národní hospodářství. *[Nár. Hosp.] ISSN: 0032-0749. Panorama*: Hálkova 1, 12072 Prague, Czechoslovakia

National Institute economic review. *[Natl. Inst. Econ. R.] ISSN: 0027-9501. National Institute of Economic and Social Research*: 2 Dean Trench Street, Smith Square, London SW1P 3HE, U.K.

National interest. *[Nat. Inter.] ISSN: 0884-9382. National Affairs*: Editorial and Business Offices, 1112 16th Street, N.W., Washington, DC. 20036, U.S.A.

National Museum papers. *[Nat. Mus. Pap.]; National Museum of the Philippines/ Concerned Citizens for the National Museum*: Executive House, P.Burgos Street, 1000 Malate, Metro-Manila, Philippines

National tax journal. *[Natl. Tax. J.] ISSN: 0028-0283. National Tax Association — Tax Institute of America*: 5310 East Main Street, Columbus, OH. 43213, U.S.A.

National Westminster Bank quarterly review. *[Nat. W. Bank] ISSN: 0028-0399. National Westminster Bank*: 41 Lothbury, London EC2P 2BP, U.K.

Natural resources forum. *[Nat. Res. For.] ISSN: 0165-0203. United Nations Department of Technical Cooperation for Development*: New York, NY. 10017, U.S.A.; **Publisher**: *Butterworth-Heinemann*: P.O. Box 63, Westbury House, Bury Street, Guildford, Surrey GU2 5BH, U.K.

Natural resources journal. *[Natur. Res. J.] ISSN: 0028-0739. University of New Mexico, School of Law*: Albuquerque, NM. 87131, U.S.A.

Nature and resources. *[Nat. Resour.] ISSN: 0028-0844. UNESCO*: 7 place de Fontenoy, 75700 Paris, France; **Publisher**: *Parthenon Publishing Group*: Casterton Hall, Carnforth, Lancashire LA6 2LA, U.K.

Negotiation journal. *[Negot. J.] ISSN: 0748-4526. Plenum Press*: 233 Spring Street, New York, N.Y. 10013, U.S.A.

NEHA-bulletin. *[NEHA-B.] ISSN: 0920-9875. Nederlandsch Economisch-Historisch Archief = Netherlands Economic History Archive*: Cruquiusweg 31, 1019 AT Amsterdam, The Netherlands

Neue Gesellschaft/ Frankfurter Hefte. *[Neue Ges. Frank.] ISSN: 0177-6738. Friedrich-Ebert-Stiftung*; **Publisher**: *Verlag J.H.W. Dietz Nachf.*: In der Raste 2, 5300 Bonn 1, Germany

Neue politische literatur. *[Neue Pol. Liter.] ISSN: 0028-3320. Verlag Peter Lang*: Eschborner Landstraße 42-50, Postfach 940225, 6000 Frankfurt 90, Germany; **Subscriptions**: *idem*: Jupiterstrasse 15, CH-3000 Bern 15, Switzerland

New England economic review. *[New Eng. Ec. Rev.]; Federal Reserve Bank of Boston, Research Department*: P.O. Box 2076, Boston, MA. 02106-2076, U.S.A.

New European. *[New Eur.] ISSN: 0953-1432. MCB University Press*: 60/62, Toller Lane, Bradford, West Yorkshire BD8 9BY, U.K.

New formations. *[New Form.] ISSN: 0950-2378. Routledge*: 11 New Fetter Lane, London EC4P 4EE, U.K.; **Subscriptions**: *idem*: House, North Way, Andover, Hants. SP10 5BE, U.K.

New left review. *[New Left R.] ISSN: 0028-6060. New Left Review*: 6 Meard Street, London W1V 3HR, U.K.

New perspectives on Turkey. *[New Persp. Turk.] ISSN: 0896-6346. Simon's Rock of Bard College*: Great Barrington, MA., U.S.A.

New technology, work and employment. *[New Tech. Work. Empl.] ISSN: 0268-1072. Basil Blackwell*: 108 Cowley Road, Oxford OX4 1JF, U.K.

New York University journal of international law and politics. *[N.Y.U. J. Int'l. L. & Pol.] ISSN: 0028-7873. New York University Law Publications*: 110 West Third Street, New York, NY. 10012, U.S.A.

New Zealand economic papers. *[N.Z. Eco. Papers.] ISSN: 0077-9954. New Zealand Association of Economists*: P.O. Box 568, Wellington, New Zealand

NFT.:*Scandinavian insurance quarterly [NFT] ISSN: 0348 6516. Forsikringsforeningen i København/ Den norske Forsikringsforening/ Försäkringsföreningen i Finland/ Svenska Föräkringsföreningen*: Amaliegade 10, DK-1256 Copenhagen, Denmark/ Hansteensgt 2, N-0253 Oslo 2, Norway/ Lönnrotsgatan 19, SF-00120 Helsingfors, Finland/ Tegeluddsvägen 100, S-115 87 Stockholm, Sweden

NIAS. *[NIAS] ISSN: 0904-597X. Nordic Institute of Asian Studies*: 84 Njalsgade, DK-2300 Copenhagen S, Denmark

Nigerian field. *[Niger. F.] ISSN: 0029-0076. Nigerian Field Society*; **Subscriptions**: *Mr. P.V. Hartley/ Mrs H. Fell*: PMB 5320, Ibadan, Oyo State, Nigeria/ Limestone House, Alma Road, Tideswell, Buxton, Derbyshire SK17 8ND, U.K.

Nigerian journal of economic and social studies. *[Nig. J. Econ. Soc. Stud.] ISSN: 0029-0092. Nigerian Economic Society*: University of Ibadan, Department of Economics, Ibadan, Nigeria

Nonprofit management and leadership. *[Non. Manag. Leader.] ISSN: 1048-6682. Jossey-Bass*: 350 Sansome Street, San Francisco, CA. 94104-1310, U.S.A.

Norsk økonomisk tidsskrift. *[Nor. Økon. Tidss.] ISSN: 0039-0720. Sosialøkonomenes Forening*: Storgt. 26 IV, 0184 Oslo 1, Norway

Nueva sociedad. *[Nueva Soc.]; Nueva Sociedad*: Apartado 61.712, Caracas 1060-A, Venezuela

Observations et diagnostics économiques. *[Obser. Diag. Econ.] ISSN: 0751-6614. Observatoire Français des Conjonctures Economiques (OFCE)*: 69 quai d'Orsay, 75007 Paris, France

Ocean development and international law. *[Ocean Dev. Int.] ISSN: 0009-8320. Taylor & Francis*: 4 John Street, London WC1N 2ET, U.K.; **Subscriptions**: *Taylor & Francis*: Rankine Road, Basingstoke, Hampshire RG24 0PR, U.K.

OECD economic studies. *[OECD Ec. Stud.] ISSN: 0255-0822. OECD*: 2 rue André-Pascal, 75775 Paris Cedex 16, France

OPEC bulletin. *[OPEC B.] ISSN: 0474-6279. Organisation of Petroleum Exporting Countries*: Obere Donaustrasse 93, 1020 Vienna, Austria

OPEC review. *[OPEC Rev.]; OPECNA*: OPEC Secretariat, Obere Donaustrasse 93, 1020 Vienna, Austria; **Publisher**: *Pergamon Press*: Headington Hill Hall, Oxford OX3 0BW, U.K.

Open economies review. *[Open Econ. R.] ISSN: 0923-7992. Kluwer Academic Publishers*: P.O. Box 17, 3300 AA Dordrecht, The Netherlands; **Subscriptions**: *idem*: P.O. Box 322, 3300 AH Dordrecht, The Netherlands/P.O. Box 358, Accord Station, Hingham, MA 02018-0358, U.S.A.

Orbis. *[Orbis] ISSN: 0030-4387. Foreign Policy Research Institute*: 3615 Chestnut Street, Philadelphia, PA. 19104, U.S.A.

Ordo. *[Ordo] ISSN: 0048-2129. Gustav Fischer Verlag*: Wollgrasweg 49, D-7000 Stuttgart, Germany

Orient. *[Orient] ISSN: 0030-5227. Deutsches Orient-Institut*: Mittelweg 150, 2000 Hamburg 13, Germany; **Publisher**: *Leske + Budrich*: Postfach 300551, 5090 Leverkusen 3, Germany

Osaka economic papers. *[Osaka Eco. P.] ISSN: 0473-4548. Osaka University, Faculty of Economics*: Toyonaka, Osaka, Japan

Österreichische Zeitschrift für öffentliches Recht und Völkerrechte. *[Öster. Z. Öffent. Völk.] ISSN: 0378-3073. Springer-Verlag*: Mölkerbastei 5, P.O. Box 367, A-1011 Vienna, Austria

Österreichische Zeitschrift für Politikwissenschaft. *[Öster. Z. Polit.]; Österreichische Gesellschaft für Politikwissenschaft*; **Publisher**: *Verlag für Gesellschaftskritik*: Kaiserstraße 91, A-1070 Vienna, Austria

Osteuropa. *[Osteuropa] ISSN: 0030-6428. Deutsche Gesellschaft für Osteuropakunde*: Schaperstraße 30, 1000 Berlin 15, Germany; **Publisher**: *Deutsche Verlags-Anstalt*: Neckarstraße 121, Postfach 1060 12, 7000 Stuttgart 10, Germany

Osteuropa Wirtschaft. *[Ost. Wirt.] ISSN: 0030-6460. Deutsche Gesellschaft für Osteuropakunde*; **Publisher**: *Deutsche Verlags-Anstalt*: Neckarstraße 121, Postfach 10 60 12, D-7000 Stuttgart 10, Germany; **Subscriptions**: *Zenit Pressevertrieb*: Postfach 810640, D-7000 Stuttgart 80, Germany

Отечественная ичтория; Otechestvennaia istoriia. *[Otechest. Istor.]; idem*: ul. Dm. Ul'ianova 19, 117036 Moscow, Russia; **Publisher**: *2-ia Tipographiia Izdatel'stva "Nauka"*: Shubinskii per., 6, 1211099 Moscow, Russia

Otemon economic studies. *[Otemon Ec. Stud.] ISSN: 0475-0756. Otemon Gakuin University, School of Economics*: Ibaraki-shi, Osaka, Japan

Oxford agrarian studies. *[Ox. Agrar. Stud.] ISSN: 0264-5491. Carfax Publishing*: P.O. Box 25, Abingdon, Oxfordshire OX14 3UE, U.K.

Oxford bulletin of economics and statistics. *[Ox. B. Econ. S.] ISSN: 0305-9049. Basil Blackwell*: 108 Cowley Road, Oxford OX4 1JF, U.K.; **Subscriptions**: *Marston Book Services, Journals Subscriptions Department*: PO Box 87, Oxford, OX23 0DT, U.K.

Oxford economic papers. *[Ox. Econ. Pap.] ISSN: 0030-7653. Oxford University Press*: Pinkhill House, Southfield Road, Eynsham, Oxford, OX8 1JJ, U.K.

Oxford review of economic policy. *[Ox. R. Econ. Pol.] ISSN: 0266-903X. Oxford University Press*: Pinkhill House, Southfield Road, Eynsham, Oxford OX8 1JJ, U.K.

Pacific affairs. *[Pac. Aff.] ISSN: 0030-851X. University of British Columbia*: Vancouver, BC., V6T 1W5 Canada

Pacific economic bulletin. *[Pac. Ec. B.] ISSN: 0817-8038. Australian National University, Research School of Pacific Studies, National Centre for Development Studies*: GPO Box 4, Canberra ACT 2601, Australia

Pacific historical review. *[Pac. Hist. R.] ISSN: 0030-8684. American Historical Association, Pacific Coast Branch*: 6339 Bunche Hall, Los Angeles, CA. 90024, U.S.A.; **Publisher**: *University of California Press*: 2120 Berkeley Way, Berkeley, CA. 94720, U.S.A.

Pacific review. *[Pac. Rev.] ISSN: 0951-2748. Oxford University Press*: Pinkhill House, Southfield Road, Eynsham OX8 1JJ, U.K.

Pakistan development review. *[Pak. Dev. R.] ISSN: 0030-9729. Pakistan Institute of Development Economics*: P.O. Box 1091, Islamabad, Pakistan

Pakistan economic and social review. *[Pak. Ec. Soc. R.]; University of the Punjab, Department of Economics*: New Campus, Lahore, Pakistan

Pakistan horizon. *[Pakis. Horiz.] ISSN: 0030-980X. Pakistan Institute of International Affairs*: Aiwan-e-Sadar Road, P.O. Box 1447, Karachi 74200, Pakistan

Państwo i prawo. *[Pań. Prawo] ISSN: 0031-0980. Polska Academia Nauk, Instytut Nauk Prawnych*: Ul. Wiejska 12, 00-490 Warsaw, Poland

Papeles de económia española. *[Pap. Econ. Esp.] ISSN: 0210-9107. Confederación Española de Cajas de Ahorros, Fundación Fondo para la Investigación Económica y Social*: Juan Hurtado de Mendoza 14, 28036 Madrid, Spain

Papers in regional science. *[Pap. Reg. Sci.] ISSN: 0486-2902. Regional Science Association International*: University of Illinois at Urbana-Champaign, 1-3 Observatory, 901 South Mathews Avenue, Urbana, IL. 61801-3682, U.S.A.

Past and present. *[Past Pres.]; Oxford University Press:* Pinkhill House, Southfield Road, Eynsham, Oxford OX8 1JJ, U.K.

Peasant studies. *[Peasant Stud.]; University of Utah:* Department of History, University of Utah, Salt Lake City, UT. 84112, U.S.A.

Pensamiento iberoamericano. *[Pen. Iber.] ISSN: 0212-0208. Sociedad Estatal Quinto Centenario:* c/ Serrano, 187-189.28002 Madrid, Spain; **Subscriptions:** *Instituto de Cooperación Iberoamericana:* Avenida de los Reyes Católicos, 4.28040 Madrid, Spain

Pénzügyi szemle. *[Pénz. Sz.] ISSN: 0031-496X. Pénzügyminisztérium:* Postafiók 481, 1269 Budapest, Hungary

Peripherie. *[Peripherie] ISSN: 0173-184X. Wissenschaftliche Vereinigung für Entwicklungstheorie und Entwicklungspolitik:* Institut für Soziologie, Scharnhorststraße 121, D-4400 Münster, Germany; **Publisher:** *Verlag Peripherie:* LN-Vertrieb, Gneisenaustraße 2, D-1000 Berlin 61, Germany

Perspectiva económica. *[Persp. Econ.] ISSN: 0100-039X. Universidade do Vale do Rio dos Sinos:* Núcleo de Publicações Unisinos, Caixa Postal 275, Avenida Unisinos 950, 93020 São Leopoldo RS, Brazil

Perspectives in energy. *[Perspect. Ener.] ISSN: 0265-8135. Moscow International Energy Club:* Izhorskaya 13/19, 127412 Moscow, U.S.S.R.; **Publisher:** *Turpion:* 207 Brondesbury Park, London NW2 5JN, U.K.; **Subscriptions:** *Turpin Transactions:* Blackhorse Road, Letchworth, Herts SG6 1HN, U.K.

Pesquisa e planejamento econômico. *[Pesq. Plan. Ec.] ISSN: 0100-0551. Instituto de Planejamento Econômico e Social (IPEA):* Av. Presidente Antônio Carlos 51, CEP 20 020, Rio de Janeiro, Brazil

Petroleum economist. *[Petrol. Econ.] ISSN: 0306-395X. Petroleum Economist:* 25-31 Ironmonger Row, London EC1V 3PN, U.K.

Philippine economic journal. *[Philip. Econ. J.]; Philippine Economic Society:* Room 302, Philippine Social Science Council Building, Don Mariano Marcos Avenue, Diliman, Quezon City, Philippines

Philippine studies. *[Phil. Stud.] ISSN: 0031-7837. Ateneo de Manila University Press:* P.O. Box 154, Manila 1099, Philippines

Philosophy & public affairs. *[Philos. Pub.] ISSN: 0048-3915. Princeton University Press:* 41 William Street, Princeton, NJ. 08540, U.S.A.; **Subscriptions:** *Johns Hopkins University Press:* Journals Division, 701 West 40th Street, Suite 275, Baltimore, MD. 21211, U.S.A.

Philosophy of the social sciences. *[Philos. S. Sc.] ISSN: 0048-3931. Sage Publications:* 2455 Teller Road, Newbury Park, CA. 91320, U.S.A.

Planeación y desarrollo. *[Plan. Desarr.] ISSN: 0034-8686. Departamento Nacional de Planeación:* Calle 26 No. 13-19 Piso 2°, Santafé de Bogota, Colombia

Planning and administration. *[Plan. Admin.] ISSN: 0304-117X. International Union of Local Authorities:* 41 Wassenaarseweg, 2596 CG The Hague, The Netherlands

Planning outlook. *[Plan. Out.] ISSN: 0032-0714. University of Newcastle-upon-Tyne, Department of Town and Country Planning:* Newcastle-upon-Tyne NE1 7RU, U.K.

Плановое Хозяйство; Planovoe khoziaistvo. *[Plan. Khoz.] ISSN: 0370-0356. Gosplan, SSSR;* **Publisher:** *Izdatel'stvo Ekonomika:* Berezhkovskaia naberezhnaia 6, 121864 Moscow, U.S.S.R.

Policy sciences. *[Policy Sci.] ISSN: 0032-2687. Kluwer Academic Publishers:* P.O. Box 17, 3300 AA Dordrecht, The Netherlands

Politica. *[Politica.] ISSN: 0105-0710. Institut for Statskundskab Universitetsparken:* 8000 Århus C, Denmark

Politica economica. *[Pol. Econ.]; Società editrice il Mulino:* Strada Maggiore 37, 40125 Bologna, Italy

Political geography. *[Pol. Geogr.] ISSN: 0962-6298. Butterworth-Heinemann:* Linacre House, Jordan Hill, Oxford OX2 8DP, U.K.

Political geography quarterly. *[Polit. Geogr. Q.] ISSN: 0260-9827. Butterworth-Heinemann:* Westbury House, Bury Street, P.O. Box 63, Guildford, Surrey GU2 5BH, U.K.

Political science quarterly. *[Pol. Sci. Q.] ISSN: 0032-3195. Academy of Political Science:* 475 Riverside Drive, Suite 1274, New York, NY. 10115-0012, U.S.A.

Politička misao. *[Pol. Misao] ISSN: 0032-3241. Facultet Političkih Nauka u Zagrebu:* 41000 Zagreb, Lepušićeva 6, Yugoslavia

Politico. *[Politico] ISSN: 0032-325X. Universita degli Studi di Pavia, Facolta' di scienze politiche;* **Publisher:** *Casa Editrice Dott. A. Giuffrè:* Servizio Pubblicità via Busto Arsizio, 40 -20151 Milano, Italy

Politics. *[Politics (U.K.)] ISSN: 0263-3957. Political Studies Association of the United Kingdom;* **Publisher:** *Whiting and Birch:* P.O. Box 872, Forest Hill, London SE23 3HL, U.K.

Politics and society in Germany, Austria and Switzerland. *[Pol. Soc. Ger. Aust. Swit.] ISSN: 0954-6030. University of Nottingham, Institute of German, Austrian and Swiss Affairs:* University Park, Nottingham NG7 2RD, U.K.

Politics and the life sciences. *[Polit. Life] ISSN: 0730-9384. Association for Politics and the Life Sciences:* Northern Illinois University, DeKalb, IL. 60115-2854, U.S.A.

Politique africaine. *[Pol. Afr.] ISSN: 0244-7827. Association des chercheurs de politique africaine*; **Publisher**: *Editions Karthala*: 22-24 boulevard Arago, 75013 Paris, France

Politique étrangère. *[Pol. Etran.] ISBN: 0032-342X. Institut Français des Relations Internationales*: 6 rue Ferrus, 75683 Paris Cedex 14, France; **Subscriptions**: *Armand Colin*: BP 22, 41353 Vineuil, France

Politique internationale. *[Polit. Int.] ISSN: 0221-2781. Politique Internationale*: 11 rue du Bois de Boulogne, 75116 Paris, France

Politiques et management public. *[Pol. Manag. Publ.] ISSN: 0758-1726. Institut de Management Public*: 14 rue Corvisart, 75013 Paris, France

Population and development review. *[Pop. Dev. Rev.] ISSN: 0098-7921. Population Council*: One Dag Hammarskjold Plaza, New York, N.Y. 10017, U.S.A.

Population and environment. *[Popul. Envir.] ISSN: 0199-0039. Human Sciences Press*: 233 Spring Street, New York, N.Y. 10013-1578, U.S.A.

Population research and policy review. *[Pop. Res. Pol. R.] ISSN: 0167-5923. Kluwer Academic Publishers*: P.O. Box 17, 3300 AH Dordrecht, The Netherlands; **Subscriptions**: *idem*: P.O. Box 322, 3300 AH Dordrecht, The Netherlands

Population studies. *[Pop. Stud.] ISSN: 0032-4728. London School of Economics, Population Investigation Committee*: Houghton Street, Aldwych, London WC2A 2AE, U.K.

Post-Soviet affairs. *[Post-Sov. Aff.] ISSN: 1060-586X. Joint Committee on Soviet Studies of the American Council of Learned Societies and the Social Science Research Council*; **Publisher**: *V.H. Winston & Son*: Silver Spring, MD., U.S.A.

Praca i zabezpieczenie społeczne. *[Pra. Zab. Społ.] ISSN: 0032-6186. Państwowe Wydawnictwo Ekonomiczne*: Ul. Niecała 4a, Warsaw, Poland

Praxis international. *[Prax. Int.] ISSN: 0260-8448. Basil Blackwell*: 108 Cowley Road, Oxford OX4 JJF, U.K.

Présence africaine. *[Prés. Afr.] ISSN: 0032-7638. Société Africaine de Culture*: 25 bis, rue des Ecoles, 75005 Paris, France

Problèmes d'Amérique latine. *[Prob. Am.Lat.] ISSN: 0765-1333. Documentation française*: 29/31 quai Voltaire, 75340 Paris Cedex 07, France

Problemi spoline trgovine I konjunkture. *[Prob. Spol. Trg. Konjunk.] ISSN: 0032-938X. Institut za Spolinu Trguvinu*: Moše Pijade 8/III, Belgrade, Yugoslavia

Problems of communism. *[Probl. Commu.] ISSN: 0032-941X. US Information Agency*: 301 4th Street SW Washington, DC. 20547, U.S.A.; **Subscriptions**: *Superintendent of Documents*: US Government Printing Office, Washington DC. 20402, U.S.A.

Proceedings. American Statistical Association. *[Proc. Am. Stat. Ass.]; American Statistical Association*: 1429 Duke Street, Alexandria, VA. 22314, U.S.A.

Professional geographer. *[Prof. Geogr.] ISSN: 0033-0124. Association of American Geographers*: 1710 Sixteenth Street, N.W., Washington, DC. 20009-3198, U.S.A.

Progress in human geography. *[Prog. H. Geog.] ISSN: 0309-1325. Edward Arnold*: Mill Road, Dunton Green, Sevenoaks, Kent TN13 2YA, U.K.; **Subscriptions**: *Subscription Department, Edward Arnold Journals*: 42 Bedford Square, London WC1B 3SL, U.K.

Progress in planning. *[Prog. Plan.] ISSN: 0305-9006. Pergamon Press*: Headington Hill Hall, Oxford OX3 0BW, U.K.

Project appraisal. *[Proj. App.] ISSN: 0268-8867. Beech Tree Publishing*: 10 Watford Close, Guildford, Surrey GU1 2EP, U.K.

Prokla.:*Probleme des Klassenkampfs [Prokla]; Vereinigung zur Kritik der politischen Ökonomie*; **Publisher**: *Rotbuch Verlag*: Potsdamer Str. 98, 1000 Berlin 30, Germany

Przegląd statystyczny. *[Prz. Staty.] ISSN: 0033-2372. Polska Akademia nauk, Komitet Statystyki i Ekonometrii*: ul. Miodowa 10, Warsaw, Poland; **Subscriptions**: *ARS Polona*: Krakowskie Przedmieście 7, 00-068 Warsaw, Poland

Public administration. *[Publ. Admin.] ISSN: 0033-3298. Royal Institute for Public Administration*: 3 Birdcage Walk, London SW1H 9JH, U.K.; **Publisher**: *Basil Blackwell*: 108 Cowley Road, Oxford OX4 1JF, U.K.

Public administration and development. *[Publ. Adm. D.] ISSN: 0271-2075. Royal Institute of Public Administration*: Regent's College, Inner Circle, Regent's Park, London NW1 4NS, U.K.; **Publisher**: *John Wiley & Sons*: Baffins Lane, Chichester, West Sussex PO19 1UD, U.K.

Public administration review. *[Publ. Adm. Re.] ISSN: 0033-3352. American Society for Public Administration*: 1120 G. Street, NW, Suite 500, Washington, DC. 20005, U.S.A.

Public affairs quarterly. *[Publ. Aff. Q.] ISSN: 0887-0373. Philosophy Documentation Center/ North American Philosophical Publications*: Bowling Green State University, Bowling Green, OH. 43403, U.S.A.

Public choice. *[Publ. Choice] ISSN: 0048-5829. Kluwer Academic Publishers*: Spuiboulevard 50, Postbus 17, 3300 AA Dordrecht, The Netherlands

Public enterprise. *[Publ. Enter.] ISSN: 0351-3564. International Center for Public Enterprises in Developing Countries*: Titova 104, 61109 Ljubljana, P.O. Box 92, Yugoslavia

Public finance; Finances publiques. *[Publ. Finan.] ISSN: 0033-3476. Public Finance/ Finances Publiques*: c/o Prof. Dieter Biehl, Institut für Öffentliche Wirtschaft, Geld und Währung, Johann Wolfgang Goethe-Universität, Postfach 111932, D-6000 Frankfurt am Main 11, Germany; **Subscriptions**: *Public Finance*: Goethestraße 13, D-6240 Königstein, Germany

Public finance quarterly. *[Publ. Fin. Q.] ISSN: 0048-5853. Sage Publications*: 2455 Teller Road, Newbury Park, CA. 91320, U.S.A.

Public interest. *[Publ. Inter.] ISSN: 0033-3557. National Affairs*: 1112 16th Street, N.W., Suite 530, Washington, D.C. 20036, U.S.A; **Subscriptions**: *Public Interest subscription office*: P.O. Box 3000, Denville, NJ. 07834, U.S.A.

Public money and management. *[Publ. Money. Manag.] ISSN: 0954-0962. Public Finance Foundation*: 3 Robert Street, London WC2N 6BH, U.K.; **Publisher**: *Basil Blackwell*: 108 Cowley Road, Oxford OX4 1JF, U.K.

Publizistik. *[Publizistik] ISSN: 0033-4006. Deutsche Gesellschaft für Publizistik- und Kommunikationswissenschaft/ Österreichische Gesellschaft für Publizistik- und Kommunikationswissenschaft/ Schweizerische Gesellschaft für Kommunikations- und Medienwissenschaft*: Martin-Legros-Straße 53, D-5300 Bonn 1, Germany; **Publisher**: *Universitätsverlag Konstanz*: Postfach 102051, D-7750 Konstanz, Germany

Quaderni di sociologia. *[Quad. Sociol.] ISSN: 0033-4952. Edizioni di Comunità*: 20090 Segrate, Milan, Italy

Quarterly bulletin. Central Bank of Ireland. *[Q. B. Ctr. Bank Ire.] ISSN: 0069-1542. Central Bank of Ireland*: Publications Section, P.O. Box No. 559, Dame Street, Dublin 2, Ireland

Quarterly economic bulletin. *[Q. Econ. Bull.] ISSN: 0952-0724. Liverpool Research Group in Macroeconomics*; **Publisher**: *Liverpool Macroeconomic Research*: University of Liverpool, Department of Economics and Accounting, P.O. Box 147, Liverpool, L69 3BX, U.K.

Quarterly economic commentary. *[Q. Eco. Comment.] ISSN: 0306-7866. The Fraser of Allander Institute*: Curran Building, 100 Cathedral Street, Glasgow G4 0LN, U.K.

Quarterly economic review. Bank of Korea. *[Q. Ec. R. Bank Korea]*; *Bank of Korea*: Seoul, Korea

Quarterly journal of agricultural economy. *[Quart. J. Agr. Ec.]*

Quarterly journal of economics. *[Q. J. Econ.] ISSN: 0033-5533. Harvard University*: Cambridge, MA. 02138, U.S.A.; **Publisher**: *MIT Press*: 55 Hayward Street, Cambridge, MA. 02142, U.S.A.

Quarterly review of economics and business. *[Q. R. Econ. Bu.] ISSN: 0033-5797. University of Illinois at Urbana-Champaign, Bureau of Economic and Business Research*: 428 Commerce West, 1206 South Sixth Street, Champaign, IL. 61820, U.S.A.

Quarterly review of economics and finance. *[Q Rev. Econ. Finan.] ISSN: 0033-5797. Midwest Economics Association, Department of Economics*: Illinois State University, Normal, Illinois 61761, U.S.A.; **Publisher**: *Bureau of Economic and Business Research*: 428 Commerce West, 1206 South Sixth Street, Champaign, IL. 61820, U.S.A.

Quarterly review. Federal Reserve Bank of New York. *[Q. R. Fed. Res. Bank N.Y.] ISSN: 0147-6580. Federal Reserve Bank of New York, Research and Statistics Group*: Public Information Department, 33 Liberty Street, New York, NY. 10045, U.S.A.

Quarterly review. Sveriges Riksbank. *[Q. Rev. Sver. Riks.] ISSN: 0346-6583. Sveriges Riksbank*: Economics Department, 103 37 Stockholm, Sweden

R&D management. *[R&D Manag.] ISSN: 0033-6807. Basil Blackwell*: 108 Cowley Road, Oxford OX4 1JF, U.K.

Race and class. *[Race Class] ISSN: 0306-3965. Institute of Race Relations*: 2-6 Leeke Street, King's Cross Road, London WC1X 9HS, U.K.

Rand journal of economics. *[Rand J. Eco.] ISSN: 0741-6261. Rand Corporation*: 1700 Main Street, P.O. Box 2138, Santa Monica, CA, 90401-3297, U.S.A.; **Subscriptions**: *Rand Journal of Economics*: P.O. Box 328, Mount Morris, Il. 61054, U.S.A.

Rassegna economica. *[Ras. Econ.]; Banco di Napoli*: Ufficio Studi, via Toledo 177-178, 80132 Naples, Italy

Rassegna italiana di sociologia. *[Rass. It. Soc.] ISSN: 0486 0349. Societá Editrice il Mulino*: Strada Maggiore 37, 40125 Bologna, Italy

Recherches économiques de Louvain. *[Rech. Ec. Louvain] ISSN: 0770-4518. Université Catholique de Louvain, Departement des Sciences Economiques*: Place Montesquieu 3, 1348 Louvain-la-Neuve, Belgium; **Publisher**: *De Boeck-Wesmael*: Av. Louise 203, Boite 1, B-1050 Brussels, Belgium

Recht der internationalen Wirtschaft. *[Recht Int. Wirst.] ISSN: 0340-7926. Verlag Recht und Wirtschaft*: Häusserstraße 14, Postfach 10 59 60, 6900 Heidelberg, Germany

Regional science and urban economics. *[Reg. Sci. Urb. Econ.] ISSN: 0166-0462. Elsevier Science Publishers (North-Holland)*: P.O. Box 1991, 1000 BZ Amsterdam, The Netherlands; **Subscriptions**: *idem*: Journals Division, P.O. Box 211, 1000 AE Amsterdam, The Netherlands

Regional studies. *[Reg. Stud.] ISSN: 0034-3404. Regional Studies Association*; **Publisher**: *Cambridge University Press*: The Edinburgh Building, Shaftesbury Road, Cambridge CB2 2RU, U.K.

Research in economic anthropology. *[Res. Eco. Anthrop.] ISSN: 0190-1281. JAI Press*: 55 Old Post Road, No.2., Greenwich, CT. 06830, U.S.A.

Research in political economy. *[Res. Pol. Econ.] ISSN: 0161-7230. JAI Press*: 55 Old Post Road, Greenwich, CT. 06830, U.S.A.

Research in population economics. *[Res. Popul. Econ.] ISSN: 0-89232-943-2. JAI Press*: 55 Old Post Road No.2, Greenwich, CT 06830, U.S.A.

Research in social stratification and mobility. *[R. Soc. Strat. Mob.] ISSN: 0276-5624. JAI Press*: 55 Old Post Road No.2, Greenwich, CT. 066830, U.S.A.

Reserve Bank bulletin. *[Res. Bank B. NZ] ISSN: 0112-871X. Reserve Bank of New Zealand*: Publications Officer, Economics Department, P.O. Box 2498, Wellington, New Zealand

Reserve Bank of India bulletin. *[Res. Bank Ind. B.] ISSN: 0034 5512. Reserve Bank of India, Department of Economic Analysis and Policy*: Amar Building, Ground Floor, P.M. Road, P.B. No. 1036 Bombay 400 001, India

Resources policy. *[Res. Pol.] ISSN: 0301-4207. Butterworth-Heinemann*: Linacre House, Jordan Hill, Oxford, OX2 8DP, U.K.

Rethinking Marxism. *[Rethink. Marx.] ISSN: 0893-5696. Association for Economic and Social Analysis*: University of Massachusetts-Amhurst, Amhurst, MA., U.S.A.; **Publisher**: *Guilford Publications*: 72 Spring Street, New York, NY. 10012, U.S.A.

Review of African political economy. *[Rev. Afr. Pol. Ec.] ISSN: 0305-6244. ROAPE Publications*: Regency House, 75-77 St. Mary's Road, Sheffield S2 4AN, U.K.

Review of Austrian economics. *[R. Austrian Econ.] ISSN: 0889-3047. Ludwig von Mises Institute*: Auburn University, Auburn, Alabama 36849, U.S.A.; **Publisher**: *Kluwer Academic Publishers*: P.O. Box 322, 3300 AH Dordrecht, The Netherlands

Review of black political economy. *[Rev. Bl. Pol. Ec.] ISSN: 0034-6446. National Economic Association/ Clark Atlanta University, Southern Center for Studies in Public Policy*: 240 Brawley Drive, S.W. Atlanta, GA. 30314, U.S.A.; **Publisher**: *Transaction Publishers*: Rutgers University, New Brunswick, NJ. 08903, U.S.A.

Review of Central and East European law. *[R. C. & E.Eur. Law] ISSN: 0925-9880. Documentation Office for East European Law*: Hugo de Grootstraat 32, P.O. Box 952i, 2300 RA Leiden, The Netherlands; **Publisher**: *Kluwer Academic Publishers*: P.O. Box 322, 3300 AH Dordrecht, The Netherlands

Review of economic conditions in Italy. *[Rev. Ec. Con. It.] ISSN: 0034-6799. Banco di Roma*: Viale U. Tupini 180, 00144 Rome, Italy

Review of economic studies. *[R. Econ. S.] ISSN: 0034-6527. Basil Blackwell*: 108 Cowley Road, Oxford OX4 1JF, U.K.; **Subscriptions**: *Marston Book Services*: P.O. Box 87, Oxford OX2 0DT, U.K.

Review of economics and statistics. *[Rev. Econ. St.] ISSN: 0034-6535. Harvard University*; **Publisher**: *Elsevier Science Publishers (North-Holland)*: P.O. Box 1991, 1000 BZ Amsterdam, The Netherlands; **Subscriptions**: *idem*: Journal Department, P.O. Box 211, 1000 AE Amsterdam, The Netherlands

Review of financial studies. *[R. Finan. Stud.] ISSN: 0893-9454. Society for Financial Studies*; **Publisher**: *Oxford University Press*: 2001 Evans Road, Cary, NC. 27513, U.S.A.

Review of income and wealth. *[R. In. Weal.] ISSN: 0034-6586. International Association for Research in Income and Wealth*: Dept. of Economics, 269 Mercer Street, Room 700, New York University, New York, NY. 10003, U.S.A.; **Subscriptions**: *The Review of Income and Wealth*: c/o J.W. Arrowsmith, Winterstoke Road, Bristol BS3 2NT, U.K.

Review of Indonesian and Malaysian affairs./*RIMA/*— *[R. Ind. Malay. Aff.] ISSN: 0034-6594. University of Sydney, Department of Indonesian and Malayan Studies*: Sydney, NSW 2001, Australia

Review of industrial organization. *[R. Indust. Organ.] ISSN: 0889-938X. Kluwer Academic Publishers*: P.O. Box 322, 3300 AH Dordrecht, The Netherlands

Review of international co-operation. *[R. Int. Co-op.] ISSN: 0034-6608. International Co-operative Alliance*: Route des Morillons 15, CH-1218 Le Grand Saconnex, Geneva, Switzerland

Review of Islamic economics. *[R. Islam. Econ.] ISSN: 0962-2055. International Association for Islamic Economics*: Review of Islamic Economics, Markfield Dawah Centre, Ratby Lane, Markfield, Leicester LE6 0RN, U.K.

Review of political economy. *[R. Pol. Econ.] ISSN: 0953-8259. Edward Arnold*: Mill Road, Dunton Green, Sevenoaks, Kent TN13 2YA, U.K.; **Subscriptions**: *idem*: Subscription Department, 42 Bedford Square, London WC1B 3SL, U.K.

Review of quantitative finance and accounting. *[R. Quant. Finan. Account.] ISSN: 0924-865X. Kluwer Academic Publishers*: P.O. Box 322, 3300 AH Dordrecht, The Netherlands/ 101 Philip Drive, Assinippi Park, Norwell, MA. 02061, U.S.A.

Review of radical political economics. *[Rev. Rad. Pol. Ec.] ISSN: 0486-6134. Union for Radical Political Economics*: c/o Dept. of Economics, University of California, Riverside, CA. 92521, U.S.A.

Review of rural and urban planning in Southern and Eastern Africa. *[R. Rur. Urb. Plan. S.& E.Afr.]; University of Zimbabwe, Department of Rural and Urban Planning*: P.O. Box MP 167, Mount Pleasant, Harare, Zimbabwe

Review of social economy. *[R. Soc. Econ.] ISSN: 0034-6764. Association for Social Economics*: c/o Department of Economics, Northern Illinois University, DeKalb, IL. 60115, U.S.A.

Review of socialist law. *[R. Soc. Law.] ISSN: 0165-0300. Kluwer Academic Publishers*: P.O. Box 17, 3300 AA Dordrecht, The Netherlands; **Subscriptions**: *idem*: P.O. Box 322, 3300 AH Dordrecht, The Netherlands

Review of the economic situation of Mexico. *[Rev. Econ. Sit. Mex.] ISSN: 0187-3407. Banco Nacional de Mexico, Department of Economic Research*: Av. Madero 21, Mexico, D.F. 06000, Mexico

Review of urban and regional development studies. *[R. Urban. Region. Dev. S.]; Applied Regional Science Conference*; **Publisher**: *Tokyo International University, Urban Development Institute*: Nakanishi Building 6F, 8-4 Takadanobaba 4-chome, Shinjuku-Ku, Tokyo 169, Japan

Review. Federal Reserve Bank of St. Louis. *[R. Fed. Resv. Bank St.Louis] ISSN: 0014-9187. Federal Reserve Bank of St. Louis, Research and Public Information Department*: P.O. Box 442, St. Louis, MO. 63166, U.S.A.

Review. Fernand Braudel Center. *[Rev. F. Braudel. Ctr.] ISSN: 0147-9032. State University of New York, Fernand Braudel Center*: P.O. Box 6000, Binghamton, NY. 13902-6000, U.S.A.

Revista brasileira de economia. *[Rev. Bras. Ec.] ISSN: 0034-7140. Fundação Getulio Vargas, Escola da Pós-Graduação em Economia*: Caixa Postal 9052, CEP 20000, Rio de Janeiro, Brazil

Revista de administración pública. *[Rev. Admin. Públ.] ISSN: 0034-7639. Centro de Estudios Constitucionales*: Fuencarral 45, 28004 Madrid, Spain

Revista de ciência política. *[Rev. Ciê. Pol.] ISSN: 0034-8023. Fundação Getulio Vargas*: Praia de Botafogo, 188-CEP 22.253 Caixa Postal 9.052, 20.000 Rio de Janeiro, Brazil

Revista de ciencias sociales. *[Rev. Cien. Soc.] ISSN: 0034-7817. Universidad de Puerto Rico, Facultad de Ciencias Sociales, Centro de Investigaciones Sociales*: Rio Piedras, Puerto Rico 00931

Revista de econometria. *[Rev. Economet.] ISSN: 0101-7012. Soceidade Brasileira de Econometria*: Universidade Federal de Pernambuco, Departamento de Economia — PIMES, Cidade Universitária, 50739 Recife, PE, Brazil

Revista de economía. *[Revis. Econ.]; Banco Central de Uruguay*: Casilla de Correo 1467, 1100 Montevideo, Uruguay

Revista de economia y estadistica. *[R. Econ. Estad.] ISSN: 0034-8066. Universidad Nacional de Cordoba, Facultad de Ciencias Economicas*: Ciudad Universitaria, Estafeta 32, 5000 Córdoba, Argentina

Revista de fomento social. *[Rev. Fom. Soc.] ISSN: 0015-6043. INSA-ETEA*: Escritor Castilla Aguayo 4, Apartado 439, 14004 Cordoba, Spain; **Publisher**: *CESI-JESPRE*: Pablo Aranda 3, 28006 Madrid, Spain

Revista de historia económica. *[Rev. Hist. Ec.] ISSN: 0212-6109. Centro de Estudios Constitucionales*: Plaza de la Marina Española 9, Apdo. 50 877, Madrid 13, Spain

Revista de planeación y desarrollo. *[Rev. Plan. Desar.] ISSN: 0034-8686. Departamento Nacional de Planeación*: Calle 26 No. 13-19 Piso 16 Biblioteca, Bogotá, Colombia

Revista del Banco de la República. *[Rev. Banco Rep.] ISSN: 0005-4828. Banco de la República*: Departamento Editorial, Calle 13, No. 35-51, Bogotá, Colombia

Revista econômica do nordeste. *[R. Eco. Nord.] ISSN: 0100-4956. Banco do Nordeste do Brasil*: Av. Paranjana 5 700, Caixa Postal 628, 60 715 Fortaleza, Brazil

Revista interamericana de planificación. *[Rev. Int.Am. Plan.] ISSN: 0037-8593. Sociedad Interamericana de Planificación*: 3a Avenida Norte No.4, Antigua Guatemala, Guatemala

Revista occidental. *[Rev. Occid.]; Instituto de Investigaciones Culturales Latinoamericanas (IICLA)*: Apartado 38, Correo Central, 22000 Tijuana, Baja California, N., Mexico

Revista paraguaya de sociología. *[Rev. Parag. Sociol.]; Centro Paraguayo de Estudios Sociológicos*: Eligio Ayala 973, Casilla no.2.157, Asunción, Paraguay

Revue algérienne des sciences juridiques économiques et politiques. *[Rev. Algér.]; Université d'Alger, Institut de Droit et des Sciences Administratives*: 2 rue Didouche Mourad, Algiers, Algeria

Revue canadienne d'études de développement; Canadian journal of development studies. *[Rev. Can. Etud. Dével.] ISSN: 0225-5189. Université d'Ottawa, Institut de développement international et de coopération/ University of Ottawa, Institute for International Development and Co-operation*: 25 University Street, Ottawa, Ontario K1N 6N5, Canada

Revue de Corée. *[Rev. Cor.]; UNESCO*; **Publisher**: *Commission Nationale Coréene*: BP 64 Poste Centrale, Seoul, Korea

Revue de droit social = Tijdschrift voor sociaal recht. *[R. Droit. Soc.] ISSN: 0035-1113. Lacier*: rue des Minimes, 1000 Brussels, Belgium

Revue de l'économie meridionale. *[R.E.M.] ISSN: 0987-3813. Université de Montpellier, Faculté de droit et des sciences économiques, Centre regional de la productivité et des études économiques*: 39 rue de l'Université, 34060 Montpellier Cedex, France; **Publisher**: *Centre national de la recherche scientifique*: 1 Place Aristide Briand, 92195 Meudon Cedex, France

Revue d'économie politique. *[Rev. Ec. Polit.] ISSN: 0373-2630. Éditions Sirey*: 22 rue Soufflot, 75005 Paris, France; **Subscriptions**: *Dalloz*: 35 rue Tournefort, 75240 Paris Cedex 05, France

Revue d'économie régionale et urbaine. *[R..Ec. Reg. Urb.] ISSN: 0180-7307. ADICUEER (Association des Directeurs d'Instituts et des Centres Universitaires d'Etudes Economiques Régionales)*: 4 Rue Michelet, 75006 Paris, France

Revue des études coopératives mutualistes et associatives. *[R. Et. Coop. Mut. Ass.] ISSN: 0035-2020. Coopérative d'Information et d'Edition Mutualiste*: 255 rue de Vaugirard, 75719 Paris Cedex 15, France

Revue d'études comparatives est-ouest. *[Rev. Et. Comp.] ISSN: 0338-0599. Institut de recherches juridiques comparatives du C.N.R.S., Centre d'études des pays socialistes/ Economie et techniques de planification des pays de l'est*; **Publisher**: *Editions de Centre national de la recherche scientifique*: 1 Place Aristide Briand, 92195 Meudon Cedex, France; **Subscriptions**: *Service des Abonnements*: 26 rue Boyer, 75020 Paris, France

Revue du financier. *[R. Finan.] ISSN: 0223-0143. Masson*: BP 22, F41353 Vineuil, France

Revue du marché commun. *[R. Mar. Comm.] ISSN: 0035-2616. Editions Techniques et Economiques*: 3 rue Soufflot, 75005 Paris, France

Revue du monde musulman et de la Méditerranée. *[R. Mon. Musul. Med.] ISSN: 0997-1327. Association pour l'étude des sciences humaines en Afrique du Nord et au Proche-Orient*; **Publisher**: *Editions EDISUD*: La Calade, 13090 Aix-en-Provence, France

Revue du travail. *[Rev. Trav.] ISSN: 0035-2705. Ministère de l'emploi et du travail*: Revue du Travail, rue Belliard 53, Brussels 1040, Belgium

Revue économique et sociale. *[R. Econ. Soc.] ISSN: 0035-2772. Société d'Études Economiques et Sociales*: Bâtiment des Facultés des Sciences Humaines (BFSH1), 1015 Lausanne-Dorigny, Switzerland

Revue européenne des sciences sociales.:*Cahiers Vilfredo Pareto* *[Rev. Eur. Sci. Soc.] ISSN: 0008-0497. Librairie DROZ*: 11 rue Massot, CH-1211 Geneva, Switzerland

Revue fiscalité européenne. *[Rev. Fisc. Eur.] ISSN: 0242-5599. Cahiers fiscaux européens*: 51 avenue Reine Victoria, 06000 Nice, France

Revue française d'administration publique. *[R. Fr. Admin. Publ.] ISSN: 0152-7401. Institut International d'Administration Publique*: 2 avenue de l'Observatoire, 75006 Paris, France; **Subscriptions**: *La Documentation Française*: 29-31 quai Voltaire, 75340 Paris Cedex 07, France

Revue française de science politique. *[R. Fr. Sci. Pol.] ISSN: 0035-2950. Fondation nationale des sciences politiques/ Association française de science politique*: 27 rue Saint-Guillame, 75341 Paris, France

Revue hellénique de droit international. *[R. Hellén. Int.] ISSN: 0035-3256. Institut Hellénique de Droit International et Etranger*: 73, rue Solonos, 106 79 Athens, Greece

Revue juridique, politique et économique du Maroc. *[R. Jur. Pol. Econ. Maroc] ISSN: 0251-4761. Faculté des Sciences Juridiques, Economiques et Sociales*: B.P. 721 Rabat-Agdal, Morocco

Revue politique et parlementaire. *[R.P.P.] ISSN: 0035-385X. Revue Politique et Parlementaire*: 110, rue de Rivoli, 75001 Paris, France

Revue roumaine des sciences sociales.:*Série des sciences économiques* *[Rev. Roumaine Sci.Soc. Série Sci. Econ.] ISSN: 0035-404X. Editura Academiei Române*: Calea Victoriei 125, 79717 Bucharest, Romania; **Subscriptions**: *Rompresfilatelia*: P.O. Box 12-201, Calea Grivitei 64-66, 78104 Bucharest, Romania

Revue Tiers-Monde. *[R. T-Monde] ISSN: 0040-7356. Université de Paris, Institut d'étude du développement économique et social*: 58 boulevard Arago, 75013 Paris, France; **Publisher**: *Presses Universitaires de France*: 108 boulevard Saint-Germain, Paris, France

Revue trimestrielle de droit commercial et de droit économique. *[R. Trim. Com. Econ.] ISSN: 0244-9358. Editions Sirey*: 22 rue Soufflot, 75005 Paris, France

Revue tunisienne de sciences sociales. *[R. Tun. Sci. Soc.] ISSN: 0035-4333. Université de Tunis, Centre d'Etudes et de Recherches Economiques et Sociales*: 23 rue d'Espagne, 1000 Tunis, Tunisia

Risparmio. *[Risparmio] ISSN: 0035-5615. Associazione fra le Casse di Risparmio Italiane*; **Publisher**: *Dott. A. Giuffrè Editore*: Via Busto Arsizio 40, Milan 20151, Italy; **Subscriptions**: *ACEACRI*: V. le di Villa Grazioli 23, 00198 Rome, Italy

Rivista di diritto finanziario e scienza delle finanze. *[Riv. Dir. Finan. Sci. Fin.] ISSN: 0035-6131. Dipartimento di Economia pubblica territoriale dell'Università/ Camera di Commercio di Pavia/ Università di Roma, Facoltà di Giurisprudenza, Istituto di diritto pubblico*: Strada Nuova 65, 27100 Pavia, Italy; **Publisher**: *A. Giuffrè Editore*: Via Busto Arsizio 40, Milan 20151, Italy

Rivista di economia agraria. *[Riv. Econ. Agrar.] ISSN: 0035-6190; ISBN: 88 15 02589 9. Istituto Nazionale di Economia Agraria/ Società Italiana di Economia Agraria*: via Barberine 36, Rome 00187, Italy; **Publisher**: *Società editrice il Mulino*: Strada Maggiore 37, 40125 Bologna, Italy

Rivista di politica economica. *[Riv. Pol. Ec.] ISSN: 0391-6170. Servizio Italiano Pubblicazioni Internazionali (SIPI)*: Viale Pasteur 6, 00144 Rome, Italy

Rivista di storia economica. *[Riv. Stor. Econ.] ISSN: 0393-3415. Giulio Einaudi editore*: Via Umberto Biancamano 2, Turin, Italy; **Subscriptions**: *Licosa, Libreria Commissionaria Sansoni*: Via Lamarmora 45, 50121 Florence, Italy

Rivista di studi politici internazionali. *[Riv. S. Pol. Int.] ISSN: 0035-6611. Giuseppe Vedovato*: 40 Lungarno del Tempio, 50121 Florence, Italy

Rivista internazionale di scienze economiche e commerciali. *[Rev. Int. Sci. Ec. Com.] ISSN: 0035-6751. Università Commerciale Luigi Bocconi/ Università degli Studi di Milano*; **Publisher**: *Casa Editrice Dott. Antonio Milani*: Via Teulià 1, 20136 Milan, Italy

Rivista internazionale di scienze sociali. *[Riv. Int. Sci. Soc.] ISSN: 0035-676X. Università Cattolica del Sacro Cuore*: Vita e Pensiero, Largo A. Gemelli, 1-1 20123 Milan, Italy

Rivista trimestrale di diritto pubblico. *[Riv. Trim. Pubbl.] ISSN: 0557-1464. A. Giuffrè Editore*: via Busto Arsizio 40, 20151 Milan, Italy

Royal Bank of Scotland review. *[R. Bank Scotl. Rev.] ISSN: 0267-1190. Royal Bank of Scotland*: 36 St. Andrew Square, Edinburgh EH2 2YE, Scotland

Rural africana. *[Rur. Afr.] ISSN: 0085-5839. Michigan State University African Studies Center*: 100 Center for International Programs, E.Lansing, MI. 48824-1035, U.S.A.

Rural development in Nigeria. *[Rural. Devel. Nig.]*; *Federal Department of Rural Development*: P.M.B. 5517, 14 Oshuntokun Avenue, Bodija, Ibadan, Nigeria

Rural history.:Economy, society, culture *[Rural Hist.] ISSN: 0956-7933. Cambridge University Press*: The Edinburgh Building, Shaftesbury Road, Cambridge CB2 2RU, U.K.

Rural sociology. *[Rural Sociol.] ISSN: 0036-0112. Rural Sociological Society*: Texas A & M University, College Station, U.S.A.; **Publisher**: *idem*: Department of Sociology, Wilson Hall, Montana State University, Bozeman, MT. 59715, U.S.A.

RWI-Mitteilungen. *[RWI-Mitt.] ISSN: 0933-0089. Rheinisch-Westfälisches Institut für Wirtschaftsforschung*: Hohenzollernstraße 1-3, 4300 Essen 1, Germany; **Publisher**: *Duncker & Humblot*: Dietrich-Schäfer-Weg 9, 1000 Berlin 41, Germany

SAIS review. *[SAIS R.] ISSN: 0036-0777. Johns Hopkins University, Paul H. Nitze School of Advanced International Studies*: 1619 Massachusetts Avenue NW, Washington, DC. 20036, U.S.A.

Sarawak gazette. *[Sara. Gaz.]; Sarawak Museum*: Kuching, Sarawak

Sarjana. *[Sarjana]; University of Malaya, Faculty of Arts and Social Sciences*: Lembah Pantai, Kuala Lumpur 22-11, Malaysia

Savanna. *[Savanna] ISSN: 0331-0523. Ahmadu Bello University Press*: PMB 1094, Zaria, Kaduna State, Nigeria

Savings and development. *[Sav. Develop.] ISSN: 0393-4551. Centre for Financial Assistance to African Countries (Finafrica)*: Via S. Vigilio 10, 20142 Milan, Italy

Scandinavian economic history review. *[Sc. Ec. Hist. R.] ISSN: 0358-5522. Scandinavian Society for Economic and Social History*: Department of Economic History, Box 7083, S-220 07 Lund, Sweden

Scandinavian housing and planning research. *[Scand. Hous. Plan. R.] ISSN: 0281-5737. Building Research Institute (Denmark)/ Ministry of Environment (Finland)/ Institute for Urban and Regional Research (Norway)/ Institute for Building Research (Sweden)*; **Publisher**: *Almqvist & Wiksell International*: P.O. Box 638, S-101 28 Stockholm, Sweden

Scandinavian journal of development alternatives. *[Scand. J. Devel. Altern.] ISSN: 0280-2791. Bethany Books*: P.O. Box 7444, S-103 91 Stockholm, Sweden

Scandinavian journal of economics. *[Sc. J. Econ.] ISSN: 0347-0520. Basil Blackwell*: 108 Cowley Road, Oxford OX4 1JF, U.K.

Schweizerische Versicherungs-Zeitschrift; Revue Suisse d'Assurances. *[Schweiz-Z.] ISSN: 0171-7200. Verlag Peter Lang*: Jupiterstrasse 15, CH-3000 Berne 15, Switzerland

Schweizerische Zeitschrift für Volkswirtschaft und Statistik; Revue suisse d'économie politique et de statistique. *[Schw. Z. Volk. Stat.]; Schweizerische Gesellschaft für Statistik und Volkswirtschaft/ Société suisse de statistique et d'économie politique*: Hallwylstraße 15, CH-3003 Berne, Switzerland; **Publisher**: *Staempfli*: Hallerstrasse 7, Postfach 8326, CH-3001 Berne, Switzerland

Science and public policy. *[Sci. Pub. Pol.] ISSN: 0302-3427. International Science Policy Foundation*: 12 Whitehall, London SW1Y 2DY, U.K.; **Publisher**: *Beech Tree Publishing*: 10 Watford Close, Guildford, Surrey GU1 2EP, U.K.

Science and society. *[Sci. Soc.] ISSN: 0036-8237. Guilford Publications*: 72 Spring Street, New York, NY. 10012, U.S.A.

Science, technology & development. *[Sc. Tech. Devel.] ISSN: 0950-0707. Frank Cass*: Gainsborough House, 11 Gainsborough Road, London E11 1RS, U.K.

Scientific American. *[Sci. Am.] ISSN: 0036-8733. Scientific American*: 415 Madison Avenue, New York, NY. 10017, U.S.A.

Scottish journal of political economy. *[Scot. J. Poli.] ISSN: 0036-9292. Scottish Economic Society*: Division of Economics, University of Stirling, Stirling FK9 4LA, U.K.; **Publisher**: *Basil Blackwell*: 108 Cowley Road, Oxford OX4 1JF, U.K.

Simulation and gaming. *[Simulat. Gam.] ISSN: 0037-5500. Sage Publications*: 2455 Teller Road, Newbury Park, CA. 91320, U.S.A.

Singapore economic review. *[Sing. Econ. R.] ISSN: 0217-5908. National University of Singapore, Department of Economics and Statistics/ Economic Society of Singapore*: 10 Kent Ridge Crescent, Singapore 0511

Skandinaviska Enskilda Banken quarterly review. *[Skan. Ensk. Bank. Q. R.] ISSN: 0349-6694. Skandinaviska Enskilda Banken*: Kungsträdgårdsgatan 8, S-106 40 Stockholm, Sweden

Slavic review. *[Slavic R.] ISSN: 0037-6779. American Association for the Advancement of Slavic Studies*: 128 Encina Commons, Stanford University, Stanford, CA. 94305, U.S.A.

Slavonic and East European review. *[Slav. E.Eur. Rev.] ISSN: 0037-6795. University of London, School of Slavonic and East European Studies*: Malet Street, London WC1E 7HU, U.K.; **Publisher**: *Modern Humanities Research Association*: King's College, Strand, London EC2R 2LS, U.K.

Sloan management review. *[Sloan Manag. R.] ISSN: 0019-848X. Massachusetts Institute of Technology, Sloan School of Management, Sloan Management Review Association*: Amherst Street, E40-292, Cambridge, MA. 02139, U.S.A.; **Subscriptions**: *Sloan Management Review*: P.O. Box 838, Farmingdale, NY. 11737, U.S.A.

Small business economics. *[Small Bus. Econ.] ISSN: 0921-898X. Kluwer Academic Publishers*: P.O. Box 322, 3300 AH Dordrecht, The Netherlands

Small enterprise development. *[Small Enter. Devel.] ISSN: 0957-1329. Intermediate Technology Publications*: 103-105 Southampton Row, London WC1B 4HH, U.K.

Social action. *[Soc. Act.] ISSN: 0037-7627. Indian Social Institute, Social Action Trust*: Lodi Road, New Delhi 130003, India

Social and economic studies. *[Soc. Econ. S.] ISSN: 0037-7651. University of the West Indies, Institute of Social and Economic Research*: Mona, Kingston 7, Jamaica

Social attitudes in Northern Ireland. *[Soc. Attit. N.Ire.]; Blackstaff Press*: 3 Galway Park, Dundonald, Belfast BT16 0AN, Northern Ireland

Social choice and welfare. *[Soc. Choice] ISSN: 0176-1714. Springer International*: Heidelberger Platz 3, W-1000 Berlin 33, Germany

Social forces. *[Soc. Forc.] ISSN: 0037-7732. University of North Carolina, Department of Sociology*: 168 Hamilton Hall, University of North Carolina, Chapel Hill, NC. 27599-3210, U.S.A.; **Publisher**: *University of North Carolina Press*: P.O. Box 2288, Chapel Hill, NC. 27515, U.S.A.

Social indicators research. *[Soc. Ind.] ISSN: 0303-8300. Kluwer Academic Publishers*: Spuiboulevard 50, P.O. Box 17, 3300 AA Dordrecht, The Netherlands

Social justice. *[Soc. Just.] ISSN: 0094-7571. Global Options*: P.O. Box 40601, San Francisco, CA. 94140, U.S.A.

Social networks. *[Soc. Networks] ISSN: 0378-8733. International Network for Social Network Analysis (INSNA)*; **Publisher**: *Elsevier Science Publishers (North-Holland)*: P.O. Box 1991, 1000 BZ Amsterdam, The Netherlands; **Subscriptions**: *idem*: Journals Division, P.O. Box 211, 1000 BZ Amsterdam, The Netherlands

Social philosophy & policy. *[Soc. Philos. Pol.] ISSN: 0265-0525. Bowling Green State University, Social Philosophy and Policy Center*: Bowling Green, Ohio 43403, U.S.A.; **Publisher**: *Basil Blackwell*: 108 Cowley Road, Oxford OX4 1JF, U.K.

Social policy and administration. *[Soc. Pol. Admin.] ISSN: 0144-5596. Basil Blackwell*: 108 Cowley Road, Oxford OX4 1JF, U.K.

Social science information. *[Soc. Sci. Info.] ISSN: 0539-0184. Maison des sciences de l'homme/ École des hautes études en science sociales*; **Publisher**: *Sage Publications*: 6 Bonhill Street, London EC2A 4PU, U.K.

Social science quarterly. *[Soc. Sci. Q.] ISSN: 0038-4941. Southwestern Social Science Association*: W.C. Hogg Building, The University of Texas at Austin, Austin, TX. 78713, U.S.A.; **Publisher**: *University of Texas Press*: P.O. Box 7819, Austin, TX. 78713, U.S.A.

Social sciences. *[Soc. Sci.] ISSN: 0134-5486. Nauka Moscow*: 33/12 Arbat, Moscow G-2. 121818, U.S.S.R.

Social sciences in China. *[Soc. Sci. China] ISSN: 0252-9203. Chinese Academy of Social Science*; **Publisher**: *China Social Sciences Publishing House*: Jia 158 Gulouxidajie, Beijing 100720, China

Social scientist. *[Soc. Scient.] ISSN: 0970-0293. Indian School of Social Sciences*: 424 Vithalbhai Patel House, Rafi Marg, New Delhi 110 001, India; **Subscriptions**: *idem*: 15/15 Sarvapriya Vihar, New Delhi 110 016, India

Social security journal. *[Soc. Sec. J.] ISSN: 0726-1195. Australian Government Publishing Service*: G.P.O. Box 84, Canberra, A.C.T. 2601, Australia

Socialisme. *[Socialisme] ISSN: 0037-8127. Institut Emile Vandervelde*: 13 boulevard de l'Empereur, Brussels 1000 , Belgium

Socialismo y participación. *[Soc. Part.]; CEDEP (Centro de Estudios para el Desarrollo y la Participación)*: Ediciones Socialismo y Participación, Av. José Faustino Sánchez Carrión 790, Lima 17, Peru

Society. *[Society] ISSN: 0147-2011. Transaction*: Rutgers — The State University, New Brunswick, NJ. 08903, U.S.A.

Socio-economic planning sciences. *[Socio. Econ.] ISSN: 0038-0121. Pergamon Press*: Journals Production Unit, Hennock Road, Marsh Barton, Exeter EX2 8NE, U.K.; **Subscriptions**: *Pergamon Press*: Headington Hill Hall, Oxford OX3 0BW, U.K.

Sociologia internationalis. *[Social. Int.] ISSN: 0038-0164. Verlag Duncker & Humblot*: Dietrich-Schäfer-Weg 9, 1000 Berlin 41, Germany

Sociological review. *[Sociol. Rev.] ISSN: 0038-0261. University of Keele*: Keele, Staffordshire ST5 5BG, U.K.; **Publisher**: *Routledge*: 11 New Fetter Lane, London EC4P 4EE, U.K.

Sociologie du travail. *[Sociol. Trav.] ISSN: 0038-0296. Dunod*: 15 rue Gossin, 92543 Montrouge Cedex, France; **Subscriptions**: *CDR — Centrale des revues*: 11 rue Gossin, 92543 Montrouge Cedex, France

Sociology of the sciences. *[Sociol. Sci.]; Kluwer Academic Publishers*: P.O. Box 17, 3300 AA Dordrecht, The Netherlands

Социологические исследования (социс); Sotsiologicheskie issledovaniia (sotsis). *[Sot. Issle.] ISSN: 0132-1625. Akademii Nauk SSSR*; **Publisher**: *Izdatel' stvo Nauka*: Profsoiuznaja ul. 90, Moscow, U.S.S.R.

South African historical journal; Suid-Afrikaanse historiese joernaal. *[S.Afr. Hist. J.] ISSN: 0258-2473. South African Historical Society*: Department of History, University of South Africa, P.O. Box 392, Pretoria 0001, South Africa

South African journal of economic history. *[S.Afr. J. Ec. Hist.]; Economic History Society of Southern Africa*: Department of History, Rand Afrikaans University, P.O. Box 524, Johannesburg 2000, South Africa

South African journal of economics; Suid-Afrikaanse tydskrif vir ekonomie. *[S. Afr. J. Econ.] ISSN: 0038 2280. Economic Society of South Africa*: P.O. Box 929, Pretoria, South Africa

South African journal of labour relations. *[S. Afr. J. Labour Relat.] ISSN: 0379-8410. University of South Africa, School of Business Leadership*: P.O. Box 392, Pretoria 0001, South Africa

South African labour bulletin. *[S.Afr. Lab. B.]; Umanyano Publications*: 700 Medical Arts Building 220 Jeppe St. (cnr. Troye Street), Johannesburg, 2001 South Africa

South African sociological review. *[S.Afr. Sociol. R.] ISSN: 1015-1370. Association for Sociology in South Africa*: Department of Sociology, University of Cape Town, 7700 Rondebosch, South Africa

South Asia bulletin. *[S.Asia B.] ISSN: 0732-3867. South Asia Bulletin*: c/o Department of History, State University of New York, Albany, NY. 12222, U.S.A.

South Asia journal. *[S.Asia. J.] ISSN: 0970-4868. Indian Council of South Asian Cooperation*; **Publisher**: *Sage Publications India*: 32 M-Block Market, Greater Kailash I, New Delhi 110 048, India

South Asia research. *[S.Asia R.] ISSN: 0262-7280. South Asia Research*: Room 472, School of Oriental and African Studies, Thornhaugh Street, Russell Square, London WC1H 0XG, U.K.

Southeast Asian affairs. *[S.E.Asian Aff.]; Institute of Southeast Asian Studies*: Heng Mui Keng Terrace, Pasir Panjang, Singapore 0511

Southern economic journal. *[S. Econ. J.] ISSN: 0038-4038. Southern Economic Association/ University of North Carolina at Chapel Hill*: CB3540, UNC, Chapel Hill, NC 27599-3540, U.S.A.

Soviet economy. *[Sov. Ec.] ISSN: 0882-6994. American Council of Learned Societies, Joint Committee on Soviet Studies/ Social Science Research Council*; **Publisher**: *V.H. Winston & Sons*: 7961 Eastern Avenue, Silver Spring, MD. 20910, U.S.A.

Soziale Welt. *[Soz. Welt.] ISSN: 0038-6073. Arbeitsgemeinschaft sozialwissenschaftlicher Institute*: Universität Bamberg, Feldkirchenstraße 21, 8600 Bamberg, Germany; **Publisher**: *Verlag Otto Schwartz*: Annastraße 7, 3400 Göttingen, Germany

Space commerce. *[Space Comm.] ISSN: 1043-934X. Gordon and Breach Science Publishers*: P.O. Box 10, Reading, Berkshire RG1 8JL, U.K.

Speaking of Japan. *[Speak. Jpn.] ISSN: 0389-3510. Keizai Koho Center, Japan Institute for Social and Economic Affairs*: 6-1 Otemachi 1-chome, Chiyoda-Ku, Tokyo 100, Japan

Spoudai. *[Spoudai]; University of Piraeus*: 98-100 Kountouriotou Str., Piraeus 185 32, Greece

Sprawy międzynarodowe. *[Spr. Między.] ISSN: 0038-853X. Polski Instytut Spraw Międzynarodowych*: ul. Warecka 1a, Warsaw 00-950, Poland

Sri Lanka journal of social sciences. *[Sri Lanka J. Soc. Sci.] ISSN: 0258-9710. Natural Resources, Energy & Science Authority of Sri Lanka*: 47/5 Maitland Place, Colombo 7, Sri Lanka

Staat und recht. *[Sta. Recht] ISSN: 0038-8858. Märkische Verlag- und Druck-Gesellschaft*: Friedrich-Engels-Straße 24, Postfach Postdam 1561, Germany

Staff papers.International Monetary Fund. *[Staff Pap. Int. Monetary] ISSN: 0020-8027. International Monetary Fund*: Publication Services, 700 19th Street, N.W., Washington DC. 20431, U.S.A.

Statistica. *[Statistica] ISSN: 0039-0380. Cooperitiva Libraria Universitaria Editrice*: Piazza G. Verdi 2/a, 40126 Bologna, Italy

Statistician. *[Statistician] ISSN: 0039-0526. Institute of Statisticians*; **Publisher**: *Carfax Publishing Company*: P.O. Box 25, Abingdon, Oxfordshire OX14 3UE, U.K.

Stato e mercato. *[Sta. Mer.]; Società Editrice il Mulino*: Strada Maggiore 37, 40125 Bologna, Italy

Studia prawno-ekonomiczne. *[Stud. Praw-Ekon.] ISSN: 0081-6841. Łódzkie Towarzystwo Naukowe*: ul. Piotrkowska 179, 90-447 Łódź, Poland; **Publisher**: *Zakład Narodowy Imienia Ossolińskich*: Wroclaw, Poland

Studies in comparative communism. *[Stud. Comp. Commun.] ISSN: 0039-3592. Butterworth-Heinemann*: Westbury House, Bury Street, P.O. Box 63, Guildford GU2 5BH, U.K.; **Subscriptions**: *Westbury Subscriptions Services*: P.O. Box 101, Sevenoaks, Kent TN15 8PL, U.K.

Studies in comparative international development. *[Stud. Comp. ID.] ISSN: 0039-3606. Transaction Periodicals Consortium*: Dept. 4010, Rutgers University, New Brunswick, NJ. 08903, U.S.A.; **Subscriptions**: *Swets-Zeitlinger Publishing Services*: Heereweg 347, 2161 CA Lisse, The Netherlands

Studies in history. *[Stud. Hist.] ISSN: 0257-6430. Sage Publications India*: 32 M-Block Market, Greater Kailash I, New Delhi 110 048, India; **Subscriptions**: *idem*: 6, Bonhill Street, London EC2A 4PU, U.K.

Studies in history and philosophy of science. *[Stud. Hist. Phil. Sci.] ISSN: 0039-3681. Pergamon Press*: Headington Hill Hall, Oxford OX3 0BW, U.K.

Studies in political economy. *[Stud. Pol. Ec.] ISSN: 0707-8552. Studies in Political Economy*: P.O. Box 4729, Station E, Ottowa, Ontario, Canada K1S 5H9

Südosteuropa Mitteilungen. *[Südosteur. Mitteil.] ISSN: 0340-174X. Südosteuropa-Gesellschaft*: Widenmayerstraße 49. D-8000 Munich 22, Germany

Свободная мысль; Svobodnaia Mysl'. *[Svobod. Mysl'] ISSN: 0131-1212. Izdatel'stvo Pravda*: Ul. Pravdy 24, 125047 Moscow, U.S.S.R.

Syrie & monde arabe. *[Syrie Mon. Arabe]; Office Arabe de presse et de documentation*: B.P. 3550, Damascus, Syria

Szigma. *[Szigma] ISSN: 0039-8128. Academiai Kiado, Publishing House of the Hungarian Academy of Sciences*: P.O. Box 24, H-1363 Budapest, Hungary

Tamkang journal of area studies. *[Tamkang J. Area Stud.]; Tamkang University*: Kinhua Street, Taipei, 10637 Taiwan

Tanzanian economic trends. *[Tanzan. Eco. Tren.] ISSN: 0856-3373. University of Dar es Salaam, Economic Research Bureau*: P.O. Box 35096, Dar es Salaam, Tanzania

Technology and culture. *[Technol. Cul.] ISSN: 0040-165X. Society for the History of Technology*; **Publisher**: *University of Chicago Press*: 5720 South Woodlawn Avenue, Chicago, IL. 60637, U.S.A.

Technology and development. *[Tech. Devel.]; Institute for International Cooperation/ Japan International Cooperation Agency*: International Cooperation Center Building, 10-5 Ichigaya-Honmura-cho, Shinjuku-ku, Tokyo 162, Japan

Telos. *[Telos] ISSN: 0090-6514. Telos Press*: 431 E. 12th Street, New York, NY. 10009, U.S.A.

Temas de economia mundial. *[Temas Econ. Mun.]; Centro de Investigaciones de la Economia Mundial*: Calle 22 No. 309, Entre 3ra y 5ta Municipio Playa, Ciudad Habana, Cuba

Temps modernes. *[Temps Mod.] ISSN: 0040-3075. Gallimard/ Les Temps Modernes*: 4, rue Férou, Paris 6e, France; **Subscriptions**: *B.S.I.*: 49, rue de la Vanne, 92120 Montrouge, France

Terra Nova. *[Ter. Nova]; International Freedom Foundation*: 200 G Street, N.E. Washington, DC., 20002, U.S.A.

Textual practice. *[Tex. Prac.] ISSN: 0950-236X. Routledge Journals*: 11 New Fetter Lane, London EC4P 4EE, U.K.

Theory and decision. *[Theory Decis.] ISSN: 0040-5833. Kluwer Academic Publishers*: P.O. Box 17, 3300 AA Dordrecht, The Netherlands; **Subscriptions**: *idem*: P.O. Box 322, 3300 AA Dordrecht, The Netherlands

Third World planning review. *[Third Wor. P.] ISSN: 0142-7849. Liverpool University Press*: P.O. Box 147, Liverpool L69 3BX, U.K.

Third World quarterly. *[Third World] ISSN: 0143-6597. Third World Foundation for Social and Economic Studies*: Third World Quarterly, Rex House, 1st Floor, 4-12 Lower Regent Street, London SW1Y 4PE, U.K.

Tijdschrift voor economie en management. *[Tijds. Econ. Manag.] ISSN: 0772-7664. Katholieke Universiteit Te Leuven, Faculteit der Economische en Toegepaste Economische Wetenschappen*: Dekenstraat 2, 3000 Leuven, Belgium

Tijdschrift voor economische en sociale geografie; Journal of economic and social geography. *[J. Econ. Soc. Geogr.] ISSN: 0040-747X. Royal Dutch Geographical Society = Koninklijk Nederlands Aardrijkskundig Genootschap*: Weteringschans 12, 1017 SG Amsterdam, The Netherlands

TRACE. *[TRACE] ISSN: 0185-6286. Centre d'Etudes Mexicaines et Centraméricaines*: Sierra Leona 330, 11000 Mexico D.F., Mexico

Transformation. *[Transformation] ISSN: 0258-7696. Transformation*: Economic History Department, University of Natal, King George V Avenue, 4001 Durban, South Africa

Transit.:*Europäische Revue [Transit] ISSN: 0938-2062. Institut für die Wissenschaften vom Menschen*: Spittelauer Lände 3, A-1090, Vienna, Austria; **Publisher**: *Verlag Neue Kritik*: Kettenhofweg 53, D-6000 Frankfurt am Main, Germany

Transition. *[Transition] ISSN: 1012-8263. University of Guyana, Faculty of Social Sciences and Institute of Development Studies*: P.O. Box 10110, Turkeyen, Georgetown, Guyana

Transportation. *[Transportation] ISSN: 0049-4438. Kluwer Academic Publishers*: P.O. Box 17, 3300 AA Dordrecht, The Netherlands

Travail et emploi. *[Trav. Emp.] ISSN: 0224-4365. Ministère du Travail, de l'Emploi et de la Formation Professionnelle, Service des études et de la statistique*: Bureau 3205A, 1 place de Fontenoy, 75700 Paris, France; **Publisher**: *Documentation Fraçaise*: 29-31 quai Voltiare, 75340 Paris Cedex 07, France

Tricontinental. *[Tricontinental] ISSN: 0864-1595. Executive Secretariat of the Organization of Solidarity of the Peoples of Africa, Asia and Latin America (OSPAAAL)*: Apartado Postale 4224 y 6130, Calle C No. 668 e/27 y 29 Vedado, Havana, Cuba

Trimestre económico. *[Trim. Econ.] ISSN: 0041-3011. Fondo de Cultura Económica*: Av Universidad 975, 03100 Mexico City, Mexico

Twentieth century British history. *[Twent. Cent. Br. Hist.] ISSN: 0955-2359. Oxford University Press*: Pinkhill House, Southfield Road, Eynsham, Oxford OX8 1JJ, United Kingdom

Unasylva. *[Unasylva] ISSN: 0041-6436. United Nations, Food and Agriculture Organization*: FAO, Via delle Terme di Caracalla, 00100 Rome, Italy

Unisa Latin American report. *[Unisa Lat.Am. Rep.] ISSN: 0256-6060. Unisa Centre for Latin American Studies*; **Publisher**: *University of South Africa*: P.O. Box 392, 0001 Pretoria, South Africa

Uniswa research journal. *[Uniswa Res. J.]; University of Swaziland*: P/ Bag, Kwaluseni, Swaziland

Unitas. *[Unitas] ISSN: 0041-7130. Union Bank of Finland*: Economic Research Department, P.O. Box 70, SF-00101 Helsinki, Finland; **Subscriptions**: *idem*: Area Management, P.O. Box 868, SF-00101 Helsinki, Finland

Universitas. *[Universitas] ISSN: 0049-5530. University of Ghana*: Department of English, P.O. Box 25, Legon, Ghana

Urban affairs quarterly. *[Urban Aff. Q.] ISSN: 0042-0816. Sage Publications*: 2455 Teller Road, Newbury Park, CA. 91320, U.S.A.

Urban geography. *[Urban Geogr.] ISSN: 0272-3638. V.H. Winston & Son*: 7961 Eastern Avenue, Silver Spring, MD. 20910, U.S.A.

Urban law and policy. *[Urban Law P.] ISSN: 0165-0068. Elsevier Science Publishers (North-Holland)*: Journals Division, P.O. Box 211, 1000 AE Amsterdam, The Netherlands

Urban studies. *[Urban Stud.] ISSN: 0042 0980. University of Glasgow, Centre for Urban and Regional Research*: Adam Smith Building, University of Glasgow, Glasgow G12 8RT, U.K.; **Publisher**: *Carfax Publishing Company*: P.O.Box 25, Abingdon, Oxfordshire OX14 3UE, U.K.

Utafiti. *[Utafiti] ISSN: 0856-096X. University of Dar es Salaam, Faculty of Arts and Social Sciences*: P.O. Box 35151, Dar es Salaam, Tanzania

Utilities policy. *[Util. Policy] ISSN: 0957-1787. Butterworth-Heinemann*: Linacre House, Jordan Hill, Oxford OX2 8DP, U.K.

Verfassung und Recht in Übersee; Law and politics in Africa, Asia and Latin America. *[Verf. Rec. Über.] ISSN: 0506-7286. Hamburger Gesellschaft für Völkerrecht und Auswärtige Politik*: Rothenbaumchaussee 21-23, D-2000 Hamburg 13, Germany; **Publisher**: *Nomos Verlagsgesellschaft*: Postfach 610, D-7570 Baden-Baden, Germany

Вестник ленинградского университета; Vestnik Leningradskogo universiteta.:Серия 5 экономика, Seriia 5 ekonomika *[Ves. Lenin. Univ. Ser. 5] ISSN: 0132-4624; ISSN: 0233-755X. Izdatel'stvo Leningradskogo Universiteta*: Universitetskaia Nab. 7/9, 199034 Leningrad, U.S.S.R.

Вестник Московского Университета; Vestnik Moskovskogo Universiteta.:Серия 6. Экономика; Seriia 6. Ekonomika *[Vest. Mosk. Univ. 6] ISSN: 0201-7385; ISSN: 0130-0105. Izdatel'stvo Moskovskogo Universiteta*: Ul. Gertsena 5/7, 103009 Moscow, U.S.S.R.

Весці Акадэмii Навук БССР; Vestsi akademii navuk BSSR.:Сурыя грамадскix навук; Seryia gramadskikh navuk *[V. Aka. BSSR] ISSN: 0321-1649. Akademii Navuk, BSSR*; **Publisher**: *Navuka i Tekhnika*: Zhodzinskaia 18, 220600 Minsk, Belorussia, U.S.S.R.

Vierteljahresberichte. *[Vierteljahresberichte] ISSN: 0936-451X. Friedrich-Ebert Stiftung*: Godesberger Alle 149, 5300 Bonn 2, Germany; **Publisher**: *J.H.W. Dietz Nachf.*: In der Raste 2, 5300 Bonn 1, Germany

Vierteljahrschrift für Sozial- und Wirtschaftsgeschichte. *[Vierteljahr. Soz. Wirt.Ges.] ISSN: 0340-8728. Franz Steiner Verlag*: Birenwaldstr. 44, D-7000 Stuttgart 1, Germany

Vierteljahrshefte zur Wirtschaftsforschung. *[Vier. Wirt.schung] ISSN: 0340-1707. Deutsches Institut für Wirtschaftsforschung*: Königin-Luise-Straße 5, D-1000 Berlin 33, Germany; **Publisher**: *Duncker & Humblot*: Dietrich-Schäfer-Weg 9, D-1000 Berlin 41, Germany

Вопросы философии; Voprosy filosofii. *[Vop. Filo.] ISSN: 0042-8744. Akademiia Nauk SSR, Institut filosofii*; **Publisher**: *Izdatel'stvo Pravda*: Ul. Pravdy 24, 125047 Moscow, U.S.S.R.

Вопросы истории; Voprosy istorii. *[Vop. Ist.] ISSN: 0042-8779. Izdatel'stvo Pravda*: Ul. Pravdy 24, 125865 Moscow, U.S.S.R.

Вопросы экономики; Voprosy ekonomiki. *[Vop. Ekon.] ISSN: 0042-8736. Akademii Nauk SSSR, Institut Ekonomiki*; **Publisher**: *Izdatel'stvo Pravda*: Ul. Pravdy 24, 125865 Moscow, U.S.S.R.

Waseda business & economic studies. *[Waseda Bus. Ec. Stud.] ISSN: 0388-1008. Graduate School of Commerce, Waseda University*: Tokyo, Japan

Waseda economic papers. *[Waseda Eco. Pap.] ISSN: 0511-1943. Waseda University, Graduate School of Economics*: Tokyo, Japan

Washington quarterly. *[Wash. Quart.] ISSN: 0163-660X. Center for Strategic and International Studies*: 1800 K. Street, NW, Suite 400, Washington DC. 20006, U.S.A.; **Publisher**: *MIT Press*: 55 Hayward Street, Cambridge, MA. 02142, U.S.A.

Weltwirtschaft. *[Weltwirt.] ISSN: 0043-2652. Universität Kiel, Institut für Welwirtschaft*: Postfach 4309, D-2300 Kiel 1, Germany; **Publisher**: *J.C.B. Mohr (Paul Siebeck)*: Postfach 2040, D-7400 Tübingen, Germany

Weltwirtschaftliches Archiv. *[Welt.liches Arc.] ISSN: 0043-2636. Institut für Weltwirtschaft*: Düsternbrooker Weg 120, D-2300 Kiel, Germany; **Publisher**: *J.C.B. Mohr (Paul Siebeck)*: Wilhelmstraße 18 Postfach 2040, D-7400 Tübingen, Germany

West European politics. *[W. Eur. Pol.] ISSN: 0140-2382. Frank Cass*: Gainsborough House, 11 Gainsborough Road, London E11 1RS, U.K.

Western political quarterly. *[West. Pol. Q.] ISSN: 0043-4078. Western Political Science Association/ Pacific Northwest Political Science Association/ Southern California Political Science Association/ Northern California Political Science Association*; **Publisher**: *University of Utah*: Salt Lake City, UT. 84112, U.S.A.

Wirtschaftsdienst. *[Wirtschaftsdienst] ISSN: 0043-6275. HWWA — Institut für Wirtschaftsforschung*; **Publisher**: *Verlag Weltarchiv*: Neuer Jungfernstieg 21, D-2000 Hamburg 36, Germany

Wirtschaftspolitische Blätter. *[Wirt. Blät.] ISSN: 0043-6291. Bundeskammer der gewerblichen Wirtschaft*: Wiedner Hauptstraße 63, 1045 Vienna, Austria; **Publisher**: *Österreichischer Wirtschaftsverlag*: Nikolsdorfer Gasse 7-11, 1050 Vienna, Austria

Wirtschaftspolitische Mitteilungen. *[Wirt.pol. Mitt.]*; *Wirtschaftsförderung Gesellschaft zur Förderung der Schweizerischen Wirtschaft*: Postfach 502, 8084-Zürich, Switzerland

Wirtschaftswissenschaft. *[Wirt.wissensch.] ISSN: 0043-633X. Verlag die Wirtschaft*: Am Friedrichchain 22, Berlin 1055, Germany

Wisconsin law review. *[Wiscon. Law R.] ISSN: 0043-650X. University of Wisconsin, Law School*: 975 Bascom Mall, Madison, WI. 53706-1399, U.S.A.

Women's studies international forum. *[Wom. St. Inter. For.] ISSN: 0277-5395. Pergamon Press*: Fairview Park, Elmsford, NY. 10523, U.S.A.

Work and occupations. *[Work Occup.] ISSN: 0730-8884. Sage Publications*: 2455 Teller Road, Newbury Park CA. 91320, U.S.A.; **Subscriptions**: *Sage Publications*: 6 Bonhill Street, London EC2A 4PU, U.K.

Work, employment and society. *[Work Emp. Soc.] ISSN: 0950-0170. British Sociological Association*: 10 Portugal Street, London WC2A 2HU, U.K.; **Subscriptions**: *Business Manager*: Work, Employment and Society, 351 Station Road, Dorridge, Solihull, West Midlands B93 8EY, U.K.

World Bank economic review. *[W.B. Econ. R.] ISSN: 0258-6770. International Bank for Reconstruction and Development*: World Bank, Washington, DC. 20433, U.S.A.; **Subscriptions**: *World Bank Publications*: Box 7247-8619, Philadelphia, PA. 19170-8619, U.S.A.

World Bank research observer. *[World Bank Res. Obser.]*; *International Bank for Reconstruction and Development/ World Bank*: 1818 II Street, N.W., Washington, DC. 20433, U.S.A.; **Subscriptions**: *Publications Sales Unit*

World development. *[World Dev.] ISSN: 0305-750X. Pergamon Press*: Headington Hill Hall, Oxford OX3 0BW, U.K.

World economy. *[World. Econ.] ISSN: 0378-5920. Trade Policy Research Centre*: 11 Grosvenor Crescent, London SW1X 7EE, U.K.; **Publisher**: *Basil Blackwell*: 108 Cowley Road, Oxford OX4 1JF, U.K.

World futures. *[Wor. Futur.] ISSN: 0260-4027. Gordon and Breach Science Publishers*: 270 8th Avenue, New York, NY. 10011, U.S.A.; **Subscriptions**: *idem*: P.O. Box 90, Reading, Berkshire, RG1 8JL, U.K.

World today. *[World Today] ISSN: 0043-9134. Royal Institute of International Affairs*: 10 St. James's Square, London SW1Y 4LE, U.K.

Yagl-Ambu. *[Yagl-Ambu] ISSN: 0254-0681. University of Papua New Guinea*: Box 320, University Post Office, Papua New Guinea

Yale law journal. *[Yale Law J.] ISSN: 0044-0094. Yale Law Journal Co.*: 401-A Yale Station, New Haven CT 06520, U.S.A.

Yapi kredi economic review. *[Yapi Kredi. Eco. Rev.]; Yapi Kredi Bank*: Economic Research Department, Yapi Kredi Bank, Levent, Istanbul

Yearbook of co-operative enterprise. *[Y. Co-op. Enter.] ISSN: 0952-5556. Plunkett Foundation*: 23 Hanborough Business Park, Long Hanborough, Oxford OX7 2LH, U.K.

Zaïre-Afrique. *[Za-Afr.] ISSN: 0049-8513. Centre d'études pour l'action sociale (CEPAS)*: Avenue Père Boka no.9, B.P. 3375 Kinshasa/Gombe, Zaire

Zambezia. *[Zambezia] ISSN: 0379-0622. University of Zimbabwe*: Publications Office, P.O. Box MP 45, Mount Pleasant, Harare, Zimbabwe

Zambia journal of history. *[Zamb. J. Hist.]; University of Zambia, Department of History*: P.O. Box 32379, Lusaka, Zambia

Zeitschrift für ausländisches öffentliches Recht und Völkerrecht. *[Z. Aus. Recht. Völk] ISSN: 0044-2348. Verlag W. Kohlhammer*: P.B. 800430, D-7000 Stuttgart 80, Germany

Zeitschrift für Energie Wirtschaft. *[Z. Energie Wirt.] ISSN: 0340-5377. Friedr. Vieweg & Sohn*: Postfach 5829, D-6200 Wiesbaden 1, Germany

Zeitschrift für Politik. *[Z. Polit.] ISSN: 0044-3360. Hochschule für Politik München*: Ludwigstraße 8, 8000 Munchen, Germany; **Publisher**: *Carl Heymanns Verlag*: Luxemburger Straße 449, 5000 Cologne 41, Germany

Zeitschrift für Unternehmensgeschichte. *[Z. Unter.gesch.] ISSN: 0342-2852. Gesellschaft für Unternehmensgeschichte*: Bonner Straße 211, 9. Etage, D-5000 Cologne 51, Germany; **Publisher**: *Franz Steiner Verlag*: Birkenwaldstraße 44, Postfach 10 15 26, D-7000 Stuttgart 1, Germany

Zeitschrift für Vergleichende Rechtswissenschft. *[Z. Vergl. Recht.] ISSN: 0044-3638. Verlag Recht und Wirtschaft*: Postfach 105960, D-6900 Heidelberg, Germany

Zeitschrift für Verkehrswissenschaft. *[Z. Verkehr.] ISSN: 0044-3670. Verkehrs-Verlag J. Fischer*: Paulusstraße 1, 4000 Düsseldorf 1, Germany

Zeitschrift für Wirtschafts- und Sozialwissenschaften. *[Z. Wirt. Soz.] ISSN: 0342-1783. Gesellschaft für Wirtschafts- und Sozialwissenschafen — Verein für Sozialpolitik*; **Publisher**: *Duncker and Humblot*: Dietrich-Schäfer-Weg 9, 1000 Berlin 41, Germany

Zeitschrift für Wirtschaftspolitik. *[Z. Wirt.pol.] ISSN: 0721-3808. Universität zu Köln, Institut für Wirtschaftspolitik*: Postfach 41 05 29, Lindenburger Allee 32, 5000 Cologne 41, Germany

Zimbabwe journal of economics. *[Zim. J. Econ.]; University of Zimbabwe, Economics Department*: P.O. Box 1516, Harare, Zimbabwe

LIST OF ABBREVIATIONS USED
LISTE DES ABBREVIATIONS UTILISÉS

A. Fond. L. Einaudi — Annali della fondazione Luigi Einaudi. — Turin: *Fondazione Luigi Einaudi*

A.J.S. — American journal of sociology. — Chicago, IL.: *University of Chicago Press*

Acad. Manag. J. — Academy of management journal. — Ohio: *Academy of management*

Acc. Bus. Finan. Hist. — Accounting, business and financial history. — London: *Routledge*

Acc. Bus. Res. — Accounting and business research. — London: *Institute of Chartered Accountants in England and Wales*

Acc. Review — Accounting review. — Sarasota, FL.: *American Accounting Association*

Acta Oecon. — Acta oeconomica. — Budapest: *Hungarian Academy of Sciences*

Acta Univ. Łódz. — Acta Universtatis Łódziensis.: *Folia oeconomica* — Łódz: *Wydawnictwo Uniwersytetu Łódzkiego*

Adm. Sci. Qua. — Administrative science quarterly. — Ithaca, NY.: *Cornell University, Johnson Graduate School of Management*

Administration — Administration. — Dublin: *Institute of Public Administration of Ireland*

Af. Spec. — Afrika Spectrum. — Hamburg: *Institut für Afrika-Kunde*

Afr. 2000 — Afrique 2000. — Brussels: *Institut panafricain de relations internationales*

Afr. Affairs — African affairs. — Oxford: *Royal African Society*

Afr. Cont. — Afrique contemporaine. — Paris: *Documentation française*

Afr. Devel. — Africa development; Afrique & developpement. — Dakar: *Council for the Development of Economic and Social Research in Africa/ Conseil pour le Développement de la Recherche Economique et Sociale en Afrique*

Afr. J. Int. Comp. Law — African journal of international and comparative law; Revue africaine de droit international et comparé. — London: *African Society of International and Comparative Law*

Afr. Q. — Africa quarterly. — New Delhi: *Indian Council for Cultural Relations*

Afr. Stud. R. — African studies review. — Atlanta, GA.: *African Studies Association*

Africa [Italy] — Africa [Italy]. — Rome, Italy: *Istituto Italo-Africano*

Age. Soc. — Ageing and society. — Cambridge: *Centre for Policy on Ageing/ British Society of Gerontology*

Agr. Soc. — Agricultura y sociedad. — Madrid: *Ministerio de Agricultura, Pesca y Alimentacion*

Agrekon — Agrekon. — Monument Park: *Landbou-Economievereniging van Suider-Afrika = Agricultural Economics Association of Southern Africa*

All. Stat. A. — Allgemeines statistisches Archiv. — Göttingen: *Deutsche Statistische Gesellschaft*

Alternatives — Alternatives. — Boulder: *Lynne Rienner Publishers*

Am. Econ. Rev. — American economic review. — Nashville, TN: *American Economic Association*

Am. J. Agr. Ec. — American journal of agricultural economics. — Ames, IA.: *American Agricultural Economics Association*

Am. J. Econ. S. — American journal of economics and sociology. — New York, NY.: *American Journal of Economics and Sociology*

Am. J. Int. Law — American journal of international law. — Washington, DC.: *American Society of International Law*

Am. J. Islam. Soc. Sci. — American journal of Islamic social sciences. — Herndon, VA.: *Association of Muslim Social Scientists/ International Institute of Islamic Thought*

Am. J. Pol. Sc. — American journal of political science. — Austin, TX: *Midwest Political Science Association*

Am. Sociol. R. — American sociological review. — Washington, D.C.: *American Sociological Association*

Ann. Afr. Nord — Annuaire de l'Afrique du Nord. — Paris: *Editions du Centre national de la recherche scientifique*

Ann. Am. Poli. — Annals of the American Academy of Political and Social Science. — Newbury Park, CA.: *American Academy of Political and Social Science*

Ann. As. Am. G. — Annals of the Association of American Geographers. — Washington, DC.: *Association of American Geographers*

Ann. R. Energy Environ. — Annual review of energy and the environment. — Palo Alto, CA.: *Annual Reviews*

Ann. R. Info. Sci. Tech. — Annual review of information science and technology. — Amsterdam: *American Society for Information Science*

Ann. R. Soc. — Annual review of sociology. — Palo Alto, CA.: *Annual Reviews*

Ann. Reg. Sci. — Annals of regional science. — Berlin: *Western Regional Science Association*

Appl. Econ. — Applied economics. — London: *Chapman and Hall*

Appl. Finan. Econ. — Applied financial economics. — London: *Chapman & Hall*

Apuntes — Apuntes. — Lima: *Revista Apuntes*

Area — Area. — London: *Institute of British Geographers*

Art. Vij. — Artha vijñāna. — Pune: *Gokhale Institute of Politics and Economics*

ASEAN Ec. B. — ASEAN economic bulletin. — Singapore: *Institute of Southeast Asian Studies*

Asian Ec. — Asian economies. — Seoul: *Research Institute of Asian Economies*

Asian Econ. J. — Asian Economic Journal. — Hong Kong: *East Asian Economic Association/ Hong Kong Institute of Asia Pacific Studies/ Chinese University of Hong Kong*

Asian J. Pub. Admin. — Asian journal of public administration. — Hong Kong: *University of Hong Kong, Department of Political Science*

Asian-Pacific Ec. Lit. — Asian-Pacific economic literature. — Guildford: *Australian National University, National Centre for Development Studies*

Asian. Afr. Stud. — Asian and African studies. — Haifa: *University of Haifa, Gustav Heinemann Institute of Middle Eastern Studies*

Aussenpolitik — Aussenpolitik. — Hamburg: *Interpress Verlag*

Aussenwirtschaft — Aussenwirtschaft. — Zürich: *Schweizerisches Institut für Aussenwirtschafts-Struktur- und Regionalforschung (SIASR)*

Aust. Ec. Rev. — Australian economic review. — Melbourne: *University of Melbourne, Institute of Applied Economic and Social Research*

Aust. Econ. P. — Australian economic papers. — Adelaide: *Flinders University of South Australia*

Aust. Geogr. — Australian geographer. — Gladesville, NSW: *Geographical Society of New South Wales*

Aust. J. Chin. Aff. — Australian journal of Chinese affairs. — Canberra: *Australian National University, Contemporary China Centre*

B. E.Carib. Aff. — Bulletin of Eastern Caribbean affairs. — Cave Hill: *Institute of Social and Economic Research (Eastern Caribbean)*

B. Econ. Res. — Bulletin of economic research. — Oxford: *Basil Blackwell*

B. Ind. Econ. St. — Bulletin of Indonesian economic studies. — Canberra: *Australian National University*

B. Int. Fiscal Docu. — Bulletin for international fiscal documentation. — Amsterdam: *International Fiscal Association*

B. Lat. Am. Res. — Bulletin of Latin American research. — Oxford: *Society for Latin American Studies*

Banca Nat. Lav. Q. Rev. — Banca Nazionale del Lavoro quarterly review. — Rome: *Banca Nazionale del Lavoro*

Bancaria — Bancaria. — Rome: *Associazione Bancaria Italiana*

Bang. Dev. Stud. — Bangladesh development studies. — Dhaka: *Bangladesh Unnayan Gobeshona Protishthan = Bangladesh Institute of Development Studies*

Bank of Engl. Q. — Bank of England quarterly bulletin. — London: *Bank of England*

Bank-Archiv — Bank-Archiv. — Vienna: *Österreichische Bankwissenschaftliche Gesellschaft*

BC. Stud. — BC studies. — Vancouver: *University of British Columbia*

Beliz. St. — Belizean studies. — Belize City: *St. John's College*

Bijdragen — Bijdragen tot de taal-, land-en volkenkunde. — Leiden: *Koninklijk Instituut voor Taal-, Land-en Volkenkunde*

Born. R. — Borneo review. — Sabah: *Institute for Development Studies (Sabah)*

Br. J. Addict. — British journal of addiction. — Abingdon: *Society for the Study of Addiction to Alcohol and Other Drugs*

Br. J. Ind. R. — British journal of industrial relations. — Oxford: *London School of Economics*

Br. J. Manag. — British journal of management. — Chichester: *British Academy of Management*

Br. J. Poli. S. — British journal of political science. — Cambridge: *Cambridge University Press*

Br. Rev. Ec. Iss. — British review of economic issues. — Stoke-on-Trent: *Association of Polytechnic Teachers in Economics*
Br. Tax Rev. — British tax review. — London: *Sweet and Maxwell*
Brookings P. — Brookings papers on economic activity. — Washington, D.C.: *Brookings Institution*
Bus. Econ. — Business economist. — Watford: *Society of Business Economists*
Cah. Sci. Hum. — Cahiers des sciences humaines. — Paris: *Editions de l'ORSTOM, Institut français de recherche scientifique pour le developpement en cooperation*
Calif. Manag. R. — California management review. — Berkeley, CA.: *University of California, Walter A. Haas School of Business*
Camb. J. Econ. — Cambridge journal of economics. — London: *University of Cambridge, Faculty of Economics and Politics*
Can. J. Afr. St. — Canadian journal of African studies; Revue canadienne des études africaines. — Ottawa: *Canadian Association of African Studies = Association canadienne des études africaines*
Can. J. Ag. Ec. — Canadian journal of agricultural economics; Revue canadienne d'économie rurale. — Ottawa: *Canadian Agricultural Economics and Farm Management Society*
Can. J. Econ. — Canadian journal of economics; Revue canadienne d'économique. — Downsview: *Canadian Economics Association*
Can. J. Poli. — Canadian journal of political science; Revue canadienne de science politique. — Ottawa: *Canadian Political Science Association = Association canadienne de science politique/ Société québécoise de science politique*
Can. J. Soc. — Canadian journal of sociology; Cahiers canadiens de sociologie. — Edmonton: *University of Alberta, Department of Sociology*
Can. Publ. Ad. — Canadian public administration; Administration publique du Canada. — Toronto: *Institute of Public Administration of Canada*
Can. R. Soc. A. — Canadian review of sociology and anthropology; Revue canadienne de sociologie et d'anthropologie. — Montreal: *Canadian Sociology and Anthropology Association*
Cap. Class — Capital and class. — London: *Conference of Socialist Economists*
Cent. Bank. — Central banking. — London: *Central Banking Publications*
Centro Est. Monet. Latinam. — Boletin. Centro de estudios monetarios latinoamericanos. — Mexico City: *Centro de Estudios Monetarios Latinoamericanos (CEMLA)*
CEPAL R. — CEPAL review. — Santiago, Chile: *United Nations Economic Commission for Latin America and the Caribbean*
Challenge — Challenge. — Armonk, N.Y.: *M.E. Sharpe*
China News. — China newsletter. — Tokyo: *Japan External Trade Organisation (JETRO)*
China Quart. — China quarterly. — London: *University of London, School of Oriental and African Studies*
China R. — China report. — New Delhi: *Sage Publications India*
Cities — Cities. — London: *Butterworth-Heinemann*
Civitas — Civitas. — Rome: *Edizioni Civitas*
Columb. J. Tr. — Columbia journal of transnational law. — New York, NY.: *Columbia Journal of Transnational Law Association*
Columb. J. W. Bus. — Columbia journal of world business. — New York, NY.: *Columbia University, Columbia Business School*
Comm. Dev. J. — Community development journal. — Oxford: *Oxford University Press*
Comm. Econ. — Communist economies. — Abingdon: *Centre for Research into Communist Economies*
Common Mkt. L. R. — Common market law review. — Dordrecht: *British Institute of International and Comparative Law/ University of Leyden, Europa Instituut*
Comp. Poli. S. — Comparative political studies. — Newbury Park, CA.: *Sage Publications*
Comp. Polit. — Comparative politics. — New York, NY.: *City University of New York*
Comp. Stud. S. — Comparative studies in society and history. — New York, NY.: *Society for the Comparative Study of Society and History*
Comun. Int. — Comunità internazionale. — Padua: *Societa Italiana per l'Organizzazione Internazionale*
Confl. Resolut. — Journal of conflict resolution. — Newbury Park, CA.: *Peace Science Society (International)*
Constit. Pol. Econ. — Constitutional political economy. — Fairfax, VA.: *Center for Study of Public Choice*

Cont. Account. Res. — Contemporary accounting research. — Toronto: *Canadian Academic Accounting Association= Association Canadienne des Professeurs de Comptabilité*

Cont. Policy — Contemporary policy issues. — Huntington Beach, CA.: *Western Economic Association International*

Cont. S.E. Asia — Contemporary Southeast Asia. — Singapore: *Institute of Southeast Asian Studies*

Contrib. Pol. Econ. — Contributions to political economy. — London: *Academic Press*

Coop. Conflict — Cooperation and conflict. — Oslo: *Nordic Cooperation Committee for International Politics*

Coy. Econ. — Coyuntura económica. — Bogotá: *Fundación para la Educación Superior y el Desarrollo (FEDESARROLLO)*

Crit. Persp. Acc. — Critical perspectives on accounting. — London: *Academic Press*

Crit. Sociol. — Critica sociologica. — Rome: *S.I.A.R.E.S.*

Cuad. Am. — Cuadernos americanos. — Mexico City: *Universidad Nacional Autónoma de México*

Curr. World Lead. — Current world leaders. — Santa Barbara, CA.: *International Academy*

Cyprus J. Econ. — Cyprus journal of economics. — Nicosia: *Cyprus Economic Society*

Cyprus Rev. — Cyprus review. — Nicosia and Indianapolis: *Intercollege/ University of Indianapolis*

Def. Econ. — Defence economics. — Reading: *Harwood Academic Publishers*

Desar. Econ. — Desarrollo económico. — Buenos Aires: *Instituto de Desarrollo Económico y Social*

Desar. Soc. — Desarrollo y sociedad. — Bogotá: *Universidad de los Andes, Facultad de Economía, Centro de Estudios Sobre Desarrollo Económico*

Deut. Arch. — Deutschland Archiv.: *Zeitschrift für das vereinigte Deutschland* — Cologne: *Verlag Wissenschaft und Politik*

Dev. Pol. R. — Development policy review. — London: *Overseas Development Institute*

Devel. & Socio-eco. Pro. — Development & socio-economic progress. — Cairo: *Afro-Asian Peoples' Solidarity Organisation (AAPSO)*

Develop. Cha. — Development and change. — London: *Sage Publications*

Develop. Eco. — Developing economies. — Tokyo: *Institute of Developing Economies*

Develop. S. Afr. — Development Southern Africa. — Halfway House: *Development Bank of Southern Africa*

Dirasat Ser. A. — Dirasat.: *Series A — the humanities* — Amman: *Deanship of Academic Research*

E & S — E & S.: *Economie et statistique* — Paris: *Institut national de la statistique et des études économiques*

E. Afr. Econ. Rev. — Eastern Africa economic review. — Nairobi: *Kenyan Economic Association*

E. Eur. Quart. — East European quarterly. — Boulder, CO.: *University of Colorado*

E.Asian R. — East Asian review. — Seoul: *Institute for East Asian Studies*

Ec. Lav. — Economia & lavoro. — Rome: *Fondazione Giacomo Brodolini*

Ec. Pap. Aust. — Economic papers. [Australia]. — Melbourne: *Economic Society of Australia*

Ec. Pros. Int. — Economie prospective internationale. — Paris: *Centre d'Etudes Prospectives et d'Informations Internationales*

Eco. Notes — Economic notes. — Siena: *Monte dei Paschi di Siena*

Ecol. Eco. — Ecological economics. — Amsterdam: *International Society for Ecological Economics*

Econ. Aff. [Calcutta] — Economic affairs [Calcutta]. — Calcutta: *Himansu Roy*

Econ. App. — Economie appliquée. — Grenoble: *Institut de Sciences Mathematiques et Economiques Appliquées*

Econ. B. Norges Bank. — Economic bulletin. Norges bank. — Oslo: *Norges Bank*

Econ. Ban. — Economia e banca. — Trento: *Banca di Trento e Bolzano*

Econ. Bull. — Economic bulletin. — Athens: *Commerical Bank of Greece*

Econ. Cen.E. — Economie du centre-est. — Dijon: *Institut d'Economie Régionale Bourgogne-Franche-Comte*

Econ. Dev. Cult. Change — Economic development and cultural change. — Chicago, IL.: *University of Chicago Press*

Econ. Devel. Q. — Economic development quarterly. — Newbury Park, CA.: *Sage Publications*

Econ. Geogr. — Economic geography. — Worcester, MA.: *Clark University*

Econ. Hist. R. — Economic history review. — Oxford: *Economic History Society*

Econ. Ind. Dem. — Economic and industrial democracy. — London: *Arbetslivscentrum (The Swedish Center for Working Life)*

Econ. Inq. — Economic inquiry. — Huntington Beach, CA.: *Western Economic Association International*
Econ. Int. — Economia internazionale. — Genova: *Istituto di Economia Internazionale*
Econ. J. — Economic journal. — Oxford: *Royal Economic Society*
Econ. Lett. — Economics letters. — Amsterdam: *Elsevier Science Publishers (North-Holland)*
Econ. Model. — Economic modelling. — Guildford: *Butterworth-Heinemann*
Econ. Papers [Warsaw] — Economic papers [Warsaw]. — Warsaw: *Central School of Planning and Statistics in Warsaw, Research Institute for Developing Countries*
Econ. Philos. — Economics and philosophy. — New York, NY.: *Cambridge University Press*
Econ. Plan. — Economics of planning. — Dordrecht: *Kluwer Academic Publishers*
Econ. Pol. — Economic policy. — Cambridge: *Centre of Economic Policy Research/ École des Hautes Etudes en Sciences Sociales*
Econ. Polit. — Economics and politics. — Oxford: *Basil Blackwell*
Econ. Rec. — Economic record. — Sydney: *Economic Society of Australia*
Econ. Rev. — Economic review. — Helsinki: *Kansallis-Osake-Pankki*
Econ. S. Quart. — Economic studies quarterly. — Tokyo: *Japan Association of Economics and Econometrics*
Econ. Soc. — Economy and society. — London: *Routledge*
Econ. Soc. R. — Economic and social review. — Dublin: *Economic and Social Studies*
Econ. Soc. Tidj. — Economisch en sociaal tijdschrift. — Antwerp: *Universtaire Faculteiten Sint-Ignatius te Antwerpen*
Econ. Sys. — Economic systems. — Heidelberg: *Osteuropa-Institut München*
Econ. Sys. Res. — Economic systems research. — Abingdon: *International Input-Output Association*
Econ. Theory — Economic theory. — Berlin: *Springer-Verlag*
Econom. R. — Econometric reviews. — New York, NY.: *Marcel Dekker*
Economet. Th. — Econometric theory. — New York, NY.: *Cambridge University Press*
Econometrica — Econometrica. — Evanston, IL.: *Econometric Society*
Economia [Lisbon] — Economia [Lisbon]. — Lisbon: *Universidade Católica Portuguesa, Faculdade de Ciências Económicas e Empresariais*
Economica — Economica. — London: *London School of Economics and Political Science*
Económica Arg — Económica. — La Plata: *Universidad Nacional de la Plata, Facultad de Ciencias Económicas, Instituto de Investigaciones Economicas*
Economics — Economics. — Haywards Heath: *Economics Association*
Economist [Leiden] — Economist [Leiden]. — Leiden: *Royal Netherlands Economic Association*
Ekon. Preg. — Ekonomski pregled. — Zagreb: *Savez Ekonimista Hrvatske*
Ener. Econ. — Energy economics. — Oxford: *Butterworth-Heinemann*
Energy Pol. — Energy policy. — Guildford: *Butterworth-Heinemann*
Envir. Plan. B. — Environment and planning B.: *Planning and design* — London: *Pion*
Envir. Plan. C. — Environment and planning C.: *Government and policy* — London: *Pion*
Envir. Plan. D — Environment and planning D.: *Society and space* — London: *Pion*
Envir. Plan.A. — Environment and planning A.: *International journal of urban and regional research* — London: *Pion*
Environ. Law — Environmental law. — Portland: *Northwestern School of Law of Lewis and Clark College*
Environ. Resour. Econ. — Environmental & resource economics. — Dordrecht: *Kluwer Academic Publishers*
Espace Géogr. — Espace géographique. — Paris: *Doin editeurs*
Est. Asia Afr. — Estudios de Ásia y África. — Mexico City: *El Colegio de México*
Est. Inter. — Estudios internacionales. — Santiago: *Universidad de Chile, Instituto de Estudios Internacionales*
Et. Int. — Etudes internationales. — Quebec: *Centre québécois de relations internationales*
Eur. Account. Rev. — European accounting review. — London: *European Accounting Association*
Eur. Bus. Econ. Develop. — European business and economic development. — Bradford: *European Research Press*
Eur. Econ. R. — European economic review. — Amsterdam: *European Economic Association*
Eur. J. Pol. Ec. — European journal of political economy. — Amsterdam: *Elsevier Science Publishers (North-Holland)*
Eur. J. Pop. — European journal of population; Revue européenne de démographie. — Amsterdam: *Elsevier Science Publishers (North Holland)*

Eur. Res. — European research. — Shipley: *European Research Press*
Eur.-Asia Stud. — Europe-Asia studies. — Abingdon: *Carfax Publishing*
Expl. Ec. His. — Explorations in economic history. — Duluth, MN.: *Academic Press*
Fed. Resv. B. — Federal Reserve bulletin. — Washington, DC.: *Board of Governors of the Federal Reserve System*
Federalist — Federalist. — Pavia: *Fondazione Europea Luciano Bolis*
Finan. Anal. J. — Financial analysts journal. — Charlottesville, VA.: *Association for Investment Management and Research*
Finan. News Anal. — Financial news analysis. — Dakar: *Africa Centre for Monetary Studies*
Finansy — Финансы СССР; Finansy SSSR. — Moscow: *Izdatel'stvo Finansy, Statistika for Ministerstvo Finansov SSSR*
Finanzarchiv — Finanzarchiv. — Tübingen: *J.C.B. Mohr (Paul Siebeck)*
Fis. Stud. — Fiscal studies. — London: *Institute for Fiscal Studies*
Foreign Aff. — Foreign affairs. — New York, NY.: *Council on Foreign Relations*
Foreign Pol. — Foreign policy. — Washington, D.C.: *Carnegie Endowment for International Peace*
Form. Emp. — Formation emploi. — Paris: *Documentation Française*
Foro Int. — Foro internacional. — Mexico City: *El Colegio de México*
Genèses — Genèses. — France: *Calman-Lévy*
Geneva Pap. Risk Insur. Theory — Geneva papers on risk and insurance theory. — Dordrecht: *Association de Genève*
Genève-Afrique — Genève-Afrique. — Geneva: *Institut Universitaire d'Études du Développement (IUED)*
Geoforum — Geoforum. — Oxford: *Pergamon Press*
Geogr. Anal. — Geographical analysis. — Columbus, OH.: *Ohio State University Press*
Geogr. J. — Geographical journal. — London: *Royal Geographical Society*
Geogr. Pol. — Geographia polonica. — Warsaw: *Polish Academy of Sciences, Institute of Geography and Spatial Organization*
Geogr. Rund. — Geographische Rundschau. — Braunschweig: *Westermann Schulbuchverlag*
Ger. Pol. — German politics. — London: *Frank Cass*
Gestion — Gestion 2000.: *Management et prospective* — Louvain: *Université Catholique de Louvain, Institut d'administration et de gestion*
Gior. Econ. A. — Giornale degli economisti e annali di economia. — Milan: *Universita Commerciale Luigi Bocconi*
Governance — Governance. — Oxford: *Basil Blackwell*
Govt. Oppos. — Government and opposition. — London: *Government and Opposition*
Gr. Econ. Rev. — Greek economic review. — Athens: *Society for Economic Research*
Group Decis. Negot. — Group decision and negotiation. — Dordrecht: *Kluwer Academic Publishers*
Harv. Bus. Re. — Harvard business review. — Boston, MA: *Harvard Business Review*
Health Pol. Plan. — Health policy and planning. — Oxford: *London School of Hygiene and Tropical Medicine*
High Tech. Law J. — High technology law journal. — Berkeley, CA.: *University of California Press*
High. Educ. — Higher education. — Dordrecht: *Kluwer Academic Publishers*
Hist. Polit. Ec. — History of political economy. — Durham, NC.: *Duke University Press*
Hito. J. Comm. Manag. — Hitotsubashi journal of commerce and management. — Tokyo: *Hitotsubashi University, Hitotsubashi Academy*
Hito. J. Econ. — Hitotsubashi journal of economics. — Tokyo: *Hitotsubashi Academy Hitotsubashi University*
Hom. Soc. — Homme et la société. — Paris: *Centre National des Lettres/ Centre National de la Recherche Scientifique*
Homines — Homines. — Hato Rey (Puerto Rico): *Universidad Interamericana de Puerto Rico*
Hous. Pol. Deb. — Housing policy debate. — Washington, D.C.: *Office of Housing Policy, Fannie Mae*
Human Relat. — Human relations. — New York, N.Y.: *Plenum Press*
Human. Org. — Human organization. — Temple Terrace, FL.: *Society for Applied Anthropology*
Ifo-Stud. — Ifo-Studien. — Berlin: *Ifo- Institut für Wirtschaftsforschung*
Impact Sci. — Impact of science on society. — Paris: *UNESCO*
Ind. Crisis Q. — Industrial crisis quarterly. — Amsterdam: *Industrial Crisis Institute*
Ind. Free China — Industry of free China. — Taipei: *Council for Economic Planning and Development*

Ind. J. Agri. Eco. — Indian journal of agricultural economics. — Bombay: *Indian Society of Agricultural Economics*

Ind. J. Eco. — Indian journal of economics. — Allahabad: *University of Allahabad, Departments of Economics and Commerce*

Ind. J. Ind. Rel. — Indian journal of industrial relations. — New Delhi: *Shri Ram Centre for Industrial Relations and Human Resources*

Ind. J. Pol. Sci. — Indian journal of political science. — Madras: *Indian Political Science Association*

Ind. J. Reg. Sci. — Indian journal of regional science. — Kharagpur: *Indian Institute of Technology, Regional Science Association*

Ind. Lab. Rel. — Industrial and labor relations review. — Ithaca, N.Y.: *Cornell University, New York State School of Industrial and Labor Relations*

Ind. Law J. — Industrial law journal. — Oxford: *Industrial Law Society*

Ind. Relat. — Industrial relations. — Oxford: *University of California, Berkeley, Institute of Industrial Relations*

Ind. Relat. J. — Industrial relations journal. — Oxford: *Basil Blackwell*

Industria — Industria. — Bologna: *Società editrice il Mulino*

Infor. Com. Esp. — Información comercial española. — Madrid: *Secretaría de Estado de Comercio*

Insur. Math. Econ. — Insurance mathematics & economics. — Amsterdam: *Elsevier Science Publishers*

Int. Aff. [London] — International affairs [London]. — London: *Royal Institute of International Affairs*

Int. Aff. Mos. — International affairs [Moscow]. — Moscow: *Progress Publishers*

Int. Asien. — Internationales Asienforum. — Cologne: *Europäisches Institut für Politische, Wirtschaftliche und Soziale Fragen*

Int. Comp. L. — International and comparative law quarterly. — London: *British Institute of International and Comparative Law*

Int. Econ. J. — International economic journal. — Seoul: *Korea International Economic Association*

Int. Econ. R. — International economic review. — Philadelphia, PA. and Osaka: *University of Pennsylvania, Department of Economics/Osaka University, Institute of Social and Economic Research Association*

Int. Inter. — International interactions. — Reading: *Gordon and Breach Science Publishers*

Int. J. — International journal. — Toronto: *Canadian Institute of International Affairs*

Int. J. Health. Ser. — International journal of health services. — Amityville, NY.: *Baywood Publishing*

Int. J. Hum. Res. Man. — International journal of human resource management. — London: *Routledge*

Int. J. Ind. O. — International journal of industrial organization. — Amsterdam: *Elsevier Science Publishers (North-Holland)*

Int. J. M.E. Stud. — International journal of Middle East studies. — New York, N.Y.: *Middle East Studies Association of North America*

Int. J. S. Law — International journal of the sociology of law. — London: *Academic Press*

Int. J. Soc. E. — International journal of social economics. — Bradford: *MCB University Press*

Int. J. Urban — International journal of urban and regional research. — Sevenoaks: *Edward Arnold*

Int. Lab. Rev. — International labour review. — Geneva: *International Labour Office (ILO)*

Int. Pol. — Internasjonal politikk. — Oslo: *Norsk Utenrikspolitisk Institutt*

Int. R. Applied Ec. — International review of applied economics. — Sevenoaks: *Edward Arnold*

Int. R. Law Econ. — International review of law and economics. — Stoneham, MA.: *Butterworth-Heinemann*

Int. R. Ret. Dist. Res. — International review of retail, distribution and consumer research. — London: *Routledge*

Int. Reg. Sci. R. — International regional science review. — Morgantown, WV.: *Regional Research Institute*

Int. Rel. — International relations. — London: *David Davies Memorial Institute of International Studies*

Int. Rev. Admin. Sci. — International review of administrative sciences. — London: *International Institute of Administrative Sciences, European Group of Public Administration*

Int. Soc. — International socialism. — London: *Socialist Workers Party*

Int. Stud. — International studies. — New Delhi: *Sage Publications India*

Int. Stud. Q. — International studies quarterly. — Stoneham, MA.: *International Studies Association*

Integ. Lat.am. — Integración latinoamericana. — Buenos Aires: *Instituto para la Integración de América Latina (INTAL)*

Inter. R. Strat. Manag. — International review of strategic management. — Chichester: *John Wiley & Sons*

Inter. Spect. — International spectator. — Rome: *Istituto Affari Internazionali*

Inter. VAT Mon. — International VAT monitor. — Amsterdam: *International Bureau of Fiscal Documentation*

Interfaces — Interfaces. — Providence, RI.: *Institute of Management Sciences and the Operations Research Society of America*

Internat. Contrib. Lab. Stud. — International contributions to labour studies. — San Diego: *Academic Press*

Invest. Econ. — Investigaciones economicas. — Madrid: *Fundacion Empresa Publica*

Irish Bank. Rev. — Irish banking review. — Dublin: *Irish Bankers' Federation*

Isr. Law R. — Israel law review. — Jerusalem: *Israel Law Review Association*

Iss. Stud. — Issues & studies. — Taipei: *National Chengchi University, Institute of International Relations*

Iz. Akad. Respub. Kazakh. — Известия Академии наук Республики Казохстан; Izvestiia Akademii nauk republik Kazakhstan.: *Seriia obshchectvennych nauk* — Alma Ata:

J. Acc. Pub. Pol. — Journal of accounting and public policy. — New York, NY.: *Elsevier Science Publishers (North-Holland)*

J. Account. E. — Journal of accounting and economics. — Amsterdam: *Elsevier Science Publishers (North Holland)*

J. Agr. Econ. — Journal of agricultural economics. — Oxford: *Agricultural Economics Society*

J. Agr. Econ. R. — Journal of agricultural economics research. — Washington, NY.: *United States Department of Agriculture, Economic Research Service*

J. Air Law Comm. — Journal of air law and commerce. — Dallas, TX.: *Southern Methodist University, School of Law*

J. Am. Plann. — Journal of the American Planning Association. — Chicago, IL.: *American Planning Association*

J. Am. Stat. Ass. — Journal of the American Statistical Association. — Alexandria, VA: *American Statistical Association*

J. Appl. Econ. — Journal of applied econometrics. — Chichester: *John Wiley and Sons*

J. Appl. Psychol. — Journal of applied psychology. — Arlington, VA.: *American Psychological Association*

J. Asian Afr. Aff. — Journal of Asian and African affairs. — Washington, DC.: *Journal of Asian and African Affairs*

J. Aust. Pol. Econ. — Journal of Australian political economy. — Sydney: *Australian Political Economy Movement*

J. Bank. Fin. — Journal of banking and finance. — Amsterdam: *Associazione Italiana Studi Finanziari (ASFI)/Association Française de Finance (AFFI)/European Finance Association (EFA)*

J. Bus. — Journal of business. — Chicago, IL.: *University of Chicago, Graduate School of Business*

J. Bus. Econ. Stat. — Journal of business & economic statistics. — Alexandria, VA.: *American Statistical Association*

J. Bus. Fin. Acc. — Journal of business finance and accounting. — Oxford: *Basil Blackwell*

J. Bus. Soc. — Journal of business and society. — Nicosia: *Cyprus College*

J. Com. Mkt. S. — Journal of common market studies. — Oxford: *University Association for Contemporary European Studies*

J. Comm. C. Pol. — Journal of Commonwealth & comparative politics. — London: *Frank Cass*

J. Comp. Econ. — Journal of comparative economics. — Duluth, MN.: *Association for Comparative Economic Studies*

J. Consum. Pol. — Journal of consumer policy. — Dordrecht: *Kluwer Academic Publishers*

J. Cont. Asia — Journal of contemporary Asia. — Manila: *Journal of Contemporary Asia Publishers*

J. Dev. Areas — Journal of developing areas. — Macomb, IL.: *Western Illinois University*

J. Dev. Econ. — Journal of development economics. — Amsterdam: *Elsevier Science Publishers (North-Holland)*
J. Dev. Soc. — Journal of developing societies. — Leiden: *E.J. Brill*
J. Dev. Stud. — Journal of development studies. — London: *Frank Cass*
J. Droit Int. — Journal du droit international. — Paris: *Editions Techniques*
J. Econ. — Journal of economics; Zeitschrift für Nationalökonomie. — Vienna: *Springer-Verlag Wien*
J. Econ. Beh. — Journal of economic behavior and organization. — Amsterdam: *Elsevier Science Publishers (North-Holland)*
J. Econ. Dyn. Cont. — Journal of economic dynamics and control. — Amsterdam: *Society of Economic Dynamics and Control*
J. Econ. Iss. — Journal of economic issues. — Lincoln, NE.: *Association for Evolutionary Economics*
J. Econ. Lit. — Journal of economic literature. — Nashville, TN.: *American Economic Association*
J. Econ. Manag. Strat. — Journal of economics & management strategy. — Cambridge, MA.: *MIT Press*
J. Econ. Pers. — Journal of economic perspectives. — Nashville, TN.: *American Economic Association*
J. Econ. Psyc. — Journal of economic psychology. — Amsterdam: *International Association for Research in Economic Psychology*
J. Econ. Soc. Geogr. — Tijdschrift voor economische en sociale geografie; Journal of economic and social geography. — Amsterdam: *Royal Dutch Geographical Society = Koninklijk Nederlands Aardrijkskundig Genootschap*
J. Econ. Stud. — Journal of economic studies. — Bradford: *MCB University Press*
J. Econ. Sur. — Journal of economic surveys. — Oxford: *Basil Blackwell*
J. Econ. Theo. — Journal of economic theory. — Brugge: *Academic Press*
J. Economet. — Journal of econometrics. — Amsterdam: *Elsevier Science Publishers (North-Holland)*
J. Entwick.pol. — Journal für Entwicklungspolitik. — Vienna: *Mattersburger Kreis für Entwicklungspolitik an den Österreichischen Universitäten*
J. Envir. Ec. Manag. — Journal of environmental economics and management. — Duluth, MN.: *Association of Environmental and Resource Economists*
J. Environ. Manag. — Journal of environmental management. — London: *Academic Press*
J. Environ. Plan. Manag. — Journal of environmental planning and management. — Abingdon: *Carfax Publishing*
J. Evolut. Econ. — Journal of evolutionary economics. — Berlin: *Springer-Verlag*
J. Fin. Qu. An. — Journal of financial and quantative analysis. — Seattle, WA.: *University of Washington, Graduate School of Business Administration*
J. Finan. Ec. — Journal of financial economics. — Amsterdam: *University of Rochester, William E. Simon Graduate School of Business Administration*
J. Finan. Ser. Res. — Journal of financial services research. — Dordrecht: *Kluwer Academic Publishers*
J. Finance — Journal of finance. — New York, NY: *American Finance Association*
J. Forecast. — Journal of forecasting. — Chichester: *John Wiley & Sons*
J. Futur. Mark. — Journal of futures markets. — New York, NY.: *Center for the Study of Futures Markets, Columbia Business School*
J. Health Econ. — Journal of health economics. — Amsterdam: *Elsevier Science Publishers (North-Holland)*
J. Hous. Res. — Journal of housing research. — Washington, D.C.: *Office of Housing Policy, Fannie Mae*
J. Hum. Res. — Journal of human resources. — Madison, WI.: *University of Wisconsin Press*
J. Ind. Econ. — Journal of industrial economics. — Oxford: *Basil Blackwell*
J. Ind. Relat. — Journal of industrial relations. — Sydney: *Journal of Industrial Relations*
J. Inst. Actuar. — Journal of the Institute of Actuaries. — Oxford: *Alden Press*
J. Inst. Theo. Ec. — *[JITE]* — Journal of institutional and theoretical economics; Zeitschrift für die gesamte Staatswissenschaft. — Tübingen: *J.C.B.Mohr (Paul Siebeck)*
J. Int. Am. St. — Journal of interamerican studies and world affairs. — Coral Gables, FL.: *Institute of Interamerican Studies*
J. Int. Bus. Stud. — Journal of international business studies. — New Orleans, LA.: *Academy of International Business/ University of South Carolina, College of Business Administration*

J. Int. Dev. — Journal of international development. — Chichester: *Institute for Development Policy and Management*

J. Int. Econ. — Journal of international economics. — Amsterdam: *Elsevier Science Publishers (North-Holland)*

J. Inter. Finan. Manag. Acc. — Journal of international financial management and accounting. — Oxford: *Basil Blackwell*

J. Interd. Ec. — Journal of interdisciplinary economics. — Bicester: *A.B. Academic Publishers*

J. Jap. Int. Ec. — Journal of the Japanese and international economies. — Duluth, MN.: *Tokyo Center for Economic Research*

J. Jpn. Stud. — Journal for Japanese studies. — Seattle, WA.: *Society for Japanese Studies*

J. Labor Ec. — Journal of labor economics. — Chicago, IL.: *Economics Research Center/NORC*

J. Labor Res. — Journal of labor research. — Fairfax, VA: *George Mason University, Department of Economics*

J. Lat. Am. St. — Journal of Latin American studies. — Cambridge: *Cambridge University Press*

J. Law Econ. — Journal of law and economics. — Chicago, IL.: *University of Chicago Press*

J. Law Soc. — Journal of law and society. — Oxford: *Basil Blackwell*

J. Macro. — Journal of macroeconomics. — Baton Rouge, LA.: *Lousiana State University, College of Business Administration*

J. Manag. Stu. — Journal of management studies. — Oxford: *Basil Blackwell*

J. Market R. — Journal of the Market Research Society. — London: *Market Research Society*

J. Math Econ. — Journal of mathematical economics. — Amsterdam: *Elsevier Science Publishers (North-Holland)*

J. Math. Sociol. — Journal of mathematical sociology. — New York: *Gordon & Breach Science Publishers*

J. Mod. Afr. S. — Journal of modern African studies. — Cambridge: *Cambridge University Press*

J. Monet. Ec. — Journal of monetary economics. — Amsterdam: *University of Rochester, William E. Simon Graduate School of Business Administration and Department of Economics*

J. Money C. B. — Journal of money, credit and banking. — Columbus, OH.: *Ohio State University Press*

J. Pacific Soc. — Journal of the Pacific Society. — Tokyo: *Pacific Society*

J. Pal. Stud. — Journal of Palestine studies. — Berkeley, CA.: *Institute for Palestine Studies*

J. Peasant Stud. — Journal of peasant studies. — London: *Frank Cass*

J. Policy M. — Journal of policy modeling. — New York, NY.: *Elsevier Science Publishing*

J. Polit. Ec. — Journal of political economy. — Chicago: *University of Chicago Press*

J. Pop. Ec. — Journal of population economics. — Berlin: *Springer-Verlag*

J. Post. Keyn. Ec. — Journal of post Keynesian economics. — Armonk, NY.: *M.E.Sharpe*

J. Prod. Anal. — Journal of productivity analysis. — Dordrecht: *Kluwer Academic Publishers*

J. Publ. Ec. — Journal of public economics. — Amsterdam: *Elsevier Science Publishers (North-Holland)*

J. Public Pol. — Journal of public policy. — Cambridge: *Cambridge University Press*

J. Real Est. Finan. Econ. — Journal of real estate finance and economics. — Dordrecht: *Kluwer Academic Publishers*

J. Reg. Pol. — Journal of regional policy. — Naples: *Isveimer*

J. Regul. Econ. — Journal of regulatory economics. — Dordrecht: *Kluwer Academic Publishers*

J. Risk Uncert. — Journal of risk and uncertainty. — Dordrecht: *Kluwer Academic Publishers*

J. Rural Devel. Admin. — Journal of rural development and administration. — Peshawar: *Academy for Rural Development*

J. Soc. Devel. Afr. — Journal of social development in Africa. — Harare: *School of Social Work*

J. Soc. Pol. — Journal of social policy. — Cambridge: *Social Policy Association*

J. Soc. Pol. E. — Journal of social, political and economic studies. — Washington, D.C.: *Council for Social and Economic Studies*

J. Soc. Stat. Paris — Journal de la Société de Statistique de Paris. — Paris: *Société de Statistique de France*

J. Theor. Pol. — Journal of theoretical politics. — London: *Sage Publications*

J. Transp. Ec. Pol. — Journal of transport economics and policy. — Bath: *University of Bath/ London School of Economics and Political Science*

J. Urban Ec. — Journal of urban economics. — Duluth, MN.: *Academic Press*

J. World Tr. — Journal of world trade. — Geneva: *Werner Publishing*

Jahr. Soz.schaft. — Jahrbuch für Sozialwissenschaft. — Göttingen: *Vandenhoeck & Ruprecht*

Jahrb. N. St. — Jahrbücher für Nationalökonomie und Statistik. — Stuttgart: *Gustav Fischer Verlag*

Jpn. Forum — Japan forum. — Oxford: *British Association for Japanese Studies*
Jpn. R. Int. Aff. — Japan review of international affairs. — Tokyo: *Japan Institute of International Affairs*
Jpn. Wor. Econ. — Japan and the world economy. — Amsterdam: *New York University*
Kasarinlan — Kasarinlan. — Quezon City: *University of the Philippines, Third World Studies Center*
Keio Econ. Stud. — Keio economic studies. — Tokyo: *Keio Economic Society*
Konjunkturpolitik — Konjunkturpolitik. — Berlin: *Duncker und Humblot*
Korea Obs. — Korea observer. — Seoul: *Institute of Korean Studies*
Közg. Sz. — Közgazdasági szemle. — Budapest: *Magyar Tudományos Akadémiai, Committee for Economic Sciences*
Kred. Kap. — Kredit und Kapital. — Berlin: *Gesellschaft zur Förderung der wissenschaftlichen Forschung über das Spar- und Girowesen*
Labour Cap. Soc. — Labour, capital and society; Travail, capital et société. — Montreal: *McGill University, Centre for Developing Area Studies*
Labour [Italy] — Labour [Italy]. — Rome: *Fondazione Giacomo Brodolini*
Land Econ. — Land economics. — Madison, WI.: *University of Wisconsin Press*
Lat. Am. Pers. — Latin American perspectives. — Newbury Park, CA.: *Sage Publishers*
Lat. Am. Res. R. — Latin American research review. — Albuquerque, NM.: *Latin American Studies Association*
Law Cont. Pr. — Law and contemporary problems. — Durham, NC: *Duke University, School of Law*
Led. Erhv. — Ledelse og Erhvervsøkonomi. — Copenhagen: *Foreningen af Danske Civiløkonomer (FDC)*
Loc. Govt. St. — Local government studies. — Croydon: *Charles Knight Publishing*
Local. Ec. — Local economy. — Harlow: *Local Economy Policy Unit*
M.East Bus. Econ. R. — Middle East business and economic review. — Australia: *International Centre for Middle East Business and Economic Research*
Maan. Econ. — Maandschrift economie. — Groningen: *Wolters-Noordhoff*
Mag. Mack. Mon. Ar. — Maghreb machrek monde arabe. — Paris: *Fondation Nationale des Sciences Politiques, Centre d'Etudes et de Recherches Internationales, Section Monde arabe/ Université de Paris, Centre d'Etudes de l'Orient contemporain*
Manag. Acc. Res. — Management accounting research. — London: *Chartered Institute of Management Accountants*
Manag. Sci. — Management science. — Providence, RI.: *Institute of Management Sciences*
Manch. Sch. E. — Manchester School of economic and social studies. — Oxford: *Basil Blackwell*
Mar. Pol. — Marine policy. — Guildford: *Butterworth-Heinemann*
Market. Lett. — Marketing letters. — Dordrecht: *Kluwer Academic Publishers*
Math. Fin. — Mathematical finance. — Oxford: *Basil Blackwell*
Math. Soc. Sc. — Mathematical social sciences. — Amsterdam: *Elsevier Science Publishers (North-Holland)*
Media Cult. Soc. — Media culture and society. — London: *Sage Publications*
Metroeconomica — Metroeconomica. — Bologna: *Nuova Casa Editrice L.Cappelli*
MI. law. R. — Michigan law review. — Ann Arbor, MI.: *Michigan Law Review*
Middle E. J. — Middle East journal. — Bloomington, IN.: *Middle East Institute*
Middle E. Stud. — Middle Eastern studies. — London: *Frank Cass*
Milbank Q. — Milbank quarterly. — New York, NY.: *Milbank Memorial Fund*
MIS Q. — MIS quarterly. — U.S.A.: *MIS Research Center*
Mod. Asian S. — Modern Asian studies. — Cambridge: *Cambridge University Press*
Mod. Chi. — Modern China. — Newbury Park, CA.: *Sage Publications*
Mod. Law R. — Modern law review. — Oxford: *Basil Blackwell*
Mon. Econ. S. — Monetary and economic studies. — Tokyo: *Bank of Japan, Institute for Monetary and Economic Studies*
Mon. R. S. Bank. Ind. — Monthly review.: *State Bank of India, Economic Research Department* — Bombay: *State Bank of India*
Mon. Rev. — Monthly review. — New York, NY.: *Monthly Review Foundation*
Monatsberichte — Monatsberichte. Österreichisches Institut für Wirtschaftsforschung. — Vienna: *Österreichisches Institut für Wirtschaftsforschung*
Monetaria — Monetaria. — Mexico City: *Centro de Estudios Monetarios Latinoamericanos*

Money Aff. — Money affairs. — Mexico City: *Centre for Latin American Studies (CEMLA)*
Nár. Hosp. — Národní hospodářství. — Prague: *Panorama*
Nat. Inter. — National interest. — Washington, D.C.: *National Affairs*
Nat. Res. For. — Natural resources forum. — Guildford: *United Nations Department of Technical Cooperation for Development*
Nat. W. Bank — National Westminster Bank quarterly review. — London: *National Westminster Bank*
Natl. Inst. Econ. R. — National Institute economic review. — London: *National Institute of Economic and Social Research*
Natl. Tax. J. — National tax journal. — Columbus, OH.: *National Tax Association — Tax Institute of America*
Natur. Res. J. — Natural resources journal. — Albuquerque, NM.: *University of New Mexico, School of Law*
Negot. J. — Negotiation journal. — New York, NY.: *Plenum Press*
New Left R. — New left review. — London: *New Left Review*
New Tech. Work. Empl. — New technology, work and employment. — Oxford: *Basil Blackwell*
Non. Manag. Leader. — Nonprofit management and leadership. — San Francisco, CA.: *Jossey-Bass*
Nor. Økon. Tidss. — Norsk økonomisk tidsskrift. — Oslo: *Sosialøkonomenes Forening*
Nueva Soc. — Nueva sociedad. — Caracas: *Nueva Sociedad*
Obser. Diag. Econ. — Observations et diagnostics économiques. — Paris: *Observatoire Français des Conjonctures Economiques (OFCE)*
Ocean Dev. Int. — Ocean development and international law. — London: *Taylor & Francis*
OECD Ec. Stud. — OECD economic studies. — Paris: *OECD*
OPEC B. — OPEC bulletin. — Vienna: *Organisation of Petroleum Exporting Countries*
OPEC Rev. — OPEC review. — Oxford: *OPECNA*
Open Econ. R. — Open economies review. — Dordrecht: *Kluwer Academic Publishers*
Orbis — Orbis. — Philadelphia, PA.: *Foreign Policy Research Institute*
Ost. Wirt. — Osteuropa Wirtschaft. — Stuttgart: *Deutsche Gesellschaft für Osteuropakunde*
Osteuropa — Osteuropa. — Stuttgart: *Deutsche Gesellschaft für Osteuropakunde*
Ox. Agrar. Stud. — Oxford agrarian studies. — Oxford: *Carfax Publishing*
Ox. B. Econ. S. — Oxford bulletin of economics and statistics. — Oxford: *Basil Blackwell*
Ox. Econ. Pap. — Oxford economic papers. — Oxford: *Oxford University Press*
Ox. R. Econ. Pol. — Oxford review of economic policy. — Oxford: *Oxford University Press*
Pac. Aff. — Pacific affairs. — Vancouver: *University of British Columbia*
Pac. Ec. B. — Pacific economic bulletin. — Canberra: *Australian National University, Research School of Pacific Studies, National Centre for Development Studies*
Pac. Rev. — Pacific review. — Oxford: *Oxford University Press*
Pak. Dev. R. — Pakistan development review. — Islamabad: *Pakistan Institute of Development Economics*
Pakis. Horiz. — Pakistan horizon. — Karachi: *Pakistan Institute of International Affairs*
Pań. Prawo — Państwo i prawo. — Warsaw: *Polska Academia Nauk, Instytut Nauk Prawnych*
Pap. Econ. Esp. — Papeles de económia española. — Madrid: *Confederación Española de Cajas de Ahorros, Fundación Fondo para la Investigación Económica y Social*
Pap. Reg. Sci. — Papers in regional science. — Urbana, IL.: *Regional Science Association International*
Pénz. Sz. — Pénzügyi szemle. — Budapest: *Pénzügyminisztérium*
Peripherie — Peripherie. — Berlin: *Wissenschaftliche Vereinigung für Entwicklungstheorie und Entwicklungspolitik*
Persp. Econ. — Perspectiva económica. — São Leopoldo: *Universidade do Vale do Rio dos Sinos*
Perspect. Ener. — Perspectives in energy. — London: *Moscow International Energy Club*
Philos. Pub. — Philosophy & public affairs. — Princeton, N.J.: *Princeton University Press*
Pol. Etran. — Politique étrangère. — Paris: *Institut Français des Relations Internationales*
Pol. Geogr. — Political geography. — Oxford: *Butterworth-Heinemann*
Pol. Manag. Publ. — Politiques et management public. — Paris: *Institut de Management Public*
Pol. Sci. Q. — Political science quarterly. — New York, NY.: *Academy of Political Science*
Policy Sci. — Policy sciences. — Dordrecht: *Kluwer Academic Publishers*
Polit. Int. — Politique internationale. — Paris: *Politique Internationale*
Politica. — Politica. — Arhus: *Institut for Statskundskab Universitetsparken*
Politico — Politico. — Milan: *Universita degli Studi di Pavia, Facolta' di scienze politiche*

Politics (U.K.) — Politics. — London: *Political Studies Association of the United Kingdom*
Pop. Dev. Rev. — Population and development review. — New York, N.Y.: *Population Council*
Pop. Res. Pol. R. — Population research and policy review. — Dordrecht: *Kluwer Academic Publishers*
Pop. Stud. — Population studies. — London: *London School of Economics, Population Investigation Committee*
Post-Sov. Aff. — Post-Soviet affairs. — Silver Spring, MD.: *Joint Committee on Soviet Studies of the American Council of Learned Societies and the Social Science Research Council*
Pra. Zab. Społ. — Praca i zabezpieczenie społeczne. — Warsaw: *Państwowe Wydawnictwo Ekonomiczne*
Prob. Am.Lat. — Problèmes d'Amérique latine. — Paris: *Documentation française*
Probl. Commu. — Problems of communism. — Washington, D.C.: *US Information Agency*
Prof. Geogr. — Professional geographer. — Washington, D.C.: *Association of American Geographers*
Prog. H. Geog. — Progress in human geography. — Sevenoaks: *Edward Arnold*
Prog. Plan. — Progress in planning. — Oxford: *Pergamon Press*
Proj. App. — Project appraisal. — Guildford: *Beech Tree Publishing*
Prokla — Prokla.: *Probleme des Klassenkampfs* — Berlin: *Vereinigung zur Kritik der politischen Ökonomie*
Prz. Staty. — Przegląd statystyczny. — Warsaw: *Polska Akademia nauk, Komitet Statystyki i Ekonometrii*
Publ. Adm. Re. — Public administration review. — Washington, DC.: *American Society for Public Administration*
Publ. Admin. — Public administration. — Oxford: *Royal Institute for Public Administration*
Publ. Choice — Public choice. — Dordrecht: *Kluwer Academic Publishers*
Publ. Fin. Q. — Public finance quarterly. — Newbury Park, CA.: *Sage Publications*
Publ. Finan. — Public finance; Finances publiques. — Frankfurt am Main: *Public Finance/ Finances Publiques*
Publ. Inter. — Public interest. — Washington, DC.: *National Affairs*
Publizistik — Publizistik. — Konstanz: *Deutsche Gesellschaft für Publizistik- und Kommunikationswissenschaft/ Österreichische Gesellschaft für Publizistik- und Kommunikationswissenschaft/ Schweizerische Gesellschaft für Kommunikations- und Medienwissenschaft*
Q Rev. Econ. Finan. — Quarterly review of economics and finance. — U.S.A.: *Midwest Economics Association, Department of Economics*
Q. B. Ctr. Bank Ire. — Quarterly bulletin. Central Bank of Ireland. — Dublin: *Central Bank of Ireland*
Q. Econ. Bull. — Quarterly economic bulletin. — Liverpool: *Liverpool Research Group in Macroeconomics*
Q. J. Econ. — Quarterly journal of economics. — Cambridge, MA.: *Harvard University*
Q. R. Fed. Res. Bank N.Y. — Quarterly review. Federal Reserve Bank of New York. — New York, NY.: *Federal Reserve Bank of New York, Research and Statistics Group*
Q. Rev. Sver. Riks. — Quarterly review. Sveriges Riksbank. — Stockholm: *Sveriges Riksbank*
Quad. Sociol. — Quaderni di sociologia. — Turin: *Edizioni di Comunità*
Quart. J. Agr. Ec. — Quarterly journal of agricultural economy. — -:
R. Austrian Econ. — Review of Austrian economics. — Dordrecht: *Ludwig von Mises Institute*
R. C. & E.Eur. Law — Review of Central and East European law. — Dordrecht: *Documentation Office for East European Law*
R. Éc. Reg. Urb. — Revue d'économie régionale et urbaine. — Paris: *ADICUEER (Association des Directeurs d'Instituts et des Centres Universitaires d'Etudes Economiques Régionales)*
R. Econ. S. — Review of economic studies. — Oxford: *Basil Blackwell*
R. Eur. Lat.am. Caribe — European review of Latin American and Caribbean studies; Revista europea de estudios latinoamericanos y del caribe. — Amsterdam: *CEDLA, Interuniversitair Centrum voor Studie en Documentatie van Latijns Amerika/ RILA, Royal Institute of Linguistics and Anthropology*
R. Fed. Resv. Bank St.Louis — Review. Federal Reserve Bank of St. Louis. — St. Louis, MO,: *Federal Reserve Bank of St. Louis, Research and Public Information Department*
R. Finan. — Revue du financier. — Vineuil: *Masson*
R. Finan. Stud. — Review of financial studies. — Cary, NC.: *Society for Financial Studies*
R. In. Weal. — Review of income and wealth. — New York, NY.: *International Association for Research in Income and Wealth*

R. Indust. Organ. — Review of industrial organization. — Dordrecht: *Kluwer Academic Publishers*

R. Islam. Econ. — Review of Islamic economics. — Leicester: *International Association for Islamic Economics*

R. Mar. Comm. — Revue du marché commun. — Paris: *Éditions Techniques et Économiques*

R. Pol. Econ. — Review of political economy. — Sevenoaks: *Edward Arnold*

R. Quant. Finan. Account. — Review of quantitative finance and accounting. — Dordrecht: *Kluwer Academic Publishers*

R. Soc. Econ. — Review of social economy. — DeKalb, IL.: *Association for Social Economics*

R. T-Monde — Revue Tiers-Monde. — Paris: *Université de Paris, Institut d'étude du développement économique et social*

R. Trim. Com. Econ. — Revue trimestrielle de droit commercial et de droit économique. — Paris: *Editions Sirey*

R. Urban. Region. Dev. S. — Review of urban and regional development studies. — Tokyo: *Applied Regional Science Conference*

R.E.M. — Revue de l'économie meridionale. — Montpellier: *Université de Montpellier, Faculté de droit et des sciences économiques, Centre regional de la productivité et des études économiques*

Race Class — Race and class. — London: *Institute of Race Relations*

Rand J. Eco. — Rand journal of economics. — Santa Monica, CA.: *Rand Corporation*

Ras. Econ. — Rassegna economica. — Naples: *Banco di Napoli*

Rech. Ec. Louvain — Recherches économiques de Louvain. — Brussels: *Université Catholique de Louvain, Departement des Sciences Economiques*

Recht Int. Wirst. — Recht der internationalen Wirtschaft. — Heidelberg: *Verlag Recht und Wirtschaft*

Reg. Sci. Urb. Econ. — Regional science and urban economics. — Amsterdam: *Elsevier Science Publishers (North-Holland)*

Reg. Stud. — Regional studies. — Cambridge: *Regional Studies Association*

Res. Bank B. NZ — Reserve Bank bulletin. — Wellington: *Reserve Bank of New Zealand*

Res. Pol. — Resources policy. — Oxford: *Butterworth-Heinemann*

Rev. Afr. Pol. Ec. — Review of African political economy. — Sheffield: *ROAPE Publications*

Rev. Algér. — Revue algérienne des sciences juridiques économiques et politiques. — Algiers: *Université d'Alger, Institut de Droit et des Sciences Administratives*

Rev. Bl. Pol. Ec. — Review of black political economy. — New Brunswick, NJ.: *National Economic Association/ Clark Atlanta University, Southern Center for Studies in Public Policy*

Rev. Bras. Ec. — Revista brasileira de economia. — Rio de Janeiro: *Fundação Getulio Vargas, Escola da Pós-Graduação em Economia*

Rev. Ec. Con. It. — Review of economic conditions in Italy. — Rome: *Banco di Roma*

Rev. Ec. Polit. — Revue d'économie politique. — Paris: *Editions Sirey*

Rev. Econ. St. — Review of economics and statistics. — Amsterdam: *Harvard University*

Rev. Et. Comp. — Revue d'études comparatives est- ouest. — Paris: *Institut de recherches juridiques comparatives du C.N.R.S., Centre d'études des pays socialistes/ Economie et techniques de planification des pays de l'est*

Rev. Fisc. Eur. — Revue fiscalité européenne. — Nice: *Cahiers fiscaux européens*

Rev. Int. Sci. Ec. Com. — Rivista internazionale di scienze economiche e commerciali. — Milan: *Università Commerciale Luigi Bocconi/ Università degli Studi di Milano*

Rev. Int.Am. Plan. — Revista interamericana de planificación. — Guatemala: *Sociedad Interamericana de Planificación*

Rev. Parag. Sociol. — Revista paraguaya de sociología. — Asunción: *Centro Paraguayo de Estudios Sociológicos*

Rev. Rad. Pol. Ec. — Review of radical political economics. — Riverside: *Union for Radical Political Economics*

Revis. Econ. — Revista de economía. — Montevideo: *Banco Central de Uruguay*

Risparmio — Risparmio. — Milan: *Associazione fra le Casse di Risparmio Italiane*

Riv. Dir. Finan. Sci. Fin. — Rivista di diritto finanziario e scienza delle finanze. — Milan: *Dipartimento di Economia pubblica territoriale dell'Università/ Camera di Commercio di Pavia/ Università di Roma, Facoltà di Giurisprudenza, Istituto di diritto pubblico*

Riv. Econ. Agrar. — Rivista di economia agraria. — Bologna: *Istituto Nazionale di Economia Agraria/ Società Italiana di Economia Agraria*

Riv. Int. Sci. Soc. — Rivista internazionale di scienze sociali. — Milan: *Università Cattolica del Sacro Cuore*

Riv. Pol. Ec. — Rivista di politica economica. — Rome: *Servizio Italiano Pubblicazioni Internazionali (SIPI)*

Riv. S. Pol. Int. — Rivista di studi politici internazionali. — Florence: *Giuseppe Vedovato*

Rural Sociol. — Rural sociology. — College Station, TX.: *Rural Sociological Society*

RWI-Mitt. — RWI-Mitteilungen. — Berlin: *Rheinisch-Westfälisches Institut für Wirtschaftsforschung*

S. Afr. J. Econ. — South African journal of economics; Suid-Afrikaanse tydskrif vir ekonomie. — Pretoria: *Economic Society of South Africa*

S. Afr. J. Labour Relat. — South African journal of labour relations. — Pretoria: *University of South Africa, School of Business Leadership*

S. Econ. J. — Southern economic journal. — Chapel Hill, NC: *Southern Economic Association/ University of North Carolina at Chapel Hill*

S.Afr. Lab. B. — South African labour bulletin. — Johannesburg: *Umanyano Publications*

S.Asia. J. — South Asia journal. — New Delhi: *Indian Council of South Asian Cooperation*

SAIS R. — SAIS review. — Washington, DC.: *Johns Hopkins University, Paul H. Nitze School of Advanced International Studies*

Sav. Develop. — Savings and development. — Milan: *Centre for Financial Assistance to African Countries (Finafrica)*

Sc. Ec. Hist. R. — Scandinavian economic history review. — Lund: *Scandinavian Society for Economic and Social History*

Sc. J. Econ. — Scandinavian journal of economics. — Oxford: *Basil Blackwell*

Scand. Hous. Plan. R. — Scandinavian housing and planning research. — Stockholm: *Building Research Institute (Denmark)/ Ministry of Environment (Finland)/ Institute for Urban and Regional Research (Norway)/ Institute for Building Research (Sweden)*

Scand. J. Devel. Altern. — Scandinavian journal of development alternatives. — Stockholm: *Bethany Books*

Schw. Z. Volk. Stat. — Schweizerische Zeitschrift für Volkswirtschaft und Statistik; Revue suisse d'économie politique et de statistique. — Bern: *Schweizerische Gesellschaft für Statistik und Volkswirtschaft/ Société suisse de statistique et d'économie politique*

Sci. Am. — Scientific American. — New York, NY.: *Scientific American*

Sci. Pub. Pol. — Science and public policy. — Guildford: *International Science Policy Foundation*

Sci. Soc. — Science and society. — New York, NY.: *Guilford Publications*

Scot. J. Poli. — Scottish journal of political economy. — Oxford: *Scottish Economic Society*

Simulat. Gam. — Simulation and gaming. — Newbury Park, CA.: *Sage Publications*

Skan. Ensk. Bank. Q. R. — Skandinaviska Enskilda Banken quarterly review. — Stockholm: *Skandinaviska Enskilda Banken*

Small Bus. Econ. — Small business economics. — Dordrecht: *Kluwer Academic Publishers*

Small Enter. Devel. — Small enterprise development. — London: *Intermediate Technology Publications*

Soc. Act. — Social action. — New Delhi: *Indian Social Institute, Social Action Trust*

Soc. Choice — Social choice and welfare. — Berlin: *Springer International*

Soc. Econ. S. — Social and economic studies. — Kingston: *University of the West Indies, Institute of Social and Economic Research*

Soc. Forc. — Social forces. — Chapel Hill, NC.: *University of North Carolina, Department of Sociology*

Soc. Ind. — Social indicators research. — Dordrecht: *Kluwer Academic Publishers*

Soc. Just. — Social justice. — San Francisco, CA.: *Global Options*

Soc. Part. — Socialismo y participación. — Lima: *CEDEP (Centro de Estudios para el Desarrollo y la Participación)*

Soc. Philos. Pol. — Social philosophy & policy. — Oxford: *Bowling Green State University, Social Philosophy and Policy Center*

Soc. Pol. Admin. — Social policy and administration. — Oxford: *Basil Blackwell*

Soc. Sci. — Social sciences. — Moscow: *Nauka Moscow*

Soc. Sci. China — Social sciences in China. — Beijing: *Chinese Academy of Social Science*

Soc. Sci. Info. — Social science information. — London: *Maison des sciences de l'homme/ Ecole des hautes études en science sociales*

Soc. Sci. Q. — Social science quarterly. — Austin, TX.: *Southwestern Social Science Association*

Society — Society. — New Brunswick, NJ.: *Transaction*

Socio. Econ. — Socio-economic planning sciences. — Exeter: *Pergamon Press*

Sociol. Trav. — Sociologie du travail. — Paris: *Dunod*

Sot. Issle. — Социологические исследования (социс); Sotsiologicheskie issledovaniia (sotsis). — Moscow: *Akademii Nauk SSSR*

Sov. Ec. — Soviet economy. — Silver Spring, MD.: *American Council of Learned Societies, Joint Committee on Soviet Studies/ Social Science Research Council*

Spoudai — Spoudai. — Piraeus: *University of Piraeus*

Spr. Między. — Sprawy międzynarodowe. — Warsaw: *Polski Instytut Spraw Międzynarodowych*

Staff Pap. Int. Monetary — Staff papers.International Monetary Fund. — Washington, DC.: *International Monetary Fund*

Stud. Comp. Commun. — Studies in comparative communism. — Guildford: *Butterworth-Heinemann*

Stud. Pol. Ec. — Studies in political economy. — Ottawa: *Studies in Political Economy*

Südosteur. Mitteil. — Südosteuropa Mitteilungen. — Munich: *Südosteuropa-Gesellschaft*

Svobod. Mysl' — Свободная мысль; Svobodnaia Mysl'. — Moscow: *Izdatel' stvo Pravda*

Tech. Devel. — Technology and development. — Tokyo: *Institute for International Cooperation/ Japan International Cooperation Agency*

Ter. Nova — Terra Nova. — Washington, DC.: *International Freedom Foundation*

Theory Decis. — Theory and decision. — Dordrecht: *Kluwer Academic Publishers*

Third Wor. P. — Third World planning review. — Liverpool: *Liverpool University Press*

Third World — Third World quarterly. — London: *Third World Foundation for Social and Economic Studies*

Tijds. Econ. Manag. — Tijdschrift voor economie en management. — Louvain: *Katholieke Universiteit Te Leuven, Faculteit der Economische en Toegepaste Economische Wetenschappen*

Transformation — Transformation. — Durban: *Transformation*

Transit — Transit.: *Europäische Revue* — Frankfurt am Main: *Institut für die Wissenschaften vom Menschen*

Transportation — Transportation. — Dordrecht: *Kluwer Academic Publishers*

Unisa Lat.Am. Rep. — Unisa Latin American report. — Pretoria: *Unisa Centre for Latin American Studies*

Urban Geogr. — Urban geography. — Silver Spring, MD.: *V.H. Winston & Son*

Urban Stud. — Urban studies. — Abingdon: *University of Glasgow, Centre for Urban and Regional Research*

Util. Policy — Utilities policy. — Oxford: *Butterworth-Heinemann*

Verf. Rec. Über. — Verfassung und Recht in Übersee; Law and politics in Africa, Asia and Latin America. — Baden- Baden: *Hamburger Gesellschaft für Völkerrecht und Auswärtige Politik*

Vest. Mosk. Univ. 6 — Вестник Московского Университета; Vestnik Moskovskogo Universiteta.: Серия 6. Экономика; Seriia 6. Ekonomika — Moscow: *Izdatel' stvo Moskovskogo Universiteta*

Vierteljahresberichte — Vierteljahresberichte. — Bonn: *Friedrich-Ebert Stiftung*

Vop. Ekon. — Вопросы экономики; Voprosy ekonomiki. — Moscow: *Akademii Nauk SSSR, Institut Ekonomiki*

W. Eur. Pol. — West European politics. — London: *Frank Cass*

Wash. Quart. — Washington quarterly. — Cambridge, MA.: *Center for Strategic and International Studies*

Welt.liches Arc. — Weltwirtschaftliches Archiv. — Tübingen: *Institut für Weltwirtschaft*

Weltwirt. — Weltwirtschaft. — Tübingen: *Universität Kiel, Institut für Welwirtschaft*

West. Pol. Q. — Western political quarterly. — Salt Lake City, UT.: *Western Political Science Association/ Pacific Northwest Political Science Association/ Southern California Political Science Association/ Northern California Political Science Association*

Wirt. Blät. — Wirtschaftspolitische Blätter. — Vienna: *Bundeskammer der gewerblichen Wirtschaft*

Wirtschaftsdienst — Wirtschaftsdienst. — Hamburg: *HWWA — Institut für Wirtschaftsforschung*

Wor. Futur. — World futures. — New York, NY.: *Gordon and Breach Science Publishers*

World Dev. — World development. — Oxford: *Pergamon Press*

World. Econ. — World economy. — Oxford: *Trade Policy Research Centre*

Y. Co- op. Enter. — Yearbook of co-operative enterprise. — Oxford: *Plunkett Foundation*

Yale Law J. — Yale law journal. — New Haven, CT: *Yale Law Journal Co.*

Yapi Kredi. Eco. Rev. — Yapi kredi economic review. — Levent, Istanbul: *Yapi Kredi Bank*

Z. Polit. — Zeitschrift für Politik. — Cologne: *Hochschule für Politik München*

Z. Verkehr. — Zeitschrift für Verkehrswissenschaft. — Düsseldorf: *Verkehrs-Verlag J. Fischer*

Z. Wirt. Soz. — Zeitschrift für Wirtschafts- und Sozialwissenschaften. — Berlin: *Gesellschaft für Wirtschafts- und Sozialwissenschafen — Verein für Sozialpolitik*

Z. Wirt.pol. — Zeitschrift für Wirtschaftspolitik. — Cologne: *Universität zu Köln, Institut für Wirtschaftspolitik*

CLASSIFICATION SCHEME
PLAN DE CLASSIFICATION

A: Preliminaries — *Préliminaires*

B: Methods — *Méthodes*

B.1: General methodology — *Méthodologie générale*

B.2: Empirical and historical methods — *Méthodes empiriques et historiques*

B.3: Mathematical methods — *Méthodes mathématiques*

B.4: Accounting method and theory — *Méthode et théorie comptables*

C: General and basic works — *Ouvrages généraux et ouvrages de base*

Decision theory *[Théorie de la décision]*; Economic theory *[Théorie économique]*; Game theory *[Théorie des jeux]*; Risk *[Risque]*

D: History of economic thought — *Histoire de la pensée économique*

18th Century *[18e siècle]*; 19th Century *[19e siècle]*; 20th Century *[20e siècle]*

E: Economic history — *Histoire économique*

F: Economic activity — *Activité économique*

F.1: Present economic conditions (since 1980) — *Conditions économiques actuelles (depuis 1980)*

Africa *[Afrique]*; Americas *[Amérique]*; Asia *[Asie]*; Europe *[Europe]*; Oceania *[Océanie]*

F.2: National income and capital (estimation and forecasting) — *Revenu capital national (évaluation et prévision)*

Forecasts *[Prévisions]*

F.3: Structures — *Structures*

F.3.1: Specific aspects — *Aspects spécifiques*

F.3.1.1: Geographical aspects — *Aspects géographiques*

Regional economics *[Économie régionale]*; Rural economics *[Économie rurale]*; Urban economics *[Economie urbaine]*

F.3.1.2: Demographical aspects — *Aspects démographiques*

F.3.1.3: Sociological aspects — *Aspects sociologiques*

F.3.1.4: Legal aspects: property rights — *Aspects juridiques : droit de propriété*

F.3.2: Underdevelopment. Economic development — *Sous-développement. Développement économique*

> Africa *[Afrique]*;Americas *[Amérique]*; Asia *[Asie]*; Europe *[Europe]*

F.3.3: Growth, maturity, stagnation — *Croissance, maturité, stagnation*

F.4: Economic equilibrium and evolution: mechanisms — *Mécanismes de l'équilibre et de l'évolution économiques*

F.5: Fluctuations, cycles and trends — *Fluctuations, cycles et tendances*

G: Organization of production — *Organisation de la production*

G.1: Productivity, output, technological progress — *Productivité, rendement, progrès technique*

> Innovation *[Innovation]*; Technological change *[Progrès technique]*

G.1.1: Productivity: functions and measurement — *Productivité: fonctions et mesure*

G.1.2: Productivity: descriptive studies — *Productivité: études descriptives*

G.1.3: Productivity policy — *Politique de productivité*

G.2: Labour — *Travail*

G.2.1: Labour forces and labour market — *Main d'oeuvre et marché du travail*

> Labour mobility *[Mobilité de la main d'oeuvre]*; Labour supply and demand *[Offre et demande de main d'oeuvre]*; Unemployment *[Chômage]*; Wage-employment relationship *[Relation salaires-emploi]*

G.2.2: Employment policy — *Politique d'emploi*

> Women's employment *[Emploi des femmes]*

G.2.3: Working conditions — *Conditions de travail*

G.2.4: Labour relations — *Relations du travail*

> Collective bargaining *[Negociation collective]*; Strikes *[Grèves]*; Trade unions *[Syndicats]*; Workers' participation *[Participation des travailleurs]*

G.2.5: Work organization — *Organisation du travail*

G.3: Business organization — *Organisation de la vie économique*

G.3.1: Professional organization of employers — *Organisation professionnelle des employeurs*

G.3.2: Economic concentration — *Concentration économique*

G.3.3: Organization of the firm — *Organisation de l'entreprise*

G.3.3.1: Entrepreneurship — *L'entrepreneur, théorie et fonction*

G.3.3.2: Capital and capital formation — *Le capital et sa formation*

G.3.3.3: Financing methods — *Méthodes de financement*

G.3.3.4: Size — *Dimension de l'entreprise*

G.3.3.5: Technical management — *Organisation technique*

> Business strategies *[Strategies d'enterprises]*; Financial management *[Gestion financière]*

G.4: Occupational structure. Occupations — *Structure professionnelle. Professions*

H: Production (goods and services) — *Production (biens et services)*

H.0: Production and conservation — *Production et conservation*

> Ecology *[Ecologie]*; Environmental protection *[Protection de l'environnement]*; Resource management *[Gestion des ressources]*; Sustainable development *[Développement soutenable]*; Waste management *[Gestion des déchets]*; Water resources *[Ressources en eau]*

H.1: Agriculture — *Agriculture*

H.1.1: Agricultural economics — *Économie agricole*

H.1.1.1: Technical factors of agricultural productivity — *Facteurs techniques de la productivité agricole*

> Soil resources *[Ressources en sol]*

H.1.1.2: Forms of agricultural enterprise and land tenure — *Formes d'entreprise agricole et tenure du sol*

H.1.1.3: Agricultural management — *Gestion agricole*

H.1.1.4: Agricultural development. Agricultural policy — *Développement agricole. Politique agricole*

> Africa *[Afrique]*; Americas *[Amérique]*; Asia *[Asie]*; Europe *[Europe]*

H.1.2: Agricultural production — *Production agricole*

H.1.2.1: Agricultural products — *Produits agricoles*

Cereals *[Céréales]*; Fish *[Poissons]*; Forests *[Forêts]*

H.2: Industry — *Industrie*

H.2.1: Industrial economics — *Économie industrielle*

Industrial management *[Gestion industrielle]*; Industrial policy *[Politique industrielle]*; Industrial productivity *[Productivité industrielle]*

H.2.2: Industrial production — *Production industrielle*

Automobile industry *[Industrie automobile]*; Energy industry *[Industrie énergétique]*; Iron and steel industry *[Industrie sidérurgique]*; Mining *[Industrie minière]*; Oil industry *[Industrie pétrolière]*

H.3: Transportation and communication — *Transports et communications*

Air transport *[Transport aérien]*; Railway transport *[Transport ferroviaire]*; Road transport *[Transport routier]*; Sea transport *[Transport maritime]*; Telecommunications *[Télécommunications]*

H.4: Trade and distribution — *Commerce et distribution*

Advertising *[Publicité]*; Marketing *[Commercialisation]*; Retail trade *[Commerce de détail]*; Service industry *[Secteur tertiaire]*

I: Prices and markets — *Prix et marchés*

I.1: Basic concepts — *Concepts de base*

I.2: Markets and price formation — *Marchés et formation du prix*

I.2.1: Theory — *Théorie*

Competition *[Concurrence]*; Pricing *[Fixation du prix]*; Supply and demand *[Offre et demande]*

I.2.2: Price levels (descriptive studies) — *Niveau des prix (études descriptives)*

I.2.3: Specific prices and markets — *Prix et marchés de produits particuliers*

Agricultural market *[Marché agricole]*; Housing market *[Marché du logement]*

J: Money and finance — *Monnaie et finance*

J.1: Money — *Monnaie*

> Demand for money *[Demande de monnaie]*; Inflation *[Inflation]*

J.2: Credit — *Crédit*

> Bank regulation and bank failure *[Règlement et faillite des banques]*; Banking *[Activité bancaire]*; Central banks *[Banques centrales]*; Indebtedness *[Endettement]*; Mortgages *[Hypothèques]*

J.3: Insurance — *Assurances*

J.4: Capital market — *Marché financier*

> Bonds *[Obligations]*; Interest rates *[Taux d'intérêt]*; Investment *[Investissements]*; Portfolio management *[Gestion de portefeuille]*; Risk *[Risque]*; Stock exchange *[Bourse]*; Stock prices and stock returns *[Prix des actions et dividendes]*

J.5: Monetary policy — *Politique monétaire*

K: Income and income distribution — *Revenu et distribution du revenu*

K.1: Income: concept and theory — *Revenu: concept et théorie*

K.2: Distribution of national income — *Répartition du revenu national*

K.3: Specific income — *Catégories de revenu*

> Profit and returns *[Profit et rendements]*; Wage determination *[Fixation du salaire]*; Wage differentials *[Eventail des salaires]*

L: Demand (use of income) — *Demande (utilisation du revenu)*

L.1: Aggregate demand — *Demande globale*

L.2: Consumer demand — *Demande de consommation*

> Consumer behaviour *[Comportement du consommateur]*; Food, drink and tobacco *[Aliments, boissons et tabac]*; Housing *[Logement]*

L.3: Investment demand — *Demande d'investissement*

M: Social economics and policy — *Économie et politique sociales*

M.1: Basic concepts: social economics, social policy and justice, welfare — *Concepts de base: économie, politique, et justice sociales, bien-être*

M.2: Standard of living — *Niveau de vie*

M.3: Social policy, welfare policy — *Politique sociale, politique de bien-être*

M.4: Social security, social assistance, occupational safety — *Sécurité sociale, assistance sociale, sécurité du travail*

> Health insurance and services *[Assurance maladie et services de santé]*; Pensions *[Pensions]*; Social security *[Sécurité sociale]*

M.5: Economics of education — *Économie de l'éducation*

N: Public economy — *Économie publique*

N.1: Economic systems and policies — *Systèmes et politiques économiques*

> Adjustment and stabilization policies *[Politiques d'adaptation et stabilisation]*; Economic management and policies *[La politique et gestion de l'économie]*; Economic reform *[Réforme économique]*; Economic systems *[Systèmes économiques]*; Planning theory and practice *[Théorie et pratique de la planification]*; Privatization *[Privatisation]*

N.2: Public finance — *Finances publiques*

> Corporate taxation *[Impôt sur les sociétés]*; Fiscal policy *[Politique fiscale]*; Income and consumption tax *[Impôts sur le revenu et sur la consommation]*; Optimal taxation *[Fiscalité optimale]*; Property tax *[Impôt sur la propriété]*; Public debt *[Dette publique]*; Public expenditure *[Dépenses publiques]*; Tax evasion and avoidance *[Evasion et fraude fiscales]*; Tax reform *[Réformes fiscales]*

N.3: Public sector, public utilities — *Secteur public, services d'utilité publique*

O: International economics — *Économie internationale*

O.1: International economic relations — *Relations économiques internationales*

O.1.1: Theory of international equilibrium and policy — *Théorie de l'équilibre international et de la politique économique internationale*

O.1.2: World economy — *Économie mondiale*

O.1.2.1: Governmental organizations — *Organisations gouvernementales*

O.1.2.2: Private international organizations (cartels, agreements) — *Organisations internationales privées (cartels, ententes)*

O.1.2.3: Market conditions — *Conditions du marché*

O.1.2.4: Economic blocs. Economic integration — *Blocs économiques. Intégration économique*

> European Communities *[Communautés européennes]*

O.1.2.5: Population movements — *Mouvements de population*

O.1.3: International economic policy — *Politique économique internationale*

> Foreign aid *[Aide à l'étranger]*; Technology transfer *[Transfert de technologie]*; Trade liberalization *[Libéralisation des échanges]*

O.2: Monetary aspects — *Aspects monétaires*

O.2.1: International monetary operations — *Opérations monétaires internationales*

> Exchange rates *[Taux de change]*

O.2.2: Balance of payments, balance of accounts — *Balance des paiements, balance des comptes*

> External debt *[Dette extérieure]*; International investment *[Investissements internationaux]*; Joint ventures *[Entreprises conjointes]*

O.2.3: Monetary policies, monetary areas — *Politiques et zones monétaires*

O.2.4: International monetary relations — *Relations monétaires internationales*

O.3: International trade — *Commerce international*

O.3.1:Theory — *Théorie*

O.3.2: Foreign trade relations — *Relations commerciales internationales*

O.3.3: Foreign trade policies — *Politique du commerce extérieur*

> Dumping *[Dumping]*; GATT *[GATT]*; Protectionism *[Protectionnisme]*

BIBLIOGRAPHY FOR 1992
BIBLIOGRAPHIE POUR 1992

A: Preliminaries — *Préliminaires*

1 Aborigines in the economy — a select annotated bibliography of policy-relevant research,1985-90. L.M. Allen; Jon C. Altman; E. Owen. Canberra: Centre for Aboriginal Economic Policy Research, Australian National University, 1991: 242 p. *ISBN: 0731511999.* [Research monograph.]

2 Better than plowing, and other personal essays. James M. Buchanan. Chicago: University of Chicago Press, 1992: ix, 184 p. *ISBN: 0226078167; LofC: 91044417. Includes bibliographical references and index.*

3 Cognitive research in information science — implications for design. Bryce L. Allen. *Ann. R. Info. Sci. Tech.* **26** 1991 pp. 3 – 37

4 Economics in Sweden — an evaluation of Swedish research in economics. Lars Engwall *[Ed.]*; Avinsh K. Dixit *[Contrib.]*; et al. London: Routledge, 1992: 284 p. *ISBN: 0415072565; LofC: 92002786. Includes bibliographical references and indexes.*

5 Economics instruction in high schools. William B. Walstad. *J. Econ. Lit.* **XXX:4** 12:1992 pp. 2019 – 2051

6 Education in economics. Jim Nettleship *[Contrib.]*; Martin Jephcote *[Contrib.]*; David Hendley *[Contrib.]*; Mike Hollis *[Contrib.]*; Linda Thomas *[Contrib.]*. *Collection of 4 articles.* **Economics** , *XXVIII:118(2),* Summer:1992 pp. 69 – 87

7 Expert systems as information intermediaries. Hilary Drenth; Anne Morris; Gwyneth Tseng. *Ann. R. Info. Sci. Tech.* **26** 1991 pp. 113 – 154

8 Information pricing. Fran Spigai. *Ann. R. Info. Sci. Tech.* **26** 1991 pp. 39 – 73

9 Information technology and services in schools. Michael B. Eisenberg; Kathleen L. Spitzer. *Ann. R. Info. Sci. Tech.* **26** 1991 pp. 243 – 285

10 Information technology in a small country — potential and practice in Cyprus. Lida Mardapitta-Hadjipandeli; Eri Nicolaides. *Sci. Pub. Pol.* **19:1** 2:1992 pp. 25 – 34

11 Information technology standards. Michael B. Spring. *Ann. R. Info. Sci. Tech.* **26** 1991 pp. 79 – 111

12 IT and accounting. B.C. Williams *[Ed.]*; Barry J. Spaul *[Ed.]*. London: Chapman & Hall, 1991: xix, 476 p. *ISBN: 0412392100.*

13 The Penguin dictionary of information technology and computer science. Tony Gunton. London: Penguin Books, 1992: 208 p. *ISBN: 0140512403.*

14 Relational databases. Barry Eaglestone. Cheltenham: Stanley Thornes, 1991: xiii, 314 p. (ill) *ISBN: 0748711767. Includes index.* [Stanley Thornes computer studies series.]

15 Trends in data collection and analysis — a new approach to the collection of global information. R. Stanat. *Inter. R. Strat. Manag.* **3** 1992 pp. 99 – 132

16 Undergraduate student research programs — are they as viable for accounting as they are in science and humanities? P.A. French; R.E. Jensen; K.R. Robertson. *Crit. Persp. Acc.* **3:4** 12:1992 pp. 337 – 357

17 Western European economic organizations — a comprehensive guide. Robert Fraser *[Ed.]*; Christopher Long. Harlow: Longman Current Affairs, 1992: ix, 448 p. *ISBN: 0582068452. Includes index.*

18 The 'wired' MNC — the role of information systems for structural change in complex organizations. Peter Hagström. Stockholm, Sweden: Institute of International Business, Stockholm School of Economics, 1991: x, 436 p. *ISBN: 9197173002. Includes bibliographical references.*

B: Methods — *Méthodes*

B.1: General methodology — *Méthodologie générale*

1 Applied econometric techniques. Keith Cuthbertson; Stephen G. Hall; Mark P. Taylor. Hemel Hempstead: Philip Allan, 1992: 274 p. *ISBN: 0860030849.*

2 Are all economic hypotheses false? J. Bradford de Lony; Kevin Lang. *J. Polit. Ec.* **100:6** 12:1992 pp. 1257 – 1272

3 Changing patterns of relative state economic growth over time — limitations on cross-sectional tests of Olson's thesis. James C. Garand. *West. Pol. Q.* **45:2** 6:1992 pp. 469 – 484

4 Comparing alleged incommensurables — institutional and Austrian economics as rivals and possible complements? Peter Wynarczyk. *R. Pol. Econ.* **4:1** 1992 pp. 18 – 36

5 The effects of macroeconomic shocks in a basic equilibrium framework. Enrique G. Mendoza. *Staff Pap. Int. Monetary* **39:4** 12:1992 pp. 855 – 889

6 Efficient score tests for heteroskedasticity in micro-econometrics. C. Orme. *Econom. R.* **11:2** 1992 pp. 235 – 252

7 Essays on the methodology and discourse of economics. Warren J. Samuels. Basingstoke: Macmillan, 1992: x, 332 p. *ISBN: 0333551737. Includes indexes.*

8 Implementing a public project and distributing its cost. Matthew Jackson; Hervé Moulin. *J. Econ. Theo.* **57:1** 6:1992 pp. 125 – 140

9 Indeterministic economics. Aron Iosifovich Katsenelinboĭgen. New York: Praeger, 1992: xiii, 315 p. *ISBN: 0275941434; LofC: 91027722. Includes bibliographical references (p. [303]-308) and indexes.*

10 The interaction between theory and observation in economics. M. Hashem Pesaran; R. Smith. *Econ. Soc. R.* **24:1** 10:1992 pp. 1 – 23

11 Interfaces in economic and social analysis. Ulf Himmelstrand. London: Routledge, 1992: 318 p. *ISBN: 041506872x; LofC: 91020580. Includes bibliographical references and index.*

12 Macroeconomic dynamics in a multi-country economy — a dynamic optimization approach. Shinsuke Ikeda; Yoshiyasu Ono. *Int. Econ. R.* **33:3** 8:1992 pp. 629 – 644

13 Macroeconomics — a survey of research strategies. Alessandro Vercelli *[Ed.]*; Nicola Dimitri *[Ed.]*. Oxford: Oxford University Press, 1992: 472 p. *ISBN: 0198773145; LofC: 92020945. Includes bibliographical refrences and indexes.*

14 Mickey Mouse numbers and inequality research in developing countries. Terence Moll. *J. Dev. Stud.* **28:4** 7:1992 pp. 689 – 704

15 New directions in economic psychology — theory, experiment, and application. Paul Webley *[Ed.]*; Brian M. Young *[Ed.]*; S.E.G. Lea *[Ed.]*. Aldershot, Hants, England: E. Elgar, 1992: 287 p. *ISBN: 1852784628; LofC: 91023879. Includes indexes.*

16 Projektionsverfahren privater Haushalte nach Haushaltsgruppen *[In German]*; Methods for projecting private households *[Summary]*. Werner Grünewald. *All. Stat. A.* **76:3** 1992 pp. 208 – 225

17 Quantification of indifference responses from business surveys with mixed data; Quantifizierung von Indifferenzaussagen in gemischten Befragungsdaten *[German summary]*. Karl-Heinz Toedtner; Max Christoph Wewel. *Jahrb. N. St.* **209:3-4** 3:1992 pp. 291 – 301

18 Seasonality in large-scale macroeconometric models. P.G. Fisher; K.F. Wallis. *J. Forecast.* **11:4** 6:1992 pp. 255 – 270

19 The sequential trading approach to disequilibrium dynamics; Ungleichgewichtsmodelle mit sequentieller Transaktionsstruktur *[German summary]*. Thomas Lux. *Jahrb. N. St.* **209:1-2** 1:1992 pp. 47 – 59

20 Testing the causal properties of economic theories — an application to a small Australian macroeconomic model. Vance Martin. *Aust. Econ. P.* **31:58** 6:1992 pp. 1 – 19

21 Themes in modern macroeconomics. Helge Brink *[Ed.]*. London: Macmillan, 1992: 185 p. *ISBN: 0333556925.*

22 Theories of political economy. James A. Caporaso; David P. Levine. New York: Cambridge University Press, 1992: viii, 243 p. *ISBN: 0521415616; LofC: 92007793. Includes bibliographical references (p. 227-237) and index.*

B.1: General methodology *[Méthodologie générale]*
23 Time consistent mixed precommitment macropolicy. Andrew P. Blake. London: National Institute of Economic and Social Research, 1992: 26 p. [Discussion paper.]
24 Towards a new research programme for post-Keynesianism and neo-Ricardianism. Marc Lavoie. *R. Pol. Econ.* **4:1** 1992 pp. 37 – 78
25 Universal economics — assessment of the achievement of the economic approach. Gerard Radnitzky *[Ed.]*. New York: Paragon House, 1991: xii, 446 p. (ill) *ISBN: 0892261021; LofC: 90025006. "An ICUS book." ; Includes index.*

B.2: Empirical and historical methods — *Méthodes empiriques et historiques*

1 How the data we make can unmake us — annals of factology. Bruce L. Gardner. *Am. J. Agr. Ec.* **74:5** 12:1992 pp. 1066 – 1075
2 Una metodología para el seguimiento de objetivos definidos sobre series históricas — el caso del control monetario en España *[In Spanish]*; [A methodology for tracking goals defined over a vector of time series — the case of monetary control in Spain] *[Summary]*. Miguel Jerez Méndez. *Invest. Econ.* **XVI:1** 1:1992 pp. 63 – 88
3 New findings in long-wave research. Alfred Kleinknecht *[Ed.]*; Ernest Mandel *[Ed.]*; Immanuel Wallerstein *[Ed.]*. New York: St. Martin's Press, 1992: 348 p. *ISBN: 0312072759; LofC: 91032752. Includes bibliographical references and index.*
4 Nonresponse in panel data — the impact on estimates of a life cycle consumption function. T. Nijman; M. Verbeek. *J. Appl. Econ.* **7:3** 7-9:1992 pp. 243 – 258

B.3: Mathematical methods — *Méthodes mathématiques*

1 ARCH models in finance. Robert F. Engle *[Ed.]*; Michael Rothschild *[Ed.]*; Tim Bollerslev *[Contrib.]*; Ray Y. Chou *[Contrib.]*; Kenneth F. Kroner *[Contrib.]*; Daniel B. Nelson *[Contrib.]*; Richard T. Baillie *[Contrib.]*; Philippe Bougerol *[Contrib.]*; Nico Picard *[Contrib.]*; Andrew Harvey *[Contrib.] and others. Collection of 12 articles.* **J. Economet.** , *52:1/2,* 4-5:1992 pp. 1 – 311
2 Artificial intelligence and economic analysis — prospects and problems. Scott J. Moss; John Rae. Aldershot, Hants, England: E. Elgar Pub, 1992: 193 p. *ISBN: 185278685x; LofC: 92008913. Includes bibliographical references and index.*
3 Ausgewählte Probleme der früheren DDR-Statistik *[In German]*; Selected problems of the former GDR-statistics *[Summary]*. Klaus Kockel. *All. Stat. A.* **76:1** 1992 pp. 1 – 14
4 Bevezetés a vintage típusú növekedési modellek elméletébe *[In Hungarian]*; Introduction into the theory of vintage-type growth models *[Summary]*. László Kónya. *Közg. Sz.* **XXXIX** 12:1992 pp. 1107 – 1125
5 Breakpoints and unit roots. Lawrence J. Christiano *[Contrib.]*; Eric Zivot *[Contrib.]*; Donald W.K. Andrews *[Contrib.]*; Anindya Banerjee *[Contrib.]*; Robin L. Lumsdaine *[Contrib.]*; James H. Stock *[Contrib.]*; Chia-Shang James Chu *[Contrib.]*; Halbert White *[Contrib.]*; Pierre Perron *[Contrib.]*; Timothy J. Vogelsang *[Contrib.] and others. Collection of 9 articles.* **J. Bus. Econ. Stat.** , *10:3,* 7:1992 pp. 237 – 374
6 A broader view of the job-shop scheduling problem. Lawrence M. Wein; Philippe B. Chevalier. *Manag. Sci.* **38:7** 7:1992 pp. 1018 – 1034
7 A comparative study of "multiproduct" vs. "single-product" household interactive variable input-output models. C.K. Liew; C.J. Liew. *Reg. Sci. Urb. Econ.* **22:2** 6:1992 pp. 285 – 290
8 A comparison of model selection criteria. J.A. Mills; K. Prasad. *Econom. R.* **11:2** 1992 pp. 201 – 234
9 A comparison of two methods for estimating income uncertainty with an application to aggregate consumption behaviour. P.R. Flacco; R.E. Parker. *Appl. Econ.* **24:7** 7:1992 pp. 701 – 707
10 Composition rules for building linear programming models from component models. Frederic H. Murphy; Edward A. Stohr; Pai-chun Ma. *Manag. Sci.* **38:7** 7:1992 pp. 948 – 963
11 A computer simulation model for the determination of Walrasian equilibrium. P.M. Turner. *Br. Rev. Ec. Iss.* **14:32** 2:1992 pp. 37 – 52

B.3: Mathematical methods *[Méthodes mathématiques]*

12 Congestion and network externalities in the short run pricing of information system services. J. Christopher Westland. *Manag. Sci.* **38:7** 7:1992 pp. 992 – 1009

13 Continuous-time econometrics — theory and applications. Giancarlo Gandolfo *[Ed.]*. London: Chapman & Hall, 1992: 267 p. *ISBN: 0412450208; LofC: 92038094. Includes index.* [International studies in economic modelling.]

14 The current state of the arbitrage pricing theory. Jay Shanken. *J. Finance* **47:4** 9:1992 pp. 1569 – 1574

15 Datenlage und Anforderungen mit Blick auf Mittel- und Osteuropa *[In German]*; Avaliable and required data with respect to Middle and Eastern Europe *[Summary]*. Doris Cornelsen. *All. Stat. A.* **76:1** 1992 pp. 53 – 61

16 Econometric software — a user's view. Jeffrey K. MacKie-Mason. *J. Econ. Pers.* **6:4** Fall:1992 pp. 165 – 187

17 Economic models, estimation and socioeconomic systems — essays in honor of Karl A.Fox. Tej.K Kaul *[Ed.]*; Karl August Fox; Jati K. Sengupta *[Ed.]*. Amsterdam: North-Holland, 1991: 645 p. *ISBN: 0444881026.* [Contributions to economic analysis. : Vol. 186]

18 Equilibrium business cycles — theory and evidence. Andy W. Mullineux; David F. Dickinson. *J. Econ. Sur.* **6:4** 1992 pp. 321 – 358

19 Estimates of systematic reporting biases in trade statistics. Marinos E. Tsigas; Thomas W. Hertel; James K. Binkley. *Econ. Sys. Res.* **4:4** 1992 pp. 297 – 310

20 An evaluation of the REMI model for the South Coast Air Quality Management District. S. Cassing; F. Giarratani. *Envir. Plan.A.* **24:11** 11:1992 pp. 1549 – 1564

21 Financial modeling. Stavros A. Zenios *[Ed.]*; William T. Ziemba *[Ed.]*; Haim Levy *[Contrib.]*; Paul A. Samuelson *[Contrib.]*; Charles Bram Cadsby *[Contrib.]*; L.C. MacLean *[Contrib.]*; G. Blazenko *[Contrib.]*; Andrew L. Turner *[Contrib.]*; Eric J. Weigel *[Contrib.]*; Hiroto Kuwahara *[Contrib.] and others. Collection of 8 articles.* **Manag. Sci.** , *38:11*, 11:1992 pp. 1525 – 1685

22 Forecasting with input-output matrices — are the coefficients stationary? John A. Sawyer. *Econ. Sys. Res.* **4:4** 1992 pp. 325 – 348

23 A forward-looking approach to learning in macroeconomic models. Peter Westaway. *Natl. Inst. Econ. R.* **:140** 5:1992 pp. 86 – 97

24 The fuzzy industry maturity grid and its application to the Singapore property sector. Danny P.H. Tay; K.W. Tham; David David K.H. Ho. *Urban Stud.* **29:8** 12:1992 pp. 1305 – 1321

25 A general-equilibrium intertemporal model of an open economy. J.S. Chipman; G. Tian. *Econ. Theory* **2:2** 1992 pp. 215 – 246

26 A generalized method of moments approach to estimating a "structural vector autoregression". Peter R. Hartley; Carl E. Walsh. *J. Macro.* **14:2** Spring:1992 pp. 199 – 232

27 Improving migration statistics — policy and conceptual issues. Paolo Garonna. *Labour [Italy]* **6:1** Spring:1992 pp. 141 – 164

28 Introduction to econometrics. C.R.S. Dougherty. New York: Oxford University Press, 1992: 399 p. *ISBN: 0195043464. Bibliography — p.386-389; Disks in pocket inside back cover (1 x 3.5"; 1 x 5.25").*

29 Keynes and probability and statistical inference and the links to Fisher. Denis Conniffe. *Camb. J. Econ.* **16:4** 12:1992 pp. 475 – 489

30 A Keynesian general equilibrium model with competitive firms and rational expectations. R. Balvers. *J. Econ.* **56:1** 1992 pp. 23 – 38

31 Managerial applications of neural networks — the case of bank failure predictions. Kar Yan Tam; Melody Y. Kiang. *Manag. Sci.* **38:7** 7:1992 pp. 926 – 947

32 The maximum entropy approach in production frontier estimation. J.K. Sengupta. *Math. Soc. Sc.* **25:1** 12:1992 pp. 41 – 57

33 Mínimos cuadrados recursivos *[In Spanish]*; Recursive least squares *[Summary]*. José L. Arrufat. *Económica Arg* **XXXVI:1-2** 1990 pp. 3 – 20

34 A mixed fan hypothesis and its implications for behavior toward risk. W.S. Neilson. *J. Econ. Beh.* **19:2** 10:1992 pp. 197 – 211

35 Un modello di sintesi per l'analisi di settori segmentati *[In Italian]*; A model for analyzing industrial sectors which are made by sections *[Summary]*. Luca Corsini. *Industria* **XIII:3** 7-9:1992 pp. 525 – 548

36 Multiple input transfer function noise modelling — a time and frequency domain algorithm. Ralf Östermark; Rune Höglund. Abo: Abo Akademi, 1991: 43, 51 p. *ISBN: 951649823x. Includes bibliographical references (p. 40-43).* [Meddelanden Fran Ekonomisk-Statsvetenskapliga Fakulteten Vid Abo Akademi.]

B.3: Mathematical methods *[Méthodes mathématiques]*

37 Multiplier analysis with flexible cost functions. Ferran Sancho. *Econ. Sys. Res.* **4:4** 1992 pp. 311 – 324

38 New perspectives on intersectoral relationships between manufacturing and services. Hans-Jürgen Engelbrecht. *Econ. Plan.* **25:2** 1992 pp. 165 – 178

39 Nonlinear dynamics and econometrics. M. Hashem Pesaran *[Ed.]*; Simon M. Potter *[Ed.]*; R.H. Day *[Contrib.]*; T. Liu *[Contrib.]*; C.W.J. Granger *[Contrib.]*; W.P. Heller *[Contrib.]*; W.D. Dechert *[Contrib.]*; R. Gencay *[Contrib.]*; B.E. Hansen *[Contrib.]*; R.J. Town *and others. Collection of 12 articles.* **J. Appl. Econ.** , *7,* 12:1992 pp. 1 – 195

40 A note on the role of survey data and expert opinion in constructing input-output tables. Randall W. Jackson; Philip R. Israilevich; Jonathan C. Comer. *Pap. Reg. Sci.* **71:1** 1:1992 pp. 87 – 93

41 The NRIES II multiregional macroeconomic model of the United States. Thomas Lienesch; John R. Kort. *Int. Reg. Sci. R.* **14:3** 1992 pp. 255 – 274

42 On persistence of shocks to economic variables — a common misconception. Marco Lippi; Lucrezia Reichlin. *J. Monet. Ec.* **29:1** 2:1992 pp. 87 – 94

43 On the methodology of constructing large econometric models of an East European country (Poland). W. Welfe; J. Gajda; E. Zóltowska. *Econ. Model.* **9:2** 4:1992 pp. 137 – 145

44 Posterior analysis of restricted seemingly unrelated regression equation models — a recursive analytical approach. M.F.J. Steel. *Econom. R.* **11:2** 1992 pp. 129 – 142

45 Probabilistic voting theory. Peter J. Coughlin. Cambridge: Cambridge University Press, 1992: xi, 252 p. *ISBN: 0521360528; LofC: 91014319. Includes bibliographical references (p.227-248) and index.*

46 Probability and the art of judgement. Richard C. Jeffrey. Cambridge: Cambridge University Press, 1992: 244 p. *ISBN: 0521394597; LofC: 91034257.* [Cambridge studies in probability, induction, and decision theory.]

47 A quantitative examination of current account dynamics in equilibrium models of barter economies. Enrique G. Mendoza. Washington, D.C.: International Monetary Fund, 1992: 34 p. *Bibliography — p.32-34.* [IMF working paper. : No. WP/92/14]

48 A Queensland input-output econometric model — an overview. Guy West. *Aust. Econ. P.* **30:57** 12:1991 pp. 221 – 240

49 Reference variables, factor structure, and the approximate multibeta representation. Haim Reisman. *J. Finance* **47:4** 9:1992 pp. 1303 – 1314

50 Representation schemes for linear programming models. Frederic H. Murphy; Edward A. Stohr; Ajay Asthana. *Manag. Sci.* **38:7** 7:1992 pp. 964 – 991

51 Similarità dei beni, scale di prezzo e «robustezza» delle stime — uno studio del mercato delle aree edificabili *[In Italian]*; Product similarity, price scales and the robustness of evaluation — a study of markets in areas suitable for building *[Summary]*. Gaetano Martino; Francesco Musotti. *Riv. Econ. Agrar.* **XLVII:2** 6:1992 pp. 265 – 295

52 Some problems with identification in parametric models and their solutions. P.A.V.B. Swamy; J.S. Mehta; P. von zur Muehlen; George S. Tavlas. *Gr. Econ. Rev.* **13:2** 12:1991 pp. 287 – 312

53 Specification and estimation of a macroeconometric model of Botswana. Xavier Malege Mhozya. Braunton: Merlin, 1992: 170 p. *ISBN: 0863035779; LofC: gb 91067258.*

54 A spectrum of statistical thought — essays in statistical theory, economics and population genetics in honour of Johan Fellman. Johan Fellman *[Ed.]*; Gunnar Rosenqvist *[Ed.]*; et al. Helsingfors: Swedish School of Economics and Business Administration, 1991: 276 p. *ISBN: 9515553512. Essays in English; pref. in Swedish and English; Includes bibliographical references.* [Ekonomi och samhälle.]

55 Das statistische Informationssystem der DDR — ein Reservoir an Erfahrungen für die Fortentwicklung der amtlichen Statistik der Bundesrepublik Deutschland *[In German]*; The statistical information system of the GDR — experiences for the development of the official statistics in Germany *[Summary]*. Markus Güttler. *All. Stat. A.* **76:2** 1992 pp. 175 – 193

56 Stochastic models of choice and reaction time. A.A.J. Marley *[Ed.]*; J.R. Busemeyer *[Contrib.]*; J.T. Townsend *[Contrib.]*; R.A. Heath *[Contrib.]*; M.J.J.M. Candel *[Contrib.]*; R. Schweickert *[Contrib.]*. *Collection of 5 articles.* **Math. Soc. Sc.** , *23:3,* 6:1992 pp. 251 – 366

57 Subjective probabilities and utility with event-dependent preferences. Edi Karni. *J. Risk Uncert.* **5:2** 1992 pp. 107 – 126

58 A test for changes in a polynomial trend function for a dynamic time series. Pierre Perron. Princeton, NJ.: Econometric Research Program, Princeton University, 1991: 28, 3, 30 p. [Research memorandum.]

B.3: Mathematical methods *[Méthodes mathématiques]*

59 Testing structural hypotheses in a multivariate cointegration analysis of the PPP and the UIP for UK. Søren Johansen; Katarina Juselius. *J. Economet.* **53**:1-3 7-9:1992 pp. 211 – 243

60 Using meta-analysis results in Bayesian updating — the empty-cell problem. Wilfried R. Vanhonacker; Lydia J. Price. *J. Bus. Econ. Stat.* **10**:4 10:1992 pp. 427 – 435

61 Using the bootstrap for improved ARIMA model identification. A.D. Aczel; N.H. Josephy. *J. Forecast.* **11**:1 1:1992 pp. 71 – 80

62 Valued opinions or opinionated values — the double aggregation problem. Kevin Roberts. London: London School of Economics and Political Science. Suntory-Toyota International Centre for Economics and Related Disciplines, 1992: 37 p. [Theoretical economics. : No. TE/92/253]

63 Wirtschaftsstatistik im vereinten Deutschland — Einheitlich, zweigeteilt oder differenziert? *[In German]*; German economic statistics after unification. Consolidation, separate or differentiated? *[Summary]*. Klaus Hanau. *All. Stat. A.* **76**:1 1992 pp. 34 – 42

B.4: Accounting method and theory — *Méthode et théorie comptables*

1 Accountancy's faulty sums. Keron Bhattacharya. London: Macmillan, 1992: 223 p. *ISBN: 0333573285.*

2 Accounting and the credibility of management forecasts; *[French summary]*. R.C. Sansing. *Cont. Account. Res.* **9**:1 Fall:1992 pp. 33 – 45

3 Accounting and the law. Michael Bromwich *[Ed.]*; Anthony G. Hopwood *[Ed.]*. Englewood Cliffs, NJ.: Prentice Hall, 1992: 253 p. *ISBN: 0130061158; LofC: 91032717. Papers presented at the Sixth Accounting and Auditing Research Symposium held at the London School of Economics and Political Science on Sept. 26-27, 1988; Includes bibliographical references and index.* [Research studies in accounting.]

4 Accounting as the master metaphor of economics. Arjo Klamer; Donald McCloskey. *Eur. Account. Rev.* **1**:1 5:1992 pp. 145 – 160

5 Accounting calculation and the shifting sphere of the economic. Anthony G. Hopwood. *Eur. Account. Rev.* **1**:1 5:1992 pp. 125 – 144

6 Accounting in the Soviet Union. Ehiel Ash; Robert Strittmatter. New York: Praeger, 1992: xii, 191 p. *ISBN: 0275930696; LofC: 90024129. Includes bibliographical references (p. [187]) and index.*

7 Accounting measurement rules in UK bank loan contracts. David B. Citron. *Acc. Bus. Res.* **23**:89 Winter:1992 pp. 21 – 30

8 Accounting recognition and the relevance of earnings as an explanatory variable for returns. Terry D. Warfield; John J. Wild. *Acc. Review* **67**:4 10:1992 pp. 821 – 842

9 Accounting — a social institution — a unified theory for the measurement of the profit and non-profit sectors. Julius Cherny; Arlene R. Gordon; Richard J.L. Herson; Joshua Ronen *[Foreword]*. New York: Quorum Books, 1992: xxvi, 211 p. *ISBN: 089930690x; LofC: 91025524 //r923. "Prepared under the auspices of the Vincent C. Ross Institute of Accounting Research, Stern School of Business, New York University."; Includes bibliographical references (p.[197]-200) and index.*

10 Adjusted accounting beta, operating leverage and financial leverage as determinants of market beta — a synthesis and empirical evaluation. Yaw M. Mensah. *R. Quant. Finan. Account.* **2**:2 6:1992 pp. 187 – 203

11 The audit expectations gap — plus ca change, plus c'est la meme chose? C. Humphrey; P. Moizer; S. Turley. *Crit. Persp. Acc.* **3**:2 6:1992 pp. 137 – 162

12 Audit policy making in the UK — the case of "the auditor's considerations in respect of going concern". Prem Sikka. *Eur. Account. Rev.* **1**:2 12:1992 pp. 349 – 392

13 Audit risk and audit evidence — the Bayesian approach to statistical auditing. Anthony Steele. London: Academic Press, 1992: 200 p. *ISBN: 0126641404.*

14 Auditor underreporting of time and moral reasoning — an experimental-lab study; La sous-évaluation du temps de travail et le raisonnement moral chez les vérificateurs — laboratoire expérimental *[In French]*. L.A. Ponemon. *Cont. Account. Res.* **9**:1 Fall:1992 pp. 171 – 211

15 The auditor's going-concern decision — interaction of task variables and the sequential processing of evidence. Stephen K. Asare. *Acc. Review* **67**:2 4:1992 pp. 379 – 393

B.4: Accounting method and theory *[Méthode et théorie comptables]*

16 Belief-function formulas for audit risk. Rajendra P. Srivastava; Glenn R. Shafer. *Acc. Review* **67:2** 4:1992 pp. 249 – 283

17 Beyond the audit expectations gap — learning from the experiences of Britain and Spain. Maria Antonia Garciá-Benau; Christopher Humphrey. *Eur. Account. Rev.* **1:2** 12:1992 pp. 303 – 331

18 Bond ratings, bond yields and financial information; *[French summary]*. D.A. Ziebart; S.A. Reiter; R. Chandra *[Discussant]*; G.D. Richardson *[Discussant]*. *Cont. Account. Res.* **9:1** Fall:1992 pp. 252 – 295

19 A classification system for economic consequences issues in accounting regulation. John Blake. *Acc. Bus. Res.* **22:88** Autumn:1992 pp. 305 – 321

20 Classification techniques in accounting research — empirical evidence of comparative performance; *[French summary]*. D.B. Kennedy. *Cont. Account. Res.* **8:2** Spring:1992 pp. 419 – 442

21 Contrasting activity-based costing with the German/Dutch cost pool method. A.A.M. Boons; H.J.E. Roberts; F.A. Roozen. *Manag. Acc. Res.* **3:2** 6:1992 pp. 97 – 117

22 Corporate governance and disclosure quality. John J. Forker. *Acc. Bus. Res.* **22:86** Spring:1992 pp. 111 – 124

23 Criticizing positive accounting theory; *[French summary]*. L.A. Boland; I.M. Gordon. *Cont. Account. Res.* **9:1** Fall:1992 pp. 142 – 170

24 A detailed social accounting matrix for the USA, 1988. Kenneth A. Reinert; David W. Roland-Holst. *Econ. Sys. Res.* **4:2** 1992 pp. 173 – 187

25 EC accounting harmonisation — an empirical study of measurement practices in France, Germany and the UK. Emmanuel N. Emenyonu; Sidney J. Gray. *Acc. Bus. Res.* **23:89** Winter:1992 pp. 49 – 58

26 The effects of line-of-business reporting on competition in oligopoly settings; *[French summary]*. G.A. Feltham; F.B. Gigler; J.S. Hughes; A. Dontoh *[Discussant]*; S. Huddart *[Discussant]*. *Cont. Account. Res.* **9:1** Fall:1992 pp. 1 – 32

27 An empirical analysis of theories on factors influencing state government accounting disclosure. Rita Hartung Cheng. *J. Acc. Pub. Pol.* **11:1** Spring:1992 pp. 1 – 42

28 An empirical investigation of the market for "single audit" services. K.K. Raman; Earl R. Wilson. *J. Acc. Pub. Pol.* **11:4** Winter:1992 pp. 271 – 295

29 Evidence on the determinants of inventory accounting policy choice. Barry E. Cushing; Marc J. LeClere. *Acc. Review* **67:2** 4:1992 pp. 355 – 366

30 Financial accounting standard setting as an institutionalized action field — constraints, opportunities and dilemmas. Timothy J. Fogarty. *J. Acc. Pub. Pol.* **11:4** Winter:1992 pp. 331 – 355

31 Formula accounting. Peter Seddon. *Acc. Bus. Res.* **22:86** Spring:1992 pp. 161 – 172

32 A forum on laboratory markets and auditing research. Nicholas Dopuch *[Contrib.]*; Ronald R. King *[Contrib.]*; David E. Wallin *[Contrib.]*; James R. Boatsman *[Contrib.]*; Lawrence P. Grasso *[Contrib.]*; Michael B. Ormiston *[Contrib.]*; J.Hal Reneau *[Contrib.]*; Douglas V. Dejong *[Contrib.]*; Robert Forsythe *[Contrib.]*. *Collection of 4 articles.* **Acc. Review** , *67:1,* 1:1992 pp. 97 – 171

33 France. Jean-Claude Scheid; Peter Walton. London: Routledge, 1992: 357 p. *ISBN: 0415061989.* [European financial reporting.]

34 Fraud detection — a theoretical foundation. Ella Mae Matsumura; Robert R. Tucker. *Acc. Review* **67:4** 10:1992 pp. 753 – 782

35 The impact of annual earnings announcements on convergence of beliefs. Lawrence D. Brown; Jerry C.Y. Han. *Acc. Review* **67:4** 10:1992 pp. 862 – 875

36 International handbook of accounting education and certification. Kwabena Anyane-Ntow *[Ed.]*. Oxford: Pergamon Press, 1992: xxxii, 556 p. *ISBN: 0080413722; LofC: 91042895.* *"Published in association with the International Association for Accounting Education and Research." ; Includes bibliographical references and index.*

37 An investigation of the behavior of accruals in the semiconductor industry — 1985; *[French summary]*. J. Rayburn; S. Lenway. *Cont. Account. Res.* **9:1** Fall:1992 pp. 237 – 251

38 Investor reaction to disclosures of 1974-75 LIFO adoption decisions. Ross Jennings; David P. Mest; Robert B. Thompson. *Acc. Review* **67:2** 4:1992 pp. 337 – 354

39 Ireland. Niamh Brennan; Francis J. O'Brien; Aileen Pierce. London: Routledge, 1992: 235 p. *ISBN: 0415063159.* [European financial reporting.]

40 Kapacitetsomkostningsstyring. Det amerikanske ABC-system versus den danske styremodel *[In Danish]*; [Capacity costing control. The American activity based costing system versus the Danish control model] *[Summary]*. Michael Anderson. *Led. Erhv.* **56:1** 1:1992 pp. 43 – 48

B.4: Accounting method and theory *[Méthode et théorie comptables]*

41 Law and accountancy — conflict and co-operation in the 1990s. Judith Freedman *[Ed.]*; Michael Power *[Ed.]*. London: Paul Chapman, 1992: 192 p. *ISBN: 1853961965.*

42 Market based accounting research — het einde van het begin of het begin van het einde? *[In Flemish]*; Market based accounting research (MBAR). The end of the beginning or the beginning of the end? *[Summary]*. Hylke Vandenbussche; Carl Reyns. *Econ. Soc. Tidj.* **46:1** 3:1992 pp. 75 – 93

43 A multidimensional analysis of selected ethical issues in accounting. Steven M. Flory; Thomas J. Phillips; R. Eric Reidenbach; Donald P. Robin. *Acc. Review* **67:2** 4:1992 pp. 284 – 302

44 The new era of auditing and the accounting system of Japan. T. Iizuka. *Jpn. Wor. Econ.* **4:1** 5:1992 pp. 69 – 75

45 On optimal choice of inventory accounting method. Sasson Bar-Yosef; Pradyot K. Sen. *Acc. Review* **67:2** 4:1992 pp. 320 – 336

46 On the history of normative accounting theory — paradigm lost, paradigm regained? Richard Mattessich. *Acc. Bus. Finan. Hist.* **2:2** 9:1992 pp. 181 – 198

47 On the methodology of a conceptual framework for financial accounting. Part I — an historical and jurisprudential analysis. Simon Archer. *Acc. Bus. Finan. Hist.* **2:2** 9:1992 pp. 199 – 228

48 Perception and attitudes of different user-groups to the role of the budget, budget pressure and budget participation. Stephen R. Lyne. *Acc. Bus. Res.* **22:88** Autumn:1992 pp. 357 – 369

49 Perspectives on financial control — essays in memory of Kenneth Hilton. Kenneth Hilton; Mahmoud Ezzamel *[Ed.]*; David F. Heathfield *[Ed.]*. London: Chapman & Hall, 1992: 333 p. *ISBN: 0412409801; LofC: 92025127. Includes index.*

50 The politics of brand accounting in the United Kingdom. Michael Power. *Eur. Account. Rev.* **1:1** 5:1992 pp. 39 – 68

51 Reasons for preferring net to gross figures of income (and product and vice versa). Frits Bos. *R. In. Weal.* **38:3** 9:1992 pp. 267 – 279

52 The reliability of perception-based annual report disclosure studies. John K. Courtis. *Acc. Bus. Res.* **23:89** Winter:1992 pp. 31 – 43

53 Research method and methodology in finance and accounting. Bob Ryan; Michael Theobald; Robert W. Scapens. London: Academic Press, 1992: 208 p. *ISBN: 0126050651.*

54 Risk preferences in participative budgeting. D.C. Kim. *Acc. Review* **67:2** 4:1992 pp. 303 – 318

55 Ritual and conflict in the audit profession. S.K. Mills; M.S. Bettner. *Crit. Persp. Acc.* **3:2** 6:1992 pp. 185 – 200

56 The role of the accounting rate of return in financial statement analysis. Richard P. Brief; Raef A. Lawson. *Acc. Review* **67:2** 4:1992 pp. 411 – 426

57 SEC communications to the independent auditors — an analysis of enforcement actions. David R. Campbell; Larry M. Parker. *J. Acc. Pub. Pol.* **11:4** Winter:1992 pp. 297 – 330

58 Segment reporting — international issues and evidence. Clive R Emmanuel; Neil Garrod. Hemel Hempstead, England: Prentice Hall in association with the Institute of Chartered Accountants in England and Wales, 1992: 170 p. *ISBN: 0137992718; LofC: 91046708. Includes bibliographical references and index.* [Research studies in accounting.]

59 Separating controllable performance from non-controllable performance — the case of optimal procurement contracting. S.I. Cohen; M.P. Loeb; A.W. Stark. *Manag. Acc. Res.* **3:4** 12:1992 pp. 291 – 306

60 The sequencing of audit evidence — its impact on the extent of audit testing and report formulation. William F. Messier. *Acc. Bus. Res.* **22:86** Spring:1992 pp. 143 – 150

61 Spain. José A. Gonzalo; José L. Gallizo. London: Routledge, 1992: 256p. *ISBN: 0415061997.* [European financial reporting.]

62 Substance over form in auditing and the auditor's position of public trust. S.C. Martens; J.E. McEnroe. *Crit. Persp. Acc.* **3:4** 12:1992 pp. 389 – 401

63 Tests of partial adjustment model of financial ratios. Chunchi Wu; Chihwa Kao; Cheng F. Lee. *Q Rev. Econ. Finan.* **32:3** Autumn:1992 pp. 96 – 111

64 Towards a framework for not-for-profit accounting; *[French summary]*. H. Falk. *Cont. Account. Res.* **8:2** Spring:1992 pp. 468 – 499

65 The use and abuse of graphs in annual reports — theoretical framework and empirical study. Vivien Beattie; Michael John Jones. *Acc. Bus. Res.* **22:88** Autumn:1992 pp. 291 – 303

66 Utjecaj pretvorbe društvenih poduzeća na promjenu obračunskog sustava; Influence of the transformation of socially-owned enterprises on changes in the accounting system

B.4: Accounting method and theory *[Méthode et théorie comptables]*
[Summary]; Влияние преобразования общественных предприятий на перемены расчётной системы *[Russian summary]*. Vladimir Lasić. *Ekon. Preg.* **43:7-8-9** 1992 pp. 511 – 526

C: General and basic works — *Ouvrages généraux et ouvrages de base*

Sub-divisions: Decision theory *[Théorie de la décision]*; Economic theory *[Théorie économique]*; Game theory *[Théorie des jeux]*; Risk *[Risque]*

1 An analysis of the impact of finite horizons on macroeconomic control. Andrew P. Blake; Peter Westaway. London: National Institute of Economic and Social Research, 1992: 37 p. [Discussion paper.]
2 Chaotic dynamics — theory and applications to economics. Alfredo Medio. Cambridge: Cambridge University Press, 1992: 344 p. *ISBN: 0521394880; LofC: 91019382. DMC software by Giampaolo Gallo; Includes index.*
3 Cooperation and contracts. Frederic Schick. *Econ. Philos.* **8:2** 10:1992 pp. 209 – 230
4 Economics and epistemology — a realist critique. Rajani K. Kanth. *Cap. Class* **:47** Summer:1992 pp. 93 – 112
5 The effect of uncertainty on interactive behaviour. M. Gradstein; S. Nitzan; S. Slutsky. *Econ. J.* **102:412** 5:1992 pp. 554 – 561
6 Efficiency criteria for optimal laws — objective standards or value judgements. Louis De Alessi. *Constit. Pol. Econ.* **3:3** Fall:1992 pp. 321 – 342
7 Essays in economic analysis and policy — a tribute to Bhabatosh Datta. Bhabatosh Datta; Dipak Banerjee *[Ed.]*. Delhi: Oxford University Press, 1991: 264 p. *ISBN: 0195627342; LofC: 91900825.*
8 Ethics in economics, business, and economic policy. Peter Koslowski *[Ed.]*. Berlin: Springer-Verlag, 1992: 188 p. *ISBN: 3540553592; LofC: 92010807. Includes index.* [Studies in economic ethics and philosophy.]
9 The future of economics. John D. Hey *[Ed.]*. Oxford: Blackwell, 1992: 162 p. *ISBN: 0631184937; LofC: 91033048. Includes bibliographical references and index.*
10 Irreversible investment with uncertainty and scale economies. Avinash K. Dixit. London: London School of Economics and Political Science. Suntory-Toyota International Centre for Economics and Related Disciplines, 1992: 23 p. [Theoretical economics. : No. TE/92/240]
11 The Nash bargaining solution manipulated by pre-donations is Talmudic. M.R. Sertel. *Econ. Lett.* **40:1** 9:1992 pp. 45 – 55
12 The nonatomic assignment model. N.E. Gretsky; J.M. Ostroy; W.R. Zame. *Econ. Theory* **2:1** 1992 pp. 103 – 128
13 Pathological rationality/rational pathologies. Roby Rajan. *Alternatives* **17:3** Summer:1992 pp. 339 – 370
14 Patinkin on Keynes and Meltzer. Allan H. Meltzer. *J. Monet. Ec.* **29:1** 2:1992 pp. 151 – 162
15 Power and wealth in a competitive capitalist economy. Samuel Bowles; Herbert Gintis. *Philos. Pub.* **21:4** Fall:1992 pp. 324 – 353
16 Quasi-rational expectations — experimental evidence. R.G. Nelson; D.A. Bessler. *J. Forecast.* **11:2** 2:1992 pp. 141 – 156
17 Rent-seeking bei Cournot-Nash Verhalten — graphische und numerische Illustrationen eines komplexen Phänomens *[In German]*; Rent-seeking under Cournot-Nash behaviour — graphic and numerical illustrations of a complex phenomenon *[Summary]*. Hans G. Monissen. *Jahrb. N. St.* **209:1-2** 1:1992 pp. 1 – 19
18 A social choice rule and its implementation in perfect equilibrium. J.V. Howard. *J. Econ. Theo.* **56:1** 2:1992 pp. 142 – 159
19 Sur l'équilibre général walrasien — les analyses de Maurice Allais et Edmond Malinvaud *[In French]*; Walrasian general equilibrium — the analyses of Maurice Allais and Edmond Malinvaud *[Summary]*. Bruno Carrier. *Rev. Int. Sci. Ec. Com.* **XXXIX:5-6** 5-6:1992 pp. 385 – 401
20 What is the matter with aggregate demand and aggregate supply? B. Bhaskarara Rao. *Aust. Econ. P.* **30:57** 12:1991 pp. 264 – 277

C: General and basic works [Ouvrages généraux et ouvrages de base] —

Decision theory [Théorie de la décision]

21 Anomalies in intertemporal choice — evidence and an interpretation. George Loewenstein; Drazen Prelec. Q. J. Econ. **CVII:2** 5:1992 pp. 573 – 597
22 Costly optimization — an experiment. M. Pingle. J. Econ. Beh. **17:1** 1:1992 pp. 3 – 30
23 Flexibility in intertemporal decision making; [French summary]; [German summary]. Armin Schmutzler. Schw. Z. Volk. Stat. **128:2** 6:1992 pp. 185 – 204
24 The market as a metaphor of politics — a critique of the foundations of economic choice theory. Andries Hoogerwerf. Int. Rev. Admin. Sci. **58:1** 3:1992 pp. 23 – 42
25 Operationality in the Shackle-Vickers approach to decision making in ignorance. Donald W. Katzner. J. Post. Keyn. Ec. **15:2** Winter:1992-1993 pp. 229 – 254
26 Revealed preference, stochastic dominance, and the expected utility hypothesis. Kim C. Border. J. Econ. Theo. **56:1** 2:1992 pp. 20 – 42
27 Stochastic models of choice and reaction time. A.A.J. Marley [Ed.]; D. Heyer [Contrib.]; R. Niederée [Contrib.]; S.A. Clark [Contrib.]; P.C. Fishburn [Contrib.]; R. Suck [Contrib.]; H. Stern [Contrib.]; S.I. Resnick [Contrib.]; R. Roy [Contrib.]. Collection of 8 articles. **Math. Soc. Sc.** , 23:1, 2:1992 pp. 1 – 145
28 Testing Bayes rule and the representativeness heuristic — some experimental evidence. D.M. Grether. J. Econ. Beh. **17:1** 1:1992 pp. 31 – 57
29 Theories of choice under ignorance and uncertainty. David Kelsey; John Quiggin. J. Econ. Sur. **6:2** 1992 pp. 133 – 154
30 The theory of choice — a critical guide. Shaun Hargreaves Heap; et al. Cambridge, MA.: Blackwell, 1992: 398 p. ISBN: 0631171746; LofC: 91025052. Includes bibliographical references and index.

Economic theory [Théorie économique]

31 Advances in economic theory — Sixth World Congress. Jean-Jacques Laffont [Ed.]. Cambridge: Cambridge University Press, 1992: 450 p. ISBN: 0521416663; LofC: 91026036. [Econometric Society monographs. : No. 21]
32 Anomalies in intertemporal choice — evidence and an interpretation. George Loewenstein; Drazen Prelec. Q. J. Econ. **CVII:2** 5:1992 pp. 573 – 597
33 Contract economics. Lars Werin [Ed.]; Hans Wijkander [Ed.]. Cambridge, MA.: Blackwell Publishers, 1992: 359 p. ISBN: 0631178937; LofC: 92006048. Proceedings of a symposium held in Aug. 1990 in Saltsjöbaden, Sweden, under the auspices of the Nobel Foundation.
34 A critique of Keynesian economics. Walter Allan [Ed.]. New York: St. Martin's Press, 1992: 247 p. ISBN: 0312085540; LofC: 92018932. Includes bibliographical references and index.
35 The development of Keynes's economics — from Marshall to Millennialism. Joseph T. Salerno. R. Austrian Econ. **6:1** 1992 pp. 3 – 64
36 [In Greek (modern)]; Economic history and economic theory — Festschrift in honour of Lazaros Th. Houmanidis. Piraeus: University of Piraeus, 1991: 751 p.
37 Economics and policy — beyond science and ideology. Rory O'Donnell. Econ. Soc. R. **24:1** 10:1992 pp. 75 – 98
38 Equilibrium unemployment in Keyne's General Theory — some recent debates. E.J. Amadeo. Contrib. Pol. Econ. **11** 1992 pp. 1 – 14
39 Essays on expectations in economic theory. Thomas Lindh. Stockholm, Sweden: Almqvist & Wikesell International, 1992: 112 p. (ill) ISBN: 9155428509. Includes bibliographical references. [Acta Universitatis Upsaliensis.]
40 European contributions to institutional thought. Anne Mayhew [Contrib.]; Sven-Erik Sjöstrand [Contrib.]; Ramana Ramaswamy [Contrib.]; Atle Midttun [Contrib.]; Otto Singer [Contrib.]; Ove K. Pedersen [Contrib.]; Niels Å. Andersen [Contrib.]; Peter Kjaer [Contrib.]. Collection of 6 articles. **J. Econ. Iss.** , XXVI:4, 12:1992 pp. 1003 – 1144
41 F.H. Knight on capitalism and freedom. R.A. Gonce. J. Econ. Iss. **XXVI:3** 9:1992 pp. 813 – 844
42 The inexact and separate science of economics. Daniel M. Hausman. Cambridge: Cambridge University Press, 1992: 376 p. ISBN: 0521415012.
43 An intransitive expectations-based Bayesian variant of prospect theory. Robert F. Bordley. J. Risk Uncert. **5:2** 1992 pp. 127 – 144

C: General and basic works *[Ouvrages généraux et ouvrages de base]* — *Economic theory [Théorie économique]*

44 Invisible-hand explanations and neoclassical economics — toward a post marginalist economics. Roger Koppl. *J. Inst. Theo. Ec.* **148:2** 6:1992 pp. 292 – 313

45 Involuntary unemployment — macroeconomics from a Keynesian perspective. James Anthony Trevithick. Hemel Hempstead: Harvester Wheatsheaf, 1992: 246 p. *ISBN: 074500055x.*

46 Leistungen und Grenzen politisch-ökonomischer Theorie — eine Kritische Bestandsaufnahme zu Mancur Olson *[In German]*; [Success and limits of political economy theory, a critical evaluation of Mancur Olson]. Klaus Schubert *[Ed.]*. Darmstadt: Wissenshaftliche Buchgesellschaft, 1992: vi, 215 p. *ISBN: 3534113616. Bibliography — p.[193]-209.*

47 Macroeconomic theories and policies for the 1990s — a Scandinavian perspective. Bruno Amoroso *[Ed.]*; Jesper Jespersen *[Ed.]*. Basingstoke: Macmillan, 1992: 156 p. *ISBN: 0333525876.*

48 The notion of equilibrium in the Kenynesian theory. Mario Sebastiani *[Ed.]*. London: Macmillan, 1992: 247 p. *ISBN: 0333523741.*

49 Paradoxa, dilemmata und Anomalien in der ökonomischen Theorie *[In German]*; Paradoxes, dilemmas, and anomalies in economic theory *[Summary]*. Joachim Güntzel; Stefan Weil. *Jahrb. N. St.* **210:3-4** 9:1992 pp. 302 – 314

50 The principles of economics — some lies my teachers told me. Lawrence A. Boland. London: Routledge, 1992: 233 p. *ISBN: 0415064333; LofC: 91031008. Includes bibliographical references and index.*

51 The quest for utilization value — economy as the good ordering of interests. P.H.L. Kloppenborg. Amsterdam: Progressio Foundation, 1991: 249 p. [Progressio civic economy series. : No. 2]

52 State-independent subjective expected lexiographic utility. Irving H. LaValle; Peter C. Fishburn. *J. Risk Uncert.* **5:3** 1992 pp. 217 – 240

53 Stochastic models of choice and reaction time. A.A.J. Marley *[Ed.]*; D. Heyer *[Contrib.]*; R. Niederée *[Contrib.]*; S.A. Clark *[Contrib.]*; P.C. Fishburn *[Contrib.]*; R. Suck *[Contrib.]*; H. Stern *[Contrib.]*; S.I. Resnick *[Contrib.]*; R. Roy *[Contrib.]*. *Collection of 8 articles.* **Math. Soc. Sc.** , *23:1,* 2:1992 pp. 1 – 145

54 Towards a neo-classical theory of institutional failure. Christos Pitelis. *J. Econ. Stud.* **19:1** 1992 pp. 14 – 28

55 Truth and meaning in economics — selected essays on economic theory and policy. Bengt-Christer Ysander; Gunnar Eliasson *[Ed.]*; Ragnar Bentzel *[Ed.]*. Stockholm: Industrial Institute for Economic and Social Research, 1991: 193 p. (ill) *ISBN: 9172043628. Includes bibliographical references.*

56 Where does subjective expected utility fail descriptively? R. Duncan Luce. *J. Risk Uncert.* **5:1** 2:1992 pp. 5 – 28

57 Wirtschaftswissenschaft und Ethik *[In German]*; [Economics and ethics] *[Summary]*. Jean-Louis Arni. *Jahr. Soz.schaft.* **43:2** 1992 pp. 149 – 170

Game theory *[Théorie des jeux]*

58 Deterrence, observability and awareness. G. Bonanno. *Eco. Notes* **21:2** 1992 pp. 307 – 315

59 Equilibrium solutions for resource dilemmas. Amnon Rapoport; Ramzi Suleiman. *Group Decis. Negot.* **1:3** 11:1992 pp. 269 – 294

60 Evaluating cooperative game theory in water resources. Ariel Dinar; Aharon Ratner; Dan Yaron. *Theory Decis.* **32:1** 1:1992 pp. 1 – 20

61 Evolutionary game theory. George J. Mailath *[Contrib.]*; Kenneth G. Binmore *[Contrib.]*; Larry Samuelson *[Contrib.]*; Jeroen M. Swinkels *[Contrib.]*; Akihiko Matsui *[Contrib.]*; Jianbo Zhang *[Contrib.]*; Eddie Dekel *[Contrib.]*; Suzanne Scotchmer *[Contrib.]*; Antonio Cabrales *[Contrib.]*; Joel Sobel *[Contrib.]* *and others. Collection of 11 articles.* **J. Econ. Theo.** , *57:2,* 8:1992 pp. 259 – 504

62 Experimental economics. W. Güth *[Contrib.]*; K.-E. Wärneryd *[Contrib.]*; S.E.G. Lea *[Contrib.]*; H. Oppewal *[Contrib.]*; E. Tougareva *[Contrib.]*; H.-D. Meyer *[Contrib.]*; A. Ostmann *[Contrib.]*; M. Sefton *[Contrib.]*; G. Ortona *[Contrib.]*; F. Scacciati *[Contrib.]* *and others. Collection of 11 articles.* **J. Econ. Psyc.** , *13:2,* 6:1992 pp. 199 – 361

63 An exploration of the eductive justifications of the rational-expectations hypothesis. Roger Guesnerie. *Am. Econ. Rev.* **82:5** 12:1992 pp. 1254 – 1278

64 Implementation via Nash equilibria. Vladimir Danilov. *Econometrica* **60:1** 1:1992 pp. 43 – 56

65 Innovation and strategic sabotage as a feedback process. W.J. Baumol. *Jpn. Wor. Econ.* **4:4** 12:1992 pp. 275 – 290

C: General and basic works *[Ouvrages généraux et ouvrages de base]* — *Game theory [Théorie des jeux]*

66 The joint exploitation of a productive asset — a game-theoretic approach. J. Benhabib; R. Radner. *Econ. Theory* **2:2** 1992 pp. 155 – 190

67 Knowledge, belief, and strategic interaction. Cristina Bicchieri *[Ed.]*; Maria Luisa Dalla Chiara *[Ed.]*. Cambridge: Cambridge University Press, 1992: xiv, 413 p. *ISBN: 0521416744; LofC: 91038415 //r92. Papers presented at the workshop on knowledge, belief, and strategic interaction which took place in Italy in June 1989; Includes bibliographical references.* [Cambridge studies in probability, induction, and decision theory.]

68 Minimal liberty. Amartya Sen. *Economica* **59:234** 5:1992 pp. 139 – 159

69 Modelling rational conflict — the limits of game theory; *[French summary]*; Modellisierung für rationalen Konflikt — die Grenzen der Spieltheorie *[In German]*; Modelización del conflicto racional — los límites de la teoría de los juegos *[In Spanish]*. Y. Varoufakis. *Econ. App.* **XLV:1** 1992 pp. 53 – 78

70 Negotiation analysis — a characterization and review. James K. Sebenius. *Manag. Sci.* **38:1** 1:1992 pp. 18 – 38

71 Organizations and games. George W.J. Hendrikse *[Contrib.]*; David Encaoua *[Contrib.]*; Philippe Michel *[Contrib.]*; Michel Moreaux *[Contrib.]*; Guillermo Owen *[Contrib.]*; Clara Ponsati- Obiols *[Contrib.]*; Jerry R. Green *[Contrib.]*; Jean-Jacques Laffont *[Contrib.]*; Claude d' Aspremont *[Contrib.]*; Jacques Crémer *[Contrib.] and others. Collection of 15 articles.* **Ann. Econ. Stat.** , :25/26, 1-6:1992 pp. 39 – 325

72 A primer in game theory. Robert Gibbons. Hemel Hempstead: Harvester-Wheatsheaf, 1992: 267 p. *ISBN: 0745011608.*

73 The principal-agent relationship with an informed principal, II — common values. Eric Maskin; Jean Tirole. *Econometrica* **60:1** 1:1992 pp. 1 – 42

74 Rationality in extensive-form games. Philip J. Reny. *J. Econ. Pers.* **6:4** Fall:1992 pp. 103 – 117

75 Recent developments in game theory. John Creedy *[Ed.]*; Jeff Borland *[Ed.]*; Jürgen Eichberger *[Ed.]*. Brookfield, VT.: Gower, 1992: 221 p. *ISBN: 1852785330; LofC: 91022144. Includes bibliographical references.*

76 Social norms and community enforcement. Michihiro Kandori. *R. Econ. S.* **59(1):198** 2:1992 pp. 63 – 80

77 Strategic delay in bargaining with two-sided uncertainty. Peter C. Cramton. *R. Econ. S.* **59(1):198** 2:1992 pp. 205 – 225

Risk *[Risque]*

78 Analytics of uncertainty and information. Jack Hirshleifer; John G. Riley. Cambridge: Cambridge University Press, 1992: 465 p. *ISBN: 0521239567.* [Cambridge surveys of economic literature.]

79 Different frames for the independence axiom — an experimental investigation in individual decision making under risk. Michele Bernasconi. *J. Risk Uncert.* **5:2** 1992 pp. 159 – 174

80 Distributive justice of bargaining and risk sensitivity. Marlies Klemisch-Ahlert. *Theory Decis.* **32:3** 5:1992 pp. 303 – 318

81 Examining risk preferences under high monetary incentives — experimental evidence from the People's Republic of China. Steven J. Kachelmeier; Mohamed Shehata. *Am. Econ. Rev.* **82:5** 12:1992 pp. 1120 – 1141

82 Investment, expectations, and uncertainty. Ciaran Driver; David Moreton. Oxford: Blackwell, 1992: 176 p. *ISBN: 063117334x; LofC: 91027566. Includes bibliographical references and index.*

83 Mastering risk — environment, markets and politics in Australian economic history. Colin White. South Melbourne, Australia: Oxford University Press, 1992: 326 p. *ISBN: 0195533518. Includes bibliographical references (p. [293]-317) and index.*

84 Measurement distortion and missing contingencies in optimal contracts. F. Allen; D. Gale. *Econ. Theory* **2:1** 1992 pp. 1 – 26

85 Strategic risk — an ordinal approach. James M. Collins; Timothy W. Ruefli. *Manag. Sci.* **38:12** 12:1992 pp. 1707 – 1731

D: History of economic thought — *Histoire de la pensée économique*

Sub-divisions: 18th Century *[18ᵉ siècle]*; 19th Century *[19ᵉ siècle]*; 20th Century *[20ᵉ siècle]*

1 The as-if view of economic motivational hypotheses. Steven Rappaport. *R. Soc. Econ.* **L:1** Spring:1992 pp. 82 – 101
2 Can economic systems be chosen? History, values and human nature. Leslie Armour. *Int. J. Soc. E.* **19:7/8/9** 1992 pp. 273 – 291
3 Capital-labour tensions and liberal economic thought. Jon D. Wisman. *Int. J. Soc. E.* **19:10/11/12** 1992 pp. 279 – 299
4 Classical theories of money, output, and inflation — a study in historical economics. Roy Green. New York: St. Martin's Press, 1992: 271 p. *ISBN: 0312085567; LofC: 92020308. Includes index.*
5 Contesting markets — analyses of ideology, discourse and practice. Roy Dilley *[Ed.]*. Edinburgh: Edinburgh University Press, 1992: 302 p. *ISBN: 0748603719.*
6 Ekonomske i političke dimenzije tranzicije *[In Serbo-Croatian]*; Экономические и политические размеры транзиции *[Russian summary]*; Economic and political dimensions of transition *[Summary]*. Dragomir Vojnić; Žarko Puhovski. *Ekon. Preg.* **43:3-4** 1992 pp. 297 – 318
7 Histoire de l'économie industrielle *[In French]*; [History of industrial economics]. R. Arena *[Contrib.]*; J.T. Ravix *[Contrib.]*; P. Fontaine *[Contrib.]*; A. Alcouffe *[Contrib.]*; J. Frayssé *[Contrib.]*; C. Schmidt *[Contrib.]*; C. Picory *[Contrib.] and others. Collection of 7 articles.* **Ec. Sociét.** , *XXVI:3,* 3:1992 pp. 3 – 194
8 Notes on neoinstitutional economics. Lars Pålsson Syll. *Sc. Ec. Hist. R.* **XL:2** 1992 p.21- 33
9 On share contracts and other economic contributions of Xenophon. L.N. Christofides. *Scot. J. Poli.* **39:1** 2:1992 pp. 111 – 121
10 On the history of economic thought. A.W. Coats. London: Routledge, 1992: 495 p. *ISBN: 0415067154; LofC: 91047898. Includes bibliographical references and index; Contents — v. 1. British and American economic essays.*
11 Previously undocumented macroeconomics from the 1680s — the analytical arguments and policy recommendations of Sir Dudley North and Roger North. George D. Choksy. *Hist. Polit. Ec.* **24:2** Summer:1992 pp. 515 – 532
12 Theoretical expositions of centralized versus decentralized strands of socialist economic systems. Abu F. Dowlah. *Int. J. Soc. E.* **19:7/8/9** 1992 pp. 210 – 258
13 Theories of regulation and the history of consumerism. John P. Tiemstra. *Int. J. Soc. E.* **19:6** 1992 pp. 3 – 27
14 Three classical economists on trouble, strife, and the "alienation" of labour; *[French summary]*. G.C. Archibald. *Can. J. Econ.* **XXV:1** 2:1992 pp. 60 – 75
15 Unequal exchange and dependency theory in George Fitzhugh. Joseph Persky. *Hist. Polit. Ec.* **24:1** Spring:1992 pp. 117 – 128

18th Century *[18ᵉ siècle]*

16 Adam Smith and conservative economics. Emma Rothschild. *Econ. Hist. R.* **XLV:1** 2:1992 pp. 74 – 96
17 Adam Smith and the market mechanism. Salim Rashid. *Hist. Polit. Ec.* **24:1** Spring:1992 pp. 129 – 152
18 Adam Smith on competitive religious markets. Charles G. Leathers; J. Patrick Raines. *Hist. Polit. Ec.* **24:2** Summer:1992 pp. 499 – 513
19 Adam Smith reviewed. Peter Jones *[Ed.]*; Andrew S. Skinner *[Ed.]*. Edinburgh: Edinburgh University Press, 1992: 252 p. *ISBN: 0748603468.*
20 Adam Smith's legacy — his place in the development of modern economics. Michael Fry *[Ed.]*. London: Routledge, 1992: 203 p. *ISBN: 0415061644; LofC: 91025698. Proceedings of a conference held in the Usher Hall, Edinburgh, on July 16-17, 1990, to mark the bicentenary of the death of Adam Smith; Includes bibliographical references and index.*
21 Commerce and the state — Turgot, Condorcet and Smith. E. Rothschild. *Econ. J.* **102:414** 9:1992 pp. 1197 – 1210

D: History of economic thought *[Histoire de la pensée économique]* — **18th Century** *[18e siècle]*

22 Ethics and the classical liberal tradition in economics. Jerry Evensky. *Hist. Polit. Ec.* **24:1** Spring:1992 pp. 61 – 78

23 Un exemple de critique philosophique appliquée à la théorie économique — Hume, Keynes et les classiques *[In French]*; An example over philosophical criticism applied to economics theory — Hume, Keynes and the classical theories *[Summary]*; (Zur philosophischen Kritik der Wirtschaftstheorie — Hume, Keynes und die Klassiker: *Title only in German*); (Un ejemplo de crítica filosófica aplicada a la teoría económica — Hume, Keynes y los clásicos: *Title only in Spanish*). Paul Chanier. *Econ. App.* **XLV:2** 7:1992 pp. 65 – 85

24 Notes on Malthus's measure of value. Pier Luigi Porta *[Ed.]*. Cambridge: Cambridge University Press, 1992: 62 p. *ISBN: 0521402980. Includes index.*

25 Il «primo» Adam Smith *[In Italian]*; [The "first" Adam Smith]. Adelino Zanini. *Ras. Econ.* **LVI:2** 4-6:1992 pp. 341 – 356

19th Century *[19e siècle]*

26 Beyond 'Capital' — Marx's political economy of the working class. Michael A. Lebowitz. London: Macmillan, 1992: 187 p. *ISBN: 0333520505. Includes index.*

27 La durata del lavoro nelle tesi di Marx, Marshall e Keynes *[In Italian]*; [The duration of work in the theses of Marx, Marshall and Keynes]. Gaetano Sabatini. *A. Fond. L. Einaudi* **XXV** 1991 pp. 189 – 211

28 Front door/back door economics — the origins of Veblenian theory in the epistemology of William James; Economia front door/back door — le origini della teoria di Veblen nella epistemologia di William James *[Italian summary]*. Robert A. Griffin. *Rev. Int. Sci. Ec. Com.* **XXXIX:7** 7:1992 pp. 569 – 584

29 J.S. Mill and the Tory school — the rhetorical value of the recantation. Evelyn L. Forget. *Hist. Polit. Ec.* **24:1** Spring:1992 pp. 31 – 60

30 Marx, Engels and economic evolution. Geoffrey M. Hodgson. *Int. J. Soc. E.* **19:7/8/9** 1992 pp. 121 – 128

31 Mechanistic physiology and institutional economics — Jacques Loeb and Thorstein Veblen. Charles T. Rasmussen; Rick Tilman. *Int. J. Soc. E.* **19:10/11/12** 1992 pp. 235 – 247

32 The models of Ricardo, Marx and Keynes on the evolution of capitalism; I modelli di Ricardo, Marx e Keynes sull'evoluzione del capitalismo *[Italian summary]*. Lazaros Th. Houmanidis. *Rev. Int. Sci. Ec. Com.* **XXXIX:5-6** 5-6:1992 pp. 403 – 418

33 On the limitations of the Marxian theory of value. V. Inosemtsev. *Soc. Sci.* **XXIII:4** 1992 pp. 110 – 125

34 Schmoller's political economy — self-interest versus the higher law. John Conway O'Brien. *Int. J. Soc. E.* **19:10/11/12** 1992 pp. 126 – 149

35 La théorie de Marx et le mode de production partitique *[In French]*; Marxist theory and the party-controlled mode of production *[Summary]*. Ali Bayar. *Rev. Ét. Comp.* **XXIII:2-3** 6-9:1992 pp. 211 – 227

20th Century *[20e siècle]*

36 Alfred Marshall on the structural and behavioural properties of social institutions. Hans E. Jensen. *Int. J. Soc. E.* **19:10/11/12** 1992 pp. 53 – 70

37 Carl Menger's theory of the evolution of money — some problems. Geoffrey M. Hodgson. *R. Pol. Econ.* **4:4** 1992 pp. 396 – 412

38 Consumption in contemporary capitalism — beyond Marx and Veblen. Richard McIntyre. *R. Soc. Econ.* **L:1** Spring:1992 pp. 40 – 60

39 Davidson and Hayek on the role of effective money in transforming the cumulative process into a real theory of growth; *[French summary]*; (Davidson und Hayek über die Rolle des Bargeldes bei der Transformation zusätzlicher Prozesse in eine reelle Wachstumstheorie: *Title only in German*); (Davidson, Hayek sobre el papel del dinero efectivo para transformar el proceso acumulativo en una teoría real del crecimiento: *Title only in Spanish*). Michael-J. Gootzeit. *Econ. App.* **XLV:2** 7:1992 pp. 87 – 104

40 La durata del lavoro nelle tesi di Marx, Marshall e Keynes *[In Italian]*; [The duration of work in the theses of Marx, Marshall and Keynes]. Gaetano Sabatini. *A. Fond. L. Einaudi* **XXV** 1991 pp. 189 – 211

41 A economia de John Hicks *[In Portuguese]*; [The economics of John Hicks]. Mario Henrique Simonsen *[Contrib.]*; Carlos M. Lopes *[Contrib.]*; Joaquim Andrade *[Contrib.]*; Fernando

D: History of economic thought *[Histoire de la pensée économique]* — **20th Century** *[20ᵉ siècle]*

J.Cardim de Carvalho *[Contrib.]*; Mauro Boianovsky *[Contrib.]*; Victoria Chick *[Contrib.]*; Edward J. Amadeo *[Contrib.]*; Ana Maria Bianchi *[Contrib.]*. *Collection of 8 articles.* **Rev. Bras. Ec.** , *46:1,* 1-3:1992 pp. 5 – 148

42 Economics, bounded rationality and the cognitive revolution. Herbert Alexander Simon; et al; M. Egidi *[Ed.]*; Robin Lapthorn Marris *[Ed.]*. Brookfield, VT.: E. Elgar Pub, 1992: 232 p. *ISBN: 1852784253; LofC: 91042473.*

43 Un exemple de critique philosophique appliquée à la théorie économique — Hume, Keynes et les classiques *[In French]*; An example over philosophical criticism applied to economics theory — Hume, Keynes and the classical theories *[Summary]*; (Zur philosophischen Kritik der Wirtschaftstheorie — Hume, Keynes und die Klassiker: *Title only in German);* (Un ejemplo de crítica filosófica aplicada a la teoría económica — Hume, Keynes y los clásicos: *Title only in Spanish).* Paul Chanier. *Econ. App.* **XLV:2** 7:1992 pp. 65 – 85

44 The fortunes of liberalism — essays on Austrian economics and the ideal of freedom. Peter G. Kleih *[Ed.]*. London: Routledge, 1992: 279 p. *ISBN: 0415035163.* [The collected works of Friedrich August Hayek. : Vol. 4]

45 Foundations of post-Keynesian economic anaylsis. Marc Lavoie. Aldershot: Edward Elgar, 1992: 461 p. *ISBN: 1852783222.* [New directions in modern economics.]

46 The "full cost" controversy of the 1940s and 1950s — a methodological assessment. Philippe Mongin. *Hist. Polit. Ec.* **24:2** Summer:1992 pp. 311 – 356

47 Gandhi and economic development. B.P. Pandey *[Ed.]*. New Delhi: Radiant Publishers, 1991: xxiv, 233 p. *ISBN: oc24332499; LofC: 91900585. Papers presented at a seminar held in the Gandhian Institute of Studies, 27-29 Aug. 1987; Includes index; Includes bibliographical references.*

48 Hayek on information and socialism. Erich Streißler. *Wirt. Blät.* **39:2** 1992 pp. 258 – 283

49 Hayek's contribution to business cycle theory — a modern assessment. G.R. Steele. *Hist. Polit. Ec.* **24:2** Summer:1992 pp. 477 – 491

50 History versus equilibrium — Joan Robinson on teaching economics. Zohreh Emami. *Int. J. Soc. E.* **19:10/11/12** 1992 pp. 83 – 94

51 The ideas of Prebisch. Ronald Sprout. *CEPAL R.* **:46** 4:1992 pp. 177 – 192

52 Jacques Le Bourva's theory of endogenous credit-money. Marc Lavoie. *R. Pol. Econ.* **4:4** 1992 pp. 436 – 446

53 John Maynard Keynes. Robert Skidelsky. London: Macmillam, 1992: 731 p. *ISBN: 0333371380. Bibliography — p. 636-52.*

54 Keynes e Kahn — un mistero nella storia della macroeconomia *[In Italian]*; [Keynes and Kahn — a mystery in the history of the macroeconomy]. Robin Marris. *Riv. Pol. Ec.* **LXXXII:7** 7:1992 pp. 3 – 38

55 Keynes on economic growth, stagnation, and structural change — new light on a 55-year controversy. William Guthrie; Vincent J. Tarascio. *Hist. Polit. Ec.* **24:2** Summer:1992 pp. 381 – 412

56 Keynes on the socialization of investment. John B. Davis. *Int. J. Soc. E.* **19:10/11/12** 1992 pp. 150 – 163

57 Kuhn's paradigms and neoclassical economics. George Argyrous. *Econ. Philos.* **8:2** 10:1992 pp. 231 – 248

58 Marshall's position in the development of economic theory. G. de Vivo. *Contrib. Pol. Econ.* **11** 1992 pp. 67 – 84

59 Maynard Keynes — an economist's biography. D. E. Moggridge. London: Routledge, 1992: 941 p. *ISBN: 041505141x.*

60 Mechanistic physiology and institutional economics — Jacques Loeb and Thorstein Veblen. Charles T. Rasmussen; Rick Tilman. *Int. J. Soc. E.* **19:10/11/12** 1992 pp. 235 – 247

61 The models of Ricardo, Marx and Keynes on the evolution of capitalism; I modelli di Ricardo, Marx e Keynes sull'evoluzione del capitalismo *[Italian summary]*. Lazaros Th. Houmanidis. *Rev. Int. Sci. Ec. Com.* **XXXIX:5-6** 5-6:1992 pp. 403 – 418

62 Modern economics and the good life — a critique. Ramashray Roy. *Alternatives* **17:3** Summer:1992 pp. 371 – 403

63 Mr. Keynes and the post Keynesians — principles of macroeconomics for a monetary production economy. Fernando J. Cardim de Carvalho. Brookfield, VT.: E. Elgar, 1992: 236 p. *ISBN: 1852786531; LofC: 92001108. Includes bibliographical references.* [New directions in modern economics.]

D: History of economic thought *[Histoire de la pensée économique]* **— 20th Century [20ᵉ siècle]**

64 The Nobel Prize economics lectures — a cross section of current thinking. William J. Zahka. Brookfield, VT.: Ashgate, 1992: 168 p. *ISBN: 1856280861; LofC: 92027358.*

65 Notes on the Sraffa-Hayek exchange. Michael Syron Lawlor; Bobbie L. Horn. *R. Pol. Econ.* **4:3** 1992 pp. 317 – 340

66 On money, method and Keynes — selected essays. Victoria Chick; Sheila C. Dow *[Ed.]*; P. Arestis *[Ed.]*. New York: St. Martin's Press, 1992: 227 p. *ISBN: 0312068158; LofC: 91025838. Includes bibliographical references and index.*

67 On political economists and modern political economy — selected essays of G.C. Harcourt. Claudio Sardoni *[Ed.]*. London: Routledge, 1992: 428 p. *ISBN: 041506158x; LofC: 91040401. Includes bibliographical references and index.*

68 On the centenary of Jacob Viner's birth — a retrospective view. Arthur I. Bloomfield. *J. Econ. Lit.* **XXX:4** 12:1992 pp. 2052 – 2085

69 On trusts and technostructures — Veblen, Berle and Means, and Galbraith. Malcolm Rutherford. *Int. J. Soc. E.* **19:10/11/12** 1992 pp. 268 – 278

70 Pigou's inconsistencies or Keynes's misconceptions? Nahid Aslanbeigui. *Hist. Polit. Ec.* **24:2** Summer:1992 pp. 413 – 434

71 The problem of order in Austrian economics — Kirzner vs. Lachmann. Karen I. Vaughn. *R. Pol. Econ.* **4:3** 1992 pp. 251 – 274

72 Questions for Kaleckians. Ian Steedman. *R. Pol. Econ.* **4:2** 1992 pp. 125 – 151

73 The relevance for social economics of Alisdair MacIntyre's conception of a practice. Joe L. Wallis. *R. Soc. Econ.* **L:1** Spring:1992 pp. 2 – 23

74 Shortage of global saving or shortage of international liquidity — should we forsake the economics of Lord Keynes? Biagio Bossone. *Gior. Econ. A.* **L:7-8** 7-8:1991 pp. 317 – 346

75 Stigler's adaptable and indivisible plant and the micro/macro schism. Wesley J. Yordon. *Hist. Polit. Ec.* **24:2** Summer:1992 pp. 455 – 470

76 Symposium on the neoclassical and post Keynesian approaches to the theory of investment. Paul Davidson *[Contrib.]*; M.J. Gordon *[Contrib.]*; Douglas Vickers *[Contrib.]*; Joel Fried *[Contrib.]*; James R. Crotty *[Contrib.]*. Collection of 4 articles. **J. Post. Keyn. Ec.** , *14:4*, Summer:1992 pp. 425 – 496

77 La théorie de Marx et le mode de production partitique *[In French]*; Marxist theory and the party-controlled mode of production *[Summary]*. Ali Bayar. *Rev. Ét. Comp.* **XXIII:2-3** 6-9:1992 pp. 211 – 227

78 Thorstein Veblen and post-Darwinian economics. Geoffrey M. Hodgson. *Camb. J. Econ.* **16:3** 9:1992 pp. 285 – 302

79 The unwritten books and papers of J.M. Keynes. Rod O'Donnell. *Hist. Polit. Ec.* **24:4** Winter:1992 pp. 767 – 817

80 A Veblenian view of Minsky's financial crisis theory. Patrick R. Kelso; Barry L. Duman. *Int. J. Soc. E.* **19:10/11/12** 1992 pp. 222 – 234

81 Walter Eucken — social economist. Siegfried G. Karsten. *Int. J. Soc. E.* **19:10/11/12** 1992 pp. 111 – 125

E: Economic history — *Histoire économique*

1 Breaking away — history of economics as history of science. Margaret Schabas. *Hist. Polit. Ec.* **24:1** Spring:1992 pp. 187 – 203

2 The British economy since 1945 — economic policy and performance, 1945-1990. Alec Cairncross. Oxford: Basil Blackwell, 1992: 338 p. *ISBN: 0631182764; LofC: 91032489. Includes bibliographical references and index.* [Making contemporary Britain.]

3 The challenge of Japan before World War II and after — a study of national growth and expansion. Nazli Choucri; Robert C. North; Susumu Yamakage. London: Routledge, 1992: 320 p. *ISBN: 0044459432.*

4 Cliometria — narrazione, alchimia o scienza? *[In Italian]*; ["Cliometria" — narrative, alchemy or science?]. Alberto Baccini. *A. Fond. L. Einaudi* **XXV** 1991 pp. 213 – 237

5 Culture evolution and the process of economic evolution. Richard L. Brinkman. *Int. J. Soc. E.* **19:10/11/12** 1992 pp. 248 – 267

6 Economic interpretations of 19th century imperialism. Stuart Jones *[Contrib.]*; John Gallagher *[Contrib.]*; Ronald Robinson *[Contrib.]*; D.K. Fieldhouse *[Contrib.]*; D.C.M. Platt *[Contrib.]*; P.J. Cain *[Contrib.]*; A.G. Hopkins *[Contrib.]*. Collection of 9 articles. **S.Afr. J. Ec. Hist.** , *7:1*, 3:1992 pp. 1 – 215

E: Economic history *[Histoire économique]*

7 The economic project of the capitalist state. John W. Barchfield. *Int. J. Soc. E.* **19:7/8/9** 1992 pp. 314 – 335

8 Eli Heckscher and natural monopoly — the nightmare that never came true. Benny Carlson. *Sc. Ec. Hist. R.* **XL:3** 1992 pp. 53 – 79

9 Financial management and manipulation in the ancient world — from pre-monetary practicalities to monetary possibilities. Keith F. Sugden. *Acc. Bus. Finan. Hist.* **2:1** 3:1992 pp. 55 – 68

10 German language precursors of the new monetary economics; *[German summary]*. Tyler Cowen; Randall Kroszner. *J. Inst. Theo. Ec.* **148:3** 9:1992 pp. 387 – 410

11 Monetary problems of post-communism — lessons from the end of the Austro-Hungarian Empire; *[German summary]*; *[French summary]*; *[Spanish summary]*. Rudiger Dornbusch. *Welt.liches Arc.* **128:3** 1992 pp. 391 – 424

12 New perspectives in economic history. Fritz Hodne. *Sc. Ec. Hist. R.* **XL:1** 1992 pp. 76 – 88

13 Organizational capabilities and the economic history of the industrial enterprise. Alfred D. Chandler. *J. Econ. Pers.* **6:3** Summer:1992 pp. 79 – 100

14 Public choice analysis in historical perspective. Alan Peacock. Cambridge: Camridge University Press, 1992: 231 p. *ISBN: 0521430070.* [Raffaele Mattioli lectures.]

15 Revised real Canadian GNP estimates and Canadian economic growth, 1870-1926. Morris Altman. *R. In. Weal.* **38:4** 12:1992 pp. 455 – 473

16 Sosial'a napravlennost' èkonomicheskogo rosta *[In Russian]*; [The social management of economic growth]. E.M. Bukhval'd; Vera Aleksandrovna Pogrebinska *[Ed.]*; V.I. Maevskiĭ *[Ed.]*. Moskva: Nauka, 1990: 132 p. *ISBN: 5020120146; LofC: 91227397. rus: eng; Summary and table of contents in English; Includes bibliographical references.*

17 The structural legacy of the Soviet-type economy. Elisabeth Winiecki; Jan Winiecki. London: Centre for Research into Communist Economies, 1992: 133 p. *ISBN: 0948027177.*

18 Systemic leadership and growth waves in the long run. William R. Thompson. *Int. Stud. Q.* **36:1** 3:1992 pp. 25 – 48

F: Economic activity — *Activité économique*

F.1: Present economic conditions (since 1980) — *Conditions économiques actuelles (depuis 1980)*

Sub-divisions: Africa *[Afrique]*; Americas *[Amérique]*; Asia *[Asie]*; Europe *[Europe]*; Oceania *[Océanie]*

1 The foundations of Islamic political economy. Masudul Alam Choudhury. Basingstoke: Macmillan, 1992: 336 p. *ISBN: 0333547047.*

2 The highest stakes — the economic foundations of the next security system. Wayne Sandholtz; et al. New York: Oxford University Press, 1992: viii, 262 p. *ISBN: 0195070356; LofC: 91043270 //r92. "A Berkeley Roundtable on the International Economy (BRIE) project on economy and security."; Includes bibliographical references (p. 207-250) and index.*

3 Measures and trends in international economic power. Irene Kyriakopoulos; Donald L. Losman. *J. Soc. Pol. E.* **17:2** Summer:1992 pp. 215 – 243

4 The political economy of small tropical islands — the importance of being small. Helen M. Hintjens *[Ed.]*; Malyn Newitt *[Ed.]*. Exeter: University of Exeter Press, 1992: 247 p. *ISBN: 0859893723.*

Africa *[Afrique]*

5 Adjusting to adjustment in Zambia — women's and young peoples's responses to a changing economy. Gabriel Banda. Oxford: Oxfam, 1991: 97 p. *ISBN: 0855981792.* [Oxfam research paper. : No. 4]

6 Commanding heights and community control — new economics for a new South Africa. Patrick Bond. Johannesburg: Ravan Press, 1991: 92 p. *ISBN: 0869754076; LofC: 91193623.*

F.1: Present economic conditions (since 1980) *[Conditions économiques actuelles (depuis 1980)]* — *Africa [Afrique]*

7 The economy of Ethiopia. Keith Griffin *[Ed.]*. New York: St. Martin's Press, 1992: 312 p. *ISBN: 0312079621; LofC: 91047751. Includes bibliographical references and index.*

8 Power and profit — politics, labour and business in South Africa. Helene Perold *[Ed.]*; Matthew Kentridge *[Ed.]*; Duncan Innes *[Ed.]*. Cape Town: Oxford University Press (South Africa), 1992: 310 p. *ISBN: 0195707567.*

Americas *[Amérique]*

9 Una aplicación del modelo de dos brechas al caso Uruguayo *[In Spanish]*; [An application of the two breach model to Uruguay]. Daniel Dominioni; José Antonio Licandro. *Revis. Econ.* **V:2-3** 12-4:1990-1991 pp. 157 – 191

10 Brazil, a new regional power in the world-economy. Bertha Becker; Claudio A.G. Egler. Cambridge: Cambridge University Press, 1992: 205 p. *ISBN: 0521370086; LofC: 91027035. Includes bibliographical references.* [Geography of the world-economy.]

11 Culture of contentment. John Kenneth Galbraith. London: Sinclair-Stevenson, 1992: 195 p. *ISBN: 1856191478.*

12 Guyana — economic recession and transition; *[Spanish summary]*. Meine Pieter van Dijk. *R. Eur. Lat.am. Caribe* **:53** 12:1992 pp. 95 – 110

13 The information economy in Canada — an "input-output" approach. Yves Rabeau. Laval, Quebec: Canadian Workplace Automation Research Centre, Organizational Research Directorate, 1990: 130 leaves *ISBN: 066218646x; LofC: cn 91072445.* "CC-CWARC-DLR-8220-111-2".

14 Latin America's economy — diversity, trends, and conflicts. Eliana Cardoso; Ann Helwege. Cambridge MA.: Massachusetts Institute of Technology Press, 1992: 326 p. *ISBN: 0262031868.*

15 Power, economics, and security — the United States and Japan in focus. Henry Bienen. Boulder: Westview Press, 1992: xii, 336 p. *ISBN: 0813384389; LofC: 92005894. Includes bibliographical references and index.* [Pew studies in economics and security.]

16 Recent U.S. economic policies and the Central Caribbean economics. Addington Coppin. *Rev. Bl. Pol. Ec.* **20:4** Spring:1992 pp. 55 – 71

17 The United States economy — performance and issues. Yusuke Horiguchi. Washington, D.C: International Monetary Fund, 1992: vii, 599 p. *ISBN: 1557752311; LofC: 92016898.*

Asia *[Asie]*

18 Accumulation of financial resources in Asian economies; Accumulation de ressources financieres dans les économies asiatiques *[French summary]*. Kui Wai Li; Michael T. Skully. *Sav. Develop.* **XVI:3** 1992 pp. 225 – 241

19 Asia, its growth and agony. Toshio Watanabe. Honolulu, Hawaii: East-West Center, 1992: xiv, 175 p. (ill) *ISBN: 0866381430; LofC: 91022946. eng; Includes index.*

20 Business systems in East Asia — firms, markets and societies. Richard Whitley. London: Sage Publications, 1992: 280 p. *ISBN: 0803987390.*

21 The Central Asian economies after independence. Michael Kaser; Santosh K. Mehrotra. London: Royal Institute of International Affairs, 1992: 73 p.

22 Country survey II — Sri Lanka. Lisa Morris Grobar. *Def. Econ.* **3:2** 1992 pp. 135 – 146

23 The Iranian economy before and after the revolution. Jahangir Amuzegar. *Middle E. J.* **46:3** Summer:1992 pp. 413 – 425

24 Japan — the coming collapse. Brian Reading. London: Weidenfeld & Nicolson, 1992: 310 p. *ISBN: 0297810200.*

25 Mainland China's new economic prospects. Te-sheng Chen. *Iss. Stud.* **28:7** 7:1992 pp. 35 – 51

26 Pacific Asia in the 1990s. Masahide Shibusawa; Zakaria bin Haji Ahmad; Brian Bridges. London: Routledge, 1992: 167 p. *ISBN: 0415021731; LofC: 91012916. Published for the Royal Institute of International Affairs; Includes bibliographical references and index.*

27 The Pacific economy — growth and external stability. Mohamed Ariff. North Sydney, NSW: Allen & Unwin in association with the Pacific Trade and Development Conference Secretariat, the Australian National University, and the Institute of Strategic and International Studies (ISIS), Malaysia, 1991: xvi, 323 p. (ill) *ISBN: 1863730354; LofC: 92125272. "Papers written for the Eighteenth Pacific Trade and Development Conference, held in Kuala Lumpur on 11-14 December 1989"--Pref; Includes bibliographical references (p. 304-312) and index.*

F.1: Present economic conditions (since 1980) *[Conditions économiques actuelles (depuis 1980)]* — **Asia** *[Asie]*

28 Perestroïka au Laos. Performances et perspectives de l'économie laotienne *[In French]*; (Perestroïka in Laos. Performances and prospects for the Laotian economy); (Perestroïka en Laos. Resultados y perspectivas de la economía laociana: *Title only in Spanish);* (Perestroïka in Laos. Leistungen und Perspektiven der laotischen Wirtschaft: *Title only in German);* (Perestroïka i Laos. Dostiženija i perspektiv laosskoj ekonomiki: *Title only in Russian).* Yves Bourdet. *R. T-Monde* **XXXIII:129** 1-3:1992 pp. 181 – 208

29 Power, economics, and security — the United States and Japan in focus. Henry Bienen. Boulder: Westview Press, 1992: xii, 336 p. *ISBN: 0813384389; LofC: 92005894. Includes bibliographical references and index.* [Pew studies in economics and security.]

30 Reform and transformation in communist systems — comparative perspectives. Ilpyong L. Kim *[Ed.];* Jane Shapiro Zacek *[Ed.].* New York: Paragon House, [1991]: viii, 380 p. (maps) *ISBN: 0887020593; LofC: 91061757. Papers presented at a conference held on Oct. 27-29, 1989 in Washington, D.C; "A Washington Institute Press book."; Includes bibliographical references (p. 369-371) and index.*

31 Survey of recent developments. Hal Hill. *B. Ind. Econ. St.* **28:2** 8:1992 pp. 3 – 42

32 The Syrian economy in the 1980s. Volker Perthes. *Middle E. J.* **46:1** Winter:1992 pp. 37 – 58

33 Taiwan — from developing to mature economy. Gustav Ranis. Boulder, CO.: Westview Press, 1992: 454 p. *ISBN: 0813384362; LofC: 91044780. Includes bibliographical references and index.*

34 Thailand's turn — profile of a new dragon. Elliott Kulick; Dick Wilson. Basingstoke: Macmillan, 1992: 212 p. *ISBN: 033359276x.*

35 The West Pacific rim — an introduction. Rupert Hodder. London: Belhaven Press, 1992: 153 p. *ISBN: 1852932104; LofC: 92027957. Includes bibliographical references and index.*

36 What kind of growth? A comparative look at the Arab economies in mandatory Palestine and in the administered territories. Jacob Metzer. *Econ. Dev. Cult. Change* **40:4** 7:1992 pp. 843 – 865

37 Women in the face of change — the Soviet Union, Eastern Europe, and China. Shirin Rai *[Ed.];* Hilary Pilkington *[Ed.];* Annie Phizacklea *[Ed.].* New York, NY.: Routledge, 1992: 227 p. *ISBN: oc25008623; LofC: 91044517. Includes bibliographical references and index.*

Europe *[Europe]*

38 Avoiding the worst — Northern Ireland in recession. Graham Gudgin; Geraldine O'Shea. *Irish Bank. Rev.* Winter:1992 pp. 17 – 32

39 Balance económico de las autonomías *[In Spanish];* [Economic aspects of self-government]. Julio Alcaide Inchausti *[Contrib.];* Gervasio Cordero Mestanza *[Contrib.];* Jean-François Drevet *[Contrib.];* Juan Ramón Cuadrado Roura *[Contrib.];* Luis Suárez-Villa *[Contrib.];* Antonio Cutanda *[Contrib.];* Joaquina Paricio *[Contrib.];* Ginés de Rus *[Contrib.];* José Luis Calvo Palacios *[Contrib.];* Angel Pueyo Campos *[Contrib.] and others. Collection of 26 articles.* **Pap. Econ. Esp.** , *51,* 1992 pp. 2 – 397

40 Bundesrepublik Deutschland — Konjunktur im Banne von Verteilungskämpfen *[In German];* [Federal Republic of Germany — economy in the grip of a conflict over distribution of the burdens] *[Summary].* Alfred Boss; Malte Fischer; Enno Langfeldt; Eckhard Nitschke; Klaus-Werner Schatz; Peter Trapp. *Weltwirt.* **:2** 1992 pp. 134 – 152

41 Centre and periphery — the Baltic states in search of economic independence. Philip Hanson. *J. Interd. Ec.* **4:3** 1992 pp. 249 – 267

42 Centre periphery relations in Czechoslovakia. Martin Myant. *J. Interd. Ec.* **4:3** 1992 pp. 269 – 280

43 Convergence and system change — the convergence hypothesis in the light of transition in Eastern Europe. Bruno Dallago *[Ed.];* Horst Dieter Brezinski *[Ed.];* Wladimir Andreff *[Ed.].* Aldershot, Hants: Dartmouth, [1991]: xii, 255 p. (ill) *ISBN: 1855212188. Includes bibliographical references and index.*

44 Eastern Europe and the former Soviet Union — economic change, social welfare and aid. Charlotte Benson; Edward J. Clay. London: Overseas Development Institute, 1992: 77 p. *ISBN: 0850031869.*

45 Economia e società in Albania *[In Italian];* [Economy and society in Albania]. L. Perrone. *Crit. Sociol.* **103** Autunno:1992 pp. 155 – 173

46 Economia irregolare e sviluppo economico in Italia e Spagna *[In Italian];* [Irregular economy and economic development in Italy and Spain]. Bruno Dallago. *Econ. Ban.* **3** 1992 pp. 311 – 346

F.1: Present economic conditions (since 1980) *[Conditions économiques actuelles (depuis 1980)]* — *Europe [Europe]*

47 Economic legacy, 1979-1992. Jonathan Michie *[Ed.]*. London: Academic Press, 1992: 365 p. *ISBN: 0124940617.*

48 Economic survey of the Baltic states. Brian van Arkadie; Mats Karlsson. London: Pinter, 1992: 344 p. *ISBN: 1855670321.*

49 Economic transition in Eastern Europe — paying the price for freedom. Leif Rosenberger. *E. Eur. Quart.* **XXVI:3** Fall:1992 pp. 261 – 278

50 Economic transition in Eastern Germany. Rudiger Dornbusch; Holger Wolf. *Brookings P.* :**1** 1992 pp. 235 – 261

51 L'économie italienne — les paradoxes d'une réussite *[In French]*; [The Italian economy — the paradoxes of a success]. Janine Menet-Genty *[Ed.]*. Paris: La Documentation française, 1992: 268 p. *ISBN: 2110027142.* [Les études de la Documentation française.]

52 The economy of Poland. Mark E. Schaffer. London: London School of Economics and Political Science. Centre for Economic Performance, 1992: 78 p.

53 The economy of united Germany — colossus at the crossroads. W.R. Smyser. London: C. Hurst, 1992: 273 p. *ISBN: 1850651531.*

54 The European economy. David A. Dyker *[Ed.]*. London: Longman, 1992: 364 p. *ISBN: 0582059194; LofC: 92-10139. Includes index.*

55 Finance in Eastern Europe. David Gowland *[Ed.]*. Aldershot: Dartmouth, 1992: 134 p. *ISBN: 185521251x.*

56 France's overseas frontier — Départements et territoires d'outre-mer. Robert Aldrich; John Connell. Cambridge: Cambridge University Press, 1992: x, 357 p. *ISBN: 0521390613; LofC: 91009067. Includes bibliographical references (p. [299]-335) and index.*

57 From stagnation to catastroika — commentaries on the Soviet economy, 1983-1991. Philip Hanson. New York: Praeger, 1992: xvii, 255 p. *ISBN: 0275942554; LofC: 91044215 //r922. Includes bibliographical references and index.* [The Washington papers.]

58 Inside the Cyprus miracle — the labours of an embattled mini-economy. Demetrios Christodoulou. Minneapolis: Iniversity of Minnesota, 1992: 352 p. [Minnesota Mediterranean and East European monographs.]

59 Is Ireland a Third World country? Therese Cahery *[Ed.]*. Belfast: Beyond the Pale Publications, 1992: 116 p. *ISBN: 0951422928. Report of a conference held in the Teachers' Club, Dublin on 20th April 1991, organised by the Centre for Research and Documentation, Belfast.*

60 Issues in contemporary economics — volume 5. The Greek economy — economic policy for the 1990s. Thanos Skouras. Basingstoke: Macmillan, [1992]: 201 p. *ISBN: 0333537262. International Economic Association. World Congress 9th. Athens, Greece 1989.* [IEA Conference volume series.]

61 Lutanja jugoslavenske privrede *[In Serbo-Croatian]*; The vagaries of the Yugoslav economy *[Summary]*; Заблуждения югославской экономики *[Russian summary]*. Banko Horvat. *Ekon. Preg.* **43:7-8-9** 1992 pp. 550 – 577

62 The market shock — an AGENDA for socio-economic reconstruction of Central and Eastern Europe. Egon Matzner *[Ed.]*; Gernot Grabher *[Ed.]*; J. A. Kregel *[Ed.]*. Vienna: Austrian Academy of Sciences, Research Institute for Socio-Economics, 1992: 132 p. *ISBN: 0472082043.*

63 MONA — a quarterly model of the Danish economy. Anders Møller Christensen; Dan Knudsen. *Econ. Model.* **9:1** 1:1992 pp. 10 – 74

64 A more perfect union — Britain and the new Europe. David Miliband *[Ed.]*. London: Institute for Public Policy Research, 1992: 153 p. *ISBN: 1872452531.*

65 MORKMON II — the Nederlandsche Bank's quarterly model of the Netherlands economy. M.M.G. Fase; P. Kramer; W.C. Boeschoten. *Econ. Model.* **9:2** 4:1992 pp. 146 – 204

66 The nature and causes of the Great Recession, 1971-199? Donald M. Ferguson. Birmingham: Wake Green Publications, 1992: 113 p.

67 Podmínky a tendence vývoje Čs. ekonomiky v roce 1991 *[In Czech]*; (Development conditions and tendencies of the Czechoslovak economy in the year 1991); (Die Bedingungen und Tendenzen der Entwicklung der tschechoslowakischen Wirtschaft im Jahre 1991: *Title only in German*). Slavoj Czesaný. *Nár. Hosp.* :**1** 1992 pp. 3 – 8

68 The post-Soviet economy — Soviet and Western perspectives. Anders Aslund *[Ed.]*. London: Pinter Publishers, 1992: 222 p. *ISBN: 1855670399.*

69 Reform and transformation in communist systems — comparative perspectives. Ilpyong L. Kim *[Ed.]*; Jane Shapiro Zacek *[Ed.]*. New York: Paragon House, [1991]: viii, 380 p.

F.1: Present economic conditions (since 1980) *[Conditions économiques actuelles (depuis 1980)]* **— Europe** *[Europe]*
(maps) *ISBN: 0887020593; LofC: 91061757. Papers presented at a conference held on Oct. 27-29, 1989 in Washington, D.C; "A Washington Institute Press book."; Includes bibliographical references (p. 369-371) and index.*

70 La regione metropolitana dello Stretto di Messina — evoluzione e caratteristiche socio-economiche *[In Italian]*; [The metropolitan region of the Straits of Messina. Socioeconomic evolution anad characteristics]. Ornello Vitali *[Ed.]*. Napoli: Edizioni Scientifiche Italiane, 1991: 128 p. *ISBN: 8871042298.* [Pubblicazioni del progetto strategico.]

71 Relative sensitivities of the Hungarian economy to internal and external shocks. J. Lew Silver; Jean Tesche. *S. Econ. J.* **59:2** 10:1992 pp. 210 – 231

72 Réunification allemande et croissance européenne — un espoir déçu? *[In French]*; German reunification and European growth — excessive expectations *[Summary]*. Hélène Harasty; Jean le Dem. *Obser. Diag. Econ.* **:39** 1:1992 pp. 195 – 218

73 La «révolution des prix» et l'effondrement de la production dans le secteur d'Etat en Pologne, 1990-1991 *[In French]*; The «price revolution» and the collapse of production in the state sector in Poland, 1990-1991 *[Summary]*. Adam Lipowski; Krystyna Szymkiewicz. *Rev. Ét. Comp.* **23:1** 1992 pp. 123 – 136

74 Russian Federation. J. C. Odling-Smee *[Ed.]*. Washington, D.C.: International Monetary Fund, 1992: 115 p. *ISBN: 1557752567.* [Economic review.]

75 Schattenwirtschaft in Ungarn — Geschöpf der alten oder Hoffnung der neuen Ökonomie? *[In German]*; [Informal economy in Hungary. Creation of the old or hope of new economies?]. István Gábor. *Transit* **:3** Winter:1992 pp. 159 – 176

76 Shock-therapy versus gradual change — economic problems and policies in Central and Eastern Europe (1989-1991). A. Köves. *Acta Oecon.* **44:1-2** 1992 pp. 13 – 36

77 The state of the economy 1992. Giles Keating; et al. London: Institute of Economic Affairs, 1992: 160 p. *ISBN: 0255363044.*

78 The UK economy. Nigel Pain. *Natl. Inst. Econ. R.* **:140** 5:1992 pp. 8 – 25

79 I vincoli di Maastricht per le imprese del Mezzogiorno *[In Italian]*; The constraints set by the Maastricht Treaty on the enterprises of the Mezzogiorno *[Summary]*. Massimo Lo Cicero. *Ras. Econ.* **LVI:3** 7-9:1992 pp. 637 – 659

80 What went wrong in Germany after unification? Peter Neckermann. *E. Eur. Quart.* **XXVI:4** Winter:1992 pp. 447 – 469

81 Women in the face of change — the Soviet Union, Eastern Europe, and China. Shirin Rai *[Ed.]*; Hilary Pilkington *[Ed.]*; Annie Phizacklea *[Ed.]*. New York, NY.: Routledge, 1992: 227 p. *ISBN: oc25008623; LofC: 91044517. Includes bibliographical references and index.*

82 Yugoslavia — a peripheral tragedy. David A. Dyker. *J. Interd. Ec.* **4:3** 1992 pp. 281 – 293

Oceania *[Océanie]*

83 Advancing into the 21st century — visions and challenges facing the downunder economy. Wolfgang Kasper. *Aust. Ec. Rev.* *4th quarter:1992* pp. 51 – 64

84 Assessing the impact of US macroeconomic policies and inflation rates on the Australian economy. Richard C.K. Burdekin. *Econ. Rec.* **68:200** 3:1992 pp. 16 – 30

85 The Australian economy in the 1990s — can it adjust to free trade? David Hale. *Ec. Pap. Aust.* **11:2** 6:1992 pp. 1 – 12

86 A briefing on the New Zealand macroeconomy 1960-1990. Paul Dalziel; R. G. Lattimore (Ralph Gerard). Auckland: Oxford University Press, 1991: x, 61 p. *ISBN: 0195582373; LofC: gb 92024983.*

87 Controlling interests — business, the state and society in New Zealand. John Deeks *[Ed.]*; Nick Perry *[Ed.]*. Auckland, NZ.: Auckland University Press, 1992: 246 p. *ISBN: 1869400666. Includes bibliographic references.*

88 Family economy. Kerreen M. Reiger. Ringwood, Victoria, Australia: McPhee Gribble, 1991: vii, 70 p. (ill) *ISBN: 0869142305.* [Themes in Australian economic and social history.]

89 Immigration and the Australian economy. William Foster; Lyle Baker. Canberra: Australian Government Publishing Service, 1991: xvi, 151 p. (ill) *ISBN: 0644147865.*

90 The Pacific economy — growth and external stability. Mohamed Ariff. North Sydney, NSW: Allen & Unwin in association with the Pacific Trade and Development Conference Secretariat, the Australian National University, and the Institute of Strategic and International Studies (ISIS), Malaysia, 1991: xvi, 323 p. (ill) *ISBN: 1863730354;*

F.1: Present economic conditions (since 1980) *[Conditions économiques actuelles (depuis 1980)]* — *Oceania [Océanie]*

LofC: 92125272. *"Papers written for the Eighteenth Pacific Trade and Development Conference, held in Kuala Lumpur on 11-14 December 1989"--Pref; Includes bibliographical references (p. 304-312) and index.*

91 The performance and prospects of the Pacific Island economies in the world economy. A.P. Thirlwall. Honolulu: East-West Center, Pacific Islands Development Program, 1991: 66p. *ISBN: 0866381309.*

92 The Western Samoan economy — prospects for recovery and long-term growth. Te'o Ian Fairbairn. Canberra: Australian Government Publishing Service, 1991: 57 p. *ISBN: 0644221089. At head of t.p.* — *Australian International Development Assistance Bureau.* [International development issues. : No. 7]

93 Where to now? New Zealand in the 1990s. Judith A. Davey; Jane Westaway. Wellington: New Zealand Planning Council, [1990]: 78 p. (ill) *ISBN: 0908601735; LofC: 91129951. With illustrations by Isabel Lowe; Includes bibliographical references.*

F.2: National income and capital (estimation and forecasting) — *Revenu capital national (évaluation et prévision)*

Sub-divisions: Forecasts *[Prévisions]*

1 Conditional asymmetries in real GNP — a seminonparametric approach. Allan D. Brunner. *J. Bus. Econ. Stat.* **10:1** 1:1992 pp. 65 – 72

2 The consequences of the 1976-79 coffee boom on the Tanzania economy — a test of the Dutch disease model. Flora Mndeme Musonda; Eliab Luvanda. *E. Afr. Econ. Rev.* **7:2** 12:1991 pp. 1 – 16

3 Dynamic efficiency and capital accumulation. G. Lang. *Eur. J. Pol. Ec.* **8:2** 5:1992 pp. 153 – 174

4 Explicando las fluctuaciones del producto en la Argentina *[In Spanish]*; Explaining output fluctuations in Argentina *[Summary]*. Frederico Sturzenegger. *Económica Arg* **XXXV:1-2** 1989 pp. 101 – 152

5 Foreign aid, capital accumulation, and developing country resource extraction. J. Strand. *J. Dev. Econ.* **38:1** 1:1992 pp. 147 – 164

6 Labor costs and manufactured exports in developing countries — an econometric analysis. L.A. Riveros. *World Dev.* **20:7** 7:1992 pp. 991 – 1008

7 Modern sector enlargement or traditional sector enrichment? GNP effects with induced migration. G.S. Fields. *J. Pop. Ec.* **5:2** 1992 pp. 101 – 112

8 A nemzetijövedelem-számítás története Magyarországon Kautz Gyulától napjainkig *[In Hungarian]*; History of national income computations in Hungary *[Summary]*. János Árvay. *Közg. Sz.* **XXXIX** 12:1992 pp. 1126 – 1143

9 Nonstationarity and level shifts with an application to purchasing power parity. Pierre Perron; Timothy J. Vogelsang. Princeton, NJ.: Econometric Research Program, Princeton University, 1991: 27, 3, 17 p. [Research memorandum.]

10 Public expenditure and national income causality — further evidence on the role of omitted variables. Syed M. Ahsan; Andy C.C. Kwan; Balbir S. Sahni. *S. Econ. J.* **58:3** 1:1992 pp. 623 – 634

11 The real domestic product of Indonesia, 1880-1989. Pierre van der Eng. *Expl. Ec. His.* **29:3** 7:1992 pp. 343 – 373

12 The relative importance of permanent and transitory components — identification and some theoretical bounds. Danny Quah. *Econometrica* **60:1** 1:1992 pp. 107 – 118

13 The role of international trade in the convergence of per capita GDP in the OECD — 1950-85. Farhad Rassekh. *Int. Econ. J.* **6:4** Winter:1992 pp. 1 – 15

14 Scenari, alternative e opportunità economiche dell'Amazzonia *[In Italian]*; [Scenario — economic alternatives and opportunities for the Amazon]. Sergio C. Buarque. *Civitas* **XLIII** 9-10:1992 pp. 55 – 74

15 Spill-over effects of supply-side changes in a two-country economy with capital accumulation. Yoshiyasu Ono; Akihisa Shibata. *J. Int. Econ.* **33:1/2** 8:1992 pp. 127 – 146

16 Why is the U.S. current account deficit so large? Evidence from vector autoregressions. Daniel David Bachman. *S. Econ. J.* **59:2** 10:1992 pp. 232 – 240

F.2: National income and capital (estimation and forecasting) *[Revenu capital national (évaluation et prévision)]*

17 Zum Zusammenhang zwischen Geldmenge und Bruttoinlandsprodukt in der Bundesrepublik Deutschland *[In German]*; [On the connection between the amount of money and the gross national product in the Federal Republic of Germany] *[Summary]*. Harmen Lehment. *Weltwirt.* :**2** 1992 pp. 153 – 171

Forecasts *[Prévisions]*

18 Co-integration, error correction and improved medium-term regional VAR forecasting. G.L. Shoesmith. *J. Forecast.* **11:2** 2:1992 pp. 91 – 110

19 Conservatism and consensus-seeking among economic forecasters. R. Batchelor; P. Dua. *J. Forecast.* **11:2** 2:1992 pp. 169 – 181

20 Efficient forecasts of measurement errors? Some evidence for revisions to United Kingdom GDP growth rates. K.D. Patterson; S.M. Heravi. *Manch. Sch. E.* **LX:3** 9:1992 pp. 249 – 263

21 Forecasting the federal budget with time-series models. H. Baghestani; R. McNown. *J. Forecast.* **11:2** 2:1992 pp. 127 – 140

22 The Liverpool forecast. Jonathan Riley. *Q. Econ. Bull.* **13:2** 6:1992 pp. 7 – 23

23 Market and survey forecasts of the three-month Treasury-bill rate. R.W. Hafer; Scott E. Hein; MacDonald S. Scott. *J. Bus.* **65:1** 1:1992 pp. 123 – 138

24 A mixture-model approach to combining forecasts. James P. LeSage; Michael Magura. *J. Bus. Econ. Stat.* **10:4** 10:1992 pp. 445 – 452

25 A model for medium term projection of the Trinidad and Tobago economy; *[French summary]*; *[Spanish summary]*. E.B.A. St. Cyr; A. Charles. *Soc. Econ. S.* **41:1** 3:1992 pp. 189 – 214

26 Mosaïque — la nouvelle version du modèle OFCE trimestriel *[In French]*; Mosaïque — the OFCE quarterly macroeconomic model *[Summary]*. Alain Gubian; Gérard Cornilleau; Catherine Mathieu; Marie-Ange Véganzones. *Obser. Diag. Econ.* :**40** 4:1992 pp. 141 – 200

27 On the problem of forecasting prior to "price" control and decontrol. N.S. Revankar. *J. Forecast.* **11:1** 1:1992 pp. 1 – 16

28 Predicting the unpredictable? Science and guesswork in financial market forecasting. T C. Mills. London: Institute of Economic Affairs, 1992: 46 p. *ISBN: 0255363109.* [IEA Occasional Paper.]

29 The relationship between forecast dispersion and forecast uncertainty — evidence from a survey data-arch model. R.W. Rich; J.E. Raymond; J.S. Butler. *J. Appl. Econ.* **7:2** 4-6:1992 pp. 131 – 148

30 The REMI economic-demographic forecasting and simulation model. George I. Treyz; Dan S. Rickman; Gang Shao. *Int. Reg. Sci. R.* **14:3** 1992 pp. 221 – 254

31 Technological forecasting with nonlinear models. J.C. Lee; K.W. Lu; S.C. Horng. *J. Forecast.* **11:3** 4:1992 pp. 195 – 206

F.3: Structures — *Structures*

F.3.1: Specific aspects — *Aspects spécifiques*

F.3.1.1: Geographical aspects — *Aspects géographiques*

Sub-divisions: Regional economics *[Économie régionale]*; Rural economics *[Économie rurale]*; Urban economics *[Économie urbaine]*

1 Applications of the expansion method. John Paul Jones *[Ed.]*; Emilio Casetti *[Ed.]*. London: Routledge, 1992: 375 p. *ISBN: 0415034949; LofC: 91011631. Includes bibliographical references and index.*

2 De bedrijfslokalisatie vanuit een transporteconomisch oogpunt *[In Flemish]*; Business location from a transport economic viewpoint *[Summary]*. Eddy Van de Voorde; Frank Witlox. *Econ. Soc. Tidj.* **46:2** 6:1992 pp. 255 – 282

3 The changing corporate head office and its spatial implications. Asu Aksoy; Neill Marshall. *Reg. Stud.* **26:2** 1992 pp. 149 – 162

4 Competing structural and institutional influences on the geography of production in Europe. A. Amin; A. Malmberg. *Envir. Plan.A.* **24:3** 3:1992 pp. 401 – 416

5 Conjectural variations and location theory. M.L. Greenhut; George Norman. *J. Econ. Sur.* **6:4** 1992 pp. 299 – 320

6 "Costs of non-Europe" and industrial location in Portugal and Spain. Christina Corado. *Economia [Lisbon]* **XV:3** 10:1991 pp. 411 – 444

7 Decentralized decision-making and capacitated facility location. G.R. Mateus; H.P.L. Luna. *Ann. Reg. Sci.* **26:4** 1992 pp. 361 – 377

8 Economic incentives in the subsistence areas of South Africa and the need for reform. R.A.A. Baber; W.L. Nieuwoudt. *Develop. S. Afr.* **9:2** 5:1992 pp. 153 – 168

9 An economic perspective on the north.*Prog. Plan.* **37:1** 1992 pp. 57 – 74

10 The economics of coastal management — a manual of benefit assessment techniques. Edmund C. Penning-Rowsell; et al. London: Belhaven Press, 1992: 380 p. *ISBN: 1852931612; LofC: 92033604. Includes bibliographical references and index.*

11 Emergence of a new oil palm belt in Ghana. Edwin Gyasi. *J. Econ. Soc. Geogr.* **83:1** 1992 pp. 39 – 49

12 Facility location modeling. John Current *[Ed.]*; Samuel Ratick *[Ed.]*; Richard L. Church *[Contrib.]*; Rhonda R. Davis *[Contrib.]*; Vladimir Marianov *[Contrib.]*; Charles ReVelle *[Contrib.]*; Jeffrey P. Osleeb *[Contrib.]*; Sara McLafferty *[Contrib.]*; Jean-Claude Thill *[Contrib.]*; Tan Miller *[Contrib.] and others. Collection of 9 articles.* **Pap. Reg. Sci.** , *71:3,* 7:1992 pp. 193 – 352

13 Firm mobility and firm location; *[French summary]*. Simon P. Anderson; André de Palma; Gap-Seon Hong. *Can. J. Econ.* **XXV:1** 2:1992 pp. 76 – 88

14 Geographical shifts in the competitive strength of mineral production since 1960, and their causes. Phillip Crowson. *Res. Pol.* **18:4** 12:1992 pp. 252 – 266

15 The geography of Europe's futures. Ian Masser; Ove Sviden; Michael Wegener. London: Belhaven Press, 1992: 225 p. *ISBN: 1852932325.*

16 The geography of housing wealth and inheritance in Britain. C. Hamnett. *Geogr. J.* **158:3** 11:1992 pp. 307 – 321

17 Income distribution and the residential density gradient. Alex Anas; Ikki Kim. *J. Urban Ec.* **31:2** 3:1992 pp. 164 – 180

18 Industrial districts — old wine in new bottles?; *[French summary]*; *[German summary]*. Bennett Harrison. *Reg. Stud.* **26:5** 1992 pp. 469 – 484

19 International trade with lumpy countries. Paul N. Courant; Alan V. Deardorff. *J. Polit. Ec.* **100:1** 2:1992 pp. 198 – 210

20 The lessons of airline regulation and deregulation — will we make the same mistakes in space? David G. Monk. *J. Air Law Comm.* **57:3** Spring:1992 pp. 715 – 754

21 Local economic development in Michigan — a reliance on the supply side. Laura A. Reese. *Econ. Devel. Q.* **6:4** 11:1992 pp. 383 – 393

22 Location and change — perspectives on economic geography. Michael Healey; Brian W Ilbery. Oxford: OUP, 1990: 381 p. *ISBN: 0198741553.*

23 The location of employment in high-technology manufacturing in Great Britain. Bernard Fingleton. *Urban Stud.* **29:8** 12:1992 pp. 1265 – 1276

24 Locational determinants of Japanese manufacturing start-ups in the United States. Douglas P. Woodward. *S. Econ. J.* **58:3** 1:1992 pp. 690 – 708

25 Lokalisatie na 1992 *[In Flemish]*; Localization after 1992 *[Summary]*. Ben Smeenk. *Econ. Soc. Tidj.* **46:2** 6:1992 pp. 299 – 317

F.3.1.1: Geographical aspects *[Aspects géographiques]*

26 Manufacturing plants in Ohio — spatial changes, 1978-1987. Howard A. Stafford; Qiutao Wu. *Econ. Devel. Q.* **6:3** 8:1992 pp. 273 – 285

27 A model of growth and migration; *[French summary]*. Gerhard Glomm. *Can. J. Econ.* **XXV:4** 11:1992 pp. 901 – 922

28 A model of rural-urban conflict in developing countries. Robert Lensink. *Economist [Leiden]* **140:1** 1992 pp. 83 – 108

29 Modern transport geography. R.D. Knowles *[Ed.]*; B.S. Hoyle *[Ed.]*. London: Belhaven Press, 1992: 276 p. *ISBN: 1852931574; LofC: 91048136.*

30 Les mutations du dispositif territorial de l'industrie électronique française *[In French]*; Changes in the territorial pattern of France's electronics industry *[Summary]*. Pierre Beckouche. *Espace Géogr.* **XXI:3** 1992 pp. 253 – 264

31 The new industrial spaces — locational logic of a new production era? Nick Henry. *Int. J. Urban* **16:3** 9:1992 pp. 375 – 396

32 On the efficiency of location decision under discriminatory pricing. M.P. Espinosa. *Int. J. Ind. O.* **10:2** 6:1992 pp. 273 – 296

33 Optimal timing and location in competitive markets. Avijit Ghosh; Vikas Tibrewala. *Geogr. Anal.* **24:4** 10:1992 pp. 317 – 334

34 Optimum producer-service location. B. Lentnek; A. MacPherson; D. Phillips. *Envir. Plan.A.* **24:4** 4:1992 pp. 467 – 479

35 The physical environment, accounting and local development. Rob Gary; Sheila Morrison. *Local. Ec.* **6:4** 2:1992 pp. 336 – 350

36 The potential contribution of Ireland's Atlantic Arc to future economic development. Bernadette Andreosso. *Administration* **40:2** Summer:1992 pp. 108 – 124

37 La production des taureaux de combat, une économie de l'image et des identités locales *[In French]*; [The production of fighting bulls — an economy of image and local identities] *[Summary]*. F. Saumade. *R.E.M.* **40:158** 2:1992 pp. 27 – 43

38 Production-location decision and free entry oligopoly. Chao-Cheng Mai; Hong Hwang. *J. Urban Ec.* **31:2** 3:1992 pp. 252 – 271

39 Les Pyrénées-Orientales — une croissance descrète et remarquable *[In French]*; [The Pyrénées-Orientales — a discreet and remarkable growth]. J. Rouzier; S. Michel. *R.E.M.* **40:1** 1992 pp. 3 – 14

40 The Roepke lecture in economic geography — the collective order of flexible production agglomerations — lessons for local economic development policy and strategic choice. Allen J. Scott. *Econ. Geogr.* **68:3** 7:1992 pp. 219 – 233

41 The role of large producers in industrial districts — a case study of high technology systems houses in southern California. Allen J. Scott. *Reg. Stud.* **26:3** 1992 pp. 265 – 276

42 The role of local sector studies — the development of sector studies in the UK. Graham Haughton; Kevin Thomas. *Local. Ec.* **7:2** 8:1992 pp. 100 – 113

43 Site selection problem and quasi-satisficing decision rule. Jacek Malczewski. *Geogr. Anal.* **24:4** 10:1992 pp. 299 – 316

44 Space and applied econometrics. Luc Anselin *[Ed.]*; H.H. Kelejian *[Contrib.]*; D.P. Robinson *[Contrib.]*; C. Nass *[Contrib.]*; D. Garfinkle *[Contrib.]*; D.A. Griffith *[Contrib.]*; D. Bolduc *[Contrib.]*; G. Santarossa *[Contrib.]*; R. Laferrière *[Contrib.]*; T.H. Barringer *[Contrib.] and others. Collection of 12 articles.* **Reg. Sci. Urb. Econ.** , *22:3*, 9:1992 pp. 307 – 536

45 The spatial linkage patterns of Israeli firms — implications for regional industrial development. Daniel Felsenstein. *J. Econ. Soc. Geogr.* **83:2** 1992 pp. 105 – 119

46 Stalking local economic development benefits — a review of evaluation issues. Robert P. Giloth. *Econ. Devel. Q.* **6:1** 2:1992 pp. 80 – 90

47 An uncertain future — a critique of post-Keynesian economic geographies. Peter Sunley. *Prog. H. Geog.* **16:1** 3:1992 pp. 58 – 70

48 Weight variations within a set of demand points, and location-allocation issues — a case studies of public libraries. H. Beguin; I. Thomas; D. Vandenbussche. *Envir. Plan.A.* **24:12** 12:1992 pp. 1769 – 1779

49 Where are they now? Some changes in firms located in UK science parks in 1986. David Storey; Adam Strange. *New Tech. Work. Empl.* **7:1** Spring:1992 pp. 15 – 28

F.3.1.1: Geographical aspects *[Aspects géographiques]* —

Regional economics *[Économie régionale]*

50 Approche dynamique du développement des régions françaises *[In French]*; [A dynamic approach to development in French regions]. V. Thireau. *R.E.M.* **40:1** 1992 pp. 59 – 76

51 Les causalités circulaires cumulatives. Le cas de l'Espagne — 1955-1987 *[In French]*; [Circular and cumulative causation — Spain 1955-1987]. J.M. Reyjulia. *R.E.M.* **40:1** 1992 pp. 77 – 96

52 Cities, regions and the new Europe — the global-local interplay and spatial development strategies. Michael Dunford *[Ed.]*; Grigorio Kafkaslas *[Ed.]*. London: Belhaven Press, 1992: 339 p. *ISBN: 185293221x.*

53 Competitiveness and regional development — the case of Northern Ireland. D.M.W.N. Hitchens; J.E. Birnie; K. Wagner. *Reg. Stud.* **26:1** 1992 pp. 106 – 114

54 Decentralisation of regional development policies in the Netherlands — a new type of state intervention? Ingeborg Tömmel. *W. Eur. Pol.* **15:2** 4:1992 pp. 107 – 125

55 Desconcentración, tecnología y localización industrial en México — los parques y ciudades industriales, 1953-1988 *[In Spanish]*; [Decentralization, technology and location of industry in Mexico — industrial parks and cities, 1953-1988]. Gustavo Garza. México, D.F.: El Colegio de México, 1992: 457 p. *ISBN: 968 12 0499 9.*

56 Development issues and strategies in the new Europe — local, regional and interregional perspectives. Markku Tykkylainen *[Ed.]*. Aldershot: Avebury, 1992: 227 p. *ISBN: 1856283267.*

57 District-level economic linkages in Kenya — evidence based on a small regional social accounting matrix. B.D. Lewis; E. Thorbecke. *World Dev.* **20:6** 6:1992 pp. 881 – 898

58 Economic impact of growth management policies surrounding the Chesapeake Bay. W. Patrick Beaton; Marcus Pollock. *Land Econ.* **68:4** 11:1992 pp. 434 – 453

59 Economic regionalization in Western Europe — Asia-Pacific economics (macroeconomic core — microeconomic optimization). M. Dutta. *Am. Econ. Rev.* **82:2** 5:1992 pp. 67 – 73

60 Estimación de la matriz de insumo-producto del estado de Nuevo León, México *[In Spanish]*; [An estimation of the consumption-production function for the state of Nuevo Leon, Mexico]. Jaime Behar. *Rev. Int.Am. Plan.* **XXV:97** 1-3:1992 pp. 104 – 123

61 Existenzgründung zwischen Elbe und Oder — Kapital - Arbeit - Leistung *[In German]*; [The founding of existence between the Elbe and Oder, capital, work, production]. Franz Käppeler. Düsseldorf: VDI-Verlag, 1991: 203 p. *ISBN: 3184010899.* [Sonderpublikation der VDI-Nachrichten.]

62 Foreign trade and regional development in China. C. Cindy Fan. *Geogr. Anal.* **24:3** 7:1992 pp. 240 – 256

63 L'intervento straordinario nel Mezzogiorno e i modelli di sviluppo regionali — il caso della Sardegna *[In Italian]*; [Regional development models and large-scale intervention in Southern Italy — the case of Sardinia]. Beniamino Moro. *Ras. Econ.* **LV:4** 10-12:1992 pp. 925 – 948

64 Local development and forms of regulation — fragmentation and hierarchy of spatial policies in Greece. P. Getimis; G. Kafkaslas. *Geoforum* **23:1** 1992 pp. 73 – 84

65 The new regionalism — developing countries and regional collaborative competition. Rebecca Morales; Carlos Quandt. *Int. J. Urban* **16:3** 9:1992 pp. 462 – 475

66 On the determination of regional base and regional base multipliers. S.J. Brown; N.E. Coulson; R.F. Engle. *Reg. Sci. Urb. Econ.* **22:4** 11:1992 pp. 619 – 636

67 An optimisation towards spatio-functional decentralisation and area development. Surendra Singh. *Ind. J. Reg. Sci.* **XXIV:2** 1992 pp. 53 – 63

68 Pathways to industrialization and regional development. Michael Storper *[Ed.]*; Allen John Scott *[Ed.]*. London: Routledge, 1992: 405 p. *ISBN: 041508752x; LofC: 92010397. Includes bibliographical references and index.*

69 La planification régionale de développement dans les économies périphériques *[In French]*; [Regional development planning in the peripheral economies]. Mieczysław Szostak. *Econ. Papers [Warsaw]* **18** 1992 pp. 152 – 176

70 Politiche economiche nazionale e disoccupazione nel Mezzogiorno *[In Italian]*; [National economic policies in Southern Italy]. Vincenzo Santandrea. *Ras. Econ.* **LVI:2** 4-6:1992 pp. 483 – 498

71 Raumwirtschaftspolitische Ansätze in den Wachstumsländern Ost-/Südostasiens. Fallbeispiele — Südkorea, Malaysia, Thailand *[In German]*; [Approaches to regional planning policy in East/Southeast Asia's rapidly developing countries. The cases of South Korea, Malaysia and Thailand]. Ludwig Schätzl. *Geogr. Rund.* **44:1** 1:1992 pp. 18 – 24

F,3.1.1: Geographical aspects *[Aspects géographiques]* — **Regional economics** *[Économie régionale]*

72 Regional and urban restructuring in Europe. Jorge Gaspar *[Contrib.]*; Arie Shachar *[Contrib.]*; Daniel Felsenstein *[Contrib.]*; William J. Coffey *[Contrib.]*; Antoine S. Bailly *[Contrib.]*; György Enyedi *[Contrib.]*; Chris Jensen-Butler *[Contrib.]*; Tomaso Pompili *[Contrib.]*; William F. Lever *[Contrib.]*; Joan-Eugeni Sánchez *[Contrib.]* *and others. Collection of 12 articles.* **Urban Stud.** , *29:6*, 8:1992 pp. 827 – 1011

73 Regional development and contemporary industrial response — extending flexible specialisation. Huib Ernste *[Ed.]*; Verena Meier *[Ed.]*. London: Belhaven Press, 1992: 296 p. *ISBN: 1852932147; LofC: 91044616. Includes bibliographical references and index.*

74 Regional development in a boom and bust petroleum economy — Indonesia since 1970. Hal Hill. *Econ. Dev. Cult. Change* **40:2** 1:1992 pp. 351 – 380

75 Regional development in the 1990s — the British Isles in transition. Peter Townroe *[Ed.]*; Ron Martin *[Ed.]*. London: Jessica Kingsley, 1992: 330 p. *ISBN: 1853021393.* [Regional policy and development. : No. 4]

76 A regional econometric (planning) model for the state of Andhra Pradesh (India). K.S.R. Murthy. *J. Dev. Areas* **26:3** 4:1992 pp. 333 – 355

77 Regional economic transformation and social overhead investments. Frank Bruinsma; Peter Nijkamp; Piet Rietveld. *J. Econ. Soc. Geogr.* **83:1** 1992 pp. 3 – 12

78 Regional evolutions. Olivier Jean Blanchard; Lawrence F. Katz. *Brookings P.* :1 1992 pp. 1 – 61

79 The regional financial sector — a Scottish case study. Sheila C. Dow. *Reg. Stud.* **26:7** 1992 pp. 619 – 631

80 Regional innovation and small high technology firms in peripheral regions. Angel Martínez Sánchez. *Small Bus. Econ.* **4:2** 6:1992 pp. 153 – 168

81 Regional paths of development. Gary Gereffi; Stephanie Fonda. *Ann. R. Soc.* **18** 1992 pp. 419 – 448

82 Regional problems and regional planning in Central and Eastern Europe. William Berentsen *[Contrib.]*; Kazimierz Zaniewski *[Contrib.]*; Boleslaw Domański *[Contrib.]*; Petr Pavlínek *[Contrib.]*; Györgyi Barta *[Contrib.]*; Pál Beluszky *[Contrib.]*; Judit Timár *[Contrib.]*; Boian Koulov *[Contrib.]*; Nikolay Tsekov *[Contrib.]*; Maria Vodenska *[Contrib.]* *and others. Collection of 10 articles.* **J. Econ. Soc. Geogr.** , *83:5*, 1992 pp. 339 – 421

83 Restructuring the local economy. Mike Geddes *[Ed.]*; John Benington *[Ed.]*. Harlow: Longman, 1992: 201 p. *ISBN: 0582091020.* [Local economic and social strategy series.]

84 Some advantages of Canadian disunity — how Quebec sovereignty might aid economic development in English-speaking Canada; *[French summary]*. Robert J. Brym. *Can. R. Soc. A.* **29:2** 5:1992 pp. 210 – 226

85 Sources of structural change in the Washington economy. An input-output perspective. D. Holland; S.C. Cooke. *Ann. Reg. Sci.* **26:2** 1992 pp. 155 – 170

86 Technology, innovation and dynamic of urban-systems. Asnoud Mouwen; Peter Nijkamp. *Ind. J. Reg. Sci.* **XXIV:1** 1992 pp. 37 – 58

87 Urban and regional restructuring within an evolving community. Martin Frost; John Shepherd. *Eur. Res.* **3:2** 3:1992 pp. 1 – 12

88 Using the RAS technique as a test of hybrid methods of regional input-output table updating; *[French summary]*; *[German summary]*. J.H.Ll. Dewhurst. *Reg. Stud.* **26:1** 1992 pp. 81 – 92

Rural economics *[Économie rurale]*

89 Agrarian law reform in the Russian federation. Mikhail I. Kozyr'. *R. C. & E.Eur. Law* **18:6** 1992 pp. 501 – 526

90 Assumptions, motivations and neutrality in rural development — the Portuguese paradigm. John H. Wolf. *Comm. Dev. J.* **27:1** 1:1992 pp. 21 – 29

91 Les espaces ruraux revisités *[In French]*; [Rural spaces revisited] *[Summary]*. A. Brun; J. Cavailhes; P. Perrier-Cornet; B. Schmitt. *R. Ec. Reg. Urb.* :1 1992 pp. 37 – 66

92 The geography of the Canadian north — issues and challenges. Robert M. Bone. Toronto: Oxford University Press, 1992: xi, 284 p. *ISBN: 0195407725; LofC: cn 91095109. Includes index; Includes bibliographical references — p. [253]-273.*

93 The impact of rural reform on economic and social stratification in a Chinese village. Yunxiang Yan. *Aust. J. Chin. Aff.* :27 1:1992 pp. 1 – 24

94 Improving rural-urban linkages through small town market-based development. Gary L. Gaile. *Third Wor. P.* **14:2** 5:1992 pp. 131 – 148

F.3.1.1: Geographical aspects *[Aspects géographiques]* — ***Rural economics*** *[Économie rurale]*

95 Lessons from abroad in rural community revitalization — the one village, one product movement in Japan. Isao Fujimoto. *Comm. Dev. J.* **27:1** 1:1992 pp. 10 – 20

96 Location analysis and rural economic development. Niles Hansen *[Contrib.]*; Poul Ove Pedersen *[Contrib.]*; Thomas R. Leinbach *[Contrib.]*. *Collection of 3 articles.* **Int. Reg. Sci. R.** , *14:3*, 1992 pp. 299 – 324

97 The renewal of Ghanaian rural economy. George J. Sefa Dei. *Can. J. Afr. St.* **26:1** 1992 pp. 24 – 54

98 Rural finance in developing countries. Jacob Yaron. Washington, D.C.: Agriculture and Rural Development Department, The World Bank, 1992: 25 p. [Policy research working papers.]

99 Rural poverty and economic change in India. V.R. Dutta. London: Sangam Books, 1992: 155 p. *ISBN: 0861322991.*

Urban economics *[Économie urbaine]*

100 Adaption and distress in the urban economy — a study of Kampala households. A. Bigsten; S. Kayizzi-Mugerwa. *World Dev.* **20:10** 10:1992 pp. 1423 – 1441

101 City and suburb — urban models with more than one employment center. John Yinger. *J. Urban Ec.* **31:2** 3:1992 pp. 181 – 205

102 The cultural imperatives of globalization — urban economic growth in the 21st century. Jack N. Behrman; Dennis A. Rondinelli. *Econ. Devel. Q.* **6:2** 5:1992 pp. 115 – 126

103 Des "garden-cities" aux "urban development corporations" — savoir-faire planificateur britannique *[In French]*; [From "garden cities" to "urban development corporations" — British planning know-how] *[Summary]*. S. Puissant. *R. Ec. Reg. Urb.* **:1** 1992 pp. 67 – 91

104 An empirical estimation of the price effects of development impact fees. Andrejs Skaburskis; Mohammad Qadeer. *Urban Stud.* **29:5** 6:1992 pp. 653 – 667

105 Gateway cities — the metropolitan sources of US producer service exports. Matthew P. Drennan. *Urban Stud.* **29:2** 4:1992 pp. 217 – 236

106 Growth in cities. Edward L. Glaeser; Hedi D. Kallal; José A. Scheinkman; Andrei Shleifer. *J. Polit. Ec.* **100:6** 12:1992 pp. 1126 – 1152

107 Improving rural-urban linkages through small town market-based development. Gary L. Gaile. *Third Wor. P.* **14:2** 5:1992 pp. 131 – 148

108 Inducing local growth — two intermediate-sized cities in the state of Paraná, Brazil. Bruce W. Ferguson. *Third Wor. P.* **14:3** 8:1992 pp. 245 – 265

109 Local economic development and the City. Tony Bovaird. *Urban Stud.* **29:3-4** 5:1992 pp. 343 – 368

110 Local economic performance in Britain during the late 1980s — the results of the third booming towns study. A.G. Champion; A.E. Green. *Envir. Plan. B.* **24:2** 2:1992 pp. 243 – 272

111 Local economic policy and job creation — a review of evaluation studies. Paul Foley. *Urban Stud.* **29:3-4** 5:1992 pp. 557 – 598

112 Malaga. Michael Barke. *Cities* **9:1** 2:1992 pp. 2 – 17

113 Market power of large cities and policy differences in metropolitan areas. W.H. Hoyt. *Reg. Sci. Urb. Econ.* **22:4** 11:1992 pp. 539 – 558

114 Measuring the industrial performance of Chinese cities by data envelopment analysis. Toshiyuki Sueyoshi. *Socio. Econ.* **26:2** 1992 pp. 75 – 88

115 Het mobiliteitsbeleid, motor in het verstedelijkingsproces — economisch-geografische verklaringen voor de lokalisatie van gezinnen *[In Flemish]*; Mobility policy and urbanization — the dynamics of household localization *[Summary]*. Ann Verhetsel. *Econ. Soc. Tijd.* **46:2** 6:1992 pp. 227 – 253

116 Nagoya. Kiyotaka Hayashi. *Cities* **9:1** 2:1992 pp. 18 – 26

117 On the birth and growth of cities — laissez-faire and planning compared. A. Anas. *Reg. Sci. Urb. Econ.* **22:2** 6:1992 pp. 243 – 258

118 On the theory of growth controls. Robert Engle; Peter Navarro; Richard Carson. *J. Urban Ec.* **32:3** 11:1992 pp. 269 – 283

119 Partnership — issues of policy and negotiation. Maureen Mackintosh. *Local. Ec.* **7:3** 11:1992 pp. 210 – 224

120 Public facility location and urban spatial structure — equilibrium and welfare analysis. Jacques-François Thisse; David E. Wildasin. *J. Publ. Ec.* **48:1** 6:1992 pp. 83 – 118

121 The Randstad today and tomorrow. Oedzge Atzema *[Contrib.]*; Bert Kruyt *[Contrib.]*; Jan van Weesep *[Contrib.]*; Piet Korteweg *[Contrib.]*; Robert Lie *[Contrib.]*; Rob Konings

F,3.1.1: Geographical aspects *[Aspects géographiques]* — *Urban economics [Économie urbaine]*
[Contrib.]; Erik Louw *[Contrib.]*; Piet Rietveld *[Contrib.]*; Cees Cortie *[Contrib.]*; Martin Dijst *[Contrib.] and others. Collection of 8 articles.* **J. Econ. Soc. Geogr.** , *83:4,* 1992 pp. 243 – 334

122 Les régions métropolitaines canadiennes et la promotion locale de l'innovation technologique *[In French]*; [Canadian metropolitan regions and the local promotion of technological innovation] *[Summary].* C.H. Davis. *R. Ec. Reg. Urb.* **:1** 1992 pp. 115 – 130

123 Science parks — a property-based initiative for urban regeneration. John Henneberry. *Local. Ec.* **6:4** 2:1992 pp. 326 – 335

124 Trade and migration in a two-city model of transportation investments. K. Sasaki. *Ann. Reg. Sci.* **26:4** 1992 pp. 305 – 317

F.3.1.2: Demographical aspects — *Aspects démographiques*

1 Alonso's discrete population model of land use — efficient allocations and competitive equilibria. Marcus Berliant; Masahisa Fujita. *Int. Econ. R.* **33:3** 8:1992 pp. 535 – 566

2 Arbeitsmarktpolitische Implikationen eines Bevölkerungsrückgangs in der Bundesrepublik Deutschland *[In German]*; [Labour market implications of population decline in the Federal Republic of Germany]. Helmut Kessler. Frankfurt am Main: Lang, 1991: x, 257 p. *ISBN: 3631444710. Bibliography — p.226-257.* [Europäische Hochschulschriften.]

3 Breaking the myth of harmony — theoretical and methodological guidelines to the study of rural Third World households. Elizabeth Katz. *Rev. Rad. Pol. Ec.* **23:3&4** Fall & Winter:1991 pp. 37 – 56

4 Catholicism and the economics of fertility. William Sander. *Pop. Stud.* **46:3** 11:1992 pp. 477 – 489

5 Cultural contingencies and economic behavior — return migration in Portugal. Allan M. Williams. *Wor. Futur.* **33:1-3** 1992 pp. 155 – 164

6 Economic development and population concentration. Gershon Alperovich. *Econ. Dev. Cult. Change* **41:1** 10:1992 pp. 63 – 74

7 Economic development in Iraq — factors underlying the relative deterioration of human capital formation. Robert E. Looney. *J. Econ. Iss.* **XXVI:2** 6:1992 pp. 615 – 622

8 The economic élite in Hungary over the last decade. J. Kisdi; R. Kulcsár. *Acta Oecon.* **44:1-2** 1992 pp. 201 – 210

9 Ethnicity and fertility differentials in Peninsular Malaysia — do policies matter?; *[French summary]*; *[Spanish summary].* Pavalavalli Govindasamy; Julie DaVanzo. *Pop. Dev. Rev.* **18:2** 6:1992 pp. 243 – 267

10 *[In Japanese]*; [Female labor force participation and fertility]. Sachiko Imada; et al. *JCER economic journal No.22 - 1992.* pp. 1 – 18

11 Fertility and the economy. G.S. Becker. *J. Pop. Ec.* **5:3** 1992 pp. 185 – 202

12 Gesamtwirtschaftliche Effekte der Zuwanderung 1988 bis 1991 *[In German]*; [The collective economic effects of migration into West Germany between 1988 and 1991] *[Summary]*; *[French summary].* György Barabas; Arne Gieseck; Ullrich Heilemann; Hans Dietrich von Loeffelholz. *RWI-Mitt.* **43:2** 1992 p. 133

13 Interprovincial migration and local public goods; *[French summary].* Kathleen M. Day. *Can. J. Econ.* **XXV:1** 2:1992 pp. 123 – 144

14 Linked migration systems — immigration and internal labor flows in the United States. Robert Walker; Mark Ellis; Richard Barff. *Econ. Geogr.* **68:3** 7:1992 pp. 234 – 248

15 Neo-classical household models and modes of household production — problems in the analysis of African agricultural households. Jeanne Koopman. *Rev. Rad. Pol. Ec.* **23:3&4** Fall & Winter:1991 pp. 148 – 173

16 Peasant patriarchy and the subversion of the collective in Vietnam. Nan Wiegersma. *Rev. Rad. Pol. Ec.* **23:3&4** Fall & Winter:1991 pp. 174 – 197

17 Population growth, density and the costs of providing public services. Helen F. Ladd. *Urban Stud.* **29:2** 4:1992 pp. 273 – 296

18 Refugees and forced migrants as development resources — the Greek Cypriot refugees from 1974. Roger Zetter. *Cyprus Rev.* **4:1** Spring:1992 pp. 7 – 39

19 Regional population development and the service sector in Austria. K. Stiglbauer. *Geogr. Pol.* **:59** 1992 pp. 7 – 20

F.3.1.2: Demographical aspects *[Aspects démographiques]*
20 Relations entre croissance démographique et environnement *[In French]*; [Relations between demographic growth and environment]. Dominique Tabutin; Evelyne Thilges. *R. T-Monde* **XXXIII:130** 4-6:1992 pp. 273 – 294
21 The role of economic growth in the fertility transition in Western Europe — econometric evidence. C.R. Winegarden; Mark Wheeler. *Economica* **59:236** 11:1992 pp. 421 – 435

F.3.1.3: Sociological aspects — *Aspects sociologiques*

1 Capital punishment and deterrence — a portfolio approach. D.O. Cloninger. *Appl. Econ.* **24:6** 6:1992 pp. 635 – 645
2 Culture et durabilité *[In French]*; [Culture and sustainability]. Lourdes Arizpe; Fernanda Paz. *R. T-Monde* **XXXIII:130** 4-6:1992 pp. 339 – 354
3 Determinants of spells of poverty following divorce. Julia A. Heath; B.F. Kiker. *R. Soc. Econ.* **L:3** Fall:1992 pp. 305 – 315
4 Economic and social consequences of restructuring in Hungary. László Csaba *[Contrib.]*; Sandor Richter *[Contrib.]*; Valentinyi Akos *[Contrib.]*; Hajna Istvanffy Lorinc *[Contrib.]*; Yudit Kiss *[Contrib.]*; Andras Toth *[Contrib.]*. *Collection of 6 articles.* **Eur.-Asia Stud.** , *44:6*, 1992 pp. 947 – 1043
5 The effects of social, political and economic constraints on the black African's allocation of time — evidence from oscillating migrants in the Republic of South Africa. David E. Ault; Gilbert L. Rutman. *Ox. Econ. Pap.* **44:1** 1:1992 pp. 135 – 155
6 Экономическая реформа: институциональный и структурный аспекты *[In Russian]*; (Economic reform — institutional and structural aspects); (La réforme économique —aspects institutennel et structurel: *Title only in French*); (Wirtschaftsreform — Institutionelle und strukturelle Aspekte: *Title only in German*); (Reforma económica — aspectos institucionales: *Title only in Spanish*). Ya. Kuz'minov; O. Anan'in; I. Prostakov; M. Korol'kov. *Svobod. Mysl'* :**18** 12:1992 pp. 50 – 59
7 Ethical aspects of the economic value of human life. Philippe van Parijs *[Contrib.]*; John Broome *[Contrib.]*; Charles Blackorby *[Contrib.]*; David Donaldson *[Contrib.]*; Jacques H. Drèze *[Contrib.]*. *Collection of 5 articles.* **Rech. Ec. Louvain** , *58:2*, 1992 pp. 121 – 171
8 Ethnic capital and intergenerational mobility. George J. Borjas. *Q. J. Econ.* **CVII:1** 2:1992 pp. 123 – 150
9 Hunting for Homo sovieticus — situational versus attitudinal factors in economic behavior. Robert J. Shiller; Maxim Boycko; Vladimir Korobov. *Brookings P.* :**1** 1992 pp. 127 – 181
10 The impact of children on married women's labor supply — black-white differentials revisited. Evelyn L. Lehrer. *J. Hum. Res.* **XXVII:3** Summer:1992 pp. 422 – 444
11 Institutionalists, radical economists, and class. Philip A. Klein. *J. Econ. Iss.* **XXVI:2** 6:1992 pp. 535 – 544
12 Intergenerational transfers within the family. H. Cremer; D. Kessler; P. Pestieau. *Eur. Econ. R.* **36:1** 1:1992 pp. 1 – 16
13 Inter-vivos transfers and intergenerational exchange. Donald Cox; Mark R. Rank. *Rev. Econ. St.* **LXXIV:2** 5:1992 pp. 305 – 314
14 Labor, gender, and the balance of productivity — South Korea and Singapore. Ralph Pettman. *J. Cont. Asia* **22:1** 1992 pp. 45 – 56
15 The life-cycle labor supply of married women and its implications for household income inequality. Kathryn L. Shaw. *Econ. Inq.* **XXX:4** 10:1992 pp. 659 – 672
16 Market orientation and the reconstitution of women's role in Philippine agriculture. Maria Sagrario Floro. *Rev. Rad. Pol. Ec.* **23:3&4** Fall & Winter:1991 pp. 106 – 128
17 На пути к рыночной экономике: социальный аспект *[In Russian]*; (On the way to the market economy — the social aspect). Yu.V. Shishkov. *Sot. Issle.* :**9** 1992 pp. 70 – 80
18 Perception and judgments of the economic system. T. Tyszka; J. Sokołowska. *J. Econ. Psyc.* **13:3** 9:1992 pp. 421 – 448
19 Public policy and the economic status of women in the United States. Janice Peterson. *J. Econ. Iss.* **XXVI:2** 6:1992 pp. 441 – 448
20 Rent seeking and social investment in taste change. Joel M. Guttman; Shmuel Nitzan; Uriel Spiegel. *Econ. Polit.* **4:1** 3:1992 pp. 31 – 42
21 Retreat from homeownership — a comparison of the generations and the states. Dowell Myers; Richard Peiser; Gregory Schwann; John Pitkin. *Hous. Pol. Deb.* **3:4** 1992 pp. 945 – 975

F.3.1.3: Sociological aspects *[Aspects sociologiques]*

22 The role of community values in modern liberal economic thought. Jerry Evensky. *Scot. J. Poli.* **39:1** 2:1992 pp. 21 – 38

23 The social economist hankers after values — a collection of essays. John Conway O'Brien. *Int. J. Soc. E.* **19:3/4/5** 1992 pp. 8 – 259

24 Social norms, savings behavior, and growth. Harold L. Cole; George J. Mailath; Andrew Postlewaite. *J. Polit. Ec.* **100:6** 12:1992 pp. 1092 – 1125

25 Social psychology, unemployment exposure and equilibrium unemployment. A.H. Goldsmith; W. Darity. *J. Econ. Psyc.* **13:3** 9:1992 pp. 449 – 471

26 The socioeconomic consequences of teen childbearing reconsidered. Arline T. Geronimus; Sanders Korenman. *Q. J. Econ.* **CVII:4** 11:1992 pp. 1187 – 1214

27 The socio-psychological aspect of reform of the Soviet economy. Grigorii Vainshtein. *Comm. Econ.* **4:3** 1992 pp. 361 – 372

28 Soviet economic culture — heritage and ways of modernization. Ya. Kuzm'inov. *Soc. Sci.* **XXIII:4** 1992 pp. 64 – 79

29 Sozialökonomische Aspekte des griechischen Wachstumsprozesses *[In German]*; [The socio-economic aspects of the process of economic growth in Greece]. Pantelis Giakoumis. *Südosteur. Mitteil.* **32:1** 1992 pp. 53 – 61

30 Symbolic interactionism and institutionalism — common roots. John T. Harvey; Michael A. Katovich. *J. Econ. Iss.* **XXVI:3** 9:1992 pp. 791 – 812

31 "What does she see in him?" — the effect of sharing on the choice of spouse. Douglas W. Allen. *Econ. Inq.* **XXX:1** 1:1992 pp. 57 – 67

32 Die wirtschaftliche Situation in Griechenland zwischen einer politisch erträglichen und wirtschaftlich notwendigen Politik *[In German]*; [The economic situation in Greece between politically bearable and economically necessary policies]. Efstathios Velissariou. *Südosteur. Mitteil.* **32:1** 1992 pp. 45 – 52

F.3.1.4: Legal aspects: property rights — *Aspects juridiques : droit de propriété*

1 Changes of corporate control and mandatory bids. Ruth Lüttmann. *Int. R. Law Econ.* **12:4** 12:1992 pp. 497 – 516

2 The choice of ownership structure. Niels Mygind. *Econ. Ind. Dem.* **13:3** 8:1992 pp. 359 – 399

3 Consumer safety under products liability and duty to disclose. Paul Burrows. *Int. R. Law Econ.* **12:4** 12:1992 pp. 457 – 478

4 Cooperative law — an instrument for development? A. Shah. *Int. Lab. Rev.* **131:4-5** 4-5:1992 pp. 513 – 524

5 Corruption as a form of insurance. L.H. Liew. *Eur. J. Pol. Ec.* **8:3** 10:1992 pp. 427 – 443

6 Economic analysis and just compensation. Daniel A. Farber. *Int. R. Law Econ.* **12:2** 6:1992 pp. 125 – 138

7 Eléments d'analyse pour une économie de la corruption *[In French]*; (Elements of analysis for a corruption economy); (Elementy analyza dlya ekonomiki korrupcii: *Title only in Russian)*; (Die Korruptionswirtschaft — versuch einer Analyse: *Title only in German)*; (Elementos de análisis para una economía de la corrupción: *Title only in Spanish)*. Jean Cartier-Bresson. *R. T-Monde* **XXXIII:131** 7-9:1992 pp. 581 – 609

8 Extraterritorial application of EC competition law — comments and reflections. Liad Whatstein. *Isr. Law R.* **26:2** Spring:1992 pp. 195 – 237

9 Farmers' rights and genetic conservation in traditional farming systems. S.B. Brush. *World Dev.* **20:11** 11:1992 pp. 1617 – 1630

10 Functional rights — private, public and collective property. Paul Phillips. *Stud. Pol. Ec.* **38** Summer:1992 pp. 61 – 84

11 Ideology, property, and groundwater resources — an exploration of relations. Jody Emel; Rebecca Roberts; David Sauri. *Pol. Geogr.* **11:1** 1:1992 pp. 37 – 55

12 Information, error costs and regulation. Anthony Ogus. *Int. R. Law Econ.* **12:4** 12:1992 pp. 411 – 421

13 The innovation diffusion through licensing — the Italian case. C. Lucioni. *Riv. Int. Sci. Soc.* **C:3** 7-9:1992 pp. 389 – 401

14 Integrating socialist public ownership with the commodity economy. Gongwen Fang. *Soc. Sci. China* **XIII:I** 1:1992 pp. 13 – 22

15 Intellectual property in Australia. J. McKeough; Andrew John Stewart. Sydney: Butterworths, 1991: xlvi, 435 p. *ISBN: 0409495816; LofC: 92100746. Includes bibliographical references and index.*

F.3.1.4: Legal aspects: property rights *[Aspects juridiques : droit de propriété]*

16 Intellectual property — litigation, legislation and education — a study of the Canadian intellectual property and litigation system. Gordon F. Henderson. [Ottawa]: Consumer and Corporate Affairs Canada, [1991]: v, 150 p. (ill) *ISBN: 066219084x; LofC: cn 92072894. Issued also in French under title — La propriété intellectuelle au Canada, contestation en justice, législation et formation; "CCAC no. 00114 91-08"--T.p. verso; Includes bibliographical references.*

17 Law as a public good — the economics of anarchy. Tyler Cowen. *Econ. Philos.* **8:2** 10:1992 pp. 249 – 268

18 Legal foundations of the market — implications for the formerly socialist countries of Eastern Europe and Africa. A. Allan Schmid. *J. Econ. Iss.* **XXVI:3** 9:1992 pp. 707 – 732

19 Materials on intellectual property. W.R. Cornish. Oxford: ESC Publishing, 1990: xxvi, 613 p. *ISBN: 090621467x.*

20 Politics of restitution in Czechoslovakia. Josef Burger. *E. Eur. Quart.* **XXVI:4** Winter:1992 pp. 485 – 498

21 Property and contract in economics — the case for economic democracy. David P. Ellerman. Cambridge, MA.: Blackwell Publishers, 1992: 275 p. *ISBN: 1557863091; LofC: 92006390. Includes bibliographical references (p.) and index.*

22 Régime des aides d'État — jurisprudence récente de la Cour de justice (1989-1992) *[In French]*; [State aid — recent legal decisions of the Court of Justice (1989-1992)]. Claude Blumann. *R. Mar. Comm.* **:361** 9-10:1992 pp. 721 – 739

23 Le régime spécial des infractions économiques *[In French]*; [The special rules of economic crime]. Rabah Kasdi. *Rev. Algér.* **XXIX:4** 1991 pp. 837 – 849

24 Renegotiation and the allocation of property rights. Piergiovanna Natale. *B. Econ. Res.* **44:3** 7:1992 pp. 241 – 248

25 Small enterprises and company law in Indonesia — a study of the limited company in Indonesian commercial practice. S. Pompe. *Bijdragen* **148:1** 1992 pp. 67 – 81

26 The social efficiency of private decisions to enforce property rights. David de Meza; J.R. Gould. *J. Polit. Ec.* **100:3** 6:1992 pp. 561 – 580

27 Some reflection on externalities, Coase theorem and endogenous determination of property rights. A. Boitani; M. Grillo. *Metroeconomica* **XLIII:3** 10:1992 pp. 309 – 326

28 The transfer and redefinition of property rights — theoretical analysis of transferring property rights and tranformational privatisation in the post-STEs. Piotr Jasiński. *Comm. Econ.* **4:2** 1992 pp. 163 – 190

29 A tulajdonjogok közgazdaságtana és versenypolitika. A magyar gazdasági átalakulás egyes piacelméleti összefüggéseiről *[In Hungarian]*; [The economics of property rights and competition policy *[Summary]*]. Ádám Török. *Közg. Sz.* **XXXIX** 6:1992 pp. 550 – 564

30 Welfare effects of global patent protection. Alan V. Deardorff. *Economica* **59:233** 2:1992 pp. 35 – 51

F.3.2: Underdevelopment. Economic development —
Sous-développement. Développement économique

Sub-divisions: Africa *[Afrique]*; Americas *[Amérique]*; Asia *[Asie]*; Europe *[Europe]*

1 Agriculture and economic development in the 1990s — a new analytical and policy agenda. Ajit Singh; Hamid Tabatabai. *Int. Lab. Rev.* **131:4-5** 4-5:1992 pp. 405 – 430

2 Biotechnology — economic and social aspects — issues for developing countries. E. J. DaSilva *[Ed.]*; Colin Ratledge *[Ed.]*; Albert Sasson *[Ed.]*. Cambridge: Cambridge University Press, 1992: 388 p. *ISBN: 0521384737; LofC: 91020767. Includes index.*

3 The community support approach (CSA) — an ABC for rural development. M. Honey; J. Thomas; J. Davidson. *Develop. S. Afr.* **9:2** 5:1992 pp. 213 – 228

4 Debt and development. Stuart Corbridge. Cambridge, MA.: Blackwell, 1992: 231 p. *ISBN: 0631179046; LofC: 92017199. Includes bibliographical references. [IBG studies in geography.]*

5 Debt, adjustment, and poverty in developing countries. David Woodward. London: Pinter Publishers, 1992 *ISBN: 1855670763; LofC: 92010936. Includes bibliographical references and indexes.*

6 Défis, savoirs, décisions dans le concept du développement durable *[In French]*; [Challenges, knowledge, decisions in the concept of sustainable development]. Abdellatif Benachenhou. *R. T-Monde* **XXXIII:130** 4-6:1992 pp. 373 – 392

F.3.2: Underdevelopment. Economic development [*Sous-développement.*

Développement économique]

7 Democracy and global economic growth. John D. Sullivan. *Wash. Quart.* **15**:2 Spring:1992 pp. 175 – 186

8 Dependency debate on the concept of the state. Elżbieta Markowska. *Econ. Papers [Warsaw]* **18** 1992 pp. 208 – 226

9 Development blocks and industrial transformation — the Dahménian approach to economic development. Bo Carlsson *[Ed.]*; Rolf G.H. Henriksson *[Ed.]*. Stockholm: Industrial Institute for Economic and Social Research, 1991: 154 p. *ISBN: 9172043725.*

10 A development model of developing economies with capital and knowledge accumulation. W.-B. Zhang. *J. Econ.* **55**:1 1992 pp. 43 – 63

11 Development planning — theory and reality.*Prog. Plan.* **37**:1 1992 pp. 46 – 56

12 Development theory and policy in the Third World. K.R. Hope. *S. Afr. J. Econ.* **60**:4 12:1992 pp. 333 – 353

13 Development with limited and unlimited supplies of capital. Ali A. Bolbol; Leslie Young. *Manch. Sch. E.* **LX**:3 9:1992 pp. 307 – 316

14 Distant obligations — speculations on NGO funding and the global market. Alan Fowler. *Rev. Afr. Pol. Ec.* **:55** 11:1992 pp. 9 – 29

15 Do rich countries grow more slowly?; Växer rika länder långsammare? *[Swedish summary]*. Pär Hansson; Magnus Henrekson. *Skan. Ensk. Bank. Q. R.* **:1-2** 1992 pp. 3 – 12

16 Gli effetti dei processi di transizione nell'Europa dell'Est sulle economie dei Paesi in via di sviluppo. Il punto di vista delle Nazioni Unite *[In Italian]*; [Effects of the transition process in Eastern Europe on the economies in developing countries. The United Nation's point of view]. Giampaolo Cantini. *Comun. Int.* **XLVI**:4 Quarto trimestre:1991 pp. 538 – 555

17 Empresa multinacional y cambio tecnológico — implicaciones para los países en desarrollo *[In Spanish]*; [Multinational industry and technology transfers — implications for developing countries]. Kurt Unger; Luz Saldaña. *Foro Int.* **XXXII**:3 1-3:1992 pp. 376 – 395

18 Environnement et développement *[In French]*; [Environment and development]. Abdellatif Benachenhou *[Ed.]*; Dominique Tabutin *[Contrib.]*; Evelyne Thilges *[Contrib.]*; Marc Dufumier *[Contrib.]*; Jan Diek van Mansvelt; Henrique Rattner *[Contrib.]*; Lourdes Arizpe *[Contrib.]*; Fernanda Paz *[Contrib.]*; Robert M. Worcester *[Contrib.]*; Michele Corrado *[Contrib.] and others. Collection of 12 articles.* **R. T-Monde** , *XXXIII:130,* 4-6:1992 pp. 243 – 469

19 Estratificación socioeconómica — aproximación conceptual y diseño metodológico *[In Spanish]*; [Socio-economic stratification — a methodological sketch]. Dario Cuervo Villafañe; Manuel Ramfrez Gómez. *Desar. Soc.* **:29** 3:1992 pp. 115 – 159

20 Explaining process and change — approaches to evolutionary economics. Ulrich Witt *[Ed.]*. Ann Arbor: University of Michigan Press, 1991: 184 p. *ISBN: 0472102915.*

21 Financial analysis for development — concepts and techniques. M.J.H. Yaffey. London: Routledge, 1992: xv, 270 p. *ISBN: 0415080959; LofC: 92022142. Includes bibliographical references (p. [263]-265) and index.*

22 Financial indicators and growth in a cross section of countries. Robert G. King; Ross Levine. Washington, D.C.: Country Economics Department, The World Bank, 1992: 50 p. [Policy research working papers.]

23 Financial structures and economic development. Ross Levine. Washington, D.C.: Country Economics Department, The World Bank, 1992: 39 p. [Policy research working papers.]

24 Four approaches to institutional development in planning. Frank van Steenbergen. *Dev. Pol. R.* **10**:1 3:1992 pp. 35 – 42

25 From the debt crisis to sustainable development — changing perspectives on north-south relationships. Gianni Vaggi *[Ed.]*. New York: St. Martin's Press, 1992: 315 p. *ISBN: 0312085427; LofC: 92010978. Includes index.*

26 The Hague Report — sustainable development — from concept to action. Jan Pronk. [New York: UNDP], 1992: 32 p.

27 Incubating high-technology firms — state economic development strategies for biotechnology. Edward J. Blakely; Nancy Nishikawa. *Econ. Devel. Q.* **6**:3 8:1992 pp. 241 – 254

28 Industrialization and development. Tom Hewitt *[Ed.]*; Hazel Johnson *[Ed.]*; David Wield *[Ed.]*. Oxford: Oxford University Press in association with the Open University, 1992: ix, 338 p. *ISBN: 0198773323. Includes index; Bibliography — p. 316-321.*

29 LDC financial requirements. C.J. Jepma. Aldershot: Avebury, 1992: 111 p. *ISBN: 1856283372.*

F.3.2: Underdevelopment. Economic development *[Sous-développement.*
Développement économique]
30 Local economic development. Michael J. Rich *[Contrib.]*; Michael A. Pagano *[Contrib.]*; Ann
O'M. Bowman *[Contrib.]*; Susan E. Clarke *[Contrib.]*; Gary L. Gaile *[Contrib.]*; Ross
Gittell *[Contrib.]*. *Collection of 5 articles.* **Econ. Devel. Q.** , *6:2*, 5:1992 pp. 148 – 210
31 The macroeconomics of development finance — a Kaleckian analysis of the semi-industrial
economy. E.V.K. FitzGerald. New York: St. Martin's Press, 1992: 222 p.
ISBN: 0312083564; LofC: 92004715. Includes index.
32 New directions in development economics. Amitava Krishna Dutt *[Ed.]*; Kenneth P. Jameson
[Ed.]. Aldershot, Hants: Edward Elgar, 1992: xvi, 191 p. *ISBN: 1852785357;*
LofC: 91021786. Includes bibliographical references and index.
33 The NICs, global accumulation and uneven development — implications of a simple
three-region model. A.K. Dutt. *World Dev.* **20:8** 8:1992 pp. 1159 – 1171
34 Outward-oriented developing economies really do grow more rapidly — evidence from 95
LDCs, 1976-1985. David Dollar. *Econ. Dev. Cult. Change* **40:3** 4:1992 pp. 523 – 544
35 Political economy, ideology, and the impact of economics on the Third World. Derrick K.
Gondwe. New York: Praeger, 1992: viii, 192 p. *ISBN: 027594025x; LofC: 91037624.*
Includes bibliographical references (p. [177]-187) and index.
36 The politics of development policy. R.W. Liddle. *World Dev.* **20:6** 6:1992 pp. 793 – 808
37 Poverty and development — economics and reality. Kishor Thanawala. *R. Soc. Econ.* **L:3**
Fall:1992 pp. 258 – 268
38 Promoting the sustainability of development institutions — a framework for strategy. D.W.
Brinkerhoff; A.A. Goldsmith. *World Dev.* **20:3** 3:1992 pp. 369 – 384
39 Role of technology in the emergence of newly industrializing countries. Hans Duller. *ASEAN*
Ec. B. **9:1** 7:1992 pp. 45 – 54
40 The role of the intellectual in economic development — a constitutional persepctive. A.D.
Lowenberg; B.T. Yu. *World Dev.* **20:9** 9:1992 pp. 1261 – 1278
41 Scenarios for growth in the 1990s. Shahrokh Fardoust; Jian-Ping Zhou. Washington, D.C.:
International Economics Department, The World Bank, 1992: 39 p. [Policy research
working papers.]
42 Schwerpunkt Strukturanpassung *[In German]*; [Focus on structural adjustment]. Adigun
Agbaje *[Contrib.]*; Heidi Willer *[Contrib.]*; Paul-Gerhardt Rösch *[Contrib.]*; Hans Jörg
Friedrich *[Contrib.]*; Siegfried Pausewang *[Contrib.]*. *Collection of 4 articles.* **Af. Spec.** ,
2, 1992 pp. 123 – 205
43 South-south aid — how developing countries help each other. Donald Bobiash. New York: St.
Martin's Press, 1992: 224 p. *ISBN: 0312068395; LofC: 91024060. Includes*
bibliographical references and index.
44 Stratégie endogène — nouvelle stratégie ou exécution différente *[In French]*; [Endogenous
strategy — a new strategy or a different execution]. Krzysztof Ners. *Econ. Papers*
[Warsaw] **18** 1992 pp. 177 – 207
45 Structural adjustment and the environment. David Reed *[Ed.]*. London: Earthscan, 1992: 209
p. *ISBN: 1853831530.*
46 Terms of trade uncertainty, savings, and the production structure. Eric van Wincoop. *J. Int.*
Econ. **33:3/4** 11:1992 pp. 305 – 325
47 Trade policy, industrialization, and development — new perspectives. G. K. Helleiner *[Ed.]*.
Oxford: Clarendon Press, 1992: 324 p. *ISBN: 0198283598; LofC: 91015325. Includes*
index. [Studies in development economics.]
48 Whatever happened to the urban informal sector? The regressive effect of "double dualism" on
the financial analysis of developing countries. J.J. Thomas. *B. Lat. Am. Res.* **11:3** 9:1992
pp. 279 – 294

Africa *[Afrique]*
49 Africa's recovery in the 1990s — from stagnation and adjustment to human development.
Giovanni Andrea Cornia; Rolph van der Hoeven; P. Thandika Mkandawire; James P. Grant
[Foreword]. New York, NY.: St. Martin's Press, 1992: 375 p. *ISBN: 0312086318;*
LofC: 92018007. Includes bibliographical references (p.) and index.
50 Aid and economic growth in LDCs — evidence from sub-Saharan Africa. Kwabena
Gyimah-Brempong. *Rev. Bl. Pol. Ec.* **20:3** Winter:1992 pp. 31 – 52
51 Alternative development strategies in Subsaharan Africa. Sanjaya Lall; Samuel Wangwe
[Ed.]; Frances Stewart *[Ed.]*. London: , 1992: 486 p. *ISBN: 0333548094. Includes index.*
52 Debt-conversion schemes in Africa — lessons from the experiences of developing countries.
African Centre for Monetary Studies. London: James Currey, 1992: 143 p.
ISBN: 085266138x.

F.3.2: Underdevelopment. Economic development *[Sous-développement.*
Développement économique] — Africa [Afrique]
53 Deindustrialization, adjustment, the World Bank and the IMF in Africa. H. Stein. *World Dev.*
20:1 1:1992 pp. 83 – 96
54 Economic crisis in sub-Saharan Africa — issues, responses and prospects for recovery. Julius
O. Ihonvbere. *Pakis. Horiz.* **44:4** 10:1991 pp. 41 – 56
55 Economic developement in a small island economy — a study of the Seychelles Marketing
Board. Rony E. Gabbay; Robin N. Ghosh. Marrickville: Academic Press International,
1992: 436 p. *ISBN: 0646075500.*
56 Economic development under structural adjustment — evidence from selected West African
countries. Akpan H. Ekpo. *J. Soc. Devel. Afr.* **7:1** 1992 pp. 25 – 44
57 Economic policies for a new South Africa. Desmond Lachman *[Ed.]*; Kenneth Bercuson
[Ed.]. Washington D.C.: IMF, 1992: 41 p. *ISBN: 1557751986.* [Occasional paper
(International Monetary Fund).]
58 Economie populaire et phenomenes informels au Zaire et en Afrique *[In French]*; [The
popular economy and informal phenomena in Zaire and Africa]. Gauthier de Villers
[Contrib.]; T. Omasombo *[Contrib.]*; Benoît Verhaegen *[Contrib.]*; Michel Willems
[Contrib.]; N. Muamba *[Contrib.]*; Hugues Leclercq *[Contrib.]*; Lokota *[Contrib.]*;
Mbwinga *[Contrib.]*; Didier de Lannoy *[Contrib.]*; Françoise Lambinet *[Contrib.]* *and*
others. Collection of 19 articles. *Cah.* CEDAF , :3-4, 1992 pp. 1 – 277
59 Environment, population growth and productivity in Kenya — a case study of Machakos
District. Mary Tiffen; Michael Mortimore. *Dev. Pol. R.* **10:4** 12:1992 pp. 359 – 387
60 Europe 1992 — a challenge to sub-Saharan African development; *[French summary]*. Kwame
Boafo-Arthur. *Afr. Devel.* **XVII:2** 1992 pp. 27 – 43
61 The extent, likely effects and implications for policy of the 1991/92 drought in countries of
the Eastern and Southern African subregion. Y.S. El Nil. *Finan. News Anal.* **5:8** 8:1992
pp. 1 – 13
62 Instruments of economic policy in Africa. Alan R. Roe; et al. Dakar: African Centre for
Monetary Studies in association with James Currey [and] Heinemann, 1992: 238 p.
ISBN: 0852551290.
63 Le Maroc à portée du million d'hectares irrigués. Éléments pour un bilan *[In French]*;
[Morocco within reach of a million hecteres of irrigated land. An overview] *[Summary]*.
Jean-Jacques Perennès. *Mag. Mack. Mon. Ar.* :**137** 7-9:1992 pp. 25 – 42
64 Policies for African development — from the 1980s to the 1990s. I.G. Patel *[Ed.]*.
Washington: International Monetary Fund, 1992: xi, 293 p. *ISBN: 155775232x;*
LofC: 92015526. Includes bibliographical references.
65 The state and development in Ethiopia. Girma Kebbede. Atlantic Highlands, NJ.: Humanities
Press, 1992: viii, 177 p. *ISBN: 0391037315; LofC: 91018846. Includes bibliographical*
references (p. 163-172) and index.
66 Undermining the political logic of African governments' poor economic policies; *[German*
summary]; *[French summary]*. S. Byron Tarr. *Genève-Afrique* **XXX:1** 1992 pp. 9 – 34
67 Urban popular attitudes towards the economic recovery programme and the PNDC
government in Ghanes. Richard Jeffries. *Afr. Affairs* **91:363** 4:1992 pp. 207 – 226
68 Zambia — Das Scheitern einer Entwicklungsstrategie als ökologische Herausforderung *[In*
German]; [The failure of a development strategy as an ecological challenge] *[Summary]*;
[French summary]. Dorothea Mezger. *Af. Spec.* :**1** 1989 pp. 25 – 46

Americas *[Amérique]*

69 Algunas falacias difundidas en la discusión sobre reestructuración productiva y empleo *[In*
Spanish]; [Some common fallacies surrounding industrial restructuring and employment]
[Summary]. Alfredo Monza. *Desar. Econ.* **32:127** 10-12:1992 pp. 439 – 450
70 América Latina — todavía en el laberinto *[In Spanish]*; [Latin America — still in the
labyrinth]. Germánico Salgado. *Cuad. Am.* **6:31** 1-2:1992 pp. 114 – 135
71 Canje de deuda por naturaleza — la necesidad de una nueva agenda *[In Spanish]*; [Latin
American external debt — the need for a new agenda]. Robert Devlin. *Desar. Soc.* :**29**
3:1992 pp. 59 – 74
72 Consideraciones sobre el desarrollo futuro de Chile *[In Spanish]*; [Considerations on Chile's
future development]. Ricardo Lagos. *Homines* **6** 1989 pp. 71 – 85
73 Contrainte extérieure et logiques endogènes de crise — l'exemple de l'Amérique latine *[In*
French]; Outside constraint and endogenous logics of crisis — the example of Latin
America *[Summary]*. Jacques Adda. *Pol. Étran.* **57:3** Automne:1992 pp. 605 – 622

F.3.2: Underdevelopment. Economic development *[Sous-développement. Développement économique] — Americas [Amérique]*

74 La dinámica del crecimiento económico en Argentina *[In Spanish]*; The dynamic of economic growth in Argentina *[Summary]*. Alfredo Visintini. *Económica Arg* **XXXVI:1-2** 1990 pp. 97 – 144

75 Economic maladjustment in Central America. Wim Pelupessy *[Ed.]*; John Weeks *[Ed.]*. New York, NY.: St Martin's Press, 1992: 198 p. *ISBN: 0312086326; LofC: 92018016. Includes bibliographical references and index.*

76 Economie de la drogue — taille, caractéristiques et impact économique *[In French]*; (The drug economy — quantitative evaluation and economic impact); (Ekonomika narkotikov — količestvennaja ocenka i ekonomičeskoe značenie: *Title only in Russian*); (Die Drogenwirtschaft — quantitative Einschätzung und wirtschaftliche Breitenwirkung: *Title only in German*); (Economía de la droga — evaluación cuantitativa e impacto económico: *Title only in Spanish*). Germàn Fonseca. *R. T-Monde* **XXXIII:131** 7-9:1992 pp. 489 – 516

77 Interamerican seminar on economics. E. Bacha *[Ed.]*; Sebastian Edwards *[Ed.]*; N. Roubini *[Contrib.]*; X. Sala-i-Martin *[Contrib.]*; J. de Gregorio *[Contrib.]*; R. Bonelli *[Contrib.]*; F.G. Morandé *[Contrib.]*; S. Özler *[Contrib.]*; D. Rodrik *[Contrib.]*; J. Aizenman *[Contrib.] and others. Collection of 8 articles.* **J. Dev. Econ.** , *39:1*, 7:1992 pp. 1 – 187

78 The last new world — the conquest of the Amazon frontier. Mac Margolis. New York: Norton, 1992: 367 p. *ISBN: 0393033791; LofC: 91037685. Includes index.*

79 Lateinamerikanische Schwellenländer — Vorbild für Osteuropa? *[In German]*; Latin American newly industrializing nations — model for Eastern Europe? *[Summary]*; *[French summary]*. Dirk Messner; Jörg Meyer-Stamer. *Vierteljahresberichte* **:129** 9:1992 pp. 219 – 233

80 Il ruolo dell'agricoltura nello sviluppo economico argentino. Applicazione di un modello strutturale di crescita in condizioni di disequilibrio *[In Italian]*; The role of agriculture in the economic development of Argentina — the application of a structural disequilibrium model economic growth *[Summary]*. Cesare Zanasi. *Riv. Econ. Agrar.* **XLVII:3** 9:1992 pp. 449 – 477

81 Structural adjustment programmes in Latin America — Mexico and Costa Rica. Flavia Rodríguez. *Money Aff.* **V:2** 7-12:1992 pp. 223 – 251

82 Sustainable development and foreign direct investment in the Eastern Caribbean — a strategy for the 1990s and beyond? Benjamin Goss; Dennis Conway. *B. Lat. Am. Res.* **11:3** 9:1992 pp. 307 – 326

83 Sustainable development in Mexico? The international politics of crisis or opportunity. Daniel Goldrich; David V. Carruthers. *Lat. Am. Pers.* **19:1(72)** Winter:1992 pp. 97 – 122

84 Tendances et perspectives du développement durable en Amérique latine *[In French]*; [Trends and perspectives on sustainable development in Latin America]. Henrique Rattner. *R. T-Monde* **XXXIII:130** 4-6:1992 pp. 329 – 338

85 Trade strategy and the dependency hypothesis — a comparison of policy, foreign investment, and economic growth in Latin America and east Asia. Simeon Hein. *Econ. Dev. Cult. Change* **40:3** 4:1992 pp. 495 – 521

Asia *[Asie]*

86 Aserbaidshan — Wirtschaftsprobleme, soziale Verwerfungen, politischer Nationalismus *[In German]*; Azerbaijan — economic problems, social rifts and political nationalism *[Summary]*. Eva-Maria Auch. *Vierteljahresberichte* **:129** 9:1992 pp. 255 – 264

87 The Asia-Pacific region and the emerging international economic order. John Wong. *Kasarinlan* **7:2/3** 4/1:1991/1992 pp. 17 – 29

88 Development and underdevelopment. Chong Yah Lim. Singapore: Longman, 1991: xi, 255 p. *ISBN: 9971898586; LofC: 92940215. Includes bibliographical references (p.237-248) and index.*

89 Development banking in India — a study of State Financial Corporation. Jaganath Panda; R.K. Dash. New Delhi: Discovery Publishing, 1991: 199 p. *ISBN: 8171411444.*

90 Development ethos and experience. M. Y. Ghorpade. Bangalore: Southern Economist Publication, 1991: 281 p.

91 Dualism and reform in China. Louis Putterman. *Econ. Dev. Cult. Change* **40:3** 4:1992 pp. 467 – 493

92 The economic development of Fujian province. Hideo Ohashi. *China News.* **:101** 11-12:1992 pp. 8 – 19

93 Economic growth strategy and urbanization policies in China, 1949-1982. Kam Wing Chan. *Int. J. Urban* **16:2** 6:1992 pp. 275 – 305

F.3.2: Underdevelopment. Economic development *[Sous-développement. Développement économique]* — *Asia [Asie]*

94 The economics of cooperation — East Asian development and the case for pro-market intervention. James A. Roumasset *[Ed.]*; Susan Barr *[Ed.]*. Boulder, CO.: Westview Press, 1992: vi, 207 p. *ISBN: 0813304547; LofC: 92003432. Includes bibliographical references.*

95 The equi-spaced optimal index formulation — and the multivariate spatial index of economic development for India. M.N. Pal; R. Mukhopadhyay. *Ind. J. Reg. Sci.* **XXIV:2** 1992 pp. 29 – 52

96 Financial development and real development in India — some contrasts. Dhirendra Nath Konar. *Econ. Aff. [Calcutta]* **37:1** 1-3:1992 pp. 49 – 58

97 Flexibility, foresight and fortuna in Taiwan's development — negotiating between Scylla and Charybdis. Steve Chan; Cal Clark. London: Routledge, 1992: 221 p. *ISBN: 0044459491.*

98 Indian industrialization — structure and policy issues. Arun Ghosh *[Ed.]*; et al. Delhi: Oxford University Press, 1992: vi, 364 p. *ISBN: 0195628225. Includes bibliographical references.*

99 Islam and economic development of Southeast Asia — the Muslim private sector in Southeast Asia. Mohamed Ariff *[Ed.]*. Singapore: ISEAS, 1992: 257 p. [Social issues in Southeast Asia.]

100 Korean economy in the 1990s — making the transition to maturity. Hyun Ohseok. *E.Asian R.* **IV:2** Summer:1992 pp. 87 – 110

101 The mechanism of economic development. Ken'ichi Inada; Sueo Sekiguchi; Yasutoyo Shōda. Oxford: Clarendon Press, 1992: 331 p. *ISBN: 0198286287; LofC: 91035067. Translation of — Keizai hatten no mekanizumu; Includes bibliographical references and index.*

102 Mobilisation of foreign savings for development. A study of the impact of external public debt on economic and human development in Bangladesh and India; Mobilitazione del risparmio estero per lo sviluppo. Studio dell'impatto dell debito pubblico estero sugli aspetti economici e umani dello sviluppo in Bangladesh e India *[Italian summary]*. Kartik C. Roy; Y.R. Vadlamudi. *Rev. Int. Sci. Ec. Com.* **XXXIX:9** 9:1992 pp. 793 – 804

103 Multilateral assistance and sustainable development — the case of an IFAD project in the pastoral region of China. C.G. Brown; J.W. Longworth. *World Dev.* **20:11** 11:1992 pp. 1663 – 1674

104 On the margin of capitalism — people and development in Mukim Plentong, Johor, Malaysia. Patrick Guinness. Singapore: Oxford University Press, 1992: xvii, 220 p. *ISBN: 0195885562; LofC: 91032455. Includes bibliographical references (p. [206]-212) and index.* [South-East Asian social science monographs.]

105 Overcoming underdevelopment — what has been learned from the East Asian and Latin American experiences? James L. Dietz. *J. Econ. Iss.* **XXVI:2** 6:1992 pp. 373 – 384

106 Political economy and east Asian economic development. Iyanatul Islam. *Asian-Pacific Ec. Lit.* **6:2** 11:1992 pp. 69 – 101

107 The political economy of discontinous development — regional disparities and inter-regional conflict. Milica Zarkovic Bookman. New York: Praeger, 1991: x, 267 p. *ISBN: 0275937771; LofC: 91010659. Includes bibliographical references (p. [257]-262) and index.*

108 The positive and negative effects of marketing on socioeconomic development — the Turkish case. Güliz Ger. *J. Consum. Pol.* **15:3** 1992 pp. 229 – 254

109 Sectoral development in India — an inter state analysis. B.S. Kantawala; A.S. Rao. *Ind. J. Reg. Sci.* **XXIV:1** 1992 pp. 27 – 36

110 The strategic dimension of the "East Asian Developmental States". Ng Chee Yuen; Sueo Sudo; Donald Crone. *ASEAN Ec. B.* **9:2** 11:1992 pp. 219 – 233

111 Die südkoreanische Erfolgsstory und der Staat — Von der Allmacht des Entwicklungsstaates zur Krise des „hierarchischen Steuerungsmodells" *[In German]*; *[French summary]*; The South Korean success story and the state — from the omnipotence of the developing state to the crisis of the "hierarchical control model" *[Summary]*. Dirk Messner. *Vierteljahresberichte* **:130** 12:1992 pp. 401 – 418

112 Sustaining economic development in Korea — lessons from Japan. Keun Lee; Chung H. Lee. *Pac. Rev.* **5:1** 1992 pp. 13 – 24

113 Trade strategy and the dependency hypothesis — a comparison of policy, foreign investment, and economic growth in Latin America and east Asia. Simeon Hein. *Econ. Dev. Cult. Change* **40:3** 4:1992 pp. 495 – 521

114 Trade, industrial restructuring and development in Hong Kong. Yin-Ping Ho. London: Macmillan, 1992: 297 p. *ISBN: 0333498828.* [Studies in the Economics of East and South-East Asia.]

F.3.2: Underdevelopment. Economic development *[Sous-développement.*
Développement économique] — Asia [Asie]
115 Uneven and combined development — dynamics of change and women's everyday forms of
resistance in Negeri, Sembilan, Malaysia. Carol McAllister. *Rev. Rad. Pol. Ec.* **23:3&4**
Fall & Winter:1991 pp. 57 – 98
116 The Western Pacific — challenge of sustainable growth. Alan Alexander Burnett. Aldershot
Hants: E. Elgar Pub, 1992: 270 p. *ISBN: 1852783672; LofC: 92010389. Includes*
bibliographical references and index.
117 Why the Philippines did not become a newly industrializing country. Leonora C. Angeles.
Kasarinlan **7:2/3** 4/1:1991/1992 pp. 90 – 120

Europe *[Europe]*
118 Baltic industry — a survey of potentials and constraints. Leif Grahm; Lennart Königson.
Vastra Frolunda, Sweden: Swedish Development Consulting Partners AB, 1991: 94 p.
[Development cooperation studies in policy and practice. : No. 1]
119 Confronting the European single market of 1992 — challenges of the ACP and ASEAN
countries. Charles O. Kwarteng. *J. Dev. Soc.* **VIII:2** 7-10:1992 pp. 223 – 239
120 Consumption and development — economic, social and technical aspects. András Hernádi
[Ed.]. Budapest, Hungary: Hungarian Scientific Council for World Economy, 1992: 142 p.
ISBN: 9633011841. Includes bibliographical references. [Trends in world economy. : No.
70]
121 Culture and development — European experiences and challenges — a special research report
of the European Culture Impact Research Consortium (EUROCIRCON). Allan M.
Williams *[Ed.]*; Paul Keating *[Contrib.]*; Martin Huber *[Contrib.]*; Dimitrije Vujadinović
[Contrib.]; Stephen Syrett *[Contrib.]*; Kazimierz Krzysztofek *[Contrib.]*; Branimir
Stojković *[Contrib.]*; Andy Griffiths *[Contrib.]*; Mária Sági *[Contrib.]*; Milena Davidović
[Contrib.] and others. Collection of 17 articles. **Wor. Futur.** , *33:1-3,* 1992 pp. 1 – 212
122 East Germany — conquest, pillage and disintegration. James Petras. *J. Cont. Asia* **22:3** 1992
pp. 340 – 359
123 Economic problems of Eastern Europe within the context of the East-West relationships.
Dmitry Smyslov. *J. Reg. Pol.* **12:2** 4-6:1992 pp 239-250
124 A fejlesztés stratégiája. Az EBRD ebő budapesti közgyűlése *[In Hungarian]*; (The strategy of
development. The first annual meeting of the EBRD, Budapest). Fodor György. *Pénz. Sz.*
36:4 4:1992 pp. 203 – 217
125 The political economy of discontinous development — regional disparities and inter-regional
conflict. Milica Zarkovic Bookman. New York: Praeger, 1991: x, 267 p.
ISBN: 0275937771; LofC: 91010659. Includes bibliographical references (p. [257]-262)
and index.
126 Red microchip — technology transfer, export control, and economic restructuring in the
Soviet Union. Daniel L. Burghart. Aldershot: Dartmouth, 1992: 250 p. *ISBN: 1855213087.*
127 Smallness, economic development and Cyprus. Michael Kammas. *Cyprus Rev.* **4:1**
Spring:1992 pp. 65 – 76
128 Wirtschaftliche Entwicklung in der Umbruchzeit — Folgen für den Informationsbereich im
ehemaligen Jugoslawien *[In German]*; [Economic development in the transition period —
results of an information report in the former Yugoslavia]. Dubravka Kunštek. *Südosteur.*
Mitteil. **32:3** 1992 pp. 225 – 233

F.3.3: Growth, maturity, stagnation — *Croissance, maturité, stagnation*

1 Balanced and unbalanced growth paths in a decomposable economy — contributions to the theory of multiple turnpikes. József Móczár; Jinkichi Tsukui. *Econ. Sys. Res.* **4:3** 1992 pp. 211 – 222

2 Basic needs and growth-welfare trade-offs. Bruce E. Moon; William J. Dixon. *Int. Stud. Q.* **36:2** 6:1992 pp. 191 – 212

3 Les causes de la lenteur de la croissance économique dans le monde islamique *[In French]*; (The causes of slow economic growth in the Islamic world); (Las causas de la lentitud del crecimiento económico en el mundo islámico: *Title only in Spanish*); (Die Ursachen für das langsame Wirtschaftswachstum in der islamischen Welt: *Title only in German*); (Pričiny medlennogo ekonomičeskogo rosta v stranakh islama: *Title only in Russian*). Denis-Clair Lambert. *R. T-Monde* **XXXIII:129** 1-3:1992 pp. 153 – 180

4 Central and Eastern Europe roads to growth — papers presented at a seminar held in Baden, Austria, April 15-18 1991. Georg Winckler. Washington, D.C.: International Monetary Fund, Austrian National Bank, 1992: 322 p. *ISBN: 1557751994.*

5 The chances of economic revival. T. Erdős. *Acta Oecon.* **44:1-2** 1992 pp. 1 – 12

6 Comparative economic growth — evidence and interpretation; *[French summary]*. James Brander. *Can. J. Econ.* **XXV:4** 11:1992 pp. 792 – 818

7 The compatibility of growth and increased equality — Korea. Jonathan Edward Leightner. *J. Dev. Stud.* **29:1** 10:1992 pp. 49 – 71

8 A contribution to the empirics of economic growth. N. Gregory Mankiw; David Romer; David N. Weil. *Q. J. Econ.* **CVII:2** 5:1992 pp. 407 – 437

9 Convergence. Robert J. Barro; Xavier Sala-i-Martin. *J. Polit. Ec.* **100:2** 4:1992 pp. 223 – 251

10 Corporatism in decline? An empirical analysis of the impact of corporatism on macroeconomic performance and industrial disputes in 18 industrialized democracies. Markus M.L. Crepaz. *Comp. Poli. S.* **25:2** 7:1992 pp. 139 – 168

11 The decline of the rate of profit in the postwar US economy — is the crisis over? Fred Moseley. *Cap. Class* **:48** Autumn:1992 pp. 115 – 130

12 Destabilizing finance worsened this recession. Robert Pollin. *Challenge* **35:2** 3/4:1992 pp. 17 – 24

13 Economic growth — theory and computations. Larry E. Jones *[Contrib.]*; Nancy L. Stokey *[Contrib.]*; John Laitner *[Contrib.]*; Rodolfo E. Manuelli *[Contrib.]*; Michele Boldrin *[Contrib.]*; Albert Marcet *[Contrib.]*; Ramon Marimon *[Contrib.]*; Xiaodong Zhu *[Contrib.]*; Thomas F. Cooley *[Contrib.]*; Gary D. Hansen *[Contrib.] and others. Collection of 12 articles.* **J. Econ. Theo.** , *58:2*, 12:1992 pp. 117 – 452

14 Efficiency in economic growth models under uncertainty. Itzhak Zilcha. *J. Econ. Dyn. Cont.* **16:1** 1:1992 pp. 27 – 38

15 Endogenous growth cycles in an open economy with fixed exchange rates. R. Sethi. *J. Econ. Beh.* **19:3** 12:1992 pp. 327 – 342

16 Endogenous innovation in neo-classical growth models — a survey. Bart Verspagen. *J. Macro.* **14:4** Fall:1992 pp. 631 – 662

17 Examining the long-run effect of money on economic growth. Ping Wang; Chong K. Yip. *J. Macro.* **14:2** Spring:1992 pp. 359 – 369

18 Explaining growth — competition and finance. Joseph E. Stiglitz. *Riv. Pol. Ec.* **LXXXII(3rd series):XI** 11:1992 pp. 169 – 225

19 Export-led growth and the center-right coalition in Turkey. John Waterbury. *Comp. Polit.* **24:2** 2:1992 pp. 127 – 146

20 Finance, growth, and public policy. Mark Gertler; Andrew K. Rose. Washington, D.C.: The World Bank. Country Economics Department, 1992: 47 p. [Policy research working papers. : No. WPS813]

21 Financial roadblocks on the route to economic prosperity. Benjamin M. Friedman. *Challenge* **35:2** 3/4:1992 pp. 25 – 34

22 The foundations of rapid economic growth — the case of the four tigers. U.C. Gulati. *Am. J. Econ. S.* **51:2** 4:1992 pp. 161 – 172

23 Growth and development — new theory and evidence. Takatoshi Ito *[Ed.]*; Hiroshi Yoshikawa *[Ed.]*; Robert J. Barro *[Contrib.]*; Xavier Sala-I-Martin; Kiminori Matsuyama *[Contrib.]*; Daniel Cohen *[Contrib.]*; Ross Levine *[Contrib.]*; Gilles Saint-Paul *[Contrib.]*; Thierry Verdier *[Contrib.]*; Jisoon Lee *[Contrib.] and others. Collection of 7 articles.* **J. Jap. Int. Ec.** , *6:4*, 12:1992 pp. 309 – 471

F.3.3: Growth, maturity, stagnation *[Croissance, maturité, stagnation]*

24 Growth effects of recent structural changes in the Canadian economy — some empirical evidence. M.I. Ansari. *Appl. Econ.* **24:11** 11:1992 pp. 1233 – 1240

25 Growth performance of the Indian economy, 1950-89 — problems of employment and poverty. Yoginder K. Alagh. *Develop. Eco.* **XXX:2** 6:1992 pp. 97 – 116

26 How much is backwardness an advantage? Further reflections on the road from backwardness advantages to convergence; In che misura l'arretratezza costituisce un vantaggio? Ulteriori riflessioni sul passaggio dai vantaggi dell' arretratezza alla convergenza *[Italian summary]*. M. Tamberi. *Econ. Int.* **XLV:1** 2:1992 pp. 59 – 76

27 Infrastructure and growth. David Canning; Marianne Fay; Roberto Perotti. *Riv. Pol. Ec.* **LXXXII(3rd series):XI** 11:1992 pp. 113 – 147

28 Institutions and economic growth — recent British experience in an international context. N.F.R. Crafts. *W. Eur. Pol.* **15:4** 10:1992 pp. 16 – 38

29 Irreversibility and the behavior of aggregate stochastic growth models. James P. Dow; Lars J. Olson. *J. Econ. Dyn. Cont.* **16:2** 4:1992 pp. 207 – 229

30 Is the export-led growth hypothesis valid for industrialized countries? Dalia Marin. *Rev. Econ. St.* **LXXIV:4** 11:1992 pp. 678 – 688

31 *[In Japanese]*; [Japan in the 1960s and after — the politics of high economic growth]. Joji Watanuki. **Research paper series, Sophia University** *No.56 - 1992*. pp. 1 – 17

32 Knowledge-based growth. Scott Freeman; Stephen Polasky. *J. Monet. Ec.* **30:1** 10:1992 pp. 3 – 24

33 Learning by doing, changes in industrial structure and trade patterns, and economic growth in a small open economy. Jota Ishikawa. *J. Int. Econ.* **33:3/4** 11:1992 pp. 221 – 244

34 Lethal model 2 — the limits to growth revisited. William D. Nordhaus. *Brookings P.* **2** 1992 pp. 1 – 43

35 Measuring Soviet economic growth — old problems and new complications. John H. Moore; Nicholas W. Balabkins *[Comments by]*; Valery S. Katkalo *[Comments by]*. *J. Inst. Theo. Ec.* **148:1** 3:1992 pp. 72 – 98

36 Mexico, the strategy to achieve sustained economic growth. Claudio Loser *[Ed.]*; Eliot Kalter *[Ed.]*. Washington, D.C: International Monetary Fund, 1992: vii, 91 p. *ISBN: 1557753121. Includes bibliographical references.* [International Monetary Fund. Occasional paper.]

37 A model of growth through creative destruction. Philippe Aghion; Peter Howitt. *Econometrica* **60:2** 3:1992 pp. 323 – 352

38 A moral hazard trap to growth. Daniel Tsiddon. *Int. Econ. R.* **33:2** 5:1992 pp. 299 – 322

39 A natureza estocástica do crescimento econômico canadense *[In Portuguese]*; [The stochastic nature of Canadian economic growth] *[Summary]*. Francisco Cribari Neto. *Rev. Bras. Ec.* **46:4** 10/12:1992 pp. 535 – 554

40 New approaches to economic growth. Colin Mayer *[Ed.]*; Andrea Boltho *[Contrib.]*; Gerald Holtham *[Contrib.]*; Frederick van der Ploeg *[Contrib.]*; Paul Tang *[Contrib.]*; Maurice Scott *[Contrib.]*; Mervyn King *[Contrib.]*; Mark Robson *[Contrib.]*; Monojit Chatterji *[Contrib.]*. *Collection of 5 articles.* **Ox. R. Econ. Pol.** , *8:4*, Winter:1992 pp. 1 – 69

41 O rozkładach inwestycji i majątku w modelach wzrostu gospodarczego *[In Polish]*; On investment and capital lag distributions in models of economic growth *[Summary]*; О распределении капитальных вложений и основных фондов в моделях экономического роста *[Russian summary]*. Witold Jurek. *Prz. Staty.* **39:2** 1992 pp. 237 – 248

42 On endogenous growth with productivity shocks. Morgan Kelly. *J. Monet. Ec.* **30:1** 10:1992 pp. 47 – 56

43 On the conditions for export-led growth; *[French summary]*. Edward F. Buffie. *Can. J. Econ.* **XXV:1** 2:1992 pp. 211 – 225

44 On the prospect of export-led growth. A.R. Bhuyan. *S.Asia. J.* **5:3** 1-3:1992 pp. 237 – 249

45 Papua New Guinea — economic recovery from the Bougainville crisis and prospects for the 1990s. Andrew Elek. *Ec. Pap. Aust.* **11:2** 6:1992 pp. 13 – 31

46 Persistence of shocks and their sources in a multisectoral model of UK output growth. K.C. Lee; M.H. Pesaran; R.G. Pierse. *Econ. J.* **102:411** 3:1992 pp. 342 – 356

47 Policies for economic growth. Robert M. Solow. *Economist [Leiden]* **140:1** 1992 pp. 1 – 15

48 Policy implications of "a new view of economic growth". M. FG. Scott. *Econ. J.* **102:412** 5:1992 pp. 622 – 632

49 Policy implications of endogenous growth theory. G.K. Shaw. *Econ. J.* **102:412** 5:1992 pp. 611 – 621

50 Possibilities and limitations of an outward-looking growth strategy in Eastern Europe — a comparative study. Valdas Samonis. *E. Eur. Quart.* **XXVI:3** Fall:1992 pp. 279 – 289

F.3.3: Growth, maturity, stagnation *[Croissance, maturité, stagnation]*

51 Pourquoi les pays en voie de développement ont-ils des rythmes de croissance aussi différents? Un survol critique de quelques orthodoxies contemporaines *[In French]*; (Why do the developing countries show such differences in growth rates? A critical view of certain contemporary orthodox approaches); (¿Porqué los países en via de desarrollo tienen ritmos de crecimiento tan diferentes? Un sobrevuelo crítico de algunas ortodoxais contemporáneas: *Title only in Spanish)*; (Warum haben die Entwicklungsländer so verschiedene Wachstumsrhythmen? Eine kritische Bestandsaufnahme einiger zeitgenössischen Orthodoxien: *Title only in German)*; (Počemu u razvivajuščikhsja stran raznye ritmy rosta? Kritičeskie zametki po povodu nekotorykh sovremennykh ortodoksal'nykh vzgljadov: *Title only in Russian)*. Gérard Grellet. *R. T-Monde* **XXXIII:129** 1-3:1992 pp. 31 – 66

52 Productivity growth reconsidered. Nicholas Crafts; Robert J. Gordon *[Comments by]*; Alan Manning *[Comments by]*. *Econ. Pol.* **:15** 10:1992 pp. 387 – 426

53 Progresso scientifico, sviluppo economico e Mezzogiorno *[In Italian]*; Advancement of science, technology and economic growth — the case of the Italian «Mezzogiorno"» *[Summary]*. Giorgio Lombardo. *Industria* **XIII:3** 7-9:1992 pp. 377 – 388

54 Razvitak ekonomske situacije u Hrvatskoj u godini 1991 *[In Serbo-Croatian]*; Development of the economic situation in Croatia in 1991 *[Summary]*; Развитие экономической ситуации в Хорватии в 1991 году *[Russian summary]*. Željko Rohatinski. *Ekon. Preg.* **43:5-6** 1992 pp. 391 – 408

55 Real or illusory growth in an oil-based economy — government expenditures and private sector investment in Saudi Arabia. R.E. Looney. *World Dev.* **20:9** 9:1992 pp. 1367 – 1376

56 Reconstructing growth theory — a survey. Theo van de Klundert; Sjak Smulders. *Economist [Leiden]* **140:2** 1992 pp. 177 – 203

57 Remarks on interrelations between internal and external growth factors. Danuta Hubner. *Econ. Papers [Warsaw]* **18** 1992 pp. 127 – 137

58 Rent seeking and growth — the case of growth through human capital accumulation; *[French summary]*. Paul Pecorino. *Can. J. Econ.* **XXV:4** 11:1992 pp. 944 – 956

59 Savings, investment and housing in Singapore's growth, 1965-90; Épargne, investissement et construction residentielle dans le contexte de la croissance de Singapour, 1965-90 *[French summary]*. Roger J. Sandilands. *Sav. Develop.* **XVI:2** 1992 pp. 119 – 143

60 Schwacher Anstieg der Produktion in den Industrieländern *[In German]*; Slow growth in the industrial countries *[Summary]*. Stefanie Bessin; Malte Fischer; Klaus-Jürgen Gern; Klaus-Werner Schatz; Peter Trapp. *Weltwirt.* **:3** 1992 pp. 227 – 243

61 Technological catch up and diverging incomes — patterns of economic growth 1960-88. S. Dowrick. *Econ. J.* **102:412** 5:1992 pp. 600 – 610

62 Testing the implications of the Olsen hypothesis. John Quiggin. *Economica* **59:235** 8:1992 pp. 261 – 278

63 Les théories de la croissance endogéne *[In French]*; The theories of endogenous growth *[Summary]*. B. Amable; D. Guellec. *Rev. Ec. Polit.* **102:3** 5-6:1992 pp. 313 – 377

64 "Unproductive" sectors and economic growth — a theoretical analysis. Amitava Krishna Dutt. *R. Pol. Econ.* **4:2** 1992 pp. 178 – 202

65 Zum Problem der kontinuierlich- dynamischen Beschreibung ökonomischer Wachstums- und Kreislaufprozesse *[In German]*; The problem of continuous-dynamic description of economic growth and circulation processes *[Summary]*. Hans Mittelbach. *Jahrb. N. St.* **210:1-2** 7:1992 pp. 47 – 63

F.4: Economic equilibrium and evolution: mechanisms — *Mécanismes de l'équilibre et de l'évolution économiques*

1 Applying general equilibrium. John B. Shoven; John Whalley. Cambridge: Cambridge University Press, 1992: vii, 299 p. *ISBN: 0521266556; LofC: 91023007. Includes bibliographical references (p. 283-289) and index.* [Cambridge surveys of economic literature.]

2 Capital and credit — a new formulation of general equilibrium theory. Michio Morishima. Cambridge: Cambridge University Press, 1992: 212 p. *ISBN: 0521418402; LofC: 91034566. Includes index.*

3 Economic convergence and the theory of factor price equalization areas. Robert A. Mundell. *Riv. Pol. Ec.* **LXXXII(3rd series):XI** 11:1992 pp. 227 – 262

4 Elasticidade de expectativas e surpresa potencial — reflexões sobre a natureza e a estabilidade do equilíbrio sob incerteza *[In Portuguese]*; [Elasticity of expectations and potential surprise — reflexions on the nature and stability of equilibrium under uncertainty]. Fernando J. Cardim de Carvalho. *Rev. Bras. Ec.* **46:1** 1-3:1992 pp. 53 – 76

5 Entry, exit, and firm dynamics in long run equilibrium. Hugo A. Hopenhayn. *Econometrica* **60:5** 9:1992 pp. 1127 – 1150

6 The ethical numeraire. Masudul Alam Choudhury. *Int. J. Soc. E.* **19:1** 1992 pp. 60 – 72

7 General equilibrium economics — space, time and money. Robert E. Kuenne. Basingstoke: Macmillan, 1992: 510 p. *ISBN: 0333566653.*

8 General equilibrium with differentiated commodities — the linear activity model without joint production. K. Podczeck. *Econ. Theory* **2:2** 1992 pp. 247 – 264

9 A geometry for non-Walrasian general equilibrium theory. Kaushik Basu. *J. Macro.* **14:1** Winter:1992 pp. 87 – 104

10 Long-run equilibria in a dynamic Heckscher-Ohlin model; *[French summary]*. Zhiqi Chen. *Can. J. Econ.* **XXV:4** 11:1992 pp. 923 – 943

11 On characterizing equilibria of economies with externalities and taxes as solutions to optimization problems. T.J. Kehoe; D.K. Levine; P.M. Romer. *Econ. Theory* **2:1** 1992 pp. 43 – 68

12 The reconstruction of economics — is there still a place for neoclassical theory? Geoffrey M. Hodgson. *J. Econ. Iss.* **XXVI:3** 9:1992 pp. 749 – 767

13 Some evidence on demand fluctuations and the increased stability of the post-war American economy; *[French summary]*. Magda Kandil. *Can. J. Econ.* **XXV:4** 11:1992 pp. 839 – 864

F.5: Fluctuations, cycles and trends — *Fluctuations, cycles et tendances*

1 Amplification des cycles — le rôle des facteurs financiers, des rigidités et des anticipations *[In French]*; Cyclical amplification — the role of financial factors, inflexibility and anticipation] *[Summary]*. Patrick Artus. *Rech. Ec. Louvain* **58:2** 1992 pp. 173 – 190

2 Anatomy of a financial crisis. F.S. Mishkin. *J. Evolut. Econ.* **2:2** 1992 pp. 115 – 130

3 Are economic fluctuations really persistent? A reinterpretation of some international evidence. D. Demery; N.W. Duck. *Econ. J.* **102:414** 9:1992 pp. 1094 – 1101

4 Are there real or monetary business cycles in the United Kingdom economy?; Nell'economia del Regno Unito i cicli economici sono reali o monetari? *[Italian summary]*. Ioannis A. Kaskarelis. *Rev. Int. Sci. Ec. Com.* **XXXIX:1** 1:1992 pp. 49 – 68

5 Business confidence and depression prevention — a micro-macroeconomic perspective. Y.-K. Ng. *Math. Soc. Sc.* **25:1** 12:1992 pp. 65 – 86

6 Business cycle indicators for the Irish economy. Gabriel Fagan; John Fell. *Q. B. Ctr. Bank Ire.* Winter:1992 pp. 71 – 88

7 Business cycles in open economies — stylized facts for Austria and Germany; Konjunkturzyklen in offenen Volkswirtschaften. Stilisierte Fakten für Österreich und Deutschland *[German summary]*; Les fluctuations conjoncturelles aux économies ouvertes. Des faits stylisés pour l'Autriche et l'Allemagne *[French summary]*; El ciclo coyuntural en las economías abiertas — hechos estilizados para Austria y Alemania *[Spanish summary]*. Peter Brandner; Klaus Neusser. *Welt.liches Arc.* **128:1** 1992 pp. 67 – 87

F.5: Fluctuations, cycles and trends *[Fluctuations, cycles et tendances]*

8 Business cycles in the United Kingdom — facts and fictions. Keith Blackburn; Morten O. Ravn. *Economica* **59:236** 11:1992 pp. 383 – 401

9 The collapse of the Yugoslav economy. Egon Žižmond. *Eur.-Asia Stud.* **44:1** 1992 pp. 101 – 112

10 A contribution to the theory of business cycles. Duncan K. Foley. *Q. J. Econ.* **CVII:3** 8:1992 pp. 1071 – 1088

11 The coordination problem and equilibrium theories of recessions. Larry E. Jones; Rodolfo E. Manuelli. *Am. Econ. Rev.* **82:3** 6:1992 pp. 451 – 471

12 Corporate leverage and the business cycle. Rama Seth. *Cont. Policy* **X:1** 1:1992 pp. 65 – 80

13 A cross country comparison of seasonal cycles and business cycles. J.J. Beaulieu; J.A. Miron. *Econ. J.* **102:413** 7:1992 pp. 772 – 788

14 Current real-business-cycle theories and aggregate labor-market fluctuations. Lawrence J. Christiano; Martin Eichenbaum. *Am. Econ. Rev.* **82:3** 6:1992 pp. 430 – 450

15 Erwartungsbildung und Konjunkturforschung — Axiomatik versus Erhebungen *[In German]*; [Rational expectations and economic research — axiomatics versus inquiry] *[Summary]*. G. Tichy. *Ifo-Stud.* **38:1** 1992 pp. 43 – 82

16 Essays on Robertsonian economics. John R. Presley. New York: St. Martin's Press, 1992: 150 p. *ISBN: 0312068263; LofC: 91038713. Includes index.*

17 Finance in a theory of the business cycle — production and distribution in a debt and equity economy. Robert E. Krainer. Cambridge, MA.: Blackwell, 1992: xx, 245 p. *ISBN: 1557863288; LofC: 91039967. Includes bibliographical references and index.*

18 History as a forecasting tool — the future of the European economy in a long-wave/long-cycle perspective. Andrew Tylecote. *R. Pol. Econ.* **4:2** 1992 pp. 226 – 248

19 How well do linear approximation methods work? The production tax case. Michael Dotsey; Ching Sheng Mao. *J. Monet. Ec.* **29:1** 2:1992 pp. 25 – 58

20 The impact of cyclical demand movements on collusive behavior. J. Haltiwanger; J.E. Harrington. *Rand J. Eco.* **22:1** Spring:1991 pp. 89 – 107

21 Imperfect competition and business cycles — an empirical investigation. David E. Lebow. *Econ. Inq.* **XXX:1** 1:1992 pp. 177 – 193

22 Income distribution and business cycles. William Van Lear. *R. Soc. Econ.* **L:3** Fall:1992 pp. 316 – 332

23 Incomplete information bargaining and business cycles. Daron Acemoglu. London: London School of Economics and Political Science. Centre for Economic Performance, 1992: 48 p.

24 International real business cycles. David K. Backus; Patrick J. Kehoe; Finn E. Kydland. *J. Polit. Ec.* **100:4** 8:1992 pp. 745 – 775

25 Is the economic cycle still alive? Paolo Annunziato *[Contrib.]*; Mario Baldassarri *[Contrib.]*; Marco Lippi *[Contrib.]*; Paolo Onofri *[Contrib.]*; Paolo Paruolo *[Contrib.]*; Bruno Salituro *[Contrib.]*; Stefano Fachin *[Contrib.]*; Andrea Gavosto *[Contrib.]*; Guido Pellegrini *[Contrib.]*; Giuseppe Schlitzer *[Contrib.] and others. Collection of 11 articles.* **Riv. Pol. Ec.** , *LXXXII:VIII-IX (3rd series)*, 8-9:1992 pp. 9 – 297

26 Misperceptions of information sets and economic performance. Tetsuro Shimamoto. *Econ. S. Quart.* **43:1** 3:1992 pp. 19 – 32

27 Les modèles du cycle économique face à la corrélation productivité — emploi *[In French]*; Business cycle theories in the light of the employment — productivity correlation *[Summary]*. Steve Ambler. *Appl. Finan. Econ.* pp. 532 – 548

28 Modelling seasonality. S. Hylleberg *[Ed.]*. New York: Clarendon Press, 1992: 476 p. *ISBN: 019877317x; LofC: 91038351. Includes bibliographical references.* [Advanced texts in econometrics.]

29 A neoclassical model of seasonal fluctuations. Satyajit Chatterjee; B. Ravikumar. *J. Monet. Ec.* **29:1** 2:1992 pp. 59 – 86

30 Nuove teorie del ciclo economico e mercato del lavoro *[In Italian]*; New theories of the economic cycle and the labour market *[Summary]*. Alberto Cucinella. *Ec. Lav.* **XXVI:2** 4-6:1992 pp. 75 – 92

31 The permanent component of GNP and consumption — results from an univariate analysis for Switzerland; *[French summary]*; *[German summary]*. Peter Kugler. *Schw. Z. Volk. Stat.* **128:1** 3:1992 pp. 21 – 34

32 Productivity convergence, profit rates and long waves of accumulation. David Arsen; Jonas Zoninsein. *Rev. Rad. Pol. Ec.* **24:2** Summer:1992 pp. 51 – 59

33 Royaume-Uni — d'une récession à l'autre *[In French]*; United Kingdom — from one recession to the next *[Summary]*. Christine Rifflart. *Obser. Diag. Econ.* **:39** 1:1992 pp. 151 – 194

F.5: Fluctuations, cycles and trends *[Fluctuations, cycles et tendances]*

34 The social causes of economic decline — organizational failure and redlining. John F. Tomer. *R. Soc. Econ.* **L:1** Spring:1992 pp. 61 – 81

35 Stochastic trends and economic fluctuations in a small open economy. E. Mellander; A. Vredin; A. Warne. *J. Appl. Econ.* **7:4** 10-12:1992 pp. 369 – 394

36 Stochastic trends in consumption and the term structure of interest rates. Lance A. Fisher; Paul A. Richardson. *J. Macro.* **14:2** Spring:1992 pp. 289 – 304

37 The synchronization of business cycles across the European Community. J.P. Formby; S.C. Norrbin; R. Sakano. *Open Econ. R.* **3:3** 1992 pp. 233 – 254

38 Testing for a unit root in Japanese GNP. Y. Iwamoto; H. Kobayashi. *Jpn. Wor. Econ.* **4:1** 5:1992 pp. 17 – 37

39 Testing the satisficing version of the political business cycle 1905-1984. L.S. Davidson; M. Fratianni; J. von Hagen. *Publ. Choice* **73:1** 1:1992 pp. 21 – 36

40 Twilight of the American dream. Sharon Smith. *Int. Soc.* **54** Spring:1992 pp. 3 – 43

41 Válság vagy visszaesés? *[In Hungarian]*; Crisis or recession? *[Summary]*. László Csaba. *Közg. Sz.* **XXXIX** 2:1992 pp. 93 – 108

42 Wage contracts and business cycle models. S. Ambler; L. Phaneuf. *Eur. Econ. R.* **36:4** 5:1992 pp. 783 – 800

43 Why do countries and industries with large seasonal cycles also have large business cycles? J. Joseph Beaulieu; Jeffrey K. MacKie-Mason; Jeffrey A. Miron. *Q. J. Econ.* **CVII:2** 5:1992 pp. 621 – 656

G: Organization of production — *Organisation de la production*

G.1: Productivity, output, technological progress — *Productivité, rendement, progrès technique*

Sub-divisions: Innovation *[Innovation]*; Technological change *[Progrès technique]*

1 Age, experience and corporate synergy — when are they sources of business unit advantage? P.J. Williamson; P.J. Verdin. *Br. J. Manag.* **3:4** 12:1992 pp. 221 – 235

2 Beyond Taylorism — computerization and the new industrial relations. Lorraine Giordano; Christopher Howe *[Foreword]*. New York: St. Martin's Press, 1992: 236 p. *ISBN: 0312075790; LofC: 91038759. Includes bibliographical references and index.*

3 Company and campus partnership — supporting technology transfer. D. Jane Bower. London: Routledge, 1992: 197 p. *ISBN: 0415070805; LofC: 91048102. Includes bibliographical references (p.) and index.*

4 Development, technology, and flexibility — Brazil faces the industrial divide. João Carlos Ferraz; Howard Rush; Ian Miles. London: Routledge, 1992: 274 p. *ISBN: 0415070899; LofC: 91038284. Includes bibliographical references and index.*

5 The emergence of technopolis — knowledge-intensive technologies and regional development. Robert W. Preer. New York: Praeger, 1992: x, 187 p. *ISBN: 027594090x; LofC: 91030616. Includes bibliographical references (p. [159]-179) and index.*

6 The human-computer interface for information retrieval. Debora Shaw. *Ann. R. Info. Sci. Tech.* **26** 1991 pp. 155 – 195

7 An index theorem for nonconvex production economies. Elyes Jouini. *J. Econ. Theo.* **57:1** 6:1992 pp. 176 – 196

8 Indian informatics in the 1980s — the changing character of state involvement. P.B. Evans. *World Dev.* **20:1** 1:1992 pp. 1 – 18

9 Is efficiency decline rent decline or capacity decline? Edward M. Miller. *S. Econ. J.* **58:3** 1:1992 pp. 635 – 643

10 Licensing and the sharing of knowledge in research joint ventures. Sudipto Bhattacharya; Jacob Glazer; David E.M. Sappington. *J. Econ. Theo.* **56:1** 2:1992 pp. 43 – 69

11 Mera för mindre — men hur? Produktivitets- och effektivitetsuppfattningar i offentlig och företagsverksamhet *[In Swedish]*; [More for less, but how? Notions of productivity and efficiency in public and business activity]. Pär Landor. Abo: Abo Akademi, 1990: 115 p.

G.1: Productivity, output, technological progress *[Productivité, rendement, progrès technique]*
(ill) *ISBN: 951649742x. Includes bibliographical references (p. 112-115).* [Meddelanden fran Ekonomisk-statsvetenskapliga fakulteten vid Abo akademi; Forskningsprojektet "Effektivitet, förvaltning och demokrati i kommuner".]

12 Mogućnost mjerenja efikasnosti organizacije predmeta rada *[In Serbo-Croatian]*; Возможности измерения эффективности организации предмета труда *[Russian summary]*; Possibilities for measuring efficiency of the organization of the means of production *[Summary]*. Marin Buble. *Ekon. Preg.* **43:3-4** 1992 pp. 247 – 268

13 Organizational equilibria and production efficiency. U. Pagano. *Metroeconomica* **XLIII:1-2** 2-6:1992 pp. 227 – 246

14 Science and technology policy for economic development in Africa. Aqueil Ahmad *[Contrib.]*; John W. Forje *[Contrib.]*; Paul B. Vitta *[Contrib.]*; Jacques Gaillard *[Contrib.]*; Roland Waast *[Contrib.]*; Thomas Owen Eisemon *[Contrib.]*; Charles H. Davis *[Contrib.]*; Scott Tiffin *[Contrib.]*; Fola Osotimehin *[Contrib.]*; John E. Udo Ndebbio *[Contrib.] and others. Collection of 9 articles.* **J. As. Afr. S.** , *XXVII:1-2*, 1-4:1992 pp. 1 – 151

15 Transaction costs, technology transfer, and in-house R & D — a study of the Indian private corporate sector. N.S. Siddharthan. *J. Econ. Beh.* **18:2** 7:1992 pp. 265 – 272

Innovation *[Innovation]*

16 Competition among techniques in the presence of increasing returns to scale. B. Amable. *J. Evolut. Econ.* **2:2** 1992 pp. 147 – 158

17 Determinants of innovative activity in oligopolistic markets. M. Stadler. *J. Econ.* **56:2** 1992 pp. 137 – 156

18 The effects of organizational culture, structure and market expectations on technical innovation — a hypothesis. I. Demirag; A. Tylecote. *Br. J. Manag.* **3:1** 3:1992 pp. 7 – 20

19 F and E-Verhalten und Gewinnentwicklung im dynamischen Wettbewerb *[In German]*; R and D expenditures, profits and dynamic competition *[Summary]*. Manfred Stadtler. *Jahrb. N. St.* **209:1-2** 1:1992 pp. 31 – 46

20 Facteurs de performance de l'innovation technologique *[In French]*; Factors of performance in the technological innovation *[Summary]*. Jean-Marie Jacques; Isabelle Husson; Jacques Bughin. *Gestion* **8:6** 1992 pp. 135 – 150

21 Innovation and technological change — an Austrian-British comparison. N. Alderman; M.M. Fischer. *Envir. Plan. B.* **24:2** 2:1992 pp. 273 – 288

22 On the equilibrium proportion of innovation and imitation. A game-theoretic approach. T. Eger; M. Kraft; P. Weise. *Econ. Lett.* **38:1** 1:1992 pp. 93 – 98

23 Technological innovation and industrial evolution — the emergence of industrial networks. Anders Lundgren. Stockholm: Stockholm School of Economics, Economic Research Institute, 1991: 1 p. *ISBN: 9172583320. Includes bibliographical references (p. 209-219).*

24 Technologie en economie — de nederlandse positie *[In Dutch]*; [Technology and the economy — the Netherlands' position. Bert Minne. 's-Gravenhage: Centraal Planbureau, 1992: 145 p. *ISBN: 9034628272.* [Onderzoeksmemorandum.]

25 Technopôle/technopole — analyse théorique *[In French]*; [A theoretical analysis of technology transfer]. C. Hugon. *Econ. Cen.E.* **34:4** 1992 pp. 205 – 224

Technological change *[Progrès technique]*

26 Changing frames — understanding technological change in organizations. Wanda J. Orlikowski; Debra C. Gash. Cambridge, MA.: Center for Information Systems Research, Sloan School of Management, Massachusetts Institute of Technology, 1992: 32 p. *ISBN: oc26145503. Includes bibliographical references (p. 26-32).* [Sloan working paper; CISR working paper. : No. 3368-92]

27 Choice of technology in small and large firms — grain milling in Tanzania. M.S.D. Bagachwa. *World Dev.* **20:1** 1:1992 pp. 97 – 108

28 Consumption, production and technological progress — a unified entropic approach. T.H. Dung. *Ecol. Eco.* **6:3** 12:1992 pp. 195 – 210

29 Diffusion of information technology — opportunities and constraints. A. Mody *[Contrib.]*; C. Dahlman *[Contrib.]*; A. Cane *[Contrib.]*; A. Moussa *[Contrib.]*; R. Schware *[Contrib.]*; D. McKendrick *[Contrib.]*; C. Frischtak *[Contrib.]*; W.B. Tan *[Contrib.]*; C.W.E. Lui *[Contrib.]*; C.M. Loh *[Contrib.] and others. Collection of 10 articles.* **World Dev.** , *20:12*, 12:1992 pp. 1703 – 1857

G.1: Productivity, output, technological progress *[Productivité, rendement, progrès technique]* — *Technological change [Progrès technique]*

30 The dilemma of technological leadership — a conceptual framework. Takeru Kusunoki. *Hito. J. Comm. Manag.* **27:1** 11:1992 pp. 63 – 79

31 The economics of hope — essays on technical change, economic growth, and the environment. Christopher Freeman. London: Pinter Publishers, 1992: 249 p. *ISBN: 1855670836; LofC: 92015155. Includes bibliographical references and index.*

32 Il fattore resa e la curva di apprendimento *[In Italian]*; The yield factor and the learning curve *[Summary]*. Harald Gruber. *Industria* **XIII:4** 10-12:1992 pp. 623 – 648

33 Forms of technical change. M. Webber; E. Sheppard; D. Rigby. *Envir. Plan.A.* **24:12** 12:1992 pp. 1679 – 1709

34 Innovation and technological change — an Austrian-British comparison. N. Alderman; M.M. Fischer. *Envir. Plan. B.* **24:2** 2:1992 pp. 273 – 288

35 New production systems — a response to critics and a re-evaluation. John Mathews. *J. Aust. Pol. Econ.* **:30** 12:1992 pp. 91 – 128

36 New technologies and enterprise development in Africa. Scott Tiffin; Fola Osotimehin; Richard Sanders. Paris: Development Centre of the Organisation for Economic Co-operation and Development, 1992: 212 p. *ISBN: 9264137505. Includes bibliographical references (p. 189-212).* [Development Centre studies.]

37 New trends in technological change — the use of general and abstract knowledge in industrial research. A. Arora; A. Gambardella. *Riv. Int. Sci. Soc.* **C:3** 7-9:1992 pp. 259 – 277

38 On dynamics with time-to-build investment technology and non-time-separable leisure. Yannis M. Ioannides; Bart Taub. *J. Econ. Dyn. Cont.* **16:2** 4:1992 pp. 225 – 242

39 Production process and technical change. Mario Morroni. Cambridge: Cambridge University Press, 1992: 224 p. *ISBN: 0521410010; LofC: 91003040. Includes bibliographical references and index.*

40 The productivity of a nation — the measurement of technical change in the total production system (example — Finland 1970-1985). Pirkko Aulin-Ahmavaara. Helsinki: Tilastokeskus, 1992: 72 p. *ISBN: 9514765273. Bibliography — p.71-72.* [Studies.]

41 Reputations in the adoption of a new technology. K. Hendricks. *Int. J. Ind. O.* **10:4** 12:1992 pp. 663 – 677

42 The rise and fall of American technological leadership — the postwar era in historical perspective. Richard R. Nelson; Gavin Wright. *J. Econ. Lit.* **XXX:4** 12:1992 pp. 1931 – 1964

43 The role of the state in technological progress. R. Mosquera. *CEPAL R.* **:45** 12:1991 pp. 61 – 70

44 Science, technology and development in the Third World — some critical notes on the North-South technology transfer debate. Parasara Mishra. *Ind. J. Pol. Sci.* **LIII:1** 1-3:1992 pp. 57 – 77

45 Spatial competition and the adoption of new technology; Concorrenza spaziale e adozione di nuova tecnologia *[Italian summary]*. Fabio Mazzola. *Rev. Int. Sci. Ec. Com.* **XXXIX:1** 1:1992 pp. 23 – 48

46 Technical change and technical adaptation to multinational firms — the case of Taiwan's electronics industry. Tain-Jy Chen. *Econ. Dev. Cult. Change* **40:4** 7:1992 pp. 867 – 881

47 Technological change at the regional level — the role of location, firm structure, and strategy. F. Tödtling. *Envir. Plan.A.* **24:11** 11:1992 pp. 1565 – 1584

48 Technological change in China. Richard Conroy. Paris: Development Centre, Organisation for Economic Co-operation and Development, 1992: 276 p. *ISBN: 9264136525.* [Development Centre studies.]

49 Technological change — the role of scientists and engineers. Derek L. Bosworth; Robert Wilson; Paul Taylor. Aldershot: Avebury, 1992: 137 p. *ISBN: 1856283224.*

50 Technological change, projection of the technology matrix and the hypothesis of negative coefficient changes — parametric and non-parametric tests with Swedish input-output data. Göran Östblom. *Econ. Sys. Res.* **4:3** 1992 pp. 235 – 244

51 Technological diffusion in primary health care. L.M. Klausen; T.E. Olsen; A.E. Risa. *J. Health Econ.* **11:4** 1992 pp. 439 – 451

52 Technologieentwicklung und Technologieprogramme — Lehren für kleine offene Volkswirtschaften *[In German]*; [Technological development and technology policy — lessons for small open economies]. Wolfgang Polt. *Wirt. Bl‰t.* **39:4** 1992 pp. 424 – 434

53 Technology and organization — power, meaning and design. Harry Scarbrough; J. Martin Corbett. New York: Routledge, 1992: 178 p. *ISBN: 0415073847; LofC: 91044793.* [Routledge series in analytical management.]

G.1: Productivity, output, technological progress *[Productivité, rendement, progrès technique] — Technological change [Progrès technique]*

54 Technology and the future of work. Paul S. Adler *[Ed.]*. New York: Oxford University Press, 1992: xiv, 336 p. *ISBN: 0195071719; LofC: 91017526. Includes bibliographical references and indexes.*

55 Technology and the wealth of nations. Nathan Rosenberg *[Ed.]*; Ralph Landau *[Ed.]*; David C. Mowery *[Ed.]*. Stanford, CA.: Stanford University Press,c, 1992: 443 p. *ISBN: 0804720827; LofC: 92024181. Includes bibliographical references and index.*

56 Technology and transition — a survey of biotechnology in Russia, Ukraine and the Baltic States. Anthony Rimmington; Rod Greenshields. London: Pinter Publishers, 1992: 227 p. *ISBN: 1855670380.*

57 Technology and US competitiveness — an institutional focus. W. Henry Lambright *[Ed.]*; Dianne Rahm *[Ed.]*. Westport, CT.: Greenwood Press, 1992: 185 p. *ISBN: 0313285608.* [Contributions in eèconomics and economic history.]

58 Technology and work in German industry. Norman Altmann *[Ed.]*; Christoph Köhler *[Ed.]*; Pamela Meil *[Ed.]*. London: Routledge, 1992: 446 p. *ISBN: 0415079268; LofC: 91041732. Includes bibliographical references and index.*

59 Technology transfer in Europe — public and private networks. David Charles; Jeremy Howells. London: Belhaven Press, 1992: 202 p. *ISBN: 1852931604.* [Studies in the information economy.]

60 Technopôle/technopole — analyse théorique *[In French]*; [A theoretical analysis of technology transfer]. C. Hugon. *Econ. Cen.E.* **34:4** 1992 pp. 205 – 224

61 Towards a dynamic theory of transactions. B. Nooteboom. *J. Evolut. Econ.* **2:4** 1992 pp. 281 – 299

62 What makes technology transfer? Small-scale hydropower in Nepal's public and private sectors. G. Cromwell. *World Dev.* **20:7** 7:1992 pp. 979 – 989

G.1.1: Productivity: functions and measurement —
Productivité: fonctions et mesure

1 Accounting for differences in aggregate state productivity. G.A. Carlino; R. Voith. *Reg. Sci. Urb. Econ.* **22:4** 11:1992 pp. 597 – 617

2 Advanced manufacturing systems and organizational choice — a sociotechnical system approach. A.B. Shani (Rami); Robert M. Grant; R. Krishnan; Eric Thompson. *Calif. Manag. R.* **34:4** Summer:1992 pp. 91 – 111

3 Adverse producer incentives and product quality when consumers are short-term players. P.B. Overgaard. *J. Econ.* **55:2** 1992 pp. 169 – 192

4 Aggregation — aggregate production functions and related topics. Franklin M. Fisher; John Monz. Hemel Hempstead: Harvester Wheatsheaf, 1992: 280 p. *ISBN: 0745011446.*

5 Asset valuation and production efficiency in an overlapping-generations model with production shocks. W. Davis Dechert; Kenji Yamamoto. *R. Econ. S.* **59:2(199)** 4:1992 pp. 389 – 406

6 Deterministic approximation to co-production problems with service constraints and random yields. Gabriel R. Bitran; Thin-Yin Leong. *Manag. Sci.* **38:5** 5:1992 pp. 724 – 742

7 An econometric study of hours and output variation with preference shocks. Valerie R. Bencivenga. *Int. Econ. R.* **33:2** 5:1992 pp. 449 – 472

8 Economic reform and product quality improvement efforts in the Soviet Union. Paul Goldberg. *Eur.-Asia Stud.* **44:1** 1992 pp. 113 – 122

9 The economics of quality, grades and brands. Peter Bowbrick. New York: Routledge, 1992: 343 p. *ISBN: 0415078482; LofC: 91041640. Includes bibliographical references and index.*

10 Eureka — a hybrid system for assembly line balancing. Thomas R. Hoffmann. *Manag. Sci.* **38:1** 1:1992 pp. 39 – 47

11 Expectations, substitution, and scrapping in a putty-clay model. E. Bjørn; P. Frenger. *J. Econ.* **56:2** 1992 pp. 157 – 184

12 Factor substitution in Greek manufacturing industries — implications for capital-skill complementarity hypothesis. Epaminondas E. Panas. *Gr. Econ. Rev.* **13:1** 6:1991 pp. 71 – 94

13 Factors contributing to productivity growth in the LDCs. R.G. Zind. *Eco. Notes* **21:1** 1992 pp. 120 – 136

G.1.1: Productivity: functions and measurement *[Productivité: fonctions et mesure]*

14 Financial capacity and output fluctuations in an economy with multi-period financial relationships. Mark Gertler. *R. Econ. S.* **59:3(200)** 7:1992 pp. 455 – 471

15 Flexible specialization — the application of theory in a poor country context — Leon, Mexico. Arthur A. Morris; Stella Lowder. *Int. J. Urban* **16:2** 6:1992 pp. 190 – 201

16 Industrial invention — a supply and demand model for the UK, 1961-1989. S. Parker. *Appl. Econ.* **24:7** 7:1992 pp. 733 – 738

17 Industrial subcontracting in the UK and Japan. John T. Thoburn; Makoto Takashima. Aldershot: Avebury, 1992: 152 p. *ISBN: 185628347x.* [The Avebury business school library.]

18 International evidence on persistence in output in the presence of an episodic change. B. Raj. *J. Appl. Econ.* **7:3** 7-9:1992 pp. 281 – 294

19 Linear programming models for firm and industry performance. Rolf Färe; Shawna Grosskopf; Sung-Ko Li. *Sc. J. Econ.* **94:4** 1992 pp. 599 – 608

20 Making noisy data sing — estimating production technologies in developing countries. James R. Tybout. *J. Economet.* **53:1-3** 7-9:1992 pp. 25 – 43

21 Manufacturing productivity and high-tech investment. Charles Steindel. *Q. R. Fed. Res. Bank N.Y.* **17:2** Summer:1992 pp. 39 – 47

22 Mäßiger Produktionsansteig in den Industrieländern *[In German]*; [Slight increase in production in industrial states] *[Summary]*. Stefanie Bessin; Malte Fischer; Klaus-Jürgen Gern; Eckhard Nitschke; Klaus-Werner Schatz; Peter Trapp. *Weltwirt.* **:2** 1992 pp. 107 – 133

23 The measurement of productivity. W.E. Diewert. *B. Econ. Res.* **44:3** 7:1992 pp. 163 – 198

24 Misure di produttività e di efficienza — una rassegna dei recenti sviluppi *[In Italian]*; (Measures of productivity and efficiency — a review of recent development). Ornella Wanda Maietta. *Riv. Econ. Agrar.* **XLVII:2** 6:1992 pp. 307 – 333

25 Modeling short-run cost and production functions in computerized business simulations. Steven C. Gold. *Simulat. Gam.* **23:4** 12:1992 pp. 417 – 430

26 Il modello di specializzazione dell'Italia nel contesto europeo *[In Italian]*; [Italy's model of specialization in the European context] *[Summary]*. Lucia Tajoli. *Riv. Pol. Ec.* **LXXXII-Serie III:X** 10:1992 pp. 173 – 207

27 Multiple output measures of returns to scale. Hirofumi Fukuyama. *Econ. S. Quart.* **43:2** 6:1992 pp. 105 – 117

28 Persistence of leadership in product innovation. Harald Gruber. *J. Ind. Econ.* **XL:4** 12:1992 pp. 359 – 375

29 Product development and competitiveness. Kim B. Clark; Takahiro Fujimoto. *J. Jap. Int. Ec.* **6:2** 6:1992 pp. 101 – 143

30 Productivity concepts and measurement problems. Charles R. Hulten *[Contrib.]*; Karl-Gustaf Löfgren *[Contrib.]*; Zvi Griliches *[Contrib.]*; Christian Hjorth-Andersen *[Contrib.]*; Dale W. Jorgenson *[Contrib.]*; Barbara M. Fraumeni *[Contrib.]*; Klaus Conrad *[Contrib.]*; Michael Intriligator *[Contrib.]*; Petter Frenger *[Contrib.]*; Jeffrey Bernstein *[Contrib.]* and others. *Collection of 14 articles.* **Sc. J. Econ.** , *94*, 1992 pp. 9 – 269

31 Productivity growth, wage setting and the equilibrium rate of unemployment. Alan Manning. London: London School of Economics and Political Science. Centre for Economic Performance, 1992: 52 p.

32 Productivity measurement from a deficient data base — an empirical study of Kenya's manufacturing sector. Eckhard Siggel. *J. Prod. Anal.* **3:4** 12:1992 pp. 365 – 380

33 Productivity measurement in common property resource industries — an application to the Pacific coast trawl fishery. D. Squires. *Rand J. Eco.* **23:2** Summer:1992 pp. 221 – 236

34 Recent developments in the theory of industrial organization. Alfredo del Monte. Basingstoke: Macmillan Academic and Professional, 1992: 246 p. *ISBN: 0333531582.*

35 Selection of auditor firms by companies in the new issue market. M. Firth; A. Smith. *Appl. Econ.* **24:2** 2:1992 pp. 247 – 256

36 Una stima degli effetti derivanti dall'applicazione di un'imposta sul valore aggiunto prodotto dalle imprese *[In Italian]*; An estimation of the effects resulting from the application of a value added tax on production *[Summary]*. Lorenzo Birindelli; Franca Crucianelli; Stefano Palmieri. *Ec. Lav.* **XXVI:1** 1-3:1992 pp. 79 – 94

37 Stochastic innovation and product market organization. S.S. Reynolds; R.M. Isaac. *Econ. Theory* **2:4** 1992 pp. 525 – 546

38 The structural implications of technological change in the manufacturing sector. Maurice D. Levi; Yimin Zhang. *J. Prod. Anal.* **3:4** 12:1992 pp. 381 – 399

G.1.1: Productivity: functions and measurement *[Productivité: fonctions et mesure]*

39 Symposium on compatibility. Richard J. Gilbert *[Ed.]*; Joseph Farrell *[Contrib.]*; Garth Saloner *[Contrib.]*; Carmen Matutes *[Contrib.]*; Pierre Regibeau *[Contrib.]*; Michael L. Katz *[Contrib.]*; Carl Shapiro *[Contrib.]*; Jeffrey Church *[Contrib.]*; Neil Gandal *[Contrib.]*; Nicholas Economides *[Contrib.] and others. Collection of 6 articles.* **J. Ind. Econ.** , *XL:1*, 3:1992 pp. 1 – 123

40 Technology and obsolescence — a reinterpretation of the specific-factor model of production. S. Marjit. *J. Econ.* **55:2** 1992 pp. 193 – 208

41 Transitory productivity shocks and long-run output. Oded Galor; Daniel Tsiddon. *Int. Econ. R.* **33:4** 11:1992 pp. 921 – 933

G.1.2: Productivity: descriptive studies — *Productivité: études descriptives*

1 Australia's industrial R&D expenditure and foreign trade. H.-J. Engelbrecht. *Appl. Econ.* **24:5** 5:1992 pp. 545 – 556

2 Conference on productivity and international competitiveness — part I. Dale W. Jorgenson *[Contrib.]*; Michael J. Boskin *[Contrib.]*; Lawrence J. Lau; Masahiro Kuroda *[Contrib.]*; Shinichiro Nakamura *[Contrib.]*; Jingwen Li *[Contrib.]*; Michael Denny *[Contrib.]*; Melvyn Fuss *[Contrib.]*; Leonard Waverman *[Contrib.]*; Jeffrey Bernstein *[Contrib.] and others. Collection of 6 articles.* **Econ. S. Quart.** , *43:4*, 12:1992 pp. 291 – 360

3 Convergence in developed countries — an empirical investigation; *[German summary]*; *[French summary]*; *[Spanish summary].* M. Shahid Alam. *Welt.liches Arc.* **128:2** 1992 pp. 189 – 201

4 Effects of foreign labour on the production pattern — the Swiss case; *[French summary]*; *[German summary].* Beat Bürgenmeier; Théo Butare; Philippe Favarger. *Schw. Z. Volk. Stat.* **128:2** 6:1992 pp. 103 – 124

5 Flexible manufacturing systems. Economic effects in Japan, United States, and Western Europe. E. Mansfield. *Jpn. Wor. Econ.* **4:1** 5:1992 pp. 1 – 16

6 The growth of US labour productivity 1950-1989. D.W. Rasmussen; I. Kim. *Appl. Econ.* **24:3** 3:1992 pp. 285 – 290

7 Improving the effectiveness of gainsharing — the role of fairness and participation. Christine Cooper; Bruno Dyck; Norman Frohlich. *Adm. Sci. Qua.* **37:3** 9:1992 pp. 471 – 490

8 Incentive effects of assigned goals and compensation schemes on budgetary performance. Victor A. Fatseas; Mark K. Hirst. *Acc. Bus. Res.* **22:88** Autumn:1992 pp. 347 – 355

9 Industrial relations and productivity growth — a comparative perspective. R. Buchele; J. Christiansen. *Internat. Contrib. Lab. Stud.* **2** 1992 pp. 77 – 97

10 Post-reform productivity performance and sources of growth in Chinese industry — 1980-1985. Robert H. McGuckin; Sang V. Nguyen; Jeffrey R. Taylor; Charles A. Waite. *R. In. Weal.* **38:3** 9:1992 pp. 249 – 266

11 Production performance. K.C. Land *[Contrib.]*; C.A. Knox Lovell *[Contrib.]*; S. Thore *[Contrib.]*; E.N. Wolff *[Contrib.]. Collection of 2 articles.* **Publ. Finan.** , *47*, 1992 pp. 109 – 137

12 Productivity growth in U.K. companies, 1975-1986. S. Nickell; S. Wadhwani; M. Wall; H. König *[Comments by].* *Eur. Econ. R.* **36:5** 6:1992 pp. 1055 – 1085

13 Regulatory reform and productivity growth in the UK's public utilities. M. Bishop; D. Thompson. *Appl. Econ.* **24:11** 11:1992 pp. 1181 – 1190

14 Research notes on the best British companies — a peer evaluation of Britain's leading firms. J. Saunders; M. Brown; S. Laverick. *Br. J. Manag.* **3:4** 12:1992 pp. 181 – 195

15 Resource use and U.S. manufacturing productivity growth. David Alexander. *J. Post. Keyn. Ec.* **14:3** Spring:1992 pp. 389 – 408

16 The spatial dynamics of Japanese manufacturing productivity — an empirical analysis by expanded verdoorn equations. Emilio Casetti; Kyoko Tanaka. *Pap. Reg. Sci.* **71:1** 1:1992 pp. 1 – 14

17 Technical change and the demand for skills by US industries. David R. Howell; Edward N. Wolff. *Camb. J. Econ.* **16:2** 6:1992 pp. 127 – 146

18 Unravelling the productivity growth slowdown in the United States, Canada, and Japan — the effects of subequilibrium, scale economies, and markups. Catherine J. Morrison. *Rev. Econ. St.* **LXXIV:3** 8:1992 pp. 381 – 393

G.1.2: Productivity: descriptive studies *[Productivité: études descriptives]*
19 Welchen Sinn haben Modellrechnungen zur Anpassung der Arbeitsproduktivität in Ost- und Westdeutschland? *[In German]*; [Model calculations and the adjustment of labour productivity levels in East and West Germany] *[Summary]*. Georg Erber; Rainer Pischner. *Konjunkturpolitik* **38:3** 1992 pp. 113 – 138

G.1.3: Productivity policy — *Politique de productivité*

1 Changes in the attitude of major Japanese corporations to research and development. Nakaoka Tetsurō. *Jpn. Forum* **4:1** 4:1992 pp. 121 – 143
2 Cooperative and noncooperative R&D in an oligopoly with spillovers. Kotaro Suzumura. *Am. Econ. Rev.* **82:5** 12:1992 pp. 1307 – 1320
3 De la bataille pour mieux produire à la bataille pour mieux concevoir *[In French]*; From the battle for better production to the battle for better design *[Summary]*. Christian Navarre. *Gestion* **8:6** 1992 pp. 13 – 30
4 The degree of spillovers and the number of rivals for maximum effective R & D. R. de Bondt; P. Slaets; B. Cassiman. *Int. J. Ind. O.* **10:1** 3:1992 pp. 35 – 54
5 Do regions matter for R & D. Alfred Kleinknecht; Tom P. Poot. *Reg. Stud.* **26:3** 1992 pp. 221 – 232
6 Dynamic R&D competition under "hazard rate" uncertainty. J.P. Choi. *Rand J. Eco.* **22:4** Winter:1991 pp. 596 – 610
7 Economic development, government policy, and the diffusion of computing in Asia-Pacific countries. Kenneth L. Kraemer; Vijay Gurbaxani; John Leslie King. *Publ. Adm. Re.* **52:2** 3-4:1992 pp. 146 – 156
8 Inducing power of Japanese technological innovation — mechanism of Japan's industrial science and technology policy. C. Watanabe; Y. Honda. *Jpn. Wor. Econ.* **3:4** 4:1992 pp. 361 – 390
9 The innovation effort of Italian pharmaceutical firms — an analysis of R&D projects. A. Grandi; M. Sobrero. *Riv. Int. Sci. Soc.* **C:3** 7-9:1992 pp. 359 – 387
10 International productivity and competitiveness. Bert G. Hickman *[Ed.]*. New York: Oxford University Press, 1992: viii, 407 p. *ISBN: 0195065158; LofC: 90039134. Includes bibliographical references and index.*
11 Investment in research and development in India. Jandhyala B.G. Tilak. *Asian Ec.* **:82** 9:1992 pp. 40 – 65
12 Issues in the design of state science- and technology-based economic development programs — the case of Pennsylvania's Ben Franklin partnership. Dianne Rahm; Thomas F. Luce. *Econ. Devel. Q.* **6:1** 2:1992 pp. 41 – 51
13 Japanese industrial science and technology policy in the 1990s. C. Watanabe; Y. Honda. *Jpn. Wor. Econ.* **4:1** 5:1992 pp. 47 – 67
14 The limits of Japanese production theory. Willard I. Zangwill. *Interfaces* **22:5** 9-10:1992 pp. 14 – 25
15 Quality choice, trade policy, and firm incentives. James D. Reitzes. *Int. Econ. R.* **33:4** 11:1992 pp. 817 – 835
16 R&D et théorie de la firme *[In French]*; R&D and the theory of the firm *[Summary]*; Forschung und Entwicklung und Theorie der Firme *[In German]*; I&D y teoría de la firma *[In Spanish]*. O. Weinstein. *Econ. App.* **XLV:1** 1992 pp. 79 – 104
17 R&D expenditures and import competition — some evidence for the US; F&E-Ausgaben und Importkonkurrenz. Einige Befunde für die USA *[German summary]*; Des dépenses pour la R&D et la concurrence de l'importation — quelques preuves pour les Etats Unis *[French summary]*; Gasto en I&D e importaciones competitvas — alguna evidencia para los EE UU *[Spanish summary]*. Joachim Zietz; Bichaka Fayissa. *Welt.liches Arc.* **128:1** 1992 pp. 52 – 66
18 Research and development trends — criteria for assessment. Grahame Walshe. *Sci. Pub. Pol.* **19:2** 4:1992 pp. 75 – 88
19 Research and development with asymmetric firm sizes. R.J. Rosen. *Rand J. Eco.* **22:3** Autumn:1991 pp. 411 – 429
20 Research joint ventures and R&D cartels. Morton I. Kamien; Eitan Muller; Israel Zang. *Am. Econ. Rev.* **82:5** 12:1992 pp. 1293 – 1306
21 The sensitivity of strategic and corrective R & D policy in battles for monopoly. Kyle Bagwell; Robert W. Staiger. *Int. Econ. R.* **33:4** 11:1992 pp. 795 – 816

G.1.3: Productivity policy *[Politique de productivité]*

22 Technological innovation and internationalisation of Australian manufacturing industry. Noreen Cooray. *Ec. Pap. Aust.* **11:2** 6:1992 pp. 47 – 63

23 Uncertainty and the standard of patentability. Robert P. Merges. *High Tech. Law J.* **7:1** Spring:1992 pp. 1 – 70

G.2: Labour — *Travail*

G.2.1: Labour forces and labour market — *Main d'oeuvre et marché du travail*

Sub-divisions: Labour mobility *[Mobilité de la main d'oeuvre]*; Labour supply and demand *[Offre et demande de main d'oeuvre]*; Unemployment *[Chômage]*; Wage-employment relationship *[Relation salaires-emploi]*

1 Accelerated failure-time regression models with a regression model of surviving fraction — an application to the analysis of "permanent employment" in Japan. Kazuo Yamaguchi. *J. Am. Stat. Ass.* **87:418** 6:1992 pp. 284 – 292

2 Ajuste estructural, mercados laborales y TLC *[In Spanish]*; [Structural adjustment, labour markets and the North American Free Trade Agreement]. México, D.F.: El Colegio de México, 1992: 400 p. *ISBN: 968 12 0528 6.*

3 Asymmetric employment cycles in Britain — evidence and an explanation. S.M. Burgess. *Econ. J.* **102:411** 3:1992 pp. 279 – 290

4 Beschäftigungswirkungen des technischen Fortschritts *[In German]*; Employment effects of technical progress *[Summary]*. Alfred E. Ott; Susanne Wied-Nebbeling. *Jahrb. N. St.* **209:1-2** 1:1992 pp. 67 – 86

5 Changing conditions in the US labor market — effects of the Immigration Reform and Control Act of 1986. K.M. Donato; J. Durand; D.S. Massey. *Pop. Res. Pol. R.* **11:2** 1992 pp. 93 – 115

6 Chaos und Stabilität in einem Beschäftigungsmodell mit rationalen Erwartungen *[In German]*; Chaos and stability in an employment model with rational expectations *[Summary]*. Carsten Lange; Markus Pasche. *Z. Wirt. Soz.* **112:1** 1992 pp. 25 – 46

7 The child care labor market. David M. Blau. *J. Hum. Res.* **XXVII:1** Winter: 1992 pp. 9 – 39

8 Coerced and free labor — property rights and the development of the labor force. Stanley L. Engerman. *Expl. Ec. His.* **29:1** 1:1992 pp. 1 – 29

9 Counter-offers in the theory of individual job search. C.J. McKenna. *Econ. Lett.* **38:4** 1992 pp. 423 – 430

10 Crime, entrepreneurship, and labor force withdrawal. Samuel L. Myers. *Cont. Policy* **X:2** 4:1992 pp. 84 – 97

11 Decline of male labor market participation — the role of declining market opportunities. Chinhui Juhn. *Q. J. Econ.* **CVII:1** 2:1992 pp. 79 – 122

12 The determinants of black-white differences in early employment careers — search, layoffs, quits, and endogenous wage growth. Kenneth I. Wolpin. *J. Polit. Ec.* **100:3** 6:1992 pp. 535 – 560

13 Differential adoption of modern rice technology and labour market adjustments in south India. Keijiro Otsuka; C. Ramasamy. *Bang. Dev. Stud.* **XX:1** 3:1992 pp. 93 – 107

14 Disability transfers, self-reported health, and the labor force attachment of older men — evidence from the historical record. John Bound; Timothy Waidmann. *Q. J. Econ.* **CVII:4** 11:1992 pp. 1393 – 1420

15 The division of labor, coordination costs, and knowledge. Gary S. Becker; Kevin M. Murphy. *Q. J. Econ.* **CVII:4** 11:1992 pp. 1137 – 1160

16 The effect of discrimination and segregation on black male migration. Tom Larson. *Rev. Bl. Pol. Ec.* **20:3** Winter:1992 pp. 53 – 74

17 Employment creation in an oil-based economy — Kuwait. Robert E. Looney. *Middle E. Stud.* **28:3** 7:1992 pp. 565 – 576

18 Employment growth and change in the Mediterranean basin during the 1980s. Bojan Popović. *Int. Lab. Rev.* **131:3** 1992/1993 pp. 297 – 311

19 Employment growth, incumbents and entrants — evidence from Germany. T. Boeri; U. Cramer. *Int. J. Ind. O.* **10:4** 12:1992 pp. 545 – 565

G.2.1: Labour forces and labour market *[Main d'oeuvre et marché du travail]*

20 Employment in manufacturing — a long-run relationship and short-run dynamics. R. MacDonald; P.D. Murphy. *J. Econ. Stud.* **19:5** 1992 pp. 3 – 18

21 Enterprise size, IT and the service sector — the employment implications. Peter Nisbet. *New Tech. Work. Empl.* **7:1** Spring:1992 pp. 61 – 70

22 Estimating a firm's age-productivity profile using the present value of workers' earnings. Laurence J. Kotlikoff; Jagadeesh Gokhale. *Q. J. Econ.* **CVII:4** 11:1992 pp. 1215 – 1242

23 European integration and the integration of labour markets. David Marsden. *Labour [Italy]* **6:1** Spring:1992 pp. 3 – 35

24 Experience, credentials, and compensation in the Japanese and U.S. managerial labor markets — evidence from new micro data. Takao Kato; Mark Rockel. *J. Jap. Int. Ec.* **6:1** 3:1992 pp. 30 – 51

25 Federal and union job queues — further evidence from the US labour market. M.S. Mohanty. *Appl. Econ.* **24:10** 10:1992 pp. 1119 – 1128

26 Gross job creation, gross job destruction, and employment reallocation. Steven J. Davis; John Haltiwanger. *Q. J. Econ.* **CVII:3** 8:1992 pp. 819 – 864

27 Housing and employment in Indonesia — prospects for employment generation in the construction materials sector. Piet Rietveld. *B. Ind. Econ. St.* **28:2** 8:1992 pp. 55 – 74

28 How the macroeconomic environment affects human resource development. Arvil van Adams; Robert Goldfarb; Terence Kelly. Washington, D.C.: Population and Human Resources Department, The World Bank, 1992: 29 p. [Policy research working papers.]

29 Imperfect labour markets, the stock market and the inefficiency of capitalism. Alan Manning. *Ox. Econ. Pap.* **44:2** 4:1992 pp. 257 – 271

30 Informal work in Hong Kong. Yin Wah Chu. *Int. J. Urban* **16:3** 9:1992 pp. 420 – 441

31 Insider-outsider theory and the case for implicit contracts. D. Leslie. *Econ. J.* **102:410** 1:1992 pp. 37 – 48

32 Job creation measures as activist fiscal policy — an empirical analysis of policy reaction behavior. H. Ohlsson. *Eur. J. Pol. Ec.* **8:2** 5:1992 pp. 269 – 280

33 Job search and immigrant assimilation — an earnings frontier approach. Nasser Daneshvary; Henry W. Herzog; Richard A. Hofler; Alan M. Schlottmann. *Rev. Econ. St.* **LXXIV:3** 8:1992 pp. 482 – 492

34 Kształtowanie sie lokalnych rynków pracy w początkowym okresie transformacji polskiej gospodarki (1990-1991) *[In Polish]*; (Формирование местных рынков рабочей силы в начале трансформации польской экономики (1990-1991): *Title only in Russian*); (Forming of local labour markets in the beginning of Polish economy tranformation (1990-1991)). Irena E. Kotowska; Marianna Kotowska-Jelonek. *Pra. Zab. Społ.* **:5-6** 5-6:1992 pp. 31 – 40

35 Labor force attitudes in the transition to the market — the Czechoslovak case. Jiří Večerník. *J. Public Pol.* **12:2** 4-6:1992 pp. 177 – 194

36 Labor market discrimination, imperfect information and self employment. Stephen Coate; Sharon Tennyson. *Ox. Econ. Pap.* **44:2** 4:1992 pp. 272 – 288

37 Labor market performance and regional types — a conceptual framework with empirical analysis of Austria. Ingrid Kubin; Michael Steiner. *Int. Reg. Sci. R.* **14:3** 1992 pp. 275 – 298

38 Labor utilization and nonwage labor costs in a disequilibrium macro framework. Horst Entorf; Heinz König; Winfried Pohlmeier. *Sc. J. Econ.* **94:1** 1992 pp. 71 – 84

39 Labour administration — the response to the crisis. Glen Sheehan. *Int. Lab. Rev.* **131:2** 1992 pp. 155 – 170

40 Labour and employment policies in Italy — report '90-'91. Renato Brunetta *[Ed.]*; Leonello Tronti *[Ed.]*. Rome: Fondazione Giacomo Brodolini, 1991: xiii, 372 p.

41 Labour and locality — uneven development and the rural labour process. Terry Marsden *[Ed.]*; Philip Lowe *[Ed.]*; Sarah Whatmore *[Ed.]*. London: David Fulton, 1992: 183 p. *ISBN: 1853461822.* [Critical perspectives on rural change series. : No. 4]

42 Labour flexibility in Europe. Tiziano Treu. *Int. Lab. Rev.* **131:4-5** 4-5:1992 pp. 497 – 512

43 Labour market regulation in France — topics and levels. L. Hoang-Ngoc; M. Lallement; F. Michon. *Internat. Contrib. Lab. Stud.* **2** 1992 pp. 1 – 15

44 Labour market segmentation, flexibility, and recession — a British Columbian case study. R. Hayter; T.J. Barnes. *Envir. Plan. C.* **10:3** 8:1992 pp. 333 – 354

45 Labour markets and the transition in Central and Eastern Europe. Tito Boeri; Mark Keese. *OECD Ec. Stud.* **:18** Spring:1992 pp. 133 – 161

46 Local labor markets. Jamie Peck *[Contrib.]*; Andrew E.G. Jonas *[Contrib.]*; Susan Hanson *[Contrib.]*; Geraldine Pratt *[Contrib.]*; Sara McLafferty *[Contrib.]*; Valerie Preston *[Contrib.]*. Collection of 4 articles. **Econ. Geogr.** , *68:4*, 10:1992 pp. 325 – 431

G.2.1: Labour forces and labour market *[Main d'oeuvre et marché du travail]*

47 The macroeconomic impact of flexible labor contracts, with an application to Spain. S. Bentolila; G. Saint-Paul; M.C. Burda *[Comments by]*; L.F. Katz *[Comments by]*. *Eur. Econ. R.* **36:5** 6:1992 pp. 1013 – 1047

48 Manpower planning in a market economy with labor market signals. Arvil van Adams; John Middleton; Adrian Ziderman. Washington, D.C.: Population and Human Resources Department, The World Bank, 1992: 27, 2 p. [Policy research working papers.]

49 Marché du travail et dynamique de l'avantage comparatif dans les nouveaux pays industrialisés d'Asie *[In French]*; Labour market and dynamic of the comparative advantage in Asian new industrialised countries *[Summary]*. B. Maximin. *Rev. Ec. Polit.* **102:3** 5-6:1992 pp. 423 – 447

50 "Market transition" in China — the case of the Jiangsu labor market, 1978-1990. Flemming Christiansen. *Mod. Chi.* **18:1** 1:1992 pp. 72 – 93

51 El mercado laboral en Japón — características y políticas sociales *[In Spanish]*; The labour market in Japan *[Summary]*. Juan José Bonilla Ramírez. *Est. Asia Afr.* **XXVII:3** 9-12:1992 pp. 442 – 471

52 Miért dolgozik az ember? *[In Hungarian]*; Why do people work? *[Summary]*. Judit Rimler. *Közg. Sz.* **XXXIX** 5:1992 pp. 448 – 459

53 Monopolistic competition, expected inflation and contract length. Giancarlo Marini; Pasquale Scaramozzino. *Labour [Italy]* **6:2** Autumn:1992 pp. 85 – 103

54 The new social economy — reworking the division of labor. Andrew Sayer; Richard Walker. Cambridge, M.A.: Blackwell, 1991: 306 p. *ISBN: 155786280x.*

55 Opening the black box — economic analyses of internal labour markets. John Creedy; Keith Whitfield. *J. Ind. Relat.* **34:3** 9:1992 pp. 455 – 471

56 The performance of the labor market during recession and structural adjustment — Costa Rica in the 1980s. T.H. Gindling; *Reviewed by:* A. Berry. *World Dev.* **20:11** 11:1992 pp. 1599 – 1616

57 A piacgazdaság kialakításának hatása a foglalkoztatottságra és ennek hosszú távú kilátásai *[In Hungarian]*; The impacts of developing a market economy on employment and its long-term prospects *[Summary]*. Sándor Türei. *Közg. Sz.* **XXXIX** 12:1992 pp. 1154 – 1174

58 R&D facilities and professional labour — labour force dynamics in high technology. Edward J. Malecki; Susan L. Bradbury. *Reg. Stud.* **26:2** 1992 pp. 123 – 136

59 The ratchet effect and the market for secondhand workers. Yoshitsugu Kanemoto; W. Bentley MacLeod. *J. Labor Ec.* **10:1** 1:1992 pp. 85 – 98

60 Simulating bias in the estimator of labor market discrimination. Lonnie K. Stevans; Charles Register; David N. Sessions. *Soc. Ind.* **27:2** 9:1992 pp. 157 – 168

61 Structural determinants of spatial labour markets — a case study of the Netherlands; *[French summary]*; *[German summary]*. Lambert van der Laan. *Reg. Stud.* **26:5** 1992 pp. 485 – 498

62 Tendenze demografiche e mercato del lavoro. Tirannia dei numeri e alternative di scelta *[In Italian]*; Demographic and labour market trends. The tiranny of numbers and alternative choices *[Summary]*. Giuseppe Gesano. *Ec. Lav.* **XXVI:2** 4-6:1992 pp. 93 – 108

63 Un test alternativo de la hipótesis de sustitución intertemporal del trabajo *[In Spanish]*; [An alternative test of the intertemporal substitution hypothesis for labour] *[Summary]*. Francisco Goerlich. *Invest. Econ.* **XVI:2** 5:1992 pp. 259 – 280

64 Transformacja rynku pracy w krajach wschodnioeuropejskich *[In Polish]*; (Labour market transformation in East European countries); (Трансформация рынка рабочей силы в странах восточной Европы: *Title only in Russian*). Urszula Sztanderska. *Pra. Zab. Społ.* **:2** 1992 pp. 1 – 9

65 Two ways to skin a cat — government policy and labour market reform in Australia and New Zealand. P. Brosnan; J. Burgess; D. Rea. *Internat. Contrib. Lab. Stud.* **2** 1992 pp. 17 – 44

66 Understanding the "informal sector" — a survey. Madhura Swaminathan. Helsinki: World Institute for Development Economics and Research of the United Nations University, 1992: 39 p. *Bibliography — p.34-39.* [WIDER working papers. : No. WP 95]

67 Until the end of time — labour market reform in Australia. Judith Sloan. *Aust. Ec. Rev.* 4th quarter:1992 pp. 65 – 78

68 Wage bargaining, public policies and underemployment of educated workers in LDCs. Asis Kumar Banerjee; Dipak Ghosh. *Aust. Econ. P.* **31:58** 6:1992 pp. 94 – 110

69 *[In Japanese]*; [What is the flexible system in Japanese labour process?]. Eiji Kyotani. *Mado* No.11 - 1992. pp. 104 – 116

G.2.1: **Labour forces and labour market** *[Main d'oeuvre et marché du travail]*
70 The workforce reconversion in the crisis of Fordism — element of break-up or element of transition? M.-C. Villeval. *Internat. Contrib. Lab. Stud.* **2** 1992 pp. 61 – 75
71 Working part-time — risks and opportunities. Barbara Warme *[Ed.]*; Katherina L. P. Lundy *[Ed.]*; Larry A. Lundy *[Ed.]*. New York: Praeger, 1992: xvi, 374 p. *ISBN: 0275931420; LofC: 91032680. Includes bibliographical references (p. [323]-357) and index.*
72 Young people and employment in the south west. David Dunkerley; Claire Wallace. *J. Interd. Ec.* **4:3** 1992 pp. 225 – 239

Labour mobility *[Mobilité de la main d'oeuvre]*
73 The choice of factor mobility in a dynamic world. O. Galor. *J. Pop. Ec.* **5:2** 1992 pp. 135 – 144
74 Economic mobility and agricultural labour in rural India — a case study. Jean Dreze; Peter Lanjouw; Nicholas Stern. London: STICERD, 1992: 65 p. [Development economics research programme.]
75 The economics of commuting and the urban labour market. Wayne Simpson; Anne van der Veen. *J. Econ. Sur.* **6:1** 1992 pp. 45 – 62
76 An empirical framework for the efficiency-wage model — use of micro data for Nigeria. Fidel Ezeala-Harrison. *J. Econ. Stud.* **19:3** 1992 pp. 18 – 35
77 International labor migration and domestic labor supply. R. Kochhar. *J. Pop. Ec.* **5:2** 1992 pp. 113 – 134
78 Investment in general and job-specific training with occupational mobility; Investition in generelles und firmenspezifisches Training bei beruflicher Mobilität *[German summary]*. Eva Pichler. *Jahrb. N. St.* **210:1-2** 7:1992 pp. 35 – 46
79 Job mobility and the careers of young men. Robert H. Topel; Michael P. Ward. *Q. J. Econ.* **CVII:2** 5:1992 pp. 439 – 479
80 Job tenure in the Dutch economy. C.C.J.M.C. Kerckhoffs; G.L.M. Wolfs. *Economist [Leiden]* **140:3** 1992 pp. 336 – 356
81 Labor migration in Europe — experiences from Germany after unification. B. Raffelhüschen. *Eur. Econ. R.* **36:7** 10:1992 pp. 1453 – 1471
82 Migration, age, and earnings — the special case of employee transfers. R.A. Nakosteen; M.A. Zimmer. *Appl. Econ.* **24:7** 7:1992 pp. 791 – 802
83 The new international migrations and the changes in the labour market. Enrico Pugliese. *Labour [Italy]* **6:1** Spring:1992 pp. 165 – 179
84 Panel estimates of male and female job turnover behavior — can female nonquitters be identified? Audrey Light; Manuelita Ureta. *J. Labor Ec.* **10:2** 4:1992 pp. 156 – 181
85 Self-selection and internal migration in the United States. George J. Borjas; Stephen G. Bronars; Stephen J. Trejo. *J. Urban Ec.* **32:2** 9:1992 pp. 159 – 185
86 A simple model of sectoral adjustment. Kiminori Matsuyama. *R. Econ. S.* **59:2(199)** 4:1992 pp. 375 – 388
87 The single European market and labour mobility. Graham Thom. *Ind. Relat. J.* **23:1** Spring:1992 pp. 14 – 25

Labour supply and demand *[Offre et demande de main d'oeuvre]*
88 L'analisi microeconomica dell'offerta di lavoro. Risultati e prospettive in Italia *[In Italian]*; A microeconomic analysis of the labour supply — results and prospects in Italy *[Summary]*. Ugo Colombino. *Ec. Lav.* **XXVI:1** 1-3:1992 pp. 157 – 174
89 Labour supply function for self employed workers. Rushidan Islam Rahman. *Bang. Dev. Stud.* **XX:1** 3:1992 pp. 75 – 92
90 The Australian experience of skilled migration — the Employer Nomination Scheme in the manufacturing and the finance, property and business services sectors. Arnold Kan. Canberra: Australian Government Publishing Service, 1991: 39 p. *ISBN: 0644139358. Includes bibliographical references.*
91 The broth and the cooks — a theory of surplus labor. K. Basu. *World Dev.* **20:1** 1:1992 pp. 109 – 118
92 The choice of factor mobility in a dynamic world. O. Galor. *J. Pop. Ec.* **5:2** 1992 pp. 135 – 144
93 Collective labor supply and welfare. Pierre-André Chiappori. *J. Polit. Ec.* **100:3** 6:1992 pp. 437 – 467
94 The coming labor shortage. John Sloan *[Contrib.]*; William B. Johnston *[Contrib.]*; Robert Polkinghorn *[Contrib.]*; Joan Davis Ratteray *[Contrib.]*; Jules Lichtenstein *[Contrib.]*;

G.2.1: Labour forces and labour market *[Main d'oeuvre et marché du travail]* — *Labour supply and demand [Offre et demande de main d'oeuvre]*

John Bishop *[Contrib.]*; Seymour Martin Lipset *[Contrib.]*; Emily S. Andrews *[Contrib.]*; June O'Neill *[Contrib.]*; Julian L. Simon *[Contrib.] and others. Collection of 10 articles.* **J. Labor Res.** , *XIII:1,* Winter:1992 pp. 1 – 78

95 The disease of direct labour — buying better for the public. Michael Ivens. London: Centre for Policy Studies, 1992: 25 p.

96 The econometrics of female labor supply and children. A. Nakamura; M. Nakamura. *Econom. R.* **11:1** 1992 pp. 1 – 72

97 The effect of social security on labor supply — a cohort analysis of the notch generation. Alan B. Krueger; Jörn-Steffen Pischke. *J. Labor Ec.* **10:4** 10:1992 pp. 412 – 437

98 Estimating labour supply disequilibrium with fixed-effects random-coefficients regression. K. Smith Conway; T.J. Kniesner. *Appl. Econ.* **24:7** 7:1992 pp. 781 – 789

99 Estimating labour supply in policy-orientated regional planning models. D.E. Fuller. *Envir. Plan.A.* **24:12** 12:1992 pp. 1781 – 1797

100 From labour shortage to labour shedding — labour markets in Central and Eastern Europe. Tito Boeri; Mark Keese. *Comm. Econ.* **4:3** 1992 pp. 373 – 394

101 Household composition, labor markets, and labor demand — testing for separation in agricultural household models. Dwayne Benjamin. *Econometrica* **60:2** 3:1992 pp. 287 – 322

102 The impact of affirmative action on labour demand — a test of some implications of the Le Chatelier principle. Peter Griffin. *Rev. Econ. St.* **LXXIV:2** 5:1992 pp. 251 – 260

103 Informal care and female labour supply. Tim Barmby; Sue Charles. *Scot. J. Poli.* **39:3** 8:1992 pp. 288 – 301

104 International labor migration and domestic labor supply. R. Kochhar. *J. Pop. Ec.* **5:2** 1992 pp. 113 – 134

105 Intertemporal substitution and labor supply in Japan. Richard Beason. *J. Hum. Res.* **XXVII:3** Summer:1992 pp. 511 – 533

106 Labor and economic growth in five Asian countries — South Korea, Malaysia, Taiwan, Thailand, and the Philippines. Walter Galenson. New York: Praeger, 1992: xi, 126 p. *ISBN: 0275942007; LofC: 91033883. Includes bibliographical references (p. [121]-126) and index.*

107 Labor flows in the corporate context — a case study of the managerial use of human resources and employee mobility. Sinikka Vanhala. Helsinki: Helsinki School of Economics and Business Administration, 1991: 263 p. *LofC: 91172217; ISBN: 9517008767. Thesis statement taken from added t.p. tipped in; Includes bibliographical references (p. 210-232).* [Acta Academiae Oeconomicae Helsingiensis.]

108 The labor market dynamics of economic restructuring — the United States and Germany in transition. Ronald Schettkat. New York: Praeger, 1992: xii, 213 p. *ISBN: 0275939103; LofC: 91023688. Includes bibliographical references and index.*

109 Labour supply and taxation — a survey. Richard Blundell. *Fis. Stud.* **13:3** 8:1992 pp. 15 – 40

110 Local labour markets — problems and policies. Mike Campbell *[Ed.]*; Katherine Duffy *[Ed.]*. Harlow: Longman, 1992: 202 p. *ISBN: 0582091039.* [Local economic and social strategy series.]

111 Modelli dinamici di domanda di lavoro nel manifatturiero italiano — un'analisi disaggregata condotta utilizzando un panel di impresa *[In Italian]*; Dynamic models of labour supply in the Italian manufacturing industry — a disaggregated analysis conducted with the use of a panel of firms *[Summary]*. Giovanni Urga. *Ec. Lav.* **XXVI:1** 1-3:1992 pp. 141 – 156

112 New technology, skills and management — human resources in the market economy. Adrian Campbell; Malcolm Warner. London: Routledge, 1992: 232 p. *ISBN: 0415055555; LofC: 92009502. Includes bibliographical references (p.221) and index.*

113 Nursing shortage crisis in New England — a test of supply and demand model; Scarsità di infermieri nel New England — verifica di un modello di domanda e offerta *[Italian summary]*. Sam Mirmirani; Richard N. Spivack. *Rev. Int. Sci. Ec. Com.* **XXXIX:4** 4:1992 pp. 325 – 340

114 Output and employment fluctuations; *[French summary]*. Klaus F. Zimmermann *[Ed.]*; Gebhard Flaig *[Contrib.]*; Friedhelm Pfeiffer *[Contrib.]*; Winfried Pohlmeier *[Contrib.]*; Lucie Merkle *[Contrib.]*; Klaus Conrad *[Contrib.]*; Helmut Seitz *[Contrib.]*; François Laisney *[Contrib.]*; Michael Lechner *[Contrib.]*; Wolfgang Franz *[Contrib.] and others. Collection of 13 articles.* **Rech. Ec. Louvain** , *58:3-4,* 1992 pp. 245 – 486

G.2.1: **Labour forces and labour market** *[Main d'oeuvre et marché du travail]* —
Labour supply and demand [Offre et demande de main d'oeuvre]

115 Pseudo-experimental estimates of labor supply functions in two Turkish state enterprises. M.R. Sertel; F. Adaman; E.Ü. Zenginobuz. *J. Econ. Beh.* **19:1** 9:1992 pp. 83 – 99

116 Separate taxation and married women's labor supply. A comparison of West Germany and Sweden. S. 'Gustefsson. *J. Pop. Ec.* **5:1** 1992 pp. 61 – 85

117 The Singapore worker — a profile. Soon Beng Chew; Rosalind Chew. Singapore: Oxford University Press, 1992: xiv, 202 p. *ISBN: 0195885783; LofC: 91035206. Includes bibliographical references (p. [193]-198) and index.*

118 Utility-based estimation of labour supply functions in the regular and irregular sectors. G. Lacroix; B. Fortin. *Econ. J.* **102:415** 11:1992 pp. 1407 – 1422

Unemployment *[Chômage]*

119 Advance notice and postdisplacement joblessness. Christopher J. Ruhm. *J. Labor Ec.* **10:1** 1:1992 pp. 1 – 32

120 Animal spirits. Peter Howitt; R. Preston McAfee. *Am. Econ. Rev.* **82:3** 6:1992 pp. 493 – 507

121 Consumer demand and equilibrium unemployment in a working model of the customer-market incentive-wage economy. Edmund S. Phelps. *Q. J. Econ.* **CVII:3** 8:1992 pp. 1003 – 1032

122 Desemprego — teorias e evidências sobre a experiência recente na OECD (I) *[In Portuguese]*; [Unemployment — theory and evidence on recent experiences in the OECD (I)] *[Summary]*. Edward J. Amadeo. *Rev. Bras. Ec.* **46:2** 4-6:1992 pp. 261 – 286

123 Desemprego — teorias e evidências sobre a experiência recente na OECD (II) *[In Portuguese]*; [Unemployment — theory and evidence on recent experiences in the OECD (II)] *[Summary]*. Edward J. Amadeo. *Rev. Bras. Ec.* **46:4** 10/12:1992 pp. 477 – 518

124 La disoccupazione in Italia e la natura dei divari territoriali *[In Italian]*; Unemployment in Italy and the nature of territorial diversities *[Summary]*. Patrizia Di Monte. *Ec. Lav.* **XXVI:2** 4-6:1992 pp. 29 – 45

125 Does unemployment lead to self-employment? Nigel Meager. *Small Bus. Econ.* **4:2** 6:1992 pp. 87 – 104

126 The duration of unemployment on the Dutch labour market   a proportional hazard model. C. Gorter; P. Nijkamp; P. Rietveld. *Reg. Sci. Urb. Econ.* **22:2** 6:1992 pp. 151 – 174

127 An efficiency-wage model with explicit monitoring — unemployment and welfare in an open economy. Richard A. Brecher. *J. Int. Econ.* **32:1/2** 2:1992 pp. 179 – 192

128 An endogenous skill loss model of long-term unemployment. Daron Acemoglu. London: London School of Economics and Political Science. Centre for Economic Performance, 1992: 27 p.

129 Estimation of mis-match and U-V analysis in Japan. K. Sakurai; T. Tachibanki. *Jpn. Wor. Econ.* **4:4** 12:1992 pp. 319 – 332

130 European unemployment — a survey. Charles R. Bean. London: London School of Economics and Political Science. Centre for Economic Performance, 1992: 116 p. [Discussion paper.]

131 Exporting jobs — the impact of import competition on employment and wages in U.S. manufacturing. Ana L. Revenga. *Q. J. Econ.* **CVII:1** 2:1992 pp. 255 – 284

132 Flow and stock analysis of Polish unemployment — January 1990-June 1991. Marek Gora; Hartmut Lehmann. *Labour [Italy]* **6:1** Spring:1992 pp. 87 – 119

133 The flow into unemployment in Britain. S.M. Burgess. *Econ. J.* **102:413** 7:1992 pp. 888 – 895

134 The impossibility of involuntary unemployment in an overlapping generations model with rational expectations. Christian Schultz. *J. Econ. Theo.* **58:1** 10:1992 pp. 61 – 76

135 Inside power as a source of hysteresis in unemployment — tests with Australian data. Nicolaas Groenewold; Leanne Taylor. *Econ. Rec.* **68:200** 3:1992 pp. 57 – 64

136 Labour market transitions of youth and prime age Italian unemployed. Patrizia Ordine. *Labour [Italy]* **6:2** Autumn:1992 pp. 123 – 143

137 Long term unemployment, hysteresis and the unemployment-vacancy relationship — a regional analysis; *[French summary]*; *[German summary]*. D.R. Jones; D.N. Manning. *Reg. Stud.* **26:1** 1992 pp. 17 – 30

138 Long-term unemployment in the OECD countries. F. Heylen. *Tijds. Econ. Manag.* **XXXVII:1** 4:1992 pp. 53 – 86

139 Loonrigiditeit en werkloosheid — de arbeidseconomie tussen markt en structuur *[In Flemish]*; Wage rigidity and unemployment *[Summary]*. Stefan Késenne. *Econ. Soc. Tidj.* **46:1** 3:1992 pp. 7 – 26

140 Loss of skill during unemployment and the persistence of employment shocks. Christopher A. Pissarides. *Q. J. Econ.* **CVII:4** 11:1992 pp. 1371 – 1392

G.2.1: Labour forces and labour market *[Main d'oeuvre et marché du travail]* — *Unemployment [Chômage]*

141 Matching and unemployment dynamics in a model of competition between employed and unemployed job searchers. Simon M. Burgess. London: London School of Economics and Political Science. Centre for Economic Performance, 1992: 28 p. [Discussion paper.]

142 Migrant unemployment and labour market programs. Roger Jones; Ian McAllister. Canberra: Australian Government Publishing Service, 1991: 141 p. *ISBN: 0644148284. On cover — Bureau of Immigration Research; Includes bibliographical references (p.130-134).*

143 Mismatch in the West German labour market? Ronald Schettkat. *Labour [Italy]* **6:1** Spring:1992 pp. 121 – 139

144 A model of regional contraction and unemployment. B. McCormick; S. Sheppard. *Econ. J.* **102:411** 3:1992 pp. 366 – 377

145 Models of unemployment in trade and economic development. Bharat R. Hazari; Pasquale M. Sgro. London: Routledge, 1992: 151 p. *ISBN: 0415022770; LofC: 91031697. Includes bibliographical references and index.*

146 Nieuwe richtingen in het economisch werkloosheidsonderzoek *[In Dutch]*; [New directions in economic research on unemployment]. H. Peer. *Maan. Econ.* **56:4** 1992 pp. 273 – 290

147 Nonfarm employment as a response to underemployment in agriculture; *[French summary]*. M. Rose Olfert. *Can. J. Ag. Ec.* **40:3** 11:1992 pp. 443 – 458

148 Output and employment fluctuations; *[French summary]*. Klaus F. Zimmermann *[Ed.]*; Gebhard Flaig *[Contrib.]*; Friedhelm Pfeiffer *[Contrib.]*; Winfried Pohlmeier *[Contrib.]*; Lucie Merkle *[Contrib.]*; Klaus Conrad *[Contrib.]*; Helmut Seitz *[Contrib.]*; François Laisney *[Contrib.]*; Michael Lechner *[Contrib.]*; Wolfgang Franz *[Contrib.] and others. Collection of 13 articles.* **Rech. Ec. Louvain** , *58:3-4*, 1992 pp. 245 – 486

149 Patterns of unemployment — an insider-outsider analysis. Assar Lindbeck; Dennis J. Snower. New York: Columbia University, Dept of Economics, [1992?]: 29 p. [Discussion paper series.]

150 Persistent unemployment, wages and hysteresis. Johannes Jakobus Graafland. Rotterdam: [s.n.], 1990: 158 p.

151 Policing the workshy — benefit controls, the labour market and the unemployed. Alex Bryson; John Jacobs. Aldershot: Avebury, 1992: 292 p. *ISBN: 1856283577.*

152 The role of the household production in models of involuntary unemployment and underemployment; Le rôle de la production domestique dans les modèles de chômage et de sous-emploi involontaires *[French summary]*. Ed Nosal; Richard Rogerson; Randall Wright. *Can. J. Econ.* **XXV:3** 8:1992 pp. 507 – 520

153 A search model with job changing costs — "Eurosclerosis" and unemployment. Simon M. Burgess. *Ox. Econ. Pap.* **44:1** 1:1992 pp. 75 – 88

154 Search unemployment with on-the-job search. Christopher A. Pissarides. London: London School of Economics and Political Science. Centre for Economic Performance, 1992: 33 p. [Discussion paper.]

155 Searching for a will o' the wisp — an empirical study of the NAIRU in Canada. M.A. Setterfield; D.V. Gordon; L. Osberg. *Eur. Econ. R.* **36:1** 1:1992 pp. 119 – 136

156 Sectoral shifts and cyclical unemployment — a reconsideration. Thomas I. Palley. *Econ. Inq.* **XXX:1** 1:1992 pp. 117 – 133

157 Structural unemployment in the United States — the effects of interindustry and interregional dispersion. Jeffrey Parker. *Econ. Inq.* **XXX:1** 1:1992 pp. 101 – 119

158 Testing a discrete switching disequilibrium model of the UK labour market. S.G. Hall; S.G.B. Henry; M. Pemberton. *J. Appl. Econ.* **7:1** 1-3:1992 pp. 83 – 92

159 Time aggregation and the distributional shape of unemployment duration. R. Bergström; P.-A. Edin. *J. Appl. Econ.* **7:1** 1-3:1992 pp. 5 – 30

160 Time-series forecasting of the German unemployment rate. M. Funke. *J. Forecast.* **11:2** 2:1992 pp. 111 – 126

161 Time-varying effects of recall expectation, a reemployment bonus, and job counseling on unemployment durations. Patricia M. Anderson. *J. Labor Ec.* **10:1** 1:1992 pp. 99 – 115

162 Unemployment effects of a fixed replacement ratio, in an economy where trade unions dominate the wage formation. C.B. Mulder. *Eur. J. Pol. Ec.* **8:1** 2:1992 pp. 89 – 104

163 Unemployment in urban China — an analysis of survey data from Shanghai. Gangzhan Fu. London: London School of Economics, 1992: 40 p. [China programme. : No. 12]

164 Unemployment rate in the civilian labor force in Guam. Chu-Tak Tseng; Dirk A. Balenndorf. *J. Pacific Soc.* **14:4(53)** 1:1992 pp. 1 – 10

165 Unemployment, discouraged workers and female labour supply. Richard Blundell; John Ham; Costas Meghir. London: Institute of Fiscal Studies, [1992]: 37 p. [Working paper series.]

G.2.1: Labour forces and labour market *[Main d'oeuvre et marché du travail]* — Unemployment *[Chômage]*

166 The "wage curve" and long-term unemployment — a cautionary note. David H. Blackaby; Lester C. Hunt. *Manch. Sch. E.* **LX:4** 12:1992 pp. 419 – 428

167 The wasteland economics of high unemployment. Elmer P. Chase. *Challenge* **35:1** 1-2:1992 pp. 23 – 29

168 De werkloosheidsdaling (1984-199) en de loonvormingshypothese *[In Dutch]*; [The drop in unemployment (1984-1990) and the wage base determination hypothesis]. A. Van Poeck; J. Van Gompel. *Maan. Econ.* **56:1** 1992 pp. 42 – 56

Wage-employment relationship *[Relation salaires-emploi]*

169 Dual labor markets, efficiency wages, and search. James W. Albrecht; Susan B. Vroman. *J. Labor Ec.* **10:4** 10:1992 pp. 438 – 461

170 Estimating the employment effects of wage discrimination. Marjorie Baldwin; William G. Johnson. *Rev. Econ. St.* **LXXIV:3** 8:1992 pp. 446 – 455

171 The profit share rate, wages and employment in collective bargaining. J.B. Schmidt-Sorensen. *Eur. J. Pol. Ec.* **8:1** 2:1992 pp. 105 – 114

172 Salaires et marchés internes — quelques évolutions récentes en France *[In French]*; Wages and internal labor markets — some recent evolutions in France *[Summary]*; (Löhne und Binnemärkte — Zu neueren Entwicklungen in Frankreich: *Title only in German*); (Salarios y mercados internos — evoluciones recientes en Francia: *Title only in Spanish*). Pierre Beret. *Econ. App.* **XLV:2** 7:1992 pp. 5 – 22

173 Wage and employment adjustment in local labor markets. Randall W. Eberts; Joe Allan Stone. Kalamazoo, Mich: W.E. Upjohn Institute for Employment Research, 1992: ix, 153 p. (ill) *ISBN: 0880991151; LofC: 91041773. Includes bibliographical references and index.*

174 The "wage curve" and long-term unemployment — a cautionary note. David H. Blackaby; Lester C. Hunt. *Manch. Sch. E.* **LX:4** 12:1992 pp. 419 – 428

175 What went wrong? The erosion of relative earnings and employment among young black men in the 1980s. John Bound; Richard B. Freeman. *Q. J. Econ.* **CVII:1** 2:1992 pp. 201 – 232

G.2.2: Employment policy — *Politique d'emploi*

Sub-divisions: Women's employment *[Emploi des femmes]*

1 Asymmetric tournaments, equal opportunity laws, and affirmative action — some experimental results. Andrew Schotter; Keith Weigelt. *Q. J. Econ.* **CVII:2** 5:1992 pp. 511 – 539

2 Disabilities, mandatory worksite modifications, and employment — some potential policy dilemmas. Paul R. Flacco; Lester A. Zeager. *Publ. Fin. Q.* **20:2** 4:1992 pp. 256 – 270

3 The divide-and-conquer and employer/employee models of discrimination — neoclassical competition as a familial defect. Patrick L. Mason. *Rev. Bl. Pol. Ec.* **20:4** Spring:1992 pp. 73 – 89

4 Do fluctuations in the Australian macroeconomy influence aboriginal employment status? Jon Altman; Anne Daly. *Ec. Pap. Aust.* **11:3** 9:1992 pp. 32 – 48

5 The economic contribution of children in peasant agriculture and the effect of education — evidence from the Philippines. George J. Mergos. *Pak. Dev. R.* **31:2** Summer:1992 pp. 189 – 201

6 The efficiency of share contracts in Ghana's cocoa industry. Fred O. Boadu. *J. Dev. Stud.* **29:1** 10:1992 pp. 108 – 120

7 Ethnic minorities, employment and labour market change. David Owen *[Contrib.]*; Anne Green *[Contrib.]*; Mohamed Pirani *[Contrib.]*; Maurice Yolles *[Contrib.]*; Ebrahim Bassa *[Contrib.]*; Mohamed Rafiq *[Contrib.]*; Shaila Srinivason *[Contrib.]*; Roger Penn *[Contrib.]*; Hilda Scattergood *[Contrib.]*; David Mason *[Contrib.] and others. Collection of 8 articles.* **New Comm.** , *19:1*, 10:1992 pp. 7 – 141

8 Expanding opportunities for older workers. Emily S. Andrews. *J. Labor Res.* **XIII:1** Winter:1992 pp. 55 – 66

9 Foreign workers in Japan. John Lie. *Mon. Rev.* **144:1** 5:1992 pp. 35 – 42

10 Full employment in the 1990s. John Grieve Smith. London: Institute for Public Policy Research, 1992: 68 p. *ISBN: 1872452485.*

11 Gender, region and work in Canadian job creation programs. Susan Heald. *Comm. Dev. J.* **27:1** 1:1992 pp. 2 – 9

G.2.2: Employment policy *[Politique d'emploi]*

12 Home work — towards a new regulatory framework? Luz Vega Ruiz. *Int. Lab. Rev.* **131:2** 1992 pp. 197 – 216

13 Impact of employment restructuring on disadvantaged groups in Hungary and Bulgaria. Gyögy Sziráczki; James Windell. *Int. Lab. Rev.* **131:4-5** 4-5:1992 pp. 471 – 496

14 An integrated model of the economic effects of right-to-work laws. Gasper A. Garofalo; Devinder M. Malhotra. *J. Labor Res.* **XIII:3** Summer:1992 pp. 293 – 306

15 International dimension of US fair employment laws — protection or interference? James M. Zimmerman. *Int. Lab. Rev.* **131:2** 1992 pp. 217 – 230

16 Introducing new process technology —implications for local employment policies. P.D. Foley; H.D. Watts; B. Wilson. *Geoforum* **23:1** 1992 pp. 61 – 72

17 Labour market segmentation and the persistance of occupational sex segregation in Australia. Martin Watts; Judith Rich. *Aust. Econ. P.* **31:58** 6:1992 pp. 58 – 76

18 Occupazione e politiche di sicurezza del rapporto di lavoro — implicazioni teoriche ed esperienza degli anni '80 *[In Italian]*; [Employment and job security policies — theoretical implications and evidence from the 1980s]. Giorgio Galeazzi. *Ras. Econ.* **LVI:2** 4-6:1992 pp. 371 – 393

19 Le politiche per il mercato del lavoro — welfare, redditi, occupazione *[In Italian]*; Labour market policies — welfare, income, employment *[Summary]*. Renato Brunetta. *Ec. Lav.* **XXVI:3** 7-9:1992 pp. 49 – 79

20 Productive employment for the poor. Jacques Gaude *[Ed.]*; Steven Miller *[Ed.]*; H. Watzlawick *[Contrib.]*; Joachim von Braun *[Contrib.]*; Tesfaye Teklu *[Contrib.]*; Patrick Webb *[Contrib.]*; José Wurgaft *[Contrib.]*; Philippe Egger *[Contrib.]*; Philippe Garnier *[Contrib.]*; Jean Majeres *[Contrib.] and others. Collection of 9 articles.* **Int. Lab. Rev.** , *131:1*, 1992 pp. 1 – 137

21 The restart effect — evaluation of a labour market programme for unemployed people. Michael White; Jane Lakey. London: Policy Studies Institute, 1992: 202 p. *ISBN: 0853745544.*

22 A specific factors approach to the analysis of labor policy in Singapore. Soo Nam Ng; Rod Tyers. *Develop. Eco.* **XXX:1** 3:1992 pp. 24 – 49

23 A structural model of labor supply and child care demand. Charles Michalopoulos; Philip K. Robins; Irwin Garfinkel. *J. Hum. Res.* **XXVII:1** Winter: 1992 pp. 166 – 203

24 The Swedish model — relevant for other European countries? Lei Delsen; Tom van Veen. *Br. J. Ind. R.* **30:1** 3:1992 pp. 83 – 105

25 Taking care of the guests — the impact of immigrants on services — an industry case study; *[French summary]*. Roger Waldinger. *Int. J. Urban* **16:1** 3:1992 pp. 97 – 113

26 Trade sensitive manufacturing employment — some new insights. Bartholomew K. Armah. *Rev. Bl. Pol. Ec.* **21:2** Fall:1992 pp. 37 – 54

27 Understanding unemployment — new perspectives on active labour market policies. Eithne McLaughlin *[Ed.]*. London: Routledge, 1992: xiv, 217 p. *ISBN: 0415078059; LofC: gb 92038571. Includes bibliographies and index.*

28 Wage and employment policies in Czechoslovakia. Luis A. Riveros. *J. Econ. Stud.* **19:5** 1992 pp. 36 – 54

Women's employment *[Emploi des femmes]*

29 Black women in the workplace — impacts of structural change in the economy. Bette Woody. New York: Greenwood Press, 1992: xii, 211 p. *ISBN: 0313255911; LofC: 91028745. Includes bibliographical references (p. [189]-197) and index.* [Contributions in women's studies.]

30 Child care and the labor supply of married women — reduced form evidence. David C. Ribar. *J. Hum. Res.* **XXVII:1** Winter: 1992 pp. 134 – 165

31 Female labour force participation, fertility and public policy in Sweden; *[French summary]*. M. Sundström; F.P. Stafford. *Eur. J. Pop.* **8:3** 1992 pp. 199 – 216

32 Female labour supply and on-the-job search — an empirical model estimated using complementary data sets. Manuel Arellano; Costas Meghir. *R. Econ. S.* **59:3(200)** 7:1992 pp. 537 – 560

33 Feminising the market — women's pay and employment in the European Community. Jane Pillinger. London: Macmillan, 1992: 212 p. *ISBN: 0333563352.*

34 A flexible work force — opportunities for women. June O'Neill. *J. Labor Res.* **XIII:1** Winter:1992 pp. 67 – 72

35 Franco-British comparisons of women's labour supply and the effects of social policies. Shirley Dex; Patricia Walters. *Ox. Econ. Pap.* **44:1** 1:1992 pp. 89 – 112

G.2.2: Employment policy *[Politique d'emploi]* — **Women's employment** *[Emploi des femmes]*

36 Lone mothers' employment and full-time work probabilities. S.P. Jenkins. *Econ. J.* **102:411** 3:1992 pp. 310 – 320

37 El nacimiento de una ocupación femenina — la enfermería en Buenos Aires *[In Spanish]*; [The birth of a feminine occupation — the nurse in Buenos Aires]. Catalina H. Wainerman; Georgina Binstock. *Desar. Econ.* **32:126** 7-8:1992 pp. 271 – 284

38 Participation of rural women in the labour force — levels and determinants. Salma Chaudhuri. *Bang. Dev. Stud.* **XIX:4** 12:1991 pp. 65 – 85

39 Perspectivas actuales de la mujer japonesa *[In Spanish]*; Perspectives on the recent outlook of the Japanese women *[Summary]*. Nonaka Masayo. *Est. Asia Afr.* **XXVII:3** 9-12:1992 pp. 472 – 481

40 Women and Japanese management — discrimination and reform. Alice Lam. London: Routledge, 1992: 281 p. *ISBN: 0415063353; LofC: 91048163. Includes bibliographical references and index.*

41 Women and the labour market. Teresa L. Rees. London: Routledge, 1992: 223 p. *ISBN: 0415038014; LofC: 92010512. Includes bibliographical references and indexes.*

42 Women, work and well-being in the Middle East — an outline of the relevant literature. Ivy Papps. *J. Dev. Stud.* **28:4** 7:1992 pp. 595 – 615

G.2.3: **Working conditions** — *Conditions de travail*

1 Economic behaviour of the firm and prevention of occupational injuries. Thierry Schneider. *Geneva Pap. Risk Insur. Theory* **17:1** 6:1992 pp. 77 – 85

2 The European Communities' health and safety legislation. Alan C. Neal *[Ed.]*; Frank B. Wright *[Ed.]*. London: Chapman & Hall, 1992: 419 p. *ISBN: 0412466902.*

3 Flexible times? Recent developments in temporal flexibility. Paul Blyton. *Ind. Relat. J.* **23:1** Spring:1992 pp. 26 – 36

4 Government breaks the law — the sabotaging of the Occupational Safety and Health Act. Harry Brill. *Soc. Just.* **19:3** Fall:1992 pp. 63 – 81

5 Harmonization and hazard — regulating health and safety in the European workplace. Robert Baldwin *[Ed.]*; Terence Daintith *[Ed.]*. London: Graham & Trotman, 1992: 283 p. *ISBN: 1853337234.*

6 Immigration wages and price stability. P.N. Junankar; David Pope. Canberra: Australian Government Publishing Sevice, 1990: 69 p. *ISBN: 0644131845. "Bureau of Immigration Research"; Includes bibliographical references (p.60-65).*

7 Incentives for protecting farm workers from pesticides. John U. Davis; Julie A. Caswell; Carolyn R. Harper. *Am. J. Agr. Ec.* **74:4** 11:1992 pp. 907 – 917

8 Labour market deregulation — a comparative study of retail industry workplaces. Suzanne Hammond. *J. Ind. Relat.* **34:1** 3:1992 pp. 31 – 47

9 The limits to employee involvement — profit sharing and disclosure of information. Stuart Ogden. *J. Manag. Stu.* **29:2** 3:1992 pp. 229 – 248

10 The new corporate health ethic — lifestyle and the social control of work. Peter Conrad; Diana Chapman Walsh. *Int. J. Health. Ser.* **22:1** 1992 pp. 89 – 111

11 The politics of reform — workers' compensation from Woodhouse to Workcare. Mark Considine. Geelong, Vic., Australia: Centre for Applied Social Research, Deakin University with the assistance of the Victorian Council of the Royal Australian Institute of Public Administration, 1991: 118 p. *ISBN: 073001472x. Includes bibliographical references (p. [113]-115) and index.* [Deakin series in public policy and administration. : No. 1]

12 La promotion de la santé au travail — une avenue d'interventions à explorer *[In French]*; The promotion of health at work — avenues of measures to be explored *[Summary]*. Jacqueline Dionne-Proulx; Jean-Claude Bernatchez. *Gestion* **8:6** 1992 pp. 101 – 113

13 Time allocation and economic welfare. Chiara Bentivogli. *Labour [Italy]* **6:2** Autumn:1992 pp. 105 – 122

14 Toward a theoretical framework of repatriation adjustment. J. Stewart Black; Hal B. Gregersen; Mark E. Mendenhall. *J. Int. Bus. Stud.* **23:4** Fourth quarter:1992 pp. 737 – 760

15 The value of job safety for railroad workers. Michael T. French; David L. Kendall. *J. Risk Uncert.* **5:2** 1992 pp. 175 – 186

16 Work and leisure in Japan. Robert E. Cole. *Calif. Manag. R.* **34:3** Spring:1992 pp. 52 – 63

17 Worker participation in health and safety regulation — some lessons from Sweden. Eric Tucker. *Stud. Pol. Ec.* :**37** Spring:1992 pp. 95 – 128

G.2.4: Labour relations — *Relations du travail*

Sub-divisions: Collective bargaining *[Negociation collective]*; Strikes *[Grèves]*; Trade unions *[Syndicats]*; Workers' participation *[Participation des travailleurs]*

1 Binding contracts, profit-sharing and the degree of centralization. Tapio Palokangas. *J. Inst. Theo. Ec.* **148:2** 6:1992 pp. 260 – 273
2 Capital and labor in American copper, 1845-1990 — linkages between product and labor markets. George H. Hildebrand; Garth L Mangum. Cambridge, Mass: Harvard University Press, 1992: xv, 334 p. (ill., maps) *ISBN: 0674094816; LofC: 91018174. Includes bibliographical references (p.301-322) and index.* [Wertheim publications in industrial relations.]
3 A comparison of interest arbitrator decision-making in experimental and field setting. Craig A. Olson; Gregory G. Dell'Omo; Paul Jarley. *Ind. Lab. Rel.* **45:4** 7:1992 pp. 711 – 723
4 Computerization and employment rights. Brian Napier. *Ind. Law J.* **21:1** 3:1992 pp. 1 – 14
5 Contemporary British industrial relations. Sidney Kessler; Fred Bayliss. Basingstoke: Macmillan Educ., 1992: 291 p. *ISBN: 0333567455.*
6 Dispute resolution in workers' compensation. Leslie I. Boden. *Rev. Econ. St.* **LXXIV:3** 8:1992 pp. 493 – 502
7 Does law matter in the Soviet economic reform process? A case study of the law governing internal transfers. Kathryn Hendley. *R. C. & E.Eur. Law* **18:2** 1992 pp. 101 – 134
8 Employee voice — a human resource management perspective. Douglas M. McCabe; David Lewin. *Calif. Manag. R.* **34:3** Spring:1992 pp. 112 – 123
9 Employee voice — a legal perspective. Benjamin Aaron. *Calif. Manag. R.* **34:3** Spring:1992 pp. 124 – 138
10 Engineers and management — international comparisons. Gloria L. Lee *[Ed.]*; Chris Smith *[Ed.]*. London: Routledge, 1992: 226 p. *ISBN: 0415064260.*
11 An experimental comparison of dispute rates in alternative arbitration systems. Orley Ashenfelter; Janet Currie; Henry S. Farber; Matthew Spiegel. *Econometrica* **60:6** 11:1992 pp. 1407 – 1433
12 Failure of conciliation — perceptions and realities. Debi S. Saini. *Ind. J. Ind. Rel.* **28:2** 10:1992 pp. 105 – 122
13 Formalization of grievance procedures — a multi-firm and industry study. Jeanette A. Davy; Greg Stewart; Joe Anderson. *J. Labor Res.* **XIII:3** Summer:1992 pp. 307 – 316
14 From theory to practice — critical choices for "mutual gains" training. Raymond A. Friedman. *Negot. J.* **8:2** 4:1992 pp. 91 – 98
15 Industrial relations and European state traditions. Colin Crouch. Oxford: Clarendon Press, 1992: 407 p. *ISBN: 0198277202; LofC: 92014645. Includes bibliographical references and index.*
16 Industrial relations and productivity — evidence from Sweden and Australia. Russell D. Lansbury; Bengt Sandkull; Olle Hammarström. *Econ. Ind. Dem.* **13:3** 8:1992 pp. 295 – 329
17 Industrial relations and the British economy in the 1990s — Mrs Thatcher's legacy. Steve Evans; Keith Ewing; Peter Nolan. *J. Manag. Stu.* **29:5** 9:1992 pp. 571 – 590
18 Industrial relations in Korea. Duk-Je Park. *Int. J. Hum. Res. Man.* **3:1** 5:1992 pp. 105 – 124
19 Labor arbitration in America — the profession and practice. Mario Frank Bognanno *[Ed.]*; Charles J. Coleman *[Ed.]*. New York: Praeger, 1992: ix, 186 p. *ISBN: 0275943755; LofC: 92-399. Includes index.*
20 Labour in transition — the labour process in Eastern Europe and China. Paul B. Thompson *[Ed.]*; Chris Smith *[Ed.]*. London: Routledge, 1992: 266 p. *ISBN: 0415082951; LofC: 92024745. Includes bibliographical references and index.* [Organization and employment studies series.]
21 Labour relations and variables of organisation dynamics — research results highlight the interplay. B.J. Swanepoel. *S. Afr. J. Labour Relat.* **16:2** 6:1992 pp. 40 – 49
22 Labour relations in Israel (part II). W. Backer. *S. Afr. J. Labour Relat.* **16:1** 3:1992 pp. 3 – 21

G.2.4: Labour relations *[Relations du travail]*

23 Labour-action in Asia — models of outcomes at national and transnational firms; *[French summary]*. David Kowalewski. *Labour Cap. Soc.* **24:2** 11:1991 pp. 208 – 222

24 The limits of autonomy — devolution, line managers and industrial relations in privatized companies. Trevor Colling; Anthony Ferner. *J. Manag. Stu.* **29:2** 3:1992 pp. 209 – 228

25 Making the link 2 — affirmative action and industrial relations. Ed Davis *[Ed.]*; Valerie Pratt *[Ed.]*. Sydney: Affirmative Action Agency and Labour-Management Studies Foundation, Graduate School of Management, Macquire University, 1991: 83 p. *ISBN: 0644145064.* *"The collection of papers which were presented at the second Women, Management and Industrial Relations Conference....held in June, 1990...organized by the Affirmative Action Agency and the Labour Management Studies Foundation..."*.

26 Managerial employees and labour legislation. Baldev R. Sharma. *Ind. J. Ind. Rel.* **28:1** 7:1992 pp. 1 – 24

27 Mandatory notice. Peter Kuhn. *J. Labor Ec.* **10:2** 4:1992 pp. 117 – 137

28 New technology and changing industrial relations in Greece — the case of the national newspaper industry 1979-85. Nicos Leandros; Colin Simmons. *Cyprus J. Econ.* **5:1** 6:1992 pp. 25 – 44

29 Ouverture commerciale, marché du travail et relations industrielles *[In French]*; Trade liberalization, the labor market and industrial relations *[Summary]*; Apertura comercial, mercado del trabajo y relaciones industriales *[Spanish summary]*. Ilán Bizberg. *Prob. Am.Lat.* **:5** 4-6:1992 pp. 55 – 80

30 Problem solving in labour negotiations — a comparative study of the United States, Israel and New Zealand. Arie Shirom; Richard B. Peterson; Lane N. Tracy. *Int. J. Hum. Res. Man.* **3:1** 5:1992 pp. 59 – 76

31 Profit sharing and employment. J.C. Eckalbar. *Econ. Model.* **9:2** 4:1992 pp. 104 – 110

32 Profit sharing in internal labour markets. G. Brunello. *Econ. J.* **102:412** 5:1992 pp. 570 – 577

33 Restrukryzacja gospodarki a ochrona trwałości stosunku pracy i roszczeń pracowniczych *[In Polish]*; (Restructurisation of economy and protection of labour agreement persistence); (Реструктуризация народного хозяйства и зашита постоянности трудового отношения и требований сотрудников: *Title only in Russian)*. Małgorzata Gersdorf-Giaro. *Pra. Zab. Społ.* **:1** 1:1992 pp. 17 – 23

34 Right and wrong at work — ethical issues in labour relations in Australia. B.N. Kaye *[Ed.]*. Kensington/NSW: New College, University of New South Wales, 1991: 78 p. *ISBN: 0733401465.*

35 Salary arbitration and pre-arbitration negotiation in major league baseball. David J. Faurot; Stephen McAllister. *Ind. Lab. Rel.* **45:4** 7:1992 pp. 697 – 710

36 Shaping the private sector — basic agreements between organised capital and organised labour. L. Douwes Dekker. *S. Afr. J. Labour Relat.* **16:1** 3:1992 pp. 22 – 48

37 A simultaneous analysis of grievance activity and outcome decisions. Richard P. Chaykowski; George A. Slotsve; J.S. Butler. *Ind. Lab. Rel.* **45:4** 7:1992 pp. 724 – 737

38 El sistema relaciones industriales brasilero — características básicas y evolución en el tiempo, 1943-1990 *[In Spanish]*; [Industrial relations in Brazil — basic characteristics and evolution from 1943-1990]. Russell E. Smith. *Rev. Parag. Sociol.* **29:83** 1-4:1992 pp. 71 – 88

39 Social institutions and economic performance — studies of industrial relations in advanced capitalist economies. Wolfgang Streeck. London: Sage, 1992: 248 p. *ISBN: 0803984758.*

40 Steel — a classic case of industrial relations change in Britain. Paul Blyton. *J. Manag. Stu.* **29:5** 9:1992 pp. 635 – 650

41 Work authority in industry — the happy demise of the ideal type. Katharyne Mitchell. *Comp. Stud. S.* **34:4** 10:1992 pp. 679 – 694

Collective bargaining *[Negociation collective]*

42 Abschlußebene und Lohndynamik. Eine vergleichende empirische Analyse von Firmen- und Branchentarifabschlüssen *[In German]*; Bargaining and wage dynamics. A comparative empirical analysis of negotiated agreements at firm and industry level *[Summary]*. Wolfgang Meyer. *Z. Wirt. Soz.* **112:1** 1992 pp. 59 – 74

43 Assessing effectiveness of joint committees in a labor-management cooperation program. Richard B. Peterson; Lane Tracy. *Human Relat.* **45:5** 5:1992 pp. 467 – 488

44 A bargaining analysis of American labor law and the search for bargaining equity and industrial peace. Kenneth G. Dau-Schmidt. *Ml. law. R.* **91:3** 12:1992 pp. 419 – 514

45 Collective bargaining and wage determination in Italian manufacturing. C. Dell'Aringa. *Banca Nat. Lav. Q. Rev.* **:180** 3:1992 pp. 21 – 34

G.2.4: Labour relations *[Relations du travail]* — *Collective bargaining [Negociation collective]*

46 Collective bargaining in state and local government. John Patrick Piskulich. New York: Praeger, 1992: xi, 127 p. *ISBN: 0275940438; LofC: 91028142. Includes bibliographical references (p. [117]-123) and index.*

47 Determinants of contract duration in collective bargaining agreements. Kevin J. Murphy. *Ind. Lab. Rel.* **45:2** 1:1992 pp. 352 – 365

48 Employers' reaction to the productivity drive — the search for labour consensus. Marino Regini. *Labour [Italy]* **6:2** Autumn:1992 pp. 31 – 47

49 Enterprise bargaining and the accord. Herb Thompson. *J. Aust. Pol. Econ.* **:30** 12:1992 pp. 42 – 60

50 The Europeanization of manufacturing and the decentralization of bargaining — multinational management strategies in the European automobile industry. Frank Mueller; John Purcell. *Int. J. Hum. Res. Man.* **3:1** 5:1992 pp. 15 – 34

51 Form of government and collective bargaining outcomes. Kevin M. O'Brien. *Publ. Fin. Q.* **20:1** 1:1992 pp. 64 – 76

52 Impala platinum — no easy road to collective bargaining. Snuki Zikalala. *S.Afr. Lab. B.* **16:3** 1:1992 pp. 26 – 39

53 Payoff divisions on coalition formation in a three-person characteristic function experiment. U. Leopold-Wildburger. *J. Econ. Beh.* **17:1** 1:1992 pp. 183 – 193

54 Social and labour issues in privatisation — an overview. C.S. Venkata Ratnam. *Ind. J. Ind. Rel.* **28:2** 10:1992 pp. 139 – 154

55 Strikes, dismissals and collective bargaining. B. Vally. *S. Afr. J. Labour Relat.* **16:1** 3:1992 pp. 49 – 55

56 Union cooperation and nontraded goods in general equilibrium. Sandemann Rasmussen. *Sc. J. Econ.* **94:4** 1992 pp. 561 – 579

57 Union of parts — labor politics in postwar Germany. Kathleen Ann Thelen. Ithaca: Cornell University Press, 1991: xii, 262 p. *ISBN: 0801425867; LofC: 91055050. Includes bibliographical references (p. 237-254) and index.* [Cornell studies in political economy.]

58 Use of joint consultation committees by large Japanese firms. Motohiro Morisihima. *Br. J. Ind. R.* **30:3** 9:1992 pp. 405 – 424

Strikes *[Grèves]*

59 Bombay textile strike, 1982-83. Hubert W. M. van Wersch. Bombay: Oxford University Press (India), 1992: 463 p. *ISBN: 0195628713; LofC: gb 92354540.*

60 An expressive voting theory of strikes. Amihai Glazer. *Econ. Inq.* **XXX:4** 10:1992 pp. 733 – 741

61 Incomes policies, inflation and strikes in Nigeria, 1950-1985 — an empirical investigation. O. Owoye. *Appl. Econ.* **24:6** 6:1992 pp. 587 – 592

62 Multivariate analysis of unionized employees' propensity to cross their union's picket line. Michael H. LeRoy. *J. Labor Res.* **XIII:3** Summer:1992 pp. 285 – 292

63 Odpowiedzialność za zorganizowanie i udział w nielegalnym strajku *[In Polish]*; (Responsibility for organization and participation in illegal strikes); (Ответственность за организование и за участие в нелегальной забастовке: *Title only in Russian*). Barbara Wagner. *Pra. Zab. Spot.* **:1** 1:1992 pp. 38 – 46

64 Sitting in. Barry Hill. Port Melbourne, Vic: W. Heinemann Australia in asociation with the Left Book Club, 1991: 338 p. *ISBN: 0855614153; LofC: 91186564. Includes bibliographical references (p. 324-338).*

65 The strike as management strategy. Ruth A. Bandzak. *J. Econ. Iss.* **XXVI:2** 6:1992 pp. 645 – 660

66 Strikes and deindustrialization in the European Community — 1970-86. Mike Ingham; Hilary Ingham. *Int. R. Applied Ec.* **6:1** 1992 pp. 93 – 113

67 Strikes as the random enforcement of asymmetric information contracts. John Leach. *J. Labor Ec.* **10:2** 4:1992 pp. 202 – 218

68 Strikes, dismissals and collective bargaining. B. Vally. *S. Afr. J. Labour Relat.* **16:1** 3:1992 pp. 49 – 55

69 The Wapping dispute — an examination of the conflict and its impact on the national newspaper industry. Suellen M. Littleton. Aldershot: Avebury, 1992: 223 p. *ISBN: 1856282015.*

G.2.4: Labour relations *[Relations du travail]* —

Trade unions *[Syndicats]*

70 Agency costs, property rights, and the evolution of labor unions. Don Bellante; Philip K. Porter. *J. Labor Res.* **XIII:3** Summer:1992 pp. 243 – 256

71 Building safety — the role of construction unions in the enforcement of OSHA. David Weil. *J. Labor Res.* **XIII:1** Winter:1992 pp. 121 – 132

72 Do unions impede or accelerate structural adjustment? Industrial versus company unions in an industrialising labour market. Guy Standing. *Camb. J. Econ.* **16:3** 9:1992 pp. 327 – 354

73 Does a trade union set a lower effort level than would be determined in a competitive labour market? George Bulkley. *B. Econ. Res.* **44:2** 4:1992 pp. 153 – 160

74 The economic effects of multiple unionism — evidence from the 1984 workplace industrial relations survey. Stephen Machin; Mark Stewart; John van Reenen. London: London School of Economics and Political Science. Centre for Economic Performance, 1992: 29 p. [Discussion paper.]

75 Education and the teacher unions. Michael Barber. London: Cassell, 1992: xiii, 145 p. *ISBN: 0304323594; LofC: 91003241. Includes bibliographical references (p. 137-139) and indexes.* [Issues in education.]

76 The future of labour movements. Marino Regini *[Ed.].* London: Sage Publications, 1992: 275 p. *ISBN: 0803987617.* [Sage studies in international sociology. : No. 43]

77 How robust is the microeconomic theory of the trade union? Alan Manning. London: London School of Economics and Political Science. Centre for Economic Performance, 1992: 52 p.

78 The impact of legislator attributes on union PAC campaign contributions. James W. Endersby; Michael C. Munger. *J. Labor Res.* **XIII:1** Winter:1992 pp. 79 – 98

79 The impact of unionization on the entry of firms — evidence from U.S. industries. William F. Chappell; Mwangi S. Kimenyi; Walter J. Mayer. *J. Labor Res.* **XIII:3** Summer:1992 pp. 273 – 284

80 The inflation-unemployment trade-offs of union members. David J. Smyth; Susan Washburn Taylor. *J. Labor Res.* **XIII:2** Spring:1992 pp. 223 – 230

81 Labor market institutions and the future role of unions. Mario F. Bognanno *[Contrib.]*; Morris M. Kleiner *[Contrib.]*; Charles McDonald *[Contrib.]*; Ray Marshall *[Contrib.]*; John T. Dunlop *[Contrib.]*; David G. Blanchflower *[Contrib.]*; Richard B. Freeman *[Contrib.]*; Jonathan S. Leonard *[Contrib.]*; Barry T. Hirsch *[Contrib.]*; Joseph D. Reid *[Contrib.]* and others. Collection of 12 articles. **Ind. Relat.** , *31:1*, Winter:1992 pp. 1 – 265

82 Margins, concentration, unions and the business cycle — theory and evidence for Britain. J. Haskel; C. Martin. *Int. J. Ind. O.* **10:4** 12:1992 pp. 611 – 632

83 Un modello previsivo della sindacalizzazione *[In Italian]*; [A forecasting model of unionization]. Davide La Valle. *Quad. Sociol.* **XXXVI:I** 1992 pp. 79 – 96

84 The new politics of British trade unionism — union power and the Thatcher legacy. David Marsh. Basingstoke: Macmillan, 1992: 268 p. *ISBN: 033349301x.*

85 On the measurement and determination of trade union power. Ian M. McDonald; Anthony Suen. *Ox. B. Econ. S.* **54:2** 5:1992 pp. 209 – 224

86 Politics and the accord. Peter Ewer; et al. Leichhardt, NSW: Pluto Press, 1991: 190 p. (ill) *ISBN: 0949138797. Includes bibliographical references (p. [179]-190).*

87 Private sector union decline and structural employment change, 1970-1988. Ethel B. Jones. *J. Labor Res.* **XIII:3** Summer:1992 pp. 257 – 272

88 Product quality improvement through employee participation — the effects of unionization and joint union-management administration. William N. Cooke. *Ind. Lab. Rel.* **46:1** 10:1992 pp. 119 – 134

89 Shaping work and technology — West German trade unions, the quality of work and industrial relations. M. Knuth. *Internat. Contrib. Lab. Stud.* **2** 1992 pp. 45 – 59

90 A shift to the "right" — legislative change and industrial relations in New Zealand. Raymond Harbridge; Kevin Hince. *Ind. J. Ind. Rel.* **28:2** 10:1992 pp. 123 – 138

91 Shifting sands? Trade unions and productivity at Rover Cars. Ed Rose; Ted Woolley. *Ind. Relat. J.* **23:4** Winter:1992 pp. 257 – 267

92 The "skill-oriented" strategies of German trade unions — their impact on efficiency and equality objectives. Birgit Mahnkopf. *Br. J. Ind. R.* **30:1** 3:1992 pp. 46 – 81

93 A study of union ability to secure the first contract in foreign-owned firms in the USA. Rajib N. Sanyal; Joao S. Neves. *J. Int. Bus. Stud.* **23:4** Fourth quarter:1992 pp. 697 – 713

94 The technological revolution at the turn of the 21st century — "new fields" of trade union activities. Leonid Veselovsky. Moscow: Profizdat Publishers, 1991: 90 p.

G.2.4: Labour relations *[Relations du travail]* — *Trade unions [Syndicats]*

95 Trade union membership and the free rider problem — the role of harassment activities. Bruno Chiarini. *Labour [Italy]* **6:2** Autumn:1992 pp. 49 – 63

96 Trade union membership in Britain, 1980-1987 — unemployment and restructuring. Jeremy Waddington. *Br. J. Ind. R.* **30:2** 6:1992 pp. 287 – 324

97 Trade union objectives, strike frequency and the Phillips Curve. A. Phipps. *Aust. Econ. P.* **31:58** 6:1992 pp. 111 – 126

98 Trade unions, collective voice and fringe benefits. Paul Miller; Charles Mulvey. *Econ. Rec.* **68:201** 6:1992 pp. 125 – 141

99 Union bargaining, wage differentials and employment. Lutz Bellmann; Knut Emmerich. *Labour [Italy]* **6:2** Autumn:1992 pp. 19 – 30

100 Union merger benefits — an empirical analysis. Kay Stratton-Devine. *J. Labor Res.* **XIII:1** Winter:1992 pp. 133 – 142

101 Union wage effects and the probability of union membership. Virginia Christie. *Econ. Rec.* **68:200** 3:1992 pp. 43 – 56

102 Unionism in a competitive industry. Glenn M. MacDonald; Chris Robinson. *J. Labor Ec.* **10:1** 1:1992 pp. 33 – 54

103 Unions and investment in British industry. K. Denny; S.J. Nickell. *Econ. J.* **102:413** 7:1992 pp. 874 – 887

104 Unions, nonwage labor costs, and the character of labor market adjustment, 1929-1987. Lonnie M. Golden. *Q Rev. Econ. Finan.* **32:2** Summer:1992 pp. 46 – 70

105 Unions, the demise of the closed shop and wage growth in the 1980s. Paul Gregg; Stephen Machin. *Ox. B. Econ. S.* **54:1** 2:1992 pp. 53 – 72

106 Unions, wages and employment — evidence from Finland. T. Tyrväinen. *Appl. Econ.* **24:12** 12:1992 pp. 1275 – 1286

107 Związki zawodowe po nowemu *[In Polish]*; (Trade unions in a new manner); (Профсюзы по новому: *Title only in Russian*). Teresa Liszcz. *Pra. Zab. Społ.* **:1** 1:1992 pp. 28 – 37

Workers' participation *[Participation des travailleurs]*

108 The American labor movement and employee ownership — objections to and use of employee stock ownership plans. Roger G. McElrath; Richard L. Rowan. *J. Labor Res.* **XIII:1** Winter:1992 pp. 99 – 120

109 Comparative dynamics in the labor-managed model of the firm. Michael R. Caputo. *J. Comp. Econ.* **16:2** 6:1992 pp. 272 – 286

110 The comparative statics of the Ward-Domar LMF — a cost function approach. Shoji Haruna. *J. Inst. Theo. Ec.* **148:2** 6:1992 pp. 326 – 331

111 The diffusion of participation in new information technology in Europe — survey results. Colin Gill; Hubert Krieger. *Econ. Ind. Dem.* **13:3** 8:1992 pp. 331 – 358

112 Division of labour, life cycle and democracy in worker co-operatives. Gerald Callan Hunt. *Econ. Ind. Dem.* **13:1** 2:1992 pp. 9 – 44

113 Employee participation and labor law in the American workplace. Raymond L. Hogler; Guillermo J. Grenier. New York: Quorum Books, 1992: x, 181 p. *ISBN: 0899307523; LofC: 91036333. Includes bibliographical references (p.[173]-176) and index.*

114 Employee participation — some Australian cases. Russell D. Lansbury; Edward M. Davis. *Int. Lab. Rev.* **131:2** 1992 pp. 231 – 248

115 ESOPS, producer co-ops, and traditional firms — are they different? Patrick Michael Rooney. *J. Econ. Iss.* **XXVI:2** 6:1992 pp. 593 – 604

116 Fødder under fælles bord *[In Danish]*; [Steps towards joint ownership] *[Summary]*. Erik Maaløe. *Led. Erhv.* **56:1** 1:1992 pp. 11 – 20

117 Information technology and workplace democracy. Martin Beirne *[Ed.]*; Harvie Ramsay *[Ed.]*. New York: Routledge, 1992: 274 p. *ISBN: 0415004179; LofC: 92001005. Includes bibliographical references.*

118 Labour — management cooperation in Indian railways. P. Subba Rao; N. Narayana. *Ind. J. Ind. Rel.* **28:1** 7:1992 pp. 37 – 48

119 On the performance of worker-managed firms — does participation only exert "technical" effects? Ottorino Chillemi; Benedetto Gui. *J. Comp. Econ.* **16:2** 6:1992 pp. 294 – 301

120 Product quality improvement through employee participation — the effects of unionization and joint union-management administration. William N. Cooke. *Ind. Lab. Rel.* **46:1** 10:1992 pp. 119 – 134

121 Systems of employee voice — theoretical and empirical perspectives. David Lewin; Daniel J.B. Mitchell. *Calif. Manag. R.* **34:3** Spring:1992 pp. 95 – 111

G.2.4: Labour relations *[Relations du travail]* — Workers' participation *[Participation des travailleurs]*

122 Theoretical and applied aspects of labor-managed firms. Yehuda Don *[Contrib.]*; Nava Kahana *[Contrib.]*; Avi Weiss *[Contrib.]*; Louis Putterman *[Contrib.]*; Gilbert L. Skillman *[Contrib.]*; Joel M. Guttman *[Contrib.]*; Hugh M. Neary *[Contrib.]*; Michael Keren *[Contrib.]*; David Levhari *[Contrib.]*; Željko Bogetić *[Contrib.] and others.* Collection of *12 articles.* **J. Comp. Econ.** , *16:4*, 12:1992 pp. 567 – 762

123 The use of cycles? Explaining employee involvement. Peter Ackers; et al. *Ind. Relat. J.* **23:4** Winter:1992 pp. 268 – 283

124 Work councils in Iran — the illusion of worker control. Saeed Rahnema. *Econ. Ind. Dem.* **13:1** 2:1992 pp. 69 – 94

125 Worker buyouts in Canada — a social networking analysis. Jack Quarter; Judith Brown. *Econ. Ind. Dem.* **13:1** 2:1992 p. 95

126 Worker-managed firms, democratic principles, and the evolution of financial relations. Charles P. Rock; Mark A. Klinedinst. *J. Econ. Iss.* **XXVI:2** 6:1992 pp. 605 – 614

G.2.5: Work organization — *Organisation du travail*

1 Absenteeism predictors — least-squares, rank-regression, and model-selection results; Les prédicteurs d'absentéisme — résultats à partir de la méthode des moindres carrés, de la régression de rangs, et de la procédure de sélection de modèle *[French summary]*. Mohammed Chaudhury; Ignace Ng. *Can. J. Econ.* **XXV:3** 8:1992 pp. 615 – 635

2 Apprentis et élèves de lycées professionnels — où sont les emplois stables? *[In French]*; Apprentices and pupils from technical schools — where are the permanent jobs? *[Summary]*; Auszubildende und Berufsfachschüler — in welchen Bereichen findet man dauerhafte Beschäftigungen? *[German summary]*. Joëlle Affichard; Marie-Christine Combes; Yvette Grelet. *Form. Emp.* :**38** 4-6:1992 pp. 9 – 28

3 Asia's port sector — the need to institutionalize training. Paul E. Kent. *Mar. Pol.* **16:5** 9:1992 pp. 371 – 378

4 Automazione flessible ed organizzazione del lavoro — alcune osservazioni *[In Italian]*; Flexible automation and labour organization — some observations *[Summary]*. Giuseppe Calabrese. *Ec. Lav.* **XXVI:3** 7-9:1992 pp. 81 – 97

5 Les choix résidentiels des employés d'un même établissement — un modèle de choix discret *[In French]*; Residential location of employees of a firm — a discrete choice model *[Summary]*. Yves van de Vyvere. *Espace Géogr.* **XXI:1** 1992 pp. 25 – 35

6 Le contrôle aérien — qualification, formation et statut *[In French]*; Air-traffic control — skill, training and status *[Summary]*; Flugverkehrskontrolle — Qualifikation, Ausbildung und Status *[German summary]*. Lucien Lavorel. *Form. Emp.* :**37** 1-3:1992 pp. 41 – 55

7 Coordination and organizational learning in the firm. L. Marengo. *J. Evolut. Econ.* **2:4** 1992 pp. 313 – 326

8 Determining cutoff scores that optimize utility — a recognition of recruiting costs. Scott L. Martin; Nambury S. Raju. *J. Appl. Psychol.* **77:1** 2:1992 pp. 15 – 23

9 The effect of distinguishing hours and workers. Ian M. Dobbs. *Scot. J. Poli.* **39:1** 2:1992 pp. 14 – 20

10 An emerging distributed work arrangement — an investigation of computer-based supplemental work at home. Alladi Venkatesh; Nicholas P. Vitalari. *Manag. Sci.* **38:12** 12:1992 pp. 1687 – 1706

11 Espoirs et désillusions de la formation au Portugal *[In French]*; Hopes and disillusionment with vocational training in Portugal *[Summary]*; Ausbildung in Portugal — Hoffnungen und Enttäuschungen *[German summary]*. Marianne Lacomblez; Isabel Freitas. *Form. Emp.* :**37** 1-3:1992 pp. 3 – 13

12 L'évaluation des personnes comme outil de développement d'acteurs institutionnels *[In French]*; The evaluation of people as development tools of institutional actors *[Summary]*. Auguste Deneumoustier. *Gestion* **8:1** 1992 pp. 139 – 148

13 La formation continue des ingénieurs pour des nouvelles organisations du travail *[In French]*; On-the-job training of engineers for new types of work organization *[Summary]*; Die Fortbildung der Ingenieure im Hinblick auf neue Arbeitsorganisationen *[German summary]*. André Rosanvallon. *Form. Emp.* :**38** 4-6:1992 pp. 29 – 42

14 Formation emploi *[In French]*; [Vocational training]. Bruno Rémond *[Contrib.]*; Pierre Cam *[Contrib.]*; Anne-Chantal Dubernet *[Contrib.]*; Maïten Bel *[Contrib.]*; Claudine Romani

G.2.5: Work organization *[Organisation du travail]*

[Contrib.]; François Beaumert *[Contrib.]*; Bernard Fourcade *[Contrib.]*; Guy Ourliac *[Contrib.]*; Maurice Ourteau *[Contrib.]*. *Collection of 6 articles*. **Form. Emp.** , *:40*, 10-12:1992 pp. 5 – 78

15 La formation permanente en gestion au Cameroun *[In French]*; [Permanent management training in Cameroon]. Jacques Boisvert; Emmanuel Kamdem. *Afr. 2000* **:10** 7-9:1992 pp. 67 – 85

16 La gestion du return on investment de la formation en entreprise *[In French]*; The management on return on investment of training in industry *[Summary]*. Jean-Marie Dujardin. *Gestion* **8:6** 1992 pp. 31 – 45

17 Human resource management in Europe — evidence from ten countries. Chris Brewster; Henrik Holt Larsen. *Int. J. Hum. Res. Man.* **3:3** 12:1992 pp. 409 – 434

18 Human resource management in Europe — text and cases. Sarah Vickerstaff *[Ed.]*. London: Chapman & Hall, 1992: 258 p. *ISBN: 0412453800.*

19 Human resource management — people and performance. Keith Bradley. Aldershot: Dartmouth, 1992: 164 p. *ISBN: 1855212935.*

20 Human resource strategies. Graeme Salaman *[Ed.]*. London: Sage Publications, 1992: 350 p. *ISBN: 0803986262.*

21 The importance of company breeding in the U.S. and Japanese managerial labor markets — a statistical comparison. T. Kato; M. Rockel. *Jpn. Wor. Econ.* **4:1** 5:1992 pp. 39 – 45

22 International comparisons in human resource management. Christopher John Brewster *[Ed.]*; Shaun James Jeremy Tyson *[Ed.]*. London: Pitman, 1991: 268 p. *ISBN: 0273033166.*

23 Labor-force-based development — a community-oriented approach to targeting job training and industrial development. David C. Ranney; John J. Betancur. *Econ. Devel. Q.* **6:3** 8:1992 pp. 286 – 296

24 Labour force transitions among low-wage married couples — a simultaneous probability model. M. Zimmer. *Appl. Econ.* **24:8** 8:1992 pp. 895 – 906

25 Learning by doing, adverse selection and firm structure. I.E. Novos. *J. Econ. Beh.* **19:1** 9:1992 pp. 17 – 40

26 Managerial objectives, capital structure, and the provision of worker incentives. Gerald T. Garvey; Peter L. Swan. *J. Labor Ec.* **10:4** 10:1992 pp. 357 – 379

27 Managing the effects of layoffs on survivors. Joel Brockner. *Calif. Manag. R.* **34:2** Winter:1992 pp. 9 – 28

28 Market failure in training — new economic analysis and evidence on training of adult employees. David Stern *[Ed.]*; J.M.M. Ritzen *[Ed.]*. London: Springer-Verlag, 1992: 233 p. *ISBN: 3540546227.* [Studies in contemporary economics.]

29 Market-based manpower planning with labour market signals. Arvil Van Adams; John Middleton; Adrian Ziderman. *Int. Lab. Rev.* **131:3** 1992/1993 pp. 261 – 279

30 Maximizing the market value of a firm to choose dynamic policies for managerial hiring, compensation, firing and tenuring. Sankarshan Acharya. *Int. Econ. R.* **33:2** 5:1992 pp. 373 – 398

31 Mentoring and the business environment — asset or liability? Richard Ernest Caruso. Aldershot: Dartmouth, 1992: 157 p. *ISBN: 1855213176.*

32 A model of layoff, search and job choice and its estimation. Rezaul K. Khandker. *Rev. Econ. St.* **LXXIV:2** 5:1992 pp. 269 – 275

33 Modèles multi-attributs et atitudes face aux offres d'emploi *[In French]*; Multi-attributes models and attitudes facing job opportunities *[Summary]*. Jean-Claude Gilardi. *Gestion* **8:4** 1992 pp. 93 – 116

34 Optimal implicit contracts and the choice between layoffs and work sharing. G.A. Jehle; M.O. Lieberman. *Eur. J. Pol. Ec.* **8:2** 5:1992 pp. 251 – 268

35 Organizational and financial correlates of a "Contrarian" human resource investment strategy. Charles R. Greer; Timothy C. Ireland. *Acad. Manag. J.* **35:5** 12:1992 pp. 956 – 984

36 Pendelzeiten und Entlohnung — eine Untersuchung mit Individualdaten für die Bundesrepublik Deutschland *[In German]*; Commuting time and wages — an analysis with individual data for the Federal Republic of Germany *[Summary]*. Knut Gerlach; Stephan Gesine. *Jahrb. N. St.* **210:1-2** 7:1992 pp. 18 – 34

37 Personnel management for the single European market. Mark Pinder. London: Pitman, 1990: 267 p. *ISBN: 0273032305.*

38 Professional liability and the licensed profession. Paul Fenn; Neil Rickman; Alistair McGuire. *Int. R. Law Econ.* **12:4** 12:1992 pp. 479 – 496

G.2.5: Work organization *[Organisation du travail]*

39 Pushing back the frontiers — management control and work intensification under JIT/TQM factory regimes. Rick Delbridge; Peter Turnbull; Barry Wilkinson. *New Tech. Work. Empl.* **7:2** Autumn:1992 pp. 97 – 106

40 The quality of employment in the nonprofit sector — an update on employee attitudes in nonprofits versus business and government. Philip H. Mirvis. *Non. Manag. Leader.* **3:1** Fall:1992 pp. 23 – 41

41 Reassessing human resource management. Paul Blyton *[Ed.]*; Peter W. Turnbull *[Ed.]*. London: Sage, 1992: 270 p. *ISBN: 0803986971.*

42 Une réduction d'effectif basée sur le volontariat — le cas d'une banque *[In French]*; Voluntary redundancy in a bank *[Summary]*; Personalabbau durch freiwilliges Ausscheiden aus dem Arbeitsverhältnis — ein Beispiel aus der Bankbranche *[German summary]*. Anne Chérain; Didier Demazière. *Form. Emp.* **:37** 1-3:1992 pp. 26 – 40

43 Selection of workers and firm heterogeneity. George W.J. Hendrikse. *Small Bus. Econ.* **4:2** 6:1992 pp. 105 – 111

44 Self-recruitment in the legal profession. David N. Laband; Bernard F. Lentz. *J. Labor Ec.* **10:2** 4:1992 pp. 182 – 201

45 Skill and consent — contemporary studies in the labour process. Andrew Sturdy *[Ed.]*; David Knights *[Ed.]*; Hugh Willmott *[Ed.]*. London: Routledge, 1992: 263 p. *ISBN: 041508671x; LofC: 92008731. Includes bibliographical references and index.* [Organization and employment studies series.]

46 Strategic hiring to deter entry by unions. A. Hollander. *J. Econ. Beh.* **18:1** 6:1992 pp. 53 – 68

47 Strategy and human resource management. Alan McKinlay; Ken Starkey. *Int. J. Hum. Res. Man.* **3:3** 12:1992 pp. 435 – 450

48 A structural dynamic analysis of job turnover and the costs associated with moving to another job. G.J. van den Berg. *Econ. J.* **102:414** 9:1992 pp. 1116 – 1133

49 The structure of authority in the firm. D.W. Katzner. *J. Econ. Beh.* **19:1** 9:1992 pp. 41 – 67

50 Traditions et innovations de formation dans le secteur financier au Québec *[In French]*; Tradition and innovation in training in the financial sector in Quebec *[Summary]*; Ausbildungstraditionen und -innovationen im Finanzsektor in Quebec *[German summary]*. Colette Bernier. *Form. Emp.* **:38** 4-6:1992 pp. 43 – 53

51 Training and technology transfer — efforts of Japanese, Mexican and American maquiladora companies in Mexico. Feraidoon Raafat (Fred); Massoud M. Saghafi; Robert J. Schlesinger; Kenichi Kiyota. *Socio. Econ.* **26:3** 1992 pp. 181 – 190

52 Training too much? A sceptical look at the economics of skill provision in the UK. J.R. Shackleton. London: Institute of Economic Affairs, 1992: 86 p. *ISBN: 0255363079.* [Hobart paper. : No. 118]

53 Vacancies and the recruitment of new employees. Jan van Ours; Geert Ridder. *J. Labor Ec.* **10:2** 4:1992 pp. 138 – 155

54 The value of communication in resource allocation decisions; *[French summary]*. R. Balakrishnan. *Cont. Account. Res.* **8:2** Spring:1992 pp. 353 – 373

55 The variation of productivity within British and German industries. P.E. Hart; A. Shipman. *J. Ind. Econ.* **XL:4** 12:1992 pp. 417 – 425

56 Vocational education and productivity in the Netherlands and Britain. Geoff Mason; S.J. Prais; Bart van Ark. *Natl. Inst. Econ. R.* **:140** 5:1992 pp. 45 – 63

57 Vocational education in India — problems and policies. Balbir Jain. *Ind. J. Ind. Rel.* **28:1** 7:1992 pp. 25 – 36

58 Vuotuinen ajankäyttö *[In Finnish]*; [Annual use of time]. Iiris Niemi; Hannu Pääkkönen. Helsinki: Tilastokeskus, 1992: 82 p. *ISBN: 9514765338. Bibliography — p.81-82.* [Tutkimuksia.]

59 Work organization and occupational qualification in CIM — the case of Swedish NC machine shops. Lars Bengtsson. *New Tech. Work. Empl.* **7:1** Spring:1992 pp. 29 – 43

60 Work organization in Brazilian data processing centres — consent and resistance; *[French summary]*. Angelo S. Soares. *Labour Cap. Soc.* **24:2** 11:1991 pp. 154 – 183

61 Workforce 2000 — the new management challenge. W. Pindur; Donoghue K.; L. Cornelius; C.D. Combs. *Inter. R. Strat. Manag.* 3 1992 pp. 205 – 223

G.3: Business organization — *Organisation de la vie économique*

G.3.1: **Professional organization of employers** — *Organisation professionnelle des employeurs*

1 Business associations in the USSR - and after — their growth and political role. S. Peregudoc; I. Semenenko; A. Zudin. Coventry: Department of Politics and International Sudies, University of Warwick, 1992: 32 p. [Working paper (University of Warwick. Department of Politics and International Studies).]
2 The impact of environmental change on the characteristics of top management teams. B. Üsdiken. *Br. J. Manag.* **3:4** 12:1992 pp. 207 – 219
3 Managerial dilemmas — the political economy of hierarchy. Gary J. Miller. Cambridge: Cambridge University Press, 1992: xv, 254 p. *ISBN: 052137281x; LofC: 91019211. Includes bibliographical references (p. 239-245) and indexes.* [The political economy of institutions and decisions.]
4 Structure and information sharing function of the Japanese Optoelectronic Industrial Association; La structure et la fonction de partage d'information de l'association industrielle optoélectronique japonaise *[French summary]*. Toshihiro Horiuchi. *Gestion* **8:3** 1992 pp. 13 – 31
5 Ustawa o organizacjach pracodawców *[In Polish]*; (Employers Associations Act); (Loi sur l'organisation de employeurs: *Title only in French*); (Устав о организациях работодателей: *Title only in Russian*). Agnieszka Wojcierowska. *Pań. Prawo* **XLVII:2(552)** 1992 pp. 36 – 45

G.3.2: **Economic concentration** — *Concentration économique*

1 Bilateral monopoly and industrial location — a cooperative outcome. D. Cheng; Y.-N. Shieh. *Reg. Sci. Urb. Econ.* **22:2** 6:1992 pp. 187 – 195
2 Canadian competition law and policy at the centenary. R.S. Khemani *[Ed.]*; W.T. Stanbury *[Ed.]*. Halifax, N.S: Institute for Research on Public Policy, 1991: xxvi, 667 p. (ill) *ISBN: 0886451353; LofC: cn 92002433. eng: fre; Companion volume to — Historical perspectives on Canadian competition policy; Includes bibliographical references.*
3 Capital and ownership structures, and the market for corporate control. Ronen Israel. *R. Finan. Stud.* **5:2** 1992 pp. 181 – 198
4 Carteis tecnológicos *[In Portuguese]*; [Technological cartels]. William Baumol. *Economia [Lisbon]* **XV:3** 10:1991 pp. 358 – 390
5 Cartel stability and product differentiation. T.W. Ross. *Int. J. Ind. O.* **10:1** 3:1992 pp. 1 – 14
6 Changes in corporate performance associated with bank acquisitions. Marcia Millon Cornett; Hassan Tehranian. *J. Finan. Ec.* **31:2** 4:1992 pp. 211 – 234
7 A comparative analysis of takeover regulation in the European Community. David J. Berger. *Law Cont. Pr.* **55:4** Autumn:1992 pp. 53 – 75
8 Competition and the EEC's ultimate aims — their relationship within the merger regulation 4064; La tutela della concorrenza e i fini ultimi della CEE — il problema del loro coordinamento nel quadro del regolamento 4064 sulle concentrazioni *[Italian summary]*. Guido Iannuzzi. *Rev. Int. Sci. Ec. Com.* **XXXIX:4** 4:1992 pp. 375 – 381
9 Concentration and profits in South Africa — monopoly or efficiency? D.F. Leach. *S. Afr. J. Econ.* **60:2** 6:1992 pp. 143 – 157
10 Does corporate performance improve after mergers? Paul M. Healy; Krishna G. Palepu; Richard S. Ruback. *J. Finan. Ec.* **31:2** 4:1992 pp. 135 – 175
11 The economics of oligopolistic competition — price and nonprice rivalry — collected papers of Robert E. Kuenne. Robert E. Kuenne. Cambridge, MA.: Basil Blackwell, 1992: 492 p. *ISBN: 1557863016; LofC: 91000767. Includes bibliographical references and index.*
12 The effect of domestic antidumping law in the presence of foreign monopoly. Robert W. Staiger; Frank A. Wolak. *J. Int. Econ.* **32:3/4** 5:1992 pp. 265 – 288

G.3.2: Economic concentration *[Concentration économique]*

13 The effect of government taxation policies on spatial monopoly. S.K. Peng. *Reg. Sci. Urb. Econ.* **22:2** 6:1992 pp. 197 – 211

14 Endogenous cartel formation with private information; *[French summary]*. Morten Hviid. *Can. J. Econ.* **XXV:4** 11:1992 pp. 972 – 982

15 Entry-deterring debt. James J. McAndrews; Leonard I. Nakamura. *J. Money C. B.* **24:1** 2:1992 pp. 98 – 110

16 Europarechtliche Aspekte der Vergabe öffentlicher Aufträge *[In German]*; [The EC's power of the right of determination with respect to businesses, using cartel law as an example]. Kay Hailbronner. *Recht Int. Wirst.* :**7** 1992 pp. 553 – 564

17 Evidence of creative destruction in the U.S. economy. Edgar Norton. *Small Bus. Econ.* **4:2** 6:1992 pp. 113 – 123

18 Filiales communes et article 85 CEE — étude des décisions récentes de la Commission des Communautés européennes *[In French]*; [Joint ventures and EEC article 85. A study of recent decisions made by the Commission of the European Communities]. Jean-Pierre Brill. *R. Trim. Com. Écon.* **45:1** 1-3:1992 pp. 87 – 107

19 Le financement des fusions-acquisitions *[In French]*; The financing of mergers and acquisitions *[Summary]*. Patrick Rousseau. *Gestion* **8:6** 1992 pp. 77 – 99

20 Historical perspectives on Canadian competition policy. R.S. Khemani *[Ed.]*; W.T. Stanbury *[Ed.]*. Halifax, N.S: Institute for Research on Public Policy, 1991: xv, 283 p. *ISBN: 0886451361; LofC: cn 92002432. eng; fre; Companion volume to — Canadian competition law and policy at the centenary; Includes bibliographical references.*

21 How anti-merger laws can reduce investment, help producers, and hurt consumers. Konstantine Gatsios; Larry Karp. *J. Ind. Econ.* **XL:3** 9:1992 pp. 339 – 348

22 Industrial groups as systems of contractual governance. W. Carl Kester. *Ox. R. Econ. Pol.* **8:3** Autumn:1992 pp. 24 – 44

23 The Japanese corporate network — a blockmodel approach. Michael L. Gerlach. *Adm. Sci. Qua.* **37:1** 3:1992 pp. 105 – 139

24 Keiretsu networks in the Japanese economy — a dyad analysis of intercorporate ties. James R. Lincoln; Michael L. Gerlach; Peggy Takahashi. *Am. Sociol. R.* **57:5** 10:1992 pp. 561 – 585

25 Management buyout announcements and securities returns — a UK study 1984-1989. R.J. Briston; B. Saadouni; C.A. Mallin; J.A. Coutts. *J. Bus. Fin. Acc.* **19:4** 6:1992 pp. 641 – 654

26 Mergers and profitability — a managerial success story? Hilary Ingham; Ingvild Kran; Andre Lovestam. *J. Manag. Stu.* **29:2** 3:1992 pp. 195 – 208

27 Mergers and the value of antitrust deterrence. B. Espen Eckbo. *J. Finance* **47:3** 7:1992 pp. 1005 – 1029

28 Mergers that harm competitors. Kenneth D. Boyer. *R. Indust. Organ.* **7:2** 1992 pp. 191 – 202

29 De micro- en macro-economische aspecten van fusies en overnames in Europa *[In Dutch]*; [The micro and macroeconomic aspects of amalgamations and take-overs in Europe]. H. van Ees; H. Garretsen; H. Nijkamp. *Maan. Econ.* **56:2** 1992 pp. 118 – 130

30 Neuere Entwicklungen auf dem österreichischen Markt für Unternehmensfusionen *[In German]*; New developments in the Austrian market for corporate mergers *[Summary]*. Kurt Bayer; Gottfried Wetzel. *Monatsberichte* **7:65** 1992 pp. 387 – 395

31 Organization theory and the market for corporate control — a dynamic analysis of the characteristics of large takeover targets, 1980-1990. Gerald F. Davis; Suzanne K. Stout. *Adm. Sci. Qua.* **37:4** 12:1992 pp. 605 – 633

32 Peer pressure and partnerships. Eugene Kandel; Edward P. Lazear. *J. Polit. Ec.* **100:4** 8:1992 pp. 801 – 817

33 Premier bilan sur la pratique décisionnelle da la Commission dans l'application du règlement relatif au contrôle des concentrations *[In French]*; [First assessment on the decision making practices of the Commissions in the application of the regulation relative to the control of mergers]. Sylvaine Poillot Peruzzetto. *R. Trim. Com. Écon.* **45:1** 1-3:1992 pp. 49 – 86

34 The probability of exit. M.A. Schary. *Rand J. Eco.* **22:3** Autumn:1991 pp. 339 – 353

35 Il progetto di direttiva comunitaria sui takeovers — un vecchio «sogno americano»? *[In Italian]*; [Community directive projects on take-overs. An old American dream?]. Nicola Pesaresi. *A. Fond. L. Einaudi* **XXV** 1991 pp. 161 – 187

36 Reasonable extraterritoriality — correcting the "balance of interests". P.M. Roth. *Int. Comp. L.* **41:2** 4:1992 pp. 245 – 286

37 Refusing to cooperate with competitors — a theory of boycotts. Timothy Brennan. *J. Law Econ.* **XXXV:2** 10:1992 pp. 247 – 264

G.3.2: Economic concentration *[Concentration économique]*

38 Le règlement du conseil des Communautés européennes relatif au contrôle des opérations de concentration entre entreprises *[In French]*; [The regulation of the Council of the European Communities relative to the control of merger deals between enterprises]. L. Gyselen. *R. Trim. Com. Écon.* **45:1** 1-3:1992 pp. 6 – 47

39 Regulating big business — antitrust in Great Britain and America, 1880 to 1990. Tony Allan Freyer. Cambridge: Cambridge University Press, 1992: 399 p. *ISBN: 052135207x; LofC: 91014033. Includes bibliographical references and index.*

40 Regulation of cartels, dominant firms and mergers. W.J. Baumol *[Contrib.]*; P.A. Geroski *[Contrib.]*; K. George *[Contrib.]*; A. Jacquemin *[Contrib.]*. Collection of 3 articles. **Econ. J.**, *102:410*, 1:1992 pp. 127 – 157

41 Strategic alliances — formation, implementation, and evolution. Peter Lorange; Johan Roos. Cambridge, MA.: Blackwell, 1992: 295 p. *ISBN: 1557861021; LofC: 91023298. Includes bibliographical references and index.*

G.3.3: Organization of the firm — *Organisation de l'entreprise*

1 The adoption of the multidivisional form of organization — a contingency model. Joseph T. Mahoney. *J. Manag. Stu.* **29:1** 1:1992 pp. 49 – 72

2 African co-operatives and the state in the 1990s. Hans-H. Münkner. *Y. Co- op. Enter.* 1992 pp. 19 – 29

3 Between government and labor — managerial decision-making in Chinese industry. Yimin Lin. *Stud. Comp. Commun.* **XXV:4** 12:1992 pp. 381 – 403

4 Between perestroika and privatisation — divided strategies and political crisis in a Soviet enterprise. Michael Burawoy; Kathryn Hendley. *Eur.-Asia Stud.* **44:3** 1992 pp. 371 – 402

5 Business ethics — a European casebook. John Donaldson *[Ed.]*; Peter Davis *[Ed.]*; et al. London: Academic Press, 1992: 293 p. *ISBN: 0122205421.*

6 Business ethics — four spheres of executive responsibility. Joseph L. Badaracco. *Calif. Manag. R.* **34:3** Spring:1992 pp. 64 – 79

7 Contrasting patterns of business organisation in Silicon Valley. A. Saxenian. *Envir. Plan. D* **10:4** 8:1992 pp. 377 – 391

8 Corporate redemption and the seven deadly sins. Andrall E. Pearson. *Harv. Bus. Re.* **70:3** 5-6:1992 pp. 65 – 75

9 Effects of bailouts, taxes, and risk-aversion on the enterprise. Stephen M. Goldfeld; Richard E. Quandt. *J. Comp. Econ.* **16:1** 3:1992 pp. 150 – 167

10 Efficiency and equity in dynamic principal-agent problems. Ramamohan T.V.S. Rao. *J. Econ.* **55:1** 1992 pp. 17 – 41

11 Enterprise response to market reforms — the case of the Chinese bicycle industry. Xunhai Zhang. *Aust. J. Chin. Aff.* **:28** 7:1992 pp. 111 – 140

12 Expertise and problem categorization — the role of expert processing in organizational sense-making. David V. Day; Robert G. Lord. *J. Manag. Stu.* **29:1** 1:1992 pp. 35 – 47

13 Extending game theoretic propositions about slack and scarcity in managerial decision making. Sandy J. Wayne; David Rubinstein. *Human Relat.* **45:5** 5:1992 pp. 525 – 536

14 Le financement de l'innovation dans les petites et moyennes entreprises industrielles — difficultés et comportements *[In French]*; The financing of innovation in small-and medium-sized industrial companies — difficulties and behaviours *[Summary]*. Mohamed Bayad; Jean-Luc Herrmann. *Gestion* **8:6** 1992 pp. 173 – 199

15 Firm cooperation and subcontracting. R. Arena; Joel-T. Ravix; Paul-M. Romani. *Metroeconomica* **XLIII:1-2** 2-6:1992 pp. 247 – 266

16 French and British top managers' understanding of the structure and the dynamics of their industries— a cognitive analysis and comparison. R. Calori; G. Johnson; P. Sarnin. *Br. J. Manag.* **3:2** 6:1992 pp. 61 – 78

17 From comparative advantage to damage control — clarifying strategic issues using SWOT analysis. Kevin P. Kearns. *Non. Manag. Leader.* **3:1** Fall:1992 pp. 3 – 22

18 Innovation, firm size and growth in a centralized organization. S. Gifford. *Rand J. Eco.* **23:2** Summer:1992 pp. 284 – 298

19 The interaction between financial and employment contracts — a formal model of Japanese corporate governance. Gerald T. Garvey; Peter L. Swan. *J. Jap. Int. Ec.* **6:3** 9:1992 pp. 247 – 274

20 The Japanese transplants — production organization and regional development. Martin Kenney; Richard Florida. *J. Am. Plann.* **58:1** Winter:1992 pp. 21 – 38

G.3.3: Organization of the firm *[Organisation de l'entreprise]*

21 The labor-managed firm under production uncertainty. L. Dean Hiebert. *J. Comp. Econ.* **16:1** 3:1992 pp. 94 – 104

22 The new boundaries of the "boundaryless" company. Larry Hirschhorn; Thomas Gilmore. *Harv. Bus. Re.* **70:3** 5-6:1992 pp. 104 – 115

23 Organizational structure and firm performance — an intertemporal perspective. Hilary Ingham. *J. Econ. Stud.* **19:5** 1992 pp. 19 – 35

24 Pre-commitment and flexibility — applications to oligopoly theory. B.J. Spencer; J.A. Brander. *Eur. Econ. R.* **36:8** 12:1992 pp. 1601 – 1626

25 Professionalizing management and managing professionalization — British management in the 1980s. Michael Reed; Peter Anthony. *J. Manag. Stu.* **29:5** 9:1992 pp. 591 – 614

26 Qualità dei managers e incentivi in un modello di duopolio con separazione tra proprietà e controllo *[In Italian]*; [The quality of managers and incentives in a duopoly model with a separation between ownership and control]. Guido Merzoni. *A. Fond. L. Einaudi* **XXV** 1991 pp. 137 – 159

27 Restructuring enterprises in Eastern Europe. Wendy Carlin; Colin Mayer; Hans-Werner Sinn *[Comments by]*; Vittorio Grilli *[Comments by]*. *Econ. Pol.* **:15** 10:1992 pp. 311 – 352

28 Strategic consequences of executive succession within diversified firms. Margarethe F. Wiersema. *J. Manag. Stu.* **29:1** 1:1992 pp. 73 – 94

29 The strategic restructuring of non-profit associations — an exploratory study. Darlyne Bailey. *Non. Manag. Leader.* **3:1** Fall:1992 pp. 65 – 80

30 Strategy and organizational development. R. Lewis. *Inter. R. Strat. Manag.* **3** 1992 pp. 225 – 238

31 Takeovers, transfers and business re-organizations. John McMullen. *Ind. Law J.* **21:1** 3:1992 pp. 15 – 30

32 Technologie, organisation et performances *[In French]*; Technology, organization and performances *[Summary]*. B. Guilhon. *Rev. Ec. Polit.* **102:4** 7-8:1992 pp. 563 – 592

33 Towards an «out of equilibrium» theory of the firm. M. Amendola; Jean Luc Gaffard. *Metroeconomica* **XLIII:1-2** 2-6:1992 pp. 267 – 288

34 Trends and policy issues in the co-operative development of Central and Eastern Europe. D. Mavrogiannis. *Y. Co- op. Enter.* 1992 pp. 1 – 18

35 Understanding power in organizations. Jeffrey Pfeffer. *Calif. Manag. R.* **34:2** Winter:1992 pp. 29 – 50

36 Why hang on to losers? Divestitures and takeovers. Arnoud W.A. Boot. *J. Finance* **47:4** 9:1992 pp. 1401 – 1423

G.3.3.1: Entrepreneurship — *L'entrepreneur, théorie et fonction*

1 African entrepreneurs — pioneers of development. Keith Marsden. *Small Enter. Devel.* **3:2** 6:1992 pp. 15 – 25

2 Chili — les nouveaux entrepreneurs *[In French]*; [Chile — the new entrepreneurs] *[Summary]*; *[Spanish summary]*. Cecillia Montero Casassus. *Prob. Am.Lat.* **:4** 1-3:1992 pp. 117 – 135

3 Constraints on development — small businesses in Saudi Arabia. Bandar Al Hajjar; John R. Presley. *Middle E. Stud.* **28:2** 4:1992 pp. 334 – 351

4 Determinants of minority business formation — a detailed industry analysis. N.F. Ekanem. *Appl. Econ.* **24:10** 10:1992 pp. 1147 – 1154

5 Directors' powers, duties and reponisbilities. Patrick Nunan. *Irish Bank. Rev.* Spring:1992 pp. 36 – 47

6 Economic and non-economic models of entrepreneurship in the UK. Allan M. Williams. *Wor. Futur.* **33:1-3** 1992 pp. 25 – 33

7 The entrepreneurial factor in economic growth. Harold Lydall. London: Macmillan Press, 1992: 104 p. (4ill) *ISBN: 0333569237.*

8 Entrepreneurship research — where are we and where should we be going? A.B. Boshoff; J.L. Schutte; H.F. Bennett. *Develop. S. Afr.* **9:1** 2:1992 pp. 47 – 64

9 Entrepreneurship support systems; *[Arabic summary]*; *[French summary]*; *[Spanish summary]*. Igor Pavlin *[Ed.]*; Li-Choy Chong *[Contrib.]*; Dwight R. Thomas *[Contrib.]*; Mark Goh *[Contrib.]*; Hashim Hassan *[Contrib.]*; Ágnes Tibor *[Contrib.]*; Pham Van Pho *[Contrib.]*; Khuyagiin Ganbaatar *[Contrib.]*; J.S. Juneja *[Contrib.]*; Darko Deškovič *[Contrib.] and others. Collection of 17 articles.* **Publ. Enter.** , *12:1-2*, 3-6:1992 pp. 3 – 167

G.3.3.1: Entrepreneurship *[L'entrepreneur, théorie et fonction]*

10 *[In Arabic]*; [The growth and development of entrepreneurship] *[Summary]*.*Dirasat Ser. A.* **18:3** 1991 pp. 64 – 98

11 Le imprese nuove nate e la legge di Gibrat *[In Italian]*; New companies and the Gibrat law *[Summary]*. Giovanni Solinas. *Ec. Lav.* **XXVI:1** 1-3:1992 pp. 117 – 140

12 The new entrepreneurs — self-employment and small business in Europe. Patricia Leighton *[Ed.]*; Alan Felstead *[Ed.]*. London: Kogan Page, 1992: 240 p. *ISBN: 0749403594.*

13 New firms and economic activity — the U.K. experience. M.T. Robson. *Eco. Notes* **21:1** 1992 pp. 137 – 147

14 The politics of entrepreneurship — affirmative-action policies for indigenous entrepreneurs. John Hailey. *Small Enter. Devel.* **3:2** 6:1992 pp. 4 – 14

15 Recenti evoluzioni del concetto di finalità aziendale — dal profitto all'eccellenza imprenditoriale *[In Italian]*; [Recent developments in the concept of business goals — from profit to entrepreneurial excellence]. Michele Andreaus. *Econ. Ban.* **3** 1992 pp. 349 – 370

16 Southeast Asian capitalists. Ruth Thomas McVey *[Ed.]*. Ithaca, N.Y: Southeast Asia Program, Cornell University, 1992: 218 p. *ISBN: 0877277087. Includes bibliographical references.* [Studies on Southeast Asia.]

17 Survival chances of newly founded business organizations. Josef Brüderl; Peter Preisendörfer; Rolf Ziegler. *Am. Sociol. R.* **57:2** 4:1992 pp. 227 – 242

18 Top team deterioration as part of the downward spiral of large corporate bankruptcies. Donald C. Hambrick; Richard A. D'Aveni. *Manag. Sci.* **38:10** 10:1992 pp. 1445 – 1466

19 Vision in Japanese entrepreneurship — the evolution of a security enterprise. Hiroshi Shimazaki. London: Routledge, 1992: 267 p. *ISBN: 0415083575; LofC: 92010995. Includes bibliographical references (p.) and index.*

20 Women-owned businesses — dimensions and policy issues. Thomas A. Clark; Franklin J. James. *Econ. Devel. Q.* **6:1** 2:1992 pp. 25 – 40

G.3.3.2: Capital and capital formation — *Le capital et sa formation*

1 Capital disadvantage — America's failing capital investment system. Michael E. Porter. *Harv. Bus. Re.* **70:5** 9-10:1992 pp. 65 – 83

2 Capital structure as an optimal contract between employees and investors. Chun Chang. *J. Finance* **47:3** 7:1992 pp. 1141 – 1158

3 Corporate capital structure and pension-funding strategy. Sheng Cheng Hu. *R. Quant. Finan. Account.* **2:2** 6:1992 pp. 145 – 168

4 Equity participation contracts and investment — some theoretical and empirical results. Abdel-Hameed M. Bashir; Ali F. Darrat. *Am. J. Islam. Soc. Sci.* **9:2** Summer:1992 pp. 219 – 232

5 Free trade and concentration of capital in Mexico. James W. Russell. *Mon. Rev.* **44:2** 6:1992 pp. 23 – 30

6 The impact of ownership and capital structure on managerial motivation and strategy in management buyouts — a cultural analysis. Sebastian Green. *J. Manag. Stu.* **29:4** 7:1992 pp. 513 – 535

7 Information leakage prior to takeover announcements — the effect of media reports. Michael Aitken; Robert Czernkowski. *Acc. Bus. Res.* **23:89** Winter:1992 pp. 3 – 20

8 Multiple objectives in the theory of the firm. Georg Hasenkamp. *J. Prod. Anal.* **3:4** 12:1992 pp. 323 – 336

9 The myth of Japan's low-cost capital. W. Carl Kester; Timothy A. Luehrman. *Harv. Bus. Re.* **70:3** 5-6:1992 pp. 130 – 138

10 Productivity of western and domestic capital in Polish industry. Katherine Terrell. *J. Comp. Econ.* **16:3** 9:1992 pp. 494 – 514

11 The role of firm-specific capital in vertical mergers. Avi Weiss. *J. Law Econ.* **XXXV:1** 4:1992 pp. 71 – 88

12 Small firm mutual funds — additional evidence on the small firm effect. S.C. Isberg; Clifford F. Thies. *Small Bus. Econ.* **4:3** 9:1992 pp. 211 – 220

13 Taxes, financial distress, and corporate capital structure. Jayant R. Kale; Thomas H. Noe. *Q Rev. Econ. Finan.* **32:1** Spring:1992 pp. 71 – 83

14 Technical and organizational progress and the turnover of capital. Jens M. Haass. *Rev. Rad. Pol. Ec.* **24:1** Spring:1992 pp. 114 – 135

15 Unproductive expenditure in manufacturing. Alexander M. Thompson. *Camb. J. Econ.* **16:2** 6:1992 pp. 147 – 168

G.3.3.2: Capital and capital formation *[Le capital et sa formation]*

16 Waluguru traders in Dar es Salaam. Jan Kees van Donge. *Afr. Affairs* **91:363**   4:1992 pp. 181 – 206

G.3.3.3: Financing methods — *Méthodes de financement*

1 Assessing the impact of inflation on business performance under conditions of limited financial disclosure — the case of firms operating in Greece. Antonios A. Papas. *Spoudai* **42:1** 1-3:1992 pp. 25 – 43

2 The audit report under going concern uncertainties — an empirical analysis. David B. Citron; Richard J. Taffler. *Acc. Bus. Res.* **22:88** Autumn:1992 pp. 337 – 345

3 Bankruptcy, warranties and the firm's capital structure. Elie Appelbaum. *Int. Econ. R.* **33:2** 5:1992 pp. 399 – 412

4 Buffer stock money and the company sector. Simon Wren-Lewis. *Ox. Econ. Pap.* **44:2** 4:1992 pp. 209 – 231

5 Buy-outs, divestment, and leverage — restructuring transactions and corporate governance. Steve Thompson; Mike Wright; Ken Robbie. *Ox. R. Econ. Pol.* **8:3** Autumn:1992 pp. 58 – 69

6 Caratteri innovativi della nuova normativa sul bilancio di esercizio *[In Italian]*; [Innovative characteristics of the new directive on the operating budget]. Sergio Manetti. *Risparmio* **XL:5** 9-10:1992 pp. 1141 – 1169

7 Common stock offerings and earnings expectations — a test of the release of unfavorable information. Peter Alan Brous. *J. Finance* **47:4** 9:1992 pp. 1517 – 1536

8 Contagion and competitive intra-industry effects of bankruptcy announcements — an empirical analysis. Larry H.P. Lang; René M. Stulz. *J. Finan. Ec.* **32:1** 8:1992 pp. 45 – 60

9 Convertible bonds as backdoor equity financing. Jeremy C. Stein. *J. Finan. Ec.* **32:1** 8:1992 pp. 3 – 22

10 Corporate debt. Garry Young. *Natl. Inst. Econ. R.* **139** 2:1992 pp. 88 – 94

11 The cost of borrowed funds by firm scale in Japan — an empirical investigation. Richard Beason. *Econ. S. Quart.* **43:1** 3:1992 pp. 57 – 66

12 Dynamics of learning and the financial instability hypothesis. R. Sethi. *J. Econ.* **56:1** 1992 pp. 39 – 70

13 Estimating the impacts of regional business assistance programs — alternative closures in a computable general equilibrium model. Dan S. Rickman. *Pap. Reg. Sci.* **71:4** 10:1992 pp. 421 – 435

14 Finance and the enterprise. Vera Negri Zamagni *[Ed.]*. London: Academic Press, 1992: 300 p. *ISBN: 0127754202.*

15 The financing of small firms in Germany. Christian Harm. Washington, D.C.: Country Economics Department The World Bank, 1992: 35 p. [Policy research working papers — financial policy and systems. : No. WPS 899]

16 Funding uncertainty and nonprofit strategies in the 1980s. Wolfgang Bielefeld. *Non. Manag. Leader.* **2:4** Summer:1992 pp. 381 – 401

17 How soft is the budget constraint for Yugoslav firms? Evan Kraft; Milan Vodopivec. *J. Comp. Econ.* **16:3** 9:1992 pp. 432 – 455

18 The impact of asset specificity on single-period contracting. G.M. Choate; S.M. Maser. *J. Econ. Beh.* **18:3** 8:1992 pp. 373 – 389

19 Information content of financial leverage — an empirical study. Il-Woon Kim; Kung H. Chen; Jon Nance. *J. Bus. Fin. Acc.* **19:1** 1:1992 pp. 133 – 152

20 Interest rate swaps and corporate financing choices. Sheridan Titman. *J. Finance* **47:4** 9:1992 pp. 1503 – 1516

21 Internalizacija proizvodnih eksternih efekata investicijskih odluka poduzeća *[In Serbo-Croatian]*; Internalization of production externalities of firms' investment decisions *[Summary]*; Интернализация производственных экстерных эффектов капиталовложительных решений предприятий *[Russian summary]*. Barbara Bojnec-Fakin. *Ekon. Preg.* **43:5-6** 1992 pp. 465 – 492

22 Investitionsvolumen und Risikoallokation. Einige Anmerkungen *[In German]*; Observations on investment volume and risk allocation *[Summary]*; Quelques remarques sur le volume des investissements et l'allocation de risques *[French summary]*. Werner Neus; Peter Nippel. *Kred. Kap.* **25:3** 1992 pp. 406 – 415

23 Investment appraisal, taxes and the security market line. Norman C. Strong; Tony R. Appleyard. *J. Bus. Fin. Acc.* **19:1** 1:1992 pp. 1 – 24

G.3.3.3: Financing methods *[Méthodes de financement]*

24 Lessons from a comparison of US and UK insolvency codes. Julian Franks; Walter Torous. *Ox. R. Econ. Pol.* **8:3** Autumn:1992 pp. 70 – 82

25 Management buyout proposals and inside information. D. Scott Lee. *J. Finance* **47:3** 7:1992 pp. 1061 – 1079

26 Management buy-outs — the sources and sharing of wealth between insiders and outside shareholders. George M. Frankfurter; Erdal Gunay. *Q Rev. Econ. Finan.* **32:3** Autumn:1992 pp. 82 – 95

27 Managerial and windfall rents in the market for corporate control. R.P. Castanias; C.E. Helfat. *J. Econ. Beh.* **18:2** 7:1992 pp. 153 – 184

28 Managerial vote ownership and shareholder wealth — evidence from employee stock ownership plans. Saeyoung Chang; David Mayers. *J. Finan. Ec.* **32:1** 8:1992 pp. 103 – 131

29 Marktkonzentration, Unsicherheit und Kapitalakkumulation *[In German]*; Oligopolistic market structure, uncertainty, and capital accumulation *[Summary]*. Manfred Stadler. *Jahrb. N. St.* **210:3-4** 9:1992 pp. 286 – 301

30 A note on a role for cost allocations in decisions concerning investment in common service facilities. Alan Gregory; R.S. Olusegun Wallace. *J. Bus. Fin. Acc.* **19:1** 1:1992 pp. 73 – 86

31 Ocena stopnia wykorzystania majątku trwałego i siły roboczej w przedsiębiorstwie. Próba pomiaru *[In Polish]*; Evaluation of utilisation of fixed capital and labour force by a firm *[Summary]*; Оценка степени использования основных фондов и рабочей силы на предприятии. Попытка измерения *[Russian summary]*. Paweł Miłobędzki; Mirosław Szreder. *Prz. Staty.* **39:2** 1992 pp. 187 – 208

32 On the price and structural efficiency in Farrell's model. Jati K. Sengupta. *B. Econ. Res.* **44:4** 10:1992 pp. 281 – 300

33 Ownership structure, value of the firm, and the bargaining power of the manager. Nicholas Mercuro; Haralambos Sourbis; Gerald Whitney. *S. Econ. J.* **59:2** 10:1992 pp. 273 – 283

34 Predictive models for annual fundraising and major gift fundraising. Wesley E. Lindahl; Christopher Winship. *Non. Manag. Leader.* **3:1** Fall:1992 pp. 43 – 64

35 Reallocation of voting rights and shareholders' wealth; Ré-allocation des droits de vote et richesse des actionnaires *[French summary]*. Elizabeth Maynes. *Can. J. Econ.* **XXV:3** 8:1992 pp. 538 – 563

36 Sources of the financing hierarchy for business investment. Stephen D. Oliner; Glenn D. Rudebusch. *Rev. Econ. St.* **LXXIV:4** 11:1992 pp. 643 – 654

37 The structure of corporate ownership in Japan. Stephen D. Prowse. *J. Finance* **47:3** 7:1992 pp. 1121 – 1140

38 La teoria degli incentivi e il problema del finanziamento dell'impresa *[In Italian]*; [The theory of incentives and the problem of enterprise financing]. Carlotta Berti Ceroni. *A. Fond. L. Einaudi* **XXV** 1991 pp. 101 – 136

39 Theory of the firm in relation to exchange rates, import substitution and export. V. Bharat-Ram; D.R. Sen. *Appl. Econ.* **24:12** 12:1992 pp. 1345 – 1356

40 Transactions, transaction costs, and vertical integration — a re-examination. Steven G. Medema; John Commons *[Subject of work]*; Oliver Williamson *[Subject of work]*. *R. Pol. Econ.* **4:3** 1992 pp. 291 – 316

G.3.3.4: Size — *Dimension de l'entreprise*

1 La competitivité des petites et moyennes entreprises *[In French]*; [Competitiveness of small and medium sized enterprises]. Alain Jenny *[Contrib.]*; Pierre Goetschin *[Contrib.]*; Francis Leonard *[Contrib.]*; Alden G. Lank *[Contrib.]*; J.-M. Blanc *[Contrib.]*; Philipp Stauber *[Contrib.]*; Véronique Jost *[Contrib.]*; Jean-Jacques Rivier *[Contrib.]*; Pierre Casse *[Contrib.]*; Antoine Andenmatten *[Contrib.] and others*. Collection of 9 articles. **R. Econ. Soc.** , 50:3, 9:1992 pp. 133 – 223

2 Credit for small firms, not dinosaurs. Barry Ickes; Randi Ryterman. *Orbis* **36:3** Summer:1992 pp. 333 – 348

3 Crise économique et petite industrie — l'exemple de la Grèce contemporaine *[In French]*; [Economic crisis and small-scale industry — contemporary Greece as an example]. Sophie Boutillier. *Soc. Sci. Info.* **31:4** 1992 pp. 735 – 772

4 Economies of scale and small firms in developing countries — theoretical and empirical issues. A. Elleithy. *J. Int. Dev.* **4:4** 7-8:1992 pp. 463 – 476

G.3.3.4: Size *[Dimension de l'entreprise]*

5 The experience of SMEs' development in Taiwan — high export-contribution and export-intensity; Lo sviluppo delle piccole e medie imprese a Formosa — il loro elevato contributo alle esportazioni e l'intensità di esportazione *[Italian summary]*. Tein-Chen Chou. *Rev. Int. Sci. Ec. Com.* **XXXIX:12** 12:1992 pp. 1067 – 1084

6 Firm size and the information content of bank loan announcements. M.B. Slovin; S.A. Johnson; J.L. Glascock. *J. Bank. Fin.* **16:6** 12:1992 pp. 1057 – 1071

7 Foreign trade potential, small enterprise development and job creation in developing countries. Dennis A. Rondinelli; John D. Kasarda. *Small Bus. Econ.* **4:4** 12:1992 pp. 253 – 265

8 The informal sector in Ghana's political economy. Kwame Akon Ninsin. Accra: Freedom Publications, 1991: x, 127 p. *ISBN: 9964910606. Includes bibliography.*

9 Ley de pequeña y microempresa — observaciones y propuestas *[In Spanish]*; [The law on small and micro-enterprises — observations and proposals]. Eliana Chávez O'Brien; Juan Chacaltana Janampa. *Soc. Part.* **:57** 3:1992 35-48

10 Microenterprise development in a sub-sector context. Donald C. Mead. *Small Enter. Devel.* **3:1** 3:1992 pp. 35 – 42

11 On the relationship between firm size and export intensity. Andrea Bonaccorsi. *J. Int. Bus. Stud.* **23:4** Fourth quarter:1992 pp. 605 – 635

12 Organizing in the small growing firm — a grounded theory approach. Tomas Brytting. Stockholm: Stockholm School of Economics, Economic Research Institute, 1991: 238 p. *ISBN: 9172583193. Includes bibliographical references (p. 227-238).*

13 Piccole e medie imprese e innovazione in Italia *[In Italian]*; Small and medium enterprises and innovation in Italy *[Summary]*. Giovanni Dosi; Massimo Moggi. *Industria* **XIII:3** 7-9:1992 pp. 429 – 453

14 The political economy of the southern African periphery — cottage industries, factories and female wage labour in Swaziland compared. Betty J. Harris. New York, NY.: St. Martin's Press, 1992: 296 p. *ISBN: 0312084714; LofC: 92012784. Includes bibliographical references and index.*

15 Private sector membership associations and support for SMEs. Jacob Levitsky. *Small Enter. Devel.* **3:1** 3:1992 pp. 22 – 34

16 Rentabilité, productivité et taille de l'entreprise *[In French]*; Profitability and productivity in relation to the size of a firm *[Summary]*; Rentabilidad, productividad y talla de la empresa *[Spanish summary]*. Gilbert Cette; Daniel Szpiro. *E & S* **:251** 2:1992 pp. 41 – 47

17 Research issues for small enterprise development. Michael Farbman; William F. Steel. *Small Enter. Devel.* **3:2** 6:1992 pp. 26 – 34

18 The role of small firms in the industrial development and transformation of Czechoslovakia. G.A. McDermott; Michal Mejstrik. *Small Bus. Econ.* **4:3** 9:1992 pp. 179 – 200

19 Scale economies in small entrepreneurial firms. Gavin C. Reid. *Scot. J. Poli.* **39:1** 2:1992 pp. 39 – 51

20 Small firm "presence" in Indian manufacturing. I.N. Gang. *World Dev.* **20:9** 9:1992 pp. 1377 – 1389

21 Small manufacturing enterprises in Egypt. Stephen P. Davies; Donald C. Mead; James L. Seale. *Econ. Dev. Cult. Change* **40:2** 1:1992 pp. 381 – 412

22 Vincoli finanziari e crescita delle piccole e medie imprese *[In Italian]*; [Financial constraints and growth in small and medium sized enterprises] *[Summary]*. E. Flaccadoro; G.B. Pittaluga. *Riv. Int. Sci. Soc.* **2** 4-6:1992 pp. 103 – 127

G.3.3.5: Technical management — *Organisation technique*

Sub-divisions: Business strategies *[Strategies d'enterprises]*; Financial management *[Gestion financière]*

1 Aktuella teman inom skandinavisk »ledelse«forskning *[In Danish]*; [Current themes in Scandinavian management research] *[Summary]*. Olof Berg. *Led. Erhv.* **56:3** 7:1992 pp. 113 – 122

2 Un brin de gerbe — d'une gestion diffuse à une gestion de projets *[In French]*; A bit of spark. From diffuse management to project management *[Summary]*. Christine Vander Borght. *Gestion* **8:1** 1992 pp. 99 – 108

3 Company directors — who cares about skill and care? Vanessa Finch. *Mod. Law R.* **55:2** 3:1992 pp. 179 – 214

4 Competition and unilateral dumping. David E. Weinstein. *J. Int. Econ.* **32:3/4** 5:1992 pp. 379 – 387

5 Competitive profits in the long run. Val Eugene Lambson. *R. Econ. S.* **59(1):198** 2:1992 pp. 125 – 142

6 Corporate control in Germany. Ellen Schneider-Lenné. *Ox. R. Econ. Pol.* **8:3** Autumn:1992 pp. 11 – 23

7 Critical management studies. Mats Alvesson *[Ed.]*; Hugh Willmott *[Ed.]*. London: Sage Publications, 1992: 230 p. *ISBN: 0803984553.*

8 Debt, financial fragility, and systemic risk. E.P. Davis. Oxford: Clarendon Press, 1992: 314 p. *ISBN: 0198287526; LofC: 92024780. Includes bibliographical references and index.*

9 Le determinanti della domanda industriale di terziario avanzato — un'indagine empirica *[In Italian]*; The determinants of high-tech firm's demand for services *[Summary]*. Piero Carducci. *Industria* **XIII:1** 1-3:1992 pp. 95 – 114

10 The economic characteristics of de-diversifying firms. C.C. Markides. *Br. J. Manag.* **3:2** 6:1992 pp. 91 – 100

11 The effect of forward markets on multinational firms. Udo Broll. *B. Econ. Res.* **44:3** 7:1992 pp. 233 – 240

12 The effect of labor cost differences on the location of economic activity under the U.S.-Canada free trade agreement. Karen Roberts; Phillip R. Smith. *Econ. Devel. Q.* **6:1** 2:1992 pp. 52 – 63

13 The effect of the Thatcher government on company liquidations — an econometric study. P. Turner; A. Coutts; S. Bowden. *Appl. Econ.* **24:8** 8:1992 pp. 935 – 943

14 Effects of board composition and stock ownership on the adoption of "poison pills". Paul Mallette; Karen L. Fowler. *Acad. Manag. J.* **35:5** 12:1992 pp. 1010 – 1035

15 The effects of competition on executive behavior. B.E. Hermalin. *Rand J. Eco.* **23:3** Autumn:1992 pp. 350 – 365

16 An empirical investigation of business financial structures in a regulated economy. A. Murphy; Z. Sabov. *Eur.-Asia Stud.* **44:2** 1992 pp. 333 – 342

17 An empirical investigation of factors affecting the earnings association coefficient. Debra C. Jeter; Paul K. Chaney. *J. Bus. Fin. Acc.* **19:6** 11:1992 pp. 839 – 863

18 Ethics in modern management. Gerald J. Williams. New York: Quorum Books, 1992: xiv, 183 p. *ISBN: 0899307078; LofC: 91044991. Includes bibliographical references (p.[173]-175) and index.*

19 The evolution of the diet model in managing food systems. Lilly M. Lancaster. *Interfaces* **22:5** 9-10:1992 pp. 59 – 68

20 Executive compensation, organizational effectiveness, social performance and firm performance — an empirical investigation. Ahmed Riahi-Belkaoui. *J. Bus. Fin. Acc.* **19:1** 1:1992 pp. 25 – 38

21 Experiences with decision conferencing in Hungary. Anna Vári; János Vecsenyi. *Interfaces* **22:6** 11-12:1992 pp. 72 – 83

22 Firm reputation and self-enforcing labor contracts. Yoshitsugu Kanemoto; W. Bentley MacLeod. *J. Jap. Int. Ec.* **6:2** 6:1992 pp. 144 – 162

23 La fonction logistique dans l'entreprise *[In French]*; Logistics in the firm *[Summary]*; Die «logistische Funktion» im Unternehmen *[German summary]*. Yann Darré. *Form. Emp.* **:39** 7-9:1992 pp. 3 – 17

24 A framework for integrated risk management in international business. Kent D. Miller. *J. Int. Bus. Stud.* **23:2** 1992 pp. 311 – 332

G.3.3.5: Technical management *[Organisation technique]*

25 Les gestionnaires face à l'efficacité *[In French]*; Managers faced with efficiency and effectiveness *[Summary]*. Jean Nizet. *Gestion* **8:1** 1992 pp. 73 – 86

26 Heathens, heretics, and cults — the religious spectrum of decision aiding. Ronald A. Howard. *Interfaces* **22:6** 11-12:1992 pp. 15 – 27

27 Hierarchy — the economics of managing. Roy Radner. *J. Econ. Lit.* **XXX:3** 9:1992 pp. 1382 – 1415

28 How entry threats induce slack. N.-H. Mørch von der Fehr. *Int. J. Ind. O.* **10:2** 6:1992 pp. 231 – 250

29 How sustainable is your competitive advantage? Jeffrey R. Williams. *Calif. Manag. R.* **34:3** Spring:1992 pp. 29 – 51

30 The human firm in the natural environment — a socio-economic analysis of its behavior. J.F. Tomer. *Ecol. Eco.* **6:2** 10:1992 pp. 119 – 138

31 The impact of ownership structure and executive team composition on firm performance — the resolution of a leadership paradox. Eva M. Meyerson. Stockholm: Industrial Institute for Economic and Social Research, 1992: 166 p. *ISBN: 9172043954.*

32 Implementing ABC — a case study of organizational and behavioural consequences. A. Bhimani; D. Pigott. *Manag. Acc. Res.* **3:2** 6:1992 pp. 119 – 132

33 Incentive compensation schemes — experimental calibration of the rationality hypothesis; *[French summary]*. A.J. Kirby. *Cont. Account. Res.* **8:2** Spring:1992 pp. 374 – 408

34 The individual and organizational culture — strategies for action in highly-ordered contexts. Karen Golden. *J. Manag. Stu.* **29:1** 1:1992 pp. 1 – 21

35 The interenterprise arrears crisis in Russia. Barry W. Ickes; Randi Ryterman. *Post-Sov. Aff.* **8:4** 10-12:1992 pp. 331 – 361

36 Intertemporal choice, hostile takeovers and the principal-agent problem — corporate managers versus political agents. Dwight R. Lee; Robert L. Sexton. *J. Soc. Pol. E.* **17:2** Summer:1992 pp. 203 – 213

37 Investment and market power. P.R. Worthington. *Int. J. Ind. O.* **10:2** 6:1992 pp. 309 – 318

38 Japanese management philosophies — from the vacuous to the brilliant. Jeremiah J. Sullivan. *Calif. Manag. R.* **34:2** Winter:1992 pp. 66 – 87

39 The key role of software make/buy decisions during the 1990s; *[French summary]*. Tony Rands. *Gestion* **8:2** 1992 pp. 155 – 175

40 Launching a viable joint venture. William H. Newman. *Calif. Manag. R.* **35:1** Fall:1992 pp. 68 – 80

41 Learning by knowledge-intensive firms. William H. Starbuck. *J. Manag. Stu.* **29:6** 11:1992 pp. 713 – 740

42 Ledelse af danske datterselskaber i Frankrig, England og Tyskland *[In Danish]*; [Executives of Danish subsidiaries in France, England and Germany] *[Summary]*. Søren Svendsen. *Led. Erhv.* **56:2** 4:1992 pp. 85 – 93

43 Logique de planification des systémes d'information — analyse de certains facteurs parasites et proposition d'un cadre méthodologique *[In French]*; [Planning scheme for information systems — study of some parasitic factors and proposal of a methodological framework]. Jean Paul Cassar. *Gestion* **8:2** 1992 pp. 139 – 154

44 The making of the corporate acolyte — some thoughts on charismatic leadership and the reality of organizational commitment. Heather Hopfl. *J. Manag. Stu.* **29:1** 1:1992 pp. 23 – 33

45 Managerial conservatism, project choice, and debt. David Hirshleifer; Anjan V. Thakor. *R. Finan. Stud.* **5:3** 1992 pp. 437 – 470

46 Managing AMT in a just-in-time environment in the UK and Japan. W.L. Currie; J.J.M. Seddon. *Br. J. Manag.* **3:3** 9:1992 pp. 123 – 136

47 Managing for quality in the US and in Japan. Barbara B. Flynn. *Interfaces* **22:5** 9-10:1992 pp. 69 – 80

48 *[In Japanese]*; Mandatory disclosure and managerial incentives — an analysis of price efficiency and social optimality *[Summary]*. Seongill Kang. *Econ. S. Quart.* **43:3** 9:1992 pp. 258 – 265

49 The market valuation implications of net periodic income cost components. Mary E. Barth; William H. Beaver; Wayne R. Landsman. *J. Account. E.* **15:1** 3:1992 pp. 27 – 62

50 A model of the socialist firm in transition to a market economy. N. Van Long; H. Siebert. *J. Econ.* **56:1** 1992 pp. 1 – 21

51 Modelling growth in the annual earnings time series. Haim A. Mozes. *J. Bus. Fin. Acc.* **19:6** 11:1992 pp. 817 – 837

G.3.3.5: Technical management *[Organisation technique]*

52 Multinational companies performance measurement systems — international perspectives. J.B. Coates; E.W. Davis; C.R. Emmanuel; S.G. Longden; R.J. Stacey. *Manag. Acc. Res.* **3:2** 6:1992 pp. 133 – 150

53 Multiple criteria decision making, multiattribute utility theory — the next ten years. James S. Dyer; Peter C. Fishburn; Ralph E. Steuer; Jyrki Wallenius; Stanley Zionts. *Manag. Sci.* **38:5** 5:1992 pp. 645 – 654

54 Optical disc technology for information management. Eugenia K. Brumm. *Ann. R. Info. Sci. Tech.* **26** 1991 pp. 197 – 240

55 Organisational capability and competitive advantage. Charles Harvey *[Ed.]*; Geoffrey Jones *[Ed.]*; Alfred D. Chandler *[Contrib.]*; Gordon Boyce *[Contrib.]*; Mira Wilkins *[Contrib.]*; Geoffrey Tweedale *[Contrib.]*; Patricia A. O'Brien *[Contrib.]*; Susan Ariel Aaronson *[Contrib.]*; Richard Roberts *[Contrib.]*. Collection of 8 articles. *Bus. Hist.* , *34:1*, 1:1992 pp. 1 – 200

56 Organizing and leading "heavyweight" development teams. Kim B. Clark; Steven C. Wheelwright. *Calif. Manag. R.* **34:3** Spring:1992 pp. 9 – 28

57 Organizzazione a rete e funzioni di organizzazione *[In Italian]*; [Network organization and organizational functioning]. Luca Solari. *Econ. Ban.* **XIV:1** 1992 pp. 9 – 32

58 An overview of methods for applied decision analysis. Craig W. Kirkwood. *Interfaces* **22:6** 11-12:1992 pp. 28 – 39

59 A partial solution to the financial risk and perverse response problems of labour-managed firms — industry-average performence bonds. Robert J. Waldmann; Stephen C. Smith. Badia Fiesolana: European University Institute, 1992: 26 p. *Bibliography — p.24-25.* [EUI working paper.]

60 Perestroika at the plant level. Daniel J. McCarthy; Sheila M. Puffer. *Columb. J. W. Bus.* **27:1** Spring:1992 p. 86

61 Performance effects of three foci in service firms. Praveen R. Nayyar. *Acad. Manag. J.* **35:5** 12:1992 pp. 985 – 1009

62 A property rights analysis of the inefficiency of investment decisions by labor-managed firms. Svetozar Pejovich; Holger Bonus *[Comments by]*; Douglas H. Ginsburg *[Comments by]*. *J. Inst. Theo. Ec.* **148:1** 3:1992 pp. 30 – 45

63 The rate of surplus value, the organic composition of capital and the rate of profit in Greek manufacturing. Theodore P. Lianos. *Rev. Rad. Pol. Ec.* **24:1** Spring:1992 pp. 136 – 145

64 The relationship between strategy, structure fit and financial performance in New Zealand — evidence of generality and validity with enhanced controls. R.T. Hamilton; G.S. Shergill. *J. Manag. Stu.* **29:1** 1:1992 p. 95

65 Research note — extending technology — the estimation and control of costs. Willis R. Greer; O. Douglas Moses. *J. Acc. Pub. Pol.* **11:1** Spring:1992 pp. 43 – 66

66 Ruolo e dimensioni del settore nonprofit in Italia — un primo tentativo di analisi *[In Italian]*; Role and dimensions of the nonprofit sector in Italy — an initial attempt at analysis *[Summary]*. Carlo Borzaga. *Ec. Lav.* **XXVI:2** 4-6:1992 pp. 47 – 61

67 Science parks as economic development policy — a case study approach. Bradley M. Braun; W. Warren McHone. *Econ. Devel. Q.* **6:2** 5:1992 pp. 135 – 147

68 Some international properties of Japanese firms. K.C. Fung. *J. Jap. Int. Ec.* **6:2** 6:1992 pp. 163 – 175

69 Takeover defences and shareholder voting. David Austen-Smith; Patricia C. O'Brien. *Economica* **59:234** 5:1992 pp. 199 – 219

70 Team concept and "Kaizen" — Japanese production management in a unionized Canadian auto plant. D. Robertson; J. Rinehart; C. Huxley. *Stud. Pol. Ec.* **:39** Autumn:1992 pp. 77 – 107

71 A theoretical relationship between equity financing and the growth rate of the firm — the case of developing countries. John Kaminarides; Andreas G. Merikas; Manolis D. Tsiritakis. *Cyprus Rev.* **4:1** Spring:1992 pp. 54 – 64

72 Transforming buyer-supplier relations — Japanese-style industrial practices in a Western context. Jonathan Morris; Rob Imrie. London: Macmillan Academic and Professional, 1992: 180 p. *ISBN: 0333512472.*

73 Two-part marginal cost pricing equilibria — existence and efficiency. Donald J. Brown; Walter P. Heller; Ross M. Starr. *J. Econ. Theo.* **57:1** 6:1992 pp. 52 – 72

74 The unifying vision process — value beyond traditional decision analysis in multiple-decision-maker environments. Michael W. Kusnic; Daniel Owen. *Interfaces* **22:6** 11-12:1992 pp. 150 – 166

G.3.3.5: Technical management *[Organisation technique]*

75 The use of operant theory in the design of performance reporting systems. L.M. Lovata. *Manag. Acc. Res.* **3:4** 12:1992 pp. 273 – 289

76 Using decision analysis and risk analysis to manage utility environmental risk. William E. Balson; Justin L. Welsh; Donald S. Wilson. *Interfaces* **22:6** 11-12:1992 pp. 126 – 139

77 The viability of employee-owned firms — evidence from France. Saul Estrin; Derek C. Jones. *Ind. Lab. Rel.* **45:2** 1:1992 pp. 323 – 338

78 The voluntary restructuring of large firms in response to performance decline. Kose John; Larry H.P. Lang; Jeffry Netter. *J. Finance* **47:3** 7:1992 pp. 891 – 917

Business strategies *[Strategies d'enterprises]*

79 CFOs and strategists — forging a common framework. Alfred Rappaport. *Harv. Bus. Re.* **70:3** 5-6:1992 pp. 84 – 91

80 Competitive intelligence and strategic group decisions — a new diagnostic tool. Benjamin Gilad; George Gordon; Ephraim Sudit. *Group Decis. Negot.* **1:1** 4:1992 pp. 5 – 26

81 Credible spatial preemption through franchising. G.K. Hadfield. *Rand J. Eco.* **22:4** Winter:1991 pp. 531 – 543

82 Development of strategic management in the Asia/Pacific Region. G.-I. Nakamura. *Inter. R. Strat. Manag.* **3** 1992 pp. 3 – 18

83 Economic globalization — labour options and business strategies in high labour cost countries. Gijsbert van Liemt. *Int. Lab. Rev.* **131:4-5** 4-5:1992 pp. 453 – 470

84 European corporate strategy — heading for 2000. Oliver L. Landreth. New York: St. Martin's Press, 1992: 183 p. *ISBN: 0312079168; LofC: 91042563. Includes index.*

85 Expert systems to support strategic management decision-making. R.J. Mockler; D.G. Dologite. *Inter. R. Strat. Manag.* **3** 1992 pp. 133 – 148

86 Game-playing agents — unobservable contracts as precommitments. M.L. Katz. *Rand J. Eco.* **22:3** Autumn:1991 pp. 307 – 328

87 Global strategy, competence-building and strategic alliances. David Lei; John W. Slocum. *Calif. Manag. R.* **35:1** Fall:1992 pp. 81 – 97

88 Growth through competition, competition through growth — strategic management and the economy in Japan. Hiroyuki Odagiri. New York, NY.: Clarendon Press, 1992: 364 p. *ISBN: 0198286554; LofC: 91020437. Includes bibliographical references and index.*

89 Information acquisition as business strategy. Chun-Hao Chang; Chi-Wen Jevons Lee. *S. Econ. J.* **58:3** 1:1992 pp. 750 – 761

90 Information systems planning and emergent strategies; *[French summary].* Robert M. Mason. *Gestion* **8:2** 1992 pp. 125 – 138

91 The knowhow company — strategy formulation in knowledge-intensive industries. K.E. Sveiby. *Inter. R. Strat. Manag.* **3** 1992 pp. 167 – 186

92 The need for strategic information systems in a world of time-based competition; *[French summary].* Reinhard Frommann. *Gestion* **8:2** 1992 pp. 109 – 124

93 Noise trading and takeovers. A.S. Kyle; J.-L. Vila. *Rand J. Eco.* **22:1** Spring:1991 pp. 54 – 71

94 Share repurchase and takeover deterrence. L.S. Bagwell. *Rand J. Eco.* **22:1** Spring:1991 pp. 72 – 88

95 Stakeholder-agency theory. Charles W.L. Hill; Thomas M. Jones. *J. Manag. Stu.* **29:2** 3:1992 pp. 131 – 154

96 Strategies of growth — maturity, recovery, and internationalization. Peter McKiernan. London: Routledge, 1992: 174 p. *ISBN: 0415073839; LofC: 91028665. Includes bibliographical references and index.* [The Routledge series in analytical management.]

97 Strategy. Arnoldo Hax *[Contrib.];* Richard Klavans *[Contrib.];* Edward B. Roberts *[Contrib.];* William F. Hamilton *[Contrib.];* Harbir Singh *[Contrib.];* James Utterback *[Contrib.];* Marc Meyer *[Contrib.];* Timothy Tuff *[Contrib.];* Lisa Richardson *[Contrib.];* William W. Cooper *[Contrib.] and others. Collection of 6 articles.* **Interfaces** , *22:4,* 7-8:1992 pp. 1 – 69

98 Gli strumenti della pianificazione aziendale per la gestione del cambiamento discontinuo *[In Italian];* Business planning tools to manage erratic changes *[Summary].* Maria Ferrara. *Ras. Econ.* **LVI:1** 1-3:1992 pp. 79 – 104

99 Top management, strategy and organizational knowledge structures. Marjorie A. Lyles; Charles R. Schwenk. *J. Manag. Stu.* **29:2** 3:1992 pp. 155 – 174

100 The UK small appliance industry — changing corporate practices and their spatial implications. Simon Milne. *J. Econ. Soc. Geogr.* **83:1** 1992 pp. 50 – 62

101 Value-focused thinking about strategic decisions at BC Hydro. Ralph L. Keeney; Timothy L. McDaniels. *Interfaces* **22:6** 11-12:1992 pp. 94 – 109

G.3.3.5: Technical management *[Organisation technique]* — **Business strategies** *[Strategies d'enterprises]*

102 Voluntary financial disclosure in an entry game with continua of types; *[French summary]*. G.A. Feltham; J.Z. Xie; E. Nosal *[Discussant]*. *Cont. Account. Res.* **9:1** Fall:1992 pp. 46 – 85

103 Writers on strategy and strategic management — the theory of strategy and the practice of strategic management at enterprise, corporate, business and functional levels. J. I. Moore. London: Penguin, 1992: 311 p. *ISBN: 0140139850.*

Financial management *[Gestion financière]*

104 Adjustment costs in production frontier analysis. J.K. Sengupta. *Eco. Notes* **21:2** 1992 pp. 316 – 329

105 Analysis and forecasting of income statement account balances. The dynamic interdependency and ARIMA approaches. W.T. Lin. *J. Forecast.* **11:4** 6:1992 pp. 283 – 307

106 An analysis of production cost inefficiency. Janet M. Thomas; Scott J. Callan. *R. Indust. Organ.* **7:2** 1992 pp. 203 – 226

107 An analysis of the profitability of business diversified companies. Thomas A. Wilson. *R. Indust. Organ.* **7:2** 1992 pp. 151 – 185

108 A case study in corporate financial reporting — Massey-Ferguson's visible accounting decisions 1970-1987. J. Amernic. *Crit. Persp. Acc.* **3:1** 3:1992 pp. 1 – 44

109 Communication of nonearnings information at the financial statements release date. Bong H. Han; Ross Jennings; James Noel. *J. Account. E.* **15:1** 3:1992 pp. 63 – 86

110 Company sector liquid asset holdings. David G. Barr; Keith Cuthbertson. *J. Money C. B.* **24:1** 2:1992 pp. 83 – 97

111 The decline of operational expertise in the knowledge-base of management accounting — an examination of some post-war trends in the qualifying requirements of the Chartered Institute of Management Accountants. P. Armstrong; C. Jones. *Manag. Acc. Res.* **3:1** 3:1992 pp. 53 – 76

112 Does debt management matter? Jonas Agell; Mats Persson; Benjamin M. Friedman. Oxford: Clarendon Press, 1992: 155 p. *ISBN: 019828361x; LofC: 91032815. Includes bibliographical references and index.* [FIEF studies in labour markets and economic policy.]

113 Economic determinants of accounting policy choice — the case of current cost accounting in the U.K. Kenneth W. Lemke; Michael J. Page. *J. Account. E.* **15:1** 3:1992 pp. 87 – 114

114 Efficiency analysis of Norwegian district courts. Sverre A.C. Kittelsen; Finn R. Førsund. *J. Prod. Anal.* **3:3** 1992 pp. 277 – 306

115 Evaluation et management dans les organisations du secteur non-marchand *[In French]*; Evaluation and management in non-profit organisations *[Summary]*. Michel Bonami. *Gestion* **8:1** 1992 pp. 57 – 72

116 Financial analysis for microenterprises. Michael Yaffey. *Small Enter. Devel.* **3:3** 9:1992 pp. 28 – 36

117 Financial reporting in Japan — regulation, practice and enviroment. M. Kikuya; T.E. Cooke. Oxford: Basil Blackwell, 1992: 356 p. *ISBN: 0631182993; LofC: 91029561. Includes index.*

118 Financial reporting, information and capital markets. Michael Bromwich. London: Pitman, 1992: 376 p. *ISBN: 0273034642.*

119 Financial statements — closing the expectation gap. Paul O'Connor. *Irish Bank. Rev. Spring:1992* pp. 27 – 35

120 Foundations as investment managers part 1 — the process. Lester M. Salamon. *Non. Manag. Leader.* **3:2** Winter:1992 pp. 117 – 137

121 Funds-flow statements and cash-flow accounting in France — evolution and significance. Daniel Boussard; Bernard Colasse. *Eur. Account. Rev.* **1:2** 12:1992 pp. 229 – 254

122 German cost accounting education and the changing manufacturing environment. N.I. Bursal. *Manag. Acc. Res.* **3:1** 3:1992 pp. 39 – 52

123 An incomplete contracts approach to financial contracting. Philippe Aghion; Patrick Bolton. *R. Econ. S.* **59:3(200)** 7:1992 pp. 473 – 494

124 Informatie-economie — ook belangrijk voor management accounting *[In Dutch]*; [Information economy — also important for management accounting]. F. Roodhooft. *Tijds. Econ. Manag.* **XXXVII:1** 4:1992 pp. 17 – 34

125 Management accounting systems in Spanish firms. Joan M. Amat Salas. *Eur. Account. Rev.* **1:1** 5:1992 pp. 1 – 26

G.3.3.5: Technical management *[Organisation technique]* — **Financial management** *[Gestion financière]*

126 The new institutional economics of the firm and lessons from Japan. F.R. FitzRoy; Z.J. Acs. *Jpn. Wor. Econ.* **4:2** 9:1992 pp. 129 – 143

127 The resurgence of cost and management accounting — a review of some recent developments in practice, theories and case research methods. B.H. Spicer. *Manag. Acc. Res.* **3:1** 3:1992 pp. 1 – 38

128 A theory of responsibility centers. Nahum Melumad; Dilip Mookherjee; Stefan Reichelstein. *J. Account. E.* **15:4** 12:1992 pp. 445 – 484

129 Why firms franchise — a search cost theory. Alanson P. Minkler. *J. Inst. Theo. Ec.* **148:2** 6:1992 pp. 240 – 259

G.4: Occupational structure. Occupations — *Structure professionnelle. Professions*

1 Atrophy rates for intermittent employment for married and never-married women — a test of the human capital theory of occupational sex segregation. Kevin C. Duncan; Mark J. Prus. *Q Rev. Econ. Finan.* **32:1** Spring:1992 pp. 27 – 37

2 Career development and specific human capital collection. Canice Prendergast. *J. Jap. Int. Ec.* **6:3** 9:1992 pp. 207 – 227

3 The effects of regulatory reform on the architectural profession in the United Kingdom. Kenneth Button; Michael Fleming. *Int. R. Law Econ.* **12:1** 3:1992 pp. 95 – 116

4 The endogenous economist — unique-model and multiple-model representation of reality. B. Gauci; T. Baumgartner. *Am. J. Econ. S.* **51:1** 1:1992 pp. 71 – 86

5 Growing pains of an indigenous accountancy profession — the Nigerian experience. R.S. Olusegun Wallace. *Acc. Bus. Finan. Hist.* **2:1** 3:1992 pp. 25 – 54

6 How do taxes affect occupational choice? Pierre Pestieau; Uri Possen. *Publ. Finan.* **47:1** 1992 pp. 108 – 119

7 The market for lawyers. Sherwin Rosen. *J. Law Econ.* **XXXV:2** 10:1992 pp. 215 – 246

8 Skill shortages — causes and consequences. Derek L. Bosworth *[Ed.]*; Patricia A. Dutton *[Ed.]*; Jackie Lewis *[Ed.]*. Aldershot: Avebury, 1992: 206 p. *ISBN: 1856283208*.

9 Three kinds of economists — memberships and characteristics. C. Copp. *Am. J. Econ. S.* **51:1** 1:1992 pp. 43 – 56

H: Production (goods and services) — *Production (biens et services)*

H.0: Production and conservation — *Production et conservation*

Sub-divisions: Ecology *[Ecologie]*; Environmental protection *[Protection de l'environnement]*; Resource management *[Gestion des ressources]*; Sustainable development *[Développement soutenable]*; Waste management *[Gestion des déchets]*; Water resources *[Ressources en eau]*

1 Accounting for Australian carbon dioxide emissions. M.S. Common; U. Salma. *Econ. Rec.* **68:200** 3:1992 pp. 31 – 42

2 Back-of-the-envelope estimates of environmental damage costs in Mexico. Sergio Margulis. Washington, D.C.: Country Department II, Latin America and the Caribbean Regional Office, The World Bank, 1992: 27 p. *Bibliography — p25-27.* [Policy research working papers.]

3 Calha Norte — military development in Brazilian Amazônia. Elizabeth Allen. *Develop. Cha.* **23:1** 1:1992 pp. 71 – 100

4 Carbon accumulations and technical progress. Dennis Anderson; Catharine D. Bird. *Ox. B. Econ. S.* **54:1** 2:1992 pp. 1 – 29

H.0: Production and conservation *[Production et conservation]*

5 Carbon taxation and global warming — domestic policy aspects. Diego Piacentino. *Riv. Dir. Finan. Sci. Fin.* **LI:4** 12:1992 pp. 636 – 654

6 Climate change and the planetary trust. Peter G. Brown. *Energy Pol.* **20:3** 3:1992 pp. 208 – 222

7 Comparison of alternative nonmarket valuation methods for an economic assessment of a public program. K.H. John; R.G. Walsh; C.G. Moore. *Ecol. Eco.* **5:2** 5:1992 pp. 179 – 196

8 The Earthscan reader in environmental economics. Anil Markandya *[Ed.]*; Julie Richardson *[Ed.]*. London: Earthscan, 1991: 469 p. *ISBN: 1853831069.*

9 Effet de serre et relations Nord-Sud *[In French]*; The greenhouse effect and North-South relations — opportunities for and threats to a global agreement *[Summary]*. Jean-Marc Burniaux; Joaquim Oliveira-Martins. *E & S* **:258-259** 10-11:1992 pp. 55 – 68

10 Electricity planning and environmental issues in selected Asian countries. Ram M. Shrestha; Mahesh P. Acharya. *Nat. Res. For.* **16:3** 8:1992 pp. 192 – 201

11 Energy and environmental challenges for developed and developing countries. Richard L. Ottinger. *Nat. Res. For.* **16:1** 2:1992 pp. 11 – 18

12 Energy efficiency and human activity — past trends, future prospects. John Holdren *[Foreword]*; Lee Schipper; Stephen Meyers. Cambridge: Cambridge University Press, 1992: xiii, 385 p. *ISBN: 0521432979; LofC: 92014112. "Sponsored by the Stockholm Environment Institute, Stockholm, Sweden."; Includes bibliographical references and index.* [Cambridge studies in energy and the environment.]

13 Energy markets and environmental issues — a European perspective. Einar Hope *[Ed.]*; Steinar Strøm *[Ed.]*. Oslo: Scandanavian University Press, 1992: 255 p.

14 Environmental concerns regarding electric power transmission in North America. Stephen S. Bernow; Jan Beyea. *Energy Pol.* **20:1** 1:1992 pp. 30 – 39

15 Environmental impact assessment in Poland — an emergent process. Ursula Rzeszot; Christopher Wood. *Proj. App.* **7:2** 6:1992 pp. 83 – 92

16 Environmental policy design and dynamic nonpoint-source pollution. A.P. Xepapadeas. *J. Envir. Ec. Manag.* **23:1** 7:1992 pp. 22 – 39

17 Environmental policy in OECD countries — lessons for ASEAN. Peter Michaelis. *ASEAN Ec. B.* **9:2** 11:1992 pp. 169 – 186

18 Environmental policy in the European Community. W. Meissner. *Metroeconomica* **XLIII:1-2** 2-6:1992 pp. 157 – 172

19 Environmental regulation — the Environment Agency proposal. Dieter Helm. *Fis. Stud.* **13:2** 5:1992 pp. 66 – 83

20 Externe Kosten durch Verkehrslärm in Stadt und Agglomeration Zürich *[In German]*; [External costs caused by traffic noise in Zurich's urban agglomeration] *[Summary]*; *[French summary]*. Rolf Iten; Markus Maibach. *Schw. Z. Volk. Stat.* **128:1** 3:1992 pp. 51 – 68

21 Giving respondents time to think in contingent valuation studies — a developing country application. Dale Whittington; V. Kerry Smith; Apai Okorafor; Augustine Okore; Jin Long Liu; Alexander McPhail. *J. Envir. Ec. Manag.* **22:3** 5:1992 pp. 205 – 225

22 Incorporating interfactor and interfuel substitutions in general equilibrium energy models. Mohammad Jaforullah. *Aust. Econ. P.* **31:58** 6:1992 pp. 177 – 202

23 Indian lands, environmental policy and military geopolitics in the development of the Brazilian Amazon — the case of the Yanomami. Bruce Albert. *Develop. Cha.* **23:1** 1:1992 pp. 35 – 70

24 Land use regulation in the Lake George basin — an ecological economic perspective. P.R. Olsen; J.M. Gowdy. *Ecol. Eco.* **6:3** 12:1992 pp. 235 – 252

25 Land-based sources of marine pollution. Douglas Cormack *[Contrib.]*; Alan E. Boyle *[Contrib.]*; Adrian Hughes *[Contrib.]*; UNEP *[Contrib.]*. Collection of 4 articles. **Mar. Pol.** , *16:1*, 1:1992 pp. 5 – 49

26 Market versus command and control environmental policies. James A. Swaney. *J. Econ. Iss.* **XXVI:2** 6:1992 pp. 623 – 634

27 Mini symposium — trade and the environment. Patrick Low *[Contrib.]*; Peter Bohm *[Contrib.]*; Piritta Sorsa *[Contrib.]*; Arvind Subramanian *[Contrib.]*; Kym Anderson *[Contrib.]*. Collection of 5 articles. **World. Econ.** , *15:1*, 1:1992 pp. 101 – 172

28 National factor markets and the macroeconomic context for environmental destruction in the Brazilian Amazon. Steven C. Kyle; Aercio S. Cunha. *Develop. Cha.* **23:1** 1:1992 pp. 7 – 34

29 National income and nature — externalities, growth and steady state. J.J. Krabbe *[Ed.]*;

H.0: Production and conservation *[Production et conservation]*
Willem Heijman *[Ed.].* Dordrecht: Kluwer Academic Publishers, 1992: viii, 232 p. (ill) *ISBN: 0792315294; LofC: 91038236. Includes bibliographical references and index.* [Economy and environment. : Vol. 5]

30 Natural resources, "vent for surplus" and the staple theory — trade and growth with an endogenous land frontier. Ronald Findlay; Mats Lundahl. New York: Columbia University, Department of Economics, 1992: 41 p. [Discussion paper series.]

31 Neoclassical and institutional approaches to development and the environment. P. Söderbaum. *Ecol. Eco.* **5:2** 5:1992 pp. 127 – 144

32 North Sea oil and the environment — developing oil and gas resources, environmental impacts, and responses. William J. Cairns *[Ed.].* London: Elsevier Applied Science, 1992: 722 p. *ISBN: 1851667040; LofC: 91025706. Includes bibliographical references and index.*

33 Nuclear power plant performance — the post Three Mile Island era. Anthony C. Krautmann; John L. Solow. *Ener. Econ.* **14:3** 7:1992 pp. 209 – 216

34 Perspectives on environmental conflict and international politics. Jyrki Käkönen *[Ed.].* London: Pinter Publishers, 1992: 162 p. *ISBN: 1855670194; LofC: 91030841. Includes bibliographical references and index.* [TAPRI studies in international relations.]

35 Political economy of the environment in Vietnam. Melanie Beresford; Lyn Fraser. *J. Cont. Asia* **22:1** 1992 pp. 3 – 19

36 Population growth and global warming; *[French summary]; [Spanish summary].* John Bongaarts. *Pop. Dev. Rev.* **18:2** 6:1992 pp. 299 – 319

37 Procédures de décision et droit international *[In French];* [Decision procedures and international law]. Ahmed Mahiou. *R. T-Monde* **XXXIII:130** 4-6:1992 pp. 429 – 454

38 Proceedings of the first international conference on "Geography in the ASEAN region", Part II. Ooi Jin Bee *[Contrib.];* Goh Ban Lee *[Contrib.];* Goh Kim Chuan *[Contrib.];* G.S. Maxwell *[Contrib.];* M.C. Cleary *[Contrib.];* Kam Ting Seong *[Contrib.];* Michael J.G. Parnwell *[Contrib.];* Jonathan Rigg *[Contrib.];* Katiman Rostam *[Contrib.];* B.J. Shaw *[Contrib.] and others. Collection of 9 articles.* **Malay. J. Trop. Geogr.** , *22:1,* 6:1991 pp. 1 – 102

39 Reconciling economics and the environment. Jeff Bennett *[Ed.];* Walter Block *[Ed.].* West Perth: Australian Institute for Public Policy, 1991: 322 p. (ill) *ISBN: 0949186457. Includes bibliographical references (p. 289-306) and index.*

40 Théorie économique et environnement *[In French];* [Economic theory and environment]. Fayçal Yachir. *R. T-Monde* **XXXIII:130** 4-6:1992 pp. 417 – 428

41 The threat at home — confronting the toxic legacy of the U.S. military. Seth Shulman. Boston: Beacon Press, 1992: xv, 254 p. *ISBN: 0807004162; LofC: 91041373. Includes bibliographical references and index.*

42 Uneven development and the tragedy of the commons — competing images for nature-society analysis. Rebecca S. Roberts; Jacque Emel. *Econ. Geogr.* **68:3** 7:1992 pp. 249 – 271

43 La ville, l'informel et l'environnement *[In French];* [The town, the informal and the environment]. Guy Pourcet. *Afr. Cont.* **:161** 1er trimestre:1992 pp. 178 – 187

44 World economy, world environment. David Pearce; Samuel Fankhauser; Neil Adger; Timothy Swanson. *World. Econ.* **15:3** 5:1992 pp. 295 – 313

45 World energy development and CO_2 emission. Igor Bashmakov. *Perspect. Ener.* **2:1** 1:1992 pp. 1 – 12

Ecology *[Ecologie]*

46 Active participants or passive observers? Mpanjilwa Pius Mulwanda. *Urban Stud.* **29:1** 2:1992 pp. 89 – 97

47 Biomass energy, forests and global warming. Frank Rosillo-Calle; David O. Hall. *Energy Pol.* **20:2** 2:1992 pp. 124 – 136

48 Deforestazione in Amazzonia e sue implicazioni globali *[In Italian];* [Deforestation in the Amazon and global implications]. Luiz Carlos Baldicero Molion. *Civitas* **XLIII** 9-10:1992 pp. 37 – 54

49 Ecologia e aspetto del sottosviluppo amazzonica *[In Italian];* [Ecology and underdevelopment in the Amazon]. Argemiro Procopio. *Civitas* **XLIII** 9-10:1992 pp. 9 – 35

50 Ecologically conscious management. Fritjof Capra. *Environ. Law* **22:2** 1992 pp. 529 – 538

51 Economics and ecology — a comparison of experimental methodologies and philosophies. J.F. Shogren; C. Nowell. *Ecol. Eco.* **5:2** 5:1992 pp. 101 – 126

H.0: Production and conservation *[Production et conservation]* — **Ecology** *[Ecologie]*

52 Fabric of the world — towards a philosophy of environment. Maurice Ash. Bideford: Green Books, 1992: 109 p. *ISBN: 1870098420.*

53 Global ecology. Colin Tudge. London: Natural History Museum Publications in association with British Petroleum, 1991: 173 p. *ISBN: 0565011731.*

54 Issues of environmental economic policy. Willem Heijman *[Ed.]*; J.J. Krabbe *[Ed.]*. Wageningen: Agricultural University, 1992: 236 p. (ill) *ISBN: 9067542059. Includes bibliographical references.* [Wageningse economische studies. : No. 24]

55 Mangroves in Taiwan — distribution management and values. L. Wester; C.T. Lee. *Geoforum* **23:4** 1992 pp. 507 – 519

56 Ökologische Dimensionen wirtschaftlicher Entwicklung *[In German]*; [Ecological dimensions of economic development]. Harald Payer. *Wirt. Blät.* **5/6:39** 1992 pp. 557 – 567

57 Ökologisch-ökonomische Verteilungskonflikte. Explorative Überlegungen zu einem vernachlässigten Forschungsgebiet *[In German]*; Eco-economic conflicts of allocation. Explorative reflections on a neglected field of research *[Summary]*. Frank Beckenbach. *Prokla* **22:1(86)** 3:1992 pp. 61 – 88

58 Ökonómia és ökológia. Környezetbarát gazdaság — tőkekorlát mellett *[In Hungarian]*; Economics and ecology — the Scylla and Charybdis of economic policy *[Summary]*. Ferenc Kozma. *Közg. Sz.* **XXXIX** 4:1992 pp. 322 – 336

59 The rainforest supply price — a tool for evaluating rainforest conservation expenditures. H.J. Ruitenbeek. *Ecol. Eco.* **6:1** 7:1992 pp. 57 – 78

60 Tropical deforestation, land degradation, and society — lessons from Rondônia, Brazil. Brent H. Millikan. *Lat. Am. Pers.* **19:1(72)** Winter:1992 pp. 45 – 72

61 Tropical forests. Exploitation, conservation and management. P.S. Ramakrishnan. *Impact Sci.* **42:2** 1992 pp. 149 – 162

62 The value of a watershed as a series of linked multiproduct assets. R.R. Gottfried. *Ecol. Eco.* **5:2** 5:1992 pp. 145 – 162

63 Zur ökologischen Wirksamkeit von CO_2-Abgaben in der Elektrizitätsversorgung *[In German]*; [On the ecological benefits from CO_2 levies in the electricity industry] *[Summary]*; *[French summary]*. Bernhard Hillebrand. *RWI-Mitt.* **43:1** 1992 pp. 1 – 18

Environmental protection *[Protection de l'environnement]*

64 Achieving environmental goals — the concept and practice of environmental performance review. Erik Lykke *[Ed.]*. London: Belhaven Press, 1992: 259 p. *ISBN: 1852932635; LofC: 92024768. Includes bibliographical references and index.*

65 Beyond compliance — a new industry view of the environment. Bruce Smart *[Ed.]*. Washington, D.C.: World Resources Institute, 1992: xiv, 285 p. *ISBN: 0915825732; LofC: 92081694.*

66 Beyond Rio — "insuring" against global warming. Christopher D. Stone. *Am. J. Int. Law* **86:3** 7:1992 pp. 445 – 488

67 Buying greenhouse insurance — the economic costs of carbon dioxide emission limits. A. S. Manne; Richard G. Richels. Cambridge, MA.: MIT Press, 1992: xii, 182 p. *ISBN: 026213280x; LofC: 91030865. Includes bibliographical references and index.*

68 Carbon emissions taxes — their comparative advantage under uncertainty. Gary W. Yohe. *Ann. R. Energy Environ.* **17** 1992 pp. 301 – 326

69 Choosing our future — a practical politics of the environment. Ann Taylor. London: Routledge, 1992: 235 p. *ISBN: 0415079454; LofC: 91042951. Includes bibliographical references and index.*

70 Climate and ecosystem protection requires burden sharing — the specific tasks after Rio (I). Wilfrid Bach; Atul K. Jain. *Perspect. Ener.* **2:1** 1:1992 pp. 67 – 93

71 Climate change — the IPCC scientific assessment. G.J. Jenkins *[Ed.]*; J.J. Ephraums *[Ed.]*; J.T. Houghton *[Ed.]*. Cambridge: Cambridge University Press, 1990: xxxix, 365 p. (ill) *ISBN: 0521407206.*

72 Competition, efficiency and emission reduction — a regulator's view. Stephen Littlechild. *Util. Policy* **2:3** 7:1992 pp. 188 – 195

73 Constitutional choice for the control of water pollution. Roger E. Meiners; Bruce Yandle. *Constit. Pol. Econ.* **3:3** Fall:1992 pp. 359 – 380

74 Controlling acid deposition — a general equilibrium assessment. Roy Boyd; Kerry Krutilla. *Environ. Resour. Econ.* **2:3** 1992 pp. 307 – 322

75 Corporate environmentalism. Frances Cairncross *[Contrib.]*; Stephan Schmidheiny *[Contrib.]*; John A. Baden *[Contrib.]*; Graciela Chichilnisky; Juan Rada *[Contrib.]*; Alex Trisoglio

H.0: Production and conservation *[Production et conservation]* — **Environmental protection** *[Protection de l'environnement]*

[Contrib.]; Richard E. Benedick *[Contrib.]*; Lawrence E. Susskind *[Contrib.]*; Joseph G. Gavin *[Contrib.]*; Charles F. Sills *[Contrib.] and others. Collection of 30 articles.* **Columb. J. W. Bus.** , *XXVII:3-4,* Fall/Winter:1992 pp. 12 – 291

76 The costs of reducing CO_2 emissions — a comparison of carbon tax curves with green. Joaquim Oliveira-Martins; et al. Paris, [France]: OECD, Economics Dept, 1992: 54 p. *ISBN: oc26562922. eng, fre; "General distribution, OCDE/GD(92)136."--Cover; Summary in English and French; Includes bibliographical references (p. 27-28).* [Working papers. : No. OECD, Economics Department]

77 The costs of reducing CO_2 emissions — evidence from green. Jean-Marc Burniaux; John P. Martin; Giuseppe Nicoletti; Joaquim Oliveira-Martins. [Paris, France]: OECD, Economics Dept, 1992: 73 p. *ISBN: oc26282515. eng, fre; "General distribution, OCDE/GD(92)117."--Cover; Summary in English and French; Includes bibliographical references.* [Working papers — OECD, Economics Department.]

78 Counting the cost of global warming. John Broome. Cambridge: White Horse Press, 1992: 147 p. *ISBN: 1874267014.*

79 Des marchés internationaux de droits à polluer pour le problème de l'effet de serre — de la recherche de l'efficacité aux enjeux de légitimité *[In French]*; [International markets of pollution rights and the greenhouse effect — from research into efficiency to the stakes of legitimacy]. Olivier Godard. *Pol. Manag. Publ.* **10:2** 6:1992 pp. 101 – 131

80 Dynamic energy-conversion and "clean" energetics. Anatoly Koroteev; Vitaly Semyonov. *Perspect. Ener.* **2:1** 1:1992 pp. 51 – 60

81 Ecologically conscious management. Fritjof Capra. *Environ. Law* **22:2** 1992 pp. 529 – 538

82 The economic costs of reducing CO_2 emissions. Andrew Dean *[Contrib.]*; Peter Hoeller *[Contrib.]*; Jean-Marc Burniaux *[Contrib.]*; Giuseppe Nicoletti *[Contrib.]*; Joaquim Oliveira-Martins *[Contrib.]*; John P. Martin *[Contrib.]*; Jonathan Coppel *[Contrib.]*. *Collection of 6 articles.* **OECD Ec. Stud.** , *:19,* Winter:1992 pp. 15 – 193

83 Economic growth and environmental preservation. Scott Barrett. *J. Envir. Ec. Manag.* **23:3** 11:1992 pp. 289 – 300

84 The economics of global warming. William R. Cline. Washington: Institute for International Economics, 1992: 399 p. *ISBN: 0881321508; LofC: 92016111. Includes bibliographical references and index.*

85 Environmental business management — an introduction. Klaus North. Geneva: International Labour Office, 1992: vii, 194 p. *ISBN: 9221072894. Includes bibliographical references (p. 157-161) and index.* [Management development series. : No. 30]

86 The environmental consequences of urban growth — cross-national perspectives on economic development, air pollution, and city size. Vibhooti Shukla; Kirit Parikh. *Urban Geogr.* **13:5** 9-10:1992 pp. 422 – 449

87 Environmental protection and free trade — are they mutually exclusive? A. Butler. *R. Fed. Resv. Bank St.Louis* **74:3** 5-6:1992 pp. 3 – 16

88 Estimating the economic and demographic effects of an air quality management plan — the case of Southern California. S. Lieu; G.I. Treyz. *Envir. Plan.A.* **24:12** 12:1992 pp. 1799 – 1811

89 La forêt en Languedoc-Roussillon — un patrimoine dévalorisé *[In French]*; [The Languedoc-Roussillon forests — a devalued inheritance]. M. Noel. *R.E.M.* **40:1** 1992 pp. 35 – 58

90 Global climate change. Richard A. Westin. *Columb. J. W. Bus.* **27:1** Spring:1992 pp. 76 – 85

91 The global environmental problems and their relationships with shipping and shipbuilding — changing industrial structures and their impacts on seaborne transport and ships. Seiji Nagatsuka. Tokyo: Japan Maritime Research Institute, 1991: 58 p. [JAMRI report. : No. 42]

92 Green globe yearbook 1992 — an independent publication on environmental and development from the Fridtjof Nansen Institute, Norway. Helge Ole Bergesen *[Ed.]*; Magnar Norderhaug *[Ed.]*; Georg Parmann *[Ed.]*. Oxford: Oxford University Press, 1992: 303 p. *ISBN: 0198233221.*

93 Green — a multi-sector, multi-region general equilibrium model for quantifying the costs of curbing CO_2 emissions — a technical manual. John P. Martin; Giuseppe Nicoletti; Jean-Marc Burniaux; Joaquim Oliveira-Martins. [Paris, France]: OECD, Dept. of Economics and Statistics, 1992: 113 p. *ISBN: oc26282726. eng, fre; "General distribution, OCDE/GD(92)118."--Cover; Summary in English and French; Includes bibliographical references.* [Working papers — OECD, Economics Departent.]

H.0: Production and conservation *[Production et conservation]* — **Environmental protection** *[Protection de l'environnement]*

94 Greenhouse earth. Annika Nilsson. Chichester: Published on behalf of the Scientific Committee on Problems of the Environment (SCOPE) of the International Council of Scientific Unions (ICSU) and the United Nations Environment Programme (UNEP) by Wiley, 1992: xvi, 219 p. *ISBN: 0471935476; LofC: 92008327.*

95 High does nothing and rising is worse — carbon taxes should keep declining to cut harmful emissions. Peter Sinclair. *Manch. Sch. E.* **LX:1** 3:1992 pp. 41 – 52

96 How much is enough? The consumer society and the future of the earth. Alan Thein Durning. London: Earthscan, 1992: 200 p. *ISBN: 1853831344.* [Worldwatch environmental alert series. : No. 2]

97 Inequality aspects of alternative CO_2 agreement designs. Heinz Welsch. *OPEC Rev.* **XVI:1** Spring:1992 pp. 23 – 36

98 Information problems in pollution control — comparing taxes and marketable permits. Ian Wills. *Ec. Pap. Aust.* **11:3** 9:1992 pp. 65 – 76

99 An investigation of the long-run relationship between pollution performance and economic performance — the case of pulp and paper firms. M. Freedman; B. Jaggi. *Crit. Persp. Acc.* **3:4** 12:1992 pp. 315 – 336

100 Land degradation impacts on tropical agricultural basins and their management — the Nigerian example. F.O. Odemerho. *Geoforum* **23:4** 1992 pp. 499 – 506

101 Market-based incentive instruments for pollution control. Glenn P. Jenkins; Ranjit Lamech. *B. Int. Fiscal Docu.* **46:11** 11:1992 pp. 523 – 538

102 Marktwirtschaftliche Instrumente der Umweltpolitik — ein Themal für die Raumordnung? *[In German]*; [Market controlling instruments for environmental policy — a subject for environmental planning?]. Dieter Ewringmann *[Contrib.]*; Karl-Heinrich Hansmeyer *[Contrib.]*; Klaus Töpfer *[Contrib.]*; Joachim Nick *[Contrib.]*; Eckhard Bergmann *[Contrib.]*; Dieter Kanzlerski *[Contrib.]*; Wolfgang Benkert *[Contrib.]*; Norbert Knauer *[Contrib.]*; Ulrich van Suntum *[Contrib.]*; Dietrich Fürst *[Contrib.] and others.* Collection of 9 articles. **Inf. Raum.** , :2-3, 1992 pp. 81 – 179

103 Marktwirtschaftliche Instrumente zur Reduktion von Luftschadstoffemissionen des Verkehrs *[In German]*; [Market economy measures to reduce air pollution from traffic] *[Summary]*. Wissenschaftlichen Beirat beim Bundesminister für Verkehr. *Z. Verkehr.* **63:2** 1992 pp. 115 – 133

104 Optimal acquisition of pollution control equipment under uncertainty. Richard F. Hartl. *Manag. Sci.* **38:5** 5:1992 pp. 609 – 622

105 Our country, the planet. Shridath S. Ramphal; Seymour Topping *[Foreword]*. Washington, D.C: Island Press, 1992: 291 p. *ISBN: 1559631651; LofC: 91043320.*

106 Point/nonpoint source pollution reduction trading — an interpretive survey. David Letson. *Natur. Res. J.* **32:2** Spring:1992 pp. 219 – 232

107 Political institutions and pollution control. Roger D. Congleton. *Rev. Econ. St.* **LXXIV:3** 8:1992 pp. 412 – 421

108 The polluter must pay. R. Valenzuela. *CEPAL R.* **:45** 12:1991 pp. 71 – 81

109 Pollution charges for environmental protection — a policy link between energy and the environment. Robert N. Stavins; Bradley W. Whitehead. *Ann. R. Energy Environ.* **17** 1992 pp. 187 – 210

110 Regulation of the environmental impacts of coal mining in the United States — market economics, cost-benefit analysis and mistakes of the past. Patrick C. McGinley. *Nat. Res. For.* **16:4** 11:1992 pp. 261 – 270

111 The right climate for carbon taxes — creating economic incentives to protect the atmosphere. Roger C. Dower; Mary Beth Zimmerman. Washington, D.C: World Resources Institute, 1992: viii, 38 p. *ISBN: 0915825783; LofC: 92085405. Includes bibliographical references.*

112 Scientific research and development facing environmental protection — needs and deontology. Gérard G. de Soete. *OPEC Rev.* **XVI:1** Spring:1992 pp. 95 – 118

113 Should environmental legislation set the rules constraining polluters? Defining the ends and assessing the means of environmental policy — an examination of the EC mercury directive. John Ashworth; Ivy Papps. *Int. R. Law Econ.* **12:1** 3:1992 pp. 79 – 94

114 Social cost of CO_2 abatement from energy efficiency and solar power in the United States. Darwin C. Hall. *Environ. Resour. Econ.* **2:5** 1992 pp. 491 – 512

115 Social project appraisal and environmental impact assessment — a necessary but complicated theoretical bridge. Diego Azqueta. *Dev. Pol. R.* **10:3** 9:1992 pp. 255 – 270

116 Stabilization of emissions of CO_2 — a computable general equilibrium assessment. Solveig Glomsrød; Haakon Vennemo; Torgeir Johnsen. *Sc. J. Econ.* **94:1** 1992 pp. 53 – 70

H.0: Production and conservation *[Production et conservation]* — **Environmental protection** *[Protection de l'environnement]*

117 Les stratégies économiques et financières de protection de l'environnement *[In French]*; Economic and financial strategies for environment protection and sustainable development — stakes and perspectives *[Summary]*. Roland Colin. *Obser. Diag. Econ.* **:40** 4:1992 pp. 101 – 140

118 Sustainable development — an imperative for environmental protection. Pauline K. Marstrand. London: Economic Affairs Division, Commonwealth Secretariat, 1991: 157 p.

119 The symmetry between controlling pollution by price and controlling it by quantity. John Pezzey. *Can. J. Econ.* **XXV:4** 11:1992 pp. 983 – 991

120 Toward a global excise on carbon. Sijbren Cnossen; Herman Vollebergh. *Natl. Tax. J.* **XLV:1** 3:1992 pp. 23 – 36

121 Tradeable emmision permits and the control of greenhouse gases. Geoffrey Bertram. *J. Dev. Stud.* **28:3** 4:1992 pp. 423 – 446

122 Umweltschutz mit Hilfe zivilrechtlicher und kollektiver Haftung *[In German]*; [Environmental protection with the help of collective liability and civil law liability]. Helmut Karl. *RWI-Mitt.* **43:3** 1992 pp. 183 – 199

123 Uneasy polygons — environment and security within the system of aims of an economy. W. Eichhorn. *Metroeconomica* **XLIII:1-2** 2-6:1992 pp. 289 – 305

124 Valuing the environment — economic approaches to environmental evaluation — proceedings of a workshop held at Ludgrove Hall, Middlesex Polytechnic, on 13 and 14 June 1990. Annabel Coker *[Ed.]*; Cathy Richards *[Ed.]*. London: Belhaven Press, 1992: 183 p. *ISBN: 1852932120; LofC: 91046605. Includes bibliographical references and index.*

125 Voluntary work and the environment — local environmental development initiatives in Europe. Nicholas Falk. Dublin, Ireland: European Foundation for the Improvement of Living and Working Conditions, 1992: 113 p. *ISBN: 928263650x. Includes bibliographical references (p. 113).*

126 When the grass is gone — development intervention in African arid lands. P.T.W. Baxter *[Ed.]*. Uppsala: Scandinavian Institute of African Studies, 1991: 214 p. (ill., maps) *ISBN: 9171063188; LofC: 91222668. Includes bibliographical references.* [Seminar proceedings from the Scandinavian Institute of African Studies. : No. 25]

Resource management *[Gestion des ressources]*

127 Accounts overdue — natural resource depreciation in Costa Rica. Raúl Solórzano; et al. San José: Tropical Science Center — Washington — World Resources Institute, 1991: 111p. *ISBN: 091582566x.*

128 Allocation, distribution, and scale — towards an economics that is efficient, just, and sustainable. H.E. Daly. *Ecol. Eco.* **6:3** 12:1992 pp. 185 – 193

129 Approach paths to the steady state — a performance test of current period decision rule solution methods for models of renewable resource management. William C. Kolberg. *Land Econ.* **68:1** 2:1992 pp. 11 – 27

130 Australia's resource sectors — challenges and opportunities in the 1990s. Ira Sohn. *Res. Pol.* **18:2** 6:1992 pp. 92 – 106

131 The bang-bang production of depletable natural resources; La produzione bang-bang delle risorse naturali esauribili *[Italian summary]*. David B. Reister; Michael A.S. Guth. *Rev. Int. Sci. Ec. Com.* **XXXIX:1** 1:1992 pp. 5 – 22

132 Conflicts and cooperation in managing environmental resources. Rüdiger Pethig *[Ed.]*. Berlin: Springer-Verlag, 1992: 338 p. *ISBN: 0387549684; LofC: 91042342. Includes bibliographical references and index.* [Microeconomic studies.]

133 Depletable resources and the economy. Willem Heijman. Wageningen: Agricultural University, 1991: xi, 267 p. (ill) *ISBN: 9067541931. Includes bibliographical references (p. [247]-262) and index.* [Wageningse economische studies.]

134 La economía de los recurso naturales. Políticas extractives y ambientales *[In Spanish]*; [The economics of natural resources — regulatory policies] *[Summary]*. Elsa Galarza; Roberto Urrunaga. *Apuntes* **30:1** 1992 pp. 45 – 61

135 Economic issues in global climate change — agriculture, forestry, and natural resources. John M. Reilly *[Ed.]*; Margot Anderson *[Ed.]*. Boulder: Westview Press, 1992: xviii, 460 p. *ISBN: 0813384354; LofC: 92002510 //r922. Includes bibliographical references and index.*

136 Economics for the wilds — wildlife, wildlands, diversity and development. Timothy M. Swanson *[Ed.]*; Edward B. Barbier *[Ed.]*. London: Earthscan Publications, 1992: 226 p. *ISBN: 1853831247.*

H.0: Production and conservation *[Production et conservation]* — *Resource management [Gestion des ressources]*

137 Economics, natural resource scarcity and development — conventional and alternative views. Edward B. Barbier. London: Earthscan, 1990: 223 p. *ISBN: 1853830720.*

138 Efficient economic growth. Stefan Homburg. Berlin: Springer-Verlag, 1992: 106 p. *ISBN: 0387549951; LofC: 91042343. Includes bibliographical references and indexes.* [Microeconomic studies.]

139 Environmental resources and the market-place. Peter Ackroyd; et al. North Sydney: Allen & Unwin Pty Ltd, 1991: 292 p. *ISBN: 1863731385. At head of title — Market and Environment Project 1991.*

140 A future for the land — organic practice from a global perspective. Philip Conford *[Ed.].* Bideford, Devon: Green Books, 1992: 244 p. *ISBN: 1870098498.*

141 Generating alternative designs for interjurisdictional natural resource development schemes in the Greater Ganges river basin. John T. Quinn; Joseph J. Harrington. *Pap. Reg. Sci.* **71:4** 10:1992 pp. 373 – 391

142 Heterogeneity, distribution, and cooperation in common property resource management. S. M. Ravi Kanbur. Washington, D.C.: Office of the Vice President, Development Economics, The World Bank, 1992: 24 p. *Bibliography — p.23-24.* [Policy research working papers.]

143 Implementing effective local management of natural resources — new roles for NGOs in Africa. Barbara P. Thomas-Slayter. *Human. Org.* **51:2** Summer:1992 pp. 136 – 143

144 Interconnections between energy and the environment — global challenges. Joel Darmstadter; Robert W. Fri. *Ann. R. Energy Environ.* **17** 1992 pp. 45 – 76

145 Marine minerals in exclusive economic zones. D.S. Cronan. London: Chapman & Hall, 1992: viii, 209 p. *ISBN: 041229270x.* [Topics in the earth sciences. : No. 5]

146 Natural resources in a high-tech economy — scarcity versus resourcefulness. Anthony Scott; Peter Pearse. *Res. Pol.* **18:3** 9:1992 pp. 154 – 166

147 Optimal management of the growth potential of renewable resources. D. Levhari; C. Withagen. *J. Econ.* **56:3** 1992 pp. 297 – 309

148 A question of balance — natural resources conflict issues in Australia. David Mercer. Sydney: Federation Press, 1991: xiv, 346 p. (ill., maps) *ISBN: 186287056x; LofC: 92183712. Includes bibliographical references (p.314-340) and index.*

149 Resource development and aboriginal land rights. Richard H. Bartlett. Calgary: Canadian Institute of Resources Law, 1991: vii, 122 p. *ISBN: 0919269338; LofC: cn 91091655. eng: fre; Includes bibliographical references.*

150 Resource management in developing countries. Peter H. Omara-Ojungu. Harlow: Longman Scientific & Technical, 1992: 256 p. *ISBN: 0582301025; LofC: gb 91085573.* [Themes in resource management. : No. 9]

151 Resource management — oil resources and the Gulf conflict. James L. Wescoat. *Prog. H. Geog.* **16:2** 6:1992 pp. 243 – 256

152 The seabed's mineral resources and the conditions affecting the regime to regulate their exploitation. Mahdi El-Baghdadi. *J. World Tr.* **26:3** 6:1992 pp. 85 – 98

153 A slow-discounting model for energy conservation. Charles M. Harvey. *Interfaces* **22:6** 11-12:1992 pp. 47 – 60

154 So much for "scarce resources". Stephen Moore. *Publ. Inter.* **:106** Winter: 1992 pp. 97 – 107

155 The time path of scarcity rent in the theory of exhaustible resources. Y.H. Farzin. *Econ. J.* **102:413** 7:1992 pp. 813 – 830

156 A troublesome legacy — the Reagan administration's conservation and renewable energy policy. David Narum. *Energy Pol.* **20:1** 1:1992 pp. 40 – 53

157 Water resources in the arid realm. Clive Agnew; E. W. Anderson. London: Routledge, 1992: xvi, 329 p. *ISBN: 0415043468; LofC: 91038302. Includes bibliographical references (p. 290-322) and index.* [Routledge physical environment series.]

Sustainable development *[Développement soutenable]*

158 Beyond the limits — global collapse or a sustainable future. D. H. Meadows; Dennis L. Meadows; Jorgen Randers. London: Earthscan Publications, 1992: 300 p. *ISBN: 1853831301.*

159 Changing course — a global business perspective on development and the environment. Stephan Schmidheiny. Cambridge, MA.: MIT Press, 1992: 374 p. *ISBN: 0262193183; LofC: 92006457. Business Council for Sustainable Development; Includes bibliographical references and index.*

160 The contribution of energy efficiency to sustainable development in developing countries. Mark D. Levine; Stephen Meyers. *Nat. Res. For.* **16:1** 2:1992 pp. 19 – 26

H.0: Production and conservation *[Production et conservation]* — *Sustainable development [Développement soutenable]*

161 Coordinated development of the economy and environment in underdeveloped areas. Yining Li. *Soc. Sci. China* :**3** 9:1992 pp. 153 – 162

162 Le copilotage du développement économique et de la biosphère *[In French]*; [Joint direction of economic development and the biosphere]. René Passet. *R. T-Monde* **XXXIII:130** 4-6:1992 pp. 393 – 416

163 Des institutions pour un développement durable *[In French]*; [Institutions for sustainable development]. Paul Streeten. *R. T-Monde* **XXXIII:130** 4-6:1992 pp. 455 – 469

164 Economic development and environment — a case study of India. K.C. Roy *[Ed.]*; C.A. Tisdell *[Ed.]*; Raj Kumar Sen *[Ed.]*. Calcutta: Oxford University Press, 1992: 164 p. *ISBN: oc26832330. Includes bibliographical references and index.*

165 Environment and development — Rio and after. Alvaro Soto *[Contrib.]*; Joan Martin-Brown *[Contrib.]*; J. Owen Saunders *[Contrib.]*; Dixon Thompson *[Contrib.]*; G.V. Buxton *[Contrib.]*; Andrew Fenton Cooper *[Contrib.]*; J.-Stefan Fritz *[Contrib.]*; Paul Sharp *[Contrib.]*. *Collection of 7 articles.* **Int. J.** , *XLVII:4*, Autumn:1992 pp. 679 – 847

166 The environmental effects of stabilization and structural adjustment programs — the Philippines case. Wilfrido Cruz; Robert C. Repetto. Washington, D.C: World Resources Institute, 1992: viii, 90 p. *ISBN: 0915825813. Includes bibliographical references (p. 85-90).*

167 The growth illusion — how economic growth has enriched the few, impoverished the many and endangered the planet. Richard Douthwaite. Bideford, Devon: Green Books, 1992: 367 p. *ISBN: 1870098412.*

168 Indicators of ecologically sustainable development — towards new fundamentals. H. Jack Ruitenbeek. Ottawa: Canadian Environmental Advisory Council, [1991]: xi, 34 p. (ill) *ISBN: 0662191366; LofC: cn 92070599. Issued also in French under title — Indicateurs d'un développement écologiquement durable — vers de nouveaux principes fondamentaux; Cover title — Towards new fundamentals; "November 1991"; Includes bibliographical references.*

169 International banks and the environment — from growth to sustainability, an unfinished agenda. Raymond F. Mikesell; Larry Williams. San Francisco: Sierra Club Books, 1992: xvi, 302 p. (ill) *ISBN: 0871566400; LofC: 91030504. Includes bibliographical references and index.*

170 Legal regulation of sustainable development in Australia — politics, economics or ethics? Helen Endre. *Natur. Res. J.* **32:3** Summer:1992 pp. 487 – 514

171 Managing sustainable development. Michael Carley; Ian Christie. London: Earthscan Publications, 1992: 303 p. *ISBN: 185383128x.*

172 Natural resources and environmentally sound sustainable development. Dunja Pastizzi-Ferencic. *Nat. Res. For.* **16:1** 2:1992 pp. 3 – 10

173 Policies for a small planet — from the International Institute for Environment and Development. Johan Holmberg *[Ed.]*; Crispin Tickell *[Foreword]*. London: Earthscan, 1992: 362 p. *ISBN: 1853831328.*

174 Regulating the global economy and environment. A. Leyshon *[Contrib.]*; S. Gill *[Contrib.]*; S. Corbridge *[Contrib.]*; P. Dicken *[Contrib.]*; K. Morgan *[Contrib.]*; T.K. Marsden *[Contrib.]*; J. Murdoch *[Contrib.]*; S. Williams *[Contrib.]*; J.A. Peck *[Contrib.]*; A. Tickell *[Contrib.] and others. Collection of 12 articles.* **Geoforum** , *23:3*, 1992 pp. 249 – 436

175 Strategic environmental assessment. N. Lee *[Contrib.]*; F. Walsh *[Contrib.]*; J. Warren Webb *[Contrib.]*; Lorene L. Sigal; Christopher Wood *[Contrib.]*; Rob Verheem *[Contrib.]*; Graham Pinfield *[Contrib.]*; John Gardiner *[Contrib.]*; W.R. Sheate *[Contrib.]*. *Collection of 8 articles.* **Proj. App.** , *7:3*, 9:1992 pp. 126 – 185

176 Les stratégies économiques et financières de protection de l'environnement *[In French]*; Economic and financial strategies for environment protection and sustainable development — stakes and perspectives *[Summary]*. Roland Colin. *Obser. Diag. Econ.* :**40** 4:1992 pp. 101 – 140

177 Struggling with Honduran poverty — the environmental consequences of natural resource-based development and rural transformations. S.C. Stonich. *World Dev.* **20:3** 3:1992 pp. 385 – 400

178 Sustainable development and the local economy. Michael Jacobs; Martin Stott. *Local. Ec.* **7:3** 11:1992 pp. 261 – 272

179 Sustainable investment. The economic challenge. Mike Young. *Impact Sci.* **42:2** 1992 pp. 111 – 120

H.0: Production and conservation *[Production et conservation]* — **Sustainable development** *[Développement soutenable]*

180 Sustainable or unsustainable development? An analysis of an environmental controversy; *[French summary]*. Joel Novek; Karen Kampen. *Can. J. Soc.* **17:3** 1992 pp. 249 – 273

181 Toward an ecological economics of sustainability. M. Common; C. Perrings. *Ecol. Eco.* **6:1** 7:1992 pp. 7 – 34

182 Transforming technology — an agenda for environmentally sustainable growth in the twenty-first century. George R. Heaton; Robert C Repetto; Rodney Sobin. Washington: World Resources Institute, 1992: 39 p. *ISBN: 0915825686.*

183 Umwelt und Entwicklung *[In German]*; Environment and development. Otmar Höll *[Ed.]*; Maurice F. Strong *[Contrib.]*; Matthew Paterson *[Contrib.]*; Renate Christ *[Contrib.]*; Laura Kelly *[Contrib.]*; Willy Kempel *[Contrib.]*; Walter Hödl *[Contrib.]*; Martin Frimmel *[Contrib.]*; J. Wagona Makoba *[Contrib.]*; Gerhard Gerster *[Contrib.] and others.* Collection of 8 articles. **J. Entwick.pol.** , *VIII:1,* 1992 pp. 211 – 303

184 Water and sustainable development. Rob Koudstaal; Frank R. Rijsberman; Hubert Savenije. *Nat. Res. For.* **16:4** 11:1992 pp. 277 – 290

185 World energy resources and global sustainable development. Peter R. Odell. *OPEC Rev.* **XVI:4** Winter:1992 pp. 369 – 381

Waste management *[Gestion des déchets]*

186 Hazardous waste sites and property values in the state of New Jersey. K. Ketkar. *Appl. Econ.* **24:6** 6:1992 pp. 647 – 659

187 Measuring hazardous waste damages with panel models. Robert Mendelsohn; Daniel Hellerstein; Michael Huguenin; Robert Unsworth; Richard Brazee. *J. Envir. Ec. Manag.* **22:3** 5:1992 pp. 259 – 271

188 Nuclear juggernaut — the transport of radioactive materials. Martin Bond. London: Earthscan Publications, 1992: 224 p. *ISBN: 1853831034.*

189 Packaging waste and the polluter pays principle — a taxation solution. David Pearce; R. Kerry Turner. *J. Environ. Plan. Manag.* **35:1** 1992 pp. 5 – 16

190 Partial static equilibrium model of newsprint recycling. D.V. Nestor. *Appl. Econ.* **24:4** 4:1992 pp. 411 – 418

191 The supply and demand for pollution control — evidence from wastewater treatment. Virginia D. McConnell; Gregory E. Schwarz. *J. Envir. Ec. Manag.* **23:1** 7:1992 pp. 54 – 77

192 Waste location — spatial aspects of waste management, hazards, and disposal. Michael Clark *[Ed.]*; Denis Smith *[Ed.]*; Andrew Blowers *[Ed.]*. London: Routledge, 1992: 257 p. *ISBN: 0415048249; LofC: 91009809. Includes bibliographical references and index.* [The Natural environment — problems and management series.]

193 Waste not, want not — the production and dumping of toxic waste. Robert Allen. London: Earthscan Publications, 1992: 224 p. *ISBN: 185383095x.*

194 World of waste — dilemmas of industrial development. K.A. Gourlay. London: Zed Books, 1992: 247 p. (Ill) *ISBN: 0862329884.*

195 Zur sektoralen Belastungswirkung der geplanten Abfallabgabe *[In German]*; [The effects of the projected production of waste of various sectors]. Peter Michaelis. *Weltwirt.* **:3** 1992 pp. 338 – 351

Water resources *[Ressources en eau]*

196 Application of state theory to ground water contamination incidents. N.L. Jackson. *Geoforum* **23:4** 1992 pp. 487 – 498

197 Community participation and rural water supply development in Sierra Leone. O.M. Bah. *Comm. Dev. J.* **27:1** 1:1992 pp. 30 – 41

198 Designing a dispute resolution system for water policy and management. Matthew McKinney. *Negot. J.* **8:2** 4:1992 pp. 153 – 164

199 Economic instruments for water management — the case for industrial water pricing. Donald M. Tate; Steven Renzetti; H.A. Shaw. Ottawa: Ecosystem Sciences and Evaluation Directorate, Economics and Conservaton Branch, 1992: 35 p. *ISBN: oc26718587; LofC: cn 92071645. eng: fre; At head of title — Environment Canada. Conservation and Protection; Includes bibliographical references (p. 35).* [Social science series. : No. 26]

200 The economics of a stock pollutant — aldicarb on Long Island. Jon M. Conrad; Lars J. Olson. *Environ. Resour. Econ.* **2:3** 1992 pp. 245 – 258

201 Environmental aspects of water price formation. An empirical investigation of the cost of ground water protection. W. Pfaffenberger; U. Scheele. *Environ. Resour. Econ.* **2:3** 1992 pp. 323 – 339

H.0: Production and conservation *[Production et conservation]* — *Water resources [Ressources en eau]*

202 Investment decisions and transferable discharge permits — an empirical study of water quality management under policy uncertainty. David Letson. *Environ. Resour. Econ.* **2:5** 1992 pp. 441 – 458

203 The last oasis — facing water scarcity. Sandra Postel. London: Earthscan Publications, 1992: 239 p. *ISBN: 1853831484.* [Worldwatch environmental alert series.]

204 Non-point source water pollution management — improving decision-making information through water quality monitoring. L.E. Reinelt; R.R. Horner; R. Castensson. *J. Environ. Manag.* **34:1** 1:1992 pp. 15 – 30

205 The problems of supplying water to Third World cities — Bulawayo's water crisis. E.L. Nel; B.B. Berry. *Develop. S. Afr.* **9:4** 11:1992 pp. 411 – 422

206 Проблемы экономической оценки подземных вод *[In Russian]*; Жер асты суларын экономикалық бағалау проблемалары *[In Kazakh]*; [Economic evaluation of underground water supplies]. T.K. Karamurztsev. *Iz. Akad. Respub. Kazakh.* **:1(181)** 1-2:1992 pp. 49 – 56

207 Valuing environmental quality changes using averting expenditures — an application to groundwater contamination. Charles W. Abdalla; Brian A. Roach; Donald J. Epp. *Land Econ.* **68:2** 5:1992 pp. 163 – 169

208 Water and instability in the Middle East — an analysis of environmental, economic and political factors influencing water management and water disputes in the Jordan and Nile basins and Tigris-Euphrates region. Natasha Beschorner. London: Brassey's, 1992: 82 p. *ISBN: 1857530586.* [Adelphi papers. : No. 273]

209 Water and sustainable development. Rob Koudstaal; Frank R. Rijsberman; Hubert Savenije. *Nat. Res. For.* **16:4** 11:1992 pp. 277 – 290

210 Water as a resource in the USSR; Le risorse idriche nell'Unione Sovietica *[Italian summary]*. Joseph A. Martellaro. *Rev. Int. Sci. Ec. Com.* **XXXIX:5-6** 5-6:1992 pp. 499 – 518

211 Water management and urban development. A call for realistic alternatives for the future. Janusz Niemczynowicz. *Impact Sci.* **42:2** 1992 pp. 131 – 147

212 Water management problems in economies in transition. Zbigniew Bochniarz. *Nat. Res. For.* **16:1** 2:1992 pp. 55 – 64

213 Water marketing in Texas — opportunities for reform. Ronald C. Griffin; Fred O. Boadu. *Natur. Res. J.* **32:2** Spring:1992 pp. 265 – 288

214 Water resources in the arid realm. Clive Agnew; E. W. Anderson. London: Routledge, 1992: xvi, 329 p. *ISBN: 0415043468; LofC: 91038302. Includes bibliographical references (p. 290-322) and index.* [Routledge physical environment series.]

215 What authority should reside in the state engineer? New Mexico as a case study. Ira Clark. *Natur. Res. J.* **32:3** Summer:1992 pp. 467 – 486

H.1: Agriculture — *Agriculture*

H.1.1: Agricultural economics — *Économie agricole*

1 L'activité agricole au sein d'un espace péri-urbain — le cas des coteaux du Lyonnais *[In French]*; [Agricultural activity at the heart of an urban space — the case of the hills of Lyonnais] *[Summary]*. C. Fougerouse. *R.E.M.* **40:158** 2:1992 pp. 91 – 108

2 Agricoltura a minor impatto ambientale ed economia dell'azienda agraria — un approccio mediante l'analisi multiobiettivo *[In Italian]*; Low input agriculture and agricultural economics — a multiobjective approach *[Summary]*. Francesco Marangon. *Riv. Econ. Agrar.* **XLVII:4** 12:1992 pp. 545 – 593

3 Agricultural credit in Nigeria — performance at farm level; Le credit agricole au Nigeria — la performance au niveau de la ferme *[French summary]*. Malachy Ezeja Obeta. *Sav. Develop.* **:2** 1992 pp. 173 – 184

4 Agricultural credit in Tanzania — the policy and operational problems of the Cooperative and Rural Development Bank; (Le credit agricole en Tanzanie — les problemes operationnels de la Cooperative and Rural Development Bank: *Title only in French*). Anacleti K. Kashuliza. *Sav. Develop.* **XVI:4** 1992 pp. 327 – 352

5 Análisis de la oferta de productos, la demanda de insumos y la tecnología del sector

H.1.1: Agricultural economics *[Économie agricole]*

agropecuario argentino empleando una función de beneficios *[In Spanish]*; A translog profit function analysis of Argentine agriculture *[Summary]*. José A. Delfino. *Económica Arg* **XXXVI:1-2** 1990 pp. 53 – 72

6 Contingent claim pricing models implied by agricultural stabilization and insurance policies; *[French summary]*. Calum G. Turvey. *Can. J. Ag. Ec.* **40:2** 7:1992 pp. 183 – 198

7 Cost structure, interfactor substitution and complementarity, and efficiency in the Canadian agricultural sector; *[French summary]*. Andreas A. Andrikopoulos; James A. Brox. *Can. J. Ag. Ec.* **40:2** 7:1992 pp. 253 – 269

8 An economic analysis of alternative farm revenue insurance policies; *[French summary]*. Calum G. Turvey. *Can. J. Ag. Ec.* **40:3** 11:1992 pp. 403 – 426

9 Economic comparison of alternative tillage system under risk; *[French summary]*. Alfons Weersink; Michael Walker; Clarence Swanton; Jim Shaw. *Can. J. Ag. Ec.* **40:2** 7:1992 pp. 199 – 217

10 Economies of scale, plot size, human capital, and productivity in Chinese agriculture. Belton M. Fleisher; Yunhua Liu. *Q Rev. Econ. Finan.* **32:3** Autumn:1992 pp. 112 – 123

11 The effects of alternative methods of crow benefit payment on economic rents of farm input suppliers in western Canada; *[French summary]*. Ghulam Sarwar; Glenn Fox. *Can. J. Ag. Ec.* **40:2** 7:1992 pp. 219 – 234

12 L'esame della congiuntura economica dell'agricoltura — quali indicatori? *[In Italian]*; Which indicators for short term economic analysis in agriculture? Carlo Aiello. *Riv. Econ. Agrar.* **XLVII:4** 12:1992 pp. 633 – 654

13 Future of institutional agricultural credit in India — likely impact of Narasimham and Khusro committee reports. M.V. Gadgil. *Ind. J. Agri. Eco.* **XLVII:2** 4-6:1992 pp. 255 – 265

14 The geography of agriculture in developed market economies. I. R. Bowler *[Ed.]*. Harlow: Longman Scientific & Technical, 1992: xvii, 317 p. *ISBN: 0582301610; LofC: 92012994. Includes bibliographical references and index.*

15 Gerarchia economica ed Agro-Industria. Sviluppi metodologici e verifica sul caso italiano *[In Italian]*; Economic hierarchy and the food industry. Methodological developments seen in relation to the Italian situation *[Summary]*. Mario Bono. *Riv. Econ. Agrar.* **XLVII:2** 6:1992 pp. 203 – 232

16 Informal finance through land pawning contracts — the Philippines. Geetha Nagarajan; Cristina C. David; Richard L. Meyer. *J. Dev. Stud.* **29:1** 10:1992 pp. 93 – 107

17 Land and labor contracts in agrarian economies — theories and facts. Keijiro Otsuka; Hiroyuki Chuma; Yujiro Hayami. *J. Econ. Lit.* **XXX:4** 12:1992 pp. 1965 – 2018

18 Macroeconomic impacts of an agro-ethanol industry in Canada; *[French summary]*. Paul J. Thomassin; John C. Henning; Laurie Baker. *Can. J. Ag. Ec.* **40:2** 7:1992 pp. 295 – 310

19 Pitfalls in the measurement of real exchange rate effects on agriculture. S. Kyle. *World Dev.* **20:7** 7:1992 pp. 1009 – 1019

20 Les prix agricoles pour 1992-1993 *[In French]*; [Agricultural prices for 1992-1993]. Pierre Baudin. *R. Mar. Comm.* **:361** 9-10:1992 pp. 683 – 697

21 Real overvaluation, terms of trade shocks, and the cost to agriculture in sub-Saharan Africa. Ibrahim A. Elbadawi. Washington, D.C.: Country Economics Department World Bank, 1992: 66 p. [Policy research working papers.]

22 The rediscovery of Alexander Chayanov. Günther Schmitt. *Hist. Polit. Ec.* **24:4** Winter:1992 pp. 925 – 965

23 State-level output supply and input demand elasticities for agricultural commodities. Pedro A. Villezca-Becerra; C. Richard Shumway. *J. Agr. Econ. R.* **44:1** 1992 pp. 22 – 34

H.1.1.1: Technical factors of agricultural productivity — *Facteurs techniques de la productivité agricole*

Sub-divisions: Soil resources *[Ressources en sol]*

1 Agricultural research bias in Nicaragua — the case of beans. R. Godoy; J. Hockenstein. *World Dev.* **20:11** 11:1992 pp. 1685 – 1696
2 Assessing the relative efficiency of agricultural production units in the Blackland Prairie, Texas. S. Haag; P. Jaska; J. Semple. *Appl. Econ.* **24:5** 5:1992 pp. 559 – 565
3 An assessment of planting flexibility options to reduce the excessive application of nitrogen fertilizer in the United States of America. W.-Y. Huang; N.D. Uri. *Envir. Plan. B.* **24:2** 2:1992 pp. 199 – 214
4 Comparison of mechanised and non-mechanised farms in Rajasthan. K.K. Saxena; P.K. Punjabi. *Ind. J. Reg. Sci.* **XXIV:1** 1992 pp. 69 – 83
5 A dynamic model of investment in the U.S. beef-cattle industry. Kenneth A. Foster; Oscar R. Burt. *J. Bus. Econ. Stat.* **10:4** 10:1992 pp. 419 – 426
6 The effect of BSE on beef fatstock revenue. D.D. Mainland; S.W. Ashworth. *J. Agr. Econ.* **43:1** 1:1992 pp. 96 – 103
7 Endogenous environmental degradation and land conservation — agricultural land use in a large region. D.W. Jones; R.V. O'Neill. *Ecol. Eco.* **6:1** 7:1992 pp. 79 – 100
8 Endogenous regional agricultural production technologies. C. Fawson; C. Richard Shumway. *Appl. Econ.* **24:11** 11:1992 pp. 1263 – 1273
9 Environment-specific rates and biases of technical change in agriculture. Ian A. Coxhead. *Am. J. Agr. Ec.* **74:3** 8:1992 pp. 592 – 604
10 Failure of irrigation projects and consequences for a different approach — a case study. R. Zwahlen. *Ecol. Eco.* **5:2** 5:1992 pp. 163 – 178
11 A farm-sizewise analysis of irrigation distribution in India. Rajan K. Sampath. *J. Dev. Stud.* **29:1** 10:1992 pp. 121 – 147
12 Fertilizer price and subsidy policies in Bangladesh. R.Z.H. Renfro. *World Dev.* **20:3** 3:1992 pp. 437 – 456
13 Fixed grants and the supply of public goods — the case of agricultural research. Jyoti Khanna. *Publ. Fin. Q.* **20:2** 4:1992 pp. 216 – 230
14 Identifying the costs and benefits of projects — an example from biotechnology. Leonie Marks; Ivy Papps. *Proj. App.* **7:1** 3:1992 pp. 21 – 30
15 Issues in irrigation pricing in developing countries. R.K. Sampath. *World Dev.* **20:7** 7:1992 pp. 967 – 977
16 Labor and production barriers to the reduction of agricultural chemical inputs. Max J. Pfeffer. *Rural Sociol.* **57:3** Fall:1992 pp. 347 – 362
17 The management of secondary consequences in dam projects — the case of drawdown agriculture in Indonesia. Y.T. Winarto. *World Dev.* **20:3** 3:1992 pp. 457 – 466
18 *[In Japanese]*; [Manualization of the rice culture]. Mitsuru Shimpo. *Agriculture and economy Vol.58; No.7 - 1992.* pp. 59 – 65
19 A nonparametric analysis of the influence of research on agricultural productivity. Jean-Paul Chavas; Thomas L. Cox. *Am. J. Agr. Ec.* **74:3** 8:1992 pp. 583 – 591
20 Obtención de planes de cultivo eficientes en el sentido de Markowits en la provincia de Córdoba *[In Spanish]*; [Obtaining a system of efficient cultivation by application of a Markowits in Córdoba Province] *[Summary]*. Antonio M. Alaejos Gutiérrez; Juan A. Cañas Madueño. *Invest. Econ.* **XVI:2** 5:1992 pp. 281 – 298
21 Organic farming as a business in Great Britain. M. C. Murphy. Cambridge: University of Cambridge. Agricultural Economics Unit, 1992: 161 p. *ISBN: 0906782856.*
22 Producer benefits from technology-induced supply shifts in the EC cotton regime. A.C. Herruzo. *J. Agr. Econ.* **43:1** 1:1992 pp. 56 – 63
23 Rainfed mechanized farming and deforestation in Central Sudan. Abdelmoneim Hashim Elnagheeb; Daniel W. Bromley. *Environ. Resour. Econ.* **2:4** 1992 pp. 359 – 371
24 Regionalization of Haryana in the context of new agricultural technology. H.S. Sidhu. *Ind. J. Reg. Sci.* **XXIV:1** 1992 pp. 85 – 97
25 Research payoff from quality improvement — the case of protein in Australian wheat. Thomas J. Voon; Geoff W. Edwards. *Am. J. Agr. Ec.* **74:3** 8:1992 pp. 564 – 572
26 Saving the seed — genetic diversity and European agriculture. Renée Vellvé. London: Earthscan Publications, 1992: 206 p. *ISBN: 1853831506.*

H.1.1.1: Technical factors of agricultural productivity *[Facteurs techniques de la productivité agricole]*

27 Technical change, productivity, and sustainability in irrigated cropping sytems of South Asia — emerging issues in the post-green revolution era. D. Byerlee. *J. Int. Dev.* **4:5** 9-10:1992 pp. 477 – 496

28 Transformation of agriculture in Central Eastern Europe and the former USSR — major policy issues and perspectives. Csaba Csáki. Washington, D.C.: Agriculture and Rural Development Department and Country Economics Department, The World Bank, 1992: 32 p. [Policy research working papers.]

29 The value of education in small-scale agriculture — some evidence from Ogun State, Nigeria. Bamidele O. Durojaiye; Fasasi A. Olanloye. *Ox. Agrar. Stud.* **20:2** 1992 pp. 107 – 115

30 Valutazione degli effetti della ricerca agricola — una rassegna *[In Italian]*; Evaluation of effects of the agriculture research — a review. Elena Viganò. *Riv. Econ. Agrar.* **XLVII:4** 12:1992 pp. 655 – 690

31 Vers une agriculture renouvelable et durable. Agriculture biologique — d'une avant-garde marginale au fer de lance d'une agriculture d'avenir *[In French]*; [Towards a renewable and sustainable agriculture. Biological agriculture — from a marginal avant-garde to the cutting edge of future agriculture]. Jan Diek van Mansvelt. *R. T-Monde* **XXXIII:130** 4-6:1992 pp. 311 – 328

Soil resources *[Ressources en sol]*

32 Economic returns to crop management research in a post-Green Revolution setting. Greg Traxler; Derek Byerlee. *Am. J. Agr. Ec.* **74:3** 8:1992 pp. 573 – 582

33 The economics of land degradation — theory and applications to Lesotho. Jan Bojö. Stockholm: Stockholm School of Economics, [1991]: iv, 352 p. *ISBN: 9172583274. Includes bibliographical references.*

34 Exploring the adoption of renewable energy — the case of biogas plants in Greek agriculture. Maria Kousis. *Perspect. Ener.* **2:1** 1:1992 pp. 99 – 108

35 Inter-regional variation in the speed of adoption of modern cereal cultivars in India. H.G.P. Jansen. *J. Agr. Econ.* **43:1** 1:1992 pp. 88 – 95

36 Modern seed-fertiliser technology and adoption of labour saving technologies in rice production — the Tamil Nadu case. C. Ramasamy; P. Paramasivam; Keijiro Otsuka. *Ind. J. Agri. Eco.* **XLVII:1** 1-3:1992 pp. 35 – 47

37 Resource management by West African farmers and the economics of shifting cultivation. Karen Ann Dvořàk. *Am. J. Agr. Ec.* **74:3** 8:1992 pp. 809 – 815

38 Soil depletion in the United States — the relationship between the loss of the American farmer's independence and the depletion of the soil. Dean Smith. *Environ. Law* **22:4** 1992 pp. 1539 – 1572

H.1.1.2: Forms of agricultural enterprise and land tenure — *Formes d'entreprise agricole et tenure du sol*

1 Agrarian reform in West Bengal — the end of an illusion. R. Mallick. *World Dev.* **20:5** 5:1992 pp. 735 – 750

2 Agricultural reform in Central and Eastern Europe — marketisation, privatisation, developing a new role for the state. Timothy N. Ash. *Comm. Econ.* **4:4** 1992 pp. 513 – 536

3 An analysis of land leasing in Bangladesh agriculture. M.A. Taslim; F.U. Ahmed. *Econ. Dev. Cult. Change* **40:3** 4:1992 pp. 615 – 628

4 Analyzing institutional successes and failures — a millennium of common mountain pastures in Iceland. Thrainn Eggertson. *Int. R. Law Econ.* **12:4** 12:1992 pp. 423 – 437

5 China's rural reform — the state and peasantry in constructing a macro-rationality. Kyung-Sup Chang. *Econ. Soc.* **21:4** 11:1992 pp. 430 – 452

6 Contract choice in modern agriculture — cash rent versus cropshare. Douglas Allen; Dean Lueck. *J. Law Econ.* **XXXV:2** 10:1992 pp. 397 – 426

7 The debate on size and productivity in developed and developing countries. Patrick Mendis. *J. Cont. Asia* **22:1** 1992 pp. 73 – 81

8 The demand for salmon in France — the effects of marketing and structural change. T. Bjørndal; K.G. Salvanes; J.H. Andreassen. *Appl. Econ.* **24:9** 9:1992 pp. 1027 – 1034

9 The determinants of farm investment and residential construction in post-reform China. Gershon Feder; Lawrence J. Lau; Justin Y. Lin; Xiaopeng Luo. *Econ. Dev. Cult. Change* **41:1** 10:1992 pp. 1 – 26

H.1.1.2: Forms of agricultural enterprise and land tenure *[Formes d'entreprise agricole et tenure du sol]*

10 Determinants of smallholder commercial tree cultivation. R.A. Godoy. *World Dev.* **20:5** 5:1992 pp. 713 – 726

11 The economics of contract choice — an agrarian perspective. Yūjirō Hayami; Keijiro Otsuka. Oxford [England]: Clarendon Press, 1991: 209 p. *ISBN: 0198283784; LofC: 91027291. Includes bibliographical references (p.) and index.*

12 Evaluating the impact of Mexico's land reform on agricultural productivity. J.R. Heath. *World Dev.* **20:5** 5:1992 pp. 695 – 712

13 Farm family pluriactivity in Western Europe. Andre Brun; Anthony M. Fuller. Oxford: Arkleton Trust (Research), 1992: 76 p. *ISBN: 0906724384.*

14 Farm structure and the economic well-being of nonmetropolitan counties. Donna Barnes; Audie Blevins. *Rural Sociol.* **57:3** Fall:1992 pp. 333 – 346

15 Green revolution, land reform, and household income distribution in the Philippines. Keijiro Otsuka; Violeta Cordova; Christina C. David. *Econ. Dev. Cult. Change* **40:4** 7:1992 pp. 719 – 741

16 A harvest of discontent — the land question in South Africa. Michael de Klerk *[Ed.].* Cape Town: IDASA, 1991: viii, 274 p. *ISBN: 087486402x; LofC: 92119029. Distributor from label on p. 2 of cover; Includes bibliographical references.*

17 Korean minifarm agriculture — from articulation to disarticulation. Larry L. Burmeister. *J. Dev. Areas* **26:2** 1:1992 pp. 145 – 168

18 Labour market dualism, threat of eviction and cropshare tenancy. M.A. Taslim. *J. Agr. Econ.* **43:1** 1:1992 pp. 43 – 53

19 Land is life — land reform and sustainable agriculture. John Madeley *[Ed.];* Sue Stolton *[Ed.];* Nigel Dudley *[Ed.].* London: Intermediate Technology Publications, 1992: 155 p. *ISBN: 1853391468.*

20 Land tenure and agricultural productivity on Indian reservations. Terry L. Anderson; Dean Lueck. *J. Law Econ.* **XXXV:2** 10:1992 pp. 427 – 454

21 Lichnoe podsobnoe khozaĭstvo — pravovoĭ rezhim imushchestva *[In Russian];* [Individual private agriculture — the legal framework for property]. V.V. Ustukova; Mikhail Ivanovich Kozyr' *[Ed.].* Moskva: Nauka, 1990: 124 p. *ISBN: 5020128996; LofC: 92106335. Includes bibliographical references.*

22 Limited liability and the existence of share tenancy. K. Basu. *J. Dev. Econ.* **38:1** 1:1992 pp. 203 – 220

23 Modern plantation agriculture — corporate wealth and labour squalor. Rene Loewenson. London: Zed Books, 1992: 147 p. *ISBN: 0862329965.*

24 Nach dem Ende der Sowjetunion — ein Neubeginn? *[In German];* [Following the end of the Soviet Union — a new beginning?]. Dirk Holtbrügge *[Contrib.];* Alexej Schulus *[Contrib.];* Georg Watzlawek *[Contrib.];* Wassilij Ja. Usun *[Contrib.];* Karl-Eugen Wädekin *[Contrib.];* Andrea Segrè *[Contrib.];* Anne-Christine Hanser *[Contrib.];* Jürgen Gneveckow *[Contrib.];* Iwan M. Potrawnij *[Contrib.].* Collection of 7 articles. **Osteuropa** , 42:9, 9:1992 pp. 727 – 809

25 *[In Japanese];* [Potentiality of family farms]. Tomoko Iwata Ishida. *Nousouken Kihou No.12 - 1992.* pp. 59 – 70

26 Private farming and agrarian reform in Russia. Stephen K. Wegren. *Probl. Commu.* **XLI** 5-6:1992 pp. 107 – 121

27 Rapporto sull'organizzazione dell'agricoltura italiana — un confronto europeo *[In Italian];* The organization of Italian agriculture — a comparison with European realities *[Summary].* Romano Prodi; Paolo De Castro. *Riv. Econ. Agrar.* **XLVII:1** 3:1992 pp. 11 – 34

28 Recent developments in the market for rural land use in China. Wenfang Zhang; Jack Makeham. *Land Econ.* **68:2** 5:1992 pp. 139 – 162

29 Restructuring of agriculture and rural society — evidence from Australia and New Zealand. Geoffrey Lawrence; Perry Share; Hugh Campbell. *J. Aust. Pol. Econ.* **:30** 12:1992 pp. 1 – 23

30 Share contracts and their rationale — lessons from marine fishing. J.-Ph. Platteau; J. Nugent. *J. Dev. Stud.* **28:3** 4:1992 pp. 386 – 422

31 Size of farm or size of family — which comes first? Daniel C. Clay; Nan E. Johnson. *Pop. Stud.* **46:3** 11:1992 pp. 491 – 505

32 Small-farm problems and group farming in Taiwan. Hsi-huang Chen. *Ind. Free China* **LXXVII:5** 5:1992 pp. 33 – 42

33 Strukturwandel der Landwirtschaft in den neuen Bundesländern — Teil I — Wandel der

H.1.1.2: Forms of agricultural enterprise and land tenure *[Formes d'entreprise agricole et tenure du sol]*

betrieblichen Struktur und der Produktionsstruktur *[In German]*; [Structural change in eastern Germany's agriculture, part I — changes in enterprise and production structures] *[Summary]*; *[French summary]*. Bernhard Lageman. *RWI-Mitt.* **43:1** 1992 pp. 61 – 92

34 La struttura delle aziende-famiglie coltivatrici attraverso una analisi tipologica multivariata *[In Italian]*; The structure of a family farm. A multivariate analysis of tipology *[Summary]*. Massimo Sabbatini; Enrico Turri. *Riv. Econ. Agrar.* **XLVII:2** 6:1992 pp. 169 – 202

35 A survey of theories of cropshare tenancy. M.A. Taslim. *Econ. Rec.* **68:202** 9:1992 pp. 254 – 275

36 A theoretical analysis of the reform of the urban land system in China. Wen Li; Jirui Yang. *Soc. Sci. China* **XIII:4** 12:1992 pp. 158 – 168

37 Wholesale- and farm- level impacts of generic advertising — the case of catfish. W. Zidack; H. Kinnucan; U. Hatch. *Appl. Econ.* **24:9** 9:1992 pp. 959 – 968

38 "The worse it got the more we laughed" — a discourse of resistance among farmers of eastern Ontario. F. Mackenzie. *Envir. Plan. D* **10:6** 12:1992 pp. 691 – 713

H.1.1.3: Agricultural management — *Gestion agricole*

1 Against the odds — managing agricultural projects in Africa. Evidence from Sierra Leone and Zambia. Steve Wiggins. *Int. Rev. Admin. Sci.* **58:1** 3:1992 pp. 79 – 92

2 *[In Japanese]*; [Agricultural advisory services in some developed countries — Japan, U.S.A., and F.R. Germany]. Tomoko Iwata; Tomoko Ishida. *Quart. J. Agr. Ec. Vol.46; No.2 - 1992.* pp. 131 – 157

3 The appropriate role of agricultural insurance in developing countries. P.B.R. Hazell. *J. Int. Dev.* **4:6** 11-12:1992 pp. 567 – 581

4 Causality between technical and allocative efficiencies — an empirical testing. K.P. Kalirajan; R.T. Shand. *J. Econ. Stud.* **19:2** 1992 pp. 3 – 17

5 The CET-CES-generalized leontief variable profit function — an application to Indian agriculture. Jere R. Behrman; C.A. Knox-Lovell; Robert A. Pollak; Robin C. Sickles. *Ox. Econ. Pap.* **44:2** 4:1992 pp. 341 – 354

6 Costs and returns for agricultural commodities — advances in concepts and measurement. Mary Ahearn *[Ed.]*; Utpal Vasavada *[Ed.]*. Boulder, CO.: Westview Press, 1992: xvii, 395 p. *ISBN: 0813303699; LofC: 92003840. Includes bibliographical references.*

7 Environmental costing for agriculture — will it be standard fare in the Farm Bill of 2000? V. Kerry Smith. *Am. J. Agr. Ec.* **74:5** 12:1992 pp. 1076 – 1088

8 Farm level models — a review of developments, concepts and applications in Canada; *[French summary]*. K.K. Klein; S.A. Narayanan. *Can. J. Ag. Ec.* **40:3** 11:1992 pp. 351 – 368

9 Farmers' wives — their contribution to the farm businss. R. Gasson. *J. Agr. Econ.* **43:1** 1:1992 pp. 74 – 87

10 Financial stress and consumption expectations among farm households — New Zealand's experience with economic liberalisation. G.A.G. Frengley; W.E. Johnston. *J. Agr. Econ.* **43:1** 1:1992 pp. 14 – 27

11 High inflation and Bolivian agriculture. Ricardo Godoy; Mario de Franco. *J. Lat. Am. St.* **24:3** 10:1992 pp. 617 – 637

12 The impact of specialised small-holder credit programmes on farmer-beneficiaries — a case study of the First Bank of Nigeria community loan scheme in Oyo State of Nigeria; L'impact des programmes de prêts aux petits agriculteurs sur les bénéficiares — une étude du programme realisé par la F.B.N. *[French summary]*. A. Osuntogun; B.O. Oramah; J.O. Olusi. *Sav. Develop.* **:1** Supplement:1992 pp. 75 – 84

13 Interdépendance partielle et sous-systèmes productifs — une application au complexe agro-industriel *[In French]*; Partial interdependence and productive sub-systems an application in the agro-industrial complex *[Summary]*; (Partielle Interdependenz und produktive Subsysteme — Anwendung bei einem agro- industriellen Komplex: *Title only in German)*; (Interdependencia parcial y subsistemas productivos — una aplicación al complejo agro-industrial: *Title only in Spanish)*. Pascal Byé; Jean-Pierre Frey. *Econ. App.* **XLV:2** 7:1992 pp. 129 – 149

H.1.1.3: Agricultural management *[Gestion agricole]*

14 Measurement of farm risk — Alberta crop production; *[Reviewed in French]*. Glen Mumey; Bob Burden; Ann Boyda. *Can. J. Ag. Ec.* **40:1** 3:1992 pp. 71 – 91

15 Optimal flex cropping and storage of spring wheat under a progressive income tax; *[French summary]*. C. Robert Taylor; F.S. Novak. *Can. J. Ag. Ec.* **40:3** 11:1992 pp. 369 – 384

16 Profit maximization, returns to scale, and measurement error. Hongil Lim; C. Richard Shumway. *Rev. Econ. St.* **LXXIV:3** 8:1992 pp. 430 – 438

17 The relationship between technical efficiency and firm size revisited; *[French summary]*. N.G. Kalaitzan-Donakes; Shunxiang Wu; Jian-chun Ma. *Can. J. Ag. Ec.* **40:3** 11:1992 pp. 427 – 442

18 Restricted estimation of crop and summerfallow acreage response in Saskatchewan; *[French summary]*. J. Stephen Clark; K.K. Klein. *Can. J. Ag. Ec.* **40:3** 11:1992 pp. 485 – 498

19 La riforma del credito agrario tra logico fondiaria e logica di mercato *[In Italian]*; *[The reform of agricultural credit — towards a market-centered approach]*. Giuseppe Muraglia. *Ras. Econ.* **LVI:2** 4-6:1992 pp. 517 – 527

20 A test of the applicability of strategic management to farm management; *[French summary]*. Kenneth F. Harling. *Can. J. Ag. Ec.* **40:1** 3:1992 pp. 129 – 139

H.1.1.4: Agricultural development. Agricultural policy —
Développement agricole. Politique agricole

Sub-divisions: Africa *[Afrique]*; Americas *[Amérique]*; Asia *[Asie]*; Europe *[Europe]*

1 Agricultural change, environment and economy. Keith Hoggart *[Ed.]*. London: Mansell, 1992: 253 p. *ISBN: 0720121272; LofC: 92001407. Includes bibliographical references and index.* [Global development and the environment.]

2 Agricultural development and environmental problems in developing countries. Tadayo Watabe; Kazuo Ando. *Tech. Devel.* **:5** 1:1992 pp. 35 – 46

3 Environnement et développement rural *[In French]*; *[Environment and rural development]*. Marc Dufumier. *R. T-Monde* **XXXIII:130** 4-6:1992 pp. 295 – 310

4 Farmers' interest groups and agricultural policy in New Zealand during the 1980s. M.M. Roche; T. Johnston; R.B. Le Heron. *Envir. Plan.A.* **24:12** 12:1992 pp. 1749 – 1767

5 From Stockholm to Rio de Janeiro — the road to sustainable agriculture. Monkombu Sambasivan Swaminathan. Madras, India: M.S. Swaminathan Research Foundation, Centre for Research on Sustainable Agricultural and Rural Development, [1991]: 68 p. (ill) *ISBN: oc26827803. Includes bibliographical references (p.53-54).*

6 Impact régional d'une libéralisation des politiques agricoles *[In French]*; *[The regional impact of liberalization of agricultural policy]* *[Summary]*. H. Becker; H. Guyomard; Y. Leon. *R. Ec. Reg. Urb.* **:1** 1992 pp. 93 – 114

7 Issues in agricultural development — sustainability and cooperation. Margot A. Bellamy *[Ed.]*; Bruce L. Greenshields *[Ed.]*. Aldershot: Dartmouth Publishing, 1992: 402 p. *ISBN: 1855213028.* [IAAE Occasional Paper. : No. 6]

8 Eine Klärung des Agrarproblems aus der sozialphilosophischen Perspektive Friedrich A. von Hayeks *[In German]*; *[An explanation of the agrarian problems from the socio-philosophical perspective of Friedrich A. von Hayek]*. Franz Kromka. *Wirt. Blät.* **5/6:39** 1992 pp. 594 – 607

9 La mutation de l'agriculture *[In French]*; *[The destruction of the agricultural industry]*. Bruno Trégouët *[Contrib.]*; Michel Cyncynatus *[Contrib.]*; Jean-Michel Floch *[Contrib.]*; Véronique Ardouin *[Contrib.]*; Laurent Bisault *[Contrib.]*; Patrick Redor *[Contrib.]*; Ahmed Barkaoui *[Contrib.]*; Jean-Christophe Bureau *[Contrib.]*; Jean-Pierre Butault *[Contrib.]*; Jean-Marc Rouselle *[Contrib.] and others. Collection of 7 articles.* E & S , :254-255, 5-6:1992 pp. 3 – 84

10 Objectives and constraints of government policy — the countercyclicity of transfers to agriculture. David S. Bullock. *Am. J. Agr. Ec.* **74:3** 8:1992 pp. 617 – 629

11 On the design of agricultural policy mechanisms. Robert G. Chambers. *Am. J. Agr. Ec.* **74:3** 8:1992 pp. 646 – 654

12 Les progrès et aléas de l'agriculture et du monde rural — les apports et les nouveaux défis de la révolution verte *[In French]*; *Performances and options for the agriculture and the rural world [Summary]*. Claude Aubert; Gilbert Etienne. *Ec. Pros. Int.* **:50** 2e trimestre:1992 pp. 31 – 65

H.1.1.4: Agricultural development. Agricultural policy *[Développement agricole. Politique agricole]*

13 Sustainable agricultural development — the role of international cooperation. G.H. Peters *[Ed.]*; Godfrey J. Tyler *[Ed.]*; B.F. Stanton *[Ed.]*. Aldershot: Dartmouth, 1992: 704 p. *ISBN: 1855212722.*

Africa *[Afrique]*

14 Aid and agriculture in Africa. Naceur Bourenane *[Ed.]*; Sam Mayo *[Ed.]*; E.E. Ekong *[Contrib.]*; Driss Khrouz *[Contrib.]*; Machioudi Dissou *[Contrib.]*; Mamadou Dansokho *[Contrib.]*; Dejene Aredo *[Contrib.]*. *Collection of 6 articles.* **Afr. Devel.**, *XVII:3,* 1992 pp. 5 – 237

15 A failed agenda? African agriculture under structural adjustment, with special reference to Kenya and Ghana. Peter Gibbon. *J. Peasant Stud.* **20:1** 10:1992 pp. 50 – 96

16 Nominal and effective protection in the Egyptian agricultural sector — a multicommodity analysis. R. Hassan; D. Greenaway; G.V. Reed. *Appl. Econ.* **24:5** 5:1992 pp. 483 – 492

17 A portfolio model for evaluating risk in economic development projects, with an application to agriculture in Niger. K.C. Schaefer. *J. Agr. Econ.* **43:3** 9:1992 pp. 412 – 423

18 Structures of intermediation and change in African agriculture — a Nigerian case study. Dickson L. Eyoh. *Afr. Stud. R.* **35:1** 4:1992 pp. 17 – 40

19 A succesful failure — integrated rural development in Zambia. A. Fenichel; B. Smith. *World Dev.* **20:9** 9:1992 pp. 1313 – 1323

Americas *[Amérique]*

20 Una ciudad agrícola — Zamora — del porfiriato a la agricultura de exportación *[In Spanish]*; [An agricultural city — Zamora — from Porfirio to export agriculture]. Gustavo Verduzco Igartúa *[Ed.]*. México, D.F./Zamora: El Colegio de México/El Colegio de Michoacán, 1992: 282 p. *ISBN: 968 12 0532 4.*

21 Compétitivité agricole et agro-alimentaire du Brésil et de l'Argentine *[In French]*; [The agricultural and agribusiness competitiveness of Brazil and Argentina] *[Summary]*; *[Spanish summary]*. Jean-Pierre Bertrand; Guillermo Hillcoat; Brigitte Jensen. *Prob. Am.Lat.* **:4** 1-3:1992 pp. 93 – 116

22 The farming frontier in northern Alberta. W. Hamley. *Geogr. J.* **158:3** 11:1992 pp. 286 – 294

23 Membership desertion as an adjustment process on Honduran agrarian reform enterprises. Bradford L. Barham; Malcolm Childress. *Econ. Dev. Cult. Change* **40:3** 4:1992 pp. 587 – 614

24 The Paraguayan agro-export model of development. R. Weisskoff. *World Dev.* **20:10** 10:1992 pp. 1531 – 1540

25 Predatory versus productive government — the case of U.S. agricultural policies. Gordon C. Rausser. *J. Econ. Pers.* **6:3** Summer:1992 pp. 133 – 158

Asia *[Asie]*

26 The adjustment of Taiwan's agricultural policy to trade liberalization. Jhi-tseng Shih; Tsu-tan Fu. *Ind. Free China* **LXXVII:1** 1:1992 pp. 57 – 76

27 The agricultural sector in China — performance and policy dilemmas during the 1990s. Robert F. Ash. *China Quart.* **:131** 9:1992 pp. 545 – 576

28 China's surplus agricultural labour force — it's size, transfer, prospects for absorption and effects of the double-track economic system. Cao Yang; C.A. Tisdell. *Asian Econ. J.* **VI:2** 7:1992 pp. 149 – 182

29 Labour use in Indian agriculture — analysis at macro level for the eighties. Sarthi Acharya. *Ind. J. Agri. Eco.* **XLVII:2** 4-6:1992 pp. 169 – 184

30 Medium-term growth prospects for Turkish agriculture — a sector model approach. Erol H. Cakmak. *Develop. Eco.* **XXX:2** 6:1992 pp. 132 – 153

31 Sustainable agricultural development in China. Cheng Xu; Han Chunru; D.C. Taylor. *World Dev.* **20:8** 8:1992 pp. 1127 – 1144

32 Vietnam — decollectivization and rice productivity growth. Prabhu L. Pingali; Vo-Tong Xuan. *Econ. Dev. Cult. Change* **40:4** 7:1992 pp. 697 – 718

H.1.1.4: Agricultural development. Agricultural policy *[Développement agricole. Politique agricole]* —

Europe *[Europe]*

33 An agricultural policy model for the UK. M. P. Burton. Aldershot: Avebury, 1992: 315 p. *ISBN: 1856282953.*

34 Agriculture française — l'ajustement forcé *[In French]*; [French agriculture — inevitable adjustment]. Eckart Guth *[Contrib.]*; Dominique Brinbaum *[Contrib.]*; André Neveu *[Contrib.]*; Jean-Pierre Carlier *[Contrib.]*; G. Lemaître *[Contrib.]*; Danielle Monsimier *[Contrib.]*; Jean-Claude Guesdon *[Contrib.]*; Marie-Claude L'Hyver *[Interviewer]*; Emile Karaïliev *[Contrib.]*; Yves Rio *[Contrib.] and others. Collection of 10 articles.* **Econ. Fin. Agr.** , :266, 1-2:1992 pp. 4 – 54

35 An analysis of 1980s dairy programs and some policy implications. Charles W. Bausell; David A. Belsley; Scott L. Smith. *Am. J. Agr. Ec.* **74:3** 8:1992 pp. 605 – 616

36 Characteristics and crisis symptoms of the Hungarian agricultural system. I. Fertő; P. Juhász; K. Mohácsi. *Acta Oecon.* **44:1-2** 1992 pp. 95 – 114

37 Economic reform, the free market and agriculture in Poland. W.B. Morgan. *Geogr. J.* **158:2** 7:1992 pp. 145 – 156

38 The effect of EC milk quotas on the milk and livestock sectors in the UK. Alison Burrell. *Ox. Agrar. Stud.* **20:1** 1992 pp. 19 – 37

39 Eléments pour une nouvelle politique agricole *[In French]*; Elements of a new agricultural policy *[Summary]*. Jacques le Cacheux; Henri Mendras. *Obser. Diag. Econ.* :42 10:1992 pp. 95 – 134

40 Das Entschädigungsgesetz von 1991 und die marktwirtschaftliche Umgestaltung des Agrarsektors in Ungarn *[In German]*; [The 1991 compensation law and market reform of the agrarian sector in Hungary]. Brigitta Fischer. *Südosteur. Mitteil.* **32:1** 1992 pp. 35 – 44

41 Factores determinantes del gasto público agrícola de las comunidades autónomas *[In Spanish]*; [Factors determining public expenditure on agriculture in the autonomous communities] *[Summary]*; *[French summary]*. José Maria García Alvarez-Coque; Barbara Möhlendick. *Agr. Soc.* :62 1-3:1992 pp. 33 – 72

42 Food regulation in a period of agricultural retreat — the British experience. A. Flynn; T. Marsden. *Geoforum* **23:1** 1992 pp. 85 – 94

43 Il governo dell'adattamento dell'agricoltura italiana — istituzioni e strumenti *[In Italian]*; [The management of Italian agricultural adjustment. Institutions and instruments]. Giuseppe de Meo *[Contrib.]*; Giuseppe Guerrieri *[Contrib.]*; Giorgio Pastori *[Contrib.]*; Secondo Tarditi *[Contrib.]*; Alessandro Romagnoli *[Contrib.]*; Gervasio Antonelli *[Contrib.]*; Franco Sotte *[Contrib.]*; Giuseppina Carrà *[Contrib.]*; Fabio Maria Santucci *[Contrib.]*; Rossella Pampanini *[Contrib.] and others. Collection of 18 articles.* **Riv. Econ. Agrar.** , :3, 9:1992 pp. 45 – 444

44 De nederlandse landbouw op de drempel van de 21ste eeuw — een beschouwing over knelpunten en perspectieven *[In Dutch]*; [Dutch agriculture on the threshold of the twentyfirst century — a review on bottlenecks and perspectives]. H.J.J. Stolwijk. 's-Gravenhage: Centraal Planbureau, 1992: 123 p. *ISBN: 9034628302.* [Onderzoeksmemorandum.]

45 The political economy of agricultural policy reform in the European Community and Australia. D. MacLaren. *J. Agr. Econ.* **43:3** 9:1992 pp. 424 – 439

46 I prodotti agroalimentari tipici e rilancio delle aree interne meridionali *[In Italian]*; Typical food products and furtherance of southern Italy's inland areas *[Summary]*. Antonella Giardiello. *Ras. Econ.* **LVI:3** 7-9:1992 pp. 661 – 675

47 Riforma della PAC e agricolture nella CEE. Un'analisi comparata delle performances nazionali negli anni Ottanta *[In Italian]*; The reform of the CAP and agriculture in the EEC. A Comparative analysis of national performance in the 80s *[Summary]*. Alessandro Bartola; Franco Sotte. *Riv. Econ. Agrar.* **XLVII:1** 3:1992 pp. 89 – 122

48 Strukturwandel der Landwirtschaft in den neuen Bundesländern — Teil 2 — Wandel der regionalen Struktur und agrarpolitische Rahmenbedingungen *[In German]*; [Structural changes in agriculture in the new federal states — part 2 — changes in the regional structure and agricultural, political limitations] *[Summary]*; *[French summary]*. Bernhard Lageman. *RWI-Mitt.* **43:2** 1992 pp. 93 – 113

49 Tschechoslowakische Landwirtschaft am Scheideweg *[In German]*; [Czechoslovakian agriculture at the crossroads]. Zdenek Lukas. *Osteuropa* **42:5** 5:1992 pp. 441 – 449

50 Verlustminderung als zentrale Aufgabe der Nahrungswirtschaft in Rußland und der GUS(SNG) *[In German]*; [Loss reduction as a central undertaking for the food economy in Russia and the CIS]. Karl-Eugen Wädekin. *Osteuropa* **42:11** 11:1992 pp. 938 – 950

H.1.2: **Agricultural production** — *Production agricole*

1 La agricultura y la alimentación *[In Spanish]*; [The agricultural and the food industries]. Jaime Lamo de Espinosa; José M.ª Sumpsi Viñas; Carlos Tió Saralegui. *Pap. Econ. Esp.* **50** 1992 pp. 80 – 122
2 Economic rents under supply controls with marketable quota. Bruce A. Babcock; William E. Foster. *Am. J. Agr. Ec.* **74:3** 8:1992 pp. 630 – 637
3 How important is organic farming in Great Britain? Frank Cudjoe; Philip Rees. *J. Econ. Soc. Geogr.* **83:1** 1992 pp. 13 – 24
4 The Ishikawa curve and agricultural productivity in Bangladesh — some new findings. Clem Tisdell; Mohammad Alauddin. *Hito. J. Econ.* **33:1** 6:1992 pp. 113 – 127
5 Total factor productivity in UK agriculture, 1967-90. C. Thirtle; P. Bottomley. *J. Agr. Econ.* **43:3** 9:1992 pp. 381 – 400

H.1.2.1: Agricultural products — *Produits agricoles*
Sub-divisions: Cereals *[Céréales]*; Fish *[Poissons]*; Forests *[Forêts]*

1 Articulaciones agroindustriales en el complejo cervecero *[In Spanish]*; [Agro-industrial relations in the brewing industry]. Rodolfo Pastore; Miguel Teubal. *Desar. Econ.* **31:124** 1-3:1992 pp. 523 – 544
2 Australian sugar industry in the 1990s — submission 91.5 to the Industry Commission. Chrysanthi Papadopoulos; Peter Connell; Patrick Whish-Wilson. Australia: Bureau of Agricultural and Resource Economics, 1991: 46 p. *ISBN: 0644220147.*
3 Les avantages comparatifs dans l'agriculture canadienne et le partage interprovincial des quotas laitiers *[In French]*; [Comparative advantages in Canadian agriculture and interprovincial sharing of dairy quotas] *[Summary]*. D.-M. Gouin; Y. Proulx. *Can. J. Ag. Ec.* **40:3** 11:1992 pp. 385 – 402
4 Colombia, Guatemala y Costa Rica — países cafeteros de la Cuenca de Caribe *[In Spanish]*; [Colombia, Guatemala and Costa Rica — coffee producing countries of the Caribbean basin]. María del Pilar Esguerra. **Coy. Econ.** *Vol.21; No.1 - 4: 1991.* pp. 111 – 138
5 Consumo e produzione di prosciutti crudi in Italia — un'analisi previsionale *[In Italian]*; Consumption and production of uncooked ham in Italy — a forecasting analysis *[Summary]*. Lorenzo Biscontin. *Riv. Econ. Agrar.* **XLVII:2** 6:1992 pp. 233 – 263
6 Dinamiche congiunturali dei prezzi delle carni ovine e suine nell'ultimo decennio un'analisi con la procedura X-11-ARIMA *[In Italian]*; The method X-11- ARIMA for the time series analysis — the case of the pork and the sheep in Italy *[Summary]*. Margherita Giannoni; Andrea Marchini. *Riv. Econ. Agrar.* **XLVII:4** 12:1992 pp. 595 – 623
7 An economic analysis of energy requirements in the production of potato crop in Biharsharif block of Nalanda district (Bihar). R.N. Yadav; R.K.P. Singh; Sarbesh Prasad. **Econ. Aff. [Calcutta]** *Vol.36; No.2 - 4-6: 1991.* pp. 112 – 119
8 Economics and the debate about preservation of species, crop varieties and genetic diversity. Clem Tisdell. **Ecol. Eco.** *Vol.2; No.1 - 4: 1990.* pp. 77 – 90
9 Economics of sheep and goat in Maharashtra. Nilakantha Rath. *Ind. J. Agri. Eco.* **XLVII:1** 1-3:1992 pp. 62 – 78
10 The effect of new price information on crop supply; *[French summary]*. J. Stephen Clark; Julia S. Taylor; John Spriggs. *Can. J. Econ.* **XXV:1** 2:1992 pp. 172 – 183
11 Le importazioni del comparto suinicolo italiano *[In Italian]*; Imports of the Italian pork sector *[Summary]*. Andrea Brugnoli; Emiro Endrighi. *Riv. Econ. Agrar.* **XLVII:3** 9:1992 pp. 425 – 448
12 An input-output analysis of agribusiness in South Africa; 'n Inset-uitset ontleding van landboubesighede in Suid-Afrika *[Afrikaans summary]*. D.E.N. van Seventer; C.S. Faux; J. van Zyl. *Agrekon* **31:1** 3:1992 pp. 12 – 21
13 Overgrazing and range degradation in Africa — is there need and scope for government control of livestock numbers? Lovell S. Jarvis. *E. Afr. Econ. Rev.* **7:1** 6:1991 pp. 95 – 116
14 The palm oil industry — issues and challenges in the 1990s. Rod Wong; Felix Golingi. *Born. R.* **III:1** 6:1992 pp. 124 – 151
15 La production camerounaise de caoutchouc naturel — evolution et perspectives de

H.1.2.1: Agricultural products *[Produits agricoles]*
commercialisation *[In French]*; [Cameroonian production of natural rubber — development and prospects for commercialization]. Dieudonné Mouafo. *Can. J. Afr. St.* **26:1** 1992 pp. 92 – 119

16 Raising cane — the political economy of sugar in western India. Donald W. Attwood. Boulder: Westview Press, 1992: xviii, 366 p. (ill) *ISBN: 0813312876; LofC: 91017330. Includes bibliographical references (p.335-349) and index.*

17 Rational expectations and output supply evidence from the sugar cane and coffee industries in Jamaica; *[French summary]*; *[Spanish summary]*. Stephen K. Pollard; Douglas H. Graham. *Soc. Econ. S.* **41:1** 3:1992 pp. 89 – 101

18 The relationship between cattle and savings — a cattle-owner perspective. M.I. Schmidt. *Develop. S. Afr.* **9:4** 11:1992 pp. 433 – 444

19 Short- and long-run adjustments in dairy production — a profit function analysis. R.E. Quiroga; B.E. Bravo-Ureta. *Appl. Econ.* **24:6** 6:1992 pp. 607 – 616

20 Spanisches Olivenöl — die Politik des Gemeinsamen Marktes und die Lebensmittelindustrie *[In German]*; Spanish olive oil. Common market policy and the agroalimentary complex *[Summary]*. Antoon Hoogveld. *Peripherie* **12:46** 5:1992 pp. 31 – 46

21 The structural transformation of Taiwan's tea industry. D.M. Etherington; K. Forster. *World Dev.* **20:3** 3:1992 pp. 401 – 422

22 The world sugar prices — an empirical analysis of long term development. Yusuf Taha Gumaa. *E. Afr. Econ. Rev.* **7:2** 12:1991 pp. 51 – 68

Cereals *[Céréales]*

23 Dynamically optimal after-tax grain storage, cash grain sale, and hedging strategies. Russell Tronstad; C. Robert Taylor. *Am. J. Agr. Ec. Vol.73; No.1 - 2: 1991.* pp. 75 – 88

24 Effects of alternative Chinese policies on the world grains market. B.H. Gunasekera; G. Rodriguez; N. Andrews. *J. Agr. Econ.* **43:3** 9:1992 pp. 440 – 451

25 Have the supply responses increased for the major crops in Bangladesh? Shamsul Alam. *Bang. Dev. Stud.* **XX:1** 3:1992 pp. 43 – 74

26 The impacts of monetary policy on the maize and beef sectors of South Africa II — model estimation and simulation results; Die impak van monetêre beleid op die mielie- en beesvleis sektore van Suid-Afrika II — modelraming en simulasie resultate *[Afrikaans summary]*. V.Y. Dushmanitch; M.A.G. Darroch. *Agrekon* **31:1** 3:1992 pp. 3 – 11

27 Implications of the growth trends in mainland China's grain production. John Wong. *Iss. Stud.* **28:1** 1:1992 pp. 39 – 52

28 Labour-saving technologies in the Javanese rice economy — recent developments and a look into the 1990s. Rosamond Naylor. *B. Ind. Econ. St.* **28:3** 12:1992 pp. 71 – 91

29 A location model of grain production and transportation. T. Heaps; J.M. Munro; C.S. Wright. *Ann. Reg. Sci.* **26:2** 1992 pp. 111 – 134

30 Market structure, quality and world wheat market; *[French summary]*. Bruno Larue; Harvey E. Lapan. *Can. J. Ag. Ec.* **40:2** 7:1992 pp. 311 – 328

31 Some maize production parameters for KwaZulu. R.M.B. Auerbach; J.D. Lea. *Develop. S. Afr.* **9:1** 2:1992 pp. 25 – 46

Fish *[Poissons]*

32 Bio-economic stability of the North Sea shrimp stock with endogenous fishing effort. A. David McDonald; Claus-Hennig Hanf. *J. Envir. Ec. Manag.* **22:1** 1:1992 pp. 38 – 56

33 The bioeconomics of resource rehabilitation — a commercial sport analysis for a Great Lakes fishery. Scott A. Milliman; Barry L. Johnson; Richard C. Bishop; Kevin J. Boyle. *Land Econ.* **68:2** 5:1992 pp. 191 – 210

34 The deterrent effect of regulatory enforcement in the fishery. William J. Furlong. ***Land Econ. Vol.67; No.1 - 2: 1991.*** pp. 116 – 129

35 Development of management measures for the groundfish fishery in Atlantic Canada — a case study of the Nova Scotia inshore fleet. R.G. Halliday; F.G. Peacock; D.L. Burke. *Mar. Pol.* **16:6** 11:1992 pp. 411 – 426

36 Efficient policies to maintain total allowable catches in ITQ fisheries with at-sea processing. Lee G. Anderson. ***Land Econ. Vol.67; No.2 - 5: 1991.*** pp. 141 – 157

37 Essays on the economics of migratory fish stocks. Ragnar Arnason *[Ed.]*; Trond Bjørndal *[Ed.]*. Berlin: Springer-Verlag, 1991: viii, 197 p. *ISBN: 3540543627. Includes bibliographical references.* [Studies in contemporary economics.]

H.1.2.1: Agricultural products *[Produits agricoles]* **— Fish** *[Poissons]*

38 Fisheries in India. N.P. Gharat; K.V. Ramani. *Mon. R. S. Bank. Ind. Vol.XXX; No.5 - 5: 1991.* pp. 231 – 242

39 Fisheries issue. Anthony Bergin *[Contrib.]*; Marcus Howard *[Contrib.]*; Peter H. Pearse *[Contrib.]*; Carl J. Walters *[Contrib.]*; Robert Nowak *[Contrib.]*; Stanley D.H. Wang *[Contrib.]*; Bing-yi Zhan *[Contrib.]*; Thorolfur Matthiasson *[Contrib.]*. *Collection of 5 articles.* **Mar. Pol.** , *16:3,* 5:1992 pp. 147 – 231

40 A fractional licensing program for fisheries. Ralph E. Townsend. *Land Econ.* **68:2** 5:1992 pp. 185 – 190

41 An inshore fishery — a commercially viable industry or an employer of last resort. William E. Schrank; Noel Roy; Rosemary Ommer; Blanca Skoda. *Ocean Dev. Int.* **23:4** 1992 pp. 335 – 367

42 Malaysian fisheries policy — search for new grounds. Ishak Hj Omar; Kusairi Mohd Noh; Nik Mustapha Raja Abdullah; K. Kuperan. *Mar. Pol.* **16:6** 11:1992 pp. 438 – 450

43 Markets for salmon in Spain and Italy. Trond Bjørndal; Daniel V. Gordon; Kjell G. Salvanes. *Mar. Pol.* **16:5** 9:1992 pp. 338 – 344

44 Strategic dynamic interaction — fish wars. Ronald D. Fischer; Leonard J. Mirman. *J. Econ. Dyn. Cont.* **16:2** 4:1992 pp. 267 – 286

45 Structural problems in the Danish fishing industry — institutional and socio-economic factors as barriers. Jesper Raakjær Nielsen. *Mar. Pol.* **16:5** 9:1992 pp. 349 – 359

46 Targeted versus nontargeted multispecies fishing. C. Costa Duarte. *Environ. Resour. Econ.* **2:3** 1992 pp. 259 – 281

47 Valuing changes in commercial fishery harvests — a general equilibrium derived demand analysis. Walter M. Thurman; J.E. Easley. *J. Envir. Ec. Manag.* **22:3** 5:1992 pp. 226 – 240

48 World marine fisheries — management and development problems. Lennox Hinds. *Mar. Pol.* **16:5** 9:1992 pp. 394 – 403

Forests *[Forêts]*

49 Communal forest management — the Honduran resin tappers. Denise L. Stanley. **Develop. Cha.** *Vol.22; No.4 - 10: 1991.* pp. 757 – 780

50 For whom the tree falls — restructuring of the global forest industry. M. Patricia Marchak. *BC. Stud. No.90 - Summer: 1991.* pp. 3 – 24

51 The impact of forestry on output in the UK and its member countries; *[French summary]*; *[German summary]*. Peter G. McGregor; Iain H. McNicoll. *Reg. Stud.* **26:1** 1992 pp. 69 – 80

52 Mark, människor och moderna skiftsreformer i Dalarna *[In Swedish]*; *[Land, people and modern shift reform in Dalarna]*. Erik Westholm. Uppsala: Uppsala University, Dept. of Social and Economic Geography, 1992: 226 p. (ill) *ISBN: 9150608975.* [Geografiska regionstudier. : No. 25]

53 National account of timber and forest environmental resources in Sweden. Lars Hultkrantz. *Environ. Resour. Econ.* **2:3** 1992 pp. 283 – 305

H.2: Industry — *Industrie*

H.2.1: Industrial economics — *Économie industrielle*

Sub-divisions: Industrial management *[Gestion industrielle]*; Industrial policy *[Politique industrielle]*; Industrial productivity *[Productivité industrielle]*

1 7as Jornadas de economia industrial — patrocinadas por la Fundación Empresa Pública — Madrid, 26 y 27 de Septiembre de 1991 *[In Spanish]*; [7th Workshop in Industrial Economics — sponsored by the Fundación Empresa Pública — Madrid, 26th and 27th September, 1991]. Julio Segura *[Contrib.]*; Xavier Freixas *[Contrib.]*; Emilio Huerta *[Contrib.]*; José M. Labeaga *[Contrib.]*; Ignacio Hernando *[Contrib.]*; Javier Vallés *[Contrib.]*; Ana Martín *[Contrib.]*; Lourdes Moreno *[Contrib.]*; J. David Pérez Castrillo *[Contrib.]*; Jordi Brandts *[Contrib.] and others. Collection of 19 articles.* **Invest. Econ.** ,Supplement:1992 pp. 7 – 154

2 Adjustment costs and factor demands in Canadian manufacturing industries. B. Carmichael; S. Ng. *Appl. Econ.* **24:8** 8:1992 pp. 845 – 857

H.2.1: Industrial economics *[Économie industrielle]*

3 Die Beihilfen für den Absatz von Kokskohle und Hochofenkoks — Grundlagen, Subventionsvolumen, Finanzierungsrisiken *[In German]*; [The protection of the supply of coking coal — foundations, volume of subsidies and financial risks]. Karl-Heinz Storchmann; Helmut Wienert. *RWI-Mitt.* **43:3** 1992 pp. 201 – 222

4 Building a strategic alliance. Robert W. Haigh. *Columb. J. W. Bus.* **27:1** Spring:1992 pp. 60 – 75

5 Classification and aggregation — an application to industrial classification in CPS data. R. Cotterman; F. Peracchi. *J. Appl. Econ.* **7:1** 1-3:1992 pp. 31 – 52

6 Competitiveness and industrial development in an international era. P. McNamee. *Inter. R. Strat. Manag.* **3** 1992 pp. 21 – 45

7 Cross licensing of complementary technologies. C. Fershtman; M.I. Kamien. *Int. J. Ind. O.* **10:3** 9:1992 pp. 329 – 348

8 Development of financial markets and the size distribution of manufacturing establishments — international comparisons. J.B. Nugent; M.K. Nabli. *World Dev.* **20:10** 10:1992 pp. 1489 – 1499

9 Dimensions of the British economy — a factor analysis. F. Green. *Br. Rev. Ec. Iss.* **14:34** 10:1992 pp. 31 – 54

10 Diversification and concentration changes in a liberalised environment — the case of New Zealand manufacturing industries. R.T. Hamilton. *Int. J. Ind. O.* **10:1** 3:1992 pp. 15 – 26

11 Dual decisions of firms, inventory stock, and quantity expectations. Chen-Min Hsu. *Econ. S. Quart.* **43:2** 6:1992 pp. 118 – 128

12 Economic analysis of a levy on sales of blank audio tape. A.J. Baker. *Br. Rev. Ec. Iss.* **14:34** 10:1992 pp. 55 – 73

13 The effects of state-societal arrangements on international competitiveness — steel, motor vehicles and semiconductors in the United States, Japan and Western Europe. Jeffery A. Hart. *Br. J. Poli. S.* **22:3** 7:1992 pp. 255 – 300

14 The efficiency-market power controversy — further evidence on the debate. C.A. Bourlakis. *Br. Rev. Ec. Iss.* **14:32** 2:1992 pp. 53 – 82

15 Egy piac működésének eltérő értelmezései *[In Hungarian]*; Different interpretations of the functioning of a market — conflicts between owners and enterprise management in buying up firms *[Summary]*. Péter Vince. *Közg. Sz.* **XXXIX** 10:1992 pp. 924 – 933

16 Entry and R & D in procurement contracting. Guofu Tan. *J. Econ. Theo.* **58:1** 10:1992 pp. 41 – 60

17 Especialización comercial y competitividad *[In Spanish]*; [Business specialization and competitiveness]. José Antonio Alonso *[Ed.]*; Paolo Guerrieri *[Contrib.]*; Kamal Abd-El-Rahman *[Contrib.]*; Rafael Myro Sánchez *[Contrib.]*; Carmela Martín *[Contrib.]*; Miguel Carrera Troyano *[Contrib.]*; Mikel Buesa *[Contrib.]*; José Molero *[Contrib.]*; Zulima Fernández *[Contrib.]*; Vicente Donoso *[Contrib.] and others. Collection of 12 articles*. **Infor. Com. Esp.** , *:705*, 5:1992 pp. 3 – 200

18 Financial structure and labour demand of West German industrial and commercial companies — a study with longitudinal data; Finanzierungsstruktur und Arbeitsnachfrage von Unternehmen in der BRD — eine Paneldaten-Analyse *[German summary]*. Kenneth Frisse; Michael Funke; Fidelis Lankes. *Jahrb. N. St.* **209:1-2** 1:1992 pp. 106 – 118

19 The four "worlds" of contemporary industry. Robert Salais; Michael Storper. *Camb. J. Econ.* **16:2** 6:1992 pp. 169 – 193

20 Growth, efficiency, and convergence in China's state and collective industry. Gary H. Jefferson; Thomas G. Rawski; Yuxin Zheng. *Econ. Dev. Cult. Change* **40:2** 1:1992 pp. 239 – 266

21 Hi tech for industrial development — lessons from the Brazilian experience in electronics and automation. Hubert Schmitz *[Ed.]*; Jose Cassiolato *[Ed.]*. London: Routledge, 1992: 322 p. *ISBN: 0415071615.*

22 Implications of post-war Japanese industrialization — government intervention and market competition. Tatsuya Ohmori. *Int. J. Soc. E.* **19:10/11/12** 1992 pp. 192 – 207

23 Implications of the state monopoly over industry and its relaxation. Barry Naughton. *Mod. Chi.* **18:1** 1:1992 pp. 14 – 41

24 The importance of small-scale industries in Indonesia. Tulus Tambunan. *J. Econ. Soc. Geogr.* **83:1** 1992 pp. 25 – 38

25 The incidence of business rates on manufacturing. Douglas Mair; Anthony J. Laramie. *Scot. J. Poli.* **39:1** 2:1992 pp. 76 – 94

26 Increasing returns to scale and trade-related industry enlargement. A generalization and new proof of welfare gains. E.L. Grinols. *Econ. Lett.* **38:1** 1:1992 pp. 61 – 66

H.2.1: Industrial economics [*Économie industrielle*]

27 Incumbents' use of preentry alliances before expansion into new technical subfields of an industry. W. Mitchell; K. Singh. *J. Econ. Beh.* **18:3** 8:1992 pp. 347 – 372

28 La industria española — evolución y perspectivas [*In Spanish*]; [Spanish industry — evolution and perspectives]. Julio Segura; Arturo González Romero. *Pap. Econ. Esp.* **50** 1992 pp. 140 – 172

29 Industrial diversification and city size — the case of Yugoslavia. Boris Begović. *Urban Stud.* **29:1** 2:1992 pp. 77 – 88

30 Industrial profitability and trade among the former Soviet republics. Claudia Senik-Leygonie; Gordon Hughes; John Flemming [*Comments by*]; Alasdair Smith [*Comments by*]. *Econ. Pol.* **:15** 10:1992 pp. 353 – 386

31 Industrial restructuring — implications for the decentralization of manufacturing to nonmetropolitan areas. David L. Barkley; Sylvain Hinschberger. *Econ. Devel. Q.* **6:1** 2:1992 pp. 64 – 79

32 Industrialization and its manifold discontents — west, east and south. A.O. Hirschman. *World Dev.* **20:9** 9:1992 pp. 1225 – 1232

33 Industrialization at bay — African experiences. Peter Anyang' Nyong'o [*Ed.*]; Peter Coughlin [*Ed.*]. Nairobi, Kenya: Academy Science Publishers, 1991: xi, 183 p. *ISBN: oc26094981; LofC: 92980360. Includes bibliographical references (p.158-170) and index.*

34 Industry income and congressional regulatory legislation — interest groups vs. median voter. Steven F. Cahan; William H. Kaempfer. *Econ. Inq.* **XXX:1** 1:1992 pp. 47 – 56

35 Infrastructural competition among jurisdictions. Leon Taylor. *J. Publ. Ec.* **49:2** 11:1992 pp. 241 – 259

36 Intensified competition, industrial restructuring and industrial relations. Werner Sengenberger. *Int. Lab. Rev.* **131:2** 1992 pp. 139 – 154

37 The interaction between game theory and theoretical industrial economics. James W. Friedman. *Scot. J. Poli.* **39:4** 11:1992 pp. 353 – 373

38 International competitiveness and policy in dynamic industries. W. Milberg; P. Gray. *Banca Nat. Lav. Q. Rev.* **:180** 3:1992 pp. 59 – 80

39 International trade; Industrial adjustment; Industrial restructuring and continental trade blocs. M. Gertler [*Contrib.*]; E. Schoenberger [*Contrib.*]; P. Dicken [*Contrib.*]; J. Howells [*Contrib.*]; A. Leyshon [*Contrib.*]; N.J. Thrift [*Contrib.*]; M. de Smidt [*Contrib.*]; J. Holmes [*Contrib.*]; A.D. MacPherson [*Contrib.*]; J.E. McConnell [*Contrib.*] and others. *Collection of 9 articles.* **Envir. Plan.A.** , *24:1,* 1:1992 pp. 2 – 170

40 De investeringsanalyse van geavanceerde flexibele produktietechnologieën [*In Flemish*]; Investment and analysis of advanced manufacturing technologies [*Summary*]. Onno Lint. *Econ. Soc. Tidj.* **46:2** 6:1992 pp. 185 – 221

41 Inward industrialisation as development strategy — a critique. B.E. Dollery. *S. Afr. J. Econ.* **60:3** 9:1992 pp. 293 – 302

42 The Japanese enterprise system — competitive strategies and cooperative structures. W. Mark Fruin. Oxford [England]: Clarendon Press, 1991: 397 p. *ISBN: 0198283180; LofC: 91033285. Includes bibliographical references and index.*

43 Künftige Aufgaben der österreichischen Technologiepolitik [*In German*]; [Future tasks for Austrian technology policy]. Gernot Hutschenreiter; Hannes Leo. *Wirt. Blät.* **39:4** 1992 pp. 453 – 460

44 The learning curve and competition — a stochastic model of duopolistic rivalry. K.F. Habermeier. *Int. J. Ind. O.* **10:3** 9:1992 pp. 369 – 392

45 The licensing of patents under asymmetric information. A.W. Beggs. *Int. J. Ind. O.* **10:2** 6:1992 pp. 171 – 192

46 Long-run output elasticities of factor demands, non-homotheticity, and scale economies in U.S. manufacturing. Chi-Chur Chao; Akira Takayama. *J. Inst. Theo. Ec.* **148:2** 6:1992 pp. 332 – 346

47 The macro impacts of Korea's heavy industry drive re-evaluated. R.M. Auty. *J. Dev. Stud.* **29:1** 10:1992 pp. 24 – 48

48 Macroeconomic implications of production bunching — factor demand linkages. Russell W. Cooper; John C. Haltiwanger. *J. Monet. Ec.* **30:1** 10:1992 pp. 107 – 128

49 Manufacturing's new economies of scale. Michael E. McGrath; Richard W. Hoole. *Harv. Bus. Re.* **70:3** 5-6:1992 pp. 94 – 102

50 Market structure and spells of employment and unemployment — evidence from the construction sector in Egypt. İ. Tunali; R. Assaad. *J. Appl. Econ.* **7:4** 10-12:1992 pp. 339 – 367

H.2.1: Industrial economics *[Économie industrielle]*
51 Market, innovation, competition — an evolutionary model of industrial dynamics. W. Kwasnicki; H. Kwasnicka. *J. Econ. Beh.* **19:3** 12:1992 pp. 343 – 368
52 The measurement of interindustry linkages — key sectors in the Netherlands. Erik Dietsenbacher. *Econ. Model.* **9:4** 10:1992 pp. 419 – 437
53 Nordic contributions in industrial economics — internal efficiency, information transmission and oligopoly competition. Rune Stenbacka *[Ed.]*. Åbo: Åbo Akademi, 1992: 287 p. *ISBN: 9516500072. Includes bibliographical references.* [Meddelanden Fran Ekonomisk-Statsvetenskapliga Fakulteten Vid Åbo Akademi.]
54 Normes de fabrication et barrières à l'entrée *[In French]*; [Manufacturing standards and entry barriers] *[Summary]*. Claude Crampes. *Appl. Finan. Econ.* pp. 567 – 581
55 The output and profit effects of horizontal joint ventures. John E. Kwoka. *J. Ind. Econ.* **XL:3** 9:1992 pp. 325 – 338
56 Potentiale der spanischen Wirtschaft und Unternehmensstrategien *[In German]*; [Spain's economic potential and enterprise strategies]. Santiago Garcia Echevarria. *Z. Wirt.pol.* **41:1** 1992 pp. 86 – 94
57 Probabilistic production costing under integrated operation agreements and joint power agency financing. Brian G. Thomas; Darwin C. Hall. *Ener. Econ.* **14:3** 7:1992 pp. 200 – 208
58 The readjustment and optimization of China's industrial structure. Wang Jiye. *Soc. Sci. China* **XIII:I** 1:1992 pp. 23 – 33
59 Reestructuración industrial y empleo. Mitos y realidades *[In Spanish]*; [Industrial restructuring and employment. Myths and realities]. Javier Lindenboim. *Desar. Econ.* **32:126** 7-8:1992 pp. 227 – 250
60 Regulation with "20-20 hindsight" — least cost rules and variable costs. Thomas P. Lyon. *J. Ind. Econ.* **XL:3** 9:1992 pp. 277 – 290
61 The relationship of industry evolution to patterns of technological linkages, joint ventures, and direct investment between U.S. and Japan. Ellen R. Auster. *Manag. Sci.* **38:6** 6:1992 pp. 778 – 792
62 Reputational spillovers, innovation, licensing, and entry. R. Jensen. *Int. J. Ind. O.* **10:2** 6:1992 pp. 193 – 212
63 La restructuración del sector urbano- industrial de Nigeria dentro de la región de África occidental, la interacción de la crisis, los eslabonamientos y la resistencia popular *[In Spanish]*; Restructuring Nigeria's urban-industrial sector within the West African region — the interplay of crisis, linkages and popular resistance *[Summary]*. Paul Lubeck. *Est. Asia Afr.* **XXVII:1** 1-4:1992 pp. 51 – 89
64 Los sectores productivos españoles ante el reto comunitario de los años noventa *[In Spanish]*; [Spanish industry before the EC threat in the nineties]. Juan Velarde Fuertes. *Pap. Econ. Esp.* **50** 1992 pp. 58 – 77
65 Strategic groups and intra-industry competition. J. McGee; H. Thomas. *Inter. R. Strat. Manag.* **3** 1992 pp. 77 – 98
66 Technologie, marktstruktuur en internationalisatie — de ontwikkeling van de industrie *[In Dutch]*; [Technology, market structure and internationalization — the development of industry]. Arnold Kusters; Bert Minne. 's-Gravenhage: Centraal Planbureau, 1992: 142 p. *ISBN: 9034629295. Bibliography — p.121-129.* [Onderzoeksmemorandum.]
67 Testing dynamic specification of factor demand equations for U.S. manufacturing. Jane Friesen. *Rev. Econ. St.* **LXXIV:2** 5:1992 pp. 240 – 250
68 Trade within an industry in the presence of vertical product differentiation and dynamic increasing returns. F. Pigliaru. *Open Econ. R.* **3:2** 1992 pp. 165 – 180
69 A transatlantic comparison of enterprise zone impacts — the British and American experience. Barry M. Rubin; Craig M. Richards. *Econ. Devel. Q.* **6:4** 11:1992 pp. 431 – 443
70 'Twixt cup and lip — organizational behaviour, technical prediction and conservation practice. Peter B. Cebon. *Energy Pol.* **20:9** 9:1992 pp. 802 – 814
71 Umsatz- oder Gewinnmaximierung? Optimale Anreizsysteme im Oligopol *[In German]*; [Sales or profit maximization? Optimal incentive schemes in oligopoly]. Brigitte Adolph. *Z. Wirt. Soz.* **112:3** 1992 pp. 401 – 418
72 Univariate methods for the analysis of the industrial sector in Spain; *[Spanish summary]*. Eduardo Morales; Antoni Espasa; María Luisa Rojo. *Invest. Econ.* **XVI:1** 1:1992 pp. 127 – 150
73 Unobservable industry characteristics and the innovation-concentration-advertising-maze — evidence from an econometric study using panel data for manufacturing industries in the FRG, 1979-1986. Joachim Wagner; J.-Matthias Graf von der Schulenburg. *Small Bus. Econ.* **4:4** 12:1992 pp. 315 – 326

H.2.1: Industrial economics *[Économie industrielle]*

74 Was Latin America too rich to prosper? Structural and political obstacles to export-led industrial growth. James E. Mahon. *J. Dev. Stud.* **28:2** 1:1992 pp. 241 – 263

75 West African industry and the debt crisis. K.P. Moseley. *J. Int. Dev.* **4:1** 1-2:1992 pp. 1 – 28

Industrial management *[Gestion industrielle]*

76 The behavior of worker cooperatives — the plywood companies of the Pacific northwest. Ben Craig; John Pencavel. *Am. Econ. Rev.* **82:5** 12:1992 pp. 1083 – 1105

77 Competition policy vs horizontal merger with public, entrepreneurial, and labor-managed firms. Flavio Delbono; Gianpaolo Rossini. *J. Comp. Econ.* **16:2** 6:1992 pp. 226 – 240

78 Costs of adjustment, the aggregation problem and investment. Gordon Stephen. *Rev. Econ. St.* **LXXIV:3** 8:1992 pp. 422 – 429

79 Deficits in Chinese industrial enterprises (I). Investigative Group on Enterprise Losses *[Contrib.]*; Minshan Zhao *[Contrib.]*; Lie Wen *[Contrib.]*; Heng Liu *[Contrib.]*; Guiliang Jing *[Contrib.]*; Qun Song *[Contrib.]*; Zhiming Lian *[Contrib.]*; Dongjiang Wang *[Contrib.]*; Guorong Lu *[Contrib.]*. *Collection of 3 articles*. **Chin. Ec. Stud.** , *26:1*, Fall: 1992 pp. 6 – 87

80 Enterprise management in the USSR — is there a productivity drive? Bruno Grancelli. *Labour [Italy]* **6:2** Autumn:1992 pp. 145 – 169

81 European industrial restructuring in the 1990s. Karen Cool *[Ed.]*; Damien J. Neven *[Ed.]*; Ingo Walter *[Ed.]*. London: Macmillan Academic and Professional, 1992: 256 p. *ISBN: 0333559061.*

82 Externes Unternehmenswachstum une externe Kontrolle *[In German]*; External growth of firms and external control *[Summary]*. Peter Liepmann. *Jahrb. N. St.* **210:1-2** 7:1992 pp. 1 – 17

83 Industrial networks — a new view of reality. Bjorn Axelsson *[Ed.]*; Geoff Easton *[Ed.]*. London: Routledge, 1992: 265 p. *ISBN: 0415025796; LofC: 91000596. Includes bibliographical references and index.*

84 Japanese targeting — successes, failure, lessons. Jon Woronoff. London: Macmillan, 1992: 286 p. *ISBN: 0333558669.*

85 Japanization at work — managerial studies for the 1990s. John Bratton; Huw Beynon *[Foreword]*. Basingstoke: Macmillan Press, 1992: 224 p. *ISBN: 0333545745.*

86 Labor-managed cooperatives and private firms in north central Italy — an empirical comparison. Will Bartlett; John Cable; Saul Estrin; Derek C. Jones; Stephen C. Smith. *Ind. Lab. Rel.* **46:1** 10:1992 pp. 103 – 118

87 Liquidation values and debt capacity — a market equilibrium approach. Andrei Shleifer; Robert W. Vishny. *J. Finance* **47:4** 9:1992 pp. 1343 – 1366

88 Lohnstückkostenposition der Industrie 1991 verbessert *[In German]*; Improvement in industrial labour cost position *[Summary]*. Alois Guger. *Monatsberichte* **7:65** 1992 pp. 381 – 386

89 Managing organisations in 1992 — strategic responses. Peter Barrar *[Ed.]*; Cary L. Cooper *[Ed.]*. London: Routledge, 1992: 308 p. *ISBN: 041506662x; LofC: 91021541. Based on papers presented at the third national conference of the British Academy of Management, held Sept. 1989 at Manchester Business School; Includes bibliographical references and index.*

90 Modern corporations and private property. Murray Weidenbaum; Mark Jensen. *Society* **30:1(201)** 11/12:1992 pp. 101 – 106

91 Multiproduct firms — a nested logit approach. Simon P. Anderson; André de Palma. *J. Ind. Econ.* **XL:3** 9:1992 pp. 261 – 276

92 Relative performance evaluation of management — the effects on industrial competition and risk sharing. V. Salas Fumas. *Int. J. Ind. O.* **10:3** 9:1992 pp. 473 – 489

93 A revelation scheme for allocating organizational resources. P.C. Brown; D.M. Buede; J.B. Miller; J.R. Thornton. *J. Econ. Beh.* **18:2** 7:1992 pp. 201 – 214

94 Technology expenditures, factor intensity, and efficiency in Indian manufacturing. Michael J. Ferrantino. *Rev. Econ. St.* **LXXIV:4** 11:1992 pp. 689 – 700

95 Twilight of the Keiretsu? A critical assessment. Michael L. Gerlach. *J. Jpn. Stud.* **18:1** Winter:1992 pp. 79 – 118

H.2.1: Industrial economics *[Économie industrielle]* —

Industrial policy *[Politique industrielle]*

96 Australian industry — what policy? Michael Costa *[Ed.]*; Michael Easson. Leichhardt, NSW: Pluto Press Australia, 1991: 414 p. (ill) *ISBN: 0949138738. Includes bibliographical references and index.*

97 Bestimmungsfaktoren des Wirtschaftswachstums in erfolgreichen Entwicklungsländern — Eine Fallstudie für Südkorea *[In German]*; [Determining factors of economic growth in successful developing countries — the case of South Korea] *[Summary]*. J. Jerger; M. Piazolo. *Ifo-Stud.* **38:1** 1992 pp. 1 – 26

98 Competition policy vs horizontal merger with public, entrepreneurial, and labor-managed firms. Flavio Delbono; Gianpaolo Rossini. *J. Comp. Econ.* **16:2** 6:1992 pp. 226 – 240

99 Competition, cooperation, and innovation — organizational arrangements for regimes of rapid technological progress. D.J. Teece. *J. Econ. Beh.* **18:1** 6:1992 pp. 1 – 25

100 Constraints on and support for industrial policy liberalization in India. Richard Heeks. *Dev. Pol. R.* **10:1** 3:1992 pp. 15 – 34

101 Eine gezielte Förderung von Schlüsselbranchen für Europa? *[In German]*; [Industrial policies targeted at key European sectors?]. Dietmar Keller. *Wirtschaftsdienst* **72:4** 4:1992 pp. 183 – 189

102 Industrial de-diversification and its consequences for productivity. F.R. Lichtenberg. *J. Econ. Beh.* **18:3** 8:1992 pp. 427 – 438

103 Industrial policy of the European Community — strategic deficits and regional dilemmas. D. Sadler. *Envir. Plan.A.* **24:12** 12:1992 pp. 1711 – 1730

104 Industrial sub-contracting — the Tunisian case. Jean Masini. *Econ. Papers [Warsaw]* **18** 1992 pp. 111 – 126

105 Der industrielle Sektor als Motor der Wohlstandsentwicklung *[In German]*; [Manufacturing as the engine behind wealth creation]. Gerhard Huemer. *Wirt. Blät.* **39:1** 1992 pp. 130 – 138

106 Industrielle Umstrukturierung in Polen. Gegenwärtiger Stand, reformpolitische Optionen *[In German]*; *[French summary]*; Industrial restructuring in Poland *[Summary]*. Klaus Grimm. *Vierteljahresberichte* **:130** 12:1992 pp. 351 – 371

107 Industrijska politika u ekonomiji tranzicije *[In Serbo-Croatian]*; Industrial policy in economies in transition *[Summary]*; *[Russian summary]*. Mato Crkvenac. *Ekon. Preg.* **43:1-2** 1992 pp. 17 – 29

108 Industry linkages, indices of variation and structure of production — an international comparison. Abdol Soofi. *Econ. Sys. Res.* **4:4** 1992 pp. 349 – 376

109 Limites de l'approche de la dominance dans un modèle input-output *[In French]*; Structure and dominance in a productive apparatus interest and limits of an approach based on the input-output model *[Summary]*; (Grenzen der Dominanzbehandlung in einem Input-Output Modell: *Title only in German*); (Límite del enfoque del dominio en un modelo de insumo-producto: *Title only in Spanish*). Bernard Lejeune. *Econ. App.* **XLV:2** 7:1992 pp. 105 – 127

110 Making it — a federal approach to industrial policy. Irene Brunskill. London: Institute for Public Policy Research, 1992: 78 p. *ISBN: 1872452507.*

111 Österreichische Industrie- und Technologiepolitik *[In German]*; [Austrian industrial and technology policy]. Wilhelmine Goldmann. *Wirt. Blät.* **39:4** 1992 pp. 461 – 468

112 Price inertia and production lags. Assar Lindbeck; Dennis J. Snower. New York: Columbia University, Dept of Economics, [1992?]: 24 p. [Discussion paper series.]

113 Quadratic spline models for producer's supply and demand functions. W.E. Diewert; T.J. Wales. *Int. Econ. R.* **33:3** 8:1992 pp. 705 – 722

114 Reflections on the nature and role of industrial policy. Malcom C. Sawyser. *Metroeconomica* **XLIII:1-2** 2-6:1992 pp. 51 – 71

115 Structural adjustment policies and productive efficiency of socialist enterprises. J. Prasnikar; J. Svejnar; M. Klinedinst. *Eur. Econ. R.* **36:1** 1:1992 pp. 179 – 200

116 Technologiepolitik, Industriepolitik und Wettbewerbsfähigkeit *[In German]*; [Technology policy, industrial policy and competitiveness]. Gunther Tichy. *Wirt. Blät.* **39:4** 1992 pp. 408 – 415

117 Trends of innovation in the world pharmaceutical industry. L.G. Thomas. *Riv. Int. Sci. Soc.* **C:3** 7-9:1992 pp. 333 – 345

118 Wages, unions, insiders and product market power. Stephen Nickell; J. Vainiomaki; Sushil B. Wadhwani. London: London School of Economics and Political Science. Centre for Economic Performance, 1992: 35 p. [Discussion paper.]

H.2.1: Industrial economics *[Économie industrielle]* — *Industrial policy [Politique industrielle]*

119 Zu einer verfügungsrechtsorientierten Strukturpolitik *[In German]*; [On a power-of-disposition oriented structural policy]. Christian Bellak. *Wirt. Blät.* **39:3** 1992 pp. 369 – 383

Industrial productivity *[Productivité industrielle]*

120 Assessing gains in efficient production among China's industrial enterprises. Gary H. Jefferson; Wenyi Xu. Washington, D.C.: Country Economics Department, The World Bank, 1992: 21 p. [Policy research working papers.]

121 Bundesrepublik Deutschland — Produktion stagniert *[In German]*; Federal Republic of Germany — production stagnates *[Summary]*. Alfred Boss; Malte Fischer; Enno Langfeldt; Klaus-Werner Schatz; Peter Trapp. *Weltwirt.* **:3** 1992 pp. 244 – 262

122 Charting strategic roles for international factories. K. Ferdows. *Inter. R. Strat. Manag.* **3** 1992 pp. 149 – 166

123 China's industrial performance since 1978. Robert Michael Field. *China Quart.* **:131** 9:1992 pp. 577 – 607

124 The economics of industrial modernization. Cristiano Antonelli; Pascal Petit; Gabriel Tahar. London: Academic Press, 1992: 224 p. *ISBN: 012059630x.*

125 Industry's response to market liberalization in China — evidence from Jiangsu Province. Penelope B. Prime. *Econ. Dev. Cult. Change* **41:1** 10:1992 pp. 27 – 50

126 Productivity dynamics in manufacturing plants. Martin Neil Baily; Charles Hulten; David Campbell. *Brookings P.* 1992 pp. 187 – 267

127 Productivity in manufacturing industries, Canada, Japan and the United States, 1953-1986 — was the "productivity slowdown" reversed?; Productivité dans les industries manufacturières, Canada, Japon, Etats-Unis, 1953-1986 — est-ce que le ralentissement de la productivité est une tendance qu'on a renversée? *[French summary]*. M. Denny; J. Bernstein; M. Fuss; S. Nakamura; L. Waverman. *Can. J. Econ.* **XXV:3** 8:1992 pp. 584 – 603

H.2.2: Industrial production — *Production industrielle*

Sub-divisions: Automobile industry *[Industrie automobile]*; Energy industry *[Industrie énergétique]*; Iron and steel industry *[Industrie sidérurgique]*; Mining *[Industrie minière]*; Oil industry *[Industrie pétrolière]*

1 Agents of change in the internationalization of the petrochemical industry. K. Chapman. *Geoforum* **23:1** 1992 pp. 13 – 28

2 Ajustamento energético dos anos 80 — a experiência da indústria cimenteira brasileira *[In Polish]*; [Energy adjustment in the 1980s — the experience of the Brazilian cement industry] *[Summary]*. Maria Cristina Pereira de Melo. *Rev. Bras. Ec.* **46:2** 4-6:1992 pp. 185 – 210

3 Amid the ruins, arms makers raise new threats. Christopher Smart. *Orbis* **36:3** Summer:1992 pp. 349 – 364

4 Antwerpen en de Belgische diamantnijverheid — een industrieel-economische benadering *[In Flemish]*; Antwerp and the Belgian diamond industry — an industrial economic approach *[Summary]*. Bart Orgaer. *Econ. Soc. Tidj.* **46:3** 9:1992 pp. 455 – 476

5 The Australian clothing industry — competition, productivity and scale. Bing Qing Zhang; Michael Webber. *Aust. Geogr.* **23:1** 5:1992 pp. 50 – 65

6 Australia's sectoral trade — manufacturing's performance declined? Bob Conlon. *Ec. Pap. Aust.* **11:1** 3:1992 pp. 32 – 41

7 Biotechnology and the political sociology of risk. E.J. Woodhouse. *Ind. Crisis Q.* **6:1** 1992 pp. 39 – 54

8 The British pottery industry — a comment on a case of industrial restructuring, labour, and locality. C. Rowley. *Envir. Plan.A.* **24:11** 11:1992 pp. 1645 – 1650

9 Città e industria tessile — il caso Prato *[In Italian]*; [City and textile industry. The case of Prato]. Marina Faccioli. Milano: Angeli, 1991: 142 p. *ISBN: 8820470268.* [Scienze geografiche. : No. 1]

10 Comparación de la industria de cómputo en Corea del Sur, México y Brasil — el papel del Estado *[In Spanish]*; [A comparison of the computer industry in South Korea, Mexico and Brazil — the role of the state]. Arturo Borja. *Foro Int.* **XXXII:3** 1-3:1992 pp. 396 – 418

H.2.2: Industrial production *[Production industrielle]*

11 The conversion of the arms industry of the Russian Federation; *[German summary]*. Michael Checinski. *Ost. Wirt.* **37:4** 12:1992 pp. 331 – 352

12 Corporate strategy, location of investments and competitiveness — the case of Trelleborg/Boliden. Bengt Löfkvist; Mati Sallert. *Res. Pol.* **18:4** 12:1992 pp. 283 – 292

13 The Cypriot clothing industry. Prodromos Panayiotopoulos. *Cyprus Rev.* **4:1** Spring:1992 pp. 77 – 123

14 Department of Defense profit policy and capital investment in the military aircraft industry. Thomas P. Frazier; Matthew S. Goldberg; Thomas R. Gulledge. *Rev. Econ. St.* **LXXIV:3** 8:1992 pp. 394 – 403

15 The drug lag issue — the debate seen from an international perspective. Frederik Andersson. *Int. J. Health. Ser.* **22:1** 1992 pp. 53 – 72

16 Economía de red y reestructuración del sector agroalimentario *[In Spanish]*; [The economic system and restructuring in the agro-food sector]. Raúl H. Green; Rosell Rocha dos Santos. *Desar. Econ.* **32:126** 7-8:1992 pp. 199 – 225

17 The economics of intellectual property in a world without frontiers — a study of computer software. Meheroo Jussawalla. New York: Greenwood Press, 1992: 158 p. *ISBN: 031327620x; LofC: 91028155. Includes bibliographical references (p. [137]-141) and index.* [Contributions in economics and economic history.]

18 The effects of 1992 on the pharmaceuticals industry in Britain and Germany. P.E. Hart. London: National Institute of Economic and Social Research, 1992: 30 p. [Discussion paper.]

19 The effects of contractual restrictions on industrial organization — the case of Swedish pulpwood transactions. Per-Olof Bjuggren. *Int. R. Law Econ.* **12:4** 12:1992 pp. 517 – 532

20 The end of Brazil's informatics policy. Jörg Meyer-Stamer. *Sci. Pub. Pol.* **19:2** 4:1992 pp. 99 – 110

21 Evidências empíricas para os condicionantes externos e internos do crescimento das empresas de Calçados do Vale do Sinos *[In Portuguese]*; [Empirical evidence for the external and internal conditions for the growth of the shoe industry in Vale de Sinos]. André Maurício dos Santos. *Persp. Econ.* **27:76** 1-3:1992 pp. 33 – 50

22 An examination of the impact of pollution performance on economic and market performance — pulp and paper firms. Bikki Jaggi; Martin Freedman. *J. Bus. Fin. Acc.* **19:5** 9:1992 pp. 697 – 714

23 Foreign manufacturing investments in resource-based industries — comparisons between Malaysia and Thailand. Mohd. Ismail Ahmad. Singapore: Institute of Southeast Asian Studies, 1990: viii, 82 p. (ill) *ISBN: 9813035692; LofC: 91942425. Includes bibliographical references (p.[81]-82).* [Research notes and discussions paper.]

24 From central planning to market systems — implications of economic reforms for the construction and building industries. David E. Dowall. *Hous. Pol. Deb.* **3:4** 1992 pp. 977 – 994

25 Hurrying through a window of opportunity — the rapid expansion of the pulp and paper industry in Alberta. N.R. Seifried. *Geoforum* **23:4** 1992 pp. 453 – 465

26 Incertezza, differenziazone del prodotto e integrazione verticale — un'analisi dell'industria dei personal computer *[In Italian]*; [Uncertainty, product differentiation and vertical integration. An analysis of personal computer industry *[Summary]*. Alfredo del Monte; Renato Passaro. *Industria* **XIII:4** 10-12:1992 pp. 649 – 683

27 India and the computer — a study of planned development. C. R. Subramanian. Delhi (India): Oxford University Press, 1992: xix, 383 p. *ISBN: 0195627350. Includes bibliographical references (p.[369]-371) and indexes.*

28 The industrial complex revisited — petrochemicals in Taiwan. D. Todd; Y. Hsueh. *Geoforum* **23:1** 1992 pp. 29 – 40

29 Input substitution, economies of scale and productivity growth in the US upholstered furniture industry. B.J. Seldon; S.H. Bullard. *Appl. Econ.* **24:9** 9:1992 pp. 1017 – 1026

30 Internationalization of Turkish construction companies — a lesson for Third World countries? Erdener Kaynak; Tevfik Dalgic. *Columb. J. W. Bus.* **XXVI:4** Winter:1992 pp. 60 – 75

31 Kapitalavkastningsraten i norsk industri. En komparativ studie *[In Norwegian]*; The profitability trend in the Norwegian manufacturing industry. A comparative study *[Summary]*. Anders Skonhoft. *Nor. Økon. Tidss.* **106:1** 1992 pp. 41 – 67

32 The material composition of product and new materials. Mark C. Roberts. *Res. Pol.* **18:2** 6:1992 pp. 122 – 136

33 The metal mining industry in Eastern Europe — its difficult reconversion and future impact on world markets. Olivier Bomsel; Christian von Hirschhausen. *Nat. Res. For.* **16:4** 11:1992 pp. 250 – 260

H.2.2: Industrial production *[Production industrielle]*

34 A micro-econometric model of capital utilization and retirement — the case of the US cement industry. Sanghamitra Das. *R. Econ. S.* **59:2(199)** 4:1992 pp. 277 – 298

35 Mineral sector technologies — policy implications for developing countries. Craig B. Andrews. *Nat. Res. For.* **16:3** 8:1992 pp. 212 – 220

36 Modern merchants of death. Tim Hewat. North Brighton: Wrightbooks, 1991: 167 p. *ISBN: 0947351361.*

37 Obstacles to "catch-up" — the case of the Indonesian aircraft industry. David McKendrick. *B. Ind. Econ. St.* **28:1** 4:1992 pp. 39 – 66

38 Perspectivas de la construcción en la década de los noventa *[In Spanish]*; [Perspectives on the construction industry in the nineties]. José Carreras Yáñez. *Pap. Econ. Esp.* **50** 1992 pp. 210 – 237

39 Price margins and capital adjustment — Canadian mill products and pulp and paper industries. J.I. Bernstein. *Int. J. Ind. O.* **10:3** 9:1992 pp. 491 – 510

40 Prices, quality, and trust — inter-firm relations in Britain and Japan. Mari Sako. Cambridge: Cambridge University Press, 1992: 270 p. *ISBN: 0521413869; LofC: 91040505. Includes bibliographical references and index.* [Cambridge studies in management. : No. 18]

41 Privatization and innovation in the pharmaceutical industry in a post-socialist economy. K. György; J. Vincze. *Riv. Int. Sci. Soc.* **C:3** 7-9:1992 pp. 403 – 417

42 Productivity levels in British and German manufacturing industry. Mary O'Mahony. *Natl. Inst. Econ. R.* **139** 2:1992 pp. 46 – 63

43 Produtividade de P&D no sector de informática — uma análise comparativa entre Brasil e EUA na década de 80 *[In Portuguese]*; [Research and development productivity in the computer sector — a comparative analysis of Brazil and the U.S.A. in the 1980s] *[Summary]*. Renata Vieira; Luiz Vieira. *Rev. Bras. Ec.* **46:2** 4-6:1992 pp. 241 – 260

44 Regional economic development strategies and the electronics industry. A.C. Pratt *[Contrib.]*; P. Totterdill *[Contrib.]*; M. Dunford *[Contrib.]*; D. Perrons *[Contrib.]*; J. Morris *[Contrib.]*; J. McCalman *[Contrib.]*; I. Brunskill *[Contrib.]*. *Collection of 5 articles.* **Envir. Plan. C.** , *10:4*, 11:1992 pp. 375 – 450

45 The regional extent of computer numerically controlled (CNC) machine tool adoption and post adoption success in small British mechanical engineering firms. R.P. Oakey; P.N. O'Farrell. *Reg. Stud.* **26:2** 1992 pp. 163 – 174

46 Regional variations in the adoption of computer-numerically-controlled machine tools by small engineering firms — a multivariate analysis. P.N. O'Farrell; R.P. Oakey. *Envir. Plan.A.* **24:6** 6:1992 pp. 887 – 902

47 Répondre à l'incertitude par la flexibilité. Le cas de 18 entreprises de la filière textile habillement *[In French]*; Answer to the uncertainty by the flexibility. The case of eighteen firms of the textile and clothes industry *[Summary]*. Jean-Luc Syssau. *Gestion* **8:4** 1992 pp. 11 – 28

48 El sector servicios *[In Spanish]*; [The service industry]. Juan R. Cuadrado Roura. *Pap. Econ. Esp.* **50** 1992 pp. 258 – 294

49 Segmented labour in the construction industry — a study of housing development in Bandung, Indonesia; *[French summary]*. Tommy Firman. *Labour Cap. Soc.* **24:2** 11:1991 pp. 184 – 206

50 Space pharmaceuticals — will the United States fumble another high technology industry? John F. Kohler. *J. Air Law Comm.* **58:2** Winter:1992 pp. 511 – 554

51 The state, the market, and competitive strategy — the housebuilding industry in the United Kingdom, France, Sweden. J. Barlow; A. King. *Envir. Plan.A.* **24:3** 3:1992 pp. 381 – 400

52 Structural adjustment and the Japanese textile industry — a production theory approach. T.A. Park; D. Pick. *Appl. Econ.* **24:4** 4:1992 pp. 437 – 444

53 Studies in international competition in semiconductors. Clement G. Krouse *[Contrib.]*; M. Therese Flaherty *[Contrib.]*; Kenneth Flamm *[Contrib.]*; W. Edward Steinmueller *[Contrib.]*. *Collection of 4 articles.* **R. Indust. Organ.** , *7:3/4,* 1992 pp. 267 – 349

54 Technological change in the Italian pharmaceutical industry. G.M. Gros-Pietro. *Riv. Int. Sci. Soc.* **C:3** 7-9:1992 pp. 319 – 332

55 Tipologie aziendali dell'artigianto manifatturiero — alcune evidenze empiriche *[In Italian]*; Typologies of manufacturing handicraft enterprises — some empirical results *[Summary]*. Sergio Brasini. *Industria* **XIII:3** 7-9:1992 pp. 455 – 471

56 The Tylenol incident, ensuing regulation, and stock prices. Thomas D. Dowdell; Suresh Govindaraj; Prem C. Jain. *J. Fin. Qu. An.* **27:2** 6:1992 pp. 283 – 302

57 Understanding the efficiency of multi-server service systems. Ward Whitt. *Manag. Sci.* **38:5** 5:1992 pp. 708 – 723

H.2.2: Industrial production *[Production industrielle]*

58 Unions and the inter-establishment adoption of new microelectronic technologies in the British private manufacturing sector. Paul L. Latreille. *Ox. B. Econ. S.* **54:1** 2:1992 pp. 31 – 51

59 What will EC membership mean for Finland's metal and engineering industries? Timo Airaksinen. *Econ. Rev.* **:1** 1992 pp. 4 – 12

Automobile industry *[Industrie automobile]*

60 L'automobile, les défis et les hommes — rapport du groupe de stratégie industrielle "automobile" *[In French]*; [Cars, challenges and people — a report by the group on "automobile industrial strategy"]. Gilbert Rutman *[Ed.]*; Daniel Bachet; et al. Paris: La documentation française, 1992: 376 p. *ISBN: 2110027762. Bibliography — p99-100.*

61 Beyond "1992" — the evolution of European Community policies towards the automobile industry. D. Sadler. *Envir. Plan. C.* **10:2** 5:1992 pp. 229 – 248

62 Das BMW-Mercedes-Duell *[In German]*; [The BMW-Mercedes duel]. Walter Junginger. Düsseldorf: ECON-Verl., 1991: 287 p. *ISBN: 3430151384.*

63 Building cars as if people mattered — the Japanese lean system vs. Volvo's Uddevalla system. Robert R. Rehder. *Columb. J. W. Bus.* **XXVII:2** Summer:1992 pp. 56 – 71

64 The changing US auto industry — a geographical analysis. James M. Rubenstein. London: Routledge, 1992: 318 p. *ISBN: 041505544x. Includes bibliography and index.*

65 Costs and productivity in automobile production — the challenge of Japanese efficiency. Melvyn Fuss; Leonard Waverman. Cambridge: Cambridge University Press, 1992: xii, 241 p. *ISBN: 0521341418; LofC: 91018785. Includes bibliographical references (p. 233-236) and index.*

66 The division of labour and industrial diversity — flexibility and mass production in the French automobile industry. Michael Storper; Robert Salais. *Int. R. Applied Ec.* **6:1** 1992 pp. 1 – 37

67 L'Europe sur l'échiquier du Japon — le cas des industries électronique et automobile *[In French]*; [Japanese production facilities in Europe — the case of electronic and automotive industry *[Summary]*. Evelyne Dourille-Feer. *Ec. Pros. Int.* **49:1** 1992 pp. 77 – 102

68 Foreign passenger car ventures and Chinese decision-making. Eric Harwit. *Aust. J. Chin. Aff.* **:28** 7:1992 pp. 141 – 166

69 The future of four wheels — government and the automobile industry in France and West Germany. Carl Cavanagh Hodge. **Governance** *Vol.4; No.1 - 1: 1991.* pp. 42 – 66

70 Just-in-time manufacturing and the spatial structure of the automobile industry — lessons from Japan. Andrew Mair. *J. Econ. Soc. Geogr.* **83:2** 1992 pp. 82 – 92

71 New procurement regimes and the spatial distribution of suppliers — the case of Ford in Europe. Peter Wells; Michael Rawlinson. *Area* **24:4** 12:1992 pp. 380 – 390

72 Procyclical labour productivity, increasing returns to labour and labour hoarding in car assembly plant employment. A.M. Aizcorbe. *Econ. J.* **102:413** 7:1992 pp. 860 – 873

73 Productivity and skills in vehicle component manufacturers in Britain, Germany, the USA and Japan. Christopher Carr. *Natl. Inst. Econ. R.* **139** 2:1992 pp. 79 – 87

74 Ramiz Sadiku — a case study in the industrialisation of Kosovo. Michael Palairet. *Eur.-Asia Stud.* **44:5** 1992 pp. 897 – 912

75 The restructuring of the automobile industry in the USA. R.D. Bingham; K.K. Sunmonu. *Envir. Plan.A.* **24:6** 6:1992 pp. 833 – 852

76 Risk absorption in Japanese subcontracting — a microeconometric study of the automobile industry. Banri Asanuma; Tatsuya Kikutani. *J. Jap. Int. Ec.* **6:1** 3:1992 pp. 1 – 29

77 Strategische Handels- und Industriepolitik in der Automobilindustrie? *[In German]*; [Strategic trade and industrial policy in the automobile industry?]. Georg Bletschacher. *Weltwirt.* **:1** 1992 pp. 68 – 84

78 US-Mexico free trade and the North American auto industry — effects on the spatial organisation of production of finished autos. Linda Hunter; James R. Markusen; Thomas F. Rutherford. *World. Econ.* **15:1** 1:1992 pp. 65 – 82

Energy industry *[Industrie énergétique]*

79 El acuerdo de libre comercio entre Canadá y Estados Unidos — factores que afectan el comercio de energía *[In Spanish]*; [The free trade agreement between Canada and the US— factors affecting energy markets]. Michel Duquette. *Foro Int.* **XXXII:3** 1-3:1992 pp. 301 – 322

80 Alternative energy in the Third World — a reappraisal of subsidies. A.V. Desai. *World Dev.* **20:7** 7:1992 pp. 959 – 965

H.2.2: Industrial production *[Production industrielle]* — *Energy industry [Industrie énergétique]*

81 Australia's North-West Shelf Gas Project — a general equilibrium analysis of its impact on the Australian economy. Peter J. Higgs; Alan A. Powell. *Res. Pol.* **18:3** 9:1992 pp. 179 – 190

82 Biomass energy — lessons from case studies in developing countries. D.O. Hall; F. Rosillo-Calle; P. de Groot. *Energy Pol.* **20:1** 1:1992 pp. 62 – 73

83 A biophysical analysis of the energy/real GDP ratio — implications for substitution and technical change. R.K. Kaufmann. *Ecol. Eco.* **6:1** 7:1992 pp. 35 – 56

84 Byproduct uranium. A.D. Owen. *Res. Pol.* **18:2** 6:1992 pp. 137 – 147

85 China's dual-thrust energy strategy — economic development and environmental protection. Qu Geping. *Nat. Res. For.* **16:1** 2:1992 pp. 27 – 32

86 China's energy system — historical evolution, current issues, and prospects. Mark D. Levine; Feng Liu; Jonathan E. Sinton. *Ann. R. Energy Environ.* **17** 1992 pp. 405 – 436

87 Clean cheap heat — the development of residential markets for natural gas in the United States. John H. Herbert. New York: Praeger, 1992: x, 190 p. *ISBN: 027594204x; LofC: 91035784 //r92. Includes bibliographical references (p. 183-184) and index.*

88 Commercial wind power — recent experience in the United States. Gerald W. Braun; Don R. Smith. *Ann. R. Energy Environ.* **17** 1992 pp. 97 – 122

89 A comparison of models for forecasting the discovery of hydrocarbon deposits. M. Power; J.D. Fuller. *J. Forecast.* **11:3** 4:1992 pp. 183 – 194

90 Competition in the British electricity spot market. Richard J. Green; David M. Newbery. *J. Polit. Ec.* **110:5** 10:1992 pp. 929 – 953

91 Competition, trading, and the reliability of electric power service. Alan T. Crane; Robin Roy. *Ann. R. Energy Environ.* **17** 1992 pp. 161 – 186

92 The cost of electric power interruptions in the industrial sector — estimates derived from interruptible service programs. Douglas W. Caves; Joseph A. Herriges; Robert J. Windle. *Land Econ.* **68:1** 2:1992 pp. 49 – 61

93 Development and production prospects for UK oil and gas post-Gulf crisis — a financial simulation. Alexander G. Kemp; David Rose; Russell Dandie. *Energy Pol.* **20:1** 1:1992 pp. 20 – 29

94 Le développement du gaz naturel — enjeux pour l'Europe *[In French]*; [The development of natural gas — what's at stake for Europe]. J.-M. Chevalier *[Contrib.]*; M. Valais *[Contrib.]*; P.-N. Giraud *[Contrib.]*; R. Lassiaille *[Contrib.]*; C. Bernardet *[Contrib.]*; J.-P. Jonchère *[Contrib.]*; I. Cadoret *[Contrib.]*; L.-M. Gaudemet *[Contrib.]*; G. Renesme *[Contrib.]*; J.-C. Hourcade *[Contrib.] and others. Collection of 15 articles.* **Ec. Sociét.** , *XXVI:1-2,* 1-2:1992 pp. 5 – 336

95 Electricity economics and planning. T. W. Berrie. London: P. Peregrinus, 1992: 276 p. *ISBN: 0863412823.* [IEE power series. : No. 16]

96 Electricity transmission pricing — the new approach. Sally Hunt; Graham Shuttleworth. *Util. Policy* **3:2** 4:1992 pp. 98 – 111

97 Elusive links — energy, value, economic growth and quality of life. Vaclav Smil. *OPEC Rev.* **XVI:1** Spring:1992 pp. 1 – 21

98 Emerging energy technologies — impacts and policy implications. Michael Grubb; et al. Aldershot: Dartmouth Publishing Company, 1992: 252 p. *ISBN: 1855211807.* [Energy and environmental programme].

99 Energetyka światowa po kryzysach *[In Polish]*; (The world energy after crises); (Мировая энергетика после кризисов: *Title only in Russian*); (L'énergétique mondiale après les crises: *Title only in French*). Jan Danielewski. *Spr. Między.* **XLV:1-2(455)** 1992 pp. 91 – 104

100 Energy and minerals in the former Soviet republics — distribution, development potential and policy issues. James P. Dorian; Vitaly T. Borisovich. *Res. Pol.* **18:3** 9:1992 pp. 205 – 229

101 Energy and the Third World. Peter Pearson *[Ed.]*; Paul Stevens *[Ed.]*; Mohan Munasinghe *[Contrib.]*; Alexander G. Kemp *[Contrib.]*; Gerald Leach *[Contrib.]*; Frank Rosillo-Calle *[Contrib.]*; David O. Hall *[Contrib.]*; John Soussan *[Contrib.]*; D. Evan Mercer *[Contrib.]*; Phil O'Keefe *[Contrib.] and others. Collection of 8 articles.* **Energy Pol.** , *20:2,* 2:1992 pp. 90 – 171

102 Energy in the long term — mobilization or laissez-faire? Part 1. Paul-Henri Bourrelier; Xavier Boy de la Tour; Jean-Jacques Lacour. *Energy Pol.* **20:3** 3:1992 pp. 192 – 207

103 Energy in the long term — mobilization or laissez-faire? Part 2. Long-term development. Paul-Henri Bourrelier; Xavier Boy de la Tour; Jean-Jacques Lacour. *Energy Pol.* **20:4** 4:1992 pp. 310 – 325

H.2.2: Industrial production *[Production industrielle]* — *Energy industry [Industrie énergétique]*

104 Energy investments and environmental implications — key policy issues in developing countries. Corazon M. Siddayao. *Energy Pol.* **20:3** 3:1992 pp. 223 – 232

105 Energy issues in sub-Saharan Africa — future directions. Ogunlade R. Davidson. *Ann. R. Energy Environ.* **17** 1992 pp. 359 – 404

106 Energy quality and energy surplus in the extraction of fossil fuels in the U.S. C.J. Cleveland. *Ecol. Eco.* **6:2** 10:1992 pp. 139 – 162

107 The energy situation in China. Tatsu Kambara. *China Quart.* :**131** 9:1992 pp. 608 – 636

108 Energy technologies for developing countries — US policies and programs for trade and investment. Samuel F. Baldwin; Sharon Burke; Joy Dunkerley; Paul Komor. *Ann. R. Energy Environ.* **17** 1992 pp. 327 – 358

109 Energy, environment and development. Maurice F. Strong *[Contrib.]*; Ahmed Zaki Yamani *[Contrib.]*; Qu Geping *[Contrib.]*; Robert Goodland *[Contrib.]*; Anastacio Juras *[Contrib.]*; Rajendra Pachauri *[Contrib.]*; C.H. Murray *[Contrib.]*; M.R. de Montalembert *[Contrib.]*; Sanga Sabhasri *[Contrib.]*; Prida Wibulswas *[Contrib.] and others*. Collection of 13 articles. **Energy Pol.** , *20:6,* 6:1992 pp. 490 – 588

110 The European power industry — characteristics and scope for deregulation. Franz Wirl. *OPEC Rev.* **XVI:2** Summer:1992 pp. 137 – 150

111 The financing of electric power projects in developing countries. Andrew Barnett. *Energy Pol.* **20:4** 4:1992 pp. 326 – 334

112 The first 50 years of nuclear power — legacy and lessons — part 1. Steve Thomas *[Ed.]*; Frans Berkhout *[Ed.]*; Michel Damian *[Contrib.]*; James G. Hewlett *[Contrib.]*; Stefan Lindström *[Contrib.]*; John Surrey *[Contrib.]*; Gordon MacKerron *[Contrib.]*; James M. Jasper *[Contrib.]*; Anders Mårtensson *[Contrib.]*; David Fischer *[Contrib.] and others*. Collection of 10 articles. **Energy Pol.** , *20:7,* 7:1992 pp. 594 – 692

113 Global and regional energy supplies — recent fictions and fallacies revisited. Peter R. Odell. *Energy Pol.* **20:4** 4:1992 pp. 284 – 296

114 Global warming and electricity demand — a study of California. Lester W. Baxter; Kevin Calandri. *Energy Pol.* **20:3** 3:1992 pp. 233 – 243

115 Information content of Canadian oil and gas companies' historic cost earnings and reserves disclosures. H.D. Teall. *Cont. Account. Res.* **8:2** Spring:1992 pp. 561 – 579

116 Integrating the power sector in India — reflections and suggestions. Philippe R. Scholtès. *Ener. Econ.* **14:2** 4:1992 pp. 119 – 131

117 Large-scale energy projects in New Zealand — whither social impact assessment? C. Cocklin; B. Kelly. *Geoforum* **23:1** 1992 pp. 41 – 60

118 Modelling peak electricity demand. R.F. Engle; C. Mustafa; J. Rice. *J. Forecast.* **11:3** 4:1992 pp. 241 – 251

119 New local diesel power stations — an economic assessment. Richard J. Wills; Bryan H. Reuben. *Util. Policy* **2:2** 4:1992 pp. 108 – 119

120 Nuclear resources and nationalism — the Brazilian case. Newton Muller Pereira. *Res. Pol.* **18:2** 6:1992 pp. 76 – 83

121 Optimal timing of transmission line investments in the face of uncertain demand — an option valuation approach. Spiros H. Martzoukos; Witold Teplitz-Sembitzky. *Ener. Econ.* **14:1** 1:1992 pp. 3 – 10

122 Optimized evaluation of ageing fossil-fueled power plants. Warren P. McNaughton; Barry Dooley. *Util. Policy* **2:2** 4:1992 pp. 120 – 134

123 Organization of the electric power sector in Mexico. Raúl Monteforte. *Util. Policy* **2:2** 4:1992 pp. 149 – 157

124 Policies for a solar economy. Chris Flavin; Nicholas Lenssen. *Energy Pol.* **20:3** 3:1992 pp. 245 – 256

125 Pricing initiatives and development of the Korean power sector — policy lessons for developing countries. Lawrence J. Hill. *Energy Pol.* **20:4** 4:1992 pp. 344 – 354

126 The process of integrating DSM and supply resources in electric utility planning. Lawrence J. Hill; Eric Hirst; Martin Schweitzer. *Util. Policy* **2:2** 4:1992 pp. 100 – 107

127 Renewables and the privatization of the UK ESI — a case study. David Elliott. *Energy Pol.* **20:3** 3:1992 pp. 257 – 268

128 Sensitivity of reserve margin to factors influencing investment behaviour in the electricity market of England and Wales. Derek W. Bunn; Erik R. Larsen. *Energy Pol.* **20:5** 5:1992 pp. 420 – 429

129 Simultaneous equation estimates of electricity demand for the rural South — revenue projection when prices are administered. J.R. McKean; W.D. Winger. *J. Forecast.* **11:3** 4:1992 pp. 225 – 240

H.2.2: Industrial production *[Production industrielle]* — **Energy industry** *[Industrie énergétique]*

130 Так кто же, собственно собственник? Электроэнергетика в Содружестве Независимых Государств *[In Russian]*; (Power industry in the Commonwealth of Independent States); (Le secteur énergétique de la Communauté des États indépendants: *Title only in French)*; (Elektroenergiewirtschaft in der Gemeinschaft Unabhängiger Staaten: *Title only in German)*; (La electroenergética en la comunidad de Estados independientes: *Title only in Spanish)*. Yu. Koryakin. *Svobod. Mysl'* **:2** 1992 pp. 8 – 16

131 World energy use in the 1970s and 1980s — exploring the changes. Stephen Meyers; Lee Schipper. *Ann. R. Energy Environ.* **17** 1992 pp. 463 – 506

Iron and steel industry *[Industrie sidérurgique]*

132 The decline and rise of the multinational corporation in the metal mineral industry. Marian Radetzki. *Res. Pol.* **18:1** 3:1992 pp. 2 – 8

133 *[In Japanese]*; Estimation of the dynamic factor demand system in the Japanese iron and steel industry *[Summary].Econ. S. Quart.* **43:2** 6:1992 pp. 165 – 176

134 Exit strategies and plant-closing decisions — the case of steel. M.E. Deily. *Rand J. Eco.* **22:2** Summer:1991 pp. 250 – 263

135 Strategic management of Japanese steel manufacturing in the changing international environment. A. Takeuchi. *Inter. R. Strat. Manag.* **3** 1992 pp. 189 – 203

136 Strukturanpassung in der eisenschaffenden Industrie. Markttheoretische Analyse und wirtschaftspolitische Strategien *[In German]*; [Structural adjustment in the iron industry. Market theoretical analysis and politico-economic strategies] *[Summary]*. Fritz Rahmeyer. *Jahr. Soz.schaft.* **43:2** 1992 pp. 243 – 266

Mining *[Industrie minière]*

137 Addictive economies — extractive industries and vulnerable localities in a changing world economy. William R. Freudenburg. *Rural Sociol.* **57:3** Fall:1992 pp. 305 – 332

138 The Bolivian mining crisis. Rolando Jordan; Alyson Warhurst. *Res. Pol.* **18:1** 3:1992 pp. 9 – 20

139 Cost specification and firm behaviour in a hotelling model of resource extraction; *[French summary]*. Denise Young. *Can. J. Econ.* **XXV:1** 2:1992 pp. 41 – 59

140 Determinants of innovation in copper mining — the Chilean experience. Juanita Gana. *Res. Pol.* **18:1** 3:1992 pp. 21 – 31

141 Dynamics of state mining enterprises during the 1980s and the outlook for the 1990s. Magnus Ericsson; Andreas Tegen. *Nat. Res. For.* **16:3** 8:1992 pp. 178 – 191

142 Environmental management in mining and mineral processing in developing countries. Alyson Warhurst. *Nat. Res. For.* **16:1** 2:1992 pp. 39 – 48

143 Financial planning and analysis techniques of mining firms — a note on Canadian practice. Huguette Blanco; Louis R. Zanibbi. *Res. Pol.* **18:2** 6:1992 pp. 84 – 91

144 Government participation in mining projects — fiscal, financial and regulatory implications for developing countries. Gerald Padmore. *Nat. Res. For.* **16:2** 5:1992 pp. 132 – 140

145 Invisible inventories — the case of copper. Marian Radetzki; John E. Tilton. *Res. Pol.* **18:1** 3:1992 pp. 32 – 44

146 Issue networks and the restructuring of the British and west German coal industries in the 1980s. Andrew J. Taylor. *Publ. Admin.* **70:1** Spring:1992 pp. 47 – 66

147 The payoff of developing a small-scale phosphate mine and beneficiating operation in the Mbeya region of Tanzania. W. van Vuuren; J.G. Hamilton. *World Dev.* **20:6** 6:1992 pp. 907 – 918

148 Returns to scale, adjustment costs and the optimal investment of the mining firm. Santiago J. Rubio. *Ener. Econ.* **14:3** 7:1992 pp. 167 – 170

149 South Africa's gold mining crisis — challenges for restructuring. Jean Leger; Martin Nicol. *Transformation* **:20** 1992 pp. 17 – 35

150 Total factor productivity vs. realism — the South African coal mining industry. B. Fine. *S. Afr. J. Econ.* **60:3** 9:1992 pp. 277 – 293

Oil industry *[Industrie pétrolière]*

151 Constraints on the oil industry in the 1990s — the financial dimension. Gerald Pollio. *OPEC Rev.* **XVI:1** Spring:1992 pp. 51 – 69

152 Discretionary disclosure of reserves by oil and gas companies — an economic analysis. A.T. Craswell; S.L. Taylor. *J. Bus. Fin. Acc.* **19:2** 1:1992 pp. 295 – 308

H.2.2: Industrial production *[Production industrielle]* — Oil industry *[Industrie pétrolière]*

153 Economic and fiscal aspects of oil and gas field abandonment — the UK contintental shelf. Alexander G. Kemp. *Energy Pol.* **20:1** 1:1992 pp. 4 – 19

154 Efficiency differences between private and state-owned enterprises in the international petroleum industry. A.M. Al-Obaidan; G.W. Scully. *Appl. Econ.* **24:2** 2:1992 pp. 237 – 246

155 The forecasting accuracy of crude oil futures prices. Manmohan S. Kumar. *Staff Pap. Int. Monetary* **39:2** 6:1992 pp. 432 – 461

156 Information content of Canadian oil and gas companies' historic cost earnings and reserves disclosures. H.D. Teall. *Cont. Account. Res.* **8:2** Spring:1992 pp. 561 – 579

157 The laws of economic rent and property — application to the oil industry. C. Bina. *Am. J. Econ. S.* **51:2** 4:1992 pp. 187 – 203

158 North Sea oil, the UK economy and macroeconomic adjustment — an overview, theoretical and simulation analysis. Charles Harvie. *OPEC Rev.* **XVI:2** Summer:1992 pp. 151 – 184

159 The oil market in the 1980s — a decade of decline. Siamack Shojai *[Ed.]*; Bernard S. Katz *[Ed.]*. New York: Praeger, 1992: xvii, 260 p. *ISBN: 0275933806; LofC: 91037625. Includes bibliographical references (p. [233]-241) and index.*

160 OPEC exploration activity in the 1980s and its implications for the future. I.A.H. Ismail. *OPEC Rev.* **XVI:1** Spring:1992 pp. 37 – 49

161 Perceptions of market efficacy, transaction costs, and vertical disintegration in offshore oil gathering. C. Paul Hallwood. *J. Econ. Stud.* **19:3** 1992 pp. 36 – 49

162 The petroleum industry — entering the 21st century. John Gault *[Ed.]*; Jack Hartshorn *[Ed.]*; Ian Seymour *[Contrib.]*; George Kowalski *[Contrib.]*; H.E. Dr. Subroto *[Contrib.]*; Peter R. Odell *[Contrib.]*; David W. Heal *[Contrib.]*; Jim Skea *[Contrib.]*; Cyrus H. Tahmassebi *[Contrib.]*; Andrew C.E. Hilton *[Contrib.] and others. Collection of 14 articles.* **Energy Pol.** , *20:10*, 10:1992 pp. 906 – 1021

163 Taxation and the optimization of oil exploration and production — the UK continental shelf. Carlo A. Favero. *Ox. Econ. Pap.* **44:2** 4:1992 pp. 187 – 208

H.3: Transportation and communication — *Transports et communications*

Sub-divisions: Air transport *[Transport aérien]*; Railway transport *[Transport ferroviaire]*; Road transport *[Transport routier]*; Sea transport *[Transport maritime]*; Telecommunications *[Télécommunications]*

1 Aggregate expenditure elasticity for transport and communication in Australia. M.O. Haque. *Transportation* **19:1** 2:1992 pp. 43 – 57

2 Appraising large-scale investments in a metropolitan transportation system. C. Anderstig; L.-G. Mattsson. *Transportation* **19:3** 1992 pp. 267 – 283

3 Die BAM — ein Großprojekt der Sowjetwirtschaft vor dem Hintergrund von Perestrojka und der Erstarkung der Republiken *[In German]*; BAM — a mammoth project of the Soviet economy under the auspices of perestroika and reenforcement of the republics *[Summary]*. Sybille Reymann. *Ost. Wirt.* **37:1** 3:1992 pp. 77 – 92

4 A benefit incidence matrix for urban transport improvement. Hisa Morisugi; Eiji Ohno. *Pap. Reg. Sci.* **71:1** 1:1992 pp. 53 – 70

5 Choice and demand in tourism. P.S. Johnson *[Ed.]*; Barry Thomas *[Ed.]*. London: Mansell, 1992: 226 p. *ISBN: 0720121183; LofC: 91028408. Includes bibliographical references and index.*

6 Controlling traffic congestion by regulating car ownership — Singapore's recent experience. Peter Smith. *J. Transp. Ec. Pol.* **XXVI:1** 1:1992 pp. 89 – 96

7 Costs of deficient infrastructure — the case of Nigerian manufacturing. Kyu Sik Lee; Alex Anas. *Urban Stud.* **29:7** 10:1992 pp. 1071 – 1092

8 Culture and tourism — the economics of nostalgia. Gareth Shaw. *Wor. Futur.* **33:1-3** 1992 pp. 199 – 212

9 The Dar es Salaam transport corridor — an appraisal. M.B. Gleave. *Afr. Affairs* **91:363** 4:1992 pp. 249 – 268

10 The economic impact of retirement tourism in Montserrat — some provisional evidence; *[French summary]*; *[Spanish summary]*. Jerome L. McElroy; Klaus de Albuquerque. *Soc. Econ. S.* **41:2** 6:1992 pp. 127 – 152

H.3: Transportation and communication *[Transports et communications]*

11 Energy use in passenger transport in OECD countries — changes since 1970. L. Schipper; R. Steiner; P. Duerr; F. An; S. Strøm. *Transportation* **19:1** 2:1992 pp. 25 – 42

12 Estimation of marginal transport costs — the flow aggregation function approach; La estimación de costes de transporte marginales — el método de la función de agregación de flujos *[Spanish summary]*; Estimation de coûts de transport marginaux — l'approche de la fonction d'agrégation de flux *[French summary]*; Zur Schätzung der Grenzkosten des Transports — Der "Flow Aggregation Function" -Ansatz *[German summary]*. Sergio R. Jara-Díaz; Pedro P. Donoso; Jorge A. Araneda. *J. Transp. Ec. Pol.* **XXVI:1** 1:1992 pp. 35 – 48

13 Evaluating the injury risk associated with all-terrain vehicles — an application of Bayes' rule. Daniel L. Rubinfeld; Gregory B. Rodgers. *J. Risk Uncert.* **5:2** 1992 pp. 145 – 158

14 Hallmark tourist events — impacts, management and planning. Colin Michael Hall. London: Belhaven, 1992: 215 p. *ISBN: 1852931477; LofC: 92028308. Includes bibliographical references and indexes.*

15 Income-generation programmes among Afghan refugees. Margaret Sinclair. *Small Enter. Devel.* **3:3** 9:1992 pp. 17 – 27

16 Infrastructure and private sector investment — the case of Pakistan's transportation and communication sector, 1972-90; Infrastrutture e investimenti nel settore privato — il caso del settore dei trasporti e comunicazioni del Pakistan, 1972- 1990 *[Italian summary]*. Robert E. Looney. *Rev. Int. Sci. Ec. Com.* **XXXIX:9** 9:1992 pp. 771 – 792

17 Japan's "resort archipelago" — creating regions of fun, pleasure, relaxation, and recreation. P.J. Rimmer. *Envir. Plan.A.* **24:11** 11:1992 pp. 1599 – 1625

18 Management science in automating postal operations — facility and equipment planning in the United States postal service. Michael E. Cebry; Anura H. deSilva; Fred J. DiLisio. *Interfaces* **22:1** 1-2:1992 pp. 110 – 130

19 Meinungsfreiheit durch viele Quellen. Nachrichtenagenturen in Deutschland *[In German]*; Freedom of opinion by means of many sources. News agencies in Germany *[Summary]*; Liberté d'opinion et diversité des sources d'information. Agences de presse en Allemagne *[French summary]*; Libertad de la opinión a través de muchas fuentes. Agencias de Prensa en Alemania *[Spanish summary]*. Hansjoachim Höhne. *Publizistik* **37:1** 1-3:1992 pp. 50 – 63

20 Modelling the demand for freight transport — a new approach; La modelización de la demanda de transporte de mercancías — un nuevo método *[Spanish summary]*; Modélisation de la demande pour le transport de fret — une nouvelle approche *[French summary]*; Nachfragemodelle für den Güterverkehr — ein neuer Ansatz *[German summary]*. Walid Abdelwahab; Michel Sargious. *J. Transp. Ec. Pol.* **XXVI:1** 1:1992 pp. 49 – 70

21 Nederland distributieland *[In Dutch]*; [The Netherlands — distribution country]. Gert Jan Koopman. 's-Gravenhage: Centraal Planbureau, 1992: 135 p. *ISBN: 903462921x. Bibliography — p.121-125.* [Onderzoeksmemorandum.]

22 Het nederlandse personenvervoer op lange termijn *[In Dutch]*; [Dutch public transport in a long term perspective]. Gert Jan Koopman. 's-Gravenhage: Centraal Planbureau, 1992: 123 p. *ISBN: 903462918x. Bibliography — p.98-106.* [Onderzoeksmemorandum.]

23 Nutzen des Verkehrs und der verschiedenen Verkehrsmittel *[In German]*; [The benefits of transport and the various means of transport] *[Summary]*. Rainer Willeke. *Z. Verkehr.* **63:3** 1992 pp. 137 – 152

24 Planning and the development of transportation in Bendel State, Nigeria, 1964-1985. J.I. Dibua. *Asian. Afr. Stud.* **25:2** 7:1991 pp. 143 – 160

25 Privatisation in the transport sector — some of the key issues; Privatisieruing in de transportsector *[Flemish summary]*. Kenneth Button. *Econ. Soc. Tidj.* **46:1** 3:1992 pp. 29 – 48

26 Productive efficiency and contract management — some evidence from public transit agencies. David H. Good. *Publ. Fin. Q.* **20:2** 4:1992 pp. 195 – 215

27 Regulation and preemptive technology adoption. M.H. Riordan. *Rand J. Eco.* **23:3** Autumn:1992 pp. 334 – 349

28 Rural tourism and development in Vojvodina — the animation of tourism-cultural relations. Vesna Djukić-Dojčinović. *Wor. Futur.* **33:1-3** 1992 pp. 189 – 197

29 Service quality, market imperfection, and intervention; Qualità dei servizi, imperfezioni del mercato e intervento *[Italian summary]*. Marco Francesconi. *Rev. Int. Sci. Ec. Com.* **XXXIX:2** 2:1992 pp. 107 – 124

H.3: Transportation and communication *[Transports et communications]*

30 Special-interest tourism. Colin Michael Hall *[Ed.]*; Betty Weiler *[Ed.]*. London: Belhaven Press, 1992: 214 p. *ISBN: 1852930721; LofC: 91040465. Includes bibliographical references and index.*

31 Taxing tourism in developing countries. R.M. Bird. *World Dev.* **20:8** 8:1992 pp. 1145 – 1158

32 Tourism and export-led growth — the case of Cyprus, 1976-1988. Michael Kammas; Haideh Salehi-Esfahani. *J. Dev. Areas* **26:4** 7:1992 pp. 489 – 506

33 A transportation-orientated interregional computable general equilibrium model of the United States. P.H. Buckley. *Ann. Reg. Sci.* **26:4** 1992 pp. 331 – 349

34 Uloga prometa i strategija njegovog razvitka *[In Serbo-Croatian]*; Роль транспортаи стратегия его развития *[Russian summary]*; The role of transport and strategy for its development *[Summary]*. Jadranka Bendeković. *Ekon. Preg.* **43:3-4** 1992 pp. 230 – 246

35 Urban transit provision in Ontario — a public/private sector cost comparison. Harry Kitchen. *Publ. Fin. Q.* **20:1** 1:1992 pp. 114 – 128

36 Die Zukunft des Verkehrs im europäischen Binnemarkt *[In German]*; [The future of transport in the single European market]. Peter Cerwenka *[Contrib.]*; Stefan Rommerskirchen *[Contrib.]*; Horst Weigelt *[Contrib.]*; Alexander Eisenkopf *[Contrib.]*; Brigitta Riebemeier *[Contrib.]*; Burkhard Stadlmann *[Contrib.]*; Roderich Regler *[Contrib.]*; Jürgen Erdmenger *[Contrib.]*. Collection of 7 articles. **Wirt. Blät.**, *39:3,* 1992 pp. 294 – 368

Air transport *[Transport aérien]*

37 Air transport in the Asian-Pacific region. Christopher Findlay; Peter Forsyth. *Asian-Pacific Ec. Lit.* **6:2** 11:1992 pp. 1 – 10

38 Airline deregulation and laissez-faire mythology. Paul Stephen Dempsey; Andrew R. Goetz. Westport, Conn: Quorum Books, 1992: xvi, 372 p. (ill) *ISBN: 0899306934; LofC: 91035688. Includes bibliographical references and index.*

39 Airlines, airports and antitrust — a proposed strategy for enchanced competition. Robert M. Hardaway; Paul Stephen Dempsey. *J. Air Law Comm.* **58:2** Winter:1992 pp. 455 – 507

40 The airport business. Rigas Doganis. London: Routledge, 1992: 226 p. *ISBN: 0415078776; LofC: 91044797. Includes bibliographical references and index.*

41 Allocative distortions, technical progress, and input demand in U.S. airlines — 1970-1984. Subal C. Kumbhakar. *Int. Econ. R.* **33:3** 8:1992 pp. 723 – 738

42 Comparability in transport evaluation. Nathaniel Lichfield *[Ed.]*; Malcolm Simpson *[Contrib.]*; William Tyson *[Contrib.]*; Christopher Nash *[Contrib.]*; Richard Smith *[Contrib.]*; Stan Abrahams *[Contrib.]*; K.M. Gwilliam *[Contrib.]*; M.J.P.F. Gommers *[Contrib.]*. Collection of 8 articles. **Proj. App.**, *7:4,* 12:1992 pp. 195 – 248

43 A conflict of interests — the European Commission's proposals for competition in the scheduled airline industry. B.J. Graham. *Area* **24:3** 9:1992 pp. 245 – 252

44 The economics of direct flights; Die Wirtschaftlichkeit von Nonstop-Flügen *[German summary]*; L'économie de vols directs *[French summary]*; El análisis económico de los vuelos directos *[Spanish summary]*. Edwin Fujii; Eric Im; James Mak. *J. Transp. Ec. Pol.* **XXVI:2** 5:1992 pp. 185 – 196

45 Entry and competitive structure in deregulated airline markets — an event study analysis of People Express. M.D. Whinston; S.C. Collins. *Rand J. Eco.* **23:4** Winter:1992 pp. 445 – 462

46 Fare determination in airline hub-and-spoke networks. J.K. Brueckner; N.J. Dyer; P.T. Spiller. *Rand J. Eco.* **23:3** Autumn:1992 pp. 309 – 333

47 Global competition in the commercial aircraft industry — positioning for advantage by the Triad nations. David W. Cravens; H. Kirk Downey; Paul Lauritano. *Columb. J. W. Bus.* **XXVI:4** Winter:1992 pp. 46 – 58

48 Market power and the Northwest-Republic airline merger — a residual demand approach. Phillip Beutal; Mark E. McBride. *S. Econ. J.* **58:3** 1:1992 pp. 709 – 720

49 A model to predict mid-air and near-mid-air collisions. K. Datta; R.M. Oliver. *J. Forecast.* **11:3** 4:1992 pp. 207 – 224

50 Opening closed skies — the prospects for further liberalization of trade in international air transport services. Bruce Stockfish. *J. Air Law Comm.* **57:3** Spring:1992 pp. 599 – 652

51 Peak-load pricing in aviation — the case of charter air fares; La fijación de precios "peak-load" en aviación — el caso de las tarifas aéreas charter *[Spanish summary]*; La tarification du transport aérien en période de pointe — le cas des prix des charters *[French summary]*; Spitzenlastgebühren im Luftverkehr — Das Beispiel der Tarife im Charterluftverkehr *[German summary]*. Matthew Bishop; David Thompson. *J. Transp. Ec. Pol.* **XXVI:1** 1:1992 pp. 71 – 82

H.3: Transportation and communication *[Transports et communications]* — **Air transport** *[Transport aérien]*

52 Something special in the fares? Regulating commercial airline advertising. Amy Nicol Marlowe. *J. Air Law Comm.* **58:2** Winter:1992 pp. 605 – 642

53 Yield management at American Airlines. Barry C. Smith; John F. Leimkuhler; Ross M. Darrow. *Interfaces* **22:1** 1-2:1992 pp. 8 – 31

Railway transport *[Transport ferroviaire]*

54 Coal rates and revenue adequacy in a quasi-regulated rail industry. A.F. Friedlaender. *Rand J. Eco.* **23:3** Autumn:1992 pp. 376 – 394

55 Comparability in transport evaluation. Nathaniel Lichfield *[Ed.]*; Malcolm Simpson *[Contrib.]*; William Tyson *[Contrib.]*; Christopher Nash *[Contrib.]*; Richard Smith *[Contrib.]*; Stan Abrahams *[Contrib.]*; K.M. Gwilliam *[Contrib.]*; M.J.P.F. Gommers *[Contrib.]*. *Collection of 8 articles.* **Proj. App.** , *7:4*, 12:1992 pp. 195 – 248

56 Evaluating alternative scenarios for high-speed rail investment in Greece. D. Tsamboulas; S. Lioukas; C. Dionelis. *Transportation* **19:3** 1992 pp. 245 – 265

57 Gesamteuropäische Eisenbahnpolitik — Konzepte zur Stärkung des Schienentransports von Personen und Gütern *[In German]*; Pan-European rail policy — concepts to boost the numbers of people and the amount of freight travelling by rail *[Summary]*; Une politique ferroviaire paneuropéenne — concepts pour conforter le statut des transports de personnes et de marchandises par voie ferrée *[French summary]*. Wilgart Schuchardt. *Vierteljahresberichte* :**127** 3:1992 pp. 43 – 50

58 Governance structure, managerial characteristics, and firm performance in the deregulated rail industry. Ann F. Friedlaender; Ernst R. Berndt; Gerard McCullough. *Brookings P.* 1992 pp. 95 – 186

59 Konkurrenz auf den europäischen Eisenbahnnetzen *[In German]*; Competition on European railway networks *[Summary]*. Günter Knieps. *Jahrb. N. St.* **209:3-4** 3:1992 pp. 283 – 290

60 Operational planing of passenger trains in Indian railways. K.V. Ramani; B.K. Mandal. *Interfaces* **22:5** 9-10:1992 pp. 39 – 51

61 Rent-seeking and property right — the Very Fast Train project in Australia. Fu-Lai Yu. *Asian Ec.* :**81** 6:1992 pp. 72 – 78

62 The use of straw men in the economic evaluation of rail transport projects. John F. Kain. *Am. Econ. Rev.* **82:2** 5:1992 pp. 487 – 493

63 What are the potential economic development impacts of high-speed rail? Chris Thompson; Tim Bawden. *Econ. Devel. Q.* **6:3** 8:1992 pp. 297 – 319

Road transport *[Transport routier]*

64 An accessibility analysis of the impact of the M25 London orbital motorway on Britain; *[French summary]*; *[German summary]*. B.J. Linneker; N.A. Spence. *Reg. Stud.* **26:1** 1992 pp. 31 – 48

65 Anlaufprobleme und Entwicklungstendenzen des Güterkraftverkehrs in den neuen Bundesländern *[In German]*; [Initial problems and development trends of road haulage transport in eastern Germany] *[Summary]*. Adolf Zobel. *Z. Verkehr.* **63:1** 1992 pp. 3 – 14

66 Automobile subsidies and land use — estimates and policy responses. Mark E. Hanson. *J. Am. Plann.* **58:1** Winter:1992 pp. 60 – 71

67 Comparability in transport evaluation. Nathaniel Lichfield *[Ed.]*; Malcolm Simpson *[Contrib.]*; William Tyson *[Contrib.]*; Christopher Nash *[Contrib.]*; Richard Smith *[Contrib.]*; Stan Abrahams *[Contrib.]*; K.M. Gwilliam *[Contrib.]*; M.J.P.F. Gommers *[Contrib.]*. *Collection of 8 articles.* **Proj. App.** , *7:4*, 12:1992 pp. 195 – 248

68 Cost benefit analysis of urban minibus operations. White P.R.; P.R. Turner; C.T. Mbara. *Transportation* **19:1** 2:1992 pp. 59 – 74

69 Development of a route level patronage forecasting method. P.R. Stopher. *Transportation* **19:3** 1992 pp. 201 – 220

70 Network economies of scale in short haul truckload operations; Economías de escala de red en las operaciones por camión de corta distancia *[Spanish summary]*; Economies d'échelle par réseau dans les opérations de camionnage de courte distance *[French summary]*; Skaleneffekte von Netzwerken im Güternahverkehr *[German summary]*. W. Thomas Walker. *J. Transp. Ec. Pol.* **XXVI:1** 1:1992 pp. 3 – 17

71 Reference points, loss aversion, and contingent values for auto safety. Timothy L. McDaniels. *J. Risk Uncert.* **5:2** 1992 pp. 187 – 200

H.3: Transportation and communication *[Transports et communications] — Road transport [Transport routier]*

72 Vehicle routing. Bruce L. Golden *[Contrib.]*; Richard T. Wong *[Contrib.]*; André van Vliet *[Contrib.]*; C. Guus E. Boender *[Contrib.]*; Alexander H.G. Rinnooy Kan *[Contrib.]*; Erhan Erkut *[Contrib.]*; Doug MacLean *[Contrib.]*; Julie Wunderlich *[Contrib.]*; Martin Collette *[Contrib.]*; Laurence Levy *[Contrib.]* *and others. Collection of 10 articles.* **Interfaces** , *22:3*, 5-6:1992 pp. 1 – 111

Sea transport *[Transport maritime]*

73 An application of core theory to the analysis of ocean shipping markets. Stephen Craig Pirrong. *J. Law Econ.* **XXXV:1** 4:1992 pp. 89 – 132

74 Het belang van de haven voor de uitstraling van Antwerpen. Of — een continu gevecht voor competitiviteit en marktaandelen *[In Flemish]*; The port of Antwerp and its significance for the economic position of the city *[Summary]*. Fernand Suykens; Eddy Van de Voorde. *Econ. Soc. Tidj.* **46:3** 9:1992 pp. 477 – 499

75 Employment regulation, state intervention and the economic performance of European ports. Peter Turnbull; Syd Weston. *Camb. J. Econ.* **16:4** 12:1992 pp. 385 – 404

76 Lokalisatie van commodity-trafieken in zeehavens *[In Flemish]*; The location of commodity traffics in seaports *[Summary]*. Fernand Suykens. *Econ. Soc. Tidj.* **46:2** 6:1992 pp. 285 – 297

77 Sea management — a theoretical approach. Adalberto Vallega. London: Elsevier Applied Science, 1992: ix, 259 p. *ISBN: 1851667725; LofC: 92008007 //r92. "Published with the collaboration of Ente Colombo '92, Genoa, Italy"--P. ii; Prepared for the International Conference on Ocean Management in Global Change, Genoa, Italy, June 22-26, 1992; Includes bibliographical references and index.*

78 Ship finance — credit expansion and the boom-bust cycle. Peter Stokes. London: Lloyd's of London Press, 1992: 236 p. *ISBN: 1850444374.*

79 VIII Anglo-Soviet symposium on the law of the sea and international shipping. W.E. Butler *[Contrib.]*; Alan E. Boyle *[Contrib.]*; N.D. Koroleva *[Contrib.]*; Catherine Redgwell *[Contrib.]*; A.V. Sorokin *[Contrib.]*; Mark W. Janis *[Contrib.]*; Paul Dickie *[Contrib.]*; M.A. Gitsu *[Contrib.]*; A.A. Makovskaia *[Contrib.]*; Michael D. Lax *[Contrib.]* *and others. Collection of 12 articles.* **Mar. Pol.** , *16:2*, 3:1992 pp. 75 – 140

Telecommunications *[Télécommunications]*

80 The crossed line — the South African telecommunications industry in transition. David Kaplan. Johannesburg: Witwatersrand University Press, 1990: 227 p. *ISBN: 1868141195. Includes bibliographical references (p.[223]-227).*

81 Deregulating telecommunications and the problem of natural monopoly — a critique of economics in telecommunications policy. Kevin G. Wilson. *Media Cult. Soc.* **14:3** 7:1992 pp. 343 – 368

82 Development strategies in the audiovisual industries — the case of North East England; *[French summary]*; *[German summary]*. James Cornford; Kevin Robins. *Reg. Stud.* **26:5** 1992 pp. 421 – 435

83 Dinamiche tecnologiche e strategie di investimento nel settore delle telecomunicazioni — un modello di simulazione *[In Italian]*; Technological dynamics and investment strategies in the telecommunications sector. A simulation model *[Summary]*. Andrea Pannone; Paolo Vicari. *Industria* **XIII:4** 10-12:1992 pp. 703 – 723

84 The economics of information networks. Cristiano Antonelli *[Ed.]*. Amsterdam: North-Holland, 1992: vii, 477 p. *ISBN: 0444886427; LofC: 91010352. Includes bibliographical references and index.*

85 The economics of television regulation — a survey with application to Australia. Allan Brown; Martin Cave. *Econ. Rec.* **68:203** 12:1992 pp. 377 – 394

86 The effects of deregulating cable television — evidence from the financial markets. Robin A. Prager. *J. Regul. Econ.* **4:4** 12:1992 pp. 347 – 363

87 Electronic byways — state policies for rural development through telecommunications. Edwin B. Parker; Heather E. Hudson; et al. Boulder: Westview Press, 1992: xiv, 306 p. (ill., maps) *ISBN: 0813315921; LofC: 92009247. Includes bibliographical references (p.281-290) and index.*

88 Global telecommunications — the technology, administration, and policies. Raymond Akwule. Boston: Focal Press, 1992: viii, 200 p. *ISBN: 024080032x; LofC: 91034813. Includes bibliographical references and index.*

H.3: Transportation and communication *[Transports et communications]* —
Telecommunications [Télécommunications]

89 Liberalization and regulation of telecommunications — some observations on the UK experience. Christopher Hurst. *Util. Policy* **2:1** 1:1992 pp. 13 – 24

90 Managing telecommunications by steering committee. Gholamreza Torkzadeh; Weidong Xia. *MIS Q.* **16:2** 6:1992 pp. 187 – 200

91 Pa Bell — A. Jean de Grandpré and the meteoric rise of Bell Canada enterprises. Lawrence Surtees. Toronto: Random House, 1992: xiii, 481 p. *ISBN: 0394221427; LofC: 92195370. Includes bibliographical references (p. [415]-481).*

92 Some spatial aspects of regulatory and technological change in telecommunication industries. P. Cooke. *Envir. Plan.A.* **24:5** 5:1992 pp. 683 – 703

93 Standard setting in high-definition television. Joseph Farrell; Carl Shapiro. *Brookings P. 1992* pp. 1 – 93

94 Telecommunications in developing countries. C.R. Dickenson. *Util. Policy* **2:1** 1:1992 pp. 43 – 50

95 Telecommunications in Europe. Eli M. Noam. New York: Oxford University Press, 1992: xii, 523 p. *ISBN: 0195070526; LofC: 90022969. Includes bibliographical references (p. 457-495) and index.* [Communication and society.]

96 The telecommunications revolution — past, present, and future. Harvey M. Sapolsky; et al. London: Routledge, 1992: 217 p. *ISBN: 0415067715; LofC: 91026477. Includes bibliographical references and index.*

97 Telephone demand over the Atlantic — evidence from country-pair data. Jan Paul Acton; Ingo Vogelsang. *J. Ind. Econ.* **XL:3** 9:1992 pp. 305 – 324

98 A test for cross subsidies in local telephone rates — do business customers subsidize residential customers? K. Palmer. *Rand J. Eco.* **23:3** Autumn:1992 pp. 415 – 431

99 Towards global localization — the computing and telecommunications industries in Britain and France. Philip Cooke; et al. London: UCL Press, 1992: 227 p. *ISBN: 1857280008.*

100 Transaction costs, telecommunications, and the microeconomics of macroeconomic growth. Seth W. Norton. *Econ. Dev. Cult. Change* **41:1** 10:1992 pp. 175 – 192

101 The US debate on integrated broadband networks. Martin C.J. Elton. *Media Cult. Soc.* **14:3** 7:1992 pp. 369 – 395

H.4: Trade and distribution — *Commerce et distribution*

Sub-divisions: Advertising *[Publicité]*; Marketing *[Commercialisation]*; Retail trade *[Commerce de détail]*; Service industry *[Secteur tertiaire]*

1 Agency theory and franchising — some empirical results. F. Lafontaine. *Rand J. Eco.* **23:2** Summer:1992 pp. 263 – 283

2 Argentine, Brésil — la distribution des produits alimentaires *[In French]*; Food distribution in Argentina and Brazil *[Summary]*; Argentina, Brasil — la distribución de los productos alimentarios *[Spanish summary]*. Raúl Green; Graciela Gutman; Roseli Rocha dos Santos. *Prob. Am.Lat.* **:6** 7-9:1992 pp. 83 – 101

3 Beatrice — a study in the creation and destruction of value. George P. Baker. *J. Finance* **47:3** 7:1992 pp. 1081 – 1119

4 The building of an industrial society — change and development in Kenya's informal (jua kali) sector — 1972 to 1991 — a summary report. Kenneth King; Charles Abuodha. Edinburgh: Centre of African Studies, Edinburgh University, 1991: 103 p. *Includes bibliography.* [Occasional papers.]

5 Company ownership vs franchising — issues and evidence. R.S. Thompson. *J. Econ. Stud.* **19:4** 1992 pp. 31 – 42

6 La comunicazione globale d'impresa come arma competitiva e come filosofia di gestione *[In Italian]*; [Global business communication as a competitive weapon and as a management philosophy]. Umberto Martini. *Econ. Ban.* **XIV:1** 1992 pp. 111 – 146

7 Concentration and buying power — the case of German food distribution. Christian Marfels. *Int. R. Ret. Dist. Res.* **2:3** 7:1992 pp. 233 – 244

8 Cooperative R & D and vertical product differentiation. M. Motta. *Int. J. Ind. O.* **10:4** 12:1992 pp. 643 – 661

9 Coordination in split award auctions. James J. Anton; Dennis A. Yao. *Q. J. Econ.* **CVII:2** 5:1992 pp. 681 – 707

H.4: Trade and distribution *[Commerce et distribution]*

10 Cost differentials among household goods carriers — network effects, operating characteristics, and shipment composition; Diferencias de costes entre los transportistas de artículos para el hogar — efectos en la red, características operativas y composición de los envíos *[Spanish summary]*; Différences de coûts entre déménageurs — effet de réseau, caractéristiques d'opération et composition de chargement *[French summary]*; Kostendifferenzen bei Transporten von Konsumgütern — Netzeffekte, Betriebscharakteristiken und Ladungszusammensetzung *[German summary]*. Scott J. Callan; Janet M. Thomas. *J. Transp. Ec. Pol.* **XXVI:1** 1:1992 pp. 19 – 34

11 Coûts irrécupérables et structure de marché endogène — les cas des marchés régis par appel d'offres *[In French]*; Sunk costs and endogenous market structure — the case of sealed bid auctions *[Summary]*. M. Mougeot; F. Naegelen. *Rev. Ec. Polit.* **102:3** 5-6:1992 pp. 379 – 399

12 Data envelopment analysis for monitoring customer-supplier relationships. Ilene K. Kleinsorge; Philip B. Schary; Ray D. Tanner. *J. Acc. Pub. Pol.* **11:4** Winter:1992 pp. 357 – 372

13 The data reduction approach to survey analysis. Martin Collins. *J. Market R.* **34:2** 4:1992 pp. 149 – 162

14 Deliverance from hunger — the public distribution system in India. K.R. Venugopal. New Delhi: Sage Publications, 1992: 223 p. *ISBN: 8170362628; LofC: 91034552.*

15 Designing call auction institutions — is double Dutch the best. K.A. McCabe; S.J. Rassenti; V.L. Smith. *Econ. J.* **102:410** 1:1992 pp. 9 – 23

16 La distribución en la CE ante el Mercado Unico. Repercusión en España *[In Spanish]*; [Distribution in the EC before the single European market. Repercussions in Spain]. Juan Antonio Trespalacios Gutiérrez. *Infor. Com. Esp.* **:707** 7:1992 pp. 109 – 125

17 La dynamique du secteur informel urbain au Mexique — le rôle de la mobilité intersectorielle *[In French]*; (The effects method thirty years on). François Roubaud. *R. T-Monde* **33:132** 10-12:1992 pp. 893 – 928

18 An economic appraisal of a South African producer co-operative. G.W. Oldham; M.M. Hickson. *Develop. S. Afr.* **9:4** 11:1992 pp. 445 – 456

19 Economic environments and differentiation — a comparative study of informal sector economies in Nigeria. H.K. Anheier. *World Dev.* **20:11** 11:1992 pp. 1573 – 1585

20 An empirical comparison of Soviet and American business negotiations. John L. Graham; Leonid I. Evenko; Mahesh N. Rajan. *J. Int. Bus. Stud.* **23:3** Third quarter:1992 pp. 387 – 418

21 Ende des Protektionismus — ökonomische Effekte der Liberalisierung des öffentlichen Beschaffungswesens in Österreich *[In German]*; [The end of protectionism — economic effects of the liberation of the public system of procurement in Austria]. Johannes M. Bauer *[Ed.]*; Markus Marterbauer *[Ed.]*. Wien: Service-Fachverl., 1991: 165 p. *ISBN: 3854281927.*

22 Fisher ideal output, input, and productivity indexes revisited. W.E. Diewert. *J. Prod. Anal.* **3:3** 1992 pp. 211 – 248

23 Gestaltung interorganisatorischer Logistiksysteme auf der Grundlage der Transaktionskostentheorie *[In German]*; [Designing interorganizational logistics systems on the basis of transaction costs theory] *[Summary]*. Hans-Christian Pfohl; Rudolf Large. *Z. Verkehr.* **63:1** 1992 pp. 15 – 51

24 Growth and employment in the UK's culture industry. Gareth Shaw. *Wor. Futur.* **33:1-3** 1992 pp. 165 – 180

25 The hidden economy of Egypt. Delwin A. Roy. *Middle E. Stud.* **28:4** 10:1992 pp. 689 – 711

26 Informal economic activity. J.J. Thomas. Hemel Hempstead: Harvester-Wheatsheaf, 1992: 371 p. *ISBN: 0745011683.* [LSE handbooks in economics.]

27 The informal sector in developing countries — a macro view point. Sarthi Acharya. *Econ. Papers [Warsaw]* **18** 1992 pp. 88 – 110

28 Intra-industry trade and investment under oligopoly — the role of market size. R.E. Rowthorn. *Econ. J.* **102:411** 3:1992 pp. 402 – 414

29 Intra-industry trade in agrofood sectors — the case of the EEC meat market. M. Christodoulou. *Appl. Econ.* **24:8** 8:1992 pp. 875 – 884

30 Kommunale Subventionen. Eine empirische Analyse ihrer Entwicklung und Struktur zwischen 1975 und 1987 *[In German]*; [Municipal subsidies — an empirical analysis of their development and structure between 1975 and 1987]. Hermann Rappen. *RWI-Mitt.* **43:3** 1992 pp. 223 – 241

H.4: Trade and distribution *[Commerce et distribution]*

31 Latent class metric conjoint analysis. Wayne S. DeSarbo; Michel Wedel; Marco Vriens; Venkatram Ramaswamy. *Market. Lett.* **3:3** 7:1992 pp. 273 – 288

32 Locational dynamics of automobile dealerships and explanations for spatial clustering. J. Dennis Lord. *Int. R. Ret. Dist. Res.* **2:3** 7:1992 pp. 283 – 308

33 A macroeconomic analysis of the underground economy. Gerasimos T. Soldatos. *Jahr. Soz.schaft.* **43:3** 1992 pp. 331 – 348

34 Market structure and R&D competition. G. Clemenz. *Eur. Econ. R.* **36:4** 5:1992 pp. 847 – 864

35 Mitigating the effect of service encounters. Ruth N. Bolton; James H. Drew. *Market. Lett.* **3:1** 1:1992 pp. 57 – 70

36 Möglichkeiten zur Intensivierung des innerdeutschen Handels. Bericht über eine Untersuchung für das Bundeswirtschaftsministerium *[In German]*; [Possibilities concerning the intensification of intra-German trade. Report on an investigation for the finance ministry]. Michael Baumann. *Deut. Arch.* **23:2** 2:1990 pp. 258 – 264

37 Moral hazard in Illyria; *[German summary]*. Thomas Wagner. *J. Inst. Theo. Ec.* **148:3** 9:1992 pp. 468 – 483

38 On efficiency and distribution. R.E. Lucas. *Econ. J.* **102:411** 3:1992 pp. 233 – 247

39 On properties of stochastic inventory systems. Yu-Sheng Zheng. *Manag. Sci.* **38:1** 1:1992 pp. 87 – 103

40 On the existence of franchise contracts and some of their implications. B.G. Katz; J. Owen. *Int. J. Ind. O.* **10:4** 12:1992 pp. 567 – 593

41 Optimal commercial policy with international returns to scale; *[French summary]*. Joseph F. Francois. *Can. J. Econ.* **XXV:1** 2:1992 pp. 184 – 195

42 Ownership structure and efficiency — an incentive mechanism approach. Liang Zou. *J. Comp. Econ.* **16:3** 9:1992 pp. 399 – 431

43 The politics of trade in Latin American development. Steven E. Sanderson. Stanford, CA.: Stanford University Press, 1992: xii, 292 p. *ISBN: 0804719837; LofC: 91039863. Includes bibliographical references (p.255-280) and index.*

44 Pooling in two-location inventory systems with non-negligible replenishment lead times. George Tagaras; Morris A. Cohen. *Manag. Sci.* **38:8** 8:1992 pp. 1067 – 1083

45 Les routes des drogues — explorations en Afrique subsaharienne *[In French]*; (Drug routes — explorations in sub-Saharan Africa); (Puti narkotikov — ekspedicija v podsakharskuju Afriku: *Title only in Russian*); (Die Drogenstraßen — Untersuchungen in Afrika südlich des Sahara: *Title only in German*); (Las rutas de drogas — exploraciones en Africa subsahariana: *Title only in Spanish*). Maria Luisa Cesoni. *R. T-Monde* **XXXIII:131** 7-9:1992 pp. 645 – 671

46 Le secteur informel, nouvel enjeu des politiques de développement? *[In French]*; The informal sector — new concern for development policies? *[Summary]*. Jacques Charmes. *Hom. Soc.* **:105-106** 3-4:1992 pp. 63 – 77

47 Le Sentier, un espace ambigu *[In French]*; [Paths, an ambiguous space]. Solange Montagné-Villette; Georges Jolles *[Foreword]*. Paris: Masson, 1990: 140 p. (ill) *ISBN: 2225820597. [Recherches en géographie.]*

48 Some characterizations of stockpiling behavior under uncertainty. Kristiaan Helsen; David C. Schmittlein. *Market. Lett.* **3:1** 1:1992 pp. 5 – 16

49 South Africa's informal economy. C.M. Rogerson *[Ed.]*; Eleanor Preston-Whyte *[Ed.]*. Cape Town: Oxford University Press, 1991: 410 p. *ISBN: 0195706331; LofC: 92117519. Includes bibliographical references and index.* [Contemporary South African debates.]

50 Tricycles, tapes and tangerines — aspects of the informal markets in Peru; *[Afrikaans summary]*; *[Spanish summary]*; *[Portuguese summary]*. Chris van Vuuren. *Unisa Lat.Am. Rep.* **8:2** 1992 pp. 16 – 24

51 A two-echelon inventory system with priority shipments. Maqbool Dada. *Manag. Sci.* **38:8** 8:1992 pp. 1140 – 1153

52 "Unfair" contractual practices and hostages in franchise contracts; *[German summary]*. Antony W. Dnes. *J. Inst. Theo. Ec.* **148:3** 9:1992 pp. 484 – 504

53 Utilization control in HMOs. Larry De Brock; Richard J. Arnould. *Q Rev. Econ. Finan.* **32:3** Autumn:1992 pp. 31 – 53

54 A vgmk-tól az aluljáró-kereskedelemig *[In Hungarian]*; From the enterprise workteams to the subway-trade — the second economy in the current of transition *[Summary]*. Ildikó Ékes. *Közg. Sz.* **XXXIX** 3:1992 pp. 226 – 243

55 Der Warenhandel Nordrhein-Westfalens mit den neuen Bundesländern — Eine Analyse mit Folgerungen zur Konstitution der nordrhein-westfälischen Wirtschaft *[In German]*; [North

H.4: Trade and distribution *[Commerce et distribution]*
Rhine-Westfalia's trade with the new federal states — an analysis of the consequences for the composition of the North Rhine Westfalian economy]. Rüdiger Hamm. *RWI-Mitt.* **43:3** 1992 pp. 223 – 241
56 Why is production more volatile than sales? Theory and evidence on the stockout-avoidance motive for inventory- holding. James A. Kahn. *Q. J. Econ.* **CVII:2** 5:1992 pp. 481 – 510

Advertising *[Publicité]*
57 Advertising effects in complete demand systems. M.R. Baye; D.W. Jansen; Jae-Woo Lee. *Appl. Econ.* **24:10** 10:1992 pp. 1087 – 1096
58 Advertising, product quality, and complex evolving marketing systems; *[German summary]*. Willem Verbeke. *J. Consum. Pol.* **15:2** 1992 pp. 143 – 158
59 Analyse, klassifikation og behandling af negative rygter *[In Danish]*; [Analysis, classification and handling of negative publicity] *[Summary]*. Jan Møller Jensen; Tage Koed Madsen. *Led. Erhv.* **56:1** 1:1992 pp. 33 – 42
60 The consumerist manifesto — advertising in post modern times. Martin P. Davidson. London: Routledge, 1992: 217 p. *ISBN: 041504619x; LofC: 91033798.* [Comedia.]
61 The effects of postexposure test expectation in advertising experiments utilizing recall and recognition measures. Robert J. Kent; Karen A. Machleit. *Market. Lett.* **3:1** 1:1992 pp. 17 – 26
62 Empirical analysis of closed-loop duopoly advertising strategies. Gary M. Erickson. *Manag. Sci.* **38:12** 12:1992 pp. 1732 – 1749
63 Optimal producer and social payoff from generic advertising — the case of the Canadian supply-managed egg sector. Mary Lou McCutcheon; Ellen Goddard. *Can. J. Ag. Ec.* **40:1** 3:1992 pp. 1 – 24
64 The return to advertising expenditure. Bruce Cooil; Timothy M. Devinney. *Market. Lett.* **3:2** 4:1992 pp. 137 – 145
65 Strategy and transaction costs — the organization of distribution in the carbonated soft drink industry. Timothy J. Muris; David T. Scheffman; Pablo T. Spiller. *J. Econ. Manag. Strat.* **1:1** Spring:1992 pp. 83 – 128

Marketing *[Commercialisation]*
66 Adapting marketing surveys to individual respondents. Jagdip Singh; Gary K. Rhoads; Roy D. Howell. *J. Market R.* **34:2** 4:1992 pp. 125 – 148
67 Administrative procedures for the control of marketing practices — theoretical rationale and perspectives; *[German summary]*. Thomas Wilhelmsson. *J. Consum. Pol.* **15:2** 1992 pp. 159 – 177
68 The agrarian origins of commerce and industry — a study of peasant marketing in Indonesia. Yujiro Hayami; Toshihiko Kawagoe; C. Peter Timmer *[Foreword]*. New York: St. Martin's Press, 1992: 202 p. *ISBN: 0312086210; LofC: 92018420. Includes bibliographical references and index.*
69 Analysis of multiple response in marketing research — estimating the degree of association. U.N. Umesh; Martin Tan; Donald E. Stem. *Market. Lett.* **3:2** 4:1992 pp. 107 – 114
70 Are null results becoming an endangered species in marketing? Raymond Hubbard; J. Scott Armstrong. *Market. Lett.* **3:2** 4:1992 pp. 127 – 136
71 A Bayesian survey technique for rare subjects. Samaradasa Weerahandi; Robert G. White. *Market. Lett.* **3:1** 1:1992 pp. 39 – 47
72 Competitive strategies for multi-establishment firms. Jean-Claude Thill. *Econ. Geogr.* **68:3** 7:1992 pp. 290 – 309
73 Contextualized representations of brand extensions — are feature lists or frames the basic components of consumer cognition? Bernd H. Schmitt; Laurette Dubé. *Market. Lett.* **3:2** 4:1992 pp. 115 – 126
74 A dimensional versus attribute approach for disaggregate choice models. Dennis H. Gensch; Sanjoy Ghose. *Market. Lett.* **3:1** 1:1992 pp. 27 – 37
75 The international licensing of branded food products — a game-theoretic analysis. I.M. Sheldon; D.R. Henderson. *J. Agr. Econ.* **43:3** 9:1992 pp. 368 – 380
76 Internationale markedsføringsstrategier for nicheprodukter *[In Danish]*; [An international marketing strategy for a Danish niche producer] *[Summary]*. Allan T. Skaalum; Brian Thostrup. *Led. Erhv.* **56:1** 1:1992 pp. 25 – 32

H.4: Trade and distribution *[Commerce et distribution]* — *Marketing [Commercialisation]*

77 Interpreting multiple correspondence analysis as a multidimensional scaling method. Donna L. Hoffman; Jan de Leeuw. *Market. Lett.* **3:3** 7:1992 pp. 259 – 272

78 Marketing and company performance — an examination of medium sized manufacturing firms in Britain. R. Brooksbank; David A. Kirby; Gillian Wright. *Small Bus. Econ.* **4:3** 9:1992 pp. 221 – 236

79 Marketing of Sabah's agricultural primary commodities — issues and challenges. Fatimah Mohd. Arshad; Mad Nasir Shamsudin. *Born. R.* **III:1** 6:1992 pp. 96 – 123

80 Le marketing social *[In French]*; Social marketing *[Summary]*. Alain Bonaventure. *Gestion* **8:1** 1992 pp. 149 – 158

81 Marketing strategy — planning and implementation. Orville C. Walker; Harper W. Boyd; Jean-Claude Larréché. Homewood, IL.: Irwin, 1992: xxiv, 503 p. *ISBN: 025609005x; LofC: 91027772. Includes bibliographical references and indexes.* [The Irwin series in marketing.]

82 Measuring the hedonic and utilitarian dimensions of attitudes toward product categories. Ayn E. Crowley; Eric R. Spangenberg; Kevin R. Hughes. *Market. Lett.* **3:3** 7:1992 pp. 239 – 249

83 Optimal policies and marketing board objectives. K. Krishna; M. Thursby. *J. Dev. Econ.* **38:1** 1:1992 pp. 1 – 15

84 Place wars — new realities of the 1990s. Donald Haider. *Econ. Devel. Q.* **6:2** 5:1992 pp. 127 – 134

85 Positioning, image and the marketing of multiple retailers. Gary Davies. *Int. R. Ret. Dist. Res.* **2:1** 1:1992 pp. 13 – 34

86 Prospects for niche marketing in South Pacific island nations. Euan Fleming; Brian Hardaker. *Pac. Ec. B.* **7:1** 6:1992 pp. 21 – 26

87 The role of image in the attraction of the out-of-town centre. Peter J. McGoldrick; Mark G. Thompson. *Int. R. Ret. Dist. Res.* **2:1** 1:1992 pp. 81 – 98

Retail trade *[Commerce de détail]*

88 The 1985 Ohio thrift crisis, the FSLIC's solvency, and rate contagion for retail CDs. Elizabeth S. Cooperman; Winson B. Lee; Glenn A. Wolfe. *J. Finance* **47:3** 7:1992 pp. 919 – 941

89 An analysis of intermarket sales inflows/outflows within a shift-share framework. Ugur Yavas; Jafar Alavi; Glen Riecken. *Int. R. Ret. Dist. Res.* **2:4** 10:1992 pp. 409 – 427

90 Antitrust regulation and the restructuring of grocery retailing in Britain and the USA. N. Wrigley. *Envir. Plan.A.* **24:5** 5:1992 pp. 727 – 749

91 Business performance in the retail sector — the experience of the John Lewis Partnership. Keith Bradley; Simon Christopher Taylor. Oxford: Clarendon Press, 1992: 194 p. *ISBN: 0198256949; LofC: 91032181. Includes bibliographical references and index.*

92 Competitive advantage in retailing. Brien Ellis; Scott W. Kelley. *Int. R. Ret. Dist. Res.* **2:4** 10:1992 pp. 381 – 396

93 The dimensions of commercial exchange. Patrick J. Kaufmann; Rajiv P. Dant. *Market. Lett.* **3:2** 4:1992 pp. 171 – 185

94 Entrepreneurs in spite of themselves? Economic and non-economic motives of booksellers in Germany. Martin Huber. *Wor. Futur.* **33:1-3** 1992 pp. 49 – 60

95 Evaluating the success of out-of-town regional shopping centres. Elizabeth Howard. *Int. R. Ret. Dist. Res.* **2:1** 1:1992 pp. 59 – 80

96 Franchising — a case-study approach. Antony W. Dnes. Aldershot: Avebury, 1992: 321 p. *ISBN: 185628221x.*

97 Import versus domestic apparel — contrasting views of Japanese and US retail buyers. Brenda Sternquist; Tomoyoshi Ogawa; Lisa Phillips. *Int. R. Ret. Dist. Res.* **2:4** 10:1992 pp. 397 – 408

98 Merchandise compatibility — an exploratory study of its measurement and effect on department store performance. Roger Dickinson; Frederick Harris; Sumit Sircar. *Int. R. Ret. Dist. Res.* **2:4** 10:1992 pp. 351 – 379

99 An opportunity-based model of customer service. William R. Swinyard. *Int. R. Ret. Dist. Res.* **2:1** 1:1992 pp. 1 – 12

100 The outputs of retail activities — French evidence. R.R. Betancourt; D.A. Gautschi. *Appl. Econ.* **24:9** 9:1992 pp. 1043 – 1052

101 Positioning, image and the marketing of multiple retailers. Gary Davies. *Int. R. Ret. Dist. Res.* **2:1** 1:1992 pp. 13 – 34

H.4: Trade and distribution *[Commerce et distribution]* — *Retail trade [Commerce de détail]*

102 Retail development in East Germany — the example of the city of Jena. Günter Meyer. *Int. R. Ret. Dist. Res.* **2:3** 7:1992 pp. 245 – 261

103 The role of image in the attraction of the out-of-town centre. Peter J. McGoldrick; Mark G. Thompson. *Int. R. Ret. Dist. Res.* **2:1** 1:1992 pp. 81 – 98

104 Slotting allowances and resale price maintenance — a comparison of facilitating practices. G. Shaffer. *Rand J. Eco.* **22:1** Spring:1991 pp. 120 – 135

105 Vertical control with bilateral contracts. D.P. O'Brien; G. Shaffer. *Rand J. Eco.* **23:3** Autumn:1992 pp. 299 – 308

Service industry *[Secteur tertiaire]*

106 Consultancy services and the urban hierarchy in Western Europe. P.W. Daniels; J.H. Van Dinteren; M.C. Monnoyer. *Envir. Plan.A.* **24:12** 12:1992 pp. 1731 – 1748

107 Estancamiento tecnológico de los servicios y terciarización en la OCDE 1964-87 *[In Spanish]*; [Technological stagnation in the service sector and service sector growth in OECD countries, 1964-1987] *[Summary]*. Pablo Gutiérrez Junquera. *Invest. Econ.* **XVI:1** 1:1992 pp. 151 – 180

108 The geography of corporate services — a case study of the New York urban region. Alex Schwartz. *Urban Geogr.* **13:1** 1-2:1992 pp. 1 – 24

109 Regolamentazione della qualità dei servizi nelle imprese publiche sottoposte a price-cap regulation — il caso della Gran Bretagna *[In Italian]*; Price cap regulated public utilities and quality regulation in the UK *[Summary]*. Laura Rovizzi; David Thompson. *Industria* **XIII:1** 1-3:1992 pp. 29 – 56

110 Small manufacturing firm business services externalization in the Chicago metropolitan region. Adrian Esparza. *Urban Geogr.* **13:1** 1-2:1992 pp. 68 – 86

111 Spatial econometrics of services. Antoine S. Bailly; et al. Aldershot, Hants, England: Avebury, 1992: 102 p. *ISBN: 185628297x; LofC: 92014782.*

112 "Unproductive" sectors and economic growth — a theoretical analysis. Amitava Krishna Dutt. *R. Pol. Econ.* **4:2** 1992 pp. 178 – 202

I: Prices and markets — *Prix et marchés*

I.1: Basic concepts — *Concepts de base*

1 Assessing the quality of expressed preference measures of value. R. Gregory; D. MacGregor; S. Lichtenstein. *J. Econ. Beh.* **17:2** 3:1992 pp. 277 – 292

2 *[In Arabic]*; Contribution of Muslim scholars in the foundation and development of the science of economics — Ibn Khaldun's thoughts on value and price *[Summary]*. Shougi Ahmed Dunia. *R. Islam. Econ.* **2:1** 1992 pp. 1 – 34

3 Our daily bread — a critical economic analysis. S.A.H.A.A Imam. Hazaribagh: Indian Heritage, 1991: 53 p.

4 The problem of international values — mainly from a Hungarian and Japanese perspective. Gabor Bakos. *Hito. J. Econ.* **33:1** 6:1992 pp. 63 – 93

I.2: Markets and price formation — *Marchés et formation du prix*

I.2.1: **Theory** — *Théorie*

Sub-divisions: Competition *[Concurrence]*; Pricing *[Fixation du prix]*; Supply and demand *[Offre et demande]*

1 Allocating priority with auctions — an experimental analysis. C. Noussair; D. Porter. *J. Econ. Beh.* **19:2** 10:1992 pp. 169 – 195
2 Arbitrage with holding costs — a utility-based approach. Bruce Tuckman; Jean-Luc Vila. *J. Finance* **47:4** 9:1992 pp. 1283 – 1302
3 Asymmetric information flows in customer markets. Hugh Sibly. *B. Econ. Res.* **44:4** 10:1992 pp. 323 – 342
4 Asymmetric information, adjustment costs and market dynamics. Andrew Caplin; John Leahy. New York: Columbia University, Dept of Economics, [1992?]: 28 p. [Discussion paper series.]
5 Attempts to monopolize and the determination of specific intent. David I. Rosenbaum; Meng-Hua Ye. *Q Rev. Econ. Finan.* **32:1** Spring:1992 pp. 50 – 70
6 Austrian views on monopoly — insights and problems. David Young. *R. Pol. Econ.* **4:2** 1992 pp. 203 – 225
7 Barrier and queue effects — a study of leading US supermarket chain entry patterns. Ronald W. Cotterill; Lawrence E. Haller. *J. Ind. Econ.* **XL:4** 12:1992 pp. 427 – 440
8 Bertrand equilibrium in a differentiated duopoly. Helmut Bester. *Int. Econ. R.* **33:2** 5:1992 pp. 433 – 448
9 Bertrand, Cournot and mixed oligopolies. Ferenc Szidarovszky; Sándor Molnár. *Keio Econ. Stud.* **XXIX:1** 1992 pp. 1 – 8
10 Bubbles and charges. Christian Gilles; Stephen F. LeRoy. *Int. Econ. R.* **33:2** 5:1992 pp. 323 – 340
11 Cartel instability and periodic price shocks. M. Rauscher. *J. Econ.* **55:2** 1992 pp. 209 – 219
12 Cartel stability in an exhaustible resource model. J. Thomas. *Economica* **59:235** 8:1992 pp. 279 – 294
13 Clean indoor air laws, addiction and cigarette smoking. F. Chaloupka. *Appl. Econ.* **24:2** 2:1992 pp. 193 – 206
14 Collusive behavior and partial ownership of rivals. D.A. Malueg. *Int. J. Ind. O.* **10:1** 3:1992 pp. 27 – 34
15 A common agency with incomplete information. E. Gal-Or. *Rand J. Eco.* **22:2** Summer:1991 pp. 274 – 286
16 A comparison of transaction costs between competitive market maker and specialist market structures. Robert Neal. *J. Bus.* **65:3** 7:1992 pp. 317 – 334
17 Competitive selection and market data — the mixed-index problem. Roger Bowden. *R. Econ. S.* **59:3(200)** 7:1992 pp. 625 – 633
18 Debt, price flexibility and aggregate stability; Dette, flexibilité des prix et stabilité économique *[French summary]*. J.P. Caskey; S.M. Fazzari. *Rev. Ec. Polit.* **102:4** 7-8:1992 pp. 519 – 543
19 Disagreement in markets with matching and bargaining. Larry Samuelson. *R. Econ. S.* **59(1):198** 2:1992 pp. 177 – 185
20 Duopoly with employee-controlled and profit-maximizing firms — Bertrand vs Cournot competition. Helmuth Cremer; Jacques Crémer. *J. Comp. Econ.* **16:2** 6:1992 pp. 241 – 258
21 Duopoly with spatial and quantity-dependent price discrimination. J.H. Hamilton; J.-F. Thisse. *Reg. Sci. Urb. Econ.* **22:2** 6:1992 pp. 175 – 185
22 Durable goods monopoly and maintenance. D.P. Mann. *Int. J. Ind. O.* **10:1** 3:1992 pp. 65 – 80
23 Durable goods monopoly with incomplete information. Lawrence M. Ausubel; Raymond J. Deneckere. *R. Econ. S.* **59:4** 10:1992 pp. 795 – 812
24 Durable goods monopoly, learning by doing and the Coase conjecture. T.E. Olsen. *Eur. Econ. R.* **36:1** 1:1992 pp. 157 – 178

I.2.1: Theory *[Théorie]*

25 Econometric tests of firm decision making under uncertainty — optimal output and hedging decisions. Timothy A. Park; Frances Antonovitz. *S. Econ. J.* **58:3** 1:1992 pp. 593 – 609

26 The economic surplus in advanced economies. John B. Davis. Aldershot: Edward Elgar Publishing, 1992: 192 p. *ISBN: 1852785551.* [New directions in modern economics.]

27 Entry, barriers, exit, and sunk costs — an analysis. D.I. Rosenbaum; F. Lamort. *Appl. Econ.* **24:3** 3:1992 pp. 297 – 304

28 L'établissement des relations fournisseur-client en milieu industriel *[In French]*; The establishment of supplier-client relations in industry *[Summary]*. Régis Goujet; Denis Bansard; Robert Salle. *Gestion* **8:6** 1992 pp. 47 – 75

29 Evolution in markets and institutions. Ulrich Witt *[Ed.]*; R. Boyer *[Contrib.]*; A. Orléan *[Contrib.]*; F.C. Englmann *[Contrib.]*; G. Hesse *[Contrib.]*; G. Laffond *[Contrib.]*; J. Lesourne *[Contrib.]*; W. Weidlich *[Contrib.]*; M. Braun *[Contrib.]*. *Collection of 6 articles.* **J. Evolut. Econ.** , *2:3,* 1992 pp. 163 – 265

30 Exclusive dealing contracts in a successive duopoly with side payments. Myong-Hun Chang. *S. Econ. J.* **59:2** 10:1992 pp. 180 – 193

31 Extracting rents with forward contracts. P. DeGraba; M. O'Hara. *Int. J. Ind. O.* **10:1** 3:1992 pp. 103 – 126

32 Inflation and efficiency in search markets. Roland Benabou. *R. Econ. S.* **59:2(199)** 4:1992 pp. 299 – 329

33 Inflation and optimal price adjustment under monopolistic competition. Ramon Caminal. *Economica* **59:234** 5:1992 pp. 179 – 197

34 Information networks and market behavior. Wayne E. Baker; Ananth V. Iyer. *J. Math. Sociol.* **16:4** 1992 pp. 305 – 332

35 Innovation and the persistence of monopoly. S.A. Lippman; J.W. Mamer. *Econ. Lett.* **38:1** 1:1992 pp. 83 – 92

36 Innovation orientation, environment and performance — a comparison of U.S. and European markets. Franklyn A. Manu. *J. Int. Bus. Stud.* **23:2** 1992 pp. 333 – 360

37 Mais qu'y a-t-il donc de différent à segmenter les marchés qui n'existent pas? *[In French]*; But what on earth is different about segmenting markets which do not exist? *[Summary]*. Paul Millier. *Gestion* **8:6** 1992 pp. 151 – 172

38 The market game — existence and structure of equilibrium. J. Peck; K. Shell; S.E. Spear. *J. Math Econ.* **21:3** 1992 pp. 271 – 299

39 Market shares and firm performance in oligopolistic markets. K. Kesteloot. *Eur. J. Pol. Ec.* **8:1** 2:1992 pp. 57 – 75

40 Market structure, sales to government, and the theory of oligopoly. W.F. Chappell; W.G. Shughart. *J. Econ. Beh.* **19:1** 9:1992 pp. 69 – 81

41 Market uncertainties and cyclical dumping. S.P. Das. *Eur. Econ. R.* **36:1** 1:1992 pp. 71 – 82

42 Markets, markets everywhere? Understanding the Cuban anomaly. C.D. Deere; M. Meurs. *World Dev.* **20:6** 6:1992 pp. 825 – 840

43 Marshallian vs. Walrasian stability in an experimental market. C.R. Plott; G. George. *Econ. J.* **102:412** 5:1992 pp. 437 – 460

44 Merger announcements, asymmetrical information, and trading volume — an empirical investigation. A.J. Keown; J.M. Pinkerton; P.J. Bolster. *J. Bus. Fin. Acc.* **19:6** 11:1992 pp. 901 – 910

45 A model of latent symmetry in cross price elasticities. Gary J. Russell. *Market. Lett.* **3:2** 4:1992 pp. 157 – 169

46 Mutual forbearance in experimental conglomerate markets. O.R. Phillips; C.F. Mason. *Rand J. Eco.* **23:3** Autumn:1992 pp. 395 – 414

47 New classical and new Keynesian macroeconomics. Howard Vane; Brian Snowdon. *Economics* **XXVIII:118(2)** Summer:1992 pp. 54 – 62

48 Non-Walrasian equilibria with speculation. S. Benninga. *J. Econ. Beh.* **17:2** 3:1992 pp. 241 – 256

49 Oligopolies and product durability. G.E. Goering. *Int. J. Ind. O.* **10:1** 3:1992 pp. 55 – 64

50 On estimating market efficiency. Brian T. Ratchford; Pola Gupta. *J. Consum. Pol.* **15:3** 1992 pp. 275 – 293

51 Optimal control theory and static optimization in economics. Daniel Leonard; Ngo van Long. Cambridge: Cambridge University Press, 1992: x, 353 p. *ISBN: 0521331587; LofC: 91014126. Includes bibliographical references (p. 345-349) and index.*

52 Optimal fiscal zoning when the local government is a discriminating monopolist. T.J. Miceli. *Reg. Sci. Urb. Econ.* **22:4** 11:1992 pp. 579 – 596

I.2.1: Theory *[Théorie]*

53 Possible adverse effects of increasing block water tariffs in developing countries. Dale Whittington. *Econ. Dev. Cult. Change* **41:1** 10:1992 pp. 75 – 87

54 Price, quality and timing of moves in markets with incomplete information — an experimental analysis. D.M. Grether; A. Schwartz; L.L. Wilde. *Econ. J.* **102:413** 7:1992 pp. 754 – 771

55 Production lags and price behaviour. Kon S. Lai; Peter Pauly. *Economica* **59:233** 2:1992 pp. 53 – 62

56 Psychological thresholds demand and price rigidity. S.A. Drakopoulos. *Manch. Sch. E.* **LX:2** 6:1992 pp. 152 – 168

57 Quasi-markets, contracts and quality. Carol Propper. Bristol: University of Bristol. School for Advanced Urban Studies, 1992: 36 p. [Studies in decentralisation and quasi-markets. : No. 9]

58 Regulation and control of monopolies and restrictive trade practices in Pakistan. M.S. Khan. Karachi, Pakistan: Royal Book, 1992: 144 p. *ISBN: 9694071275. Includes bibliographical references (p. 143-144).*

59 Risk reduction and umbrella branding. Cynthia A. Montgomery; Birger Wernerfelt. *J. Bus.* **65:1** 1:1992 pp. 31 – 50

60 Sequential entry with brand loyalty caused by consumer learning-by-using. Jean Gabszewicz; Lynne Pepall; Jacques-François Thisse. *J. Ind. Econ.* **XL:4** 12:1992 pp. 397 – 416

61 Taxation and welfare in an oligopoly with strategic commitment. Timothy Besley; Kotaro Suzumura. *Int. Econ. R.* **33:2** 5:1992 pp. 413 – 432

62 Technology adoption under price uncertainty. T.-K. Kim; D.J. Hayes; A. Hallam. *J. Dev. Econ.* **38:1** 1:1992 pp. 245 – 253

63 The uses and abuses of stand-alone costs. Mark E. Meitzen; Alexander C. Larson. *Util. Policy* **2:2** 4:1992 pp. 135 – 148

64 Vertical product differentiation with entry. S. Donnenfeld; S. Weber. *Int. J. Ind. O.* **10:3** 9:1992 pp. 449 – 472

65 A Walrasian theory of markets with adverse selection. Douglas Gale. *R. Econ. S.* **59:2(199)** 4:1992 pp. 229 – 255

66 Welfare implications of entry deterrence in a spatial market. D.S. Priyarsono. *Ann. Reg. Sci.* **26:4** 1992 pp. 319 – 330

67 Who deters entry? Evidence on the use of strategic entry deterrents. David S. Bunch; Robert Smiley. *Rev. Econ. St.* **LXXIV:3** 8:1992 pp. 509 – 521

Competition *[Concurrence]*

68 Antitrust, innovation, and competitiveness. Thomas M. Jorde *[Ed.]*; David J. Teece *[Ed.]*. New York: Oxford University Press, 1992: viii, 244 p. *ISBN: 019506769x; LofC: 91016148. Includes bibliographical references and index.*

69 Coalitional fair allocations in smooth mixed markets with an atomless sector. B. Shitovitz. *Math. Soc. Sc.* **25:1** 12:1992 pp. 27 – 40

70 Collusion in finitely-repeated oligopolies. K. Basu. *Int. J. Ind. O.* **10:4** 12:1992 pp. 595 – 609

71 Competition among mutually dependent sellers. Friedel Bolle; Werner Güth. *J. Inst. Theo. Ec.* **148:2** 6:1992 pp. 209 – 239

72 Competition law and policy in New Zealand. Rex J. Ahdar *[Ed.]*; Ivor Richardson *[Foreword]*. Sydney: Law Book Company, 1991: xvi, 321 p. *ISBN: 0455210144. Includes bibliographical references.*

73 The competitive outcome as the equilibrium in an Edgeworthian price-quantity model. H.D. Dixon. *Econ. J.* **102:411** 3:1992 pp. 301 – 309

74 Concentration control in the European Economic Community. Pierre V.F. Bos; Jules Stuyck; Peter Wytinck; David Leibman *[Ed.]*; Derek Ridyard. London: Graham & Trotman, 1992: 488 p. *ISBN: 1853335703.* [European business law and practice series.]

75 Contestability in the presence of an alternate market — an experimental examination. J.L. Brown-Kruse. *Rand J. Eco.* **22:1** Spring:1991 pp. 136 – 147

76 Contestable markets, das neoklassische Marktmodell und die Wettbewerbstheorie *[In German]*; Contestable markets, the neoclassical market model and the theory of competition *[Summary]*. Chrysostomos Mantzavinos. *Jahrb. N. St.* **209:1-2** 1:1992 pp. 60 – 66

77 Cost competition — new evidence on an old issue. E. Woodrow Eckard. *Appl. Econ.* **24:11** 11:1992 pp. 1241 – 1250

78 Credible entry threats into contestable markets — a symmetric multi-market model of contestability. Marc Van Wegberg; Arjen Van Witteloostuijn. *Economica* **59:236** 11:1992 pp. 437 – 452

I.2.1: Theory *[Théorie]* — Competition *[Concurrence]*
79 Credible spatial preemption through reputation extension. C.J. Choi; C. Scarpa. *Int. J. Ind. O.* **10:3** 9:1992 pp. 439 – 447
80 Culture and competition — a laboratory market comparison between China and the West. S.J. Kachelmeier; M. Shehata. *J. Econ. Beh.* **19:2** 10:1992 pp. 145 – 168
81 An empirical model of mark-ups in a quality-differentiated export market. Bee Yan Aw. *J. Int. Econ.* **33:3/4** 11:1992 pp. 327 – 344
82 Endogenous availability in search equilibrium. A.F. Daughety; J.F. Reinganum. *Rand J. Eco.* **22:2** Summer:1991 pp. 287 – 306
83 Imperfect competition and basing-point pricing — evidence from the softwood plywood industry. Thomas W. Gilligan. *Am. Econ. Rev.* **82:5** 12:1992 pp. 1106 – 1119
84 Imperfect competition and Pareto-improving strategic trade policy. Aslam H. Anis; Thomas W. Ross. *J. Int. Econ.* **33:3/4** 11:1992 pp. 363 – 371
85 Imperfect competition and the theory of the falling rate of profit. Peter Skott. *Rev. Rad. Pol. Ec.* **24:1** Spring:1992 pp. 101 – 113
86 Imperfect competition, differential information, and microfoundations of macroeconomics. Kiyohiko Nishimura. Oxford: New York, 1992: 231 p. *ISBN: 0198286171; LofC: 91035239. Includes bibliographical references and index.*
87 Imperfect competition, expectations and the multiple effects of monetary growth. N. Rankin. *Econ. J.* **102:413** 7:1992 pp. 743 – 752
88 Increasing returns and competitive equilibrium — the content and development of Marshall's theory. Renee Prendergast. *Camb. J. Econ.* **16:4** 12:1992 pp. 447 – 462
89 Industrial clusters and the competitiveness of the Netherlands. Dany Jacobs; Mark W. de Jong. *Economist [Leiden]* **140:2** 1992 pp. 233 – 252
90 Industrial structures components of finance theory's CAPM. John G. Greenhut; Melvin L. Greenhut. *R. Indust. Organ.* **7:3/4** 1992 pp. 361 – 373
91 Information, incentives, and the economics of control. George Christopher Archibald. Cambridge: Cambridge University Press, 1992: 173 p. *ISBN: 0521330459; LofC: 91043850. Includes index.*
92 Market concentration and competition in Eastern Europe. David M. Newbery; Paul Kattuman. *World. Econ.* **15:3** 5:1992 pp. 315 – 333
93 The meanings of competition in economic analysis. J.E. Stiglitz. *Riv. Int. Sci. Soc.* **2** 4-6:1992 pp. 191 – 211
94 Measures of external and internal competitiveness. U. Schoefisch. *Res. Bank B. NZ* **55:1** 1992 pp. 27 – 38
95 Minimum quality standards, fixed costs, and competition. U. Ronnen. *Rand J. Eco.* **22:4** Winter:1991 pp. 490 – 504
96 Monopolistic competition and preference diversity. Raymond Deneckere; Michael Rothschild. *R. Econ. S.* **59:2(199)** 4:1992 pp. 361 – 373
97 Monopolistic competition when price and quality are imperfectly observable. D. Dranove; M.A. Satterthwaite. *Rand J. Eco.* **23:4** Winter:1992 pp. 518 – 534
98 Nonuniform Bertrand competition. David M. Mandy. *Econometrica* **60:6** 11:1992 pp. 1293 – 1330
99 Oligopoly and dynamic competition — firm, market, and economic system. Mario Baldassarri *[Ed.]*. New York, NY.: St. Martin's Press in association with Rivisita di politica economica, SIPI, Rome, 1992: 368 p. *ISBN: 0312079850; LofC: 92000738. Includes index.* [Central issues in contemporary economic theory and policy.]
100 On hierarchical spatial competition. Shlomo Weber. *R. Econ. S.* **59:2(199)** 4:1992 pp. 407 – 425
101 Optimal licensing of cost-reducing innovation. M.I. Kamien; S.S. Oren. *J. Math Econ.* **21:5** 1992 pp. 483 – 508
102 Preemptive investment, toehold entry, and the mimicking principle. D.A. Malueg; M. Schwartz. *Rand J. Eco.* **22:1** Spring:1991 pp. 1 – 13
103 Sources of competitiveness of the United States and its multinational firms. Irving B. Kravis; Robert E. Lipsey. *Rev. Econ. St.* **LXXIV:2** 5:1992 pp. 193 – 201
104 Technology adoption, learning spillovers, and the optimal duration of patent-based monopolies. P.A. David; T.E. Olsen. *Int. J. Ind. O.* **10:4** 12:1992 pp. 517 – 543
105 Theories of competition and market performance. Arjen van Witteloostuijn. *Economist [Leiden]* **140:1** 1992 pp. 109 – 139

I.2.1: Theory *[Théorie]* —

Pricing *[Fixation du prix]*

106 Adjustment costs and pricing-to-market — theory and evidence. Kenneth Kasa. *J. Int. Econ.* **32:1/2** 2:1992 pp. 1 – 30

107 Aggregation and optimization with state-dependent pricing. Andrew Caplin; John Leahy. New York: Columbia University, Dept of Economics, 1992: 31 p. [Discussion paper series.]

108 Basing point pricing — competition versus collusion. Jacques-François Thisse; Xavier Vives. *J. Ind. Econ.* **XL:3** 9:1992 pp. 249 – 260

109 Bertrand equilibrium and price competition. H. Salonen. *Eur. J. Pol. Ec.* **8:1** 2:1992 pp. 41 – 55

110 Commodity taxation with administered and free market prices — theory and an application to China. Christopher J. Heady; Pradeep K. Mitra. *J. Publ. Ec.* **47:2** 3:1992 pp. 207 – 226

111 Conduct in spatial markets — an empirical analysis of spatial pricing behavior. Bruce L. Benson; Merle D. Faminow; Timothy J. Fik. *Pap. Reg. Sci.* **71:1** 1:1992 pp. 15 – 30

112 Dynamic price competition, briefly sunk costs, and entry deterrence. S.M. Davies. *Rand J. Eco.* **22:4** Winter:1991 pp. 519 – 530

113 The efficiency of advance-purchase discounts in the presence of aggregate demand uncertainty. I.L. Gale; T.J. Holmes. *Int. J. Ind. O.* **10:3** 9:1992 pp. 413 – 437

114 An empirical model of mark-ups in a quality-differentiated export market. Bee Yan Aw. *J. Int. Econ.* **33:3/4** 11:1992 pp. 327 – 344

115 Evidence on price adjustment costs in U.S. manufacturing industry. John M. Roberts. *Econ. Inq.* **XXX:3** 7:1992 pp. 399 – 417

116 Expectations and retail profit margins. René G den Hertog; A. Roy Thurik. *Int. R. Ret. Dist. Res.* **2:3** 7:1992 pp. 263 – 282

117 Experience goods, expectations and pricing. Jae-Cheol Kim. *Econ. Rec.* **68:200** 3:1992 pp. 7 – 15

118 Factor price shocks, factor substitution and their implication for policy. Zafar Mahmood. *Int. Econ. J.* **6:4** Winter:1992 pp. 63 – 73

119 The fate of an errant hypothesis — the doctrine of normal-cost prices. F.S. Lee; J. Irving-Lessmann. *Hist. Polit. Ec.* **24:2** Summer:1992 pp. 273 – 309

120 Futures markets — price discovery and price determination. Jerome L. Stein *[Ed.]*; Barry A. Goss *[Ed.]*; Basil S. Yamey *[Contrib.]*; S. Gulay Avsar *[Contrib.]*; Siang-Choo Chan *[Contrib.]*; Raymond M. Leuthold *[Contrib.]*; Philip Garcia *[Contrib.]*; Nabil Chaherli *[Contrib.]*; Glenn W. Harrison *[Contrib.]*; Anne E. Peck *[Contrib.] and others. Collection of 12 articles.* **Econ. Rec.** , pp. 1 – 140

121 History's role in coordinating decentralized allocation decisions. Donald J. Meyer; John B. van Huyck; Raymond C. Battalio; Thomas R. Saving. *J. Polit. Ec.* **100:2** 4:1992 pp. 292 – 316

122 How to measure price progression — a first axiomatic approach. C. Weinhardt. *Eur. J. Pol. Ec.* **8:1** 2:1992 pp. 115 – 130

123 Index number biases during price liberalization. Kent Osband. *Staff Pap. Int. Monetary* **39:2** 6:1992 pp. 287 – 309

124 Influence of interindustrial relationships on prices in Czechoslovakia. Pavol Karasz. *Econ. Sys. Res.* **4:4** 1992 pp. 377 – 384

125 An intertemporal model of asset prices in a Markov economy with a limiting stationary distribution. Hossein B. Kazemi. *R. Finan. Stud.* **5:1** 1992 pp. 85 – 104

126 Intertemporal speculation, shortages and the political economy of price reform. S. Van Wijnbergen. *Econ. J.* **102:415** 11:1992 pp. 1395 – 1406

127 Iterated elimination of dominated strategies in a Bertrand-Edgeworth model. Tilman Börgers. *R. Econ. S.* **59(1):198** 2:1992 pp. 163 – 176

128 Levels and disparities of retail prices in Slovenia; Livelli e disparità dei prezzi al dettaglio in Slovenia *[Italian summary]*. Egon Žižmond. *Rev. Int. Sci. Ec. Com.* **XXXIX:5-6** 5-6:1992 pp. 519 – 530

129 Levels of disparities of producer prices in Yugoslavia. Egon Žižmond. *Comm. Econ.* **4:2** 1992 pp. 249 – 258

130 Long-term contracting and multiple-price systems. R. Glenn Hubbard; Robert J. Weiner. *J. Bus.* **65:2** 4:1992 pp. 177 – 198

131 Marchandises non fondamentales et système étalon en présence de terres *[In French]*; Non-basic commodities, the standard system and the presence of land *[Summary]*. G. Erreygers. *Rev. Ec. Polit.* **102:5** 9-10:1992 pp. 687 – 702

I.2.1: Theory *[Théorie]* — *Pricing [Fixation du prix]*

132 The mechanisms of price control. D.R. Glynn. *Util. Policy* **2:2** 4:1992 pp. 90 – 99

133 Mixed pricing in oligopoly with consumer switching costs. A.J. Padilla. *Int. J. Ind. O.* **10:3** 9:1992 pp. 393 – 411

134 Nomial price stickiness as a rational expectations equilibrium. Roger E.A. Farmer. *J. Econ. Dyn. Cont.* **16:2** 4:1992 pp. 317 – 338

135 Oligopolistic pricing and the effects of aggregate demand on economic activity. Julio Rotemberg; Michael Woodford. *J. Polit. Ec.* **100:6** 12:1992 pp. 1153 – 1207

136 Oligopoly limit pricing. K. Bagwell; G. Ramey. *Rand J. Eco.* **22:2** Summer:1991 pp. 155 – 172

137 On the behaviour of commodity prices. Angus Deaton; Guy Laroque. *R. Econ. S.* **59(1):198** 2:1992 pp. 1 – 23

138 On the efficiency of ex ante and ex post pricing institution. M. Peters. *Econ. Theory* **2:1** 1992 pp. 85 – 102

139 On the estimation of beta-pricing models. Jay Shanken. *R. Finan. Stud.* **5:1** 1992 pp. 1 – 34

140 On the welfare effects of regulating price discrimination. Norman J. Ireland. *J. Ind. Econ.* **XL:3** 9:1992 pp. 237 – 248

141 Optimal control of price and investment policies in a dynamic deterministic model. Christoph Weiser. *J. Inst. Theo. Ec.* **148:2** 6:1992 pp. 274 – 291

142 Output fluctuations as entry deterrence — a model of predatory pricing; *[French summary]*. Leslie Young; Ali Bolbol. *Can. J. Econ.* **XXV:1** 2:1992 pp. 89 – 110

143 Price control versus quantity control — the implication of stabilizing intervention. Christopher K. Ma; Morgan J. Lynge. *Q Rev. Econ. Finan.* **32:1** Spring:1992 pp. 84 – 102

144 Price cycles and booms — dynamic search equilibrium. Chaim Fershtman; Arthur Fishman. *Am. Econ. Rev.* **82:5** 12:1992 pp. 1221 – 1233

145 Price discrimination in competitive markets. Luis Locay; Alvaro Rodriguez. *J. Polit. Ec.* **110:5** 10:1992 pp. 954 – 965

146 Price dynamics in UK manufacturing — a microeconomic view. P.A. Geroski. *Economica* **59:236** 11:1992 pp. 403 – 419

147 Price leadership. Raymond J. Deneckere; Dan Kovenock. *R. Econ. S.* **59(1):198** 2:1992 pp. 143 – 162

148 Price reform in China, 1979-86. Jiann-Jong Guo. New York: St Martin's Press, 1992: 205 p. *ISBN: 0312068190; LofC: 91024332. Includes bibliographical references and index.*

149 Price responsiveness in socialist industry — a generalized restricted cost function approach; *[German summary]*. Mark A. Reimann. *Econ. Sys.* **16:2** 10:1992 pp. 205 – 226

150 Price-cap versus rate-of-return regulation in a stochastic-cost model. E.M. Pint. *Rand J. Eco.* **23:4** Winter:1992 pp. 564 – 578

151 Price-cost margins in Dutch manufacturing. Y.M. Prince; A.R. Thurik. *Economist [Leiden]* **140:3** 1992 pp. 310 – 335

152 Prices and knowledge — a market process perspective. Esteban F. Thomsen. London: Routledge, 1992: 150 p. *ISBN: 0415068657; LofC: 91028388. Includes bibliographical references and index.* [Foundations of the market economy.]

153 Prices of state contingent claims with insider traders, and the favourite-longshot bias. H.S. Shin. *Econ. J.* **102:411** 3:1992 pp. 426 – 435

154 Pricing and capacity decisions for a service facility — stability and multiple local optima. Shaler Stidham. *Manag. Sci.* **38:8** 8:1992 pp. 1121 – 1139

155 Pricing in Australian manufacturing. Harry Bloch. *Econ. Rec.* **68:203** 12:1992 pp. 365 – 376

156 Pricing strategies in markets with dynamic elasticities. Philip Parker. *Market. Lett.* **3:3** 7:1992 pp. 227 – 237

157 Product differentiation and price collusion. P. Jehiel. *Int. J. Ind. O.* **10:4** 12:1992 pp. 633 – 641

158 Production prices and dynamic stability results and open questions. Luciano Boggio. *Manch. Sch. E.* **LX:3** 9:1992 pp. 264 – 294

159 Регулирование цен в условиях перехода к рынку *[In Russian]*; (Price regulation in transition to market). T.K. Kondrasheva; A.A. Nikiphorov. *Vest. Mosk. Univ.* 6 **:5** 9-10:1992 pp. 3 – 12

160 Relation between finance statement information and prices. Ray Ball *[Contrib.]*; Thomas L. Stober *[Contrib.]*; Robert W. Holthausen *[Contrib.]*; David F. Larcker *[Contrib.]*; Anthony C. Greig *[Contrib.]*. *Collection of 4 articles.* **J. Account. E.** , *15:2/3*, 6/9:1992 pp. 319 – 442

161 Search costs and prices. L. Samuelson; J. Zhang. *Econ. Lett.* **38:1** 1:1992 pp. 55 – 60

I.2.1: Theory *[Théorie]* — *Pricing [Fixation du prix]*

162 Selling costs and switching costs — explaining retail gasoline margins. S. Borenstein. *Rand J. Eco.* **22:**3 Autumn:1991 pp. 354 – 369

163 Signalling strength — limit pricing and predatory pricing. G. LeBlanc. *Rand J. Eco.* **23:**4 Winter:1992 pp. 493 – 506

164 Some evidence on option prices as predictors of volatility. Malcolm Edey; Graham Elliot. *Ox. B. Econ. S.* **54:**4 11:1992 pp. 567 – 578

165 Special offers and clustering under symmetric monopoly. N. Schulz. *J. Econ.* **56:**3 1992 pp. 311 – 334

166 Staggered and synchronized price policies under inflation — the multiproduct monopoly case. Eytan Sheshinski; Yoram Weiss. *R. Econ. S.* **59:**2(199) 4:1992 pp. 331 – 359

167 Sunspot-like effects of random endowments. Rodolfo Manuelli; James Peck. *J. Econ. Dyn. Cont.* **16:**2 4:1992 pp. 193 – 206

168 Transfer pricing reconsidered. Joshua Ronen. *J. Publ. Ec.* **47:**1 2:1992 pp. 125 – 136

169 Uncertainty, information, and hedonic pricing. S.B. Kask; S.A. Maani. *Land Econ.* **68:**2 5:1992 pp. 170 – 184

170 Valuing goods' characteristics — an application of the hedonic price method to environmental attributes. G.D. Garrod; K.G. Willis. *J. Environ. Manag.* **34:**1 1:1992 pp. 59 – 76

171 Vertical price fixing in Australia. Philip H. Clarke. Sydney: Federation Press, 1991: xviii, 244 p. (ill) *ISBN: 1862870543. Includes bibliographical references (p. 235-238) and index.*

172 Violations of dominance in pricing judgements. Barbara Mellers; Robin Weiss; Michael Birnbaum. *J. Risk Uncert.* **5:**1 2:1992 pp. 73 – 90

173 Voting, spatial monopoly, and spatial price regulation. Meng-Hua Ye; Anthony M.J. Yezer. *Econ. Inq.* **XXX:**1 1:1992 pp. 29 – 39

174 When more is less — defense profit policy in a competitive environment. A.G. Bower; K. Osband. *Rand J. Eco.* **22:**1 Spring:1991 pp. 107 – 119

Supply and demand *[Offre et demande]*

175 A behavioural approach to kinked demand curves. Stavros Drakopoulos. *Cyprus J. Econ.* **5:**1 6:1992 pp. 1 – 14

176 Demand and shortage of durable consumer goods in socialist countries. X. Yin. *Appl. Econ.* **24:**2 2:1992 pp. 219 – 226

177 The dual role of user cost in the derivation of Keynes's aggregate supply function. Christopher Torr. *R. Pol. Econ.* **4:**1 1992 pp. 1 – 17

178 Duality and modern economics. Richard Cornes. Cambridge: Cambridge University Press, 1992: xii, 290 p. *ISBN: 0521332915; LofC: 91018054. Includes bibliographical references (p. 267-281) and indexes.*

179 Income variability, homeownership, and housing demand. Donald R. Haurin. *Journal of social distress and the homeless Vol.1; No.1 - 3: 1991.* pp. 60 – 74

180 The informational role of upstairs and downstairs trading. Sanford J. Grossman. *J. Bus.* **65:**4 10:1992 pp. 509 – 528

181 Market forms and effective demand — Keynesian results with perfect competition. Claudio Sardoni. *R. Pol. Econ.* **4:**4 1992 pp. 377 – 395

182 Multimarket cooperation with scope effects in demand. K. Kesteloot. *J. Econ.* **55:**3 1992 pp. 245 – 264

183 A review of new demand elasticities with special reference to short and long run effects of price change; Ein Überblick über neuere Schätzungen von Nachfrageelastizitäten mit spezieller Berücksichtigung kurz- und langfristiger Effekte von Preisänderungen *[German summary]*; Etude d'élasticités de demande nouvelles avec référence spéciale aux effets à court terme et à long terme de changements de prix *[French summary]*; Una síntesis de nuevas elasticidades de demanda con especial referencia a los efectos a corto y largo plazo de cambios en los precios *[Spanish summary]*. P.B. Goodwin. *J. Transp. Ec. Pol.* **XXVI:**2 5:1992 pp. 155 – 170

I.2.2: Price levels (descriptive studies) — *Niveau des prix (études descriptives)*

1 ARIMA models of the price level — an assessment of the multilevel adaptive learning process in the USA. P. Dua; S.C. Ray. *J. Forecast.* **11:6** 9:1992 pp. 507 – 516

2 Estimating price trends for residential property — a comparison of repeat sales and assessed value methods. John M. Clapp; Carmelo Giaccotto. *J. Real Est. Finan. Econ.* **5:4** 12:1992 pp. 357 – 374

3 Inflação e variabilidade dos preços relativos no Brasil — a questão da causalidade *[In Portuguese]*; [Inflation and relative price variability in Brazil — the issue of causality] *[Summary]*. Marcelo Resende; Rodolfo Grandi. *Rev. Bras. Ec.* **46:4** 10/12:1992 pp. 595 – 604

4 Price levels and price disparities in Slovenia; *[Italian summary]*. E. Žižmond. *Econ. Int.* **XLV:3-4** 8-11:1992 pp. 364 – 377

5 Product quality, attributes, and brand name as determinants of price — the case of consumer electronics. Morris B. Holbrook. *Market. Lett.* **3:1** 1:1992 pp. 71 – 83

6 The resale price maintenance struggle — its legislative updating. A.J. Greco. *Am. J. Econ. S.* **51:2** 4:1992 pp. 173 – 186

7 The response of domestic prices to expected exchange rates. Robert M. Feinberg; Seth Kaplan. *J. Bus.* **65:2** 4:1992 pp. 267 – 280

I.2.3: Specific prices and markets — *Prix et marchés de produits particuliers*

Sub-divisions: Agricultural market *[Marché agricole]*; Housing market *[Marché du logement]*

1 Les analyses formelles des marchés de la drogue *[In French]*; (Formal analyses of drug markets); (Formal'nyj analiz rynka narkotikov: *Title only in Russian*); (Analyse des Drogenhandels: *Title only in German*); (Los análisis formales de los mercados de la droga: *Title only in Spanish*). Pierre Kopp. *R. T-Monde* **XXXIII:131** 7-9:1992 pp. 565 – 579

2 Applying Margrabe's exchange option model to pricing proxy contests. G.D. Hancock; T.K. Mukherjee. *J. Bus. Fin. Acc.* **19:6** 11:1992 pp. 889 – 900

3 Auslandspreise und Inlandskonjunktur bei Wechselkursflexibilität *[In German]*; Foreign prices and domestic economy under flexible exchange rates *[Summary]*. Hans-Joachim Jarchow. *Z. Wirt. Soz.* **112:1** 1992 pp. 1 – 23

4 The behavior of prices and inflation — an empirical analysis of disaggregated price data. Saul Lach; Daniel Tsiddon. *J. Polit. Ec.* **100:2** 4:1992 pp. 349 – 389

5 Bundling subscription TV channels — a case of natural bundling. S. Chae. *Int. J. Ind. O.* **10:2** 6:1992 pp. 213 – 230

6 Co-integration analysis and the determinants of land prices. D. Hallam; F. Machado; G. Rapsomanikis. *J. Agr. Econ.* **43:1** 1:1992 pp. 28 – 37

7 The commercialization of the land market? Land ownership patterns in the Mexican city of Puebla. Gareth Jones. *Third World Vol.13; No.2 - 5: 1991.* pp. 129 – 154

8 A comparison of electricity and natural gas markets and regulation in the USA. Richard O'Neill; Charles Whitmore; Gary J. Mahrenholz. *Util. Policy* **2:3** 7:1992 pp. 204 – 227

9 Competition in New Zealand's electricity business. Clark W. Gellings. *Util. Policy* **2:3** 7:1992 pp. 178 – 184

10 Concepts of price elasticities of transport demand and recent empirical estimates; Konzepte der Preiselastizitäten der Verkehrsnachfrage und neuere empirische Schätzansätze *[German summary]*; Concepts d'élasticité des prix de la demande de transport et estimations empiriques récentes *[French summary]*; Los conceptos de elasticidades-precio de la demanda de transporte y estimaciones empíricas recientes *[Spanish summary]*. Tae Hoon Oum; W.G. Waters; Jong-Say Yong. *J. Transp. Ec. Pol.* **XXVI:2** 5:1992 pp. 139 – 154

11 Consumer price perceptions and expectations. Peter Simmons; Daniel Weiserbs. *Ox. Econ. Pap.* **44:1** 1:1992 pp. 35 – 50

12 The crude oil market mechanism in the light of the 1990-91 price crisis. Mohammad Sadegh Memarian. *OPEC Rev.* **XVI:4** Winter:1992 pp. 419 – 439

I.2.3: Specific prices and markets *[Prix et marchés de produits particuliers]*

13 De la pratique du marketing direct dans le secteur des services financiers *[In French]*; Direct marketing practice in the financial services sector *[Summary]*. Jean-Charles Chebat; George Sani. *Gestion* **8:1** 1992 pp. 41 – 50

14 The demand for cider in the United Kingdom. David Blake; Sean Boyle. *Ox. B. Econ. S.* **54:1** 2:1992 pp. 73 – 86

15 Demand, pricing and regulation — evidence from the cable TV industry. J.W. Mayo; Y. Otsuka. *Rand J. Eco.* **22:3** Autumn:1991 pp. 396 – 410

16 The determinants of commercial property prices and rents. S.M. Dobson; J.A. Goddard. *B. Econ. Res.* **44:4** 10:1992 pp. 301 – 322

17 A disaggregated nonhomothetic modeling of responsiveness to residential time-of-use electricity rates. Dean C. Mountain; Evelyn L. Lawson. *Int. Econ. R.* **33:1** 2:1992 pp. 181 – 208

18 Domestic content requirements with bilateral monopoly. John C. Beghin; Daniel C. Sumner. *Ox. Econ. Pap.* **44:2** 4:1992 pp. 306 – 316

19 Due diligence and the demand for electricity — a cautionary tale. Franklin M. Fisher; Peter S. Fox-Penner; Joen E. Greenwood; William G. Moss; Almarin Phillips. *R. Indust. Organ.* **7:2** 1992 pp. 117 – 149

20 The economic effects of minimum import prices with an application to Uruguay. Federico Changanaquí; Patrick A. Messerlin. Washington, D.C.: Country Economics Department, The World Bank, 1992: 23 p. [Policy research working papers.]

21 Une économie européenne des marchés de l'art *[In French]*; [A European economy in the art markets]. Bruno Claverie. *R. Mar. Comm.* :**361** 9-10:1992 pp. 698 – 716

22 Effects of urban transportation system change on land prices in the setting of owner-occupied residence. Se-il Mun; Komei Sasaki. *J. Urban Ec.* **32:3** 11:1992 pp. 351 – 366

23 Energy issues for the 1990s. His Excellency Subroto *[Contrib.]*; Walter J. Hickel *[Contrib.]*; Donald Behrend *[Contrib.]*; Saadalla A. Al-Fathi *[Contrib.]*; Scott Goldsmith *[Contrib.]*; Arlon R. Tussing *[Contrib.]*; Michael J. Harris *[Contrib.]*; Roger Marks *[Contrib.]*; Bright E. Okogu *[Contrib.]*; Charles L. Logsdon *[Contrib.] and others. Collection of 15 articles.* **OPEC Rev.** , *XVI:4,* Winter:1992 pp. 1 – 261

24 The energy supply and demand outlook in the Asia-Pacific region. Fereidun Fesharaki; Nancy Yamaguchi. *OPEC Rev.* **XVI:2** Summer:1992 pp. 119 – 136

25 Energy use in an era of rapidly changing oil price — how OPEC did not save the world from the greenhouse effect. H. Neuburger. *Envir. Plan.A.* **24:7** 7:1992 pp. 1039 – 1049

26 Estimating loyalty and switching with an application to the automobile market. Patrick S. McCarthy; P.K. Kannan; Radha Chandrasekharan; Gordon P. Wright. *Manag. Sci.* **38:10** 10:1992 pp. 1371 – 1393

27 Estimating the effects of consumer incentive programs on domestic automobile sales. Patrick A. Thompson; Thomas Noordewier. *J. Bus. Econ. Stat.* **10:4** 10:1992 pp. 409 – 417

28 Estimating VAR models under non-stationarity and cointegration — alternative approaches for forecasting cattle prices. P. Franchon; J. Wendel. *Appl. Econ.* **24:2** 2:1992 pp. 207 – 218

29 Flessibilità dei prezzi e struttura indutriale — un'analisi relativa ai mercati italiani *[In Italian]*; Price flexibility and industrial structure — a survey on the Italian markets *[Summary]*. Vincenzo Testa. *Industria* **XIII:1** 1-3:1992 pp. 57 – 78

30 The food situation in the ex-Soviet republics. Susan Senior Nello. *Eur.-Asia Stud.* **44:5** 1992 pp. 857 – 880

31 Forecasting rough diamond prices — a non-linear optimization model of dominant firm behaviour. Michael von Saldern. *Res. Pol.* **18:1** 3:1992 pp. 45 – 58

32 Forward looking price setting in UK manufacturing. S. Price. *Econ. J.* **102:412** 5:1992 pp. 497 – 505

33 Freedom of speech vs. efficient regulation in markets for ideas. A. Breton; R. Wintrobe. *J. Econ. Beh.* **17:2** 3:1992 pp. 217 – 240

34 Government-introduced price distortions and growth — evidence from twenty-nine developing countries. R.D. Singh. *Publ. Choice* **73:1** 1:1992 pp. 83 – 100

35 Hierarchical spline models for conditional quantiles and the demand for electricity. Wallace Hendricks; Roger Koenker. *J. Am. Stat. Ass.* **87:417** 3:1992 pp. 58 – 68

36 The housing system of the former Soviet Union — why do the Soviets need housing markets? Betrand Renaud. *Hous. Pol. Deb.* **3:3** 1992 pp. 877 – 899

37 The impact of excise duty changes on retail prices in the UK. Paul Baker; Vanessa Brechling. *Fis. Stud.* **13:2** 5:1992 pp. 48 – 65

I.2.3: Specific prices and markets *[Prix et marchés de produits particuliers]*

38 Intercommodity price transmittal — analysis of food markets in Ghana. Harold Alderman. Washington, D.C.: Western Africa Department and Agriculture and Rural Development Department, The World Bank, 1992: 36 p. *Bibliography* — *p.34-36.* [Policy research working papers.]

39 Land taxation and its impact on land prices — the case of Japan in the 1990s. Koichi Mera. *R. Urban. Region. Dev. S.* **4:2** 7:1992 pp. 130 – 146

40 Localized competition and organizational failure in the Manhattan hotel industry, 1898-1990. Joel A.C. Baum; Stephen J. Mezias. *Adm. Sci. Qua.* **37:4** 12:1992 pp. 580 – 604

41 Markups in U.S. and Japanese manufacturing — a short-run econometric analysis. Catherine J. Morrison. *J. Bus. Econ. Stat.* **10:1** 1:1992 pp. 51 – 64

42 A mezőgazdasági termőföld komplex értékelése *[In Hungarian]*; Complex valuation of the cultivable land area *[Summary]*. Aladár Sipos; István Szücs. *Közg. Sz.* **XXXIX** 12:1992 pp. 1144 – 1153

43 A model of the electricity market in the province of Québec — overview and results. Danny Bélanger; Jean-Thomas Bernard. *Ener. Econ.* **14:2** 4:1992 pp. 107 – 118

44 Modelling and testing the effect of market structure on price — the case of international air transport; Ein Modell zu den Auswirkungen der Marktstruktur auf den Preis — Das Beispiel des internationalen Luftverkehrs *[German summary]*; Modèles et essais des effets sur les prix de la structure du marché. Le cas du transport aérien international *[French summary]*; La modelización y evaluación de los efectos de la estructura de mercado en los precios — el caso del transporte aéreo internacional *[Spanish summary]*. Martin Dresner; Michael W. Tretheway. *J. Transp. Ec. Pol.* **XXVI:2** 5:1992 pp. 171 – 184

45 Multi-product incumbent and a puppy dog entrant — some simulations for the Norwegian cement market. L. Sørgard. *Int. J. Ind. O.* **10:2** 6:1992 pp. 251 – 272

46 Oil futures and spot markets. Massood V. Samii. *OPEC Rev.* **XVI:4** Winter:1992 pp. 409 – 417

47 Az oligopóliumoktól a monopolisztikus versenyig *[In Hungarian]*; From oligopolies to the monopolistic competition. A microeconomic and institutional analysis — based on the investigation of the taxi, book and flower markets *[Summary]*. Szabó Katalin. *Közg. Sz.* **XXXIX:** 7-8:1992 pp. 667 – 690

48 Pool prices, contracts and regulation in the British electricity supply industry. Dieter Helm; Andrew Powell. *Fis. Stud.* **13:1** 2:1992 pp. 89 – 105

49 Preserving oil's competitiveness in the face of the environmental regulations. John V. Mitchell. *OPEC B.* **XXIII:5** 5:1992 pp. 13 – 22

50 The prices of alcoholic beverages in the Nordic countries; *[French summary]*; *[Spanish summary]*. Øyvind Horverak; Esa Österberg. *Br. J. Addict.* **87:10** 10:1992 pp. 1393 – 1408

51 Pricing, patent loss and the market for pharmaceuticals. Richard G. Frank; David S. Salkever. *S. Econ. J.* **59:2** 10:1992 pp. 165 – 179

52 Relações dinâmicas entre oferta monetária, preços agrícolas e preços industriais — testes de co-integração e causalidade *[In Portuguese]*; [Dynamic relations between money supply, agricultural prices and industrial prices — co-integration and causality tests] *[Summary]*. Antonio Cordeiro de Santana; Sergio Alberto Brandt. *Rev. Bras. Ec.* **46:2** 4-6:1992 pp. 223 – 240

53 Residential energy demand modelling in developing regions — the use of multivariate statistical techniques. V. Assimakopoulos. *Ener. Econ.* **14:1** 1:1992 pp. 57 – 64

54 Retail pricing and the costs of clearance sales — the formalisation of a rule of thumb. B. van Praag; B. Bode. *Eur. Econ. R.* **36:4** 5:1992 pp. 945 – 963

55 Soft budget constraints, firm commitments, and the social safety net. Daniel C. Hardy. *Staff Pap. Int. Monetary* **39:2** 6:1992 pp. 310 – 329

56 Subsidization policies in Egypt — neither economic growth nor distribution. Iliya Harik. *Int. J. M.E. Stud.* **24:3** 8:1992 pp. 481 – 499

57 Supply functioning equilibria and the danger of tacit collusion — the case of spot markets for electricity. Friedel Bolle. *Ener. Econ.* **14:2** 4:1992 pp. 94 – 102

58 Symmetric or asymmetric price adjustments in the oil market — an empirical analysis of the relations between international and domestic prices in the Federal Republic of Germany, 1972-89. Gebhard Kirchgässner; Knut Kübler. *Ener. Econ.* **14:3** 7:1992 pp. 171 – 185

59 Tarifas óptimas en dos partes — el caso de la energía eléctrica residencial en España *[In Spanish]*; [Optimal two part tariffs — the case of household electrical energy in Spain] *[Summary]*. Ana C. Buisán. *Invest. Econ.* **XVI:1** 1:1992 pp. 99 – 125

60 A theory of land prices when land is supplied publicly — the case of the Netherlands. Barrie Needham. *Urban Stud.* **29:5** 6:1992 pp. 669 – 686

I.2.3: Specific prices and markets *[Prix et marchés de produits particuliers]*
61 The US retail demand for fish products — an application of the almost ideal demand system. K.F. Wellman. *Appl. Econ.* **24:4** 4:1992 pp. 445 – 458
62 Vancouver's gasoline-price wars — an empirical exercise in uncovering supergame strategies. Margaret E. Slade. *R. Econ. S.* **59:2(199)** 4:1992 pp. 257 – 276
63 Wage and rent capitalization in the commercial real estate market. Rena Sivitanidou; William C. Wheaton. *J. Urban Ec.* **31:2** 3:1992 pp. 206 – 229
64 A welfare analysis of the site value taxation model. Chin W. Yang; Dwight B. Means. *J. Real Est. Finan. Econ.* **5:3** 9:1992 pp. 281 – 290
65 Wettbewerbspolitik in Österreich *[In German]*; [Competition policy in Austria]. Elisabeth Czachay *[Contrib.]*; Gerhard Karsch *[Contrib.]*; Hanspeter Hanreich *[Contrib.]*; Wolfgang Pollan *[Contrib.]*; Joachim Lamel *[Contrib.]*; Manfred E. Streit *[Contrib.]*; Meinhard Ciresa *[Contrib.]*; Dieter Birkenmaier *[Contrib.]*; Ingfried F. Hochbaum *[Contrib.]*; Johann Farnleitner *[Contrib.] and others. Collection of 12 articles.* **Wirt. Blät.** , *39:1*, 1992 pp. 16 – 122
66 Wissensnutzung in Märkten *[In German]*; [Use of information in markets] *[Summary]*. Gerhard Wegner. *Jahr. Soz.schaft.* **43:1** 1992 pp. 44 – 64

Agricultural market *[Marché agricole]*

67 Agricultural pricing and public investment. David M. Newbery. *J. Publ. Ec.* **47:2** 3:1992 pp. 253 – 272
68 Australia's recent experience with the collapse of its wool buffer stock scheme — some key lessons. H. Don; B.H. Gunasekera; Brian S. Fisher. *World. Econ.* **15:2** 3:1992 pp. 251 – 269
69 An economic analysis of a cross-market subsidy scheme for Morocco's food grain sector. Azzeddine M. Azzam; Amal Britel. *J. Econ. Stud.* **19:5** 1992 pp. 55 – 72
70 Economies of scope and the cash crop — food crop debate in Senegal. S.J. Goetz. *World Dev.* **20:5** 5:1992 pp. 727 – 734
71 Effect of institutional realities on dynamic hedging performance for a grain producer. Steve Martinez; Kelly D. Zering. *J. Futur. Mark.* **12:2** 4:1992 pp. 237 – 251
72 The effect of price reduction and direct income support policies on agricultural input markets in Austria. Chr. R. Weiss. *J. Agr. Econ.* **43:1** 1:1992 pp. 1 – 13
73 Hypotheses testing concerning relationships between spot prices of various types of coffee. E. Vogelvang. *J. Appl. Econ.* **7:2** 4-6:1992 pp. 191 – 201
74 Logique de filière et logique territoriale — analyse comparée des productions animales de Midi-Pyrénées dans la concurrence *[In French]*; [Channel logic and territorial logic a comparative analysis of the market position of Midi-Pyrénées meat products]. D. Coquart; L. Mazenc. *R.E.M.* **40:1** 1992 pp. 15 – 34
75 The nature and extent of the market for high-quality beef in Japan before the abolition of import quotas. H. Mori; B.-H. Lin; N.D. Uri. *Appl. Econ.* **24:7** 7:1992 pp. 761 – 773
76 Price distortions and resource-use efficiency in Indian agriculture — a restricted profit function approach. Subal C. Kumbhakar; Arunava Bhattacharyya. *Rev. Econ. St.* **LXXIV:2** 5:1992 pp. 231 – 239
77 La relazione domanda-prezzo nei prodotti dell'agricoltura ecologica *[In Italian]*; Demand-price relationships for the produce from organic farming *[Summary]*. Lorella Marchesini. *Riv. Econ. Agrar.* **XLVII:1** 3:1992 pp. 35 – 66
78 Soviet feedgrain consumption — a stable long-run relationship? Mark Denbaly. *J. Comp. Econ.* **16:2** 6:1992 pp. 259 – 271
79 Spatial pricing efficiency in groundnut markets in Tamil Nadu. D. Jayaraj. *Ind. J. Agri. Eco.* **XLVII:1** 1-3:1992 pp. 79 – 89
80 Sugar prices and high-fructose corn syrup consumption in the United States. A.R. Barros. *J. Agr. Econ.* **43:1** 1:1992 pp. 64 – 73

Housing market *[Marché du logement]*

81 Adjustable rate mortgages and housing demand — the impact of initial rate discounts. Richard A. Phillips; James H. VanderHoff. *J. Real Est. Finan. Econ.* **5:3** 9:1992 pp. 269 – 279
82 Aging and housing market dynamics — a case study of local supply and demand. F. Filius; L. Lundin. *Scand. Hous. Plan. R.* **9:2** 5:1992 pp. 79 – 92
83 Consumer durables spending and housing market activity. Alan Carruth; Andrew Henley. *Scot. J. Poli.* **39:3** 8:1992 pp. 261 – 271

I.2.3: Specific prices and markets *[Prix et marchés de produits particuliers]* — **Housing market** *[Marché du logement]*

84 Development of standardized indices for measuring house price inflation incorporating physical and locational characteristics. M.C. Fleming; J.G. Nellis. *Appl. Econ.* **24:9** 9:1992 pp. 1067 – 1085

85 Discrimination in the housing and mortgage markets. Margery Austin Turner *[Contrib.]*; Ronald E. Wienk *[Contrib.]*; Glenn B. Canner *[Contrib.]*; Stuart A. Gabriel *[Contrib.]*; Susan M. Wachter *[Contrib.]*; Isaac F. Megbolugbe *[Contrib.]*; John F. Kain *[Contrib.]*; Meryl Finkel *[Contrib.]*; Stephen D. Kennedy *[Contrib.]*; Mittie Olion Chandler *[Contrib.]* and others. Collection of 11 articles. **Hous. Pol. Deb.** , *3:2,* 1992 pp. 185 – 745

86 The distribution of the benefits of tax arbitrage in the housing market. Andrew Narwold. *J. Urban Ec.* **32:3** 11:1992 pp. 367 – 376

87 Dynamic housing market equilibrium with taste heterogeneity, idiosyncratic perfect foresight, and stock conversions. Alex Anas; Richard J. Arnott. *Journal of social distress and the homeless Vol.1; No.1 - 3: 1991.* pp. 2 – 32

88 The effect of coastal land use restrictions on housing prices — a repeat sale analysis. George R. Parsons. *J. Envir. Ec. Manag.* **22:1** 1:1992 pp. 25 – 37

89 Explaining UK house price inflation 1971-89. D. Stern. *Appl. Econ.* **24:12** 12:1992 pp. 1327 – 1333

90 House prices, arrears and possessions.*Bank of Engl. Q.* **32:2** 5:1992 pp. 173 – 179

91 Housing and employment in Indonesia — prospects for employment generation in the construction materials sector. Piet Rietveld. *B. Ind. Econ. St.* **28:2** 8:1992 pp. 55 – 73

92 Housing markets, consumption and financial liberalisation in the major economies. D. Miles; M. Sebastián *[Comments by]*; S.P. Zeldes *[Comments by]*. *Eur. Econ. R.* **36:5** 6:1992 pp. 1093 – 1127

93 The impact of hazardous waste superfund sites on the value of houses sold in New Jersey. M. Greenberg; J. Hughes. *Ann. Reg. Sci.* **26:2** 1992 pp. 147 – 154

94 Income inequality as an indicator of discrimination in housing markets. Robert Kaestner; Wendy Fleischer. *Rev. Bl. Pol. Ec.* **21:2** Fall:1992 pp. 55 – 80

95 Increasing access or widening choice — the role of resold public-sector dwellings in the housing market. N.J. Williams; F.E. Twine. *Envir. Plan.A.* **24:11** 11:1992 pp. 1585 – 1598

96 Integrating auction and search markets — the slow Dutch auction. Paul D. Adams; Brian D. Kluger; Steve B. Wyatt. *J. Real Est. Finan. Econ.* **5:3** 9:1992 pp. 239 – 253

97 Land values and housing rents in urban Japan. Louis A. Rose. *J. Urban Ec.* **31:2** 3:1992 pp. 230 – 251

98 Legyenek-e bérlakások? *[In Hungarian]*; Should rented flats exist? Problems of the Hungarian rented flats sector as reflected by foreign experience *[Summary]*. Zsuzsa Dániel. *Közg. Sz.* **XXXIX** 2:1992 pp. 109 – 122

99 Local market and national components in house price appreciation. Joseph Gyourko; Richard Voith. *J. Urban Ec.* **32:1** 7:1992 pp. 52 – 69

100 Markets, states and housing provision — four European growth regions compared. J. Barlow; S. Duncan. *Prog. Plan.* **38:2** 1992 pp. 97 – 177

101 A model of rental housing choices in the Korean market. Seon-Jae Kim. *Urban Stud.* **29:8** 12:1992 pp. 1247 – 1263

102 Un modelo para el análisis del gasto en vivienda *[In Spanish]*; [A model for the analysis of the housing market]. Luis Angel Hiero Recio; Ana María Carrillo Vargas; María Luisa Ridao Carlini; Mercedes Morillo Moreno. *Infor. Com. Esp.* :707 7:1992 pp. 89 – 97

103 Overlapping neighborhoods and housing externalities. William Strange. *J. Urban Ec.* **32:1** 7:1992 pp. 17 – 39

104 The racial housing price differential and racially transitional neighborhoods. Daniel N. Chambers. *J. Urban Ec.* **32:2** 9:1992 pp. 214 – 232

105 The real estate cycle and the economy — consequences of the Massachusetts boom of 1984-87. Karl E. Case. *Urban Stud.* **29:2** 4:1992 pp. 171 – 184

106 The role of co-skewness in the pricing of real estate. Crocker H. Liu; David J. Hartzell; Terry V. Grissom. *J. Real Est. Finan. Econ.* **5:3** 9:1992 pp. 299 – 319

107 The role of the list price in housing markets — theory and an econometric model. J.L. Horowitz. *J. Appl. Econ.* **7:2** 4-6:1992 pp. 115 – 129

108 Search, hedonic prices and housing demand. Sunwoong Kim. *Rev. Econ. St.* **LXXIV:3** 8:1992 pp. 503 – 508

109 A second look at the Bangkok land and housing market. David E. Dowall. *Urban Stud.* **29:1** 2:1992 pp. 25 – 38

I.2.3: Specific prices and markets *[Prix et marchés de produits particuliers]* — Housing market *[Marché du logement]*

110 Taxes and speculative behavior in land and real estate markets. Karl Case. *R. Urban. Region. Dev. S.* **4:2** 7:1992 pp. 226 – 239

111 Timing of bids at pooled real estate auctions. Bruce Vanderporten. *J. Real Est. Finan. Econ.* **5:3** 9:1992 pp. 255 – 267

112 Why should Ghanaians build houses in urban areas? An introduction to private sector housing supply in Ghana. Graham A. Tipple; Kenneth G. Willis. *Cities* **9:1** 2:1992 pp. 60 – 74

J: Money and finance — *Monnaie et finance*

J.1: Money — *Monnaie*

Sub-divisions: Demand for money *[Demande de monnaie]*; Inflation *[Inflation]*

1 An application of the Girton-Roper monetary model of exchange market pressure — the Japanese experience, 1959-1991; Una applicazione del modello monetario Girton-Roper di pressione del mercato dei cambi — l'esperienza giapponese, 1959-1991 *[Italian summary]*. Mark E. Wohar; Bun Song Lee. *Rev. Int. Sci. Ec. Com.* **XXXIX:12** 12:1992 pp. 993 – 1013

2 Arfolyampolitika a stabilizációs programokban *[In Hungarian]*; (Currency policy in the programmes of stabilization). Gáspár Pál. *Pénz. Sz.* **36:4** 4:1992 pp. 218 – 234

3 Asymmetric effects of positive and negative money supply shocks. James Peery Cover. *Q. J. Econ.* **CVII:4** 11:1992 pp. 1261 – 1282

4 Behavior and determinants of the currency to demand deposits ration in Egypt. Mokhlis Y. Zaki. *J. Dev. Areas* **26:3** 4:1992 pp. 357 – 370

5 The changing effect of money on aggregate output in the U.S.; *[German summary]*; *[French summary]*; *[Spanish summary]*. H. Sonmez Atesoglu; Donald H. Dutkowsky. *Welt.liches Arc.* **128:2** 1992 pp. 221 – 236

6 Les chemins escarpés de la hausse des prix en Amérique latine *[In French]*; (The precipitous paths of price rises in Latin America); (Las vías escarpadas del alza de precios en América Latina: *Title only in Spanish*); (Die steilen Wege der Preiserhöhung in Lateinamerika: *Title only in German*); (Krutye dorogi povyšenija cen v Latinskoj Amerike: *Title only in Russian*). Pierre Salma; Jacques Valier. *R. T-Monde* **XXXIII:129** 1-3:1992 pp. 137 – 152

7 The determination of sterling M_3, 1963-88 — an evolutionary macroeconomic approach. J. Foster. *Econ. J.* **102:412** 5:1992 pp. 481 – 496

8 Endogenous market participation and the general equilibrium value of money. Satyajit Chatterjee; Dean Corbae. *J. Polit. Ec.* **100:3** 6:1992 pp. 615 – 646

9 Endogenous money supply and the long-run stability of a neoclassical growth model. Vijay K. Bhasin. *Gr. Econ. Rev.* **13:1** 6:1991 pp. 135 – 156

10 Endogenous transfer institutions in overlapping generations. Merwan Engineer; Dan Bernhardt. *J. Monet. Ec.* **29:3** 6:1992 pp. 445 – 474

11 External supply shocks and stagflation. H. Frisch. *Eco. Notes* **21:2** 1992 pp. 225 – 237

12 How well does the IS-LM model fit postwar U.S. data? Jordi Galí. *Q. J. Econ.* **CVII:2** 5:1992 pp. 709 – 738

13 In search of the liquidity effect. Eric M. Leeper; David B. Gordon. *J. Monet. Ec.* **29:3** 6:1992 pp. 341 – 369

14 Intertemporal complementarity and money in an economy out of equilibrium. M. Amendola; J.L. Gaffard. *J. Evolut. Econ.* **2:2** 1992 pp. 131 – 145

15 The liquidity premium in average interest rates. Wilbur John Coleman; Christian Gilles; Pamela Labadie. *J. Monet. Ec.* **30:3** 12:1992 pp. 449 – 465

16 A model of the BFH payments system. W. William Woolsey. *S. Econ. J.* **59:2** 10:1992 pp. 260 – 272

17 Modelling the monetary system of Greece. Nicholas C. Garganas. *Gr. Econ. Rev.* **13:1** 6:1991 pp. 11 – 50

18 Modelling the yield curve. M.P. Taylor. *Econ. J.* **102:412** 5:1992 pp. 524 – 537

19 Monedas fuertes y monedas débiles *[In Spanish]*; [Strong currencies and weak currencies]. Maxwell J. Fry. *Monetaria* **XV:1** 1-3:1992 pp. 1 – 38

J.1: Money *[Monnaie]*

20 Monetary dependency in the Southern Cone — the case of Paraguay. Donald G. Richards. *Develop. Eco.* **XXX:1** 3:1992 pp. 50 – 62

21 Money and capital markets — pricing, yields and analysis. Michael Sherris. North Sydney, NSW: Allen & Unwin, 1991: xiii, 200 p. *ISBN: 0044422393. Includes index; Includes bibliographical references (p. 198).*

22 Money and credit or a never ending story; Geld und Kredit oder Eine endlose Geschichte *[German summary].* Arne Heise. *Jahrb. N. St.* **210:3-4** 9:1992 pp. 266 – 278

23 Money in the People's Republic of China — a comparative perspective. Gavin Peebles. Sydney: Allen & Unwin, 1991: xiii, 289 p. (ill) *ISBN: 1863730338; LofC: 92103647. Includes bibliographical references (p. 252-282) and index.*

24 Money, income, prices, and interest rates. Benjamin M. Friedman; Kenneth N. Kuttner. *Am. Econ. Rev.* **82:3** 6:1992 pp. 472 – 492

25 La monnaie est-elle intrinsèque ou extrinsèque? *[In French];* [Is money intrinsic or extrinsic?]. Jean Remy. *R. Finan.* **:86** 4-5:1992 pp. 37 – 43

26 A new test of money/income causality. James M. Holmes; Patricia A. Hutton. *J. Money C. B.* **24:3** 8:1992 pp. 338 – 355

27 The non-neutrality of money and the optimal monetary growth rule when preferences are recursive — cash-in-advance vs. money in the utility function. Hiroaki Hayakawa. *J. Macro.* **14:2** Spring:1992 pp. 233 – 266

28 Nouvelles considérations sur le motif de «finance» de John Maynard Keynes *[In French];* Further thoughts on John Maynard Keyne's "finance" motive *[Summary];* Neue Betrachtungen zum "Finanzmotif" bei John Maynard Keynes *[In German];* Nuevas consideraciones sobre el tema de "finanzas" de John Maynard Keynes *[In Spanish].* J.-L. Bailly. *Econ. App.* **XLV:1** 1992 pp. 105 – 127

29 On the creation of money and the accumulation of bank-capital. Mike Hall. *Cap. Class* **:48** Autumn:1992 pp. 89 – 114

30 A pénzforgalom egy input-output modellje *[In Hungarian];* An input-output model of money circulation — an attempt at generalization of the multiplier theory and at computing the multipliers *[Summary].* András Bródy. *Közg. Sz.* **XXXIX** 3:1992 pp. 197 – 207

31 A pénzügyi egyensúlyról *[In Hungarian];* On monetary equilibrium *[Summary].* András Bródy. *Közg. Sz.* **XXXIX** 5:1992 pp. 389 – 400

32 The persistence of real interest differentials — a Kalman filtering approach. Stefano Cavaglia. *J. Monet. Ec.* **29:3** 6:1992 pp. 429 – 443

33 The program of transition to the convertibility of the rouble; *[German summary].* V. Belkin; A. Kazmin; A. Tsimailo. *Bank-Archiv* **38** 3:1990 pp. 585 – 595

34 Russia's money — towards a market-based monetary system. Jeffrey Sachs; David Lipton. *Cent. Bank.* **3:1** Summer:1992 pp. 29 – 53

35 Samuelson's model of money with n-period lifetimes. J. Bullard. *R. Fed. Resv. Bank St.Louis* **74:3** 5-6:1992 pp. 67 – 82

36 Seigniorage in the United States — how much does the U.S. government make from money production? M. Neumann. *R. Fed. Resv. Bank St.Louis* **74:2** 3/4:1992 pp. 29 – 40

37 Seignorage and resource mobilization in socialist Ethiopia. John Roberts. *Dev. Pol. R.* **10:3** 9:1992 pp. 271 – 288

38 Should buffer stock theorists be broad- or narrow-minded? Some answers from aggregate U.K. data — 1966-1989. Paul Mizen. *Manch. Sch. E.* **LX:4** 12:1992 pp. 403 – 418

39 The source of fluctuations in money — evidence from trade credit. Valerie A. Ramey. *J. Monet. Ec.* **30:2** 11:1992 pp. 171 – 193

40 Specialization, transactions technologies, and money growth. Harold L. Cole; Alan C. Stockman. *Int. Econ. R.* **33:2** 5:1992 pp. 283 – 298

41 Stable, unstable, and persistent cyclical behaviour in a Keynes-Wicksell monetary growth model. Reiner Franke. *Ox. Econ. Pap.* **44:2** 4:1992 pp. 242 – 256

42 The substitutability of financial assets in the U.K. and the implications for monetary aggregation. Leigh Drake. *Manch. Sch. E.* **LX:3** 9:1992 pp. 221 – 248

43 Symposium on money. George S. Alogoskoufis *[Contrib.];* James Robertson *[Contrib.];* Lothar Müller *[Contrib.]. Collection of 3 articles.* **New Eur.** , *5:2,* 1992 pp. 13 – 30

44 Unemployment, money growth and interest rate volatility in Italy and the United Kingdom; Disoccupazione, crescita della moneta e volatilità del tasso d'interesse in Italia e nel Regno Unito *[Italian summary].* Amer K. Al-Saji. *Rev. Int. Sci. Ec. Com.* **XXXIX:7** 7:1992 pp. 607 – 616

J.1: Money *[Monnaie]* —

Demand for money *[Demande de monnaie]*

45 The connectedness of the set of equilibrium money prices demands on the choice of the numeraire. Rod Garratt. *J. Econ. Theo.* **56:1** 2:1992 pp. 206 – 217

46 Consumer theory and the demand for money. William A. Barnett; Douglas Fisher; Apostolos Serletis. *J. Econ. Lit.* **XXX:4** 12:1992 pp. 2086 – 2119

47 The currency substitution hypothesis and relative money demand in Mexico and Canada. John H. Rogers. *J. Money C. B.* **24:3** 8:1992 pp. 300 – 318

48 The demand for large bank notes. Willem C. Boeschoten; Martin M.G. Fase. *J. Money C. B.* **24:3** 8:1992 pp. 319 – 337

49 The demand for M1 in the USA — 1960-1988. Yoshihisa Baba; David F. Hendry; Ross M. Starr. *R. Econ. S.* **59(1):198** 2:1992 pp. 25 – 61

50 La demanda por medios de pago, revisitada *[In Spanish]*; [The demand for money revisited] *[Summary]*. Umberto della Mea. *Revis. Econ.* **V:2-3** 12-4:1990-1991 pp. 85 – 106

51 An econometric analysis of money demand in Ghana. Kelfala M. Kallon. *J. Dev. Areas* **26:4** 7:1992 pp. 475 – 488

52 An error-correction approach to demand for money in five African developing countries. Robert Simmons. *J. Econ. Stud.* **19:1** 1992 pp. 29 – 47

53 The financial transactions motive in the Dutch money demand function; Das Motiv für Finanztransaktionen in der niederländischen Geldnachfragefunktion *[German summary]*; Les motifs de transactions financiéres dans la fonction de demande monétaire hollandaise *[French summary]*. Elmer Sterken. *Kred. Kap.* **25:3** 1992 pp. 386 – 405

54 The functional form of the money demand equation — evidence from selected OECD countries. Abdur R. Chowdhury. *Q Rev. Econ. Finan.* **32:3** Autumn:1992 pp. 16 – 30

55 The impact of financial innovations on the demand for money in the UK and Canada. P. Arestis; G. Hadjimatheou; G. Zis. *Appl. Finan. Econ.* **2:2** 6:1992 pp. 115 – 123

56 Interest rates, inflation and the stability of the demand for M3 in South Africa. A.S. Hurn. *Gr. Econ. Rev.* **13:2** 12:1991 pp. 251 – 268

57 Is it possible to find an econometric law that works well in explanation and prediction? The case of Australian money demand. P.A.V.B. Swamy; G.S. Tavlas. *J. Forecast.* **11:1** 1:1992 pp. 17 – 34

58 The long-run properties of the demand for M3 in South Africa. A.S. Hurn. *S. Afr. J. Econ.* **60:2** 6:1992 pp. 158 – 172

59 Monetary anticipations and the demand for money — further tests of shock-absorber price equations. P. Dorian Owen; Kevin J. Fox. *J. Macro.* **14:1** Winter:1992 pp. 1 – 14

60 Money demand in an open economy. C.R. McKenzie. *J. Jap. Int. Ec.* **6:2** 6:1992 pp. 176 – 198

61 Optimal reserve requirements, deposit taxation, and the demand for money. Alex Mourmouras; Steven Russell. *J. Monet. Ec.* **30:1** 10:1992 pp. 129 – 142

62 Pénz a hiánygazdaságban *[In Hungarian]*; Money in economies of shortage *[Summary]*. András Simon. *Közg. Sz.* **XXXIX** 4:1992 pp. 309 – 321

63 Price smoothing policies — a welfare analysis. Fabio Canova. *J. Monet. Ec.* **30:2** 11:1992 pp. 255 – 275

64 Rational expectations and the demand for money — a nonparametric approach. Douglas Fisher; Myra McCrickard. *J. Macro.* **14:4** Fall:1992 pp. 573 – 591

65 Speculative attacks — the roles of intertemporal substitution and the interest elasticity of the demand for money. Kent P. Kimbrough. *J. Macro.* **14:4** Fall:1992 pp. 689 – 710

66 Structural change in the demand for money. Seungmook Choi; Kim Sosin. *J. Money C. B.* **24:2** 5:1992 pp. 226 – 238

67 Testing superexogeneity — the demand for broad money in the UK. A.S. Hurn; V.A. Muscatelli. *Ox. B. Econ. S.* **54:4** 11:1992 pp. 543 – 556

68 U.S. money demand — structural shifts or heterogeneous agents. Stuart Landon. *Econ. Inq.* **XXX:3** 7:1992 pp. 496 – 510

69 U.S. money demand — surprising cross-sectional estimates. Casey B. Mulligan; Xavier Sala-I-Martin. *Brookings P.* **2** 1992 pp. 285 – 329

Inflation *[Inflation]*

70 Asset returns and inflation in a cash-in-advance economy. Ashraf Nakibullah. *J. Macro.* **14:1** Winter:1992 pp. 155 – 164

J.1: Money *[Monnaie]* — *Inflation [Inflation]*

71 A bargaining model of partisan appointments to the central bank. Christopher J. Waller. *J. Monet. Ec.* **29:3** 6:1992 pp. 411 – 428

72 Capital mobility and anticipated inflation with cash-in-advance constraints. Sanjay Banerji; Sugata Marjit. *J. Macro.* **14:1** Winter:1992 pp. 143 – 154

73 Conflito distributivo e inflação — um enfoque intersetorial *[In Portuguese]*; [Distributive conflict and inflation — an intersectorial focus] *[Summary]*. Manuel Alcino R. da Fonseca. *Rev. Bras. Ec.* **46:2** 4-6:1992 pp. 167 – 184

74 Dinámica de la inflación en una economía cerrada *[In Spanish]*; [Inflation dynamics in a closed economy]. Ricardo H. Arriazu. *Revis. Econ.* **V:2-3** 12-4:1990-1991 pp. 107 – 156

75 Dollarization in Latin America — Gresham's law in reverse? Pablo E. Guidotti; Carlos A. Rodriguez. *Staff Pap. Int. Monetary* **39:3** 9:1992 pp. 518 – 544

76 A dynamic specific-factors model with money; Epargnes, richesse et le legs motivé par la logique de l'echange *[French summary]*. Jorge E. Roldos. *Can. J. Econ.* **XXV:3** 8:1992 pp. 729 – 742

77 Evaluating inflation forecasts derived from interest rate and time-series models. G.H. Hafer; R.W. Hafer; S.E. Hein. *Appl. Finan. Econ.* **2:4** 12:1992 pp. 229 – 236

78 Indexación, rezagos fiscales e inflación *[In Spanish]*; [Indexation, fiscal logs and inflation]. Alfredo Canavese; Daniel Heymann. *Revis. Econ.* **V:2-3** 12-4:1990-1991 pp. 3 – 18

79 Az infláció mechanizmusa a fejlett nyugati országokban *[In Hungarian]*; The mechanism of inflation in the developed western countries *[Summary]*. György Simon. *Közg. Sz.* **XXXIX** 11:1992 pp. 1036 – 1049

80 Inflation and social pacts in Brazil and Mexico. Ian Roxborough. *J. Lat. Am. St.* **24:3** 10:1992 pp. 639 – 664

81 Inflation and stabilization in Yugoslavia. Roberto De Rezende Rocha. *Cont. Policy* **X:4** 10:1992 pp. 21 – 38

82 Inflation convergence with realignments in a two-speed Europe. L. Lambertini; M. Miller; A. Sutherland. *Econ. J.* **102:411** 3:1992 pp. 333 – 341

83 The inflation discipline of currency substitution. M.B. Canzoneri; B.T. Diba. *Eur. Econ. R.* **36:4** 5:1992 pp. 827 – 846

84 Inflation in the transformation phase of the Chinese economic system — its prevalence, causes and effects. Ruilong Yang; Clem Tisdell. *Asian Ec.* **:81** 6:1992 pp. 25 – 41

85 L'inflation par les actifs non-renouvelables *[In French]*; Inflation through non-renewable assets *[Summary]*. Bernard Godement; Nicolas Pless. *Ec. Pros. Int.* **49:1** 1992 pp. 5 – 28

86 Inflation stabilization in Turkey — an application of the RMSM-X Model. Luc Everaert. Washington, D.C.: Country Department I, Europe and Central Asia Region, The World Bank, 1992: 51 p. [Policy research working papers].

87 Inflationary effects of changes in effective exchange rates — LDCs experience. M. Bahmani-Oskooee; M. Malixi. *Appl. Econ.* **24:4** 4:1992 pp. 465 – 471

88 Инфляция: причины и закономерности *[In Russian]*; [Inflation — reasons and degree of conformity to natural laws]. S. Lushin *[Contrib.]*; V. Pashkovskii *[Contrib.]*; A. Amosov *[Contrib.]*; L. Lykova *[Contrib.]*; A. Martynov *[Contrib.]*; I. Bobkov *[Contrib.]*; S. Zhuravlev *[Contrib.]*; A. Ivanter *[Contrib.]*; N. Brusilovskaia *[Contrib.]*. *Collection of 7 articles.* **Vop. Ekon.** , :2, 1992 pp. 3 – 61

89 Interest rates, inflation and the stability of the demand for M3 in South Africa. A.S. Hurn. *Gr. Econ. Rev.* **13:2** 12:1991 pp. 251 – 268

90 Is the Fisher effect for real? A reexamination of the relationship between inflation and interest rates. Frederic S. Mishkin. *J. Monet. Ec.* **30:2** 11:1992 pp. 195 – 215

91 Libéralisme et hyperinflation *[In French]*; (Liberalism and hyperinflation); (Liberalismo e hiperinflación: *Title only in Spanish*); (Liberalismus und Hyperinflation: *Title only in German*); (Liberalizm i sverkhinfljacija: *Title only in Russian*). Celia Himelfarb. *R. T-Monde* **XXXIII:129** 1-3:1992 pp. 101 – 112

92 Market power in an non-monetarist inflation model for Greece. D. Dogas. *Appl. Econ.* **24:3** 3:1992 pp. 367 – 378

93 Medusektorski efekti inflatorskih dobitaka i gubitaka u jugoslavenskom gospodarstvu u razdoblju 1980-1989 *[In Serbo-Croatian]*; Междусекторые эффекты инфляционных прибылей и убытков в югославском хозяйстве в периоде 1980-1989 гг *[Russian summary]*; Intersectoral effects of inflationary gains and losses in the Yugoslav economy in 1980-1989 *[Summary]*. Neven Mates. *Ekon. Preg.* **43:3-4** 1992 pp. 207 – 222

94 Modèles monétaristes de l'hyperinflation *[In French]*; (Monetarist models of hyperinflation); (Modelos monetaristas de la hiperinflación: *Title only in Spanish*); (Monetaristische

J.1: Money *[Monnaie]* — *Inflation [Inflation]*

Modelle der Hyperinflation: *Title only in German)*; (Denežnaja model' i sverinfljacija: *Title only in Russian)*. Gérard Kremer; Ali Bouhaili. *R. T-Monde* **XXXIII:129** 1-3:1992 pp. 113 – 136

95 Models of inflation and the costs of disinflation. Bankim Chadha; Paul R. Masson; Guy Meredith. *Staff Pap. Int. Monetary* **39:2** 6:1992 pp. 395 – 431

96 Money supply and inflation in Morocco; L'offre de monnaie et l'inflation au Maroc *[French summary]*. Ahmed Zejli. *Sav. Develop.* **XVI:2** 1992 pp. 145 – 158

97 Money, inflation and untested common factors. J. Gibson. *Appl. Econ.* **24:6** 6:1992 pp. 581 – 585

98 On the formation of expected inflation under various conditions — some survey evidence. Hamid Baghestani. *J. Bus.* **65:2** 4:1992 pp. 281 – 293

99 Optimal anti-inflation programs in semi-industrialized economies — orthodox versus heterodox policies. S. Ambler; E. Cardia. *J. Dev. Econ.* **38:1** 1:1992 pp. 41 – 61

100 Politiques libérales et fin des processus hyperinflationnistes *[In French]*; Liberal politics and the end of the hyperinflationary process *[Summary]*; Políticas liberales y fin de los procesos hiperinflacionistas *[In Spanish]*. Pierre Salama; Jacques Valier. *Prob. Am.Lat.* **:5** 4-6:1992 pp. 3 – 28

101 Pricing and inflation in India. Pulapre Balakrishnan. Delhi: Oxford University Press, 1991: xix, 271 p. *ISBN: 0195628330; LofC: 91900841. Includes bibliographical references (p. [247]-264) and index.*

102 The resilience of high inflation — recent Brazilian failures with stabilization policies. Carmem Aparecida Feijo; Fernando J. Cardim de Carvalho. *J. Post. Keyn. Ec.* **15:1** Fall:1992 pp. 109 – 124

103 Sectoral inflation in Yugoslavia. James H. Gapinski. *J. Dev. Areas* **27:1** 10:1992 pp. 33 – 48

104 Seigniorage and the welfare cost of inflation — evidence from an inter-temporal model of money and consumption. Zvi Eckstein; Leonardo Leiderman. *J. Monet. Ec.* **29:3** 6:1992 pp. 389 – 410

105 Seigniorage und Inflationsdynamik. Einige grundlegende Zusammenhänge *[In German]*; Seigniorage and the dynamism of inflation — certain basic interrelationships *[Summary]*; Seigniorage et dynamique de l'inflation — quelques rapports fondamentaux *[French summary]*. Helmut Wagner. *Kred. Kap.* **25:3** 1992 pp. 335 – 358

106 The Soviet hyperinflation — its origin and impact throughout the former republics. Igor Filatochev; Roy Bradshaw. *Eur.-Asia Stud.* **44:5** 1992 pp. 739 – 759

107 Stopping high inflation — an analytical overview. Carlos A. Végh. *Staff Pap. Int. Monetary* **39:3** 9:1992 pp. 626 – 695

108 Survey evidence on the Muthian rationality of the inflation forecasts of US consumers. Hamid Baghestani. *Ox. B. Econ. S.* **54:2** 5:1992 pp. 173 – 186

109 Term structure forecasts of inflation. D. Robertson. *Econ. J.* **102:414** 9:1992 pp. 1083 – 1093

110 Wage inflation, electoral uncertainty and the exchange rate regime — theory and UK evidence. G.S. Alogoskoufis; B. Lockwood; A. Philippopoulos. *Econ. J.* **102:415** 11:1992 pp. 1370 – 1394

111 The welfare cost of inflation under imperfect insurance. Ayşe Imrohoroğlu. *J. Econ. Dyn. Cont.* **16:1** 1:1992 pp. 79 – 92

112 ¿Es aplicable la hipótesis de Fischer en Colombia? *[In Spanish]*; [Is Fischer's hypothesis applicable to Colombia?]. Alberto Carrasquilla; Carlos A. Rodríguez. *Desar. Soc.* **:29** 3:1992 pp. 101 – 114

J.2: Credit — *Crédit*

Sub-divisions: Bank regulation and bank failure *[Règlement et faillite des banques]*; Banking *[Activité bancaire]*; Central banks *[Banques centrales]*; Indebtedness *[Endettement]*; Mortgages *[Hypothèques]*

1 Analyse des données et credit scoring *[In French]*; [Data analysis and credit scoring]. Jacques D'Hoeraene. *R. Finan.* :**86** 4-5:1992 pp. 44 – 54
2 Applications of finance. Fischer Black *[Contrib.]*; André F. Perold *[Contrib.]*; Zvi Bodie *[Contrib.]*; Robert C. Merton *[Contrib.]*; William F. Samuelson *[Contrib.]*; William A. Brock *[Contrib.]*; Allan W. Kleidon *[Contrib.]*; John C. Cox *[Contrib.]*; Chi-fu Huang *[Contrib.]*; Jean-Pierre Danthine *[Contrib.] and others. Collection of 15 articles.* **J. Econ. Dyn. Cont.** , *16:3/4*, 7-10:1992 pp. 403 – 790
3 Approccio ad una valutazione dei progetti d'integrazione banca/assicurazione *[In Italian]*; [Advances to a valuation of bank/insurance integration projects]. Stefano Ratti. *Bancaria* **48:7-8** 7-8:1992 pp. 17 – 27
4 Assessing the employment effectiveness of small business financing schemes — some evidence from Israel. Daniel Felsenstein. *Small Bus. Econ.* **4:4** 12:1992 pp. 273 – 285
5 Le banche estere nella RFT — hanno vita difficile e molte fanno perdite *[In Italian]*; [Foreign banks in the FRG — they are having problems and many are suffering losses]. Giovanni Lovato. *Bancaria* **48:3** 3:1992 pp. 59 – 67
6 Bank financing of industries in India. Asha Ram Tripathi. Delhi, India: Tiwari Publications, 1991: xx, 232 p. *ISBN: 8185535078. Includes bibliographical references (p.[227]-232).*
7 Building durable rural financial markets in Africa; Des marchés financiers ruraux durables en Afrique *[French summary]*. Dale W. Adams. *Sav. Develop.* :**1** Supplement:1992 pp. 5 – 16
8 Calcolo dell'indicatore cui rapportare il premio di produttività nelle aziende di credito *[In Italian]*; [Estimating the productivity bonus indicator in credit institutions]. Antonio Rigon. *Risparmio* **XL:1** 1-2:1992 pp. 1 – 32
9 Capital in the payments system. Milton H. Marquis; Kevin L. Reffett. *Economica* **59:235** 8:1992 pp. 351 – 364
10 Centralization in international financial intermediation — theory, practice, and evidence for the European Community. L.J.R. Scholtens. *Banca Nat. Lav. Q. Rev.* :**182** 9:1992 pp. 255 – 304
11 Commercial banks in macroeconomic theory. Arne Heise. *J. Post. Keyn. Ec.* **14:3** Spring:1992 pp. 285 – 296
12 Concorrenza europea e globale dei sistemi bancari *[In Italian]*; [Global and European competition in the banking system]. Uwe H. Schneider. *Ras. Econ.* **LVI:2** 4-6:1992 pp. 499 – 516
13 Contract costs, bank loans, and the cross-monitoring hypothesis. James R. Booth. *J. Finan. Ec.* **31:1** 2:1992 pp. 25 – 41
14 Credit for small firms, not dinosaurs. Barry Ickes; Randi Ryterman. *Orbis* **36:3** Summer:1992 pp. 333 – 348
15 Credit rationing, implicit contracts, risk aversion, and the variability of interest rates. Nilss Olekalns; Hugh Sibly. *J. Macro.* **14:2** Spring:1992 pp. 337 – 347
16 Credit rationing, involuntary unemployment, and financial collapse in general equilibrium. Philip N. Jefferson. New York: Columbia University, Department of Economics, 1992: 18 p. [Discussion paper series.]
17 Credit recovery through payments related to borrower income in unstable economies — the Mexican experience, 1984-1989. José Manuel Agudo Roldán; Manuel Campos Spoor. *Hous. Pol. Deb.* **3:1** 1992 pp. 157 – 175
18 The credit view, financial announcements and interest rate responses. S.E. Hein; J. Mercado-Mendez. *J. Bank. Fin.* **16:4** 8:1992 pp. 743 – 756
19 The crisis in the Norwegian financial industry — action taken in 1991. Morten Jonassen; Audun Gleinsvik. *Econ. B. Norges Bank.* **LXIII:1** 3:1992 pp. 44 – 53
20 Demand for consumer borrowing in the UK, 1969-90. A. Hartropp. *Appl. Finan. Econ.* **2:1** 3:1992 pp. 11 – 20
21 The determinants of cross-border non-bank deposits and the competitiveness of financial market centres. Julian S. Alworth; S. Andersen. *Money Aff.* **V:2** 7-12:1992 pp. 105 – 133
22 The determinants of tendering rates in interfirm and self-tender offers. David T. Brown; Michael D. Ryngaert. *J. Bus.* **65:4** 10:1992 pp. 529 – 556

J.2: Credit *[Crédit]*

23 Developments in the pricing of credit card services. Glenn B. Canner; Charles A. Luckett. *Fed. Resv. B.* **78:9** 9:1992 pp. 652 – 666

24 DIDMCA and bank market risk — theory and evidence. T.P. Bundt; T.F. Cosimano; J.A. Halloran. *J. Bank. Fin.* **16:6** 12:1992 pp. 1179 – 1193

25 Economic survey — Section 1 — main picture. Annex to section 1 — borrowing costs in Norway and abroad. Section 2 — recent developments — monetary, credit and foreign exchange situation.*Econ. B. Norges Bank.* **LXIII:2** 6:1992 pp. 107 – 134

26 Economie di informazione e conflitti di interesse — gli effetti del nuovo quadro normativo in Italia *[In Italian]*; [Information economies and conflicts of interest. The effects of the new regulatory situation in Italy]. Elisabetta Gualandri; Andrea Landi. *Risparmio* **:6** 11-12:1992 pp. 1421 – 1450

27 Economie et religion. Le projet financier islamiste *[In French]*; Economy and religion. The Islamic project *[Summary]*. Michel Galloux. *Hom. Soc.* **:105-106** 3-4:1992 pp. 79 – 91

28 The effect of base rate change announcements on interest rates. N.P. Tessaromatis; P.E. Triantafillou. *Spoudai* **42:1** 1-3:1992 pp. 11 – 24

29 Les effets du taux d'intérêt réel sur l'activité en France *[In French]*; The effects of the real interest rate on French activity *[Summary]*. Alexandre Mathis; Lucrezia Reichlin. *Obser. Diag. Econ.* **:41** 7:1992 pp. 195 – 216

30 Efficienza organizzativa e sviluppo della rete distributiva delle aziende di credito *[In Italian]*; [Organizational efficiency and development in the distribution network of credit institutions]. Francesco Paoletti; Andrea Pontiggia; Luca Solari. *Bancaria* **48:9** 9:1992 pp. 27 – 38

31 Die Entstehung des Bankenmarkts in der ČSFR *[In German]*; The development of the banking market in Czechoslovakia *[Summary]*. Jörg Borrmann; Andrea Manzotti; Frank A. Schmid. *Ost. Wirt.* **37:4** 12:1992 pp. 298 – 308

32 Estructura temporal de los tipos de interés — hipótesis teóricas y resultados empíricos *[In Spanish]*; [The term structure of interest rates — theoretical hypotheses and empirical results] *[Summary]*. Xavier Freixas. *Invest. Econ.* **XVI:2** 5:1992 pp. 187 – 204

33 Evolución del sistema financiero mexicano hacia la banca universal; [Progress of the Mexican financial system towards the multi-functional bank]. José-Ramón Palencia Gómez. *Monetaria* **XV:1** 1-3:1992 pp. 67 – 80

34 Factors influencing the decisions of bank managers — the evidence from investment portfolios. A.A. Heggestad; J.F. Houston. *J. Bank. Fin.* **16:4** 8:1992 pp. 813 – 830

35 Factors that affect short-term commercial bank lending to developing countries. Sudarshan Gooptu; Maria Soledad Martinez Peria. Washington, D.C.: Office of the Vice President, Cofinancing and Financial Advisory Services, The World Bank, 1992: 5 p. [Policy research working papers.]

36 Finance companies, bank competition, and niche markets. Eli M. Remolona; Kurt C. Wulfekuhler. *Q. R. Fed. Res. Bank N.Y.* **17:2** Summer:1992 pp. 25 – 38

37 Le financement de l'informatique *[In French]*; [The financing of data-processing]. Frédérique Dupuis-Toubol. *R. Finan.* **:86** 4-5:1992 pp. 12 – 18

38 Financial institutions in 1991. Knut Eeg; Inger Anne Nordal. *Econ. B. Norges Bank.* **LXIII:1** 3:1992 pp. 54 – 72

39 Financial institutions or asset markets — alternative trading and banking arrangements as risk sharing mechanisms. B. Drees. *Eur. J. Pol. Ec.* **8:2** 5:1992 pp. 175 – 200

40 Financial ratio covenants in UK bank loan contracts and accounting policy choice. David B. Citron. *Acc. Bus. Res.* **22:88** Autumn:1992 pp. 322 – 335

41 Financial services for microenterprises — principles and institutions. E. Rhyne; M. Otero. *World Dev.* **20:11** 11:1992 pp. 1561 – 1571

42 Financial structure in Indian economy. R. K. Jadhav. Bombay: J. Enterprise, 1991: 140 p.

43 Finite horizons, infinite horizons, and the real interest rate. Paul Evans. *Econ. Inq.* **XXX:1** 1:1992 pp. 14 – 28

44 Fixed versus variable rate financing — the influence of borrower, lender, and market characteristics. Lawrence G. Goldberg; Andrea J. Heuson. *J. Finan. Ser. Res.* **6:1** 5:1992 pp. 49 – 60

45 Fixed-rate deposit insurance and risk-shifting behavior at commercial banks. J.-C. Duan; A.F. Moreau; C.W. Sealey. *J. Bank. Fin.* **16:4** 8:1992 pp. 715 – 742

46 A flow of funds test of the capital inflow hypothesis. William R. Hosek; Frank Zahn. *J. Macro.* **14:1** Winter:1992 pp. 165 – 178

47 Gesellschaftsrechtliche Fragen der Gründung von Sparkassenaktiengesellschaften *[In German]*; [Social and legal questions regarding the founding of savings banks as public limited companies]. Peter Jabornegg. *Bank-Archiv* **38** 2:1990 pp. 82 – 101

J.2: Credit *[Crédit]*

48 The good work of financial crises. Menahem Prywes. *Columb. J. W. Bus.* **27:1** Spring:1992 pp. 14 – 21

49 How the 1992 legislation will affect European financial services. K. Chrystal; C. Coughlin. *R. Fed. Resv. Bank St.Louis* **74:2** 3/4:1992 pp. 62 – 77

50 Hungary — the initial stages in the financial sector reform of a socialist economy in transition. M.I. Blejer; S.B. Sagari. *Appl. Finan. Econ.* **2:1** 3:1992 pp. 33 – 42

51 The impact and cost of Philippine agricultural credit risk guarantee schemes; L'impact et le cout des schemas de garantie contre les risques de crédit en agriculture aux Philippines *[French summary]*. Ernesto D. Bautista. *Sav. Develop.* **XVI:2** 1992 pp. 199 – 217

52 Impact of monetary policy on the profitability of commercial banks in India. Minakshi Malhotra; Gian Kaur. *Art. Vij.* **XXXIV:1** 3:1992 pp. 57 – 68

53 Implementation of the BIS "rules" on capital adequacy assessment. M.J.B. Hall. *Banca Nat. Lav. Q. Rev.* **:180** 3:1992 pp. 35 – 57

54 Income distribution, transaction costs and market fragmentation in informal credit markets. Pan A. Yotopoulos; Sagrario L. Floro. *Camb. J. Econ.* **16:3** 9:1992 pp. 303 – 326

55 Inefficient information aggregation as a source of asset price bubbles. Daniel Friedman; Masanao Aoki. *B. Econ. Res.* **44:4** 10:1992 pp. 251 – 280

56 Informal finance in a semi-rural area of the Philippines; La finance informelle dans une zone semi-rurale des Philippines *[French summary]*. Dale W. Adams; Virginia Nazarea-Sandoval. *Sav. Develop.* **XVI:2** 1992 pp. 159 – 168

57 Informal finance in low-income countries. Dale W. Adams *[Ed.]*; Delbert A. Fitchett *[Ed.]*. Boulder: Westview Press, 1992: xii, 393 p. (ill) *ISBN: 0813315042; LofC: 91043702. Revised versions of papers presented at the seminar held Oct. 18-20, 1989; Includes bibliographical references and index.*

58 The informal financial sector in Bangladesh — an appraisal of its role in development. Atiq Rahman. *Develop. Cha.* **23:1** 1:1992 pp. 147 – 167

59 Das Informations- und das Inhaltsschrankenmodell beim konsumentenkredit *[In German]*; [The information and contents limitation model for consumer credit]. Claus-Willhelm Canaris. *Bank-Archiv* **38** 11:1990 pp. 882 – 898

60 Innovazione finanziaria in Francia *[In Italian]*; [Financial innovation in France]. Marina Damilano. *Econ. Ban.* **XIV:1** 1992 pp. 33 – 72

61 Interaction between the formal and informal financial sectors — the Asian experience. P.B. Ghate. *World Dev.* **20:6** 6:1992 pp. 859 – 872

62 Is there light at the end of the Indonesian interest rate tunnel? Miron Mushkat. *Asian Ec.* **:81** 6:1992 pp. 42 – 71

63 Kiinduló megközelítés a banki kamatlábkockázat kezeléséhez *[In Hungarian]*; (Opening approach to the management of interest risks); (Ausgangs Annäerung zur Handhabung des Zinssarzrisikos der Banken: *Title only in German*). Péter Szabadhegy. *Pénz. Sz.* **36:1** 1:1992 pp. 3 – 10

64 Lebanon development bank — a proposal for action; Banque de developpement du Liban — un plan d'action *[French summary]*. Eghbal Mostofi-Zadeh; Rahmat Niknam. *Sav. Develop.* **XVI:3** 1992 pp. 287 – 304

65 Managing consumer credit delinquency in the US economy — a multi-billion dollar management science application. William M. Makuch; Jeffrey L. Dodge; Joseph G. Ecker; Donna C. Granfors; Gerald J. Hahn. *Interfaces* **22:1** 1-2:1992 pp. 90 – 109

66 Market structure and the nature of price rigidity — evidence from the market for consumer deposits. David Neumark; Steven A. Sharpe. *Q. J. Econ.* **CVII:2** 5:1992 pp. 657 – 680

67 Merkmale der persönlichen Kreditwürdigkeit bei Kreditanträgen mittelständischer Unternehmen *[In German]*; [Characteristics of personal credit worthiness of those applying for credit — medium-sized enterprises]. H. Rommelfanger; T. Bagus; E. Himmelsbach. *Bank-Archiv* **38** 10:1990 pp. 786 – 797

68 Microenterprise credit programs — déja vu. D.W. Adams; J.D. von Pischke. *World Dev.* **20:10** 10:1992 pp. 1463 – 1470

69 Monetaire transmissie en de kredietmarkt — een aangepaste IS/LM-analyse *[In Dutch]*; [Monetary transmission and the credit market — a modified IS/LM analysis]. H. van Gemert; L. van Veldhuizen. *Maan. Econ.* **56:4** 1992 pp. 309 – 324

70 Monetary shocks and the nominal interest rate. Giancarlo Marini. *Economica* **59:235** 8:1992 pp. 365 – 372

71 The national bank note controversy reexamined. Michael Kuehlwein. *J. Money C. B.* **24:1** 2:1992 pp. 111 – 126

J.2: Credit *[Crédit]*

72 New issues in financial services. Ray Kinsella *[Ed.]*. Oxford: Blackwell Publishers, 1992: 240 p. *ISBN: 0631183183; LofC: 92015592. Includes index.*

73 Una nota sobre la evolución competitiva en el sector de las sociedades de inversión mobiliaria *[In Spanish]*; [A note on the competitive developments in the building society sector]. Camilo José Vázquez Ordás. *Infor. Com. Esp.* **:707** 7:1992 pp. 153 – 162

74 Nutzung der Pfandsache durch den Pfandgläubiger? *[In German]*; [Utilization of securities through the holder?]. Georg Graf. *Bank-Archiv* **38** 10:1990 pp. 798 – 810

75 Payments systems in New Zealand. John Tait. *Res. Bank B. NZ* **55:1** 1992 pp. 9 – 17

76 Performance of the Ghanaian rural banks — a canonical correlation analysis. James Obben. *Ox. Agrar. Stud.* **20:1** 1992 pp. 39 – 50

77 Pourquoi des banques? *[In French]*; Why do we need banks? *[Summary]*. Th. Chevallier-Farat. *Rev. Ec. Polit.* **102:5** 9-10:1992 pp. 633 – 685

78 Presupposti e limiti della despecializzazione creditizia — alcune considerazioni sulla ristrutturazione degli ICS *[In Italian]*; [Assumptions and limits of the despecialization of credit. Some considerations on the restructuring of the ICS]. Paolo Nardi. *Bancaria* **48:11** 11:1992 pp. 9 – 23

79 A private bank in China — Hui Tong urban co-operative bank. On Kit Tam. *China Quart.* **:131** 9:1992 pp. 766 – 777

80 Privatisation and financial structure in Eastern and Central European countries. Andy Mullineux. *Nat. W. Bank* **5:**1992 pp. 12 – 25

81 Problems in the Japanese financial system in the early 1990s. Yoshinori Shimizu. *Hito. J. Comm. Manag.* **27:1** 11:1992 pp. 29 – 49

82 Problems of financial analysis in institutional lending operations — some lessons from Tanzania. Kami S.P. Rwegasira. Aldershot, Hants, England: Avebury, 1992: 228 p. *ISBN: 1856282996; LofC: 92033657. Includes bibliographical references.*

83 Qualità dei prestiti ed equilibri di gestione delle aziende di credito *[In Italian]*; [Quality of loans and balances of management of credit companies]. Claudio Cacciamani. *Risparmio* **XL:4** 7-8:1992 pp. 743 – 810

84 Le rationnement du crédit bancaire — causes et conséquences *[In French]*; The economics of credit rationing *[Summary]*. Frédéric Lobez. *Gestion* **8:3** 1992 pp. 33 – 45

85 The recent credit crunch — the neglected dimensions. K. Klieson; J. Tatom. *R. Fed. Resv. Bank St.Louis* **74:5** 9-10:1992 pp. 18 – 36

86 The regional consequence of completion of the EC internal market for financial services — an overview and a case study of Scotland. Iain Begg. *Int. Econ. J.* **6:1** Spring:1992 pp. 17 – 43

87 Regulatory change, corporate restructuring and the spatial development of the British financial sector; *[French summary]*; *[German summary]*. J.N. Marshall; C.J.S. Gentle; S. Raybould; M. Coombes. *Reg. Stud.* **26:5** 1992 pp. 453 – 467

88 The relation of judgment, personal involvement, and experience in the audit of bank loans. Cynthia Jeffrey. *Acc. Review* **67:4** 10:1992 pp. 802 – 819

89 La ristrutturazione del sistema degli intermediari creditizi e finanziari *[In Italian]*; [The reconstruction of the credit and financial intermediary system]. Tancredi Bianchi. *Bancaria* **48:7-8** 7-8:1992 pp. 71 – 87

90 The role of non-bank financial intermediaries in savings mobilization in Jamaica 1981-1990. Pauline Batchelor. *Money Aff.* **V:2** 7-12:1992 pp. 135 – 153

91 Rural banks and rural credit. V. Balamohandas; J.V. Prabhakara Rao; P. Hrushikesava Rao. New Delhi: Discovery Pub. House, 1991: xvi, 300 p. *ISBN: 8171411207; LofC: 90909040. Evaluation of the performance of regional rural banks in India since their inception in 1975; Includes index; Includes bibliographical references.*

92 La segmentación del mercado y su aplicación al mercado bancario minorista *[In Spanish]*; [Market segmentation in the financial services sector]. Asunción Beerli Palacio; Juan Manuel Garciá Falcón. *Infor. Com. Esp.* **:707** 7:1992 pp. 143 – 151

93 Segmentation in rural financial markets — the case of Nepal. S. Yadav; K. Otsuka; C.C. David. *World Dev.* **20:3** 3:1992 pp. 423 – 436

94 Some evidence on the empirical significance of credit rationing. Allen N. Berger; Gregory F. Udell. *J. Polit. Ec.* **110:5** 10:1992 pp. 1047 – 1077

95 Some international evidence on the exogeneity of the ex-ante real rate of interest and the rationality of expectations. Mark A. Thoma. *J. Macro.* **14:1** Winter:1992 pp. 33 – 46

96 Supervision of registered banks' large credit risks. C. Heppleston; B. White. *Res. Bank B. NZ* **55:1** 1992 pp. 18 – 26

J.2: Credit *[Crédit]*

97 The Swedish credit market in 1991. Marianne Biljer. *Q. Rev. Sver. Riks.* **2** 1992 pp. 13 – 20

98 Technical and scale efficiency in UK building societies. L. Drake; T.G. Weyman-Jones. *Appl. Finan. Econ.* **2:1** 3:1992 pp. 1 – 9

99 Los tipos de interés y las sorpresas monetarias *[In Spanish]*; [Interest rates and monetary surprises] *[Summary]*. Marta Campillo. *Invest. Econ.* **XVI:2** 5:1992 pp. 205 – 224

100 Transaction costs and the use of cash and credit. S.L. Schreft. *Econ. Theory* **2:2** 1992 pp. 283 – 297

101 Two faces of financial innovation. M. Flood. *R. Fed. Resv. Bank St.Louis* **74:5** 9-10:1992 pp. 3 – 17

102 Umfeldanalyse für Finanzintermediäre *[In German]*; [An analysis of the situation for financial intermediaries]. Werner Schicklgruber. *Bank-Archiv* **38** 7:1990 pp. 509 – 523

103 Underwriter compensation and corporate monitoring. Robert S. Hansen; Paul Torregrosa. *J. Finance* **47:4** 9:1992 pp. 1537 – 1555

104 Universal banking, US banking reform and financial competition in the EEC. J.A. Kregel. *Banca Nat. Lav. Q. Rev.* **:182** 9:1992 pp. 231 – 253

105 US business credit sources, demand deposits, and the "missing money". J.V. Duca. *J. Bank. Fin.* **16:3** 6:1992 pp. 567 – 583

106 Welfare-improving credit controls. Stacey L. Schreft. *J. Monet. Ec.* **30:1** 10:1992 pp. 57 – 72

Bank regulation and bank failure *[Règlement et faillite des banques]*

107 Bank insolvency and stabilization in Eastern Europe. Daniel C. Hardy; Ashok Kumar Lahiri. *Staff Pap. Int. Monetary* **39:4** 12:1992 pp. 778 – 800

108 Bank regulation as an antidote to price level instability — a "real bills" model that yields "quantity theory" prescriptions. Alex Mourmouras; Steven Russell. *J. Monet. Ec.* **29:1** 2:1992 pp. 125 – 150

109 Banking and deregulation. Stephen Martin; John Hawkins. *Ec. Pap. Aust.* **11:1** 3:1992 pp. 1 – 13

110 Banking deregulation — allocational consequences of relaxing entry barriers. D. Besanko; A.V. Thakor. *J. Bank. Fin.* **16:5** 9:1992 pp. 909 – 932

111 Did financial deregulation help consumers? Access to market-yield instruments. N.A. Jianakoplos; F.O. Irvine. *Appl. Econ.* **24:8** 8:1992 pp. 813 – 832

112 Differential impact on bank valuation of interstate banking law changes. L.G. Goldberg; G.A. Hanweck; T.F. Sugrue. *J. Bank. Fin.* **16:6** 12:1992 pp. 1143 – 1158

113 An ecology of agency arrangements — mortality of savings and loan associations, 1960-1987. Hayagreeva Rao; Eric H. Neilsen. *Adm. Sci. Qua.* **37:3** 9:1992 pp. 448 – 470

114 Evaluation du risque de défaillance bancaire en Europe *[In French]*; An empirical investigation of bank risk in Europe *[Summary]*. D. Goyeau; A. Tarazi. *Rev. Ec. Polit.* **102:2** 3-4:1992 pp. 249 – 280

115 Institutional responses to bank failure — a comparative case study of the Home Bank (1923) and Canadian Commercial Bank (1985) failures. B. Lew; A.J. Richardson. *Crit. Persp. Acc.* **3:2** 6:1992 pp. 163 – 184

116 International banking deregulation — the great banking experiment. Richard Dale. Oxford: Blackwell, 1992: 211 p. *ISBN: 0631160574; LofC: 91046139. Includes index.*

117 Liberalizzazione del mercato dei capitali e struttura bancaria del Mezzogiorno *[In Italian]*; [Deregulation of the capital markets and banking structure of Southern Italy]. Michele Bagella. *Ras. Econ.* **LVI:2** 4-6:1992 pp. 469 – 481

118 Modeling the bank regulator's closure option — a two-step logit regression approach. James B. Thomson. *J. Finan. Ser. Res.* **6:1** 5:1992 pp. 5 – 23

119 On the eve of the second bank reform. Z. Spéder; É. Várhegyi. *Acta Oecon.* **44:1-2** 1992 pp. 53 – 76

120 Turmoil among depository institutions — implications for the U.S. real estate market. James R. Barth; R. Dan Brumbaugh; Sarah K. Bryant *[Comments by]*; Martha L. Carter *[Comments by]*; William B. Brueggeman *[Comments by]*. *Hous. Pol. Deb.* **3:4** 1992 pp. 901 – 943

Banking *[Activité bancaire]*

121 Analysis of the determinants of the Nigerian banking system's profits and profitability performance; (Une analyse de la performance du systeme bancaire Nigerien: *Title only in French*). Cletus C. Agu. *Sav. Develop.* **XVI:4** 1992 pp. 353 – 370

J.2: Credit *[Crédit]* — Banking *[Activité bancaire]*

122 Australian banking performance in an era of deregulation. Ross Milbourne; Matthew Cumberworth. *Aust. Econ. P.* **30:57** 12:1991 pp. 171 – 191

123 La banca e il management per segnali deboli *[In Italian]*; [The bank and the management of signs of weakness]. Francesco Ramunni. *Risparmio* **XL:3** 5-6:1992 pp. 565 – 582

124 Bank computerization and organizational innovations — the long and winding road to the bank of the future. Rob Bilderbeek; Wout Buitelaar. *New Tech. Work. Empl.* **7:1** Spring:1992 pp. 54 – 60

125 Bank heterogeneity, reputation and debt renegotiation. Raquel Fernandez; David Kaaret. *Int. Econ. R.* **33:1** 2:1992 pp. 61 – 78

126 Bank nationalization, financial savings, and economic development — a case study of India. Kusum W. Ketkar; Suhas L. Ketkar. *J. Dev. Areas* **27:1** 10:1992 pp. 69 – 84

127 Bank size portfolio behaviour — cross-sectional estimates for Nigerian commercial banks; La taille de banque et le comportement de portefeuille — des prévisions à travers les secteurs pour les banques commerciales nigérianes *[French summary]*. M.O. Odedokun. *Sav. Develop.* **:1** Supplement:1992 pp. 29 – 48

128 Bank window dressing — theory and evidence. L. Allen; A. Saunders. *J. Bank. Fin.* **16:3** 6:1992 pp. 585 – 623

129 Banken und Wirtschaftskreislauf *[In German]*; Banks and economic activity *[Summary]*. Rainer Klump. *Jahrb. N. St.* **210:3-4** 9:1992 pp. 203 – 218

130 Banken-, Gesellschafter- und Konzernleitungshaftung nach den "Eumig"-Erkenntnissen *[In German]*; [Banking, social and business management liability according to "Eumig" decisions]. Martin Karollus. *Bank-Archiv* **38** 5:1990 pp. 337 – 359

131 Bank-firm customer relationships as dynamic game equilibria; Relazioni di clientela tra banca e impresa come equilibri di giochi dinamici *[Italian summary]*. Angelo Baglioni. *Rev. Int. Sci. Ec. Com.* **XXXIX:10-11** 10-11:1992 pp. 943 – 957

132 Banking and deregulation. Stephen Martin; John Hawkins. *Ec. Pap. Aust.* **11:1** 3:1992 pp. 1 – 13

133 Banking and finance in Eastern Europe. Andreas R. Prindl *[Ed.]*. London: Woodhead-Faulkner, 1992: 199 p. *ISBN: 0859417832.*

134 Banking for people. Udo Reifner *[Ed.]*; Janet Ford *[Ed.]*. Berlin: Walter de Gruyter, 1992: 672 p. *ISBN: 3110126753; LofC: 92004171. Includes bibliographical references and index; Contents — v. 1. Social banking and new poverty -- v. 2. Consumer debts and unemployment in Europe--national reports.*

135 The "banking group" in Italy and in the European context. R. la Tella. *Rev. Ec. Con. It.* **:1** 1-4:1992 pp. 77 – 93

136 Banking in Central and Eastern Europe. Brendan Twomey. *Irish Bank. Rev.* Spring:1992 pp. 14 – 26

137 Banking in transition — development and current problems in Hungary. Saul Estrin; Paul Hare; Marta Surányi. *Eur.-Asia Stud.* **44:5** 1992 pp. 785 – 808

138 Banking in transition — development and current problems in Hungary. Saul Estrin; Paul Hare; Marta Suranyi. London: London School of Economics and Political Science. Centre for Economic Performance, 1992: 59 p. [Discussion paper.]

139 Banking markets and the use of financial services by households. G. Elliehausen; J. Wolken. *Fed. Resv. B.* **78:3** 3:1992 pp. 169 – 181

140 Banking on flexibility — a comparison of the use of flexible employment strategies in the retail banking sector in Britain and France. Jacqueline O'Reilly. *Int. J. Hum. Res. Man.* **3:1** 5:1992 pp. 35 – 58

141 The banking system and financial reform in Taiwan. Kuo-shu Liang. *Ind. Free China* **LXXVIII:3** 9:1992 pp. 25 – 46

142 Banks as information specialists — the case of hospital lending. P.S. Calem; J.A. Rizzo. *J. Bank. Fin.* **16:6** 12:1992 pp. 1123 – 1141

143 La BERS una banca per l'Est europeo *[In Italian]*; [European monitor — the European Bank for Reconstruction and Development — a bank for Eastern European countries]. Myrta Merlino. *Ras. Econ.* **LVI:2** 4-6:1992 pp. 417 – 449

144 Bewertung festverzinslicher Forderungen und Verbindlichkeiten in der Bankbilanz bei Änderungen des Marktzinssatzes *[In German]*; [The evaluation of claims with fixed interest and of liabilities in a bank balance sheet through changes in the market interest rate]. Philip Göth; Michael Tumpel. *Bank-Archiv* **38** 8:1990 pp. 600 – 611

145 Branch bank operating costs — evidence from savings banks in Finland. J. Kolari; A. Zardkoohi; T. Santalainen; A. Suvanto. *Appl. Econ.* **24:4** 4:1992 pp. 401 – 410

J.2: Credit *[Crédit]* — Banking *[Activité bancaire]*

146 Capital requirements and the behaviour of commercial banks. J.-C. Rochet; C. Mayer *[Comments by]*; R. Repullo *[Comments by]*. *Eur. Econ. R.* **36:5** 6:1992 pp. 1137 – 1170

147 Changing patterns of banks' liabilities policies — the Italian case. M. Di Giovanni; G.B. Pittaluga; A. Tamagnini. *Eco. Notes* **21:2** 1992 pp. 291 – 306

148 Competition between banks and building societies in the retailing of financial services. P.J. McGoldrick; S.J. Greenland. *Br. J. Manag.* **3:3** 9:1992 pp. 169 – 179

149 The competitiveness of Finnish banks in the 1990s. Kaisa Vikkula. *Econ. Rev.* **:1** 1992 pp. 13 – 24

150 A composite cost function for multiproduct firms with an application to economies of scope in banking. Lawrence B. Pulley; Yale M. Braunstein. *Rev. Econ. St.* **LXXIV:2** 5:1992 pp. 221 – 230

151 A computation of interest equivalences for nonprice characteristics of bank products. Shelagh A. Heffernan. *J. Money C. B.* **24:2** 5:1992 pp. 162 – 172

152 Considérations quantitatives sur le ratio Cooke et sur ses conséquences *[In French]*; Quantitative considerations on the Cooke ration and its consequences *[Summary]*. Claude Dufloux; Laurent Margulici. *Gestion* **8:4** 1992 pp. 41 – 56

153 Il cuore finanziario italiano e le sue alleanze con i gruppi francesi *[In Italian]*; The Italian financial heart and its alliances with French groups *[Summary]*. François Morin. *Industria* **XIII:1** 1-3:1992 pp. 13 – 28

154 Determinants of bilateral operations of Canadian and US commercial banks. J.W. Harrington. *Envir. Plan.A.* **24:1** 1:1992 pp. 137 – 152

155 Developments in international banking and capital markets in 1991.*Bank of Engl. Q.* **32:2** 5:1992 pp. 190 – 198

156 The dilemma of black banking — lending risks vs. community service (Westerfield lecture). Andrew F. Brimmer. *Rev. Bl. Pol. Ec.* **20:3** Winter:1992 pp. 5 – 30

157 Do Belgian banks have power vis-a-vis the minister of finance. H. Degryse. *Tijds. Econ. Manag.* **XXXVII:2** 6:1992 pp. 117 – 136

158 Does the debt market assess large banks' risk? Time series evidence from money center CDs. David M. Ellis; Mark J. Flannery. *J. Monet. Ec.* **30:3** 12:1992 pp. 481 – 502

159 Le economie di scala nel settore bancario — il caso delle banche popolari *[In Italian]*; [Economies of scale in the banking sector — the example of "popular banks"]. Gianandrea Goisis; Paola Parravicini; Donatella Porrini. *Risparmio* **XL:3** 5-6:1992 pp. 533 – 564

160 The Euro money market — a strategic analysis of bank operations. Andreas Haindl. Bern: Verlag Paul Haupt, 1991: x, 307 p. (ill) *ISBN: 3258045186. Includes bibliographical references (p. 293-306)*. [Bank- und finanzwirtschaftliche Forschungen. : Vol. 139]

161 European banking. A. W. Mullineux *[Ed.]*. Oxford: Blackwell, 1992: 222 p. *ISBN: 0631197968; LofC: 91026706. Includes bibliographical references and index.*

162 Evidence on the size of banking markets from mortgage loan rates in twenty cities. Stephen A. Rhoades. Washington, DC: Board of Governors of the Federal Reserve System, 1992: 11 p. [Staff study.]

163 The evolution of credit terms — an empirical study of commercial bank lending to developing countries. Ş. Özler. *J. Dev. Econ.* **38:1** 1:1992 pp. 79 – 97

164 The experience of free banking. Kevin Dowd *[Ed.]*. London: Routledge, 1992: 275 p. *ISBN: 0415048087.*

165 Financial deregulation — disarming the nation state. Manfred Bienefeld. *Stud. Pol. Ec.* **:37** Spring:1992 pp. 31 – 58

166 Financial markets liberalization and the role of banks. Vittorio Conti *[Ed.]*; Rony Hamaui *[Ed.]*. Cambridge: Cambridge University Press, 1992: 376 p. *ISBN: 0521419824; LofC: 92006551. Includes index.*

167 Das Finanzsystem Spaniens *[In German]*; [Spain's financial system]. Lygum; Perée; Steinherr. *Bank-Archiv* **38** 11:1990 pp. 899 – 911

168 Geographic deregulation of the U.S. banking industry and spatial transfers of corporate control. J. Dennis Lord. *Urban Geogr.* **13:1** 1-2:1992 pp. 25 – 48

169 L'impatto dei coefficienti BRI sulle politiche patrimoniali delle banche *[In Italian]*; [The impact of the "BRI" factor on the capital policies of the banks]. Vittorio Conti; Mauro Maccarinelli. *Bancaria* **48:2** 2:1992 pp. 13 – 24

170 Le implicazioni organizzative della disciplina gruppi creditizi *[In Italian]*; [Organizational implications of the discipline of credit groups]. Maurizio Baravelli. *Risparmio* **XL:5** 9-10:1992 pp. 1011 – 1047

171 Indonesia's new banking law. Ross H. McLeod. *B. Ind. Econ. St.* **28:3** 12:1992 pp. 107 – 122

J.2: Credit *[Crédit]* — *Banking [Activité bancaire]*

172 The international political economy of bank nationalization — Mexico in comparative perspective. Sylvia Maxfield. *Lat. Am. Res. R.* **27:1** 1992 pp. 75 – 104

173 Issues in reforming financial systems in Eastern Europe — the case of Bulgaria. Alfredo Thorne. Washington, D.C.: Technical Department Europe and Central Asia and Middle East and North Africa Regions, The World Bank, 1992: 42 p. [Policy research working papers.]

174 Malmquist indices of productivity growth during the deregulation of Norwegian banking. Sigbjørn Atle Berg; Finn R. Førsund; Eilev S. Jansen. *Sc. J. Econ.* **94** 1992 pp. 211 – 228

175 Models of banking instability — a partial review of the literature. Kevin Dowd. *J. Econ. Sur.* **6:2** 1992 pp. 107 – 132

176 The monetary economics of Henry Meulen. Kevin Dowd. *J. Money C. B.* **24:2** 5:1992 pp. 173 – 183

177 A "new view" of the role of banking firms in Keynesian monetary theory. Gary A. Dymski. *J. Post. Keyn. Ec.* **14:3** Spring:1992 pp. 311 – 320

178 Norway's banking sector and economy — current situation and outlook. Hermod Skånland. *Econ. B. Norges Bank.* **LXIII:2** 6:1992 pp. 135 – 141

179 Note sul sistema creditizio italiano — assetti strutturali e strategie aziendali *[In Italian]*; The Italian banking system — structures and business strategies *[Summary]*. Massimo lo Cicero. *Ras. Econ.* **LVI:1** 1-3:1992 pp. 45 – 78

180 Le nouveau paysage bancaire européen *[In French]*; The new European banking system *[Summary]*. Bernand Marois. *Gestion* **8:4** 1992 pp. 81 – 92

181 On matching book — a problem in banking and corporate finance. M. Shubik; M.J. Sobel. *Manag. Sci.* **38:6** 6:1992 pp. 827 – 839

182 On the financial management of credit institutions — banking risks, deposit guarantee and solvency ratio. Nicoletta Hadjiyannis. *Econ. Bull.* **:147** 1-3:1991 pp. 10 – 27

183 Operating efficiency of Canadian banks. Alli Nathan; Edwin H. Neave. *J. Finan. Ser. Res.* **6:3** 9:1992 pp. 265 – 276

184 Osservatorio europeo — i principali sistemi bancari europei in vista del '93 *[In Italian]*; European monitor — the main European banking systems on the eve of 1993 *[Summary]*. Myrta Merlino. *Ras. Econ.* **LVI:3** 7-9:1992 pp. 619 – 636

185 Output and productivity in banking. R.J. Colwell; E.P. Davis. *Sc. J. Econ.* **94** 1992 pp. 111 – 130

186 Ownership structure and performance in the banking industry in Nigeria; (Structure de la propriéte et performance du secteur bancaire au Nigeria: *Title only in French*). Aforka C. Ibe. *Sav. Develop.* **XVI:3** 1992 pp. 243 – 254

187 Pénzpiaci szegmensek — szegmentált irányítás *[In Hungarian]*; Money market segments — segmented management *[Summary]*. Király Júlia. *Közg. Sz.* **XXXIX:** 7-8:1992 pp. 642 – 653

188 People that count — the forgotten faces of rotating savings and credit associations in Indonesia; Les gens qui comptent — les faces oubliees des associations rotatoires d'epargne et de credit en Indonesie *[French summary]*. Otto Hospes. *Sav. Develop.* **XVI:4** 1992 pp. 371 – 401

189 Performance control in banking; *[German summary]*. Albertus Bruggink. *Bank-Archiv* **38** 8:1990 pp. 612 – 620

190 A political logjam still blocks banking reform. R. Dan Brumbaugh; Kenneth E. Scott. *Challenge* **35:2** 3/4:1992 pp. 35 – 41

191 Prinzipien des US- Bankrechts *[In German]*; [Principles of US banking law]. Michael Gruson; Thomas Herndl. *Bank-Archiv* **38** 1:1990 pp. 6 – 18

192 Il processo di ricomposizione del portafoglio crediti delle banche — una ricostruzione dell'evoluzione recente e delle principali tendenze *[In Italian]*; [Reconstruction of credit portfolios in banks. Recent developments and main trends]. Mauro Maccarinelli; Andrea Resti. *Risparmio* **:6** 11-12:1992 pp. 1451 – 1491

193 Productive efficiency performance of minority and nonminority-owned banks — a nonparametric approach. E. Elyasiani; S. Mehdian. *J. Bank. Fin.* **16:5** 9:1992 pp. 933 – 948

194 The productivity of the Spanish banking system in the 80s — international comparison. F. Pérez García; R. Doménech Vilariño. *Banca Nat. Lav. Q. Rev.* **:181** 6:1992 pp. 147 – 169

195 The proposals of BIS and EEC capital adequacy of credit institutions. Nikos Mihopoulos; Nikos Troullinos. *Econ. Bull.* **:147** 1-3:1991 pp. 28 – 42

196 Qualità in banca — un processo già avviato? *[In Italian]*; [Quality in the banks — a process that has already started?]. Cesare Rossi. *Bancaria* **48:2** 2:1992 pp. 57 – 66

J.2: Credit *[Crédit]* — *Banking [Activité bancaire]*

197 A question of interest — the paralysis of Saudi banking. Peter W. Wilson. Boulder: Westview Press, 1991: viii, 296 p. *ISBN: 081338107x; LofC: 90021793. Includes bibliographical references (p. [293]-296).*

198 Las reformas del sector bancario y financiero en América Latina *[In Spanish]*; [Reform in the banking and financial sectors in Latin America]. Manfred Nitsch. *Homines* **6** 1989 pp. 86 – 91

199 The regional distribution of bank closings in the United States from 1982-1988. Orley M. Amos. *S. Econ. J.* **58:3** 1:1992 pp. 805 – 815

200 Il ruolo dei gruppi creditizi nella realizzazione dei grandi progetti infrastrutturali *[In Italian]*; [The role of banking groups in the implementation of infrastructural projects]. Dario Simoncini. *Ras. Econ.* **LVI:2** 4-6:1992 pp. 395 – 415

201 Scale and scope economies in Portuguese commercial banking — the years 1965-88. Victor Mendes. *Economia [Lisbon]* **XV:3** 10:1991 pp. 453 – 490

202 Sequential banking. David S. Bizer; Peter DeMarzo. *J. Polit. Ec.* **100:1** 2:1992 pp. 41 – 61

203 Strategic planning and goal setting in the banking sector. Paraskeri Boulfounau. *Econ. Bull.* **:146** 10-12:1990 pp. 9 – 21

204 Traditional and nontraditional banking — an information-theoretic approach. L.J. Mester. *J. Bank. Fin.* **16:3** 6:1992 pp. 545 – 566

205 U.S. deposit insurance reform. T.F. Cargill; T. Mayer. *Cont. Policy* **X:3** 7:1992 pp. 95 – 103

206 Überlegungen zur globalen Analyse der Banken-Geschäftsstruktur *[In German]*; [Considerations of a global analysis of banking business structure]. Josef Stockinger. *Bank-Archiv* **38** 12:1990 pp. 990 – 998

207 What should banks really do? L.J. White. *Cont. Policy* **X:3** 7:1992 pp. 104 – 112

208 Why are banks dying? David O. Beim. *Columb. J. W. Bus.* **27:1** Spring:1992 pp. 6 – 12

209 Women's access to credit facilities from commercial banks in Nigeria — challenges for the 1990s; L'acces des femmes au credit des banques commerciales au Nigeria — un defi pour les annees '90 *[French summary]*. John C. Anyanwu. *Sav. Develop.* **XVI:4** 1992 pp. 421 – 440

210 Zukunftsstrategien der Schweizer Banken — Konzepte für Österreich? *[In German]*; [Future strategies of the Swiss banks — concepts for Austria?]. I. Wagner; M. Zimmermann; E. Antensteiner. *Bank-Archiv* **38** 6:1990 pp. 428 – 437

211 Zusammenschluss einer Sparkassen-Aktiengesellschaft mit einer bankgeschäftlich tätigen Sparkasse *[In German]*; [Merger of a savings bank — public limited company with a savings bank also carrying out banking business]. Waldemar Jud; Alfons Grünwald. *Bank-Archiv* **38** 9:1990 pp. 690 – 707

Central banks *[Banques centrales]*

212 Abhängigkeit versus Autonomie der Notenbank *[In German]*; Dependence versus autonomy of the central bank *[Summary]*. Heinz-Peter Spahn; Georg Ziemes. *Jahrb. N. St.* **210:3-4** 9:1992 pp. 219 – 232

213 Can a central bank go bust? Maxwell J. Fry. *Manch. Sch. E.* **LX** 1992 pp. 85 – 98

214 The case for central bank independence. J. de Haan; J.E. Sturm. *Banca Nat. Lav. Q. Rev.* **:182** 9:1992 pp. 305 – 327

215 Commercial banks, the central bank, and endogenous money. L. Randall Wray. *J. Post. Keyn. Ec.* **14:3** Spring:1992 pp. 297 – 310

216 The effects of monetary targeting on business activity and financial market stability in the United Kingdom. S.W. Barnhart; A.F. Darrat. *J. Bank. Fin.* **16:3** 6:1992 pp. 523 – 543

217 Establishing a central bank — issues in Europe and lessons from the US. Matthew B. Canzoneri *[Ed.]*; Vittorio U. Grilli *[Ed.]*; Paul R. Masson *[Ed.]*. Cambridge: Cambridge University Press, 1992: 307 p. *ISBN: 0521420989; LofC: 91046674. Papers presented at the conference — "Designing a central bank," held May 1-2, 1991 at Georgetown University and sponsored by the Centre for Economic Policy Research, the Center for German and European Studies at Georgetown University, et al; Includes index.*

218 The European Central Bank and monetary policy in stage III of EMU. Peter B. Kenen. *Int. Aff. [London]* **68:3** 7:1992 pp. 457 – 474

219 Die geldpolitischen Konzeptionen der Bank von England und der Deutschen Bundesbank — eine Analyse über den Einfluss des monetaristischen Paradigmas *[In German]*; [Monetary policy concepts of the Bank of England and the German federal bank — an analysis of the influence of monetary paradigms]. Maria Paprotzki. Bern: Lang, 1991: 341 p. *ISBN: 363143782x. [Europäische Hochschulschriften.]*

J.2: Credit *[Crédit]* — Central banks *[Banques centrales]*

220 The Japanese financial system and monetary policy — a descriptive review. S. Eijffinger; A. van Rixtel. *Jpn. Wor. Econ.* **4:4** 12:1992 pp. 291 – 309

221 Monetary sovereignty — the politics of central banking in Western Europe. John B. Goodman. Ithaca, N.Y: Cornell University Press, 1992: xii, 239 p. *ISBN: 0801480132; LofC: 91057897. Includes bibliographical references and index.* [Cornell studies in political economy; Cornell paperbacks.]

222 Planteamientos sobre un posible Banco Central Europeo *[In Spanish]*; [Plans for a possible European Central Bank]. Philip Arestis. *Infor. Com. Esp.* **:701** 1:1992 pp. 47 – 58

223 Political economy and comparative central banking. Gerald Epstein. *Rev. Rad. Pol. Ec.* **24:1** Spring:1992 pp. 1 – 30

224 Regional autonomy in central banking. Patrick Honohan. *Irish Bank. Rev.* *Spring:1992* pp. 3 – 13

225 The regional representation of federal reserve bank presidents. John A. Gildea. *J. Money C. B.* **24:2** 5:1992 pp. 215 – 225

Indebtedness *[Endettement]*

226 American influences on European consumer bankruptcy law; *[German summary]*. Nick Huls. *J. Consum. Pol.* **15:2** 1992 pp. 125 – 142

227 Credit and debt — the PSI report. Richard Berthoud; Elaine Kempson. London: Policy Studies Institute, 1992: 226 p. *ISBN: 0853744971.* [PSI research report. : No. 728]

228 Does the government have to clean bank balance sheets in transitional economies? Neven Mates. *Comm. Econ.* **4:3** 1992 pp. 395 – 409

229 How can debt swaps be used for development? Mohua Mukherjee. Washington, D.C.: Cofinancing and Financial Advisory Services, The World Bank, 1992: 24 p. [Policy research working papers.]

230 Insiders and outsiders — the choice between informed and arm's-length debt. Raghuram G. Rajan. *J. Finance* **47:4** 9:1992 pp. 1367 – 1400

231 A note on burden sharing among creditors. Michael P. Dooley; Richard D. Haas; Steven A. Symansky. Washington, D.C.: International Monetary Fund, Research Department, 1992: 19 p. [IMF working paper. : No. WP/92/21]

232 Research note — debt covenant disclosures and the impact of SEC rule 144A. Eric Press; Joseph Weintrop. *J. Acc. Pub. Pol.* **11:1** Spring:1992 pp. 67 – 82

233 The timing of intergenerational transfers, tax policy, and aggregate savings. David Altig; Steven J. Davis. *Am. Econ. Rev.* **82:5** 12:1992 pp. 1199 – 1220

234 Überschuldungssituation und Schuldnerberatung in der Bundesrepublik Deutschland — Studie im Auftrag des Bundesministeriums für Familie und Senioren und des Bundesministeriums der Justiz *[In German]*; [Debt situation and advice to debtors in Germany — a study sponsored by the Federal Department for Family and Elderly and by the Federal Ministry of Law]. Dieter Korczak; Gabriela Pfefferkorn. Stuttgart: Kohlhammer, 1992: lxvii, 336 p. *ISBN: 3170121189. Bibliography — p.311-333.* [Schriftenreihe des Bundesministeriums für Familie und Senioren. : Vol. 3]

Mortgages *[Hypothèques]*

235 Adopting spatially flexible lending strategies — building society mortgage lending in Dublin during the 1980s. Laurence Murphy. *Area* **24:1** 3:1992 pp. 30 – 35

236 Can retail depositories fund mortgages profitably? Wayne Passmore. *J. Hous. Res.* **3:2** 1992 pp. 305 – 340

237 Coping with the legacies of subsidized mortgage credit in Hungary. Silvia B. Sagari; Loic Chiquier. Washington, D.C.: Country Economics Department, The World Bank, 1992: 26 p. [Policy research working papers.]

238 Dual-indexed mortgages in reforming socialist economics — evaluating the risks and institutional requirements. Gwendolyn Ball. *Hous. Pol. Deb.* **3:3** 1992 pp. 855 – 876

239 Estimating the marginal contribution of adjustable-rate mortgage selection to termination probabilities in a nested model. Charles A. Capone; Donald F. Cunningham. *J. Real Est. Finan. Econ.* **5:4** 12:1992 pp. 333 – 356

240 Evidence on the size of banking markets from mortgage loan rates in twenty cities. Stephen A. Rhoades. Washington, DC: Board of Governors of the Federal Reserve System, 1992: 11 p. [Staff study.]

241 A generalized valuation model for fixed-rate residential mortgages. James B. Kau; Donald C. Keenan; Walter J. Muller; James F. Epperson. *J. Money C. B.* **24:3** 8:1992 pp. 279 – 299

J.2: Credit *[Crédit]* — *Mortgages [Hypothèques]*

242 Indexált kölcsönök és várakozások matematikai clemzése *[In Hungarian]*; Mathematical analysis of indexed mortgages and expectations *[Summary]*. András Simonovits. *Közg. Sz.* **XXXIX** 3:1992 pp. 262 – 278

243 Points, risk and structure in the mortgage market. Robert E. Martin; David J. Smyth. *S. Econ. J.* **58:3** 1:1992 pp. 779 – 789

244 Prepayment, default, and the valuation of mortgage pass-through securities. Eduardo S. Schwartz; Walter N. Torous. *J. Bus.* **65:2** 4:1992 pp. 221 – 239

245 Le prêt immobilier cautionné — an innovative substitute for the French mortgage. Charles Austin Stone; Anne Zissu. *J. Hous. Res.* **3:2** 1992 pp. 401 – 421

246 Residential mortgage default — a review of the literature. Roberto G. Quercia; Michael A. Stegman. *J. Hous. Res.* **3:2** 1992 pp. 341 – 379

247 When will residential mortgage underwriting come of age? Jack M. Guttentag. *Hous. Pol. Deb.* **3:1** 1992 pp. 143 – 156

J.3: Insurance — *Assurances*

1 Adverse selection and equilibrium in liability insurance markets. Lawrence A. Berger; J. David Cummins. *J. Risk Uncert.* **5:3** 1992 pp. 273 – 288

2 Automobile insurance ratemaking in the presence of asymmetrical information. G. Dionne; C. Vanasse. *J. Appl. Econ.* **7:2** 4-6:1992 pp. 149 – 165

3 Corporate demand for insurance — some empirical and theoretical results. Wallace N. Davidson; Mark L. Cross; John H. Thornton. *J. Finan. Ser. Res.* **6:1** 5:1992 pp. 61 – 72

4 Dynamic equilibrium and the structure of premiums in a reinsurance market. Knut K. Aase. *Geneva Pap. Risk Insur. Theory* **17:2** 12:1992 pp. 93 – 136

5 Earthquake insurance — mandated disclosure and homeowner response in California. Risa Palm; Michael Hodgson. *Ann. As. Am. G.* **82:2** 6:1992 pp. 207 – 222

6 Economie di scala e della diversificazione produttiva nel settore assicurativo italiano *[In Italian]*; [Economies of scale and scope in the Italian insurance sector]. Dario Focarelli. *Riv. Pol. Ec.* **LXXXII:III** 4:1992 pp. 23 – 44

7 Executive compensation in the life insurance industry. David Mayers; Clifford W. Smith. *J. Bus.* **65:1** 1:1992 pp. 51 – 74

8 The impact of stabilization and interim audits on the pricing of deposit insurance. Brian Smith; Robert White. *J. Bus. Fin. Acc.* **19:1** 1:1992 pp. 113 – 132

9 The insurance effect of groups. Canice Prendergast. *Int. Econ. R.* **33:3** 8:1992 pp. 567 – 582

10 The life insurance industry in the United States — an analysis of economic and regulatory issues. Kenneth M. Wright. Washington, D.C.: Country Economics Department, The World Bank, 1992: 46 p. [Policy research working papers.]

11 Optimistic reporting in the property-casualty insurance industry. Kathy Ruby Petroni. *J. Account. E.* **15:4** 12:1992 pp. 485 – 508

12 Price adjustment in an automobile insurance market — a test of the Sheshinski-Weiss model; Ajustement de prix dans un marché d'assurance-automobile — un test du modèle Sheshinski-Weiss *[French summary]*. Bev Dahlby. *Can. J. Econ.* **XXV:3** 8:1992 pp. 564 – 583

13 Pricing insurance and warranties — ambiguity and correlated risks. Robin M. Hogarth; Howard Kunreuther. *Geneva Pap. Risk Insur. Theory* **17:1** 6:1992 pp. 35 – 60

14 Private insurance reform in the 1990s — can it solve the health care crisis? Thomas Bodenheimer. *Int. J. Health. Ser.* **22:2** 1992 pp. 197 – 216

15 Reinsurance and the liability insurance crisis. Lawrence A. Berger; J. David Cummins; Sharon Tennyson. *J. Risk Uncert.* **5:3** 1992 pp. 253 – 272

16 Should earthquake mitigation measures be voluntary or required? Howard Kunreuther; Anne E. Kleffner. *J. Regul. Econ.* **4:4** 12:1992 pp. 321 – 333

17 A stochastic approach to insurance cycles. M.J. Goovaerts; F. de Vylder; R. Kaas. *Insur. Math. Econ.* **11:2** 8:1992 pp. 97 – 108

18 The valuation of multiple claim insurance contracts. David C. Shimko. *J. Fin. Qu. An.* **27:2** 6:1992 pp. 229 – 246

19 Versicherungswirtschaft überwindet Wachstumsschwäche *[In German]*; Insurance industry overcomes stagnation period *[Summary]*. Peter Brandner. *Monatsberichte* **7:65** 1992 pp. 375 – 380

20 Una versión de la teoría del arrepentimiento — aplicación a la demanda de seguro *[In Spanish]*; [A version of regret theory — an application to insurance demand] *[Summary]*. Ramón Sirvent; Josefa Tomás. *Invest. Econ.* **XVI:1** 1:1992 pp. 43 – 62

J.4: Capital market — *Marché financier*

Sub-divisions: Bonds *[Obligations]*; Interest rates *[Taux d'intérêt]*; Investment *[Investissements]*; Portfolio management *[Gestion de portefeuille]*; Risk *[Risque]*; Stock exchange *[Bourse]*; Stock prices and stock returns *[Prix des actions et dividendes]*

1 An alternative approach for determining hedge ratios for futures contracts. Allan Hodgson; John Okunev. *J. Bus. Fin. Acc.* **19:2** 1:1992 pp. 211 – 224
2 Alternative characterizations of American put options. Peter Carr; Robert Jarrow; Ravi Myneni. *Math. Fin.* **2:2** 4:1992 pp. 87 – 106
3 An analysis of the process of capital liberalization in Italy. Leonardo Bartolini; Gordon M. Bodnar. Washington, D.C.: International Monetary Fund, European I Department, 1992: 23 p. *Bibliography — p.21-23.* [IMF working paper. : No. WP/92/27]
4 Arbitrage and price behavior of the Nikkei stock index futures. Kian-Guan Lim. *J. Futur. Mark.* **12:2** 4:1992 pp. 151 – 162
5 The arbitrage pricing theory and multifactor models of asset returns. Gregory Connor; Robert A. Korajczyk. London: LSE Financial Markets Group, 1992: 94 p. [LSE Financial Markets Group discussion paper series. : No. 149]
6 Are negative option prices possible? The callable U.S. treasury-bond puzzle. Francis A. Longstaff. *J. Bus.* **65:4** 10:1992 pp. 571 – 592
7 Asset pricing with stochastic differential utility. Darrell Duffie; Larry G. Epstein. *R. Finan. Stud.* **5:3** 1992 pp. 411 – 436
8 Die Bewertung von Stillhalter Optionen *[In German]*; [The pricing of covert warrants] *[Summary]*; *[French summary]*. Walter Wasserfallen; Thomas Stucki; Andreas Jacobs. *Schw. Z. Volk. Stat.* **128:1** 3:1992 pp. 35 – 49
9 Buyers' strategies, entry barriers, and competition. David T. Scheffman; Pablo T. Spiller. *Econ. Inq.* **XXX:3** 7:1992 pp. 418 – 436
10 Capital markets in the development process — the case of Brazil. John H. Welch. Basingstoke: Macmillan Press, 1992: 231 p. *ISBN: 0333513290.*
11 Capital markets — institution and instruments. Frank J. Fabozzi; Franco Modigliani. : Prentice Hall, 1992: 726 p. *ISBN: 0135911168.*
12 Cijena kapitala *[In Serbo-Croatian]*; Цена капитала *[Russian summary]*; The price of capital *[Summary]*. Ivan. Teodorović. *Ekon. Preg.* **43:3-4** 1992 pp. 172 – 188
13 A comparative analysis of merchant and broker intermediation. S.C. Hackett. *J. Econ. Beh.* **18:3** 8:1992 pp. 299 – 316
14 Consumer reaction to measures of poor quality — evidence from the mutual fund industry. Richard A. Ippolito. *J. Law Econ.* **XXXV:1** 4:1992 pp. 45 – 70
15 Денежно-кредитное регулирование и рынок ссудных капиталов *[In Russian]*; [Monetary-credit regulation and the loan capital market]. I.Ya. Noskova. *Finansy* :12 1992 pp. 60 – 65
16 Derivative asset pricing with transaction costs. Bernard Bensaid; Jean-Philippe Lesne; Henri Pagès; José Scheinkman. *Math. Fin.* **2:2** 4:1992 pp. 63 – 86
17 The derived demand with hedging cost uncertainty in the futures markets. J. Paroush; A. Wolf. *Econ. J.* **102:413** 7:1992 pp. 831 – 844
18 A direct examination of the dividend clientele hypothesis. John Karl Scholz. *J. Publ. Ec.* **49:3** 12:1992 pp. 261 – 285
19 Diversification returns and asset contributions. David G. Booth; Eugene F. Fama. *Finan. Anal. J.* *5/6:1992* pp. 26 – 32
20 Do futures markets react efficiently to predictable errors in government announcements? David E. Runkle. *J. Futur. Mark.* **12:6** 12:1992 pp. 635 – 643
21 Does the S & P 500 futures mispricing series exhibit nonlinear dependence across time? Ravi Vaidyanathan; Tim Krehbiel. *J. Futur. Mark.* **12:6** 12:1992 pp. 659 – 677
22 Dual listings and shareholders' wealth — evidence from UK and Japanese firms. Insup Lee. *J. Bus. Fin. Acc.* **19:2** 1:1992 pp. 243 – 252
23 Dual-class shares — a review. Kristian Rydqvist. *Ox. R. Econ. Pol.* **8:3** Autumn:1992 pp. 45 – 57
24 An earnings prediction approach to examing intercompany information transfers. Robert Freeman; Senyo Tse. *J. Account. E.* **15:4** 12:1992 pp. 509 – 523

J.4: Capital market *[Marché financier]*

25 Economic effects of EEC insider trading regulation applied to Germany. Hans-Bernd Schäfer; Claus Ott. *Int. R. Law Econ.* **12:3** 9:1992 pp. 357 – 378

26 The effect of asset class maintenance costs on optimal asset allocation. G. Leslie Smith-Britto; Richard A. Crowell. *Finan. Anal. J.* *5/6:1992* pp. 40 – 43

27 The effect of contemporaneous reserve accounting on the market for federal funds. D.J. Lasser. *J. Bank. Fin.* **16:6** 12:1992 pp. 1047 – 1056

28 The effect of futures trading on spot price volatility — evidence for Brent Crude Oil using GARCH. Antonios Antoniou; Andrew J. Foster. *J. Bus. Fin. Acc.* **19:4** 6:1992 pp. 473 – 484

29 The effect of two-tier collective bargaining agreements on shareholder equity. Steven L. Thomas; Morris M. Kleiner. *Ind. Lab. Rel.* **45:2** 1:1992 pp. 339 – 351

30 Empirical analysis of pricing efficiency in the Hungarian capital markets. A. Murphy; Z. Sabov. *Appl. Finan. Econ.* **2:2** 6:1992 pp. 63 – 78

31 An empirical investigation of the role of accounting in the valuation of unseasoned equity issues. Kevin Keasey; Paul McGuinness. *Acc. Bus. Res.* **22:86** Spring:1992 pp. 133 – 142

32 The empirical significance of tax effects on the valuation of dividends — the UK evidence. Alice Chui; Norman Strong; John Cadle. *J. Bus. Fin. Acc.* **19:4** 6:1992 pp. 515 – 532

33 Equity issues and changes in expectations of earnings by financial analysts. Prem C. Jain. *R. Finan. Stud.* **5:4** 1992 pp. 669 – 683

34 Equity issues with time-varying asymmetric information. Robert A. Korajczyk; Deborah J. Lucas; Robert L. McDonald. *J. Fin. Qu. An.* **27:3** 9:1992 pp. 397 – 417

35 Die ersten vier Wochen der deutschen Terminbörse (Teil II) *[In German]*; The first four weeks of the German Futures Exchange (Deutsche Terminbörse (DTB)) (Part II) *[Summary]*; Les quatre premières semaines de la bourse à terme allemande (Deutsche Terminbörse) (Partie II) *[French summary]*. Jens Spudy. *Kred. Kap.* **25:1** 1992 pp. 135 – 174

36 European capital markets. F. de Jong *[Contrib.]*; A. Kemna *[Contrib.]*; T. Kloek *[Contrib.]*; S.-H. Poon *[Contrib.]*; S.J. Taylor *[Contrib.]*; A. Corhay *[Contrib.]*; S. Beckers *[Contrib.]*; R. Grinold *[Contrib.]*; A. Rudd *[Contrib.]*; D. Stefek *[Contrib.] and others. Collection of 12 articles.* **J. Bank. Fin.** , *16:1,* 2:1992 pp. 11 – 272

37 Evaluating benchmark quality. Jeffery V. Bailey. *Finan. Anal. J.* *5/6:1992* pp. 33 – 39

38 An examinatioin of the underpricing of initial public offerings in Hong Kong — 1980-90. Paul McGuinness. *J. Bus. Fin. Acc.* **19:2** 1:1992 pp. 165 – 186

39 La experiencia de Japón con la liberalización financiera y cuestiones anexas *[In Spanish]*; [Japan's experience of financial liberalization and related questions]. Shigyo Kimura. *Monetaria* **XV:3** 7-10:1992 pp. 213 – 232

40 Financial and capital markets in Asia. Foundation for Advanced Information and Research (Japan); Committee for the Development of Financial and Capital Markets in the Asia-Pacific Region. Tokyo: Foundation for Advanced Information and Research, 1991: 385 p.

41 Financial markets in the Pacific basin — an inside view. Samuel C. Shieh. *Ind. Free China* **LXXVIII:1** 7:1992 pp. 31 – 52

42 Finanzmarktliberalisierung und politökonomische Reformgrenzen in Entwicklungsländern am Beispiel der Philippinen *[In German]*; [Liberalization of financial markets and politico-economic limitations of reform in developing countries — the example of the Philippines] *[Summary]*. Lukas Menkhoff. *Konjunkturpolitik* **38:2** 1992 pp. 69 – 85

43 Formal and informal financial markets, and the neo-structuralist critique of the financial liberalization strategy in less developed countries. B.K. Kapur. *J. Dev. Econ.* **38:1** 1:1992 pp. 63 – 77

44 Futures manipulation with "cash settlement". Praveen Kumar; Duane J. Seppi. *J. Finance* **47:4** 9:1992 pp. 1485 – 1502

45 Handelsbeschränkungen und „finanzielle Protektion". Zur sektoralen Struktur von Finanzmarktregulierungen am Beispiel Brasilien und Peru *[In German]*; Trade restrictions and "financial protection" — the sectoral structure of financial market regulations demonstrated by the Brazilian and Peruvian examples *[Summary]*; Restrictions dans les échanges commerciaux et «protection financière» — la structure sectorielle des règlementations des marchés financiers — l'exemple du Brésil et du Perou *[French summary]*. Markus Diehl. *Kred. Kap.* **25:4** 1992 pp. 528 – 544

46 Herd on the street — informational inefficiencies in a market with short-term speculation. Kenneth A. Froot; David S. Scharfstein; Jeremy C. Stein. *J. Finance* **47:4** 9:1992 pp. 1461 – 1484

J.4: Capital market *[Marché financier]*

47 How financial markets affect long-run growth — a cross-country study. Ejaz Ghani. Washington, D.C.: Eastern Africa Department, Africa Regional Office, The World Bank, 1992: 30 p. [Policy research working papers.]

48 Imperfect capital markets and persistence of initial wealth inequalities. Thomas Pilketty. London: London School of Economics and Political Science. Suntory-Toyota International Centre for Economics and Related Disciplines, 1992: 53 p. [Theoretical economics. : No. TE/92/255]

49 The implications of knowledge-based growth for the optimality of open capital markets; *[French summary]*. Meir Kohn; Nancy Marion. *Can. J. Econ.* **XXV:4** 11:1992 pp. 865 – 883

50 Information and diversity of analyst opinion. Christopher B. Barry; Robert H. Jennings. *J. Fin. Qu. An.* **27:2** 6:1992 pp. 169 – 184

51 Information, asset prices, and the volume of trade. Gregory W. Huffman. *J. Finance* **47:4** 9:1992 pp. 1575 – 1590

52 Initial public offerings of equity securities — anomalous evidence using REITs. Ko Wang; Su Han Chan; George W. Gau. *J. Finan. Ec.* **31:3** 6:1992 pp. 381 – 410

53 Insider trading and the cost of capital in a multi-period economy. Jurgen Dennert. London: LSE Financial Markets Group, 1992: 35 p. [LSE Financial Markets Group discussion paper series. : No. 128]

54 Insider trading in a globalizing market — who should regulate what? Merritt B. Fox. *Law Cont. Pr.* **55:4** Autumn:1992 pp. 263 – 302

55 Insider trading in continuous time. Kerry Back. *R. Finan. Stud.* **5:3** 1992 pp. 387 – 409

56 Insider trading in financial signaling models. Mark Bagnoli; Naveen Khanna. *J. Finance* **47:5** 12:1992 pp. 1905 – 1934

57 Insider trading — should it be prohibited? Hayne E. Leland. *J. Polit. Ec.* **100:4** 8:1992 pp. 859 – 887

58 Inter-currency transmission of volatility in foreign exchange futures. Mohammad Najand; Hamid Rahman; Kenneth Yung. *J. Futur. Mark.* **12:6** 12:1992 pp. 609 – 620

59 The Irish unit fund industry — structure and performance. Martin Kenneally; Liam Gallagher. *Econ. Soc. R.* **23:4** 7:1992 pp. 397 – 422

60 Issue costs and regulated returns — a general approach. Keith M. Howe; William Beranek. *J. Regul. Econ.* **4:4** 12:1992 pp. 365 – 378

61 Liberalisation and consolidation — the single European market and the remaking of European financial capital. A. Leyshon; N.J. Thrift. *Envir. Plan.A.* **24:1** 1:1992 pp. 49 – 82

62 The limited future of unlimited liability — a capital markets perspective. Joseph A. Grundfest. *Yale Law J.* **102:2** 11:1992 pp. 387 – 426

63 Liquidity, loanable funds, and real activity. Timothy S. Fuerst. *J. Monet. Ec.* **29:1** 2:1992 pp. 3 – 24

64 The market impact of UK company news announcements. David Brookfield; Richard Morris. *J. Bus. Fin. Acc.* **19:4** 6:1992 pp. 585 – 602

65 The market value of information — some experimental results. Thomas E. Copeland; Daniel Friedman. *J. Bus.* **65:2** 4:1992 pp. 241 – 266

66 Markttechnische "Trading Rules" kontra Buy und Hold-Strategien *[In German]*; Market-based (technical) trading rules versus buy and hold strategies *[Summary]*. Stöttner Rainer. *Jahrb. N. St.* **209:3-4** 3:1992 pp. 266 – 282

67 A Martingale representation result and an application to incomplete financial markets. S.D. Jacka. *Math. Fin.* **2:4** 10:1992 pp. 239 – 250

68 Measuring the agency cost of debt. Antonio S. Mello; John E. Parsons. *J. Finance* **47:5** 12:1992 pp. 1887 – 1904

69 Memories, heteroscedasticity, and price limit in currency futures markets. G. Wenchi Kao; Christopher K. Ma. *J. Futur. Mark.* **12:6** 12:1992 pp. 679 – 692

70 Mercados e instituciones financieras *[In Spanish]*; [Markets and financial institutions]. Juan José Durán Herrera *[Contrib.]*; Prosper Lamothe Fernández *[Contrib.]*; J. Ignacio Peña *[Contrib.]*; Manuel Monjas Barroso *[Contrib.]*; Anunciación Martínez Rego *[Contrib.]*; Francisco Mochón Morcillo *[Contrib.]*; Ernesto R. Gallardo Jiménez *[Contrib.]*; Sofía de la Maza Arroyo *[Contrib.]*; Pilar Morán Reyero *[Contrib.]*. *Collection of 9 articles.* **Infor. Com. Esp.** , :704, 4:1992 pp. 3 – 93

71 Mercato efficiente ed effetto gennaio *[In Italian]*; [Market efficiency and January effect]. Franco Caparrelli; Dora de Simone; Ugo Calcagnini. *Risparmio* **XL:1** 1-2:1992 pp. 33 – 74

J.4: Capital market *[Marché financier]*

72 Il mercato italiano dei futures (MIF) — problematiche di avvio e prospettive *[In Italian]*; [On the Italian futures market (MIF) — problems and prospects]. Bruno Bianchi. *Ras. Econ.* **LVI:2** 4-6:1992 pp. 357 – 369

73 Moneylenders and informal financial markets in Malawi. B.R. Bolnick. *World Dev.* **20:1** 1:1992 pp. 57 – 68

74 The monotonicity of the term premium — another look. Matthew Richardson; Paul Richardson; Tom Smith. *J. Finan. Ec.* **31:1** 2:1992 pp. 97 – 105

75 The new European financial marketplace. Alfred Steinherr *[Ed.]*. London: Longman, 1992: 298 p. *ISBN: 0582089360.*

76 Notes on dynamic factor pricing models. Bruce N. Lehmann. *R. Quant. Finan. Account.* **2:1** 3:1992 pp. 69 – 87

77 One market? Stocks, futures, and options during October 1987. Allan W. Kleidon; Robert E. Whaley. *J. Finance* **47:3** 7:1992 pp. 851 – 877

78 The performance of credit markets under asymmetric information about project means and variances. Brian Hillier; M.V. Ibrahimo. *J. Econ. Stud.* **19:3** 1992 pp. 3 – 17

79 Performance-Messung schweizerischer Aktienfonds — Markt- Timing und Selektivität *[In German]*; [Measuring the performance of Swiss share funds — market timing and selectivity] *[Summary]*; *[French summary]*. Heinz Zimmermann; Claudia Zogg-Wetter. *Schw. Z. Volk. Stat.* **128:2** 6:1992 pp. 133 – 160

80 Policy issues in financial regulation. Dimitri Vittas. Washington, D.C.: Country Economics Department, The World Bank, 1992: 38 p. [Policy research working papers.]

81 Private market financing for developing countries. Charles Collyns. Washington, D.C.: International Monetary Fund, 1992: 80 p. *ISBN: 1557753180.* [World economic and financial surveys.]

82 The probability of a trade at the ask — an examination of interday and intraday behavior. David C. Porter. *J. Fin. Qu. An.* **27:2** 6:1992 pp. 209 – 228

83 Promise keeping in the great society — a model of credit information sharing. Daniel B. Klein. *Econ. Polit.* **4:2** 7:1992 pp. 117 – 136

84 Reading the regulatory text — regulation and the new stock issue process. D. Neu. *Crit. Persp. Acc.* **3:4** 12:1992 pp. 359 – 388

85 Real effects of the 1992 financial deregulation; *[French summary]*; *[German summary]*; *[Spanish summary]*. Jean-Marie Viaene. *Welt.liches Arc.* **4:128** 1992 pp. 615 – 638

86 The relation between the value line enigma and post-earnings-announcement drift. John Affleck-Graves; Richard R. Mendenhall. *J. Finan. Ec.* **31:1** 2:1992 pp. 75 – 96

87 Representing Martingale measures when asset prices are continuous and bounded. Freddy Delbaen. *Math. Fin.* **2:2** 4:1992 pp. 107 – 130

88 The robustness of risk-return nonlinearities to the normality assumption. Carolyn Carroll; Paul D. Thistle; K.C. John Wei. *J. Fin. Qu. An.* **27:3** 9:1992 pp. 419 – 435

89 Serious money — legitimation of deviancy in the financial markets. C. Stanley. *Int. J. S. Law* **20:1** 3:1992 pp. 43 – 60

90 Signal facilitation — a policy response to asymmetric information. Thomas E. Cooper. *J. Bus.* **65:3** 7:1992 pp. 431 – 450

91 The size effect — a multiperiod analysis. Wai Mun Fong. *Appl. Finan. Econ.* **2:2** 6:1992 pp. 87 – 92

92 Some considerations on the causes of structural change in financial markets. J.A. Kregel. *J. Econ. Iss.* **XXVI:3** 9:1992 pp. 733 – 747

93 Specialist vs. saitori — market-making in New York and Tokyo. Richard R. Lindsey; Ulrike Schaede. *Finan. Anal. J.* **48:4** 7-8:1992 pp. 48 – 57

94 The structure and performance of the money management industry. Josef Lakonishok; Andrei Shleifer; Robert W. Vishny. *Brookings P.* *1992* pp. 339 – 391

95 Survivorship bias in performance studies. Stephen J. Brown; William Goetzmann; Roger G. Ibbotson; Stephen A. Ross. *R. Finan. Stud.* **5:4** 1992 pp. 553 – 579

96 Swedish stocks, bonds, bills and inflation (1919-1990). P. Frennberg; B. Hansson. *Appl. Finan. Econ.* **2:2** 6:1992 pp. 79 – 86

97 Technological choice, financial markets and economic development. G. Saint-Paul. *Eur. Econ. R.* **36:4** 5:1992 pp. 763 – 782

98 A test for the winner-loser anomaly in the Australian equity market — 1958-87. Tim Brailsford. *J. Bus. Fin. Acc.* **19:2** 1:1992 pp. 225 – 242

99 Testing financial market equilibrium under asymmetric information. Larry H.P. Lang; Robert H. Litzenberger; Vicente Madrigal. *J. Polit. Ec.* **100:2** 4:1992 pp. 317 – 348

J.4: Capital market *[Marché financier]*

100 The theory of futures markets. Paul Weller *[Ed.]*. Oxford: Blackwell, 1992: 313 p. *ISBN: 063117172x; LofC: 91040410. Includes bibliographical references and index.* [Applied economic theory and econometrics.]

101 Trading noise, adverse selection, and intraday bid-ask spreads in future markets. Christopher K. Ma; Richard L. Peterson; R. Stephen Sears. *J. Futur. Mark.* **12:5** 10:1992 pp. 519 – 538

102 Valoración de activos financieros por el método de las martingalas *[In Spanish]*; [Valuation of financial assets through the Martingale method] *[Summary]*. Miguel A. Ariño; Pablo Fernández. *Invest. Econ.* **XVI:1** 1:1992 pp. 89 – 96

103 Variability in soybean futures prices — an integrated framework. Deborah H. Streeter; William G. Tomek. *J. Futur. Mark.* **12:6** 12:1992 pp. 705 – 728

Bonds *[Obligations]*

104 Alternative bond market indexes. Frank K. Reilly; G. Wenchi Kao; David J. Wright. *Finan. Anal. J.* *5/6:1992* pp. 44 – 58

105 Bond pricing and the term structure of interest rates — a new methodology for contingent claims valuation. David Heath; Robert Jarrow; Andrew Morton. *Econometrica* **60:1** 1:1992 pp. 77 – 106

106 The case for mandatory municipal disclosure — do seasoned municipal bond yields impound publicly available information? R. Penny Marquette; Earl R. Wilson. *J. Acc. Pub. Pol.* **11:3** Fall:1992 pp. 181 – 206

107 Credit quality spreads, bond market efficiency and financial fragility. E.P. Davis. *Manch. Sch. E.* **LX** 1992 pp. 21 – 46

108 Deregulation and market efficiency — evidence from the gilt-edged market. J.M. Steeley. *Appl. Finan. Econ.* **2:3** 9:1992 pp. 125 – 144

109 Determinants of the call option on corporate bonds. R.J. Kish; M. Livingston. *J. Bank. Fin.* **16:4** 8:1992 pp. 687 – 704

110 The dilemmas of market socialism — capital market reform in China — part I — bonds. Paul Bowles; Gordon White. *J. Dev. Stud.* **28:3** 4:1992 pp. 363 – 385

111 Does the bond market predict bankruptcy settlements? Allan C. Eberhart; Richard J. Sweeney. *J. Finance* **47:3** 7:1992 pp. 943 – 980

112 The equity premium — stock and bond return since 1802. Jeremy J. Siegel. *Finan. Anal. J.* **48:1** 1-2:1992 pp. 28 – 38

113 The implications of corporate bond ratings drift. Edward I. Altman; Duen Li Kao. *Finan. Anal. J.* *5/6:1992* pp. 64 – 75

114 Institutional bond pricing and information arrival — the case of bond rating changes. James W. Wansley; John L. Glascock; Terence M. Clauretie. *J. Bus. Fin. Acc.* **19:5** 9:1992 pp. 733 – 756

115 Is there a global market for convertible bonds? Yong-Cheol Kim; René M. Stulz. *J. Bus.* **65:1** 1:1992 pp. 75 – 91

116 Market segmentation and the residual demand for tax-exempt bonds — empirical evidence from the elimination of interest deductions. Michael Joseph McCue; Jerry L. Stevens. *J. Bus. Fin. Acc.* **19:5** 9:1992 pp. 777 – 788

117 A multiple-objective programming technique for structuring tax-exempt serial revenue debt issues. Amy Puelz. v; Sang M. Lee. *Manag. Sci.* **38:8** 8:1992 pp. 1186 – 1200

118 The optimal currency composition of government debt. Tsutomu Watanabe. *Mon. Econ. S.* **10:2** 11:1992 pp. 31 – 62

119 The relationship between accounting earnings and bond returns. Jong-Dae Jin. *J. Acc. Pub. Pol.* **11:3** Fall:1992 pp. 245 – 267

120 Stock prices and bond yields — can their comovements be explained in terms of present value models? Robert J. Shiller; Andrea E. Beltratti. *J. Monet. Ec.* **30:1** 10:1992 pp. 25 – 46

121 Tests of the nominal contracting hypothesis using stocks and bonds of the same firms. E.C. Chang; G.R. McQueen; J.M. Pinegar. *J. Bank. Fin.* **16:3** 6:1992 pp. 477 – 496

122 Time-varying term premia on U.S. treasury bills and bonds. Robert C. Klemkosky; Eugene A. Pilotte. *J. Monet. Ec.* **30:1** 10:1992 pp. 87 – 106

123 The valuation and management of bonds with sinking fund provisions. Andrew J. Kalotay; George O. Williams. *Finan. Anal. J.* **48:1** 3/4:1992 pp. 59 – 67

124 De zwakke variant van de efficiënte markthypothese en de Nederlandse staatsobligatiemarkt *[In Dutch]*; [The weak variant of the efficient market hypothesis and the Dutch state bond market]. E.P. Kroon. *Maan. Econ.* **56:2** 1992 pp. 84 – 104

J.4: Capital market *[Marché financier]* —

Interest rates *[Taux d'intérêt]*

125 Alternative approaches to money and interest rates. L. Randall Wray. *J. Econ. Iss.* **XXVI:4** 12:1992 pp. 1145 – 1178

126 Bond pricing and the term structure of interest rates — a new methodology for contingent claims valuation. David Heath; Robert Jarrow; Andrew Morton. *Econometrica* **60:1** 1:1992 pp. 77 – 106

127 Causal relations among stock returns, interest rates, real activity, and inflation. Bong-Soo Lee. *J. Finance* **47:4** 9:1992 pp. 1591 – 1603

128 The design of an interest rate rule with staggered contracting and costly transacting. Vincent Reinhart. *J. Macro.* **14:4** Fall:1992 pp. 663 – 688

129 The determinants of the tax-adjusted real interest rate. Stuart D. Allen. *J. Macro.* **14:1** Winter:1992 pp. 15 – 32

130 An empirical comparison of alternative models of the short-term interest rate. K.C. Chan; G. Andrew Karolyi; Francis A. Longstaff; Anthony B. Sanders. *J. Finance* **47:3** 7:1992 pp. 1209 – 1227

131 Equilibrium interest-rate determination under adjustment costs. Alfonso Novales. *J. Econ. Dyn. Cont.* **16:1** 1:1992 pp. 1 – 26

132 Die Fristigkeitsstruktur der Zinssätze — Theoretisches Konstrukt und empirische Evaluierung. Untersuchung mit Daten des Kapitalmarktes der Bundesrepublik Deutschland *[In German]*; The term structure of interest rates — theoretical construct and empirical evaluation *[Summary]*; La structure des échéances des taux d'intérêt — construction théretique et évaluation empirique *[French summary]*. Jochen Wilhelm; Lars Brüning. *Kred. Kap.* **25:2** 1992 pp. 259 – 294

133 Interest rate liberalization, savings, investment and growth — the case of Kenya; Liberalisation des taux d'interet, epargne, investissement et croissance — le cas du Kenya *[French summary]*. T.W. Oshikoya. *Sav. Develop.* **XVI:3** 1992 pp. 305 – 320

134 Interest rate variability and economic performance — some international evidence. M. Kandil. *Appl. Econ.* **24:2** 2:1992 pp. 175 – 192

135 Interest rate volatility and the term structure — a two-factor general equilibrium model. Francis A. Longstaff; Eduardo S. Schwartz. *J. Finance* **47:4** 9:1992 pp. 1259 – 1282

136 Interpreting the movements in short-term interest rates. Martin Evans; Paul Wachtel. *J. Bus.* **65:3** 7:1992 pp. 395 – 429

137 The interrelationship between money and interest rates in Hong Kong — a causality analysis. Yu-Hon Lui; G. Yu-Nan Tang; R.C.Y. Leung. *Br. Rev. Ec. Iss.* **14:33** 6:1992 pp. 57 – 75

138 Il paradosso di Fisher alla luce di un modello mediavarianza *[In Italian]*; [The Fisher paradox in the light of a mean-variance model]. Maria Monti. *Risparmio* **XL:5** 9-10:1992 pp. 1109 – 1139

139 Presidential address — swaps — plain and fanciful. Robert H. Litzenberger. *J. Finance* **47:3** 7:1992 pp. 831 – 850

140 Pricing interest rate options in a two-factor Cox-Ingersoll-Ross model of the term structure. Ren-Raw Chen; Louis Scott. *R. Finan. Stud.* **5:4** 1992 pp. 613 – 636

141 Pricing options on risky assets in a stochastic interest rate economy. Kaushik I. Amin; Robert A. Jarrow. *Math. Fin.* **2:4** 10:1992 pp. 217 – 238

142 Real and nominal interest rates — a discrete-time model and its continuous-time limit. Tong-sheng Sun. *R. Finan. Stud.* **5:4** 1992 pp. 581 – 611

143 The response of market interest rates to discount rate changes. *R. Fed. Resv. Bank St.Louis* **74:4** 7/8:1992 pp. 78 – 91

144 The sensitivity of bank stock returns to market, interest and exchange rate risks. J.J. Choi; E. Elyasiani; K.J. Kopecky. *J. Bank. Fin.* **16:5** 9:1992 pp. 983 – 1004

145 Taux d'intérêt élevés — peut-on agir sur le taux de change? *[In French]*; Fighting against high interest rates — is it possible to use the exchange rate? *[Summary]*. P. Artus. *Rev. Ec. Polit.* **102:5** 9-10:1992 pp. 703 – 725

146 Treasury bill rates in the 1970s and 1980s. Patric H. Hendershott; Joe Peek. *J. Money C. B.* **24:2** 5:1992 pp. 195 – 214

147 Understanding the term structure of interest rates — the expectations theory. *R. Fed. Resv. Bank St.Louis* **74:4** 7/8:1992 pp. 36 – 50

148 La valutazione delle interest rate options — un'analisi comparata *[In Italian]*; [An evaluation of interest rate options. A comparative analysis]. Mauro Camelia. *Risparmio* **XL:5** 9-10:1992 pp. 1073 – 1107

J.4: Capital market *[Marché financier]* — *Interest rates [Taux d'intérêt]*

149 Zinsrisikopotential. Kennziffer für das Risikomanagement von Zinsinstrumenten *[In German]*; Interest rate variation risk potential — a concept for managing the interest rate variation risk of interest rate-linked financial instruments *[Summary]*; Potentiel de risque des intérêts indice pour le management des risques d'instruments d'intérêts *[French summary]*. Raoul Oberman. *Kred. Kap.* **25:4** 1992 pp. 558 – 583

Investment *[Investissements]*

150 Accuracy versus efficiency when modelling investment. B. Smith. *Econ. Model.* **9:2** 4:1992 pp. 98 – 103

151 Automation of securities markets and the European Community's proposed investment services directive. Norman S. Poser. *Law Cont. Pr.* **55:4** Autumn:1992 pp. 29 – 51

152 Bid-ask spreads in financial futures. Paul A. Laux; A.J. Senchack. *J. Futur. Mark.* **12:6** 12:1992 pp. 621 – 634

153 A cross-sectional analysis of mutual funds' market timing and security selection skill. Carl R. Chen; Cheng F. Lee; Shafiqur Rahman; Anthony Chan. *J. Bus. Fin. Acc.* **19:5** 9:1992 pp. 659 – 676

154 Evolution and market behavior. Lawrence Blume; David Easley. *J. Econ. Theo.* **58:1** 10:1992 pp. 9 – 40

155 The impact of a capital investment on a subregional level — research note on an extended input-output approach. B.J. van der Merwe; D.E.N. van Seventer. *Develop. S. Afr.* **9:2** 5:1992 pp. 233 – 242

156 International investments and the European challenge. M. de Smidt. *Envir. Plan.A.* **24:1** 1:1992 pp. 83 – 94

157 Investment barriers and international asset pricing. Prasad Padmanabhan. *R. Quant. Finan. Account.* **2:3** 9:1992 pp. 299 – 319

158 New issues in the theory of investment — modernization and persistance effects. Marcel Savioz. London: Springer, 1992: 216 p. *ISBN: 354054979x.* [Studies in contemporary economics.]

159 Opening the capital account — a survey of issues and results. James A. Hanson. Washington, D.C.: Country Economics Department and Country Department IV, Latin America and the Caribbean Region, The World Bank, 1992: 37, 6 p. *Bibliography — p.31-37.* [Policy research working papers.]

160 Predictability, trends and seasonalities — an empirical analysis of UK investment trust portfolios 1970-1989. P. Fraser; D.M. Power. *Appl. Finan. Econ.* **2:3** 9:1992 pp. 161 – 172

161 Relationship-specific assets and the pricing of underwriter services. Christopher James. *J. Finance* **47:5** 12:1992 pp. 1865 – 1885

162 The use and misuse of value investing. Eric H. Sorensen; Chee Y. Thum. *Finan. Anal. J.* **48:1** 3/4:1992 pp. 51 – 58

163 Waiting to invest — investment and uncertainty. Jonathan E. Ingersoll; Stephen A. Ross. *J. Bus.* **65:1** 1:1992 pp. 1 – 29

Portfolio management *[Gestion de portefeuille]*

164 Asymptotically optimal portfolios. Farshid Jamshidian. *Math. Fin.* **2:2** 4:1992 pp. 131 – 150

165 Etude empirique de la stabilité inter-temporelle de la structure des rentabilités obligataires internationales *[In French]*; [An empirical study of the stability of returns on international portfolios]. Hubert de la Bruslerie. *J. Soc. Stat. Paris* **133:2** 2e trimestre:1992 pp. 24 – 49

166 An exploratory study of portfolio objectives and asset holdings. S.N. Ramaswami; R.K. Srivastava; T.H. McInish. *J. Econ. Beh.* **19:3** 12:1992 pp. 285 – 306

167 Factor representing portfolios in large asset markets. Enrique Sentana. London: LSE Financial Markets Group, 1992: 57 p. [LSE Financial Markets Group discussion paper series. : No. 135]

168 Global portfolio optimization. Fischer Black; Robert Litterman. *Finan. Anal. J.* **48:5** 9/10:1992 pp. 28 – 43

169 An instantaneous control model of bank reserves and federal funds management. A.H. Chen; S.C. Mazumdar. *J. Bank. Fin.* **16:6** 12:1992 pp. 1073 – 1095

170 International portfolio selection and efficiency analysis. K. Victor Chow; William B. Riley; John P. Formby. *R. Quant. Finan. Account.* **2:1** 3:1992 pp. 47 – 67

171 L'internationalisation des portefeuilles français de titres de placement et l'«hexagonalisation» des portefeuilles étrangers dans les années 80 *[In French]*; The

J.4: Capital market *[Marché financier]* — **Portfolio management** *[Gestion de portefeuille]*
international diversification of French portfolios and the «Frenchization» of foreign portfolios in the 80s *[Summary]*. A. Parent; J. Issoulié. *Rev. Ec. Polit.* **102:3** 5-6:1992 pp. 401 – 422

172 Un modello di programmazione lineare per la gestione dinamica di un portafoglio azionario *[In Italian]*; [A linear programming model for dynamic portfolio management]. Arturo Capasso. *Ras. Econ.* **LV:4** 10-12:1992 pp. 841 – 862

173 Optimal consumption-portfolio policies with habit formation. Jerome B. Detemple; Fernando Zapatero. *Math. Fin.* **2:4** 10:1992 pp. 251 – 274

174 Optimal dynamic trading with leverage constraints. Sandra J. Grossman; Jean-Luc Vila. *J. Fin. Qu. An.* **27:2** 6:1992 pp. 151 – 168

175 Optimal hedging with futures contracts — the case for fixed-income portfolios. Eric Briys; Dan Pieptea. *J. Futur. Mark.* **12:6** 12:1992 pp. 693 – 703

176 Optimal investment strategies with investor liabilities. E.J. Elton; M.J. Gruber. *J. Bank. Fin.* **16:5** 9:1992 pp. 869 – 890

177 Portfolio diversification — a pictorial analysis of the UK stock market. S. Poon; S.J. Taylor; C.W.R. Ward. *J. Bus. Fin. Acc.* **19:1** 1:1992 pp. 87 – 102

178 Portfolio insurance, dynamic portfolio strategies and market equilibrium; Portföljförsäkring, dynamiska portföljstrategier och marknadsjämvikt *[Swedish summary]*. Ragnar Lindgren. *Skan. Ensk. Bank. Q. R.* **:1-2** 1992 pp. 33 – 40

179 Portfolio redistribution impacts within the narrow monetary aggregate. Jean Gauger. *J. Money C. B.* **24:2** 5:1992 pp. 239 – 257

180 Risk reduction by diversification in the Nordic stock markets. Tarmo Haavisto; Björn Hansson. *Sc. J. Econ.* **94:4** 1992 pp. 581 – 588

181 Risk-adjusted performance attribution. Ernest M. Ankrim. *Finan. Anal. J.* **48:1** 3/4:1992 pp. 75 – 86

182 Underestimation of portfolio insurance and the crash of October 1987. Charles J. Jacklin; Allan W. Kleidon; Paul Pfleiderer. *R. Finan. Stud.* **5:1** 1992 pp. 35 – 64

183 When will mean-variance efficient portfolios be well diversified? Richard C. Green; Burton Hollifield. *J. Finance* **47:5** 12:1992 pp. 1785 – 1809

Risk *[Risque]*

184 An assessment of risk and return — some empirical findings from the Hong Kong exchange. Yan-Leung Cheung; Ka-Tai Wong. *Appl. Finan. Econ.* **2:2** 6:1992 pp. 105 – 114

185 Cash position, credit risk and hedging. Glenn W. Boyle. *J. Inter. Finan. Manag. Acc.* **4:1** Spring:1992 pp. 1 – 12

186 The cost of equity capital and the risk premium on equities. M.F.G. Scott. *Appl. Finan. Econ.* **2:1** 3:1992 pp. 21 – 32

187 The currency risk factor in international equity pricing. Manoj Gupta; Joseph E. Finnerty. *R. Quant. Finan. Account.* **2:3** 9:1992 pp. 245 – 257

188 Does market risk really explain the size effect? Narasimhan Jegadeesh. *J. Fin. Qu. An.* **27:3** 9:1992 pp. 337 – 351

189 Equity risk premia and the pricing of foreign exchange risk. Robert A. Korajczyk; Claude J. Viallet. *J. Int. Econ.* **33:3/4** 11:1992 pp. 199 – 219

190 Global financial markets and the risk premium on U.S. equity. K.C. Chan; G. Andrew Karolyi; René M. Stulz. *J. Finan. Ec.* **32:2** 10:1992 pp. 137 – 168

191 Hedge effectiveness — basis risk and minimum-variance hedging. Mark G. Castelino. *J. Futur. Mark.* **12:2** 4:1992 pp. 187 – 202

192 Information risk and initial public offerings — an empirical investigation. Swee-Sum Lam. *Appl. Finan. Econ.* **2:2** 6:1992 pp. 93 – 98

193 The market's perception of the riskiness of large U.S. bank commercial letters of credit. M. Kabir Hassan. *J. Finan. Ser. Res.* **6:3** 9:1992 pp. 207 – 221

194 Pricing options on risky assets in a stochastic interest rate economy. Kaushik I. Amin; Robert A. Jarrow. *Math. Fin.* **2:4** 10:1992 pp. 217 – 238

195 Risk aversion and stock market volatility. Glenn W. Boyle; Leslie Young. *J. Macro.* **14:4** Fall:1992 pp. 593 – 606

196 Risk reduction by diversification in the Nordic stock markets. Tarmo Haavisto; Björn Hansson. *Sc. J. Econ.* **94:4** 1992 pp. 581 – 588

197 Le rôle de l'estimation des variables rentabilité et risque dans les anomalies boursières

J.4: Capital market *[Marché financier]* — **Risk** *[Risque]*
liées à la taille et au P.E.R. *[In French]*; [The role of estimation of changing profit and risk in stock market anomalies]. Isabelle Girerd-Potin. *J. Soc. Stat. Paris* **133:3** 3rd trimester:1992 pp. 3 – 33

198 Systematic risk, hedging pressure, and risk premiums in futures markets. Hendrik Bessembinder. *R. Finan. Stud.* **5:4** 1992 pp. 637 – 667

199 Time stationarity of systematic risk — some Australian evidence. Robert W. Faff; John H.H. Lee; Tim R.L. Fry. *J. Bus. Fin. Acc.* **19:2** 1:1992 pp. 253 – 270

200 Time-varying risk premia and forecastable returns in futures markets. Hendrik Bessembinder; K. Chan. *J. Finan. Ec.* **32:2** 10:1992 pp. 169 – 194

201 Zinsrisikopotential. Kennziffer für das Risikomanagement von Zinsinstrumenten *[In German]*; Interest rate variation risk potential — a concept for managing the interest rate risk of interest rate-linked financial instruments *[Summary]*; Potentiel de risque des intérêts indice pour le management des risques d'instruments d'intérêts *[French summary]*. Raoul Oberman. *Kred. Kap.* **25:4** 1992 pp. 558 – 583

Stock exchange *[Bourse]*

202 Adverse selection and large trade volume — the implication for market efficiency. David Easley; Maureen O'Hara. *J. Fin. Qu. An.* **27:2** 6:1992 pp. 185 – 208

203 An assessment of risk and return — some empirical findings from the Hong Kong exchange. Yan-Leung Cheung; Ka-Tai Wong. *Appl. Finan. Econ.* **2:2** 6:1992 pp. 105 – 114

204 Block trading and information revelation around quarterly earnings announcements. Duane J. Seppi. *R. Finan. Stud.* **5:2** 1992 pp. 281 – 306

205 Business as usual, market crashes and wisdom after the fact. Andrew Caplin; John Leahy. New York: Columbia University, Dept of Economics, 1992: 23 p. [Discussion paper series.]

206 Clearance and settlement in U.S. securities markets. Patrick M. Parkinson; et al. Washington, D.C.: Board of Governors of the Federal Reserve System, 1992: 37 p. [Staff study.]

207 The contrarian investment strategy does not work in Canadian markets. Lawrence Kryzanowski; Hao Zhang. *J. Fin. Qu. An.* **27:3** 9:1992 pp. 383 – 395

208 Corporate disclosure and price discovery associated with NYSE temporary trading halts; *[French summary]*. R. King; G. Pownall; G. Waymire. *Cont. Account. Res.* **8:2** Spring:1992 pp. 509 – 531

209 Day-of-the-week effects — evidence from developing stock markets. K.A. Wong; T.K. Hui; C.Y. Chan. *Appl. Finan. Econ.* **2:1** 3:1992 pp. 49 – 56

210 ECU securities markets. *Bank of Engl. Q.* **32:2** 5:1992 pp. 180 – 189

211 The effect of futures trading on the stability of Standard and Poor 500 returns. Avraham Kamara; Thomas W. Miller; Andrew F. Siegel. *J. Futur. Mark.* **12:6** 12:1992 pp. 645 – 658

212 L'effet jour de la semaine à la Bourse de Paris — un effet transactionnel *[In French]*; [The transactional effect of the day-of-the-week syndrome on the Paris stock exchange]. Pascal Louvet; Olivier Taramasco. *J. Soc. Stat. Paris* **133:2** 2e trimestre:1992 pp. 50 – 76

213 An empirical analysis of the interrelationships between the stock market and the economy; Una analisi empirica delle interrelazioni tra il mercato azionario e l'economia *[Italian summary]*. Giorgio Canarella; Stephen K. Pollard. *Rev. Int. Sci. Ec. Com.* **XXXIX:2** 2:1992 pp. 125 – 147

214 An empirical test of the CAPM on the stocks listed on the Tokyo Stock Exchange. Y. Yonezawa; K.H. Tio. *Jpn. Wor. Econ.* **4:2** 9:1992 pp. 145 – 161

215 A further analysis of the lead-lag relationship between the cash market and stock index futures market. Kalok Chan. *R. Finan. Stud.* **5:1** 1992 pp. 123 – 152

216 General equilibrium in an economy with incomplete stock markets. Takaki Abe. *Econ. S. Quart.* **43:2** 6:1992 pp. 139 – 153

217 The impact of institutional trading on stock prices. Josef Lakonishok; Andrei Shleifer; Robert W. Vishny. *J. Finan. Ec.* **32:1** 8:1992 pp. 23 – 44

218 Implied volatilities and transaction costs. Steve Swidler; J. David Diltz. *J. Fin. Qu. An.* **27:3** 9:1992 pp. 437 – 447

219 Informed speculation and hedging in a noncompetitive securities market. Matthew Spiegel; Avanidhar Subrahmanyam. *R. Finan. Stud.* **5:2** 1992 pp. 307 – 330

220 The international transmission of stock market fluctuation between the developed markets and the Asian-Pacific markets. Y.-L. Cheung; S.-C. Mak. *Appl. Finan. Econ.* **2:1** 3:1992 pp. 43 – 47

J.4: Capital market *[Marché financier]* — *Stock exchange [Bourse]*

221 Looks can be deceiving — a comparison of initial public offering procedures under Japanese and U.S. securities laws. Alan L. Beller; Tsunemasa Terai; Richard M. Levine. *Law Cont. Pr.* **55:4** Autumn:1992 pp. 77 – 118

222 Margin requirements, speculative trading, and stock price fluctuations — the case of Japan. Gikas A. Hardouvelis; Stavros Peristiani. *Q. J. Econ.* **CVII:4** 11:1992 pp. 1333 – 1370

223 Market manipulation. Bubbles, corners, and short squeezes. Robert A. Jarrow. *J. Fin. Qu. An.* **27:3** 9:1992 pp. 311 – 336

224 The market valuation effects of the financial institutions reform, recovery and enforcement act of 1989. S. Sundaram; N. Rangan; W.M. Davidson. *J. Bank. Fin.* **16:6** 12:1992 pp. 1097 – 1122

225 Market volatility prediction and the efficiency of the S & P 100 index option market. Campbell R. Harvey; Robert E. Whaley. *J. Finan. Ec.* **31:1** 2:1992 pp. 43 – 73

226 Il mercato finanziario italiano nel processo di integrazione economica europea *[In Italian]*; [The Italian financial market in the process of European economic integration]. Fabio Panetta. *Risparmio* **XL:5** 9-10:1992 pp. 1049 – 1072

227 Monetary growth innovations in a simple cash-in-advance asset-pricing model. M. Bianconi. *Eur. Econ. R.* **36:8** 12:1992 pp. 1501 – 1521

228 Le muraglie cinesi. Aspetti di separazione organizzativa nell'intermediazione mobiliare *[In Italian]*; [Chinese walls. Aspects of organizational separation in intermediation in stock-exchange securities]. Mauro Vigolini. *Risparmio* **XL:4** 7-8:1992 pp. 811 – 834

229 Noise traders permanence in stock markets — a tâtonnement approach. 1 — informational dynamics for the two-dimensional case. Pier Luigi Sacco. Badia Fiesolana: European University Institute, 1992: 37 p. *Bibliography — p.34-35*. [EUI working paper.]

230 Options trading and the bid-ask spread of the underlying stocks. Mark Fedenia; Theoharry Grammatikos. *J. Bus.* **65:3** 7:1992 pp. 335 – 351

231 Le opzioni sull'indice e incertezza nel mercato azionario *[In Italian]*; [Floating-rate options and uncertainty in the capital market]. Antonio Roma. *Risparmio* **XL:1** 1-2:1992 pp. 89 – 104

232 Portfolio diversification — a pictorial analysis of the UK stock market. S. Poon; S.J. Taylor; C.W.R. Ward. *J. Bus. Fin. Acc.* **19:1** 1:1992 pp. 87 – 102

233 Pricing options with curved boundaries. Naoto Kunitomo; Masayuki Ikeda. *Math. Fin.* **2:4** 10:1992 pp. 275 – 298

234 Principles of trading market structure. Hans R. Stoll. *J. Finan. Ser. Res.* **6:1** 5:1992 pp. 75 – 106

235 La réaction des titres canadiens aux changements dans les prévisions de bénéfices comptables *[In French]*; The reaction of Canadian securities to revisions of earnings forecasts. J.-M. Suret; J.-F. L' Her. *Cont. Account. Res.* **7:2** Spring:1991 pp. 347 – 406

236 Regulation of securities markets — some recent trends and their implications for emerging markets. Terry M. Chuppe; Michael Atkin. Washington, D.C.: Economics Department, International Finance Corporation, The World Bank, 1992: 40 p. *Bibliography — p.38-40*. [Policy research working papers.]

237 Le rôle de l'estimation des variables rentabilité et risque dans les anomalies boursières liées à la taille et au P.E.R. *[In French]*; [The role of estimation of changing profit and risk in stock market anomalies]. Isabelle Girerd-Potin. *J. Soc. Stat. Paris* **133:3** 3rd trimester:1992 pp. 3 – 33

238 Die Rolle der Regionalbörsen am deutschen Kapitalmarkt heute und morgen (Teil I) *[In German]*; The role of regional stock exchanges on the German capital market today and tomorrow (part I) *[Summary]*; Les bourses régionales sur le marché allemand des capitaux aujord'hui et demain (Partie I) *[French summary]*. Hartmut Schmidt. *Kred. Kap.* **25:1** 1992 pp. 110 – 134

239 Die Rolle der Regionalbörsen am deutschen Kapitalmarkt heute und morgen (Teil II) *[In German]*; The role of regional stock exchanges on the German capital market today and tomorrow *[Summary]*; Le rôle des borses régionales sur le marché des capitaux allemand aujourd'hui et demain *[French summary]*. Hartmut Schmidt. *Kred. Kap.* **25:2** 1992 pp. 233 – 258

240 Securities markets and systemic risks in dynamic Asian economies. S. Ghon Rhee. Paris: Organisation for Economic Co-operation and Development, 1992: 95 p. *ISBN: 926413638x. Includes bibliographical references.*

241 Sources of wealth loss in new equity issues. J.D. Diltz; L.J. Lockwood; S. Min. *J. Bank. Fin.* **16:3** 6:1992 pp. 511 – 522

J.4: Capital market *[Marché financier]* **— Stock exchange** *[Bourse]*

242 Stock index futures listing and structural change in time-varying volatility. Sang Bin Lee; Ki Yool Ohk. *J. Futur. Mark.* **12:5** 10:1992 pp. 493 – 510

243 The stock market reaction to performance plan adoptions. Jennifer J. Gaver; Kenneth M. Gaver; George P. Battistel. *Acc. Review* **67:1** 1:1992 pp. 172 – 182

244 Stock market seasonality — some evidence from the Pacific-Basin countries. Insup Lee. *J. Bus. Fin. Acc.* **19:2** 1:1992 pp. 199 – 210

245 Strong-form efficiency on the Toronto stock exchange — an examination of analyst price forecasts. L.D. Brown; G.D. Richardson; C.A. Trzcinka. *Cont. Account. Res.* **7:2** Spring:1991 pp. 323 – 346

246 Trading rules and excess volatility. George Bulkley; Ian Tonks. *J. Fin. Qu. An.* **27:3** 9:1992 pp. 365 – 382

247 Trading volumes and stock market prices. Andy Snell; Ian Tonks. London: LSE Financial Markets Group, 1992: 35 p. [LSE Financial Markets Group discussion paper series. : No. 130]

248 What's special about the specialist? J. Wilhelm Benveniste; Alan J. Marcus; William J. Wilhelm. *J. Finan. Ec.* **32:1** 8:1992 pp. 61 – 86

Stock prices and stock returns *[Prix des actions et dividendes]*

249 Analysts' forecast revisions and stock price movements. W.P. Forbes; L.C.L. Skerratt. *J. Bus. Fin. Acc.* **19:4** 6:1992 pp. 555 – 570

250 The behavior of option price around large block transactions in the underlying security. Raman Kumar; Atulya Sarin; Kuldeep Shastri. *J. Finance* **47:3** 7:1992 pp. 879 – 889

251 The black and scholes option price as a random variable. Mthuli Ncube; Stephen Ellwood Satchell. Cambridge: University of Cambridge. Department of Applied Economics, 1991: 34 p. [DAE working paper.]

252 Cross-sectional variation in common stock returns. Richard W. McEnally; Rebecca B. Todd. *Finan. Anal. J.* 5/6:1992 pp. 59 – 63

253 The currency risk factor in international equity pricing. Manoj Gupta; Joseph E. Finnerty. *R. Quant. Finan. Account.* **2:3** 9:1992 pp. 245 – 257

254 Determinantes de la distribución de dividendos *[In Spanish]*; [Determinants of dividend payouts] *[Summary]*. Maria Arrazola; José Hevía; Gonzalo Mato. *Invest. Econ.* **XVI:2** 5:1992 pp. 235 – 258

255 Les determinants du coût de la liquidité immédiate sur le marché canadien des options *[In French]*; Determinants of the "bid asked" spread on the Canadian option market *[Summary]*. Nabil Khoury; Pierre Yourougou; Gilles Vigneau. *Appl. Finan. Econ.* pp. 499 – 516

256 Differential information, the variability of UK stock returns and earnings announcements. Peter Pope; Charles G. Inyangete. *J. Bus. Fin. Acc.* **19:4** 6:1992 pp. 603 – 624

257 Dividend surprises inferred from option and stock prices. Sasson Bar-Yosef; Oded H. Sarig. *J. Finance* **47:4** 9:1992 pp. 1623 – 1640

258 Dividend yields and expected stock returns — alternative procedures for inference and measurement. Robert J. Hodrick. *R. Finan. Stud.* **5:3** 1992 pp. 357 – 386

259 Dividends and losses. Harry DeAngelo; Linda DeAngelo; Douglas J. Skinner. *J. Finance* **47:5** 12:1992 pp. 1837 – 1863

260 Dividends and S & P 100 index option valuation. Campbell R. Harvey; Robert E. Whaley. *J. Futur. Mark.* **12:2** 4:1992 pp. 123 – 137

261 Economic forces and seasonality in security returns. Lawrence Kryzanowski; Hao Zhang. *R. Quant. Finan. Account.* **2:3** 9:1992 pp. 227 – 244

262 The effects of predictability on stock price response to the financing decision. Frederick P. Schadler; William T. Moore. *J. Bus. Fin. Acc.* **19:6** 11:1992 pp. 865 – 875

263 An empirical analysis of illegal insider trading. Lisa K. Meulbroek. *J. Finance* **47:5** 12:1992 pp. 1661 – 1699

264 The equilibrium price of futures contracts — a result drawn from capital asset pricing model. Robert H. Deans; Thomas A. Rhee. *R. Quant. Finan. Account.* **2:3** 9:1992 pp. 259 – 272

265 Family control and return covariation in Hong Kong's common stocks. Henry M.K. Mok; Kin Lam; Iris Cheung. *J. Bus. Fin. Acc.* **19:2** 1:1992 pp. 277 – 294

266 Forecasting the correlation structure of share prices — a test of new models. C.S. Eun; B.G. Resnick. *J. Bank. Fin.* **16:3** 6:1992 pp. 643 – 656

267 Fundamentals-dependent bubbles in stock prices. Shinsuke Ikeda; Akihisa Shibata. *J. Monet. Ec.* **30:1** 10:1992 pp. 143 – 168

J.4: Capital market *[Marché financier]* **— Stock prices and stock returns** *[Prix des actions et dividendes]*

268 Futures-trading activity and stock price volatility. Hendrik Bessembinder; Paul J. Seguin. *J. Finance* **47:5** 12:1992 pp. 2015 – 2034

269 Growth opportunities and the stock price response to new financing. Eugene Pilotte. *J. Bus.* **65:3** 7:1992 pp. 371 – 394

270 How learning in financial markets generates excess volatility and predictability in stock prices. Allan Timmermann. London: Birbeck College, 1992: 32 p.

271 The impact of option listing on underlying stock returns — the UK evidence. Wing H. Watt; Pradeep K. Yadav; Paul Draper. *J. Bus. Fin. Acc.* **19:4** 6:1992 pp. 485 – 504

272 Improving the Parkinson method of estimating security price volatilities. Naoto Kunitomo. *J. Bus.* **65:2** 4:1992 pp. 295 – 302

273 The information content of prices in derivative security markets. Louis O. Scott. *Staff Pap. Int. Monetary* **39:3** 9:1992 pp. 596 – 625

274 Informational externalities of seasoned equity issues — differences between banks and industrial firms. Myron B. Slovin; Marie E. Sushka; John A. Polonchek. *J. Finan. Ec.* **32:1** 8:1992 pp. 87 – 102

275 The intra-industry transfer of information inferred from announcements of corporate security offerings. Samuel H. Szewczyk. *J. Finance* **47:5** 12:1992 pp. 1935 – 1945

276 Liquidity costs and stock price response to convertible security calls. Michael A. Mazzeo; William T. Moore. *J. Bus.* **65:3** 7:1992 pp. 353 – 369

277 Market recognition of differences in earnings persistence — UK evidence. J. O'Hanlon; S. Poon; R.A. Yaansah. *J. Bus. Fin. Acc.* **19:4** 6:1992 pp. 625 – 640

278 Measuring abnormal performance — do stocks over-react? Navin Chopra; Josef Lakonishok; Jay R. Ritter. *J. Finan. Ec.* **31:2** 4:1992 pp. 235 – 268

279 A model of information aggregation with a simultaneous determination of stock prices and dividends. Allan Timmermann. London: Birkbeck College, 1992: 37 p.

280 Modelling abnormal returns — a review article. Norman Strong. *J. Bus. Fin. Acc.* **19:4** 6:1992 pp. 533 – 554

281 New product innovations and stock price performance. Paul K. Chaney; Timothy M. Devinney. *J. Bus. Fin. Acc.* **19:5** 9:1992 pp. 677 – 696

282 No news is good news — an asymmetric model of changing volatility in stock returns. John Y. Campbell; Ludger Hentschel. *J. Finan. Ec.* **31:3** 6:1992 pp. 281 – 318

283 Persistence in UK stock market returns — some evidence using high-frequency data. Ronald MacDonald; David Power. *J. Bus. Fin. Acc.* **19:4** 6:1992 pp. 505 – 514

284 Portfolio selection and matching — a synthesis. M. Sherris. *J. Inst. Actuar.* **119:I(472)** 6:1992 pp. 87 – 106

285 The post-merger performance of acquiring firms — a re-examination of an anomaly. Anup Agrawal; Jeffrey F. Jaffe; Gershon N. Mandelker. *J. Finance* **47:4** 9:1992 pp. 1605 – 1621

286 The prepayment option on mortgage securities — a random coefficient approach. James B. Kau; Thomas M. Springer. *R. Quant. Finan. Account.* **2:1** 3:1992 pp. 33 – 45

287 The reaction of investors and stock prices to insider trading. Bradford Cornell; Erik R. Sirri. *J. Finance* **47:3** 7:1992 pp. 1031 – 1059

288 A reexamination of finite- and infinite-variance distributions as models of daily stock returns. Alan L. Tucker. *J. Bus. Econ. Stat.* **10:1** 1:1992 pp. 73 – 82

289 Reputation and performance among security analysts. Scott E. Stickel. *J. Finance* **47:5** 12:1992 pp. 1811 – 1836

290 Seasonalities in NYSE bid-ask spreads and stock returns in January. Robert A. Clark; John J. McConnell; Manoj Singh. *J. Finance* **47:5** 12:1992 pp. 1999 – 2014

291 Share prices and pension funding — an empirical test of the joint effect of pension insurance and the pension tax shield. Paul Grier; Edward J. Zychowicz. *R. Quant. Finan. Account.* **2:3** 9:1992 pp. 273 – 289

292 Simultaneous determination of insider ownership, debt, and dividend policies. Gerald R. Jensen; Donald P. Solberg; Thomas S. Zorn. *J. Fin. Qu. An.* **27:2** 6:1992 pp. 247 – 264

293 Some relations between volatility and serial correlations in stock market returns. Blake LeBaron. *J. Bus.* **65:2** 4:1992 pp. 199 – 219

294 The specification and power of the sign test in event study hypothesis tests using daily stock returns. Charles J. Corrado; Terry L. Zivney. *J. Fin. Qu. An.* **27:3** 9:1992 pp. 465 – 478

295 Stock price dynamics and firm size — an empirical investigation. Yin-Wong Cheung; Lilian K. Ng. *J. Finance* **47:5** 12:1992 pp. 1985 – 1997

296 Stock price informativeness of accounting numbers — evidence on earnings, book values, and their components. John J. Wild. *J. Acc. Pub. Pol.* **11:2** Summer:1992 pp. 119 – 154

J.4: Capital market *[Marché financier]* — Stock prices and stock returns *[Prix des actions et dividendes]*

297 Stock price response to accounting information in oligopoly. Gun-Ho Joh; Chi-Wen Jevons Lee. *J. Bus.* **65:3** 7:1992 pp. 451 – 472

298 Stock prices and volume. A. Ronald Gallant; Peter E. Rossi; George Tauchen. *R. Finan. Stud.* **5:2** 1992 pp. 199 – 242

299 Stock return variation and expected dividends — a time-series and cross-sectional analysis. S.P. Kothari; Jay Shanken. *J. Finan. Ec.* **31:2** 4:1992 pp. 177 – 210

300 Stock-price manipulation. Franklin Allen; Douglas Gale. *R. Finan. Stud.* **5:3** 1992 pp. 503 – 529

301 Sulla formazione dei corsi azionari — analisi delle variabili endogene *[In Italian]*; Stock pricing — an analysis of the endogenous variables *[Summary]*. Pietro Giovannini. *Ras. Econ.* **LVI:1** 1-3:1992 pp. 5 – 44

302 Targeted repurchases and common stock returns. W.H. Mikkelson; R.S. Ruback. *Rand J. Eco.* **22:4** Winter:1991 pp. 544 – 561

303 Taux implicite d'impôt et détachement du dividende *[In French]*; [Tax rates on dividends] *[Summary]*. Jean-Marc Suret; Jean-Marie Gagnon. *Appl. Finan. Econ.* pp. 482 – 498

304 Term structure estimation and pricing of callable treasury bonds. Thomas S.Y. Ho; Sang-bin Lee; Kyu-hyun Son. *R. Quant. Finan. Account.* **2:2** 6:1992 pp. 127 – 143

305 Tests of analysts' overreaction/underreaction to earnings information as an explanation for anomalous stock price behavior. Jeffery S. Abarbanell; Victor L. Bernard. *J. Finance* **47:3** 7:1992 pp. 1181 – 1207

306 The treasury yield curve as a cointegrated system. Michael G. Bradley; Stephen A. Lumpkin. *J. Fin. Qu. An.* **27:3** 9:1992 pp. 449 – 463

307 Turn-of-month and pre-holiday effects on stock returns — some international evidence. C.B. Cadsby; M. Ratner. *J. Bank. Fin.* **16:3** 6:1992 pp. 497 – 509

308 Using privileged information to manipulate markets — insiders, gurus, and credibility. Roland Benabou; Guy Laroque. *Q. J. Econ.* **CVII:3** 8:1992 pp. 921 – 958

309 Using the capital market as a monitor — corporate spinoffs in an agency framework. D.J. Aron. *Rand J. Eco.* **22:4** Winter:1991 pp. 505 – 518

310 Why does aggragate insider trading predict future stock returns? H. Nejat Seyhun. *Q. J. Econ.* **CVII:4** 11:1992 pp. 1303 – 1332

J.5: Monetary policy — *Politique monétaire*

1 Los agregados monetarios en la transición a la unión monetaria europea *[In Spanish]*; [Monetary aggregates in the transition to European monetary union]. Giorgio Gomel. *Monetaria* **XV:2** 4-6:1992 pp. 111 – 132

2 Announcement effects of anticipated monetary-fiscal policies at home and abroad. Victor Argy. *Aust. Econ. P.* **31:58** 6:1992 pp. 20 – 46

3 The appropriate intermediate target for monetary policy in less developed countries — empirical evidence. W. Naudé. *Develop. S. Afr.* **9:2** 5:1992 pp. 121 – 138

4 Aspectos operativos e instrumentales de la programación monetaria en Alemania *[In Spanish]*; [Operational and instrumental aspects of monetary policy in Germany]. André Bartholomae. *Monetaria* **XV:1** 1-3:1992 pp. 39 – 66

5 Die Ausgestaltung von Geldpolitiken unter dem Einfluss von Unsicherheit beim Geldangebotsprozess der Zentralbank *[In German]*; [The formulation of monetary policies under uncertainty as to the central bank's money supply policy] *[Summary]*; *[French summary]*. Volker Bieta. *Schw. Z. Volk. Stat.* **128:2** 6:1992 pp. 161 – 183

6 The Bundesbank — the bank that rules Europe. David Marsh. London: Heinemann, 1992: 359 p. *ISBN: 0434451169.*

7 Can monetary policy be make to work? Papers presented at the IPA Melbourne. Des Moore. Melbourne: Institute of Public Affairs, 1992: 116 p. *ISBN: 0909536287.*

8 Canadian monetary policy — will the check-list approach ever get us to price stability?; *[French summary]*. Daniel Racette; Jacques Raynauld. *Can. J. Econ.* **XXV:4** 11:1992 pp. 819 – 838

9 Capital accumulation, price stability, and base drift. Milton H. Marquis. *J. Macro.* **14:2** Spring:1992 pp. 321 – 335

10 Changes in monetary policy effectiveness — evidence from large macroeconometric models. *Q. R. Fed. Res. Bank N.Y.* **17:1** Spring:1992 pp. 36 – 51

J.5: Monetary policy *[Politique monétaire]*

11 A comparison of monetary policy operating procedures in six industrial countries. Bruce Kasman. *Q. R. Fed. Res. Bank N.Y.* **17:2** Summer:1992 pp. 5 – 24

12 Current issues in financial and monetary economics. Kevin Dowd *[Ed.]*; Mervyn K. Lewis *[Ed.]*. London: Macmillan, 1992: 232 p. *ISBN: 0333516400.*

13 Dynamic implications of chaotic monetary policy. Gregory P. DeCoster; Douglas W. Mitchell. *J. Macro.* **14:2** Spring:1992 pp. 267 – 287

14 Economic and monetary policy in Aruba. Frank Dubbeld. *Money Aff.* **V:1** 1-6:1992 pp. 43 – 56

15 The equilibrium rate of inflation with discretion and some reputation. V. Argy. *Banca Nat. Lav. Q. Rev.* **:182** 9:1992 pp. 329 – 347

16 Financial deregulation and the monetary transmission mechanism. Jerome Fahrer; Thomas Rohling. *Aust. Ec. Rev.* **:1(97)** 1-3:1992 pp. 33 – 43

17 Financial innovation and divisia monetary aggregates. J.L. Ford; W.S. Peng; A.W. Mullineux. *Ox. B. Econ. S.* **54:1** 2:1992 pp. 87 – 102

18 Financial openness and national autonomy — opportunities and constraints. Tariq Banuri *[Ed.]*; Juliet Schor *[Ed.]*. Oxford: Clarendon Press, 1992: 288 p. *ISBN: 0198283644; LofC: 91029916. "A Study prepared for the World Institute for Development Economics Research (WIDER) of the United Nations University."; Includes bibliographical references and index.*

19 Financial sector reforms in Egypt. Y.S. El Nil. *Finan. News Anal.* **5:7** 7:1992 pp. 14 – 36

20 The FOMC in 1991 — an elusive recovery. J. Bullard. *R. Fed. Resv. Bank St.Louis* **74:2** 3/4:1992 pp. 41 – 61

21 Gradual output adjustment and expansionary monetary policy. Phillip Lawler. *J. Econ. Stud.* **19:1** 1992 pp. 48 – 62

22 How has monetary policy influenced the French economy? Jacques de Larosière. *Cent. Bank.* **2:4** Spring:1992 pp. 14 – 24

23 Incomplete information, stabilization, and the relationship between inflation and unemployment. Arto Kovanen. *J. Macro.* **14:2** Spring:1992 pp. 305 – 319

24 Interest rate control and nonconvergence to rational expectations. Peter Howitt. *J. Polit. Ec.* **100:4** 8:1992 pp. 776 – 800

25 International accumulation and the contradictions of monetary policy. Dick Bryan. *Sci. Soc.* **56:3** Fall:1992 pp. 324 – 352

26 Interpreting the macroeconomic time series facts — the effects of monetary policy. C.A. Sims; M. Eichenbaum *[Comments by]*. *Eur. Econ. R.* **36:5** 6:1992 pp. 975 – 1000

27 Irrationalitäten und Anomalien als Bestimmungsfaktoren währungspolitischer Entscheidungen *[In German]*; Irrationalities and anomalies as determinants of monetary policy decisions *[Summary]*; Facteurs déterminant les décisions de politique monétaire — irrationalités et anomalies *[French summary]*. Beate Reszat. *Kred. Kap.* **25:1** 1992 pp. 94 – 109

28 La liberalización financiera en los países en desarrollo — un enfoque neokeynesiano *[In Spanish]*; [Financial liberalization in developing countries — a neo-Keynesian focus]. Yilmaz Akyuz. *Centro Est. Monet. Latinam.* **XXXVIII:2** 3-4:1992 pp. 85 – 94

29 Liberalización financiera y control monetario en Japón *[In Spanish]*; [Financial liberalization and monetary control in Japan]. Bruce Kasman; Anthony Rodrigues. *Monetaria* **XV:3** 7-10:1992 pp. 233 – 274

30 Liquidity effects and the monetary transmission mechanism. Lawrence J. Christiano; Martin Eichenbaum. *Am. Econ. Rev.* **82:2** 5:1992 pp. 346 – 353

31 Monetarism and monetary policy. Anna Jacobson Schwartz. London: Institute of Economic Affairs, 1992: 40 p. *ISBN: 0255363028.* [Occasional paper.]

32 Monetary aggregates as monetary targets. William Roberds; Charles H. Whiteman. *J. Money C. B.* **24:2** 5:1992 pp. 141 – 161

33 Monetary and banking reform in postcommunist economies. David M. Kemme *[Ed.]*; Andrzej Rudka *[Ed.]*; Institute for East-West Security Studies. New York: Institute for East-West Security Studies, 1992: 165 p. *ISBN: 0813385725. A compendium of papers presented at the Institute for East-West Security Studies conference on money, banking and credit in Eastern Europe and the Soviet Union co-hosted by the Mitsui Marine Research Institute and the Japan Center for International Finance ... .*

34 Monetary and foreign exchange policy in 1991. *Q. Rev. Sver. Riks.* **:1** 1992 pp. 5 – 12

35 Monetary neutrality in a dynamic macroeconomic model under alternative monetary regimes. Lawrence J. Belcher. *J. Macro.* **14:1** Winter:1992 p. 179

36 Monetary policy and open market operations during 1991. *Q. R. Fed. Res. Bank N.Y.* **17:1** Spring:1992 pp. 72 – 96

J.5: Monetary policy *[Politique monétaire]*

37 Monetary policy in a game — theoretic framework; Spieltheoretische Ansätze zur Geldpolitik *[German summary]*. Jac J. Sijben. *Jahrb. N. St.* **210:3-4** 9:1992 pp. 233 – 253

38 Monetary stabilization with interest rates instruments in Japan — a linear quadratic control analysis. Paul McNelis; Naoyuki Yoshino. *Mon. Econ. S.* **10:2** 11:1992 pp. 79 – 106

39 Nominal effects of fiscal and monetary policies in Greece; Nominale Effekte der griechischen Fiskal- und Geldpolitik *[German summary]*; Effets nominaux des politiques fiscale et monétaire en Grèce *[French summary]*. Georgios Karras. *Kred. Kap.* **25:3** 1992 pp. 416 – 427

40 Operation of monetary policy.*Bank of Engl. Q.* **32:2** 5:1992 pp. 155 – 164

41 Optimal monetary policy with an interest-equalization tax in a two-country macroeconomic model. Arthur Benavie; Richard Froyen. *J. Macro.* **14:3** Summer:1992 pp. 449 – 466

42 Overlapping structures as a model of money — an analytical review. Bruno Schönfelder. Berlin: Springer-Verlag, 1992: 242 p. *ISBN: 038755274x; LofC: 92012919.* [Microeconomic studies.]

43 La política monetaria en una economía en proceso de estabilización — el caso venezolano *[In Spanish]*; [Monetary policy in an economy in the process of stabilization — the Venezuelan case]. Agustín Díaz; Roberto d'Empaire. *Monetaria* **XV:3** 7-10:1992 pp. 275 – 299

44 Políticas monetarias de tasas de interés, con expectativas racionales *[In Spanish]*; [Monetary policy on interest rates, with rational expectations]. Elías Salama. *Monetaria* **XV:2** 4-6:1992 pp. 133 – 150

45 The potency of monetary and fiscal policies in sub-Saharan countries — St. Louis model estimates; L'impact des politiques monétaires et fiscales en Afrique sub-saharienne — une évaluation de l'équation de Saint Louis *[French summary]*. David W.H. Orsmond. *Sav. Develop.* :1 Supplement:1992 pp. 17 – 28

46 Preliminary evidence on the determinants of Federal Reserve open market operations. H. Singh; P. Zak. *Publ. Choice* **74:3** 10:1992 pp. 317 – 338

47 Price and currency reform in Russia and the C.I.S. Brigitte Granville. London: Royal Institute of International Affairs, 1992: 45 p. [Post-Soviet Business Forum publication.]

48 Secondary currencies and high inflation — implications for monetary theory and policy. Paul Auerbach; G. Davison; Jacek Rostowski. London: London School of Economics and Political Science. Centre for Economic Performance, 1992: 34 p.

49 Small time deposits and the recent weakness in M2.*Q. R. Fed. Res. Bank N.Y.* **17:1** Spring:1992 pp. 21 – 35

50 Some evidence on the potential role of commodity prices in the formulation of monetary policy. Patricia Fraser; Christopher D. Rogers. *Manch. Sch. E.* **LX:4** 12:1992 pp. 377 – 389

51 Specialization, the terms of trade, and the international transmission of monetary policies; *[French summary]*. Kent P. Kimbrough. *Can. J. Econ.* **XXV:4** 11:1992 pp. 884 – 900

52 Stabilization policy can lead to chaos. Gerald P. Dwyer. *Econ. Inq.* **XXX:1** 1:1992 pp. 40 – 46

53 Stabilizing a previously centrally planned economy — Poland 1990. Guillermo A. Calvo; Fabrizio Coricelli. *Econ. Pol.* :14 4:1992 pp. 175 – 226

54 Targeting M2 — the issue of monetary control.*R. Fed. Resv. Bank St.Louis* **74:4** 7/8:1992 pp. 23 – 35

55 Teoria della politica monetaria e costituzionalismo economico *[In Italian]*; The theory of monetary policy and economic constitutionalism *[Summary]*. Donato Masciandaro. *Gior. Econ. A.* **L:7-8** 7-8:1991 pp. 347 – 371

56 A theory of Fed watching in a macroeconomic policy game. Nathan S. Balke; Joseph H. Haslag. *Int. Econ. R.* **33:3** 8:1992 pp. 619 – 628

57 Time inconsistency problems and commitments of monetary and fiscal policies. H. Jensen. *J. Econ.* **56:3** 1992 pp. 247 – 266

58 Two nations, one money? — Canada's monetary system following a Quebec secession. David E.W. Laidler; William B.P. Robson; et al. Toronto: C.D. Howe Institute, 1991: xv, 88 p. *ISBN: 0888062869; LofC: cn 91095368. Includes bibliographical references.* [The Canada round.]

59 U.S. monetary policy and financial markets. Ann-Marie Meulendyke. New York: Federal Reserve Bank of New York, [1990]: 231 p.

60 Why does high inflation raise inflation uncertainty? Laurence Ball. *J. Monet. Ec.* **29:3** 6:1992 pp. 371 – 388

J.5: Monetary policy *[Politique monétaire]*
61 Die Zinsstruktur als Indikator der Geldpolitik? *[In German]*; The interest rate structure as a monetary policy indicator *[Summary]*; La structure des intérêts est-elle un indicateur de la politique monétaire? *[French summary]*. Helmut Hesse; Gisela Roth. *Kred. Kap.* **25:1** 1992 pp. 1 – 25

K: Income and income distribution — *Revenu et distribution du revenu*

K.1: Income: concept and theory — *Revenu: concept et théorie*

1 Household work and national income accounting — to include or not to include? Euston Quah. *Asian Econ. J.* **VI:1** 3:1992 pp. 25 – 41
2 Measuring income from family enterprises with household surveys. Wim P.M. Vijverberg. *Small Bus. Econ.* **4:4** 12:1992 pp. 287 – 305
3 On shortages and the "monetary overhang"; *[German summary]*. Richard L. Carson. *Econ. Sys.* **16:2** 10:1992 pp. 227 – 245
4 On the rank, generalized Lorenz and overtaking criteria for evaluating stochastic income regimes. Rubin Saposnik; Roger Tutterow. *S. Econ. J.* **58:3** 1:1992 pp. 583 – 592
5 A re-examination of the doctrine of relative purchasing power parity. E.D. Beach; N.H. Cottrell; N.D. Uri. *Eco. Notes* **21:2** 1992 pp. 341 – 360
6 Strictly fair allocations in large exchange economies. Lin Zhou. *J. Econ. Theo.* **57:1** 6:1992 pp. 158 – 175
7 Wealth, income, and consumption in a developing economy. Prem S. Laumas; Susan Porter-Hudak. *J. Macro.* **14:2** Spring:1992 pp. 349 – 358

K.2: Distribution of national income — *Répartition du revenu national*

1 Adjustment and income distribution — a micro-macro model for counter-factual analysis. F. Bourguignon; W.H. Branson; J. de Melo. *J. Dev. Econ.* **38:1** 1:1992 pp. 17 – 39
2 The changing composition of income transfer programmes — a public choice analysis. C.B. Colburn. *Appl. Econ.* **24:2** 2:1992 pp. 161 – 168
3 Conflict, inflation and the distribution of income. Peter Skott *[Ed.]*; F.A.G. den Butter *[Contrib.]*; R.F. van de Wijngaert *[Contrib.]*; F. Green *[Contrib.]*; S. Bowles *[Contrib.]*; A.K. Dutt *[Contrib.]*; R. Franke *[Contrib.]*; M. Rao *[Contrib.]*; K. Futagami *[Contrib.]*. Collection of 8 articles. **Eur. J. Pol. Ec.** , *8:4*, 12:1992 pp. 521 – 650
4 Creating and transforming households — the constraints of the world-economy. Joan Smith *[Comp.]*; Immanuel Wallerstein *[Comp.]*. Cambridge: Cambridge University Press, 1992: 311 p. *ISBN: 0521415527; LofC: 91029344. Includes bibliographical references and index.* [Studies in modern capitalism.]
5 Credit markets and the distribution of income. Anup Shah. London: Academic Press, 1992: 191 p. *ISBN: 0126381305.*
6 Cross-national determinants of income inequality — a replication and extension using ecological-evolutionary theory. Edward Crenshaw. *Soc. Forc.* **71:2** 12:1992 pp. 339 – 363
7 Cyclical and political influences on the size distribution of income in the US (1959-1989). P. van Wijck. *Appl. Econ.* **24:2** 2:1992 pp. 169 – 174
8 Decomposition of income inequality in rural Bangladesh. Pk. Md. Motiur Rahman; S. Huda. *Mod. Asian S.* **26:1** 2:1992 pp. 83 – 94
9 Differences in needs and assessment of income distributions. Fiona Coulter; Frank Cowell; Stephen Jenkins. *B. Econ. Res.* **44:2** 4:1992 pp. 77 – 124
10 Distribution of economic resources — implications of including the household production. Jens Bonke. *R. In. Weal.* **38:3** 9:1992 pp. 281 – 293
11 The distribution of income and wealth in Japan. John Bauer; Andrew Mason. *R. In. Weal.* **38:4** 12:1992 pp. 403 – 428

K.2: Distribution of national income *[Répartition du revenu national]*

12 Distribuzione dei guadagni di produttività e livelli della contrattazione *[In Italian]*; Distribution of productivity earnings and bargaining levels *[Summary]*. Leonello Tronti. *Ec. Lav.* **XXVI:1** 1-3:1992 pp. 51 – 66

13 An explanation for the recent behavior of income and transaction velocities in the United Kingdom. Peter Howells; Iris Beifang-Frisancho Mariscal. *J. Post. Keyn. Ec.* **14:3** Spring:1992 pp. 367 – 388

14 Impacto distributivo del gasto social *[In Spanish]*; [The distributive impact of social expenditure]. Alberto Porto; Leonardo Gasparini. *Desar. Econ.* **31:124** 1-3:1992 pp. 487 – 502

15 Income distribution and poverty. G.S. Fields *[Contrib.]*; L. Haddad *[Contrib.]*; R. Kanbur *[Contrib.]*; E. Ahmad *[Contrib.]*. Collection of 3 articles. **Publ. Finan.** , 47, 1992 pp. 59 – 106

16 Income distribution in the dynamic two-factor trade model. Ronald Fischer. *Economica* **59:234** 5:1992 pp. 221 – 233

17 Income tax progression and redistributive effect — the influence of changes in the pre-tax income distribution. Peter J. Lambert; Wilhelm Pfähler. *Publ. Finan.* **47:1** 1992 pp. 1 – 16

18 Inflation, corruption, and income distribution — the recent price reform in China. Kar-Yiu Wong. *J. Macro.* **14:1** Winter:1992 pp. 105 – 124

19 Interstate income inequality in the United States — measurement, modelling and some characteristics. Rati Ram. *R. In. Weal.* **38:1** 3:1992 pp. 39 – 48

20 Kuznets' curve and Asian income distribution trends. Harry T. Oshima. *Hito. J. Econ.* **33:1** 6:1992 pp. 95 – 111

21 Labor force participation, race, and human capital — influence on earnings distributions across states. Daniel J. Slottje; Kathy J. Hayes; Joyce Shackett. *R. In. Weal.* **38:1** 3:1992 pp. 27 – 38

22 Labor mobility and wages distribution under the dual-track infrastructure. Yuanchen Dai; Hanming Li. *Soc. Sci. China* **:3** 9:1992 pp. 141 – 152

23 Measurement of income inequality. Experimental test by questionnaire. Yoram Amiel; Frank A. Cowell. *J. Publ. Ec.* **47:1** 2:1992 pp. 3 – 26

24 Political determinants of income changes for African-American women and men. Kimberly Christensen. *Rev. Rad. Pol. Ec.* **24:1** Spring:1992 pp. 52 – 70

25 Regional income disparity and fiscal-monetary policy. An interregional macroeconomic model of Japan. M. Fujita; S. Takahashi. *Ann. Reg. Sci.* **26:3** 1992 pp. 231 – 256

26 Relative income determination in the United States — a social accounting perspective. David W. Roland-Holst; Ferran Sancho. *R. In. Weal.* **38:3** 9:1992 pp. 311 – 327

27 Revenue neutral value added tax (VAT) in Bangladesh — some general equilibrium illustrations. Osman Haider Chowdhury. *Bang. Dev. Stud.* **XIX:4** 12:1991 pp. 49 – 63

28 Rising earnings inequality and returns to skills in the United Kingdom labour market. Terence Moll. *Labour [Italy]* **6:3** Winter:1992 pp. 45 – 69

29 Sectoral shifts and interindustry wage differentials. Jean Helwege. *J. Labor Ec.* **10:1** 1:1992 pp. 55 – 84

30 A simple imperfectly competitive model of the distribution of income. Howard F. Naish. *Scot. J. Poli.* **39:4** 11:1992 pp. 439 – 456

31 The simple macroeconomic TIP model — a world of Keynesian unemployment. Masahiro Yabuta. *Econ. S. Quart.* **43:2** 6:1992 pp. 129 – 138

32 Simultaneous density estimation of several income distributions. J.S. Marron; H.P. Schmitz. *Economet. Th.* **8:4** 12:1992 pp. 476 – 488

33 Some reflections on the sensitivity of income distribution in the Kaldor-Pasinetti model. Rob Ph.G. Walsteijn. *J. Post. Keyn. Ec.* **15:2** Winter:1992-1993 pp. 193 – 210

34 Status, the distribution of wealth, private and social attitudes to risk. Arthur J. Robson. *Econometrica* **60:4** 7:1992 pp. 837 – 857

35 Taxation, time use and the value of unpaid labor — policy implications for the redistribution of income. Iulie Aslaksen; Charlotte Koren. *Rev. Rad. Pol. Ec.* **24:2** Summer:1992 pp. 8 – 16

36 The through-time redistributive effect of income taxation — the intermediate inequality view. P. Moyes. *Math. Soc. Sc.* **24:1** 1992 pp. 59 – 71

37 Unemployment, participation and family incomes in the 1980s. Bruce Bradbury. *Econ. Rec.* **68:203** 12:1992 pp. 328 – 342

38 Uneven tides — rising inequality in the 1980s. Sheldon Danziger *[Ed.]*; Peter Gottschalk *[Ed.]*. New York: Russell Sage Foundation, 1992: 287 p. *ISBN: 0871542226; LofC: 92014233. Includes bibliographical references and index.*

K.2: Distribution of national income *[Répartition du revenu national]*

39 The vintage schooling hypothesis and racial differences in earnings and on-the-job training — a longitudinal analysis. Kevin C. Duncan. *Rev. Bl. Pol. Ec.* **20:3** Winter:1992 pp. 99 – 118

40 Wages and wage policies in market economies — lessons for Central and Eastern Europe. Robert J. Flanagan. *OECD Ec. Stud.* :18 Spring:1992 pp. 105 – 132

41 Welfare evaluations of state income distributions. John A. Bishop; John P. Formby; Lester A. Zeager. *Soc. Sci. Q.* **73:1** 3:1992 pp. 166 – 176

42 De "zero-sum-crisis" — een verklaring voor de stabiliteit van de inkomens- en welvaartsverdeling in periode van economische crisis *[In Dutch]*; [The "zero sum crisis" — an interpretation of the stable distribution of incomes and prosperity in a period of economic crisis]. B. Cantillon. *Maan. Econ.* **56:1** 1992 pp. 57 – 73

K.3: Specific income — *Catégories de revenu*

Sub-divisions: Profit and returns *[Profit et rendements]*; Wage determination *[Fixation du salaire]*; Wage differentials *[Eventail des salaires]*

1 Aggregation, unit roots and the time series structure of manufacturing real wages. Robert J. Rossana; John J. Seater. *Int. Econ. R.* **33:1** 2:1992 pp. 159 – 180

2 Can wage increases pay for themselves? Tests with a production function. D.I. Levine. *Econ. J.* **102:414** 9:1992 pp. 1102 – 1115

3 Centralisation, employment and wage dispersion. R.E. Rowthorn. *Econ. J.* **102:412** 5:1992 pp. 506 – 523

4 Changes in relative wages, 1963-1987 — supply and demand factors. Lawrence F. Katz; Kevin M. Murphy. *Q. J. Econ.* **CVII:1** 2:1992 pp. 35 – 78

5 Changes in the structure of wages in the 1980s — an evaluation of alternative explanations. John Bound; George Johnson. *Am. Econ. Rev.* **82:3** 6:1992 pp. 371 – 392

6 Closed shops and relative pay — institutional arrangements or high density? David Metcalf; Mark Stewart. *Ox. B. Econ. S.* **54:4** 11:1992 pp. 503 – 516

7 Comparable worth — Canada's experience. M. Gunderson; W.C. Riddell. *Cont. Policy* **X:3** 7:1992 pp. 85 – 94

8 Constraints on the choice of work hours — agency versus specific-capital. Shulamit Kahn; Kevin Lang. *J. Hum. Res.* **XXVII:4** Fall:1992 pp. 661 – 678

9 Copra revenues as a parameter of male income in the outer islands of the Republic of the Marshall Islands. Dirk H.R. Spennemann. *J. Pacific Soc.* **15:55-56 and 2-3** 9:1992 pp. 43 – 54

10 Desiderabilità di un contratto indicizzato e variabilità dell'inflazione *[In Italian]*; The desirability of an indexed contract and inflation variability *[Summary]*. Corrado Benassi; Andrea Ichino. *Ec. Lav.* **XXVI:1** 1-3:1992 pp. 23 – 35

11 Distribution of lifetime income allowing for varying mortality rates among women, men, blacks, and whites. J. Paul Leigh. *J. Econ. Iss.* **XXVI:4** 12:1992 pp. 1191 – 1220

12 Does the baseball labor market contradict the human capital model of investment? Asher A. Blass. *Rev. Econ. St.* **LXXIV:2** 5:1992 pp. 261 – 268

13 Economic crisis in a shortage economy. Kent Osband. *J. Polit. Ec.* **100:4** 8:1992 pp. 673 – 690

14 The economics of earnings. S. W. Polachek; W. Stanley Siebert. Cambridge: Cambridge University Press, 1992: 367 p. *ISBN: 0521364760; LofC: 91038731. Includes bibliographical references and index.*

15 The effect of ex ante earnings uncertainty on earnings response coefficients. Eugene A. Imhoff; Gerald J. Lobo. *Acc. Review* **67:2** 4:1992 pp. 427 – 439

16 The effect of mandatory retirement on earnings profiles in Japan. Robert L. Clark; Naohiro Ogawa. *Ind. Lab. Rel.* **45:2** 1:1992 pp. 258 – 266

17 The effect of size on the magnitude of long-window earnings response coefficients; *[French summary]*. P.K. Chaney; D.C. Jeter. *Cont. Account. Res.* **8:2** Spring:1992 pp. 540 – 560

18 The effects of trade unions on the distribution of earnings — a sample selectivity approach. P.D. Murphy; P.J. Sloane; D.H. Blackaby. *Ox. B. Econ. S.* **54:4** 11:1992 pp. 517 – 542

19 The effects of Trinidad and Tobago's oil boom on relative prices, wages and labour flows; *[French summary]*; *[Spanish summary]*. Alvin Hilaire. *Soc. Econ. S.* **41:2** 6:1992 pp. 45 – 82

20 An empirical analysis of sales-force compensation plans. Anne T. Coughlan; Chakravarthi Narasimhan. *J. Bus.* **65:1** 1:1992 pp. 93 – 121

K.3: Specific income *[Catégories de revenu]*

21 Employee wage growth within the firm — a deferred payment or human capital investment. R. Kaestner; L. Solnick. *Appl. Econ.* **24:3** 3:1992 pp. 347 – 362

22 Expected inflation and output variability in flexible price and contracting models. Giancarlo Marini; Pasquale Scaramozzino. *Ox. Econ. Pap.* **44:2** 4:1992 pp. 232 – 241

23 The heterogeneity of labor, wage indexation and welfare. A. Kovanen. *Eur. Econ. R.* **36:1** 1:1992 pp. 37 – 50

24 In search of a stylised fact — do real wages exhibit a consistent pattern of cyclical variability? Andrea Brandolini. London: London School of Economics and Political Science, Centre for Economic Performance, 1992: 98 p.

25 In search of excess — the overcompensation of the American executive. Graef S. Crystal. New York: W.W. Norton, 1992: 272 p. *ISBN: 039303089x; LofC: 91025569. Includes bibliographical references and index.*

26 An income-satiation model of efficiency wages. Eric Rasmusen. *Econ. Inq.* **XXX:3** 7:1992 pp. 467 – 477

27 Individuelle Einkommensdynamik und Humankapitaleffekte nach Erwerbsunterbrechungen *[In German]*; Individual income dynamics, human capital effects and non-employment spells *[Summary]*. Georg Licht; Viktor Steiner. *Jahrb. N. St.* **209:3-4** 3:1992 pp. 241 – 265

28 Industry wage effects of horizontal acquisitions in the USA. J. Peoples. *Appl. Econ.* **24:5** 5:1992 pp. 519 – 528

29 Insiders, outsiders, and nominal wage contracts. Nils Gottfries. *J. Polit. Ec.* **100:2** 4:1992 pp. 252 – 270

30 Intergenerational income mobility in the United States. Gary R. Solon. *Am. Econ. Rev.* **82:3** 6:1992 pp. 393 – 408

31 International comparisons of earnings inequality for men in the 1980s. Gordon Green; John Coder; Paul Ryscavage. *R. In. Weal.* **38:1** 3:1992 pp. 1 – 16

32 Labor's share and market power — evidence from the Greek manufacturing industries. Vassilis Droucopoulos; Theodore P. Lianos. *J. Post. Keyn. Ec.* **15:2** Winter:1992-1993 pp. 263 – 280

33 The law and economics of the minimum wage. Simon Deakin; Frank Wilkinson. *J. Law Soc.* **19:3** Autumn:1992 pp. 379 – 392

34 Linkage, heterogeneity and income determinants in petty trading — the case of Calcutta. N. Dasgupta. *World Dev.* **20:10** 10:1992 pp. 1443 – 1461

35 Low-wage workers in a high-technology manufacturing complex — the southern Californian electronics assembly industry. Allen J. Scott. *Urban Stud.* **29:8** 12:1992 pp. 1231 – 1246

36 Modeling earnings distorting government intervention — the case of Singapore's managerial earnings. K.P. Kalirajan. *J. Comp. Econ.* **16:1** 3:1992 pp. 105 – 117

37 A national minimum wage for Britain? Les Simpson; Ian Peterson. *Economics* **XXVIII:117(1)** Spring:1992 pp. 12 – 17

38 New minimum wage research — a symposium. Ronald G. Ehrenberg *[Contrib.]*; Lawrence F. Katz *[Contrib.]*; Alan B. Krueger *[Contrib.]*; David Card *[Contrib.]*; David Neumark *[Contrib.]*; William Wascher *[Contrib.]*; Ralph E. Smith *[Contrib.]*; Bruce Vavrichek *[Contrib.]*. Collection of 6 articles. **Ind. Lab. Rel.** , *46:1,* 10:1992 pp. 3 – 88

39 Nominal wage flexibility in a partly unionized economy. Huw Dixon. *Manch. Sch. E.* **LX:3** 9:1992 pp. 295 – 306

40 Non scholae sed vitae discimus! Wilhelm Lorenz; Joachim Wagner. *Jahr. Soz.schaft.* **43:1** 1992 pp. 25 – 43

41 On the efficiency of stock-based compensation. Jonathan M. Paul. *R. Finan. Stud.* **5:3** 1992 pp. 471 – 502

42 Patterns of intergenerational mobility in income and earnings. H. Elizabeth Peters. *Rev. Econ. St.* **LXXIV:3** 8:1992 pp. 456 – 466

43 Pay and benefits. Pete Burgess *[Ed.]*. London: Institute of Personnel Management, 1992: 235 p. *ISBN: 0852924542.* [European management guides.]

44 Piece rates, output restriction, and conformism. D.I. Levine. *J. Econ. Psyc.* **13:3** 9:1992 pp. 473 – 489

45 Post-layoff earnings among semiconductor workers. Paul M. Ong; Don Mar. *Ind. Lab. Rel.* **45:2** 1:1992 pp. 366 – 379

46 A preliminary investigation into farm labourer remuneration. M.W. van Wyk; F.W. Greef. *S. Afr. J. Labour Relat.* **16:4** 12:1992 pp. 3 – 12

47 Regional earnings and unemployment — a simultaneous approach. D.H. Blackaby; D.N. Manning. *Ox. B. Econ. S.* **54:4** 11:1992 pp. 481 – 501

K.3: Specific income *[Catégories de revenu]*

48 Remunerating general practitioners in Western Europe. Peter P. Groenewegen; Jouke van der Zee; Rene van Haaften. Aldershot: Avebury, 1991: vi, 125 p. *ISBN: 1856281620. Includes bibliographies.*

49 Le revenu minimum d'insertion *[In French]*; [The guaranteed minimum income]. Vincent Poubelle *[Contrib.]*; Michel Villac *[Contrib.]*; Eric Maurin *[Contrib.]*; Constance Torelli *[Contrib.]*; Cédric Afsa *[Contrib.]*; Christine Catteau *[Contrib.]*; Jean-Claude Hautcoeur *[Contrib.]*; René Squarzoni *[Contrib.]*; Alain Tran Ap *[Contrib.]*. *Collection of 6 articles.* **E & S** , :252, 3:1992 pp. 11 – 71

50 Les rigidités nominales — développements récents — 2 *[In French]*; Nominal rigidities — new approaches — 2 *[Summary]*. H. Kempf. *Rev. Ec. Polit.* **102:2** 3-4:1992 pp. 155 – 206

51 Schooling, ability, and earnings in Colombia, 1988. George Psacharopoulos; Eduardo Velez. *Econ. Dev. Cult. Change* **40:3** 4:1992 pp. 629 – 644

52 Search from an unknown distribution — an explicit solution. Gabriel Talmain. *J. Econ. Theo.* **57:1** 6:1992 pp. 141 – 157

53 Searching for the opportunity cost of an individual's time. W. Douglass Shaw. *Land Econ.* **68:1** 2:1992 pp. 107 – 115

54 Seniority wage system in the Far East — Confucian influence over Japan and South Korea. Byung Whan Kim. Aldershot, Hants, England: Avebury, 1992: xv, 206 p. *ISBN: 1856282937; LofC: 92028699. Includes bibliographical references (p. 190-206).*

55 Sources of income inequality in rural Pakistan — a decomposition analysis. Richard H. Adams; Harold Alderman. *Ox. B. Econ. S.* **54:4** 11:1992 pp. 591 – 608

56 The structure of wages. Kevin M. Murphy; Finis Welch. *Q. J. Econ.* **CVII:1** 2:1992 pp. 285 – 326

57 La struttura retributiva dei lavoratori alle dipendenze — evidenza empirica dagli osservatori INPS *[In Italian]*; The pay structure of employed workers — empirical evidence of the INPS observers *[Summary]*. Massimo Ferrero; Dino Invernizzi. *Ec. Lav.* **XXVI:1** 1-3:1992 pp. 95 – 116

58 Swedish wage-earner funds — an experiment in economic democracy. Jonas Pontusson; Sarosh Kuruvilla. *Ind. Lab. Rel.* **45:4** 7:1992 pp. 779 – 791

59 Technical change and wage-share fluctuations in a regime-switching model. P. Ferri; E. Greenberg. *J. Econ. Beh.* **19:3** 12:1992 pp. 369 – 377

60 A time series analysis of regional income inequalities and migration in Japan, 1955-1985. Howard L. Gauthier; Kyoko Tanaka; W. Randy Smith. *Geogr. Anal.* **24:4** 10:1992 pp. 283 – 298

61 Trade regimes and wages. M.A. Webb; M.C. Berger. *J. Dev. Econ.* **38:1** 1:1992 pp. 119 – 131

62 U.S. earnings levels and earnings inequality — a review of recent trends and proposed explanations. Frank Levy; Richard J. Murnane. *J. Econ. Lit.* **XXX:3** 9:1992 pp. 1333 – 1381

63 Unemployment, institutions and the living standard in the classical theory of wages. A. Stirati. *Contrib. Pol. Econ.* **11** 1992 pp. 41 – 66

64 Union egalitarianism as income insurance. Jonas Agell; Kjell Erik Lommerud. *Economica* **59:235** 8:1992 pp. 295 – 310

65 Una valutazione quantitativa della scala mobile modello «chimici» *[In Italian]*; A quantitative valuation of the «scala mobile» (indexation mechanism) for the chemical sector *[Summary]*. Federico Rappelli. *Ec. Lav.* **XXVI:1** 1-3:1992 pp. 37 – 50

66 Die Verbindlichkeit von Lohntarifverträgen aus arbeitsmarkttheoretischer Perspektive *[In German]*; [The binding quality of wage rate agreements from a labour market theoretical perspective] *[Summary]*. Lutz Bellmann; Knut Emmerich. *Jahr. Soz.schaft.* **43:2** 1992 pp. 227 – 242

67 Wage dynamics in Israel — market forces and spillover effects. Y. Artstein; Z. Sussman. *Appl. Econ.* **24:9** 9:1992 pp. 969 – 980

68 Wage generosity. Ekkehart Schlicht. *J. Inst. Theo. Ec.* **148:3** 9:1992 pp. 437 – 451

69 Wage inflation and the two-tier labour market. Ioannis Theodossiou. Aldershot: Avebury, 1992: 253 p. *ISBN: 1856282686.*

70 Wage levels and method of pay. C. Brown. *Rand J. Eco.* **23:3** Autumn:1992 pp. 366 – 375

71 Wage profiles and imperfect capital markets — a positive analysis; Profils de salaires et marchés de capitaux imparfaits — une analyse positive *[French summary]*. B. Mak Arvin; Richard J. Arnott. *Can. J. Econ.* **XXV:3** 8:1992 pp. 521 – 537

72 Wages and unemployment in Poland — recent developments and policy issues. Fabrizio Coricelli; Ana Revenga. Washington, D.C.: Country Economics Department World Bank, 1992: 45 p. [Policy research working papers.]

K.3: Specific income *[Catégories de revenu]*

73 Why Britain needs a minimum wage. Frank Wilkinson. London: Institute for Public Policy Research, 1992: 52 p. *ISBN: 1872452442.*

74 Work location, residence location, and the intraurban wage gradient. Daniel P. McMillen; Larry D. Singell. *J. Urban Ec.* **32:2** 9:1992 pp. 195 – 213

75 Workers and their wages — changing patterns in the United States. Marvin H. Kosters *[Ed.].* Washington, D.C.: AEI Press, 1991: 207 p. *ISBN: 084473747x.*

Profit and returns *[Profit et rendements]*

76 The comparative institutions of profit sharing — the U.S. computer industry. Michael D. Bradley; Stephen C. Smith. *J. Econ. Iss.* **XXVI:2** 6:1992 pp. 573 – 582

77 Contingent compensation — (how) does it affect company performance? Michael Conte. *J. Econ. Iss.* **XXVI:2** 6:1992 pp. 583 – 592

78 Economic democracy and financial participation — a comparative study. Daryl J d' Art. New York: Routledge, Chapman and Hall, 1992: 355 p. *ISBN: 0415062152; LofC: 91024195. Includes bibliographical references and index.*

79 Manoeuvres stratégiques et rentabilité *[In French]*; [Strategic manoeuvres and profitability rate]. Jacques Liouville. *Gestion* **8:2** 1992 pp. 83 – 92

80 On differential rent and landed property; *[French summary].* Alan W. Evans. *Int. J. Urban* **16:1** 3:1992 pp. 81 – 96

81 Profit sharing and productivity — microeconomic evidence from United States. D.L. Kruse. *Econ. J.* **102:410** 1:1992 pp. 24 – 36

82 Profit sharing in the British retail trade sector — the relative performance of the John Lewis Partnership. Keith Bradley; Saul Estrin. *J. Ind. Econ.* **XL:3** 9:1992 pp. 291 – 304

83 Profit-sharing and employment; *[German summary].* Kornelius Kraft. *Jahr. Soz.schaft.* **43:3** 1992 pp. 349 – 363

84 Profit-sharing in a unionized Cournot duopoly. J.R. Sørensen. *J. Econ.* **55:2** 1992 pp. 151 – 168

85 Smith on the falling rate of profit. Francisco Verdera. *Scot. J. Poli.* **39:1** 2:1992 pp. 100 – 110

86 Support for profit sharing and organizational commitment — a path analysis. Gary W. Florkowski; Michael H. Schuster. *Human Relat.* **45:5** 5:1992 pp. 507 – 523

87 A theory of predictable excess returns in real estate. Matthew Spiegel; William Strange. *J. Real Est. Finan. Econ.* **5:4** 12:1992 pp. 375 – 392

88 Unions and firm profits. Brian E. Becker; Craig A. Olson. *Ind. Relat.* **31:3** Fall:1992 pp. 395 – 415

Wage determination *[Fixation du salaire]*

89 Bargaining power and wage-employment contracts in a unionized industry. Denise J. Doiron. *Int. Econ. R.* **33:3** 8:1992 pp. 583 – 606

90 Collective bargaining and wage determination in Italian manufacturing. C. Dell'Aringa. *Banca Nat. Lav. Q. Rev.* **:180** 3:1992 pp. 21 – 34

91 Firm-specific determinants of the real wage. Janet Currie; Sheena McConnell. *Rev. Econ. St.* **LXXIV:2** 5:1992 pp. 297 – 304

92 La formation des salaires *[In French]*; [Wage determination]. Pierre Morin *[Contrib.]*; Jean-Louis L'Heritier *[Contrib.]*; Nathalie Greenan *[Contrib.]*; Pierre Cahuc *[Contrib.]*; Brigitte Dormont; Véronique Sandoval *[Contrib.].* *Collection of 6 articles.* **E & S** , *:257,* 9:1992 pp. 3 – 65

93 An investigation into the power of insiders in wage determination. S. Nickell; P. Kong. *Eur. Econ. R.* **36:8** 12:1992 pp. 1573 – 1599

94 Local pay determination. Ian Molho. *J. Econ. Sur.* **6:2** 1992 pp. 155 – 194

95 Net employment reserves and occupational wage rate determination. David Gleicher; Lonnie K. Stevans. *J. Post. Keyn. Ec.* **15:1** Fall:1992 pp. 125 – 146

96 New pay — linking employee and organizational performance. Jay Schuster; Patricia K. Zingheim. New York: Lexington Books, 1992: 366 p. *ISBN: 0669153583.*

97 Optimal allocation of time and estimation of market wage functions. B.F. Kiker; M. Mendes de Oliveira. *J. Hum. Res.* **XXVII:3** Summer:1992 pp. 445 – 471

98 Private sector pay possibilities for synchronisation. Fred Bayliss. London: Campaign for Work, 1992: 26 p.

99 Real wage determination and rent-sharing in collective bargaining agreements. Louis N. Christofides; Andrew J. Oswald. *Q. J. Econ.* **CVII:3** 8:1992 pp. 985 – 1002

K.3: Specific income *[Catégories de revenu]* — Wage determination *[Fixation du salaire]*

100 Les règles salariales au concret *[In French]*; [Concrete rules regarding wages]. Vladimir Najman; Bénédicte Reynaud. Paris: La Documentation française, 1992: 163 p. *ISBN: 2110027657. Bibliography — p.139-152.* [Document travail emploi.]

101 Relation between earnings and prices. Peter D. Easton *[Contrib.]*; Trevor S. Harris *[Contrib.]*; James A. Ohlson *[Contrib.]*; S.P. Kothari *[Contrib.]*; Richard G. Sloan *[Contrib.]*; Joseph H. Anthony *[Contrib.]*; K. Ramesh *[Contrib.]*; Sung K. Choi *[Contrib.]*; Debra C. Jeter *[Contrib.]*; Ashiq Ali *[Contrib.] and others. Collection of 8 articles.* **J. Account. E.** , *15:2/3,* 6/9:1992 pp. 119 – 318

102 Sindicatos y negociaciones salariales. El caso argentino *[In Spanish]*; Trade unions and wage bargaining. The Argentine case *[Summary]*. Luisa Montuschi. *Económica Arg* **XXXV:1-2** 1989 pp. 15 – 36

103 Underpaid and overworked — measuring the effect of imperfect information on wages. Richard A. Hofler; Kevin J. Murphy. *Econ. Inq.* **XXX:3** 7:1992 pp. 511 – 529

104 Wage bargaining and the Phillips curve — the identification and specification of aggregate wage equations. Alan Manning. London: London School of Economics and Political Science. Centre for Economic Performance, 1992: 49 p. [Discussion paper.]

105 Wage determination in low income, surplus labour economies — a review of theories and evidence. Rushidan Islam Rahman. Canberra: National Centre for Development Studies, Australian National University, 1991: 28 p. *ISBN: 0731509366.*

106 Wage rivalry and insider-outsider relations — evidence for skilled and unskilled men in Denmark. Ole Risager. *Sc. J. Econ.* **94:4** 1992 pp. 543 – 559

107 Who should set CEO pay? The press? Congress? Shareholders? Andrew R. Brownstein; Morris J. Panner. *Harv. Bus. Re.* **70:3** 5-6:1992 pp. 28 – 38

Wage differentials *[Eventail des salaires]*

108 An analysis of wage differentials by gender and ethnicity in the public sector. Todd L. Idson; Hollis F. Price. *Rev. Bl. Pol. Ec.* **20:3** Winter:1992 pp. 75 – 98

109 Black-white earnings over the 1970s and 1980s — gender differences in trends. Francine D. Blau; Andrea H. Beller. *Rev. Econ. St.* **LXXIV:2** 5:1992 pp. 276 – 286

110 Compensating wage differentials and unobserved productivity. Hae-shin Hwang; W. Robert Reed; Carlton Hubbard. *J. Polit. Ec.* **100:4** 8:1992 pp. 835 – 858

111 The contribution of intermittent labour force participation to the gender wage differential. Sarah Rummery. *Econ. Rec.* **68:203** 12:1992 pp. 351 – 364

112 Does unmeasured ability explain inter-industry wage differentials? Robert Gibbons; Lawrence Katz. *R. Econ. S.* **59:3(200)** 7:1992 pp. 515 – 536

113 The earnings of top executives — compensating differentials for risky business. Robin L. Bartlett; James H. Grant; Timothy I. Miller. *Q Rev. Econ. Finan.* **32:1** Spring:1992 pp. 38 – 49

114 The effects of college education on the male-female wage differential. Kwabena Gyimah-Brempong; Rudy Fichtenbaum; Gregory Willis. *S. Econ. J.* **58:3** 1:1992 pp. 790 – 804

115 An empirical analysis of university choice and earnings. Hessel Oosterbeek; Wim Groot; Joop Hartog. *Economist [Leiden]* **140:3** 1992 pp. 293 – 309

116 Gender discrimination and compensating differentials in Sweden. M.O. Palme; R.E. Wright. *Appl. Econ.* **24:7** 7:1992 pp. 751 – 759

117 Intersektorale Lohndifferentiale. Eine mikroökonomische Untersuchung mit Paneldaten für die Bundesrepublik Deutschland *[In German]*; [Intersectoral wage differentials. A microeconomic investigation with data from Germany]. Elke Maria Schmidt. *Z. Wirt. Soz.* **112:2** 1992 pp. 201 – 218

118 Intraurban wage gradients — evidence by race, gender, occupational class, and sector. Keith R. Ihlanfeldt. *J. Urban Ec.* **32:1** 7:1992 pp. 70 – 91

119 The law of the shrinking middle — inequality of earnings in Australia. J.E. King; R.J. Rimmer; S.M. Rimmer. *Scot. J. Poli.* **39:4** 11:1992 pp. 391 – 412

120 Salary dispersion, location in the salary distribution, and turnover among college administrators. Jeffrey Pfeffer; Alison Davis-Blake. *Ind. Lab. Rel.* **45:4** 7:1992 pp. 753 – 763

121 Sex segregated employment, wage inequality and labor intensive production — a study of 33 U.S. manufacturing industries. Jayne Dean. *Rev. Rad. Pol. Ec.* **23:3&4** Fall & Winter:1991 pp. 244 – 268

122 Wage linkages between private and public sectors in Sweden. bertil Holmlund; Henry Ohlsson. *Labour [Italy]* **6:2** Autumn:1992 pp. 3 – 17

123 Wage structure, incomes policy and decentralised bargaining — the case of Greece. Christos Ioannou. *Labour [Italy]* **6:3** Winter:1992 pp. 23 – 44

124 Wages, incentive schemes, and the role of gender. Dale Belman; John S. Heywood. *R. Soc. Econ.* **L:2** Summer:1992 pp. 149 – 162

125 Women and the union wage gap. B.G.M. Main; B. Reilly. *Econ. J.* **102:410** 1:1992 pp. 49 – 66

L: Demand (use of income) — *Demande (utilisation du revenu)*

L.1: Aggregate demand — *Demande globale*

1 An alternative framework of estimating investment and saving functions for developing countries — an application to time-series data for sub-Saharan African countries. M.O. Odedokun. *Int. Econ. J.* **6:3** Autumn:1992 pp. 49 – 74

2 The buffer-stock theory of saving — some macroeconomic evidence. Christopher D. Carroll. *Brookings P.* **2** 1992 pp. 61 – 135

3 Capital market imperfections, taxation and household saving. E. Koskela; M. Virén. *Eur. J. Pol. Ec.* **8:1** 2:1992 pp. 77 – 88

4 Les conséquences du chômage sur la consommation *[In French]*; How unemployment affects consumption *[Summary]*; Las consecuencias del desempleo sobre el consumo *[Spanish summary]*. Nicolas Herpin. *E & S* **:256** 7-8:1992 pp. 43 – 57

5 Crowding out in open economies — results from a simulation study; Effet d'encombrement dans des économies ouvertes — résultats d'une étude de simulation *[French summary]*. Emanuela Cardia. *Can. J. Econ.* **XXV:3** 8:1992 pp. 708 – 728

6 Developments in the Republic of Ireland savings and lending markets. Des Drew. *Irish Bank. Rev. Autumn:1992* pp. 11 – 26

7 Do individuals optimize in intertemporal consumption/savings decisions? A liberal method to encourage savings. Y.-K. Ng. *J. Econ. Beh.* **17:1** 1:1992 pp. 101 – 114

8 Dynamic savings behaviour in an oil-dependent economy — the case of Trinidad and Tobago. R.C. Craigwell; L.L. Rock. *J. Dev. Econ.* **39:2** 10:1992 pp. 247 – 261

9 Earnings uncertainty and precautionary saving. Luigi Guiso; Tullio Jappelli; Daniele Terlizzese. *J. Monet. Ec.* **30:2** 11:1992 pp. 307 – 337

10 L'economia in presenza di una domanda nominale esogenamente data *[In Italian]*; [The economy when nominal demand is exogenous]. Piero Garbero. *Ras. Econ.* **LV:4** 10-12:1992 pp. 819 – 840

11 Erklärungsansätze zum Rückgang der Sparquote der privaten Haushalte in den USA während der 1980er Jahre *[In German]*; [Towards an explanation of the decrease in private household savings in the USA in the eighties] *[Summary]*. Carl-Ludwig Holtfrerich. *Ifo-Stud.* **38:2** 1992 pp. 227 – 247

12 An estimate of resource expenditures on transfer activity in the United States. David N. Laband; John P. Sophocleus. *Q. J. Econ.* **CVII:3** 8:1992 pp. 959 – 984

13 An evaluation of co-operative capital management in Rift Valley province, Kenya; Une evaluation de la gestion du capital des cooperatives dans la Rift Valley province, Kenya *[French summary]*. F.O.C. Nwonwu. *Sav. Develop.* **:2** 1992 pp. 159 – 172

14 Factors influencing the demand for rural deposits in Bangladesh — a test for functional form. M.A. Baqui Khalily; Richard L. Meyer. *J. Dev. Areas* **26:3** 4:1992 pp. 371 – 382

15 A flow-of-funds approach to savings mobilisation using Nigerian data; L'approche des flux de caisse dans la mobilisation de l'épargne sur la base de données du Nigeria *[Summary]*. I.O. Taiwo. *Sav. Develop.* **XVI:2** 1992 pp. 169 – 182

16 Forced saving and repressed inflation in the Soviet Union, 1986-90 — some empirical results. Carlo Cottarelli; Mario I. Blejer. *Staff Pap. Int. Monetary* **39:2** 6:1992 pp. 256 – 286

17 Future trends in Japan's saving rate and the implications thereof for Japan's external imbalance. C.Y. Horioka. *Jpn. Wor. Econ.* **3:4** 4:1992 pp. 307 – 330

L.1: Aggregate demand *[Demande globale]*

18 Government saving and private saving in Brazil; *[Portuguese summary]*. Daniel Luiz Gleizer. *Rev. Bras. Ec.* **46:3** 7-9:1992 pp. 291 – 317

19 The informal financial sector in Malawi; Le secteur financier non officiel au Malawi *[French summary]*. C. Chipeta; M.L.C. Mkandawire. *Sav. Develop.* :2 1992 pp. 121 – 157

20 Interdependency of personal savings and labour force participation of the elderly, and social wealth — a time series analysis. T. Yamada; G. Liu. *Appl. Econ.* **24:4** 4:1992 pp. 379 – 388

21 De internationale verschillen in het aggregatief gezinsspaargedrag, 1971-1985 — omvang, aard en verklaring *[In Flemish]*; Household saving rates of twelve OECD countries, 1971-1985 *[Summary]*. Guido Peersman. *Econ. Soc. Tidj.* **46:1** 3:1992 pp. 49 – 72

22 A lakossági megtakarítások portfóliószerkezete *[In Hungarian]*; Portfolio structure of personal savings *[Summary]*. Ábel István; John P. Bonin; Székely P. István. *Közg. Sz.* **XXXIX:** 7-8:1992 pp. 654 – 666

23 Liquidity constraints and aggregate consumption behavior. Matthew J. Cushing. *Econ. Inq.* **XXX:1** 1:1992 pp. 134 – 153

24 Measuring personal savings, consumption, and disposable income in Canada; La mesure de l'épargne personnelle, de la consommation, et du revenu disponible des Canadiens *[French summary]*. Marcel G. Dagenais. *Can. J. Econ.* **XXV:3** 8:1992 pp. 681 – 707

25 La modélisation de la consommation des ménages en France *[In French]*; Modelling aggregate households' consumption and saving behavior in France *[Summary]*. P. Allard. *Rev. Ec. Polit.* **102:5** 9-10:1992 pp. 727 – 768

26 Modelling savings behaviour in centrally planned developing countries — the case of Algeria 1963 to 1984; Comment construire un modele sur le comportement des epargnants dans une économie planifée d'un pays en voie de developpement — le cas de l'Algerie *[French summary]*. B. Laabas; P.R.D. Wilson. *Sav. Develop.* **XVI:3** 1992 pp. 255 – 273

27 On the reduction of interest rate margins in developing countries and implicated welfare effects for private households; La reduction des marges des taux d'interet dans les pays en voie de developpement et ses effets economiques sur les menages *[French summary]*. Friedrich L. Sell; Silke Wohlgemuth. *Sav. Develop.* **XVI:4** 1992 pp. 403 – 420

28 Private saving and terms of trade shocks — evidence from developing countries. Jonathan D. Ostry; Carmen M. Reinhart. *Staff Pap. Int. Monetary* **39:3** 9:1992 pp. 495 – 517

29 Private saving in Mexico, 1980-90. Patricio Arrau; Daniel F. Oks. Washington, D.C.: The World Bank, 1992: 48 p. [Policy research working papers.]

30 Relatively stable lifetime consumption as evidence of positive time preference. James A. Yunker. *J. Post. Keyn. Ec.* **14:3** Spring:1992 pp. 347 – 366

31 The role of savings in economic development — the U.S. and Japanese experiences. D. Dhakal; R. Grabowski; M.P. Shields. *Jpn. Wor. Econ.* **3:4** 4:1992 pp. 331 – 340

32 Saving and investment under Muḍārabah finance; *[Arabic summary]*. Shamim Ahmed Siddiqui; Mohsen Fardmanesh. *R. Islam. Econ.* **2:1** 1992 pp. 31 – 51

33 Saving behavior and Soviet reform. M. Alexeev. *Cont. Policy* **X:3** 7:1992 pp. 39 – 48

34 Saving under uncertainty — a bivariate non-expected utility approach. Fanny Demers; Michel Demers. *Geneva Pap. Risk Insur. Theory* **17:1** 6:1992 pp. 61 – 76

35 Saving-investment correlations and capital mobility — on the evidence from annual data. S. Sinn. *Econ. J.* **102:414** 9:1992 pp. 1162 – 1170

36 Savings behavior — theory, international evidence and policy implications. Jeffrey R. Shafer *[Contrib.]*; Jorgen Elmeskov *[Contrib.]*; Warren Tease *[Contrib.]*; Edmond Malinvaud *[Comments by]*; Angus Maddison *[Contrib.]*; Luigi Guiso *[Contrib.]*; Tullio Jappelli *[Contrib.]*; Daniele Terlizzese *[Contrib.]*; Erkki Koskela *[Contrib.]*; Matti Virén *[Contrib.] and others. Collection of 18 articles.* **Sc. J. Econ.** , *94:2*, 1992 pp. 155 – 372

37 Savings behavior — theory, international evidence and policy implications. Erkki Koskela *[Ed.]*; Jouko Paunio *[Ed.]*. Oxford: Blackwell, 1992: 223 p. *ISBN: 0631182667.* [Scandinavian Journal of Economics special issues.]

38 Savings-and-investment and other myths. Peter L. Bernstein. *Publ. Inter.* :107 Spring:1992 pp. 87 – 94

39 The social opportunity cost of consumption for Australia, 1960-61 to 1988-89. Ian M. McDonald; Luca Tacconi; Ravjeet Kaur. *Aust. Ec. Rev.* :1(97) 1-3:1992 pp. 44 – 53

40 Social security investment and capital formation. W. Thorbecke. *Cont. Policy* **X:3** 7:1992 pp. 26 – 38

41 Symposium on saving and age structure. A. Cigno *[Ed.]*; D.T. Greenwood *[Contrib.]*; E.N. Wolff *[Contrib.]*; A. Börsch-Supan *[Contrib.]*; S. Perelman *[Contrib.]*; P. Pestieau *[Contrib.]*; F.C. Rosati *[Contrib.]. Collection of 5 articles.* **J. Pop. Ec.** , *5:4*, 1992 pp. 257 – 341

L.1: Aggregate demand *[Demande globale]*

42 A systems approach to the relationship between consumption and wealth. S.G. Hall; K.D. Patterson. *Appl. Econ.* **24:10** 10:1992 pp. 1165 – 1172

43 Transformations of the commodity space, behavioral heterogenity, and the aggregation problem. Jean-Michel Grandmont. *J. Econ. Theo.* **57:1** 6:1992 pp. 1 – 35

L.2: Consumer demand — *Demande de consommation*

Sub-divisions: Consumer behaviour *[Comportement du consommateur]*; Food, drink and tobacco *[Aliments, boissons et tabac]*; Housing *[Logement]*

1 The construction of a continuous demand function for uniformly rotund preferences. D.S. Bridges. *J. Math Econ.* **21:3** 1992 pp. 217 – 227

2 Consumption and living standards in China. Joseph C.H. Chai. *China Quart.* **:131** 9:1992 pp. 721 – 749

3 Copper consumption in the USA — main determinants and structural changes. Joaquin Vial. *Res. Pol.* **18:2** 6:1992 pp. 107 – 121

4 The cult[ure] of the customer. Paul du Gay; Gaeme Salaman. *J. Manag. Stu.* **29:5** 9:1992 pp. 615 – 634

5 The demand for retail products and the household production model — new views on complementarity and substitutability. R.R. Betancourt; D. Gautschi. *J. Econ. Beh.* **17:2** 3:1992 pp. 257 – 276

6 A dynamic model for correcting quarterly electricity consumption data. Thalassinos El. *Ener. Econ.* **14:3** 7:1992 pp. 186 – 191

7 Economics of information and heterogeneous products. R.L. Andrews. *J. Econ. Psyc.* **13:3** 9:1992 pp. 399 – 420

8 Engel's law and cointegration. Masao Ogaki. *J. Polit. Ec.* **110:5** 10:1992 pp. 1027 – 1046

9 Estimating consumer surplus in the censored linear model. Daniel Hellerstein. *Land Econ.* **68:1** 2:1992 pp. 83 – 92

10 Exact and superlative welfare change indicators. W.E. Diewert. *Econ. Inq.* **XXX:4** 10:1992 pp. 565 – 582

11 Forecasting residential electricity consumption in Greece using monthly and quarterly data. E. Dikaios Tserkezos. *Ener. Econ.* **14:3** 7:1992 pp. 226 – 232

12 Government expenditures and consumption crowding out. George Tridimas. *Economia [Lisbon]* **XV:3** 10:1991 pp. 391 – 410

13 Household formation by the young in the United States. R.J. Kent. *Appl. Econ.* **24:10** 10:1992 pp. 1129 – 1138

14 Housework time in Bulgaria and Finland. Leena M. Kirjavainen; et al. Helsinki: Tilastokeskus, 1992: 132 p. *ISBN: 9514760085.* [Tutkimiksia.]

15 Impact of league restructuring on team sport attendance — the case of rugby league. B. Burkitt; S. Cameron. *Appl. Econ.* **24:2** 2:1992 pp. 265 – 272

16 Integration and consumer protection — the case of Latin America; *[German summary]*. Jean Michel Arrighi. *J. Consum. Pol.* **15:2** 1992 pp. 179 – 190

17 The intertemporal elasticity of substitution in consumption in the United States and the United Kingdom. Kerry D. Patterson; Bahram Pesaran. *Rev. Econ. St.* **LXXIV:4** 11:1992 pp. 573 – 584

18 Is the extended family altruistically linked? Direct tests using micro data. Joseph G. Altonji; Fumio Hayashi; Laurence J. Kotlikoff. *Am. Econ. Rev.* **82:5** 12:1992 pp. 1177 – 1198

19 Kernel smoothed consumption-age quantiles; Estimation des quantiles de la distribution de la consommation selon les groupes d'âges obtenue par lissage du noyau *[French summary]*. A.L. Robb; L. Magee; J.B. Burbidge. *Can. J. Econ.* **XXV:3** 8:1992 pp. 669 – 680

20 The logit as a model of product differentiation. Simon P. Anderson; Andre de Palma. *Ox. Econ. Pap.* **44:1** 1:1992 pp. 51 – 67

21 Lucas's signal-extraction model — a finite state exposition with aggregate real shocks. Neil Wallace. *J. Monet. Ec.* **30:3** 12:1992 pp. 433 – 447

22 Market responses to publicly-provided information — the case of automotive safety. G.E. Hoffer; S.W. Pruitt; R.J. Reilly. *Appl. Econ.* **24:7** 7:1992 pp. 661 – 667

23 Maximum score estimates of the determinants of residential mobility — implications for the value of residential attachment and neighborhood amenities. Timothy J. Bartik; J.S. Butler; Jin-Tan Liu. *J. Urban Ec.* **32:2** 9:1992 pp. 233 – 256

L.2: Consumer demand *[Demande de consommation]*

24 Measuring quality perceptions. Chakravarthi Narasimhan; Subrata Sen. *Market. Lett.* **3:2** 4:1992 pp. 147 – 156

25 Measuring the consumer welfare effects of carbon penalties — theory and applications to household energy demand. Jesus C. Dumagan; Timothy D. Mount. *Ener. Econ.* **14:2** 4:1992 pp. 82 – 93

26 Military spending as a burden on growth — an "underconsumptionist" critique. Massimo Pivetti. *Camb. J. Econ.* **16:4** 12:1992 pp. 373 – 384

27 Modelling household car ownership in the Gulf States — the case of Kuwait; Mikroökonomische Modelle des Pkw- Besitzes in den Golf-Staaten — Der Fall Kuwait *[German summary]*; Modélisation de la propriété des voitures des ménages des Etats du Golfe. Le cas du Kuwait *[French summary]*; La modelización de la tenencia familiar de automóviles en los Estados del Golfo — el caso de Kuwait *[Spanish summary]*. Galal M. Said. *J. Transp. Ec. Pol.* **XXVI:2** 5:1992 pp. 121 – 138

28 On efficient distribution with private information. Andrew Atkeson; Robert E. Lucas. *R. Econ. S.* **59:3(200)** 7:1992 pp. 427 – 454

29 Optimal nonlinear pricing and contingent contracts. Daniel F. Spulber. *Int. Econ. R.* **33:4** 11:1992 pp. 747 – 772

30 Overheidsfinanciering en private consumptie — heeft Barro ongelijk? *[In Dutch]*; [Government financing and private consumption — is Barro wrong?]. F. Vanhorebeek. *Tijds. Econ. Manag.* **XXXVII:1** 4:1992 pp. 35 – 52

31 Preferences and nonreversibility of indifference curves. J.K. Knetsch. *J. Econ. Beh.* **17:1** 1:1992 pp. 131 – 139

32 The rational expectations approach to the study of consumption-income dynamics — the case of Greece 1953-1988; L'approccio delle aspettative razionali allo studio della dinamica reddito-consumo — il caso della Grecia 1953-1988 *[Italian summary]*. John M. Paleologos; Spiros E. Georgantelis. *Rev. Int. Sci. Ec. Com.* **XXXIX:5-6** 5-6:1992 pp. 485 – 498

33 Reform of the law of product liability in Australia; *[German summary]*. David Harland. *J. Consum. Pol.* **15:2** 1992 pp. 191 – 206

34 Rural landlords and rental housing energy efficiency. Joseph Laquatra. *Energy Pol.* **20:9** 9:1992 pp. 815 – 824

35 Separability, partial demand systems, and consumer's surplus measures. Michael Hanemann; Edward Morey. *J. Envir. Ec. Manag.* **22:3** 5:1992 pp. 241 – 258

36 The service flow from consumption goods with an application to Friedman's permanent income hypothesis. K.D. Patterson. *Ox. Econ. Pap.* **44:2** 4:1992 pp. 289 – 305

37 Social security, uncertainty adjustments and the consumption decision. Dean R. Leimer; David H. Richardson. *Economica* **59:235** 8:1992 pp. 311 – 336

38 Surplus from publicness in consumption and its equitable distribution. Mikiro Otsuki. *J. Publ. Ec.* **47:1** 2:1992 pp. 107 – 124

39 Survey expectations in the times series consumption function. Roy Batchelor; Pami Dua. *Rev. Econ. St.* **LXXIV:4** 11:1992 pp. 598 – 606

40 Testing the constancy of relative risk aversion — an analysis of Japanese household financial asset data. Seki Asano; Toshiaki Tachibanaki. *J. Jap. Int. Ec.* **6:1** 3:1992 pp. 52 – 70

41 Towards a model of use of remittances for social ceremonies and luxury items — a case study of a village in the North West Frontier province of Pakistan. Mohammad Idris; A.J. Sofranko. *J. Rural Devel. Admin.* **XXIV:3** 7-9:1992 pp. 32 – 56

42 Two kinds of consumer switching costs. T. Nilssen. *Rand J. Eco.* **23:4** Winter:1992 pp. 579 – 589

43 Understanding consumption. Angus Deaton. Oxford: Clarendon Press, 1992: 242 p. *ISBN: 0198287593; LofC: 92030783. Includes bibliographical references and index.*

44 The use and cost of child care in Australia. Francis Teal. *Aust. Ec. Rev.* **:1(97)** 1-3:1992 pp. 3 – 14

45 Wealth effects and exogeneity — the Norwegian consumption function 1966(1)-1984(4). P. Anders Brodin; Ragnar Nymoen. *Ox. B. Econ. S.* **54:3** 8:1992 pp. 431 – 454

46 What is households' non-market production worth? Ann Chadeau. *OECD Ec. Stud.* **:18** Spring:1992 pp. 85 – 104

47 Working, shopping, and house rents. Robert W. Bacon. *Geogr. Anal.* **24:3** 7:1992 pp. 268 – 280

48 Der Zusammenhang zwischen Konsum und Einkommen — Alternative ökonometrische Ansätze *[In German]*; [The connection between consumption and income — alternative econometric approach] *[Summary]*; *[French summary]*. Jürgen Wolters. *RWI-Mitt.* **43:2** 1992 pp. 115 – 132

L.2: Consumer demand *[Demande de consommation]* —

Consumer behaviour *[Comportement du consommateur]*

49 Accomodating the effects of brand unfamiliarity in the multidimensional scaling of preference data. Rabikar Chatterjee; Wayne S. DeSarbo. *Market. Lett.* **3:1** 1:1992 pp. 85 – 99

50 Analyse des décisions spatiales et du processus de choix des consommateurs — théorie, méthodes et exemples d'applications *[In French]*; The analysis of consumer spatial decision-making and choice processes — theory, methods, and examples of applications *[Summary]*. Jean-Claude Thill; Harry Timmermans. *Espace Géogr.* **XXI:2** 1992 pp. 143 – 166

51 Approximately rational consumer demand and ville cycles. David Jerison; Michael Jerison. *J. Econ. Theo.* **56:1** 2:1992 pp. 100 – 120

52 Bestedingseffecten van het stelsel van sociale zekerheid — de gevolgen voor bedrijfstakken van wijzigingen in het consumptiepakket *[In Dutch]*; [The effects on spending of the social security system — the consequences of changes in consumer spending for branches of industry and commerce]. D. van der Vuurst; C. Petersen; A.E. Steenge; A. van der Veen. *Maan. Econ.* **56:2** 1992 pp. 105 – 117

53 Children and household economic behavior. Martin Browning. *J. Econ. Lit.* **XXX:3** 9:1992 pp. 1434 – 1475

54 Choice experiments versus revealed choice models — a before-after study of consumer spatial shopping behaviour. Harry Timmermans; Aloys Borgers; Peter van der Waerden. *Prof. Geogr.* **44:4** 11:1992 pp. 406 – 416

55 Demand system specification and estimation. Robert A. Pollak; Terence J. Wales. New York: Oxford University Press, 1992: xiii, 217 p. *ISBN: 0195069412; LofC: 91016054. Includes bibliographical references (p. 197-207) and indexes.*

56 Discrete choice theory of product differentiation. Simon P. Anderson; Jacques Francois Thisse; André de Palma. Cambridge, MA.: The MIT Press, 1992: xviii, 423 p. *ISBN: 026201128x; LofC: 92015791. Includes bibliographical references and index.*

57 Effects of consumer preferences for foreign sourced products. Victor V. Cordell. *J. Int. Bus. Stud.* **23:2** 1992 pp. 251 – 270

58 Effects of physical contact on customers' shopping time and behavior. Jacob Hornik. *Market. Lett.* **3:1** 1:1992 pp. 49 – 55

59 Effects of rationing on the consumption behavior of Chinese urban households during 1981-1987. Zhi Wang; Wen S. Chern. *J. Comp. Econ.* **16:1** 3:1992 pp. 1 – 26

60 An empirically oriented demand system with improved regularity properties; Un système de demande empiriquement orienté avec des propriétés de régularité améliorées *[French summary]*. Russel J. Cooper; Keith R. MacLaren. *Can. J. Econ.* **XXV:3** 8:1992 pp. 652 – 668

61 Estimating the efficiency of consumer choices of new automobiles. P. Gupta; B.T. Ratchford. *J. Econ. Psyc.* **13:3** 9:1992 pp. 375 – 398

62 Estimation of a continuous-time dynamic demand system. M.J. Chambers. *J. Appl. Econ.* **7:1** 1-3:1992 pp. 53 – 64

63 Explaining buyer behavior — central concepts and philosophy of science issues. John O'Shaughnessy. New York: Oxford University Press, 1992: 385 p. *ISBN: 0195071085; LofC: 91022140. Includes bibliographical references and index.*

64 Keynes' economic thought and the theory of consumer behaviour. S.A. Drakopoulos. *Scot. J. Poli.* **39:3** 8:1992 pp. 318 – 336

65 Norms, sovereignty and regulation. Keith Cowling; Robin Naylor. Coventry: University of Warwick, Dept. of Economics, 1992: 27 p. [Warwick economic research papers. : No. 390]

66 Потребительское поведение населения в кризисных ситуациях *[In Russian]*; [Consumption behaviour of the population in crisis situations].*Vop. Ekon.* **:1** 1992 pp. 74 – 82

67 Recall in consumer search. C.A. Kogut. *J. Econ. Beh.* **17:1** 1:1992 pp. 141 – 151

68 The role of loyalty discounts when consumers are uncertain of the value of repeat purchases. G. Bulkley. *Int. J. Ind. O.* **10:1** 3:1992 pp. 91 – 102

69 Social utility and fashion behavior. Shelby H. McIntyre; Christopher M. Miller. *Market. Lett.* **3:4** 10:1992 pp. 371 – 382

70 Spatial duopolistic competition with multipurpose and multistop shopping. J.-C. Thill. *Ann. Reg. Sci.* **26:3** 1992 pp. 287 – 304

71 Veblen effects and their impact on the new European Community and some of their trading partners. K.J. Hayes; D.J. Slottje; M.J. Ferrantino; J. Wagner. *Eur. Econ. R.* **36:1** 1:1992 pp. 51 – 70

L.2: Consumer demand *[Demande de consommation]* —

Food, drink and tobacco *[Aliments, boissons et tabac]*

72 Flexible demand systems with serially correlated errors — fat and oil consumption in the United States. Steven T. Yen; Wen S. Chern. *Am. J. Agr. Ec.* **74:3** 8:1992 pp. 689 – 697

73 Food security in a South Pacific context — the case of rice in Vanuatu. Tim Foy; Kevin Parton *[Comments by]*; Euan Fleming *[Comments by]*. *Pac. Ec. B.* **7:1** 6:1992 pp. 32 – 40

74 Frequency of purchase and the estimation of demand systems. Costas Meghir; Jean-Marc Robin. *J. Economet.* **53:1-3** 7-9:1992 pp. 53 – 85

75 Functional forms and habit effects in the US demand for coffee. A.A. Okunade. *Appl. Econ.* **24:11** 11:1992 pp. 1203 – 1212

76 Housing affordability — myth or reality? Peter D. Linneman; Isaac F. Megbolugbe. *Urban Stud.* **29:3-4** 5:1992 pp. 369 – 392

77 Imported foods in a British supermarket chain — buyer decisions in Safeway. S.A. Shaw; J.A. Dawson; L.M.A. Blair. *Int. R. Ret. Dist. Res.* **2:1** 1:1992 pp. 35 – 58

78 Regional economic impact of a reduction of resident expenditure on cigarettes — a case study of Glasgow. I. McNicoll; S. Boyle. *Appl. Econ.* **24:3** 3:1992 pp. 291 – 296

79 Self-sufficiency and food security in the UK and EC. I.M. Sturgess. *J. Agr. Econ.* **43:3** 9:1992 pp. 311 – 326

80 U.S. cigarette consumption — the case of low-income women. James R. Blaylock; W. Noel Blisard. *Am. J. Agr. Ec.* **74:3** 8:1992 pp. 698 – 705

Housing *[Logement]*

81 Algunos aspectos de la economía y la política de la vivienda *[In Spanish]*; [Some aspects of housing economics and policy]. Miguel Angel López García. *Invest. Econ.* **XVI:1** 1:1992 pp. 3 – 41

82 Analyse empirique des comportements de localisation résidentielle dans les espaces urbains multicentriques *[In French]*; [Empirical analysis of the behaviour of residential localization in multicentric urban spaces] *[Summary]*. C. Maurice-Baumont. *R. Ec. Reg. Urb.* **:1** 1992 pp. 11 – 35

83 Analysis of the process of dwelling rehabilitation in Auckland. Martin Putterill. *Soc. Ind.* **26:2** 3:1992 pp. 159 – 181

84 Bidding, auctions, and house purchase. K. Gibb. *Envir. Plan.A.* **24:6** 6:1992 pp. 853 – 869

85 Consequences juridiques et fiscales du marche unique dans le secteur immobilier en espagne *[In French]*; [Fiscal and legal consequences of the single European market on the Spanish housing market]. Pierre Fontaneau. *Rev. Fisc. Eur.* **23:2** 1992 pp. 3 – 26

86 Consumer preferences and willingness-to-pay for water-related residences in non-urban settings — a vignette analysis; *[French summary]*; *[German summary]*. Eran Feitelson. *Reg. Stud.* **26:1** 1992 pp. 49 – 68

87 Demographic change and housing demand in Spain — projections up to the year 2010. José L. Curbelo; Victoria Martin. *Pap. Reg. Sci.* **71:1** 1:1992 pp. 31 – 44

88 An empirical analysis of the demand for housing attributes in a Third World city. Ben C. Arimah. *Land Econ.* **68:4** 11:1992 pp. 366 – 379

89 Financing multifamily rental housing — the changing role of lenders and investors. Denise DiPasquale; Jean L. Cummings. *Hous. Pol. Deb.* **3:1** 1992 pp. 77 – 116

90 A general equilibrium model of housing, taxes, and portfolio choice. James Berkovec; Don Fullerton. *J. Polit. Ec.* **100:2** 4:1992 pp. 390 – 429

91 Hedonic prices and the demand for housing attributes in a Third World city — the case of Ibadan, Nigeria. Ben C. Arimah. *Urban Stud.* **29:5** 6:1992 pp. 639 – 651

92 Housing affordability — myth or reality? Peter D. Linneman; Isaac F. Megbolugbe. *Urban Stud.* **29:3-4** 5:1992 pp. 369 – 392

93 Housing and the wider economy in the short and long run. David Miles. *Natl. Inst. Econ. R.* **139** 2:1992 pp. 64 – 78

94 Housing finance in developed countries — an international comparison of efficiency. Douglas B. Diamond; Michael J. Lea. *J. Hous. Res.* **3:1** 1992 pp. 1 – 260

95 The inevitable crisis of the Brazilian housing finance system. Márcio M. Valença. *Urban Stud.* **29:1** 2:1992 pp. 39 – 56

96 Introducing risky housing and endogenous tenure choice into a portfolio-based general equilibrium model. Patric H. Hendershott; Yunhi Won. *J. Publ. Ec.* **48:3** 8:1992 pp. 293 – 316

L.2: Consumer demand *[Demande de consommation]* — Housing *[Logement]*

97 Location, housing, and leisure demand under local employment. Geoffrey K. Turnbull. *Land Econ.* **68:1** 2:1992 pp. 62 – 71

98 On the use of auctions as a disposition strategy for RTC real estate assets — a policy perspective. Kerry D. Vandell; Timothy J. Riddiough. *Hous. Pol. Deb.* **3:1** 1992 pp. 117 – 141

99 Owner-occupied housing, capital gains, and the Tax Reform Act of 1986. William H. Hoyt; Stuart S. Rosenthal. *J. Urban Ec.* **32:2** 9:1992 pp. 119 – 139

100 Quasi-exact equivalence scales for Poland. A. Szulc. *Eco. Notes* **21:1** 1992 pp. 175 – 183

101 Racial differences in homeownership and housing wealth, 1970-1986. James E. Long; Steven B. Caudill. *Econ. Inq.* **XXX:1** 1:1992 pp. 83 – 100

102 Renovation of public housing — suggestions from a simple model. Michael E. Gleeson. *Manag. Sci.* **38:5** 5:1992 pp. 655 – 666

103 Rental vacancy rates — a policy primer. Eric S. Belsky. *Hous. Pol. Deb.* **3:3** 1992 pp. 793 – 813

104 A Ricardian interpretation of the provision of public housing services in Hong Kong. P. Sai-Wing Ho. *Camb. J. Econ.* **16:2** 6:1992 pp. 207 – 225

105 The role of pension funds in housing finance — the South African scenario. P.S. Reddy; P. Brijlal. *Develop. S. Afr.* **9:2** 5:1992 pp. 187 – 198

106 A simulation model of consumer spending and housing demand. Peter Westaway. London: National Institute of Economic Research, 1992: 24 p. [Discussion paper.]

107 Testing the standard urban model of residential choice — an implicit markets approach. William E. Herrin; Clifford R. Kern. *J. Urban Ec.* **31:2** 3:1992 pp. 145 – 163

108 Time for mortgage benefits. Steven Webb; Steve Wilcox. *Fis. Stud.* **13:1** 2:1992 pp. 71 – 88

109 To whom should limited housing resources be directed? Kathryn P. Nelson; Jill Khadduri; Michael A. Stegman; Gordon Cavanaugh. *Hous. Pol. Deb.* **3:1** 1992 pp. 1 – 76

110 What price housing? Valuing "voluntary transfers" of council housing. Karen Gardiner; John Hills. *Fis. Stud.* **13:1** 2:1992 pp. 54 – 70

L.3: Investment demand — *Demande d'investissement*

1 Adjustment and private investment in Kenya. Kazi M. Matin; Bernard Wasow. Washington, D.C.: Country Economics Department, The World Bank, 1992: 45 p. *Bibliography* — p.43-45. [Policy research working papers.]

2 Collusive pricing with capacity constraints in the presence of demand uncertainty. R.W. Staiger; F.A. Wolak. *Rand J. Eco.* **23:2** Summer:1992 pp. 203 – 220

3 Competitors or collaborators? The structure of inward investment promotion in Northern England. P. Dicken; A. Tickell. *Reg. Stud.* **26:1** 1992 pp. 99 – 106

4 Did the debt crisis cause the investment crisis? Andrew M. Warner. *Q. J. Econ.* **CVII:4** 11:1992 pp. 1161 – 1186

5 Dynamics of the composition of household asset portfolios and the life cycle. Y.M. Ioannides. *Appl. Finan. Econ.* **2:3** 9:1992 pp. 145 – 160

6 Equipment investment and economic growth — how strong is the nexus? J. Bradford de Long; Lawrence H. Summers. *Brookings P. 2* 1992 pp. 157 – 199

7 Europe 1992 and the liberalization of direct investment flows — services versus manufacturing. Francisco Rivera-Batiz; Luis Rivera-Batiz. *Int. Econ. J.* **6:1** Spring:1992 pp. 45 – 57

8 Explaining home improvement in the context of household investment in residential housing. Claire Montgomery. *J. Urban Ec.* **32:3** 11:1992 pp. 326 – 350

9 Le financement de l'industrialisation — investissement, épargne, croissance *[In French]*; The financing of industrialization *[Summary]*. Jean-Joseph Boillot; Françoise Lemoine. *Ec. Pros. Int.* **:50** 2ᵉ trimestre:1992 pp. 67 – 98

10 Foreign and domestic divestments — evidence on valuation effects of plant closings. George P. Tsetsekos; Michael J. Gombola. *J. Int. Bus. Stud.* **23:2** 1992 pp. 203 – 224

11 Foreign direct and private local sector investment shares in developing countries — the impact on investment efficiency; *[German summary]*. Herbert Oberhänsli. *Aussenwirtschaft* **47:1** 2:1992 pp. 31 – 54

12 Industrie stützt Investitionskonjunktur *[In German]*; Results of the spring 1992 investment survey — manufacturing industry boosts investment cycle *[Summary]*. Karl Aiginger; Margarete Czerny; Wolfgang Klameth; Karl Musil. *Monatsberichte* **7:65** 1992 pp. 357 – 369

L.3: Investment demand *[Demande d'investissement]*

13 An interest rate shock on a small debtor economy with installation costs of investment. Baekin Cha. *Int. Econ. J.* **6:3** Autumn:1992 pp. 21 – 36

14 Intermediation and the equilibrium allocation of investment capital — implications for economic development. John H. Boyd; Bruce D. Smith. *J. Monet. Ec.* **30:3** 12:1992 pp. 409 – 432

15 Internal net worth and the investment process — an application to U.S. agriculture. R. Glenn Hubbard; Anil K. Kashyap. *J. Polit. Ec.* **100:3** 6:1992 pp. 506 – 534

16 Investissement, profitabilité et croissance dans les années quatre-vingt *[In French]*; Investment, profitability and growth in the eighties *[Summary]*. Pierre-Alain Muet; Marie-Ange Véganzones. *Obser. Diag. Econ.* **:41** 7:1992 pp. 119 – 150

17 Modeling private investment in Egypt. N. Shafik. *J. Dev. Econ.* **39:2** 10:1992 pp. 263 – 277

18 Neoklassische und keynesianische Investitionstheorien. Synopse und Synthese *[In German]*; Neoclassical and Keynesian investment theories. Survey and synthesis *[Summary]*. Martin Klein. *Jahrb. N. St.* **209:3-4** 3:1992 pp. 207 – 222

19 The new Cambridge private expenditure model — a theoretical modification and empirical testing for Canada. Abu N.M. Wahid. *Econ. Aff. [Calcutta]* **37:4** 10-12:1992 pp. 199 – 216

20 Optimal internal investment in a labor-managed firm with heterogeneous membership — an overlapping generations approach. Meng-Hua Ye; Stephen C. Smith; Michael A. Conte. *J. Comp. Econ.* **16:3** 9:1992 pp. 479 – 493

21 Private investment, relative prices and business cycle in Malaysia; Investimento privato, prezzi relativi ciclo economico in Malaysia *[Italian summary]*. Gang Wee Beng. *Rev. Int. Sci. Ec. Com.* **XXXIX:9** 9:1992 pp. 753 – 769

22 Private saving in Mexico, 1980-90. Patricio Arrau; Daniel F. Oks. Washington, D.C.: International Economics Department and Country Department I, Latin America and the Caribbean, The World Bank, 1992: 47 p. [Policy research working papers.]

23 A regional comparison of the impact of changes in input prices on input demand for U.S. manufacturing. G.A. Garofalo; D.M. Malhotra. *Reg. Sci. Urb. Econ.* **22:2** 6:1992 pp. 213 – 228

24 The responsiveness of domestic investment to foreign economic conditions. Timothy Koechlin. *J. Post. Keyn. Ec.* **15:1** Fall:1992 pp. 63 – 84

25 Sequential-equilibrium investment by regulated firms. D. Besanko; D.F. Spulber. *Rand J. Eco.* **23:2** Summer:1992 pp. 153 – 170

26 Transitory variation in investment and output. Eugene F. Fama. *J. Monet. Ec.* **30:3** 12:1992 pp. 467 – 480

27 What happens to investment under structural adjustment — results from a simulation model. N.C. Benjamin. *World Dev.* **20:9** 9:1992 pp. 1335 – 1344

M: Social economics and policy — *Économie et politique sociales*

M.1: Basic concepts: social economics, social policy and justice, welfare — *Concepts de base: économie, politique, et justice sociales, bien-être*

1 Diamonds are forever (?) — Nassau Senior and utility theory. Michael V. White. *Manch. Sch. E.* **LX:1** 3:1992 pp. 64 – 78

2 Economía del bienestar — teoría y política económica *[In Spanish]*; Theory and policy in welfare economics *[Summary]*. Alberto Porto. *Económica Arg* **XXXV:1-2** 1989 pp. 71 – 100

3 Economía, ética social y escogencia colectiva — ¿Domando al leviatán? *[In Spanish]*; [Economics, social ethics and collective responsibility — The need for a leviation?]. Luis Fernando Medina Sierra. *Desar. Soc.* **:29** 3:1992 pp. 75 – 100

4 Economic policy precommitment and social welfare. Robin P. Cubitt. *J. Publ. Ec.* **49:2** 11:1992 pp. 191 – 201

5 The effect of information on health risk valuations. Alan J. Krupnick; Maureen L. Cropper. *J. Risk Uncert.* **5:1** 2:1992 pp. 29 – 48

M.1: Basic concepts: social economics, social policy and justice, welfare *[Concepts de base: économie, politique, et justice sociales, bien-être]*

6 The endogenous public choice theorist. U. Witt. *Publ. Choice* **73:1** 1:1992 pp. 117 – 130

7 Equity, efficiency, and incentives in a large economy. Yingyi Qian. *J. Comp. Econ.* **16:1** 3:1992 pp. 27 – 46

8 Fashion dynamics and the economic theory of clubs. Roy D. Adam; Ken McCormick. *R. Soc. Econ.* **L:1** Spring:1992 pp. 24 – 39

9 Generalized expected utility analysis and preference reversals — some initial results in the loss domain. D.N. MacDonald; W.L. Huth; P.M. Taube. *J. Econ. Beh.* **17:1** 1:1992 pp. 115 – 130

10 Hierarchical Arrow social welfare functions. T.E. Armstrong. *Econ. Theory* **2:1** 1992 pp. 27 – 42

11 Inequality and welfare in EEC countries. Panos Tsakloglou. *B. Econ. Res.* **44:1** 1:1992 pp. 21 – 38

12 The older the more valuable — divergence between utility and dollar values of life as one ages. Y.-K. Ng. *J. Econ.* **55:1** 1992 pp. 1 – 16

13 On measuring the quality of life. P. Dasgupta; M. Weale. *World Dev.* **20:1** 1:1992 pp. 119 – 132

14 Paternalistic altruism and the value of statistical life. M.W. Jones-Lee. *Econ. J.* **102:410** 1:1992 pp. 80 – 90

15 Precedence, privilege, preferences, plus Pareto principle — some examples on egalitarian ethics and economic efficiency. B.-A. Wickström. *Publ. Choice* **73:1** 1:1992 pp. 101 – 116

16 Principles and instruments of the social market economy. Karl Fasbender *[Ed.]*; Manfred Holthus *[Ed.]*; Eberhard Thiel *[Ed.]*. Hamburg: Verlag Weltarchiv, 1992: 310 p. *ISBN: 3878954352.* [Publication of HWWA-Institut für Wirtschaftsforschung Hamburg.]

17 Quadratic social welfare functions. Larry G. Epstein; Uzi Segal. *J. Polit. Ec.* **100:4** 8:1992 pp. 691 – 712

18 Schwierige Gleichheit — Prozedurale Gleichheit, materiale Gerechtigkeit und Leistungsfähigkeitsprinzip *[In German]*; [Difficult equality — procedural equality material justice and the principle of efficiency]. Richard Sturn. *Wirt. Blät.* **5/6:39** 1992 pp. 626 – 639

19 The second theorem of the second best. Karla Hoff. London: London School of Economics and Political Science. Suntory-Toyota International Centre for Economics and Related Disciplines, 1992: 47 p.

20 Sharpening the tools — a provisional 1988 social accounting matrix for South Africa. J.B. Eckert; D.E.N. van Seventer; A. Roukens de Lange. *Develop. S. Afr.* **9:2** 5:1992 pp. 243 – 256

21 The social viability of money — competitive equilibria and the core of overlapping generations economies. Joan Esteban. London: Springer, 1992: 202 p. *ISBN: 3540546499.* [Lecture notes in economics. : No. 372]

22 Social welfare in a common property oligopoly. Larry Karp. *Int. Econ. R.* **33:2** 5:1992 pp. 353 – 372

23 Strategy-proofness of social welfare functions — the use of the Kemeny distance between preference orderings. W. Bossert; T. Storcken. *Soc. Choice* **9:4** 1992 pp. 345 – 360

24 Transitive social choice in economic environments. Donald E. Campbell. *Int. Econ. R.* **33:2** 5:1992 pp. 341 – 352

25 Understanding welfare stigma — taxpayer resentment and statistical discrimination. Timothy Besley; Stephen Coate. *J. Publ. Ec.* **48:2** 7:1992 pp. 165 – 183

26 When Jack and Jill make a deal. Daniel M. Hausman. *Soc. Philos. Pol.* **9:1** Winter:1992 pp. 95 – 113

27 Where are the welfare losses of imperfect competition large? J. Willner; L. Ståhl. *Eur. J. Pol. Ec.* **8:3** 10:1992 pp. 477 – 491

M.2: Standard of living — *Niveau de vie*

1 Are estimates of calorie-income elasticities too high? A recalibration of the plausible range. H.E. Bouis; L.J. Haddad. *J. Dev. Econ.* **39:2** 10:1992 pp. 333 – 364

2 Die Auswirkungen des wirtschaftlichen Umbaus auf den Lebensstaadard in Polen (1990-1991) *[In German]*; (The impacts of economic transformation on the standard of living in Poland). Elzbieta Czarny; Bogusław Czarny. *Ost. Wirt.* **3** 1992 pp. 237 – 254

3 Basic needs, subsistence, and government; Bisogni fondamentali, sussistenza e governo *[Italian summary]*. Panayiotis C. Afxentiou. *Rev. Int. Sci. Ec. Com.* **XXXIX:3** 3:1992 pp. 193 – 210

4 Below the poverty line — poverty in Latin America. E. Cardoso; A. Helwege. *World Dev.* **20:1** 1:1992 pp. 19 – 38

5 Culture, cash and housing — community and tradition in low-income building. Maurice Mitchell; Andy Bevan. London: VSO/Intermediate Technology Publications, 1992: 130 p. *ISBN: 1853391530.*

6 Down and out in North America — recent trends in poverty rates in the United States and Canada. Maria J. Hanratty; Rebecca M. Blank. *Q. J. Econ.* **CVII:1** 2:1992 pp. 233 – 254

7 Economic aspects of global civilization — the unmet challenges of world poverty. Richard A. Falk. Princeton, NJ.: Center of International Studies, Princeton University, 1992: 43 p. *ISBN: oc26740006. Sequel to Positive prescriptions for the near future; Includes bibliographical references.* [World Order Studies Program occasional paper.]

8 Equivalence scale relativities and the extent of inequality and poverty. F.A.E. Coulter; F.A. Cowell; S.P. Jenkins. *Econ. J.* **102:414** 9:1992 pp. 1067 – 1082

9 Family time use — leisure, home production, market work, and work related travel. Eric J. Solberg; David C. Wong. *J. Hum. Res.* **XXVII:3** Summer:1992 pp. 485 – 510

10 A feminization of poverty in Great Britain? Robert E. Wright. *R. In. Weal.* **38:1** 3:1992 pp. 17 – 26

11 The future of the Survey of Income and Program Participation. C.F. Citro *[Contrib.]*; G. Kalton *[Contrib.]*; M.H. David *[Contrib.]*; G.G. Cain *[Contrib.]*; M.E. Manser *[Contrib.]*; M.S. Hill *[Contrib.]*; M. Adler *[Contrib.]*; M.P. Laplante *[Contrib.]*; R.M. Blank *[Contrib.]*; P. Ruggles *[Contrib.] and others. Collection of 17 articles.* **J. Econ. Soc.** , *18:1-4*, 1992 pp. 1 – 374

12 A gazdagság mérése *[In Hungarian]*; The measurement of wealth *[Summary]*. Katalin Martinás. *Közg. Sz.* **XXXIX** 2:1992 pp. 159 – 171

13 Homeownership affordability in England. Glen Bramley. *Hous. Pol. Deb.* **3:3** 1992 pp. 815 – 853

14 Hunger and poverty in Iraq, 1991. J. Drèze; H. Gazdar. *World Dev.* **20:7** 7:1992 pp. 921 – 945

15 Income distribution and infant mortality. Robert J. Waldmann. *Q. J. Econ.* **CVII:4** 11:1992 pp. 1283 – 1302

16 Income taxation, labor supply and the theory of income-based cost-of-living indices. M.R. Baye; D.A. Black. *Eur. Econ. R.* **36:1** 1:1992 pp. 83 – 100

17 Intercountry inequalities in income and basic-needs indicators — a recent perspective. R. Ram. *World Dev.* **20:6** 6:1992 pp. 899 – 906

18 Living decently. Peter Travers; Sue Richardson. *Aust. Ec. Rev.* **3rd quarter** 7-9:1992 pp. 29 – 42

19 Matching and a technology-induced skewness in income distributions. Y.J. Lin; F.T. Lui. *Math. Soc. Sc.* **25:1** 12:1992 pp. 1 – 13

20 Measures of economic well-being as predictors of psychological well-being. Randolph J. Mullis. *Soc. Ind.* **26:2** 3:1992 pp. 119 – 135

21 Measuring living standards. Helen Brownlee. Melbourne: Australian Institute of Family Studies, 1991: 65 p. *ISBN: 0642163596.* [AIFS Australian living standards study.]

22 Measuring poverty and differences in family composition. A.B. Atkinson. *Economica* **59:233** 2:1992 pp. 1 – 16

23 Methods of estimating house equivalence scales — an empirical investigation. Julie A. Nelson. *R. In. Weal.* **38:3** 9:1992 pp. 295 – 310

24 Micro-economic definitions of poverty. Klaas de Vos. Rotterdam: Universiteits Drukkerij, 1991: 252 p.

25 New budget standard poverty lines for Malaysia. Muniappan Perumal. *R. In. Weal.* **38:3** 9:1992 pp. 341 – 353

M.2: Standard of living *[Niveau de vie]*

26 On the chronically poor in rural India. R. Gaiha. *J. Int. Dev.* **4:3** 5-6:1992 pp. 273 – 289

27 On the measurement of poverty — conceptual issues and estimation problems. Markus Jäntti. Åbo: Åbo Akademi, 1990: ii, 81, 30 p. ill *ISBN: oc23708300. Includes bibliographical references (p. 78-81).* [Meddelanden Fran Ekonomisk-Statsvetenskapliga Fakulteten Vid Abo Akademi.]

28 La política económica neoliberal y sus efectos socioeconómicos. El caso de Chile *[In Spanish]*; [Neoliberal economic policy and its socio-economic effects — the case of Chile]. José A. Déniz Espinós. *Cuad. Am.* **2:32** 3-4:1992 pp. 77 – 87

29 Political democracy, military size and income inequality. John Mukum Mbaku. *Ind. J. Pol. Sci.* **LIII:2** 4-6:1992 pp. 127 – 151

30 Poverty in Poland, 1978-88. Branko Milanovic. *R. In. Weal.* **38:3** 9:1992 pp. 329 – 340

31 Prices, infrastructure, household characteristics and child height. D. Thomas; J. Strauss. *J. Dev. Econ.* **39:2** 10:1992 pp. 301 – 331

32 Real life economics — understanding wealth creation. Paul Ekins *[Ed.]*; Manfred A. Max-Neef *[Ed.]*. London: Routledge, 1992: 460 p. *ISBN: 0415079764; LofC: 92008827. Includes bibliographical references and index.*

33 The relationship between meures of subjective and economic well-being — a new look. Robin A. Douthitt; Maurice Macdonald; Randolph Mullins. *Soc. Ind.* **26:4** 6:1992 pp. 407 – 422

34 Rural poverty and its measurement — a comparative study of villages in Nusa Penida, Bali. Carunia Firdausy; Clem Tisdell. *B. Ind. Econ. St.* **28:2** 8:1992 pp. 75 – 94

35 Rural poverty in India — an analysis of inter-state differences. Rohini Nayyar. Bombay: Oxford University Press, 1991: x, 297 p. *ISBN: 0195625579. Includes bibliographical references (p. [284]-291) and index.*

36 The state of world rural poverty. Idris Jazairy; Mohiuddin Alamgir; Theresa Panuccio. London: Intermediate Technology Publications for International Fund for Agricultural Development, 1992: 515 p.

37 Why the U.S. antipoverty system doesn't work very well. Timothy M. Smeeding. *Challenge* **35:1** 1-2:1992 pp. 30 – 35

M.3: Social policy, welfare policy — *Politique sociale, politique de bien-être*

1 Economic theory and the welfare state — a survey and interpretation. Nicholas Barr. *J. Econ. Lit.* **XXX:2** 6:1992 pp. 741 – 803

2 The economics of poverty alleviation — the Janasaviya programme in Sri Lanka. Patrick Mendis. *S.Asia. J.* **5:3** 1-3:1992 pp. 289 – 298

3 The economics of social responsibility in the European Community. Peter Curwen. *Economics* **XXVIII:4(120)** Winter:1992 pp. 156 – 162

4 Identifying welfare state regimes — the links between politics, instruments and outcomes. Deborah Mitchell; Francis G. Castles. *Governance* **5:1** 1:1992 pp. 1 – 26

5 The intergenerational transfer of welfare dependency — some statistical evidence. John J. Antel. *Rev. Econ. St.* **LXXIV:3** 8:1992 pp. 467 – 473

6 Making sense of the mixed economy of welfare. Robert Pinker. *Soc. Pol. Admin.* **26:4** 12:1992 pp. 273 – 284

7 The mixed economy of welfare. Linda Hantrais *[Ed.]*; Margaret O'Brien *[Ed.]*; Stephen P. Mangen *[Ed.]*. Loughborough: Cross-National Research Group,European Research Group,Loughborough University, 1992: 68 p. [Cross-National research papers.]

8 Needs and targeting. M. Keen. *Econ. J.* **102:410** 1:1992 pp. 67 – 79

9 *[In Japanese]*; On the tax reform — from the viewpoint of economic welfare *[Summary]*. Haruhiko Korekawa. *Econ. S. Quart.* **43:3** 9:1992 pp. 246 – 257

10 Paying for or providing welfare? Julian le Grand. Bristol: University of Bristol, School for Advanced Urban Studies, 1992: 27 p. *ISBN: 1873575378.* [Studies in decentralisation & quasi-markets.]

11 The politics of protecting the poor during adjustment — Bolivia's emergency social fund. C. Graham. *World Dev.* **20:9** 9:1992 pp. 1233 – 1252

12 Tax expenditures on health in Australia — 1960-61 to 1988-89. J.R.G. Butler; J.P. Smith. *Aust. Ec. Rev.* **3rd quarter** 7-9:1992 pp. 43 – 58

M.3: Social policy, welfare policy *[Politique sociale, politique de bien-être]*

13 Velferdsstaten — offentlig politikk og private incitamenter *[In Norwegian]*; The welfare state — public policies and private incentives *[Summary]*. Agnar Sandimo. *Nor. Økon. Tidss.* **106:1** 1992 pp. 1 – 16

14 The welfare state — alternative strategies for the 1990s. Dexter Whitfield. London: Pluto Press, 1992: 545 p. *ISBN: 074530608x; LofC: 91035959. Includes bibliographical references and index.*

M.4: Social security, social assistance, occupational safety — *Sécurité sociale, assistance sociale, sécurité du travail*

Sub-divisions: Health insurance and services *[Assurance maladie et services de santé]*; Pensions *[Pensions]*; Social security *[Sécurité sociale]*

1 Alternative delivery systems in the provision of social services. Patricia Brown. *Int. Rev. Admin. Sci.* **58:2** 6:1992 pp. 201 – 214

2 Child care. David M. Blau *[Contrib.]*; James R. Walker *[Contrib.]*; Sandra L. Hofferth *[Contrib.]*; Douglas A. Wissoker *[Contrib.]*; Arleen Leibowitz *[Contrib.]*; Jacob Alex Klerman *[Contrib.]*; Linda J. Waite *[Contrib.]*; David C. Ribar *[Contrib.]*; Charles Michalopoulos *[Contrib.]*; Philip K. Robins *[Contrib.] and others. Collection of 8 articles.* **J. Hum. Res.** , *XXVII:1*, Winter: 1992 pp. 9 – 230

3 The consequences and costs of maternal substance abuse in New York City — a pooled time-series, cross-section analysis. T. Joyce; A.D. Racine; N. Mocan. *J. Health Econ.* **11:3** 10:1992 pp. 297 – 314

4 Cost effectiveness/utility analyses — do current decision rules lead us to where we want to be? S. Birch; A. Gafni. *J. Health Econ.* **11:3** 10:1992 pp. 279 – 296

5 The evaluation of rural development projects using the social accounting matrix approach; *[Portuguese summary]*. Manuel J. Rojas Buvinich. *Rev. Bras. Ec.* **46:4** 10/12:1992 pp. 555 – 594

6 Older peoples' experiences of community care. David Barrett. *Soc. Pol. Admin.* **26:4** 12:1992 pp. 296 – 312

7 Population ageing and intergenerational conflict — a post-Keynesian view. William A. Jackson. *J. Econ. Stud.* **19:2** 1992 pp. 26 – 37

8 Professional versus consumer interests in regulation — the case of the U.S. child care industry. A.D. Lowenberg; T.D. Tinnin. *Appl. Econ.* **24:6** 6:1992 pp. 571 – 580

9 Reassessing federal disability insurance. Carolyn L. Weaver. *Publ. Inter.* **:106** Winter: 1992 pp. 108 – 121

10 Substitution between unemployment insurance and workers' compensation — an analysis applied to the risk of workplace accidents. Bernard Fortin; Paul Lanoie. *J. Publ. Ec.* **49:3** 12:1992 pp. 287 – 312

Health insurance and services *[Assurance maladie et services de santé]*

11 Adverse selection with a multiple choice among health insurance plans — a simulation analysis. M.S. Marquis. *J. Health Econ.* **11:2** 8:1992 pp. 129 – 152

12 Advertising and the price, quantity, and quality of primary care physician services. John A. Rizzo; Richard J. Zeckhauser. *J. Hum. Res.* **XXVII:3** Summer:1992 pp. 381 – 421

13 An alternative framework for evaluating welfare losses in the health care market. T. Rice. *J. Health Econ.* **11:1** 1992 pp. 85 – 92

14 Assessing the impact of economic reform in medical services in the Netherlands. W. Zant. *Appl. Econ.* **24:2** 2:1992 pp. 227 – 236

15 Budgetkonsolidierung und Krankenhausreform *[In German]*; [Budgetary consolidation and hospital reform]. Andreas Altmann; Engelbert Theurl. *Wirt. Blät.* **39:2** 1992 pp. 202 – 215

16 Can the poor afford "free" health services? A case study of Tanzania. Brian Abel-Smith; Pankaj Rawal. *Health Pol. Plan.* **7:4** 1992 pp. 329 – 341

17 Case mix adjusted nursing-home reimbursement — a critical review of the evidence. William G. Weissert; Melissa Constable Musliner. *Milbank Q.* **70:3** 1992 pp. 455 – 490

18 Cigarette smoking and lifetime medical expenditures. Thomas A. Hodgson. *Milbank Q.* **70:1** 1992 pp. 81 – 126

M.4: Social security, social assistance, occupational safety *[Sécurité sociale, assistance sociale, sécurité du travail] — Health insurance and services [Assurance maladie et services de santé]*

19 Commitment problems justify subsidies for medical insurance. Amihai Glazer; Esko Niskanen. *Geneva Pap. Risk Insur. Theory* **17:2** 12:1992 pp. 137 – 145

20 Cost containment and new priorities in the European Community. Brian Abel-Smith. *Milbank Q.* **70:3** 1992 pp. 393 – 416

21 The costs of hospital at home — the case of the New Brunswick extra-mural hospital. B. Ferguson; S. Barry. *Appl. Econ.* **24:10** 10:1992 pp. 1107 – 1118

22 Determinanten des Gesundheitszustands. Ein empirischer Ansatz zur Outputmessung im Gesundheitswesen bei partieller Information *[In German]*; [The determinants of health. An empirical estimate of the output rate in the health service on partial information]. Winfried Pohlmeier; Volker Ulrich. *Z. Wirt. Soz.* **112:2** 1992 pp. 219 – 238

23 Determinants of health expenditures in Greece in the postwar period — an empirical investigation; Le determinanti delle spese sanitarie in Grecia nel periodo postbellico —uno studio empirico *[Italian summary]*. George Karatzas. *Rev. Int. Sci. Ec. Com.* **XXXIX:1** 1:1992 pp. 69 – 90

24 An econometric analysis of health care expenditure — a cross-section study of the OECD countries. U.-G. Gerdtham; J Søgaard; F. Andersson; B. Jönsson. *J. Health Econ.* **11:1** 1992 pp. 63 – 84

25 L'economia sanitaria nella formazione manageriale — prospettive e problemi *[In Italian]*; [Health economics in management development — prospects and problems] *[Summary]*. A. Brenna. *Riv. Int. Sci. Soc.* **C:1** 1-3:1992 pp. 29 – 40

26 The economics of AIDS-related health insurance regulations — interest group influence and ideology. R.L. Ohsfeldt; S.F. Gohmann. *Publ. Choice* **74:1** 7:1992 pp. 105 – 126

27 The effect of per-item fees on the behaviour of general practitioners. D. Hughes; B. Yule. *J. Health Econ.* **11:4** 1992 pp. 413 – 437

28 The effect of the medicaid program on welfare participation and labor supply. Robert Moffitt; Barbara Wolfe. *Rev. Econ. St.* **LXXIV:4** 11:1992 pp. 615 – 626

29 The effects of market structure and bargaining position on hospital prices. G.A. Melnick; J. Zwanziger; A. Bamezai; R. Pattison. *J. Health Econ.* **11:3** 10:1992 pp. 217 – 233

30 Empirische Ergebnisse zur Ausgabenbelastung der Gesetzlichen Krankenversicherung durch einzelne Mitgliedsgruppen *[In German]*; Some empirical evidence of the expenditures caused by different categories of persons in the German statutory health insurance system *[Summary]*. Holger Mühlenkamp. *Jahrb. N. St.* **209:3-4** 3:1992 pp. 302 – 322

31 Equity in the delivery of health care — some international comparisons. E. van Doorslaer; A. Wagstaff. *J. Health Econ.* **11:4** 1992 pp. 389 – 411

32 Equity in the finance of health care — some international comparisons. A. Wagstaff; E. van Doorslaer. *J. Health Econ.* **11:4** 1992 pp. 361 – 387

33 Estimating the indirect costs of teaching. J.A. Rogowski; J.P. Newhouse. *J. Health Econ.* **11:2** 8:1992 pp. 153 – 172

34 Финансовый контроль в здравоохранении *[In Russian]*; [Financial control and public health care]. I.D. Serdyukova. *Finansy* **:12** 1992 pp. 51 – 55

35 Finding the optimal allocation to a health-care reimbursement account. T.S. Nunnikhoven. *Insur. Math. Econ.* **11:3** 10:1992 pp. 223 – 236

36 La gestion et l'évaluation dans le secteur des soins de santé *[In French]*; Management and evaluation in the medical sector *[Summary]*. Bernard Morell. *Gestion* **8:1** 1992 pp. 87 – 98

37 The growth of public health care expenditure. David Whynes. *Soc. Pol. Admin.* **26:4** 12:1992 pp. 285 – 295

38 Health care finance — economic incentives and productivity enhancement. Steven R. Eastaugh. Westport CT: Auburn House, 1992: 540 p. *ISBN: 0865690499.*

39 Health economics — efficiency, quality, and equity. Steven R. Eastaugh. Westport, CO.: Auburn House, 1992: xiv, 465 p. (ill) *ISBN: 0865691967; LofC: 91026275. Companion v. to — Health care finance. 1992; Includes bibliographical references and indexes.*

40 Health, wealth and time preference. John Cairns. *Proj. App.* **7:1** 3:1992 pp. 31 – 40

41 Hospital expenditures in the United States and Canada — do hospital worker wages explain the differences? S.G. Haber; J. Zwanziger; G.M. Anderson; K.E. Thorpe; J.P. Newhouse. *J. Health Econ.* **11:4** 1992 pp. 453 – 465

42 Hospitals in developing countries — in the perspective of limited resources. Naruo Uehara; Takashi Wagatsuma. *Tech. Devel.* **:5** 1:1992 pp. 17 – 34

43 Impacy of varying Medigap insurance coverage on the use of medical services of the elderly. W.S. Cartwright; T.-W. Hu; L.-F. Huang. *Appl. Econ.* **24:5** 5:1992 pp. 529 – 539

M.4: Social security, social assistance, occupational safety *[Sécurité sociale, assistance sociale, sécurité du travail]* **— Health insurance and services** *[Assurance maladie et services de santé]*

44 Indigent health care in Texas. Jung-Woo Kim. *Asian Ec.* :**82** 9:1992 pp. 66 – 88

45 The interaction between forms of insurance contract and types of technical change in medical care. J.R. Baumgardner. *Rand J. Eco.* **22:1** Spring:1991 pp. 36 – 53

46 Is hospital competition wasteful? D. Dranove; M. Shanley; C. Simon. *Rand J. Eco.* **23:2** Summer:1992 pp. 247 – 262

47 Issues regarding health plan payments under Medicare and recommendations for reform. Bryan Dowd; Jon Christianson; Roger Feldman; Catherine Wisner; John Klein. *Milbank Q.* **70:3** 1992 pp. 423 – 453

48 Medical care costs — how much welfare loss? Joseph P. Newhouse. *J. Econ. Pers.* **6:3** Summer:1992 pp. 3 – 22

49 Medical cost inflation and the evaluation of preventive health care; Inflazione da costi per spese sanitarie e stima delle cure preventive *[Italian summary]*. M.S. Marzouk. *Rev. Int. Sci. Ec. Com.* **XXXIX:5-6** 5-6:1992 pp. 439 – 456

50 The mystique of markets — public and private health care in developing countries. Sara Bennett. London: London School of Hygiene and Tropical Medicine, 1991: 70 p. [PHP departmental publication.]

51 Need, equity and the NHS — the distribution of health care expenditure 1974-87. Carol Propper; Richard Upward. *Fis. Stud.* **13:2** 5:1992 pp. 1 – 21

52 Organizing the health insurance market. Peter Diamond. *Econometrica* **60:6** 11:1992 pp. 1233 – 1254

53 The political economy of health and medical care — the Ghanaian experience. Randolph Quaye. *Scand. J. Devel. Altern.* **XI:1** 3:1992 pp. 5 – 26

54 Private insurance reform in the 1990s — can it solve the health care crisis? Thomas Bodenheimer. *Int. J. Health. Ser.* **22:2** 1992 pp. 197 – 216

55 Quality-adjusted cost functions and policy evaluation in the nursing home industry. Paul J. Gertler; Donald M. Waldman. *J. Polit. Ec.* **100:6** 12:1992 pp. 1232 – 1256

56 Reconciling increasing capability and decreasing flexibility in medical care — information infrastructure requirements for professional work in an era of cost containment. R.A. Greenes. *Jpn. Wor. Econ.* **4:3** 11:1992 pp. 251 – 271

57 Relevance of social market conditions in the German health care system to the United States. Francis D. Powell. *R. Soc. Econ.* **L:3** Fall:1992 pp. 269 – 296

58 Riforma del salario, finanziamento del servizio sanitario nazionale e crescita economica *[In Italian]*; Wage reform, functioning of the national health service and economic growth *[Summary]*. Alberto Heimler; Carlo Milana. *Ec. Lav.* **XXVI:1** 1-3:1992 pp. 67 – 78

59 A risk-based prospective payment system that integrates patient, hospital and national costs. C. Siegel; K. Jones; E. Laska; M. Meisner; S. Lin. *J. Health Econ.* **11:1** 1992 pp. 1 – 42

60 Sensitivity analysis for DEA models — an empirical example using public vs. NFP hospitals. Vivian Valdmanis. *J. Publ. Ec.* **48:2** 7:1992 pp. 185 – 205

61 Smoking, health costs and public policy. J.V. Koch; R.J. Cebula. *Am. J. Econ. S.* **51:2** 4:1992 pp. 159 – 160

62 Sociological and economic theories of markets and nonprofits — evidence from home health organizations. Lee Clarke; Carroll L. Estes. *A.J.S.* **97:4** 1:1992 pp. 945 – 969

63 Some economic implications of a universal national health insurance program in the Republic of China. Peter C. Lin. *Ind. Free China* **LXXVIII:4** 10:1992 pp. 35 – 44

64 State mandated benefits and the small firm's decision to offer insurance. Gail A. Jensen; Jon R. Gabel. *J. Regul. Econ.* **4:4** 12:1992 pp. 379 – 404

65 The supply of charity services by nonprofit hospitals — motives and market structure. R.G. Frank; D.S. Salkever. *Rand J. Eco.* **22:3** Autumn:1991 pp. 430 – 445

66 Who pays for measles? The economic arguments for sustained immunization. Neil Andersson; Sergio Paredes; Jose Legorreta; Robert J. Ledogar. *Health Pol. Plan.* **7:4** 1992 pp. 352 – 363

Pensions *[Pensions]*

67 Analysis of a national private pension scheme — the case of Chile. Colin Gillion; Alejandro Bonilla. *Int. Lab. Rev.* **131:2** 1992 pp. 171 – 196

68 Characteristics of early and late adopters of pension accounting standard; *[French summary]*. H. Sami; M.J. Welsh. *Cont. Account. Res.* **9:1** Fall:1992 pp. 212 – 236

69 A critical perspective on pension accounting, pension research and pension terminations. S.A. Reiter; T. Omer. *Crit. Persp. Acc.* **3:1** 3:1992 pp. 61 – 86

M.4: Social security, social assistance, occupational safety *[Sécurité sociale, assistance sociale, sécurité du travail]* — *Pensions [Pensions]*

70 Decision making on pension schemes under rational expectations. H. Verbon; M.J.M. Verhoeven. *J. Econ.* **56:1** 1992 pp. 71 – 97

71 Does a public pension system reduce savings rates and birth rates? Bernhard Felderer. *J. Inst. Theo. Ec.* **148:2** 6:1992 pp. 314 – 325

72 The economics of flexible retirement. A.T. Mallier; T.A.C. Shafto. London: Academic Press, 1992: 180 p. *ISBN: 0124666108.*

73 Financing state pensions in alternative pay-as-you-go schemes. John Creedy; Richard Disney. *B. Econ. Res.* **44:1** 1:1992 pp. 39 – 54

74 Fiscal implications of an aging population. Dieter Bös *[Ed.]*; Sijbren Cnossen *[Ed.]*. Berlin: Springer-Verlag, 1992: 191 p. *ISBN: 0387550720; LofC: 92008110.* [Population economics.]

75 The future of pensions in the European Community. Jorgen Mortensen *[Ed.]*. London: Brassey's, 1992: 231 p. *ISBN: 1857530578.*

76 How pension investment policy drains American economic strength. Herbert A. Whitehouse. *Columb. J. W. Bus.* **27:1** Spring:1992 pp. 22 – 37

77 Issues in pension funding. David Blake. London: Routledge, 1992: 127 p. *ISBN: 0415075319; LofC: 92005053. Includes bibliographical references and index.*

78 Life-cycle valuation of social security and pension wealth. Thad W. Mirer. *J. Publ. Ec.* **48:3** 8:1992 pp. 377 – 384

79 Mennyibe kerül egy társadalombiztosítási nyugdíjrendszer működtetése? I. Biztosítástechnikai alapfogalmak *[In Hungarian]*; What is the cost of a pension system operating in the frame work of social insurance? Part I. Basic notions of insurance techniques *[Summary]*. Péter Bod. *Közg. Sz.* **XXXIX** 2:1992 pp. 123 – 145

80 Mennyibe kerül egy társadalombiztosítási nyugdíjrendszer működtetése? II. A finanszírozási típusokról *[In Hungarian]*; What is the cost of a pension system operating in the framework of social insurance? II. On the types of financing *[Summary]*. Péter Bod. *Közg. Sz.* **XXXIX** 3:1992 pp. 244 – 261

81 Modelling pension fund investment behaviour. David Blake. London: Routledge, 1992: 282 p. *ISBN: 0415009898; LofC: 91025719. Includes bibliographical references and index.*

82 A nyugdíjrendszer válsága *[In Hungarian]*; The crisis of the pension system *[Summary]*. Augusztinovics Mária. *Közg. Sz.* **XXXIX:** 7-8:1992 pp. 624 – 641

83 Pay-as-you-go public pensions with endogenous fertility. Kazuo Nishimura; Junsen Zhang. *J. Publ. Ec.* **48:2** 7:1992 pp. 239 – 258

84 Paying for early retirement. Bernard Casey. *J. Soc. Pol.* **21:3** 7:1992 pp. 303 – 324

85 Pension and tax structures in an ageing population. John Creedy; Margaret H. Morgan. *J. Econ. Stud.* **19:3** 1992 pp. 50 – 65

86 Pension reversions and worker-stockholder wealth transfers. Mitchell A. Petersen. *Q. J. Econ.* **CVII:3** 8:1992 pp. 1033 – 1056

87 Pensions and wages — an hedonic price theory approach. Edward Montgomery; Kathryn Shaw; Mary Ellen Benedict. *Int. Econ. R.* **33:1** 2:1992 pp. 111 – 128

88 Personal pensions and the review of the contracting-out terms. Richard Disney; Edward Whitehouse. *Fis. Stud.* **13:1** 2:1992 pp. 38 – 53

89 The personal pensions stampede. Richard Disney; Edward Whitehouse. London: Institute for Fiscal Studies, 1992: 46 p. *ISBN: 1873357141.*

90 Public debt and pension policy. Lans Bovenberg; Carel Petersen. *Fis. Stud.* **13:3** 8:1992 pp. 1 – 14

91 The rationale and performance of personal pensions plans in Chile. Dimitri Vittas; Augusto Iglesias. Washington, D.C.: Country Economics Department, The World Bank, 1992: 38 p. [Policy research working papers.]

92 Retirement decisions in a discrete choice model and implications for the government budget. The case of Belgium. G. Pepermans. *J. Pop. Ec.* **5:3** 1992 pp. 229 – 243

93 Retraites et évolutions démographiques en France *[In French]*; Pensions and demographics in France — a long-run perspective *[Summary]*. Sandrine Cazes; Thierry Chauveau; Jacques le Cacheux; Rahim Loufir. *Obser. Diag. Econ.* **:39** 1:1992 pp. 93 – 150

94 The rise and rise of occupational superannuation. Rhonda Sharpe. *J. Aust. Pol. Econ.* **:30** 12:1992 pp. 24 – 41

95 Il ruolo della previdenza integrativa negli USA — interpretazioni teoriche *[In Italian]*; [The role of integrative foresight in the USA — theoretical interpretations]. Clara Busana Banterle. *Riv. Dir. Finan. Sci. Fin.* **LI:2** 6:1992 pp. 185 – 228

M.4: Social security, social assistance, occupational safety *[Sécurité sociale, assistance sociale, sécurité du travail]* — **Pensions** *[Pensions]*

96 Saving for the future — a comparative study of "saving policies" in Singapore and Australia. Georgina Carnegie; Daryl Dixon. Carlton South, Vic: Australian Commission for the Future, 1991: 64 p. (ill) *ISBN: 1875637001. Includes bibliographical references (p. 61-63).*

97 What pension should the state provide? Andrew Dilnot; Paul Johnson. *Fis. Stud.* **13:4** 11:1992 pp. 1 – 20

98 Workers as owners — the ideology and practice of personal pensions. Barbara Waine. *Econ. Soc.* **21:1** 2:1992 pp. 27 – 44

Social security *[Sécurité sociale]*

99 Alternative proposals on tax and social security. Evan Davis; et al. London: Institute for Fiscal Studies, 1992: 45 p. *ISBN: 1873357168.* [IFS commentary. : No. 29]

100 Child support, routine income withholding, and post-divorce income. Marieka M. Klawitter; Irwin Garfinkel. *Cont. Policy* **X:1** 1:1992 pp. 52 – 64

101 A critical perspective on pension accounting, pension research and pension terminations. S.A. Reiter; T. Omer. *Crit. Persp. Acc.* **3:1** 3:1992 pp. 61 – 86

102 Immigrant welfare recipiency — recent trends and future implications. Stephen J. Trejo. *Cont. Policy* **X:2** 4:1992 pp. 44 – 53

103 Life-cycle valuation of social security and pension wealth. Thad W. Mirer. *J. Publ. Ec.* **48:3** 8:1992 pp. 377 – 384

104 Lone mothers, family credit and paid work. Andrew Dilnot; Alan Duncan. *Fis. Stud.* **13:1** 2:1992 pp. 1 – 21

105 Mennyibe kerül egy társadalombiztosítási nyugdíjrendszer működtetése? I. Biztosítástechnikai alapfogalmak *[In Hungarian]*; What is the cost of a pension system operating in the frame work of social insurance? Part I. Basic notions of insurance techniques *[Summary]*. Péter Bod. *Közg. Sz.* **XXXIX** 2:1992 pp. 123 – 145

106 Mennyibe kerül egy társadalombiztosítási nyugdíjrendszer működtetése? II. A finanszírozási típusokról *[In Hungarian]*; What is the cost of a pension system operating in the framework of social insurance? II. On the types of financing *[Summary]*. Péter Bod. *Közg. Sz.* **XXXIX** 3:1992 pp. 244 – 261

107 On the time consistency of the government's social security benefit policy. Raymond G. Batina. *J. Monet. Ec.* **29:3** 6:1992 pp. 475 – 486

108 Pay-as-you-go public pensions with endogenous fertility. Kazuo Nishimura; Junsen Zhang. *J. Publ. Ec.* **48:2** 7:1992 pp. 239 – 258

109 Paying for welfare — the 1990s. Howard Glennerster. Hemel Hempstead: Harvester-Wheatsheaf, 1992: 315 p. *ISBN: 0745009972.*

110 The politics of universalism — the case of Finnish sickness insurance. Olli Kangas. *J. Soc. Pol.* **21:1** 1:1992 pp. 25 – 52

111 Privatizing social security — the Chilean case. Marco Santamaria. *Columb. J. W. Bus.* **27:1** Spring:1992 pp. 38 – 51

112 Racjonalizacja gospodarki finansowej świadczeń społecznych *[In Polish]*; [Rationalizing the financing of social benefits]. Janusz Chechliński *[Contrib.]*; Jan Sobiech *[Contrib.]*; Janusz Wierzbicki *[Contrib.]*; Krystyna Piotrowska-Marczak *[Contrib.]*; Wiktor Rutkowski *[Contrib.]*; Johannes Gurtz *[Contrib.]*; Vladimir Kylink *[Contrib.]*; Lila Mackiewicz-Golnik *[Contrib.]*; Anatoli Zawiałow *[Contrib.]*; Janusz A. Indulski *[Contrib.] and others. Collection of 18 articles.* **Acta Univ. Łódz.**, *115*, 1992 pp. 5 – 228

113 The role of unemployment insurance in an economy with liquidity constraints and moral hazard. Gary D. Hansen; Ayşe Imrohoroğlu. *J. Polit. Ec.* **100:1** 2:1992 pp. 118 – 142

114 Social insurance. A. B. Atkinson. London: STICERD, 1991: 31 p. [Discussion paper.]

115 Social insurance in developing countries — are there net benefits to program participation? Matthew N. Murray; Donna S. Bueckman. *J. Dev. Areas* **26:2** 1:1992 pp. 193 – 212

116 The social safety net. A. B. Atkinson. London: STICERD, 1991: 43 p. [Discussion paper.]

117 Social security in transition economies. J. Micklewright *[Contrib.]*; D. Blanchet *[Contrib.]*; D. Kessler *[Contrib.]*; W. Schmähl *[Contrib.]*. **Publ. Finan.**, *47*, 1992 pp. 1 – 56

118 Social security rules and marginal tax rates. Martin Feldstein; Andrew Samwick. *Natl. Tax. J.* **XLV:1** 3:1992 pp. 1 – 22

119 Social security, longevity, and moral hazard. James B. Davies; Peter Kuhn. *J. Publ. Ec.* **49:1** 10:1992 p.91-106

120 A szociális védőháló közgazdaságtana és a kelet-közép-európai átmenet *[In Hungarian]*; The economics of social safety nets and the transition in Eastern and Central Europe *[Summary]*. Kálmán Rupp. *Közg. Sz.* **XXXIX** 5:1992 pp. 425 – 447

M.4: Social security, social assistance, occupational safety *[Sécurité sociale, assistance sociale, sécurité du travail]* — *Social security [Sécurité sociale]*

121 Unemployment benefits and labour market transitions in Britain. Jonathan Wadsworth. London: London School of Economics and Political Science. Centre for Economic Performance, 1992: 34 p. [Discussion paper.]

122 Vermindert die bestehende Sozialhilfe das Arbeitsangebot? *[In German]*; [The labour supply effects of German social assistance for the needy] *[Summary]*. Joachim Weeber. *Konjunkturpolitik* **38:2** 1992 pp. 55 – 68

M.5: Economics of education — *Économie de l'éducation*

1 An analysis of the probability of default on federally guaranteed student loans. Laura Greene Knapp; Terry G. Seaks. *Rev. Econ. St.* **LXXIV:3** 8:1992 pp. 404 – 411

2 Basic education and national development — lessons from China and India. Manzoor Ahmed; et al. Paris: UNICEF, 1992: 265 p. *ISBN: 9280610627.*

3 Benefits of compensatory preschool education. W. Steven Barnett. *J. Hum. Res.* **XXVII:2** Spring:1992 pp. 279 – 312

4 Changing patterns of finance in higher education. Gareth L. Willams. Buckingham [England]: Society for Research into Higher Education, 1992: 173 p. *ISBN: 0335156649; LofC: 91046669. Includes bibliographical references and index.*

5 A contractual approach to higher education performance — with an application to Australia. James M. Ferris. *High. Educ.* **24:4** 12:1992 pp. 503 – 516

6 The demand for education with "power equalizing" aid — estimation and simulation. Paul Rothstein. *J. Publ. Ec.* **49:2** 11:1992 pp. 135 – 162

7 La direction d'un établissement d'enseignement secondaire *[In French]*; Running a secondary school *[Summary]*. Michéle Garant. *Gestion* **8:1** 1992 pp. 109 – 124

8 Does school quality matter? Returns to education and the characteristics of public schools in the United States. David Card; Alan B. Krueger. *J. Polit. Ec.* **100:1** 2:1992 pp. 1 – 40

9 Earnings and education among self-employed males in Colombia. George Psacharopoulos; Ana Maria Arriagada; Eduardo Velez. *B. Lat. Am. Res.* **11:1** 1:1992 pp. 69 – 89

10 Economic incentives and political institutions — spending and voting in school budget referenda. Thomas Romer; Howard Rosenthal; Vincent G. Munley. *J. Publ. Ec.* **49:1** 10:1992 pp. 1 – 33

11 The economic relevance of Irish education — an emerging debate. John Sheehan. *Irish Bank. Rev.* Autumn:1992 pp. 27 – 42

12 The economics of public investment in education in Papua New Guinea. Timothy Curtin. Waigani: University of Papua New Guinea Press, 1991: v, 164 p. *ISBN: 998084034x. Includes bibliographical references (p.130-136) and index; Faculty of Education occasional paper.* [Occasional paper.]

13 Education in Asia — a comparative study of cost and financing. Jee-Peng Tan; Alain Mingat. Washington, DC: The World Bank, 1992: xvii, 204 p. *ISBN: 082132098x; LofC: 92011537. Includes bibliographical references (p. 198-204).* [World Bank regional and sectoral studies.]

14 Educational attainment and earnings determination in Colombia. Noel Gaston; Jaime Tenjo. *Econ. Dev. Cult. Change* **41:1** 10:1992 pp. 125 – 139

15 Effect of class size on economies of scale and marginal costs in higher education. R. Nelson; K.T. Hevert. *Appl. Econ.* **24:5** 5:1992 pp. 473 – 482

16 The effect of subsidies in kind on the choice of a college. Philip T. Ganderton. *J. Publ. Ec.* **48:3** 8:1992 pp. 269 – 292

17 Esquemos alternativos de transferências e qualidade do ensino universitário *[In Portuguese]*; [Alternative payment schemes and their impact on university-level education] *[Summary]*. Pedro Pitta Barros. *Economia [Lisbon]* **XV:3** 10:1991 pp. 445 – 452

18 Has federal student aid contributed to equality in higher education? G.W. Sazama. *Am. J. Econ. S.* **51:2** 4:1992 pp. 129 – 146

19 High tuition, financial aid, and cross-subsidization — do needy students really benefit? David C. Rose; Robert L. Sorensen. *S. Econ. J.* **59:1** 7:1992 pp. 66 – 76

20 Higher education. Martin Cave *[Contrib.]*; Martin Weale *[Contrib.]*; Geraint Johnes *[Contrib.]*; Paul Hare *[Contrib.]*; Geoffrey Wyatt *[Contrib.]*; Ewart Keep *[Contrib.]*; Keith Sisson *[Contrib.]*; Ruth Dodsworth *[Contrib.]*; David Thompson *[Contrib.]*; Peter Dolton *[Contrib.] and others. Collection of 9 articles.* **Ox. R. Econ. Pol.** , *8:2,* Summer:1992 pp. 1 – 158

M.5: Economics of education *[Économie de l'éducation]*

21 Higher education and market economy in Mongolia. Seth Spaulding. *J. Asian Afr. Aff.* **IV:1** Fall:1992 pp. 1 – 33

22 Higher education and progressive taxation — equity, efficiency and majority voting. John Creedy; Patrick François. *J. Econ. Stud.* **19:4** 1992 pp. 17 – 30

23 Higher education in a world market. An historical look at the global context of international study. Mary E. McMahon. *High. Educ.* **24:4** 12:1992 pp. 465 – 482

24 Immigration and its impact on the incidence of training in Australia. Meredith Baker; Mark Wooden. *Aust. Ec. Rev.* **:98(2nd quarter)** 4-6:1992 pp. 39 – 53

25 Investment in education and U.S. economic growth. Dale W. Jorgenson; Barbara M. Fraumeni; Klaus Conrad *[Comments by]*. *Sc. J. Econ.* **94** 1992 pp. 51 – 71

26 Lifetime inequality and higher education grants — a public choice approach. John Creedy; Patrick Francois. *Aust. Econ. P.* **31:58** 6:1992 pp. 146 – 157

27 Oktatásfinanszírozas — szempontok egy reformhoz *[In Hungarian]*; Financing education — viewpoints to a reform *[Summary]*. András Semjén. *Közg. Sz.* **XXXIX** 12:1992 pp. 1091 – 1106

28 On social rates of return to investment in education. S.G. Hosking. *S. Afr. J. Econ.* **60:2** 6:1992 pp. 221 – 232

29 On the political economy of skill in the advanced industrial nations. Francis Green. *R. Pol. Econ.* **4:4** 1992 pp. 413 – 435

30 Optimal localized production experience and schooling. Charles van Marrewijk; Casper G. de Vries; Cees Withagen. *Int. Econ. R.* **33:1** 2:1992 pp. 91 – 110

31 The political construction of education — the state, school expansion, and economic change. Bruce Fuller *[Ed.]*; Richard Rubinson *[Ed.]*. New York: Praeger, 1992: xiii, 261 p. *ISBN: 027593831x; LofC: 91-33893. Bibliography — p[239]-254. - Includes index.*

32 Post-secondary education — preparation for the world of work — proceedings of a Canada/UK colloquium, November 21-22, 1988, Mississauga, Ontario, Canada. Ronald L. Watts *[Ed.]*; Jeff Greenberg *[Ed.]*. Aldershot: Dartmouth, 1990: xv, 216 p. *ISBN: 0886450918; LofC: 90187067. Includes bibliographical references.*

33 Private school enrollment in metropolitan areas. Amy B. Schmidt. *Publ. Fin. Q.* **20:3** 7:1992 pp. 298 – 320

34 Public expenditure on higher education — a comparative study in the member states of the European Community. Frans Kaiser; et al. London: Jessica Kingsley, 1992: 252 p. *ISBN: 1853025321.* [Higher education policy series. : No. 18]

35 The pure human capital investment model — a test and applications using LDC data. Tafah-Edokat. *Scand. J. Devel. Altern.* **XI:1** 3:1992 pp. 63 – 80

36 The quality and cost in early childhood education. Irene Powell; James Cosgrove. *J. Hum. Res.* **XXVII:3** Summer:1992 pp. 472 – 484

37 School quality and black-white relative earnings — a direct assessment. David Card; Alan B. Krueger. *Q. J. Econ.* **CVII:1** 2:1992 pp. 151 – 200

38 Sharks and splashes — the future of education and employment. Christopher Ball; G.R. Hawke *[Ed.]*. Wellington: Institute of Policy Studies, Victoria University of Wellington, 1991: 102 p. *ISBN: 0908935730.*

39 Student emigration and the willingness to pay for public schools — a test of the publicness of public high schools in the U.S. Lori L. Taylor. *Publ. Finan.* **47:1** 1992 pp. 131 – 152

40 Student loans in developing countries. Maureen Woodhall *[Contrib.]*; Douglas Albrecht *[Contrib.]*; Adrian Ziderman *[Contrib.]*; Li Shouxin *[Contrib.]*; Mark Bray *[Contrib.]*; Jandhyala B.G. Tilak *[Contrib.]*; G. Shantakumar *[Contrib.]*; G.M.G. Mokgwathi *[Contrib.]*; W. Senteza Kajubi *[Contrib.]*; E.J. Chuta *[Contrib.]* and others. Collection of 9 articles. **High. Educ.** , *23:4*, 6:1992 pp. 345 – 460

41 Underinvestment, low economic returns to education, and the schooling of rural children — some new evidence from Brazil. Ram D. Singh. *Econ. Dev. Cult. Change* **40:3** 4:1992 pp. 645 – 664

42 The university — a regional booster? Raymond Florax. Aldershot: Avebury, 1992: 330 p. *ISBN: 1856283429.*

43 What does a university add to its local economy? M.F. Bleaney; M.R. Binks; D. Greenaway; G.V. Reed; D.K. Whynes. *Appl. Econ.* **24:3** 3:1992 pp. 305 – 312

N: Public economy — *Économie publique*

N.1: Economic systems and policies — *Systèmes et politiques économiques*

Sub-divisions: Adjustment and stabilization policies *[Politiques d'adaptation et stabilisation]*; Economic management and policies *[La politique et gestion de l'économie]*; Economic reform *[Réforme économique]*; Economic systems *[Systèmes économiques]*; Planning theory and practice *[Théorie et pratique de la planification]*; Privatization *[Privatisation]*

1 Amid the ruins, arms makers raise new threats. Christopher Smart. *Orbis* **36:3** Summer:1992 pp. 349 – 364
2 Applications of decision analysis to the military systems acquisition process. Dennis M. Buede; Terry A. Bresnick. *Interfaces* **22:6** 11-12:1992 pp. 110 – 125
3 Australian economic nationalism — old and new. Dick Bryan. *Aust. Econ. P.* **30:57** 12:1991 pp. 290 – 309
4 L'avenir de l'Etat dans une économie de marché *[In French]*; [The future of the state in a market economy]. Michel Franc *[Contrib.]*; Marceau Long *[Contrib.]*; Abdou Diouf *[Contrib.]*; Jean-Pierre Soisson *[Contrib.]*; Jean-Claude Paye *[Contrib.]*; Abdou Aziz Diop *[Contrib.]*; Jean-Michel Séverino *[Contrib.]*; Jean-Pierre Gonon *[Contrib.]*; Jean-Baptiste Kristiadi *[Contrib.]*; Carlos Maroto Perez Del Rio *[Contrib.] and others. Collection of 32 articles.* **R. Fr. Admin. Publ.** , :61, 1-3:1992 pp. 7 – 182
5 Building a peace economy — opportunities and problems of post-cold war defense cuts. Betty G. Lall; John Tepper Marlin; Eugene Chollick; Domenick Bertelli; et al. Boulder: Westview Press, 1992: x, 294 p. *ISBN: 0813384338; LofC: 91041072. Includes bibliographical references.*
6 Central appraisal and financing of local projects — physiology and pathology. Gilberto Muraro. *Riv. Dir. Finan. Sci. Fin.* **LI:4** 12:1992 pp. 617 – 635
7 China and Japan — politics versus economics. Allen S. Whiting. *Ann. Am. Poli.* **519** 1:1992 pp. 39 – 51
8 The Chinese mirror of transition. Guilhem Fabre. *Comm. Econ.* **4:2** 1992 pp. 259 – 268
9 Collapse of the state and competitiveness — evidence from African and post-socialist countries. Olivier Bomsel. *Res. Pol.* **18:4** 12:1992 pp. 270 – 281
10 Competition between local governments as a discovery procedure. Martti Vihanto. *J. Inst. Theo. Ec.* **148:3** 9:1992 pp. 411 – 436
11 Converting resources from military to non-military uses. Jurgen Brauer; John Tepper Marlin. *J. Econ. Pers.* **6:4** Fall:1992 pp. 145 – 164
12 Defense spending and unemployment rates — empirical analysis disaggregated by race and gender. J.D. Abell. *Am. J. Econ. S.* **51:1** 1:1992 pp. 27 – 42
13 Des économies et des états en Afrique francophone — pour comprendre l'interventionnisme *[In French]*; The economies and states of French-speaking Africa *[Summary]*. Bernard Contamin; Yves-André Fauré. *Cah. Sci. Hum.* **28:2** 1992 pp. 305 – 326
14 Eastern Europe goes to market. Mark Kramer. *Foreign Pol.* :86 Spring:1992 pp. 134 – 157
15 Economia politica e analisi della burocrazia pubblica *[In Italian]*; [Political economy and analysis of public bureaucracy]. Silvia Fedeli. *A. Fond. L. Einaudi* **XXV** 1991 pp. 51 – 99
16 Economic growth and military spending in South Africa. Susan M. McMillan. *Int. Inter.* **18:1** 1992 pp. 35 – 50
17 Economic liberalization in India; *[French summary]*; *[German summary]*. Jean A. Bernard. *Vierteljahresberichte* :129 9:1992 pp. 289 – 301
18 The emergence of market economies in Eastern Europe. Christopher K. Clague *[Ed.]*; Gordon C. Rausser *[Ed.]*. Cambridge, MA.: Blackwell Publishers, 1992: x, 352 p. *ISBN: 1557863334; LofC: 91040746.*
19 Etica e governo locale *[In Italian]*; [Ethics and local government]. Amedeo Fossati. *Riv. Dir. Finan. Sci. Fin.* **LI:4** 12:1992 pp. 589 – 616
20 Formalizing the informal sector in a changing South Africa — small-scale manufacturing on the Witwatersrand. D. Simon; S.L. Birch. *World Dev.* **20:7** 7:1992 pp. 1029 – 1045

N.1: Economic systems and policies *[Systèmes et politiques économiques]*

21 A forum on accounting for defense contracts. William P. Rogerson *[Contrib.]*; Jacob K. Thomas *[Contrib.]*; Samuel Tung *[Contrib.]*; Stefan Reichelstein *[Contrib.]*; Joel S. Demski *[Contrib.]*; Robert P. Magee *[Contrib.]*; Frank R. Lichtenberg. *Collection of 5 articles*. **Acc. Review** , *67:4*, 10:1992 pp. 671 – 752

22 From boom to bust — trial and error in British economic policy. David Smith. London: Penguin, 1992: 255 p. *ISBN: 0140165495*.

23 From the second to the informed economy. Endre Sik. *J. Public Pol.* **12:2** 4-6:1992 pp. 153 – 175

24 The future of the U.S. defense industry. Murray Weidenbaum. *Cont. Policy* **X:2** 4:1992 pp. 27 – 34

25 Government relief for risk associated with government action. Louis Kaplow. *Sc. J. Econ.* **94:4** 1992 pp. 525 – 541

26 Das grüne Denken der Väter der sozialen Marktwirtschaft *[In German]*; [Green thinking of the fathers of the social market economy] *[Summary]*. Franz Kromka. *Z. Polit.* **39:3** 9:1992 pp. 264 – 285

27 Die kommune als Gestaltungsfaktor — Einflussmöglichkeiten der ostdeutschen Kommunen auf den wirtschaftlichen Umstrukturierungsprozess der Region in Ostdeutschland *[In German]*; [Local authority districts as a formational factor — possibilities for East German local authorities districts in influencing the economic process of restructuring in East German regions]. Okyta A'Walela. Berlin: Forschungsstelle für Gesamtdeutsche Wirtschaftliche und Soziale Fragen, 1992: iv, 70 p. [FS Analysen. : No. 1992/3]

28 Market socialism — a case for rejuvenation. Pranab Bardhan; John E. Roemer. *J. Econ. Pers.* **6:3** Summer:1992 pp. 101 – 116

29 Market socialism — a historical view and a retrospective assessment; *[German summary]*. Alberto Chilosi. *Econ. Sys.* **16:1** 4:1992 p.171-185

30 The market — practice and policy. F.H. Hahn *[Ed.]*. Basingstoke: Macmillan, 1992: 178 p. *ISBN: 0333556518. "Proceedings of Section F (Economics) of the British Association for the Advancement of Science, Swansea, 1990"*.

31 Markets and democracy — lessons from Chile. Alejandra Cox Edwards; Sebastian Edwards. *World. Econ.* **15:2** 3:1992 pp. 203 – 220

32 Markets and states in development — the search continues for an optimal mix. Krishnamurthy Sriram. *Scand. J. Devel. Altern.* **XI:1** 3:1992 pp. 41 – 52

33 Memos to the president — a guide through macroeconomics for the busy policymaker. Charles L. Schultze. Washington, DC: Brookings Institution, 1992: xiv, 334 p. *ISBN: 0815777787; LofC: 92013098*.

34 Mineral endowment, public policy and competitiveness — a survey of the issues. John E. Tilton. *Res. Pol.* **18:4** 12:1992 pp. 237 – 249

35 A miracle without end? Japanese capitalism and the world economy. Costas Kossis. *Int. Soc.* **54** Spring:1992 pp. 105 – 132

36 Modernization in mainland China — self-reliance and dependence. C.-H. Chen. *Am. J. Econ. S.* **51:1** 1:1992 pp. 57 – 67

37 Mon pays, c'est l'hiver — reflections of a market populist. Thomas Courchene. *Can. J. Econ.* **XXV:4** 11:1992 pp. 759 – 791

38 Myths and realities — Latin America's free markets. James Petras; Steve Vieux. *Mon. Rev.* **144:1** 5:1992 pp. 9 – 20

39 North Korea inches toward economic liberalization. Teruo Komaki. *Jpn. R. Int. Aff.* **6:2** Summer:1992 pp. 155 – 174

40 Ordnungsethik — Versuch einer Klärung ihres Gegenstandes und der Dimension ihres Anliegens *[In German]*; [Structural ethics — towards an explanation of the subject matter and its scope]. Wolfgang Schmitz. *Z. Wirt.pol.* **41:3** 1992 pp. 213 – 230

41 Organizational dynamics of market transition — hybrid forms, property rights, and mixed economy in China. Victor Nee. *Adm. Sci. Qua.* **37:1** 3:1992 pp. 1 – 27

42 Political cycles in OECD economics. Alberto Alesina; Nouriel Roubini. *R. Econ. S.* **59:4** 10:1992 pp. 663 – 687

43 The political economy of Latin America — the Colombian experience during the 1980s. Alberto Supelano. *J. Econ. Iss.* **XXVI:3** 9:1992 pp. 845 – 864

44 Post-socialist transition from a neo-Schumpeterian perspective — the case of the former Soviet Union. Evgenii Kuznetsov. *Comm. Econ.* **4:4** 1992 pp. 469 – 499

45 Les prises de participation publiques et le régime communautaire des aides d'etat *[In French]*; [The prices of public participation and the community regime of state aids]. Robert Kovar. *R. Trim. Com. Écon.* **45:1** 1-3:1992 pp. 109 – 157

N.1: Economic systems and policies *[Systèmes et politiques économiques]*

46 Private enterprise and the state in modern Nepal. Laurie Zivetz. Madras: Oxford University Press, 1992: 248 p. *ISBN: 0195628721; LofC: gb 92030643. Includes index; Bibliography — p. 235-241.*

47 Public rules and private profits — recent assessments of private enterprise regulation in Africa. Andrew Stone. *Finan. News Anal.* **5:2** 2:1992 pp. 1 – 16

48 Russia beyond perestroika. László Csaba. *Comm. Econ.* **4:3** 1992 pp. 333 – 359

49 Soviet political economy in transition — from Lenin to Gorbachev. A. F. Dowlah. New York: Greenwood Press, 1992: vi, 287 p. *ISBN: 0313279446; LofC: 91028147 //r922. Includes bibliographical references (p. [251]-274) and index.* [Contributions in economics and economic history.]

50 Strategies for revamping the Nigerian economy. Wale Oyemakinde. Ibadan: Sunlight Institute, 1991: 84 p. *ISBN: 9783117807. Includes bibliographical references (p. 81) and index.*

51 The Syrian private industrial and commercial sectors and the state. Volker Perthes. *Int. J. M.E. Stud.* **24:2** 5:1992 pp. 207 – 230

52 Technological change in the USSR and the return to a market economy. Priyatosh Maitra. *Int. J. Soc. E.* **19:1** 1992 pp. 27 – 46

53 Toward a civil economy? Richard Rose. Glasgow: Centre for the Study of Public Policy, University of Strathclyde, 1992: 23 p. [Studies in public policy. : No. 200]

54 The transition from central planning to a market economy — a computable general equilibrium model. J.M. Pogodzinski; Claudia Antes. *Econ. Plan.* **25:2** 1992 pp. 139 – 164

55 Tržišno gospodarstvo i tranzicija prijašnjih socijalistčkih društava *[In Serbo-Croatian]*; Рыночная экономика и транзиция раньших социалистических обществ *[Russian summary]*; Market economy and the transition of former socialist societies *[Summary]*. Dušan Ćalić. *Ekon. Preg.* **43:3-4** 1992 pp. 189 – 206

56 The virtues of gradualism and legitimacy in the transition to a market economy. M. Dewatripont; G. Roland. *Econ. J.* **102:411** 3:1992 pp. 291 – 300

57 A vision for Australia — indicators from Singapore. Clive T. Edwards. *Aust. Ec. Rev.* **:98(2nd quarter)** 4-6:1992 pp. 16 – 30

58 Volksrepublik China — ein neuer Konflktherd im Osten Asiens *[In German]*; People's Republic of China — a new hearth of conflict in Eastern Asia? *[Summary]*. Thomas Heberer. *Ost. Wirt.* **37:4** 12:1992 pp. 277 – 297

59 Zu transformationstheoretischen Ansätzen der ordoliberalen Schule und der amerikanischen Institutionenökonomik *[In German]*; [Towards transformation-theoretical attempts of the ordoliberal school and of American institutional economics]. Jürgen Schulz. *Z. Wirt.pol.* **41:3** 1992 pp. 231 – 268

60 Zur Diskussion Technologiepolitik und Wettbewerbsfähigkeit *[In German]*; [Discussion point — technology policy and competitiveness]. Karl Heinz Steinhöfler. *Wirt. Blät.* **39:4** 1992 pp. 483 – 497

Adjustment and stabilization policies *[Politiques d'adaptation et stabilisation]*

61 Adjustment and equity in Chile. Patricio Meller; Christian Morrisson *[Ed.]*. Paris: Development Centre of the Organisation for Economic Co-operation and Development, 1992: 102 p. *ISBN: 9264136193. Includes bibliographical references.* [Adjustment and equity in developing countries; Development Centre studies.]

62 The analytical aspects of adjustment programs; Gli aspetti analitici dei programmi di riequilibrio *[Italian summary]*. P.K. Mitra. *Econ. Int.* **XLV:1** 2:1992 pp. 26 – 41

63 Beyond import substitution — the restructuring projects of Brazil and Mexico. Diana Alarcón; Terry McKinley. *Lat. Am. Pers.* **19:2(73)** Spring:1992 pp. 72 – 87

64 Beyond structural adjustment in Africa. Stanley Please. *Dev. Pol. R.* **10:3** 9:1992 pp. 289 – 308

65 Beyond structural adjustment in Africa — the political economy of sustainable and democratic development. Julius Edo Nyang'oro *[Ed.]*; Timothy M. Shaw *[Ed.]*. New York: Praeger, 1992: 190 p. *ISBN: 027594221x; LofC: 91047087. Includes bibliographical references (p. [179]-182) and index.*

66 The challenge of structural adjustment in the Commonwealth Caribbean. Ramesh F. Ramsaran. New York: Praeger, 1992: xiv, 206 p. *ISBN: 0275942090; LofC: 91037505 //r92. Includes bibliographical references (p. [195]-201) and index.*

67 Debito estero e aggiustamento economico in America Latina *[In Italian]*; [Foreign debt and economic adjustment in Latin America]. Fabio Fossati. *Comun. Int.* **XLVI:4** Quarto trimestre:1991 pp. 556 – 577

N.1: Economic systems and policies *[Systèmes et politiques économiques]* —
Adjustment and stabilization policies [Politiques d'adaptation et stabilisation]

68 Development finance and policy reform — essays in the theory and practice of conditionality in less developed countries. Paul Mosley *[Ed.]*. New York: St. Martin's Press, 1992: 338 p. *ISBN: 031207915x; LofC: 91042578. Includes bibliographical references and index.* [International political economy series.]

69 Development strategy and the economy of Sierra Leone. John Weeks. New York: St. Martin's Press, 1992: xi, 191 p. *ISBN: 0312072120; LofC: 91039069. Includes bibliographical references (p.) and index.*

70 A gazdaság stabilizálásáról *[In Hungarian]*; On the stabilization of the Hungarian economy *[Summary]*. Tibor Erdős. *Közg. Sz.* **XXXIX** 11:1992 pp. 985 – 1000

71 How to realize an "economic miracle" in a socialist country — a stabilization plan for Poland. Anghel N. Rugina. *Int. J. Soc. E.* **19:7/8/9** 1992 pp. 160 – 171

72 Liberalization and integration in Africa. Youssouf Dembele. *Finan. News Anal.* **5:8** 8:1992 pp. 14 – 28

73 Macroeconomic stabilisation under transition in Laos. Yves Bourdet. *Comm. Econ.* **4:4** 1992 pp. 537 – 555

74 Макроэкономическое планирование и стабилизация финансов *[In Russian]*; [Macroeconomic planning and the stabilization of finance]. G.Ya. Shakhova. *Finansy* :**6** 1992 pp. 10 – 20

75 Openness and the scope for macroeconomic policy in micro states. Malcolm L. Treadgold. *Cyprus J. Econ.* **5:1** 6:1992 pp. 15 – 24

76 Peruvian economic policy in the 1980s — from orthodoxy to heterodoxy and back. Manuel Pastor; Carol Wise. *Lat. Am. Res. R.* **27:2** 1992 pp. 83 – 117

77 Policy-making without facts — a note on the assessment of structural adjustment policies in Nigeria 1985-1990. Paul Mosley. *Afr. Affairs* **91:363** 4:1992 pp. 227 – 240

78 President Babangida's structural adjustment programme and inflation in Nigeria. John C. Anyanwu. *J. Soc. Devel. Afr.* **7:1** 1992 pp. 5 – 24

79 Stabilizáció és növekedés Magyarországon — néhány ehméleti megfontolás *[In Hungarian]*; Stabilization and growth in Hungary — some theoretical considerations *[Summary]*. Ákos Valentinyi. *Közg. Sz.* **XXXIX** 10:1992 pp. 908 – 923

80 Stabilization and growth recovery in Mexico — lessons and dilemmas. Daniel F. Oks. Washington, D.C.: Country Department II, Latin America and the Caribbean Regional Office, The World Bank, 1992: 23 p. [Policy research working papers.]

81 Stabilization and reform in Eastern Europe — a preliminary evaluation. Michael Bruno. *Staff Pap. Int. Monetary* **39:4** 12:1992 pp. 741 – 777

82 Structural reform in the Australian economy — conference proceedings. Tim Riley *[Ed.]*. St. Leonards/NSW: Economics Education Resource Centre, 1991: 230 p. *ISBN: 094976972x.*

83 Strukturanpassung und Armutsbekämpfung in Entwicklungsländern *[In German]*; [Structural adjustment and the war on poverty in developing countries] *[Summary]*. Marco Ferroni. *Scot. J. Poli.* **47:III** 1992 pp. 389 – 411

84 Testing for credibility effects. Pierre-Richard Agénor; Mark P. Taylor. *Staff Pap. Int. Monetary* **39:3** 9:1992 pp. 545 – 571

85 Things fall apart again — structural adjustment programmes in sub-Saharan Africa. J. Barry Riddell. *J. Mod. Afr. S.* **30:1** 3:1992 pp. 53 – 68

86 Understanding the investment cycle in adjustment programs — evidence from reforming economies. Andrés Solimano. Washington, D.C.: Country Economics Department, The World Bank, 1992: 43 p. *Bibliography — p.41-43.* [Policy research working papers.]

Economic management and policies *[La politique et gestion de l'économie]*

87 Authoritarian versus nonauthoritarian approaches to economic development — update and additional evidence. A. Pourgerami. *Publ. Choice* **74:3** 10:1992 pp. 365 – 377

88 Business and government under Labor. Brian Galligan *[Ed.]*; Gwynneth Singleton *[Ed.]*. Melbourne, Australia: Longman Cheshire, 1991: xvi, 212 p. *ISBN: 0582871409. Includes bibliographical references.*

89 Changing aims in economics. T. W. Hutchison. Oxford: Blackwell, 1992: 186 p. *ISBN: 0631184988; LofC: 91038301. Includes bibliographical references and index.*

90 Decentralization in infinite horizon economies. Mukul Majumdar *[Ed.]*. Boulder, Colorado: Westview Press, 1992: 190 p. *ISBN: 0813380901.*

91 The development of the nationwide econometric model. Mitsuo Saito. *Econ. S. Quart.* **43:1** 3:1992 pp. 1 – 18

N.1: Economic systems and policies *[Systèmes et politiques économiques]* — *Economic management and policies [La politique et gestion de l'économie]*

92 Dynamics of policy-making in Malaysia — the formulation of the new economic policy and the national development policy. Ho Khai Leong. *Asian J. Pub. Admin.* **14:2** 12:1992 pp. 204 – 227

93 Economic cooperation between Guangdong and inland areas. Kazuo Yukawa. *China News.* **:100** 9-10:1992 pp. 9 – 16

94 Economic development in the context of China — policy issues and analysis. C.A. Tisdell. New York, NY.: St. Martin's Press, 1992: 218 p. *ISBN: 0312086709; LofC: 92024485. Includes index.*

95 The economic policy framework in transition — resistance to and strategy for change in Eastern Europe. Karl-Ernst Schenk; Rudolf Andorka *[Comments by]*; Bruno S. Frey *[Comments by]*. *J. Inst. Theo. Ec.* **148:1** 3:1992 pp. 103 – 122

96 Economic policy reform in developing countries — the Kuznets memorial lectures of the Economic Growth Center, Yale University. Anne O. Krueger. Cambridge, MA.: B. Blackwell, 1992: xiii, 184 p. *ISBN: 1557862745; LofC: 91025959. Includes bibliographical references and index.*

97 Eficiencia de la intervención estatal en la economía brasileña *[In Spanish]*; [Efficiency of state intervention in the Brazilian economy]. Fernando de Holanda Barbosa. *Monetaria* **XV:2** 4-6:1992 pp. 171 – 194

98 Engineers of the transition (interventionist temptations in Eastern European economic thought). J.M. Kovács. *Acta Oecon.* **44:1-2** 1992 pp. 37 – 52

99 Evaluación y perspectivas de la apertura *[In Spanish]*; [Evaluation and perspectives on liberalization]. Eduardo Sarmiento Palacio. *Desar. Soc.* **:29** 3:1992 pp. 11 – 23

100 Financial programming and policy — the case of Hungary. Karen Swiderski *[Ed.]*. Washington, D.C: IMF Institute, International Monetary Fund, 1992: v, 205 p. *ISBN: 1557753040; LofC: 92020734. Includes bibliographical references.*

101 Foundations of India's political economy — towards an agenda for the 1990s. Subroto Roy *[Ed.]*; William E. James *[Ed.]*. New Delhi: Sage Publications, 1992: 339 p. *ISBN: 0803994117; LofC: 91041195. Includes bibliographical references and index.*

102 Implementing Thatcherite policies — audit of an era. David Marsh *[Ed.]*; R.A.W. Rhodes *[Ed.]*. Buckingham, England: Open University Press, 1992: 212 p. *ISBN: 0335156835; LofC: 91044913. Includes bibliogaraphical references and index.* [Public policy and management series.]

103 Industrialization and China's rural modernization. Dong Fureng. New York: St. Martin's Press, 1992: 113 p. *ISBN: 0312084072; LofC: 92011894. Includes bibliographical references (p.) and index.*

104 Judging the performance of an economy with an application to the Netherlands. M. Peter van der Hoek. *R. Pol. Econ.* **4:1** 1992 pp. 79 – 94

105 Macroeconomic issues in China in the 1990s. K.C. Yeh. *China Quart.* **:131** 9:1992 pp. 501 – 544

106 Macroeconomic management and the black market for foreign exchange in Sudan. Ibrahim A. Elbadawi. Washington, D.C.: Country Economics Department, The World Bank, 1992: 88 p. [Policy research working papers.]

107 Macroeconomic policy. Gus Hooke *[Ed.]*; Ron Reilly *[Ed.]*. North Sydney NSW: Allen & Unwin, 1991: xii, 251 p. *ISBN: 0044422237; LofC: 90055034. Includes bibliographical references.*

108 Modelo macroeconómico y políticas de reactivación para la economía peruana *[In Spanish]*; [A macroeconomic model and policies to stimulate the Peruvian economy]. Félix Jiménez; Juan Pichigua. *Soc. Part.* **:57** 3:1992 pp. 73 – 84

109 National economic policies. Dominick Salvatore *[Ed.]*. Amsterdam: North-Holland, 1991: xii, 399 p. *ISBN: 0444986928; LofC: gb 92011273. Includes index; Bibliography — p.387-389.* [Studies in comparative economic policies. : Vol. 1]

110 Objections to economic restructuring and the strategies of coercion — an analytical evaluation of policies and practices in Australia and the United States. Gordon L. Clark; John McKay; Geoff Missen; Michael Webber. *Econ. Geogr.* **68:1** 1:1992 pp. 43 – 59

111 The oil boom and after — Indonesian economic policy and performance in the Soeharto era. Anne Booth *[Ed.]*. Singapore: Oxford University Press, 1992: xxvi, 448 p. *ISBN: 019588969x; LofC: 91-23712.*

112 Persistência de inovações e política econômica — a experiência do II PND *[In Portuguese]*; [Persistence of innovations and economic policy — the experience of the Second National Development Plan] *[Summary]*. Francisco Cribari Neto. *Rev. Bras. Ec.* **46:3** 7-9:1992 pp. 413 – 428

N.1: Economic systems and policies *[Systèmes et politiques économiques]* — *Economic management and policies [La politique et gestion de l'économie]*
113 Planlægning, modeller og politik *[In Danish]*; Planning, economic models and politics *[Summary]*. Kim Viborg Andersen. *Politica.* **24:2** 1992 pp. 206 – 218
114 Policy choice and political constraints. S.M.R. Kanbur; G.D. Myles. *Eur. J. Pol. Ec.* **8:1** 2:1992 pp. 1 – 29
115 The Polish economy — legacies from the past, prospects for the future. Raphael Shen. New York: Praeger, 1992: xvi, 226 p. *ISBN: 0275938867; LofC: 91016683. Includes bibliographical references (p. [217]-219) and index.*
116 The politics of economic stagnation in the Soviet Union — the role of local party organs in economic management. Peter Rutland. New York: Cambridge University Press, 1992: 297 p. *ISBN: 0521392411; LofC: 91048028 //r922. Includes bibliographical references and index.* [Soviet and East European studies. : No. 88]
117 The politics of German regulation. Kenneth H.F. Dyson *[Ed.]*. Aldershot: Dartmouth, 1992: 279 p. *ISBN: 1855212730.*
118 Regulación económica y teoría del monopolio natural *[In Spanish]*; Economic regulations and theory of natural monopoly *[Summary]*. Héctor J.C. Grupe. *Económica Arg* **XXXVI:1-2** 1990 pp. 73 – 96
119 The rise and fall of the Swedish model. Rudolf Meidner. *Stud. Pol. Ec.* **:39** Autumn:1992 pp. 159 – 171
120 Robertson on economic policy. S. R. Dennison *[Ed.]*; John R. Presley *[Ed.]*. New York: St. Martin's Press, 1992: 228 p. *ISBN: 0312079133; LofC: 91044082. Includes bibliographical references and index.*
121 Das Sequenzing-Problem der Systemtransformation in Mittel- und Osteuropa *[In German]*; The problem of sequencing the system transformation in Central and Eastern Europe *[Summary]*; Le problème séquentiel de la transformation des systèmes en Europe centrale et en Europe de l'Est *[French summary]*. Eirik Svindland. *Kred. Kap.* **25:1** 1992 pp. 65 – 93
122 Should rules be simple? Paul Levine. *Econ. Plan.* **25:2** 1992 pp. 113 – 138
123 Structural adjustment and macroeconomic policy issues — papers presented at a seminar held in Lahore, Pakistan, October 26-28, 1991. V.A. Jafarey. Washington: International Monetary Fund, 1992: x, 137 p. *ISBN: 1557753024; LofC: 92022648. Includes bibliographical references.*
124 The Thatcher years — macroeconomic policy and performance of the UK economy, 1979-1988. Howard Vane. *Nat. W. Bank* **5:***1992* pp. 26 – 43
125 Towards a macrometric policy model of a semi-industrial economy — the case of Egypt. S. El-Sheikh. *Econ. Model.* **9:1** 1:1992 pp. 75 – 95
126 The transition from command to market economies in East-Central Europe. Sandor Richter *[Ed.]*. Boulder: Westview, 1992: 321 p. *ISBN: 0813385598.* [Vienna Institute for Comparative Economic Studies yearbook. : No. 4]
127 Der Weg aus der Knechtschaft — Probleme des Übergangs von der Planwirtschaft zur Marktwirtschaft *[In German]*; [The escape from servitude — the problems of the transition from a planned to a free market economy]. Herbert Matis *[Ed.]*; Dieter Stiefel *[Ed.]*. Wien: Ueberreuter, 1992: 215 p. *ISBN: 3800034328. Papers from a conference held in Vienna in Spring, 1991, sponsored by the Schumpeter Gesellschaft; Includes bibliographical references and index.* [Ueberreuter Wirtschaft.]
128 Die wirtschaftspolitischen Herausforderungen der Umwandlung der ostdeutschen Wirtschaft *[In German]*; [Challenges for economic policy posed by the transformation of eastern Germany's economy]. Peter Nunnenkamp. *Z. Wirt.pol.* **41:1** 1992 pp. 51 – 70

Economic reform *[Réforme économique]*
129 Adjustment and equity in Indonesia. Erik Thorbecke; Roger Downey; et al. Paris: Development Centre, Organisation for Economic Co-operation and Development, 1992: 264 p. *ISBN: 9264136517.* [Adjustment and equity in developing countries; Development Centre studies.]
130 Adjustment and equity in Malaysia. David Demery; Christian Morrisson. Paris: Development Centre of the Organisation for Economic Co-operation and Development, 1992: 148 p. *ISBN: 9264136010. "Development Centre studies"--Cover; Includes bibliographical references (p. 147-148).* [Adjustment and equity in developing countries.]
131 Building a market economy in Poland. Jeffrey Sachs. *Sci. Am.* **266:3** 3:1992 pp. 20 – 27
132 Bulgarie — les difficultés d'une transition balkanique *[In French]*; Bulgaria — difficulties of a transition in the Balkans *[Summary]*. Jacky Fayolle. *Obser. Diag. Econ.* **:42** 10:1992 pp. 159 – 198

N.1: Economic systems and policies *[Systèmes et politiques économiques]* —
Economic reform [Réforme économique]

133 Can perestroika still be reformed? Elisabeth Tamedly Lenches. *Int. J. Soc. E.* **19:1** 1992 pp. 3 – 26

134 Capitalism in Poland. David Ost *[Contrib.]*; Zygmunt Bauman *[Contrib.]*; Janine R. Wedel *[Contrib.]*; Kazimierz Kloc *[Contrib.]*; Piotr Marciniak *[Contrib.]*; Teresa Kuczyńska *[Contrib.]. Collection of 6 articles.* **Telos** , *:92,* Summer:1992 pp. 107 – 163

135 Capitalist reforms in sub-Saharan Africa — some questions and issues; *[German summary]*; *[French summary]*. April Gordon. *Genève-Afrique* **XXX:1** 1992 pp. 35 – 53

136 The challenges of Nigeria's economic reform. Oladele Olashore. Ibadan, Nigeria: Fountain Publications, 1991: xiv, 330 p. (ill) *ISBN: 9782679496; LofC: 91210038. Includes bibliographical references and index.*

137 China's economic reform — the role and significance of SEZs. Ram Dev Bhardwaj. *Ind. J. Pol. Sci.* **LIII:3** 7-9:1992 pp. 332 – 373

138 La Chine à la recherche du néo-autoritarisme ou la revanche de Zhao Ziyang *[In French]*; China on the way to neo-authoritarianism, or the revenge of Zhao Ziyang *[Summary]*. Jean-Pierre Cabestan. *Rev. Ét. Comp.* **23:1** 1992 pp. 5 – 27

139 Die chinesische Finanzsystemreform *[In German]*; (The Chinese finance reform). Armin Bohnet; Zhong Hong. *Ost. Wirt.* **3** 1992 pp. 255 – 273

140 Contrasting styles of industrial reform — China and India in the 1980s. George Rosen. Chicago: University of Chicago Press, 1992: xiii, 168 p. *ISBN: 0226726460; LofC: 91031762. Includes bibliographical references (p. 149-157) and index.*

141 Crisis and reform in Eastern Europe. Ferenc Fehér *[Ed.]*; Andrew Arato *[Ed.]*. New Brunswick: Transaction Publishers, 1991: ix, 531 p. *ISBN: 0887383114.*

142 Cuba's free-market experiment — los mercados libres campesinos, 1980-1986. Jonathan Rosenberg. *Lat. Am. Res. R.* **27:3** 1992 pp. 51 – 89

143 La débâcle de l'expérience soviétique. De la tentative de réformer l'irréformable à la «thérapie de choc» *[In French]*; The collapse of the Soviet system. From the attempt to reform the unreformable to «shock therapy» *[Summary]*. Serge Métais. *Rev. Ét. Comp.* **23:1** 1992 pp. 29 – 59

144 Debate a la revolución pacífica *[In Spanish]*; [Debate on the peaceful revolution]. Armando Montenegro T. *[Contrib.]*; Eduardo Lora *[Contrib.]*; Guillermo Perry *[Contrib.]*; Jorge Armando Rodríguez *[Contrib.]*; Manuel Ramírez G. *[Contrib.]*; Juan Luis Londoño *[Contrib.]*; Alvaro Reyes Posada *[Contrib.]*; Miguel Urrutia M. *[Contrib.]*; Jaime Maldonado F. *[Contrib.]*; Jorge Ramírez V. *[Contrib.] and others. Collection of 21 articles.* **Plan. Desarr.** , *XXIII:1,* 5:1992 pp. 6 – 336

145 The dilemmas of market socialism — capital market reform in China — part II — shares. Paul Bowles; Gordon White. *J. Dev. Stud.* **28:4** 7:1992 pp. 575 – 594

146 The disintegration of the Soviet economic system. Michael Ellman; Vladimir Kontorovich. London: Routledge, 1992: 281 p. *ISBN: 0415063493.*

147 The Eastern transition to a market economy — a global perspective. John Williamson. London: London School of Economics and Political science, 1992: 52 p. [Occasional paper.]

148 Economic reform and dynamic political constraints. M. Dewatripont; G. Roland. *R. Econ. S.* **59:4** 10:1992 pp. 703 – 730

149 Economic reform and population control in rural mainland China in the 1980s. Ze Hong; G. Edward Ebanks. *Iss. Stud.* **28:9** 9:1992 pp. 22 – 46

150 Economic reform and social change in China. Andrew Watson *[Ed.]*. London: Routledge, 1992: 259 p. *ISBN: 0415069734; LofC: 91044804. Includes bibliographical references and index.*

151 Economic reform and Third-World socialism — a political economy of food policy in post-revolutionary societies. Peter Utting. London: Macmillan, 1992: 320 p. *ISBN: 0333559185.* [Macmillan international political economy series.]

152 Economic reform in Eastern Europe. Graham Bird *[Ed.]*. Brookfield, VT.: E. Elgar Pub, 1992: 187 p. *ISBN: 1852785942; LofC: 91038474. "Based on a conference held by the Department of Economics at the University of Surrey, in February 1991."; Includes index.*

153 Economic reform in Russia. Peter M. Oppenheimer. *Natl. Inst. Econ. R.* **:141** 8:1992 pp. 48 – 61

154 The economic reform of North Korea — the strategy of hidden and assimilable reforms. Hy-Sang Lee. *Korea Obs.* **XXIII:1** Spring:1992 pp. 45 – 78

155 Economic reforms in Shanghai. Sorab Sadri; Bala Ramaswamy. *China R.* **28:1** 1-3:1992 pp. 1 – 12

N.1: Economic systems and policies *[Systèmes et politiques économiques]* — *Economic reform [Réforme économique]*

156 Economic transition in Eastern Europe. Michael Ellman; E. T. Gaĭdar; Grzegorz W Kołodko. Cambridge, MA.: Blackwell, 1992: 99 p. *ISBN: 0631187790; LofC: 92025470. Collection of essays from the F. de Vries seminar held at the Erasmus University in the fall of 1991; Includes index.* [De Vries lectures in economics.]

157 Economics and politics of transition. Christopher T Saunders *[Ed.].* London: Macmillan, 1992: 419 p. *ISBN: 0333575423.* [East-West European economic interaction. : No. 13]

158 Eltsine, le dernier rempart *[In French]*; [Yeltsin — the last stand] *[Summary]; [Spanish summary].* Michael Tatu. *Polit. Int.* :57 Autumn:1992 pp. 225 – 239

159 Экономические преобразования в странах Восточной Европы (опыт анализа формальных аспектов) *[In Russian]*; [Economic reforms in the countries of Eastern Europe (the experience of analysis formal aspects)]. A. Nesterenko; A. Lukovenko. *Vop. Ekon.* :1 1992 pp. 118 – 125

160 The failure of supply response in transition — a market-based explanation; *[German summary].* Adi Schnytzer; Avi Weiss. *Econ. Sys.* **16:2** 10:1992 pp. 189 – 203

161 Hindernisse für Wirtschaftsreformen in den Ländern Osteuropas *[In German]*; Obstacles to economic reform in the countries of Eastern Europe *[Summary]*; Les obstacles aux réformes économiques dans les pays d'Europe de l'Est *[French summary].* Wolfram Schrettl. *Vierteljahresberichte* :128 6:1992 pp. 139 – 148

162 Hungary's transition to the market — the case against a "big-bang". Paul Hare; Tamás Révész. *Econ. Pol.* :14 4:1992 pp. 227 – 264

163 Una ilustración sobre la operación de las fuerzas del mercado *[In Spanish]*; [An illustration of market forces]. Lauchlin Currie. *Desar. Soc.* :29 3:1992 pp. 49 – 58

164 Industrial reform in socialist countries — from restructuring to revolution. Ian Jeffries *[Ed.].* Aldershot, Hants, England: Edward Elgar Pub, 1992: 294 p. *ISBN: 185278380x; LofC: 91034962.*

165 Industrial systems and reform in North Korea — a comparison with China. M.-K. Kang; K. Lee. *World Dev.* **20:7** 7:1992 pp. 947 – 958

166 Institutional boundaries, structural change, and economic reform in China, part I. Louis Putterman *[Ed.]*; Barry Naughton *[Contrib.]*; Gary H. Jefferson *[Contrib.]*; Thomas G. Rawski *[Contrib.]*; Flemming Christiansen *[Contrib.]. Collection of 4 articles.* **Mod. Chi.** , *18:1,* 1:1992 pp. 3 – 93

167 Jump-starting a market economy — a critique of the radical strategy for economic reform in light of the East German experience. Andreas Pickel. *Stud. Comp. Commun.* **XXV:2** 6:1992 pp. 177 – 191

168 Koncepcija razvitka i prijelaz na tržišno gospodarstvo *[In Serbo-Croatian]*; Концепт развития и переход на рыночную экономику *[Russian summary]*; The concept of economic development and transition to a market economy *[Summary].* Rikard Lang. *Ekon. Preg.* **43:3-4** 1992 pp. 157 – 171

169 Labour and the failure of reform in China. Michael Korzec. New York: St. Martin's Press, 1992: 108 p. *ISBN: 0312075928; LofC: 91040232. Includes bibliographical references and index.*

170 Lessons from China's economic reform. Kang Chen; Gary H. Jefferson; Inderjit Singh. *J. Comp. Econ.* **16:2** 6:1992 pp. 201 – 225

171 Libéralisation, changements structurels et chute de la production dans les économies en transition *[In French]*; Liberalization, structural changes and fall in output in transition economies *[Summary].* Daniel Linotte. *Rev. Ét. Comp.* **XXIII:2-3** 6-9:1992 pp. 193 – 210

172 The limits on effective transition from centrally-planned to market-oriented economies — experiences from Asia. Paul Cook; Martin Minogue. *Asian J. Pub. Admin.* **14:2** 12:1992 pp. 186 – 203

173 Market institutions, East European reform, and economic theory. Rey Koslowski. *J. Econ. Iss.* **XXVI:3** 9:1992 pp. 673 – 705

174 Market liberalization policies in a reforming socialist economy. Elias Dinopoulos; Timothy D. Lane. *Staff Pap. Int. Monetary* **39:3** 9:1992 pp. 465 – 494

175 Microeconomic efficiency and macroeconomic policy effectiveness in China's transformation phase. Clem A. Tisdell. *Int. J. Soc. E.* **19:10/11/12** 1992 pp. 181 – 191

176 Mongolia's struggle to create a market economy. Ryokichi Hirono. *Jpn. R. Int. Aff.* **6:2** Summer:1992 pp. 107 – 133

177 The New Economic System, the New Economic Mechanism, and the Yugoslav LMF — bureaucratic limits to reform; *[German summary].* Michael Keren. *Econ. Sys.* **16:1** 4:1992 pp. 89 – 111

N.1: Economic systems and policies *[Systèmes et politiques économiques]* — *Economic reform [Réforme économique]*

178 Perestroika — a catastrophic change of economic reform policy. Alexander D. Smirnov; Emil B. Ershov. *Confl. Resolut.* **36:3** 9:1992 pp. 415 – 453

179 Perestrojka in der sowjetischen Wirtschaft —Bilanz einer widerspruchsvollen Entwicklung *[In German]*; Perestroika in the Soviet economy — results of a contradictory development *[Summary]*. Vladimir Korovkin. *Ost. Wirt.* **37:1** 3:1992 pp. 52 – 65

180 Peruvian economic policy in the 1980s — from orthodoxy to heterodoxy and back. Manuel Pastor; Carol Wise. *Lat. Am. Res. R.* **27:2** 1992 pp. 83 – 117

181 Piecemeal reforms in planned economies — currency auctions in the Soviet Union. Giancarlo Perasso. *Comm. Econ.* **4:4** 1992 pp. 557 – 566

182 Polish economic reform, 1990-91 — principles, policies and outcomes. Stanislaw Gomulka. *Camb. J. Econ.* **16:3** 9:1992 pp. 355 – 372

183 The Polish transition programme — underpinnings, results, interpretations. Jan Winiecki. *Eur.-Asia Stud.* **44:5** 1992 pp. 809 – 835

184 The political economy of left and right during China's decade of reform. Peter M. Lichenstein. *Int. J. Soc. E.* **19:10/11/12** 1992 pp. 164 – 180

185 The politics and economics of German unification — from currency union to economic dichotomy. Otto Singer. *Ger. Pol.* **1:1** 4:1992 pp. 78 – 94

186 The politics of economic reform in the Middle East. Henri J. Barkey *[Ed.]*. New York: St. Martin's Press, 1992: 262 p. *ISBN: 0312052766; LofC: 92010698. Includes bibliographical references (p. [237]-249) and index.*

187 The politics of economic restructuring in India — the paradox of state strength and policy weakness. Baldev Raj Nayar. *J. Comm. C. Pol.* **XXX:2** 7:1992 pp. 145 – 171

188 The postsocialist transition and the state — reflections in the light of Hungarian fiscal problems. János Kornai. Cambridge, MA.: Harvard Institute of Economic Research, Harvard University, [1992]: 46 p. *ISBN: oc25321397. "Richard Ely Lecture, American Economic Association meeting, New Orleans, January 3, 1992."; "Forthcoming in American Economic Review, papers and proceedings, 1992."; Includes bibliographical references (p. 43-46).* [Discussion paper.]

189 Problems of the Polish transformation. Jan Krzysztof Bielecki. *Comm. Econ.* **4:3** 1992 pp. 321 – 332

190 Il programma di riforme economiche in Zimbabwe *[In Italian]*; [The economic reform programme in Zimbabwe] *[Summary]*. Alessandro Rocchi. *Africa [Italy]* **XLVII:4** 12:1992 pp. 531 – 562

191 Prospects for Russia's economic reforms. David Lipton; Jeffrey D. Sachs. *Brookings P.* **2** 1992 pp. 213 – 265

192 Reform and transformation in Eastern Europe — Soviet-type economics on the threshold of change. Janos Kovacs *[Ed.]*; Marton Tardos *[Ed.]*. London: Routledge, 1992: 345 p. *ISBN: 0415066301.*

193 Reform from below — the private economy and local politics in the rural industrialization of Wenzhou. Yia-Ling Liu. *China Quart.* **:130** 6:1992 pp. 293 – 316

194 Reform in Eastern Europe and the developing country dimension. Christopher Stevens *[Ed.]*; Jane Kennan *[Ed.]*. : Overseas Development Institute, 1992: 158 p. *ISBN: 0850031702.* [Overseas Development Institute development policy studies.]

195 La réforme économique radicale en Russie — bilan de la première étape *[In French]*; Radical economic reform in Russia — an assessment of the first stage *[Summary]*. Vladimir Korovkin. *Rev. Ét. Comp.* **XXIII:2-3** 6-9:1992 pp. 137 – 156

196 Reformen in Osteuropa II *[In German]*; [Reform in Eastern Europe II]. Friedrich Levcik; et al. Wien: Jugend und Volk, 1991: 155 p. [Gemeinwirtschaft. : Vol. 91]

197 Reforming finance in transitional socialist economies. Gerard Caprio; Ross Levine. Washington, D.C.: Country Economics Department The World Bank, 1992: 37 p. [Policy research working papers — financial policy and systems. : No. WPS 898]

198 Reforming Laos' economic system; *[German summary]*. Yves Bourdet. *Econ. Sys.* **16:1** 4:1992 pp. 63 – 88

199 Das Ringen um die Wirtschaftsreform in der DDR *[In German]*; [The struggle for economic reform in the GDR]. Jürgen Becher. *Deut. Arch.* **23:5** 5:1990 pp. 687 – 696

200 Russia in transition — perils of the fast track to capitalism. Thomas E. Weisskopf. *Challenge* **35:6** 11/12:1992 pp. 28 – 37

201 The Russian economic reform — progress and prospects. James H. Noren. *Sov. Ec.* **8:1** 1-3:1992 pp. 3 – 41

N.1: Economic systems and policies *[Systèmes et politiques économiques]* — *Economic reform [Réforme économique]*

202 La Russie en transition *[In French]*; Russia in transition *[Summary]*. Frédéric Lerais. *Obser. Diag. Econ.* :**42** 10:1992 pp. 135 – 158

203 The shift to market economies in Eastern Europe. Yoshiaki Nishimura. *Jpn. R. Int. Aff.* **6:1** Spring: 1992 pp. 22 – 42

204 "Shock therapy" in Poland — experience and conclusions. Sergei Matytsin; Irina Sinitsina; Natalya Chudakova. *Int. Aff. Mos.* :**7** 7:1992 pp. 50 – 58

205 Socialist economies in transition — appraisals of the market mechanism. Mark Knell *[Ed.]*; Christine Rider *[Ed.]*. Aldershot, Hants: E. Elgar Pub, 1992: 245 p. *ISBN: 1852784385; LofC: 92026137.*

206 Sokkterápia vagy fokozatosság *[In Hungarian]*; Shock therapy or gradual measures *[Summary]*. András Köves. *Közg. Sz.* **XXXIX** 1:1992 pp. 1 – 18

207 Some highlights of Malawi's experience with financial liberalization. Y.S. El Nil. *Finan. News Anal.* **5:1** 1:1992 pp. 1 – 15

208 Stabilization and economic reform in Russia. Stanley Fischer. *Brookings P.* :**1** 1992 pp. 77 – 111

209 The state central economic bureaucracies and the outcome of systemic economic reform — an institutional explanation for the Soviet and Chinese experiences. Baohui Zhang. *Governance* **5:3** 7:1992 pp. 312 – 341

210 The theory of social cost and China's economic reforms. Renliang Niu; Ruoxian He. *Soc. Sci. China* **XIII:4** 12:1992 pp. 147 – 157

211 Towards a new economic order in the countries of central and eastern Europe. Tomas J.F. Riha. *Int. J. Soc. E.* **19:7/8/9** 1992 pp. 172 – 194

212 Trade, investment, and the fear of "peaceful evolution". Roger W. Sullivan. *Iss. Stud.* **28:2** 2:1992 pp. 51 – 66

213 Tradition und Modernisierung in Ostmitteleuropa, Südostasien und Lateinamerika. Drei vergleichende Kommentare *[In German]*; [Tradition and modernization in East Central Europe, Southeast Asia and Latin America. Comparisons in three commentaries]. Peter L. Berger; Robert P. Weller; Barry B. Levine. *Transit* :**3** Winter:1992 pp. 206 – 220

214 La transition de l'économie roumaine vers l'économie de marché — réformes économiques et institutionnelles *[In French]*; The Rumanian economy in transition to a market economy — economic and institutional reforms *[Summary]*. Daniel Labaronne. *Rev. Ét. Comp.* **XXIII:2-3** 6-9:1992 pp. 105 – 136

215 Transition en Europe de l'est — les nouveaux rivages du marché *[In French]*; [Transition in Eastern Europe — the new market horizons]. M. Lavigne *[Contrib.]*; M. Jackson *[Contrib.]*; R. Lantner *[Contrib.]*; E. Fauchart *[Contrib.]*; A.M. Vacic *[Contrib.]*; J. Ch. Asselain *[Contrib.]*; W. Trzeciakowski *[Contrib.]*; J. Kreuter *[Contrib.]*; D. Daianu *[Contrib.]*; V. Kouznetsov *[Contrib.]* and others. *Collection of 18 articles.* Ec. Sociét. , *XXVI:4-5*, 1992 pp. 9 – 381

216 Transition from planned to market economy — Hungary and Poland. Andrzej K. Kozminski. *Stud. Comp. Commun.* **XXV:4** 12:1992 pp. 315 – 333

217 The transition to a market economy — pitfalls of partial reform. Kevin M. Murphy; Andrei Shleifer; Robert W. Vishny. *Q. J. Econ.* **CVII:3** 8:1992 pp. 889 – 906

218 Trials of transition — economic reform in the former Communist bloc. Michael Keren *[Ed.]*; Gur Ofer *[Ed.]*. Boulder, CO.: Westview Press, 1992: xx, 308 p. *ISBN: 0813315646; LofC: 92026065. Includes bibliographical references and indexes.*

219 Van planeconomie naar markteconomie *[In Dutch]*; [From planned economy to market economy]. N.J. van der Lijn. *Maan. Econ.* **56:4** 1992 pp. 325 – 340

220 Western aid and economic reform in the former Soviet Union. Jim Leitzel. *World. Econ.* **15:3** 5:1992 pp. 357 – 374

221 With axes in their eyes — rentierism and market reform in Yugoslavia. Boris Young. *Stud. Comp. Commun.* **XXV:3** 9:1992 pp. 274 – 286

222 Yeltsin's economic reform course and its critics. Roland Goetz. *Aussenpolitik* **43:3** 1992 pp. 267 – 276

Economic systems *[Systèmes économiques]*

223 La Commissione economica per la Costituente quarantasette anni dopo *[In Italian]*; The economic commission for the Italian Constituent Assembly forty-seven years after *[Summary]*. Giovanni Demaria. *Rev. Int. Sci. Ec. Com.* **XXXIX:4** 4:1992 pp. 289 – 302

224 Demokrácia és piacgazdaság. I *[In Hungarian]*; Democracy and market economy, part I *[Summary]*. Péter Gedeon. *Közg. Sz.* **XXXIX** 5:1992 pp. 401 – 424

N.1: Economic systems and policies *[Systèmes et politiques économiques]* — *Economic systems [Systèmes économiques]*

225 Demokrácia és piacgazdaság. II. A rendszertranszformáció tipológiájához *[In Hungarian]*; Democracy and market economy II. To the typology of industrial societies *[Summary]*. Péter Gedeon. *Közg. Sz.* **XXXIX** 6:1992 pp. 525 – 537

226 The endogenous stability of economic systems. Larry S. Karp. *J. Econ. Dyn. Cont.* **16:1** 1:1992 pp. 117 – 138

227 European business systems — firms and markets in their national contexts. Richard Whitley *[Ed.]*. London: Sage Publications, 1992: 291 p. *ISBN: 0803987323. Includes bibliographies.*

228 Fra stat til privat *[In Norwegian]*; From state to private *[Summary]*. Kåre Dahl Martinsen. *Int. Pol.* **50:3** 1992 pp. 291 – 304

229 From a Ricardian to a Marxian ranking of economic goals and means (a case of the Soviet Union). Ernest Raiklin. *Int. J. Soc. E.* **19:7/8/9** 1992 pp. 90 – 107

230 A gazdasági rendszerváltás dilemmái — válságban *[In Hungarian]*; Dilemmas of the change of economic system — in a crisis *[Summary]*. Miklós Mandel; József Veress. *Közg. Sz.* **XXXIX** 1:1992 pp. 19 – 32

231 Islam and the economic system; *[Arabic summary]*. Mohsin S. Khan; Abbas Mirakhor. *R. Islam. Econ.* **2:1** 1992 pp. 1 – 30

232 Islamic economic alternatives — critical perspectives and new directions. Jomo K.S. *[Ed.]*. London: Macmillan Academic and Professional, 1992: 180 p. *ISBN: 0333549201.*

233 Macrosystems — the dynamics of economic policy. Elias Karakitsos. Oxford: Blackwell, 1992: 335 p. *ISBN: 0631172971; LofC: 91045207. Includes index.*

234 New strategists who demand the old economy. Stephen Blank. *Orbis* **36:3** Summer:1992 pp. 365 – 378

235 Social corporatism — a superior economic system? Jukka Pekkarinen *[Ed.]*; Matti Pohjoka *[Ed.]*; Bob Rowthorn *[Ed.]*. Oxford: Clarendon Press, 1992: 430 p. *ISBN: 0198283806; LofC: 91005027. "A Study prepared for the World Institute for Development Economics Research (WIDER) of the United Nations University."; Includes bibliographical references and index.* [Studies in development economics.]

236 Socialism — alternative visions and models. David Schweickart *[Contrib.]*; Michael Albert *[Contrib.]*; Robin Hahnel *[Contrib.]*; David Laibman *[Contrib.]*; Diane Flaherty *[Contrib.]*. Collection of 4 articles. *Sci. Soc.* , *56:1,* Spring:1992 pp. 9 – 108

237 *[In Japanese]*; [Swedish model or Japanese model?]. Tetsuo Kaio. *Keizai Hyoron Vol.8; No.1992* pp. 23 – 33

238 Systemic transformation in Central and Eastern Europe — general framework, specific features and prospects; *[German summary]*. Aleksandar M. Vacic. *Ost. Wirt.* **37:1** 3:1992 pp. 1 – 18

239 Understanding the market economy. Arne J. Isachsen; Thorvaldur Gylfason; Carl B. Hamilton. Oxford: Oxford University Press, 1992: 243 p. *ISBN: 0198773560; LofC: 92024790. Includes bibliographical references and index.*

240 When higher incomes reduce welfare — queues, labor supply, and macro equilibrium in socialist economies. Maxim Boycko. *Q. J. Econ.* **CVII:3** 8:1992 pp. 907 – 920

241 Zum gegenwärtigen Stand der Transformationstheorie — eine Literaturstudie *[In German]*; [On current approaches in transformation theory — a review of the literature]. Armin Bohnet; Claudia Ohly. *Z. Wirt.pol.* **41:1** 1992 pp. 27 – 49

Planning theory and practice *[Théorie et pratique de la planification]*

242 Economic planning in Iran — roots, processes and prospects. A.A. Banouei; A. Aryafar. *Asian. Afr. Stud.* **25:2** 7:1991 pp. 161 – 178

243 Enterprise reforms in a centrally planned economy — the case of the Chinese bicycle industry. Xun-Hai Zhang. New York: St. Martin's Press, 1992: 219 p. *ISBN: 0312075936; LofC: 91041239. Includes bibliographical references (p.) and index.*

244 An explanation of coexistence of taut planning and hidden reserves in centrally planned economies. Huizhong Zhou. *J. Comp. Econ.* **16:3** 9:1992 pp. 456 – 478

245 Financial innovation and planning in a capitalist economy. P. Auerbach; P. Skott. *Metroeconomica* **XLIII:1-2** 2-6:1992 pp. 75 – 96

246 Indian planning at the crossroads. Bhabatosh Datta. Delhi: Oxford University Press, 1992: viii, 251 p. *ISBN: 0195629582.*

247 The Iranian economy after the revolution — an economic appraisal of the five-year plan. M.R. Ghasimi. *Int. J. M.E. Stud.* **24:4** 11:1992 pp. 599 – 614

N.1: Economic systems and policies *[Systèmes et politiques économiques]* — **Planning theory and practice** *[Théorie et pratique de la planification]*

248 The measurement of localisation performance and the industrial labour absorption function for regional planning of human resources in India. Prasanta Pathak; Vaskar Saha. *Ind. J. Reg. Sci.* **XXIV:1** 1992 pp. 1 – 14

249 La méthode des effets trente ans après *[In French]*; (The effects method thirty years on); *[Title only in German]*; *[Title only in Spanish]*. Marc Chervel. *R. T-Monde* **33:132** 10-12:1992 pp. 873 – 891

250 Permanent chaos without a market — the non-Latinamericanization of the USSR. Hillel H. Ticktin. *Stud. Comp. Commun.* **XXV:3** 9:1992 pp. 242 – 256

251 Pervasive shortages under socialism. A. Shleifer; R. Vishny. *Rand J. Eco.* **23:2** Summer:1992 pp. 237 – 246

252 La planificación venezolana en los noventa *[In Spanish]*; [Venezuelan economic planning in the 1990s]. Jorge A. Giordani C.; Hercilio Castellano B.; Jésus López. Valencia: Cendes, [1992?]: 141 p. *ISBN: 9802121355*. [Colección Jorge Ahumada.]

253 Planning and development under the monarchy and the Islamic government of Iran — a critical assessment. A.A. Banouei. *Int. Stud.* **29:1** 1-3:1992 pp. 41 – 54

254 Trade and the collapse of central planning in Europe. Eleftherios Botsas. *E. Eur. Quart.* **XXVI:2** Summer:1992 pp. 239 – 259

255 Varying data quality and effects in economic analysis and planning. Jan A. Eklof. Stockholm: Stockholm School of Economics. Economic Research Institute, 1992: 300 p. *ISBN: 917258341x*.

Privatization *[Privatisation]*

256 Adjusting privatization — case studies from developing countries. Christopher Adam; William Cavendish; Percy S. Mistry. London: James Currey, 1992: 400 p. *ISBN: 0852551320*.

257 Autogestion et privatisations en Yougoslavie *[In French]*; Self-management and privatization in Yugoslavia *[Summary]*. Michel Drouet. *Rev. Ét. Comp.* **XXIII:2-3** 6-9:1992 pp. 59 – 103

258 British privatization — taking capitalism to the people. John Moore. *Harv. Bus. Re.* **70:1** 1-2:1992 pp. 115 – 124

259 Commodity exchanges and the privatization of the agricultural sector in the Commonwealth of Independent States — needed steps in creating a market economy. Alexander Belozertsev; Jerry W. Markham. *Law Cont. Pr.* **55:4** Autumn:1992 pp. 119 – 155

260 Development of the private sector in Poland in 1989-90 — the early phase of structural transformation. Maria Ciechocinska. *Comm. Econ.* **4:2** 1992 pp. 215 – 236

261 Does sequencing of privatization matter in reforming planned economies? Aasim M. Husain; Ratna Sahay. *Staff Pap. Int. Monetary* **39:4** 12:1992 pp. 801 – 824

262 Eastern Europe and the Soviet Union — recent developments and prospects. Jonathan Riley. *Q. Econ. Bull.* **13:2** 6:1992 pp. 24 – 32

263 Les fermes d'État de la Basse Silésie au seuil de la privatisation *[In French]*; State farms of Lower Silesia, on the threshold of privatization *[Summary]*. Izabela Ferens; Barbara A. Despiney Zochowska. *R. Pol. Econ.* **4:3** 1992 pp. 173 – 191

264 Les fermes d'État de la Basse Silésie au seuil de la privatisation *[In French]*; State farms of Lower Silesia, on the threshold of privatization *[Summary]*. Izabela Ferens; Barbara A. Despiney Zochowska. *Stud. Comp. Commun.* **XXV:3** 9:1992 pp. 173 – 191

265 Les fermes d'État de la Basse Silésie au seuil de la privatisation *[In French]*; State farms of Lower Silesia, on the threshold of privatization *[Summary]*. Izabela Ferens; Barbara A. Despiney Zochowska. *Util. Policy* **2:4** 10:1992 pp. 173 – 191

266 Les fermes d'État de la Basse Silésie au seuil de la privatisation *[In French]*; State farms of Lower Silesia, on the threshold of privatization *[Summary]*. Izabela Ferens; Barbara A. Despiney Zochowska. *Nord. Ny. Taiwan and the geopolitics of the Asian-American dilemma* pp. 173 – 191

267 Les fermes d'État de la Basse Silésie au seuil de la privatisation *[In French]*; State farms of Lower Silesia, on the threshold of privatization *[Summary]*. Izabela Ferens; Barbara A. Despiney Zochowska. *Nord. Ny. IMF working paper* pp. 173 – 191

268 Foreign direct investment and privatisation in Central and Eastern Europe. Gábor Hunya. *Comm. Econ.* **4:4** 1992 pp. 501 – 511

269 Fosztogatás — osztogatás — fosztogatás (az állami tulajdon tündöklése és bukása) *[In Hungarian]*; Splendour and fall of the state property *[Summary]*. Péter Mihályi. *Közg. Sz.* **XXXIX** 11:1992 pp. 1001 – 1017

N.1: Economic systems and policies *[Systèmes et politiques économiques]* —
Privatization [Privatisation]

270 How and how not to desocialize. Murray N. Rothbard. *R. Austrian Econ.* **6:1** 1992 pp. 65 – 77
271 The Hungarian public on the advance of private economy. E. Hann; M. Laki. *Acta Oecon.* **44:1-2** 1992 pp. 191 – 200
272 Is the World Bank approach to structural reform supported by experience of electricity privatization in the UK? Adilson de Oliveira; Gordon MacKerron. *Energy Pol.* **20:2** 2:1992 pp. 153 – 162
273 Kooperáció és privatizáció *[In Hungarian]*; Cooperation and privatization *[Summary]*. Fekete Ferenc. *Közg. Sz.* **XXXIX:** 7-8:1992 pp. 713 – 723
274 Legal development and privatization in Russia — a case study. Kathryn Hendley. *Sov. Ec.* **8:2** 4-7:1992 pp. 130 – 157
275 Moral economy and the expansion of the privatisation constituency in Nigeria. Pita Ogaba Agbese. *J. Comm. C. Pol.* **XXX:3** 11:1992 pp. 335 – 357
276 Not even the contrary is true — the transfigurations of centralization and decentralization. É. Voszka. *Acta Oecon.* **44:1-2** 1992 pp. 77 – 94
277 Old debts and new beginnings — a policy choice in transitional socialist economies. Ross Levine; David Scott. Washington, D.C.: Country Economics Department, The World Bank, 1992: 27 p. [Policy research working papers.]
278 Política económica conservadora en América Latina y Europa Occidental — las fuentes políticas de la privatización *[In Spanish]*; [Conservative economic policy in Latin America and Western Europe — the political roots of privatization]. Héctor E. Schamis. *Est. Inter.* **XXV:99** 7-9:1992 pp. 341 – 364
279 Post-privatisation regulation in Britain. William A. Maloney; Jeremy J. Richardson. *Politics (U.K.)* **12:2** 10:1992 pp. 14 – 20
280 Pretvorba vlasništva — dokle smo stigli i kako dalje? *[In Serbo-Croatian]*; Преобразование собственности — до куда мы дошли и как дальше? *[Russian summary]*; Ownership transformation — how far have we come and what next? *[Summary]*. Gorazd Nikić. *Ekon. Preg.* **43:3-4** 1992 pp. 223 – 229
281 Privatisation and buy-outs in the USSR. Igor Filatochev; Trevor Buck; Mike Wright. *Eur.-Asia Stud.* **44:2** 1992 pp. 265 – 282
282 Privatisation and entrepreneurship in the break-up of the USSR. Igor Filatochev; Trevor Buck; Mike Wright. *World. Econ.* **15:4** 7:1992 pp. 505 – 524
283 La privatisation en Europe de l'Est *[In French]*; Privatization in Eastern Europe *[Summary]*. Morris Bornstein. *Rev. Ét. Comp.* **XXIII:2-3** 6-9:1992 pp. 5 – 58
284 Privatisation everywhere — the world's adoption of the British experience. John Moore. London: Centre for Policy Studies, 1992: 36 p. *ISBN: 186999020x.*
285 Privatisation in Eastern Europe. Morris Bornstein. *Comm. Econ.* **4:3** 1992 pp. 283 – 320
286 Privatisation in Eastern Europe — a comparative study of Poland and Hungary. Kálmán Mizsei. *Eur.-Asia Stud.* **44:2** 1992 pp. 283 – 296
287 Privatisation of public transit — lessons from the wider experience. David Hensher; Michael Beesley. *Ec. Pap. Aust.* **11:3** 9:1992 pp. 49 – 56
288 Privatisation of the Polish economy — problems of transition. Kazimierz Z. Poznanski. *Eur.-Asia Stud.* **44:4** 1992 pp. 641 – 664
289 Privatisation options for Eastern Europe — the irrelevance of Western experience. Paul R. Ferguson. *World. Econ.* **15:4** 7:1992 pp. 487 – 504
290 Privatisation — a global perspective. V.V. Ramanadham *[Ed.]*. London: Routledge, 1992: 610 p. *ISBN: 0415075661; LofC: 92030813. Includes bibliographical references and index.*
291 Privatisation — the road to a market economy. Veselin Vukotić. *Comm. Econ.* **4:3** 1992 pp. 411 – 423
292 Privatisierung in Polen 1990/91 *[In German]*; [Privatisation in Poland 1990-1991]. Christoph G. Bandyk. *Osteuropa* **42:5** 5:1992 pp. 431 – 440
293 Privatisierung in Polen, Ungarn und der ČSFR — eine Bestandsaufnahme *[In German]*; [Privatization in Poland, Hungary and Czechoslovakia — an evaluation]. Ralph Heinrich. *Weltwirt.* **:3** 1992 pp. 295 – 316
294 Privatisierungsstrategien in der CSFR, Ostdeutschland, Polen und Ungarn. Ein Vergleich *[In German]*; [Privatization strategies in Czechoslovakia, East Germany, Poland and Hungary. A comparison]. David Stark. *Transit* **:3** Winter:1992 pp. 177 – 192
295 Privatising the British energy industries — the lessons to be learned. C. Robinson. *Metroeconomica* **XLIII:1-2** 2-6:1992 pp. 103 – 129
296 A privatizáció makroökonómiai hatásai zárt gazdaságban *[In Hungarian]*; Macroeconomic impacts of privatization in a closed economy *[Summary]*. Valentinyi Ákos. *Közg. Sz.* **XXXIX** 3:1992 pp. 208 – 225

N.1: Economic systems and policies *[Systèmes et politiques économiques] — Privatization [Privatisation]*

297 Privatización de empresas estatales *[In Spanish]*; [The privatization of state enterprises]. Guillermo de la Dehesa *[Contrib.]*; John Driffill *[Contrib.]*; Carlo Favero *[Contrib.]*; Matthew Bishop *[Contrib.]*; John Kay *[Contrib.]*; Robert Delorme *[Contrib.]*. Collection *of 6 articles*. **Infor. Com. Esp.** , *:707*, 7:1992 pp. 3 – 88

298 Privatización y cambios en los costos sociales de la inflación — el caso de ENT el Argentina *[In Spanish]*; [Privatization and change in the social costs of inflation — the case of the Argentinian ENT] *[Summary]*. Manuel Angel Abdala. *Desar. Econ.* **32:127** 10-12:1992 pp. 357 – 380

299 Privatization. Horst Siebert; Herbert Giersch. Tübingen: Mohr, 1992: 230 p. *ISBN: 3161459644.*

300 Privatization and entrepreneurship in post-socialist countries — economy, law, and society. Bruno Dallago *[Ed.]*; Gianmaria Ajani *[Ed.]*; Bruno Grancelli *[Ed.]*. New York, NY.: St. Martin's, 1992: 360 p. *ISBN: 0312081006; LofC: 92007252.*

301 Privatization and private sector development in Nepal. Narayan Khadka. *Asian Ec.* **:82** 9:1992 pp. 12 – 39

302 Privatization and regulation in Turkey — an assessment. C. Karataş. *J. Int. Dev.* **4:6** 11-12:1992 pp. 583 – 606

303 Privatization and the development of capitalism in Russia. Simon Clarke. *New Left R.* **:196** 11/12:1992 pp. 3 – 27

304 Privatization and the Soviet economy. Patrick Flaherty. *Mon. Rev.* **43:8** 1:1992 pp. 1 – 14

305 Privatization complicates the fresh start. Peter Murrell. *Orbis* **36:3** Summer:1992 pp. 323 – 332

306 Privatization in Eastern European countries. Yali Peng. *E. Eur. Quart.* **XXVI:4** Winter:1992 pp. 471 – 484

307 Privatization in Europe — West and East experiences. F. Targetti *[Ed.]*. Aldershot: Dartmouth Publishing, 1992: 236 p. *ISBN: 1855212757.*

308 Privatization in the ASEAN states — who gets what, why, and with what effect. R.S. Milne. *Pac. Aff.* **65:1** Spring:1992 pp. 7 – 29

309 Privatization in the Asian-Pacific region. Ng Chee Yuen; Toh Kin Woon. *Asian-Pacific Ec. Lit.* **6:2** 11:1992 pp. 42 – 68

310 Privatization issues. G. Jenkins *[Contrib.]*; H.-W. Sinn *[Contrib.]*; G.E. Metcalf *[Contrib.]*; L. Ambrus-Lakatos *[Contrib.]*. Collection of 3 articles. **Publ. Finan.** , 47, 1992 pp. 141 – 183

311 Privatization policies in Central and Eastern Europe. Patrick Bolton; Gérard Roland; John Vickers *[Comments by]*; Michael Burda *[Comments by]*. Econ. Pol. **:15** 10:1992 pp. 275 – 309

312 Privatization — financial choices and opportunities. Amnuay Viravan. Bangkok: Per Jacobsson Foundation, 1991: 28 p. [Per Jacobsson Lecture. : No. 1991]

313 Privatization, public ownership, and the regulation of natural monopoly. C. D. Foster. Oxford: Blackwell, 1992: 458 p. *ISBN: 0631184864; LofC: 91047004. Includes bibliographical references and index.*

314 Privatizing and rolling back the Latin American state. David Félix. *CEPAL R.* **:46** 4:1992 pp. 31 – 46

315 Proces rynkowej reformy gospodarczej w Polsce i we wschodnich krajach Republiki Federalnej Niemiec ze szczególnym uwzględnieniem prywatyzacji *[In Polish]*; Der marktwirtschaftliche Reformenprozess in Polen und den östlichen Ländern der Bundesrepublik Deutschland unter besonderer Berücksichtigung der Privatisierung *[In German]*; [The market economy process of reform in Poland and the Eastern German states, with special reference to privatization]. Mattan Ostrowski *[Contrib.]*; Gerhard Fels *[Contrib.]*; Manfred Lennings *[Contrib.]*; Entz Knauss *[Contrib.]*; Barbara Błaszczyk *[Contrib.]*; Ewa Balcerowicz *[Contrib.]*; Marek Dąbrowski *[Contrib.]*; Urzula Wojciechowska *[Contrib.]*; Tomasz Stankiewicz *[Contrib.]*; Jerzy Drygalski *[Contrib.]* and others. Collection of 10 articles. **Gosp. Nar.** , *:7-8*, 1991 pp. 2 – 29

316 The promise of privatization; La promessa della privatizzazione *[Italian summary]*. Robert H. Wessel. *Rev. Int. Sci. Ec. Com.* **XXXIX:4** 4:1992 pp. 303 – 323

317 Prospects for privatisation in OECD countries. Barrie Stevens. *Nat. W. Bank* 8:1992 pp. 2 – 22

318 Recent controversies in political economy. Russell Lewis *[Ed.]*. London: Routledge, 1992: 346 p. *ISBN: 0415061636; LofC: 91045321. Includes bibliographical references and index.*

N.1: Economic systems and policies *[Systèmes et politiques économiques]* — **Privatization** *[Privatisation]*

319 The role of entrepreneurship in desocialization. Jeffrey M. Herbener. *R. Austrian Econ.* **6:1** 1992 pp. 79 – 93

320 Romania's evolving legal framework for private sector development. Cheryl Williamson Gray; Rebecca J. Hanson; Peter G. Ianachkov. Washington, D.C.: Country Economics Department and the Legal Department, The World Bank, 1992: 27 p. [Policy research working papers.]

321 Tecniche ed esperienze di privatizzazione in Francia — un modello per l'Europa dell'Est? *[In Italian]*; [Techniques and experiences of privatization in France — a model for Eastern Europe?]. Wladimir Andreff. *Econ. Ban.* **3** 1992 pp. 373 – 399

322 Transformation of ownership in Czechoslovakia. Martin Kupka. *Eur.-Asia Stud.* **44:2** 1992 pp. 297 – 312

323 Transforming the economies of East Central Europe. David Stark *[Contrib.]*; Peter Murrell *[Contrib.]*; László Bruszt *[Contrib.]*; David Bartlett *[Contrib.]*. Collection of 4 articles. **E.Eur. Pol. Soc.** , *6:1*, Winter:1992 pp. 1 – 118

324 Transition en Europe de l'est — les nouveaux rivages du marché *[In French]*; [Transition in Eastern Europe — the new market horizons]. M. Lavigne *[Contrib.]*; M. Jackson *[Contrib.]*; R. Lantner *[Contrib.]*; E. Fauchart *[Contrib.]*; A.M. Vacic *[Contrib.]*; J. Ch. Asselain *[Contrib.]*; W. Trzeciakowski *[Contrib.]*; J. Kreuter *[Contrib.]*; D. Daianu *[Contrib.]*; V. Kouznetsov *[Contrib.] and others.* Collection of 18 articles. **Ec. Sociét.** , *XXVI:4-5*, 1992 pp. 9 – 381

325 La Treuhandanstalt dans la privatisation de l'agriculture est-allemande *[In French]*; The Treuhandanstalt's role in the privatization of East-German agriculture *[Summary]*. Benoît Petit; Florent Gerbaud. *Rev. Ét. Comp.* **XXIII:2-3** 6-9:1992 pp. 157 – 171

326 A vállalatokat eladják, ugye? *[In Hungarian]*; The entreprises are sold — are they not? *[Summary]*. István Ábel; Richard A. Miller. *Közg. Sz.* **XXXIX** 1:1992 pp. 33 – 45

327 What is privatisation? Stephen King. *Ec. Pap. Aust.* **11:3** 9:1992 pp. 57 – 64

328 Wieviel Staat braucht der Markt? *[In German]*; [How much state does the market need?]. Roman Frydman; Andrzej Rapaczynski. *Transit* **:3** Winter:1992 pp. 193 – 205

N.2: Public finance — *Finances publiques*

Sub-divisions: Corporate taxation *[Impôt sur les sociétés]*; Fiscal policy *[Politique fiscale]*; Income and consumption tax *[Impôts sur le revenu et sur la consommation]*; Optimal taxation *[Fiscalité optimale]*; Property tax *[Impôt sur la propriété]*; Public debt *[Dette publique]*; Public expenditure *[Dépenses publiques]*; Tax evasion and avoidance *[Evasion et fraude fiscales]*; Tax reform *[Réformes fiscales]*

1 Az államháztartás a kilenevenes évek Magyarországán *[In Hungarian]*; Public finances in Hungary in the nineties *[Summary]*. László Muraközy. *Közg. Sz.* **XXXIX** 11:1992 pp. 1050 – 1066

2 Approccio pigouviano e approccio volontaristico nelle politiche ambientali — valutazione critica attraverso i risultati di una ricerca diretta *[In Italian]*; Pigouvian approach and voluntary approach in environmental policies — a critical evaluation through a direct survey *[Summary]*. Giorgio Casoni; Fabio Nuti. *Industria* **XIII:3** 7-9:1992 pp. 473 – 501

3 Are the treasury's tax revenue forecasts rational? Barry Reilly; Robert Witt. *Manch. Sch. E.* **LX:4** 12:1992 pp. 390 – 402

4 Budget policy and the decline of national saving revisited. Michael M. Hutchison. Basle: Bank for International Settlements, Monetary and Economic Department, 1992: 65 p. *Bibliography — p.58-62p.* [BIS economic papers. : No. 33]

5 Budgetary reform — a capital budget? J.S. v.d. Heyns. *S. Afr. J. Econ.* **60:4** 12:1992 pp. 354 – 372

6 Budgetary rules to minimize societal poverty in a general equilibrium context. E. Thorbecke; D. Berrian. *J. Dev. Econ.* **39:2** 10:1992 pp. 189 – 205

7 Budgettaire politiek, interdependentie en sectoranalyse *[In Dutch]*; [Budgetary politics, interdependence and sector analysis]. R.J. de Groof; M.A. van Tuijl. *Maan. Econ.* **56:1** 1992 pp. 24 – 41

8 Capital account effects on optimum international reserves and the speed of adjustment. G.C. Anayiotos. *Eco. Notes* **21:2** 1992 pp. 330 – 340

N.2: Public finance *[Finances publiques]*

9 Central and local finances in developing countries — the trend toward decentralization. Reeitsu Kojima *[Contrib.]*; Hiroshi Satō *[Contrib.]*; Hiroyoshi Kanō *[Contrib.]*; Kazuhisa Itō *[Contrib.]*; Keiko Imai *[Contrib.]*; Sobhi Moharram *[Contrib.]*. *Collection of 6 articles*. **Develop. Eco.** , *XXX:4*, 12:1992 pp. 315 – 481

10 Competitive tax theory in open economies — constrained inefficiency and a Pigovian remedy. R. Krelove. *J. Publ. Ec.* **48:3** 8:1992 pp. 361 – 375

11 Discovery assessments — cenlon, olin and statement of practice. David F. Williams. *Br. Tax Rev.* **:5** 1992 pp. 323 – 333

12 Does a government save from capital controls? The case of Japan; Trae vantaggio lo stato dai controlli sui capital? Il caso del Giappone *[Italian summary]*. Reiko Nakamura. *Rev. Int. Sci. Ec. Com.* **XXXIX:12** 12:1992 pp. 1025 – 1051

13 Economic psychological perspectives on taxation. P. Webley *[Ed.]*; D.J. Hessing *[Ed.]*; F.A. Cowell *[Contrib.]*; H. Elffers *[Contrib.]*; H.S.J. Robben *[Contrib.]*; B. Kazemier *[Contrib.]*; R. van Eck *[Contrib.]*; E.A.G. Groenland *[Contrib.]*; R.A. Sommerhalder *[Contrib.]*; A.M. Eling *[Contrib.] and others*. *Collection of 14 articles*. **J. Econ. Psyc.** , *13:4*, 12:1992 pp. 515 – 755

14 Efficiency inducing tax for a common property oligopoly. L. Karp. *Econ. J.* **102:411** 3:1992 pp. 321 – 332

15 Equilibrio alla Nash e variazioni congetturali in un modello di concorrenza fiscale *[In Italian]*; [The Nash balance and conjectural variations in a model of fiscal competition]. Francesca Stroffolini. *Riv. Dir. Finan. Sci. Fin.* **LI:1** 3:1992 pp. 39 – 50

16 Equity release schemes and equity extraction by elderly households in Britain. Beverley Mullings; Chris Hamnett. *Age. Soc.* **12:4** 12:1992 pp. 413 – 442

17 Évolution et perspectives du corps analytique des innovations financières *[In French]*; A critical assessment of financial innovation theories *[Summary]*. P. Geoffron. *Rev. Ec. Polit.* **102:6** 11-12:1992 pp. 843 – 872

18 The evolution of the managed economy in Europe. Grahame Thompson. *Econ. Soc.* **21:2** 5:1992 pp. 129 – 151

19 Experimental evidence on an economic model of taxpayer aggression under strategic and non-strategic audits; *[French summary]*. P.J. Beck; J.S. Davis; W-O. Jung. *Cont. Account. Res.* **9:1** Fall:1992 pp. 86 – 112

20 Exploring the tax revolt. Harold W. Elder. *Publ. Fin. Q.* **20:1** 1:1992 pp. 47 – 63

21 Federal-state financial relations — a priority for reform? Des Moore. *Ec. Pap. Aust.* **11:1** 3:1992 pp. 70 – 82

22 Finances publiques — l'émergence de la crise fiscale dans les années 80 — les causes, tant du point de vue des dépenses et recettes, que de la répartition Etat-périphérie *[In French]*; The public sector finances — the development of the crisis of the tax system in the 1980s *[Summary]*. Jean-Joseph Boillot; Françoise Lemoine. *Ec. Pros. Int.* **:50** 2e trimestre:1992 pp. 99 – 121

23 Financial markets and public finance in the transformation process. Vito Tanzi. Washington, D.C.: International Monetary Fund, Fiscal Affairs Department, 1992: 29 p. *Bibliography* — p.27-29. [IMF working paper. : No. WP/92/29]

24 Financing state and local government in the 1990s. William H. Oakland *[Ed.]*; Roy Bahl *[Contrib.]*; Jorge Martinez-Vazquez *[Contrib.]*; David L. Sjoquist *[Contrib.]*; Ronald C. Fisher *[Contrib.]*; John C. Navin *[Contrib.]*; Helen F. Ladd *[Contrib.]*; Thomas A. Downes *[Contrib.]*; Thomas F. Pogue *[Contrib.]*; Andrew Reschovsky *[Contrib.] and others*. *Collection of 12 articles*. **Publ. Fin. Q.** , *20:4*, 10:1992 pp. 413 – 585

25 The first Pacific region conference. Veerinderjeet Singh *[Contrib.]*; Anthony J. Lines *[Contrib.]*; Graham G. Tubb; Sai Ree Yun *[Contrib.]*; Yoong Neung Kee *[Contrib.]*; Anthony Au-Yeung *[Contrib.]*; Michael Abrutyn *[Contrib.]*; Paul Ellard *[Contrib.]*; R.A. Oser *[Contrib.]*; Koichi Uno *[Contrib.] and others*. *Collection of 8 articles*. **B. Int. Fiscal Docu.** , *46:1/2*, 1-2:1992 pp. 3 – 64

26 Fiscal illusion, uncertainty, and the flypaper effect. Geoffrey K. Turnbull. *J. Publ. Ec.* **48:2** 7:1992 pp. 207 – 223

27 Fiscal lags and the high inflation drop. Alfredo J. Canavese; Daniel Heymann. *Q Rev. Econ. Finan.* **32:2** Summer:1992 pp. 100 – 109

28 Fiscal policy in an endogenous growth model. Gilles Saint-Paul. *Q. J. Econ.* **CVII:4** 11:1992 pp. 1243 – 1260

29 Form and substance under schedule E. John Ward. *Br. Tax Rev.* **:3** 1992 pp. 139 – 147

30 From the static to the dynamic — some problems in the theory of taxation. Nicholas Stern. *J. Publ. Ec.* **47:2** 3:1992 pp. 273 – 296

N.2: Public finance *[Finances publiques]*

31 Gasoline tax policy, carbon emissions and the global environment; Mineralölsteuer, Kohlenstoff-Emissionen und globale Umweltprobleme *[German summary]*; Politique de taxation de carburant, émission de carbone et l'environnement global *[French summary]*; La política impositiva de las gasolinas, las emisiones de carbón y el medio ambiente global *[Spanish summary]*. Thomas Sterner; Carol Dahl; Mikael Franzén. *J. Transp. Ec. Pol.* **XXVI:2** 5:1992 pp. 109 – 120

32 Global tax progressivity. Udo Ebert. *Publ. Fin. Q.* **20:1** 1:1992 pp. 77 – 92

33 Hierarchical and contractual approaches to budgetary reform. Jørgen Grønnegård Christensen. *J. Theor. Pol.* **4:1** 1:1992 pp. 67 – 92

34 The impact of taxation on investments — an analysis through effective tax rates — the case of Greece; L'impatto delle imposte sugli investimenti — analisi delle aliquote fiscali effettive — il caso della Grecia *[Italian summary]*. Anastasia Maggina. *Rev. Int. Sci. Ec. Com.* **XXXIX:3** 3:1992 pp. 267 – 286

35 The implications of a switch to locally varying business rates. Kevin Denny; Michael Ridge. *Fis. Stud.* **13:1** 2:1992 pp. 22 – 37

36 Improving tax administration in developing countries. Richard Miller Bird *[Ed.]*; Milka Casanegra de Jantscher *[Ed.]*. Washington, D.C: International Monetary Fund, 1992: xii, 403 p. *ISBN: 1557753172; LofC: 92034718. Includes bibliographical references.*

37 Incentive regulation in oligopoly industry — welfare effects of the ex post adjustment system. Jae-Cheol Kim; Byong-Kook Yoo. *Econ. S. Quart.* **43:3** 9:1992 pp. 193 – 209

38 Increasing local government revenue and the concept of financial equalisation. Phang Siew Nooi. *Born. R.* **III:1** 6:1992 pp. 73 – 95

39 The influence of culture on budget control practices in the USA and Japan — an empirical study. Susumu Ueno; Uma Sekaran. *J. Int. Bus. Stud.* **23:4** Fourth quarter:1992 pp. 659 – 674

40 International public finance — a new perspective on global relations. Ruben P. Mendez. New York: Oxford University Press, 1992: xxii, 339 p. *ISBN: 0195071948; LofC: 91024763. Includes bibliographical references and index.*

41 Ipotesi di «rientro» della finanza pubblica *[In Italian]*; [The hypothesis of the public finance "comeback"]. Stefano Micossi. *Riv. Pol. Ec.* **LXXXII:III** 4:1992 pp. 99 – 115

42 Is tax-discounting stable over time? Giuseppe Nicoletti. *Ox. B. Econ. S.* **54:2** 5:1992 pp. 121 – 144

43 Kommunale Unternehmensbesteuerung. Grundsätzliche Anmerkungen zur Verwirklichung eines effizienten Systems *[In German]*; [Local government taxation of enterprises. Comments on the realization of an efficient system] *[Summary]*. Wolfram F. Richter. *Z. Wirt. Soz.* **112:4** 1992 pp. 567 – 586

44 Limitations of the budget as an instrument of macroeconomic policy in 1992-93. Philip D. Adams; Peter B. Dixon. *Aust. Ec. Rev.* 4th quarter:1992 pp. 41 – 50

45 Local government economics in theory and practice. David N. King *[Ed.]*. London: Routledge, 1992: 184 p. *ISBN: 0415062209; LofC: 91024979. Papers presented at a conference held in Ferrara, Italy in 1988, and organized by the Inter-University Centre for the Study of Regional and Local Finance; Includes bibliographical references and index.*

46 Local government finance and equilisation — the case of Ireland. Michael Ridge. *Fis. Stud.* **13:3** 8:1992 pp. 54 – 73

47 Macroeconomic stabilisation in the former Soviet Republics — dream or reality? Sergei Aleksashenko. *Comm. Econ.* **4:4** 1992 pp. 439 – 467

48 A magyar gazdaság és a művelődésfinanszírozás *[In Hungarian]*; (The financing of the Hungarian economy and education). András Rupp. *Pénz. Sz.* **36:4** 4:1992 pp. 284 – 293

49 Managing Greenland's mineral revenues — a trust fund approach. Graham R. Poole; Michael Pretes; Knud Sinding. *Res. Pol.* **18:3** 9:1992 pp. 191 – 204

50 Measuring the size and distributional effects of homeowner tax preferences. David C. Ling; Gary A. McGill. *J. Hous. Res.* **3:2** 1992 pp. 273 – 303

51 Mestnye budzhety *[In Russian]*; [Local budgets]. N.A. Shirkevich. Moskva: Finansy i statistika, 1991: 126 p. *ISBN: 5279005991.* [Iz istorii sovetskikh finansov.]

52 Die neue Institutionenökomie — Ein Überblick über wichtige Elemente und Probleme der Weiterentwicklung *[In German]*; [The new institutionalism — an overview of important elements and problems of further development]. K.-E. Schenk. *Z. Wirt. Soz.* **112:3** 1992 pp. 337 – 378

53 On the fair division of a heterogeneous commodity. M. Berliant; W. Thomson; K. Dunz. *J. Math Econ.* **21:3** 1992 pp. 201 – 216

N.2: Public finance *[Finances publiques]*

54 On the superiority of the destination over the origin principle of taxation for intra-union trade. T. Georgakopoulos; T. Hitiris. *Econ. J.* **102:410** 1:1992 pp. 117 – 126

55 Peasants versus city-dwellers — taxation and the burden of economic development. Raaj Kumar Sah *[Ed.]*; Joseph E. Stiglitz *[Ed.]*. Oxford: Clarendon Press, 1992: 223 p. *ISBN: 0198285817; LofC: 91033923. Includes bibliographical references and index.*

56 Petty smuggling and lost revenue at Santa Elena. Bruce Wiegand. *Beliz. St.* **20:1** 5:1992 pp. 14 – 20

57 Planning and evaluation of projects in countries with high inflation rates. Axel Sell. *Proj. App.* **7:1** 3:1992 pp. 11 – 20

58 Planning and the regulatory role of the Indian state. Dilip K. Dutta. *J. Cont. Asia* **22:1** 1992 pp. 82 – 93

59 Population dependency rates and savings rates — stability of estimates. Linda D. Shumaker; Robert L. Clark. *Econ. Dev. Cult. Change* **40:2** 1:1992 pp. 319 – 332

60 Precommitment and financial structure — an analysis of the effects of taxes. Varouj A. Aivazian; Michael K. Berkowitz. *Economica* **59:233** 2:1992 pp. 93 – 106

61 Profili tributari della cessione gratuita dei beni relativi all'impresa *[In Italian]*; [Financial profiles of the free transfer of relative goods to businesses]. Marco Versiglioni. *Riv. Dir. Finan. Sci. Fin.* **LI:3** 9:1992 pp. 481 – 548

62 Public finance in models of economic growth. Robert J. Barro; Xavier Sala-i-Martin. *R. Econ. S.* **59:4** 10:1992 pp. 661 – 645

63 Public finance in the Thatcher era — a critical assessment. Arthur F. Midwinter. Glasgow: Department of Government, University of Strathclyde, 1992: 32 p. [Strathclyde Papers on Government and Politics. : No. 84]

64 Q and the tax bias theory. The role of depreciation tax shields. Thomas W. Downs. *J. Publ. Ec.* **47:1** 2:1992 pp. 59 – 84

65 Reassessing the role for wealth transfer taxes. Henry J. Aaron; Alicia H. Munnell. *Natl. Tax. J.* **XLV:2** 6:1992 pp. 119 – 143

66 Reserve requirements on bank deposits as implicit taxes — a case study of Italy. Lazaros E. Molho. Washington, D.C.: International Monetary Fund, 1992: 20 p. [IMF working paper. : No. WP/92/18]

67 Setting domestic priorities — what can government do? Henry J. Aaron *[Ed.]*; Charles L. Schultze *[Ed.]*. Washington, DC: The Brookings Institution, 1992: xii, 318 p. *ISBN: 0815700547; LofC: 92028464. Includes bibliographical references and index.*

68 The short-period incidence of taxation revisited. R. Damania; D. Mair. *Camb. J. Econ.* **16:2** 6:1992 pp. 195 – 206

69 Some tests of the incentive effects of the research and experimentation tax credit. C.W. Swenson. *J. Publ. Ec.* **49:2** 11:1992 pp. 203 – 218

70 Squilibri di bilancio, distorsioni economiche e performance di lungo periodo dell'economia italiana *[In Italian]*; [Unbalanced budgets, economic distortions and long-term performances in the Italian economy]. Stefano Micossi; Giuseppe Tullio. *Riv. Pol. Ec.* **LXXXII:7** 7:1992 pp. 39 – 92

71 Surplus and stagnation in Jamaica — further notes; *[French summary]*; *[Spanish summary]*. Anders Danielson. *Soc. Econ. S.* **41:1** 3:1992 pp. 45 – 66

72 Sustained growth in the model of overlapping generations. Eric O'N. Fisher. *J. Econ. Theo.* **58:1** 10:1992 pp. 77 – 92

73 Tax collection with agency costs — private contracting or government bureaucrats? Eugenia Froedge Toma; Mark Toma. *Economica* **59:233** 2:1992 pp. 107 – 120

74 Tax innovation in the states — capitalizing on political opportunity. Frances Stokes Berry; William D. Berry. *Am. J. Pol. Sc.* **36:3** 8:1992 pp. 715 – 742

75 Tax neutrality under parallel tax systems. Andrew B. Lyon. *Publ. Fin. Q.* **20:3** 7:1992 pp. 338 – 358

76 Tax options for 1992 — the green budget. Gavyn Davies; et al. London: Institute of Fiscal Studies, 1992: 118 p. *ISBN: 1873357133.* [IFS commentary. : No. 28]

77 Tax preferences and employment-based health insurance. Leonard E. Burman; Jack Rodgers. *Natl. Tax. J.* **XLV:3** 9:1992 pp. 331 – 346

78 Tax treatment of financial instruments in the UK — new treatment proposed by the Inland Revenue Consultative Document. Stephen Edge. *Fis. Stud.* **13:2** 5:1992 pp. 122 – 129

79 Taxation and economic growth — the case of Taiwan. P. Wang; C.K. Yip. *Am. J. Econ. S.* **51:3** 7:1992 pp. 317 – 331

80 Taxation and inflation — a new explanation for current account imbalances. Tamim Bayoumi; Joseph E. Gagnon. [Washington, D.C.]: Board of Governors of the Federal Reserve System, 1992: 41 p. [International finance discussion papers. : No. 420]

N.2: Public finance *[Finances publiques]*

81 Taxation in decentralizing socialist economies — the case of China. Christopher John Heady; Pradeep K. Mitra. Washington, D.C.: Country Department I, Asia Regional Office, The World Bank, 1992: 33 p. [Policy research working papers.]

82 Taxation in empirical labour supply models — lone mothers in the UK. R. Blundell; A. Duncan; C. Meghir. *Econ. J.* **102:411** 3:1992 pp. 265 – 278

83 Taxes, fringe benefits and faculty. Stephen A. Woodbury; Daniel S. Hamermesh. *Rev. Econ. St.* **LXXIV:2** 5:1992 pp. 287 – 296

84 Tax-free manufacturing in Fiji — an evaluation. A. Haroon Akram-Lodhi. *J. Cont. Asia* **22:3** 1992 pp. 373 – 393

85 The treatment of transfers in the measurement of sales tax incidence — the case of Canada's manufacturers' sales tax. Giuseppe C. Ruggeri; Kelly A. Bluck. *Publ. Fin. Q.* **20:1** 1:1992 pp. 24 – 46

86 The trial of Chaka Dlamini — an economic scenario for the new South Africa. Stephen Meintjes; Michael Jacques; Thami Mazwai *[Foreword]*. Norwood, South Africa: Amagi Books, 1990: 114 p. *ISBN: 0958310513; LofC: 91148677. Includes bibliographical references (p.114).*

87 Turnover tax on foreign investment in China — the consolidated industrial and commercial tax. Jinyan Li. *Inter. VAT Mon.* **:5** 5:1992 pp. 2 – 17

88 Umsatzbesteuerung im EG-Binnenmarkt — Von der Mehrwertsteuer zur Verkaufssteuer? *[In German]*; [Sales taxation in the EC internal market — from value added tax to the sales tax]. Jürgen Stehn. *Weltwirt.* **:3** 1992 pp. 274 – 294

89 Understanding local economic development in a comparative context. Harold Wolman; Gerry Stoker. *Econ. Devel. Q.* **6:4** 11:1992 pp. 406 – 417

90 Utilización del impuesto inflacionario en Colombia *[In Spanish]*; [Use of the inflationary tax in Colombia]. Hernán Rincón; Luz A. Saavedra; Roberto Steiner. *Monetaria* **XV:2** 4-6:1992 pp. 195 – 212

91 Valeur ajoutée et taxe professionnelle *[In French]*; [Added value and professional taxation]. Jérôme Bogaert; Hervé Utheza. Paris: La Documentation française, 1992: 143 p. *ISBN: 2110026839.* [Collection études et recherches.]

92 Why do people pay taxes? James Alm; Gary H. McClelland; William D. Schulze. *J. Publ. Ec.* **48:1** 6:1992 pp. 21 – 38

93 Zur Ökonomie der Gemeinschaftsbedürfnisse — Neuere Versuche einer ethischen Begründung der Theorie meritorischer Güter *[In German]*; [On the economy of community needs — new attempts towards an ethical basis for the theory of merit goods]. Birger P. Priddat. *Z. Wirt. Soz.* **112:2** 1992 pp. 239 – 259

Corporate taxation *[Impôt sur les sociétés]*

94 Allgemeine Finanzzuweisungen und kommunale Leistungen bei alternativen kommunalen Unternehmenssteuern *[In German]*; Regional fiscal policy with alternative business taxes *[Summary]*. Dietmar Wellisch; Uwe Walz. *Jahrb. N. St.* **210:1-2** 7:1992 pp. 86 – 104

95 Allokations- und Wohlfahrtseffekte der Besteuerung — Die Vorschläge zur Reform der Unternehmensbesteuerung *[In German]*; The excess burden of taxation — the proposals for a reform of company taxation *[Summary]*; Effets d'allocation et d'assistance de l'imposition — les propositions de réforme de l'imposition des entreprises *[French summary]*. Klaus Conrad. *Kred. Kap.* **25:3** 1992 pp. 359 – 385

96 Foreign government's response to recent U.S. tax legislation affecting foreign-controlled U.S.-based corporations. B. Anthony Billings; John R. McGowan; Foaud K. AlNajjar. *J. World Tr.* **26:1** 2:1992 pp. 85 – 98

97 The interactions of corporate tax between the EC, Japan and the United States. Michael Devereux; Mark Pearson. *B. Int. Fiscal Docu.* **46:8** 8:1992 pp. 367 – 383

98 International business taxation — a study in the internationalization of business regulation. Sol Picciotto. London: Weidenfeld & Nicolson, 1992: 400 p. *ISBN: 0297821067.* [Law in context.]

99 Kommunale Subventionen. Eine empirische Analyse ihrer Entwicklung und Struktur zwischen 1975 und 1987 *[In German]*; [Municipal subsidies — an empirical analysis of their development and structure between 1975 and 1987]. Hermann Rappen. *RWI-Mitt.* **43:3** 1992 pp. 223 – 241

100 Neutralità dell'imposta problemi finanziari dell'impresa e sistemi fiscali complessi — l'approccio "generale" del modello di Sinn *[In Italian]*; Taxation neutrality, financial problems of the firm and complex tax systems — the "general" approach of Sinn's model *[Summary]*. Luca Errico. *Rev. Int. Sci. Ec. Com.* **XXXIX:4** 4:1992 pp. 341 – 363

N.2: Public finance *[Finances publiques]* — *Corporate taxation [Impôt sur les sociétés]*

101 A new approach to modelling corporation tax. Garry Young. *Natl. Inst. Econ. R.* :**140** 5:1992 pp. 98 – 105

102 Problems with integrating corporate and personal income taxes in an open economy. Robin Boadway; Neil Bruce. *J. Publ. Ec.* **48:1** 6:1992 pp. 39 – 66

103 Reforming corporate taxation — an evaluation of the United States Treasury integration proposals and other corporate tax systems in an international context — part 1. Malcolm Gammie. *Br. Tax Rev.* :**3** 1992 pp. 148 – 173

104 Reforming corporate taxation — an evaluation of the United States Treasury integration proposals and other corporate tax systems in an international context — part 2. Malcolm Gammie. *Br. Tax Rev.* :**4** 1992 pp. 243 – 276

105 Symposium on the Ruding Committee report. Franz Vanistendael *[Contrib.]*; Michael Devereux *[Contrib.]*; Malcolm Gammie *[Contrib.]*. Collection of 3 articles. **Fis. Stud.** , *13:2*, 5:1992 pp. 84 – 121

106 Taxes and capital structure — evidence from firms' response to the Tax Reform Act of 1986. Dan Givoly; Carla Hayn; Aharon R. Ofer; Oded Sarig. *R. Finan. Stud.* **5:2** 1992 pp. 331 – 355

107 Taxes and organizational form — a comparison of corporations and master limited partnerships. David A. Guenther. *Acc. Review* **67:1** 1:1992 pp. 17 – 45

Fiscal policy *[Politique fiscale]*

108 Act on taxation procedures. Budapest: Ministry of Finance, 1992: 88 p. [Public finance in Hungary. : No. 96]

109 Az adóhatóság nyomozási jogköre Ausztriában és Hollandiában *[In Hungarian]*; (The investigation right of the tax authority in Austria and in Netherlands). Imre Zoltán Nagy. *Pénz. Sz.* **36:4** 4:1992 pp. 310 – 318

110 Allgemeine Finanzzuweisungen und kommunale Leistungen bei alternativen kommunalen Unternehmenssteuern *[In German]*; Regional fiscal policy with alternative business taxes *[Summary]*. Dietmar Wellisch; Uwe Walz. *Jahrb. N. St.* **210:1-2** 7:1992 pp. 86 – 104

111 Approcci valutativi e trattamento delle imposte indirette nell'analisi costi benefici *[In Italian]*; [Evaluative approaches to, and handling of, the indirect taxes in cost benefit analyses]. Cesare Dosi. *Riv. Dir. Finan. Sci. Fin.* **LI:1** 3:1992 pp. 16 – 38

112 Besteuerung, intertemporale Neutralität und zeitliche Inkonsistenz *[In German]*; [Taxation, intertemporal neutrality and time inconsistency] *[Summary]*. Bernd Huber. *Finanzarchiv* **49:4** 1991/1992 pp. 423 – 456

113 Capital gains redux — why holding periods matter. Eric W. Cook; John F. O'Hare. *Natl. Tax. J.* **XLV:1** 3:1992 pp. 53 – 76

114 Capital gains taxation, growth, and fairness. J.J. Minarik. *Cont. Policy* **X:3** 7:1992 pp. 16 – 25

115 Carbon taxes and economic welfare. Dale W. Jorgenson; Daniel T. Slesnick; Peter J. Wilcoxen. *Brookings P.* 1992 pp. 393 – 454

116 A comparative analysis of tax reforms in Singapore and Hong Kong. Mukul G. Asher. *B. Int. Fiscal Docu.* **46:4** 4:1992 pp. 181 – 191

117 The comparison between ad valorem and specific taxation under imperfect competition. Sofia Delipalla; Michael Keen. *J. Publ. Ec.* **49:3** 12:1992 pp. 351 – 367

118 Competitive externalities and the optimal seigniorage segmentation. Joshua Aizenman. *J. Money C. B.* **24:1** 2:1992 pp. 61 – 71

119 Corruption in tax administration. Parkash Chander; Louis Wilde. *J. Publ. Ec.* **49:3** 12:1992 pp. 333 – 349

120 Crise financière et système fiscal — analyse qualitative et quantitative du cas ivoirien (1980-1990) *[In French]*; [Financial crisis and fiscal system — qualitative and quantitative analysis of the Ivory Coast (1980-1990)] *[Summary]*. Zogbélémou Togba. *Afr. J. Int. Comp. Law* **4:1** 3:1992 pp. 84 – 130

121 Definitive issues of the English council tax legislation. Peter Sparkes. *Br. Tax Rev.* :**5** 1992 pp. 305 – 322

122 Det norske skattesystemet 1992 *[In Norwegian]*; [The Norwegian tax system]. Inger Gabrielsen. Oslo: Statistisk Sentralbyra, 1992: 171 p. *ISBN: 8253737289. Bibliography —* p.171. [Sosiale og økonomiske studier. : No. 79]

123 Development in the United Kingdom. Colin Farrington. *R. Urban. Region. Dev. S.* **4:2** 7:1992 pp. 179 – 192

N.2: Public finance *[Finances publiques]* — Fiscal policy *[Politique fiscale]*

124 A discredited tax — the capital gains tax problem and its solution. Bruce Sutherland; John F. Chown; Barry Bracewell-Milnes. London: Institute of Economic Affairs, 1992: 90 p. *ISBN: 0255363095.*

125 Distortionary taxes and the provision of public goods. Charles L. Ballard; Don Fullerton. *J. Econ. Pers.* **6:3** Summer:1992 pp. 117 – 131

126 Economía política del federalismo fiscal español *[In Spanish]*; [The political economy of federal taxation in Spain]. Javier Salinas Sanchez. Madrid: Instituto de Estudios Fiscales, 1991: 167 p. *ISBN: 8471969319. Bibliography — p.159-167.* [Monografía.]

127 Economic change and the evolving state tax structure — the case of the sales tax. William Duncombe. *Natl. Tax. J.* **XLV:3** 9:1992 pp. 299 – 313

128 Economic effects of a carbon tax in Belgium — application with the macrosectoral model HERMES. F. Bossier; R. De Rous. *Ener. Econ.* **14:1** 1:1992 pp. 33 – 42

129 Economic effects of a carbon tax — with a general equilibrium illustration for Belgium. S. Proost; D. van Regemorter. *Ener. Econ.* **14:2** 4:1992 pp. 136 – 149

130 Economic reform and institutional innovation. Glenn P. Jenkins. *B. Int. Fiscal Docu.* **46:12** 12:1992 pp. 588 – 597

131 Effective tax rates and Tobin's q. Yasushi Iwamoto. *J. Publ. Ec.* **48:2** 7:1992 pp. 225 – 237

132 The effects of systematic and surprise fiscal policy actions on cyclical movements of research output in a developing economy — evidence from Nigeria. M.O. Odedokun. *E. Afr. Econ. Rev.* **7:1** 6:1991 pp. 1 – 11

133 Efficient tax exporting; *[French summary]*. Russell Krelove. *Can. J. Econ.* **XXV:1** 2:1992 pp. 145 – 155

134 Evaluating the sustainability of fiscal deficits. A.M. Gagales. *Gr. Econ. Rev.* **13:2** 12:1991 pp. 215 – 250

135 Events affecting the deduction of trading losses from capital gains. David Stopforth. *Br. Tax Rev.* **:6** 1992 pp. 384 – 394

136 Exploring the information gap — the taxation of portfolio stock investments in foreign corporations. Nancy H. Kaufman. *Columb. J. Tr.* **30:2** 1992 pp. 251 – 325

137 Finanzpolitik und Steuerverwaltung in Tansania während der "verlorenen Entwicklungsdekade" *[In German]*; [Fiscal policy and tax administration in Tanzania during the "lost decade" of economic development] *[Summary]*. Ulrich Fanger. *Verf. Rec. Über.* **25:3** 1992 pp. 303 – 326

138 Fiscal adjustment and the real exchange rate — the case of Bangladesh. Kazi M. Martin. Washington, D.C.: The World Bank, 1992: 42 p. [Policy research working papers.]

139 Fiscal crisis and UK local tax reform. Douglas Mair; Richard Damania. *Loc. Govt. St.* **18:3** Autumn:1992 pp. 179 – 190

140 The fiscal dimensions of adjustment in low-income countries. Karim Nashashibi. Washington, D.C.: International Monetary Fund, 1992: 59 p. *ISBN: 155775229x.* [Occasional paper.]

141 Fiscal implications of the transition from planned to market economy. R. Sean Craig; Catherine L. Mann. [Washington, D.C.]: Board of Governors of the Federal Reserve System, 1992: 33 p. [International finance discussion papers. : No. 424]

142 Fiscal policies to control pollution — international experience. Glenn P. Jenkins; Ranjit Lamech. *B. Int. Fiscal Docu.* **46:10** 10:1992 pp. 483 – 502

143 Fiscal policy and economic reconstruction in Latin America. V. Tanzi. *World Dev.* **20:5** 5:1992 pp. 641 – 658

144 Fiscal policy — an introduction. Graham C. Hockley. London: Routledge, 1992: xx, 277 p. *ISBN: 0415062764; LofC: 91031161. Includes bibliographical references (p. [258]-265) and indexes.*

145 A framework for intergovernmental fiscal relations in South Africa. J.A. Döckel; O. Somers. *Develop. S. Afr.* **9:2** 5:1992 pp. 139 – 152

146 Fringe benefits and employee expenses — tax planning and neutral tax policy; *[French summary]*. A. Macnaughton; D. Thornton *[Discussant]*. *Cont. Account. Res.* **9:1** Fall:1992 pp. 113 – 141

147 In-kind distribution, uncertainty, and merit wants — a simple model. Alistair Munro. *Publ. Fin. Q.* **20:2** 4:1992 pp. 175 – 194

148 Interactions of land policy and land-based tax policy — the Vermont land gains tax. Dennis Robinson; Elizabeth Chant. *R. Urban. Region. Dev. S.* **4:2** 7:1992 pp. 147 – 161

149 Intergovernmental fiscal relations in China. Roy W. Bahl; Christine Wallich. Washington, D.C.: Country Economics Department, The World Bank, 1992: 48 p. [Policy research working papers.]

N.2: Public finance *[Finances publiques]* — Fiscal policy *[Politique fiscale]*

150 International fiscal policy coordination and economic growth. Michael B. Devereux; Arman Mansoorian. *Int. Econ. R.* **33:2** 5:1992 pp. 249 – 268

151 Investment behaviour and government tax policy — a survey of the largest UK firms. Eleanor J. Morgan. *J. Bus. Fin. Acc.* **19:6** 11:1992 pp. 789 – 815

152 Key questions in considering a value-added tax for Central and Eastern European countries. Sijbren Cnossen. *Inter. VAT Mon.* **:11** 11:1992 pp. 2 – 21

153 Korea. Sung Chul Moon. *Inter. VAT Mon.* **:5** 5:1992 pp. 18 – 27

154 Land development timing — effects of uncertainty in income and tax policy. John E. Anderson. *Pap. Reg. Sci.* **71:1** 1:1992 pp. 45 – 52

155 A model of local fiscal choice. Shyam Nath; Brijesh C. Purohit. *Publ. Finan.* **47:1** 1992 pp. 93 – 107

156 National fiscal policy within EMU — the fiscal implications of Maastricht. C. A.E. Goodhart. London: London School of Economics and Political Science, 1992: 31 p. [LSE Financial Markets Group special paper series. : No. 45]

157 A note on the effect of tax brackets on non-renewable resource extraction. John Livernois. *J. Envir. Ec. Manag.* **22:3** 5:1992 pp. 272 – 280

158 Oil prices, macroeconomic disequilibrium, and fiscal policy. Saraswati P. Singh; T.V.S. Ramamohan Rao. *Publ. Finan.* **47:1** 1992 pp. 120 – 130

159 On efficiency-inducing taxation for a non-renewable resource monopolist. Larry Karp; John Livernois. *J. Publ. Ec.* **49:2** 11:1992 pp. 219 – 239

160 On the definition of tax neutrality — distributional and welfare implications of policy alternatives. John P. Formby; W. James Smith; Paul D. Thistle. *Publ. Fin. Q.* **20:1** 1:1992 pp. 3 – 23

161 On the demographic realism of the Ricardian theory of public finance. Hendrik P. van Dalen. *Economist [Leiden]* **140:2** 1992 pp. 204 – 232

162 On the effects of commodity tax under free entry oligopoly in the presence of export market. Yasuhito Tanaka. *Int. Econ. J.* **6:3** Autumn:1992 pp. 83 – 92

163 Petroleum taxation under uncertainty — contigent claims analysis with an application to Norway. Diderik Lund. *Ener. Econ.* **14:1** 1:1992 pp. 23 – 32

164 The postsocialist transition and the state — reflections in the light of Hungarian fiscal problems. János Kornai. *Am. Econ. Rev.* **82:2** 5:1992 pp. 1 – 21

165 Pour défendre le quotient familial *[In French]*; In defence of the family quotient tax system *[Summary]*; Para defender el cociente familiar *[Spanish summary]*. Henri Sterdyniak. *E & S* **:256** 7-8:1992 pp. 5 – 24

166 Property prices, tax and expenditure levels and local fiscal performance. N. Topham; R. Ward. *Appl. Econ.* **24:11** 11:1992 pp. 1225 – 1232

167 Property tax abatement and the simultaneous determination of local fiscal variables in a metropolitan area. Robert W. Wassmer. *Land Econ.* **68:3** 8:1992 pp. 263 – 282

168 Public sector debt, fiscal deficits, and economic adjustment — a comparative study of six EMENA countries. Alfredo E. Thorne; Azita Dastgheib. Washington, D.C.: Technical Department, Europe, Middle East, and North Africa Regional Office, The World Bank, 1992: 68 p. *Bibliography* — *p.67-68.* [Policy research working papers.]

169 Residence- and source-based taxation of capital income in an overlapping generations model. A.L. Bovenberg. *J. Econ.* **56:3** 1992 pp. 267 – 295

170 Revenue and progressivity neutral changes in the tax mix. John Creedy. *Aust. Ec. Rev.* **:98(2nd quarter)** 4-6:1992 pp. 31 – 38

171 La riforma fiscale svedese *[In Italian]*; [Swedish fiscal reform]. Luisa Rimini. *Riv. Dir. Finan. Sci. Fin.* **LI:4** 12:1992 pp. 686 – 710

172 Sentieri di rientro del debito pubblico in Italia — ottimalità e gradualità *[In Italian]*; Curbing Italy's public debt. Gradual and optimal paths *[Summary]*. Franco Sartori; Pasquale Lucio Scandizzo. *Ras. Econ.* **LVI:3** 7-9:1992 pp. 565 – 594

173 Substituting consumption-based direct taxation for income taxes as the international norm. Charles E. McLure. *Natl. Tax. J.* **XLV:2** 6:1992 pp. 145 – 154

174 Supply policies in an open economy with centralised wage setting. Beniamino Quintieri; Furio Camillo Rosati. *Labour [Italy]* **6:3** Winter:1992 pp. 71 – 88

175 The supply-side consequences of U.S. fiscal policy in the 1980s. *Q. R. Fed. Res. Bank N.Y.* **17:1** Spring:1992 pp. 1 – 20

176 Supply-side tax policies for developing countries — a survey and synthesis. P.C. Kumar. *Dev. Pol. R.* **10:1** 3:1992 pp. 5 – 14

177 The sustainability of current fiscal policy — fiscal policy from a medium term perspective. *Res. Bank B. NZ* **55:3** 9:1992 pp. 224 – 245

N.2: Public finance *[Finances publiques]* — *Fiscal policy [Politique fiscale]*

178 Tax credits for debt reduction. Michael P. Dooley; Elhanan Helpman. *J. Int. Econ.* **32:**1/2 2:1992 pp. 165 – 178

179 The tax dilemma of married women in Germany. Paul Bernd Spahn; Helmut Kaiser; Thomas Kassella. *Fis. Stud.* **13:**2 5:1992 pp. 22 – 47

180 Tax neutrality and the tax treatment of purchased intangibles. Jane G. Gravelle; Jack Taylor. *Natl. Tax. J.* **XLV:**1 3:1992 pp. 77 – 88

181 Tax policy and business fixed investment in the United States. Alan J. Auerbach; Kevin Hassett. *J. Publ. Ec.* **47:**2 3:1992 pp. 141 – 170

182 Tax policy and the dividend puzzle. B.D. Bernheim. *Rand J. Eco.* **22:**4 Winter:1991 pp. 455 – 476

183 Eine theoretische Analyse zur Kontroverse um Unabhängigkeit versus Koordination der Fiskalpolitik in einer Währungsunion *[In German]*; [On the controversy about independent vs. co-ordinated fiscal policy in a monetary union — a theoretical analysis] *[Summary]*. Michael Frenkel; Martin Klein. *Jahr. Soz.schaft.* **43:**1 1992 pp. 65 – 84

184 Time consistency of government financial policy in a small open economy. B. Huber. *Eur. Econ. R.* **36:**8 12:1992 pp. 1545 – 1555

185 Time-consistent income taxation. Raymond G. Batina. *Q Rev. Econ. Finan.* **32:**3 Autumn:1992 pp. 68 – 81

186 Union wage responses to a shift from direct to indirect taxation. John Creedy; Ian M. McDonald. *B. Econ. Res.* **44:**3 7:1992 pp. 221 – 232

187 Wealth effects and fiscal policy in the National Institute global econometric model. Ray Barrell; Jan Willem in't Veld. *Natl. Inst. Econ. R.* **:**140 5:1992 pp. 78 – 85

Income and consumption tax *[Impôts sur le revenu et sur la consommation]*

188 Can capital income taxes survive in open economies? Roger H. Gordon. *J. Finance* **47:**3 7:1992 pp. 1159 – 1180

189 Capital income taxation in a growing world economy. S.B. Nielsen. *J. Econ.* **55:**1 1992 pp. 77 – 100

190 Company cars and the consultative document. Kevin Paterson. *Br. Tax Rev.* **:**6 1992 pp. 368 – 383

191 Comparison between the EC sixth VAT directive and the Italian VAT law. Rosamund Barr. *Inter. VAT Mon.* **:**1 1:1992 pp. 2 – 12

192 A cross-country analysis of the tax-push hypothesis. Fiorella Padoa Schioppa Kostoris. Washington, D.C.: International Monetary Fund, 1992: 43 p. [IMF working paper. : No. WP/92/11]

193 The effects of income tax rate uncertainty in a dynamic setting. Harry Watson. *S. Econ. J.* **58:**3 1:1992 pp. 682 – 689

194 Empirical application of optimal commodity tax theory to taxation of alcoholic beverages. Pasi Holm; Ilpo Suoniemi. *Sc. J. Econ.* **94:**1 1992 pp. 85 – 102

195 An evaluation of alternative methods of taxing social security benefits. Philip J. Harmelink; Janet Furman Speyrer. *J. Post. Keyn. Ec.* **15:**1 Fall:1992 pp. 3 – 30

196 From shockmania to tax therapy. Tatyana Ryzhenkova. *Int. Aff. Mos.* **10** 1992 pp. 40 – 49

197 The impact of a hybrid personal tax system on capital accumulation and economic welfare. R.A. Androkovich; M.J. Daly; F.M. Naqib. *Eur. Econ. R.* **36:**4 5:1992 pp. 801 – 814

198 Income tax changes and trade union wage demands. John Creedy; Ian McDonald. *Aust. Econ. P.* **31:**58 6:1992 pp. 47 – 57

199 Income tax policy for the Russian Republic. Charles E. McLure. *Comm. Econ.* **4:**3 1992 pp. 425 – 436

200 Income tax — a critical analysis. Stan D. Ross; Philip Burgess; Richard E. Krever. Sydney: Law Book Co, 1991: xxii, 236 p. *ISBN: 0455210268; LofC: 91179385 //r92. Includes index.*

201 Income taxation and supply of labour in West Germany; Einkommensbesteuerung und Arbeitsangebot in der Bundesrepublik Deutschland *[German summary]*. Helmut Kaiser; Ulrich van Essen; P. Bernd Spahn. *Jahrb. N. St.* **209:**1-2 1:1992 pp. 87 – 105

202 Indirect tax harmonization in Denmark; *[French summary]*; *[German summary]*; *[Spanish summary]*. Nathan Wajsman. *Welt.liches Arc.* **4:**128 1992 pp. 727 – 741

203 Institutionelle Überlegungen zu einer schrittweisen Reform der indirekten Steuern *[In German]*; [Institutional considerations on piecemeal reform of indirect taxation] *[Summary]*. Hugo Mann. *Jahr. Soz.schaft.* **43:**2 1992 pp. 211 – 226

204 Japan's VAT and its aftermath. Hiromitsu Ishi. *Hito. J. Econ.* **33:**1 6:1992 pp. 19 – 48

N.2: Public finance *[Finances publiques]* — Income and consumption tax *[Impôts sur le revenu et sur la consommation]*

205 Key questions in considering a value-added tax for Central and Eastern European countries. Sijbren Cnossen. *Staff Pap. Int. Monetary* **39:2** 6:1992 pp. 211 – 255

206 Local income tax — a study of the options. A.J.G. Isaac. York: Joseph Rowntree Foundation, 1992: 91 p. *ISBN: 1872470629.*

207 "A natural safeguard" — the General Commissioners of Income Tax. Chantal Stebbings. *Br. Tax Rev.* :**6** 1992 pp. 398 – 406

208 On income taxation and the core. Marcus Berliant. *J. Econ. Theo.* **56:1** 2:1992 pp. 121 – 141

209 Recent activity in the United States involving value added tax. Alan Schenk. *Inter. VAT Mon.* **8/9** 1992 pp. 2 – 12

210 Some economic effects of value-added tax substitution in Greece — a first ex-post assessment. Theodore A. Georgakopoulos. *Gr. Econ. Rev.* **13:1** 6:1991 pp. 117 – 134

211 State income tax amnesties — causes. Jeffrey A. Dubin; Michael J. Graetz; Louis L. Wilde. *Q. J. Econ.* **CVII:3** 8:1992 pp. 1057 – 1070

212 State taxation of interest income and municipal borrowing costs. Mary E. Lovely; Michael J. Wasylenko. *Natl. Tax. J.* **XLV:1** 3:1992 pp. 37 – 52

213 Taxing imputed income from owner-occupation — distributional implications of alternative packages. Tim Callan. *Fis. Stud.* **13:4** 11:1992 pp. 58 – 70

214 Tobacco taxation in Australia. Terry Alchin. *Ec. Pap. Aust.* **11:3** 9:1992 pp. 77 – 90

215 Die Überwindung von Kapitalfehlallokationen durch eine Besteuerung von Sollzinseinkommen *[In German]*; Overcoming misallocations of capital by means of a tax on potential interest earnings *[Summary]*; L'élimination des mauvaises allocations de capitaux par um impôt sur les revenus potentiels des intérêts *[French summary]*. Johannes Hackmann. *Kred. Kap.* **25:4** 1992 pp. 491 – 527

216 Withholding position and income tax compliance — some experimental evidence. Jorge Martinez-Vazquez; Gordon B. Harwood; Ernest R. Larkins. *Publ. Fin. Q.* **20:2** 4:1992 pp. 152 – 174

217 Zu den Nutzungsdauerwirkungen der Einkommensbesteuerung *[In German]*; [On the effect of income taxes on the duration and use]. Johannes Hackmann. *Z. Wirt. Soz.* **112:2** 1992 pp. 169 – 186

Optimal taxation *[Fiscalité optimale]*

218 Grandfather rules and the theory of optimal tax reform. George R. Zodrow. *J. Publ. Ec.* **49:2** 11:1992 pp. 163 – 190

219 Optimal extractive taxes under demand uncertainty. James R. Fain; Mary N. Gade. *Publ. Fin. Q.* **20:2** 4:1992 pp. 243 – 255

220 Optimal taxation and debt in an open economy. James E. Anderson; Leslie Young. *J. Publ. Ec.* **47:1** 2:1992 pp. 27 – 58

221 Optimal taxation in a life-cycle model; *[French summary]*. Yvette Alvarez; John Burbidge; Ted Farrell; Leigh Palmer. *Can. J. Econ.* **XXV:1** 2:1992 pp. 111 – 122

222 The optimal taxation of risky capital income — an elasticity rule. W.F. Richter. *J. Econ.* **55:1** 1992 pp. 101 – 112

223 Public goods, self-selection and optimal income taxation. Robin W. Boadway; M. J. Keen. London: Institute for Fiscal Studies, 1992: 20 p. [IFS working paper series. : No. W92/10]

224 Tariffs, optimal taxes, and collection costs. Dubravko Mihaljek. Washington, D.C.: International Monetary Fund, European I Department, 1992: 30 p. *Bibliography — p.27-30.* [IMF working paper. : No. WP/92/28]

Property tax *[Impôt sur la propriété]*

225 Building-tax abatements — an approximation to land value taxation. A.K. Severn. *Am. J. Econ. S.* **51:2** 4:1992 pp. 237 – 246

226 Composite area linked system for property tax reform in India. R.M. Kapoor; P.K. Ghosh. *R. Urban. Region. Dev. S.* **4:2** 7:1992 pp. 209 – 225

227 The council tax — the distributional implications of returning to a tax on property. Kenneth Gibb. *Scot. J. Poli.* **39:3** 8:1992 pp. 302 – 317

228 Implementing property tax reform in developing countries — lessons from the property tax in Indonesia. Roy Kelly. *R. Urban. Region. Dev. S.* **4:2** 7:1992 pp. 193 – 208

229 The interaction of stamp duty and value added tax on land transactions. Yvonne M. Metcalfe; R.S. Nock. *Br. Tax Rev.* :**3** 1992 pp. 174 – 187

N.2: Public finance *[Finances publiques]* — **Property tax** *[Impôt sur la propriété]*

230 Optimal property taxation in California — is greater reliance on land values feasible and desirable? Marion Beaumont. *R. Urban. Region. Dev. S.* **4:2** 7:1992 pp. 162 – 178

231 Property tax abatement and the simultaneous determination of local fiscal variables in a metropolitan area. Robert W. Wassmer. *Land Econ.* **68:3** 8:1992 pp. 263 – 282

232 Property tax assessment rates and residential abandonment — policy for New York City. D. Arsen. *Am. J. Econ. S.* **51:3** 7:1992 pp. 361 – 377

233 Property tax auction sales. Larry DeBoer; James Conrad; Kevin T. McNamara. *Land Econ.* **68:1** 2:1992 pp. 72 – 82

Public debt *[Dette publique]*

234 Budget deficits and economic performance. Richard C.K. Burdekin; Farrokh K. Langdana; Thomas D. Willet *[Foreword]*. London: Routledge, 1992: 226 p. *ISBN: 041507262x; LofC: 92005393. Includes bibliographical references and index.*

235 Buy now pay later — trends in state indebtedness, 1950-1989. James L. Regens; Thomas P. Lauth. *Publ. Adm. Re.* **52:2** 3-4:1992 pp. 157 – 161

236 Central government budget deficits and ex ante real long term interest rates in the United Kingdom — an empirical note; Deficit pubblico e tassi d'interesse reali ex ante a lungo termine nel Regno Unito — nota empirica *[Italian summary]*. Richard J. Cebula; Ira S. Saltz. *Rev. Int. Sci. Ec. Com.* **XXXIX:5-6** 5-6:1992 pp. 479 – 484

237 Commodity prices and debt crisis in sub-Saharan Africa. I.O. Toiwo. *E. Afr. Econ. Rev.* **7:2** 12:1991 pp. 39 – 50

238 Debt financing and tax status — tests of the substitution effect and the tax exhaustion hypothesis using firms' responses to the Economic Recovery Tax Act of 1981. Robert Trezevant. *J. Finance* **47:4** 9:1992 pp. 1557 – 1568

239 Debt, deficits, and inflation — an application to the public finances of India. Willem H. Buiter; Urjit R. Patel. *J. Publ. Ec.* **47:2** 3:1992 pp. 171 – 205

240 Default risk on government debt in OECD countries. Alberto Alesina; Mark de Broeck; Alessandro Prati; Guido Tabellini; Maurice Obstfeld *[Comments by]*; Sergio Rebelo *[Comments by]*. *Econ. Pol.* **:15** 10:1992 pp. 427 – 463

241 Government budget deficits and interest rates — an empirical analysis for the United States and Canada; Deficit del bilancio statale e tassi di interesse — analisi empirica per gli Stati Uniti e il Canada *[Italian summary]*. Richard J. Cebula; Chao-Shun Hung. *Rev. Int. Sci. Ec. Com.* **XXXIX:10-11** 10-11:1992 pp. 917 – 927

242 Growth via external public debt and capital controls. Harris Dellas; Oded Galor. *Int. Econ. R.* **33:2** 5:1992 pp. 269 – 282

243 L'impôt ou l'emprunt? Vrai ou faux débat? Suggestions pour une révision du financement public *[In French]*; Tax increase or public loan? True or false predicament — proposals for a revision of public finance *[Summary]*; (Steuererhöhung oder Staatsanleihe — Wahre oder falsche Debatte? Für eine Revision der öffentlichen Finanzierung: *Title only in German*); (El impuesto y el empréstito — ¿Verdàdero o falso debate? Sugestiones para una revisión de la financiación pública: *Title only in Spanish*). Jean-Pierre Galavielle. *Econ. App.* **XLV:2** 7:1992 pp. 23 – 64

244 Innovations récentes dans la restructuration de la dette *[In French]*; [Recent innovations in debt restructuring]. Carsten Thomas Ebenroth. *J. Droit Int.* **119:4** 10-12:1992 pp. 859 – 905

245 Optimal maturity of nominal government debt — an infinite-horizon model. Guillermo A. Calvo; Pablo E. Guidotti. *Int. Econ. R.* **33:4** 11:1992 pp. 895 – 919

246 *[In Arabic]*; The problem of budget deficit in Islamic economics *[Summary]*. Mohamed A. Elgari Bin Eid. *R. Islam. Econ.* **2:1** 1992 pp. 35 – 68

247 Public debt and private wealth — debt, capital flight and the IMF in Sudan. Richard P.C. Brown. Basingstoke: Macmillan, 1992: 334 p. *ISBN: 0333575431.* [Macmillan international political economy series.]

248 Research note — debt financing, the Darby effect, and the inflation-induced penalty in historical cost depreciation. Jacques A. Schnabel; Rashmi Thakkar. *J. Acc. Pub. Pol.* **11:1** Spring:1992 pp. 83 – 92

249 Secondary debt market fundamentals and policy implications for debt conversion — the Algerian case. Mohammed Akacem. *OPEC Rev.* **XVI:4** Winter:1992 pp. 383 – 408

250 Sentieri di rientro del debito pubblico in Italia — ottimalità e gradualità *[In Italian]*; Curbing Italy's public debt. Gradual and optimal paths *[Summary]*. Franco Sartori; Pasquale Lucio Scandizzo. *Ras. Econ.* **LVI:3** 7-9:1992 pp. 565 – 594

N.2: Public finance *[Finances publiques]* — Public debt *[Dette publique]*

251 Sovereign debt — a primer. Jonathan Eaton. Washington, D.C.: International Economics Department, The World Bank, 1992: 68 p. *Bibliography — p.66-68.* [Policy research working papers.]

252 Les spécificités de la dette africaine *[In French]*; [The specifics of the African debt burden]. Bénédicte Chatel. *Afr. Cont.* **:164** 10-12:1992 pp. 120 – 142

253 Squilibri di finanza pubblica e crescita del debito pubblico — occasioni mancate, sfide ed opportunità presenti *[In Italian]*; [Public finance disequilibria and growth of public debt — missed opportunities, challenges, and present opportunities]. Paolo Roberti; Mauro Visaggio. *Riv. Pol. Ec.* **LXXXII:III** 4:1992 pp. 3 – 22

254 Die steigende Verschuldung Indiens und ihre wirtschaftlichen Konsequenzen *[In German]*; [The Indian public debt and its economic consequences] *[Summary]*. Michael von Hauff. *Int. Asien.* **23:3-4** 11:1992 pp. 213 – 226

255 Trade, taxes and debt repayment in Sri Lanka. Daniel V. Gordon; Wimal Rankaduwa. *J. Dev. Stud.* **29:1** 10:1992 pp. 148 – 165

Public expenditure *[Dépenses publiques]*

256 Alternative forms of government expenditure financing — a comparative welfare analysis. Stephen J. Turnovsky. *Economica* **59:234** 5:1992 pp. 235 – 252

257 Biudzhet i ekonomika — vremia otvetstvennykh reshenii *[In Russian]*; [The budget and the economy — the times of responsible decisions]. V.S. Pavlov. Moskva: Finansy i statistika, 1991: 96 p. *ISBN: 5279009490.*

258 Budgetary deficits and government expenditure growth — towards a more accurate empirical specification. George Tridimas. *Publ. Fin. Q.* **20:3** 7:1992 pp. 275 – 297

259 Donor-determined intergovernmental grants structure. Dennis Patrick Leyden. *Publ. Fin. Q.* **20:3** 7:1992 pp. 321 – 337

260 The effects of systematic and surprise fiscal policy actions on cyclical movements of research output in a developing economy — evidence from Nigeria. M.O. Odedokun. *E. Afr. Econ. Rev.* **7:1** 6:1991 pp. 1 – 11

261 Effects of taxation in economic models — a survey. Anthonie Knoester; André Kolodziejak. *Econ. Model.* **9:4** 10:1992 pp. 352 – 364

262 Empirical tests for allocative efficiency in the local public sector. Anwar Shah. *Publ. Fin. Q.* **20:3** 7:1992 pp. 359 – 377

263 Finance commissions and centre state financial relations. Muppidi Sarojini. Allahabad: Chugh Publications, 1991: 243 p.

264 Financing government spending in the Netherlands. C. den Broeder; C.C.A. Winder. *Economist [Leiden]* **140:1** 1992 pp. 65 – 82

265 Friedman tax cuts vs. Buchanan deficit reduction as the best way of constraining government. Dwight R. Lee; Richard K. Vedder. *Econ. Inq.* **XXX:4** 10:1992 pp. 722 – 732

266 Government purchasing — some policy implications; *[Italian summary]*. Ilde Rizzo. *Politico* **LVII:1** 1-3:1992 pp. 109 – 126

267 The impact of the IMF on government expenditures — a study of African LDCs. G. Harris; N. Kusi. *J. Int. Dev.* **4:1** 1-2:1992 pp. 73 – 86

268 Interregional allocation of resources — the case of Indonesia. Iwan J. Azis. *Pap. Reg. Sci.* **71:4** 10:1992 pp. 393 – 404

269 Is public spending determined by voter choice or fiscal capacity? Leonard Dudley; Claude Montmarquette. *Rev. Econ. St.* **LXXIV:3** 8:1992 pp. 522 – 529

270 Local authority expenditure decisions — a maximum likelihood analysis of budget setting in the face of piecewise linear budget constraints. Richard R. Barnett; Rosella Levaggi; Peter Smith. *Ox. Econ. Pap.* **44:1** 1:1992 pp. 113 – 134

271 Modeling the relationship between output and government expenditure in Canada. Panos C. Afxentiou; Apostolos Serletis. *Keio Econ. Stud.* **XXIX:1** 1992 pp. 17 – 44

272 Modelling public expenditure — empirical evidence from five countries. George Hadjimatheou; Alex Tackie. *Int. R. Applied Ec.* **6:1** 1992 pp. 65 – 92

273 The output, employment, and interest rate effects of government consumption. S. Rao Aiyagari; Lawrence J. Christiano; Martin Eichenbaum. *J. Monet. Ec.* **30:1** 10:1992 pp. 73 – 86

274 Planning and controlling public expenditure in the UK, part I — the Treasury's Public Expenditure Survey. Colin Thain; Maurice Wright. *Publ. Admin.* **70:1** Spring:1992 pp. 3 – 24

275 Private profit and public capital. Catherine Lynde. *J. Macro.* **14:1** Winter:1992 pp. 125 – 142

N.2: Public finance *[Finances publiques]* — **Public expenditure** *[Dépenses publiques]*

276 Public expenditures in sub-Saharan Africa during a period of economic reforms. D.E. Sahn. *World Dev.* **20:5** 5:1992 pp. 673 – 694

277 Regulatory controls as barriers to entry in government procurement. William E. Kovacic. *Policy Sci.* **25:1** 2:1992 pp. 29 – 42

278 Sorting out state expenditure pressures. Richard F. Dye; Therese J. McGuire. *Natl. Tax. J.* **XLV:3** 9:1992 pp. 315 – 329

279 Tax discounting vs. crowding out. Stephen Mathis; Hamid Bastin. *Cont. Policy* **X:2** 4:1992 pp. 54 – 62

280 Tax reform with variable public expenditure. Kazuhiuko Mikami. *Publ. Finan.* **47:1** 1992 pp. 82 – 92

281 Tax regimes, tariff revenues and government spending. Grant W. Gardner; Kent P. Kimbrough. *Economica* **59:233** 2:1992 pp. 75 – 92

Tax evasion and avoidance *[Evasion et fraude fiscales]*

282 Adócsalás és adónyomozás... *[In Hungarian]*; (Tax fraud and tax investigations); (Steuernetrug und Steuerfahndung: *Title only in German).* Nagy Imre Zoltán. *Pénz. Sz.* **36:1** 1:1992 pp. 12 – 19

283 An econometric analysis of income tax evasion and its detection. J.S. Feinstein. *Rand J. Eco.* **22:1** Spring:1991 pp. 14 – 35

284 The effect of different sanction communications on hypothetical taxpayer compliance — policy implications from New Zealand. John Hasseldine; Steven E. Kaplan. *Publ. Finan.* **47:1** 1992 pp. 45 – 60

285 Estimates of cash-based income tax evasion in Australia. Glen Hepburn. *Aust. Ec. Rev.* **:98(2nd quarter)** 4-6:1992 pp. 54 – 62

286 Evading the use tax on cross-border sales — pricing and welfare effects. Gregory A. Trandel. *J. Publ. Ec.* **49:3** 12:1992 pp. 313 – 331

287 Evasione fiscale — aspetti teorici e suggerimenti practici *[In Italian]*; [Tax evasion — theoretical aspects and practical suggestions] *[Summary]*. M. Bordignon. *Riv. Int. Sci. Soc.* **C:1** 1-3:1992 pp. 3 – 28

288 Factor taxes and evasion in general equilibrium. P. Thalmann. *Reg. Sci. Urb. Econ.* **22:2** 6:1992 pp. 259 – 283

289 Fringe benefits and employee expenses — tax planning and neutral tax policy; *[French summary]*. A. Macnaughton; D. Thornton *[Discussant]*. *Cont. Account. Res.* **9:1** Fall:1992 pp. 113 – 141

290 Income tax evasion — theory and measurement. Henk Elffers. Deventer: Kluwer, 1991: ix, 239 p. (ill) *ISBN: 9020014315. Summary in Dutch; Includes bibliographical references (p.223-232).* [Burger en belastingen. : No. 9]

291 Pigouvian taxation, risk aversion, and avoidance. Robert E. Kohn. *Publ. Fin. Q.* **20:1** 1:1992 pp. 103 – 113

292 Social contract, taxation and the standing of deadweight loss. Richard A. Musgrave. *J. Publ. Ec.* **49:3** 12:1992 pp. 369 – 381

293 Steuerhinterziehung — Einige romantische, realistische und nicht zuletzt empirische Befunde *[In German]*; [Tax evasion — some romantic, realistic and not least empirical findings]. Werner W. Pommerehne; Hannelore Weck-Hannemann. *Z. Wirt. Soz.* **112:3** 1992 pp. 433 – 466

294 Una stima « prudenziale» dell'evasione dell'IVA nel settore del commercio *[In Italian]*; [A "cautious" evaluation of VAT evasion in the commercial sector]. Gianfranco Cerea. *Riv. Dir. Finan. Sci. Fin.* **LI:2** 6:1992 pp. 157 – 184

295 Tax evasion and compliance under different environments. H. Cremer *[Contrib.]*; F. Gahvari *[Contrib.]*; S. Scotchmer *[Contrib.]*; S.C. Wadhawan *[Contrib.]*; B.W. Ickes *[Contrib.]*; J. Slemrod *[Contrib.]*. *Collection of 4 articles.* **Publ. Finan.** *, 47,* 1992 pp. 351 – 399

Tax reform *[Réformes fiscales]*

296 Across group Pareto efficiency and the 1986 tax reform — a general equilibrium assessment. R.G. Boyd; L. Gallaway; R. Vedder. *Eco. Notes* **21:1** 1992 pp. 60 – 72

297 Centralization versus decentralization. M.E. Bell *[Contrib.]*; J. Regulska *[Contrib.]*; J.M. Quigley *[Contrib.]*; E. Smolensky *[Contrib.]*; D.E. Wildasin *[Contrib.]*. *Collection of 3 articles.* **Publ. Finan.** *, 47,* 1992 pp. 187 – 230

N.2: Public finance *[Finances publiques]* — *Tax reform [Réformes fiscales]*

298 A comparative analysis of tax reforms in Singapore and Hong Kong. Mukul G. Asher. *B. Int. Fiscal Docu.* **46:4** 4:1992 pp. 181 – 191

299 Composite area linked system for property tax reform in India. R.M. Kapoor; P.K. Ghosh. *R. Urban. Region. Dev. S.* **4:2** 7:1992 pp. 209 – 225

300 Ecological tax reform — a policy proposal for sustainable development. Ernst U. von Weizsacker; Jochen Jesinghaus. London: Zed Books, 1992: 90 p. *ISBN: 1856490955.*

301 Fiscal crisis and UK local tax reform. Douglas Mair; Richard Damania. *Loc. Govt. St.* **18:3** Autumn:1992 pp. 179 – 190

302 Fiscal problems of transition. A. Hussain *[Contrib.]*; N. Stern *[Contrib.]*; G. Ofer *[Contrib.]*; B. Genser *[Contrib.]*; Ch. John *[Contrib.]*. *Collection of 3 articles.* **Publ. Finan.** , *47*, 1992 pp. 289 – 348

303 Grandfather rules and the theory of optimal tax reform. George R. Zodrow. *J. Publ. Ec.* **49:2** 11:1992 pp. 163 – 190

304 Implementing property tax reform in developing countries — lessons from the property tax in Indonesia. Roy Kelly. *R. Urban. Region. Dev. S.* **4:2** 7:1992 pp. 193 – 208

305 Incidence effects of a state fiscal policy shift — the Florio inititatives in New Jersey. William T. Bogart; David F. Bradford; Michael G. Williams. *Natl. Tax. J.* **XLV:4** 12:1992 pp. 371 – 387

306 Income tax reform in Colombia and Venezuela — a comparative history. C.E. McLure. *World Dev.* **20:3** 3:1992 pp. 351 – 368

307 The interventionist state and taxation reforms — how are the redistribution issues handled? Francesco Kjellberg. *Ind. J. Pol. Sci.* **LIII:1** 1-3:1992 pp. 14 – 23

308 La riforma fiscale svedese *[In Italian]*; [Swedish fiscal reform]. Luisa Rimini. *Riv. Dir. Finan. Sci. Fin.* **LI:4** 12:1992 pp. 686 – 710

309 Sales taxes, investment, and the Tax Reform Act of 1986. David Joulfaian; James Mackie. *Natl. Tax. J.* **XLV:1** 3:1992 pp. 89 – 105

310 Seigniorage and political instability. Alex Cukierman; Sebastian Edwards; Guido Tabellini. *Am. Econ. Rev.* **82:3** 6:1992 pp. 537 – 555

311 Steuerliche Investitionsförderung in den fünf neuen Bundesländern — Maßnahmen und Auswirkungen *[In German]*; [The impact of tax reform measures on capital formation in the five eastern German states] *[Summary]*. Michael Funke; Dirk Willenbockel. *Finanzarchiv* **49:4** 1991/1992 pp. 457 – 480

312 Tax reform. R. Holzmann *[Contrib.]*; D. van de Gaer *[Contrib.]*; E. Schokkaert *[Contrib.]*; G. de Bruyne *[Contrib.]*; T. Tachibanaki *[Contrib.]*. *Collection of 3 articles.* **Publ. Finan.** , *47*, 1992 pp. 233 – 285

313 Tax reform 1986 and marginal welfare changes for labor. Sally Wallace; Michael Wasylenko. *S. Econ. J.* **59:1** 7:1992 pp. 39 – 48

314 Tax reform in Latin America — a review of some recent experiences. Richard M. Bird. *Lat. Am. Res. R.* **27:1** 1992 pp. 7 – 36

315 Tax reform with altruistic bequests. William Lord; Peter Rangazas. *Publ. Finan.* **47:1** 1992 pp. 61 – 81

316 Tax reform with variable public expenditure. Kazuhiuko Mikami. *Publ. Finan.* **47:1** 1992 pp. 82 – 92

317 The valuation of the deferred tax liability — evidence from the stock market. Dan Givoly; Carla Hayn. *Acc. Review* **67:2** 4:1992 pp. 394 – 410

318 Worldwide tax reform "how does Australia compare?". Cedric Sandford. *Aust. Ec. Rev.* **:1(97)** 1-3:1992 pp. 22 – 32

N.3: Public sector, public utilities — *Secteur public, services d'utilité publique*

1 Ansätze zur Erfassung der Präferenzen für öffentliche Güter — ein Überblick *[In German]*; [Approaches designed to estimate the preferences for public goods — an overview] *[Summary]*. Werner W. Pommerehne; Anselm U. Römer. *Jahr. Soz.schaft.* **43:2** 1992 pp. 171 – 210

2 Arbitrary values, good causes, and premature verdicts. V. Kerry Smith. *J. Envir. Ec. Manag.* **22:1** 1:1992 pp. 71 – 89

3 Cases in public sector accounting. B.A. Rutherford; Michael Sherer; R.T. Wearing. London: Paul Chapman Publishing, 1992: 256 p. *ISBN: 1853960721.*

4 A comparative analysis of methods for regulating public utilities. M. Waterson. *Metroeconomica* **XLIII:1-2** 2-6:1992 pp. 205 – 222

5 Comparative statics for the private provision of public goods in a conjectural variations model with heterogeneous agents. Dipanker Dasgupta; Jun-ichi Itaya. *Publ. Finan.* **47:1** 1992 pp. 17 – 31

6 Competition in government-financed services. John C. Hilke. New York: Quorum Books, 1992: viii, 212 p. (ill) *ISBN: 0899307507; LofC: 91036409. Includes bibliographical references (p.[187]-208) and index.*

7 Les contrats programme entre l'Etat nigérien et les entreprises publiques *[In French]*; [Programme contracts between the Nigerian state and public enterprises]. Amadou Tankoano. *Afr. J. Int. Comp. Law* **4:4** 12:1992 pp. 854 – 873

8 The contribution of publicly provided inputs to states' economies. T. Garcia-Milà; T.J. McGuire. *Reg. Sci. Urb. Econ.* **22:2** 6:1992 pp. 229 – 241

9 Current utility regulatory practice from a historical perspective. Robert L. Swartwout. *Natur. Res. J.* **32:2** Spring:1992 pp. 289 – 343

10 Demande, marchés publics et innovation *[In French]*; [Demand, public markets and innovation]. Yves Terrasse *[Contrib.]*; Robert Dalpé *[Contrib.]*; Philippe Nell *[Contrib.]*; Michel Mougeot *[Contrib.]*; Florence Naegelen *[Contrib.]*; Augusto Ninni *[Contrib.]*; Olivier Godard *[Contrib.]*; Antoinette Catrice-Lorey *[Contrib.]*; Marie-Chantal L'Huillier *[Contrib.]*. *Collection of 7 articles.* **Pol. Manag. Publ.** , *10:2,* 6:1992 pp. 3 – 183

11 Descentralización fiscal y crecimiento del sector público *[In Spanish]*; [Financial decentralization and growth in the public sector]. Elías M. Amor Bravo. *Infor. Com. Esp.* **:707** 7:1992 pp. 98 – 108

12 An East-West tug of water — water services in united Germany. R. Andreas Kraemer. *Util. Policy* **2:1** 1:1992 pp. 25 – 35

13 The effects of resource distribution, voice, and decision framing on the provision of public goods. Karl Aquino; Victoria Steisel; Avi Kay. *Confl. Resolut.* **36:4** 12:1992 pp. 665 – 687

14 An empirical analysis of public enterprises's performance in Tanzania's manufacturing sector and some suggestions for improvement. Laurean W. Rustayisire. *E. Afr. Econ. Rev.* **7:1** 6:1991 pp. 13 – 30

15 Fiscal decentralization and public sector size in Australia. Philip J. Grossman. *Econ. Rec.* **68:202** 9:1992 pp. 240 – 246

16 The fiscal effect of community composition on public services and welfare. Charles A.M. de Bartolome. *J. Urban Ec.* **32:2** 9:1992 pp. 140 – 158

17 From overindustrialization to the reform of public enterprises in Algeria. Salah Mouhoubi. *Finan. News Anal.* **5:3** 3:1992 pp. 1 – 12

18 The government sector in Kaldor-Pasinetti models of growth and income distribution. Jorge Thompson Araújo. *J. Post. Keyn. Ec.* **15:2** Winter:1992-1993 pp. 211 – 228

19 Government subsidies to private spending on public goods. R.D. Roberts. *Publ. Choice* **74:2** 9:1992 pp. 133 – 152

20 The Harambee movement and efficient public good provision in Kenya. L.S. Wilson. *J. Publ. Ec.* **48:1** 6:1992 pp. 1 – 19

21 Impure public goods and transfers in a three-agent model. Toshihiro Ihori. *J. Publ. Ec.* **48:3** 8:1992 pp. 385 – 401

22 Incentives for conservation and quality-improvement by public utilities. Tracy R. Lewis; David E.M. Sappington. *Am. Econ. Rev.* **82:5** 12:1992 pp. 1321 – 1340

23 Indivisibility and preference for collective provision. J.H.Y. Edwards. *Reg. Sci. Urb. Econ.* **22:4** 11:1992 pp. 559 – 577

N.3: Public sector, public utilities *[Secteur public, services d'utilité publique]*

24 Information systems on public enterprises in developing countries; *[French summary]*; *[Spanish summary]*; *[Arabic summary]*. Anthony Bennett *[Ed.]*; Pavle Sicherl *[Ed.]*; Dominique Babini *[Contrib.]*; M. Abul Kalam Mazumdar *[Contrib.]*; Xinzheng Wang *[Contrib.]*; Lucas Y. Chigabatia *[Contrib.]*; Asif A. Shah *[Contrib.]*; E. Arumugam *[Contrib.]*; Maritza Lara Vasquez *[Contrib.]*; Nuria Cunill *[Contrib.]* and others. *Collection of 10 articles.* **Publ. Enter.** , *12:3-4*, 9-12:1992 pp. 177 – 326

25 A közmûszektor privatizációs lehetőségei *[In Hungarian]*; Privatization possibilities of the public utilities sector *[Summary]*. Tamás Masztis. *Közg. Sz.* **XXXIX** 2:1992 pp. 172 – 183

26 Malaysia's public enterprises — a performance evaluation. Abdul Hafeez Shaikh. *ASEAN Ec. B.* **9:2** 11:1992 pp. 207 – 218

27 Mandating utility competition — one option for promoting energy efficiency. Edward Vine; et al. *Util. Policy* **2:1** 1:1992 pp. 51 – 61

28 Measuring public sector size in the advanced market economy countries — the problem of deflators. Vincent A. Mahler. *Soc. Ind.* **27:4** 12:1992 pp. 311 – 325

29 A model of expropriation with asymmetric information. Horst Raff. *J. Int. Econ.* **33:3/4** 11:1992 pp. 245 – 265

30 Nationalisation — beyond the slogans. Keith Coleman. Johannesburg: Ravan Press, 1991: xii, 179 p. (ill) *ISBN: 0869754130; LofC: 91228900. Includes bibliographical references and index.*

31 A note on contestability and the government supply of public goods in a post-apartheid economy. R.E. Dollery. *Develop. S. Afr.* **9:1** 2:1992 pp. 3 – 10

32 On the public good provision rule under a nonlinear income tax. Hideo Konishi. *Econ. S. Quart.* **43:2** 6:1992 pp. 97 – 104

33 Optimum supply of international public goods. Katsushi Terasaki. *Keio Econ. Stud.* **XXIX:1** 1992 pp. 45 – 62

34 Ownership versus competition — efficiency in public enterprise. A.R. Vining; A.E. Boardman. *Publ. Choice* **73:2** 1992 pp. 205 – 239

35 Policy changes in Indonesian public enterprises during the old order and new order governments. Iketut Mardjana. *ASEAN Ec. B.* **9:2** 11:1992 pp. 187 – 206

36 The pricing of capital services under regulation. Anna P. Della Valle; G. Campbell Watkins. *Util. Policy* **2:1** 1:1992 pp. 36 – 42

37 Production efficiency in local government — a parametric approach. Steven C. Deller. *Publ. Finan.* **47:1** 1992 pp. 32 – 44

38 Productividad global de los factorès teoría y aplicación al caso de una empresa pública argentina *[In Spanish]*; Global factor productivity — theory and application to the case of an Argentine public enterprise *[Summary]*. German Coloma. *Económica Arg* **XXXVI:1-2** 1990 pp. 21 – 52

39 Productivity analysis in the public sector — the case of the fire service. Geert Bouckaert. *Int. Rev. Admin. Sci.* **58:2** 6:1992 pp. 175 – 200

40 Public enterprise reform in Papua New Guinea. A. Whitworth. *World Dev.* **20:1** 1:1992 pp. 69 – 82

41 Rational conjectures equilibria in the private provision of public goods. Allen J. Scafuri. *Publ. Fin. Q.* **20:2** 4:1992 pp. 139 – 151

42 Reconciling public entrepreneurship and democracy. Carl J. Bellone; George Frederick Goerl. *Publ. Adm. Re.* **52:2** 3-4:1992 pp. 130 – 134

43 Regular public good economies. D. Diamantaras. *J. Math Econ.* **21:6** 1992 pp. 523 – 542

44 The regulation of product quality in the public utilities and the Citizen's Charter. Laura Rovizzi; David Thompson. *Fis. Stud.* **13:3** 8:1992 pp. 74 – 95

45 Residential demand for water and the pricing of municipal water services. Randolph C. Martin; Ronald P. Wilder. *Publ. Fin. Q.* **20:1** 1:1992 pp. 93 – 102

46 Servizi di pubblica utilità *[In Italian]*; [Public services]. Alfred E. Kahn *[Contrib.]*; Sabino Cassese *[Contrib.]*; Luigi Prosperetti *[Contrib.]*; Giuliano Graziosi *[Contrib.]*; Fabio Gobbo *[Contrib.]*; Gabriella Utili *[Contrib.]*; Alberto Clô *[Contrib.]*; Giovanni Fraquelli *[Contrib.]*; Graziella Fornengo *[Contrib.]*; Enzo Pontarollo *[Contrib.]* and others. *Collection of 10 articles.* **Industria** , *XIII:2*, 4-6:1992 pp. 147 – 368

47 Sharing among clubs — a club of clubs theory. Frederic P. Sterbenz; Todd Sandler. *Ox. Econ. Pap.* **44:1** 1:1992 pp. 1 – 19

48 Social contracts and pipe dreams. Jerome Ellig; Jack High. *Cont. Policy* **X:1** 1:1992 pp. 39 – 51

49 State enterprise and employment generation in Brazil. Benedict J. Clements. *Econ. Dev. Cult. Change* **41:1** 10:1992 pp. 51 – 62

N.3: Public sector, public utilities *[Secteur public, services d'utilité publique]*

50 State-owned enterprise reform in Latin America. Antonio Martín del Campo; Donald R. Winkler. *CEPAL R.* :**46** 4:1992 pp. 47 – 68

51 Unanimity and exclusion as mechanisms to eliminate free riding in public goods — diagrammatical illustrations. D. Bigman. *J. Econ. Beh.* **19:1** 9:1992 pp. 101 – 117

52 Valuing public goods — the purchase of moral satisfaction. Daniel Kahneman; Jack L. Knetsch. *J. Envir. Ec. Manag.* **22:1** 1:1992 pp. 57 – 70

53 The voluntary contributions mechanism with real time revisions. R.E. Dorsey. *Publ. Choice* **73:3** 1992 pp. 261 – 282

54 Voluntary provision of public goods. The multiple unit case. Mark Bagnoli; Shaul Ben-David; Michael McKee. *J. Publ. Ec.* **47:1** 2:1992 pp. 85 – 106

55 A welfare comparison of private and public monopoly. John E. Roemer; Joaquim Silvestre. *J. Publ. Ec.* **48:1** 6:1992 pp. 67 – 81

O: International economics — *Économie internationale*

O.1: International economic relations — *Relations économiques internationales*

O.1.1: Theory of international equilibrium and policy — *Théorie de l'équilibre international et de la politique économique internationale*

1 Changing fortunes — the world's money and the threat to American leadership. Paul A. Volcker; Toyoo Gyohten. New York: Times Books, 1992: xix, 394 p., 8 p. of plates (ill) *ISBN: 081292018x; LofC: 91051035. Includes bibliographical references and index.*

2 The internationalization of Japan. Glenn D. Hook *[Ed.]*; Michael A. Weiner *[Ed.]*. London: Routledge, 1992: 325 p. *ISBN: 0415071380; LofC: 91037474. Selection of papers originally presented at the two-day Silver Jubilee Conference of the Centre for Japanese Studies at the University of Sheffield, held in Sept. 1989; Includes bibliographical references and index.* [Sheffield Centre for Japanese Studies. Routledge series.]

3 Pays développés et développement mondial équilibré — défis et responsabilités *[In French]*; [Developed countries and balanced world development — challenges and responsibilities]. Nana Sinkam. *Afr. 2000* :**11** 10-12:1992 pp. 25 – 38

4 Sprawiedliwość międzynarodowa gospodarcza *[In Polish]*; (International economic justice); (La justice économique internationale: *Title only in French*); (Международная экономическая справедливость: *Title only in Russian*). Janusz Gilas. *Spr. Między.* **XLV:3(456)** 1992 pp. 51 – 64

O.1.2: World economy — *Économie mondiale*

1 Cyprus and the international economy. Rodney Wilson. New York: St. Martin's Press, 1992: 156 p. *ISBN: 0312075103; LofC: 91031687. Includes bibliographical references and index.*

2 Europe and the new world economic order. Dario Velo. *Federalist* **XXXIV:1** 1992 pp. 44 – 53

3 European macro-econometric modelling of the world economy. R. Barrell *[Ed.]*; J. Le Dem *[Ed.]*; M. Artis *[Contrib.]*; S. Holly *[Contrib.]*; G.P. Meen *[Contrib.]*; J.W.In't Veld *[Contrib.]*; A. Gurney *[Contrib.]*; P. Richardson *[Contrib.]*; J.D. Whitley *[Contrib.]*; G.A. Horn *[Contrib.]* and others. Collection of 7 articles. **J. Forecast.** , *11*:5, 8:1992 pp. 331 – 506

4 Free or forced riders? Small states in the international political economy — the example of Sweden. Anders Ahnlid. *Coop. Conflict* **27:3** 9:1992 pp. 241 – 276

5 Global disequilibrium in the world economy. Mario Baldassarri *[Ed.]*; John C. P. McCallum

O.1.2: World economy *[Économie mondiale]*
[Ed.]; R.A. Mundell *[Ed.]*. New York, NY.: St Martin's Press, 1992: 472 p.
ISBN: 0312079842; LofC: 92000065. Includes index. [Central issues in contemporary economic theory and policy.]
6 The global economy in the 90s — a user's guide. Bill Orr. Basingstoke: Macmillan, 1992: 330 p. (figs.tabs) *ISBN: 0333579771.*
7 The impact of response measures by industrialized countries on the world economy. Mohammad S. Al-Sabban. *OPEC B.* **XXIII:5** 5:1992 pp. 4 – 12
8 International aspects of economic development. Graham Bird *[Ed.]*. London: Surrey University Press in association with Academic Press, 1992: 250 p. *ISBN: 0120997428.*
9 Latin America and the internationalization of the world economy. Mikio Kuwayama. *CEPAL R.* **:46** 4:1992 pp. 9 – 30
10 Patterns of convergence and divergence among industrialized nations — 1960-1988. C. Samuel Craig; Susan P. Douglas; Andreas Grein. *J. Int. Bus. Stud.* **23:4** Fourth quarter:1992 pp. 773 – 787
11 The spectre of capitalism — the future of the world economy after the fall of communism. William Keegan. London: Radius, 1992: 221 p. *ISBN: 0091745969.*
12 Stochastic behavior of the world economy under alternative policy regimes. Joseph E. Gagnon; Ralph W. Tryon. [Washington, D.C.]: Board of Governors of the Federal Reserve System, 1992: 38 p. [International finance discussion papers. : No. 428]
13 The taming of Leviathan — competition among governments. Stefan Sinn. *Constit. Pol. Econ.* **3:2** Spring-Summer:1992 pp. 177 – 196
14 Trends in the world economy — implications for fiscal choices. Roy Bahl. *B. Int. Fiscal Docu.* **46:12** 12:1992 pp. 576 – 587
15 Wastes, the environment and the international economy. Nigel Harris. *Cities* **9:3** 8:1992 pp. 177 – 185
16 The world economy after the Cold War. C. Fred Bergsten. *Calif. Manag. R.* **34:2** Winter:1992 pp. 51 – 65
17 A world economy — paradigms lost and found. Robert Wuliger. *Challenge* **35:1** 1-2:1992 pp. 4 – 22
18 Zur Reintegration der baltischen Staaten in die Weltwirtschaft *[In German]*; [On the reintegration of the Baltic States into the world economy]. Claus-Friedrich Laaser; Klaus Schrader. *Weltwirt.* **:2** 1992 pp. 189 – 211

O.1.2.1: Governmental organizations — *Organisations gouvernementales*

O.1.2.2: Private international organizations (cartels, agreements) — *Organisations internationales privées (cartels, ententes)*

1 Barefoot in the boardroom — venture and misadventure in the People's Republic of China. Bill Purves. North Sydney, NSW, Australia: Allen & Unwin, 1991: 178 p. *ISBN: 1863730389. Includes index.*
2 Differential British and U.S. adoption rates of investment project post-completion auditing. C.W. Neale; Peter J. Buckley. *J. Int. Bus. Stud.* **23:3** Third quarter:1992 pp. 443 – 459
3 Dynamic effects of foreign tax credits on multinational corporations. Rosanne Altshuler; Paolo Fulghieri. New York: Columbia University, Dept of Economics, 1992: 27 p. [Discussion paper series.]
4 The effects of government policies in a macromodel with multinational corporations. T. Moutos. *Eco. Notes* **21:1** 1992 pp. 1 – 14
5 Europe and the multinationals — issues and responses for the 1990s. Stephen Young *[Ed.]*; James Hamill *[Ed.]*. Aldershot: Edward Elgar, 1992: 320 p. *ISBN: 1852785349; LofC: 91034822. Includes index.* [New horizons in international business.]
6 The European Community and multinational enterprises — lessons in the social control of industry. Anthony Scaperlanda. *J. Econ. Iss.* **XXVI:2** 6:1992 pp. 421 – 432
7 Foreign and domestic multinational presence in the UK. K. Hughes; C. Oughton. *Appl. Econ.* **24:7** 7:1992 pp. 745 – 749

O.1.2.2: Private international organizations (cartels, agreements) *[Organisations internationales privées (cartels, ententes)]*

8 Global or stateless corporations are national firms with international operations. Yao-Su Hu. *Calif. Manag. R.* **34:2** Winter:1992 pp. 107 – 126

9 Implementing global strategy — characteristics of global subsidiary mandates. Kendall Roth; Allen J. Morrison. *J. Int. Bus. Stud.* **23:4** Fourth quarter:1992 pp. 715 – 735

10 Internalization vs. cooperation of MNC's business. Kiyoshi Kojima. *Hito. J. Econ.* **33:1** 6:1992 pp. 1 – 18

11 International business and global integration — empirical studies. Mark Casson *[Ed.]*. Basingstoke: Macmillan in association with the Graduate School of European and International Studies, University of Reading, 1992: xiii, 271 p. *ISBN: 0333560353. Bibliography — p.252-261. Includes index.*

12 International investment location decisions — the case of U.S. firms. David Wheeler; Ashoka Mody. *J. Int. Econ.* **33:1/2** 8:1992 pp. 57 – 76

13 International management control in multinational corporations — the case of Japanese consumer electronics firms in Asia. Schon Beechler. *ASEAN Ec. B.* **9:2** 11:1992 pp. 149 – 168

14 The internationalization process of the firm — searching for new patterns and explanations. Kjell A. Nordström. Stockholm, Sweden: Institute of International Business, Stockholm School of Economics, 1991: 228 p. *ISBN: 9197100579. Bibliography — p. 185-192.*

15 Internationalization — an event study test. Randall Morck; Bernard Yeung. *J. Int. Econ.* **33:1/2** 8:1992 pp. 41 – 56

16 Japan's global reach — the influences, strategies and weaknesses of Japan's multinational companies. Bill Emmott. London: Century, 1991, c1992: xi, 244 p. *ISBN: 071264928x; LofC: gb 92040130. Includes index; Bibliography — p. 233-235.*

17 Large multinational enterprises based in a small economy — effects on domestic investment; *[German summary]*; *[French summary]*; *[Spanish summary]*. René A. Belderbos. *Welt.liches Arc.* **128:3** 1992 pp. 543 – 557

18 Multinational enterprise and strikes. F. Carmichael. *Scot. J. Poli.* **39:1** 2:1992 pp. 52 – 68

19 Multinationale Konzerne in der petrochemischen Industrie Brasiliens *[In German]*; Multinational corporations in the petrochemical industry of Brazil — the importance of foreign firm origin in the transfer of technology *[Summary]*. Wilma Roos. *Peripherie* **12:46** 5:1992 pp. 5 – 17

20 Les multinationales hors de la tourmente? *[In French]*; The untouchable multinationals *[Summary]*. Jean Masini. *Hom. Soc.* **:105-106** 3-4:1992 pp. 51 – 61

21 Multinationals in the new Europe and global trade. Michael W. Klein *[Ed.]*; Paul J.J. Welfens *[Ed.]*. Berlin: Springer, 1992: 281 p. *ISBN: 3540546340.*

22 The structure of European stock returns. Martin Drummen; Heinz Zimmermann. *Finan. Anal. J.* **48:4** 7-8:1992 pp. 15 – 26

23 Studies in international business. Peter J. Buckley; Raymond Vernon *[Foreword]*. New York: St. Martin's Press, 1992: 167 p. *ISBN: 0312076010; LofC: 91044083. Includes index.*

24 Transnationals and foreign trade — evidence from Brazil. Larry Willmore. *J. Dev. Stud.* **28:2** 1:1992 pp. 314 – 335

25 Welfare and protection in the presence of endogenous transfer prices. Vibhas Madan. *Int. Econ. J.* **6:3** Autumn:1992 pp. 1 – 20

O.1.2.3: Market conditions — *Conditions du marché*

1 America and the new economy. First part — the new market standards; L'Amérique et la nouvelle économie *[French summary]*. Anthony P. Carnevale *[Contrib.]*. Collection of 4 articles. *Gestion* , *8:3,* 1992 pp. 127 – 170

2 The behavior of oil futures returns around OPEC conferences. Richard Deaves; Itzhak Krinsky. *J. Futur. Mark.* **12:5** 10:1992 pp. 563 – 574

3 Can the UK exploit the international oil market? A game theoretic approach. A. Johannsen; E. Karakitsos. *Appl. Econ.* **24:2** 2:1992 pp. 143 – 152

4 Cargill — trading the world's grain. Wayne G. Broehl. Hanover, New Hampshire: Dartmouth College, 1992: xx, 1007 p. (ill) *ISBN: 0874515726; LofC: 91031608. Includes index.*

5 Commodity development measures. Józef M. Toczek. *Econ. Papers [Warsaw]* **18** 1992 pp. 60 – 87

6 Competition in global markets — a case study of American and Japanese competition in the British market. Peter Doyle; John Saunders; Veronica Wong. *J. Int. Bus. Stud.* **23:3** Third quarter:1992 pp. 419 – 442

O.1.2.3: Market conditions *[Conditions du marché]*
7 Competition policy and the competitive process — Europe in the 1990s. A. Hughes. *Metroeconomica* **XLIII:1-2** 2-6:1992 pp. 1 – 46
8 The dynamic stability of OPEC's oil price mechanism. Shawkat Hammoudeh; Vibhas Madan. *Ener. Econ.* **14:1** 1:1992 pp. 65 – 72
9 The economics of globalism. H.W. Arndt. *Banca Nat. Lav. Q. Rev.* **:180** 3:1992 pp. 103 – 111
10 Effects of alternative Chinese policies on the world grains market. B.H. Gunasekera; G. Rodriguez; N. Andrews. *J. Agr. Econ.* **43:3** 9:1992 pp. 440 – 451
11 EG 92 — Der Gemeinsame Bankenmarkt und seine Auswirkungen auf Österreich *[In German]*; [EC 92 — the single banking market and its effects on Austria]. Maria Peubey-Kronsteiner. *Bank-Archiv* **38** 2:1990 pp. 102 – 111
12 End-use performance uncertainty and competition in international wheat markets. William W. Wilson; Todd Preszler. *Am. J. Agr. Ec.* **74:3** 8:1992 pp. 556 – 563
13 Energy swaps as profit motive instruments in oil markets. Ali Asghar Arshi. *OPEC Rev.* **XVI:2** Summer:1992 pp. 201 – 216
14 Die Entwicklung der Weltmarktpreise für Rohstoffe von 1960/61 bis 1982/83 *[In German]*; [The development of raw materials prices on the world market in 1960/61 to 1982/83 *[Summary]*. John-ren Chen. *J. Entwick.pol.* **VIII:4** 1992 pp. 387 – 411
15 Foreign direct investment in a strategically competitive environment — Coca-Cola, Belize, and the international citrus industry. B.L. Barham. *World Dev.* **20:6** 6:1992 pp. 841 – 858
16 How to service a foreign market under uncertainty — a real option approach. J. Capel. *Eur. J. Pol. Ec.* **8:3** 10:1992 pp. 455 – 475
17 Impact of the price adjustment process and trading noise on return patterns of grain futures. Shi-Miin Liu; Sarahelen Thompson; Paul Newbold. *J. Futur. Mark.* **12:5** 10:1992 pp. 575 – 585
18 Industrie mondiale — trois scénarios pour l'an 2000 *[In French]*; World industry — three scenarios for the year 2000 *[Summary]*; Industria mundial — tres escenarios para el año 2000 *[Spanish summary]*. Gérard Lafay. *E & S* **:256** 7-8:1992 pp. 59 – 67
19 An internal insurance market before the turn of the century? A. Ottow. *Common Mkt. L. R.* **29:3** :1992 pp. 511 – 536
20 The international arms market — a structural analysis. Andrew L. Ross. *Int. Inter.* **18:1** 1992 pp. 63 – 83
21 International configuration and coordination archetypes for medium-sized firms in global industries. Kendall Roth. *J. Int. Bus. Stud.* **23:3** Third quarter:1992 pp. 533 – 549
22 International high-technology competition. F.M. Scherer. Cambridge, Mass: Harvard University Press, 1992: viii, 196 p. (ill) *ISBN: 0674458451; LofC: 91044479. Includes bibliographical references and indexes.*
23 Japan, the Middle East and the world economy — a note on the oil triangle. Sugihara Kaoru. *Jpn. Forum* **4:1** 4:1992 pp. 21 – 32
24 Krigen om oljeprisen — oljen og konflikten ved Den persiske gulf *[In Norwegian]*; The oil price war — oil and the conflict in the Persian Gulf area *[Summary]*. Ole Gunnar Austvik. *Int. Pol.* **50:3** 1992 pp. 277 – 290
25 Market integration and regulation — Europe after 1992. G. Majone. *Metroeconomica* **XLIII:1-2** 2-6:1992 pp. 131 – 156
26 Market structure, excess capacity and price movement — implications for the world oil market in the 1990s. Akin Iwayemi. *OPEC Rev.* **XVI:3** Autumn:1992 pp. 299 – 307
27 Modelling the link between commodity prices and exchange rates — the tale of daily data; *[French summary]*. Peter S. Sephton. *Can. J. Econ.* **XXV:1** 2:1992 pp. 156 – 171
28 Oil and gas in Russian foreign policy.*Int. Aff. Mos.* **11** 1992 pp. 57 – 66
29 OPEC and the international financial system. Kofi A. Amoateng. *OPEC Rev.* **XVI:2** Summer:1992 pp. 185 – 200
30 Petroleum perestroika. Robert D. Kase. *Columb. J. W. Bus.* **XXVI:4** Winter:1992 pp. 16 – 28
31 Protecting markets — U.S. policy and the world grain trade. Ronald T. Libby. Ithaca: Cornell University Press, 1992: xvii, 152 p. (ill) *ISBN: 0801426170; LofC: 91055536. Includes bibliographical references (p. 140-145) and index.*
32 Recent writings on competitiveness — boxing the compass. Richard R. Nelson. *Calif. Manag. R.* **34:2** Winter:1992 pp. 127 – 137
33 The ROC's role in building a global economy. Jan Prybyla. *Iss. Stud.* **28:11** 11:1992 pp. 1 – 29
34 Servicing international markets — competitive strategies of firms. Peter J. Buckley *[Ed.]*; Kate Prescott *[Ed.]*; C. L. Pass *[Ed.]*. Cambridge, MA.: Blackwell Publishers, 1992: xii, 336 p. *ISBN: 063118189x; LofC: 92008133. Includes bibliographical references and index.*

O.1.2.3: Market conditions *[Conditions du marché]*
35 The single European energy market — the politics of realization. Stephen Padgett. *J. Com. Mkt. S.* **XXX:1** 3:1992 pp. 53 – 76
36 La structuration de l'offre de drogue en réseaux *[In French]*; (The structure of the drug supply network); (Strukturnoe postroenie predloženija narkotikov po seti: *Title only in Russian)*; (Die Strukturierung des Drogenangebots im Verteilernetz: *Title only in German)*; (La estructuración de la oferta de droga en redes: *Title only in Spanish)*. Pierre Kopp. *R. T-Monde* **XXXIII:131** 7-9:1992 pp. 517 – 536
37 The trade trap — poverty and the global commodity markets. Belinda Coote. Oxford: Oxfam, 1992: 214 p. *ISBN: 0855981342.*
38 Transfer prices and the excess cost of Canadian oil imports — new evidence on Bertrand versus Rugman; *[French summary]*. Jean-Thomas Bernard; Robert J. Weiner. *Can. J. Econ.* **XXV:1** 2:1992 pp. 22 – 40
39 Two-step testing procedure for price discovery role of future prices. Jing Quan. *J. Futur. Mark.* **12:2** 4:1992 pp. 139 – 150
40 The world economy. R. Anderton; R. Barrell; J. W. in't Veld. *Natl. Inst. Econ. R.* **:140** 5:1992 pp. 26 – 44

O.1.2.4: Economic blocs. Economic integration — *Blocs économiques. Intégration économique*

Sub-divisions: European Communities *[Communautés européennes]*

1 1980-1990 — du plan d'action de Lagos à la déclaration d'Abuja *[In French]*; [1980-1990 — from the Lagos Plan of action to the Abuja declaration]. Bruno E. Koffi. *Afr. 2000* **:9** 4-6:1992 pp. 59 – 72
2 Africa's experiences with regional co-operation and integration — assessing some groupings; *[French summary]*; *[Italian summary]*. Ahmed Aghrout. *Africa [Italy]* **XLVII:4** 12:1992 pp. 563 – 586
3 Una agenda democrática frente al Mercosur *[In Spanish]*; [A democratic agenda, fronted by "Mercosur"]. Héctor Alimonda. *Nueva Soc.* **:121** 9-10:1992 pp. 26 – 34
4 The agreement on a European Economic Area. S. Norberg. *Common Mkt. L. R.* **29:6** 1992 pp. 1171 – 1198
5 Amériques latines — quelles intétegrations? *[In French]*; [Latin America — which integrations?]. Jean Revel-Mouroz *[Ed.]*; Paule Arnaud-Ameller *[Contrib.]*; Brigitte Jensen *[Contrib.]*; Nelson Delgado *[Contrib.]*; Lena Lavinas *[Contrib.]*; Renato S. Maluf *[Contrib.]*; Jorge O. Romano *[Contrib.]*; Carlos Alba Vega *[Contrib.]*; Gabriel Szekely *[Contrib.]*; Oscar Vera *[Contrib.] and others. Collection of 8 articles.* **Cah. Amer. Lat.** , *12, 1992* pp. 45 – 176
6 Antecedentes y perspectivas económicas del programa de integración entre Argentina-Brasil-Uruguay *[In Spanish]*; [Background and economic prospects for the programme for the integration of Argentina, Brazil and Uruguay]. Dora Isabel Nieva; Hugo Omar Andrade. *Cuad. Am.* **VI:3 (33)** 5-6:1992 pp. 210 – 239
7 ASEAN and the Pacific. Mohamed Ariff *[Contrib.]*; Joseph L.H. Tan *[Contrib.]*; Tan Eu Chye *[Contrib.]*; F.A. Alburo *[Contrib.]*; C.C. Bautista *[Contrib.]*; M.S.H. Gochoco *[Contrib.]*; Tan Kong Yam *[Contrib.]*; Toh Mun Heng *[Contrib.]*; Linda Low *[Contrib.]*; Mari Pangestu *[Contrib.] and others. Collection of 6 articles.* **ASEAN Ec. B.** , *8:3,* 3:1992 pp. 251 – 375
8 ASEAN economic cooperation — status and challenges. Chien-nan Wang. *Ind. Free China* **LXXVII:5** 5:1992 pp. 43 – 54
9 Britain in the new Europe. Geoffrey Smith. *Foreign Aff.* **71:4** Fall:1992 pp. 155 – 170
10 Centripetal and centrifugal forces in the CMEA — prospects for the future. Lee Kendall Metcalf. *Stud. Comp. Commun.* **XXV:2** 6:1992 pp. 123 – 138
11 Circling the wagons — the trend toward economic regionalism and its consequences for Asia. Karl J. Fields. *Iss. Stud.* **28:12** 12:1992 pp. 73 – 96
12 Defesa da concorrência no Mercosul *[In Portuguese]*; [In defence of competition in Mercosul]. Werter R. Faria. Brasília: Associação Brasileira de Estudos da Integração, 1992: 300 p. *ISBN: 8570180969. Bibliography — p.63.* [Estudos da integração. : Vol. 1]
13 Economic integration and regionalism in East Asia. Luigi Narbone. *Inter. Spect.* **XXVII:4** 10-12:1992 pp. 25 – 40

O.1.2.4: Economic blocs. Economic integration *[Blocs économiques. Intégration économique]*

14 Economic integration as competitive discipline. K.C. Fung. *Int. Econ. R.* **33:4** 11:1992 pp. 837 – 847

15 Economic integration in Africa from speech to reality. Mohamed Haddar. *Devel. & Socio-eco. Pro.* **:53** 1:1992 pp. 5 – 14

16 Economic integration — Latin American and Southern African experiences; *[Portuguese summary]*; *[Spanish summary]*; *[Afrikaans summary]*. Gavin Maasdorp. *Unisa Lat.Am. Rep.* **8:1** 1992 pp. 7 – 19

17 The economics of German reunification — a review of the literature. Phillip J. Bryson. *J. Comp. Econ.* **16:1** 3:1992 pp. 118 – 149

18 Effects of economic integration in industrial countries on ASEAN and the Asian NIEs. M.E. Kreinin; M.G. Plummer. *World Dev.* **20:9** 9:1992 pp. 1345 – 1366

19 Die Energiewirtschaft als Klammer gegen das wirtschaftliche Auseinanderfallen der ehemaligen UdSSR *[In German]*; Energy economics as a clamp against economic disintegration of the former USSR *[Summary]*. Alois K. Fischer. *Ost. Wirt.* **37:1** 3:1992 pp. 66 – 76

20 Europa, Raum wirtschaftlicher Begegnung *[In German]*; [Europe, an area of economic relations]. Hermann Kellenbenz. Stuttgart: Franz Steiner, 1991: 115 p. *ISBN: 3515058052. ger, fre; Includes bibliographical references.* [Vierteljahrschrift für Sozial- und Wirtschaftsgeschichte; Kleine Schriften.]

21 The European Central Bank — a full-fledged scheme or just a "fledgeling"? M. Sarcinelli. *Banca Nat. Lav. Q. Rev.* **:181** 6:1992 pp. 119 – 145

22 A game model of Asia Pacific economic cooperation. Tom Jackson. *Asian Econ. J.* **VI:2** 7:1992 pp. 131 – 147

23 German unification and systemic transition — towards a new German economic miracle? P.J.J. Welfens. *Acta Oecon.* **44:1-2** 1992 pp. 115 – 140

24 A "greater China economic sphere" — reality and prospects. Charng Kao. *Iss. Stud.* **28:11** 11:1992 pp. 49 – 64

25 Implicit trade subsidies within the CMEA — a historical perspective; *[German summary]*. Michael Marrese; Lauren Wittenberg. *Econ. Sys.* **16:1** 4:1992 pp. 1 – 32

26 La integración económica de Argentina, Brasil y Uruguay. Brasil — ¿integración o expansionismo? *[In Spanish]*; [The economic integration of Argentina, Brazil and Uruguay. Brazil — integration or expansionism]. Wilson Fernández. *Cuad. Am.* **VI:3 (33)** 5-6:1992 pp. 240 – 264

27 Die Integration des Wirtschaftsgebietes der ehemaligen DDR in den EG-Binnenmarkt. Chancen und Risiken *[In German]*; [The integration of the former GDR's economic area into the EC single market. Opportunities and risks]. Christine Kulke-Fiedler. *Deut. Arch.* **23:12** 12:1990 pp. 1873 – 1879

28 International economic integration. David Henderson. *Int. Aff. [London]* **68:4** 10:1992 pp. 633 – 653

29 International economic integration. Miroslav N. Jovanović. London: New York, 1992: 302 p. *ISBN: 0415038197; LofC: 91010671. Includes bibliographical references and index.*

30 International integration and labour market organization. Alberto Castro *[Ed.]*; Phillippe Mehaut *[Ed.]*; Jill Rubery *[Ed.]*. London: Academic Press, 1992: 268 p. *ISBN: 0121638707.*

31 Joining the future — economic integration and co-operation in Africa. Oliver S. Saasa *[Ed.]*. Nairobi, Kenya: ACTS Press, 1991: 168 p. *ISBN: 9966410368. Includes bibliographical references (p.157-164) and index.* [African Centre for Technology Studies policy series. : No. 2]

32 Maghreb — quelle intégration à la lumière des expériences dans le Tiers Monde? *[In French]*; (The Maghreb — what forms of integration in view of experience in the Third World?); (Maghreb — ¿Que tipos de integración a la luz de las experiencias del Tercer Mundo?: *Title only in Spanish*); (Maghreb — Welche Integration im Lichte der Erfahrungen in der Dritten Welt?: *Title only in German*); (Magrib — kakaja integracija v svete opyta stran Tret'ego mira?: *Title only in Russian*). Abdelkader Sid-Ahmed. *R. T-Monde* **XXXIII:129** 1-3:1992 pp. 67 – 97

33 Nationale Politik versus internationale Koordination *[In German]*; National economic policy versus international coordination *[Summary]*. Ulrich Schempp. *Jahrb. N. St.* **210:1-2** 7:1992 pp. 105 – 116

34 Norge og den europeiske økonomiske integrasjonen — fra den andre verdenskrig til EØS *[In Norwegian]*; Norway and the European economic integration — from World War II to the EEA *[Summary]*. Margarida Ponte Ferreira. *Int. Pol.* **50:3** 1992 pp. 313 – 322

O.1.2.4: Economic blocs. Economic integration [*Blocs économiques. Intégration économique*]

35 North American integration. D.K. Brown; A.V. Deardorff; R.M. Stern. *Econ. J.* **102:415** 11:1992 pp. 1507 – 1518

36 Nuevo concepto de integración [*In Spanish*]; [A new concept of integration]. Guillermo Ondarts [*Contrib.*]; Pedro da Motta Veiga [*Contrib.*]; Mónica Hirst [*Contrib.*]; Marcelo Halperin [*Contrib.*]. *Collection of 4 articles.* **Integ. Lat.am.** , *17:175*, 1-2:1992 pp. 1 – 40

37 Ökonomische Integrationsforschung in Vergangenheit und Zukunft [*In German*]; [Research on economic integration in the past and in the future]. Fritz Breuss. *Wirt. Blät.* **5/6:39** 1992 pp. 608 – 625

38 Policy issues regarding inter-Korean economic cooperation. Yeon Hacheong. *E.Asian R.* **IV:3** Autumn:1992 pp. 55 – 79

39 The political implications of regional co-operation — South American pointers for Southern Africa; [*Portuguese summary*]; [*Spanish summary*]; [*Afrikaans summary*]. Maxie van Aardt. *Unisa Lat.Am. Rep.* **8:1** 1992 pp. 20 – 29

40 The problem of "globalization" — international economic relations, national economic management and the formation of trading blocs. Paul Hirst; Grahame Thompson. *Econ. Soc.* **21:4** 11:1992 pp. 357 – 396

41 El proceso de armonización de políticas nacionales en el Grupo Andino [*In Spanish*]; [The process of harmonization of national policy within the Andean Group]. Drago Kisic W.. *Integ. Lat.am.* **17:176** 3:1992 pp. 13 – 25

42 The regional and international implications of the south China economic zone. Ting Wai. *Iss. Stud.* **28:12** 12:1992 pp. 46 – 72

43 Regional integration and economic prospects of the developing countries to the south of the Mediterranean. Franco Zallio. *Inter. Spect.* **XXVII:2** 4-6:1992 pp. 51 – 66

44 Regional integration in Europe. A. Sapir. *Econ. J.* **102:415** 11:1992 pp. 1491 – 1506

45 Reorientation of Central American integration. Rómulo Caballeros. *CEPAL R.* **:46** 4:1992 pp. 125 – 138

46 A review of and the prospects for inter-Korean economic exchanges. Yoon Kikwan. *E.Asian R.* **IV:1** Spring:1992 pp. 71 – 98

47 The single European market and industrial relations. Howard F. Gospel [*Contrib.*]; John T. Addison [*Contrib.*]; W. Stanley Siebert [*Contrib.*]; John Grahl [*Contrib.*]; Paul Teague [*Contrib.*]; Paul Marginson [*Contrib.*]; Mark Hall [*Contrib.*]; Andrew Henley [*Contrib.*]; Euclid Tsakalotos [*Contrib.*]; David Marsden [*Contrib.*] *and others. Collection of 9 articles.* **Br. J. Ind. R.** , *30:4*, 12:1992 pp. 483 – 638

48 South Asian regional economic cooperation in the 1990's — challenges and prospect. Debapriya Bhattacharya. *Devel. & Socio-eco. Pro.* **:53** 1:1992 pp. 48 – 55

49 Southern Africa/South America — the physical framework for regional development; [*Portuguese summary*]; [*Spanish summary*]; [*Afrikaans summary*]. Mike Muller. *Unisa Lat.Am. Rep.* **8:1** 1992 pp. 30 – 34

50 Theoretical and empirical considerations on the dimension of an optimum integration area in Europe; [*German summary*]. Gunther Tichy. *Aussenwirtschaft* **47:1** 2:1992 pp. 107 – 137

51 Towards forming a northeast Asian community — a perspective analysis. Sung-Hoon Kim. *Asian Ec.* **:81** 6:1992 pp. 5 – 14

52 Trade and investment in the Caribbean basin since the CBI; [*French summary*]; [*Spanish summary*]. Addington Coppin. *Soc. Econ. S.* **41:1** 3:1992 pp. 21 – 43

53 Trade flows and economic integration in Latin America. Ferruccio Maggiora. *Inter. Spect.* **XXVII:3** 7-9:1992 pp. 87 – 100

54 The Treaty of Asunción — an analysis. Charles Chatterjee. *J. World Tr.* **26:1** 2:1992 pp. 63 – 72

55 Las ventajas de ser pequeño [*In Spanish*]; [The advantages of being small]. Nora Berretta. *Rev. Parag. Sociol.* **29:83** 1-4:1992 pp. 89 – 105

56 Die wirtschaftliche Vereinigung Deutschlands. Europäische und deutsche Aspekte [*In German*]; [The economic unification of Germany. European and German aspects]. Michael Baumann. *Deut. Arch.* **23:6** 6:1990 pp. 890 – 896

57 Die Wirtschaftsverfassung der Schweiz und der EWR-Vertrag [*In German*]; [Switzerland's economic constitution and the EEA-treaty]. Ernst-Ulrich Petersmann. *Scot. J. Poli.* **47:III** 1992 pp. 295 – 322

O.1.2.4: Economic blocs. Economic integration *[Blocs économiques. Intégration économique]* —

European Communities *[Communautés européennes]*

58 Armonización financiera en la Comunidad Europea *[In Spanish]*; [Financial harmonization in the European Community]. Antonio Carrascosa Morales *[Ed.]*; Joaquín de la Herrán Mendívil *[Contrib.]*; José Pérez Fernández *[Contrib.]*; Gloria Hernández García *[Contrib.]*; Nicolás Hernández Castilla *[Contrib.]*; Vicente Javier Fernández Rodríguez *[Contrib.]*; José Manuel Gómez de Miguel *[Contrib.]*; Fernando Vargas Bohamonde; Antonio Carrascosa Morales *[Contrib.]*; Pedro Antonio Merino García *[Contrib.]* and others. Collection of 13 articles. **Infor. Com. Esp.** , *:703*, 3:1992 pp. 3 – 180

59 La batalla de Maastricht y los problemas fundamentales de la economía española *[In Spanish]*; [The battle of Maastricht and fundamental problems in the Spanish economy]. José Luis Raymond *[Contrib.]*; Antonio Argandoña *[Contrib.]*; Juan F. Jimeno Serrano *[Contrib.]*; Luis Toharia Cortés *[Contrib.]*; Manuel J. Lagares *[Contrib.]*; José M. González-Páramo *[Contrib.]*; J.M. Roldán Alegre *[Contrib.]*; Francisco Pérez *[Contrib.]*; Enrique Giménez-Reyna Rodriguez *[Contrib.]*; Ignacio Zurdo *[Contrib.]* and others. Collection of 37 articles. **Pap. Econ. Esp.** , *:52/53*, 1992 pp. 2 – 423

60 Building the new Europe — I. Single market and monetary unification in the EEC countries. Mario Baldassarri *[Contrib.]*; James Meade *[Contrib.]*; Robert Mundell *[Contrib.]*; Silvio Borner *[Contrib.]*; Martino Lo Cascio *[Contrib.]*; Richard S. Eckaus *[Contrib.]*; Giovanni Caravale *[Contrib.]*; Jürgen Kröger *[Contrib.]*; Robert Triffin *[Contrib.]*; Michele Fratianni *[Contrib.]* and others. Collection of 26 articles. **Riv. Pol. Ec.** , *LXXXI(3rd series):V*, 5:1991 pp. 5 – 675

61 Economia sovranazionale — il caso dell'Europa *[In Italian]*; [Supernational economy — the European case]. Alberto Quadrio Curzio. *Riv. S. Pol. Int.* **LIX:3** 7-9:1992 pp. 365 – 383

62 Economic and monetary union in Europe. Charles R. Bean. *J. Econ. Pers.* **6:4** Fall:1992 pp. 31 – 52

63 Economic integration and financial liberalization — prospects for southern Europe. Heather D. Gibson *[Ed.]*; Euclid Tsakalotos *[Ed.]*. London: Macmillan in associatioon with St.Antony's College, 1992: 209 p. *ISBN: 0333544447.*

64 Europäische Forschungspolitik und Wettbewerbsfähigkeit *[In German]*; [European research policy and competitiveness]. Christoph Schlüter. *Wirt. Blät.* **39:4** 1992 pp. 446 – 452

65 Europäische Industriepolitik nach Maastricht *[In German]*; [European industrial policy following Maastricht]. Henning Klodt. *Weltwirt.* **:3** 1992 pp. 263 – 273

66 The European Community and COMECON — models of success and failure in European integration. Jack G. Kaikati. *E. Eur. Quart.* **XXVI:3** Fall:1992 pp. 291 – 307

67 European economic integration. Frank MacDonald; Stephen Dearden. London: Longman, 1992: 241 p. *ISBN: 0582082269; LofC: 91032574. Includes bibliographical references and index.* [Longman economics series.]

68 European economic integration and its relevance to the economy of Cyprus — a political economy approach. Philip Arestis. *Cyprus Rev.* **4:1** Spring:1992 pp. 40 – 53

69 European international economic integration of 1992. André Sapir *[Contrib.]*; Iain Begg *[Contrib.]*; Francisco Rivera-Batiz *[Contrib.]*; Luis Rivera-Batiz *[Contrib.]*; John H. Dunning *[Contrib.]*; Polly Reynolds Allen *[Contrib.]*; Paul de Grauwe *[Contrib.]*. Collection of 6 articles. **Int. Econ. J.** , *6:1*, Spring:1992 pp. 1 – 120

70 The external relations of the European Community — the international response to 1992. John Redmond *[Ed.]*. New York: St. Martin's Press, 1992: 186 p. *ISBN: 0312080514; LofC: 92004253. Includes index.*

71 Financing the European Community — a review of options for the future. Stephen Smith. *Fis. Stud.* **13:4** 11:1992 pp. 98 – 127

72 Forschungs-, Technologie- und Industriepolitik der Europäischen Gemeinschaft — Bestandsaufnahme und Perspektive *[In German]*; [The EC's research, technology and industrial policies — evaluation and outlook]. Michel Carpentier. *Wirt. Blät.* **39:4** 1992 pp. 435 – 445

73 La France et l'Union économique et monétaire européenne *[In French]*; France and European economic and monetary union *[Summary]*. Rudiger Dornbusch; Pierre Jacquet. *Obser. Diag. Econ.* **:39** 1:1992 pp. 31 – 74

74 La integración europea — consecuencias para América Latina *[In Spanish]*; [European integration — consequences for Latin America]. Wolf Grabendorff. *Integ. Lat.am.* **17:180** 7:1992 pp. 16 – 42

O.1.2.4: Economic blocs. Economic integration *[Blocs économiques. Intégration économique] — European Communities [Communautés européennes]*

75 Integration and co-operation in Europe. Brigid Laffan. London: Routledge, 1992: 235 p. *ISBN: 0415063388; LofC: 91041474. Includes bibliographical references and index.* [The Routledge University Association for Contemporary European Studies series.]

76 Integration v. regulation? On the dynamics of regulation in the European Community. Renaud Dehousse. *J. Com. Mkt. S.* **XXX:4** 12:1992 pp. 383 – 402

77 Measuring convergence of the EC economies. S.G. Hall; D. Robertson; M.R. Wickens. *Manch. Sch. E.* **LX** 1992 pp. 99 – 111

78 "Mutual recognition" and cross-border financial services in the European Community. E. Waide Warner. *Law Cont. Pr.* **55:4** Autumn:1992 pp. 7 – 28

79 Un nuovo blocco commerciale — il NAFTA *[In Italian]*; [A new commercial block — NAFTA]. Sergio Alesandrini. *Risparmio* **XL:4** 7-8:1992 pp. 913 – 924

80 The politics of 1992 — fiscal policy and European integration. Torsten Persson; Guido Tabellini. *R. Econ. S.* **59:4** 10:1992 pp. 689 – 702

81 Product markets and 1992 — full integration, large gains? Harry Flam. *J. Econ. Pers.* **6:4** Fall:1992 pp. 7 – 30

82 Real interest parity, dynamic convergence and the European Monetary System. A.G. Haldane; Mahmood Pradhan. London: Bank of England, 1992: 18 p. *ISBN: 185730070x.* [Working paper series.]

83 The realities behind the European single market. David G. Mayes. *Bus. Econ.* **23:2** Spring:1992 pp. 20 – 32

84 Reflexiones sobre la union económica y monetaria *[In Spanish]*; [Reflections on economic and monetary union]. Miguel Angel Feito Hernández *[Contrib.]*; Manuel Conthe *[Contrib.]*; Shirley Williams *[Contrib.]*; José Luis Feito Higueruela *[Contrib.]*; Guillermo de la Dehesa *[Contrib.]*; José Alberto Zaragoza Rameau *[Contrib.]*; Carlos Sebastián *[Contrib.]*; José Antonio Zamora *[Contrib.]*; M. Carmen Gallastegui *[Contrib.]*; Charles A.E. Goodhart *[Contrib.] and others. Collection of 12 articles.* **Infor. Com. Esp.** , :710, 10:1992 pp. 3 – 138

85 The single European market and beyond — a study of the wider implications of the Single European Act. Dennis Swann *[Ed.]*. London: Routledge, 1992: 299 p. *ISBN: 0415061601.*

86 The single European market — prospects for economic integration. R. W. Vickerman. London: Harvester Wheatsheaf, 1992: 224 p. *ISBN: 0860038165.*

87 Tax harmonization and financial liberalization in Europe — proceedings of a conference held by the Confederation of European Economic Associations at Vienna, Austria, 1989. Georg Winckler *[Ed.]*. New York: St Martin's Press in association with the Confederation of European Economic Associations, 1992: 312 p. *ISBN: 0312075162; LofC: 91034311. Includes index.*

88 Tax harmonization in the European Community — policy issues and analysis. George Kopits *[Ed.]*. Washington, D.C: International Monetary Fund, 1992: viii, 115 p. *ISBN: 1557752257; LofC: 91044899. Includes bibliographical references.* [Occasional paper.]

89 Testing real interest parity in the European Monetary System. A.G. Haldane; Mahmood Pradhan. London: Bank of England, 1992: 34 p. *ISBN: 1857300807.* [Working paper series.]

90 Umsatzbesteuerung im EG-Binnenmarkt — Von der Mehrwertsteuer zur Verkaufssteuer? *[In German]*; [Sales taxation in the EC internal market — from value added tax to the sales tax]. Jürgen Stehn. *Weltwirt.* :3 1992 pp. 274 – 294

91 Whose champions? Multinationals, labour and industry policy in the European Community after 1992. Harvie Ramsay. *Cap. Class* **:48** Autumn:1992 pp. 17 – 39

92 Die Wirtschaften Mittel- und Osteuropas auf dem Weg in die EG *[In German]*; (The economies of Middle and Eastern Europe on their way into the EC). Harald Zschiedrich. *Ost. Wirt.* **3** 1992 pp. 201 – 214

O.1.2.5: Population movements — *Mouvements de population*

1 Brain drain in East Asia. Parris Chang *[Contrib.]*; Bang-Soon L. Yoon *[Contrib.]*; Shirley L. Chang *[Contrib.]*; Zhiduan Deng *[Contrib.]*. *Collection of 3 articles.* **Stud. Comp. ID.** , *27:1,* Spring:1992 pp. 3 – 60
2 Income inequality and international migration. J.B. Davies; I. Wooton. *Econ. J.* **102:413** 7:1992 pp. 789 – 802
3 International migration and welfare in the presence of non-traded goods — an interconnected markets approach. Bharati Basu. *Int. Econ. J.* **6:4** Winter:1992 pp. 33 – 45
4 Labour mobility in Europe as a result of changes in Central and Eastern Europe. Alexander Samorodov. *Labour [Italy]* **6:3** Winter:1992 pp. 3 – 21
5 Migration from Nicaragua — some recent evidence. E. Funkhouser. *World Dev.* **20:8** 8:1992 pp. 1209 – 1218
6 Savings, remittances, and return migration. L. Merkle; K.F. Zimmermann. *Econ. Lett.* **38:1** 1:1992 pp. 77 – 82
7 The spatial pattern of international labour flows from and to Pakistan — a preliminary analysis. Mir Anjum Altaf; Obaidullah. *Pak. Dev. R.* **31:2** Summer:1992 pp. 145 – 164

O.1.3: International economic policy — *Politique économique internationale*

Sub-divisions: Foreign aid *[Aide à l'étranger]*; Technology transfer *[Transfert de technologie]*; Trade liberalization *[Libéralisation des échanges]*

1 L'Acte unique européen et l'avenir des pays ACP *[In French]*; [The Single European Act and the future of the ACP countries]. Christian N'Dombi. *Afr. 2000* **:8** 1-3:1992 pp. 17 – 28
2 Britain in a cold climate. Will Hutton. *Int. Aff. [London]* **68:4** 10:1992 pp. 619 – 632
3 Can Europe and Japan compete? Gianni Fodella. *Jpn. Forum* **4:1** 4:1992 pp. 1 – 14
4 Le commerce international *[In French]*; [International commerce]. Jean-Yves Capul *[Ed.]*. Paris: La Documentation française, 1992: 124 p. [Cahiers français. : No. 253]
5 Commodity exports and Latin American development. J.M. Benavente. *CEPAL R.* **:45** 12:1991 pp. 41 – 60
6 Commodity stabilization funds. Patricio Arrau. Washington, D.C.: International Economics Department, The World Bank, 1992: 36 p. *Bibliography* — *p.24-25.* [Policy research working papers.]
7 La cooperación internacional para América Central y los proyectos regionales *[In Spanish]*; [International cooperation in Central America and regional projects]. Edgar J. Chamorro Marín. *Integ. Lat.am.* **17:179** 6:1992 pp. 28 – 43
8 Cooperación internacional para el desarrollo *[In Spanish]*; [International cooperation for development]. Luis Portillo *[Contrib.]*; Francisco Alburquerque *[Contrib.]*; Alfonso Lasso de la Vega *[Contrib.]*; Manuel Gómez Galán *[Contrib.]*; Francisca Segundo *[Contrib.]*; Manuel Marín *[Contrib.]*; Luis López Moreno *[Contrib.]*; Carlos Camino Muñoz *[Contrib.]*; José Antonio Nieto Solís *[Contrib.]* and others. *Collection of 15 articles.* **Infor. Com. Esp.** , *:702,* 2:1992 pp. 21 – 201
9 Coordinación de políticas económicas *[In Spanish]*; [Economic policy coordination]. Miguel Angel Galindo *[Contrib.]*; Jesús Paúl Gutiérrez *[Contrib.]*; Keith Bain *[Contrib.]*; Peter Lowe *[Contrib.]*; Juan A. de Castro Arespacochaga *[Contrib.]*; Pilar Fernández-Baca Gutiérrez del Alamo *[Contrib.]*; Philip Arestis *[Contrib.]*; Miguel Angel Galindo Martín *[Contrib.]*; Antonio Calvo Bernardino *[Contrib.]*. *Collection of 7 articles.* **Infor. Com. Esp.** , *:701,* 1:1992 pp. 3 – 78
10 Coping with global debt crises — debt settlements, 1820-1986. Christian Suter; Hanspeter Stamm. *Comp. Stud. S.* **34:4** 10:1992 pp. 645 – 678
11 The debt/equity swap in Latin America — in whose interest? Robert Grosse. *J. Inter. Finan. Manag. Acc.* **4:1** Spring:1992 pp. 13 – 39
12 Det østlige Europas reintegration i den internationale politiske økonomi *[In Danish]*; Reintegrating Eastern Europe into the international political economy *[Summary]*. Mette Skak. *Politica.* **24:2** 1992 pp. 151 – 168
13 Die deutsch-polnischen Wirtschaftsbeziehungen vor und nach Erreichen der Deutschen Einheit *[In German]*; (German-Polish economic relations before and after the German reunification). Jozef Misala. *Ost. Wirt.* **3** 1992 pp. 225 – 236

O.1.3: International economic policy *[Politique économique internationale]*

14 Economic liberalization — openness and integration — but what kind? Edith T. Penrose. *Dev. Pol. R.* **10:3** 9:1992 pp. 237 – 254

15 Economic summit declarations, 1975-1989 — examining the written record of international cooperation. George M. von Furstenberg; Joseph P. Daniels. Princeton, NJ.: International Finance Section, Dept. of Economics, Princeton University, 1992: 60 p. *ISBN: 088165244x; LofC: 92003756. Includes bibliographical refernces.* [Princeton studies in international finance.]

16 Economic, industrial and managerial coordination between Japan and the USA. Kiyoshi Abe *[Ed.]*; William Gunther *[Ed.]*; Harold See *[Ed.]*. New York: St. Martin's Press, 1992: 408 p. *ISBN: 0312079877; LofC: 92002539. Papers presented at a conference held at the East-West Center in 1990, and sponsored by the Chiba University and University of Alabama, Tuscaloosa; Includes index.*

17 Emerging South African perspectives on regional cooperation and integration after apartheid. Robert Davies. *Transformation* **:20** 1992 pp. 75 – 87

18 Экономические связи между республиками *[In Russian]*; [Economic links between republics]. Gertrude Shreder. *Vop. Ekon.* **:1** 1992 pp. 83 – 91

19 ESPRIT and the politics of international collective action. Wayne Sandholtz. *J. Com. Mkt. S.* **XXX:1** 3:1992 pp. 1 – 22

20 The European Central Bank — constitutional dimensions and political limits. Daniel Wincott. *Int. Rel.* **XI:2** 8:1992 pp. 111 – 126

21 Freihandel der EG und EFTA mit Ost- Mitteleuropa *[In German]*; Free trade of EC and EFTA with East Central Europe *[Summary]*. Jan Stankovsky. *Monatsberichte* **7:65** 1992 pp. 370 – 374

22 From liberal continentalism to neoconservatism — North American free trade and the politics of the C.D. Howe Institute. Alan Ernst. *Stud. Pol. Ec.* **:39** Autumn:1992 pp. 109 – 140

23 From the CMEA to the "Europe agreements" — trade and aid in the relations between the European Community and Eastern Europe; *[German summary]*. Renzo Daviddi. *Econ. Sys.* **16:2** 10:1992 pp. 269 – 294

24 International economic responses to reform in Vietnam — an overview of obstacles and progress. Nick J. Freeman. *Stud. Comp. Commun.* **XXV:3** 9:1992 pp. 287 – 302

25 International monetary and fiscal policy cooperation in the presence of wage inflexibilities — are both counterproductive? Jeffery Sheen. *J. Econ. Dyn. Cont.* **16:2** 4:1992 pp. 359 – 388

26 Interrepublican economic relations after the disintegration of the USSR. James H. Noren; Robin Watson. *Sov. Ec.* **8:2** 4-7:1992 pp. 89 – 129

27 Japan's foreign investment and Asian economic interdependence — production, trade, and financial systems. Shōjirō Tokunaga *[Ed.]*. Tokyo: University of Tokyo Press, 1992: ix, 294 p. *ISBN: 4130470531. Includes bibliographical references and index.*

28 Law and economics. Ruth Taplin *[Ed.]*; Terry Burke *[Contrib.]*; J.R. Shackleton *[Contrib.]*; Nico Spiegel *[Contrib.]*; Chong Ju Choi *[Contrib.]*; Konosuke Kimura *[Contrib.]*. *Collection of 5 articles.* **J. Interd. Ec.** , *4:4*, 1992 pp. 299 – 362

29 Macroeconomic policy coordination and integration. A. Schwidrowski. *CEPAL R.* **:45** 12:1991 pp. 83 – 98

30 The need for a global partnership. Mark Griffith. *B. E.Carib. Aff.* **17:1-2** 1-6:1992 pp. 60 – 67

31 The new international political economy of East Europe. Ronald H. Linden. *Stud. Comp. Commun.* **XXV:1** 3:1992 pp. 3 – 22

32 North American free trade — issues and recommendations. Gary Clyde Hufbauer; Jeffrey J. Schott. Washington, DC: Institute for International Economics, 1992: 369 p. *ISBN: 0881321451; LofC: 92008206. "March 1992."; Includes bibliographical references and index.*

33 Osteuropa auf dem Weg zur Marktwirtschaft — Gedanken zur Unterstützung des Übergangs *[In German]*; Eastern Europe on the way to the market economy —reflections on possible support of the transition *[Summary]*. Rolf Urs Egger; Alex Melzer Kappel. *Ost. Wirt.* **37:1** 3:1992 pp. 19 – 51

34 Policy interactions between the OECD countries and Latin America in the 1980s. Chris Allen; David Currie; T.G. Srinivasan; David Vines. *Manch. Sch. E.* **LX** 1992 pp. 1 – 20

35 The political impact of free trade on Mexico. Peter H. Smith. *J. Int. Am. St.* **34:1** Spring:1992 pp. 1 – 25

36 Post-apartheid South Africa's economic ties with neighbouring countries. E. Leistner. *Develop. S. Afr.* **9:2** 5:1992 pp. 169 – 186

O.1.3: International economic policy *[Politique économique internationale]*
37 President Bush's southern strategy — the Enterprise for the Americas Initiative. Peter Hakim. *Wash. Quart.* **15:2** Spring:1992 pp. 93 – 106
38 Prospects of trade expansion in the SAARC region. Mangat Ram Aggarwal; Posh Raj Pandey. *Develop. Eco.* **XXX:1** 3:1992 pp. 3 – 23
39 Recent international economic developments — the implications for the South African economy. Wilma Viviers; Derik Steyn; Bettina Hurni. *Wirt. Blät.* **5/6:39** 1992 pp. 645 – 653
40 Regionalism and multilateralism — an overview. Jagdish N. Bhagwati. New York: Columbia University, Dept of Economics, 1992: 43 p. [Discussion paper series.]
41 Regionalism versus multilateralism. Jagdish Bhagwati. *World. Econ.* **15:5** 9:1992 pp. 535 – 555
42 Relazioni economiche dell'India con il terzo mondo — difficoltà della cooperazione Sud-Sud *[In Italian]*; [India's economic relations with the Third World — difficulty with south-south cooperation]. Sandro Sideri. *Econ. Ban.* **3** 1992 pp. 275 – 308
43 The restrictiveness of the multi-fibre arrangement on Eastern European trade. Refik Erzan; Christopher Holmes. Washington, D.C.: International Economics Department, The World Bank, 1992: 33 p. [Policy research working papers.]
44 Restructurations industrielles et coopération entre firmes en Europe de l'Est *[In French]*; The reorganization of industry and cooperation between firms in Eastern Europe *[Summary]*. Xavier Richet. *Sociol. Trav.* **2** 1992 pp. 263 – 274
45 Rules and discretion in international economic policy. Manuel Guitián. Washington, DC: International Monetary Fund, 1992: v, 52 p. *ISBN: 1557752370; LofC: 92012943. Includes bibliographical references (p.45-50).* [Occasional paper International Monetary Fund.]
46 Sanctions. Jonathan Eaton; Maxim Engers. *J. Polit. Ec.* **110:5** 10:1992 pp. 899 – 928
47 Small industry and economic cooperation between India and Nepal. Anjana Chatterjee. *S.Asia. J.* **5:3** 1-3:1992 pp. 299 – 312
48 Son of Garnaut — accelerating change? Geoff Raby *[Contrib.]*; David Lim *[Contrib.]*; H.W. Arndt *[Contrib.]*; Paul Ivory *[Contrib.]*; John Ravenhill *[Contrib.]*; Clem Tisdell *[Contrib.]*. Collection of 6 articles. **Asian Stud. R.** , *16:2*, 11:1992 pp. 1 – 38
49 Southeast Asia's "growth triangle" — a subregional response to global transformation. James Parsonage. *Int. J. Urban* **16:2** 6:1992 pp. 307 – 317
50 The Soviet Union and Eastern Europe in the global economy. Marie Lavigne *[Ed.]*. Cambridge: Cambridge University Press, 1992: 219 p. *ISBN: 0521414172; LofC: 91030816. "Selected papers from the Fourth World Congress for Soviet and East European Studies, Harrogate, July 1990".*
51 The Soviet Union and international economic organizations and arrangements. Sumitra Chishti. *Int. Stud.* **29:1** 1-3:1992 pp. 1 – 15
52 The Soviets and the Pacific challenge. Peter Drysdale *[Ed.]*; Martin O'Hare *[Ed.]*. North Sydney, NSW: Allen & Unwin in association with the Australia-Japan Research Centre, Australian National University, 1991: xxii, 160 p. *ISBN: 1863730117. Revised versions of papers presented at an international conference organized by the Australia-Japan Research Centre, the Australian National University, in Feb. 1990 in Canberra; Includes bibliographical references (p. 149-153) and index.*
53 Stosunki ekonomiczne Stanów Zjednoczonych z krajami rozwijającymi się *[In Polish]*; U.S. economic relations with the developing countries *[Summary]*. Paweł Samecki. *Acta Univ. Łódz.* **114** 1992 pp. 3 – 115
54 The United States and the European Community in a transfomed world. Michael Smith; Stephen Woolcock. London: Pinter, 1992: 121 p. *ISBN: 0861870980.* [Chatham House papers.]
55 The welfare effects of imperfect harmonisation of trade and industrial policy. K. Gatsios; L. Karp. *Econ. J.* **102:410** 1:1992 pp. 107 – 116
56 Zur künftigen Einbindung der osteuropäischen Reformländer in die Weltwirtschaft *[In German]*; [On the future integration of the Eastern European countries currently undergoing reform into the world economy] *[Summary]*; *[French summary]*. Roland Döhrn; Antoine-Richard Milton. *RWI-Mitt.* **43:1** 1992 pp. 19 – 40

Foreign aid *[Aide à l'étranger]*

57 Aid and the Dutch disease — macroeconomic management when everybody loves you. S.D. Younger. *World Dev.* **20:11** 11:1992 pp. 1587 – 1598
58 Britain's Third World charities in a changing world. Peter J. Burnell. Coventry: Department of Politics and International Studies, 1992: 52 p. [Working Paper (University of Warwick. Department of Politics and International Studies).]

O.1.3: International economic policy *[Politique économique internationale]* — *Foreign aid [Aide à l'étranger]*

59 EC aid to associated countries — distribution and determinants; *[German summary]*; *[French summary]*; *[Spanish summary]*. Enzo Grilli; Markus Riess. *Welt.liches Arc.* **128:2** 1992 pp. 202 – 220

60 The ethics of aid and trade — U.S. food policy, foreign competition, and the social contract. Paul B. Thompson. Cambridge: Cambridge University Press, 1992: x, 233 p. *ISBN: 0521414687; LofC: 92001036. Includes bibliographical references (p. 215-229) and index.* [Cambridge studies in philosophy and public policy.]

61 European Community development assistance to Asia — policies, programs and performance. Martin Rudner. *Mod. Asian S.* **26:1** 2:1992 pp. 1 – 30

62 Evaluating development assistance — policies and performance. Olav Stokke *[Ed.]*. London: Frank Cass, 1992: 298 p. *ISBN: 0714634468; LofC: 91029762.* [EADI book series. : No. 12]

63 Foreign aid and payments agreements in Central and Eastern Europe. R. Daviddi; E. Espa. *Eco. Notes* **21:1** 1992 pp. 15 – 38

64 Foreign aid in ROC diplomacy. Tuan Y. Cheng. *Iss. Stud.* **28:9** 9:1992 pp. 67 – 84

65 Foreign assistance and economic policies in Laos, 1976-86. Dorothea Arndt. *Cont. S.E. Asia* **14:2** 9:1992 pp. 188 – 210

66 The geographic allocation of the European development fund under the Lomé Conventions. M.K. Anyadike-Danes; M.N. Anyadike-Danes. *World Dev.* **20:11** 11:1992 pp. 1647 – 1661

67 Growth and catch-up in Central and Eastern Europe — macroeconomic effects on western countries. Alessandro Giustiniani; Francesco Papadia; Daniela Porciani. Princeton, NJ.: International Finance Section, Dept. of Economics, Princeton University, 1992: 48 p. *ISBN: 0881650935; LofC: 92013314. "April 1992."; Includes bibliographical references.* [Essays in international finance.]

68 The impact of foreign assistance on agricultural growth. George W. Norton; Jaime Ortiz; Philip G. Pardey. *Econ. Dev. Cult. Change* **40:4** 7:1992 pp. 775 – 786

69 Inducing efficiency in the use of foreign aid — the case for incentive mechanisms. Carlo Pietrobelli; Carlo Scarpa. *J. Dev. Stud.* **29:1** 10:1992 pp. 72 – 92

70 The integrated approach to project cycle management. Hellmut Eggers. *Proj. App.* **7:1** 3:1992 pp. 3 – 10

71 International justice and the Third World — studies in the philosophy of development. Robin Attfield *[Ed.]*; Barry Wilkins *[Ed.]*. London: Routledge, 1992: 207 p. *ISBN: oc2485419; LofC: 91038394. Includes bibliographical references and index.*

72 The macroeconomic impact of development aid — a critical survey. Howard White. *J. Dev. Stud.* **28:2** 1:1992 pp. 163 – 240

73 Multilateral and non-payable nature of foreign aid. Mieczysław Gulcz. *Econ. Papers [Warsaw]* **18** 1992 pp. 48 – 59

74 Paltry aid to Central Europe. Richard E. Feinberg. *Challenge* **35:1** 1-2:1992 pp. 36 – 43

75 Repenser le soutien de la communauté internationale à l'Europe de l'Est *[In French]*; Rethinking on international aid for Eastern Europe *[Summary]*. Michel Aglietta; Michèle Bailly; Christian de Boisseau; Jean-Michel Charpin; Jean-Paul Dessertine; Etienne Lakits; Georges Mink; Jean-Pierre Pagé; Jacques Sapir; Jean Pisani-Ferry *and others.Obser. Diag. Econ.* **:42** 10:1992 pp. 199 – 248

76 Rhetoric and reality — the management of Botswana's 1982-88 drought relief programme. C. Simmons; S. Lyons. *J. Int. Dev.* **4:6** 11-12:1992 pp. 607 – 631

77 A two-part sample selection model of British bilateral foreign aid allocation. M. McGillivray; E. Oczkowski. *Appl. Econ.* **24:12** 12:1992 pp. 1311 – 1319

78 World food in the 1990s — production, trade, and aid. Lehman B. Fletcher *[Ed.]*. Boulder: Westview Press, 1992: xv, 368 p. (ill) *ISBN: 0813380499; LofC: 90044542. "Based on materials prepared for a four-session workshop held September 20-22, 1989, in Washington, D.C."--Pref; Includes bibliographical references.*

Technology transfer *[Transfert de technologie]*

79 Chronique d'un transfert dans la transition hongroise *[In French]*; Chronicles of a transfer during the transitional phase in Hungary *[Summary]*. Daniel Chave; Peter Simon. *Sociol. Trav.* **2** 1992 pp. 275 – 288

80 The clever city — Japan, Australia, and the multifunction polis. Ian Inkster. South Melbourne, Australia: Sydney University Press, 1991: xi, 180 p. *ISBN: 0424001829; LofC: 91192700. Includes bibliographical references (p. 172-175) and index.*

O.1.3: International economic policy *[Politique économique internationale]* —
Technology transfer [Transfert de technologie]
81 Economic and technical co-operation between India and Africa. Tabassum Jamal. London: Sangam Books, 1992: 165 p. *ISBN: 0861323076.*
82 Exploiting a technological edge — voluntary and involuntary dissemination of technology. Udo Zander. Stockholm: Akademisk Avhandling, 1991: xx, 253 p. *ISBN: 9197100552. Errata t.p; Thesis - Stockholm School of Economics; Includes bibliographical references (p. 207-228).*
83 Minimum terms and conditions of access — responsible fisheries management measures in the South Pacific Region. Michael Lodge. *Mar. Pol.* **16:4** 7:1992 pp. 277 – 305
84 Pacific economic co-operation — policy choices for the 1990s. Andrew Elek. *Asian-Pacific Ec. Lit.* **6:1** 5:1992 pp. 1 – 15
85 Transfer of Japanese technology and management to the ASEAN countries. Shoichi Yamashita *[Ed.].* Tokyo: University of Tokyo Press, 1991: 312 p. *ISBN: 0860084639.*
86 Un transfert de technologie dans les télécommunications en Chine *[In French]*; A transfer of telecommunications technology to China *[Summary].* François Gipouloux. *Sociol. Trav.* **2** 1992 pp. 245 – 261

Trade liberalization *[Libéralisation des échanges]*

87 Auf dem Weg zur Nordamerikanischen Freihandelszone *[In German]*; On the way to a North American Free Trade zone Area *[Summary].* Hans-Joachim Lauth. *Vierteljahresberichte* **:129** 9:1992 pp. 265 – 278
88 The Canada-USA free trade agreement and Canadian trade patterns — some ex ante results. A. Antoniou. *S. Afr. J. Econ.* **60:4** 12:1992 pp. 373 – 385
89 Free trade agreements with the United States — what's in it for Latin America? Refik Erzan; Alexander J. Yeats. Washington, D.C.: International Economics Department, The World Bank, 1992: 66 p. [Policy research working papers.]
90 Free trade area or common capital market? Notes on Mexico-US economic integration and current NAFTA negotiations. Jaime Ros. *J. Int. Am. St.* **34:2** Summer:1992 pp. 53 – 91
91 Free trade — why did it happen?; *[French summary].* R. Jack Richardson. *Can. R. Soc. A.* **29:3** 8:1992 pp. 307 – 328
92 Libre comercio y frontera — el acuerdo México-Estados Unidos *[In Spanish]*; [Free trade and the border — the Mexico-United States agreement]. Joseph Grunwald *[Contrib.]*; Gerardo M. Bueno *[Contrib.]*; Eugenio O. Valenciano *[Contrib.]*; David J. Molina *[Contrib.]*; Mary E. Kelly *[Contrib.]*; Dick Kamp *[Contrib.]*; Michael Gregory *[Contrib.]*; Jan Rich *[Contrib.]. Collection of 5 articles.* **Integ. Lat.am.** , *17:181-182*, 8-9:1992 pp. 3 – 72
93 Libre-échange en Amérique latine — les perspectives de succès *[In French]*; Free trade in Latin America — the outlook for success *[Summary]*; Libre comercio en América Latina — las perspectivas de éxito *[Spanish summary].* Diana Brand. *Prob. Am.Lat.* **:7** 10-12:1992 pp. 3 – 25
94 México ante el libre comercio con América del norte *[In Spanish]*; [Mexico and free trade with North America]. Gustavo Vega Cánovas *[Ed.].* México, D.F.: El Colegio de México/ Universidad Tecnológica de México, 1991: 507 p. *ISBN: 968 12 0474 3.*
95 Modelling North American free trade. Leonard Waverman *[Contrib.]*; Drusilla K. Brown *[Contrib.]*; Alan V. Deardorff *[Contrib.]*; Robert M. Stern *[Contrib.]*; David Cox *[Contrib.]*; Richard G. Harris *[Contrib.]*; Irene Trela *[Contrib.]*; John Whalley *[Contrib.]*; Linda Hunter *[Contrib.]*; James R. Markusen *[Contrib.] and others. Collection of 6 articles.* **World. Econ.** , *15:1*, 1:1992 pp. 1 – 100
96 North American free trade area. William G. Watson *[Ed.].* Kingston, Ont: John Deutsch Institute for the Study of Economic Policy, 1991: vi, 157 p. *ISBN: 0889116148; LofC: cn 92093052. Papers presented at the Policy Forum on the North American Free Trade Area held Oct. 25, 1991, at Queen's University; Includes bibliographical references.* [Policy forum series. : No. 24]
97 North American free trade — assessing the impact. Robert Z. Lawrence *[Ed.]*; Nora Lustig *[Ed.]*; Barry Bosworth *[Ed.].* Washington DC: Brookings Institute, 1992: 274 p. *ISBN: 0815753160.*
98 North American free trade — opportunities and pitfalls. William C. Gruben. *Cont. Policy* **X:4** 10:1992 pp. 1 – 10
99 Perspectivas de la inciativa para las Américas *[In Spanish]*; [Perspectives on the "Enterprise for the Americas" initiative] *[Summary].* Victor Torres. *Apuntes* **30:1** 1992 pp. 63 – 79
100 Reconciling subregional and hemispheric integration. J.A. Fuentes. *CEPAL R.* **:45** 12:1991 pp. 99 – 120

O.1.3: International economic policy *[Politique économique internationale]* — **Trade liberalization** *[Libéralisation des échanges]*

101 The urban economy and regional trade liberalization. Peter Karl Kresl. New York: Praeger, 1992: 214 p. *ISBN: 0275942899; LofC: 91045611. Includes bibliographical references (p. [201]-208) and index.*

102 US-Mexico free trade — implications for the United States. Sidney Weintraub. *J. Int. Am. St.* **34:2** Summer:1992 pp. 29 – 52

103 Vista preliminar del acuerdo de libre comercio entre Canadá, Estados Unidos y México *[In Spanish]*; [Preliminary look at the free trade agreement between Canada, the U.S.A. and Mexico]. Brenda González H.; Kate Langdon; Brian O'Reilly. *Monetaria* **XV:1** 1-3:1992 pp. 81 – 109

O.2: Monetary aspects — *Aspects monétaires*

O.2.1: International monetary operations — *Opérations monétaires internationales*

Sub-divisions: Exchange rates *[Taux de change]*

1 Capital controls and foreign exchange market crises in the EMS. D. Gros. *Eur. Econ. R.* **36:8** 12:1992 pp. 1533 – 1544

2 Causes of the forward bias — non-rational expectations versus risk premia. N. Pittis. *Appl. Econ.* **24:3** 3:1992 pp. 317 – 326

3 Colombia's black market in foreign exchange. R. Grosse. *World Dev.* **20:8** 8:1992 pp. 1193 – 1207

4 Credibility, capital controls, and the EMS. Timothy Lane; Liliana Rojas-Suarez. *J. Int. Econ.* **32:3/4** 5:1992 pp. 321 – 338

5 Currency risk management in multinational companies. Edward W. Davis; et al. Hemel Hempstead: Prentice Hall International — in association with Institute of Chartered Accountants in England and Wales, 1991: ix, 108 p. *ISBN: 0136053122.* [Research studies in accounting series.]

6 Developments in international exchange and payments systems. Hans M. Flickenschild. Washington, D.C: International Monetary Fund, [1992]: 79 p. *ISBN: 1557752338; LofC: 92015993.* [World economic and financial surveys.]

7 Dominant interest and inflation differentials within the EMS. K.G. Koedijk; C.J.M. Kool. *Eur. Econ. R.* **36:4** 5:1992 pp. 925 – 944

8 Du système monétaire européen à l'union monétaire européenne — une transition malaisée *[In French]*; [From the European monetary system to European monetary union — a blighted system]. Luigi A.M. Spaventa. Grenoble: Presses universitaires de Grenoble, 1992: 48 p. *ISBN: 2706104570.*

9 Economie financière internationale — les interventions du Trésor *[In French]*; [International finances — treasury intervention]. Dov Zerah. Paris: La Documentation française, 1992: 299 p. *ISBN: 2110027134. Bibliography — p229-[230].* [Les études de la Documentation française.]

10 The effect of the ERM on participating economies. Tamim Bayoumi. *Staff Pap. Int. Monetary* **39:2** 6:1992 pp. 330 – 356

11 L'efficience et la formation des anticipations sur le marché des changes *[In French]*; Efficiency and formation of expectations in exchange markets *[Summary]*. Catherine Bruno; Pascal Jacquinot; Rahim Loufir. *Obser. Diag. Econ.* **:42** 10:1992 pp. 249 – 282

12 Efficiency in German and Japanese foreign exchange markets — evidence from cointegration techniques; Effizienz auf deutschen und japanischen Devisenmärkten. Einige Ergebnisse der Kointegrationstechnik *[German summary]*; L'efficience des marchés des changes de l'Allemagne et du Japon. Des preuves des techniques de co-intégration *[French summary]*; La eficiencia de los mercados de cambio alemanes y japoneses — resultados de la aplicación de técnicas de cointegración *[Spanish summary]*. Marco Tronzano. *Welt.liches Arc.* **128:1** 1992 pp. 1 – 20

13 Euromärkte, Leistungsbilanz und Geldmenge *[In German]*; Eurocurrency markets, current account balances and money supply *[Summary]*. Dimitrios Malliaropulos. *Z. Wirt. Soz.* **112:1** 1992 pp. 47 – 58

O.2.1: International monetary operations *[Opérations monétaires internationales]*

14 Das Europäische Währungssystem (EWS) im Zielkonflikt zwischen Stabilität und Konvergenz *[In German]*; [The European Monetary System (EMS) in a conflict of objectives between stability and convergence]. Jürgen Schiemann. *Z. Wirt.pol.* **41:3** 1992 pp. 269 – 299

15 Feedback Trading auf Devisenmärkten *[In German]*; Feedback trading on foreign exchange markets *[Summary]*. Lukas Menkhoff. *Jahrb. N. St.* **210:1-2** 7:1992 pp. 127 – 144

16 Fiscal policy and the term structure of interest rates. Walter H. Fisher; Stephen J. Turnovsky. *J. Money C. B.* **24:1** 2:1992 pp. 1 – 26

17 Foreign exchange intervention by the United States — a review and assessment of 1985-89.R. *Fed. Resv. Bank St.Louis* **74:3** 5/6:1992 pp. 32 – 51

18 The foreign exchange risk premium in a target zone with devaluation risk. Lars E.O. Svensson. *J. Int. Econ.* **33:1/2** 8:1992 pp. 21 – 40

19 Innovations in interest rates, duration transformation, and bank stock returns. Srinivas R. Akella; Stuart I. Greenbaum. *J. Money C. B.* **24:1** 2:1992 pp. 27 – 42

20 Interest rate causality and asymmetry in the EMS. K. Biltoft; C. Boersch. *Open Econ. R.* **3:3** 1992 pp. 297 – 306

21 International contracts and payments. Petar Sarcevic *[Ed.]*; Paul Volken *[Ed.]*. London: Graham & Trotman, 1992: 144 p. *ISBN: 1853336157; LofC: 91036836. Includes index.*

22 International finance. Keith Pilbeam. Basingstoke: Macmillan, 1992: 446 p. *ISBN: 0333545281.* [Macmillan texts in economics.]

23 International macroeconomic interdependence, currency substitution, and price stickiness. Athina Zervoyianni. *J. Macro.* **14:1** Winter:1992 pp. 59 – 86

24 Investigating the correlation of unobserved expectations — expected returns in equity and foreign exchange markets and other examples. Robert E. Cumby; John Huizinga. *J. Monet. Ec.* **30:2** 11:1992 pp. 217 – 253

25 La liberalizzazione valutaria e lo «spread» sui finanziamenti in divisa *[In Italian]*; [Monetary liberalization and the spread of loans across currencies]. Armando Spinella. *Risparmio* **XL:1** 1-2:1992 pp. 105 – 114

26 Managerial perceptions of the net benefits of foreign listing — Canadian evidence. Usha R. Mittoo. *J. Inter. Finan. Manag. Acc.* **4:1** Spring:1992 pp. 40 – 62

27 A monetary constitution case for an independent European central bank. Richard C.K. Burdekin; Clas Wihlborg; Thomas D. Willett. *World. Econ.* **15:2** 3:1992 pp. 231 – 249

28 On designing an international monetary system. John Williamson. *J. Post. Keyn. Ec.* **15:2** Winter:1992-1993 pp. 181 – 192

29 On the foreign exchange risk premium in a general equilibrium model. Charles Engel. *J. Int. Econ.* **32:3/4** 5:1992 pp. 305 – 320

30 Parallel currency markets in developing countries — theory, evidence, and policy implications. Pierre-Richard Agénor. Princeton, NJ.: International Finance Section, Dept. of Economics, Princeton University, 1992: 40 p. *ISBN: 0881650951; LofC: 92032099. Includes bibliographical references.* [Essays in international finance. : No. 188]

31 Profit-making speculation in foreign exchange markets. Patachara Surajaras; Richard J. Sweeney. Boulder: Westview Press, 1992: xiv, 280 p. (ill) *ISBN: 0813380766; LofC: 90024417 //r92. Includes bibliographical references (p.263-272) and index.* [Political economy of global interdependence.]

32 Purchasing power parity in Latin America — a co-integration analysis; *[French summary]*; *[German summary]*; *[Spanish summary]*. Peter C. Liu. *Welt.liches Arc.* **4:128** 1992 pp. 662 – 680

33 Random walk or bandwagon — some evidence from foreign exchanges in the 1980s. K.S. Lai; P. Pauly. *Appl. Econ.* **24:7** 7:1992 pp. 693 – 700

34 A re-examination of the doctrine of relative purchasing power parity. M.T.H. Miah; M.R. Islam. *Econ. Aff. [Calcutta]* **37:2** 4-6:1992 pp. 83 – 99

35 Reforming the world's money. Paul Davidson. *J. Post. Keyn. Ec.* **15:2** Winter:1992-1993 pp. 153 – 180

36 Seasonality estimation in the UK foreign exchange market. Nathan L. Joseph; Robin D. Hewins. *J. Bus. Fin. Acc.* **19:1** 1:1992 pp. 39 – 72

37 A survey of recent empirical tests of the purchasing power parity hypothesis. G. Giovannetti. *Banca Nat. Lav. Q. Rev.* **:180** 3:1992 pp. 81 – 101

38 Time-consistency, foreign exchange market intervention, and the welfare effects of exogenous variability. Shin-ichi Fukuda. *Econ. S. Quart.* **43:1** 3:1992 pp. 33 – 51

39 Ungedeckte Zinsparität im Europäischen Währungssystem *[In German]*; Uncovered interest parity in the European Monetary System *[Summary]*; Parité des taux d'intérêt non-couverts dans le système monétaire européen *[French summary]*. Eckhard Freimann. *Kred. Kap.* **25:4** 1992 pp. 545 – 557

O.2.1: International monetary operations *[Opérations monétaires internationales]*
40 Unification of foreign exchange markets. Pierre-Richard Agénor; Robert P. Flood. *Staff Pap. Int. Monetary* **39:4** 12:1992 pp. 923 – 947
41 What are the microfoundations of the demand for foreign exchanges? R. Tamborini. *Eco. Notes* **21:1** 1992 pp. 148 – 156
42 Where does the meteor shower come from? The role of stochastic policy coordination. Takatoshi Ito; Robert F. Engle; Wen-Ling Lin. *J. Int. Econ.* **32:3/4** 5:1992 pp. 221 – 240
43 Why don't individuals speculate in forward foreign exchange? Charles A.E. Goodhart; Mark P. Taylor. *Scot. J. Poli.* **39:1** 2:1992 pp. 1 – 13

Exchange rates *[Taux de change]*

44 Adjustment under fixed exchange rates — application to the European Monetary Union. A. Steven Englander; Thomas Egedo. Paris: Organisation for Economic Co-operation and Development, 1992: 87 p. *ISBN: oc26391800. Summary in English and French; Includes bibliographical references (p. 35-41).* [Working papers — economics department. : No. 17]
45 An analysis of the determination of Deutsche Mark/French franc exchange rate in a discrete-time target-zone model. M.H. Pesaran; H. Samiei. *Econ. J.* **102:411** 3:1992 pp. 388 – 401
46 Asian-Pacific real exchange rates. K.G. Koedijk; R.J. Mahieu. *Appl. Econ.* **24:11** 11:1992 pp. 1255 – 1262
47 Britain's future in the EMS. Theodor Schonebeck. *Bus. Econ.* **23:2** Spring:1992 pp. 11 – 19
48 Chaos in the Dornbusch model of the exchange rate; Chaos im Dornbusch-Modell für den Wechselkurs *[German summary]*; Chaos dans le modèle du cours du change de Dornbusch *[French summary]*. Paul de Grauwe; Hans Dewachter. *Kred. Kap.* **25:1** 1992 pp. 26 – 54
49 A class of nonlinear ARCH models. M.L. Higgins; A.K. Bera. *Int. Econ. R.* **33:1** 2:1992 pp. 137 – 158
50 De la flexibilité des taux de change et de ses conséquences macroéconomiques *[In French]*; Exchange rate flexiblity and its macroeconomic consequences — modelization of the financial variables in the MIMOSA model *[Summary]*. Agnès Bénassy; Murielle Fiole; Emmanuel Fourmann; Henri Sterdyniak. *Obser. Diag. Econ.* **:40** 4:1992 pp. 201 – 248
51 Dual and multiple exchange rate systems in developing countries — some empirical evidence. Nita Ghei; Miguel Alberto Kiguel. Washington, D.C.: Country Economics Department, The World Bank, 1992: 31 p. [Policy research working papers.]
52 Dynamic equilibrium and the rural exchange rate in a spatially separated world. Bernard Dumas. *R. Finan. Stud.* **5:2** 1992 pp. 153 – 180
53 Empirical evidence on the insulation properties of fixed and flexible exchange rates — the Japanese experience. Michael Hutchison; Carl E. Walsh. *J. Int. Econ.* **32:3/4** 5:1992 pp. 241 – 264
54 Equilibrium real exchange rates. Stephen Wright. *Manch. Sch. E.* **LX** 1992 pp. 63 – 84
55 Equities and the UK exchange rate. C.E. Smith. *Appl. Econ.* **24:3** 3:1992 pp. 327 – 336
56 Exchange rate flexibility, volatility and the patterns of domestic and foreign direct investment. Joshua Aizenman. Washington, D.C.: International Monetary Fund, Research Department, 1992: 21 p. *Bibliography — p.20-21.* [IMF working paper. : No. WP/92/20]
57 Exchange rate flexibility, volatility, and domestic and foreign direct investment. Joshua Aizenman. *Staff Pap. Int. Monetary* **39:4** 12:1992 pp. 890 – 922
58 Exchange rate survey data — a disaggregated G-7 perspective. Ronald MacDonald. *Manch. Sch. E.* **LX** 1992 pp. 47 – 62
59 Exchange rate uncertainty, futures markets and the multinational firm. U. Broll; I. Zilcha. *Eur. Econ. R.* **36:4** 5:1992 pp. 815 – 826
60 Exchange rates and prices of Australian manufactured exports; *[French summary]*; *[German summary]*; *[Spanish summary]*. Jayant Menon. *Welt.liches Arc.* **4:128** 1992 pp. 695 – 710
61 Exchange rates, prices, and world trade — new methods, evidence, and implications. Meher Manzur. New York: Routledge, 1992: 206 p. *ISBN: 0415085896; LofC: 92019785. Includes bibliographical references and index.*
62 Exchange rates, trade liberalization and aid — the Sri Lankan experience. H. White; G. Wignaraja. *World Dev.* **20:10** 10:1992 pp. 1471 – 1480
63 Exchange-rate regimes and currency unions — proceedings of a conference held by the Confederation of European Economic Associations at Frankfurt, Germany, 1990. Ernst Baltensperger *[Ed.]*; Hans-Werner Sinn *[Ed.]*. New York: St. Martins Press, 1992: 296 p. *ISBN: 0312081014; LofC: 92007179. Includes bibliographical references and index.*
64 Federal budget deficits, money, and exchange rates. Keivan Deravi; Philip Gregorowicz; Charles E. Hegji. *Cont. Policy* **X:1** 1:1992 pp. 81 – 90

O.2.1: International monetary operations *[Opérations monétaires internationales]*
— *Exchange rates [Taux de change]*

65 Fiscal adjustment and the real exchange rate — the case of Bangladesh. Kazi M. Matin. Washington, D.C.: Country Economics Department, The World Bank, 1992: 42 p. [Policy research working papers.]

66 Fixed parity of the exchange rate and economic performance in the CFA Zone — a comparative study. Ibrahim A. Elbadawi; Nader Majd. Washington, D.C.: Country Economics Department World Bank, 1992: 46 p. [Policy research working papers.]

67 The impact of jump risks on nominal interest rates and foreign exchange rates. Chang Mo Ahn; Howard E. Thompson. *R. Quant. Finan. Account.* **2:1** 3:1992 pp. 17 – 31

68 Influences of imperfect capital mobility and asset substitutability on exchange rate volatility — money market shocks. Saziye Gazioglu. *Gr. Econ. Rev.* **13:2** 12:1991 pp. 313 – 330

69 An interpretation of recent research on exchange rate target zones. Lars E.O. Svensson. *J. Econ. Pers.* **6:4** Fall:1992 pp. 119 – 140

70 Intramarginal intervention in the EMS and the target-zone model of exchange-rate behavior. K.M. Dominguez; P.B. Kenen. *Eur. Econ. R.* **36:8** 12:1992 pp. 1523 – 1532

71 Liquidity and exchange rates. Vittorio Grilli; Nouriel Roubini. *J. Int. Econ.* **32:3/4** 5:1992 pp. 339 – 352

72 The long-run behavior of the real exchange rate. Joseph A. Whitt. *J. Money C. B.* **24:1** 2:1992 pp. 72 – 82

73 Long-run purchasing power parity and mean-reversion in real exchange rates — a further assessment; Parità dei poteri d'acquisto e riequilibrio dei cambi reali nel lungo periodo — una nuova verifica empirica *[Italian summary]*. M. Tronzano. *Econ. Int.* **XLV:1** 2:1992 pp. 77 – 100

74 May exchange rate volatility cause dumping injury? Steven M. Hoffer. *J. World Tr.* **26:3** 6:1992 pp. 61 – 72

75 The monetary model of exchange rates and cointegration — estimation, testing and prediction. Javier Gardeazabal; Marta Regulez. Berlin: Springer-Verlag, 1992: 194 p. *ISBN: 3540556354.* [Lecture notes in economics and mathematical systems. : No. 385]

76 Nachfrageschocks und Wechselkursvolatilität *[In German]*; Demand shocks and exchange rate volatility *[Summary]*; Chocs de demande et volatilité des cours du change *[French summary]*. Franco Reither. *Kred. Kap.* **25:1** 1992 pp. 55 – 64

77 Nonfundamental uncertainty and exchange rates. Robert G. King; Neil Wallace; Warren E. Weber. *J. Int. Econ.* **32:1/2** 2:1992 pp. 83 – 108

78 Pakistan's exchange rate policy — an econometric investigation. Mohammad Ahmed. *Pak. Dev. R.* **31:1** Spring:1992 pp. 49 – 74

79 Parallel markets, the foreign exchange auction, and exchange rate unification in Zambia. Janine Aron. Washington, D.C.: Country Economics Department, The World Bank, 1992: 115 p. *Bibliography — p.105-107.* [Policy research working papers.]

80 Real exchange rate overshooting and persistent trade effects — the case of New Zealand. Isabelle Joumard; Helmut Reisen. *World. Econ.* **15:3** 5:1992 pp. 375 – 388

81 Real exchange rates in the short, medium, and long run. Jack D. Glen. *J. Int. Econ.* **33:1/2** 8:1992 pp. 147 – 166

82 Response of the equilibrium real exchange rate to real disturbances in developing countries. M.S. Khan; J.D. Ostry. *World Dev.* **20:9** 9:1992 pp. 1325 – 1334

83 Robust, non-parametric measures of exchange rate variability. M. Anderson; D.A. Grier. *Appl. Econ.* **24:9** 9:1992 pp. 951 – 958

84 Some evidence in favor of a monetary rational expectations exchange rate model with imperfect capital substitutability. Robert A. Driskill; Nelson C. Mark; Steven M. Sheffrin. *Int. Econ. R.* **33:1** 2:1992 pp. 223 – 238

85 Speculation, incomplete currency market participation, and nonfundamental movements in nominal and real exchange rates. Richard C. Barnett. *J. Int. Econ.* **33:1/2** 8:1992 pp. 167 – 186

86 Stock markets and the exchange rate — a multi-country approach. C.E. Smith. *J. Macro.* **14:4** Fall:1992 pp. 607 – 629

87 Stock prices and the effective exchange rate of the dollar. M. Bahmani-Oskooee; A. Sohrabian. *Appl. Econ.* **24:4** 4:1992 pp. 459 – 464

88 Tail estimates of East European exchange rates. Kees G. Koedijk; J.M. Kool. *J. Bus. Econ. Stat.* **10:1** 1:1992 pp. 83 – 96

89 Target zones and forward rates in a model with repeated realignments. Leonardo Bartolini; Gordon M. Bodnar. *J. Monet. Ec.* **30:3** 12:1992 pp. 373 – 408

O.2.1: International monetary operations *[Opérations monétaires internationales]*
— *Exchange rates [Taux de change]*

90 Target zones and international policy coordination — the contrast between the necessary and sufficient conditions for success. A.J. Hughes Hallett. *Eur. Econ. R.* **36:4** 5:1992 pp. 893 – 914

91 Target zones and realignments. Giuseppe Bertola; Ricardo J. Caballero. *Am. Econ. Rev.* **82:3** 6:1992 pp. 520 – 536

92 Testing for the fundamental determinants of the long run real exchange rate. G.C. Lim. *J. Bank. Fin.* **16:3** 6:1992 pp. 625 – 642

93 Traded goods consumption smoothing and the random walk behavior of the real exchange rate. Kenneth Rogoff. *Mon. Econ. S.* **10:2** 11:1992 pp. 1 – 29

94 Unanticipated exchange rate variability and the growth of international trade; *[German summary]*; *[French summary]*; *[Spanish summary]*. Andreas Savvides. *Welt.liches Arc.* **128:3** 1992 pp. 446 – 463

95 Variance ratio tests of random walk for foreign exchange rates. J.L. Urrutia. *Econ. Lett.* **38:4** 1992 pp. 457 – 466

96 Verfahren zur Schätzung fundamental determinierter Wechselkurse — Purchasing-Power-Parity-Approach versus Trade-Balance-Approach? *[In German]*; [An estimation method for fundamentally determined exchange rates — purchasing-power-parity approach vs. trade-balance approach?] *[Summary]*. Margarete Wagner-Braun. *Jahr. Soz.schaft.* **43:1** 1992 pp. 85 – 107

O.2.2: Balance of payments, balance of accounts — *Balance des paiements, balance des comptes*

Sub-divisions: External debt *[Dette extérieure]*; International investment *[Investissements internationaux]*; Joint ventures *[Entreprises conjointes]*

1 An analysis of the potential externalities affecting the borrowing behaviour of developing countries. Amnon Levy. *Aust. Econ. P.* **31:58** 6:1992 pp. 164 – 176

2 Asian debt scenarios for the 1990s. Rameshwar Tandon. *J. Entwick.pol.* **VIII:1** 1992 pp. 81 – 89

3 The balance of payments and economic performance. Tony Thirlwall. *Nat. W. Bank* 5:1992 pp. 2 – 11

4 The Brady plan — theoretical foundations and application; Il Plano Brady — fondamenti teorici ed applicazione *[Italian summary]*. Giancarlo Perasso. *Rev. Int. Sci. Ec. Com.* **XXXIX:3** 3:1992 pp. 221 – 238

5 Capital controls and distribution of income — empirical evidence for Great Britain, Japan and Australia; *[German summary]*; *[French summary]*; .Daniele Checchi. *Welt.liches Arc.* **128:3** 1992 pp. 558 – 587

6 Capital controls and distribution of income — empirical evidence for Great Britain, Japan and Australia; *[German summary]*; *[French summary]*; *[Spanish summary]*. Daniele Checchi. *Welt.liches Arc.* **128:3** 1992 pp. 558 – 587

7 Capital controls and international trade finance. Alberto Giovannini; Jae Won Park. *J. Int. Econ.* **33:3/4** 11:1992 pp. 285 – 304

8 Capital flows to South Asian and ASEAN countries — trends, determinants, and policy implications. Ishrat Zafar Husain; Kwang W. Jun. Washington, D.C.: International Economics Department, The World Bank, 1992: 48 p. [Policy research working papers.]

9 Changes in the extent of financial interdependence between the G7 countries in the 1970s and 1980s. M.J. Holmes; J. Pentecost. *Int. Econ. J.* **6:4** Winter:1992 pp. 95 – 105

10 Common stochastic trends in international stock markets. Kenneth Kasa. *J. Monet. Ec.* **29:1** 2:1992 pp. 95 – 124

11 Corporate risk shifts resulting from international acquisition; Spostamenti del rischio delle imprese determinati da acquisizioni internazionali *[Italian summary]*. Stephen F. Borde; Jeff Madura. *Rev. Int. Sci. Ec. Com.* **XXXIX:3** 3:1992 pp. 259 – 266

12 Cyclical balance of the current account; Zyklischer Ausgleich der Leistungsbilanz *[German summary]*. Michael Carlberg. *Jahrb. N. St.* **209:3-4** 3:1992 pp. 193 – 206

13 Demand and supply factors in the determination of NIE exports — a simultaneous error-correction model for Hong Kong. V.A. Muscatelli; T.G. Srinivasan; D. Vines. *Econ. J.* **102:415** 11:1992 pp. 1467 – 1477

O.2.2: Balance of payments, balance of accounts *[Balance des paiements, balance des comptes]*

14 Do economic sanctions work? Makio Miyagawa. New York: St. Martin's Press, 1992: 240 p. *ISBN: 0312085443; LofC: 92014516. Includes bibliographical references and index.*

15 Do self-fulfilling expectations of currency devaluation improve the balance of payments? Ching-chong Lai; Wen-ya Chang. *J. Econ. Stud.* **19:4** 1992 pp. 48 – 57

16 The economic impact of the Israeli loan guarantees. Sheldon L. Richman. *J. Pal. Stud.* **XXI:2** Winter:1992 pp. 88 – 95

17 Economic restructuring and the debt problem — the Greek case. Takis Fotopoulos. *Int. R. Applied Ec.* **6:1** 1992 pp. 38 – 64

18 Economic sanctions and econometric policy evaluation — a cautionary note. Rajeev H. Dehejia; Bernard Wood. *J. World Tr.* **26:1** 2:1992 pp. 73 – 84

19 Effects of exchange rate changes on capital flows. S. Sundararajan. *Art. Vij.* **XXXIV:1** 3:1992 pp. 12 – 40

20 Equity control of multinational firms by less developed countries — a general equilibrium analysis. John K. Hill; José A. Méndez. *Manch. Sch. E.* **LX:1** 3:1992 pp. 53 – 63

21 Exchange rate dynamics and capital mobility. L. Bini Smaghi. *Eco. Notes* **21:1** 1992 pp. 73 – 84

22 Export credit insurance under present world conditions with special reference to the countries of East Europe. Roberto Ruberti. *Rev. Ec. Con. It.* **:1** 1-4:1992 pp. 53 – 76

23 External financial flows — the case of Africa; Les flux financiers extérieurs — le cas de l'Afrique *[French summary]*. S. Sideri. *Sav. Develop.* :1 Supplement:1992 pp. 89 – 115

24 Fiscal solvency in Europe — budget deficits and government debt under European monetary union. Guglielmo Maria Caporale. *Natl. Inst. Econ. R.* **:140** 5:1992 pp. 69 – 77

25 Foreign bank credit to U.S. corporations — the implications of offshore loans. *Q. R. Fed. Res. Bank N.Y.* **17:1** Spring:1992 pp. 52 – 64

26 Foreign-owned companies in the United States — malign or benign? C. Coughlin. *R. Fed. Resv. Bank St.Louis* **74:3** 5-6:1992 pp. 17 – 31

27 The globalization of service multinationals in the "Triad" regions — Japan, Western Europe and North America. Jiatao Li; Stephen Guisinger. *J. Int. Bus. Stud.* **23:4** Fourth quarter:1992 pp. 675 – 696

28 Gulf War reparations — Iraq, OPEC, and the transfer problem. R.J. Morrison. *Am. J. Econ. S.* **51:4** 10:1992 pp. 385 – 399

29 High noon in Washington — the shootout over the loan guarantees. Leon T. Hadar. *J. Pal. Stud.* **XXI:2** Winter:1992 pp. 72 – 87

30 International capital and the oil-producing states in Africa — an analysis of Angola, Nigeria, and Algeria. Catherine V. Scott. *J. Dev. Soc.* **VIII:2** 7-10:1992 pp. 179 – 193

31 International capital market, currency forward contract and the export decision; *[French summary]*; *[German summary]*. Udo Broll. *Schw. Z. Volk. Stat.* **128:2** 6:1992 pp. 125 – 131

32 International capital markets — developments and prospects, and policy issues. Morris Goldstein; et al. Washington D.C.: International Monetary Fund, 1991: 81 p. *ISBN: 1557753091. "September 1992"--t.p.. [World economic and financial surveys.]*

33 International financial markets — the performance of Britain and its rivals. A. D. Smith. New York, NY.: Cambridge University Press, 1992: 190 p. *ISBN: 0521431034; LofC: 92005882. Includes bibliographical references and index. [Occasional papers.]*

34 Liberalization of capital movements and of the domestic financial system. Philippe Bacchetta. *Economica* **59:236** 11:1992 pp. 465 – 474

35 Macroeconomic adjustments, economic growth and the balance of payments in Ghana 1983-88. N.K. Kusi. *J. Int. Dev.* **4:5** 9-10:1992 pp. 541 – 560

36 Macroeconomic interdependence under capital controls — a two-country model of dual exchange rates. Pablo E. Guidotti; Carlos A. Végh. *J. Int. Econ.* **32:3/4** 5:1992 pp. 353 – 368

37 Multinational corporations and the balance on current account. Evan Jones. *J. Aust. Pol. Econ.* **:30** 12:1992 pp. 61 – 90

38 Production and trade with international capital movements and payments. Henry Thompson. *S. Econ. J.* **58:3** 1:1992 pp. 743 – 749

39 Reducing official debt via market-based techniques. Bernard Hoekman; Pierre Sauvé. *Aussenwirtschaft* **47:2** 7:1992 pp. 207 – 226

40 Reviving private investment in developing countries — empirical studies and policy lessons. Ajay Chhibber *[Ed.]*; Mansoor Dailami *[Ed.]*; Nemat Shafik *[Ed.]*. Amsterdam: North-Holland, 1992: 245 p. *ISBN: 0444893954; LofC: 92012342. [Contributions to economic analysis. : No. 208]*

O.2.2: Balance of payments, balance of accounts *[Balance des paiements, balance des comptes]*

41 Scarcity of capital and the reconstruction of Eastern Europe — a challenge and a role for the EBRD. Mario Sarcinelli. *Rev. Ec. Con. It.* :**1** 1-4:1992 pp. 9 – 24

42 Speculative attacks and models of balance of payments crises. Pierre-Richard Agenor; Jagdeep S. Bhandari; Robert P. Flood. *Staff Pap. Int. Monetary* **39:2** 6:1992 pp. 357 – 394

43 Towards an EC policy on export financing subsidies — lessons from the 1980s and prospects for future reform. Filip Abraham; Inge Couwenberg; Gerda Dewit. *World. Econ.* **15:3** 5:1992 pp. 389 – 405

44 The tragedy of the commons and economic growth — why does capital flow from poor to rich countries? Aarón Tornell; Andrés Velasco. *J. Polit. Ec.* **100:6** 12:1992 pp. 1208 – 1231

45 Unit root tests of the current account balance — implications for international capital mobility. E. Gundlach; S. Sinn. *Appl. Econ.* **24:6** 6:1992 pp. 617 – 625

46 What are the long-run determinants of the U.S. trade balance? Mohsen Bahmani-Oskooee. *J. Post. Keyn. Ec.* **15:1** Fall:1992 pp. 85 – 97

47 Why current account deficits still matter. Menzie David Chinn. *World. Econ.* **15:2** 3:1992 pp. 221 – 230

External debt *[Dette extérieure]*

48 Australia's foreign debt — searching for the benefits. Peter Daniels. *Ec. Pap. Aust.* **11:1** 3:1992 pp. 14 – 31

49 Dealing with developing country debt in the 1990s. Kenneth Rogoff. *World. Econ.* **15:4** 7:1992 pp. 475 – 486

50 Debt and ecological disaster in Latin America. Elizabeth Dore. *Race Class* **34:1** 7-9:1992 pp. 73 – 88

51 Debt arrears in Latin America — do political variables matter? Carmen A. Li. *J. Dev. Stud.* **28:4** 7:1992 pp. 668 – 688

52 The debt boomerang — how Third World debt harms us all. Susan George. London: Pluto Press with the Transnational Institute (TNI), 1992: 202 p. *ISBN: 0745305946.*

53 Debt crisis in sub-Saharan countries. R.L. Chawla. *Afr. Q.* **30:3-4** 1990 pp. 41 – 64

54 Debt management objectives for a small open economy. Paul Boothe; Bradford Reid. *J. Money C. B.* **24:1** 2:1992 pp. 43 – 60

55 Debt relief for Eastern Europe — its costs and the distribution of proceeds — some preliminary results; *[French summary]*; *[German summary]*; *[Spanish summary]*. Stephan Koren. *Welt.liches Arc.* **4:128** 1992 pp. 639 – 661

56 Debt relief through debt conversion — a critical analysis of the Chilean debt conversion programme. Ricardo A. Lagos. *J. Dev. Stud.* **28:3** 4:1992 pp. 473 – 499

57 A debt to the West — recent developments in the international financial situation of East-Central Europe. Wieslaw Z. Michalak; Richard A. Gibb. *Prof. Geogr.* **44:3** 8:1992 pp. 260 – 271

58 Debt-equity conversions, debt-for-nature swaps, and the continuing world debt crisis. Daniel H. Cole. *Columb. J. Tr.* **30:1** 1992 pp. 57 – 88

59 L'échange dette-nature — la nécessité d'un nouveau calendrier *[In French]*; The "debt for nature" swap — the need for a new agenda *[Summary]*; El intercambio deuda-naturaleza — la necesidad de un nuevo calendario *[Spanish summary]*. Robert Devlin. *Prob. Am.Lat.* :**6** 7-9:1992 pp. 69 – 81

60 An evaluation of some options for the entry of Argentina in the Brady Plan. José-Luis Maia. *Money Aff.* **V:2** 7-12:1992 pp. 155 – 171

61 External debt and economic adjustment in Guyana. Elmer Harris. *Money Aff.* **V:2** 7-12:1992 pp. 173 – 197

62 External debt, net transfers, and growth in developing countries. E.L. Bacha. *World Dev.* **20:8** 8:1992 pp. 1183 – 1192

63 The IMF and Paris club debt rescheduling — a conflicting role? R.P.C. Brown. *J. Int. Dev.* **4:3** 5-6:1992 pp. 291 – 313

64 The IMF, the World Bank and Africa's adjustment and external debt problems — an unofficial view. G.K. Helleiner. *World Dev.* **20:6** 6:1992 pp. 779 – 792

65 The impact of privatization on the Latin American debt problem. Ravi Ramamurti. *J. Int. Am. St.* **34:2** Summer:1992 pp. 93 – 125

66 India's economic crisis, new dispensations and the poor. Basudeb Sahoo. *Soc. Act.* **42:1** 1-3:1992 pp. 64 – 78

67 Jamaica — stories of poverty. James Ferguson. *Race Class* **34:1** 7-9:1992 pp. 61 – 72

O.2.2: Balance of payments, balance of accounts *[Balance des paiements, balance des comptes] — External debt [Dette extérieure]*

68 Külső adósságfelhalmozás és az adósságkezelés makroökonómiai problémái Magyarországon. I. A külső adósság felhalmozása, erőforrás-transzfer és a hazai adósságstratégia kritikái *[In Hungarian]*; Foreign debt accumulation and macroeconomic problems of debt management in Hungary. I. Debt accumulation, resource transfers and criticism of the present debt strategy *[Summary]*. Oblath Gábor. *Közg. Sz.* **XXXIX:** 7-8:1992 pp. 605 – 621

69 Latin American debt moratoria and the British banks — the stock market response; Moratoria dei debiti latino-americani e banche britanniche — la risposta del mercato azionario *[Italian summary]*. S.V. Jayanti; G. Geoffrey Booth. *Rev. Int. Sci. Ec. Com.* **XXXIX:10-11** 10-11:1992 pp. 849 – 863

70 Orígenes históricos y la gran crisis de endeudamiento en América Latina *[In Spanish]*; [Historical origins to the Latin American debt crisis]. Aline Frambes-Buxeda. *Homines* **6** 1989 pp. 103 – 134

71 Perspectivas para o financiamento externo da América Latina e do Caribe no início da década de 90 *[In Portuguese]*; [Prospects of external financing for Latin America and the Caribbean at the beginning of the 1990s] *[Summary]*. Arno Meyer. *Rev. Bras. Ec.* **46:3** 7-9:1992 pp. 339 – 376

72 Political instability, country risk and probability of default. E.M. Balkan. *Appl. Econ.* **24:9** 9:1992 pp. 999 – 1008

73 The revolving door? External debt and capital flight — a Philippine case study. J.K. Boyce. *World Dev.* **20:3** 3:1992 pp. 335 – 350

74 Sovereign debt — optimal contract, underinvestment, and forgiveness. Eduardo S. Schwartz; Salvador Zurita. *J. Finance* **47:3** 7:1992 pp. 981 – 1004

75 Sub-Saharan Africa's dilemma of indebtedness. Feraidoon Shams. *J. Asian Afr. Aff.* **III:2** Spring:1992 pp. 192 – 204

76 Sustaining lender commitment to sovereign debtors. Derek Asiedu-Akrofi. *Columb. J. Tr.* **30:1** 1992 pp. 1 – 56

77 Trade and payments after Soviet disintegration. John Williamson. Washington, D.C: Insitute for International Economics, 1992: 76 p. *ISBN: 0881321737; LofC: 92021821.* "*July 1992.*"; *Includes bibliographical references and index.* [Policy analyses in international economics. : No. 37]

78 Transfers, economic structure, and vulnerability of the African economy. Gerald E. Scott. *J. Dev. Areas* **26:2** 1:1992 pp. 213 – 238

79 Verschuldung und Umwelt — Ökologische Aspekte der Schuldenkrise in Entwicklungsländern *[In German]*; [Indebtedness and the environment — ecological aspects of the debt crisis in developing countries] *[Summary]*. Richard Gerster. *Aussenwirtschaft* **47:2** 7:1992 pp. 227 – 252

International investment *[Investissements internationaux]*

80 Les capitaux étrangers à l'Est *[In French]*; Foreign investments in Central Europe *[Summary]*. Patricia Lormeau. *Rev. Ét. Comp.* **23:1** 1992 pp. 109 – 122

81 Changements structurels et investissement multidimensionnel *[In French]*; Cambiamenti strutturali e investimento multidimensionale *[Italian summary]*; Structural change and multidimensional investment *[Summary]*. B. Carrier. *Econ. Int.* **XLV:1** 2:1992 pp. 1 – 25

82 Changing determinants of Japanese foreign investment in the United States. Tracey A. Drake; Richard E. Caves. *J. Jap. Int. Ec.* **6:3** 9:1992 pp. 228 – 246

83 China's experiences and lessons from the utilisation of foreign capital. Lei Qihuai. *China R.* **28:3** 7-9:1992 pp. 183 – 192

84 China's "open door" and the United States — foreign investment and national autonomy. Ranbir Vohra. *China R.* **28:3** 7-9:1992 pp. 193 – 214

85 Competitive advantages, two-way foreign investment, and capital accumulation in Korea. Keun Lee; Michael G. Plummer. *Asian Econ. J.* **VI:2** 7:1992 pp. 93 – 113

86 The decentralization of Peking's economic management and its impact on foreign investment. Feng-Cheng Fu. *Iss. Stud.* **28:2** 2:1992 pp. 67 – 83

87 Desarrollo económico e inserción externa en América Latina — un proyecto elusivo *[In Spanish]*; [Economic development and external investment — an elusive project]. Luciano Tomassini. *Est. Inter.* **XXV:97** 1-3:1992 pp. 73 – 116

88 The determinants of Korean foreign direct investment in manufacturing industries; *[German summary]*; *[French summary]*; *[Spanish summary]*. Yoong-Deok Jeon. *Welt.liches Arc.* **128:3** 1992 pp. 527 – 542

O.2.2: Balance of payments, balance of accounts *[Balance des paiements, balance des comptes]* — *International investment [Investissements internationaux]*

89 The development of the international bond market. Richard Benzie. Basle: Bank for International Settlements, 1992: 95 p. [BIS economic papers. : No. 32]

90 Evidence of risk premiums in foreign currency futures markets. Thomas H. McCurdy; Ieuan Morgan. *R. Finan. Stud.* **5:1** 1992 pp. 65 – 84

91 The expansion of foreign direct investments — discrete rational location choices or a cultural learning process? Gabriel R.G. Benito; Geir Gripsrud. *J. Int. Bus. Stud.* **23:3** Third quarter:1992 pp. 461 – 476

92 Le financement interne des engagements extérieurs du secteur public brésilien *[In French]*; The financing of the external indebtedness of the public sector in Brazil *[Summary]*. Jérôme Trotignon. *Ec. Pros. Int.* **49:1** 1992 pp. 57 – 76

93 Foreign direct investment and host country conditions — looking from the other side now. Steve Chan; Melanie Mason. *Int. Inter.* **17:3** 1992 pp. 215 – 232

94 Foreign direct investment in Asia — developing country versus developed country firms; *[French summary]*. Edward K.Y. Chen. *Gestion* **8:2** 1992 pp. 31 – 58

95 Foreign investment and economic change in China. Y.Y. Kueh. *China Quart.* **:131** 9:1992 pp. 637 – 689

96 Foreign investment and technological development in Silicon Valley. David J. Teece. *Calif. Manag. R.* **34:2** Winter:1992 pp. 88 – 106

97 Foreign investment and technology transfer — a simple model. J.-Y. Wang; M. Blomström. *Eur. Econ. R.* **36:1** 1:1992 pp. 137 – 156

98 Foreign investment in East European countries. Zbigniew Dobosiewicz. London: Routledge, 1992: 134 p. *ISBN: 0415056888; LofC: 91005093. Includes bibliographical references and index.*

99 Hedge period length and ex-ante futures hedging effectiveness — the case of foreign-exchange risk cross hedges. Bruce A. Benet. *J. Futur. Mark.* **12:2** 4:1992 pp. 163 – 176

100 How successfully do we measure capital flight? The empirical evidence from five developing countries. Myrvin L. Anthony; Andrew J. Hughes Hallett. *J. Dev. Stud.* **28:3** 4:1992 pp. 538 – 556

101 The impact of exchange rate risk on the foreign direct investment of U.S. multinational manufacturing companies. Some further results. G. Clare. *Open Econ. R.* **3:2** 1992 pp. 143 – 164

102 Institutional developments in the globalization of securities and futures markets. Jodi G. Scarlata. *R. Fed. Resv. Bank St.Louis* **74:1** 1/2: 1992 pp. 17 – 30

103 International investments and exchange rate risk. U. Broll; J.E. Wahl. *Eur. J. Pol. Ec.* **8:1** 2:1992 pp. 31 – 40

104 La inversión extranjera directa en España y su contribución al equilibrio de la economía española en el período 1986-90 *[In Spanish]*; [Direct external investment in Spain and its contributions to a balanced Spanish economy between 1986 and 1990]. Eloísa Ortega. *Monetaria* **XV:3** 7-10:1992 pp. 301 – 320

105 Investissement étranger direct et développement économique *[In French]*; Direct foreign investment and economic development *[Summary]*; Inversión extranjera directa y desarollo económico *[Spanish summary]*. Alexandre Minda. *Prob. Am.Lat.* **:5** 4-6:1992 pp. 105 – 124

106 Inwestycje zagraniczne w Polsce — ewolucja uwarunkowań i możliwości *[In Polish]*; (Foreign investment in Poland — evolution of conditions and prospects); (Иностранные капиталовложения в Польше - эволюция обусловлений и возможностей: *Title only in Russian*); (L'évolution des conditions et des possibilités pour les investissements étrangers en Pologne: *Title only in French*). Marian Małecki. *Spr. Między.* **XLV:1-2(455)** 1992 pp. 71 – 90

107 Japanese direct investment in EC. John Cramer. *Gestion* **8:1** 1992 pp. 29 – 40

108 Japanese direct investment in the US. George C. Georgiou; Sharon Weinhold. *World. Econ.* **15:6** 11:1992 pp. 761 – 778

109 A külföldi működő tőke hazánkban *[In Hungarian]*; Direct foreign investment in Hungary *[Summary]*. Katalin Falusné-Szikra; Zsuzsa Mosolygó. *Közg. Sz.* **XXXIX** 1:1992 pp. 59 – 71

110 Liberalizing foreign direct investment regimes — the vestigial screen. A.G. Wint. *World Dev.* **20:10** 10:1992 pp. 1515 – 1529

111 The negative correlation between foreign direct investment and economic growth in the Third World — theory and evidence; La correlazione negativa tra investimento diretto estero e crescita economica nel terzo mondo — teoria e evidenza *[Italian summary]*. Ira S. Saltz. *Rev. Int. Sci. Ec. Com.* **XXXIX:7** 7:1992 pp. 617 – 634

O.2.2: Balance of payments, balance of accounts *[Balance des paiements, balance des comptes]* — International investment *[Investissements internationaux]*

112 A note on foreign investment in India's "new" economy. Paul Birtill. *Race Class* **34:1** 7-9:1992 pp. 17 – 22

113 Optimal weights and international portfolio hedging with U.S. dollar index futures — an empirical investigation. Steven Krull; Anoop Rai. *J. Futur. Mark.* **12:5** 10:1992 pp. 549 – 562

114 Overseas investments, capital gains and the balance of payments. C. F. Pratten. London: Institute of Economic Affairs, 1992: 121 p. *ISBN: 0255363036.* [Research monographs.]

115 Private foreign asset accumulation, not just capital flight — evidence from the Philippines. Rob Vos. *J. Dev. Stud.* **28:3** 4:1992 pp. 500 – 537

116 Privatization and investment in sub-Saharan Africa. Rexford A. Ahene *[Ed.]*; Bernard S. Katz *[Ed.]*. New York: Praeger, 1992: xiv, 244 p. *ISBN: 0275933741; LofC: 91037511 //r92.* *Includes bibliographical references (p. [219]-226) and index.*

117 Protection, terms of technology transfer and foreign investment — a welfare analysis. M. Anam; A.B. Supapol. *Int. Econ. J.* **6:4** Winter:1992 pp. 75 – 83

118 Le protectionnisme et les investissements directs manufacturiers japonais dans la CEE *[In French]*; The determinants of Japanese foreign investments in manufacturing industries in the ECC *[Summary]*. N. Fabry. *Rev. Ec. Polit.* **102:5** 9-10:1992 pp. 769 – 788

119 Quid pro quo foreign investment and vers — a Nash bargaining approach. Elias Dinopoulos. *Econ. Polit.* **4:1** 3:1992 pp. 43 – 60

120 Saving and investment in the world economy and Italy's place. Mario Arcelli; Stefano Micossi. *Rev. Ec. Con. It.* **:1** 1-4:1992 pp. 25 – 52

121 The scope and prospects of foreign investment in Vietnam. Hoang N. Nguyen. *Cont. S.E. Asia* **14:3** 12:1992 pp. 244 – 256

122 Une situation préoccupante — les investissements canadiens au Brésil dans les années 70 et 80 *[In French]*; A disturbing situation — Canadian investment in Brazil in the 70's and the 80's *[Summary]*; (Una situación preocupante — las inversiones canadienses en el Brasil en los años 70 y 80: *Title only in Spanish*). Daniel Holly. *Ét. Int.* **XXIII:2** 6:1992 pp. 349 – 375

123 Takeover or makeover? Japanese investment in America. Gregory W. Noble. *Calif. Manag. R.* **34:4** Summer:1992 pp. 127 – 147

124 Tests of integration, mild segmentation and segmentation hypotheses. V. Errunza; E. Losq; P. Padmanabhan. *J. Bank. Fin.* **16:5** 9:1992 pp. 949 – 972

125 Trans-Atlantic foreign direct investment and the European economic community. John H. Dunning. *Int. Econ. J.* **6:1** Spring:1992 pp. 59 – 81

126 Two-sided expropriation and international equity contracts. Harold L. Cole; William B. English. *J. Int. Econ.* **33:1/2** 8:1992 pp. 77 – 104

127 US policy debate towards inward investment. David Bailey; George Harte; Roger Sugden. *J. World Tr.* **26:4** 8:1992 pp. 65 – 93

128 We are all "us". Stephen Thomsen. *Columb. J. W. Bus.* **XXVI:4** Winter:1992 pp. 6 – 14

129 Western investment in East-Central Europe — emerging patterns and implications for state stability. Alexander B. Murphy. *Prof. Geogr.* **44:3** 8:1992 pp. 249 – 259

Joint ventures *[Entreprises conjointes]*

130 Joint ventures and a special economic zone in North Korea. Toshio Miyatsuka. *China News.* **96:1-2** 1992 pp. 15 – 21

131 Joint-ventures et modernisation de l'industrie électronique Chinoise *[In French]*; Joint ventures and modernisation of the electronics industry in China *[Summary]*. Jean-François Huchet; Zhaoxi Li. *Sociol. Trav.* **2** 1992 pp. 209 – 228

132 Soviet joint ventures and the West — a process of learning by joining; *[German summary]*. Silvana Malle. *Econ. Sys.* **16:1** 4:1992 pp. 33 – 62

133 Valuation effects of joint ventures in Eastern Bloc countries; Effetti delle attese di joint ventures nei paesi dell'Europa Orientale *[Italian summary]*. Armand Picou; John M. Cheney. *Rev. Int. Sci. Ec. Com.* **XXXIX:2** 2:1992 pp. 97 – 105

O.2.3: Monetary policies, monetary areas — *Politiques et zones monétaires*

1 Achieving monetary union in Europe. Andrew Britton; David G. Mayes. London: Sage Publications, 1992: 144 p. *ISBN: 0803987196.*

2 Big effects of small interventions — the informational role of intervention in exchange rate policy. M.W. Klein. *Eur. Econ. R.* **36:4** 5:1992 pp. 915 – 924

3 Canadian foreign exchange policies — intervention, control, cointegration; Kanadische Wechselkurspolitik — Invertention, Kontrolle, Kointegration *[German summary]*; Les politiques canadiennes du taux de change — intervention, contrôle, et co-intégration *[French summary]*; Las políticas de cambio canadienses — intervención, control, cointegración *[Spanish summary]*. G. Geoffrey Booth; Mustafa Chowdhury. *Welt.liches Arc.* **128:1** 1992 pp. 21 – 33

4 A critical evaluation of exchange rate policy in Turkey. Y. Asikoglu; M. Uctum. *World Dev.* **20:10** 10:1992 pp. 1501 – 1514

5 Die D-Mark als Leitwährung in Europa? *[In German]*; [The DM as leading currency in Europe] *[Summary]*. Gebhard Mayer. *Konjunkturpolitik* **38:3** 1992 pp. 153 – 173

6 EC monetary integration and its ramifications for non-member countries — a Nordic perspective. Patrik Anckar. Åbo: Åbo Akademi, 1992: 108 p. *ISBN: 9516500315.* [Meddelanden fran Ekonomisk-Statsvetenskapliga Fakulteten vid Åbo Akademi.]

7 The economics of monetary integration. Paul de Grauwe. Oxford: Oxford University Press, 1992: 193 p. *ISBN: 0198773471; LofC: 91042193. Includes bibliographical references.*

8 ECU — the currency of Europe. Christopher Johnson *[Ed.]*. London: Euromoney Publications PLC, 1991: 259 p. *ISBN: 1855640090.*

9 Die ECU-Wirtschaft. Ein Modell zu den Konsequenzen der Europäischen Währungsunion *[In German]*; The ECU-economy — modelling the implications of European currency union *[Summary]*; Une économie ECU — un modèle sur les conséquences de l'Union monétaire européenne *[French summary]*. Heinz-Peter Spahn. *Kred. Kap.* **25:4** 1992 pp. 469 – 490

10 L'emergence de la monnaie européenne *[In French]*; [The emergence of a European currency]. Michel Aglietta; Christian de Boissieu. *Genèses* :8 6:1992 pp. 4 – 24

11 EMU after Maastricht. Peter B. Kenen. Washington, D.C: Group of Thirty, 1992: 123 p. *ISBN: 1567080367. Includes bibliographical references.*

12 EMU and ESCB after Maastricht. C.A.E. Goodhart *[Ed.]*. London: London School of Economics, Financial Markets Group, 1992: 335 p.

13 EMU — progress, problems and prospects. Barry Harrison. *Economics* **XXVIII:4(120)** Winter:1992 pp. 149 – 155

14 Estimating limited-dependent rational expectations models with an application to exchange rate determination in a target zone. M. Hashem Pesaran; Hossein Samiei. *J. Economet.* **53:1-3** 7-9:1992 pp. 141 – 164

15 European monetary integration — from the European Monetary System to monetary union. Daniel Gros; Niels Thygesen. Harlow: Longman, 1992: 494 p. *ISBN:0582079225.*

16 The European monetary system and European monetary union. Michele Fratianni; Jürgen von Hagen. Boulder, CO: Westview Press, 1992: xvi, 248 p. (ill) *ISBN: 0813379954; LofC: 92001348. Includes bibliographical references and index.* [Political economy of global interdependence.]

17 European Monetary Union and "1992" — opportunities for Africa. Paul Collier. *World. Econ.* **15:5** 9:1992 pp. 633 – 643

18 European monetary union — institutional structure and economic performance. D. Currie. *Econ. J.* **102:411** 3:1992 pp. 248 – 264

19 Exchange rate policy, the real exchange rate, and inflation — lessons from Latin America. Miguel Alberto Kiguel. Washington, D.C.: Country Economics Department, The World Bank, 1992: 22 p. [Policy research working papers.]

20 The experience with monetary policy in an environment with strong microeconomic distortions; *[German summary]*. Peter Bofinger. *Econ. Sys.* **16:2** 10:1992 pp. 247 – 268

21 The federal funds rate and the arbitrage pricing theory — evidence that monetary policy matters. Willem Thorbecke; Tarik Alami. *J. Macro.* **14:4** Fall:1992 pp. 731 – 744

22 Fédéralisme budgétaire et unification économique européenne *[In French]*; Fiscal federalism and EMU *[Summary]*. Dominique Bureau; Paul Champsaur. *Obser. Diag. Econ.* :**40** 4:1992 pp. 87 – 100

O.2.3: Monetary policies, monetary areas *[Politiques et zones monétaires]*

23 Financial liberalization and its impact on domestic stabilization policies — Singapore and Malaysia. Emil-Maria Claassen. *Welt.liches Arc.* **128:1** 1992 pp. 136 – 167

24 Fiscal stabilisation and monetary integration in Europe — a short-run analysis. Frederick van der Ploeg. *Economist [Leiden]* **140:1** 1992 pp. 16 – 44

25 Foreign banking in Spain — challenges and opportunities. Louis Eduardo Rivera-Solis. *J. Bus. Soc.* **5:1-2** 1992 pp. 59 – 67

26 Geld- und Wechselkurspolitik in Argentinien und Chile 1970- 1988 — ein Vergleich *[In German]*; [Monetary and exchange rate policy in Argentina and Chile, 1970- 1988 — a comparative study]. Rainer Schweickert. *Weltwirt.* **:1** 1992 pp. 85 – 106

27 German unification and the European monetary system — a quantitative analysis. Gwyn Adams; Lewis S. Alexander; Joseph E. Gagnon. [Washington, D.C.]: Board of Governors of the Federal Reserve System, 1992: 40 p. [International finance discussion papers. : No. 421]

28 Has the EMS reduced the cost of capital? Enrique Sentana; Sushil B. Wadhwani; Mushtaq Shah. London: LSE Financial Markets Group, 1992: 35 p. [LSE Financial Markets Group discussion paper series. : No. 134]

29 How can European monetary union be made to work in practice? David B. Smith. *Bus. Econ.* **23:3** Summer:1992 pp. 17 – 32

30 Inflationary expectations, political parties and the exchange rate regime — Greece 1958-1989. G.S. Alogoskoufis; A. Philippopoulos. *Eur. J. Pol. Ec.* **8:3** 10:1992 pp. 375 – 399

31 Institutional commitments and policy credibility — a critical survey and empirical evidence from the ERM. Thomas Egedo; A. Steven Englander. *OECD Ec. Stud.* **:18** Spring:1992 pp. 45 – 84

32 Institutional developments towards a single European monetary policy. Lorenzo Smaghi. *Gr. Econ. Rev.* **13:2** 12:1991 pp. 173 – 200

33 Integrativer Rückschritt mit Tücken — Überlegungen zu einem Vorschlag von James Tobin *[In German]*; Integrative retrogression with problems — thoughts on a suggestion by James Tobin *[Summary]*. Ulrich Schempp. *Jahrb. N. St.* **209:3-4** 3:1992 pp. 231 – 240

34 The international transmission of Eurodollar and US interest rates — a cointegration analysis. H.-G. Fung; S.C. Isberg. *J. Bank. Fin.* **16:4** 8:1992 pp. 757 – 770

35 The Iranian foreign exchange policy and the black market for dollars. M. Hashem Pesaran. *Int. J. M.E. Stud.* **24:1** 2:1992 pp. 101 – 125

36 Is it signalling? Exchange intervention and the dollar-Deutschemark rate. Atish R. Ghosh. *J. Int. Econ.* **32:3/4** 5:1992 pp. 201 – 220

37 Japanese financial markets and the role of the yen. C. R. McKenzie *[Ed.]*; Michael Stutchbury *[Ed.]*. North Sydney, NSW Australia: Allen & Unwin in association with Australia-Japan Research Centre, Australian National University, 1992: 173 p. *ISBN: 186373239x. Papers from a conference held Nov., 1987 in Canberra and Sydney, Australia; Includes bibliographical references (p. 160-167) and index.*

38 The Maastricht way to EMU. Michele Fratianni; Jürgen von Hagen; Christopher Waller. Princton, N.J: International Finance Section, Dept. of Economics, Princeton University, 1992: 50p. *ISBN: 0881650943; LofC: 92021840. Includes bibliographical references.* [Essays in international finance.]

39 Monetary accomodation, exchange rate regimes and inflation persistence. G.S. Alogoskoufis. *Econ. J.* **102:412** 5:1992 pp. 461 – 480

40 Monetary union — a theoretical perspective. F. Cesarano. *Banca Nat. Lav. Q. Rev.* **:182** 9:1992 pp. 349 – 361

41 Necesidades de financiamiento del gobierno y régimenes cambiarios duales *[In Spanish]*; [Public finance needs and dual exchange rate regimes]. Omar O. Chisari; Guillermo Rozenwurcel. *Revis. Econ.* **V:2-3** 12-4:1990-1991 pp. 19 – 48

42 The new Swedish ecu basket; Den nya svenska ecu-korgen *[Swedish summary]*. Marianne Nessén. *Skan. Ensk. Bank. Q. R.* **:1-2** 1992 pp. 22 – 32

43 Oil price, capital mobility and oil importers — a general equilibrium macro analysis. Arturo González Romero. *Ener. Econ.* **14:1** 1:1992 pp. 11 – 22

44 On the way to the EMU — testing convergence of the European economies. P.G. Ardeni. *Eco. Notes* **21:2** 1992 pp. 238 – 257

45 One market, one money — an evaluation of the potential benefits and costs of forming an economic and monetary union. Michael Emerson; et al. Oxford: Oxford University Press, 1992: 354 p. *ISBN: 0198773234; LofC: 91034734. Includes bibliographical references.*

46 Optimal international reserves and sovereign risk. Avraham Ben-Bassat; Daniel Gottlieb. *J. Int. Econ.* **33:3/4** 11:1992 pp. 345 – 362

O.2.3: Monetary policies, monetary areas *[Politiques et zones monétaires]*

47 Optimum currency area theory and European monetary integration. I. Maes. *Tijds. Econ. Manag.* **XXXVII:2** 6:1992 pp. 137 – 152

48 Policy issues in the evolving international monetary system. Morris Goldstein; et al. Washington, DC: International Monetary Fund, 1992: vii, 74 p. *ISBN: 1557752346; LofC: 92017080. Includes bibliographical references (p. 68-72).* [Occasional paper. International Monetary Fund.]

49 Policy-delegation and fixed exchange rates. Jürgen von Hagen. *Int. Econ. R.* **33:4** 11:1992 pp. 849 – 870

50 The political economy of European monetary union. A.R. Nobay. *Gr. Econ. Rev.* **13:2** 12:1991 pp. 201 – 214

51 Possible evolution of African multi-lateral payments arrangements in the prospect of the pan-African economic community. François Yao. *Finan. News Anal.* **5:7** 7:1992 pp. 1 – 13

52 La problématique de la monnaie unique et son application au cas de l'Europe *[In French]*; The problem of a single currency and its application in the European context *[Summary]*. Ph. Narassiguin. *Rev. Ec. Polit.* **102:6** 11-12:1992 pp. 799 – 842

53 Quel avenir pour la zone franc? *[In French]*; The future of the franc zone *[Summary]*. Bruno Coquet; Jean-Marc Daniel. *Obser. Diag. Econ.* **:41** 7:1992 pp. 241 – 292

54 Regulation of international banking — a review of the issues. Charles W. Hultman. *J. World Tr.* **26:5** 10:1992 pp. 79 – 92

55 Second thoughts on EMU. P. Krugman. *Jpn. Wor. Econ.* **4:3** 11:1992 pp. 187 – 200

56 Seigniorage flows in the West African monetary union, 1976-89; *[German summary]*; *[French summary]*; *[Spanish summary]*. Rohinton Medhora. *Welt.liches Arc.* **128:3** 1992 pp. 513 – 526

57 The sovereignty of money — legal problems of European monetary integration. R. Knieper. *Int. J. S. Law Vol.19; No.2 - 5: 1991.* pp. 121 – 148

58 Structural adjustment and international trade in Eastern Europe — the case of Poland. Andrew Berg; Jeffrey Sachs. *Econ. Pol.* **:14** 4:1992 pp. 117 – 173

59 Symposium on money. George S. Alogoskoufis *[Contrib.]*; James Robertson *[Contrib.]*; Lothar Müller *[Contrib.]*. *Collection of 3 articles.* New Eur. , *5:2,* 1992 pp. 13 – 30

60 Target zones and forward rates in a model with repeated realignments. Leonardo Bartolini; Gordon M. Bodnar. Washington, D.C.: International Monetary Fund, Research Department, 1992: 28 p. *Bibliography — p.26-28.* [IMF working paper. : No. WP/92/22]

61 Testing for long run purchasing power parity — an examination of Korean won. M. Bahmani-Oskooee; H.J. Rhee. *Int. Econ. J.* **6:3** Autumn:1992 pp. 93 – 103

62 The theory of optimum currency areas and monetary integration in Africa; (La theorie de la "zone monetaire optimale" et l'integration monetaire en Afique). Ben E. Aigbokhan. *Sav. Develop.* **XVI:3** 1992 pp. 275 – 286

63 Überlegungen zu einem optimalen DM- Währungsraum *[In German]*; [Thoughts on an optimal DM-currency area]. Lukas Menkhoff; Friedrich L. Sell. *Z. Wirt. Soz.* **112:3** 1992 pp. 379 – 400

64 Unpleasant monetarist arithmetic revisited — central bank independence, fiscal policy and European Monetary Union. Nigel M. Healey; Paul Levine. *Nat. W. Bank* *8:1992* pp. 23 – 37

65 Währungspolitik in der Übergangsphase zur Europäischen Währungsunion *[In German]*; Monetary policy in the phase of transition to European Monetary Union *[Summary]*; Politique monétaire pendant la phase transitoire jusqu'à l'Union monétaire Européenne *[French summary]*. Bernhard Herz. *Kred. Kap.* **25:2** 1992 pp. 185 – 210

66 Wandel währungspolitischer Arrangements. Was tragen Multinationale Unternehmungen dazu bei? *[In German]*; Changes in monetary policy arrangements — what do multinational enterprises contribute thereto? *[Summary]*; Changement dans les dispositions de politique monétaire. Comment y contribuent les entreprises multinationales? *[French summary]*. Norbert Berthold. *Kred. Kap.* **25:2** 1992 pp. 211 – 232

67 Der Weg zur Europäischen Währungsunion — Überwindbare Hindernisse? *[In German]*; [The way towards European monetary union — are there insurmountable obstacles?] *[Summary]*. Norbert Berthold. *Aussenwirtschaft* **47:2** 7:1992 pp. 175 – 205

68 What has held the Australian dollar up? Tom Valentine. *Ec. Pap. Aust.* **11:2** 6:1992 pp. 32 – 46

69 Why are Japanese industries immune to devaluation of the dollar? Chong K. Liew; Chung J. Liew. *Econ. Sys. Res.* **4:2** 1992 pp. 189 – 200

70 Will an EC currency harm outsiders? Richard N. Cooper. *Orbis* **36:4** Fall:1992 pp. 517 – 529

O.2.4: International monetary relations — *Relations monétaires internationales*

1 Arab-European monetary relations and the emergence of the single European market. Osama Faquih. *OPEC B.* **XXIII:2** 2:1992 pp. 9 – 15
2 Country experiences with IMF programmes in the 1980s. Tony Killick; Moazzam Malik. *World. Econ.* **15:5** 9:1992 pp. 599 – 632
3 Desirable rules of monetary coordination and intervention among a large number of countries — a new method to analyze the N-country world. Shin-ichi Fukuda. *Econ. S. Quart.* **43:3** 9:1992 pp. 230 – 245
4 Finance and the international economy. Richard O'Brien *[Ed.].* Oxford: Oxford University Press for the AMEX Bank Review, 1992: 160 p. *ISBN: 0198287968.* [AMEX Bank Review Prize Essays. : No. 6]
5 International Monetary Fund. Anne C.M. Salda *[Ed.].* Oxford: Clio Press, 1992: 295 p. *ISBN: 1851091491.* [International Organizations Series. : Vol. 4]
6 The International Monetary Fund and the dilemmas of adjustment in Eastern Europe — lessons from the 1980s and prospects for the 1990s. A. Henderson. *J. Int. Dev.* **4:3** 5-6:1992 pp. 245 – 271
7 The International Monetary Fund in the 1990s. A.D. Crockett. *Govt. Oppos.* **27:3** Summer:1992 pp. 267 – 282
8 International Monetary Fund lending and Third World sovereignty. Alison Brysk. *Curr. World Lead.* **35:6** 12:1992 pp. 1031 – 1052
9 Japan and the changing global financial order. Eric Helleiner. *Int. J.* **XLVII:2** Spring:1992 pp. 420 – 444
10 Ein „Konzert der Institutionen"? IWF, Weltbank und EBRD unter Koordinierungs- und Anpassungsdruck in Osteuropa *[In German]*; A "concert of institutions"? IMF, World Bank and EBRD under the necessity to coordinate and adapt in Eastern Europe *[Summary].* Philip v. Schoppenthau. *Ost. Wirt.* **37:4** 12:1992 pp. 309 – 330
11 Local versus global convergence across national economies. Steven N. Durlauf; Paul A. Johnson. London: LSE Financial Markets Group, 1992: 31 p. [LSE Financial Markets Group discussion paper series. : No. 131]
12 Official creditor seniority and burden-sharing in the former Soviet bloc. Jeremy Bulow; Kenneth Rogoff; Afonso S. Bevilaqua. *Brookings P.* **:1** 1992 pp. 195 – 221
13 Reaction of bank share prices to the Third-World debt reduction plan. J. Madura; A.L. Tucker; E. Zarruk. *J. Bank. Fin.* **16:5** 9:1992 pp. 853 – 868
14 The reconquest of India — the victory of international monetary fundamentalism. Jeremy Seabrook. *Race Class* **34:1** 7-9:1992 pp. 1 – 16
15 The role of the World Bank in sub-Saharan Africa in the 1980s. Asutosh Satpathy. *Afr. Q.* **31:1-2** 1991 pp. 59 – 75
16 The unique nature of the responsibilities of the International Monetary Fund. Manuel Guitián. Washington, DC: International Monetary Fund, 1992: v, 64 p. *ISBN: 1557752281. Includes bibliographical references (p.55-64).* [Pamphlet series — International Monetary Fund.]
17 Valuación de algunas opciones del ingreso argentino al Plan Brady *[In Spanish]*; [Valuation of some of the options for Argentine entry to the Brady Plan]. José-Luis Maia. *Monetaria* **XV:2** 4-6:1992 pp. 151 – 170
18 Die Vereinheitlichung der Bankenaufsicht in Europa *[In German]*; [The standardization of bank supervision in Europe]. Klaus-Peter Follak. *Bank-Archiv* **38** 3:1990 pp. 151 – 161
19 What can we know about the effects of IMF programmes? Tony Killick; Moazzam Malik; Marcus Manuel. *World. Econ.* **15:5** 9:1992 pp. 575 – 597
20 The World Bank and African poverty, 1973-91. Peter Gibbon. *J. Mod. Afr. S.* **30:2** 6:1992 pp. 193 – 220
21 The World Bank and education in Africa. Committee for Academic Freedom in Africa. *Race Class* **34:1** 7-9:1992 pp. 51 – 60

O.3: International trade — *Commerce international*

O.3.1: Theory — *Théorie*

1 After the Soviet Union — the international trading environment. David A. Dyker. London: Royal Institute of International Affairs, 1992: 33 p. [Post-Soviet Business Forum publication.]

2 The autonomy of trade elasticities — choice and consequences. Jaime R. Marquez. [Washington, D.C.]: Board of Governors of the Federal Reserve System, 1992: 36 p. [International finance discussion papers. : No. 422]

3 Cost differential and welfare effects on interventionist trade policies in oligopolistic international trade. S. Tsutsui. *Jpn. Wor. Econ.* **3:4** 4:1992 pp. 341 – 355

4 Countertrade revisited — the Nigerian experience. Michael I. Obadan. *OPEC Rev.* **XVI:2** Summer:1992 pp. 217 – 234

5 Countertrade transactions — theory and evidence. R.E. Caves; D. Marin. *Econ. J.* **102:414** 9:1992 pp. 1171 – 1183

6 Countervailing the effects of subsidies — an economic analysis. Joseph F. Francois. *J. World Tr.* **26:1** 2:1992 pp. 5 – 13

7 Declining hegemony and rising international trade — moving beyond hegemonic stability theory. Curtis Peet. *Int. Inter.* **18:2** 1992 pp. 101 – 127

8 Determinants of export performance of Bangladesh. Dilip Kumar Roy. *Bang. Dev. Stud.* **XIX:4** 12:1991 pp. 27 – 48

9 The determinants of West German exports of manufactures — an integrated demand and supply approach; *[German summary]*; *[French summary]*; *[Spanish summary]*. Michael Funke; Sean Holly. *Welt.liches Arc.* **128:3** 1992 pp. 498 – 512

10 Differential impacts of export expansion on economic growth in the LDCs — a comparison of evidences across regional income groups and between the decades of 1970s and 1980s. M.O. Odedokun. *E. Afr. Econ. Rev.* **7:2** 12:1991 pp. 69 – 93

11 Domestic market structure and international trade in an open economy. Don P. Clark; David L. Kaserman; Francois Melese. *Q Rev. Econ. Finan.* **32:3** Autumn:1992 pp. 3 – 15

12 Dynamique cyclique et stabilisation sous contrainte *[In French]*; Cyclical dynamics and stabilisation under conditions of constraint *[Summary]*; (Zyklische Dynamik und erzwungene Stabilisierung: *Title only in German)*; (Dinámica cíclica y estabilización con coacción: *Title only in Spanish*). Blaise Mukoko. *Econ. App.* **XLV:2** 7:1992 pp. 151 – 172

13 Econometric analysis of industrial country commodity exports. Manmohan S. Kumar. Washington, D.C.: International Monetary Fund, 1992: 29 p. [IMF working paper. : No. WP/92/4]

14 The economics of international trade — an independent view. David Z. Rich. New York: Quorum Books, 1992: viii, 206 p. *ISBN: 0899307531; LofC: 91033600. Includes bibliographical references (p.[199]-201) and index.*

15 Effect of export instability on economic growth in Africa. Augustin Kwasi Fosu. *J. Dev. Areas* **26:3** 4:1992 pp. 323 – 332

16 Effects of exchange rate risk on exports — crosscountry analysis. M. Bahmani-Oskooee; N. Ltaifa. *World Dev.* **20:8** 8:1992 pp. 1173 – 1181

17 Endogenous market structures in international trade (natura facit saltum). Ignatius J. Horstmann; James R. Markusen. *J. Int. Econ.* **32:1/2** 2:1992 pp. 109 – 130

18 Endogenous probability of protection and firm behavior. Ronald D. Fischer. *J. Int. Econ.* **32:1/2** 2:1992 pp. 149 – 164

19 Environmental and labour standards in trade. Steve Charnovitz. *World. Econ.* **15:3** 5:1992 pp. 335 – 356

20 Estrategias empresariales y desempeño exportador *[In Spanish]*; [Business strategies and export performance] *[Summary]*. Adriana Cassoni; Marcel Vaillant. *Revis. Econ.* **VI:1** 8:1991 pp. 15 – 76

21 Europe 1992 — the external trade implications. André Sapir. *Int. Econ. J.* **6:1** Spring:1992 pp. 1 – 16

22 Exchange rates, market structure, prices and imports. Anne Sibert. *Econ. Rec.* **68:202** 9:1992 pp. 233 – 239

O.3.1: Theory *[Théorie]*

23 Export growth and Canadian economic development. A. Serletis. *J. Dev. Econ.* **38:1** 1:1992 pp. 133 – 145

24 Exportables, importables and the terms of trade. Tony Makin. *Ec. Pap. Aust.* **11:1** 3:1992 pp. 42 – 52

25 Exports and economic growth in developing countries — the case of Latin America; Esportazioni e crescita economica nei paesi in via di sviluppo — il caso dell'America Latina *[Italian summary]*. Jong H. Park. *Rev. Int. Sci. Ec. Com.* **XXXIX:3** 3:1992 pp. 239 – 258

26 External imbalances and policy constraints in the 1990s — papers of the Fifteenth Annual Conference of the International Economics Study Group. Chris Milner *[Ed.]*; P.N. Snowden *[Ed.]*. New York: St. Martin's Press, 1992: 300 p. *ISBN: 0312079788; LofC: 92002783. Conference held at the University of Nottingham in 1990; Includes bibliographical references and index.*

27 Facteurs spécifiques, changements de techniques et spécialisation internationale *[In French]*; Specific factors, technical changes and international trade *[Summary]*. D. Delgay-Troïse. *Rev. Ec. Polit.* **102:4** 7-8:1992 pp. 545 – 561

28 Factor mobility, trade and welfare — a North-South analysis with economies of scale. A. Panagariya. *J. Dev. Econ.* **39:2** 10:1992 pp. 229 – 245

29 The fallacy of composition argument — is it relevant for LDCs' manufactures exports? R. Faini; F. Clavijo; A. Senhadji-Semlali. *Eur. Econ. R.* **36:4** 5:1992 pp. 865 – 882

30 Finland and the new international division of labour. Kimmo Kiljunen. London: Mcmillan, 1992: 240 p. *ISBN: 0333458818.*

31 First and second-best factor comparative advantages and international trade. Roy J. Ruffin. *Economica* **59:236** 11:1992 pp. 453 – 463

32 Fiscal policy, specialization, and trade in the two-sector model — the return of Ricardo? Marianne Baxter. *J. Polit. Ec.* **100:4** 8:1992 pp. 713 – 744

33 Fiscal policy, the terms of trade, and the external balance. Atish R. Ghosh. *J. Int. Econ.* **33:1/2** 8:1992 pp. 105 – 125

34 Foreign trade reforms and development strategy. Jean-Marc Fontaine *[Ed.]*. London: Routledge, 1992: 304 p. *ISBN: 0415072948.*

35 Free international trade and protection of the environment — irreconcilable conflict? Thomas J. Schoenbaum. *Am. J. Int. Law* **86:4** 10:1992 pp. 700 – 727

36 Global shakeout — world market competition - the challenges for business and government. Louis Turner; Michael Hodges. London: Century Business, 1992: 234 p. *ISBN: 0091748097.*

37 Global trade prospects for the developing countries. Anne O. Krueger. *World. Econ.* **15:4** 7:1992 pp. 457 – 474

38 Growth and trade prospects for Central and Eastern Europe. J.M.C. Rollo; J. Stern. *World. Econ.* **15:5** 9:1992 pp. 645 – 668

39 A Heckscher-Ohlin approach to changing comparative advantage in Singapore's manufacturing sector; *[German summary]*; *[French summary]*; *[Spanish summary]*. Lin-Yeok Tan. *Welt.liches Arc.* **128:2** 1992 pp. 288 – 309

40 The impact of oil price shocks and exchange rate changes on import demand elasticities; *[German summary]*; *[French summary]*; *[Spanish summary]*. Joachim Zietz. *Welt.liches Arc.* **128:2** 1992 pp. 237 – 248

41 Imports, output and the demand for manufactures. Bob Anderton; Bahram Pesaran; Simon Wren-Lewis. *Ox. Econ. Pap.* **44:2** 4:1992 pp. 175 – 186

42 International competitiveness and specialization. O. Mandeng. *CEPAL R.* **:45** 12:1991 pp. 25 – 40

43 International trade and Cournot equilibrium — existence, uniqueness and comparative statics. David Collie. *B. Econ. Res.* **44:1** 1:1992 pp. 55 – 66

44 International trade and factor intensity uniformity — an empirical assessment; *[German summary]*; *[French summary]*; *[Spanish summary]*. Bruce Elmslie; William Milberg. *Welt.liches Arc.* **128:3** 1992 pp. 464 – 486

45 International trade modelling. Marcel G. Dagenais *[Ed.]*; Pierre Alain Muet *[Ed.]*. London: Chapman & Hall, 1992: 357 p. *BNB: 91034278; LofC: 91034278. Includes bibliographical references and index.* [International studies in economic modelling.]

46 Interstate differences in relative export performance — a test of factor endowments theory. Rodney A. Erickson; David J. Hayward. *Geogr. Anal.* **24:3** 7:1992 pp. 223 – 239

47 Judging factor abundance. Harry P. Bowen; Leo Sveikauskas. *Q. J. Econ.* **CVII:2** 5:1992 pp. 599 – 620

O.3.1: Theory *[Théorie]*

48 Matching product category and country image perceptions — a framework for managing country-of-origin effects. Martin S. Roth; Jean B. Romeo. *J. Int. Bus. Stud.* **23:3** Third quarter:1992 pp. 477 – 497

49 Measurable dynamic gains from trade. Richard E. Baldwin. *J. Polit. Ec.* **100:1** 2:1992 pp. 162 – 174

50 Measure and interpretation of effective protection in the presence of high capital costs — evidence from India. Francois M. Ettori. Washington, D.C.: Country Department IV, Asia Regional Office, The World Bank, 1992: 11 p. [Policy research working papers.]

51 Measurement of net import substitution in the food and fibre and manufacturing sectors of Pakistan's economy. Abdul Qayyum Khan. *Econ. Sys. Res.* **4:3** 1992 pp. 269 – 274

52 Modelling imports when variables are stochastically trending. Nicholas G. Zonzilos. *Gr. Econ. Rev.* **13:2** 12:1991 pp. 269 – 286

53 New economic principles in America — competition and cooperation — a comparative study of the U.S. and Japan. Kosaku Yoshida. *Columb. J. W. Bus.* **XXVI:4** Winter:1992 pp. 30 – 44

54 Nouvelle actualité de la théorie weillérienne de l'échange international *[In French]*; Recent development of Jean Weiller's contribution to the theory of international trade *[Summary]*; Aktuelles Interesse an der Weiller'schen Theorie des Welthandels *[In German]*; La nueva actualidad de la teoría weilleriana del intercambio internacional *[In Spanish]*. B. Carrier. *Econ. App.* **XLV:1** 1992 pp. 129 – 140

55 Opening up international trade with Eastern Europe. Carl B. Hamilton; L. Alan Winters. *Econ. Pol.* **:14** 4:1992 pp. 77 – 116

56 Production, foreign trade, and global curvature conditions — Switzerland, 1948-1988; *[French summary]*; *[German summary]*. Ulrich Kohli. *Schw. Z. Volk. Stat.* **128:1** 3:1992 pp. 3 – 20

57 Rethinking international trade theory — a methodological appraisal; *[German summary]*; *[French summary]*; *[Spanish summary]*. Terrence Bensel; Bruce T. Elmslie. *Welt.liches Arc.* **128:2** 1992 pp. 249 – 265

58 Ricardo's international trade theory — beyond the comparative cost example. Andrea Maneschi. *Camb. J. Econ.* **16:4** 12:1992 pp. 421 – 437

59 Rival capitalists — international competitiveness in the United States, Japan, and Western Europe. Jeffrey A. Hart. Ithaca, NY.: Cornell University Press, 1992: 305 p. *ISBN: 0801426499; LofC: 92052757. Includes bibliographical references and index.* [Cornell studies in political economy.]

60 Rivals beyond trade — America versus Japan in global competition. Dennis J. Encarnation. Ithaca: Cornell University Press, 1992: xvi, 222 p. (ill) *ISBN: 0801427339; LofC: 91057900. Includes bibliographical references and index.* [Cornell studies in political economy.]

61 Strategic trade theory in the context of small, less developed countries — some considerations. Ronald Ramkissoon. *J. World Tr.* **26:3** 6:1992 pp. 73 – 84

62 Structure and dynamics of the global economy — network analysis of international trade 1965-1980. David A. Smith; Douglas R. White. *Soc. Forc.* **70:4** 6:1992 pp. 857 – 893

63 The structure of Swedish international trade and specialization — "old" and "new" explanations; *[German summary]*; *[French summary]*; *[Spanish summary]*. Lars Lundberg. *Welt.liches Arc.* **128:2** 1992 pp. 266 – 287

64 A systems approach to the demand for imports and domestic output in the UK. Nigel Pain; Bob Anderton; Peter Westaway. London: National Institute of Economic and Social Research, 1992: 30 p. [Discussion paper.]

65 Tariffs, terms of trade, unemployment and the real exchange rate. Bharat R. Hazari; Sisira Jayasuriya; Pasquale M. Sgro. *S. Econ. J.* **58:3** 1:1992 pp. 721 – 731

66 Teoria normativa del commercio internazionale — un riesame critico *[In Italian]*; The normative theory of international trade. A reappraisal *[Summary]*. Tito Cordella. *Industria* **XIII:4** 10-12:1992 pp. 597 – 621

67 Terms of trade disturbances, real exchange rates, and welfare — the role of capital controls and labor market distortions. Sebastian Edwards; Jonathan Ostry. *Ox. Econ. Pap.* **44:1** 1:1992 pp. 20 – 34

68 Terms of trade fluctuation and stabilization of producer prices by compensatory taxation. J.-P. Azam. *Eur. Econ. R.* **36:1** 1:1992 pp. 101 – 118

69 The threats to the world trading system. Jagdish Bhagwati. *World. Econ.* **15:4** 7:1992 pp. 443 – 456

O.3.1: Theory *[Théorie]*
70 Trade and protection in vertically related markets. Barbara J. Spencer; Ronald W. Jones. *J. Int. Econ.* **32:1/2** 2:1992 pp. 31 – 56
71 Trade liberalisation with imperfect competition — the large and the small of it. T.T. Nguyen; R.M. Wigle. *Eur. Econ. R.* **36:1** 1:1992 pp. 17 – 36
72 Trade patterns and gains from trade with an intermediate good produced under increasing returns to scale. Jota Ishikawa. *J. Int. Econ.* **32:1/2** 2:1992 pp. 57 – 82
73 The value-added chain approach as a method of assessing business strategies — case — the Finnish food-processing industry. Leo Vilen. Helsinki: Helsinki School of Economics and Business Administration, 1991: 176 p. *ISBN: 9517008708. Includes bibliographical references (p. 168-176).* [Helsingin kauppakorkeakoulun julkaisuja. B. : No. 108]
74 De visie van Keynes op de internationale handel en het protectionisme — een actueel dilemma? *[In Dutch]*; [Keynes' view on international trade and protectionism — a current dilemma]. Fr. Buelens. *Maan. Econ.* **56:1** 1992 pp. 6 – 23
75 Wybrane problemy handlu światowego *[In Polish]*; [Problems of world trade]. Bogdan Mirosław Buczkowski *[Contrib.]*; Janina Dzikowska-Zawirska *[Contrib.]*; Wiesława Włodarczyk-Guzek *[Contrib.]*; Jerzy Nacewski *[Contrib.]*; Jolanta Osowska *[Contrib.]*; Maciej Stalmaszczyk *[Contrib.]*; Marek Kudła *[Contrib.]*; Aleksander Legatowicz *[Contrib.]*; Mirosław F. Zieliński *[Contrib.]*; Andrzej Miciński *[Contrib.] and others. Collection of 9 articles.* **Acta Univ. Łódz.** , *116*, 1992 pp. 5 – 152

O.3.2: Foreign trade relations — *Relations commerciales internationales*

1 Agriculture and trade in the Pacific — toward the twenty-first century. William T. Coyle *[Ed.]*; Dermot James Hayes *[Ed.]*; Hiroshi Yamauchi *[Ed.]*. Boulder: Westview Press, 1992: 344 p. *ISBN: 0813382777; LofC: 91048043. Includes index.*
2 The American Pacific — from the old China trade to the present. Arthur Power Dudden. New York: Oxford University Press, 1992: xi, 314 p. *ISBN: 0195058216; LofC: 91017372. Includes bibliographical references (p. 273-292) and index.*
3 An analysis of the growth of Jordan's balance of trade deficit. Charles R. Chittle; Wassel Al-Mashagbeh. *J. Bus. Soc.* **5:1-2** 1992 pp. 18 – 32
4 Eine asymmetrische, dynamische Importfunktion für die deutschen Kraftfahrzeugimporte *[In German]*; [An asymmetric, dynamic import function for German automobile imports] *[Summary]*. Horst Kräger. *Jahr. Soz.schaft.* **43:1** 1992 pp. 130 – 140
5 The Atlantic economy after German unification — cooperation or the rise of "fortress Europe". James Sperling. *Ger. Pol.* **1:2** 8:1992 pp. 200 – 222
6 Der Außenhandel der neuen deutschen Bundesländer mit Osteuropa *[In German]*; [Eastern Germany's foreign trade with Eastern Europe]. Klaus Werner. *Wirtschaftsdienst* **72:4** 4:1992 pp. 206 – 214
7 Banana libre *[In Spanish]*; [Banana trade]. Alvaro Martínez Cuenca. Managua, Nicaragua: Editorial Nueva Nicaragua, [1991]: 212 p. (ill) *ISBN: oc25486136. Includes bibliographical references.*
8 Britain's trade in invisibles. R. Ayres. *Br. Rev. Ec. Iss.* **14:32** 2:1992 pp. 1 – 36
9 Buyer-seller links in export development. M.L. Egan; A. Mody. *World Dev.* **20:3** 3:1992 pp. 321 – 334
10 Can a manufactured good cease to be a manufactured good merely by crossing a national frontier? Alexander J. Yeats. *B. Econ. Res.* **44:3** 7:1992 pp. 199 – 220
11 Canadian adjustment to trade with developing countries — the case of the textile and clothing sectors — prepared for the North-South Institute's project on "Canada's commercial relations with developing countries into the 1990s". Tim Hazledine; Bernard Lapointe. [Ottawa]: The Institue, 1991: v, 50 p. *ISBN: 0921942338; LofC: cn 91090463. Includes bibliographical references — p. 49-50.*
12 Capital markets and trade — the United States faces a united Europe. Mark Perlman *[Ed.]*; Claude E. Barfield *[Ed.]*. Washington, D.C.: AEI Press, 1991: 311 p. *ISBN: 0844737518.* [AEI studies. : No. 522]
13 Casting blame, erecting barriers — U.S.-Japan trade conflicts. James Bovard. *Ter. Nova* **1:3** Spring (North), Autumn (South):1992 pp. 5 – 19
14 The changing role of oil in Chinese exports, 1974-89. Larry Chuen-ho Chow. *China Quart.* **:131** 9:1992 pp. 750 – 765

O.3.2: Foreign trade relations *[Relations commerciales internationales]*

15 China's exports since 1979. Hong Wang. New York, NY.: St. Martin's Press, 1992: 262 p. *ISBN: 0312083971; LofC: 92009325. Includes bibliographical references and index.* [Studies on the Chinese economy.]

16 Chinese foreign trade. Nicholas R. Lardy. *China Quart.* :**131** 9:1992 pp. 691 – 720

17 Coffee — the political economy of an export industry in Papua New Guinea. Randal G. Stewart. Boulder: Westview Press, 1992: x, 316 p. *ISBN: 0813385253; LofC: 91037452. Includes bibliographical references (p. [287]-309) and index.*

18 Commodities in crisis — the commodity crises of the 1980s and the political economy of international commodity policies. Alfred Maizels. Oxford: Clarendon Press, 1992: 307 p. *ISBN: 0198283873; LofC: 91026887. "A study prepared for the World Institute for Development Economics Research (WIDER) of the United Nations University." ; Includes bibliographical references and index.* [Studies in development economics.]

19 The competitive consequences of Japan's export cartel associations. Andrew R. Dick. *J. Jap. Int. Ec.* **6:3** 9:1992 pp. 275 – 298

20 Contrasting US and German attitudes to Soviet trade, 1917-91 — politics by economic means. Hélène Seppain. New York, NY.: St. Martin's Press, 1992: 349 p. *ISBN: 0312079761; LofC: 92006810. Includes bibliographical references and index.*

21 Curbing Beijing's arms sales. R. Bates Gill. *Orbis* **36:3** Summer:1992 pp. 379 – 396

22 The current account and the budget deficit in an interdependent world. L. Bosco. *Eur. J. Pol. Ec.* **8:2** 5:1992 pp. 213 – 230

23 The determinants of intra-industry trade — the case of the automobile industry; Die Bestimmungsgründe für den intra-industriellen Handel. Der Fall der Automobilindustrie *[German summary]*; Les déterminants du commerce intra-branche — le cas du secteur de l'automobile *[French summary]*; Las determinantes del comercio intraindustrial — el caso de la industria automotriz *[Spanish summary]*. Stéphane Becuwe; Claude Mathieu. *Welt.liches Arc.* **128:1** 1992 pp. 34 – 51

24 Devaluation, national output and the trade balance — some evidence from Colombia; *[German summary]*; *[French summary]*; *[Spanish summary]*. Linda Kamas. *Welt.liches Arc.* **128:3** 1992 pp. 425 – 445

25 Disarray in world food markets — a quantitative assessment. Rodney Tyers; Kym Anderson. Cambridge: Cambridge University Press, 1992: 444 p. *ISBN: 0521351057; LofC: 91037329. Includes bibliographical references and index.* [Trade and development.]

26 EC bananarama 1992. Brent Borrell; Maw-Cheng Yang. *Develop. Eco.* **XXX:3** 9:1992 pp. 259 – 283

27 Economic aspects of North-South interaction — analytical macroeconomic issues. Syed Mansoob Murshed. London: Academic Press, 1992: 202 p. *ISBN: 0125120702.*

28 Economic development and international transactions in services. Bernard Hoekman; Guy Karsenty. *Dev. Pol. R.* **10:3** 9:1992 pp. 211 – 236

29 Effects of foreign direct investment on trade flows — the case of Greece; Effetti degli investimenti diretti esteri sui flussi commerciali — il caso della Grecia *[Italian summary]*. Dimitrios Kyrkilis; Pantelis Pantelidis. *Rev. Int. Sci. Ec. Com.* **XXXIX:4** 4:1992 pp. 365 – 373

30 European presence in Japan. Maurice Bourène *[Contrib.]*; CEC Japan *[Contrib.]*; Philippe Debroux *[Contrib.]*; Ali M. El Agraa *[Contrib.]*; Masumi Hakogi *[Contrib.]*; Constantin Kinias *[Contrib.]*; Wolfgang Pape *[Contrib.]*; Margarete Sawada *[Contrib.]*; Arie van der Steenhoven *[Contrib.]*. *Collection of 9 articles.* **Gestion** , *8:5*, 1992 pp. 17 – 190

31 Exchange rates, pass-through, and Canadian export competitiveness — an analysis using vector autoregressions. D.W. Rockerbie. *Appl. Econ.* **24:6** 6:1992 pp. 627 – 634

32 A gazdasági nöekedés külgazdasági összefüggései *[In Hungarian]*; Foreign trade interrelations of economic growth *[Summary]*. Béla Káddár. *Közg. Sz.* **XXXIX** 10:1992 pp. 934 – 945

33 Growth and instability of Latin American primary commodity exports to the EC; Crescita e instabilità delle esportazioni latinoamericane di prodotti primari alla CE *[Italian summary]*. Stefano Mainardi. *Rev. Int. Sci. Ec. Com.* **XXXIX:9** 9:1992 pp. 807 – 822

34 High-technology exports of EEC countries — persistence and diversity of specialization patterns. E. Papagni. *Appl. Econ.* **24:8** 8:1992 pp. 925 – 933

35 Holes and loopholes in regional trade arrangements and the multilateral trading system; *[German summary]*. Bernard M. Hoekman; Michael P. Leidy. *Scot. J. Poli.* **47:III** 1992 pp. 325 – 360

36 Hungary — foreign trade in a transitional economy. Karen Bahnick. *Eur. Bus. Econ. Develop.* **1:3** 11:1992 pp. 18 – 23

O.3.2: Foreign trade relations *[Relations commerciales internationales]*

37 Hungary's export prospects in the EC market. A. Tovias; S. Laird. *Open Econ. R.* **3:2** 1992 pp. 181 – 202

38 The improvement in Indonesia's real resource balance, 1986-89 — absorption, switching and growth effects. M.L. Treadgold; E.M. Treadgold. *B. Ind. Econ. St.* **28:3** 12:1992 pp. 93 – 106

39 International economic interdependence, patterns of trade balances and economic policy coordination. Mario Baldassarri *[Ed.]*; Luigi Paganetto *[Ed.]*; Edmund S. Phelps *[Ed.]*. New York: St. Martin's Press in association with Rivista di Politica Economica, SIPI, Rome, 1992: 441 p. *ISBN: 0312079834; LofC: 92000044. Includes index.* [Central issues in contemporary economic theory and policy.]

40 International economic interdependence and export development — the case of Chile. Alejandra Mizala. *CEPAL R.* **:46** 4:1992 pp. 151 – 176

41 International trade relations and regional industrial adjustment — the implications of the 1982-86 Canadian-US softwood lumber dispute for British Columbia. R. Hayter. *Envir. Plan.A.* **24:1** 1:1992 pp. 153 – 170

42 International transfers and defense expenditures in allied and adversarial relationship — Japan and the United States. T. Ihori. *Jpn. Wor. Econ.* **4:2** 9:1992 pp. 89 – 101

43 The internationalization of the German political economy — evolution of a hegemonic project. William David Graf *[Ed.]*. New York: St. Martin's Press, 1992: 358 p. *ISBN: 0312080999; LofC: 92003189. Includes index.* [International political economy series.]

44 Intertemporal prices and the U.S. trade balance. Michael C. Burda; Stefan Gerlach. *Am. Econ. Rev.* **82:5** 12:1992 pp. 1234 – 1253

45 Intra-industry trade in manufactured products between the European Economic Community and the Eastern European countries. Dimitri Mardas. *J. World Tr.* **26:5** 10:1992 pp. 5 – 23

46 Intra-industry trade — the Australian experience. R. Ratnayake; P. Athukorala. *Int. Econ. J.* **6:4** Winter:1992 pp. 47 – 62

47 Like-minded nations and contrasting diplomatic styles — Australian and Canadian approaches to agricultural trade; *[French summary]*. Andrew Fenton Cooper. *Can. J. Poli.* **XXV:2** 6:1992 pp. 349 – 379

48 The limits to globalization — technology districts and international trade. Michael Storper. *Econ. Geogr.* **68:1** 1:1992 pp. 60 – 93

49 The Maquilas in Mexico — a global perspective. Leslie Sklair. *B. Lat. Am. Res.* **11:1** 1:1992 pp. 91 – 107

50 Measuring the degree of market power exerted by government trade agencies. H. Alan Love; Endah Murniningtyas. *Am. J. Agr. Ec.* **74:3** 8:1992 pp. 546 – 555

51 Nontraditional agricultural exports in Latin America. Bradford Barham; Mary Clark; Elizabeth Katz; Rachel Schurman. *Lat. Am. Res. R.* **27:2** 1992 pp. 43 – 82

52 On the design of invoicing practices in international trade. J.-M. Viaene; C.G. de Vries. *Open Econ. R.* **3:2** 1992 pp. 133 – 142

53 OPEC natural gas exports — past, present and future. Simon Adewole. *OPEC Rev.* **XVI:1** Spring:1992 pp. 71 – 94

54 Perspectives on tourism policy. Barry Thomas *[Ed.]*; P.S. Johnson *[Ed.]*. London: Mansell, 1992: 240 p. *ISBN: 0720121213; LofC: 91031208. Includes bibliographical references and index.*

55 Political implications of illegal arms exports from the United States. Edward J. Laurance. *Pol. Sci. Q.* **107:3** Fall:1992 pp. 501 – 533

56 The potential for an export-oriented growth strategy in Central Europe. Harry Oldersma; Peter A.G. van Bergeijk. *J. World Tr.* **26:4** 8:1992 pp. 47 – 63

57 The power of the cultural element in international trade — learning from American weaknesses in exporting to China. Pavlos Michaels. *J. Bus. Soc.* **5:1-2** 1992 pp. 33 – 44

58 Produktionsstruktur und Außenhandelsverflechtung der Nachfolgestaaten der Sowjetunion *[In German]*; [Production structure and foreign trade interrelationships between the former states of the Soviet Union]. Matthias Lücke. *Weltwirt.* **:3** 1992 pp. 317 – 337

59 Qatar prepares to move into gas export market.*OPEC B.* **XXIII:8** 9:1992 pp. 20 – 33

60 R&D reactions to high-technology import competition. F.M. Scherer; Keun Huh. *Rev. Econ. St.* **LXXIV:2** 5:1992 pp. 202 – 212

61 Rearranging the deck chairs — a political economy approach to foreign policy management in Canada; *[French summary]*. Ernie Keenes. *Can. Publ. Ad.* **35:3** Fall:1992 pp. 381 – 401

62 Regional trade arrangements. Augusto de la Torre; Margaret R. Kelly. Washington, D.C.: International Monetary Fund, 1992: 54 p. *ISBN: 1557752273.* [Occasional paper.]

O.3.2: Foreign trade relations *[Relations commerciales internationales]*

63 Regionalization of trade in the Asia-Pacific — a statistical approach. Torsten Amelung. *ASEAN Ec. B.* **9:2** 11:1992 pp. 133 – 148

64 Les relations économiques entre la CEE et les pays du Maghreb *[In French]*; [Economic relations between the EC and the countries of the Maghreb]. Benoît Parisot; Louis Blin. *Ann. Afr. Nord* **XXVIII** 1990 pp. 57 – 98

65 The response of UK retailers to the single European market. David G. Mayes; Alan Shipman. London: National Institute of Economic and Social Research, 1992: 62 p. [Discussion paper.]

66 Returns to scale, imperfect competition and aggregate demand and trade policy effects in a two-country model. H. Molana; T. Moutos. *Open Econ. R.* **3:3** 1992 pp. 271 – 296

67 Revision to the components of the trade balance for the United Kingdom. K.D. Patterson. *Ox. B. Econ. S.* **54:1** 2:1992 pp. 103 – 120

68 Risk sharing markets and international trade; Risikomärkte und internationaler Handel *[German summary]*. Udo Broll; Jack Wahl. *Jahrb. N. St.* **210:1-2** 7:1992 pp. 64 – 71

69 Salient features of trade among former Soviet Union republics — facts, flaws and findings. Rolf J. Langhammer. *Aussenwirtschaft* **47:2** 7:1992 pp. 253 – 276

70 Short changed — Africa and world trade. Michael Barratt Brown; Pauline Tiffen; Susan George *[Foreword]*. London: Pluto Press, 1992: 220 p. *ISBN: 0745306993.*

71 South-south trade and development — manufacturers in the new international division of labour. Steen Folke; Niels Fold; Thyge Enevoldsen. New York: St. Martin's Press, 1992: 267 p. *ISBN: 0312083726; LofC: 92009127. Includes bibliographical references and index.*

72 Structural roots of U.S. trade problems — income elasticities, secular trends, and hysteresis. Robert A. Blecker. *J. Post. Keyn. Ec.* **14:3** Spring:1992 pp. 321 – 346

73 Trade and the poor — the impact of international trade on developing countries. John Madeley. London: Intermediate Technology Pubs, 1992: 209 p. *ISBN: 1853391212.*

74 Trade experience of Indian agriculture — behaviour of net export supply functions for dominant commodities. V. Ratna Reddy; K. Badri Narayanan. *Ind. J. Agri. Eco.* **XLVII:1** 1-3:1992 pp. 48 – 61

75 Trade patterns and trends in the African-European trading area — lessons for sub-Saharan Africa from the era of the Lome accords 1975-1988; *[French summary]*. Lawrence M. Sommers; Assefa Mehretu. *Afr. Devel.* **XVII:2** 1992 pp. 5 – 26

76 Trade performance of the main EC economies relative to the USA and Japan in 1992-sensitive sectors. Kirsty S. Hughes. *J. Com. Mkt. S.* **XXX:4** 12:1992 pp. 437 – 454

77 Trade relationship between Australia and Middle Eastern countries. M.M. Metwally; R. Vadlamudi. *M.East Bus. Econ. R.* **4:2** 7:1992 pp. 6 – 13

78 Trade wars — Japan versus the West. Phillip Oppenheim. London: Weidenfeld & Nicolson, 1992: 241 p. *ISBN: 029782144x.*

79 Trade, payments and adjustments in Central and Eastern Europe. John Flemming *[Ed.]*; J.M.C. Rollo *[Ed.]*. London: Royal Institute of International Affairs, 1992: 242 p. *ISBN: 0905031504.*

80 U.K. exports of manufacturers — testing for the effects of non-price competitiveness using stochastic trends and profitability measures. R. Anderton. *Manch. Sch. E.* **LX:1** 3:1992 pp. 23 – 40

81 United States demand for Indonesian plywood. Ida-Bagus Parthama; Jeffrey R. Vincent. *B. Ind. Econ. St.* **28:1** 4:1992 pp. 101 – 112

82 Urban tourism and its contribution to economic regeneration. Christopher M. Law. *Urban Stud.* **29:3-4** 5:1992 pp. 599 – 618

83 US-Japan trade relations — the ASEAN dimension. Richard Stubbs. *Pac. Rev.* **5:1** 1992 pp. 60 – 67

84 The visible hand — the United States, Japan, and the management of trade disputes. Renée Marlin-Bennett; Alan Rosenblatt; Jianxin Wang. *Int. Inter.* **17:3** 1992 pp. 191 – 214

85 Whither long-term Canada-U.S. natural gas trade? A view from the (modelling) trenches. John Rowse. *Socio. Econ.* **26:1** 1992 pp. 43 – 55

86 Zur Veränderung des ostdeutschen Handels mit Stahl und stahlhaltigen Gütern — Druck aus dem Westen, Rückzug im Osten *[In German]*; [On the changes in eastern German trade in steel and goods containing steel — western pressure, eastern retreat] *[Summary]*; *[French summary]*. Helmut Wienert; Hans-Karl Starke. *RWI-Mitt.* **43:1** 1992 pp. 41 – 60

O.3.3: Foreign trade policies — *Politique du commerce extérieur*
Sub-divisions: Dumping *[Dumping]*; GATT *[GATT]*; Protectionism *[Protectionnisme]*

1 Agricultural impediments to global free trade. Jean-Marc Lucq. *Ter. Nova* **1:3** Spring (North), Autumn (South):1992 pp. 39 – 46
2 Alternative quota and VER allocation schemes — a welfare comparison. Mordechai E. Kreinin; Elias Dinopoulos. *Economica* **59:235** 8:1992 pp. 337 – 350
3 Are economists' traditional trade policy views still valid? Robert E. Baldwin. *J. Econ. Lit.* **XXX:2** 6:1992 pp. 804 – 829
4 Assessing the fair trade and safeguards laws in terms of modern trade and political economy analysis. Robert E. Baldwin. *World. Econ.* **15:2** 3:1992 pp. 185 – 202
5 Beyond import substitution and export promotion — a new typology of trade strategies. Neng Liang. *J. Dev. Stud.* **28:3** 4:1992 pp. 447 – 472
6 China's foreign trade behaviour in the 1980's — an empirical analysis. Adi Brender. Washington, D.C.: International Monetary Fund, 1992: 60 p. *Bibliography — p.57-60.* [IMF working paper. : No. WP/92/5]
7 Comercio, apertura, y desarrollo — casos seleccionados *[In Spanish]*; [Trade, liberalization and development — case studies]. Manuel R. Agosin *[Contrib.]*; Ricardo Ffrench-Davis *[Contrib.]*; Patricio Leiva *[Contrib.]*; Roberto Madrid *[Contrib.]*; Adriaan Ten Kate *[Contrib.]*; Fernando de Mateo *[Contrib.]*; Mario Damill *[Contrib.]*; Saúl Keifman *[Contrib.]*; Winston Fritsch *[Contrib.]*; Gustavo H.B. Franco *[Contrib.] and others*. *Collection of 11 articles.* **Pen. Iber.** , *21*, 1-6:1992 pp. 9 – 257
8 Comparing quotas with VERs — a three-region, North-South NICs macroeconomic analysis. S.M. Murshed. *Open Econ. R.* **3:3** 1992 pp. 255 – 270
9 Conceptual issues in the design of trade policy for industrialization. D. Rodrik. *World Dev.* **20:3** 3:1992 pp. 309 – 320
10 Conflict among nations — trade policies in the 1990s. Thomas R. Howell *[Ed.]*; et al. Boulder: Westview Press, 1992: xiv, 633 p. *ISBN: 0813312558; LofC: 92003846. Includes bibliographical references and index.* [Economic competition among nations].
11 The customs union issue reopened. Paul Wonnacott; Ronald Wonnacott. *Manch. Sch. E.* **LX:2** 6:1992 pp. 119 – 135
12 Des mécanismes de paiement pour les échanges entre les Républiques de l'ex-URSS *[In French]*; New payments mechanisms for trade between the Republics of the former USSR *[Summary]*. Michel Aglietta. *Ec. Pros. Int.* **49:1** 1992 pp. 29 – 56
13 Diplomatic barriers to trade. Peter A.G. van Bergeijk. *Economist [Leiden]* **140:1** 1992 pp. 45 – 64
14 The discipline of imports — the case of Sweden. Pär Hansson. *Sc. J. Econ.* **94:4** 1992 pp. 589 – 597
15 Does the new trade theory require a new trade policy? Paul Krugman. *World. Econ.* **15:4** 7:1992 pp. 423 – 442
16 Dynamically consistent oil import tariffs; *[French summary]*. Larry Karp; David M. Newbery. *Can. J. Econ.* **XXV:1** 2:1992 pp. 1 – 21
17 Economic dependence and changes in Taiwan's trade policy, 1984-89. Yujen Chou. *Iss. Stud.* **28:1** 1:1992 pp. 96 – 118
18 Evaluation of trade policies in Peninsular Malaysia, 1965-85. Hooi Eng Phang. *Develop. Eco.* **XXX:2** 6:1992 pp. 117 – 131
19 Export controls in transition — perspectives, problems, and prospects. Gary K. Bertsch *[Ed.]*; Steven Elliott-Gower *[Ed.]*. Durham: Duke University Press, 1992: vi, 355 p. *ISBN: 0822311917; LofC: 91014463. Includes bibliographical references (p. [337]-341) and index.*
20 Export diversification strategies and community welfare. J. Love. *J. Int. Dev.* **4:5** 9-10:1992 pp. 531 – 540
21 Export response to trade reform — recent Mexican experience. John Weiss. *Dev. Pol. R.* **10:1** 3:1992 pp. 43 – 60
22 Export subsidies, entry deterrence and countervailing tariffs. David Collie. *Manch. Sch. E.* **LX:2** 6:1992 pp. 136 – 151
23 Foreign trade and economic reform in China, 1978-1990. Nicholas R. Lardy. Cambridge: Cambridge University press, 1992: x, 197 p. *ISBN: 0521414954; LofC: 91015693. Includes bibliographical references (p. [171]-189) and index.*

O.3.3: Foreign trade policies *[Politique du commerce extérieur]*

24 Fortress Europe — problems and prospects for Franco-Nigerian entente. Bola A. Akinterinwa. *J. Asian Afr. Aff.* **III:2** Spring:1992 pp. 123 – 145

25 Freiwillige Exportselbstbeschränkungsabkommen und internationale Wettbewerbsfähigkeit der europäischen Automobilindustrie *[In German]*; [Voluntary export restraints agreements and the international competitiveness of the European automobile industry] *[Summary]*. Heinz Gert Preuße. *Scot. J. Poli.* **47:III** 1992 pp. 361 – 388

26 Goals and own goals in European trade policy. L. Alan Winters. *World. Econ.* **15:5** 9:1992 pp. 557 – 574

27 Government, trade, and economic integration. Anne O. Krueger. *Am. Econ. Rev.* **82:2** 5:1992 pp. 109 – 114

28 How EC 1992 and reforms of the Common Agricutural Policy would affect developing countries' grain trade. Merlinda D. Ingco; Donald O. Mitchell. Washington, D.C.: International Economics Department, The World Bank, 1992: 35 p. [Policy research working papers.]

29 The impact of EC-92 on developing countries' trade — a dissenting view. Andrew Hughes Hallett. Washington, D.C.: International Economics Department, The World Bank, 1992: 41 p. [Policy research working papers.]

30 The impact of foreign patents on national economy — a case of the United States, Japan, Germany and Britain. M. Kotabe. *Appl. Econ.* **24:12** 12:1992 pp. 1335 – 1343

31 Import price adjustments with staggered import contracts. Tryphon Kollintzas; Ruilin Zhou. *J. Econ. Dyn. Cont.* **16:2** 4:1992 pp. 289 – 316

32 Increasing export diversification in commodity exporting countries — a theoretical analysis. Dean A. Derosa. *Staff Pap. Int. Monetary* **39:3** 9:1992 pp. 572 – 595

33 Indonesian trade reform in close-up — the steel and footwear experiences. Ross Chapman. *B. Ind. Econ. St.* **28:1** 4:1992 pp. 67 – 84

34 Input tariffs, duty drawbacks, and tariff reforms. Arvind Panagariya. *J. Int. Econ.* **32:1/2** 2:1992 pp. 131 – 148

35 International trade policy — benevolent dictators and optimizing politicians. A.L. Hillman. *Publ. Choice* **74:1** 7:1992 pp. 1 – 15

36 Interventionism, microeconomic reform and the external deficit. Tony Makin. *Aust. Ec. Rev.* **:1(97)** 1-3:1992 pp. 15 – 21

37 An investigation of the export expansion hypothesis. William L. Wilbur; Mohammed Z. Haque. *J. Dev. Stud.* **28:2** 1:1992 pp. 297 – 313

38 Is there a case for an optimal export tax on perennial crops? Takamasa Akiyama. Washington, D.C.: International Economics Department, The World Bank, 1992: 39 p. [Policy research working papers.]

39 Latin American integration and the Enterprise for the Americas Initiative. Eduardo Gitli; Gunilla Ryd. *J. World Tr.* **26:4** 8:1992 pp. 25 – 45

40 La libéralisation des relations économiques extérieures en Hongrie, Pologne et Tchécoslovaquie *[In French]*; The liberalization of foreign economic relations in Hungary, Poland and Czechoslovakia *[Summary]*. Petr Hanel. *Rev. Ét. Comp.* **23:1** 1992 pp. 77 – 108

41 Liberalization and industrialization — the Sri Lankan experience of the 1980s. Saman Kelegama. *S.Asia. J.* **5:3** 1-3:1992 pp. 251 – 287

42 Machine tool industry — the policy frame work. P.I. Suvrathan. *Ind. J. Eco.* **LXXII:286** 1:1992 pp. 281 – 300

43 Measuring trade policy intervention — a cross-country index of relative price dispersion. Brian J. Aitken. Washington, D.C.: Country Economics Department, The World Bank, 1992: 48 p. [Policy research working papers.]

44 A methodology for tariffication of commodity trade in the presence of quality differences — the case of peanuts. David G. Raboy; Teri Simpson. *World. Econ.* **15:2** 3:1992 pp. 271 – 282

45 The Multi-Fibre Arrangement and Eastern European trade in textiles and clothing. Refik Erzan; Christopher Holmes. *Yapi Kredi. Eco. Rev.* **5:2** 1:1992 pp. 3 – 40

46 Multilateral negotiations and trade barriers in service trade — a case study of U.S. shipping services. Neela Mukherjee. *J. World Tr.* **26:5** 10:1992 pp. 45 – 58

47 Multinational firms and the tariff-jumping argument — a game theoretic analysis with some unconventional conclusions. M. Motta. *Eur. Econ. R.* **36:8** 12:1992 pp. 1557 – 1571

48 The myth of export pessimism (even) under the MFA — evidence from Indonesia and Thailand; *[German summary]*; *[French summary]*; *[Spanish summary]*. Hal Hill; Suphat Suphachalasai. *Welt.liches Arc.* **128:2** 1992 pp. 310 – 329

O.3.3: Foreign trade policies *[Politique du commerce extérieur]*

49 National trade policies. Dominick Salvatore *[Ed.]*. Amsterdam: Greenwood Press, 1992: xvi, 574 p. *ISBN: 0313264899; LofC: gb 92041786. Includes bibliographical references and index.* [Studies in comparative economic policies. : Vol. 2]

50 Nonprimary exports of African LDCs — have trade preferences helped? Dale B. Truett; Lila J. Truett. *J. Dev. Areas* **26:4** 7:1992 pp. 457 – 473

51 Non-tariff measures and industrial nation imports of GSP-covered products. Don P. Clark; Simonetta Zarrilli. *S. Econ. J.* **59:2** 10:1992 pp. 284 – 293

52 Norges importrestriksjoner mot tredje verden — En gjennomgag og vurdering *[In Norwegian]*; Norway trade barriers against the Third World. An overview and an evaluation *[Summary]*. Carl-Erik Schulz. *Int. Pol.* **50:3** 1992 pp. 335 – 348

53 A note on the time inconsistency of strategic trade policy. P. Welzel. *Open Econ. R.* **3:2** 1992 pp. 203 – 214

54 On the theory of piecemeal tariff reform — the case of pure imported intermediate inputs. Ramón López; Arvind Panagariya. *Am. Econ. Rev.* **82:3** 6:1992 pp. 615 – 625

55 The optimal revenue tariffs for public input provision. J.P. Feehan. *J. Dev. Econ.* **38:1** 1:1992 pp. 221 – 231

56 Optimal tariffs and capital taxes when capital movements are sluggish — an extension and synthesis. Michael S. Michael; Stephen M. Miller. *Gr. Econ. Rev.* **13:1** 6:1991 pp. 157 – 165

57 Optimal trade policy in a distorted economy. T. Palokangas. *Eur. J. Pol. Ec.* **8:2** 5:1992 pp. 201 – 212

58 Optimum tariffs — North-South. C.C. Yang; Tzong-rong Tsai. *J. Int. Econ.* **32:3/4** 5:1992 pp. 369 – 378

59 Policy forum — trade and fiscal adjustment in developing countries. Rod Falvey *[Contrib.]*; Cha Dong Kim *[Contrib.]*; Paul Collier *[Contrib.]*; Jan Willem Gunning *[Contrib.]*; Christopher Bliss *[Contrib.]*. Collection of 3 articles. **Econ. J.** , *102:413*, 7:1992 pp. 906 – 951

60 The political economy of international market access. Robert E. Baldwin *[Contrib.]*; Douglas Nelson *[Contrib.]*; J. David Richardson; Thomas O. Bayard *[Contrib.]*; Kimberly A. Elliott *[Contrib.]*; Bernard Hoekman *[Contrib.]*; Michael Mastanduno *[Contrib.]*. Collection of 4 articles. **World. Econ.** , *15:6*, 11:1992 pp. 679 – 753

61 Problems of India's export promotion — an anxiety for social scientists. B.N.P. Singh. *Econ. Aff. [Calcutta]* **37:1** 1-3:1992 pp. 9 – 20

62 Protection and export performance in sub-Saharan Africa; Protektion und Exportleistung in Schwarzafrika *[German summary]*; La protection et les exportations en Afrique noire *[French summary]*; Protección y performance exportadora en el Africa del Sub-Sahara *[Spanish summary]*. Dean A. DeRosa. *Welt.liches Arc.* **128:1** 1992 pp. 88 – 124

63 Public sector marketing and production assistance to South Korea's manufacturing exporters — did it make a difference? Michael T. Rock. *Dev. Pol. R.* **10:4** 12:1992 pp. 339 – 357

64 Quantitative restrictions and tariffs with endogenous firm behavior. C. Syropoulos. *Eur. Econ. R.* **36:8** 12:1992 pp. 1627 – 1646

65 Quotas as commitment in Stackelberg trade equilibrium; Quoten als Selbstbindungsmechanismus im Stackelberg Handelsgleichgewicht *[German summary]*. Michael R. Baye. *Jahrb. N. St.* **209:1-2** 1:1992 pp. 20 – 30

66 Regional economic integration schemes in Southern Africa — options for independent Namibia. Nglla Mwase. *E. Afr. Econ. Rev.* **7:1** 6:1991 pp. 51 – 68

67 Regionalisation and world trade. Peter J. Lloyd. *OECD Ec. Stud.* **:18** Spring:1992 pp. 7 – 44

68 Restrictive trade practices — commentary and materials. Anne Hurley. North Ryde/NSW: Law Book Company, 1991: 615 p. *ISBN: 045521008x.*

69 Second-best rates of effective protection with imperfect substitution. Chris Milner. *J. Econ. Stud.* **19:1** 1992 pp. 3 – 13

70 The Southern African Customs Union in a changing economic and political environment. Colin McCarthy. *J. World Tr.* **26:4** 8:1992 pp. 5 – 24

71 State government promotion of manufacturing exports — a gap analysis. Masaaki Kotabe; Michael R. Czinkota. *J. Int. Bus. Stud.* **23:4** Fourth quarter:1992 pp. 637 – 658

72 The state, organized interests and Canadian agricultural trade policy — the impact of institutions; *[French summary]*. Grace Skogstad. *Can. J. Poli.* **XXV:2** 6:1992 pp. 319 – 347

73 Strategic trade practices in the presence of a VER. Judith M. Dean; Shubhashis Gangopadhyay. *Int. Econ. R.* **33:3** 8:1992 pp. 645 – 660

O.3.3: Foreign trade policies *[Politique du commerce extérieur]*

74 Sunk costs and trade liberalisation. M. Motta. *Econ. J.* **102:412** 5:1992 pp. 578 – 587

75 Supply management and import concessions; *[French summary]*. James Vercammen; Andrew Schmitz. *Can. J. Econ.* **XXV:4** 11:1992 pp. 957 – 971

76 Tariff design and reform in a revenue-constrained economy — theory and an illustration from India. Pradeep K. Mitra. *J. Publ. Ec.* **47:2** 3:1992 pp. 227 – 252

77 Tariff reform in a small open economy with public production. Kenzo Abe. *Int. Econ. R.* **33:1** 2:1992 pp. 209 – 222

78 Tax smoothing and tariff behavior in the United States. Grant W. Gardner; Kent P. Kimbrough. *J. Macro.* **14:4** Fall:1992 pp. 711 – 729

79 The terms-of-trade effects from the elimination of state trading in Soviet-Hungarian trade. Gabor Oblath; David Tarr. *J. Comp. Econ.* **16:1** 3:1992 pp. 75 – 93

80 Terms-of-trade uncertainty, incomplete markets and unemployment. Raquel Fernandez. *Int. Econ. R.* **33:4** 11:1992 pp. 881 – 894

81 Testing the efficiency of thin forward foreign exchange markets — an application of instrumental variable multiple regression with integrated, I(1), variables. Yerima L. Ngama. *Manch. Sch. E.* **LX:2** 6:1992 pp. 169 – 180

82 Trade liberalization and agricultural prices. Pasquale Lucio Scandizzo. *J. Policy M.* **14:5** 10:1992 pp. 561 – 582

83 Trade liberalization and economic stabilization in Mexico — lessons of experience. A. Ten Kate. *World Dev.* **20:5** 5:1992 pp. 659 – 672

84 Trade policy and exchange rate issues in the former Soviet Union. W.M. Corden. Washington, D.C.: Country Economics Department, The World Bank, 1992: 53 p. *Bibliography — p.52-53.* [Policy research working papers.]

85 Trade policy and the legalization of drugs. Martin Richardson. *S. Econ. J.* **58:3** 1:1992 pp. 655 – 670

86 Trade policy reform and performance in manufacturing — Mexico 1975-88. John Weiss. *J. Dev. Stud.* **29:1** 10:1992 pp. 1 – 23

87 Trade reform with quotas, partial rent retention, and tariffs. James E. Anderson; J. Peter Neary. *Econometrica* **60:1** 1:1992 pp. 57 – 76

88 Trade reform, policy uncertainty, and the current account — a non-expected-utility. Sweder van Wijnbergen. *Am. Econ. Rev.* **82:3** 6:1992 pp. 626 – 633

89 The trade restrictiveness index — an application to Mexican agriculture. James E. Anderson; Geoffrey Bannister. Washington, D.C.: International Economics Department, The World Bank, 1992: 50 p. [Policy research working papers.]

90 Trading American interests. Alfred E. Eckes. *Foreign Aff.* **71:4** Fall:1992 pp. 135 – 154

91 U.S. export subsidies in wheat — strategic trade policy or expensive beggar-thy-neighbor tactic? Giovanni Anania; Mary Bohman; Colin Carter. *Am. J. Agr. Ec.* **74:3** 8:1992 pp. 534 – 545

92 The U.S. leadership role in world trade — past, present, and future. Ernest H. Preeg. *Wash. Quart.* **15:2** Spring:1992 pp. 81 – 92

93 Variable labor supply and the theory of customs union. S. Michael Michael; Panos Hatzipanayotou. *Keio Econ. Stud.* **XXIX:1** 1992 pp. 63 – 72

94 Welfare effects of tariffs in free-entry oligopoly under integrated markets. Yasuhito Tanaka. *Econ. S. Quart.* **43:3** 9:1992 pp. 210 – 229

Dumping *[Dumping]*

95 The ambiguous consequences of anti-dumping laws. Michael Webb. *Econ. Inq.* **XXX:3** 7:1992 pp. 437 – 448

96 L'anti-dumping (II) *[In French]*; Anti-dumping (II). Thiébaut Flory *[Contrib.]*; Michel Kostecki *[Contrib.]*; Jean-Louis Delvolve *[Contrib.]*; Onno Brouwer *[Contrib.]*; Fiona Carlin *[Contrib.]*; Dominique Berlin *[Contrib.]*. *Collection of 5 articles.* **Dr. Prat. Commer. Int.** , *17:2*, 1991 pp. 198 – 296

97 Cascading contingent protection. B.M. Hoekman; M.P. Leidy. *Eur. Econ. R.* **36:4** 5:1992 pp. 883 – 892

98 A decade of European Community anti-dumping law and practice applicable to imports from China. Edwin A. Vermulst; Folkert Graafsma. *J. World Tr.* **26:3** 6:1992 pp. 5 – 60

99 Rules or politics? An empirical analysis of ITC antidumping decisions. Michael O. Moore. *Econ. Inq.* **XXX:3** 7:1992 pp. 449 – 466

100 A shot across the bow — South Korea's first test of its antidumping law. Corinne M. Krupp. *J. World Tr.* **26:3** 6:1992 pp. 111 – 124

O.3.3: Foreign trade policies *[Politique du commerce extérieur]* — **Dumping**
[Dumping]
101 Why are so many antidumping petitions withdrawn? Thomas J. Prusa. *J. Int. Econ.* **33:1/2** 8:1992 pp. 1 – 20

GATT *[GATT]*

102 L'anti-dumping (II) *[In French]*; Anti-dumping (II). Thiébaut Flory *[Contrib.]*; Michel Kostecki *[Contrib.]*; Jean-Louis Delvolve *[Contrib.]*; Onno Brouwer *[Contrib.]*; Fiona Carlin *[Contrib.]*; Dominique Berlin *[Contrib.]*. *Collection of 5 articles.* **Dr. Prat. Commer. Int.** , *17:2, 1991* pp. 198 – 296
103 Challenges to the liberal international trading system, GATT and the Uruguay Round. E.R. Grilli. *Banca Nat. Lav. Q. Rev.* :**181** 6:1992 pp. 191 – 224
104 China and GATT — implications of international norms for China. Thomas C.W. Chiu. *J. World Tr.* **26:6** 12:1992 pp. 5 – 18
105 China's GATT membership — selected legal and political issues. Wenguo Cai. *J. World Tr.* **26:1** 2:1992 pp. 35 – 61
106 Do rules control power? GATT articles and arrangements in the Uruguay Round. J. Michael Finger; Sumana Dhar. Washington, D.C.: Country Economics Department, The World Bank, 1992: 51 p. *Bibliography — p.44-51.* [Policy research working papers.]
107 The EEC and free trade agreements — stretching the limits of GATT exceptions to non-discriminatory trade? Frank Schoneveld. *J. World Tr.* **26:5** 10:1992 pp. 59 – 78
108 Environmental and agricultural policy linkages and reforms in the United States under the GATT. Richard E. Just; Gordon C. Rausser. *Am. J. Agr. Ec.* **74:3** 8:1992 pp. 766 – 774
109 Fixing the rules — North-South issues in international trade and the GATT Uruguay Round. Kevin Watkins. London: Catholic Institute for International Relations, 1992: 144 p. *ISBN: 1852871040.*
110 GATT and environment. Piritta Sorsa. *World. Econ.* **15:1** 1:1992 pp. 115 – 134
111 GATT and the environment — rules changes to minimize adverse trade and environmental effects. Eliza Patterson. *J. World Tr.* **26:3** 6:1992 pp. 99 – 109
112 GATT and the Third World — fixing the rules. Kevin Watkins. *Race Class* **34:1** 7-9:1992 pp. 23 – 40
113 GATT customs union provisions and the Uruguay Round — the European Community experience. Youri Devuyst. *J. World Tr.* **26:1** 2:1992 pp. 15 – 34
114 GATT, dispute settlement and cooperation. Dan Kovenock; Marie Thursby. *Econ. Polit.* **4:2** 7:1992 pp. 151 – 170
115 How agriculture blocked the Uruguay Round. Robert L. Paarlberg. *SAIS R.* **12:1** Winter-Spring:1992 pp. 27 – 42
116 Intellectual property in international trade law and policy — the GATT connection; *[German summary]*. Thomas Cottier. *Aussenwirtschaft* **47:1** 2:1992 pp. 79 – 105
117 The level of development and GSP treatment — an empirical investigation into the differential impacts of export expansion. Robert E. Moore. *J. World Tr.* **26:6** 12:1992 pp. 19 – 30
118 Mercantilism and global security. Michael Borrus; Steve Weber; John Zysman; Joseph Willihnganz. *Nat. Inter.* :**29** Fall:1992 pp. 21 – 29
119 Multilateral trade agreements and U.S. states — an analysis of potential GATT Uruguay Round agreements. Matt Schaefer; Thomas Singer. *J. World Tr.* **26:6** 12:1992 pp. 31 – 59
120 The non-violation procedure of Article XXIII:2 GATT — its operational rationale. Armin von Bogdandy. *J. World Tr.* **26:4** 8:1992 pp. 95 – 111
121 Political economy of the Uruguay Round of negotiations — a perspective. B.S. Chimni. *Int. Stud.* **29:2** 4-6:1992 pp. 135 – 158
122 Politik som sædvanlig? EF i den internationale politiske økonomi 1985-1991 *[In Danish]*; Politics as usual? EC in the international political economy 1985-1991 *[Summary]*. Jens Henrik Haahr. *Politica.* **24:2** 1992 pp. 169 – 187
123 Some reflections on the GATT TPRM, in the light of the trade policy review of the European Communities — a legal perspective. Asif H. Qureshi. *J. World Tr.* **26:6** 12:1992 pp. 103 – 120
124 Toward extension of the GATT standards code to production processes. George Foy. *J. World Tr.* **26:6** 12:1992 pp. 121 – 131
125 Will the GATT system survive? Gerd Langguth. *Aussenpolitik* **43:3** 1992 pp. 220 – 229

O.3.3: **Foreign trade policies** *[Politique du commerce extérieur]* —

Protectionism *[Protectionnisme]*

126 Comparative advantage and protection in Indonesia. Peter G. Warr. *B. Ind. Econ. St.* **28:3** 12:1992 pp. 41 – 70

127 Consumer protection and protectionism in Japan. David Vogel. *J. Jpn. Stud.* **18:1** Winter:1992 pp. 119 – 154

128 The decline of free trade and U.S. trade policy today. Biswajit Dhar. *J. World Tr.* **26:6** 12:1992 pp. 133 – 154

129 Développment technologique et protectionnisme au Brésil *[In French]*; Technological development and protection in Brazil *[Summary]*. Hubert Drouvot. *Sociol. Trav.* **2** 1992 pp. 153 – 170

130 Dismantling the barriers — tariff policy in New Zealand. Ian Duncan; Ralph Gerard Lattimore; Alan Bollard. Wellington: NZ Institute of Economic Research, 1992: vii, 94 p. (ill) *ISBN: 0908969007. Includes bibliographical references (p. 91-94).* [Research monograph / New Zealand Institute of Economic Research. : No. 57]

131 Effective rates of protection when domestic and foreign goods are imperfect substitutes — the case of Thailand. Shantayanan Devarajan; Chalongphob Sussangkarn. *Rev. Econ. St.* **LXXIV:4** 11:1992 pp. 701 – 711

132 Exchange rates, protectionism and commercial policy — alternative strategies for coordinating the G3 economies. A.J. Hughes Hallett. *Jpn. Wor. Econ.* **4:3** 11:1992 pp. 215 – 237

133 How costly is protectionism? Robert C. Feenstra. *J. Econ. Pers.* **6:3** Summer:1992 pp. 159 – 178

134 Institutional structure in the political economy of protection — legislated v. administered protection. H. Keith Hall; Douglas Nelson. *Econ. Polit.* **4:1** 3:1992 pp. 61 – 77

135 Macro-commercial policy revisited — a global, North-South analysis. S. Mansoob Murshed. *Gr. Econ. Rev.* **13:1** 6:1991 pp. 51 – 70

136 Models of endogenous protection. L. de Benedictis. *Eco. Notes* **21:1** 1992 pp. 85 – 119

137 The political economy of protectionism in Indonesia — a computable general equilibrium analysis. Eva Elisabet Rutström. Stockholm: Stockholm School of Economics, Economic Research Institute, [1991]: 414 p. *ISBN: 9172583258. Revision of the author's doctoral thesis (Stockholm School of Economics, 1990); Includes bibliographical references (p. 406-414).*

138 Rules of origin as commercial policy instruments — revisited. Edwin A. Vermulst. *J. World Tr.* **26:6** 12:1992 pp. 61 – 102

139 Short- and long-run incidence of protection — the case of Madagascar. C. Milner. *Appl. Econ.* **24:2** 2:1992 pp. 257 – 264

140 La soluzione della crisi dei paesi latino-americani negli anni '80 — protezionismo o necessità di cooperazione come gioco di scelte? *[In Italian]*; [Solution for the crisis of the Latin American countries in the 1980s — protectionism or the need for cooperation as a game of choice?]. Antonella Rotunno. *Econ. Ban.* **XIV:1** 1992 pp. 73 – 110

141 Strategische Handels- und Industriepolitik in der Automobilindustrie? *[In German]*; [Strategic trade and industrial policy in the automobile industry?]. Georg Bletschacher. *Weltwirt.* **:1** 1992 pp. 68 – 84

142 Struktur und Bestimmungsgründe der Agrarprotektion — food crops versus cash crops *[In German]*; [The structure and determinants of agricultural protection — food crops versus cash crops] *[Summary]*. Patricia Gorn. *Konjunkturpolitik* **38:2** 1992 pp. 86 – 108

AUTHOR INDEX
INDEX DES AUTEURS

Arizpe, L: **F.3.1.3**: 2. **F.3.2**: 18.
Arkadie, van, B: **F.1**: 48.
Ark, van, B: **G.2.5**: 56.
Armah, B: **G.2.2**: 26.
Armour, L: **D**: 2.
Armstrong, J: **H.4**: 70.
Armstrong, P: **G.3.3.5**: 111.
Armstrong, T: **M.1**: 10.
Arnason, R: **H.1.2.1**: 37.
Arnaud-Ameller, P: **O.1.2.4**: 5.
Arndt, D: **O.1.3**: 65.
Arndt, H: **O.1.2.3**: 9. **O.1.3**: 48.
Arni, J: **C**: 57.
Arnott, R: **I.2.3**: 87. **K.3**: 71.
Arnould, R: **H.4**: 53.
Aron, D: **J.4**: 309.
Aron, J: **O.2.1**: 79.
Arora, A: **G.1**: 37.
Arrau, P: **L.1**: 29. **L.3**: 22. **O.1.3**: 6.
Arrazola, M: **J.4**: 254.
Arriagada, A: **M.5**: 9.
Arriazu, R: **J.1**: 74.
Arrighi, J: **L.2**: 16.
Arrufat, J: **B.3**: 33.
Arsen, D: **F.5**: 32. **N.2**: 232.
Arshad, F: **H.4**: 79.
Arshi, A: **O.1.2.3**: 13.
Art, d', D: **K.3**: 78.
Artis, M: **O.1.2**: 3.
Artstein, Y: **K.3**: 67.
Artus, P: **F.5**: 1. **J.4**: 145.
Arumugam, E: **N.3**: 24.
Arvay, J: **F.2**: 8.
Arvin, B: **K.3**: 71.
Aryafar, A: **N.1**: 242.
Asano, S: **L.2**: 40.
Asanuma, B: **H.2.2**: 76.
Asare, S: **B.4**: 15.
Ash, E: **B.4**: 6.
Ash, M: **H.0**: 52.
Ash, R: **H.1.1.4**: 27.
Ash, T: **H.1.1.2**: 2.
Ashenfelter, O: **G.2.4**: 11.
Asher, M: **N.2**: 298.
Ashworth, J: **H.0**: 113.
Ashworth, S: **H.1.1.1**: 6.

Asiedu-Akrofi, D: **O.2.2**: 76.
Asikoglu, Y: **O.2.3**: 4.
Aslaksen, I: **K.2**: 35.
Aslanbeigui, N: **D**: 70.
Aslund, A: **F.1**: 68.
Aspremont, d', C: **C**: 71.
Assaad, R: **H.2.1**: 50.
Asselain, J: **N.1**: 324.
Assimakopoulos, V: **I.2.3**: 53.
Asthana, A: **B.3**: 50.
Atesoglu, H: **J.1**: 5.
Athukorala, P: **O.3.2**: 46.
Atkeson, A: **L.2**: 28.
Atkin, M: **J.4**: 236.
Atkinson, A: **M.2**: 22. **M.4**: 114, 116.
Attfield, R: **O.1.3**: 71.
Attwood, D: **H.1.2.1**: 16.
Atzema, O: **F.3.1.1**: 121.
Au-Yeung, A: **N.2**: 25.
Aubert, C: **H.1.1.4**: 12.
Auch, E: **F.3.2**: 86.
Auerbach, A: **N.2**: 181.
Auerbach, P: **J.5**: 48. **N.1**: 245.
Auerbach, R: **H.1.2.1**: 31.
Aulin-Ahmavaara, P: **G.1**: 40.
Ault, D: **F.3.1.3**: 5.
Austen-Smith, D: **G.3.3.5**: 69.
Auster, E: **H.2.1**: 61.
Austvik, O: **O.1.2.3**: 24.
Ausubel, L: **I.2.1**: 23.
Auty, R: **H.2.1**: 47.
Avsar, S: **I.2.1**: 120.
Aw, B: **I.2.1**: 114.
Axelsson, B: **H.2.1**: 83.
Ayres, R: **O.3.2**: 8.
Azam, J: **O.3.1**: 68.
Azis, I: **N.2**: 268.
Azqueta, D: **H.0**: 115.
Azzam, A: **I.2.3**: 69.
Baba, Y: **J.1**: 49.
Babcock, B: **H.1.2**: 2.
Baber, R: **F.3.1.1**: 8.
Babini, D: **N.3**: 24.
Bacchetta, P: **O.2.2**: 34.
Baccini, A: **E**: 4.
Bach, W: **H.0**: 70.
Bacha, E: **F.3.2**: 77. **O.2.2**: 62.

Bachet, D: **H.2.2**: 60.
Bachman, D: **F.2**: 16.
Back, K: **J.4**: 55.
Backer, W: **G.2.4**: 22.
Backus, D: **F.5**: 24.
Bacon, R: **L.2**: 47.
Badaracco, J: **G.3.3**: 6.
Baden, J: **H.0**: 75.
Bagachwa, M: **G.1**: 27.
Bagella, M: **J.2**: 117.
Baghestani, H: **F.2**: 21. **J.1**: 98, 108.
Baglioni, A: **J.2**: 131.
Bagnoli, M: **J.4**: 56. **N.3**: 54.
Bagus, T: **J.2**: 67.
Bagwell, K: **G.1.3**: 21. **I.2.1**: 136.
Bagwell, L: **G.3.3.5**: 94.
Bah, O: **H.0**: 197.
Bahl, R: **N.2**: 24, 149. **O.1.2**: 14.
Bahmani-Oskooee, M: **J.1**: 87. **O.2.1**: 87. **O.2.2**: 46. **O.2.3**: 61. **O.3.1**: 16.
Bahnick, K: **O.3.2**: 36.
Bailey, D: **G.3.3**: 29. **O.2.2**: 127.
Bailey, J: **J.4**: 37.
Baillie, R: **B.3**: 1.
Bailly, A: **F.3.1.1**: 72. **H.4**: 111.
Bailly, J: **J.1**: 28.
Bailly, M: **O.1.3**: 75.
Baily, M: **H.2.1**: 126.
Bain, K: **O.1.3**: 9.
Baker, A: **H.2.1**: 12.
Baker, G: **H.4**: 3.
Baker, L: **F.1**: 89. **H.1.1**: 18.
Baker, M: **M.5**: 24.
Baker, P: **I.2.3**: 37.
Baker, W: **I.2.1**: 34.
Bakos, G: **I.1**: 4.
Balabkins, N: **F.3.3**: 35.
Balakrishnan, P: **J.1**: 101.
Balakrishnan, R: **G.2.5**: 54.
Balamohandas, V: **J.2**: 91.
Balcerowicz, E: **N.1**: 315.
Baldassarri, M: **F.5**: 25. **I.2.1**: 99. **O.1.2**: 5. **O.1.2.4**: 60. **O.3.2**: 39.
Baldwin, M: **G.2.1**: 170.
Baldwin, R: **G.2.3**: 5. **O.3.1**: 49. **O.3.3**: 3–4, 60.
Baldwin, S: **H.2.2**: 108.
Balenndorf, D: **G.2.1**: 164.

Balkan, E: **O.2.2**: 72.
Balke, N: **J.5**: 56.
Ball, C: **M.5**: 38.
Ball, G: **J.2**: 238.
Ball, L: **J.5**: 60.
Ball, R: **I.2.1**: 160.
Ballard, C: **N.2**: 125.
Balson, W: **G.3.3.5**: 76.
Baltensperger, E: **O.2.1**: 63.
Balvers, R: **B.3**: 30.
Bamezai, A: **M.4**: 29.
Banda, G: **F.1**: 5.
Bandyk, C: **N.1**: 292.
Bandzak, R: **G.2.4**: 65.
Banerjee, A: **B.3**: 5. **G.2.1**: 68.
Banerjee, D: **C**: 7.
Banerji, S: **J.1**: 72.
Bannister, G: **O.3.3**: 89.
Banouei, A: **N.1**: 242, 253.
Bansard, D: **I.2.1**: 28.
Banterle, C: **M.4**: 95.
Banuri, T: **J.5**: 18.
Bar-Yosef, S: **B.4**: 45. **J.4**: 257.
Barabas, G: **F.3.1.2**: 12.
Baravelli, M: **J.2**: 170.
Barber, M: **G.2.4**: 75.
Barbier, E: **H.0**: 136–137.
Barbosa, F: **N.1**: 97.
Barchfield, J: **E**: 7.
Bardhan, P: **N.1**: 28.
Barff, R: **F.3.1.2**: 14.
Barfield, C: **O.3.2**: 12.
Barham, B: **H.1.1.4**: 23. **O.1.2.3**: 15. **O.3.2**: 51.
Barkaoui, A: **H.1.1.4**: 9.
Barke, M: **F.3.1.1**: 112.
Barkey, H: **N.1**: 186.
Barkley, D: **H.2.1**: 31.
Barlow, J: **H.2.2**: 51. **I.2.3**: 100.
Barmby, T: **G.2.1**: 103.
Barnes, D: **H.1.1.2**: 14.
Barnes, T: **G.2.1**: 44.
Barnett, A: **H.2.2**: 111.
Barnett, R: **N.2**: 270. **O.2.1**: 85.
Barnett, W: **J.1**: 46. **M.5**: 3.
Barnhart, S: **J.2**: 216.
Barr, D: **G.3.3.5**: 110.

Bono, M: **H.1.1**: 15.
Bonus, H: **G.3.3.5**: 62.
Bookman, M: **F.3.2**: 125.
Boons, A: **B.4**: 21.
Boot, A: **G.3.3**: 36.
Booth, A: **N.1**: 111.
Booth, D: **J.4**: 19.
Booth, G: **O.2.2**: 69. **O.2.3**: 3.
Booth, J: **J.2**: 13.
Boothe, P: **O.2.2**: 54.
Borde, S: **O.2.2**: 11.
Border, K: **C**: 26.
Bordignon, M: **N.2**: 287.
Bordley, R: **C**: 43.
Borenstein, S: **I.2.1**: 162.
Borgers, A: **L.2**: 54.
Börgers, T: **I.2.1**: 127.
Borght, Vander, C: **G.3.3.5**: 2.
Borisovich, V: **H.2.2**: 100.
Borja, A: **H.2.2**: 10.
Borjas, G: **F.3.1.3**: 8. **G.2.1**: 85.
Borland, J: **C**: 75.
Borner, S: **O.1.2.4**: 60.
Bornstein, M: **N.1**: 283, 285.
Borrell, B: **O.3.2**: 26.
Borrmann, J: **J.2**: 31.
Borrus, M: **O.3.3**: 118.
Börsch-Supan, A: **L.1**: 41.
Borzaga, C: **G.3.3.5**: 66.
Bös, D: **M.4**: 74.
Bos, F: **B.4**: 51.
Bos, P: **I.2.1**: 74.
Bosco, L: **O.3.2**: 22.
Boshoff, A: **G.3.3.1**: 8.
Boskin, M: **G.1.2**: 2.
Boss, A: **F.1**: 40. **H.2.1**: 121.
Bossert, W: **M.1**: 23.
Bossier, F: **N.2**: 128.
Bossone, B: **D**: 74.
Bosworth, B: **O.1.3**: 97.
Bosworth, D: **G.1**: 49. **G.4**: 8.
Botsas, E: **N.1**: 254.
Bottomley, P: **H.1.2**: 5.
Bouckaert, G: **N.3**: 39.
Bougerol, P: **B.3**: 1.
Bouhaili, A: **J.1**: 94.

Bouis, H: **M.2**: 1.
Boulfounau, P: **J.2**: 203.
Bound, J: **G.2.1**: 14, 175. **K.3**: 5.
Bourdet, Y: **F.1**: 28. **N.1**: 73, 198.
Bourenane, N: **H.1.1.4**: 14.
Bourène, M: **O.3.2**: 30.
Bourguignon, F: **K.2**: 1.
Bourlakis, C: **H.2.1**: 14.
Bourrelier, P: **H.2.2**: 102–103.
Boussard, D: **G.3.3.5**: 121.
Boutillier, S: **G.3.3.4**: 3.
Bovaird, T: **F.3.1.1**: 109.
Bovard, J: **O.3.2**: 13.
Bovenberg, A: **N.2**: 169.
Bovenberg, L: **M.4**: 90.
Bowbrick, P: **G.1.1**: 9.
Bowden, R: **I.2.1**: 17.
Bowden, S: **G.3.3.5**: 13.
Bowen, H: **O.3.1**: 47.
Bower, A: **I.2.1**: 174.
Bower, D: **G.1**: 3.
Bowler, I: **H.1.1**: 14.
Bowles, P: **J.4**: 110. **N.1**: 145.
Bowles, S: **C**: 15. **K.2**: 3.
Bowman, A: **F.3.2**: 30.
Boyce, G: **G.3.3.5**: 55.
Boyce, J: **O.2.2**: 73.
Boycko, M: **F.3.1.3**: 9. **N.1**: 240.
Boyd, H: **H.4**: 81.
Boyd, J: **L.3**: 14.
Boyd, R: **H.0**: 74. **N.2**: 296.
Boyda, A: **H.1.1.3**: 14.
Boyer, K: **G.3.2**: 28.
Boyer, R: **I.2.1**: 29.
Boyle, A: **H.0**: 25. **H.3**: 79.
Boyle, G: **J.4**: 185, 195.
Boyle, K: **H.1.2.1**: 33.
Boyle, S: **I.2.3**: 14. **L.2**: 78.
Bracewell-Milnes, B: **N.2**: 124.
Bradbury, B: **K.2**: 37.
Bradbury, S: **G.2.1**: 58.
Bradford, D: **N.2**: 305.
Bradley, K: **G.2.5**: 19. **H.4**: 91. **K.3**: 82.
Bradley, M: **J.4**: 306. **K.3**: 76.
Bradshaw, R: **J.1**: 106.
Brailsford, T: **J.4**: 98.
Bramley, G: **M.2**: 13.

275

Brand, D: **O.1.3**: 93.
Brander, J: **F.3.3**: 6. **G.3.3**: 24.
Brandner, P: **F.5**: 7. **J.3**: 19.
Brandolini, A: **K.3**: 24.
Brandt, S: **I.2.3**: 52.
Brandts, J: **H.2.1**: 1.
Branson, W: **K.2**: 1.
Brasini, S: **H.2.2**: 55.
Bratton, J: **H.2.1**: 85.
Brauer, J: **N.1**: 11.
Braun, B: **G.3.3.5**: 67.
Braun, G: **H.2.2**: 88.
Braun, M: **I.2.1**: 29.
Braunstein, Y: **J.2**: 150.
Braun, von, J: **G.2.2**: 20.
Bravo-Ureta, B: **H.1.2.1**: 19.
Bray, M: **M.5**: 40.
Brazee, R: **H.0**: 187.
Brecher, R: **G.2.1**: 127.
Brechling, V: **I.2.3**: 37.
Brender, A: **O.3.3**: 6.
Brenna, A: **M.4**: 25.
Brennan, N: **B.4**: 39.
Brennan, T: **G.3.2**: 37.
Bresnick, T: **N.1**: 2.
Breton, A: **I.2.3**: 33.
Breuss, F: **O.1.2.4**: 37.
Brewster, C: **G.2.5**: 17, 22.
Brezinski, H: **F.1**: 43.
Bridges, B: **F.1**: 26.
Bridges, D: **L.2**: 1.
Brief, R: **B.4**: 56.
Brijlal, P: **L.2**: 105.
Brill, H: **G.2.3**: 4.
Brill, J: **G.3.2**: 18.
Brimmer, A: **J.2**: 156.
Brinbaum, D: **H.1.1.4**: 34.
Brink, H: **B.1**: 21.
Brinkerhoff, D: **F.3.2**: 38.
Brinkman, R: **E**: 5.
Briston, R: **G.3.2**: 25.
Britel, A: **I.2.3**: 69.
Britton, A: **O.2.3**: 1.
Briys, E: **J.4**: 175.
Brock, W: **J.2**: 2.
Brock, De, L: **H.4**: 53.

Brockner, J: **G.2.5**: 27.
Brodin, P: **L.2**: 45.
Bródy, A: **J.1**: 30–31.
Broeck, de, M: **N.2**: 240.
Broeder, den, C: **N.2**: 264.
Broehl, W: **O.1.2.3**: 4.
Broll, U: **G.3.3.5**: 11. **O.2.1**: 59. **O.2.2**: 31, 103. **O.3.2**: 68.
Bromley, D: **H.1.1.1**: 23.
Bromwich, M: **B.4**: 3. **G.3.3.5**: 118.
Bronars, S: **G.2.1**: 85.
Brookfield, D: **J.4**: 64.
Brooksbank, R: **H.4**: 78.
Broome, J: **F.3.1.3**: 7. **H.0**: 78.
Brosnan, P: **G.2.1**: 65.
Brous, P: **G.3.3.3**: 7.
Brouwer, O: **O.3.3**: 96.
Brown, A: **H.3**: 85.
Brown, C: **F.3.2**: 103. **K.3**: 70.
Brown, D: **G.3.3.5**: 73. **J.2**: 22. **O.1.2.4**: 35. **O.1.3**: 95.
Brown, J: **G.2.4**: 125.
Brown, L: **B.4**: 35. **J.4**: 245.
Brown, M: **G.1.2**: 14.
Brown, P: **H.0**: 6. **H.2.1**: 93. **M.4**: 1.
Brown, R: **N.2**: 247. **O.2.2**: 63.
Brown, S: **F.3.1.1**: 66. **J.4**: 95.
Brown-Kruse, J: **I.2.1**: 75.
Browning, M: **L.2**: 53.
Brownlee, H: **M.2**: 21.
Brownstein, A: **K.3**: 107.
Brox, J: **H.1.1**: 7.
Bruce, N: **N.2**: 102.
Brueckner, J: **H.3**: 46.
Brüderl, J: **G.3.3.1**: 17.
Brueggeman, W: **J.2**: 120.
Brüning, L: **J.4**: 132.
Bruggink, A: **J.2**: 189.
Brugnoli, A: **H.1.2.1**: 11.
Bruinsma, F: **F.3.1.1**: 77.
Brumbaugh, R: **J.2**: 120, 190.
Brumm, E: **G.3.3.5**: 54.
Brun, A: **F.3.1.1**: 91. **H.1.1.2**: 13.
Brunello, G: **G.2.4**: 32.
Brunetta, R: **G.2.1**: 40. **G.2.2**: 19.
Brunner, A: **F.2**: 1.
Bruno, C: **O.2.1**: 11.

Case, K: **I.2.3**: 105, 110.
Casetti, E: **F.3.1.1**: 1. **G.1.2**: 16.
Casey, B: **M.4**: 84.
Caskey, J: **I.2.1**: 18.
Casoni, G: **N.2**: 2.
Cassar, J: **G.3.3.5**: 43.
Casse, P: **G.3.3.4**: 1.
Cassese, S: **N.3**: 46.
Cassiman, B: **G.1.3**: 4.
Cassing, S: **B.3**: 20.
Cassiolato, J: **H.2.1**: 21.
Casson, M: **O.1.2.2**: 11.
Cassoni, A: **O.3.1**: 20.
Castanias, R: **G.3.3.3**: 27.
Castelino, M: **J.4**: 191.
Castellano B., H: **N.1**: 252.
Castensson, R: **H.0**: 204.
Castles, F: **M.3**: 4.
Castro, A: **O.1.2.4**: 30.
Castro, De, P: **H.1.1.2**: 27.
Caswell, J: **G.2.3**: 7.
Catrice-Lorey, A: **N.3**: 10.
Catteau, C: **K.3**: 49.
Caudill, S: **L.2**: 101.
Cavaglia, S: **J.1**: 32.
Cavailhes, J: **F.3.1.1**: 91.
Cavanaugh, G: **L.2**: 109.
Cave, M: **H.3**: 85. **M.5**: 20.
Cavendish, W: **N.1**: 256.
Caves, D: **H.2.2**: 92.
Caves, R: **O.2.2**: 82. **O.3.1**: 5.
Cazes, S: **M.4**: 93.
Cebon, P: **H.2.1**: 70.
Cebry, M: **H.3**: 18.
Cebula, R: **M.4**: 61. **N.2**: 236, 241.
CEC Japan: **O.3.2**: 30.
Cerea, G: **N.2**: 294.
Ceroni, C: **G.3.3.3**: 38.
Cerwenka, P: **H.3**: 36.
Cesarano, F: **O.2.3**: 40.
Cesoni, M: **H.4**: 45.
Cette, G: **G.3.3.4**: 16.
Cha, B: **L.3**: 13.
Chacaltana Janampa, J: **G.3.3.4**: 9.
Chadeau, A: **L.2**: 46.
Chadha, B: **J.1**: 95.

Chae, S: **I.2.3**: 5.
Chaherli, N: **I.2.1**: 120.
Chai, J: **L.2**: 2.
Chaloupka, F: **I.2.1**: 13.
Chambers, D: **I.2.3**: 104.
Chambers, M: **L.2**: 62.
Chambers, R: **H.1.1.4**: 11.
Chamorro Marín, E: **O.1.3**: 7.
Champion, A: **F.3.1.1**: 110.
Champsaur, P: **O.2.3**: 22.
Chan, A: **J.4**: 153.
Chan, C: **J.4**: 209.
Chan, K: **F.3.2**: 93. **J.4**: 130, 190, 200, 215.
Chan, S: **F.3.2**: 97. **I.2.1**: 120. **J.4**: 52. **O.2.2**: 93.
Chander, P: **N.2**: 119.
Chandler, A: **E**: 13. **G.3.3.5**: 55.
Chandler, M: **I.2.3**: 85.
Chandra, R: **B.4**: 18.
Chandrasekharan, R: **I.2.3**: 26.
Chaney, P: **G.3.3.5**: 17. **J.4**: 281. **K.3**: 17.
Chang, C: **G.3.3.2**: 2. **G.3.3.5**: 89.
Chang, E: **J.4**: 121.
Chang, K: **H.1.1.2**: 5.
Chang, M: **I.2.1**: 30.
Chang, P: **O.1.2.5**: 1.
Chang, S: **G.3.3.3**: 28. **O.1.2.5**: 1.
Chang, W: **O.2.2**: 15.
Changanaquí, F: **I.2.3**: 20.
Chanier, P: **D**: 23.
Chant, E: **N.2**: 148.
Chao, C: **H.2.1**: 46.
Chapman, K: **H.2.2**: 1.
Chapman, R: **O.3.3**: 33.
Chappell, W: **G.2.4**: 79. **I.2.1**: 40.
Charles, A: **F.2**: 25.
Charles, D: **G.1**: 59.
Charles, S: **G.2.1**: 103.
Charmes, J: **H.4**: 46.
Charnovitz, S: **O.3.1**: 19.
Charpin, J: **O.1.3**: 75.
Chase, E: **G.2.1**: 167.
Chatel, B: **N.2**: 252.
Chatterjee, A: **O.1.3**: 47.
Chatterjee, C: **O.1.2.4**: 54.
Chatterjee, R: **L.2**: 49.
Chatterjee, S: **F.5**: 29. **J.1**: 8.
Chatterji, M: **F.3.3**: 40.

Chaudhuri, S: **G.2.2**: 38.
Chaudhury, M: **G.2.5**: 1.
Chauveau, T: **M.4**: 93.
Chavas, J: **H.1.1.1**: 19.
Chave, D: **O.1.3**: 79.
Chawla, R: **O.2.2**: 53.
Chaykowski, R: **G.2.4**: 37.
Chebat, J: **I.2.3**: 13.
Checchi, D: **O.2.2**: 5–6.
Chechliński, J: **M.4**: 112.
Checinski, M: **H.2.2**: 11.
Chen, A: **J.4**: 169.
Chen, C: **J.4**: 153. **N.1**: 36.
Chen, E: **O.2.2**: 94.
Chen, H: **H.1.1.2**: 32.
Chen, J: **O.1.2.3**: 14.
Chen, K: **G.3.3.3**: 19. **N.1**: 170.
Chen, R: **J.4**: 140.
Chen, T: **F.1**: 25. **G.1**: 46.
Chen, Z: **F.4**: 10.
Cheney, J: **O.2.2**: 133.
Cheng, D: **G.3.2**: 1.
Cheng, R: **B.4**: 27.
Cheng, T: **O.1.3**: 64.
Chérain, A: **G.2.5**: 42.
Chern, W: **L.2**: 59, 72.
Cherny, J: **B.4**: 9.
Chervel, M: **N.1**: 249.
Cheung, I: **J.4**: 265.
Cheung, Y: **J.4**: 184, 220, 295.
Chevalier, J: **H.2.2**: 94.
Chevalier, P: **B.3**: 6.
Chevallier-Farat, T: **J.2**: 77.
Chew, R: **G.2.1**: 117.
Chew, S: **G.2.1**: 117.
Chhibber, A: **O.2.2**: 40.
Chiappori, P: **G.2.1**: 93.
Chiara, Dalla, M: **C**: 67.
Chiarini, B: **G.2.4**: 95.
Chichilnisky, G: **H.0**: 75.
Chick, V: **D**: 41, 66.
Chigabatia, L: **N.3**: 24.
Childress, M: **H.1.1.4**: 23.
Chillemi, O: **G.2.4**: 119.
Chilosi, A: **N.1**: 29.
Chimni, B: **O.3.3**: 121.

Chinn, M: **O.2.2**: 47.
Chipeta, C: **L.1**: 19.
Chipman, J: **B.3**: 25.
Chiquier, L: **J.2**: 237.
Chisari, O: **O.2.3**: 41.
Chishti, S: **O.1.3**: 51.
Chittle, C: **O.3.2**: 3.
Chiu, T: **O.3.3**: 104.
Choate, G: **G.3.3.3**: 18.
Choi, C: **I.2.1**: 79. **O.1.3**: 28.
Choi, J: **G.1.3**: 6. **J.4**: 144.
Choi, S: **J.1**: 66. **K.3**: 101.
Choksy, G: **D**: 11.
Chollick, E: **N.1**: 5.
Chong, L: **G.3.3.1**: 9.
Chopra, N: **J.4**: 278.
Chou, R: **B.3**: 1.
Chou, T: **G.3.3.4**: 5.
Chou, Y: **O.3.3**: 17.
Choucri, N: **E**: 3.
Choudhury, M: **F.1**: 1. **F.4**: 6.
Chow, K: **J.4**: 170.
Chow, L: **O.3.2**: 14.
Chowdhury, A: **J.1**: 54.
Chowdhury, M: **O.2.3**: 3.
Chown, J: **N.2**: 124.
Christ, R: **H.0**: 183.
Christensen, A: **F.1**: 63.
Christensen, J: **N.2**: 33.
Christensen, K: **K.2**: 24.
Christiano, L: **B.3**: 5. **F.5**: 14. **J.5**: 30. **N.2**: 273.
Christiansen, F: **G.2.1**: 50. **N.1**: 166.
Christiansen, J: **G.1.2**: 9.
Christianson, J: **M.4**: 47.
Christie, I: **H.0**: 171.
Christie, V: **G.2.4**: 101.
Christodoulou, D: **F.1**: 58.
Christodoulou, M: **H.4**: 29.
Christofides, L: **D**: 9. **K.3**: 99.
Chrystal, K: **J.2**: 49.
Chu, C: **B.3**: 5.
Chu, Y: **G.2.1**: 30.
Chuan, G: **H.0**: 38.
Chudakova, N: **N.1**: 204.
Chui, A: **J.4**: 32.
Chuma, H: **H.1.1**: 17.
Chunru, H: **H.1.1.4**: 31.

Chuppe, T: **J.4**: 236.
Church, J: **G.1.1**: 39.
Church, R: **F.3.1.1**: 12.
Chuta, E: **M.5**: 40.
Chye, T: **O.1.2.4**: 7.
Cicero, Lo, M: **F.1**: 79. **J.2**: 179.
Ciechocinska, M: **N.1**: 260.
Cigno, A: **L.1**: 41.
Ciresa, M: **I.2.3**: 65.
Citro, C: **M.2**: 11.
Citron, D: **B.4**: 7. **G.3.3.3**: 2. **J.2**: 40.
Claassen, E: **O.2.3**: 23.
Clague, C: **N.1**: 18.
Clapp, J: **I.2.2**: 2.
Clare, G: **O.2.2**: 101.
Clark, C: **F.3.2**: 97.
Clark, D: **O.3.1**: 11. **O.3.3**: 51.
Clark, G: **N.1**: 110.
Clark, I: **H.0**: 215.
Clark, J: **H.1.1.3**: 18. **H.1.2.1**: 10.
Clark, K: **G.1.1**: 29. **G.3.3.5**: 56.
Clark, M: **H.0**: 192. **O.3.2**: 51.
Clark, R: **J.4**: 290. **K.3**: 16. **N.2**: 59.
Clark, S: **C**: 27.
Clark, T: **G.3.3.1**: 20.
Clarke, L: **M.4**: 62.
Clarke, P: **I.2.1**: 171.
Clarke, S: **F.3.2**: 30. **N.1**: 303.
Clauretie, T: **J.4**: 114.
Claverie, B: **I.2.3**: 21.
Clavijo, F: **O.3.1**: 29.
Clay, D: **H.1.1.2**: 31.
Clay, E: **F.1**: 44.
Cleary, M: **H.0**: 38.
Clements, B: **N.3**: 49.
Clemenz, G: **H.4**: 34.
Cleveland, C: **H.2.2**: 106.
Cline, W: **H.0**: 84.
Clô, A: **N.3**: 46.
Cloninger, D: **F.3.1.3**: 1.
Cnossen, S: **H.0**: 120. **M.4**: 74. **N.2**: 152, 205.
Coate, S: **G.2.1**: 36. **M.1**: 25.
Coates, J: **G.3.3.5**: 52.
Coats, A: **D**: 10.
Cocklin, C: **H.2.2**: 117.
Coder, J: **K.3**: 31.

Coffey, W: **F.3.1.1**: 72.
Cohen, D: **F.3.3**: 23.
Cohen, M: **H.4**: 44.
Cohen, S: **B.4**: 59.
Coker, A: **H.0**: 124.
Colasse, B: **G.3.3.5**: 121.
Colburn, C: **K.2**: 2.
Cole, D: **O.2.2**: 58.
Cole, H: **F.3.1.3**: 24. **J.1**: 40. **O.2.2**: 126.
Cole, R: **G.2.3**: 16.
Coleman, C: **G.2.4**: 19.
Coleman, K: **N.3**: 30.
Coleman, W: **J.1**: 15.
Colin, R: **H.0**: 117.
Collette, M: **H.3**: 72.
Collie, D: **O.3.1**: 43. **O.3.3**: 22.
Collier, P: **O.2.3**: 17. **O.3.3**: 59.
Colling, T: **G.2.4**: 24.
Collins, J: **C**: 85.
Collins, M: **H.4**: 13.
Collins, S: **H.3**: 45.
Collyns, C: **J.4**: 81.
Coloma, G: **N.3**: 38.
Colombino, U: **G.2.1**: 88.
Colwell, R: **J.2**: 185.
Combes, M: **G.2.5**: 2.
Combs, C: **G.2.5**: 61.
Comer, J: **B.3**: 40.
Committee for Academic Freedom in Africa: **O.2.4**: 21.
Committee for the Development of Financial and Capital Markets in the Asia-Pacific Region: **J.4**: 40.
Common, M: **H.0**: 1, 181.
Conford, P: **H.0**: 140.
Congleton, R: **H.0**: 107.
Conlon, B: **H.2.2**: 6.
Connell, J: **F.1**: 56.
Connell, P: **H.1.2.1**: 2.
Conniffe, D: **B.3**: 29.
Connor, G: **J.4**: 5.
Conrad, J: **H.0**: 200. **N.2**: 233.
Conrad, K: **G.1.1**: 30. **G.2.1**: 114. **M.5**: 25. **N.2**: 95.
Conrad, P: **G.2.3**: 10.
Conroy, R: **G.1**: 48.
Considine, M: **G.2.3**: 11.
Contamin, B: **N.1**: 13.

Conte, M: **K.3**: 77. **L.3**: 20.
Conthe, M: **O.1.2.4**: 84.
Conti, V: **J.2**: 166, 169.
Conway, D: **F.3.2**: 82.
Conway, K: **G.2.1**: 98.
Cooil, B: **H.4**: 64.
Cook, E: **N.2**: 113.
Cook, P: **N.1**: 172.
Cooke, P: **H.3**: 92, 99.
Cooke, S: **F.3.1.1**: 85.
Cooke, T: **G.3.3.5**: 117.
Cooke, W: **G.2.4**: 120.
Cool, K: **H.2.1**: 81.
Cooley, T: **F.3.3**: 13.
Coombes, M: **J.2**: 87.
Cooper, A: **H.0**: 165. **O.3.2**: 47.
Cooper, C: **G.1.2**: 7. **H.2.1**: 89.
Cooper, R: **H.2.1**: 48. **L.2**: 60. **O.2.3**: 70.
Cooper, T: **J.4**: 90.
Cooper, W: **G.3.3.5**: 97.
Cooperman, E: **H.4**: 88.
Cooray, N: **G.1.3**: 22.
Coote, B: **O.1.2.3**: 37.
Copeland, T: **J.4**: 65.
Copp, C: **G.4**: 9.
Coppel, J: **H.0**: 82.
Coppin, A: **F.1**: 16. **O.1.2.4**: 52.
Coquart, D: **I.2.3**: 74.
Coquet, B: **O.2.3**: 53.
Corado, C: **F.3.1.1**: 6.
Corbae, D: **J.1**: 8.
Corbett, J: **G.1**: 53.
Corbridge, S: **F.3.2**: 4. **H.0**: 174.
Cordell, V: **L.2**: 57.
Cordella, T: **O.3.1**: 66.
Corden, W: **O.3.3**: 84.
Cordero Mestanza, G: **F.1**: 39.
Cordova, V: **H.1.1.2**: 15.
Corhay, A: **J.4**: 36.
Coricelli, F: **J.5**: 53. **K.3**: 72.
Cormack, D: **H.0**: 25.
Cornelius, L: **G.2.5**: 61.
Cornell, B: **J.4**: 287.
Cornelsen, D: **B.3**: 15.
Cornes, R: **I.2.1**: 178.
Cornett, M: **G.3.2**: 6.

Cornford, J: **H.3**: 82.
Cornia, G: **F.3.2**: 49.
Cornilleau, G: **F.2**: 26.
Cornish, W: **F.3.1.4**: 19.
Corrado, C: **J.4**: 294.
Corrado, M: **F.3.2**: 18.
Corsini, L: **B.3**: 35.
Cortie, C: **F.3.1.1**: 121.
Cosgrove, J: **M.5**: 36.
Cosimano, T: **J.2**: 24.
Costa, M: **H.2.1**: 96.
Cottarelli, C: **L.1**: 16.
Cotterill, R: **I.2.1**: 7.
Cotterman, R: **H.2.1**: 5.
Cottier, T: **O.3.3**: 116.
Cottrell, N: **K.1**: 5.
Coughlan, A: **K.3**: 20.
Coughlin, C: **J.2**: 49. **O.2.2**: 26.
Coughlin, P: **B.3**: 45. **H.2.1**: 33.
Coulson, N: **F.3.1.1**: 66.
Coulter, F: **K.2**: 9. **M.2**: 8.
Courant, P: **F.3.1.1**: 19.
Courchene, T: **N.1**: 37.
Courtis, J: **B.4**: 52.
Coutts, A: **G.3.3.5**: 13.
Coutts, J: **G.3.2**: 25.
Couwenberg, I: **O.2.2**: 43.
Cover, J: **J.1**: 3.
Cowell, F: **K.2**: 9, 23. **M.2**: 8. **N.2**: 13.
Cowen, T: **E**: 10. **F.3.1.4**: 17.
Cowling, K: **L.2**: 65.
Cox, D: **F.3.1.3**: 13. **O.1.3**: 95.
Cox, J: **J.2**: 2.
Cox, T: **H.1.1.1**: 19.
Coxhead, I: **H.1.1.1**: 9.
Coyle, W: **O.3.2**: 1.
Crafts, N: **F.3.3**: 28, 52.
Craig, B: **H.2.1**: 76.
Craig, C: **O.1.2**: 10.
Craig, R: **N.2**: 141.
Craigwell, R: **L.1**: 8.
Cramer, J: **O.2.2**: 107.
Cramer, U: **G.2.1**: 19.
Crampes, C: **H.2.1**: 54.
Cramton, P: **C**: 77.
Crane, A: **H.2.2**: 91.
Craswell, A: **H.2.2**: 152.

Cravens, D: **H.3**: 47.
Creedy, J: **C**: 75. **G.2.1**: 55. **M.4**: 73, 85. **M.5**: 22, 26. **N.2**: 170, 186, 198.
Cremer, H: **F.3.1.3**: 12. **I.2.1**: 20. **N.2**: 295.
Crémer, J: **C**: 71. **I.2.1**: 20.
Crenshaw, E: **K.2**: 6.
Crepaz, M: **F.3.3**: 10.
Crkvenac, M: **H.2.1**: 107.
Crockett, A: **O.2.4**: 7.
Cromwell, G: **G.1**: 62.
Cronan, D: **H.0**: 145.
Crone, D: **F.3.2**: 110.
Cropper, M: **M.1**: 5.
Cross, M: **J.3**: 3.
Crotty, J: **D**: 76.
Crouch, C: **G.2.4**: 15.
Crowell, R: **J.4**: 26.
Crowley, A: **H.4**: 82.
Crowson, P: **F.3.1.1**: 14.
Crucianelli, F: **G.1.1**: 36.
Cruz, W: **H.0**: 166.
Crystal, G: **K.3**: 25.
Csaba, L: **F.3.1.3**: 4. **F.5**: 41. **N.1**: 48.
Csáki, C: **H.1.1.1**: 28.
Cuadrado Roura, J: **H.2.2**: 48.
Cubitt, R: **M.1**: 4.
Cucinella, A: **F.5**: 30.
Cudjoe, F: **H.1.2**: 3.
Cuervo Villafañe, D: **F.3.2**: 19.
Cukierman, A: **N.2**: 310.
Cumberworth, M: **J.2**: 122.
Cumby, R: **O.2.1**: 24.
Cummings, J: **L.2**: 89.
Cummins, J: **J.3**: 1, 15.
Cunha, A: **H.0**: 28.
Cunill, N: **N.3**: 24.
Cunningham, D: **J.2**: 239.
Curbelo, J: **L.2**: 87.
Current, J: **F.3.1.1**: 12.
Currie, D: **O.1.3**: 34. **O.2.3**: 18.
Currie, J: **G.2.4**: 11. **K.3**: 91.
Currie, L: **N.1**: 163.
Currie, W: **G.3.3.5**: 46.
Curtin, T: **M.5**: 12.
Curwen, P: **M.3**: 3.
Curzio, A: **O.1.2.4**: 61.
Cushing, B: **B.4**: 29.

Cushing, M: **L.1**: 23.
Cutanda, A: **F.1**: 39.
Cuthbertson, K: **B.1**: 1. **G.3.3.5**: 110.
Cyncynatus, M: **H.1.1.4**: 9.
Czachay, E: **I.2.3**: 65.
Czarny, B: **M.2**: 2.
Czarny, E: **M.2**: 2.
Czernkowski, R: **G.3.3.2**: 7.
Czerny, M: **L.3**: 12.
Czesaný, S: **F.1**: 67.
Czinkota, M: **O.3.3**: 71.
D'Aveni, R: **G.3.3.1**: 18.
d'Empaire, R: **J.5**: 43.
D'Hoeraene, J: **J.2**: 1.
Dąbrowski, M: **N.1**: 315.
Dada, M: **H.4**: 51.
Dagenais, M: **L.1**: 24. **O.3.1**: 45.
Dahl, C: **N.2**: 31.
Dahlby, B: **J.3**: 12.
Dahlman, C: **G.1**: 29.
Dai, Y: **K.2**: 22.
Daianu, D: **N.1**: 324.
Dailami, M: **O.2.2**: 40.
Daintith, T: **G.2.3**: 5.
Dale, R: **J.2**: 116.
Dalen, van, H: **N.2**: 161.
Dalgic, T: **H.2.2**: 30.
Dallago, B: **F.1**: 43, 46. **N.1**: 300.
Dalpé, R: **N.3**: 10.
Daly, A: **G.2.2**: 4.
Daly, H: **H.0**: 128.
Daly, M: **N.2**: 197.
Dalziel, P: **F.1**: 86.
Damania, R: **N.2**: 68, 139.
Damian, M: **H.2.2**: 112.
Damilano, M: **J.2**: 60.
Damill, M: **O.3.3**: 7.
Dandie, R: **H.2.2**: 93.
Daneshvary, N: **G.2.1**: 33.
Daniel, J: **O.2.3**: 53.
Dániel, Z: **I.2.3**: 98.
Danielewski, J: **H.2.2**: 99.
Daniels, J: **O.1.3**: 15.
Daniels, P: **H.4**: 106. **O.2.2**: 48.
Danielson, A: **N.2**: 71.
Danilov, V: **C**: 64.

Doiron, D: **K.3**: 89.
Dollar, D: **F.3.2**: 34.
Dollery, B: **H.2.1**: 41.
Dollery, R: **N.3**: 31.
Dologite, D: **G.3.3.5**: 85.
Dolton, P: **M.5**: 20.
Domański, B: **F.3.1.1**: 82.
Dominguez, K: **O.2.1**: 70.
Dominioni, D: **F.1**: 9.
Don, H: **I.2.3**: 68.
Don, Y: **G.2.4**: 122.
Donaldson, D: **F.3.1.3**: 7.
Donaldson, J: **G.3.3**: 5.
Donato, K: **G.2.1**: 5.
Donge, van, J: **G.3.3.2**: 16.
Donnenfeld, S: **I.2.1**: 64.
Donoghue K.: **G.2.5**: 61.
Donoso, P: **H.3**: 12.
Donoso, V: **H.2.1**: 17.
Dontoh, A: **B.4**: 26.
Dooley, B: **H.2.2**: 122.
Dooley, M: **J.2**: 231. **N.2**: 178.
Doorslaer, van, E: **M.4**: 31–32.
Dopuch, N: **B.4**: 32.
Dore, E: **O.2.2**: 50.
Dorian, J: **H.2.2**: 100.
Dormont, B: **K.3**: 92.
Dornbusch, R: **E**: 11. **F.1**: 50. **O.1.2.4**: 73.
Dorsey, R: **N.3**: 53.
Dosi, C: **N.2**: 111.
Dosi, G: **G.3.3.4**: 13.
Dotsey, M: **F.5**: 19.
Dougherty, C: **B.3**: 28.
Douglas, S: **O.1.2**: 10.
Dourille-Feer, E: **H.2.2**: 67.
Douthitt, R: **M.2**: 33.
Douthwaite, R: **H.0**: 167.
Dow, J: **F.3.3**: 29.
Dow, S: **D**: 66. **F.3.1.1**: 79.
Dowall, D: **H.2.2**: 24. **I.2.3**: 109.
Dowd, B: **M.4**: 47.
Dowd, K: **J.2**: 164, 175–176. **J.5**: 12.
Dowdell, T: **H.2.2**: 56.
Dower, R: **H.0**: 111.
Dowlah, A: **D**: 12. **N.1**: 49.
Downes, T: **N.2**: 24.

Downey, H: **H.3**: 47.
Downey, R: **N.1**: 129.
Downs, T: **N.2**: 64.
Dowrick, S: **F.3.3**: 61.
Doyle, P: **O.1.2.3**: 6.
Drake, L: **J.1**: 42. **J.2**: 98.
Drake, T: **O.2.2**: 82.
Drakopoulos, S: **I.2.1**: 56, 175. **L.2**: 64.
Dranove, D: **I.2.1**: 97. **M.4**: 46.
Draper, P: **J.4**: 271.
Drees, B: **J.2**: 39.
Drennan, M: **F.3.1.1**: 105.
Drenth, H: **A**: 7.
Dresner, M: **I.2.3**: 44.
Drevet, J: **F.1**: 39.
Drew, D: **L.1**: 6.
Drew, J: **H.4**: 35.
Drèze, J: **F.3.1.3**: 7. **G.2.1**: 74. **M.2**: 14.
Driffill, J: **N.1**: 297.
Driskill, R: **O.2.1**: 84.
Driver, C: **C**: 82.
Droucopoulos, V: **K.3**: 32.
Drouet, M: **N.1**: 257.
Drouvot, H: **O.3.3**: 129.
Drummen, M: **O.1.2.2**: 22.
Drygalski, J: **N.1**: 315.
Drysdale, P: **O.1.3**: 52.
Dua, P: **F.2**: 19. **I.2.2**: 1. **L.2**: 39.
Duan, J: **J.2**: 45.
Duarte, C: **H.1.2.1**: 46.
Dubbeld, F: **J.5**: 14.
Dubé, L: **H.4**: 73.
Dubernet, A: **G.2.5**: 14.
Dubin, J: **N.2**: 211.
Duca, J: **J.2**: 105.
Duck, N: **F.5**: 3.
Dudden, A: **O.3.2**: 2.
Dudley, L: **N.2**: 269.
Dudley, N: **H.1.1.2**: 19.
Duerr, P: **H.3**: 11.
Duffie, D: **J.4**: 7.
Duffy, K: **G.2.1**: 110.
Dufloux, C: **J.2**: 152.
Dufumier, M: **F.3.2**: 18. **H.1.1.4**: 3.
Dujardin, J: **G.2.5**: 16.
Duller, H: **F.3.2**: 39.
Dumagan, J: **L.2**: 25.

Ekpo, A: **F.3.2**: 56.

El, T: **L.2**: 6.

El Nil, Y: **F.3.2**: 61. **J.5**: 19. **N.1**: 207.

El-Baghdadi, M: **H.0**: 152.

El-Sheikh, S: **N.1**: 125.

Elbadawi, I: **H.1.1**: 21. **N.1**: 106. **O.2.1**: 66.

Elder, H: **N.2**: 20.

Elek, A: **F.3.3**: 45. **O.1.3**: 84.

Elffers, H: **N.2**: 13, 290.

Elgari Bin Eid, M: **N.2**: 246.

Eliasson, G: **C**: 55.

Eling, A: **N.2**: 13.

Ellard, P: **N.2**: 25.

Elleithy, A: **G.3.3.4**: 4.

Ellerman, D: **F.3.1.4**: 21.

Elliehausen, G: **J.2**: 139.

Ellig, J: **N.3**: 48.

Elliot, G: **I.2.1**: 164.

Elliott, D: **H.2.2**: 127.

Elliott, K: **O.3.3**: 60.

Elliott-Gower, S: **O.3.3**: 19.

Ellis, B: **H.4**: 92.

Ellis, D: **J.2**: 158.

Ellis, M: **F.3.1.2**: 14.

Ellman, M: **N.1**: 146, 156.

Elmeskov, J: **L.1**: 36.

Elmslie, B: **O.3.1**: 44, 57.

Elnagheeb, A: **H.1.1.1**: 23.

Elton, E: **J.4**: 176.

Elton, M: **H.3**: 101.

Elyasiani, E: **J.2**: 193. **J.4**: 144.

Emami, Z: **D**: 50.

Emel, J: **F.3.1.4**: 11. **H.0**: 42.

Emenyonu, E: **B.4**: 25.

Emerson, M: **O.2.3**: 45.

Emmanuel, C: **B.4**: 58. **G.3.3.5**: 52.

Emmerich, K: **G.2.4**: 99. **K.3**: 66.

Emmott, B: **O.1.2.2**: 16.

Encaoua, D: **C**: 71.

Encarnation, D: **O.3.1**: 60.

Endersby, J: **G.2.4**: 78.

Endre, H: **H.0**: 170.

Endrighi, E: **H.1.2.1**: 11.

Enevoldsen, T: **O.3.2**: 71.

Engel, C: **O.2.1**: 29.

Engelbrecht, H: **B.3**: 38. **G.1.2**: 1.

Engerman, S: **G.2.1**: 8.

Engers, M: **O.1.3**: 46.

Engineer, M: **J.1**: 10.

Englander, A: **O.2.1**: 44. **O.2.3**: 31.

Engle, R: **B.3**: 1. **F.3.1.1**: 66, 118. **H.2.2**: 118. **O.2.1**: 42.

English, W: **O.2.2**: 126.

Englmann, F: **I.2.1**: 29.

Eng, van der, P: **F.2**: 11.

Engwall, L: **A**: 4.

Entorf, H: **G.2.1**: 38.

Enyedi, G: **F.3.1.1**: 72.

Ephraums, J: **H.0**: 71.

Epp, D: **H.0**: 207.

Epperson, J: **J.2**: 241.

Epstein, G: **J.2**: 223.

Epstein, L: **J.4**: 7. **M.1**: 17.

Erber, G: **G.1.2**: 19.

Erdmenger, J: **H.3**: 36.

Erdős, T: **F.3.3**: 5. **N.1**: 70.

Erickson, G: **H.4**: 62.

Erickson, R: **O.3.1**: 46.

Ericsson, M: **H.2.2**: 141.

Erkut, E: **H.3**: 72.

Ernst, A: **O.1.3**: 22.

Ernste, H: **F.3.1.1**: 73.

Erreygers, G: **I.2.1**: 131.

Errico, L: **N.2**: 100.

Errunza, V: **O.2.2**: 124.

Ershov, E: **N.1**: 178.

Erzan, R: **O.1.3**: 43, 89. **O.3.3**: 45.

Esguerra, M: **H.1.2.1**: 4.

Espa, E: **O.1.3**: 63.

Esparza, A: **H.4**: 110.

Espasa, A: **H.2.1**: 72.

Espinosa, M: **F.3.1.1**: 32.

Espinosa, de, J: **H.1.2**: 1.

Essen, van, U: **N.2**: 201.

Esteban, J: **M.1**: 21.

Estes, C: **M.4**: 62.

Estrin, S: **G.3.3.5**: 77. **H.2.1**: 86. **J.2**: 137–138. **K.3**: 82.

Etherington, D: **H.1.2.1**: 21.

Etienne, G: **H.1.1.4**: 12.

Ettori, F: **O.3.1**: 50.

Eun, C: **J.4**: 266.

Evans, A: **K.3**: 80.

Evans, M: **J.4**: 136.
Evans, P: **G.1**: 8. **J.2**: 43.
Evans, S: **G.2.4**: 17.
Evenko, L: **H.4**: 20.
Evensky, J: **D**: 22. **F.3.1.3**: 22.
Everaert, L: **J.1**: 86.
Ewer, P: **G.2.4**: 86.
Ewing, K: **G.2.4**: 17.
Ewringmann, D: **H.0**: 102.
Eyoh, D: **H.1.1.4**: 18.
Ezeala-Harrison, F: **G.2.1**: 76.
Ezzamel, M: **B.4**: 49.
Fabozzi, F: **J.4**: 11.
Fabre, G: **N.1**: 8.
Fabry, N: **O.2.2**: 118.
Faccioli, M: **H.2.2**: 9.
Fachin, S: **F.5**: 25.
Faff, R: **J.4**: 199.
Fagan, G: **F.5**: 6.
Fahrer, J: **J.5**: 16.
Fain, J: **N.2**: 219.
Faini, R: **O.3.1**: 29.
Fairbairn, T: **F.1**: 92.
Falk, H: **B.4**: 64.
Falk, N: **H.0**: 125.
Falk, R: **M.2**: 7.
Falusné-Szikra, K: **O.2.2**: 109.
Falvey, R: **O.3.3**: 59.
Fama, E: **J.4**: 19. **L.3**: 26.
Faminow, M: **I.2.1**: 111.
Fan, C: **F.3.1.1**: 62.
Fang, G: **F.3.1.4**: 14.
Fanger, U: **N.2**: 137.
Fankhauser, S: **H.0**: 44.
Faquih, O: **O.2.4**: 1.
Farber, D: **F.3.1.4**: 6.
Farber, H: **G.2.4**: 11.
Farbman, M: **G.3.3.4**: 17.
Fardmanesh, M: **L.1**: 32.
Fardoust, S: **F.3.2**: 41.
Färe, R: **G.1.1**: 19.
Faria, W: **O.1.2.4**: 12.
Farmer, R: **I.2.1**: 134.
Farnleitner, J: **I.2.3**: 65.
Farrell, J: **G.1.1**: 39. **H.3**: 93.
Farrell, T: **N.2**: 221.

Farrington, C: **N.2**: 123.
Farzin, Y: **H.0**: 155.
Fasbender, K: **M.1**: 16.
Fase, M: **F.1**: 65. **J.1**: 48.
Fatseas, V: **G.1.2**: 8.
Fauchart, E: **N.1**: 324.
Fauré, Y: **N.1**: 13.
Faurot, D: **G.2.4**: 35.
Faux, C: **H.1.2.1**: 12.
Favarger, P: **G.1.2**: 4.
Favero, C: **H.2.2**: 163. **N.1**: 297.
Fawson, C: **H.1.1.1**: 8.
Fay, M: **F.3.3**: 27.
Fayissa, B: **G.1.3**: 17.
Fayolle, J: **N.1**: 132.
Fazzari, S: **I.2.1**: 18.
Fedeli, S: **N.1**: 15.
Fedenia, M: **J.4**: 230.
Feder, G: **H.1.1.2**: 9.
Feehan, J: **O.3.3**: 55.
Feenstra, R: **O.3.3**: 133.
Fehér, F: **N.1**: 141.
Fehr, von der, N: **G.3.3.5**: 28.
Feijo, C: **J.1**: 102.
Feinberg, R: **I.2.2**: 7. **O.1.3**: 74.
Feinstein, J: **N.2**: 283.
Feitelson, E: **L.2**: 86.
Feito Hernández, M: **O.1.2.4**: 84.
Feito Higueruela, J: **O.1.2.4**: 84.
Felderer, B: **M.4**: 71.
Feldman, R: **M.4**: 47.
Feldstein, M: **M.4**: 118.
Félix, D: **N.1**: 314.
Fell, J: **F.5**: 6.
Fellman, J: **B.3**: 54.
Fels, G: **N.1**: 315.
Felsenstein, D: **F.3.1.1**: 45, 72. **J.2**: 4.
Felstead, A: **G.3.3.1**: 12.
Feltham, G: **B.4**: 26. **G.3.3.5**: 102.
Fenichel, A: **H.1.1.4**: 19.
Fenn, P: **G.2.5**: 38.
Ferdows, K: **H.2.1**: 122.
Ferenc, F: **N.1**: 273.
Ferens, I: **N.1**: 263–267.
Ferguson, B: **F.3.1.1**: 108. **M.4**: 21.
Ferguson, D: **F.1**: 66.
Ferguson, J: **O.2.2**: 67.

Friedman, R: **G.2.4**: 14.
Friedrich, H: **F.3.2**: 42.
Friesen, J: **H.2.1**: 67.
Frimmel, M: **H.0**: 183.
Frisch, H: **J.1**: 11.
Frischtak, C: **G.1**: 29.
Frisse, K: **H.2.1**: 18.
Fritsch, W: **O.3.3**: 7.
Fritz, J: **H.0**: 165.
Frohlich, N: **G.1.2**: 7.
Frommann, R: **G.3.3.5**: 92.
Froot, K: **J.4**: 46.
Frost, M: **F.3.1.1**: 87.
Froyen, R: **J.5**: 41.
Fruin, W: **H.2.1**: 42.
Fry, M: **D**: 20. **J.1**: 19. **J.2**: 213.
Fry, T: **J.4**: 199.
Frydman, R: **N.1**: 328.
Fu, F: **O.2.2**: 86.
Fu, G: **G.2.1**: 163.
Fu, T: **H.1.1.4**: 26.
Fuentes, J: **O.1.3**: 100.
Fürst, D: **H.0**: 102.
Fuerst, T: **J.4**: 63.
Fuertes, J: **H.2.1**: 64.
Fujii, E: **H.3**: 44.
Fujimoto, I: **F.3.1.1**: 95.
Fujimoto, T: **G.1.1**: 29.
Fujita, M: **F.3.1.2**: 1. **K.2**: 25.
Fukuda, S: **O.2.1**: 38. **O.2.4**: 3.
Fukuyama, H: **G.1.1**: 27.
Fulghieri, P: **O.1.2.2**: 3.
Fuller, A: **H.1.1.2**: 13.
Fuller, B: **M.5**: 31.
Fuller, D: **G.2.1**: 99.
Fuller, J: **H.2.2**: 89.
Fullerton, D: **L.2**: 90. **N.2**: 125.
Fumas, V: **H.2.1**: 92.
Fung, H: **O.2.3**: 34.
Fung, K: **G.3.3.5**: 68. **O.1.2.4**: 14.
Funke, M: **G.2.1**: 160. **H.2.1**: 18. **N.2**: 311. **O.3.1**: 9.
Funkhouser, E: **O.1.2.5**: 5.
Fureng, D: **N.1**: 103.
Furlong, W: **H.1.2.1**: 34.
Furstenberg, von, G: **O.1.3**: 15.
Fuss, M: **G.1.2**: 2. **H.2.1**: 127. **H.2.2**: 65.

Futagami, K: **K.2**: 3.
Gabbay, R: **F.3.2**: 55.
Gabel, J: **M.4**: 64.
Gábor, I: **F.1**: 75.
Gábor, O: **O.2.2**: 68.
Gabriel, S: **I.2.3**: 85.
Gabrielsen, I: **N.2**: 122.
Gabszewicz, J: **I.2.1**: 60.
Gade, M: **N.2**: 219.
Gadgil, M: **H.1.1**: 13.
Gaer, van de, D: **N.2**: 312.
Gaffard, J: **G.3.3**: 33. **J.1**: 14.
Gafni, A: **M.4**: 4.
Gagales, A: **N.2**: 134.
Gagnon, J: **J.4**: 303. **N.2**: 80. **O.1.2**: 12. **O.2.3**: 27.
Gahvari, F: **N.2**: 295.
Gaïdar, E: **N.1**: 156.
Gaiha, R: **M.2**: 26.
Gaile, G: **F.3.1.1**: 94. **F.3.2**: 30.
Gaillard, J: **G.1**: 14.
Gajda, J: **B.3**: 43.
Gal-Or, E: **I.2.1**: 15.
Galán, M: **O.1.3**: 8.
Galarza, E: **H.0**: 134.
Galavielle, J: **N.2**: 243.
Galbraith, J: **F.1**: 11.
Gale, D: **C**: 84. **I.2.1**: 65. **J.4**: 300.
Gale, I: **I.2.1**: 113.
Galeazzi, G: **G.2.2**: 18.
Galenson, W: **G.2.1**: 106.
Galí, J: **J.1**: 12.
Galindo, M: **O.1.3**: 9.
Gallagher, J: **E**: 6.
Gallagher, L: **J.4**: 59.
Gallant, A: **J.4**: 298.
Gallastegui, M: **O.1.2.4**: 84.
Gallaway, L: **N.2**: 296.
Galligan, B: **N.1**: 88.
Gallizo, J: **B.4**: 61.
Galloux, M: **J.2**: 27.
Galor, O: **G.1.1**: 41. **G.2.1**: 92. **N.2**: 242.
Gambardella, A: **G.1**: 37.
Gammie, M: **N.2**: 103–105.
Gana, J: **H.2.2**: 140.
Ganbaatar, K: **G.3.3.1**: 9.
Gandal, N: **G.1.1**: 39.

Ganderton, P: **M.5**: 16.
Gandolfo, G: **B.3**: 13.
Gang, I: **G.3.3.4**: 20.
Gangopadhyay, S: **O.3.3**: 73.
Gapinski, J: **J.1**: 103.
Garand, J: **B.1**: 3.
Garant, M: **M.5**: 7.
Garbero, P: **L.1**: 10.
García, F: **J.2**: 194.
Garcia, P: **I.2.1**: 120.
García Alvarez-Coque, J: **H.1.1.4**: 41.
Garciá Falcón, J: **J.2**: 92.
Garciá-Benau, M: **B.4**: 17.
Garcia-Milà, T: **N.3**: 8.
Gardeazabal, J: **O.2.1**: 75.
Gardiner, J: **H.0**: 175.
Gardiner, K: **L.2**: 110.
Gardner, B: **B.2**: 1.
Gardner, G: **N.2**: 281. **O.3.3**: 78.
Garfinkel, I: **G.2.2**: 23. **M.4**: 100.
Garfinkle, D: **F.3.1.1**: 44.
Garganas, N: **J.1**: 17.
Garnier, P: **G.2.2**: 20.
Garofalo, G: **G.2.2**: 14. **L.3**: 23.
Garonna, P: **B.3**: 27.
Garratt, R: **J.1**: 45.
Garretsen, H: **G.3.2**: 29.
Garrod, G: **I.2.1**: 170.
Garrod, N: **B.4**: 58.
Garvey, G: **G.2.5**: 26. **G.3.3**: 19.
Gary, R: **F.3.1.1**: 35.
Garza, G: **F.3.1.1**: 55.
Gash, D: **G.1**: 26.
Gaspar, J: **F.3.1.1**: 72.
Gasparini, L: **K.2**: 14.
Gasson, R: **H.1.1.3**: 9.
Gaston, N: **M.5**: 14.
Gatsios, K: **G.3.2**: 21. **O.1.3**: 55.
Gau, G: **J.4**: 52.
Gauci, B: **G.4**: 4.
Gaude, J: **G.2.2**: 20.
Gaudemet, L: **H.2.2**: 94.
Gauger, J: **J.4**: 179.
Gault, J: **H.2.2**: 162.
Gauthier, H: **K.3**: 60.
Gautschi, D: **H.4**: 100. **L.2**: 5.
Gaver, J: **J.4**: 243.

Gaver, K: **J.4**: 243.
Gavin, J: **H.0**: 75.
Gavosto, A: **F.5**: 25.
Gay, du, P: **L.2**: 4.
Gazdar, H: **M.2**: 14.
Gazioglu, S: **O.2.1**: 68.
Geddes, M: **F.3.1.1**: 83.
Gedeon, P: **N.1**: 224–225.
Gellings, C: **I.2.3**: 9.
Gemert, van, H: **J.2**: 69.
Gencay, R: **B.3**: 39.
Gensch, D: **H.4**: 74.
Genser, B: **N.2**: 302.
Gentle, C: **J.2**: 87.
Geoffron, P: **N.2**: 17.
Georgakopoulos, T: **N.2**: 54, 210.
Georgantelis, S: **L.2**: 32.
George, G: **I.2.1**: 43.
George, K: **G.3.2**: 40.
George, S: **O.2.2**: 52. **O.3.2**: 70.
Georgiou, G: **O.2.2**: 108.
Geping, Q: **H.2.2**: 85, 109.
Ger, G: **F.3.2**: 108.
Gerbaud, F: **N.1**: 325.
Gerdtham, U: **M.4**: 24.
Gereffi, G: **F.3.1.1**: 81.
Gerlach, K: **G.2.5**: 36.
Gerlach, M: **G.3.2**: 23–24. **H.2.1**: 95.
Gerlach, S: **O.3.2**: 44.
Gern, K: **F.3.3**: 60. **G.1.1**: 22.
Geronimus, A: **F.3.1.3**: 26.
Geroski, P: **G.3.2**: 40. **I.2.1**: 146.
Gersdorf-Giaro, M: **G.2.4**: 33.
Gerster, G: **H.0**: 183.
Gerster, R: **O.2.2**: 79.
Gertler, M: **F.3.3**: 20. **G.1.1**: 14. **H.2.1**: 39.
Gertler, P: **M.4**: 55.
Gesano, G: **G.2.1**: 62.
Gesine, S: **G.2.5**: 36.
Getimis, P: **F.3.1.1**: 64.
Ghani, E: **J.4**: 47.
Gharat, N: **H.1.2.1**: 38.
Ghasimi, M: **N.1**: 247.
Ghate, P: **J.2**: 61.
Ghei, N: **O.2.1**: 51.
Ghorpade, M: **F.3.2**: 90.

Ghose, S: **H.4**: 74.
Ghosh, A: **F.3.1.1**: 33. **F.3.2**: 98. **O.2.3**: 36. **O.3.1**: 33.
Ghosh, D: **G.2.1**: 68.
Ghosh, P: **N.2**: 226.
Ghosh, R: **F.3.2**: 55.
Giaccotto, C: **I.2.2**: 2.
Giakoumis, P: **F.3.1.3**: 29.
Giannoni, M: **H.1.2.1**: 6.
Giardiello, A: **H.1.1.4**: 46.
Giarratani, F: **B.3**: 20.
Gibb, K: **L.2**: 84. **N.2**: 227.
Gibb, R: **O.2.2**: 57.
Gibbon, P: **H.1.1.4**: 15. **O.2.4**: 20.
Gibbons, R: **C**: 72. **K.3**: 112.
Gibson, H: **O.1.2.4**: 63.
Gibson, J: **J.1**: 97.
Giersch, H: **N.1**: 299.
Gieseck, A: **F.3.1.2**: 12.
Gifford, S: **G.3.3**: 18.
Gigler, F: **B.4**: 26.
Gilad, B: **G.3.3.5**: 80.
Gilardi, J: **G.2.5**: 33.
Gilas, J: **O.1.1**: 4.
Gilbert, R: **G.1.1**: 39.
Gildea, J: **J.2**: 225.
Gill, C: **G.2.4**: 111.
Gill, R: **O.3.2**: 21.
Gill, S: **H.0**: 174.
Gilles, C: **I.2.1**: 10. **J.1**: 15.
Gilligan, T: **I.2.1**: 83.
Gillion, C: **M.4**: 67.
Gilmore, T: **G.3.3**: 22.
Giloth, R: **F.3.1.1**: 46.
Giménez-Reyna Rodriguez, E: **O.1.2.4**: 59.
Gindling, T: **G.2.1**: 56.
Ginsburg, D: **G.3.3.5**: 62.
Gintis, H: **C**: 15.
Giordani C., J: **N.1**: 252.
Giordano, L: **G.1**: 2.
Giovannetti, G: **O.2.1**: 37.
Giovanni, Di, M: **J.2**: 147.
Giovannini, A: **O.2.2**: 7.
Giovannini, P: **J.4**: 301.
Gipouloux, F: **O.1.3**: 86.
Giraud, P: **H.2.2**: 94.
Girerd-Potin, I: **J.4**: 197.

Gitli, E: **O.3.3**: 39.
Gitsu, M: **H.3**: 79.
Gittell, R: **F.3.2**: 30.
Giustiniani, A: **O.1.3**: 67.
Givoly, D: **N.2**: 106, 317.
Glaeser, E: **F.3.1.1**: 106.
Glascock, J: **G.3.3.4**: 6. **J.4**: 114.
Glazer, A: **G.2.4**: 60. **M.4**: 19.
Glazer, J: **G.1**: 10.
Gleave, M: **H.3**: 9.
Gleeson, M: **L.2**: 102.
Gleicher, D: **K.3**: 95.
Gleinsvik, A: **J.2**: 19.
Gleizer, D: **L.1**: 18.
Glen, J: **O.2.1**: 81.
Glennerster, H: **M.4**: 109.
Glomm, G: **F.3.1.1**: 27.
Glomsrød, S: **H.0**: 116.
Glynn, D: **I.2.1**: 132.
Gneveckow, J: **H.1.1.2**: 24.
Gobbo, F: **N.3**: 46.
Gochoco, M: **O.1.2.4**: 7.
Godard, O: **H.0**: 79. **N.3**: 10.
Goddard, E: **H.4**: 63.
Goddard, J: **I.2.3**: 16.
Godement, B: **J.1**: 85.
Godoy, R: **H.1.1.1**: 1. **H.1.1.2**: 10. **H.1.1.3**: 11.
Goering, G: **I.2.1**: 49.
Goerl, G: **N.3**: 42.
Goerlich, F: **G.2.1**: 63.
Goetschin, P: **G.3.3.4**: 1.
Goetz, A: **H.3**: 38.
Goetz, R: **N.1**: 222.
Goetz, S: **I.2.3**: 70.
Goetzmann, W: **J.4**: 95.
Goh, M: **G.3.3.1**: 9.
Gohmann, S: **M.4**: 26.
Goisis, G: **J.2**: 159.
Gokhale, J: **G.2.1**: 22.
Gold, S: **G.1.1**: 25.
Goldberg, L: **J.2**: 44, 112.
Goldberg, M: **H.2.2**: 14.
Goldberg, P: **G.1.1**: 8.
Golden, B: **H.3**: 72.
Golden, K: **G.3.3.5**: 34.
Golden, L: **G.2.4**: 104.

Goldfarb, R: **G.2.1**: 28.
Goldfeld, S: **G.3.3**: 9.
Goldmann, W: **H.2.1**: 111.
Goldrich, D: **F.3.2**: 83.
Goldsmith, A: **F.3.1.3**: 25. **F.3.2**: 38.
Goldsmith, S: **I.2.3**: 23.
Goldstein, M: **O.2.2**: 32. **O.2.3**: 48.
Golingi, F: **H.1.2.1**: 14.
Gombola, M: **L.3**: 10.
Gomel, G: **J.5**: 1.
Gómez de Miguel, J: **O.1.2.4**: 58.
Gommers, M: **H.3**: 67.
Gompel, Van, J: **G.2.1**: 168.
Gomulka, S: **N.1**: 182.
Gonce, R: **C**: 41.
Gondwe, D: **F.3.2**: 35.
Gonon, J: **N.1**: 4.
González H., B: **O.1.3**: 103.
González Romero, A: **H.2.1**: 28. **O.2.3**: 43.
González-Páramo, J: **O.1.2.4**: 59.
Gonzalo, J: **B.4**: 61.
Good, D: **H.3**: 26.
Goodhart, C: **N.2**: 156. **O.1.2.4**: 84. **O.2.1**: 43. **O.2.3**: 12.
Goodland, R: **H.2.2**: 109.
Goodman, J: **J.2**: 221.
Goodwin, P: **I.2.1**: 183.
Gooptu, S: **J.2**: 35.
Gootzeit, M: **D**: 39.
Goovaerts, M: **J.3**: 17.
Gora, M: **G.2.1**: 132.
Gordon, A: **B.4**: 9. **N.1**: 135.
Gordon, D: **G.2.1**: 155. **H.1.2.1**: 43. **J.1**: 13. **N.2**: 255.
Gordon, G: **G.3.3.5**: 80.
Gordon, I: **B.4**: 23.
Gordon, M: **D**: 76.
Gordon, R: **F.3.3**: 52. **N.2**: 188.
Gorn, P: **O.3.3**: 142.
Gorter, C: **G.2.1**: 126.
Gospel, H: **O.1.2.4**: 47.
Goss, B: **F.3.2**: 82. **I.2.1**: 120.
Göth, P: **J.2**: 144.
Gottfried, R: **H.0**: 62.
Gottfries, N: **K.3**: 29.
Gottlieb, D: **O.2.3**: 46.
Gottschalk, P: **K.2**: 38.

Gouin, D: **H.1.2.1**: 3.
Goujet, R: **I.2.1**: 28.
Gould, J: **F.3.1.4**: 26.
Gourlay, K: **H.0**: 194.
Govindaraj, S: **H.2.2**: 56.
Govindasamy, P: **F.3.1.2**: 9.
Gowdy, J: **H.0**: 24.
Gowland, D: **F.1**: 55.
Goyeau, D: **J.2**: 114.
Graafland, J: **G.2.1**: 150.
Graafsma, F: **O.3.3**: 98.
Grabendorff, W: **O.1.2.4**: 74.
Grabher, G: **F.1**: 62.
Grabowski, R: **L.1**: 31.
Gradstein, M: **C**: 5.
Graetz, M: **N.2**: 211.
Graf, G: **J.2**: 74.
Graf, W: **O.3.2**: 43.
Graham, B: **H.3**: 43.
Graham, C: **M.3**: 11.
Graham, D: **H.1.2.1**: 17.
Graham, J: **H.4**: 20.
Grahl, J: **O.1.2.4**: 47.
Grahm, L: **F.3.2**: 118.
Grammatikos, T: **J.4**: 230.
Grancelli, B: **H.2.1**: 80. **N.1**: 300.
Grandi, A: **G.1.3**: 9.
Grandi, R: **I.2.2**: 3.
Grand, le, J: **M.3**: 10.
Grandmont, J: **L.1**: 43.
Granfors, D: **J.2**: 65.
Granger, C: **B.3**: 39.
Grant, J: **F.3.2**: 49. **K.3**: 113.
Grant, R: **G.1.1**: 2.
Granville, B: **J.5**: 47.
Grasso, L: **B.4**: 32.
Grauwe, de, P: **O.1.2.4**: 69. **O.2.1**: 48. **O.2.3**: 7.
Gravelle, J: **N.2**: 180.
Gray, C: **N.1**: 320.
Gray, P: **H.2.1**: 38.
Gray, S: **B.4**: 25.
Graziosi, G: **N.3**: 46.
Greco, A: **I.2.2**: 6.
Greef, F: **K.3**: 46.
Green, A: **F.3.1.1**: 110. **G.2.2**: 7.
Green, F: **H.2.1**: 9. **K.2**: 3. **M.5**: 29.

Hamilton, R: **G.3.3.5**: 64. **H.2.1**: 10.
Hamilton, W: **G.3.3.5**: 97.
Hamley, W: **H.1.1.4**: 22.
Hamm, R: **H.4**: 55.
Hammarström, O: **G.2.4**: 16.
Hammond, S: **G.2.3**: 8.
Hammoudeh, S: **O.1.2.3**: 8.
Hamnett, C: **F.3.1.1**: 16. **N.2**: 16.
Han, B: **G.3.3.5**: 109.
Han, J: **B.4**: 35.
Hanau, K: **B.3**: 63.
Hancock, G: **I.2.3**: 2.
Hanel, P: **O.3.3**: 40.
Hanemann, M: **L.2**: 35.
Hanf, C: **H.1.2.1**: 32.
Hann, E: **N.1**: 271.
Hanratty, M: **M.2**: 6.
Hanreich, H: **I.2.3**: 65.
Hansen, B: **B.3**: 39.
Hansen, G: **F.3.3**: 13. **M.4**: 113.
Hansen, N: **F.3.1.1**: 96.
Hansen, R: **J.2**: 103.
Hanser, A: **H.1.1.2**: 24.
Hansmeyer, K: **H.0**: 102.
Hanson, J: **J.4**: 159.
Hanson, M: **H.3**: 66.
Hanson, P: **F.1**: 41, 57.
Hanson, R: **N.1**: 320.
Hanson, S: **G.2.1**: 46.
Hansson, B: **J.4**: 96, 196.
Hansson, P: **F.3.2**: 15. **O.3.3**: 14.
Hantrais, L: **M.3**: 7.
Hanweck, G: **J.2**: 112.
Haque, M: **H.3**: 1. **O.3.3**: 37.
Harasty, H: **F.1**: 72.
Harbridge, R: **G.2.4**: 90.
Hardaker, B: **H.4**: 86.
Hardaway, R: **H.3**: 39.
Hardouvelis, G: **J.4**: 222.
Hardy, D: **I.2.3**: 55. **J.2**: 107.
Hare, P: **J.2**: 137–138. **M.5**: 20. **N.1**: 162.
Hargreaves Heap, S: **C**: 30.
Harik, I: **I.2.3**: 56.
Harland, D: **L.2**: 33.
Harling, K: **H.1.1.3**: 20.
Harm, C: **G.3.3.3**: 15.
Harmelink, P: **N.2**: 195.

Harper, C: **G.2.3**: 7.
Harrington, J: **F.5**: 20. **H.0**: 141. **J.2**: 154.
Harris, B: **G.3.3.4**: 14.
Harris, E: **O.2.2**: 61.
Harris, F: **H.4**: 98.
Harris, G: **N.2**: 267.
Harris, M: **I.2.3**: 23.
Harris, N: **O.1.2**: 15.
Harris, R: **O.1.3**: 95.
Harris, T: **K.3**: 101.
Harrison, B: **F.3.1.1**: 18. **O.2.3**: 13.
Harrison, G: **I.2.1**: 120.
Hart, J: **H.2.1**: 13. **O.3.1**: 59.
Hart, P: **G.2.5**: 55. **H.2.2**: 18.
Harte, G: **O.2.2**: 127.
Hartl, R: **H.0**: 104.
Hartley, P: **B.3**: 26.
Hartog, J: **K.3**: 115.
Hartropp, A: **J.2**: 20.
Hartshorn, J: **H.2.2**: 162.
Hartzell, D: **I.2.3**: 106.
Haruna, S: **G.2.4**: 110.
Harvey, A: **B.3**: 1.
Harvey, C: **G.3.3.5**: 55. **H.0**: 153. **J.4**: 225, 260.
Harvey, J: **F.3.1.3**: 30.
Harvie, C: **H.2.2**: 158.
Harwit, E: **H.2.2**: 68.
Harwood, G: **N.2**: 216.
Hasenkamp, G: **G.3.3.2**: 8.
Haskel, J: **G.2.4**: 82.
Haslag, J: **J.5**: 56.
Hassan, H: **G.3.3.1**: 9.
Hassan, M: **J.4**: 193.
Hassan, R: **H.1.1.4**: 16.
Hasseldine, J: **N.2**: 284.
Hassett, K: **N.2**: 181.
Hatch, U: **H.1.1.2**: 37.
Hatzipanayotou, P: **O.3.3**: 93.
Hauff, von, M: **N.2**: 254.
Haughton, G: **F.3.1.1**: 42.
Haurin, D: **I.2.1**: 179.
Hausman, D: **C**: 42. **M.1**: 26.
Hautcoeur, J: **K.3**: 49.
Hawke, G: **M.5**: 38.
Hawkins, J: **J.2**: 132.
Hax, A: **G.3.3.5**: 97.

Hayakawa, H: **J.1**: 27.
Hayami, Y: **H.1.1**: 17. **H.1.1.2**: 11. **H.4**: 68.
Hayashi, F: **L.2**: 18.
Hayashi, K: **F.3.1.1**: 116.
Hayes, D: **I.2.1**: 62. **O.3.2**: 1.
Hayes, K: **K.2**: 21. **L.2**: 71.
Hayn, C: **N.2**: 106, 317.
Hayter, R: **G.2.1**: 44. **O.3.2**: 41.
Hayward, D: **O.3.1**: 46.
Hazari, B: **G.2.1**: 145. **O.3.1**: 65.
Hazell, P: **H.1.1.3**: 3.
Hazledine, T: **O.3.2**: 11.
He, R: **N.1**: 210.
Heady, C: **I.2.1**: 110. **N.2**: 81.
Heal, D: **H.2.2**: 162.
Heald, S: **G.2.2**: 11.
Healey, M: **F.3.1.1**: 22.
Healey, N: **O.2.3**: 64.
Healy, P: **G.3.2**: 10.
Heaps, T: **H.1.2.1**: 29.
Heath, D: **J.4**: 105.
Heath, J: **F.3.1.3**: 3. **H.1.1.2**: 12.
Heath, R: **B.3**: 56.
Heathfield, D: **B.4**: 49.
Heaton, G: **H.0**: 182.
Heberer, T: **N.1**: 58.
Heeks, R: **H.2.1**: 100.
Heffernan, S: **J.2**: 151.
Heggestad, A: **J.2**: 34.
Hegji, C: **O.2.1**: 64.
Heijman, W: **H.0**: 29, 54, 133.
Heilemann, U: **F.3.1.2**: 12.
Heimler, A: **M.4**: 58.
Hein, S: **F.2**: 23. **F.3.2**: 85. **J.1**: 77. **J.2**: 18.
Heinrich, R: **N.1**: 293.
Heise, A: **J.1**: 22. **J.2**: 11.
Helfat, C: **G.3.3.3**: 27.
Helleiner, E: **O.2.4**: 9.
Helleiner, G: **F.3.2**: 47. **O.2.2**: 64.
Heller, W: **B.3**: 39. **G.3.3.5**: 73.
Hellerstein, D: **H.0**: 187. **L.2**: 9.
Helm, D: **H.0**: 19. **I.2.3**: 48.
Helpman, E: **N.2**: 178.
Helsen, K: **H.4**: 48.
Helwege, A: **F.1**: 14. **M.2**: 4.
Helwege, J: **K.2**: 29.
Hendershott, P: **J.4**: 146. **L.2**: 96.

Henderson, A: **O.2.4**: 6.
Henderson, D: **H.4**: 75. **O.1.2.4**: 28.
Henderson, G: **F.3.1.4**: 16.
Hendley, D: **A**: 6.
Hendley, K: **G.2.4**: 7. **G.3.3**: 4. **N.1**: 274.
Hendricks, K: **G.1**: 41.
Hendricks, W: **I.2.3**: 35.
Hendrikse, G: **C**: 71. **G.2.5**: 43.
Hendry, D: **J.1**: 49.
Heng, T: **O.1.2.4**: 7.
Henley, A: **I.2.3**: 83. **O.1.2.4**: 47.
Henneberry, J: **F.3.1.1**: 123.
Henning, J: **H.1.1**: 18.
Henrekson, M: **F.3.2**: 15.
Henriksson, R: **F.3.2**: 9.
Henry, N: **F.3.1.1**: 31.
Henry, S: **G.2.1**: 158.
Hensher, D: **N.1**: 287.
Hentschel, L: **J.4**: 282.
Hepburn, G: **N.2**: 285.
Heppleston, C: **J.2**: 96.
Heravi, S: **F.2**: 20.
Herbener, J: **N.1**: 319.
Herbert, J: **H.2.2**: 87.
Her, L', J: **J.4**: 235.
Hermalin, B: **G.3.3.5**: 15.
Hernádi, A: **F.3.2**: 120.
Hernández Castilla, N: **O.1.2.4**: 58.
Hernández García, G: **O.1.2.4**: 58.
Hernando, I: **H.2.1**: 1.
Herndl, T: **J.2**: 191.
Heron, Le, R: **H.1.1.4**: 4.
Herpin, N: **L.1**: 4.
Herrán Mendívil, de la, J: **O.1.2.4**: 58.
Herrera, J: **J.4**: 70.
Herriges, J: **H.2.2**: 92.
Herrin, W: **L.2**: 107.
Herrmann, J: **G.3.3**: 14.
Herruzo, A: **H.1.1.1**: 22.
Herson, R: **B.4**: 9.
Hertel, T: **B.3**: 19.
Hertog, den, R: **I.2.1**: 116.
Herz, B: **O.2.3**: 65.
Herzog, H: **G.2.1**: 33.
Hesse, G: **I.2.1**: 29.
Hesse, H: **J.5**: 61.

Ishikawa, J: **F.3.3**: 33. **O.3.1**: 72.
Islam, I: **F.3.2**: 106.
Islam, M: **O.2.1**: 34.
Ismail, I: **H.2.2**: 160.
Israel, R: **G.3.2**: 3.
Israilevich, P: **B.3**: 40.
Issoulié, J: **J.4**: 171.
István, A: **L.1**: 22.
István, S: **L.1**: 22.
Itaya, J: **N.3**: 5.
Iten, R: **H.0**: 20.
Itō, K: **N.2**: 9.
Ito, T: **F.3.3**: 23. **O.2.1**: 42.
Ivanter, A: **J.1**: 88.
Ivens, M: **G.2.1**: 95.
Ivory, P: **O.1.3**: 48.
Iwamoto, Y: **F.5**: 38. **N.2**: 131.
Iwata, T: **H.1.1.3**: 2.
Iwata Ishida, T: **H.1.1.2**: 25.
Iwayemi, A: **O.1.2.3**: 26.
Iyer, A: **I.2.1**: 34.
Jabornegg, P: **J.2**: 47.
Jacka, S: **J.4**: 67.
Jacklin, C: **J.4**: 182.
Jackson, M: **B.1**: 8. **N.1**: 324.
Jackson, N: **H.0**: 196.
Jackson, R: **B.3**: 40.
Jackson, T: **O.1.2.4**: 22.
Jackson, W: **M.4**: 7.
Jacobs, A: **J.4**: 8.
Jacobs, D: **I.2.1**: 89.
Jacobs, J: **G.2.1**: 151.
Jacobs, M: **H.0**: 178.
Jacquemin, A: **G.3.2**: 40.
Jacques, J: **G.1**: 20.
Jacques, M: **N.2**: 86.
Jacquet, P: **O.1.2.4**: 73.
Jacquinot, P: **O.2.1**: 11.
Jadhav, R: **J.2**: 42.
Jafarey, V: **N.1**: 123.
Jaffe, J: **J.4**: 285.
Jaforullah, M: **H.0**: 22.
Jaggi, B: **H.0**: 99. **H.2.2**: 22.
Jain, A: **H.0**: 70.
Jain, B: **G.2.5**: 57.
Jain, P: **H.2.2**: 56. **J.4**: 33.

Jamal, T: **O.1.3**: 81.
James, C: **J.4**: 161.
James, F: **G.3.3.1**: 20.
James, W: **N.1**: 101.
Jameson, K: **F.3.2**: 32.
Jamshidian, F: **J.4**: 164.
Janis, M: **H.3**: 79.
Jansen, D: **H.4**: 57.
Jansen, E: **J.2**: 174.
Jansen, H: **H.1.1.1**: 35.
Jäntti, M: **M.2**: 27.
Jappelli, T: **L.1**: 9, 36.
Jara-Díaz, S: **H.3**: 12.
Jarchow, H: **I.2.3**: 3.
Jarley, P: **G.2.4**: 3.
Jarrow, R: **J.4**: 2, 105, 194, 223.
Jarvis, L: **H.1.2.1**: 13.
Jasiński, P: **F.3.1.4**: 28.
Jaska, P: **H.1.1.1**: 2.
Jasper, J: **H.2.2**: 112.
Jayanti, S: **O.2.2**: 69.
Jayaraj, D: **I.2.3**: 79.
Jayasuriya, S: **O.3.1**: 65.
Jazairy, I: **M.2**: 36.
Jefferson, G: **H.2.1**: 20, 120. **N.1**: 166, 170.
Jefferson, P: **J.2**: 16.
Jeffrey, C: **J.2**: 88.
Jeffrey, R: **B.3**: 46.
Jeffries, I: **N.1**: 164.
Jeffries, R: **F.3.2**: 67.
Jegadeesh, N: **J.4**: 188.
Jehiel, P: **I.2.1**: 157.
Jehle, G: **G.2.5**: 34.
Jenkins, G: **H.0**: 71, 101. **N.1**: 310. **N.2**: 130, 142.
Jenkins, S: **G.2.2**: 36. **K.2**: 9. **M.2**: 8.
Jennings, R: **B.4**: 38. **G.3.3.5**: 109. **J.4**: 50.
Jenny, A: **G.3.3.4**: 1.
Jensen, B: **H.1.1.4**: 21. **O.1.2.4**: 5.
Jensen, G: **J.4**: 292. **M.4**: 64.
Jensen, H: D: 36. **J.5**: 57.
Jensen, J: **H.4**: 59.
Jensen, M: **H.2.1**: 90.
Jensen, R: **A**: 16. **H.2.1**: 62.
Jensen-Butler, C: **F.3.1.1**: 72.
Jeon, Y: **O.2.2**: 88.
Jephcote, M: **A**: 6.
Jepma, C: **F.3.2**: 29.

Jerez Méndez, M: **B.2**: 2.
Jerger, J: **H.2.1**: 97.
Jerison, D: **L.2**: 51.
Jerison, M: **L.2**: 51.
Jesinghaus, J: **N.2**: 300.
Jespersen, J: **C**: 47.
Jeter, D: **G.3.3.5**: 17. **K.3**: 17, 101.
Jianakoplos, N: **J.2**: 111.
Jiménez, E: **J.4**: 70.
Jiménez, F: **N.1**: 108.
Jimeno Serrano, J: **O.1.2.4**: 59.
Jin, J: **J.4**: 119.
Jing, G: **H.2.1**: 79.
Jiye, W: **H.2.1**: 58.
Joh, G: **J.4**: 297.
Johannsen, A: **O.1.2.3**: 3.
Johansen, S: **B.3**: 59.
John, C: **N.2**: 302.
John, K: **G.3.3.5**: 78. **H.0**: 7.
Johnes, G: **M.5**: 20.
Johnsen, T: **H.0**: 116.
Johnson, B: **H.1.2.1**: 33.
Johnson, C: **O.2.3**: 8.
Johnson, G: **G.3.3**: 16. **K.3**: 5.
Johnson, H: **F.3.2**: 28.
Johnson, N: **H.1.1.2**: 31.
Johnson, P: **H.3**: 5. **M.4**: 97. **O.2.4**: 11. **O.3.2**: 54.
Johnson, S: **G.3.3.4**: 6.
Johnson, W: **G.2.1**: 170.
Johnston, T: **H.1.1.4**: 4.
Johnston, W: **G.2.1**: 94. **H.1.1.3**: 10.
Jolles, G: **H.4**: 47.
Jomo K.S.: **N.1**: 232.
Jonas, A: **G.2.1**: 46.
Jonassen, M: **J.2**: 19.
Jonchère, J: **H.2.2**: 94.
Jones, C: **G.3.3.5**: 111.
Jones, D: **G.2.1**: 137. **G.3.3.5**: 77. **H.1.1.1**: 7. **H.2.1**: 86.
Jones, E: **G.2.4**: 87. **O.2.2**: 37.
Jones, G: **G.3.3.5**: 55. **I.2.3**: 7.
Jones, J: **F.3.1.1**: 1.
Jones, K: **M.4**: 59.
Jones, L: **F.3.3**: 13. **F.5**: 11.
Jones, M: **B.4**: 65.
Jones, P: **D**: 19.
Jones, R: **G.2.1**: 142. **O.3.1**: 70.

Jones, S: **E**: 6.
Jones, T: **G.3.3.5**: 95.
Jones-Lee, M: **M.1**: 14.
Jong, de, F: **J.4**: 36.
Jong, de, M: **I.2.1**: 89.
Jönsson, B: **M.4**: 24.
Jordan, R: **H.2.2**: 138.
Jorde, T: **I.2.1**: 68.
Jorgenson, D: **G.1.1**: 30. **G.1.2**: 2. **M.5**: 25. **N.2**: 115.
Joseph, N: **O.2.1**: 36.
Josephy, N: **B.3**: 61.
Jost, V: **G.3.3.4**: 1.
Jouini, E: **G.1**: 7.
Joulfaian, D: **N.2**: 309.
Joumard, I: **O.2.1**: 80.
Jovanović, M: **O.1.2.4**: 29.
Joyce, T: **M.4**: 3.
Jud, W: **J.2**: 211.
Juhász, P: **H.1.1.4**: 36.
Juhn, C: **G.2.1**: 11.
Júlia, K: **J.2**: 187.
Jun, K: **O.2.2**: 8.
Junankar, P: **G.2.3**: 6.
Juneja, J: **G.3.3.1**: 9.
Jung, W: **N.2**: 19.
Junginger, W: **H.2.2**: 62.
Juras, A: **H.2.2**: 109.
Jurek, W: **F.3.3**: 41.
Juselius, K: **B.3**: 59.
Jussawalla, M: **H.2.2**: 17.
Just, R: **O.3.3**: 108.
Kaaret, D: **J.2**: 125.
Kaas, R: **J.3**: 17.
Kachelmeier, S: **C**: 81. **I.2.1**: 80.
Káddár, B: **O.3.2**: 32.
Kaempfer, W: **H.2.1**: 34.
Kaestner, R: **I.2.3**: 94. **K.3**: 21.
Kafkaslas, G: **F.3.1.1**: 52, 64.
Kahana, N: **G.2.4**: 122.
Kahn, A: **N.3**: 46.
Kahn, J: **H.4**: 56.
Kahn, S: **K.3**: 8.
Kahneman, D: **N.3**: 52.
Kaikati, J: **O.1.2.4**: 66.
Kain, J: **H.3**: 62. **I.2.3**: 85.
Kaio, T: **N.1**: 237.

Kaiser, F: **M.5**: 34.
Kaiser, H: **N.2**: 179, 201.
Kajubi, W: **M.5**: 40.
Käkönen, J: **H.0**: 34.
Kalaitzan-Donakes, N: **H.1.1.3**: 17.
Kale, J: **G.3.3.2**: 13.
Kalirajan, K: **H.1.1.3**: 4. **K.3**: 36.
Kallal, H: **F.3.1.1**: 106.
Kallon, K: **J.1**: 51.
Kalotay, A: **J.4**: 123.
Kalter, E: **F.3.3**: 36.
Kalton, G: **M.2**: 11.
Kamara, A: **J.4**: 211.
Kamas, L: **O.3.2**: 24.
Kambara, T: **H.2.2**: 107.
Kamdem, E: **G.2.5**: 15.
Kamien, M: **G.1.3**: 20. **H.2.1**: 7. **I.2.1**: 101.
Kaminarides, J: **G.3.3.5**: 71.
Kammas, M: **F.3.2**: 127. **H.3**: 32.
Kamp, D: **O.1.3**: 92.
Kampen, K: **H.0**: 180.
Kan, A: **G.2.1**: 90. **H.3**: 72.
Kanbur, R: **K.2**: 15.
Kanbur, S: **H.0**: 142. **N.1**: 114.
Kandel, E: **G.3.2**: 32.
Kandil, M: **F.4**: 13. **J.4**: 134.
Kandori, M: **C**: 76.
Kanemoto, Y: **G.2.1**: 59. **G.3.3.5**: 22.
Kang, M: **N.1**: 165.
Kang, S: **G.3.3.5**: 48.
Kangas, O: **M.4**: 110.
Kannan, P: **I.2.3**: 26.
Kanō, H: **N.2**: 9.
Kantawala, B: **F.3.2**: 109.
Kanth, R: **C**: 4.
Kanzlerski, D: **H.0**: 102.
Kao, C: **B.4**: 63. **O.1.2.4**: 24.
Kao, D: **J.4**: 113.
Kao, G: **J.4**: 69, 104.
Kaoru, S: **O.1.2.3**: 23.
Kaplan, D: **H.3**: 80.
Kaplan, S: **I.2.2**: 7. **N.2**: 284.
Kaplow, L: **N.1**: 25.
Kapoor, R: **N.2**: 226.
Kappel, A: **O.1.3**: 33.
Käppeler, F: **F.3.1.1**: 61.

Kapur, B: **J.4**: 43.
Karaïliev, E: **H.1.1.4**: 34.
Karakitsos, E: **N.1**: 233. **O.1.2.3**: 3.
Karamurztsev, T: **H.0**: 206.
Karasz, P: **I.2.1**: 124.
Karatas, C: **N.1**: 302.
Karatzas, G: **M.4**: 23.
Karl, H: **H.0**: 122.
Karlsson, M: **F.1**: 48.
Karni, E: **B.3**: 57.
Karollus, M: **J.2**: 130.
Karolyi, G: **J.4**: 130, 190.
Karp, L: **G.3.2**: 21. **M.1**: 22. **N.1**: 226. **N.2**: 14, 159. **O.1.3**: 55. **O.3.3**: 16.
Karras, G: **J.5**: 39.
Karsch, G: **I.2.3**: 65.
Karsenty, G: **O.3.2**: 28.
Karsten, S: **D**: 81.
Kasa, K: **I.2.1**: 106. **O.2.2**: 10.
Kasarda, J: **G.3.3.4**: 7.
Kasdi, R: **F.3.1.4**: 23.
Kase, R: **O.1.2.3**: 30.
Kaser, M: **F.1**: 21.
Kaserman, D: **O.3.1**: 11.
Kashuliza, A: **H.1.1**: 4.
Kashyap, A: **L.3**: 15.
Kask, S: **I.2.1**: 169.
Kaskarelis, I: **F.5**: 4.
Kasman, B: **J.5**: 11, 29.
Kasper, W: **F.1**: 83.
Kassella, T: **N.2**: 179.
Katalin, S: **I.2.3**: 47.
Kate, A: **O.3.3**: 7, 83.
Katkalo, V: **F.3.3**: 35.
Kato, T: **G.2.1**: 24. **G.2.5**: 21.
Katovich, M: **F.3.1.3**: 30.
Katsenelinboĭgen, A: **B.1**: 9.
Kattuman, P: **I.2.1**: 92.
Katz, B: **H.2.2**: 159. **H.4**: 40. **O.2.2**: 116.
Katz, E: **F.3.1.2**: 3. **O.3.2**: 51.
Katz, L: **F.3.1.1**: 78. **G.2.1**: 47. **K.3**: 4, 38, 112.
Katz, M: **G.1.1**: 39. **G.3.3.5**: 86.
Katzner, D: **C**: 25. **G.2.5**: 49.
Kau, J: **J.2**: 241. **J.4**: 286.
Kaufman, N: **N.2**: 136.
Kaufmann, P: **H.4**: 93.
Kaufmann, R: **H.2.2**: 83.

Kroon, E: **J.4**: 124.
Kroszner, R: **E**: 10.
Krouse, C: **H.2.2**: 53.
Krueger, A: **G.2.1**: 97. **K.3**: 38. **M.5**: 8, 37. **N.1**: 96. **O.3.1**: 37. **O.3.3**: 27.
Krugman, P: **O.2.3**: 55. **O.3.3**: 15.
Krull, S: **O.2.2**: 113.
Krupnick, A: **M.1**: 5.
Krupp, C: **O.3.3**: 100.
Kruse, D: **K.3**: 81.
Krutilla, K: **H.0**: 74.
Kruyt, B: **F.3.1.1**: 121.
Kryzanowski, L: **J.4**: 207, 261.
Krzysztofek, K: **F.3.2**: 121.
Kubin, I: **G.2.1**: 37.
Kuczyńska, T: **N.1**: 134.
Kudła, M: **O.3.1**: 75.
Kübler, K: **I.2.3**: 58.
Kueh, Y: **O.2.2**: 95.
Kuehlwein, M: **J.2**: 71.
Kuenne, R: **F.4**: 7. **G.3.2**: 11.
Kugler, P: **F.5**: 31.
Kuhn, P: **G.2.4**: 27. **M.4**: 119.
Kulcsár, R: **F.3.1.2**: 8.
Kulick, E: **F.1**: 34.
Kulke-Fiedler, C: **O.1.2.4**: 27.
Kumar, M: **H.2.2**: 155. **O.3.1**: 13.
Kumar, P: **J.4**: 44. **N.2**: 176.
Kumar, R: **J.4**: 250.
Kumar Roy, D: **O.3.1**: 8.
Kumbhakar, S: **H.3**: 41. **I.2.3**: 76.
Kunitomo, N: **J.4**: 233, 272.
Kunreuther, H: **J.3**: 13, 16.
Kunštek, D: **F.3.2**: 128.
Kuperan, K: **H.1.2.1**: 42.
Kupka, M: **N.1**: 322.
Kuroda, M: **G.1.2**: 2.
Kuruvilla, S: **K.3**: 58.
Kusi, N: **N.2**: 267. **O.2.2**: 35.
Kusnic, M: **G.3.3.5**: 74.
Kusters, A: **H.2.1**: 66.
Kusunoki, T: **G.1**: 30.
Kuttner, K: **J.1**: 24.
Kuwahara, H: **B.3**: 21.
Kuwayama, M: **O.1.2**: 9.
Kuz'minov, Y: **F.3.1.3**: 6.
Kuzm'inov, Y: **F.3.1.3**: 28.

Kuznetsov, E: **N.1**: 44.
Kwan, A: **F.2**: 10.
Kwarteng, C: **F.3.2**: 119.
Kwasnicka, H: **H.2.1**: 51.
Kwasnicki, W: **H.2.1**: 51.
Kwoka, J: **H.2.1**: 55.
Kydland, F: **F.5**: 24.
Kyle, A: **G.3.3.5**: 93.
Kyle, S: **H.0**: 28. **H.1.1**: 19.
Kylink, V: **M.4**: 112.
Kyotani, E: **G.2.1**: 69.
Kyriakopoulos, I: **F.1**: 3.
Kyrkilis, D: **O.3.2**: 29.
L'Heritier, J: **K.3**: 92.
L'Huillier, M: **N.3**: 10.
L'Hyver, M: **H.1.1.4**: 34.
Laabas, B: **L.1**: 26.
Laan, van der, L: **G.2.1**: 61.
Laaser, C: **O.1.2**: 18.
Labadie, P: **J.1**: 15.
Laband, D: **G.2.5**: 44. **L.1**: 12.
Labaronne, D: **N.1**: 214.
Labeaga, J: **H.2.1**: 1.
Lach, S: **I.2.3**: 4.
Lachman, D: **F.3.2**: 57.
Lacomblez, M: **G.2.5**: 11.
Lacour, J: **H.2.2**: 102–103.
Lacroix, G: **G.2.1**: 118.
Ladd, H: **F.3.1.2**: 17. **N.2**: 24.
Lafay, G: **O.1.2.3**: 18.
Laferrière, R: **F.3.1.1**: 44.
Laffan, B: **O.1.2.4**: 75.
Laffond, G: **I.2.1**: 29.
Laffont, J: **C**: 31, 71.
Lafontaine, F: **H.4**: 1.
Lagares, M: **O.1.2.4**: 59.
Lageman, B: **H.1.1.2**: 33. **H.1.1.4**: 48.
Lagos, R: **F.3.2**: 72. **O.2.2**: 56.
Lahiri, A: **J.2**: 107.
Lai, C: **O.2.2**: 15.
Lai, K: **I.2.1**: 55. **O.2.1**: 33.
Laibman, D: **N.1**: 236.
Laidler, D: **J.5**: 58.
Laird, S: **O.3.2**: 37.
Laisney, F: **G.2.1**: 114.
Laitner, J: **F.3.3**: 13.

Lakey, J: **G.2.2**: 21.
Laki, M: **N.1**: 271.
Lakits, E: **O.1.3**: 75.
Lakonishok, J: **J.4**: 94, 217, 278.
Lall, B: **N.1**: 5.
Lall, S: **F.3.2**: 51.
Lallement, M: **G.2.1**: 43.
Lam, A: **G.2.2**: 40.
Lam, K: **J.4**: 265.
Lam, S: **J.4**: 192.
Lambert, D: **F.3.3**: 3.
Lambert, P: **K.2**: 17.
Lambertini, L: **J.1**: 82.
Lambinet, F: **F.3.2**: 58.
Lambright, W: **G.1**: 57.
Lambson, V: **G.3.3.5**: 5.
Lamech, R: **H.0**: 101. **N.2**: 142.
Lamel, J: **I.2.3**: 65.
Lamort, F: **I.2.1**: 27.
Lancaster, L: **G.3.3.5**: 19.
Land, K: **G.1.2**: 11.
Landau, R: **G.1**: 55.
Landi, A: **J.2**: 26.
Landon, S: **J.1**: 68.
Landor, P: **G.1**: 11.
Landreth, O: **G.3.3.5**: 84.
Landsman, W: **G.3.3.5**: 49.
Lane, T: **N.1**: 174. **O.2.1**: 4.
Lang, G: **F.2**: 3.
Lang, K: **B.1**: 2. **K.3**: 8.
Lang, L: **G.3.3.3**: 8. **G.3.3.5**: 78. **J.4**: 99.
Lang, R: **N.1**: 168.
Langdana, F: **N.2**: 234.
Langdon, K: **O.1.3**: 103.
Lange, C: **G.2.1**: 6.
Lange, de, A: **M.1**: 20.
Langfeldt, E: **F.1**: 40. **H.2.1**: 121.
Langguth, G: **O.3.3**: 125.
Langhammer, R: **O.3.2**: 69.
Lanjouw, P: **G.2.1**: 74.
Lank, A: **G.3.3.4**: 1.
Lankes, F: **H.2.1**: 18.
Lannoy, de, D: **F.3.2**: 58.
Lanoie, P: **M.4**: 10.
Lansbury, R: **G.2.4**: 16, 114.
Lantner, R: **N.1**: 324.
Lapan, H: **H.1.2.1**: 30.

Laplante, M: **M.2**: 11.
Lapointe, B: **O.3.2**: 11.
Laquatra, J: **L.2**: 34.
Laramie, A: **H.2.1**: 25.
Larcker, D: **I.2.1**: 160.
Lardy, N: **O.3.2**: 16. **O.3.3**: 23.
Large, R: **H.4**: 23.
Larkins, E: **N.2**: 216.
Laroque, G: **I.2.1**: 137. **J.4**: 308.
Larosière, de, J: **J.5**: 22.
Larréché, J: **H.4**: 81.
Larsen, E: **H.2.2**: 128.
Larsen, H: **G.2.5**: 17.
Larson, A: **I.2.1**: 63.
Larson, T: **G.2.1**: 16.
Larue, B: **H.1.2.1**: 30.
Lasić, V: **B.4**: 66.
Laska, E: **M.4**: 59.
Lasser, D: **J.4**: 27.
Lassiaille, R: **H.2.2**: 94.
Latreille, P: **H.2.2**: 58.
Lattimore, R: **F.1**: 86. **O.3.3**: 130.
Lau, L: **G.1.2**: 2. **H.1.1.2**: 9.
Laumas, P: **K.1**: 7.
Laurance, E: **O.3.2**: 55.
Lauritano, P: **H.3**: 47.
Lauth, H: **O.1.3**: 87.
Lauth, T: **N.2**: 235.
Laux, P: **J.4**: 152.
LaValle, I: **C**: 52.
Laverick, S: **G.1.2**: 14.
Lavigne, M: **N.1**: 324. **O.1.3**: 50.
Lavinas, L: **O.1.2.4**: 5.
Lavoie, M: **B.1**: 24. **D**: 45, 52.
Lavorel, L: **G.2.5**: 6.
Law, C: **O.3.2**: 82.
Lawler, P: **J.5**: 21.
Lawlor, M: **D**: 65.
Lawrence, G: **H.1.1.2**: 29.
Lawrence, R: **O.1.3**: 97.
Lawson, E: **I.2.3**: 17.
Lawson, R: **B.4**: 56.
Lax, M: **H.3**: 79.
Lazear, E: **G.3.2**: 32.
Lea, J: **H.1.2.1**: 31.
Lea, M: **L.2**: 94.

Levitsky, J: **G.3.3.4**: 15.
Levy, A: **O.2.2**: 1.
Levy, F: **K.3**: 62.
Levy, H: **B.3**: 21.
Levy, L: **H.3**: 72.
Lew, B: **J.2**: 115.
Lewin, D: **G.2.4**: 8, 121.
Lewis, B: **F.3.1.1**: 57.
Lewis, J: **G.4**: 8.
Lewis, M: **J.5**: 12.
Lewis, R: **G.3.3**: 30. **N.1**: 318.
Lewis, T: **N.3**: 22.
Leyden, D: **N.2**: 259.
Leyshon, A: **H.0**: 174. **H.2.1**: 39. **J.4**: 61.
Li, C: **O.2.2**: 51.
Li, H: **K.2**: 22.
Li, J: **G.1.2**: 2. **N.2**: 87. **O.2.2**: 27.
Li, K: **F.1**: 18.
Li, S: **G.1.1**: 19.
Li, W: **H.1.1.2**: 36.
Li, Y: **H.0**: 161.
Li, Z: **O.2.2**: 131.
Lian, Z: **H.2.1**: 79.
Liang, K: **J.2**: 141.
Liang, N: **O.3.3**: 5.
Lianos, T: **G.3.3.5**: 63. **K.3**: 32.
Libby, R: **O.1.2.3**: 31.
Licandro, J: **F.1**: 9.
Lichenstein, P: **N.1**: 184.
Lichfield, N: **H.3**: 67.
Licht, G: **K.3**: 27.
Lichtenberg, F: **H.2.1**: 102. **N.1**: 21.
Lichtenstein, J: **G.2.1**: 94.
Lichtenstein, S: **I.1**: 1.
Liddle, R: **F.3.2**: 36.
Lie, J: **G.2.2**: 9.
Lie, R: **F.3.1.1**: 121.
Lieberman, M: **G.2.5**: 34.
Liemt, van, G: **G.3.3.5**: 83.
Lienesch, T: **B.3**: 41.
Liepmann, P: **H.2.1**: 82.
Lieu, S: **H.0**: 88.
Liew, C: **B.3**: 7. **O.2.3**: 69.
Liew, L: **F.3.1.4**: 5.
Light, A: **G.2.1**: 84.
Lijn, van der, N: **N.1**: 219.

Lim, C: **F.3.2**: 88.
Lim, D: **O.1.3**: 48.
Lim, G: **O.2.1**: 92.
Lim, H: **H.1.1.3**: 16.
Lim, K: **J.4**: 4.
Lin, B: **I.2.3**: 75.
Lin, J: **H.1.1.2**: 9.
Lin, P: **M.4**: 63.
Lin, S: **M.4**: 59.
Lin, W: **G.3.3.5**: 105. **O.2.1**: 42.
Lin, Y: **G.3.3**: 3. **M.2**: 19.
Lincoln, J: **G.3.2**: 24.
Lindahl, W: **G.3.3.3**: 34.
Lindbeck, A: **G.2.1**: 149. **H.2.1**: 112.
Linden, R: **O.1.3**: 31.
Lindenboim, J: **H.2.1**: 59.
Lindgren, R: **J.4**: 178.
Lindh, T: **C**: 39.
Lindsey, R: **J.4**: 93.
Lindström, S: **H.2.2**: 112.
Lines, A: **N.2**: 25.
Ling, D: **N.2**: 50.
Linneker, B: **H.3**: 64.
Linneman, P: **L.2**: 76.
Linotte, D: **N.1**: 171.
Lint, O: **H.2.1**: 40.
Lioukas, S: **H.3**: 56.
Liouville, J: **K.3**: 79.
Lipowski, A: **F.1**: 73.
Lippi, M: **B.3**: 42. **F.5**: 25.
Lippman, S: **I.2.1**: 35.
Lipset, S: **G.2.1**: 94.
Lipsey, R: **I.2.1**: 103.
Lipton, D: **J.1**: 34. **N.1**: 191.
Liszcz, T: **G.2.4**: 107.
Litterman, R: **J.4**: 168.
Littlechild, S: **H.0**: 72.
Littleton, S: **G.2.4**: 69.
Litzenberger, R: **J.4**: 99, 139.
Liu, C: **I.2.3**: 106.
Liu, F: **H.2.2**: 86.
Liu, G: **L.1**: 20.
Liu, H: **H.2.1**: 79.
Liu, J: **H.0**: 21. **L.2**: 23.
Liu, P: **O.2.1**: 32.
Liu, S: **O.1.2.3**: 17.
Liu, T: **B.3**: 39.

Malecki, E: **G.2.1**: 58.
Małecki, M: **O.2.2**: 106.
Malhotra, D: **G.2.2**: 14. **L.3**: 23.
Malhotra, M: **J.2**: 52.
Malik, M: **O.2.4**: 2, 19.
Malinvaud, E: **L.1**: 36.
Malixi, M: **J.1**: 87.
Malle, S: **O.2.2**: 132.
Mallette, P: **G.3.3.5**: 14.
Malliaropulos, D: **O.2.1**: 13.
Mallick, R: **H.1.1.2**: 1.
Mallier, A: **M.4**: 72.
Mallin, C: **G.3.2**: 25.
Malmberg, A: **F.3.1.1**: 4.
Maloney, W: **N.1**: 279.
Malueg, D: **I.2.1**: 14, 102.
Maluf, R: **O.1.2.4**: 5.
Mamer, J: **I.2.1**: 35.
Mandal, B: **H.3**: 60.
Mandel, E: **B.2**: 3.
Mandel, M: **N.1**: 230.
Mandelker, G: **J.4**: 285.
Mandeng, O: **O.3.1**: 42.
Mandy, D: **I.2.1**: 98.
Maneschi, A: **O.3.1**: 58.
Manetti, S: **G.3.3.3**: 6.
Mangen, S: **M.3**: 7.
Mangum, G: **G.2.4**: 2.
Mankiw, N: **F.3.3**: 8.
Mann, C: **N.2**: 141.
Mann, D: **I.2.1**: 22.
Mann, H: **N.2**: 203.
Manne, A: **H.0**: 67.
Manning, A: **F.3.3**: 52. **G.1.1**: 31. **G.2.1**: 29. **G.2.4**: 77. **K.3**: 104.
Manning, D: **G.2.1**: 137. **K.3**: 47.
Manser, M: **M.2**: 11.
Mansfield, E: **G.1.2**: 5.
Mansoob Murshed, S: **O.3.3**: 135.
Mansoorian, A: **N.2**: 150.
Mansvelt, van, J: **F.3.2**: 18. **H.1.1.1**: 31.
Mantzavinos, C: **I.2.1**: 76.
Manu, F: **I.2.1**: 36.
Manuel, M: **O.2.4**: 19.
Manuelli, R: **F.3.3**: 13. **F.5**: 11. **I.2.1**: 167.
Manzotti, A: **J.2**: 31.
Manzur, M: **O.2.1**: 61.

Mao, C: **F.5**: 19.
Mar, D: **K.3**: 45.
Marangon, F: **H.1.1**: 2.
Marcet, A: **F.3.3**: 13.
Marchak, M: **H.1.2.1**: 50.
Marchesini, L: **I.2.3**: 77.
Marchini, A: **H.1.2.1**: 6.
Marciniak, P: **N.1**: 134.
Marcus, A: **J.4**: 248.
Mardapitta-Hadjipandeli, L: **A**: 10.
Mardas, D: **O.3.2**: 45.
Mardjana, I: **N.3**: 35.
Marengo, L: **G.2.5**: 7.
Marfels, C: **H.4**: 7.
Marginson, P: **O.1.2.4**: 47.
Margolis, M: **F.3.2**: 78.
Margulici, L: **J.2**: 152.
Margulis, S: **H.0**: 2.
Mária, A: **M.4**: 82.
Marianov, V: **F.3.1.1**: 12.
Marimon, R: **F.3.3**: 13.
Marin, D: **F.3.3**: 30. **O.3.1**: 5.
Marín, M: **O.1.3**: 8.
Marini, G: **G.2.1**: 53. **J.2**: 70. **K.3**: 22.
Marion, N: **J.4**: 49.
Marjit, S: **G.1.1**: 40. **J.1**: 72.
Mark, N: **O.2.1**: 84.
Markandya, A: **H.0**: 8.
Markham, J: **N.1**: 259.
Markides, C: **G.3.3.5**: 10.
Markowska, E: **F.3.2**: 8.
Marks, L: **H.1.1.1**: 14.
Marks, R: **I.2.3**: 23.
Markusen, J: **H.2.2**: 78. **O.1.3**: 95. **O.3.1**: 17.
Marley, A: **B.3**: 56. **C**: 27.
Marlin, J: **N.1**: 5, 11.
Marlin-Bennett, R: **O.3.2**: 84.
Marlowe, A: **H.3**: 52.
Marois, B: **J.2**: 180.
Maroto Perez Del Rio, C: **N.1**: 4.
Marquette, R: **J.4**: 106.
Marquez, J: **O.3.1**: 2.
Marquis, M: **J.2**: 9. **J.5**: 9. **M.4**: 11.
Marrese, M: **O.1.2.4**: 25.
Marrewijk, van, C: **M.5**: 30.
Marris, R: **D**: 42, 54.

Marron, J: **K.2**: 32.
Marsden, D: **G.2.1**: 23. **O.1.2.4**: 47.
Marsden, K: **G.3.3.1**: 1.
Marsden, T: **G.2.1**: 41. **H.0**: 174. **H.1.1.4**: 42.
Marsh, D: **G.2.4**: 84. **J.5**: 6. **N.1**: 102.
Marshall, J: **J.2**: 87.
Marshall, N: **F.3.1.1**: 3.
Marshall, R: **G.2.4**: 81.
Marstrand, P: **H.0**: 118.
Martellaro, J: **H.0**: 210.
Martens, S: **B.4**: 62.
Mårtensson, A: **H.2.2**: 112.
Marterbauer, M: **H.4**: 21.
Martín, A: **H.2.1**: 1.
Martin, C: **G.2.4**: 82. **H.2.1**: 17.
Martin, J: **H.0**: 77, 82, 93.
Martin, K: **N.2**: 138.
Martín, M: **O.1.3**: 9.
Martin, R: **F.3.1.1**: 75. **J.2**: 243. **N.3**: 45.
Martin, S: **G.2.5**: 8. **J.2**: 132.
Martin, V: **B.1**: 20. **L.2**: 87.
Martin-Brown, J: **H.0**: 165.
Martinás, K: **M.2**: 12.
Martinez, S: **I.2.3**: 71.
Martínez Cuenca, A: **O.3.2**: 7.
Martinez Peria, M: **J.2**: 35.
Martinez-Vazquez, J: **N.2**: 24, 216.
Martini, U: **H.4**: 6.
Martino, G: **B.3**: 51.
Martinsen, K: **N.1**: 228.
Martynov, A: **J.1**: 88.
Martzoukos, S: **H.2.2**: 121.
Marzouk, M: **M.4**: 49.
Masayo, N: **G.2.2**: 39.
Masciandaro, D: **J.5**: 55.
Maser, S: **G.3.3.3**: 18.
Masini, J: **H.2.1**: 104. **O.1.2.2**: 20.
Maskin, E: **C**: 73.
Mason, A: **K.2**: 11.
Mason, C: **I.2.1**: 46.
Mason, D: **G.2.2**: 7.
Mason, G: **G.2.5**: 56.
Mason, M: **O.2.2**: 93.
Mason, P: **G.2.2**: 3.
Mason, R: **G.3.3.5**: 90.
Masser, I: **F.3.1.1**: 15.
Massey, D: **G.2.1**: 5.

Masson, P: **J.1**: 95. **J.2**: 217.
Mastanduno, M: **O.3.3**: 60.
Masztis, T: **N.3**: 25.
Mateo, de, F: **O.3.3**: 7.
Mates, N: **J.1**: 93. **J.2**: 228.
Mateus, G: **F.3.1.1**: 7.
Mathews, J: **G.1**: 35.
Mathieu, C: **F.2**: 26. **O.3.2**: 23.
Mathis, A: **J.2**: 29.
Mathis, S: **N.2**: 279.
Matin, K: **L.3**: 1. **O.2.1**: 65.
Matis, H: **N.1**: 127.
Mato, G: **J.4**: 254.
Matsui, A: **C**: 61.
Matsumura, E: **B.4**: 34.
Matsuyama, K: **F.3.3**: 23. **G.2.1**: 86.
Mattessich, R: **B.4**: 46.
Matthiasson, T: **H.1.2.1**: 39.
Mattsson, L: **H.3**: 2.
Matutes, C: **G.1.1**: 39.
Matytsin, S: **N.1**: 204.
Matzner, E: **F.1**: 62.
Maurice-Baumont, C: **L.2**: 82.
Maurin, E: **K.3**: 49.
Mavrogiannis, D: **G.3.3**: 34.
Max-Neef, M: **M.2**: 32.
Maxfield, S: **J.2**: 172.
Maximin, B: **G.2.1**: 49.
Maxwell, G: **H.0**: 38.
Mayer, C: **F.3.3**: 40. **G.3.3**: 27. **J.2**: 146.
Mayer, G: **O.2.3**: 5.
Mayer, T: **J.2**: 205.
Mayer, W: **G.2.4**: 79.
Mayers, D: **G.3.3.3**: 28. **J.3**: 7.
Mayes, D: **O.1.2.4**: 83. **O.2.3**: 1. **O.3.2**: 65.
Mayhew, A: **C**: 40.
Maynes, E: **G.3.3.3**: 35.
Mayo, J: **I.2.3**: 15.
Mayo, S: **H.1.1.4**: 14.
Maza Arroyo, de la, S: **J.4**: 70.
Mazenc, L: **I.2.3**: 74.
Mazumdar, M: **N.3**: 24.
Mazumdar, S: **J.4**: 169.
Mazwai, T: **N.2**: 86.
Mazzeo, M: **J.4**: 276.
Mazzola, F: **G.1**: 45.

Mbaku, J: **M.2**: 29.
Mbara, C: **H.3**: 68.
Mbwinga: **F.3.2**: 58.
McAfee, R: **G.2.1**: 120.
McAllister, C: **F.3.2**: 115.
McAllister, I: **G.2.1**: 142.
McAllister, S: **G.2.4**: 35.
McAndrews, J: **G.3.2**: 15.
McBride, M: **H.3**: 48.
McCabe, D: **G.2.4**: 8.
McCabe, K: **H.4**: 15.
McCallum, J: **O.1.2**: 5.
McCalman, J: **H.2.2**: 44.
McCarthy, C: **O.3.3**: 70.
McCarthy, D: **G.3.3.5**: 60.
McCarthy, P: **I.2.3**: 26.
McClelland, G: **N.2**: 92.
McCloskey, D: **B.4**: 4.
McConnell, J: **H.2.1**: 39. **J.4**: 290.
McConnell, S: **K.3**: 91.
McConnell, V: **H.0**: 191.
McCormick, B: **G.2.1**: 144.
McCormick, K: **M.1**: 8.
McCrickard, M: **J.1**: 64.
McCue, M: **J.4**: 116.
McCullough, G: **H.3**: 58.
McCurdy, T: **O.2.2**: 90.
McCutcheon, M: **H.4**: 63.
McDaniels, T: **G.3.3.5**: 101. **H.3**: 71.
McDermott, G: **G.3.3.4**: 18.
McDonald, A: **H.1.2.1**: 32.
McDonald, C: **G.2.4**: 81.
McDonald, I: **G.2.4**: 85. **L.1**: 39. **N.2**: 186, 198.
McDonald, R: **J.4**: 34.
McElrath, R: **G.2.4**: 108.
McElroy, J: **H.3**: 10.
McEnally, R: **J.4**: 252.
McEnroe, J: **B.4**: 62.
McGee, J: **H.2.1**: 65.
McGill, G: **N.2**: 50.
McGillivray, M: **O.1.3**: 77.
McGinley, P: **H.0**: 110.
McGoldrick, P: **H.4**: 103. **J.2**: 148.
McGowan, J: **N.2**: 96.
McGrath, M: **H.2.1**: 49.
McGregor, P: **H.1.2.1**: 51.
McGuckin, R: **G.1.2**: 10.

McGuinness, P: **J.4**: 31, 38.
McGuire, A: **G.2.5**: 38.
McGuire, T: **N.2**: 278. **N.3**: 8.
McHone, W: **G.3.3.5**: 67.
McInish, T: **J.4**: 166.
McIntyre, R: **D**: 38.
McIntyre, S: **L.2**: 69.
McKay, J: **N.1**: 110.
McKean, J: **H.2.2**: 129.
McKee, M: **N.3**: 54.
McKendrick, D: **G.1**: 29. **H.2.2**: 37.
McKenna, C: **G.2.1**: 9.
McKenzie, C: **J.1**: 60. **O.2.3**: 37.
McKeough, J: **F.3.1.4**: 15.
McKiernan, P: **G.3.3.5**: 96.
McKinlay, A: **G.2.5**: 47.
McKinley, T: **N.1**: 63.
McKinney, M: **H.0**: 198.
McLafferty, S: **F.3.1.1**: 12. **G.2.1**: 46.
McLaughlin, E: **G.2.2**: 27.
McLeod, R: **J.2**: 171.
McLure, C: **N.2**: 173, 199, 306.
McMahon, M: **M.5**: 23.
McMillan, S: **N.1**: 16.
McMillen, D: **K.3**: 74.
McMullen, J: **G.3.3**: 31.
McNamara, K: **N.2**: 233.
McNamee, P: **H.2.1**: 6.
McNaughton, W: **H.2.2**: 122.
McNelis, P: **J.5**: 38.
McNicoll, I: **H.1.2.1**: 51. **L.2**: 78.
McNown, R: **F.2**: 21.
McPhail, A: **H.0**: 21.
McQueen, G: **J.4**: 121.
McVey, R: **G.3.3.1**: 16.
Mead, D: **G.3.3.4**: 10, 21.
Meade, J: **O.1.2.4**: 60.
Mea, della, U: **J.1**: 50.
Meadows, D: **H.0**: 158.
Meager, N: **G.2.1**: 125.
Means, D: **I.2.3**: 64.
Medema, S: **G.3.3.3**: 40.
Medhora, R: **O.2.3**: 56.
Medina Sierra, L: **M.1**: 3.
Medio, A: **C**: 2.
Meen, G: **O.1.2**: 3.

Megbolugbe, I: **I.2.3**: 85. **L.2**: 76.
Meghir, C: **G.2.1**: 165. **G.2.2**: 32. **L.2**: 74. **N.2**: 82.
Mehaut, P: **O.1.2.4**: 30.
Mehdian, S: **J.2**: 193.
Mehretu, A: **O.3.2**: 75.
Mehrotra, S: **F.1**: 21.
Mehta, J: **B.3**: 52.
Meidner, R: **N.1**: 119.
Meier, V: **F.3.1.1**: 73.
Meil, P: **G.1**: 58.
Meiners, R: **H.0**: 73.
Meintjes, S: **N.2**: 86.
Meisner, M: **M.4**: 59.
Meissner, W: **H.0**: 18.
Meitzen, M: **I.2.1**: 63.
Mejstrik, M: **G.3.3.4**: 18.
Melese, F: **O.3.1**: 11.
Mellander, E: **F.5**: 35.
Meller, P: **N.1**: 61.
Mellers, B: **I.2.1**: 172.
Mello, A: **J.4**: 68.
Melnick, G: **M.4**: 29.
Melo, de, J: **K.2**: 1.
Melo, de, M: **H.2.2**: 2.
Meltzer, A: **C**: 14.
Melumad, N: **G.3.3.5**: 128.
Memarian, M: **I.2.3**: 12.
Mendelsohn, R: **H.0**: 187.
Mendenhall, M: **G.2.3**: 14.
Mendenhall, R: **J.4**: 86.
Mendes, V: **J.2**: 201.
Mendes de Oliveira, M: **K.3**: 97.
Méndez, J: **O.2.2**: 20.
Mendez, R: **N.2**: 40.
Mendis, P: **H.1.1.2**: 7. **M.3**: 2.
Mendoza, E: **B.1**: 5. **B.3**: 47.
Mendras, H: **H.1.1.4**: 39.
Menet-Genty, J: **F.1**: 51.
Menkhoff, L: **J.4**: 42. **O.2.1**: 15. **O.2.3**: 63.
Menon, J: **O.2.1**: 60.
Mensah, Y: **B.4**: 10.
Meo, de, G: **H.1.1.4**: 43.
Mera, K: **I.2.3**: 39.
Mercado-Mendez, J: **J.2**: 18.
Mercer, D: **H.0**: 148. **H.2.2**: 101.
Mercuro, N: **G.3.3.3**: 33.
Meredith, G: **J.1**: 95.

Merges, R: **G.1.3**: 23.
Mergos, G: **G.2.2**: 5.
Merikas, A: **G.3.3.5**: 71.
Merino García, P: **O.1.2.4**: 58.
Merkle, L: **G.2.1**: 114. **O.1.2.5**: 6.
Merlino, M: **J.2**: 143, 184.
Merton, R: **J.2**: 2.
Merwe, van der, B: **J.4**: 155.
Merzoni, G: **G.3.3**: 26.
Messerlin, P: **I.2.3**: 20.
Messier, W: **B.4**: 60.
Messner, D: **F.3.2**: 79, 111.
Mest, D: **B.4**: 38.
Mester, L: **J.2**: 204.
Métais, S: **N.1**: 143.
Metcalf, D: **K.3**: 6.
Metcalf, G: **N.1**: 310.
Metcalf, L: **O.1.2.4**: 10.
Metcalfe, Y: **N.2**: 229.
Metwally, M: **O.3.2**: 77.
Metzer, J: **F.1**: 36.
Meulbroek, L: **J.4**: 263.
Meulendyke, A: **J.5**: 59.
Meurs, M: **I.2.1**: 42.
Meyer, A: **O.2.2**: 71.
Meyer, D: **I.2.1**: 121.
Meyer, G: **H.4**: 102.
Meyer, H: **C**: 62.
Meyer, M: **G.3.3.5**: 97.
Meyer, R: **H.1.1**: 16. **L.1**: 14.
Meyer, W: **G.2.4**: 42.
Meyer-Stamer, J: **F.3.2**: 79. **H.2.2**: 20.
Meyers, S: **H.0**: 12, 160. **H.2.2**: 131.
Meyerson, E: **G.3.3.5**: 31.
Meza, de, D: **F.3.1.4**: 26.
Mezger, D: **F.3.2**: 68.
Mezias, S: **I.2.3**: 40.
Mhozya, X: **B.3**: 53.
Miah, M: **O.2.1**: 34.
Miceli, T: **I.2.1**: 52.
Michael, M: **O.3.3**: 56.
Michael, S: **O.3.3**: 93.
Michaelis, P: **H.0**: 17, 195.
Michaels, P: **O.3.2**: 57.
Michalak, W: **O.2.2**: 57.
Michalopoulos, C: **G.2.2**: 23. **M.4**: 2.

Michel, P: **C**: 71.
Michel, S: **F.3.1.1**: 39.
Michie, J: **F.1**: 47.
Michon, F: **G.2.1**: 43.
Miciński, A: **O.3.1**: 75.
Micklewright, J: **M.4**: 117.
Micossi, S: **N.2**: 41, 70. **O.2.2**: 120.
Middleton, J: **G.2.1**: 48. **G.2.5**: 29.
Midttun, A: **C**: 40.
Midwinter, A: **N.2**: 63.
Mihaljek, D: **N.2**: 224.
Mihályi, P: **N.1**: 269.
Mihopoulos, N: **J.2**: 195.
Mikami, K: **N.2**: 316.
Mikesell, R: **H.0**: 169.
Mikkelson, W: **J.4**: 302.
Milana, C: **M.4**: 58.
Milanovic, B: **M.2**: 30.
Milberg, W: **H.2.1**: 38. **O.3.1**: 44.
Milbourne, R: **J.2**: 122.
Miles, D: **I.2.3**: 92. **L.2**: 93.
Miles, I: **G.1**: 4.
Miliband, D: **F.1**: 64.
Miller, C: **L.2**: 69.
Miller, E: **G.1**: 9.
Miller, G: **G.3.1**: 3.
Miller, J: **H.2.1**: 93.
Miller, K: **G.3.3.5**: 24.
Miller, M: **J.1**: 82.
Miller, P: **G.2.4**: 98.
Miller, R: **N.1**: 326.
Miller, S: **G.2.2**: 20. **O.3.3**: 56.
Miller, T: **F.3.1.1**: 12. **J.4**: 211. **K.3**: 113.
Millier, P: **I.2.1**: 37.
Millikan, B: **H.0**: 60.
Milliman, S: **H.1.2.1**: 33.
Mills, J: **B.3**: 8.
Mills, S: **B.4**: 55.
Mills, T: **F.2**: 28.
Milne, R: **N.1**: 308.
Milne, S: **G.3.3.5**: 100.
Milner, C: **O.3.1**: 26. **O.3.3**: 69, 139.
Miłobędzki, P: **G.3.3.3**: 31.
Milton, A: **O.1.3**: 56.
Min, S: **J.4**: 241.
Minarik, J: **N.2**: 114.
Minda, A: **O.2.2**: 105.

Mingat, A: **M.5**: 13.
Mink, G: **O.1.3**: 75.
Minkler, A: **G.3.3.5**: 129.
Minne, B: **G.1**: 24. **H.2.1**: 66.
Minogue, M: **N.1**: 172.
Mirakhor, A: **N.1**: 231.
Mirer, T: **M.4**: 103.
Mirman, L: **H.1.2.1**: 44.
Mirmirani, S: **G.2.1**: 113.
Miron, J: **F.5**: 13, 43.
Mirvis, P: **G.2.5**: 40.
Misala, J: **O.1.3**: 13.
Mishkin, F: **F.5**: 2. **J.1**: 90.
Mishra, P: **G.1**: 44.
Missen, G: **N.1**: 110.
Mistry, P: **N.1**: 256.
Mitchell, D: **G.2.4**: 121. **J.5**: 13. **M.3**: 4. **O.3.3**: 28.
Mitchell, J: **I.2.3**: 49.
Mitchell, K: **G.2.4**: 41.
Mitchell, M: **M.2**: 5.
Mitchell, W: **H.2.1**: 27.
Mitra, P: **I.2.1**: 110. **N.1**: 62. **N.2**: 81. **O.3.3**: 76.
Mittelbach, H: **F.3.3**: 65.
Mittoo, U: **O.2.1**: 26.
Miyagawa, M: **O.2.2**: 14.
Miyatsuka, T: **O.2.2**: 130.
Mizala, A: **O.3.2**: 40.
Mizen, P: **J.1**: 38.
Mizsei, K: **N.1**: 286.
Mkandawire, M: **L.1**: 19.
Mkandawire, P: **F.3.2**: 49.
Mocan, N: **M.4**: 3.
Mockler, R: **G.3.3.5**: 85.
Móczár, J: **F.3.3**: 1.
Modigliani, F: **J.4**: 11.
Mody, A: **G.1**: 29. **O.1.2.2**: 12. **O.3.2**: 9.
Moffitt, R: **M.4**: 28.
Moggi, M: **G.3.3.4**: 13.
Moggridge, D: **D**: 59.
Mohácsi, K: **H.1.1.4**: 36.
Mohanty, M: **G.2.1**: 25.
Moharram, S: **N.2**: 9.
Möhlendick, B: **H.1.1.4**: 41.
Moizer, P: **B.4**: 11.
Mok, H: **J.4**: 265.
Mokgwathi, G: **M.5**: 40.

Mowery, D: **G.1**: 55.
Moyes, P: **K.2**: 36.
Mozes, H: **G.3.3.5**: 51.
Muamba, N: **F.3.2**: 58.
Mühlenkamp, H: **M.4**: 30.
Muehlen, von zur, P: **B.3**: 52.
Mueller, F: **G.2.4**: 50.
Müller, L: **O.2.3**: 43.
Münkner, H: **G.3.3**: 2.
Muet, P: **L.3**: 16. **O.3.1**: 45.
Mukherjee, M: **J.2**: 229.
Mukherjee, N: **O.3.3**: 46.
Mukherjee, T: **I.2.3**: 2.
Mukhopadhyay, R: **F.3.2**: 95.
Mukoko, B: **O.3.1**: 12.
Mulder, C: **G.2.1**: 162.
Muller, E: **G.1.3**: 20.
Muller, M: **O.1.2.4**: 49.
Muller, W: **J.2**: 241.
Mulligan, C: **J.1**: 69.
Mullineux, A: **B.3**: 18. **J.2**: 80, 161. **J.5**: 17.
Mullings, B: **N.2**: 16.
Mullins, R: **M.2**: 33.
Mullis, R: **M.2**: 20.
Mulvey, C: **G.2.4**: 98.
Mulwanda, M: **H.0**: 46.
Mumey, G: **H.1.1.3**: 14.
Mun, S: **I.2.3**: 22.
Munasinghe, M: **H.2.2**: 101.
Mundell, R: **F.4**: 3. **O.1.2**: 5. **O.1.2.4**: 60.
Munger, M: **G.2.4**: 78.
Munley, V: **M.5**: 10.
Munnell, A: **N.2**: 65.
Muñoz, C: **O.1.3**: 8.
Munro, A: **N.2**: 147.
Munro, J: **H.1.2.1**: 29.
Muraglia, G: **H.1.1.3**: 19.
Muraközy, L: **N.2**: 1.
Muraro, G: **N.1**: 6.
Murdoch, J: **H.0**: 174.
Muris, T: **H.4**: 65.
Murnane, R: **K.3**: 62.
Murniningtyas, E: **O.3.2**: 50.
Murphy, A: **G.3.3.5**: 16. **J.4**: 30. **O.2.2**: 129.
Murphy, F: **B.3**: 10, 50.
Murphy, K: **G.2.1**: 15. **G.2.4**: 47. **K.3**: 4, 56, 103. **N.1**: 217.

Murphy, L: **J.2**: 235.
Murphy, M: **H.1.1.1**: 21.
Murphy, P: **G.2.1**: 20. **K.3**: 18.
Murray, C: **H.2.2**: 109.
Murray, M: **M.4**: 115.
Murrell, P: **N.1**: 305, 323.
Murshed, S: **O.3.2**: 27. **O.3.3**: 8.
Murthy, K: **F.3.1.1**: 76.
Muscatelli, V: **J.1**: 67. **O.2.2**: 13.
Musgrave, R: **N.2**: 292.
Mushkat, M: **J.2**: 62.
Musil, K: **L.3**: 12.
Musliner, M: **M.4**: 17.
Musonda, F: **F.2**: 2.
Musotti, F: **B.3**: 51.
Mustafa, C: **H.2.2**: 118.
Mwase, N: **O.3.3**: 66.
Myant, M: **F.1**: 42.
Myers, D: **F.3.1.3**: 21.
Myers, S: **G.2.1**: 10.
Mygind, N: **F.3.1.4**: 2.
Myles, G: **N.1**: 114.
Myneni, R: **J.4**: 2.
Myro Sánchez, R: **H.2.1**: 17.
N'Dombi, C: **O.1.3**: 1.
Nabli, M: **H.2.1**: 8.
Nacewski, J: **O.3.1**: 75.
Naegelen, F: **H.4**: 11. **N.3**: 10.
Nagarajan, G: **H.1.1**: 16.
Nagatsuka, S: **H.0**: 91.
Nagy, I: **N.2**: 109.
Naish, H: **K.2**: 30.
Najand, M: **J.4**: 58.
Najman, V: **K.3**: 100.
Nakamura, A: **G.2.1**: 96.
Nakamura, G: **G.3.3.5**: 82.
Nakamura, L: **G.3.2**: 15.
Nakamura, M: **G.2.1**: 96.
Nakamura, R: **N.2**: 12.
Nakamura, S: **G.1.2**: 2. **H.2.1**: 127.
Nakibullah, A: **J.1**: 70.
Nakosteen, R: **G.2.1**: 82.
Nance, J: **G.3.3.3**: 19.
Napier, B: **G.2.4**: 4.
Naqib, F: **N.2**: 197.
Narasimhan, C: **K.3**: 20. **L.2**: 24.

Narassiguin, P: **O.2.3**: 52.
Narayana, N: **G.2.4**: 118.
Narayanan, K: **O.3.2**: 74.
Narayanan, S: **H.1.1.3**: 8.
Narbone, L: **O.1.2.4**: 13.
Nardi, P: **J.2**: 78.
Narum, D: **H.0**: 156.
Narwold, A: **I.2.3**: 86.
Nash, C: **H.3**: 67.
Nashashibi, K: **N.2**: 140.
Nass, C: **F.3.1.1**: 44.
Natale, P: **F.3.1.4**: 24.
Nath, S: **N.2**: 155.
Nathan, A: **J.2**: 183.
Naudé, W: **J.5**: 3.
Naughton, B: **H.2.1**: 23. **N.1**: 166.
Navarre, C: **G.1.3**: 3.
Navarro, P: **F.3.1.1**: 118.
Navin, J: **N.2**: 24.
Nayar, B: **N.1**: 187.
Naylor, R: **H.1.2.1**: 28. **L.2**: 65.
Nayyar, P: **G.3.3.5**: 61.
Nayyar, R: **M.2**: 35.
Nazarea-Sandoval, V: **J.2**: 56.
Ncube, M: **J.4**: 251.
Ndebbio, J: **G.1**: 14.
Neal, A: **G.2.3**: 2.
Neal, R: **I.2.1**: 16.
Neale, C: **O.1.2.2**: 2.
Neary, H: **G.2.4**: 122.
Neary, J: **O.3.3**: 87.
Neave, E: **J.2**: 183.
Neckermann, P: **F.1**: 80.
Nee, V: **N.1**: 41.
Needham, B: **I.2.3**: 60.
Negri Zamagni, V: **G.3.3.3**: 14.
Neilsen, E: **J.2**: 113.
Neilson, W: **B.3**: 34.
Nel, E: **H.0**: 205.
Nell, P: **N.3**: 10.
Nellis, J: **I.2.3**: 84.
Nello, S: **I.2.3**: 30.
Nelson, D: **B.3**: 1. **O.3.3**: 60, 134.
Nelson, J: **M.2**: 23.
Nelson, K: **L.2**: 109.
Nelson, R: **C**: 16. **G.1**: 42. **M.5**: 15. **O.1.2.3**: 32.
Ners, K: **F.3.2**: 44.

Nessén, M: **O.2.3**: 42.
Nesterenko, A: **N.1**: 159.
Nestor, D: **H.0**: 190.
Neto, F: **F.3.3**: 39. **N.1**: 112.
Netter, J: **G.3.3.5**: 78.
Nettleship, J: **A**: 6.
Neu, D: **J.4**: 84.
Neuburger, H: **I.2.3**: 25.
Neumann, M: **J.1**: 36.
Neumark, D: **J.2**: 66. **K.3**: 38.
Neus, W: **G.3.3.3**: 22.
Neusser, K: **F.5**: 7.
Neven, D: **H.2.1**: 81.
Neves, J: **G.2.4**: 93.
Neveu, A: **H.1.1.4**: 34.
Newbery, D: **H.2.2**: 90. **I.2.1**: 92. **I.2.3**: 67. **O.3.3**: 16.
Newbold, P: **O.1.2.3**: 17.
Newhouse, J: **M.4**: 33, 41, 48.
Newitt, M: **F.1**: 4.
Newman, W: **G.3.3.5**: 40.
Ng, I: **G.2.5**: 1.
Ng, L: **J.4**: 295.
Ng, S: **G.2.2**: 22. **H.2.1**: 2.
Ng, Y: **F.5**: 5. **L.1**: 7. **M.1**: 12.
Ngama, Y: **O.3.3**: 81.
Nguyen, H: **O.2.2**: 121.
Nguyen, S: **G.1.2**: 10.
Nguyen, T: **O.3.1**: 71.
Nick, J: **H.0**: 102.
Nickell, S: **G.1.2**: 12. **G.2.4**: 103. **H.2.1**: 118. **K.3**: 93.
Nicol, M: **H.2.2**: 149.
Nicolaides, E: **A**: 10.
Nicoletti, G: **H.0**: 77, 82, 93. **N.2**: 42.
Niederée, R: **C**: 27.
Nielsen, J: **H.1.2.1**: 45.
Nielsen, S: **N.2**: 189.
Niemczynowicz, J: **H.0**: 211.
Niemi, I: **G.2.5**: 58.
Nieuwoudt, W: **F.3.1.1**: 8.
Nieva, D: **O.1.2.4**: 6.
Nijkamp, H: **G.3.2**: 29.
Nijkamp, P: **F.3.1.1**: 77, 86. **G.2.1**: 126.
Nijman, T: **B.2**: 4.
Nikić, G: **N.1**: 280.
Nikiphorov, A: **I.2.1**: 159.

Niknam, R: **J.2**: 64.
Nilssen, T: **L.2**: 42.
Nilsson, A: **H.0**: 94.
Ninni, A: **N.3**: 10.
Ninsin, K: **G.3.3.4**: 8.
Nippel, P: **G.3.3.3**: 22.
Nisbet, P: **G.2.1**: 21.
Nishikawa, N: **F.3.2**: 27.
Nishimura, K: **I.2.1**: 86. **M.4**: 83.
Nishimura, Y: **N.1**: 203.
Niskanen, E: **M.4**: 19.
Nitsch, M: **J.2**: 198.
Nitschke, E: **F.1**: 40. **G.1.1**: 22.
Nitzan, S: **C**: 5. **F.3.1.3**: 20.
Niu, R: **N.1**: 210.
Nizet, J: **G.3.3.5**: 25.
Noam, E: **H.3**: 95.
Nobay, A: **O.2.3**: 50.
Noble, G: **O.2.2**: 123.
Nock, R: **N.2**: 229.
Noe, T: **G.3.3.2**: 13.
Noel, J: **G.3.3.5**: 109.
Noel, M: **H.0**: 89.
Noh, K: **H.1.2.1**: 42.
Nolan, P: **G.2.4**: 17.
Nooi, P: **N.2**: 38.
Noordewier, T: **I.2.3**: 27.
Nooteboom, B: **G.1**: 61.
Norberg, S: **O.1.2.4**: 4.
Nordal, I: **J.2**: 38.
Norderhaug, M: **H.0**: 92.
Nordhaus, W: **F.3.3**: 34.
Nordström, K: **O.1.2.2**: 14.
Noren, J: **N.1**: 201. **O.1.3**: 26.
Norman, G: **F.3.1.1**: 5.
Norrbin, S: **F.5**: 37.
North, K: **H.0**: 85.
North, R: **E**: 3.
Norton, E: **G.3.2**: 17.
Norton, G: **O.1.3**: 68.
Norton, S: **H.3**: 100.
Nosal, E: **G.2.1**: 152. **G.3.3.5**: 102.
Noskova, I: **J.4**: 15.
Noussair, C: **I.2.1**: 1.
Novak, F: **H.1.1.3**: 15.
Novales, A: **J.4**: 131.

Novek, J: **H.0**: 180.
Novos, I: **G.2.5**: 25.
Nowak, R: **H.1.2.1**: 39.
Nowell, C: **H.0**: 51.
Nugent, J: **H.1.1.2**: 30. **H.2.1**: 8.
Nunan, P: **G.3.3.1**: 5.
Nunnenkamp, P: **N.1**: 128.
Nunnikhoven, T: **M.4**: 35.
Nuti, F: **N.2**: 2.
Nwonwu, F: **L.1**: 13.
Nyang'oro, J: **N.1**: 65.
Nymoen, R: **L.2**: 45.
Nyong'o, P: **H.2.1**: 33.
O'Brien, D: **H.4**: 105.
O'Brien, E: **G.3.3.4**: 9.
O'Brien, F: **B.4**: 39.
O'Brien, J: **D**: 34. **F.3.1.3**: 23.
O'Brien, K: **G.2.4**: 51.
O'Brien, M: **M.3**: 7.
O'Brien, P: **G.3.3.5**: 55, 69.
O'Brien, R: **O.2.4**: 4.
O'Connor, P: **G.3.3.5**: 119.
O'Donnell, R: **C**: 37. **D**: 79.
O'Farrell, P: **H.2.2**: 45–46.
O'Hanlon, J: **J.4**: 277.
O'Hara, M: **I.2.1**: 31. **J.4**: 202.
O'Hare, J: **N.2**: 113.
O'Hare, M: **O.1.3**: 52.
O'Keefe, P: **H.2.2**: 101.
O'Mahony, M: **H.2.2**: 42.
O'Neill, J: **G.2.1**: 94. **G.2.2**: 34.
O'Neill, R: **H.1.1.1**: 7. **I.2.3**: 8.
O'Reilly, B: **O.1.3**: 103.
O'Reilly, J: **J.2**: 140.
O'Shaughnessy, J: **L.2**: 63.
O'Shea, G: **F.1**: 38.
Oakey, R: **H.2.2**: 45–46.
Oakland, W: **N.2**: 24.
Obadan, M: **O.3.1**: 4.
Obaidullah: **O.1.2.5**: 7.
Obben, J: **J.2**: 76.
Oberhänsli, H: **L.3**: 11.
Oberman, R: **J.4**: 201.
Obeta, M: **H.1.1**: 3.
Oblath, G: **O.3.3**: 79.
Obstfeld, M: **N.2**: 240.
Oczkowski, E: **O.1.3**: 77.

Odagiri, H: **G.3.3.5**: 88.
Odedokun, M: **J.2**: 127. **L.1**: 1. **N.2**: 132. **O.3.1**: 10.
Odell, P: **H.0**: 185. **H.2.2**: 113, 162.
Odemerho, F: **H.0**: 100.
Odling-Smee, J: **F.1**: 74.
Ofer, A: **N.2**: 106.
Ofer, G: **N.1**: 218. **N.2**: 302.
Ogaki, M: **L.2**: 8.
Ogawa, N: **K.3**: 16.
Ogawa, T: **H.4**: 97.
Ogden, S: **G.2.3**: 9.
Ogus, A: **F.3.1.4**: 12.
Ohashi, H: **F.3.2**: 92.
Ohk, K: **J.4**: 242.
Ohlson, J: **K.3**: 101.
Ohlsson, H: **G.2.1**: 32. **K.3**: 122.
Ohly, C: **N.1**: 241.
Ohmori, T: **H.2.1**: 22.
Ohno, E: **H.3**: 4.
Ohseok, H: **F.3.2**: 100.
Ohsfeldt, R: **M.4**: 26.
Okogu, B: **I.2.3**: 23.
Okorafor, A: **H.0**: 21.
Okore, A: **H.0**: 21.
Oks, D: **L.1**: 29. **L.3**: 22. **N.1**: 80.
Okunade, A: **L.2**: 75.
Okunev, J: **J.4**: 1.
Olanloye, F: **H.1.1.1**: 29.
Olashore, O: **N.1**: 136.
Oldersma, H: **O.3.2**: 56.
Oldham, G: **H.4**: 18.
Olekalns, N: **J.2**: 15.
Olfert, M: **G.2.1**: 147.
Oliner, S: **G.3.3.3**: 36.
Oliveira-Martins, J: **H.0**: 9, 76–77, 82, 93.
Oliveira, de, A: **N.1**: 272.
Oliver, R: **H.3**: 49.
Olsen, P: **H.0**: 24.
Olsen, T: **G.1**: 51. **I.2.1**: 24, 104.
Olson, C: **G.2.4**: 3. **K.3**: 88.
Olson, L: **F.3.3**: 29. **H.0**: 200.
Olusi, J: **H.1.1.3**: 12.
Omar, I: **H.1.2.1**: 42.
Omara-Ojungu, P: **H.0**: 150.
Omasombo, T: **F.3.2**: 58.
Omer, T: **M.4**: 69.

Ommer, R: **H.1.2.1**: 41.
Ondarts, G: **O.1.2.4**: 36.
Ong, P: **K.3**: 45.
Ono, Y: **B.1**: 12. **F.2**: 15.
Onofri, P: **F.5**: 25.
Oosterbeek, H: **K.3**: 115.
Oppenheim, P: **O.3.2**: 78.
Oppenheimer, P: **N.1**: 153.
Oppewal, H: **C**: 62.
Oramah, B: **H.1.1.3**: 12.
Ordine, P: **G.2.1**: 136.
Oren, S: **I.2.1**: 101.
Orgaer, B: **H.2.2**: 4.
Orléan, A: **I.2.1**: 29.
Orlikowski, W: **G.1**: 26.
Orme, C: **B.1**: 6.
Ormiston, M: **B.4**: 32.
Orr, B: **O.1.2**: 6.
Orsmond, D: **J.5**: 45.
Ortega, E: **O.2.2**: 104.
Ortiz, J: **O.1.3**: 68.
Ortona, G: **C**: 62.
Osband, K: **I.2.1**: 123, 174. **K.3**: 13.
Osberg, L: **G.2.1**: 155.
Oser, R: **N.2**: 25.
Oshikoya, T: **J.4**: 133.
Oshima, H: **K.2**: 20.
Osleeb, J: **F.3.1.1**: 12.
Osotimehin, F: **G.1**: 14, 36.
Osowska, J: **O.3.1**: 75.
Ost, D: **N.1**: 134.
Östblom, G: **G.1**: 50.
Österberg, E: **I.2.3**: 50.
Östermark, R: **B.3**: 36.
Ostmann, A: **C**: 62.
Ostrowski, M: **N.1**: 315.
Ostroy, J: **C**: 12.
Ostry, J: **L.1**: 28. **O.2.1**: 82. **O.3.1**: 67.
Osuntogun, A: **H.1.1.3**: 12.
Oswald, A: **K.3**: 99.
Otero, M: **J.2**: 41.
Otsuka, K: **G.2.1**: 13. **H.1.1**: 17. **H.1.1.1**: 36. **H.1.1.2**: 11, 15. **J.2**: 93.
Otsuka, Y: **I.2.3**: 15.
Otsuki, M: **L.2**: 38.
Ott, A: **G.2.1**: 4.
Ott, C: **J.4**: 25.

Ottinger, R: **H.0**: 11.
Ottow, A: **O.1.2.3**: 19.
Oughton, C: **O.1.2.2**: 7.
Oum, T: **I.2.3**: 10.
Ourliac, G: **G.2.5**: 14.
Ours, van, J: **G.2.5**: 53.
Ourteau, M: **G.2.5**: 14.
Overgaard, P: **G.1.1**: 3.
Owen, A: **H.2.2**: 84.
Owen, D: **G.2.2**: 7. **G.3.3.5**: 74.
Owen, E: **A**: 1.
Owen, G: **C**: 71.
Owen, J: **H.4**: 40.
Owen, P: **J.1**: 59.
Owoye, O: **G.2.4**: 61.
Oyemakinde, W: **N.1**: 50.
Özler, S: **F.3.2**: 77. **J.2**: 163.
Pääkkönen, H: **G.2.5**: 58.
Paarlberg, R: **O.3.3**: 115.
Pachauri, R: **H.2.2**: 109.
Padgett, S: **O.1.2.3**: 35.
Padilla, A: **I.2.1**: 133.
Padmanabhan, P: **J.4**: 157. **O.2.2**: 124.
Padmore, G: **H.2.2**: 144.
Paganetto, L: **O.3.2**: 39.
Pagano, M: **F.3.2**: 30.
Pagano, U: **G.1**: 13.
Pagé, J: **O.1.3**: 75.
Page, M: **G.3.3.5**: 113.
Pagès, H: **J.4**: 16.
Pain, N: **F.1**: 78. **O.3.1**: 64.
Pál, G: **J.1**: 2.
Pal, M: **F.3.2**: 95.
Palairet, M: **H.2.2**: 74.
Palencia Gómez, J: **J.2**: 33.
Paleologos, J: **L.2**: 32.
Palepu, K: **G.3.2**: 10.
Palley, T: **G.2.1**: 156.
Palm, R: **J.3**: 5.
Palma, de, A: **F.3.1.1**: 13. **H.2.1**: 91. **L.2**: 20, 56.
Palme, M: **K.3**: 116.
Palmer, K: **H.3**: 98.
Palmer, L: **N.2**: 221.
Palmieri, S: **G.1.1**: 36.
Palokangas, T: **G.2.4**: 1. **O.3.3**: 57.
Pampanini, R: **H.1.1.4**: 43.

Panagariya, A: **O.3.1**: 28. **O.3.3**: 34, 54.
Panas, E: **G.1.1**: 12.
Panayiotopoulos, P: **H.2.2**: 13.
Panda, J: **F.3.2**: 89.
Pandey, B: **D**: 47.
Pandey, P: **O.1.3**: 38.
Panetta, F: **J.4**: 226.
Pangestu, M: **O.1.2.4**: 7.
Panner, M: **K.3**: 107.
Pannone, A: **H.3**: 83.
Pantelidis, P: **O.3.2**: 29.
Panuccio, T: **M.2**: 36.
Paoletti, F: **J.2**: 30.
Papadia, F: **O.1.3**: 67.
Papadopoulos, C: **H.1.2.1**: 2.
Papagni, E: **O.3.2**: 34.
Papas, A: **G.3.3.3**: 1.
Pape, W: **O.3.2**: 30.
Papps, I: **G.2.2**: 42. **H.0**: 113. **H.1.1.1**: 14.
Paprotzki, M: **J.2**: 219.
Paramasivam, P: **H.1.1.1**: 36.
Pardey, P: **O.1.3**: 68.
Paredes, S: **M.4**: 66.
Parent, A: **J.4**: 171.
Paricio, J: **F.1**: 39.
Parijs, van, P: **F.3.1.3**: 7.
Parikh, K: **H.0**: 86.
Parisot, B: **O.3.2**: 64.
Park, D: **G.2.4**: 18.
Park, J: **O.2.2**: 7. **O.3.1**: 25.
Park, T: **H.2.2**: 52. **I.2.1**: 25.
Parker, E: **H.3**: 87.
Parker, J: **G.2.1**: 157.
Parker, L: **B.4**: 57.
Parker, P: **I.2.1**: 156.
Parker, R: **B.3**: 9.
Parker, S: **G.1.1**: 16.
Parkinson, P: **J.4**: 206.
Parmann, G: **H.0**: 92.
Parnwell, M: **H.0**: 38.
Paroush, J: **J.4**: 17.
Parravicini, P: **J.2**: 159.
Parsonage, J: **O.1.3**: 49.
Parsons, G: **I.2.3**: 88.
Parsons, J: **J.4**: 68.
Parthama, I: **O.3.2**: 81.
Parton, K: **L.2**: 73.

Paruolo, P: **F.5**: 25.
Pasche, M: **G.2.1**: 6.
Pashkovskii, V: **J.1**: 88.
Pass, C: **O.1.2.3**: 34.
Passaro, R: **H.2.2**: 26.
Passet, R: **H.0**: 162.
Passmore, W: **J.2**: 236.
Pastizzi-Ferencic, D: **H.0**: 172.
Pastor, M: **N.1**: 76.
Pastore, R: **H.1.2.1**: 1.
Pastori, G: **H.1.1.4**: 43.
Patel, I: **F.3.2**: 64.
Patel, U: **N.2**: 239.
Paterson, K: **N.2**: 190.
Paterson, M: **H.0**: 183.
Pathak, P: **N.1**: 248.
Patterson, E: **O.3.3**: 111.
Patterson, K: **F.2**: 20. **L.1**: 42. **L.2**: 17, 36. **O.3.2**: 67.
Pattison, R: **M.4**: 29.
Paul, J: **K.3**: 41.
Pauly, P: **I.2.1**: 55. **O.2.1**: 33.
Paunio, J: **L.1**: 37.
Pausewang, S: **F.3.2**: 42.
Pavlin, I: **G.3.3.1**: 9.
Pavlínek, P: **F.3.1.1**: 82.
Pavlov, V: **N.2**: 257.
Paye, J: **N.1**: 4.
Payer, H: **H.0**: 56.
Paz, F: **F.3.1.3**: 2. **F.3.2**: 18.
Peacock, A: **E**: 14.
Peacock, F: **H.1.2.1**: 35.
Pearce, D: **H.0**: 44, 189.
Pearse, P: **H.0**: 146. **H.1.2.1**: 39.
Pearson, A: **G.3.3**: 8.
Pearson, M: **N.2**: 97.
Pearson, P: **H.2.2**: 101.
Peck, A: **I.2.1**: 120.
Peck, J: **G.2.1**: 46. **H.0**: 174. **I.2.1**: 38, 167.
Pecorino, P: **F.3.3**: 58.
Pedersen, O: **C**: 40.
Pedersen, P: **F.3.1.1**: 96.
Peebles, G: **J.1**: 23.
Peek, J: **J.4**: 146.
Peer, H: **G.2.1**: 146.
Peersman, G: **L.1**: 21.
Peet, C: **O.3.1**: 7.

Peiser, R: **F.3.1.3**: 21.
Pejovich, S: **G.3.3.5**: 62.
Pekkarinen, J: **N.1**: 235.
Pellegrini, G: **F.5**: 25.
Pelupessy, W: **F.3.2**: 75.
Pemberton, M: **G.2.1**: 158.
Peña, J: **J.4**: 70.
Pencavel, J: **H.2.1**: 76.
Peng, S: **G.3.2**: 13.
Peng, W: **J.5**: 17.
Peng, Y: **N.1**: 306.
Penn, R: **G.2.2**: 7.
Penning-Rowsell, E: **F.3.1.1**: 10.
Penrose, E: **O.1.3**: 14.
Pentecost, J: **O.2.2**: 9.
Peoples, J: **K.3**: 28.
Pepall, L: **I.2.1**: 60.
Pepermans, G: **M.4**: 92.
Peracchi, F: **H.2.1**: 5.
Perasso, G: **N.1**: 181. **O.2.2**: 4.
Perée: **J.2**: 167.
Peregudoc, S: **G.3.1**: 1.
Pereira, N: **H.2.2**: 120.
Perelman, S: **L.1**: 41.
Perennès, J: **F.3.2**: 63.
Pérez, F: **O.1.2.4**: 59.
Pérez Castrillo, J: **H.2.1**: 1.
Pérez Fernández, J: **O.1.2.4**: 58.
Peristiani, S: **J.4**: 222.
Perlman, M: **O.3.2**: 12.
Perold, A: **J.2**: 2.
Perold, H: **F.1**: 8.
Perotti, R: **F.3.3**: 27.
Perrier-Cornet, P: **F.3.1.1**: 91.
Perrings, C: **H.0**: 181.
Perron, P: **B.3**: 5, 58. **F.2**: 9.
Perrone, L: **F.1**: 45.
Perrons, D: **H.2.2**: 44.
Perry, G: **N.1**: 144.
Perry, N: **F.1**: 87.
Persky, J: **D**: 15.
Persson, M: **G.3.3.5**: 112.
Persson, T: **O.1.2.4**: 80.
Perthes, V: **F.1**: 32. **N.1**: 51.
Perumal, M: **M.2**: 25.
Pesaran, B: **L.2**: 17. **O.3.1**: 41.

Pesaran, M: **B.1**: 10. **B.3**: 39. **F.3.3**: 46. **O.2.1**: 45. **O.2.3**: 14, 35.

Pesaresi, N: **G.3.2**: 35.

Pestieau, P: **F.3.1.3**: 12. **G.4**: 6. **L.1**: 41.

Peters, G: **H.1.1.4**: 13.

Peters, H: **K.3**: 42.

Peters, M: **I.2.1**: 138.

Petersen, C: **L.2**: 52. **M.4**: 90.

Petersen, M: **M.4**: 86.

Petersmann, E: **O.1.2.4**: 57.

Peterson, I: **K.3**: 37.

Peterson, J: **F.3.1.3**: 19.

Peterson, R: **G.2.4**: 30, 43. **J.4**: 101.

Pethig, R: **H.0**: 132.

Petit, B: **N.1**: 325.

Petit, P: **H.2.1**: 124.

Petras, J: **F.3.2**: 122. **N.1**: 38.

Petroni, K: **J.3**: 11.

Pettman, R: **F.3.1.3**: 14.

Peubey-Kronsteiner, M: **O.1.2.3**: 11.

Pezzey, J: **H.0**: 119.

Pfaffenberger, W: **H.0**: 201.

Pfähler, W: **K.2**: 17.

Pfeffer, J: **G.3.3**: 35. **K.3**: 120.

Pfeffer, M: **H.1.1.1**: 16.

Pfefferkorn, G: **J.2**: 234.

Pfeiffer, F: **G.2.1**: 114.

Pfleiderer, P: **J.4**: 182.

Pfohl, H: **H.4**: 23.

Phaneuf, L: **F.5**: 42.

Phang, H: **O.3.3**: 18.

Phelps, E: **G.2.1**: 121. **O.3.2**: 39.

Philippopoulos, A: **J.1**: 110. **O.2.3**: 30.

Phillips, A: **I.2.3**: 19.

Phillips, D: **F.3.1.1**: 34.

Phillips, L: **H.4**: 97.

Phillips, O: **I.2.1**: 46.

Phillips, P: **F.3.1.4**: 10.

Phillips, R: **I.2.3**: 81.

Phillips, T: **B.4**: 43.

Phipps, A: **G.2.4**: 97.

Phizacklea, A: **F.1**: 81.

Pho, P: **G.3.3.1**: 9.

Piacentino, D: **H.0**: 5.

Piazolo, M: **H.2.1**: 97.

Picard, N: **B.3**: 1.

Picciotto, S: **N.2**: 98.

Pichigua, J: **N.1**: 108.

Pichler, E: **G.2.1**: 78.

Pick, D: **H.2.2**: 52.

Pickel, A: **N.1**: 167.

Picory, C: **D**: 7.

Picou, A: **O.2.2**: 133.

Pieptea, D: **J.4**: 175.

Pierce, A: **B.4**: 39.

Pierse, R: **F.3.3**: 46.

Pietrobelli, C: **O.1.3**: 69.

Pigliaru, F: **H.2.1**: 68.

Pigott, D: **G.3.3.5**: 32.

Pilbeam, K: **O.2.1**: 22.

Pilketty, T: **J.4**: 48.

Pilkington, H: **F.1**: 81.

Pillinger, J: **G.2.2**: 33.

Pilotte, E: **J.4**: 122, 269.

Pinder, M: **G.2.5**: 37.

Pindur, W: **G.2.5**: 61.

Pinegar, J: **J.4**: 121.

Pinfield, G: **H.0**: 175.

Pingali, P: **H.1.1.4**: 32.

Pingle, M: **C**: 22.

Pinker, R: **M.3**: 6.

Pinkerton, J: **I.2.1**: 44.

Pint, E: **I.2.1**: 150.

Piotrowska-Marczak, K: **M.4**: 112.

Pirani, M: **G.2.2**: 7.

Pirrong, S: **H.3**: 73.

Pisani-Ferry, J: **O.1.3**: 75.

Pischke, J: **G.2.1**: 97.

Pischke, von, J: **J.2**: 68.

Pischner, R: **G.1.2**: 19.

Piskulich, J: **G.2.4**: 46.

Pissarides, C: **G.2.1**: 140, 154.

Pitelis, C: **C**: 54.

Pitkin, J: **F.3.1.3**: 21.

Pittaluga, G: **G.3.3.4**: 22. **J.2**: 147.

Pittis, N: **O.2.1**: 2.

Pivetti, M: **L.2**: 26.

Platt, D: **E**: 6.

Platteau, J: **H.1.1.2**: 30.

Please, S: **N.1**: 64.

Pless, N: **J.1**: 85.

Ploeg, van der, F: **F.3.3**: 40. **O.2.3**: 24.

Plott, C: **I.2.1**: 43.

Procopio, A: **H.0**: 49.
Prodi, R: **H.1.1.2**: 27.
Pronk, J: **F.3.2**: 26.
Proost, S: **N.2**: 129.
Propper, C: **I.2.1**: 57. **M.4**: 51.
Prosperetti, L: **N.3**: 46.
Prostakov, I: **F.3.1.3**: 6.
Proulx, Y: **H.1.2.1**: 3.
Prowse, S: **G.3.3.3**: 37.
Pruitt, S: **L.2**: 22.
Prus, M: **G.4**: 1.
Prusa, T: **O.3.3**: 101.
Prybyla, J: **O.1.2.3**: 33.
Prywes, M: **J.2**: 48.
Psacharopoulos, G: **K.3**: 51. **M.5**: 9.
Puelz. v, A: **J.4**: 117.
Pueyo Campos, A: **F.1**: 39.
Puffer, S: **G.3.3.5**: 60.
Pugliese, E: **G.2.1**: 83.
Puhovski, Z: **D**: 6.
Puissant, S: **F.3.1.1**: 103.
Pulley, L: **J.2**: 150.
Punjabi, P: **H.1.1.1**: 4.
Purcell, J: **G.2.4**: 50.
Purohit, B: **N.2**: 155.
Purves, B: **O.1.2.2**: 1.
Putterill, M: **L.2**: 83.
Putterman, L: **F.3.2**: 91. **G.2.4**: 122. **N.1**: 166.
Qadeer, M: **F.3.1.1**: 104.
Qian, Y: **M.1**: 7.
Qihuai, L: **O.2.2**: 83.
Quah, D: **F.2**: 12.
Quah, E: **K.1**: 1.
Quan, J: **O.1.2.3**: 39.
Quandt, C: **F.3.1.1**: 65.
Quandt, R: **G.3.3**: 9.
Quarter, J: **G.2.4**: 125.
Quaye, R: **M.4**: 53.
Quercia, R: **J.2**: 246.
Quiggin, J: **C**: 29. **F.3.3**: 62.
Quigley, J: **N.2**: 297.
Quinn, J: **H.0**: 141.
Quintieri, B: **N.2**: 174.
Quiroga, R: **H.1.2.1**: 19.
Qureshi, A: **O.3.3**: 123.
Raafat, F: **G.2.5**: 51.
Rabeau, Y: **F.1**: 13.

Raboy, D: **O.3.3**: 44.
Raby, G: **O.1.3**: 48.
Racette, D: **J.5**: 8.
Racine, A: **M.4**: 3.
Rada, J: **H.0**: 75.
Radetzki, M: **H.2.2**: 132, 145.
Radner, R: **C**: 66. **G.3.3.5**: 27.
Radnitzky, G: **B.1**: 25.
Rae, J: **B.3**: 2.
Raff, H: **N.3**: 29.
Raffelhüschen, B: **G.2.1**: 81.
Rafiq, M: **G.2.2**: 7.
Rahm, D: **G.1**: 57. **G.1.3**: 12.
Rahman, A: **J.2**: 58.
Rahman, H: **J.4**: 58.
Rahman, P: **K.2**: 8.
Rahman, R: **G.2.1**: 89. **K.3**: 105.
Rahman, S: **J.4**: 153.
Rahmeyer, F: **H.2.2**: 136.
Rahnema, S: **G.2.4**: 124.
Rai, A: **O.2.2**: 113.
Rai, S: **F.1**: 81.
Raiklin, E: **N.1**: 229.
Rainer, S: **J.4**: 66.
Raines, J: **D**: 18.
Raj, B: **G.1.1**: 18.
Rajan, M: **H.4**: 20.
Rajan, R: **C**: 13. **J.2**: 230.
Raju, N: **G.2.5**: 8.
Ram, R: **K.2**: 19. **M.2**: 17.
Ramakrishnan, P: **H.0**: 61.
Ramamurti, R: **O.2.2**: 65.
Raman, K: **B.4**: 28.
Ramanadham, V: **N.1**: 290.
Ramani, K: **H.1.2.1**: 38. **H.3**: 60.
Ramasamy, C: **G.2.1**: 13. **H.1.1.1**: 36.
Ramaswami, S: **J.4**: 166.
Ramaswamy, B: **N.1**: 155.
Ramaswamy, R: **C**: 40.
Ramaswamy, V: **H.4**: 31.
Ramesh, K: **K.3**: 101.
Ramey, G: **I.2.1**: 136.
Ramey, V: **J.1**: 39.
Ramfrez Gómez, M: **F.3.2**: 19.
Ramírez G., M: **N.1**: 144.
Ramírez V., J: **N.1**: 144.

Ramkissoon, R: **O.3.1**: 61.
Ramón Cuadrado Roura, J: **F.1**: 39.
Ramphal, S: **H.0**: 105.
Ramsaran, R: **N.1**: 66.
Ramsay, H: **G.2.4**: 117. **O.1.2.4**: 91.
Ramunni, F: **J.2**: 123.
Randers, J: **H.0**: 158.
Rands, T: **G.3.3.5**: 39.
Rangan, N: **J.4**: 224.
Rangazas, P: **N.2**: 315.
Ranis, G: **F.1**: 33.
Rank, M: **F.3.1.3**: 13.
Rankaduwa, W: **N.2**: 255.
Rankin, N: **I.2.1**: 87.
Ranney, D: **G.2.5**: 23.
Rao, A: **F.3.2**: 109.
Rao, B: **C**: 20.
Rao, H: **J.2**: 113.
Rao, J: **J.2**: 91.
Rao, M: **K.2**: 3.
Rao, P: **G.2.4**: 118. **J.2**: 91.
Rao, R: **G.3.3**: 10.
Rao, T: **N.2**: 158.
Rapaczynski, A: **N.1**: 328.
Rapoport, A: **C**: 59.
Rappaport, A: **G.3.3.5**: 79.
Rappaport, S: **D**: 1.
Rappelli, F: **K.3**: 65.
Rappen, H: **H.4**: 30.
Rapsomanikis, G: **I.2.3**: 6.
Rashid, S: **D**: 17.
Rasmusen, E: **K.3**: 26.
Rasmussen, C: **D**: 31.
Rasmussen, D: **G.1.2**: 6.
Rasmussen, S: **G.2.4**: 56.
Rassekh, F: **F.2**: 13.
Rassenti, S: **H.4**: 15.
Ratchford, B: **I.2.1**: 50. **L.2**: 61.
Rath, N: **H.1.2.1**: 9.
Ratick, S: **F.3.1.1**: 12.
Ratledge, C: **F.3.2**: 2.
Ratnam, C: **G.2.4**: 54.
Ratnayake, R: **O.3.2**: 46.
Ratner, A: **C**: 60.
Ratner, M: **J.4**: 307.
Ratteray, J: **G.2.1**: 94.
Ratti, S: **J.2**: 3.

Rattner, H: **F.3.2**: 18, 84.
Rauscher, M: **I.2.1**: 11.
Rausser, G: **H.1.1.4**: 25. **N.1**: 18. **O.3.3**: 108.
Ravenhill, J: **O.1.3**: 48.
Ravikumar, B: **F.5**: 29.
Ravix, J: **D**: 7. **G.3.3**: 15.
Ravn, M: **F.5**: 8.
Rawal, P: **M.4**: 16.
Rawlinson, M: **H.2.2**: 71.
Rawski, T: **H.2.1**: 20. **N.1**: 166.
Ray, S: **I.2.2**: 1.
Raybould, S: **J.2**: 87.
Rayburn, J: **B.4**: 37.
Raymond, J: **F.2**: 29. **O.1.2.4**: 59.
Raynauld, J: **J.5**: 8.
Rea, D: **G.2.1**: 65.
Reading, B: **F.1**: 24.
Rebelo, S: **N.2**: 240.
Reddy, P: **L.2**: 105.
Reddy, V: **O.3.2**: 74.
Redgwell, C: **H.3**: 79.
Redmond, J: **O.1.2.4**: 70.
Redor, P: **H.1.1.4**: 9.
Reed, D: **F.3.2**: 45.
Reed, G: **H.1.1.4**: 16. **M.5**: 43.
Reed, M: **G.3.3**: 25.
Reed, W: **K.3**: 110.
Reenen, van, J: **G.2.4**: 74.
Rees, P: **H.1.2**: 3.
Rees, T: **G.2.2**: 41.
Reese, L: **F.3.1.1**: 21.
Reffett, K: **J.2**: 9.
Regemorter, van, D: **N.2**: 129.
Regens, J: **N.2**: 235.
Regibeau, P: **G.1.1**: 39.
Regini, M: **G.2.4**: 48, 76.
Register, C: **G.2.1**: 60.
Regler, R: **H.3**: 36.
Rego, A: **J.4**: 70.
Regulez, M: **O.2.1**: 75.
Regulska, J: **N.2**: 297.
Rehder, R: **H.2.2**: 63.
Reichelstein, S: **G.3.3.5**: 128. **N.1**: 21.
Reichlin, L: **B.3**: 42. **J.2**: 29.
Reid, B: **O.2.2**: 54.
Reid, G: **G.3.3.4**: 19.

Reid, J: **G.2.4**: 81.
Reidenbach, R: **B.4**: 43.
Reifner, U: **J.2**: 134.
Reiger, K: **F.1**: 88.
Reilly, B: **K.3**: 125. **N.2**: 3.
Reilly, F: **J.4**: 104.
Reilly, J: **H.0**: 135.
Reilly, R: **L.2**: 22. **N.1**: 107.
Reimann, M: **I.2.1**: 149.
Reinelt, L: **H.0**: 204.
Reinert, K: **B.4**: 24.
Reinganum, J: **I.2.1**: 82.
Reinhart, C: **L.1**: 28.
Reinhart, V: **J.4**: 128.
Reisen, H: **O.2.1**: 80.
Reisman, H: **B.3**: 49.
Reister, D: **H.0**: 131.
Reiter, S: **B.4**: 18. **M.4**: 69.
Reither, F: **O.2.1**: 76.
Reitzes, J: **G.1.3**: 15.
Remolona, E: **J.2**: 36.
Rémond, B: **G.2.5**: 14.
Remy, J: **J.1**: 25.
Renaud, B: **I.2.3**: 36.
Reneau, J: **B.4**: 32.
Renesme, G: **H.2.2**: 94.
Renfro, R: **H.1.1.1**: 12.
Reny, P: **C**: 74.
Renzetti, S: **H.0**: 199.
Repetto, R: **H.0**: 166, 182.
Repullo, R: **J.2**: 146.
Reschovsky, A: **N.2**: 24.
Resende, M: **I.2.2**: 3.
Resnick, B: **J.4**: 266.
Resnick, S: **C**: 27.
Resti, A: **J.2**: 192.
Reszat, B: **J.5**: 27.
Reuben, B: **H.2.2**: 119.
Revankar, N: **F.2**: 27.
Revel-Mouroz, J: **O.1.2.4**: 5.
ReVelle, C: **F.3.1.1**: 12.
Revenga, A: **G.2.1**: 131. **K.3**: 72.
Révész, T: **N.1**: 162.
Reyero, P: **J.4**: 70.
Reyes Posada, A: **N.1**: 144.
Reyjulia, J: **F.3.1.1**: 51.
Reymann, S: **H.3**: 3.

Reynaud, B: **K.3**: 100.
Reynolds, S: **G.1.1**: 37.
Reyns, C: **B.4**: 42.
Rezende Rocha, De, R: **J.1**: 81.
Rhee, H: **O.2.3**: 61.
Rhee, S: **J.4**: 240.
Rhee, T: **J.4**: 264.
Rhoades, S: **J.2**: 162.
Rhoads, G: **H.4**: 66.
Rhodes, R: **N.1**: 102.
Rhyne, E: **J.2**: 41.
Riahi-Belkaoui, A: **G.3.3.5**: 20.
Ribar, D: **G.2.2**: 30. **M.4**: 2.
Rice, J: **H.2.2**: 118.
Rice, T: **M.4**: 13.
Rich, D: **O.3.1**: 14.
Rich, J: **G.2.2**: 17. **O.1.3**: 92.
Rich, M: **F.3.2**: 30.
Rich, R: **F.2**: 29.
Richards, C: **H.0**: 124. **H.2.1**: 69.
Richards, D: **J.1**: 20.
Richardson, A: **J.2**: 115.
Richardson, D: **L.2**: 37.
Richardson, G: **B.4**: 18. **J.4**: 245.
Richardson, I: **I.2.1**: 72.
Richardson, J: **H.0**: 8. **N.1**: 279. **O.3.3**: 60.
Richardson, L: **G.3.3.5**: 97.
Richardson, M: **J.4**: 74. **O.3.3**: 85.
Richardson, P: **F.5**: 36. **J.4**: 74. **O.1.2**: 3.
Richardson, R: **O.1.3**: 91.
Richardson, S: **M.2**: 18.
Richels, R: **H.0**: 67.
Richet, X: **O.1.3**: 44.
Richman, S: **O.2.2**: 16.
Richter, S: **F.3.1.3**: 4. **N.1**: 126.
Richter, W: **N.2**: 43, 222.
Rickman, D: **F.2**: 30. **G.3.3.3**: 13.
Rickman, N: **G.2.5**: 38.
Ridao Carlini, M: **I.2.3**: 102.
Riddell, J: **N.1**: 85.
Riddell, W: **K.3**: 7.
Ridder, G: **G.2.5**: 53.
Riddiough, T: **L.2**: 98.
Rider, C: **N.1**: 205.
Ridge, M: **N.2**: 35, 46.
Ridyard, D: **I.2.1**: 74.

Riebemeier, B: **H.3**: 36.
Riecken, G: **H.4**: 89.
Riess, M: **O.1.3**: 59.
Rietveld, P: **F.3.1.1**: 77, 121. **G.2.1**: 27, 126. **I.2.3**: 91.
Rifflart, C: **F.5**: 33.
Rigby, D: **G.1**: 33.
Rigg, J: **H.0**: 38.
Rigon, A: **J.2**: 8.
Riha, T: **N.1**: 211.
Rijsberman, F: **H.0**: 209.
Riley, J: **C**: 78. **F.2**: 22. **N.1**: 262.
Riley, T: **N.1**: 82.
Riley, W: **J.4**: 170.
Rimini, L: **N.2**: 308.
Rimler, J: **G.2.1**: 52.
Rimmer, P: **H.3**: 17.
Rimmer, R: **K.3**: 119.
Rimmer, S: **K.3**: 119.
Rimmington, A: **G.1**: 56.
Rincón, H: **N.2**: 90.
Rinehart, J: **G.3.3.5**: 70.
Rio, Y: **H.1.1.4**: 34.
Riordan, M: **H.3**: 27.
Risa, A: **G.1**: 51.
Risager, O: **K.3**: 106.
Ritter, J: **J.4**: 278.
Ritzen, J: **G.2.5**: 28.
Rivera-Batiz, F: **L.3**: 7. **O.1.2.4**: 69.
Rivera-Batiz, L: **L.3**: 7. **O.1.2.4**: 69.
Rivera-Solis, L: **O.2.3**: 25.
Riveros, L: **F.2**: 6. **G.2.2**: 28.
Rivier, J: **G.3.3.4**: 1.
Rixtel, van, A: **J.2**: 220.
Rizzo, I: **N.2**: 266.
Rizzo, J: **J.2**: 142. **M.4**: 12.
Roach, B: **H.0**: 207.
Robb, A: **L.2**: 19.
Robben, H: **N.2**: 13.
Robbie, K: **G.3.3.3**: 5.
Roberds, W: **J.5**: 32.
Roberti, P: **N.2**: 253.
Roberts, E: **G.3.3.5**: 97.
Roberts, H: **B.4**: 21.
Roberts, J: **I.2.1**: 115. **J.1**: 37.
Roberts, K: **B.3**: 62. **G.3.3.5**: 12.
Roberts, M: **H.2.2**: 32.

Roberts, R: **F.3.1.4**: 11. **G.3.3.5**: 55. **H.0**: 42. **N.3**: 19.
Robertson, D: **G.3.3.5**: 70. **J.1**: 109. **O.1.2.4**: 77.
Robertson, J: **O.2.3**: 43.
Robertson, K: **A**: 16.
Robin, D: **B.4**: 43.
Robin, J: **L.2**: 74.
Robins, K: **H.3**: 82.
Robins, P: **G.2.2**: 23. **M.4**: 2.
Robinson, C: **G.2.4**: 102. **N.1**: 295.
Robinson, D: **F.3.1.1**: 44. **N.2**: 148.
Robinson, R: **E**: 6.
Robson, A: **K.2**: 34.
Robson, M: **F.3.3**: 40. **G.3.3.1**: 13.
Robson, W: **J.5**: 58.
Rocchi, A: **N.1**: 190.
Rocha dos Santos, R: **H.2.2**: 16. **H.4**: 2.
Roche, M: **H.1.1.4**: 4.
Rochet, J: **J.2**: 146.
Rock, C: **G.2.4**: 126.
Rock, L: **L.1**: 8.
Rock, M: **O.3.3**: 63.
Rockel, M: **G.2.1**: 24. **G.2.5**: 21.
Rockerbie, D: **O.3.2**: 31.
Rodgers, G: **H.3**: 13.
Rodgers, J: **N.2**: 77.
Rodrigues, A: **J.5**: 29.
Rodriguez, A: **I.2.1**: 145.
Rodriguez, C: **J.1**: 75, 112.
Rodríguez, F: **F.3.2**: 81.
Rodriguez, G: **H.1.2.1**: 24.
Rodríguez, J: **N.1**: 144.
Rodrik, D: **F.3.2**: 77. **O.3.3**: 9.
Roe, A: **F.3.2**: 62.
Roemer, J: **N.1**: 28. **N.3**: 55.
Rogers, C: **J.5**: 50.
Rogers, J: **J.1**: 47.
Rogerson, C: **H.4**: 49.
Rogerson, R: **G.2.1**: 152.
Rogerson, W: **N.1**: 21.
Rogoff, K: **O.2.1**: 93. **O.2.2**: 49. **O.2.4**: 12.
Rogowski, J: **M.4**: 33.
Rohatinski, Z: **F.3.3**: 54.
Rohling, T: **J.5**: 16.
Rojas-Suarez, L: **O.2.1**: 4.
Rojo, M: **H.2.1**: 72.
Roland, G: **N.1**: 56, 148, 311.

Rubio, S: **H.2.2**: 148.
Rudd, A: **J.4**: 36.
Rudebusch, G: **G.3.3.3**: 36.
Rudka, A: **J.5**: 33.
Rudner, M: **O.1.3**: 61.
Ruefli, T: **C**: 85.
Ruffin, R: **O.3.1**: 31.
Ruggeri, G: **N.2**: 85.
Ruggles, P: **M.2**: 11.
Rugina, A: **N.1**: 71.
Ruhm, C: **G.2.1**: 119.
Ruitenbeek, H: **H.0**: 59, 168.
Rummery, S: **K.3**: 111.
Runkle, D: **J.4**: 20.
Rupp, A: **N.2**: 48.
Rupp, K: **M.4**: 120.
Rus, de, G: **F.1**: 39.
Rush, H: **G.1**: 4.
Russell, G: **I.2.1**: 45.
Russell, J: **G.3.3.2**: 5.
Russell, S: **J.1**: 61. **J.2**: 108.
Rustayisire, L: **N.3**: 14.
Rutherford, B: **N.3**: 3.
Rutherford, M: **D**: 69.
Rutherford, T: **H.2.2**: 78.
Rutkowski, W: **M.4**: 112.
Rutland, P: **N.1**: 116.
Rutman, G: **F.3.1.3**: 5. **H.2.2**: 60.
Rutström, E: **O.3.3**: 137.
Rwegasira, K: **J.2**: 82.
Ryan, B: **B.4**: 53.
Ryd, G: **O.3.3**: 39.
Rydqvist, K: **J.4**: 23.
Ryngaert, M: **J.2**: 22.
Ryscavage, P: **K.3**: 31.
Ryterman, R: **G.3.3.4**: 2. **G.3.3.5**: 35.
Ryzhenkova, T: **N.2**: 196.
Rzeszot, U: **H.0**: 15.
Saadouni, B: **G.3.2**: 25.
Saasa, O: **O.1.2.4**: 31.
Saavedra, L: **N.2**: 90.
Sabatini, G: **D**: 27.
Sabbatini, M: **H.1.1.2**: 34.
Sabhasri, S: **H.2.2**: 109.
Sabov, Z: **G.3.3.5**: 16. **J.4**: 30.
Sacco, P: **J.4**: 229.

Sachs, J: **J.1**: 34. **N.1**: 131, 191. **O.2.3**: 58.
Sadler, D: **H.2.1**: 103. **H.2.2**: 61.
Sadri, S: **N.1**: 155.
Sagari, S: **J.2**: 50, 237.
Saghafi, M: **G.2.5**: 51.
Sági, M: **F.3.2**: 121.
Sah, R: **N.2**: 55.
Saha, V: **N.1**: 248.
Sahay, R: **N.1**: 261.
Sahn, D: **N.2**: 276.
Sahni, B: **F.2**: 10.
Sahoo, B: **O.2.2**: 66.
Said, G: **L.2**: 27.
Saini, D: **G.2.4**: 12.
Saint-Paul, G: **F.3.3**: 23. **G.2.1**: 47. **J.4**: 97. **N.2**: 28.
Saito, M: **N.1**: 91.
Sakano, R: **F.5**: 37.
Sako, M: **H.2.2**: 40.
Sakurai, K: **G.2.1**: 129.
Sala-i-Martin, X: **F.3.2**: 77. **F.3.3**: 9, 23. **J.1**: 69. **N.2**: 62.
Salais, R: **H.2.1**: 19. **H.2.2**: 66.
Salama, E: **J.5**: 44.
Salama, P: **J.1**: 100.
Salaman, G: **G.2.5**: 20. **L.2**: 4.
Salamon, L: **G.3.3.5**: 120.
Salas, J: **G.3.3.5**: 125.
Salda, A: **O.2.4**: 5.
Saldaña, L: **F.3.2**: 17.
Saldern, von, M: **I.2.3**: 31.
Salehi-Esfahani, H: **H.3**: 32.
Salerno, J: **C**: 35.
Salgado, G: **F.3.2**: 70.
Salinas Sanchez, J: **N.2**: 126.
Salituro, B: **F.5**: 25.
Salkever, D: **I.2.3**: 51. **M.4**: 65.
Salle, R: **I.2.1**: 28.
Sallert, M: **H.2.2**: 12.
Salma, P: **J.1**: 6.
Salma, U: **H.0**: 1.
Salonen, H: **I.2.1**: 109.
Saloner, G: **G.1.1**: 39.
Saltz, I: **N.2**: 236. **O.2.2**: 111.
Salvanes, K: **H.1.1.2**: 8. **H.1.2.1**: 43.
Salvatore, D: **N.1**: 109. **O.3.3**: 49.
Samecki, P: **O.1.3**: 53.

Sami, H: **M.4**: 68.
Samiei, H: **O.2.1**: 45. **O.2.3**: 14.
Samii, M: **I.2.3**: 46.
Samonis, V: **F.3.3**: 50.
Samorodov, A: **O.1.2.5**: 4.
Sampath, R: **H.1.1.1**: 11, 15.
Samuels, W: **B.1**: 7.
Samuelson, L: **C**: 61. **I.2.1**: 19, 161.
Samuelson, P: **B.3**: 21.
Samuelson, W: **J.2**: 2.
Samwick, A: **M.4**: 118.
Sánchez, A: **F.3.1.1**: 80.
Sánchez, J: **F.3.1.1**: 72.
Sancho, F: **B.3**: 37. **K.2**: 26.
Sander, W: **F.3.1.2**: 4.
Sanders, A: **J.4**: 130.
Sanders, R: **G.1**: 36.
Sanderson, S: **H.4**: 43.
Sandford, C: **N.2**: 318.
Sandholtz, W: **F.1**: 2. **O.1.3**: 19.
Sandilands, R: **F.3.3**: 59.
Sandimo, A: **M.3**: 13.
Sandkull, B: **G.2.4**: 16.
Sandler, T: **N.3**: 47.
Sandoval, V: **K.3**: 92.
Sani, G: **I.2.3**: 13.
Sansing, R: **B.4**: 2.
Santalainen, T: **J.2**: 145.
Santamaria, M: **M.4**: 111.
Santana, de, A: **I.2.3**: 52.
Santandrea, V: **F.3.1.1**: 70.
Santarossa, G: **F.3.1.1**: 44.
Santos, dos, A: **H.2.2**: 21.
Santucci, F: **H.1.1.4**: 43.
Sanyal, R: **G.2.4**: 93.
Sapir, A: **O.1.2.4**: 44, 69. **O.3.1**: 21.
Sapir, J: **O.1.3**: 75.
Sapolsky, H: **H.3**: 96.
Saposnik, R: **K.1**: 4.
Sappington, D: **G.1**: 10. **N.3**: 22.
Sarcevic, P: **O.2.1**: 21.
Sarcinelli, M: **O.1.2.4**: 21. **O.2.2**: 41.
Sardoni, C: **D**: 67. **I.2.1**: 181.
Sargious, M: **H.3**: 20.
Sarig, O: **J.4**: 257. **N.2**: 106.
Sarin, A: **J.4**: 250.

Sarmiento Palacio, E: **N.1**: 99.
Sarnin, P: **G.3.3**: 16.
Sarojini, M: **N.2**: 263.
Sartori, F: **N.2**: 250.
Sarwar, G: **H.1.1**: 11.
Sasaki, K: **F.3.1.1**: 124. **I.2.3**: 22.
Sasson, A: **F.3.2**: 2.
Satchell, S: **J.4**: 251.
Satō, H: **N.2**: 9.
Satpathy, A: **O.2.4**: 15.
Satterthwaite, M: **I.2.1**: 97.
Saumade, F: **F.3.1.1**: 37.
Saunders, A: **J.2**: 128.
Saunders, C: **N.1**: 157.
Saunders, J: **G.1.2**: 14. **H.0**: 165. **O.1.2.3**: 6.
Sauri, D: **F.3.1.4**: 11.
Sauvé, P: **O.2.2**: 39.
Savenije, H: **H.0**: 209.
Saving, T: **I.2.1**: 121.
Savioz, M: **J.4**: 158.
Savvides, A: **O.2.1**: 94.
Sawada, M: **O.3.2**: 30.
Sawyer, J: **B.3**: 22.
Sawyser, M: **H.2.1**: 114.
Saxena, K: **H.1.1.1**: 4.
Saxenian, A: **G.3.3**: 7.
Sayer, A: **G.2.1**: 54.
Sazama, G: **M.5**: 18.
Scacciati, F: **C**: 62.
Scafuri, A: **N.3**: 41.
Scandizzo, P: **N.2**: 250. **O.3.3**: 82.
Scapens, R: **B.4**: 53.
Scaperlanda, A: **O.1.2.2**: 6.
Scaramozzino, P: **G.2.1**: 53. **K.3**: 22.
Scarbrough, H: **G.1**: 53.
Scarlata, J: **O.2.2**: 102.
Scarpa, C: **I.2.1**: 79. **O.1.3**: 69.
Scattergood, H: **G.2.2**: 7.
Schabas, M: **E**: 1.
Schadler, F: **J.4**: 262.
Schaede, U: **J.4**: 93.
Schaefer, K: **H.1.1.4**: 17.
Schaefer, M: **O.3.3**: 119.
Schäfer, H: **J.4**: 25.
Schaffer, M: **F.1**: 52.
Schamis, H: **N.1**: 278.
Scharfstein, D: **J.4**: 46.

Schary, M: **G.3.2**: 34.
Schary, P: **H.4**: 12.
Schatz, K: **F.1**: 40. **F.3.3**: 60. **G.1.1**: 22. **H.2.1**: 121.
Schätzl, L: **F.3.1.1**: 71.
Scheele, U: **H.0**: 201.
Scheffman, D: **H.4**: 65. **J.4**: 9.
Scheid, J: **B.4**: 33.
Scheinkman, J: **F.3.1.1**: 106. **J.4**: 16.
Schempp, U: **O.1.2.4**: 33. **O.2.3**: 33.
Schenk, A: **N.2**: 209.
Schenk, K: **N.1**: 95. **N.2**: 52.
Scherer, F: **O.1.2.3**: 22. **O.3.2**: 60.
Schettkat, R: **G.2.1**: 108, 143.
Schick, F: **C**: 3.
Schicklgruber, W: **J.2**: 102.
Schiemann, J: **O.2.1**: 14.
Schipper, L: **H.0**: 12. **H.2.2**: 131. **H.3**: 11.
Schlesinger, R: **G.2.5**: 51.
Schlicht, E: **K.3**: 68.
Schlitzer, G: **F.5**: 25.
Schlottmann, A: **G.2.1**: 33.
Schlüter, C: **O.1.2.4**: 64.
Schmähl, W: **M.4**: 117.
Schmid, A: **F.3.1.4**: 18.
Schmid, F: **J.2**: 31.
Schmidheiny, S: **H.0**: 75, 159.
Schmidt, A: **M.5**: 33.
Schmidt, C: **D**: 7.
Schmidt, E: **K.3**: 117.
Schmidt, H: **J.4**: 238–239.
Schmidt, M: **H.1.2.1**: 18.
Schmidt-Sorensen, J: **G.2.1**: 171.
Schmitt, B: **F.3.1.1**: 91. **H.4**: 73.
Schmitt, G: **H.1.1**: 22.
Schmittlein, D: **H.4**: 48.
Schmitz, A: **O.3.3**: 75.
Schmitz, H: **H.2.1**: 21. **K.2**: 32.
Schmitz, W: **N.1**: 40.
Schmutzler, A: **C**: 23.
Schnabel, J: **N.2**: 248.
Schneider, T: **G.2.3**: 1.
Schneider, U: **J.2**: 12.
Schneider-Lenné, E: **G.3.3.5**: 6.
Schnytzer, A: **N.1**: 160.
Schoefisch, U: **I.2.1**: 94.
Schoenbaum, T: **O.3.1**: 35.

Schoenberger, E: **H.2.1**: 39.
Schokkaert, E: **N.2**: 312.
Scholtens, L: **J.2**: 10.
Scholtès, P: **H.2.2**: 116.
Scholz, J: **J.4**: 18.
Schonebeck, T: **O.2.1**: 47.
Schoneveld, F: **O.3.3**: 107.
Schönfelder, B: **J.5**: 42.
Schoppenthau, P: **O.2.4**: 10.
Schor, J: **J.5**: 18.
Schott, J: **O.1.3**: 32.
Schotter, A: **G.2.2**: 1.
Schrader, K: **O.1.2**: 18.
Schrank, W: **H.1.2.1**: 41.
Schreft, S: **J.2**: 100, 106.
Schrettl, W: **N.1**: 161.
Schubert, K: **C**: 46.
Schuchardt, W: **H.3**: 57.
Schulenburg, von der, J: **H.2.1**: 73.
Schultz, C: **G.2.1**: 134.
Schultze, C: **N.1**: 33. **N.2**: 67.
Schulus, A: **H.1.1.2**: 24.
Schulz, C: **O.3.3**: 52.
Schulz, J: **N.1**: 59.
Schulz, N: **I.2.1**: 165.
Schulze, W: **N.2**: 92.
Schurman, R: **O.3.2**: 51.
Schuster, J: **K.3**: 96.
Schuster, M: **K.3**: 86.
Schutte, J: **G.3.3.1**: 8.
Schwann, G: **F.3.1.3**: 21.
Schware, R: **G.1**: 29.
Schwartz, A: **H.4**: 108. **I.2.1**: 54. **J.5**: 31.
Schwartz, E: **J.2**: 244. **J.4**: 135. **O.2.2**: 74.
Schwartz, M: **I.2.1**: 102.
Schwarz, G: **H.0**: 191.
Schweickart, D: **N.1**: 236.
Schweickert, R: **B.3**: 56. **O.2.3**: 26.
Schweitzer, M: **H.2.2**: 126.
Schwenk, C: **G.3.3.5**: 99.
Schwidrowski, A: **O.1.3**: 29.
Scotchmer, S: **C**: 61. **N.2**: 295.
Scott, A: **F.3.1.1**: 40–41, 68. **H.0**: 146. **K.3**: 35.
Scott, C: **O.2.2**: 30.
Scott, D: **N.1**: 277.
Scott, G: **O.2.2**: 78.

Shaw, G: **F.3.3**: 49. **H.3**: 8. **H.4**: 24.
Shaw, H: **H.0**: 199.
Shaw, J: **H.1.1**: 9.
Shaw, K: **F.3.1.3**: 15. **M.4**: 87.
Shaw, S: **L.2**: 77.
Shaw, T: **N.1**: 65.
Shaw, W: **K.3**: 53.
Sheate, W: **H.0**: 175.
Sheehan, G: **G.2.1**: 39.
Sheehan, J: **M.5**: 11.
Sheen, J: **O.1.3**: 25.
Sheffrin, S: **O.2.1**: 84.
Shehata, M: **C**: 81. **I.2.1**: 80.
Sheldon, I: **H.4**: 75.
Shell, K: **I.2.1**: 38.
Shen, R: **N.1**: 115.
Shepherd, J: **F.3.1.1**: 87.
Sheppard, E: **G.1**: 33.
Sheppard, S: **G.2.1**: 144.
Sherer, M: **N.3**: 3.
Shergill, G: **G.3.3.5**: 64.
Sherris, M: **J.1**: 21. **J.4**: 284.
Sheshinski, E: **I.2.1**: 166.
Shibata, A: **F.2**: 15. **J.4**: 267.
Shibusawa, M: **F.1**: 26.
Shieh, S: **J.4**: 41.
Shieh, Y: **G.3.2**: 1.
Shields, M: **L.1**: 31.
Shih, J: **H.1.1.4**: 26.
Shiller, R: **F.3.1.3**: 9. **J.4**: 120.
Shimamoto, T: **F.5**: 26.
Shimazaki, H: **G.3.3.1**: 19.
Shimizu, Y: **J.2**: 81.
Shimko, D: **J.3**: 18.
Shimpo, M: **H.1.1.1**: 18.
Shin, H: **I.2.1**: 153.
Shipman, A: **G.2.5**: 55. **O.3.2**: 65.
Shirkevich, N: **N.2**: 51.
Shirom, A: **G.2.4**: 30.
Shishkov, Y: **F.3.1.3**: 17.
Shitovitz, B: **I.2.1**: 69.
Shleifer, A: **F.3.1.1**: 106. **H.2.1**: 87. **J.4**: 94, 217. **N.1**: 217, 251.
Shōda, Y: **F.3.2**: 101.
Shoesmith, G: **F.2**: 18.
Shogren, J: **H.0**: 51.
Shojai, S: **H.2.2**: 159.

Shouxin, L: **M.5**: 40.
Shoven, J: **F.4**: 1.
Shreder, G: **O.1.3**: 18.
Shrestha, R: **H.0**: 10.
Shubik, M: **J.2**: 181.
Shughart, W: **I.2.1**: 40.
Shukla, V: **H.0**: 86.
Shulman, S: **H.0**: 41.
Shumaker, L: **N.2**: 59.
Shumway, C: **H.1.1**: 23. **H.1.1.1**: 8. **H.1.1.3**: 16.
Shuttleworth, G: **H.2.2**: 96.
Sibert, A: **O.3.1**: 22.
Sibly, H: **I.2.1**: 3. **J.2**: 15.
Sicherl, P: **N.3**: 24.
Sickles, R: **H.1.1.3**: 5.
Sid-Ahmed, A: **O.1.2.4**: 32.
Siddayao, C: **H.2.2**: 104.
Siddharthan, N: **G.1**: 15.
Siddiqui, S: **L.1**: 32.
Sideri, S: **O.1.3**: 42. **O.2.2**: 23.
Sidhu, H: **H.1.1.1**: 24.
Siebert, H: **G.3.3.5**: 50. **N.1**: 299.
Siebert, W: **K.3**: 14. **O.1.2.4**: 47.
Siegel, A: **J.4**: 211.
Siegel, C: **M.4**: 59.
Siegel, J: **J.4**: 112.
Sigal, L: **H.0**: 175.
Siggel, E: **G.1.1**: 32.
Sijben, J: **J.5**: 37.
Sik, E: **N.1**: 23.
Sikka, P: **B.4**: 12.
Sills, C: **H.0**: 75.
Silver, J: **F.1**: 71.
Silvestre, J: **N.3**: 55.
Simmons, C: **G.2.4**: 28. **O.1.3**: 76.
Simmons, P: **I.2.3**: 11.
Simmons, R: **J.1**: 52.
Simon, A: **J.1**: 62.
Simon, C: **M.4**: 46.
Simon, D: **N.1**: 20.
Simon, G: **J.1**: 79.
Simon, H: **D**: 42.
Simon, J: **G.2.1**: 94.
Simon, P: **O.1.3**: 79.
Simoncini, D: **J.2**: 200.
Simone, de, D: **J.4**: 71.

Simonovits, A: **J.2**: 242.

Simonsen, M: **D**: 41.

Simpson, L: **K.3**: 37.

Simpson, M: **H.3**: 67.

Simpson, T: **O.3.3**: 44.

Simpson, W: **G.2.1**: 75.

Sims, C: **J.5**: 26.

Sinclair, M: **H.3**: 15.

Sinclair, P: **H.0**: 95.

Sinding, K: **N.2**: 49.

Singell, L: **K.3**: 74.

Singer, O: **C**: 40. **N.1**: 185.

Singer, T: **O.3.3**: 119.

Singh, A: **F.3.2**: 1.

Singh, B: **O.3.3**: 61.

Singh, H: **G.3.3.5**: 97. **J.5**: 46.

Singh, I: **N.1**: 170.

Singh, J: **H.4**: 66.

Singh, K: **H.2.1**: 27.

Singh, M: **J.4**: 290.

Singh, R: **H.1.2.1**: 7. **I.2.3**: 34. **M.5**: 41.

Singh, S: **F.3.1.1**: 67. **N.2**: 158.

Singh, V: **N.2**: 25.

Singleton, G: **N.1**: 88.

Sinitsina, I: **N.1**: 204.

Sinkam, N: **O.1.1**: 3.

Sinn, H: **G.3.3**: 27. **N.1**: 310. **O.2.1**: 63.

Sinn, S: **L.1**: 35. **O.1.2**: 13. **O.2.2**: 45.

Sinton, J: **H.2.2**: 86.

Sipos, A: **I.2.3**: 42.

Sircar, S: **H.4**: 98.

Sirri, E: **J.4**: 287.

Sirvent, R: **J.3**: 20.

Sisson, K: **M.5**: 20.

Sivitanidou, R: **I.2.3**: 63.

Sjoquist, D: **N.2**: 24.

Sjöstrand, S: **C**: 40.

Skaalum, A: **H.4**: 76.

Skaburskis, A: **F.3.1.1**: 104.

Skak, M: **O.1.3**: 12.

Skånland, H: **J.2**: 178.

Skea, J: **H.2.2**: 162.

Skerratt, L: **J.4**: 249.

Skidelsky, R: **D**: 53.

Skillman, G: **G.2.4**: 122.

Skinner, A: **D**: 19.

Skinner, D: **J.4**: 259.

Sklair, L: **O.3.2**: 49.

Skoda, B: **H.1.2.1**: 41.

Skogstad, G: **O.3.3**: 72.

Skonhoft, A: **H.2.2**: 31.

Skott, P: **I.2.1**: 85. **K.2**: 3. **N.1**: 245.

Skouras, T: **F.1**: 60.

Skully, M: **F.1**: 18.

Slade, M: **I.2.3**: 62.

Slaets, P: **G.1.3**: 4.

Slemrod, J: **N.2**: 295.

Slesnick, D: **N.2**: 115.

Sloan, J: **G.2.1**: 67, 94.

Sloan, R: **K.3**: 101.

Sloane, P: **K.3**: 18.

Slocum, J: **G.3.3.5**: 87.

Slotsve, G: **G.2.4**: 37.

Slottje, D: **K.2**: 21. **L.2**: 71.

Slovin, M: **G.3.3.4**: 6. **J.4**: 274.

Slutsky, S: **C**: 5.

Smaghi, L: **O.2.2**: 21. **O.2.3**: 32.

Smart, B: **H.0**: 65.

Smart, C: **H.2.2**: 3.

Smeeding, T: **M.2**: 37.

Smeenk, B: **F.3.1.1**: 25.

Smidt, de, M: **H.2.1**: 39. **J.4**: 156.

Smil, V: **H.2.2**: 97.

Smiley, R: **I.2.1**: 67.

Smirnov, A: **N.1**: 178.

Smith, A: **G.1.1**: 35. **H.2.1**: 30. **O.2.2**: 33.

Smith, B: **H.1.1.4**: 19. **H.3**: 53. **J.3**: 8. **J.4**: 150. **L.3**: 14.

Smith, C: **G.2.4**: 10, 20. **J.3**: 7. **O.2.1**: 55, 86.

Smith, D: **H.0**: 192. **H.1.1.1**: 38. **H.2.2**: 88. **N.1**: 22. **O.2.3**: 29. **O.3.1**: 62.

Smith, G: **O.1.2.4**: 9.

Smith, J: **K.2**: 4. **M.3**: 12.

Smith, M: **O.1.3**: 54.

Smith, P: **G.3.3.5**: 12. **H.3**: 6. **N.2**: 270. **O.1.3**: 35.

Smith, R: **B.1**: 10. **G.2.4**: 38. **H.3**: 67. **K.3**: 38.

Smith, S: **F.5**: 40. **G.3.3.5**: 59. **H.1.1.4**: 35. **H.2.1**: 86. **K.3**: 76. **L.3**: 20. **O.1.2.4**: 71.

Smith, T: **J.4**: 74.

Smith, V: **H.0**: 21. **H.1.1.3**: 7. **H.4**: 15. **N.3**: 2.

Smith, W: **K.3**: 60. **N.2**: 160.

Smith-Britto, G: **J.4**: 26.

Smolensky, E: **N.2**: 297.

Smulders, S: **F.3.3**: 56.

Stafford, H: **F.3.1.1**: 26.
Ståhl, L: **M.1**: 27.
Staiger, R: **G.1.3**: 21. **G.3.2**: 12. **L.3**: 2.
Stalmaszczyk, M: **O.3.1**: 75.
Stamm, H: **O.1.3**: 10.
Stanat, R: **A**: 15.
Stanbury, W: **G.3.2**: 2, 20.
Standing, G: **G.2.4**: 72.
Stankiewicz, T: **N.1**: 315.
Stankovsky, J: **O.1.3**: 21.
Stanley, C: **J.4**: 89.
Stanley, D: **H.1.2.1**: 49.
Stanton, B: **H.1.1.4**: 13.
Starbuck, W: **G.3.3.5**: 41.
Stark, A: **B.4**: 59.
Stark, D: **N.1**: 294, 323.
Starke, H: **O.3.2**: 86.
Starkey, K: **G.2.5**: 47.
Starr, R: **G.3.3.5**: 73. **J.1**: 49.
Stauber, P: **G.3.3.4**: 1.
Stavins, R: **H.0**: 109.
Stebbings, C: **N.2**: 207.
Steedman, I: **D**: 72.
Steel, M: **B.3**: 44.
Steel, W: **G.3.3.4**: 17.
Steele, A: **B.4**: 13.
Steele, G: **D**: 49.
Steeley, J: **J.4**: 108.
Steenbergen, van, F: **F.3.2**: 24.
Steenge, A: **L.2**: 52.
Steenhoven, van der, A: **O.3.2**: 30.
Stefek, D: **J.4**: 36.
Stegman, M: **J.2**: 246. **L.2**: 109.
Stehn, J: **N.2**: 88.
Stein, H: **F.3.2**: 53.
Stein, J: **G.3.3.3**: 9. **I.2.1**: 120. **J.4**: 46.
Steindel, C: **G.1.1**: 21.
Steiner, M: **G.2.1**: 37.
Steiner, R: **H.3**: 11. **N.2**: 90.
Steiner, V: **K.3**: 27.
Steinherr: **J.2**: 167.
Steinherr, A: **J.4**: 75.
Steinhöfler, K: **N.1**: 60.
Steinmueller, W: **H.2.2**: 53.
Steisel, V: **N.3**: 13.
Stem, D: **H.4**: 69.

Stenbacka, R: **H.2.1**: 53.
Stephen, G: **H.2.1**: 78.
Sterbenz, F: **N.3**: 47.
Sterdyniak, H: **N.2**: 165. **O.2.1**: 50.
Sterken, E: **J.1**: 53.
Stern, D: **G.2.5**: 28. **I.2.3**: 89.
Stern, H: **C**: 27.
Stern, J: **O.3.1**: 38.
Stern, N: **G.2.1**: 74. **N.2**: 30, 302.
Stern, R: **O.1.2.4**: 35. **O.1.3**: 95.
Sterner, T: **N.2**: 31.
Sternquist, B: **H.4**: 97.
Steuer, R: **G.3.3.5**: 53.
Stevans, L: **G.2.1**: 60. **K.3**: 95.
Stevens, B: **N.1**: 317.
Stevens, C: **N.1**: 194.
Stevens, J: **J.4**: 116.
Stevens, P: **H.2.2**: 101.
Stewart, A: **F.3.1.4**: 15.
Stewart, F: **F.3.2**: 51.
Stewart, G: **G.2.4**: 13.
Stewart, M: **G.2.4**: 74. **K.3**: 6.
Stewart, R: **O.3.2**: 17.
Steyn, D: **O.1.3**: 39.
Stickel, S: **J.4**: 289.
Stidham, S: **I.2.1**: 154.
Stiefel, D: **N.1**: 127.
Stiglbauer, K: **F.3.1.2**: 19.
Stiglitz, J: **F.3.3**: 18. **I.2.1**: 93. **N.2**: 55.
Stirati, A: **K.3**: 63.
Stober, T: **I.2.1**: 160.
Stock, J: **B.3**: 5.
Stockfish, B: **H.3**: 50.
Stockinger, J: **J.2**: 206.
Stockman, A: **J.1**: 40.
Stohr, E: **B.3**: 10, 50.
Stojković, B: **F.3.2**: 121.
Stoker, G: **N.2**: 89.
Stokes, P: **H.3**: 78.
Stokey, N: **F.3.3**: 13.
Stokke, O: **O.1.3**: 62.
Stoll, H: **J.4**: 234.
Stolton, S: **H.1.1.2**: 19.
Stolwijk, H: **H.1.1.4**: 44.
Stone, A: **N.1**: 47.
Stone, C: **H.0**: 66. **J.2**: 245.
Stone, J: **G.2.1**: 173.

Teague, P: **O.1.2.4**: 47.
Teal, F: **L.2**: 44.
Teall, H: **H.2.2**: 115.
Tease, W: **L.1**: 36.
Teece, D: **H.2.1**: 99. **I.2.1**: 68. **O.2.2**: 96.
Tegen, A: **H.2.2**: 141.
Tehranian, H: **G.3.2**: 6.
Teklu, T: **G.2.2**: 20.
Tella, la, R: **J.2**: 135.
Tenjo, J: **M.5**: 14.
Tennyson, S: **G.2.1**: 36. **J.3**: 15.
Teodorović, I: **J.4**: 12.
Teplitz-Sembitzky, W: **H.2.2**: 121.
Terai, T: **J.4**: 221.
Terasaki, K: **N.3**: 33.
Terlizzese, D: **L.1**: 9, 36.
Terrasse, Y: **N.3**: 10.
Terrell, K: **G.3.3.2**: 10.
Tesche, J: **F.1**: 71.
Tessaromatis, N: **J.2**: 28.
Testa, V: **I.2.3**: 29.
Tetsurō, N: **G.1.3**: 1.
Teubal, M: **H.1.2.1**: 1.
Thain, C: **N.2**: 274.
Thakkar, R: **N.2**: 248.
Thakor, A: **G.3.3.5**: 45. **J.2**: 110.
Thalmann, P: **N.2**: 288.
Tham, K: **B.3**: 24.
Thanawala, K: **F.3.2**: 37.
Thelen, K: **G.2.4**: 57.
Theobald, M: **B.4**: 53.
Theodossiou, I: **K.3**: 69.
Theurl, E: **M.4**: 15.
Thiel, E: **M.1**: 16.
Thies, C: **G.3.3.2**: 12.
Thilges, E: **F.3.1.2**: 20. **F.3.2**: 18.
Thill, J: **F.3.1.1**: 12. **H.4**: 72. **L.2**: 50, 70.
Thireau, V: **F.3.1.1**: 50.
Thirlwall, A: **F.1**: 91.
Thirlwall, T: **O.2.2**: 3.
Thirtle, C: **H.1.2**: 5.
Thisse, J: **F.3.1.1**: 120. **I.2.1**: 21, 60, 108. **L.2**: 56.
Thistle, P: **J.4**: 88. **N.2**: 160.
Thoburn, J: **G.1.1**: 17.
Thom, G: **G.2.1**: 87.
Thoma, M: **J.2**: 95.

Thomas, B: **H.2.1**: 57. **H.3**: 5. **O.3.2**: 54.
Thomas, D: **G.3.3.1**: 9. **M.2**: 31.
Thomas, H: **H.2.1**: 65.
Thomas, I: **F.3.1.1**: 48.
Thomas, J: **F.3.2**: 3, 48. **G.3.3.5**: 106. **H.4**: 10, 26. **I.2.1**: 12. **N.1**: 21.
Thomas, K: **F.3.1.1**: 42.
Thomas, L: **A**: 6. **H.2.1**: 117.
Thomas, S: **H.2.2**: 112. **J.4**: 29.
Thomas-Slayter, B: **H.0**: 143.
Thomassin, P: **H.1.1**: 18.
Thompson, A: **G.3.3.2**: 15.
Thompson, C: **H.3**: 63.
Thompson, D: **G.1.2**: 13. **H.0**: 165. **H.3**: 51. **H.4**: 109. **M.5**: 20. **N.3**: 44.
Thompson, E: **G.1.1**: 2.
Thompson, G: **N.2**: 18. **O.1.2.4**: 40.
Thompson, H: **G.2.4**: 49. **O.2.1**: 67. **O.2.2**: 38.
Thompson, M: **H.4**: 103.
Thompson, P: **G.2.4**: 20. **I.2.3**: 27. **O.1.3**: 60.
Thompson, R: **B.4**: 38. **H.4**: 5.
Thompson, S: **G.3.3.3**: 5. **O.1.2.3**: 17.
Thompson, W: **E**: 18.
Thomsen, E: **I.2.1**: 152.
Thomsen, S: **O.2.2**: 128.
Thomson, J: **J.2**: 118.
Thomson, W: **N.2**: 53.
Thorbecke, E: **F.3.1.1**: 57. **N.1**: 129. **N.2**: 6.
Thorbecke, W: **L.1**: 40. **O.2.3**: 21.
Thore, S: **G.1.2**: 11.
Thorne, A: **J.2**: 173. **N.2**: 168.
Thornton, D: **N.2**: 289.
Thornton, J: **H.2.1**: 93. **J.3**: 3.
Thorpe, K: **M.4**: 41.
Thostrup, B: **H.4**: 76.
Thrift, N: **H.2.1**: 39. **J.4**: 61.
Thum, C: **J.4**: 162.
Thurik, A: **I.2.1**: 116, 151.
Thurman, W: **H.1.2.1**: 47.
Thursby, M: **H.4**: 83. **O.3.3**: 114.
Thygesen, N: **O.2.3**: 15.
Tian, G: **B.3**: 25.
Tibor, A: **G.3.3.1**: 9.
Tibrewala, V: **F.3.1.1**: 33.
Tichy, G: **F.5**: 15. **H.2.1**: 116. **O.1.2.4**: 50.
Tickell, A: **H.0**: 174. **L.3**: 3.
Tickell, C: **H.0**: 173.

Ticktin, H: **N.1**: 250.
Tiemstra, J: **D**: 13.
Tiffen, M: **F.3.2**: 59.
Tiffen, P: **O.3.2**: 70.
Tiffin, S: **G.1**: 14, 36.
Tilak, J: **G.1.3**: 11. **M.5**: 40.
Tilman, R: **D**: 31.
Tilton, J: **H.2.2**: 145. **N.1**: 34.
Timár, J: **F.3.1.1**: 82.
Timmer, C: **H.4**: 68.
Timmermann, A: **J.4**: 270, 279.
Timmermans, H: **L.2**: 50, 54.
Tinnin, T: **M.4**: 8.
Tio, K: **J.4**: 214.
Tió Saralegui, C: **H.1.2**: 1.
Tipple, G: **I.2.3**: 112.
Tirole, J: **C**: 73.
Tisdell, C: **H.0**: 164. **H.1.1.4**: 28. **H.1.2**: 4. **H.1.2.1**: 8. **J.1**: 84. **M.2**: 34. **N.1**: 94, 175. **O.1.3**: 48.
Titman, S: **G.3.3.3**: 20.
Toczek, J: **O.1.2.3**: 5.
Todd, D: **H.2.2**: 28.
Todd, R: **J.4**: 252.
Tödtling, F: **G.1**: 47.
Toedtner, K: **B.1**: 17.
Togba, Z: **N.2**: 120.
Toharia Cortés, L: **O.1.2.4**: 59.
Toiwo, I: **N.2**: 237.
Tokunaga, S: **O.1.3**: 27.
Toma, E: **N.2**: 73.
Toma, M: **N.2**: 73.
Tomás, J: **J.3**: 20.
Tomassini, L: **O.2.2**: 87.
Tomek, W: **J.4**: 103.
Tomer, J: **F.5**: 34. **G.3.3.5**: 30.
Tömmel, I: **F.3.1.1**: 54.
Tonks, I: **J.4**: 246–247.
Topel, R: **G.2.1**: 79.
Töpfer, K: **H.0**: 102.
Topham, N: **N.2**: 166.
Topping, S: **H.0**: 105.
Torelli, C: **K.3**: 49.
Torkzadeh, G: **H.3**: 90.
Tornell, A: **O.2.2**: 44.
Török, A: **F.3.1.4**: 29.
Torous, W: **G.3.3.3**: 24. **J.2**: 244.
Torr, C: **I.2.1**: 177.

Torre, de la, A: **O.3.2**: 62.
Torregrosa, P: **J.2**: 103.
Torres, V: **O.1.3**: 99.
Toth, A: **F.3.1.3**: 4.
Totterdill, P: **H.2.2**: 44.
Tougareva, E: **C**: 62.
Tour, de la, X: **H.2.2**: 102–103.
Tovias, A: **O.3.2**: 37.
Town, R: **B.3**: 39.
Townroe, P: **F.3.1.1**: 75.
Townsend, J: **B.3**: 56.
Townsend, R: **H.1.2.1**: 40.
Tracy, L: **G.2.4**: 30, 43.
Trandel, G: **N.2**: 286.
Trapp, P: **F.1**: 40. **F.3.3**: 60. **G.1.1**: 22. **H.2.1**: 121.
Travers, P: **M.2**: 18.
Traxler, G: **H.1.1.1**: 32.
Treadgold, E: **O.3.2**: 38.
Treadgold, M: **N.1**: 75. **O.3.2**: 38.
Trégouët, B: **H.1.1.4**: 9.
Trejo, S: **G.2.1**: 85. **M.4**: 102.
Trela, I: **O.1.3**: 95.
Trespalacios Gutiérrez, J: **H.4**: 16.
Tretheway, M: **I.2.3**: 44.
Treu, T: **G.2.1**: 42.
Trevithick, J: **C**: 45.
Treyz, G: **F.2**: 30. **H.0**: 88.
Trezevant, R: **N.2**: 238.
Triantafillou, P: **J.2**: 28.
Tridimas, G: **L.2**: 12. **N.2**: 258.
Triffin, R: **O.1.2.4**: 60.
Tripathi, A: **J.2**: 6.
Trisoglio, A: **H.0**: 75.
Tronstad, R: **H.1.2.1**: 23.
Tronti, L: **G.2.1**: 40. **K.2**: 12.
Tronzano, M: **O.2.1**: 12, 73.
Trotignon, J: **O.2.2**: 92.
Troullinos, N: **J.2**: 195.
Truett, D: **O.3.3**: 50.
Truett, L: **O.3.3**: 50.
Tryon, R: **O.1.2**: 12.
Trzcinka, C: **J.4**: 245.
Trzeciakowski, W: **N.1**: 324.
Tsai, T: **O.3.3**: 58.
Tsakalotos, E: **O.1.2.4**: 47, 63.
Tsakloglou, P: **M.1**: 11.

Tsamboulas, D: **H.3**: 56.
Tse, S: **J.4**: 24.
Tsekov, N: **F.3.1.1**: 82.
Tseng, C: **G.2.1**: 164.
Tseng, G: **A**: 7.
Tserkezos, E: **L.2**: 11.
Tsetsekos, G: **L.3**: 10.
Tsiddon, D: **F.3.3**: 38. **G.1.1**: 41. **I.2.3**: 4.
Tsigas, M: **B.3**: 19.
Tsimailo, A: **J.1**: 33.
Tsiritakis, M: **G.3.3.5**: 71.
Tsukui, J: **F.3.3**: 1.
Tsutsui, S: **O.3.1**: 3.
Tubb, G: **N.2**: 25.
Tucker, A: **J.4**: 288. **O.2.4**: 13.
Tucker, E: **G.2.3**: 17.
Tucker, R: **B.4**: 34.
Tuckman, B: **I.2.1**: 2.
Tudge, C: **H.0**: 53.
Türei, S: **G.2.1**: 57.
Tuff, T: **G.3.3.5**: 97.
Tuijl, van, M: **N.2**: 7.
Tullio, G: **N.2**: 70.
Tumpel, M: **J.2**: 144.
Tunali, I: **H.2.1**: 50.
Tung, S: **N.1**: 21.
Turley, S: **B.4**: 11.
Turnbull, G: **L.2**: 97. **N.2**: 26.
Turnbull, P: **G.2.5**: 39, 41. **H.3**: 75.
Turner, A: **B.3**: 21.
Turner, L: **O.3.1**: 36.
Turner, M: **I.2.3**: 85.
Turner, P: **B.3**: 11. **G.3.3.5**: 13. **H.3**: 68.
Turner, R: **H.0**: 189.
Turnovsky, S: **N.2**: 256. **O.2.1**: 16.
Turri, E: **H.1.1.2**: 34.
Turvey, C: **H.1.1**: 6, 8.
Tussing, A: **I.2.3**: 23.
Tutterow, R: **K.1**: 4.
Tweedale, G: **G.3.3.5**: 55.
Twine, F: **I.2.3**: 95.
Twomey, B: **J.2**: 136.
Tybout, J: **G.1.1**: 20.
Tyers, R: **G.2.2**: 22. **O.3.2**: 25.
Tykkylainen, M: **F.3.1.1**: 56.
Tylecote, A: **F.5**: 18. **G.1**: 18.
Tyler, G: **H.1.1.4**: 13.

Tyrväinen, T: **G.2.4**: 106.
Tyson, S: **G.2.5**: 22.
Tyson, W: **H.3**: 67.
Tyszka, T: **F.3.1.3**: 18.
Uctum, M: **O.2.3**: 4.
Udell, G: **J.2**: 94.
Uehara, N: **M.4**: 42.
Ueno, S: **N.2**: 39.
Üsdiken, B: **G.3.1**: 2.
Ulrich, V: **M.4**: 22.
Umesh, U: **H.4**: 69.
UNEP: **H.0**: 25.
Unger, K: **F.3.2**: 17.
Uno, K: **N.2**: 25.
Unsworth, R: **H.0**: 187.
Upward, R: **M.4**: 51.
Ureta, M: **G.2.1**: 84.
Urga, G: **G.2.1**: 111.
Uri, N: **H.1.1.1**: 3. **I.2.3**: 75. **K.1**: 5.
Urrunaga, R: **H.0**: 134.
Urrutia, J: **O.2.1**: 95.
Urrutia M., M: **N.1**: 144.
Urs Egger, R: **O.1.3**: 33.
Ustukova, V: **H.1.1.2**: 21.
Usun, W: **H.1.1.2**: 24.
Utheza, H: **N.2**: 91.
Utili, G: **N.3**: 46.
Utterback, J: **G.3.3.5**: 97.
Utting, P: **N.1**: 151.
Vacic, A: **N.1**: 238, 324.
Vadlamudi, R: **O.3.2**: 77.
Vadlamudi, Y: **F.3.2**: 102.
Vaggi, G: **F.3.2**: 25.
Vaidyanathan, R: **J.4**: 21.
Vaillant, M: **O.3.1**: 20.
Vainiomaki, J: **H.2.1**: 118.
Vainshtein, G: **F.3.1.3**: 27.
Valais, M: **H.2.2**: 94.
Valdmanis, V: **M.4**: 60.
Valença, M: **L.2**: 95.
Valenciano, E: **O.1.3**: 92.
Valentine, T: **O.2.3**: 68.
Valentinyi, A: **N.1**: 79.
Valenzuela, R: **H.0**: 108.
Valier, J: **J.1**: 6, 100.
Valle, A: **N.3**: 36.

Vallega, A: **H.3**: 77.
Valle, La, D: **G.2.4**: 83.
Vallés, J: **H.2.1**: 1.
Vally, B: **G.2.4**: 68.
Vanasse, C: **J.3**: 2.
Vandell, K: **L.2**: 98.
Vandenbussche, D: **F.3.1.1**: 48.
Vandenbussche, H: **B.4**: 42.
VanderHoff, J: **I.2.3**: 81.
Vanderporten, B: **I.2.3**: 111.
Vane, H: **I.2.1**: 47. **N.1**: 124.
Vanhala, S: **G.2.1**: 107.
Vanhonacker, W: **B.3**: 60.
Vanhorebeek, F: **L.2**: 30.
Vanistendael, F: **N.2**: 105.
Vargas Bohamonde, F: **O.1.2.4**: 58.
Várhegyi, E: **J.2**: 119.
Vári, A: **G.3.3.5**: 21.
Varoufakis, Y: **C**: 69.
Vasavada, U: **H.1.1.3**: 6.
Vasquez, M: **N.3**: 24.
Vaughn, K: **D**: 71.
Vavrichek, B: **K.3**: 38.
Vázquez Ordás, C: **J.2**: 73.
Večerník, J: **G.2.1**: 35.
Vecsenyi, J: **G.3.3.5**: 21.
Vedder, R: **N.2**: 265, 296.
Veen, van, T: **G.2.2**: 24.
Veen, van der, A: **G.2.1**: 75. **L.2**: 52.
Vega, C: **O.1.2.4**: 5.
Vega Cánovas, G: **O.1.3**: 94.
Vega Ruiz, L: **G.2.2**: 12.
Vega, de la, A: **O.1.3**: 8.
Véganzones, M: **F.2**: 26. **L.3**: 16.
Végh, C: **J.1**: 107. **O.2.2**: 36.
Velasco, A: **O.2.2**: 44.
Veld, J: **O.1.2**: 3.
Veldhuizen, van, L: **J.2**: 69.
Veld, in't, J: **N.2**: 187. **O.1.2.3**: 40.
Velez, E: **K.3**: 51. **M.5**: 9.
Velissariou, E: **F.3.1.3**: 32.
Vellvé, R: **H.1.1.1**: 26.
Velo, D: **O.1.2**: 2.
Venkatesh, A: **G.2.5**: 10.
Vennemo, H: **H.0**: 116.
Venugopal, K: **H.4**: 14.
Vera, O: **O.1.2.4**: 5.

Verbeek, M: **B.2**: 4.
Verbeke, W: **H.4**: 58.
Verbon, H: **M.4**: 70.
Vercammen, J: **O.3.3**: 75.
Vercelli, A: **B.1**: 13.
Verdera, F: **K.3**: 85.
Verdier, T: **F.3.3**: 23.
Verdin, P: **G.1**: 1.
Verduzco Igartúa, G: **H.1.1.4**: 20.
Veress, J: **N.1**: 230.
Verhaegen, B: **F.3.2**: 58.
Verheem, R: **H.0**: 175.
Verhetsel, A: **F.3.1.1**: 115.
Verhoeven, M: **M.4**: 70.
Vermulst, E: **O.3.3**: 98, 138.
Vernon, R: **O.1.2.2**: 23.
Versiglioni, M: **N.2**: 61.
Verspagen, B: **F.3.3**: 16.
Veselovsky, L: **G.2.4**: 94.
Viaene, J: **J.4**: 85. **O.3.2**: 52.
Vial, J: **L.2**: 3.
Viallet, C: **J.4**: 189.
Vicari, P: **H.3**: 83.
Vickerman, R: **O.1.2.4**: 86.
Vickers, D: **D**: 76.
Vickers, J: **N.1**: 311.
Vickerstaff, S: **G.2.5**: 18.
Vieira, L: **H.2.2**: 43.
Vieira, R: **H.2.2**: 43.
Vieux, S: **N.1**: 38.
Viganò, E: **H.1.1.1**: 30.
Vigneau, G: **J.4**: 255.
Vigolini, M: **J.4**: 228.
Vihanto, M: **N.1**: 10.
Vijverberg, W: **K.1**: 2.
Vikkula, K: **J.2**: 149.
Vila, J: **G.3.3.5**: 93. **I.2.1**: 2. **J.4**: 174.
Vilariño, R: **J.2**: 194.
Vilen, L: **O.3.1**: 73.
Villac, M: **K.3**: 49.
Villers, de, G: **F.3.2**: 58.
Villeval, M: **G.2.1**: 70.
Villezca-Becerra, P: **H.1.1**: 23.
Vince, P: **H.2.1**: 15.
Vincent, J: **O.3.2**: 81.
Vincze, J: **H.2.2**: 41.

Vine, E: **N.3**: 27.
Vines, D: **O.1.3**: 34. **O.2.2**: 13.
Vining, A: **N.3**: 34.
Viravan, A: **N.1**: 312.
Virén, M: **L.1**: 3, 36.
Visaggio, M: **N.2**: 253.
Vishny, R: **H.2.1**: 87. **J.4**: 94, 217. **N.1**: 217, 251.
Visintini, A: **F.3.2**: 74.
Vitalari, N: **G.2.5**: 10.
Vitali, O: **F.1**: 70.
Vitta, P: **G.1**: 14.
Vittas, D: **J.4**: 80. **M.4**: 91.
Vives, X: **I.2.1**: 108.
Viviers, W: **O.1.3**: 39.
Vivo, de, G: **D**: 58.
Vliet, van, A: **H.3**: 72.
Vodenska, M: **F.3.1.1**: 82.
Vodopivec, M: **G.3.3.3**: 17.
Vogel, D: **O.3.3**: 127.
Vogelsang, I: **H.3**: 97.
Vogelsang, T: **B.3**: 5. **F.2**: 9.
Vogelvang, E: **I.2.3**: 73.
Vohra, R: **O.2.2**: 84.
Voith, R: **G.1.1**: 1. **I.2.3**: 99.
Vojnić, D: **D**: 6.
Volcker, P: **O.1.1**: 1.
Volken, P: **O.2.1**: 21.
Vollebergh, H: **H.0**: 120.
Voon, T: **H.1.1.1**: 25.
Voorde, Van de, E: **F.3.1.1**: 2. **H.3**: 74.
Vos, R: **O.2.2**: 115.
Vos, de, K: **M.2**: 24.
Voszka, E: **N.1**: 276.
Vredin, A: **F.5**: 35.
Vriens, M: **H.4**: 31.
Vries, de, C: **M.5**: 30. **O.3.2**: 52.
Vroman, S: **G.2.1**: 169.
Vujadinović, D: **F.3.2**: 121.
Vukotić, V: **N.1**: 291.
Vuuren, van, C: **H.4**: 50.
Vuuren, van, W: **H.2.2**: 147.
Vuurst, van der, D: **L.2**: 52.
Vylder, de, F: **J.3**: 17.
Vyvere, van de, Y: **G.2.5**: 5.
Waast, R: **G.1**: 14.
Wachtel, P: **J.4**: 136.
Wachter, S: **I.2.3**: 85.

Waddington, J: **G.2.4**: 96.
Wädekin, K: **H.1.1.2**: 24. **H.1.1.4**: 50.
Wadhawan, S: **N.2**: 295.
Wadhwani, S: **G.1.2**: 12. **H.2.1**: 118. **O.2.3**: 28.
Wadsworth, J: **M.4**: 121.
Waerden, van der, P: **L.2**: 54.
Wagatsuma, T: **M.4**: 42.
Wagner, B: **G.2.4**: 63.
Wagner, H: **J.1**: 105.
Wagner, I: **J.2**: 210.
Wagner, J: **H.2.1**: 73. **K.3**: 40. **L.2**: 71.
Wagner, K: **F.3.1.1**: 53.
Wagner, T: **H.4**: 37.
Wagner-Braun, M: **O.2.1**: 96.
Wagstaff, A: **M.4**: 31–32.
Wahid, A: **L.3**: 19.
Wahl, J: **O.2.2**: 103. **O.3.2**: 68.
Wai, T: **O.1.2.4**: 42.
Waidmann, T: **G.2.1**: 14.
Waine, B: **M.4**: 98.
Wainerman, C: **G.2.2**: 37.
Waite, C: **G.1.2**: 10.
Waite, L: **M.4**: 2.
Wajsman, N: **N.2**: 202.
Waldinger, R: **G.2.2**: 25.
Waldman, D: **M.4**: 55.
Waldmann, R: **G.3.3.5**: 59. **M.2**: 15.
Wales, T: **H.2.1**: 113. **L.2**: 55.
Walker, J: **M.4**: 2.
Walker, M: **H.1.1**: 9.
Walker, O: **H.4**: 81.
Walker, R: **F.3.1.2**: 14. **G.2.1**: 54.
Walker, W: **H.3**: 70.
Wall, M: **G.1.2**: 12.
Wallace, C: **G.2.1**: 72.
Wallace, N: **L.2**: 21. **O.2.1**: 77.
Wallace, R: **G.3.3.3**: 30. **G.4**: 5.
Wallace, S: **N.2**: 313.
Wallenius, J: **G.3.3.5**: 53.
Waller, C: **J.1**: 71. **O.2.3**: 38.
Wallerstein, I: **B.2**: 3. **K.2**: 4.
Wallich, C: **N.2**: 149.
Wallin, D: **B.4**: 32.
Wallis, J: **D**: 73.
Wallis, K: **B.1**: 18.
Walsh, C: **B.3**: 26. **O.2.1**: 53.

Walsh, D: **G.2.3**: 10.
Walsh, F: **H.0**: 175.
Walsh, R: **H.0**: 7.
Walshe, G: **G.1.3**: 18.
Walstad, W: **A**: 5.
Walsteijn, R: **K.2**: 33.
Walter, I: **H.2.1**: 81.
Walters, C: **H.1.2.1**: 39.
Walters, P: **G.2.2**: 35.
Walton, P: **B.4**: 33.
Walz, U: **N.2**: 94.
Wang, C: **O.1.2.4**: 8.
Wang, D: **H.2.1**: 79.
Wang, H: **O.3.2**: 15.
Wang, J: **O.2.2**: 97. **O.3.2**: 84.
Wang, K: **J.4**: 52.
Wang, P: **F.3.3**: 17. **N.2**: 79.
Wang, S: **H.1.2.1**: 39.
Wang, X: **N.3**: 24.
Wang, Z: **L.2**: 59.
Wangwe, S: **F.3.2**: 51.
Wansley, J: **J.4**: 114.
Ward, C: **J.4**: 177.
Ward, J: **N.2**: 29.
Ward, M: **G.2.1**: 79.
Ward, R: **N.2**: 166.
Warfield, T: **B.4**: 8.
Warhurst, A: **H.2.2**: 138, 142.
Warme, B: **G.2.1**: 71.
Warne, A: **F.5**: 35.
Warner, A: **L.3**: 4.
Warner, E: **O.1.2.4**: 78.
Warner, M: **G.2.1**: 112.
Wärneryd, K: **C**: 62.
Warr, P: **O.3.3**: 126.
Wascher, W: **K.3**: 38.
Wasow, B: **L.3**: 1.
Wasserfallen, W: **J.4**: 8.
Wassmer, R: **N.2**: 231.
Wasylenko, M: **N.2**: 212, 313.
Watabe, T: **H.1.1.4**: 2.
Watanabe, C: **G.1.3**: 8, 13.
Watanabe, T: **F.1**: 19. **J.4**: 118.
Watanuki, J: **F.3.3**: 31.
Waterbury, J: **F.3.3**: 19.
Waters, W: **I.2.3**: 10.
Waterson, M: **N.3**: 4.

Watkins, G: **N.3**: 36.
Watkins, K: **O.3.3**: 109, 112.
Watson, A: **N.1**: 150.
Watson, H: **N.2**: 193.
Watson, R: **O.1.3**: 26.
Watson, W: **O.1.3**: 96.
Watt, W: **J.4**: 271.
Watts, H: **G.2.2**: 16.
Watts, M: **G.2.2**: 17.
Watts, R: **M.5**: 32.
Watzlawek, G: **H.1.1.2**: 24.
Watzlawick, H: **G.2.2**: 20.
Waverman, L: **G.1.2**: 2. **H.2.1**: 127. **H.2.2**: 65.
    O.1.3: 95.
Waymire, G: **J.4**: 208.
Wayne, S: **G.3.3**: 13.
Weale, M: **M.1**: 13. **M.5**: 20.
Wearing, R: **N.3**: 3.
Weaver, C: **M.4**: 9.
Webb, J: **H.0**: 175.
Webb, M: **K.3**: 61. **O.3.3**: 95.
Webb, P: **G.2.2**: 20.
Webb, S: **L.2**: 108.
Webber, M: **G.1**: 33. **H.2.2**: 5. **N.1**: 110.
Weber, S: **I.2.1**: 64, 100. **O.3.3**: 118.
Weber, W: **O.2.1**: 77.
Webley, P: **B.1**: 15. **N.2**: 13.
Weck-Hannemann, H: **N.2**: 293.
Wedel, J: **N.1**: 134.
Wedel, M: **H.4**: 31.
Weeber, J: **M.4**: 122.
Weeks, J: **F.3.2**: 75. **N.1**: 69.
Weerahandi, S: **H.4**: 71.
Weersink, A: **H.1.1**: 9.
Weesep, van, J: **F.3.1.1**: 121.
Wegberg, Van, M: **I.2.1**: 78.
Wegener, M: **F.3.1.1**: 15.
Wegner, G: **I.2.3**: 66.
Wegren, S: **H.1.1.2**: 26.
Wei, K: **J.4**: 88.
Weidenbaum, M: **H.2.1**: 90. **N.1**: 24.
Weidlich, W: **I.2.1**: 29.
Weigel, E: **B.3**: 21.
Weigelt, H: **H.3**: 36.
Weigelt, K: **G.2.2**: 1.
Weil, D: **F.3.3**: 8. **G.2.4**: 71.
Weil, S: **C**: 49.

Ziderman, A: **G.2.1**: 48. **G.2.5**: 29. **M.5**: 40.
Ziebart, D: **B.4**: 18.
Ziegler, R: **G.3.3.1**: 17.
Zieliński, M: **O.3.1**: 75.
Ziemba, W: **B.3**: 21.
Ziemes, G: **J.2**: 212.
Zietz, J: **G.1.3**: 17. **O.3.1**: 40.
Zikalala, S: **G.2.4**: 52.
Zilcha, I: **F.3.3**: 14. **O.2.1**: 59.
Zimmer, M: **G.2.1**: 82. **G.2.5**: 24.
Zimmerman, J: **G.2.2**: 15.
Zimmerman, M: **H.0**: 111.
Zimmermann, H: **J.4**: 79. **O.1.2.2**: 22.
Zimmermann, K: **G.2.1**: 114. **O.1.2.5**: 6.
Zimmermann, M: **J.2**: 210.
Zind, R: **G.1.1**: 13.
Zingheim, P: **K.3**: 96.
Zionts, S: **G.3.3.5**: 53.
Zis, G: **J.1**: 55.
Zissu, A: **J.2**: 245.
Zivetz, L: **N.1**: 46.
Zivney, T: **J.4**: 294.
Zivot, E: **B.3**: 5.
Žižmond, E: **F.5**: 9. **I.2.1**: 128–129. **I.2.2**: 4.
Zobel, A: **H.3**: 65.
Zodrow, G: **N.2**: 303.
Zogg-Wetter, C: **J.4**: 79.
Zoltán, N: **N.2**: 282.
Zóltowska, E: **B.3**: 43.
Zoninsein, J: **F.5**: 32.
Zonzilos, N: **O.3.1**: 52.
Zorn, T: **J.4**: 292.
Zou, L: **H.4**: 42.
Zschiedrich, H: **O.1.2.4**: 92.
Zudin, A: **G.3.1**: 1.
Zurdo, I: **O.1.2.4**: 59.
Zurita, S: **O.2.2**: 74.
Zwahlen, R: **H.1.1.1**: 10.
Zwanziger, J: **M.4**: 29, 41.
Zychowicz, E: **J.4**: 291.
Zyl, van, J: **H.1.2.1**: 12.
Zysman, J: **O.3.3**: 118.

PLACENAME INDEX
INDEX DES ENDROITS

Bolivia
F.3.2: 76. H.1.1.3: 11. H.2.2: 138. J.1: 100.
M.3: 11.

Botswana
M.5: 40. O.1.3: 76.

Brazil
Entries also appear under:

PARAIBA; PARANA; RIO GRANDE DO SUL
F.1: 10. G.1: 4, 29. G.2.4: 38. G.2.5: 60. H.0: 3,
23, 28, 60. H.1.1.4: 21. H.2.1: 21. H.2.2: 2,
10, 20, 43, 120. H.4: 2. I.2.2: 3. J.1: 80, 102.
J.4: 10, 45. L.1: 18. L.2: 95. M.5: 41. N.1: 63,
84, 97. N.3: 49. O.1.2.2: 19, 24. O.1.2.4: 6,
26, 54. O.2.2: 92, 122. O.3.3: 7, 129.

British Columbia
G.2.1: 44. I.2.3: 62.

Bulgaria
F.3.1.1: 82. G.2.2: 13. J.2: 173. L.2: 14. N.1:
81, 132.

C.I.S.
Entries also appear under:

U.S.S.R.
H.1.1.1: 28. H.1.1.4: 50. H.2.2: 130. J.5: 47.
N.1: 259. O.3.2: 58.

California
F.3.1.1: 41. G.3.3: 7. H.0: 88. J.3: 5. K.3: 35,
38. N.2: 230. O.2.2: 96.

Cameroon
G.2.5: 15. H.1.2.1: 15. L.3: 27.

Canada
Entries also appear under:

ALBERTA; BRITISH COLUMBIA; MANITOBA;
NEWFOUNDLAND; NOVA SCOTIA;
ONTARIO; QUEBEC; SASKATCHEWAN
E: 15. F.1: 13. F.3.1.1: 84, 92, 122. F.3.1.2: 13.
F.3.1.4: 16. F.3.3: 24, 39. G.1.1: 18. G.1.2: 2,
18. G.2.1: 155. G.2.2: 11. G.2.4: 125. G.3.2:
2, 20, 27. G.3.3.3: 35. G.3.3.5: 12, 70. H.0:
149, 199. H.1.1: 7, 11, 18. H.1.1.3: 8.
H.1.2.1: 3, 10. H.2.1: 2, 127. H.2.2: 39, 65,
79, 115, 143. H.3: 91. H.4: 63. J.1: 47, 55.
J.2: 154, 183. J.4: 207, 235, 303. J.5: 8, 11,
58. K.3: 7. L.1: 24. L.3: 19. M.4: 41. M.5: 32.
N.1: 37. N.2: 85, 158, 241, 271. N.3: 10.
O.1.2.2: 9. O.1.2.3: 38. O.1.3: 87–88, 91,
96–97, 101, 103. O.2.1: 26. O.2.2: 122.
O.2.3: 3. O.3.1: 23. O.3.2: 11, 31, 41, 61, 85.
O.3.3: 72.

Caribbean
F.1: 16. N.1: 66. O.1.2.4: 52. O.2.2: 71.

Central America
F.3.2: 75. O.1.2.4: 45. O.1.3: 7.

Central Asia
F.1: 21.

Central Europe
F.1: 62, 76. F.3.3: 4. G.2.1: 45, 100. G.3.3:
34. H.1.1.2: 2. J.2: 80, 136. K.2: 40. M.4:

Central Europe continued
120. N.1: 121, 126, 238, 268, 300, 323. N.2:
152, 205. O.1.2.4: 92. O.1.3: 21, 63, 67, 74.
O.2.2: 57, 80, 129. O.3.2: 56.

Chile
F.3.2: 72. G.1.1: 20. G.3.3.1: 2. H.2.2: 140.
M.2: 28. M.4: 67, 91, 111. N.1: 61. O.2.2: 56.
O.2.3: 26. O.3.2: 40. O.3.3: 7.

China
C: 81. F.1: 25, 81. F.3.1.1: 62, 93, 114.
F.3.2: 91–93, 103. G.1: 48. G.1.2: 2, 10.
G.2.1: 50, 163. G.2.4: 20, 41. G.3.3: 3, 11.
G.3.3.4: 20. H.1.1: 10. H.1.1.2: 5, 9, 28, 36.
H.1.1.4: 12, 27–28, 31. H.1.2.1: 24, 27.
H.2.1: 20, 58, 79, 120, 123, 125. H.2.2: 68,
85–86, 107. I.2.1: 80, 110, 148. J.1: 23, 84.
J.2: 79. J.4: 110. K.2: 18. L.2: 2, 59. L.3: 9.
M.5: 2, 40. N.1: 7–8, 36, 41, 58, 93–94, 103,
105, 137–140, 145, 149–150, 155, 165–166,
169–170, 175, 184, 193, 217, 243. N.2: 9, 22,
81, 87, 149, 302. N.3: 24. O.1.2.2: 1. O.1.2.3:
24. O.1.2.4: 24, 42. O.1.3: 86. O.2.2: 83–84,
95, 131. O.3.2: 14–16, 21, 57. O.3.3: 6, 23,
104–105.

Colombia
F.3.2: 76. H.1.2.1: 4. J.1: 112. K.3: 51. M.5:
9, 14. N.1: 43, 144. N.2: 90, 306, 314. O.2.1:
3. O.3.2: 24. O.3.3: 7.

Congo
J.1: 52.

Costa Rica
F.3.2: 81. G.2.1: 56. H.0: 127. H.1.2.1: 4.
O.3.3: 7.

Croatia
F.3.3: 54.

Cuba
I.2.1: 42. N.1: 142.

Cyprus
A: 10. F.1: 58. F.3.2: 127. H.2.2: 13. H.3: 32.
N.2: 272. O.1.2: 1. O.1.2.4: 68.

Czechoslovakia
F.1: 42, 67. F.3.1.1: 82. F.3.1.4: 20. G.2.1:
35. G.2.2: 28. G.3.3.4: 18. H.1.1.4: 49. I.2.1:
124. J.2: 31. N.1: 81, 293–294, 311, 322.
O.2.2: 80. O.3.3: 40.

Denmark
B.4: 40. C: 40. F.1: 63. F.3.1.1: 72. G.1.1:
18. G.3.3.5: 42. H.1.2.1: 45. H.4: 76. K.3:
106. L.2: 94. N.1: 113. N.2: 33, 202.

East Asia
F.3.2: 106.

Eastern Europe
B.3: 15. F.1: 43–44, 49, 55, 62, 76, 81.
F.3.1.4: 18. F.3.2: 16, 79, 123. F.3.3: 4, 50.
G.2.1: 45, 64, 100. G.2.4: 20. G.3.3: 27, 34.
G.3.3.4: 2. H.1.1.1: 28. H.1.1.2: 2. H.2.2: 24,
33, 41. I.2.1: 92. I.2.3: 55. J.2: 2, 80, 107,
133, 136, 143, 173. J.5: 33. K.2: 40. M.4:
112, 120. N.1: 14, 18, 53, 81, 95, 98, 121,

Eastern Europe continued
127, 141, 147, 152, 156–157, 159–161, 164,
167, 173, 177, 192, 194, 196–197, 203, 206,
211, 213, 218, 228, 262, 268, 270, 277, 283,
285, 289, 300, 305–306, 315, 319, 321, 324.
N.2: 23, 152, 205, 297, 302. **O.1.2.4**: 10.
O.1.2.5: 4. **O.1.3**: 12, 23, 31, 33, 43–44, 50,
56, 63, 75. **O.2.1**: 88. **O.2.2**: 22, 41, 55, 57,
98, 129. **O.2.3**: 58. **O.2.4**: 6, 10, 12. **O.3.1**:
38, 55. **O.3.2**: 6, 45, 79. **O.3.3**: 45.

Egypt
    G.3.3.4: 21. **H.1.1.4**: 16. **H.2.1**: 50. **H.4**: 25.
I.2.3: 56. **J.1**: 4. **J.5**: 19. **L.3**: 17. **N.1**: 125.
N.2: 9.

England
    G.2.1: 151. **G.2.3**: 8. **G.2.4**: 69. **G.3.3.5**: 42.
H.2.2: 128. **H.3**: 82. **I.2.3**: 100. **L.3**: 3. **M.2**:
13. **M.5**: 43. **N.2**: 121. **O.1.3**: 28.

Ethiopia
    F.1: 7. **F.3.2**: 42, 65. **H.1.1.4**: 14. **J.1**: 37.

Europe
    Entries also appear under:

    BALTIC STATES; CENTRAL EUROPE;
EASTERN EUROPE; SCANDINAVIA;
SOUTHERN EUROPE; WESTERN EUROPE

C: 40. **F.1**: 54, 64. **F.3.1.1**: 4, 15, 52, 56, 72.
F.3.2: 119, 121. **F.3.3**: 52. **F.5**: 18. **G.1**: 59.
G.1.1: 26. **G.2.1**: 42, 81, 130. **G.2.2**: 18.
G.2.4: 15, 50, 111. **G.2.5**: 17–18, 37. **G.3.2**:
19, 29. **G.3.3**: 5. **G.3.3.1**: 12. **H.0**: 13, 125.
H.1.1.1: 26. **H.1.1.2**: 27. **H.2.1**: 81, 85. **H.2.2**:
67, 71, 110. **H.3**: 43, 57, 59, 75, 95. **I.2.1**: 36.
J.1: 82. **J.2**: 12, 59, 114, 134–135, 160, 180,
184, 191, 203, 222, 226. **J.4**: 36, 75, 156.
K.3: 92. **N.1**: 227, 307. **N.2**: 18, 45, 192.
O.1.2: 2–3. **O.1.2.2**: 21–22. **O.1.2.3**: 11, 25.
O.1.2.4: 9, 20–21, 34, 37, 44, 50, 61, 65, 81,
84. **O.1.3**: 3, 20, 23. **O.2.1**: 27, 63. **O.2.3**: 5,
11, 27–28, 47, 52. **O.2.4**: 18. **O.3.2**: 23, 65,
75. **O.3.3**: 24, 26.

Fiji
    N.2: 84.

Finland
    F.3.1.1: 72. **G.1**: 40. **G.2.1**: 107. **G.2.4**: 106.
G.2.5: 58. **H.2.2**: 59. **J.2**: 145, 149. **L.2**: 14.
M.4: 110. **O.3.1**: 30, 73.

France
    B.4: 25, 33. **F.1**: 56. **F.2**: 26. **F.3.1.1**: 30, 39,
50, 72. **F.5**: 1. **G.1.1**: 18. **G.2.1**: 43, 172.
G.2.2: 35. **G.3.3**: 16. **G.3.3.5**: 42, 77, 121.
H.0: 89. **H.1.1**: 1. **H.1.1.2**: 8. **H.1.1.3**: 13.
H.1.1.4: 34, 39. **H.2.1**: 17. **H.2.2**: 47, 60, 66,
69. **H.4**: 47, 100. **I.2.3**: 74, 100. **J.2**: 29, 60,
140, 153, 245. **J.4**: 212. **J.5**: 22. **K.3**: 100.
L.2: 74, 94. **M.4**: 93. **N.1**: 321. **N.2**: 91, 165,
272. **N.3**: 10. **O.1.2.2**: 9. **O.1.2.4**: 73. **O.3.3**:
24.

Francophone Africa
    N.1: 13. **O.2.1**: 66.

Germany
    B.3: 3, 55, 63. **B.4**: 25. **F.1**: 40, 50, 53, 72,
80. **F.2**: 17. **F.3.1.1**: 61. **F.3.1.2**: 2, 12.
F.3.1.4: 1. **F.5**: 7. **G.1**: 58. **G.1.2**: 19. **G.2.1**:
19, 81, 108, 114, 116, 143, 160. **G.2.4**: 57,
89, 92–93. **G.2.5**: 36, 55. **G.3.3.3**: 15.
G.3.3.5: 6, 42. **H.0**: 195. **H.1.1.2**: 33. **H.1.1.3**:
2. **H.1.1.4**: 48. **H.2.1**: 18, 73, 121. **H.2.2**: 18,
42, 62, 65, 69, 73, 146. **H.3**: 19, 65. **H.4**: 7,
36, 55, 94. **I.2.3**: 58. **J.1**: 91. **J.2**: 5, 12, 59,
104, 219, 234. **J.4**: 25, 35, 238–239. **J.5**: 4,
6, 11. **K.3**: 117. **L.1**: 41. **L.2**: 94. **M.4**: 57,
117, 122. **N.1**: 117, 128, 167, 185, 294, 311,
315. **N.2**: 179, 201, 311. **N.3**: 12. **O.1.2**: 3.
O.1.2.2: 9. **O.1.2.4**: 17, 27, 56. **O.1.3**: 13.
O.2.1: 12. **O.2.3**: 27. **O.3.1**: 9. **O.3.2**: 4–6, 20,
43, 86. **O.3.3**: 30.

Germany (East)
    F.3.2: 122. **H.4**: 102. **N.1**: 27, 199, 310, 325.
N.2: 302.

Ghana
    F.3.1.1: 11, 97. **F.3.2**: 67. **G.2.2**: 6. **G.3.3.4**:
4, 8. **H.1.1.4**: 15. **I.2.3**: 38, 112. **J.1**: 51. **J.2**:
76. **M.4**: 53. **M.5**: 40. **N.3**: 24. **O.2.2**: 35.

Greece
    F.1: 60. **F.3.1.1**: 64. **F.3.1.3**: 29, 32. **G.1.1**:
12. **G.2.4**: 28. **G.3.3.3**: 1. **G.3.3.4**: 3. **G.3.3.5**:
63. **H.1.1.1**: 34. **H.2.1**: 14. **H.3**: 56. **J.1**: 17,
92. **J.5**: 39. **K.3**: 32, 123. **L.2**: 11–12, 32. **M.4**:
23. **N.2**: 34, 210, 272. **O.2.2**: 17. **O.2.3**: 30.
O.3.2: 29.

Greenland
    N.2: 49.

Guatemala
    H.1.2.1: 4.

Guyana
    F.1: 12. **O.2.2**: 61.

Haryana
    H.1.1.1: 24.

Holland
    Entries also appear under:

    NETHERLANDS

Honduras
    H.0: 177. **H.1.1.4**: 23. **H.1.2.1**: 49.

Hong Kong
    F.3.2: 114. **G.2.1**: 30. **J.4**: 38, 137, 184, 244,
265. **L.2**: 104. **N.2**: 298. **O.1.2.4**: 24, 42.
O.2.2: 13.

Hungary
    F.1: 71. **F.2**: 8. **F.3.1.1**: 82. **F.3.1.2**: 8. **F.3.2**:
120. **F.5**: 41. **G.2.2**: 13. **G.3.3.5**: 21. **H.1.1.4**:
36, 40. **H.2.2**: 41. **H.4**: 54. **I.1**: 4. **I.2.1**: 149.
I.2.3: 98. **J.2**: 50, 137–138, 187, 237–238.
J.4: 30. **L.1**: 22. **M.4**: 82, 117. **N.1**: 70, 79, 81,
100, 149, 162, 188, 216, 224, 230, 269, 271,
273, 286, 293–294, 311. **N.2**: 1, 48, 108, 164.
O.1.3: 79. **O.2.2**: 68, 80, 109. **O.3.2**: 36–37.
O.3.3: 40, 79.

Iceland
H.1.1.2: 4.

Illinois
F.3.1.1: 46. H.4: 110. I.2.3: 104.

India
Entries also appear under:

ANDHRA PRADESH; BIHAR; HARYANA; MAHARASHTRA; TAMIL NADU; WEST BENGAL

D: 47. F.3.1.1: 86. F.3.2: 89–90, 95–96, 98, 102, 109, 125. F.3.3: 25. G.1: 8, 15. G.1.3: 11. G.2.1: 13, 74. G.2.4: 59, 118. G.2.5: 57. H.0: 141, 164. H.1.1: 13. H.1.1.1: 4, 11, 35. H.1.1.3: 4–5. H.1.1.4: 12, 29. H.1.2.1: 16, 38. H.2.1: 94, 100. H.2.2: 27, 116. H.3: 60. H.4: 14. I.2.3: 76. J.1: 101. J.2: 6, 42, 52, 91, 126. L.3: 9. M.2: 26, 35. M.5: 2, 40. N.1: 17, 101, 140, 187, 246. N.2: 9, 58, 226, 239, 254, 263. O.1.3: 42, 47, 81. O.2.2: 66, 112. O.2.4: 14. O.3.1: 50. O.3.3: 42, 61, 76.

Indonesia
Entries also appear under:

BALI; JAVA

F.2: 11. F.3.1.1: 74, 96. G.1: 29. G.2.1: 27. H.1.1.1: 17. H.2.1: 24. H.2.2: 37, 49. H.4: 68. I.2.3: 91. J.2: 62, 171, 188. N.1: 111, 129. N.2: 9, 228, 268. N.3: 35. O.1.3: 49. O.3.2: 38, 81. O.3.3: 33, 48, 126, 137.

Iran
F.1: 23. G.2.4: 124. N.1: 242, 247, 253. O.2.3: 35.

Iraq
F.3.1.2: 7. M.2: 14. O.2.2: 28.

Ireland
B.4: 39. F.1: 59. F.3.1.1: 36. F.5: 6. J.2: 235. J.4: 59. L.1: 6. M.5: 11. N.2: 46. O.3.1: 48.

Israel
Entries also appear under:

ISRAELI OCCUPIED TERRITORIES

F.3.1.1: 45. G.2.4: 22, 30, 122. I.2.3: 4. J.1: 104. J.2: 4. K.3: 67. O.2.2: 16, 29.

Israeli Occupied Territories
F.1: 36.

Italy
F.1: 46, 51, 70, 79. F.3.1.1: 63, 70, 72. F.3.1.4: 13. F.3.3: 53. G.1.1: 26. G.1.3: 9. G.2.1: 40, 62, 88, 111, 124, 136. G.2.4: 45. G.3.3.4: 11, 13. G.3.3.5: 66. H.1.1: 15. H.1.1.2: 27. H.1.1.3: 19. H.1.1.4: 43, 46. H.1.2.1: 5–6, 11, 43. H.2.1: 17, 86. H.2.2: 9, 54–55. H.3: 83. I.2.2: 4. I.2.3: 29. J.1: 44. J.2: 117, 135, 147, 153, 179, 184, 200. J.3: 6. J.4: 3, 72. K.3: 45. L.1: 41. N.1: 223. N.2: 2, 66, 70, 191, 250. O.2.2: 120.

Ivory Coast
J.1: 52. N.2: 120.

Jamaica
H.1.2.1: 17. J.2: 90. N.2: 71. O.2.2: 67.

Japan
B.3: 38. B.4: 37. E: 3. F.1: 15, 24, 26. F.3.1.1: 24, 95, 116. F.3.2: 88, 101, 112. F.3.3: 23, 31. F.5: 38. G.1.1: 17. G.1.2: 2, 5, 16, 18. G.1.3: 1, 8, 13–14. G.2.1: 1, 24, 51, 69, 105, 129. G.2.2: 9, 39–40. G.2.3: 16. G.2.4: 58, 93. G.2.5: 21, 51. G.3.1: 4. G.3.2: 23–24. G.3.3: 19–20. G.3.3.1: 19. G.3.3.2: 9. G.3.3.3: 11, 37. G.3.3.5: 38, 46–47, 68, 70, 72, 88, 117, 126. H.1.1.2: 25. H.1.1.3: 2. H.2.1: 13, 22, 42, 61, 84–85, 127. H.2.2: 40, 50, 52–53, 65, 67, 70, 73, 76, 133, 135. H.3: 17. H.4: 97. I.1: 4. I.2.1: 29. I.2.3: 39, 41, 75, 97. J.1: 1. J.2: 81, 220. J.4: 4, 22, 39, 93, 214, 221–222. J.5: 11, 29, 38. K.2: 11, 25. K.3: 16, 54, 60. L.1: 17, 31. L.2: 40. N.1: 7, 35, 237. N.2: 12, 39, 97, 204, 312. O.1.1: 2. O.1.2.2: 9, 13, 16. O.1.2.3: 6, 23. O.1.3: 3, 16, 27–28, 80, 85. O.2.1: 12, 53. O.2.2: 5–6, 27, 33, 82, 107–108, 118, 123. O.2.3: 37, 69. O.2.4: 9. O.3.1: 53, 59–60. O.3.2: 13, 19, 30, 76, 78, 83–84. O.3.3: 25, 30, 60, 127.

Java
H.1.2.1: 28.

Jordan
O.3.2: 3.

Kenya
F.3.1.1: 57, 94. F.3.2: 59. G.1.1: 32. H.1.1.4: 15. H.4: 4. J.4: 133. L.1: 13. L.3: 1. N.3: 20.

Korea
Entries also appear under:

NORTH KOREA; SOUTH KOREA

F.3.2: 100. F.3.3: 7. G.1: 29. G.2.4: 18. H.2.1: 47. N.2: 9, 153. O.1.2.4: 38, 46. O.1.3: 28. O.2.2: 85, 88.

Kuwait
G.2.1: 17. L.2: 27.

Laos
F.1: 28. N.1: 73, 198.

Latin America
F.1: 14. F.3.2: 70–71, 73, 77, 79, 81, 84–85, 105. H.2.1: 74. H.4: 43. J.1: 6, 75. J.2: 198. K.2: 15. L.2: 16. M.2: 4. N.1: 38, 43, 278, 314. N.2: 143, 314. N.3: 24, 50. O.1.2: 9. O.1.2.3: 36. O.1.2.4: 5, 12, 16, 36, 53, 74. O.1.3: 5, 11, 29, 34, 37, 89, 93, 99. O.2.1: 32. O.2.2: 50–51, 59, 65, 69–71, 87. O.2.3: 19. O.3.1: 25. O.3.2: 33. O.3.3: 7, 39, 140.

Lebanon
J.2: 64.

Lesotho
H.1.1.1: 33.

Madagascar
O.3.3: 139.

Maharashtra
H.1.2.1: 9.

Malawi
J.4: 73. L.1: 19. N.1: 207.

Malaysia
Entries also appear under:
SABAH
F.3.1.1: 71. **F.3.2**: 104, 115. **G.2.4**: 72. **H.1.2.1**: 42. **H.2.2**: 23. **L.3**: 21. **M.2**: 25. **N.1**: 92, 130. **N.3**: 26. **O.1.3**: 49. **O.2.3**: 23. **O.3.3**: 18.

Manitoba
H.0: 180.

Marshall Islands
K.3: 9.

Maryland
L.2: 86.

Massachusetts
I.2.3: 105.

Mauritius
J.1: 52.

Mediterranean Region
G.2.1: 18.

Mexico
F.3.1.1: 55, 60. **F.3.1.4**: 11. **F.3.2**: 81, 83. **F.3.3**: 36. **G.1.1**: 15. **G.2.4**: 29. **G.2.5**: 51. **G.3.3.2**: 5. **H.0**: 2. **H.1.1.2**: 12. **H.1.1.4**: 20. **H.2.2**: 10, 123. **H.4**: 17. **I.2.3**: 7. **J.1**: 47, 80, 100. **J.2**: 17, 33, 172. **L.1**: 29. **L.3**: 22. **N.1**: 63, 80. **N.2**: 56, 314. **O.1.3**: 35, 87, 90, 92, 94, 96–97, 103. **O.2.2**: 105. **O.3.1**: 48. **O.3.2**: 49. **O.3.3**: 7, 21, 83, 86, 88–89.

Michigan
F.3.1.1: 21.

Middle East
F.1: 36. **G.2.2**: 42. **H.0**: 157, 208. **N.1**: 186. **O.1.2.3**: 23–24. **O.1.2.4**: 43. **O.3.2**: 77.

Mongolia
M.5: 21. **N.1**: 176.

Montserrat
H.3: 10.

Morocco
F.3.2: 63. **H.1.1.4**: 14. **I.2.3**: 69. **J.1**: 52, 96. **N.1**: 249.

Namibia
O.3.3: 66.

Nepal
G.1: 62. **N.1**: 46, 301.

Netherlands
F.1: 65. **F.3.1.1**: 54, 77, 82, 121. **G.1**: 24. **G.2.1**: 61, 80, 126. **G.2.2**: 7. **G.2.5**: 56. **H.1.1.4**: 44. **H.2.1**: 52, 66. **H.3**: 21–22. **I.2.1**: 89, 151. **I.2.3**: 60. **J.1**: 53. **J.4**: 124. **K.3**: 115. **M.4**: 14. **N.1**: 104. **N.2**: 109, 264.

New Jersey
H.0: 186. **I.2.3**: 93. **N.2**: 305.

New Mexico
H.0: 215.

New York
F.3.1.1: 105. **H.0**: 200. **H.4**: 108. **J.4**: 93. **N.2**: 232.

New Zealand
F.1: 83, 86–87, 93. **G.2.1**: 65. **G.2.4**: 30, 90. **G.3.3.5**: 64. **H.0**: 139. **H.1.1.2**: 29. **H.1.1.3**: 10. **H.1.1.4**: 4. **H.2.1**: 10. **H.2.2**: 117. **I.2.1**: 72, 94. **I.2.3**: 9. **J.2**: 75. **L.2**: 83. **M.5**: 38. **N.2**: 284. **O.2.1**: 80. **O.3.3**: 130.

Newfoundland
H.1.2.1: 41.

Nicaragua
H.1.1.1: 1. **O.1.2.5**: 5. **O.3.2**: 7.

Nigeria
F.3.2: 42. **G.2.1**: 76. **G.2.4**: 61. **G.4**: 5. **H.0**: 21, 100. **H.1.1**: 3. **H.1.1.1**: 29. **H.1.1.3**: 12. **H.1.1.4**: 14, 18. **H.2.1**: 63. **H.3**: 7, 24. **H.4**: 19. **J.2**: 121, 127, 186, 209. **L.1**: 15. **L.2**: 91. **M.5**: 40. **N.1**: 50, 77–78, 136, 275. **N.2**: 132. **N.3**: 7. **O.2.2**: 30. **O.3.1**: 4. **O.3.3**: 24.

North Africa
O.1.2.4: 32, 43.

North America
G.2.1: 2. **H.0**: 14. **H.2.2**: 78. **M.2**: 6. **O.1.2.4**: 35. **O.1.3**: 22, 32, 94–98. **O.2.2**: 27.

North Korea
N.1: 39, 154, 165. **O.2.2**: 130.

North Sea
H.1.2.1: 32. **H.2.2**: 158.

Northeast Asia
O.1.2.4: 51.

Northern Ireland
F.1: 38. **F.3.1.1**: 53.

Norway
G.1: 51. **G.3.3.5**: 114. **H.0**: 116. **H.2.2**: 31. **I.2.3**: 45. **J.2**: 19, 25, 174, 178. **K.2**: 35. **L.2**: 45. **N.2**: 122, 163. **O.1.2.4**: 34. **O.3.3**: 52.

Nova Scotia
H.1.2.1: 35.

Ohio
F.3.1.1: 26. **H.4**: 88.

Ontario
H.1.1.2: 38. **H.3**: 35. **I.2.3**: 17. **J.4**: 245.

Pacific Region
F.1: 26–27, 35, 91. **F.3.2**: 87, 116. **G.1.3**: 7. **G.2.1**: 164. **G.3.3.5**: 82. **H.4**: 86. **I.2.3**: 24. **J.4**: 41, 220. **N.1**: 309. **N.2**: 25. **O.1.2.4**: 7, 22. **O.1.3**: 52, 80, 83–84. **O.2.1**: 46. **O.3.2**: 1–2, 63.

Pakistan
H.3: 15–16. **I.2.1**: 58. **K.3**: 55. **L.2**: 41. **N.3**: 24. **O.1.2.5**: 7. **O.2.1**: 78. **O.3.1**: 51.

Papua New Guinea
F.3.3: 45. **M.5**: 12. **N.3**: 40. **O.3.2**: 17.

Paraguay
H.1.1.4: 24. **J.1**: 20. **O.1.2.4**: 54.

Paraiba
M.4: 5.

Parana
    F.3.1.1: 108.

Pennsylvania
    F.3.1.1: 66. **G.1.3**: 12.

Peru
    F.3.2: 76. **H.4**: 50. **J.4**: 45. **N.1**: 76, 108.

Philippines
    F.3.1.3: 16. **F.3.2**: 117. **G.2.2**: 5. **H.0**: 166.
    H.1.1: 16. **H.1.1.2**: 15. **J.2**: 51, 56. **J.4**: 42.
    K.2: 15. **M.2**: 1. **O.2.2**: 73, 115.

Poland
    B.3: 43. **F.1**: 52, 73. **G.2.1**: 34, 132. **G.3.3.2**:
    10. **H.0**: 15. **H.1.1.4**: 37. **H.2.1**: 106. **J.5**: 53.
    K.3: 72. **L.2**: 100. **M.2**: 2, 30. **N.1**: 71, 81,
    115, 131, 134, 149, 182–183, 189, 204, 216,
    260, 263–267, 286, 288, 292–294, 311, 315.
    N.2: 297. **O.1.3**: 13. **O.2.2**: 80, 106. **O.3.3**:
    40.

Portugal
    F.3.1.1: 6, 90. **F.3.1.2**: 5. **G.2.5**: 11. **J.2**: 201.
    M.5: 17.

Qatar
    O.3.2: 59.

Quebec
    F.3.1.1: 84. **G.2.5**: 50. **I.2.3**: 43. **J.5**: 58. **N.3**:
    10.

Queensland
    B.3: 48.

Rio Grande Do Sul
    H.2.2: 21.

Romania
    N.1: 81, 214, 320.

Russia
    F.1: 74. **F.3.1.1**: 89. **F.3.1.3**: 6. **G.1**: 56.
    G.3.3.5: 35. **H.1.1.2**: 21, 26. **H.1.1.4**: 50.
    H.2.2: 11. **J.1**: 34, 88. **J.5**: 47. **N.1**: 48, 153,
    158, 191, 195, 200–202, 208, 217, 222, 274,
    303. **N.2**: 199. **O.1.2.3**: 28.

Sabah
    H.1.2.1: 14. **H.4**: 79.

Samoa
    Entries also appear under:
    WESTERN SAMOA

Saskatchewan
    G.2.1: 147. **H.1.1.3**: 18.

Saudi Arabia
    F.3.3: 55. **G.3.3.1**: 3. **J.2**: 197.

Scandinavia
    C: 47. **G.3.3.5**: 1. **I.2.3**: 50. **J.4**: 196. **O.2.3**:
    6.

Scotland
    F.3.1.1: 72, 79, 88. **H.0**: 32.

Senegal
    H.1.1.4: 14. **I.2.3**: 70.

Seychelles
    F.3.2: 55.

Sierra Leone
    H.0: 197. **H.1.1.3**: 1. **N.1**: 69.

Singapore
    B.3: 24. **F.3.1.3**: 14. **F.3.3**: 59. **G.1**: 29.
    G.2.1: 117. **G.2.2**: 22. **H.3**: 6. **K.3**: 36. **M.4**:
    96. **M.5**: 40. **N.1**: 57. **N.2**: 298. **O.1.3**: 49.
    O.2.3: 23. **O.3.1**: 39.

Slovenia
    I.2.1: 128. **I.2.2**: 4.

South Africa
    F.1: 6, 8. **F.3.1.1**: 8. **F.3.1.3**: 5. **F.3.2**: 57.
    G.2.4: 52. **G.3.2**: 9. **G.3.3.4**: 14. **H.1.1.2**: 16.
    H.1.2.1: 12, 31. **H.2.2**: 149. **H.3**: 80. **H.4**: 18,
    49. **J.1**: 58, 89. **L.2**: 105. **M.1**: 20. **N.1**: 16, 20.
    N.2: 5, 86, 145. **N.3**: 30–31. **O.1.3**: 17, 36,
    39.

South America
    Entries also appear under:
    AMAZON
    O.1.2.4: 39, 49.

South Asia
    H.1.1.1: 27.

South Korea
    F.3.1.1: 71. **F.3.1.3**: 14. **F.3.2**: 111–112.
    H.1.1.2: 17. **H.2.1**: 97. **H.2.2**: 10, 125. **I.2.3**:
    101. **K.3**: 54. **O.2.3**: 61. **O.3.3**: 7, 63, 100.

Southeast Asia
    F.3.2: 99. **G.2.1**: 106. **G.3.3.1**: 16. **H.0**: 38.
    J.4: 209. **N.1**: 308. **O.1.2.4**: 8. **O.1.3**: 49, 85.
    O.2.2: 8.

Southern Africa
    G.1: 36. **O.1.2.4**: 16, 39, 49. **O.3.3**: 66, 70.

Southern Europe
    O.1.2.4: 63.

Spain
    B.2: 2. **B.4**: 17, 61. **F.1**: 46. **F.3.1.1**: 6, 37,
    51, 72, 80, 112. **G.2.1**: 47. **G.3.3.5**: 125.
    H.1.1.1: 20. **H.1.1.4**: 41. **H.1.2.1**: 20, 43.
    H.2.1: 1, 17, 28, 56, 72. **H.4**: 16. **I.2.3**: 59.
    J.2: 167, 194. **J.4**: 70. **L.2**: 85, 87. **N.2**: 126.
    O.1.2.4: 59, 84. **O.2.2**: 104. **O.2.3**: 25.

Sri Lanka
    F.1: 22. **M.3**: 2. **N.2**: 255. **O.2.1**: 62. **O.3.3**:
    41.

Sub-Saharan Africa
    F.3.2: 49–51, 54, 60, 62. **H.1.1**: 21. **H.2.2**:
    105. **H.4**: 45. **J.5**: 45. **L.1**: 1. **N.1**: 85, 135.
    N.2: 237, 276. **O.2.2**: 53, 75, 116. **O.2.4**: 15.
    O.3.2: 75. **O.3.3**: 62.

Sudan
    H.1.1.1: 23. **N.1**: 106. **N.2**: 247.

Sweden
    A: 4. **C**: 40. **F.5**: 35. **G.1**: 23, 50. **G.2.1**: 116.
    G.2.2: 24, 31. **G.2.3**: 17. **G.2.4**: 16. **G.2.5**: 59.
    G.3.3.4: 12. **G.3.3.5**: 31. **H.1.2.1**: 52–53.
    H.2.2: 12, 19. **J.2**: 97. **J.4**: 96. **K.3**: 58, 116,
    122. **N.1**: 119, 235, 237. **N.2**: 308. **O.1.2.2**:
    14. **O.1.3**: 82. **O.2.3**: 42. **O.3.1**: 63. **O.3.3**: 14.

United Kingdom continued
274. **N.3**: 3, 44. **O.1.2**: 3. **O.1.2.2**: 2, 7, 9.
O.1.2.3: 3, 6. **O.1.2.4**: 9. **O.1.3**: 2, 58, 77.
O.2.1: 36, 47, 55. **O.2.2**: 5–6, 33, 69, 114.
O.3.1: 64, 75. **O.3.2**: 8, 65, 67.

Uruguay
F.1: 9. **I.2.3**: 20. **J.1**: 50. **O.1.2.4**: 6, 26, 54.

Vanuatu
L.2: 73.

Venezuela
J.5: 43. **N.1**: 252. **N.2**: 306. **N.3**: 24.

Vermont
N.2: 148.

Victoria
G.2.3: 8, 11.

Vietnam
F.3.1.2: 16. **H.0**: 35. **H.1.1.4**: 32. **O.1.3**: 24.
O.2.2: 121.

Wales
H.2.2: 128. **O.1.3**: 28.

Washington
F.3.1.1: 85.

West Africa
F.3.2: 56. **H.1.1.1**: 37. **H.2.1**: 75. **O.2.1**: 66.
O.2.3: 56.

West Bengal
H.1.1.2: 1. **K.3**: 34.

Western Europe
A: 17. **F.3.1.1**: 59. **F.3.1.2**: 21. **G.1.2**: 5.
H.1.1.2: 13. **H.2.1**: 13. **H.3**: 97. **H.4**: 106. **J.2**:
221. **K.3**: 48. **N.1**: 278. **O.2.2**: 27, 33. **O.3.1**:
59. **O.3.2**: 76.

Western Samoa
F.1: 92.

Yugoslavia
Entries also appear under:

CROATIA; SLOVENIA
F.1: 61, 82. **F.3.2**: 125, 128. **F.5**: 9. **G.3.3.3**: 17.
H.2.1: 29, 115. **H.2.2**: 74. **H.3**: 28. **I.2.1**: 129.
J.1: 81, 93, 103. **N.1**: 177, 221, 236, 257.

Zaire
F.3.2: 58.

Zambia
F.1: 5. **H.1.1.3**: 1. **H.1.1.4**: 19. **O.2.1**: 79.

Zimbabwe
F.3.1.1: 96. **F.3.2**: 42. **H.0**: 205. **H.1.1.2**: 23.
N.1: 190.

SUBJECT INDEX

Ability **K.3**: 51, 112.

Aborigines **A**: 1. **G.2.2**: 4.

Absenteeism **G.2.5**: 1.

Academic achievement **M.5**: 14.

Access to education **O.3.3**: 26.

Access to information **A**: 7. **B.4**: 2. **F.3.1.4**: 12. **G.2.5**: 38. **I.2.1**: 15. **J.4**: 65, 78, 204. **N.3**: 29.

Accident insurance **J.3**: 9.

Accidents
Entries also appear under:
OCCUPATIONAL ACCIDENTS

Accountants **G.4**: 5.

Accounting
Entries also appear under:
AGRICULTURAL ACCOUNTING; BUSINESS ACCOUNTING; COMMERCIAL ACCOUNTING; COST ACCOUNTING; FINANCIAL ACCOUNTING; INDUSTRIAL ACCOUNTING; NATIONAL ACCOUNTING; SOCIAL ACCOUNTING
A: 12, 16. **B.4**: 1–6, 21, 23, 25, 27, 29, 31, 33, 36, 39, 41, 50, 53, 56, 61, 64, 66. **F.3.1.1**: 35. **F.3.2**: 21. **G.1.1**: 1. **G.3.3.3**: 6. **G.3.3.5**: 105, 117–118, 122. **J.4**: 31, 296–297. **M.4**: 68–69. **N.3**: 3.

Accounting methods **B.4**: 10, 16, 19, 43, 45, 48. **J.2**: 40. **J.4**: 27.

Accounting models **J.4**: 119.

Accounting research **B.4**: 20, 42.

Accounting standards **B.4**: 12.

Accounting theory **B.4**: 30, 44, 46.

Achievement motivation
Entries also appear under:
ACADEMIC ACHIEVEMENT

Addiction **I.2.1**: 13.

Adjustment costs **H.1.1.3**: 16.

Administration
Entries also appear under:
DEVELOPMENT ADMINISTRATION; FISCAL ADMINISTRATION; LABOUR ADMINISTRATION

Administrative decentralization **N.3**: 15.

Administrative efficiency **M.5**: 22.

Administrative organization **H.4**: 67.

Administrative reform **N.2**: 130.

Adults **G.2.5**: 28.

Advertising **H.1.1.2**: 37. **H.4**: 57–58, 60–65. **I.2.1**: 67. **M.4**: 12.

Aerospace industry
Entries also appear under:
AIRCRAFT INDUSTRY

Affirmative action **G.2.1**: 102. **G.2.2**: 1. **G.2.4**: 25. **G.3.3.1**: 14.

Afghans **H.3**: 15.

Age groups **L.2**: 19. **M.4**: 7.

Aged
Entries also appear under:
CARE OF THE AGED
K.3: 54. **L.1**: 41. **M.4**: 43. **N.2**: 16.

Ageing **I.2.3**: 82. **M.1**: 12. **M.4**: 7, 74, 85.

Aggregate demand **C**: 20. **F.5**: 5. **I.2.1**: 18, 113, 135. **L.1**: 10, 17. **O.3.2**: 66.

Aggregate expenditure **H.3**: 1.

Aggregate supply **C**: 20. **I.2.1**: 177.

Agrarian problems **H.1.1.4**: 8.

Agrarian reform **F.3.1.1**: 89. **H.1.1.2**: 1–2, 5, 24, 26. **H.1.1.4**: 23, 40.

Agricultural accounting **H.1.1.3**: 10.

Agricultural change **H.1.1.1**: 28.

Agricultural cooperatives **H.1.1.2**: 35. **H.1.1.4**: 7.

Agricultural credit **F.3.1.1**: 98. **H.1.1**: 3–4, 13, 16. **H.1.1.3**: 12, 19. **J.2**: 51, 57, 91, 93.

Agricultural development
Entries also appear under:
GREEN REVOLUTION
F.3.2: 63. **H.1.1.1**: 31. **H.1.1.4**: 2, 5, 12, 18, 20, 22, 31, 36, 45. **O.1.3**: 68.

Agricultural economics **H.1.1**: 2, 6, 17, 19, 22. **H.1.1.4**: 24.

Agricultural enterprises
Entries also appear under:
COLLECTIVE FARMS; FAMILY FARMS; SMALL FARMS
G.2.1: 147. **H.1.1**: 3, 8, 11. **H.1.1.1**: 4, 11. **H.1.1.2**: 7, 9, 14, 33, 37. **H.1.1.3**: 8, 14, 17–18, 20. **H.1.1.4**: 21. **H.1.2.1**: 12. **I.2.3**: 77.

Agricultural equipment
Entries also appear under:
FERTILIZERS

Agricultural exports **H.1.1.4**: 20. **O.3.2**: 17.

Agricultural imports **O.3.2**: 26.

Agricultural income **H.1.1.1**: 6.

Agricultural industry **F.3.1.1**: 11. **G.2.2**: 6. **H.1.1.3**: 11, 13, 16. **H.1.1.4**: 9. **O.1.2.3**: 15.

Agricultural insurance **H.1.1**: 8. **H.1.1.3**: 3.

Agricultural labour **G.2.1**: 74. **H.1.1.3**: 9. **H.1.1.4**: 28.

Agricultural management **H.1.1.1**: 38. **H.1.1.3**: 5. **H.1.1.4**: 43.

Agricultural market **I.2.3**: 74.

Agricultural mechanization **H.1.1.1**: 4.

Agricultural methods **H.0**: 100. **H.1.1.4**: 15.

Agricultural policy **H.1.1.3**: 7. **H.1.1.4**: 4, 6, 8, 11, 14, 17, 25–27, 30, 33–36, 38–39, 41–42, 45, 47–48, 50. **H.1.2.1**: 20. **O.3.3**: 1, 108.

Agricultural prices **H.1.1**: 20. **H.1.1.4**: 47. **I.2.3**: 28, 52, 77, 80. **O.3.3**: 82.

Agricultural pricing **I.2.3**: 67.

Agricultural production **F.3.1.2**: 15. **F.3.2**: 59. **H.0**: 74. **H.1.1.1**: 2, 8, 22, 29, 36. **H.1.1.2**: 24. **H.1.2.1**: 27, 29, 31. **H.4**: 63, 68.

Agricultural productivity **H.1.1**: 5, 10. **H.1.1.1**: 10, 19–20, 25, 27, 32. **H.1.1.2**: 12, 20. **H.1.1.4**: 32. **H.1.2**: 4–5. **I.2.3**: 76.

Agricultural products **H.1.1**: 18. **H.1.2.1**: 17, 21, 24–25. **H.4**: 79. **I.2.3**: 79. **K.3**: 9. **O.1.2.3**: 24. **O.3.3**: 38.

Agricultural projects **H.1.1.3**: 1.

Agricultural protection **O.3.3**: 142.

Agricultural reform **N.1**: 263–267, 325.

Agricultural research **H.1.1.1**: 1, 13, 30.

Agricultural sector **H.1.1**: 7. **H.1.1.4**: 16, 27. **N.1**: 259.

Agricultural technology **G.2.1**: 13. **H.1.1.1**: 14, 24, 34–35. **H.1.2.1**: 28.

Agricultural trade **O.3.2**: 47, 74. **O.3.3**: 72.

Agricultural workers **G.2.1**: 41. **K.3**: 46.

Agriculture **F.3.1.3**: 16. **F.3.2**: 1, 80, 91. **G.2.1**: 101, 147. **H.0**: 126, 148, 173. **H.1.1**: 1, 12, 21. **H.1.1.1**: 9, 17–18, 26, 33. **H.1.1.2**: 3, 6, 11, 17, 19, 27, 29. **H.1.1.3**: 2, 4, 6. **H.1.1.4**: 1, 10, 13, 34, 37, 44, 49. **H.1.2.1**: 52. **L.3**: 15. **O.3.2**: 1, 25. **O.3.3**: 89, 115.

Agrofood industry **H.1.1**: 5, 15. **H.1.1.4**: 46. **H.1.2**: 1. **H.2.2**: 16. **H.4**: 29. **I.2.3**: 69.

Aid
Entries also appear under:
  DEVELOPMENT AID; ECONOMIC AID; FINANCIAL AID; FOOD AID; FOREIGN AID; STATE AID
  F.3.2: 119.

AIDS **M.4**: 26.

Air pollution **H.0**: 4, 74, 84, 86, 88, 103. **N.2**: 115.

Air traffic **H.3**: 49.

Air transport **H.3**: 37, 44, 51, 67. **I.2.3**: 44.

Aircraft industry **H.2.2**: 14, 37. **H.3**: 47.

Airlines **F.3.1.1**: 20. **H.3**: 38, 41, 43, 45–46, 48, 50, 53.

Airports **G.2.5**: 6. **H.3**: 39–40.

Alcoholic beverages **I.2.3**: 14, 50. **N.2**: 194.

Algorithms **B.3**: 36.

Alienation **D**: 14.

Alliances **G.3.3.5**: 87.

Alonso, W. **F.3.1.2**: 1.

Altruism **L.2**: 18. **M.1**: 14.

Amerindians
Entries also appear under:
  NORTH AMERINDIANS; SOUTH AMERINDIANS

Anarchy **F.3.1.4**: 17.

Ancient economies **E**: 9.

Andean Group **O.1.2.4**: 41.

Animals
Entries also appear under:
  SHEEP

Anti-dumping law **G.3.2**: 12. **O.1.3**: 28. **O.3.3**: 96–97, 100.

Anti-dumping policy **O.3.3**: 95, 99, 101.

Anti-inflation policy **J.1**: 99.

Anti-trust legislation **G.3.2**: 2, 20–22, 27, 36–37, 39. **H.2.2**: 50. **H.3**: 39. **H.4**: 90. **I.2.1**: 68, 72. **O.1.3**: 28. **O.3.2**: 19.

Apartheid **O.1.3**: 17.

Applied economics **B.2**: 1.

Applied general equilibrium models **G.3.3.3**: 13. **H.3**: 33.

Apprentices **G.2.5**: 2.

Arab countries **O.2.4**: 1.

Arbitrage **B.3**: 14, 49. **I.2.1**: 2. **J.4**: 4–5, 189. **O.2.3**: 21.

Arbitration **G.2.4**: 3, 6, 11, 13, 19, 35, 37.

Architecture **G.4**: 3.

Armaments industry **H.2.2**: 3, 11. **N.1**: 3, 11.

Armed forces **H.0**: 41.

Arms procurement **N.1**: 21.

Arms trade **O.1.2.3**: 20. **O.3.2**: 21, 55.

Art market **I.2.3**: 21.

Artificial intelligence **B.3**: 2, 31.

ASEAN **H.0**: 17. **N.1**: 308. **O.1.2.4**: 7–8, 18. **O.1.3**: 85. **O.2.2**: 8. **O.3.2**: 83.

Asset valuation **B.3**: 21. **G.1.1**: 5. **J.4**: 7, 16, 19, 26, 32, 46, 50–51, 69, 87–88, 102, 152, 154, 157, 194–195, 227, 261, 264.

Assets

Commodity market **O.1.2.3**: 5, 37. **O.1.3**: 5. **O.3.2**: 18.

Commodity money **O.1.3**: 6.

Commodity prices **B.3**: 37. **I.2.1**: 137. **J.4**: 103. **O.1.2.3**: 27.

Common market **O.1.2.4**: 54.

Commons, John **G.3.3.3**: 40.

Communication
Entries also appear under:
BUSINESS COMMUNICATIONS
G.2.5: 54. **H.3**: 1, 16.

Communication policy **H.3**: 3, 92.

Communism **F.1**: 69.

Community
Entries also appear under:
BUSINESS COMMUNITY; LOCAL COMMUNITIES; RURAL COMMUNITIES
C: 76. **F.3.1.3**: 22. **M.2**: 5. **N.2**: 93. **O.3.3**: 20.

Community care **M.4**: 6.

Community development **F.3.1.1**: 52.

Community law **G.2.3**: 2. **G.3.2**: 18, 35.

Community participation **H.0**: 197. **N.1**: 45.

Community services **J.2**: 156.

Commuting **G.2.1**: 75. **G.2.5**: 36.

Company law **F.3.1.4**: 25.

Company management
Entries also appear under:
BUSINESS MANAGEMENT

Comparative advantage **G.3.3**: 17. **H.1.2.1**: 3. **I.1**: 4. **O.1.2.3**: 22. **O.3.1**: 31, 39, 73. **O.3.3**: 126.

Comparative analysis **F.1**: 69. **F.3.3**: 6. **G.2.3**: 8. **G.2.4**: 30. **G.2.5**: 22. **H.1.1**: 9. **H.2.2**: 31. **H.4**: 19. **J.2**: 223. **N.2**: 192, 298. **O.2.3**: 26.

Comparative costs **O.3.1**: 58.

Compensation **F.3.1.4**: 6. **G.2.3**: 11. **G.2.4**: 6. **G.3.3.5**: 20, 33. **H.1.1.4**: 40. **J.2**: 103. **J.3**: 7. **K.3**: 25, 41, 116.

Competition
Entries also appear under:
IMPERFECT COMPETITION; INTERNATIONAL COMPETITION; MONOPOLISTIC COMPETITION; PERFECT COMPETITION; PRICE COMPETITION; UNFAIR COMPETITION
B.4: 37. **E**: 3. **F.3.1.1**: 33. **F.3.3**: 18. **G.1**: 16, 19, 29, 45. **G.1.1**: 28. **G.1.3**: 2, 19. **G.2.1**: 131. **G.3.3.5**: 4, 15, 88. **H.0**: 72. **H.2.1**: 1, 22, 35–36, 44, 51, 53, 65, 92. **H.2.2**: 5, 53, 90–91. **H.3**: 43, 45, 59. **H.4**: 84. **I.2.1**: 68–72, 74–79, 90–91, 93, 95, 98–100, 102, 104–105, 108, 112, 114, 162, 174. **I.2.3**: 9, 40. **J.2**: 12, 36, 104, 148. **N.1**: 10, 287, 318. **N.2**: 15. **N.3**: 6, 27, 34. **O.1.2.3**: 1, 6, 12, 22. **O.1.2.4**: 14. **O.2.2**: 85. **O.3.1**: 8, 53.

Competition law **F.3.1.4**: 8, 22. **G.3.2**: 2, 20. **I.2.1**: 72.

Competition policy **F.3.1.4**: 29. **G.3.2**: 8. **H.2.1**: 77, 99. **H.2.2**: 94. **I.2.1**: 92, 101. **I.2.3**: 65. **O.1.2.3**: 7.

Competitive equilibrium **F.3.1.2**: 1. **I.2.1**: 80, 88.

Competitive firms **B.3**: 30. **G.3.3.5**: 55, 68.

Competitiveness **F.3.1.1**: 53. **G.1.1**: 29. **G.2.4**: 73, 102. **G.3.2**: 11, 28. **G.3.3.4**: 1. **G.3.3.5**: 5, 13, 29. **H.1.1.4**: 21. **H.2.1**: 6, 13, 38, 116. **H.2.2**: 12. **I.2.1**: 73, 89, 94, 103. **J.2**: 21, 149. **J.5**: 21. **N.1**: 34, 60. **O.1.2.3**: 32. **O.1.2.4**: 64. **O.3.2**: 31, 80. **O.3.3**: 25.

Computer industry **H.2.1**: 13. **H.2.2**: 10, 20, 26–27, 43. **H.3**: 99. **K.3**: 76.

Computer programmes **F.3.3**: 13. **H.2.2**: 17.

Computer science **A**: 13.

Computerization **G.2.4**: 4. **J.2**: 124.

Computers **B.3**: 11. **G.1.3**: 7. **G.2.5**: 10. **H.2.2**: 45.

Condorcet, M. **D**: 21.

Conflict **C**: 69. **F.3.1.1**: 28. **J.2**: 26. **K.2**: 3. **N.1**: 58. **O.1.2.3**: 24. **O.2.1**: 14.

Conflict resolution **F.1**: 1. **G.2.4**: 11–12. **H.0**: 198. **O.3.3**: 114.

Confucianism **K.3**: 54.

Conglomerates **I.2.1**: 46.

Conservation
Entries also appear under:
ENERGY CONSERVATION; RESOURCE CONSERVATION; SOIL CONSERVATION
F.3.1.4: 9. **H.0**: 59, 61, 130, 153, 156. **H.1.1.1**: 7. **H.1.2.1**: 13. **H.2.1**: 70.

Conservatism **D**: 16. **F.2**: 19. **G.3.3.5**: 45.

Conservatives **D**: 29.

Constitution **M.1**: 18. **O.1.2.4**: 57.

Construction industry **G.2.4**: 71. **H.2.1**: 50. **H.2.2**: 24, 30, 38, 51. **I.2.3**: 91. **J.2**: 73.

Consumer behaviour **B.3**: 9. **H.4**: 48, 60, 73, 82. **I.2.1**: 60, 178. **J.1**: 46, 108. **L.1**: 36. **L.2**: 49, 54–59, 63–66, 69, 71. **O.3.3**: 77.

Consumer credit **J.2**: 20, 59, 65, 134, 234.

Consumer demand **G.2.1**: 121. **H.4**: 97. **I.2.3**: 14. **L.2**: 5, 19, 23, 27, 29–30, 32, 35–36, 48, 51, 57, 60–62, 68, 72, 87.

Consumer expenditure **I.2.3**: 83. **L.2**: 12, 52, 106.

Consumer goods **I.2.1**: 176. **N.2**: 147. **O.3.1**: 75.

Consumer preferences **C**: 30. **G.1.1**: 9. **I.2.1**: 91. **L.2**: 86.

Consumer protection **F.3.1.4**: 3. **L.2**: 16, 33. **O.3.3**: 127.

Consumer surplus **L.2**: 9.

Consumerism **D**: 13.

Consumers **F.3.2**: 108. **G.1.1**: 3. **G.3.2**: 21. **H.4**: 35, 93. **I.2.1**: 133, 165, 180. **I.2.3**: 11. **J.2**: 66, 111, 226. **J.4**: 14. **L.2**: 4, 7, 10, 20, 24, 42, 50, 67–68. **M.4**: 8.

Consumption
Entries also appear under:
> ENERGY CONSUMPTION; FOOD CONSUMPTION; HOUSEHOLD CONSUMPTION; WATER CONSUMPTION
B.3: 9. **D**: 38. **F.3.2**: 120. **F.5**: 31, 36. **G.1**: 28. **H.0**: 96. **H.1.1.3**: 10. **H.1.2.1**: 5. **I.2.3**: 80, 92. **J.2**: 2. **J.4**: 173. **K.1**: 7. **L.1**: 2, 16, 23–25, 30, 39, 42. **L.2**: 2–3, 6, 11, 17, 21, 26, 28, 31, 38–39, 43, 48, 72, 80, 106. **L.3**: 26. **M.1**: 8. **N.2**: 279. **O.2.1**: 93.

Consumption functions **B.2**: 4. **L.2**: 37, 45.

Consumption patterns **H.1.2.1**: 11. **H.2.2**: 145.

Continental shelf **H.2.2**: 163.

Contracts
Entries also appear under:
> LABOUR CONTRACT; PUBLIC CONTRACTS; SOCIAL CONTRACT
B.4: 59. **C**: 3, 33, 73, 84. **D**: 9. **F.5**: 42. **G.2.1**: 31, 53. **G.2.4**: 47, 67, 93. **G.3.3.2**: 2, 4. **G.3.3.5**: 22, 123. **H.1.1.2**: 6, 11, 30. **H.4**: 40. **I.2.1**: 30–31, 57. **I.2.3**: 48. **J.2**: 13, 40. **J.4**: 1, 13. **K.3**: 10, 89. **L.2**: 29. **M.5**: 5. **N.3**: 7. **O.2.2**: 31.

Control theory **I.2.1**: 51.

Convertibility **J.1**: 33. **O.2.3**: 58.

Co-operative banks **H.1.1**: 4.

Co-operative sector **G.2.4**: 122.

Cooperatives
Entries also appear under:
> AGRICULTURAL COOPERATIVES; COOPERATIVE BANKS; COOPERATIVE SECTOR; INDUSTRIAL COOPERATIVES; PRODUCTION COOPERATIVES
F.3.1.4: 4. **G.2.4**: 112. **G.3.3**: 2. **H.2.1**: 86. **H.4**: 8, 18. **L.1**: 13. **N.1**: 273.

Copper **G.2.4**: 2. **H.2.2**: 145. **L.2**: 3.

Copper mines **H.2.2**: 140.

Corporate debt **G.3.3.3**: 10. **G.3.3.5**: 8.

Corporate finance **G.3.3.2**: 3.

Corporate income **J.4**: 208.

Corporate planning **G.3.3.5**: 36, 84, 96, 98. **J.4**: 243.

Corporate power **G.3.2**: 3, 23–24. **I.2.1**: 79. **J.2**: 168.

Corporate taxation **N.2**: 94–98, 100–107.

Corporation law **B.4**: 3. **F.3.1.4**: 1, 12. **G.3.2**: 7. **G.3.3.5**: 117. **J.4**: 62.

Corporatism **F.3.3**: 10.

Corruption **F.3.1.4**: 5. **K.2**: 18.

Cost accounting **B.4**: 40. **D**: 75.

Cost analysis **N.2**: 159.

Cost of living **M.2**: 16, 21.

Cost prices **G.3.3.5**: 73. **I.2.1**: 119.

Cost-benefit analysis **F.3.1.4**: 12. **H.3**: 68. **I.2.1**: 146. **M.4**: 4. **N.2**: 111.

Costs
Entries also appear under:
> CAPITAL COSTS; COMPARATIVE COSTS; HOSPITAL COSTS; LABOUR COSTS; PRODUCTION COSTS; SOCIAL COSTS; TRANSPORT COSTS; WELFARE COSTS
D: 46. **F.3.1.2**: 17. **G.1**: 15. **G.1.1**: 25. **G.2.1**: 15, 153. **G.3.3.5**: 104. **H.1.1.3**: 6. **H.2.1**: 2, 60, 78, 88. **H.2.2**: 65, 115, 148. **H.4**: 11. **I.2.1**: 2, 15–16, 63, 77, 95, 106, 115, 133, 149, 161. **J.2**: 145, 150. **J.4**: 16, 68, 131. **K.3**: 53. **L.1**: 39. **L.2**: 42, 44. **L.3**: 13. **M.4**: 3, 20, 55–56. **M.5**: 15. **O.3.3**: 74.

Cotton **H.1.1.1**: 22.

Counselling **G.2.1**: 161.

Countertrade **O.3.1**: 4–5.

Countries
Entries also appear under:
> ARAB COUNTRIES; WESTERN COUNTRIES

Cournot, Augustin **D**: 7.

Courts **G.3.3.5**: 114.

Credit
Entries also appear under:
> AGRICULTURAL CREDIT; CONSUMER CREDIT; EXPORT CREDIT; MONEY AND CREDIT; RURAL CREDIT; TAX CREDITS
D: 4. **G.3.3.4**: 2. **H.3**: 78. **J.1**: 22, 29, 39. **J.2**: 1–2, 8, 16, 18, 25, 30, 41, 44, 46, 57, 67–68, 78, 89, 96–97, 163, 170, 182, 188, 192, 195, 202, 209, 227, 235. **J.4**: 73, 78, 83, 107, 185. **L.2**: 94. **O.2.2**: 25. **O.2.3**: 20. **O.2.4**: 8.

Credit control **J.2**: 106. **K.2**: 5.

Credit market **J.2**: 54, 69. **J.5**: 16, 53.

Credit policy **J.2**: 17.

Credit rationing **J.2**: 15, 84–85.

Credit systems **J.2**: 23.

Criminality
Entries also appear under:
> ECONOMIC CRIMINALITY

Critical theory **G.3.3.5**: 7.

Crops
Entries also appear under:
> CASH CROPS
H.1.1.1: 24, 32. **H.1.1.3**: 18. **H.1.2.1**: 8, 25. **I.2.3**: 70.

Cultural change **E**: 5.

Cultural differentiation **O.3.2**: 57.

Cultural heritage **H.3**: 8.

Cultural identity **F.3.1.2**: 5.

Cultural industry **H.4**: 24.

Deregulation **G.2.3**: 8. **H.2.2**: 110. **H.3**: 39, 45, 52, 58, 81, 96. **J.2**: 24, 110–111, 116–117, 122, 132, 164, 168, 174. **J.4**: 85, 108. **M.3**: 14. **N.1**: 47. **N.3**: 11.

Desert **H.0**: 157.

Deterrence **C**: 58.

Deutsche Mark **O.2.1**: 45. **O.2.3**: 5, 14, 36.

Devaluation **O.2.1**: 18. **O.2.2**: 15. **O.2.3**: 69. **O.3.2**: 24.

Developed countries **F.3.3**: 60. **H.0**: 11. **H.1.1.2**: 7. **J.1**: 54. **L.2**: 94. **N.2**: 65. **O.1.1**: 3. **O.2.2**: 44.

Developing areas **I.2.3**: 53.

Developing countries
Entries also appear under:
    LESS DEVELOPED COUNTRIES
    F.1: 59. **F.2**: 5–6. **F.3.1.1**: 12, 28, 65, 69, 71, 98. **F.3.1.2**: 3. **F.3.2**: 1–2, 4–5, 10, 12, 15–17, 21, 23, 25, 28–29, 35, 41, 43–50, 61–62, 71, 73, 119. **F.3.3**: 51. **G.1**: 29, 44. **G.1.1**: 15, 20. **G.2.1**: 28. **G.3.3.4**: 4, 7. **G.3.3.5**: 71. **H.0**: 11, 21, 150, 160, 165, 169, 205. **H.1.1.1**: 14–15. **H.1.1.2**: 7, 11, 19. **H.1.1.3**: 3. **H.1.1.4**: 2. **H.2.1**: 97. **H.2.2**: 30, 35, 80, 82, 104, 108, 111, 125, 142, 144. **H.3**: 7, 15, 31, 94. **H.4**: 27. **I.2.1**: 53. **I.2.3**: 34. **J.1**: 52. **J.2**: 35, 41, 57, 68, 163, 229. **J.4**: 47, 81, 159. **J.5**: 3, 28. **K.1**: 7. **L.1**: 1, 26–28. **L.2**: 88. **L.3**: 11. **M.2**: 5. **M.4**: 42, 50, 115. **M.5**: 40. **N.1**: 83, 86, 96, 151, 256. **N.2**: 9, 36, 55, 132, 140, 168, 176, 228, 244, 254. **N.3**: 24. **O.1.1**: 3. **O.1.2.3**: 5, 37. **O.1.2.4**: 32, 43. **O.1.3**: 1, 6, 42, 53, 58, 62, 69, 71, 78. **O.2.1**: 30, 51, 82. **O.2.2**: 1, 40, 44, 49, 52–53, 62, 75, 79, 88, 94, 100, 110–111. **O.2.4**: 8, 13. **O.3.1**: 25, 29, 34, 37, 61. **O.3.2**: 11, 18, 71, 73. **O.3.3**: 20, 28–29, 38, 52, 59, 112.

Development
Entries also appear under:
    ECONOMIC DEVELOPMENT; RURAL DEVELOPMENT; SOCIO-ECONOMIC DEVELOPMENT; SUSTAINABLE DEVELOPMENT; URBAN DEVELOPMENT

Development administration **N.2**: 137.

Development aid **H.1.1.4**: 14. **O.1.3**: 61, 70, 72.

Development banks **H.0**: 169. **H.1.1**: 4. **J.2**: 64.

Development economics **B.1**: 14. **F.3.2**: 77. **H.0**: 43. **H.1.1**: 22.

Development financing **F.3.2**: 13, 31, 89. **N.1**: 68.

Development models **F.3.2**: 10.

Development planning **F.3.2**: 11, 51. **N.1**: 69.

Development policy **F.3.2**: 12, 36. **H.4**: 46. **N.1**: 57, 92.

Development potential **H.2.2**: 100.

Development programmes **G.1.3**: 12.

Development projects **H.0**: 169. **H.1.1.4**: 17. **M.4**: 5.

Development strategies **F.3.2**: 27, 44, 68, 110. **H.3**: 82.

Development theory **F.3.2**: 12.

Diamonds **H.2.2**: 4. **I.2.3**: 31.

Diet **G.3.3.5**: 19.

Diplomacy **O.1.3**: 64. **O.3.3**: 13.

Direct taxation **N.2**: 173.

Disability **G.2.2**: 2. **M.4**: 9.

Disasters
Entries also appear under:
    NATURAL DISASTERS

Discrimination
Entries also appear under:
    PRICE DISCRIMINATION; RACIAL DISCRIMINATION; SEX DISCRIMINATION; WAGE DISCRIMINATION
    I.2.1: 145.

Diseases
Entries also appear under:
    AIDS
    M.4: 66.

Disequilibrium
Entries also appear under:
    ECONOMIC DISEQUILIBRIUM
    B.1: 19. **F.3.2**: 80. **G.2.1**: 38, 98.

Disequilibrium models **G.2.1**: 158.

Dismissals **G.2.1**: 12. **G.2.4**: 27, 68. **G.2.5**: 27, 32, 34. **K.3**: 45.

Distribution **F.3.3**: 41. **H.0**: 55. **H.3**: 9, 20–21. **H.4**: 2, 7, 10, 14, 16, 32, 38, 44–45, 65, 105. **I.2.1**: 125. **I.2.3**: 56, 86. **J.2**: 30. **K.2**: 10. **L.2**: 28. **M.2**: 23. **N.2**: 160. **N.3**: 13. **O.1.3**: 59. **O.2.2**: 55.

Distribution economics **M.4**: 118.

Distributive justice **C**: 80. **L.2**: 38.

Diversification
Entries also appear under:
    EXPORT DIVERSIFICATION; PRODUCTION DIVERSIFICATION
    H.2.1: 10, 29. **J.4**: 19, 177, 196.

Divestment **G.3.3.3**: 5. **L.3**: 10.

Division of labour
Entries also appear under:
    INTERNATIONAL DIVISION OF LABOUR
    G.2.1: 15, 54. **G.2.4**: 112. **H.2.2**: 66. **K.3**: 35.

Divorce **F.3.1.3**: 3. **M.4**: 100.

Dollar **O.2.1**: 11, 87. **O.2.2**: 113. **O.2.3**: 35–36, 69.

Domestic market **O.3.1**: 11.

Domestic policy **H.0**: 5.

Drought **O.1.3**: 76.

Drug trafficking **O.2.1**: 3.

Drugs **G.2.1**: 10. **H.4**: 45. **I.2.3**: 1. **O.3.3**: 85.

Dual economy **F.3.2**: 91.

Dumping **G.3.3.5**: 4. **I.2.1**: 41. **O.2.1**: 74. **O.3.3**: 98.

Duopolistic competition **I.2.1**: 82. **L.2**: 70.

Duopoly **G.3.3**: 26. **H.4**: 62. **I.2.1**: 8, 20–21, 30. **K.3**: 84.

Durable goods **I.2.1**: 22–24. **I.2.3**: 27, 83.

Duty **F.3.1.4**: 3. **I.2.3**: 37. **O.3.3**: 34.

Dyad **G.3.2**: 24.

Dynamic models **F.4**: 10. **G.2.1**: 111. **J.1**: 76. **J.4**: 51. **J.5**: 35. **L.2**: 6.

Dynamics **B.1**: 12. **G.1**: 38. **H.3**: 83. **J.1**: 74. **J.2**: 131. **J.4**: 295.

Early childhood **M.5**: 36.

Early motherhood **F.3.1.3**: 26.

Earnings **B.4**: 35. **F.3.1.3**: 26. **G.2.1**: 33, 82, 175. **G.3.3.3**: 7. **G.3.3.5**: 17, 51. **H.2.2**: 115. **J.4**: 24, 33, 119, 235, 289, 296, 305. **K.2**: 12, 28, 39. **K.3**: 15–18, 31, 36, 42, 45, 47, 51, 62, 109, 113, 119. **L.1**: 9. **M.4**: 107. **M.5**: 9, 14, 37.

Earthquakes **J.3**: 5, 16.

East-West relations **F.3.2**: 123. **N.1**: 324. **O.3.2**: 20.

Eastern bloc **O.2.2**: 133.

Ecology **H.0**: 24, 49–50, 52–54, 56–58. **H.1.1.1**: 33. **N.2**: 300.

Econometric models **B.1**: 18. **B.3**: 17, 20, 41, 43, 53. **C**: 10. **F.3.1.1**: 44, 76. **F.3.2**: 41. **H.4**: 111. **I.2.1**: 178. **I.2.3**: 107. **J.4**: 5, 47, 53, 119. **J.5**: 10. **K.3**: 24, 104. **M.1**: 21. **N.1**: 91. **N.2**: 80, 187, 192. **O.1.2**: 12. **O.2.1**: 44, 75. **O.2.3**: 60. **O.3.1**: 2, 13, 45.

Econometrics **B.1**: 1, 6. **B.3**: 13, 28, 32, 48. **E**: 4. **F.3.1.2**: 21. **F.3.3**: 30. **G.1.1**: 7. **G.2.1**: 96. **H.2.1**: 73. **I.2.1**: 25. **I.2.3**: 41. **J.1**: 51, 57, 112. **L.2**: 48. **M.4**: 24. **O.2.1**: 78. **O.2.2**: 18.

Economic aid **F.1**: 44. **O.1.3**: 62, 67.

Economic analysis **B.3**: 34, 59. **C**: 11. **F.3.1.4**: 6–7. **H.1.1**: 8, 12. **H.1.1.1**: 23. **H.2.1**: 12. **I.2.1**: 93.

Economic behaviour **C**: 17, 76. **F.3.1.2**: 5. **F.3.1.3**: 9. **G.2.3**: 1. **I.2.1**: 64. **M.4**: 118.

Economic calculations **B.4**: 19.

Economic change **D**: 6. **E**: 5, 11. **F.1**: 12, 50, 75. **F.3.1.3**: 28. **F.3.1.4**: 18. **F.3.2**: 16, 42, 122. **F.3.3**: 4. **G.2.1**: 34–35, 67. **G.3.1**: 1. **G.3.3.5**: 50. **H.0**: 212. **H.2.2**: 11. **J.2**: 31, 238. **M.2**: 2. **M.4**: 120. **M.5**: 31. **N.1**: 8, 17, 23, 27, 39, 44, 53, 55–56, 58–59, 98, 127, 132, 147, 156, 188, 204, 259, 262, 270, 277, 293, 310. **N.2**: 127, 295, 312. **O.1.2**: 16. **O.1.3**: 44, 48. **O.2.2**: 95.

Economic choice **C**: 24.

Economic concentration
Entries also appear under:

CAPITAL CONCENTRATION
G.3.2: 9–10, 23. **H.3**: 39.

Economic conditions **A**: 1. **B.3**: 47. **C**: 83. **E**: 2–3. **F.1**: 1, 4–8, 10–11, 14, 17, 19–22, 24, 26–27, 31–35, 40, 43–48, 51–53, 55–60, 64–65, 68, 71, 73–78, 80–81, 83, 85, 88–89, 91–93. **F.3.1.1**: 61, 75, 92. **F.3.1.2**: 12. **F.3.1.3**: 28, 32. **F.3.2**: 57, 88, 114, 116. **F.3.3**: 5, 21, 26, 36, 54, 60. **G.1**: 55. **G.2.4**: 20. **H.2.1**: 66. **J.1**: 23. **J.2**: 178. **J.4**: 213. **L.3**: 24. **M.2**: 20. **M.5**: 2. **N.1**: 13, 46, 61, 124, 141, 152, 164, 188, 205, 213, 227. **N.2**: 247. **N.3**: 31. **O.1.2**: 1. **O.1.2.2**: 5. **O.1.2.4**: 20, 68, 92. **O.1.3**: 39. **O.2.1**: 14, 66, 78. **O.3.2**: 73.

Economic control **N.1**: 118.

Economic cooperation **N.1**: 93. **O.1.2.4**: 3, 8, 22, 31, 42, 46, 48. **O.1.3**: 13, 42, 47, 81, 84. **O.2.2**: 131. **O.2.4**: 10.

Economic criminality **F.3.1.4**: 5, 7, 23.

Economic crisis **F.1**: 82. **F.3.2**: 54, 73. **F.5**: 9, 41. **G.3.3.4**: 3. **K.2**: 42. **K.3**: 13. **L.2**: 66. **N.1**: 146. **O.2.2**: 66. **O.2.4**: 15. **O.3.3**: 61.

Economic decline **F.3.3**: 11, 54.

Economic dependence **O.3.3**: 17.

Economic development **C**: 55. **D**: 47. **F.1**: 67. **F.2**: 2, 14. **F.3.1.1**: 9, 21, 35–36, 39–40, 46, 84, 109, 119, 121. **F.3.1.2**: 6–7. **F.3.1.4**: 23. **F.3.2**: 1, 4, 9, 13, 15, 20, 23, 26–27, 30, 32, 39–40, 47, 56, 60, 64, 72, 78, 88, 90, 92, 94–97, 99–102, 106, 111–112, 116, 118, 120, 124, 127–128. **F.3.3**: 23. **F.4**: 2. **G.1**: 14, 29, 31. **G.1.3**: 7, 12. **G.2.1**: 145. **G.3.3.5**: 67. **H.0**: 29, 34, 56, 69, 86, 92, 105, 118, 158, 161–162, 164, 171, 173, 180, 182. **H.1.1.4**: 17. **H.2.1**: 69. **H.2.2**: 85. **J.2**: 58, 64, 126, 143. **J.4**: 97. **J.5**: 22. **L.1**: 31. **L.3**: 14. **M.2**: 32. **N.1**: 17, 32, 65, 87, 93, 99, 168. **N.2**: 89, 237. **O.1.2**: 8. **O.1.3**: 71–72. **O.2.2**: 87, 105. **O.3.1**: 23. **O.3.2**: 28.

Economic disequilibrium **N.2**: 158. **O.1.2**: 5.

Economic dynamics **B.1**: 19. **F.2**: 3. **N.1**: 41.

Economic efficiency **C**: 6. **G.1**: 9. **G.1.1**: 24. **G.3.3**: 3. **H.1.1.3**: 4. **H.1.2.1**: 41. **H.2.1**: 14, 53. **J.2**: 89. **J.4**: 111. **M.1**: 15. **M.5**: 22. **N.1**: 287. **N.2**: 159, 185, 303. **N.3**: 15, 20.

Economic elites **F.3.1.2**: 8.

Economic equilibrium **C**: 38. **D**: 71. **F.4**: 10. **F.5**: 11. **I.2.1**: 38. **J.1**: 14. **N.1**: 61. **O.2.1**: 52. **O.3.3**: 137.

Economic equilibrium theory **C**: 48. **F.4**: 5, 9.

Economic fluctuations **F.5**: 3, 35.

Economic forces **J.4**: 261.

Economic forecasts **B.3**: 22. **F.2**: 19, 22, 25–26, 30. **F.5**: 18. **H.2.2**: 155. **I.2.3**: 28. **J.1**: 108–109. **L.2**: 11. **N.2**: 3.

Economic geography **F.3.1.1**: 1, 22, 29, 40, 47. **H.1.1**: 14.

48, 54, 65, 105, 117, 167, 175, 178. **J.4**: 92, 138. **J.5**: 55. **K.3**: 105. **L.2**: 8. **M.1**: 3. **M.3**: 1. **M.4**: 7. **N.1**: 173. **N.3**: 46. **O.1.2.4**: 55. **O.3.1**: 44. **O.3.3**: 3.

Economic thought
Entries also appear under:
  HISTORY OF ECONOMIC THOUGHT
  D: 3, 28, 62, 64. **F.3.1.3**: 22. **L.2**: 64. **N.1**: 98.

Economics **C**: 9.

Economics of education **M.5**: 8, 11, 13, 25–28, 31, 36–37, 41. **N.2**: 147.

Economies of scale **G.3.3.4**: 4, 19. **H.2.1**: 49. **H.2.2**: 29, 148. **H.3**: 70. **J.3**: 6. **M.5**: 15.

Economists **A**: 2. **C**: 14. **D**: 41, 51, 68. **F.3.1.3**: 11. **G.4**: 4, 9.

Ecosystems **H.0**: 62, 70.

Education
Entries also appear under:
  ACCESS TO EDUCATION; ECONOMICS OF EDUCATION; HIGHER EDUCATION; PRESCHOOL EDUCATION; SECONDARY EDUCATION; VOCATIONAL EDUCATION
  F.3.2: 58. **G.2.2**: 5. **G.2.4**: 75. **G.3.3.5**: 122. **H.1.1.1**: 29. **M.5**: 2, 6, 9, 35. **O.2.4**: 21.

Education policy **M.5**: 3, 19, 31. **N.2**: 48.

Education reform **M.5**: 27.

Educational expenditure **M.5**: 4, 12, 34, 39.

Effective demand **I.2.1**: 181.

Effects
Entries also appear under:
  ENVIRONMENTAL EFFECTS
EFTA **O.1.2.4**: 4. **O.1.3**: 21.

Egalitarianism **K.3**: 64. **M.1**: 15.

Electoral mandates **N.2**: 269.

Electric power **H.0**: 14. **H.2.2**: 91, 111, 123, 126.

Electric power plants **H.2.2**: 92.

Electrical industries **G.3.3.5**: 100. **H.2.2**: 127.

Electricity **H.0**: 10, 63, 72. **H.2.2**: 90, 96, 114, 118, 128–129. **I.2.3**: 8–9, 17, 19, 35, 43, 48, 57. **L.2**: 6, 11. **N.1**: 272.

Electronic equipment **I.2.2**: 5.

Electronics **F.3.1.1**: 30.

Electronics industry **B.4**: 37. **G.1**: 46. **H.2.2**: 40, 44, 53, 67. **K.3**: 35, 45. **O.1.2.2**: 13. **O.2.2**: 131.

Elites
Entries also appear under:
  ECONOMIC ELITES
Emigration **F.1**: 89. **G.2.1**: 90. **G.2.3**: 6.

Empirical research **J.1**: 13, 32. **J.4**: 130.

Empirical tests **J.4**: 214, 291.

Empiricism **F.3.3**: 8.

Employees **G.1**: 58. **G.2.1**: 82. **G.2.4**: 2, 64, 114. **G.2.5**: 5, 28, 40. **G.3.3**: 10. **G.3.3.2**: 2. **K.3**: 21, 106.

Employers **G.2.4**: 48.

Employers' organizations **G.3.1**: 5.

Employment
Entries also appear under:
  FULL EMPLOYMENT; PARTTIME EMPLOYMENT; RURAL EMPLOYMENT; SECTORAL EMPLOYMENT; URBAN EMPLOYMENT
  F.3.1.1: 23, 121. **F.3.2**: 69. **F.3.3**: 25. **G.2.1**: 3–4, 12, 17, 20–21, 27, 57, 72. **G.2.2**: 4, 13, 20, 36, 40. **G.2.4**: 4, 31, 99. **G.2.5**: 40. **G.4**: 1. **H.1.1.4**: 29. **H.2.1**: 50. **H.3**: 75. **H.4**: 24. **I.2.1**: 29. **I.2.3**: 91. **J.2**: 4, 140. **K.3**: 3, 54, 66, 95. **L.2**: 97. **N.2**: 273.

Employment creation **F.3.1.1**: 111. **G.2.1**: 19, 26, 32. **G.2.2**: 11. **G.3.3.4**: 7. **N.3**: 49.

Employment level **G.2.1**: 18. **K.3**: 59.

Employment opportunities **G.2.5**: 33.

Employment policy **G.2.1**: 40. **G.2.2**: 1–2, 7, 15–16, 18, 22, 24, 27–28. **K.3**: 121. **N.1**: 169.

Employment situation **G.2.1**: 25.

Employment stability **G.2.1**: 170.

Employment theory **F.5**: 27.

Energy
Entries also appear under:
  BIOMASS ENERGY; NUCLEAR ENERGY; SOLAR ENERGY; WIND ENERGY
  H.0: 11, 22, 109, 144, 153. **H.2.2**: 2, 86, 97, 99–102, 104–106, 108, 117, 131. **I.2.3**: 24, 53, 59.

Energy conservation **H.0**: 12. **N.3**: 22.

Energy consumption **H.0**: 12. **H.1.2.1**: 7.

Energy economics **L.2**: 25.

Energy efficiency **H.0**: 12, 80. **L.2**: 34. **N.3**: 27.

Energy industry **H.0**: 13. **H.2.2**: 79, 98, 107, 116, 125, 130. **N.1**: 295. **O.1.2.3**: 13.

Energy market **I.2.3**: 43. **O.1.2.3**: 35. **O.3.2**: 59.

Energy planning **H.0**: 45. **H.2.2**: 95.

Energy policy **H.0**: 13. **H.2.2**: 80, 85, 87, 109, 124, 162. **I.2.3**: 8. **O.1.2.4**: 19.

Energy prices **I.2.3**: 48.

Energy resources **H.2.2**: 106. **I.2.3**: 23.

Energy sources
Entries also appear under:
  RENEWABLE ENERGY SOURCES
Energy taxes **N.2**: 31, 115, 128–129, 157, 163.

Energy utilization **H.3**: 11. **I.2.3**: 25.

Engels, Friedrich **D**: 30.

Engineering **H.2.2**: 59.

Engineers **G.1**: 49. **G.2.4**: 10.

Enterprises

Federalism **F.3.2**: 109. **N.2**: 297. **O.1.2.4**: 62. **O.2.3**: 22.

Fellman, Johan **B.3**: 54.

Female labour **F.3.1.2**: 10. **G.2.1**: 96, 103. **G.2.2**: 31–32.

Fertility **F.3.1.2**: 4, 9–11, 21. **G.2.2**: 31.

Fertilizers **H.1.1.1**: 3, 12.

Festivals **H.3**: 14.

Finance
Entries also appear under:
INDUSTRIAL FINANCE; INTERNATIONAL FINANCE; LOCAL FINANCE; PUBLIC FINANCE
B.4: 10, 53. **F.1**: 55. **F.3.2**: 29. **F.3.3**: 12, 18, 20. **F.5**: 1, 17. **G.3.3.3**: 14, 19. **G.3.3.5**: 8. **H.1.1**: 16. **H.2.1**: 18. **H.3**: 78. **H.4**: 36. **I.2.1**: 90. **J.1**: 28. **J.2**: 2, 16, 36, 48, 56, 133, 153, 160, 166. **J.4**: 240, 270, 279. **J.5**: 12. **L.1**: 19. **L.2**: 94. **N.1**: 74, 117, 197. **O.1.2.4**: 63. **O.2.3**: 37.

Financial accounting **B.4**: 7, 18, 30, 47, 57. **G.3.3.5**: 121.

Financial aid **O.1.3**: 23.

Financial analysis **F.3.2**: 48. **G.3.3.5**: 116. **J.4**: 78.

Financial assets **J.1**: 42, 85. **J.4**: 65, 102. **L.2**: 40. **N.2**: 309.

Financial centres **J.2**: 21.

Financial control **M.4**: 34.

Financial crisis **D**: 80. **F.5**: 2. **G.3.3.2**: 13. **N.2**: 120.

Financial incentives **G.1.3**: 15. **H.0**: 101.

Financial information **B.4**: 18. **F.2**: 23. **G.3.3.3**: 1. **G.3.3.5**: 102. **H.1.2.1**: 10. **J.4**: 64, 256.

Financial innovation **J.1**: 55. **J.2**: 60, 101. **J.4**: 171. **J.5**: 17. **N.1**: 245. **N.2**: 17.

Financial institutions **J.2**: 8, 10, 38–39, 42, 57, 73, 83, 87, 89, 188. **J.4**: 70, 75, 80, 92, 224. **N.1**: 207. **N.2**: 23. **O.1.2.4**: 87. **O.2.2**: 33.

Financial management **B.4**: 2. **E**: 9. **G.3.3**: 19. **G.3.3.5**: 112, 128. **J.4**: 95. **N.2**: 244.

Financial models **B.3**: 1, 21. **N.2**: 155. **N.3**: 5.

Financial planning **H.2.2**: 143.

Financial policy **J.4**: 43. **N.2**: 184. **O.1.2.4**: 58.

Financial reforms **I.2.3**: 92. **J.2**: 50, 141, 165, 198. **J.5**: 28. **O.2.3**: 23.

Financial reporting **B.4**: 26, 56, 65. **G.3.3.5**: 108–109, 118–119. **J.4**: 208.

Financial resources **F.1**: 18.

Financial risks **G.3.3.3**: 22. **H.2.1**: 3. **J.4**: 88.

Financial services **F.3.1.1**: 79. **G.2.5**: 50. **I.2.3**: 13. **J.2**: 19, 49, 58, 72, 86, 92, 111, 139, 148. **J.4**: 94, 161. **O.1.2.2**: 11. **O.1.2.4**: 78. **O.2.3**: 54.

Financial speculation **I.2.3**: 110. **J.1**: 65. **J.4**: 46. **O.2.1**: 31, 43, 85.

Financial systems **J.2**: 33, 41, 61, 81, 167, 173, 220. **J.5**: 16. **N.2**: 60. **O.1.2.3**: 29. **O.2.2**: 34.

Fire services **N.3**: 39.

Firm theory **G.1.3**: 16. **G.2.4**: 109. **G.3.3**: 33. **G.3.3.2**: 8. **G.3.3.3**: 39.

Firm value **H.2.1**: 82.

Fiscal administration **N.2**: 3, 36, 47, 109, 119, 137, 269.

Fiscal law **J.4**: 303. **N.2**: 96, 120, 180, 309.

Fiscal policy **F.3.1.2**: 13. **F.3.3**: 13. **G.2.1**: 32. **G.3.2**: 13. **J.2**: 217, 233. **J.5**: 2, 39, 45, 57. **L.2**: 85. **M.4**: 74. **N.1**: 144, 188, 318. **N.2**: 94, 127, 130, 132, 134, 137–140, 142–144, 147–152, 154–156, 158, 160–161, 164–165, 168, 170, 173–177, 181–185, 187, 199, 231, 250, 289, 297–298. **N.3**: 15. **O.1.2**: 14. **O.1.2.4**: 80, 84, 88. **O.1.3**: 25. **O.2.1**: 16, 65. **O.2.3**: 24, 48, 64. **O.3.1**: 33.

Fiscal theory **N.2**: 117, 292.

Fiscal transfer **N.3**: 21.

Fish **I.2.3**: 61.

Fish farming **H.1.1.2**: 37.

Fisheries **H.1.2.1**: 33, 38–40, 47.

Fishery economics **H.1.2.1**: 32, 37.

Fishery industry **G.1.1**: 33. **H.1.1.2**: 8. **H.1.2.1**: 41, 44–46, 48.

Fishery management **H.1.2.1**: 34–35, 43. **O.1.3**: 83.

Fishery policy **H.1.2.1**: 36, 42, 45.

Fishery resources **H.1.2.1**: 37.

Fitzhugh, George **D**: 15.

Fixed assets **G.3.3.3**: 31.

Fixed exchange rates **O.2.1**: 44, 53. **O.2.3**: 49.

Flexible exchange rates **I.2.3**: 3. **O.2.1**: 37, 53.

Flexible specialization **G.1.1**: 15.

Food **H.1.1**: 15. **H.1.2.1**: 5. **I.2.3**: 70. **O.3.1**: 51. **O.3.3**: 142.

Food aid **O.1.3**: 60.

Food consumption **L.2**: 73–74. **M.2**: 1.

Food industry **H.1.1.1**: 26. **H.1.2.1**: 11. **H.4**: 2, 7. **L.2**: 75. **O.3.1**: 73. **O.3.2**: 25.

Food policy **H.1.1.4**: 42. **N.1**: 151.

Food price policy **G.3.3.5**: 19.

Food prices **I.2.3**: 38. **O.3.2**: 25.

Food products **H.4**: 75.

Food security **H.1.1.4**: 50. **L.2**: 73, 79.

Food supply **F.3.2**: 61. **H.4**: 14. **I.2.3**: 30. **O.1.3**: 78. **O.3.3**: 28.

Forecasting techniques **F.2**: 24. **H.3**: 69.

Forecasts
Entries also appear under:

Indonesians **F.3.1.4**: 25.

Industrial accounting **B.4**: 37. **H.2.1**: 1.

Industrial adjustment **H.2.1**: 31, 36, 63, 81.

Industrial co-operatives **H.2.1**: 76.

Industrial development **F.3.1.1**: 45. **G.2.5**: 23. **G.3.3.4**: 18. **H.2.1**: 6, 21, 28, 61, 66, 74, 124. **O.3.2**: 30.

Industrial economics **H.2.1**: 47, 68, 82, 102, 119. **H.2.2**: 147, 151.

Industrial enterprises **E**: 13. **H.2.1**: 120. **N.2**: 151.

Industrial exports **H.2.1**: 1.

Industrial finance **J.2**: 6.

Industrial geography **F.3.1.1**: 26.

Industrial innovations **H.2.1**: 7.

Industrial investment **H.4**: 28. **L.3**: 9.

Industrial labour **H.2.1**: 88. **N.1**: 248.

Industrial management **G.1**: 4, 26, 58. **G.2.3**: 2. **G.3.1**: 3. **G.3.3.5**: 18, 88. **H.0**: 65, 85. **H.2.1**: 77, 79, 83–85, 89. **N.1**: 116, 164. **O.1.3**: 16.

Industrial organization **F.3.1.1**: 73. **G.1**: 23. **G.1.1**: 34. **G.3.3.5**: 72. **H.2.1**: 42, 53. **H.2.2**: 19.

Industrial policy **F.3.1.1**: 83, 123. **F.3.2**: 55. **G.1.3**: 13. **G.3.2**: 22. **H.2.1**: 77, 97, 100–101, 103–104, 106–107, 110–111, 114, 116–117. **H.2.2**: 20, 61, 77. **O.1.2.4**: 65, 72. **O.1.3**: 55. **O.3.3**: 77.

Industrial prices **I.2.3**: 52.

Industrial production **F.3.1.1**: 31. **H.0**: 63. **H.2.2**: 28, 32, 78, 145.

Industrial productivity **B.3**: 24. **F.3.1.1**: 114. **G.1.1**: 19. **G.1.3**: 10, 14. **H.2.1**: 122–123, 125, 127.

Industrial products **H.2.1**: 54, 122.

Industrial profit **K.3**: 88.

Industrial property **H.2.1**: 15.

Industrial psychology **G.3.1**: 3.

Industrial research **G.1**: 31, 37, 55.

Industrial sector **B.3**: 35. **H.2.1**: 64, 72. **H.2.2**: 92, 116.

Industrial society **H.4**: 4. **M.5**: 29. **N.1**: 225.

Industrial sociology **G.1**: 58. **G.2.5**: 45.

Industrial structure **F.3.3**: 33. **H.2.1**: 19, 36, 58. **I.2.1**: 90. **I.2.3**: 29. **N.1**: 165. **O.1.2**: 18. **O.1.3**: 44.

Industrialization **F.3.1.1**: 68. **F.3.2**: 28, 47, 98. **G.1.1**: 22. **G.2.4**: 72. **H.2.1**: 22, 32–33, 41, 47. **H.3**: 99. **N.1**: 103, 193. **N.3**: 17. **O.3.3**: 9, 41, 63.

Industrialized countries **F.3.2**: 15. **F.3.3**: 30. **G.1.2**: 3. **J.5**: 11. **O.1.2**: 7. **O.1.2.4**: 18.

Industry

Entries also appear under:

AGRICULTURAL INDUSTRY; AGROFOOD INDUSTRY; AIRCRAFT INDUSTRY; ARMAMENTS INDUSTRY; AUTOMOBILE INDUSTRY; CEMENT INDUSTRY; CHEMICAL INDUSTRY; CLOTHING INDUSTRY; COAL INDUSTRY; COMPUTER INDUSTRY; CONSTRUCTION INDUSTRY; CULTURAL INDUSTRY; DAIRY INDUSTRY; ELECTRICAL INDUSTRIES; ELECTRONICS INDUSTRY; ENERGY INDUSTRY; EXPORT-ORIENTED INDUSTRY; FISHERY INDUSTRY; FOOD INDUSTRY; FORESTRY INDUSTRY; FURNITURE INDUSTRY; HEAVY INDUSTRY; HOTEL INDUSTRY; IRON AND STEEL INDUSTRY; LIGHT INDUSTRY; LOCATION OF INDUSTRY; METAL INDUSTRY; MILLING INDUSTRY; NATIONALIZED INDUSTRY; OIL INDUSTRY; PETROCHEMICAL INDUSTRY; PHARMACEUTICAL INDUSTRY; POTTERY INDUSTRY; PULP AND PAPER INDUSTRY; RECORD INDUSTRY; SERVICE INDUSTRY; SHOE INDUSTRY; SMALL-SCALE INDUSTRY; SUGAR INDUSTRY; TELECOMMUNICATIONS INDUSTRY; TEXTILE INDUSTRY; TOBACCO INDUSTRY

B.4: 65. **F.3.2**: 17, 91. **G.1**: 3. **G.1.1**: 16. **G.1.2**: 10. **G.1.3**: 22. **G.2.1**: 111, 157. **G.2.4**: 102. **G.2.5**: 16. **G.3.3**: 24. **G.3.3.2**: 10. **G.3.3.3**: 18. **G.3.3.4**: 14. **G.3.3.5**: 91. **H.0**: 85. **H.1.1**: 18. **H.2.1**: 5, 8, 18, 20, 26, 29, 34–35, 75, 78, 96–97, 108. **H.2.2**: 23. **H.4**: 28, 68. **I.2.1**: 28, 101, 124, 149. **J.4**: 59, 274. **K.3**: 28. **L.2**: 52. **M.5**: 32, 38. **N.1**: 21, 88. **N.2**: 37. **O.1.2.3**: 18, 21. **O.1.2.4**: 91. **O.2.2**: 118. **O.2.3**: 69. **O.3.3**: 42.

Inflation

Entries also appear under:

HYPERINFLATION

D: 4. **F.1**: 84. **G.2.1**: 53, 155. **G.2.3**: 6. **G.2.4**: 61. **G.3.3.3**: 1. **H.1.1.3**: 11. **I.2.1**: 32–33, 123, 166. **I.2.2**: 3. **I.2.3**: 4, 84. **J.1**: 70–89, 92–93, 95–98, 101–105, 108–112. **J.2**: 29. **J.4**: 96, 127. **J.5**: 15, 23, 48, 53, 60. **K.2**: 3, 18. **K.3**: 10, 22, 69. **L.1**: 16. **M.2**: 2. **M.4**: 49. **N.1**: 42, 78, 298. **N.2**: 27, 57, 80, 239. **O.2.1**: 7, 37. **O.2.3**: 19, 30, 39.

Inflation controls **O.2.3**: 31.

Inflation rate **N.2**: 269.

Informal sector **F.1**: 46, 75. **F.3.2**: 48. **G.2.1**: 66. **G.3.3.4**: 8. **H.0**: 43. **H.4**: 4, 17, 19, 26–27, 33, 46–47, 49–50. **J.2**: 57–58, 61. **J.4**: 73. **L.1**: 19. **N.1**: 20.

Information

Entries also appear under:

ACCESS TO INFORMATION; ASYMMETRIC INFORMATION; BUSINESS INFORMATION; IMPERFECT INFORMATION

A: 15. **B.4**: 26, 35. **D**: 48. **F.5**: 23, 26. **G.1.3**: 6. **G.3.2**: 14. **G.3.3.3**: 19. **G.3.3.4**: 6. **G.3.3.5**: 124. **H.0**: 98. **I.2.1**: 34, 91, 152, 160, 169. **I.2.3**: 66. **J.2**: 26, 55, 59, 142, 204. **J.3**: 2. **J.4**: 24, 34, 46, 51, 83, 106, 192, 273, 275, 297, 305. **J.5**: 23. **L.2**: 22. **M.1**: 5. **N.1**: 122. **N.2**: 136.

International integration **M.3**: 3. **O.1.2.3**: 18. **O.1.2.4**: 29–30, 32–33, 59. **O.1.3**: 100. **O.2.3**: 44. **O.3.3**: 124.

International investment **J.4**: 156. **O.1.2.2**: 12. **O.2.2**: 80–84, 86–88, 91–98, 101, 103–109, 111–112, 114, 117–120, 123, 125–128.

International law **H.0**: 37. **O.1.3**: 28. **O.3.3**: 116.

International loans **N.2**: 251.

International market **O.1.2.3**: 12, 34. **O.2.2**: 89.

International migration **G.2.1**: 77, 83. **O.1.2.5**: 2–4.

International monetary operations **O.2.1**: 12, 18, 25, 27, 38, 42, 58, 82, 90. **O.2.3**: 2, 36, 39.

International monetary relations **O.2.4**: 3, 6, 17.

International monetary system **O.2.1**: 28, 35. **O.2.3**: 48.

International payments **O.2.1**: 35. **O.2.2**: 38, 77.

International politics **F.3.2**: 83.

International relations **F.1**: 1. **M.2**: 7. **O.1.2.4**: 42. **O.1.3**: 54.

International trade
Entries also appear under:
    EXPORTS; IMPORTS
B.3: 47. **B.4**: 37. **F.2**: 13. **F.3.1.1**: 19. **F.3.2**: 46, 114. **G.1.3**: 22. **H.1.2.1**: 22. **I.2.1**: 84. **O.1.2**: 6. **O.1.2.2**: 21. **O.1.3**: 27, 39–40. **O.2.1**: 94. **O.2.2**: 81. **O.2.3**: 58. **O.3.1**: 1, 3, 7, 14, 17, 19–20, 27, 31–32, 34, 38, 43–45, 49, 54, 56–58, 60, 62–63, 70, 72, 74. **O.3.2**: 1–2, 7, 15, 20, 35–36, 42, 46, 48, 52, 57, 62, 68, 71, 73, 79, 81. **O.3.3**: 1, 10, 14, 32, 43, 95, 107, 114, 125–126, 135.

Internationalism **H.2.1**: 6.

Internationalization **H.2.1**: 122. **H.2.2**: 1, 30. **O.1.2**: 9–10. **O.1.2.2**: 14–15. **O.1.2.3**: 9.

Interpersonal relations **B.3**: 62.

Interventionism **N.1**: 13.

Inventions **G.1.1**: 16. **G.1.3**: 23.

Inventories **B.4**: 29, 45. **H.2.1**: 11. **H.4**: 39, 44, 51, 56.

Investment
Entries also appear under:
    BUSINESS INVESTMENT; FOREIGN INVESTMENT; INDUSTRIAL INVESTMENT; INTERNATIONAL INVESTMENT; PRIVATE INVESTMENT; PUBLIC INVESTMENT; SAVINGS AND INVESTMENT
B.4: 18. **C**: 10, 82. **D**: 56, 74. **F.3.1.3**: 20. **F.3.3**: 21, 40–41, 55, 59. **G.1**: 38, 51. **G.1.3**: 11. **G.2.1**: 78. **G.2.5**: 16. **G.3.3.2**: 1, 4, 9. **G.3.3.3**: 22, 36. **G.3.3.5**: 37. **H.0**: 101. **H.1.1.1**: 5. **H.1.1.2**: 9. **H.2.1**: 65, 78. **H.2.2**: 12, 14, 104, 121, 128. **H.3**: 2, 56, 83. **J.2**: 21, 34. **J.4**: 133, 150–151, 154–158, 161–163. **L.1**: 1, 13. **L.3**: 5–6, 11, 13–16, 18–19, 26–27. **M.4**: 77, 81. **M.5**: 25, 28, 35. **N.1**: 86, 212. **N.2**: 34, 72,

136, 151, 309. **O.1.2.2**: 17. **O.1.2.4**: 52. **O.1.3**: 11, 85. **O.2.1**: 56–57. **O.2.2**: 40, 74, 81, 87–88.

Investment analysis **B.3**: 21. **G.3.3.3**: 23.

Investment banks **J.2**: 103.

Investment decision **B.4**: 52. **G.3.3.3**: 21, 30. **G.3.3.5**: 62. **H.0**: 202. **J.4**: 152.

Investment demand **G.3.2**: 21. **L.3**: 12, 25.

Investment expenditure **L.3**: 4.

Investment incentives **J.4**: 166.

Investment policy **H.0**: 179. **I.2.1**: 141. **L.3**: 20.

Investment promotion **I.2.3**: 27.

Investment rates **L.3**: 24.

Investment returns
Entries also appear under:
    RENT
J.4: 303.

Investment strategies **H.2.1**: 56. **J.4**: 9, 176, 207.

Investment theory **D**: 76.

Investment trusts **J.4**: 153, 160, 265.

Investments abroad **O.2.2**: 91.

Investors **B.4**: 38. **J.4**: 176, 287.

Invisible transactions **O.3.2**: 8.

Iron and steel industry **G.2.4**: 40. **H.2.1**: 3, 13. **H.2.2**: 133–136.

Irrationality **J.5**: 27.

Irrigation **H.1.1.1**: 10–11, 15.

Islam **F.3.2**: 99. **I.2.1**: 58. **J.2**: 27, 197. **N.1**: 231.

Islamic countries **F.3.3**: 3.

Islamic economics **F.1**: 1. **N.1**: 232. **N.2**: 246.

Islands **F.1**: 4.

Issue of money **J.2**: 71.

James, William **D**: 28.

Job change **G.2.1**: 153. **G.2.5**: 48.

Job search **G.2.1**: 9, 12, 33, 140–141, 153. **G.2.5**: 32.

Job security **G.2.2**: 18.

Job vacancies **G.2.5**: 53.

Joint committees **G.2.4**: 43.

Joint consultation **G.2.4**: 58.

Joint ventures **G.1**: 10. **G.1.3**: 2, 20. **G.3.2**: 4, 18, 41. **G.3.3.5**: 40. **H.2.1**: 55–56, 61. **O.1.2.2**: 1. **O.1.3**: 50. **O.2.2**: 130–133. **O.3.1**: 75. **O.3.2**: 40.

Judgement **B.3**: 46. **C**: 6. **I.2.1**: 172.

Jurisprudence **N.2**: 292.

Justice
Entries also appear under:
    DISTRIBUTIVE JUSTICE; ECONOMIC JUSTICE; SOCIAL JUSTICE
M.1: 3, 18.

Leasing **H.1.1.2**: 3.

Least-squares estimation **B.3**: 33.

Left **N.1**: 184.

Legal aspects **F.3.1.4**: 18, 22. **G.2.4**: 9. **H.3**: 75. **J.2**: 74. **J.4**: 224, 228. **L.2**: 85. **N.1**: 274, 320. **N.2**: 52.

Legal profession **G.2.5**: 44.

Legislation
Entries also appear under:
    ANTI-TRUST LEGISLATION; CAPITAL MARKET LEGISLATION
H.0: 113. **N.2**: 207.

Legislature **H.2.1**: 34.

Legitimacy **H.0**: 79. **N.1**: 56.

Legitimation **J.4**: 89.

Leisure **H.3**: 14, 17. **L.2**: 47. **M.2**: 9.

Leisure time **L.2**: 97.

Less developed countries **F.3.2**: 34, 82. **F.3.3**: 57. **G.1.1**: 13. **G.2.1**: 68. **J.1**: 87. **J.4**: 43. **M.5**: 35. **N.1**: 68. **N.2**: 267. **O.2.2**: 20. **O.3.1**: 10. **O.3.3**: 50.

Liability **F.3.1.4**: 3. **G.3.3.3**: 12. **H.0**: 122. **H.1.1.2**: 22. **J.2**: 130, 144, 147. **J.3**: 1, 15. **J.4**: 62. **L.2**: 33.

Liberalism
Entries also appear under:
    ECONOMIC LIBERALISM; NEOLIBERALISM
D: 22, 44. **F.3.1.3**: 22. **J.1**: 91, 100.

Liberalization
Entries also appear under:
    TRADE LIBERALIZATION
H.1.1.4: 6. **H.2.1**: 125. **H.3**: 89. **H.4**: 21. **J.2**: 166. **J.4**: 42–43, 133. **J.5**: 19, 28. **N.1**: 171. **O.1.3**: 14. **O.2.1**: 62. **O.2.2**: 34. **O.2.3**: 23.

Liberalization policy **H.2.1**: 100. **J.4**: 39. **J.5**: 29. **N.1**: 99.

Libraries **F.3.1.1**: 48.

Licenses **H.1.2.1**: 40. **H.2.1**: 45. **I.2.1**: 101.

Life cycles **B.2**: 4. **G.2.4**: 112. **L.3**: 5. **M.4**: 103.

Life insurance **J.3**: 7.

Life styles **G.2.3**: 10.

Light industry **H.2.1**: 30.

Linear models **F.4**: 8. **G.1.1**: 19. **L.2**: 9.

Linear programming **B.3**: 10, 50. **G.1.1**: 19. **J.4**: 172.

Liquidity **D**: 74. **J.1**: 13, 15. **J.4**: 63, 276. **J.5**: 30. **L.1**: 23. **M.4**: 113. **O.2.1**: 71.

Livestock **H.1.2.1**: 11.

Livestock industry **H.1.1.1**: 5.

Livestock production **H.1.2.1**: 13.

Loans
Entries also appear under:

BANK LOANS; INTERNATIONAL LOANS; MORTGAGE LOANS
H.1.1.3: 12. **J.2**: 35, 113, 233. **J.4**: 15. **L.1**: 6. **M.5**: 1, 40. **N.2**: 251. **O.2.2**: 1, 16, 25, 29.

Local communities **G.2.1**: 46.

Local finance **I.2.1**: 52. **N.1**: 6. **N.2**: 9, 45–46, 51, 133, 155, 166, 206, 315.

Local government **F.3.1.1**: 83. **G.2.4**: 46, 51. **H.1.1.4**: 41. **H.4**: 30. **I.2.1**: 52. **M.5**: 10. **N.1**: 10, 19, 27, 116. **N.2**: 24, 30, 38, 43, 46, 89, 270, 297. **N.3**: 37.

Local taxes **H.2.1**: 25. **N.2**: 20, 35, 121, 123.

Location of enterprises **F.3.1.1**: 2, 5, 7, 12, 18, 25, 32, 49, 120–121, 123. **H.4**: 32. **O.2.2**: 91.

Location of industry **F.3.1.1**: 4, 6, 11, 13, 24, 31, 33, 38, 43, 55. **G.1**: 47. **G.3.2**: 1. **H.2.1**: 31. **H.2.2**: 64.

Lockouts **G.2.4**: 69.

Loeb, Jacques **D**: 31.

Long waves **F.5**: 18.

Low income **G.2.5**: 24. **K.3**: 34, 105. **L.2**: 80. **M.2**: 5.

Loyalty **I.2.3**: 26. **L.2**: 68.

Machine tools **H.2.2**: 45. **O.3.3**: 42.

MacIntyre, Alisdair **D**: 73.

Macroeconomic policy **F.1**: 84. **J.5**: 43, 56. **N.1**: 75, 105, 107, 123–125, 175. **O.1.3**: 29.

Macroeconomics **B.1**: 5, 12–13, 18, 20–21, 23. **B.3**: 23. **C**: 1, 45, 47. **D**: 11, 54, 63. **F.1**: 86. **F.2**: 26. **F.3.1.1**: 59. **F.3.3**: 10, 40. **G.2.1**: 28, 47. **G.2.2**: 4. **G.3.2**: 29. **H.0**: 28. **H.1.1**: 18. **H.2.1**: 48. **H.2.2**: 158. **H.3**: 100. **H.4**: 33. **I.2.1**: 47, 86. **J.1**: 7, 69. **J.2**: 11. **J.5**: 26. **K.2**: 31. **L.1**: 2. **L.2**: 17. **N.1**: 33, 73–74, 108, 233, 296. **N.2**: 44, 47. **O.1.3**: 57, 72. **O.2.1**: 50. **O.2.2**: 36, 68. **O.3.2**: 27.

Maize **H.1.2.1**: 26, 31.

Malthus, T. R. **D**: 24.

Management
Entries also appear under:
    AGRICULTURAL MANAGEMENT; BUSINESS MANAGEMENT; DEMAND MANAGEMENT; ECONOMIC MANAGEMENT; ENVIRONMENTAL MANAGEMENT; FARM MANAGEMENT; FINANCIAL MANAGEMENT; FISHERY MANAGEMENT; FOREST MANAGEMENT; HOSPITAL MANAGEMENT; INDUSTRIAL MANAGEMENT; MIDDLE MANAGEMENT; PERSONNEL MANAGEMENT; PORTFOLIO MANAGEMENT; PRODUCT MANAGEMENT; PRODUCTION MANAGEMENT; PUBLIC MANAGEMENT; RESOURCE MANAGEMENT; RISK MANAGEMENT; STOCK MANAGEMENT; SUPPLY MANAGEMENT; TOP MANAGEMENT; WASTE MANAGEMENT; WATER MANAGEMENT

Monetary growth **J.1**: 27, 40–41. **J.4**: 227.

Monetary history **D**: 37.

Monetary models **B.3**: 44. **J.1**: 1, 41, 94. **O.2.1**: 84.

Monetary policy
Entries also appear under:
INTEREST RATE POLICY
B.2: 2. **F.3.3**: 13. **F.4**: 2. **H.1.2.1**: 26. **J.1**: 11, 13, 20, 23, 37, 71, 89, 101. **J.2**: 52, 129, 216, 219–220. **J.4**: 171. **J.5**: 2–8, 10–11, 13–22, 25–27, 30–37, 39–51, 53–55, 57, 59–61. **K.2**: 25. **N.1**: 207. **O.1.2**: 3, 12. **O.1.2.4**: 85. **O.2.1**: 8, 25, 44. **O.2.2**: 9. **O.2.3**: 3, 6–7, 11–13, 15–16, 20–21, 23, 26, 32, 47–49, 65–66.

Monetary reform **O.2.1**: 35.

Monetary relations **O.2.4**: 1.

Monetary reserves **O.2.3**: 46.

Monetary systems
Entries also appear under:
INTERNATIONAL MONETARY SYSTEM
J.1: 17, 34. **J.2**: 75. **O.2.1**: 28.

Monetary theory **D**: 52. **J.1**: 8, 16, 39. **J.2**: 177. **L.1**: 16. **O.2.3**: 40.

Monetary unification **O.2.3**: 47, 52.

Monetary unions
Entries also appear under:
EUROPEAN MONETARY UNION
J.1: 43. **N.1**: 185. **N.2**: 183. **O.1.2.4**: 62. **O.2.1**: 63. **O.2.3**: 7, 40, 43, 45, 48, 51, 56.

Money
Entries also appear under:
COMMODITY MONEY; DEMAND FOR MONEY; ISSUE OF MONEY
D: 4, 37, 39. **F.3.3**: 17. **F.4**: 7. **F.5**: 16. **I.1**: 3. **J.1**: 5, 14, 22, 25–27, 35–36, 50, 52, 69, 76, 97, 104. **J.2**: 158, 215. **J.4**: 125. **J.5**: 12, 58. **M.1**: 21. **O.1.2.4**: 89. **O.2.1**: 64.

Money and credit **D**: 52.

Money market **J.1**: 21. **J.2**: 187. **J.5**: 59.

Money supply **I.2.3**: 52. **J.1**: 7, 9, 37, 96. **J.4**: 137. **J.5**: 5, 9, 49. **K.1**: 3. **K.2**: 13. **O.2.1**: 13.

Monopolies **G.1.3**: 21. **G.3.2**: 1, 12–13. **H.3**: 81. **I.2.1**: 6, 22–24, 35, 58, 66, 74, 102, 165–166, 173. **I.2.3**: 18. **N.1**: 118, 313. **N.2**: 159. **N.3**: 55.

Monopolistic competition **G.2.1**: 53. **I.2.1**: 33, 96–97. **I.2.3**: 47.

Monopoly power **I.2.1**: 113.

Morals **H.4**: 37. **M.4**: 119.

Mortality **K.3**: 11.

Mortgage loans **J.2**: 237.

Mortgages **I.2.3**: 81, 85, 90. **J.2**: 162, 235–236, 238–239, 241–247. **J.4**: 286. **L.2**: 108.

Mothers

Entries also appear under:
EARLY MOTHERHOOD;   WORKING MOTHERS
M.4: 3, 104. **N.2**: 82.

Motivation **F.3.1.1**: 90. **F.4**: 6.

Motorways **H.3**: 64.

Multidimensional analysis **B.4**: 43.

Multilateral trade **O.3.3**: 119.

Multilateralism **O.1.3**: 41.

Multinational enterprises **A**: 18. **F.3.2**: 17. **G.1**: 46. **G.2.4**: 23, 50. **G.2.5**: 51. **G.3.3.5**: 11, 52. **H.0**: 159. **H.2.2**: 27, 132. **I.2.1**: 103. **N.3**: 29. **O.1.2.2**: 1, 3–21, 23–25. **O.1.2.4**: 91. **O.2.1**: 5, 59. **O.2.2**: 20, 27, 37, 101. **O.2.3**: 66. **O.3.3**: 47.

Multiplier **B.3**: 37. **J.1**: 30.

Multivariate analysis **G.2.4**: 62. **H.1.1.2**: 34.

Muslims **I.1**: 2.

Nation state **J.2**: 165.

National accounting **B.4**: 51.

National budget **M.4**: 92. **N.2**: 33.

National income **B.4**: 51. **F.2**: 2, 7–8, 10, 17. **H.0**: 29. **K.1**: 1.

National planning **N.2**: 58.

National product
Entries also appear under:
GROSS NATIONAL PRODUCT

National security **F.1**: 2.

Nationalism
Entries also appear under:
ECONOMIC NATIONALISM
F.3.2: 86. **H.2.2**: 120.

Nationalization **J.2**: 126, 172. **N.3**: 29–30.

Nationalized industry **H.2.1**: 23.

Natural disasters **H.0**: 46.

Natural gas **H.2.2**: 87, 94, 152–153, 162. **I.2.3**: 8. **N.3**: 48. **O.3.2**: 53, 85.

Natural resources **F.3.1.1**: 92. **G.1.1**: 33. **H.0**: 30, 34, 38, 42, 126–127, 131–135, 137, 139, 141–143, 146, 149–150, 172, 177, 185. **H.1.1.2**: 4. **H.1.2.1**: 13. **H.2.2**: 23. **I.2.1**: 131. **N.2**: 86.

Nature **H.0**: 29.

Needs
Entries also appear under:
HOUSING NEEDS

Neighbourhoods **I.2.3**: 104.

Neoclassical economics **C**: 44, 50. **D**: 42, 76. **F.3.2**: 35. **F.4**: 12. **H.0**: 31. **I.2.1**: 76. **L.3**: 18.

Neoconservatism **O.1.3**: 22.

Neoinstitutionalism **D**: 8.

Neoliberalism **N.1**: 163.

Network analysis **B.3**: 12, 31. **H.2.1**: 83.

Neutrality **F.3.1.1**: 90. **J.5**: 35. **N.2**: 75, 100, 112, 180, 289.

New technology **G.1**: 23, 45. **G.2.1**: 112. **G.2.2**: 16. **G.2.4**: 28. **G.3.3.5**: 65. **H.2.1**: 7, 27, 40. **H.2.2**: 58. **H.4**: 107.

Newly industrializing countries **F.3.2**: 33, 39, 79, 87. **G.2.1**: 49. **H.2.1**: 104. **O.1.2.4**: 18. **O.2.2**: 13. **O.3.3**: 8.

News **G.2.4**: 69.

Noise **H.0**: 20.

Non-governmental organizations **H.0**: 143.

Non-linear models **O.2.1**: 49.

Non-profit organizations **B.4**: 9, 64. **G.2.5**: 40. **G.3.3**: 29. **G.3.3.5**: 66, 115. **M.4**: 62, 65.

Non-renewable resources **H.0**: 138, 155. **I.2.1**: 12. **N.2**: 157, 159, 219.

North Amerindians **F.3.1.1**: 92. **H.0**: 149. **H.1.1.2**: 20.

North-South relations **F.3.2**: 25, 73. **H.0**: 165, 183. **O.1.1**: 3. **O.1.3**: 10, 30. **O.3.1**: 28. **O.3.2**: 27. **O.3.3**: 109, 135.

North-South trade **O.3.3**: 58.

Nuclear energy **H.0**: 33. **H.2.2**: 112.

Nuclear fuels **H.2.2**: 120.

Nurses **G.2.1**: 113. **G.2.2**: 37.

Nutrition **N.1**: 151.

OAU **O.1.2.4**: 1.

Observation **B.1**: 10.

Obstacles to development **H.2.1**: 74.

Occupational accidents **M.4**: 10.

Occupational choice **G.4**: 6.

Occupational mobility **G.2.1**: 78–80, 84. **G.2.5**: 38. **K.2**: 22.

Occupational qualification **G.2.5**: 50, 59.

Occupational safety **G.2.3**: 1–2, 5, 7, 10, 12, 15, 17.

Occupational segregation **G.4**: 1.

Occupations
Entries also appear under:
LEGAL PROFESSION
G.4: 2–3, 8. **K.3**: 14.

OECD **F.2**: 13. **G.2.1**: 122–123, 138. **H.0**: 17. **H.3**: 11. **H.4**: 107. **J.1**: 54. **L.1**: 21. **M.4**: 24. **N.1**: 42, 317. **N.2**: 240. **O.1.3**: 34.

Oil
Entries also appear under:
VEGETABLE OILS
F.3.1.1: 74. **H.0**: 151. **H.2.2**: 93. **J.4**: 28. **K.3**: 19. **L.2**: 72. **N.2**: 163. **O.1.2.3**: 2, 28. **O.2.2**: 30.

Oil companies **H.2.2**: 115, 152.

Oil exploration **H.2.2**: 89, 153, 160, 163.

Oil industry **F.3.3**: 55. **G.2.1**: 17. **H.0**: 32. **H.2.1**: 30. **H.2.2**: 151, 154–155, 157–159, 161–163. **I.2.3**: 49. **O.3.2**: 14. **O.3.3**: 16.

Oil market **I.2.3**: 12, 23, 46, 58. **O.1.2.3**: 3, 13, 23, 26.

Oil policy **L.1**: 8.

Oil price **I.2.3**: 25, 62. **N.2**: 158. **O.1.2.3**: 8, 24, 38–39. **O.2.3**: 43. **O.3.1**: 40.

Older workers **G.2.1**: 14. **G.2.2**: 8.

Oligopoly **B.4**: 26. **F.3.1.1**: 38. **G.1.3**: 2. **G.3.2**: 11, 17. **G.3.3**: 24. **G.3.3.3**: 29. **H.2.1**: 53, 71. **H.4**: 28. **I.2.1**: 9, 12, 14–15, 39–40, 49, 61, 69–70, 99, 133, 135. **I.2.3**: 47. **J.4**: 297. **M.1**: 22. **N.2**: 14, 37, 162. **O.3.1**: 3. **O.3.3**: 94.

One-parent families **F.3.1.3**: 3. **M.4**: 104. **N.2**: 82.

On-the-job training **G.2.5**: 13. **K.2**: 39.

OPEC **H.2.2**: 160, 162. **I.2.3**: 23, 25. **O.1.2.3**: 2, 8, 29. **O.2.2**: 28. **O.2.3**: 43. **O.3.2**: 53.

Open economies **B.3**: 25. **F.3.3**: 15, 33. **F.5**: 7, 35. **G.1**: 52. **G.2.1**: 127. **J.1**: 60. **L.1**: 5. **N.2**: 10, 102, 174, 184, 188, 220. **O.1.2.5**: 3. **O.2.2**: 54. **O.3.1**: 11. **O.3.3**: 77.

Opinion
Entries also appear under:
FREEDOM OF OPINION; PUBLIC OPINION

Optimal taxation **N.2**: 219–224, 303. **O.3.3**: 38.

Option pricing **I.2.1**: 164. **I.2.3**: 2. **J.4**: 193–194, 233, 250–251, 255, 272, 304.

Options on stocks **J.4**: 140, 225, 230–231.

Organization
Entries also appear under:
ADMINISTRATIVE ORGANIZATION; BUSINESS ORGANIZATION; ECONOMIC ORGANIZATION; INDUSTRIAL ORGANIZATION; WORK ORGANIZATION
G.3.3: 20. **G.3.3.5**: 57.

Organization theory **G.3.2**: 31. **G.3.3**: 17. **H.4**: 3. **J.4**: 309.

Organizational analysis **G.2.4**: 21. **G.3.3**: 30.

Organizational behaviour **C**: 40. **D**: 42. **G.3.1**: 3. **G.3.3.5**: 32. **H.2.1**: 70. **K.3**: 86.

Organizational change **G.1**: 26, 58. **G.3.3.2**: 14. **J.2**: 124.

Organizational effectiveness **E**: 13. **G.3.3**: 32. **G.3.3.5**: 20, 54–55, 128. **J.2**: 30, 170.

Organizational size **G.3.3.4**: 16.

Organizational structure **G.2.5**: 4, 7, 25. **G.3.1**: 2. **G.3.3**: 23. **G.3.3.5**: 99. **H.4**: 42. **N.2**: 107.

Organizations
Entries also appear under:
NON-PROFIT ORGANIZATIONS; PROFESSIONAL ORGANIZATIONS; VOLUNTARY ORGANIZATIONS
A: 17. **C**: 71. **G.1**: 26. **G.3.3**: 35. **G.3.3.1**: 17. **G.3.3.5**: 34. **H.2.1**: 83.

Regional development **F.3.1.1**: 50–51, 53–54, 62–65, 67, 69, 72–74, 78, 81–82. **F.3.2**: 92, 109. **G.1**: 5, 47. **G.3.3**: 20. **H.0**: 141. **H.3**: 17. **N.1**: 137. **O.1.2.4**: 2, 49. **O.1.3**: 100. **O.3.3**: 66.

Regional disparities **F.3.1.1**: 75, 83. **F.3.2**: 125. **G.1**: 5. **G.1.1**: 1. **K.2**: 25. **M.2**: 17.

Regional economic development **F.3.1.1**: 45.

Regional economics **B.3**: 41. **F.2**: 30. **F.3.1.1**: 57, 66, 79, 86. **G.2.1**: 144. **G.2.2**: 11. **G.3.3**: 7. **H.1.1.1**: 24. **J.2**: 199. **L.2**: 78. **M.5**: 43. **O.1.2.4**: 48. **O.2.3**: 51.

Regional integration **O.1.2.4**: 15, 35, 37, 43–44. **O.1.3**: 17, 102.

Regional markets **O.1.3**: 41.

Regional planning **F.3.1.1**: 52, 55–56, 58, 68, 71, 73, 75. **G.2.1**: 99. **H.0**: 102. **N.1**: 248.

Regional policy **F.3.1.1**: 87.

Regional variation **H.2.2**: 46.

Regionalism **F.3.2**: 125. **H.1.1.4**: 7. **H.2.1**: 103. **H.2.2**: 44. **J.2**: 224–225. **O.1.2.4**: 11, 13. **O.1.3**: 41, 49.

Regionalization **F.3.1.1**: 59. **H.1.1.1**: 24. **O.3.2**: 63.

Regions **G.1.3**: 5.

Regression analysis **B.3**: 5, 44. **B.4**: 63. **G.2.1**: 1. **K.2**: 32.

Regulation
Entries also appear under:
  CAPITAL MARKET REGULATION; MARKET REGULATION; PRICE REGULATION
  F.3.1.1: 64. **F.3.1.4**: 3. **G.1.2**: 13. **G.2.1**: 43. **G.2.3**: 5. **G.3.2**: 7–8, 33, 38, 40. **H.0**: 24, 72, 110, 170, 196. **H.1.1.4**: 42. **H.2.1**: 34, 60. **H.3**: 27, 75, 85, 89. **H.4**: 90. **I.1.2.1**: 58, 150, 159. **I.2.3**: 8, 15, 33, 48. **J.2**: 87, 108. **J.3**: 10. **J.4**: 15, 45, 54, 60, 66, 80, 84, 211, 236. **M.4**: 8. **N.1**: 117, 279, 302, 313. **N.2**: 37, 98, 266. **N.3**: 4, 9, 36, 44. **O.1.2.4**: 76. **O.2.3**: 54.

Regulatory policy **H.0**: 134, 174. **N.2**: 58.

Reinsurance **J.3**: 4, 15.

Relative prices **I.2.2**: 3. **K.3**: 19. **L.3**: 21.

Reliability **H.2.2**: 91.

Religion **D**: 18.

Remittances **O.1.2.5**: 6.

Renewable energy sources **H.0**: 114, 156. **H.1.1.1**: 34. **H.2.2**: 127.

Renewable resources **H.0**: 129, 147.

Rent
Entries also appear under:
  LAND RENT
  G.1: 9. **H.1.1**: 11. **H.1.1.2**: 6. **H.1.2**: 2. **H.2.2**: 157. **I.2.1**: 31. **I.2.3**: 16, 63, 98. **K.3**: 80. **L.2**: 89. **O.3.3**: 87.

Rents **I.2.3**: 97.

Rent-seeking **C**: 17. **F.3.1.3**: 20. **F.3.3**: 58. **H.3**: 61.

Research
Entries also appear under:
  ACCOUNTING RESEARCH; AGRICULTURAL RESEARCH; ECONOMIC RESEARCH; EMPIRICAL RESEARCH; INDUSTRIAL RESEARCH; MANAGEMENT RESEARCH; SCIENTIFIC RESEARCH; SOCIAL SCIENCE RESEARCH; SOCIOLOGICAL RESEARCH
  B.1: 24. **F.3.2**: 121. **G.1.3**: 22. **G.3.3.1**: 8. **G.3.3.5**: 127. **H.0**: 57. **H.1.1.1**: 19. **N.2**: 132. **O.1.2.4**: 72.

Research and development **G.1**: 6, 10, 15, 17, 19. **G.1.2**: 1. **G.1.3**: 1–2, 4–6, 9, 11, 16, 18, 20–23. **G.2.1**: 58. **H.2.1**: 16, 94. **H.2.2**: 43. **H.4**: 8, 34. **O.3.2**: 60.

Research methods **A**: 11. **B.2**: 1. **B.4**: 53.

Research policy **G.1.3**: 17. **G.3.3.4**: 17. **O.1.2.4**: 64.

Research programmes **A**: 16.

Residence **K.3**: 74.

Residential mobility **G.2.5**: 5. **L.2**: 23, 82.

Resource allocation **C**: 6. **G.1**: 51. **G.1.2**: 15. **G.2.5**: 54. **G.3.3**: 32. **G.3.3.3**: 17. **G.3.3.5**: 120. **H.0**: 57, 128, 196. **H.1.1.2**: 4. **H.2.1**: 93. **I.2.1**: 69. **J.4**: 147. **M.2**: 29. **M.5**: 10. **N.1**: 90, 137. **N.2**: 268. **O.2.2**: 68. **O.2.3**: 54. **O.2.4**: 8.

Resource conservation **H.0**: 140, 146.

Resource depletion **H.0**: 131.

Resource exploitation **F.2**: 5. **H.0**: 137. **H.2.2**: 139.

Resource exploration **N.1**: 34.

Resource management **C**: 59. **H.0**: 127, 129, 142, 147, 150–151, 157, 215. **H.1.1.1**: 37.

Resource utilization **H.0**: 154.

Responsibility
Entries also appear under:
  STATE RESPONSIBILITY
  G.2.4: 63. **G.3.3.5**: 128. **M.3**: 3.

Restriction **I.2.3**: 88.

Retail prices **H.4**: 105. **I.2.1**: 128. **I.2.3**: 37.

Retail trade **G.2.3**: 8. **H.4**: 72, 88–93, 95, 97–105. **I.2.1**: 162. **I.2.2**: 6. **I.2.3**: 54, 61. **K.3**: 82. **L.2**: 5, 70. **O.3.2**: 65.

Retirement **H.3**: 10. **K.3**: 16. **M.4**: 72, 74, 92.

Retirement pensions **M.4**: 85.

Return migration **F.3.1.2**: 5. **O.1.2.5**: 6.

Returns to scale **G.1**: 16. **G.1.1**: 27. **H.2.1**: 26. **H.4**: 41. **O.3.1**: 72. **O.3.2**: 66.

Revealed preferences **C**: 26. **L.1**: 43.

Ricardo, David **D**: 24. **N.1**: 229.

Rice **G.2.1**: 13. **H.1.1.1**: 18, 36. **H.1.2.1**: 28.

Right **N.1**: 184.

Right to work **G.2.2**: 14.

Rights
Entries also appear under:
 PROPERTY RIGHTS
 F.3.1.4: 9. **H.0**: 79.

Risk
Entries also appear under:
 FINANCIAL RISKS
 B.3: 21, 34. **B.4**: 10, 16, 54. **C**: 78–85. **G.3.3**: 9.
 G.3.3.5: 24, 59. **H.1.1**: 9. **H.1.1.4**: 17. **H.2.1**:
 92. **H.2.2**: 7, 76. **I.2.1**: 59. **J.2**: 15, 45, 114,
 158, 165, 182, 243, 246. **J.3**: 13. **J.4**: 88,
 181, 184–201, 240. **L.1**: 34. **L.2**: 40. **M.4**: 10.
 N.2: 240, 291. **O.2.1**: 2, 29, 43. **O.2.2**: 11, 72,
 90, 101, 103. **O.2.3**: 46. **O.3.2**: 68.

Risk management **G.3.3.5**: 26, 58, 76. **H.0**: 66.
 J.2: 63. **J.4**: 195. **N.1**: 25.

Risk theory **J.4**: 170. **O.2.1**: 67.

Rivers **H.0**: 141.

Road traffic **H.3**: 6.

Road transport **H.3**: 65, 67, 70.

Roads **N.3**: 37.

Robertson, Dennis Holme **F.5**: 16. **N.1**: 120.

Robinson, Joan **D**: 50.

Rubber **H.1.2.1**: 15.

Rural areas **F.3.1.1**: 82, 91. **F.3.1.3**: 4. **F.3.2**: 48.
 G.2.1: 74. **H.1.1.2**: 14. **J.2**: 56. **K.2**: 8. **K.3**:
 55. **L.1**: 14.

Rural communities **F.3.1.1**: 95. **F.3.1.2**: 3.

Rural credit **J.2**: 57, 76, 91. **L.1**: 27.

Rural development **F.3.1.1**: 90, 96, 99. **F.3.2**: 3.
 H.0: 38, 177, 197. **H.1.1.2**: 5. **H.1.1.4**: 3, 19,
 24. **H.3**: 28, 87. **M.4**: 5. **N.1**: 103, 193.

Rural economics **F.3.1.1**: 89, 97. **H.3**: 28. **J.2**: 7,
 93.

Rural employment **G.2.1**: 41.

Rural housing **L.2**: 34.

Rural policy **F.3.1.1**: 93.

Rural poverty **M.2**: 26, 34–36.

Rural schools **M.5**: 41.

Rural society **H.1.1.2**: 29.

Rural women **G.2.2**: 38.

Rural-urban migration **F.3.1.1**: 67.

Rural-urban relations **F.3.1.1**: 28, 94.

Safety
Entries also appear under:
 OCCUPATIONAL SAFETY; PRODUCT
 SAFETY
 G.2.4: 71. **H.3**: 71.

Sales **I.2.3**: 88.

Sales taxes **N.2**: 85, 88, 127, 309. **O.1.2.4**: 88.

Samples **K.3**: 18.

Samuelson, Paul **J.1**: 35.

Sanctions
Entries also appear under:
 ECONOMIC SANCTIONS

Savings
Entries also appear under:
 HOUSEHOLD SAVINGS
 D: 74. **F.3.1.3**: 24. **F.3.2**: 46, 102. **F.3.3**: 59. **J.2**:
 90, 113, 126, 145, 188, 211, 233. **L.1**: 1–2,
 7–8, 14–18, 20, 22, 24–26, 28, 30–31,
 33–34, 36, 41. **L.3**: 22. **M.4**: 71. **N.2**: 59.
 O.1.2.5: 6. **O.2.2**: 120.

Savings and investment **F.3.3**: 13. **J.2**: 120. **J.4**:
 159. **L.1**: 5, 9, 27, 29, 32, 35, 37–39. **M.4**: 96.
 N.2: 4. **O.1.2.4**: 59.

Savings banks **H.4**: 88. **J.2**: 47, 235.

Scarcity **G.3.3**: 13. **H.0**: 146, 155.

Schmoller, von, Gustav **D**: 34.

Schooling **K.2**: 39. **K.3**: 51. **M.5**: 30.

Schools
Entries also appear under:
 PRIVATE SCHOOLS; RURAL SCHOOLS;
 SECONDARY SCHOOLS; TECHNICAL
 SCHOOLS
 A: 9. **M.5**: 10, 37.

Science
Entries also appear under:
 COMPUTER SCIENCE; HISTORY OF
 SCIENCE; INFORMATION SCIENCES;
 PHILOSOPHY OF SCIENCE
 C: 37. **F.3.1.1**: 49, 123. **F.3.3**: 53. **G.1**: 44.
 G.1.3: 12.

Science policy **G.1**: 14. **G.1.3**: 13. **G.3.3.5**: 67.

Scientific and technical progress **G.1**: 43. **G.1.3**:
 23.

Scientific cooperation **G.1.3**: 2.

Scientific research **H.0**: 112.

Scientists **G.1**: 49.

Sea **H.3**: 73, 77.

Sea traffic **H.3**: 76.

Sea transport **H.0**: 91. **H.3**: 78. **O.3.3**: 46.

Seabed **H.0**: 152.

Seasonal fluctuations **F.5**: 28–29, 43.

Seasonality **B.1**: 18. **G.2.1**: 114. **J.4**: 160, 244,
 261, 290. **O.2.1**: 36.

Secondary education **A**: 5.

Secondary schools **M.5**: 7–8, 39.

Sectoral development **F.3.2**: 109.

Sectoral employment **K.2**: 29.

Securities issues **J.4**: 34, 52.

Segregation
Entries also appear under:
 OCCUPATIONAL SEGREGATION; RACIAL
 SEGREGATION

Self **D**: 34.

Self-employed workers **G.2.1**: 36, 89, 114, 125. **G.3.3.1**: 12. **M.5**: 9.

Self-government **F.1**: 39.

Self-management **N.1**: 257.

Self-reliance **N.1**: 36.

Service industry **F.3.3**: 64. **G.2.1**: 21. **G.2.2**: 25. **G.3.3.5**: 61. **H.4**: 64, 106–108, 111. **I.2.3**: 40. **L.3**: 7. **O.1.2.2**: 11. **O.3.2**: 28.

Sex differentiation **G.2.2**: 17.

Sex discrimination **G.2.2**: 40–41. **K.3**: 116.

Sex inequality **K.3**: 121.

Sheep **H.1.2.1**: 6, 9.

Shifting cultivation **H.1.1.1**: 37.

Shipbuilding **H.0**: 91.

Shoe industry **H.2.2**: 21. **O.3.2**: 9.

Shortage
Entries also appear under:
   CAPITAL SHORTAGE; LABOUR SHORTAGE
I.2.1: 126, 176. **J.1**: 62. **N.1**: 174, 251.

Simulation **B.3**: 11. **G.1.1**: 25. **H.2.2**: 158. **H.3**: 83. **M.4**: 11.

Single European Act **O.1.2.4**: 85. **O.1.3**: 1.

Single European market
Entries also appear under:
   SINGLE EUROPEAN ACT
F.3.1.1: 25. **F.3.2**: 119. **G.1.1**: 26. **G.2.1**: 87. **G.2.5**: 37. **H.3**: 36. **H.4**: 16. **J.2**: 86, 161, 184, 189, 210. **J.4**: 61. **L.2**: 85. **L.3**: 7. **N.2**: 88. **O.1.2.3**: 35. **O.1.2.4**: 27, 37, 47, 60, 78, 83–84, 86, 88. **O.2.4**: 1, 18. **O.3.1**: 21. **O.3.2**: 65.

Siting decisions **F.3.1.1**: 7.

Size of enterprise **G.1**: 27. **G.1.3**: 9, 19. **G.2.1**: 21. **G.2.5**: 43. **G.3.3.4**: 11. **G.3.3.5**: 113. **J.4**: 295.

Skilled workers **G.2.1**: 85, 90. **G.2.5**: 45. **G.4**: 8.

Skills **G.1.1**: 12. **G.1.2**: 17. **G.2.1**: 140. **G.2.5**: 52. **G.3.3.5**: 3. **H.2.2**: 73. **K.2**: 28. **M.5**: 29.

Small and medium sized enterprises **F.3.1.4**: 25. **G.3.3**: 14. **G.3.3.1**: 3, 12, 17. **G.3.3.2**: 12. **G.3.3.3**: 15. **G.3.3.4**: 1–2, 4–9, 12–15, 18–20, 22. **H.2.2**: 46. **H.4**: 78. **J.2**: 2, 4, 67–68. **J.4**: 91. **K.3**: 34. **M.4**: 64. **O.1.2.3**: 21. **O.1.3**: 47.

Small farms **H.1.1.2**: 17, 32.

Small states **F.1**: 4. **F.3.2**: 55, 127.

Small towns **F.3.1.1**: 94.

Small-scale farming **H.1.1.2**: 10.

Small-scale industry **G.3.3.4**: 3, 21. **H.2.1**: 24. **H.2.2**: 45.

Smith, Adam **D**: 7, 14, 16–22, 25. **K.3**: 85.

Smoking **I.2.1**: 13. **M.4**: 18, 61.

Smuggling **N.2**: 56.

Social accounting **B.4**: 9, 24. **F.3.1.1**: 57. **K.2**: 26. **M.1**: 20. **M.4**: 5.

Social action **F.3.1.4**: 26.

Social change **F.3.2**: 86, 111. **N.1**: 58, 150, 319.

Social conditions **E**: 16. **F.1**: 8, 34, 45, 56, 59, 70, 81, 88, 93. **N.1**: 61, 141.

Social contract **N.2**: 292. **N.3**: 48.

Social control **G.2.3**: 10. **O.1.2.2**: 6.

Social costs **H.0**: 114. **K.2**: 14. **M.2**: 28. **N.1**: 210.

Social disadvantage **G.2.2**: 13.

Social economics **D**: 36, 73, 81. **F.5**: 34. **M.1**: 8, 21, 24. **N.1**: 26.

Social factors **H.2.2**: 117.

Social housing **L.2**: 102, 104, 109–110.

Social infrastructure **N.1**: 144.

Social justice **O.1.3**: 71.

Social networks **G.2.4**: 125.

Social norms **C**: 76. **F.3.1.3**: 24.

Social philosophy **C**: 41.

Social planning **J.1**: 80.

Social policy **F.1**: 62. **G.2.2**: 35. **I.2.3**: 55. **M.3**: 3–4, 7–8. **N.1**: 102. **N.2**: 67.

Social psychology **F.3.1.3**: 25.

Social science research **A**: 3, 8.

Social security **G.2.1**: 97. **L.1**: 40–41. **L.2**: 37, 52. **M.1**: 25. **M.2**: 37. **M.4**: 69, 79–80, 83, 99–100, 102–104, 107, 110–111, 113–122. **N.2**: 195.

Social security financing **M.4**: 109, 112.

Social services **M.4**: 1.

Social stratification **F.3.1.1**: 93. **F.3.2**: 19.

Social utility **L.2**: 69.

Social values **M.1**: 3.

Social welfare **F.1**: 44. **M.1**: 4, 10, 22. **M.2**: 15.

Socialism
Entries also appear under:
   MARKET SOCIALISM; STATE SOCIALISM
D: 12, 48. **F.3.1.1**: 82. **F.3.1.4**: 14, 21. **G.1.2**: 11. **J.1**: 37. **N.1**: 151, 236.

Socialist countries **F.1**: 69, 81. **N.1**: 164, 251. **N.2**: 81.

Socialist economies **D**: 12. **I.2.1**: 149, 176. **I.2.3**: 36. **J.2**: 50, 238. **J.4**: 110. **N.1**: 55, 145, 174, 205, 240.

Socialist enterprises **G.3.3**: 3. **G.3.3.5**: 50. **H.2.1**: 115.

Socialization **D**: 56.

Society
Entries also appear under:
   CAPITALIST SOCIETY; INDUSTRIAL SOCIETY; RURAL SOCIETY

Socio-economic development **F.3.1.3**: 27. **F.3.1.4**: 4. **F.3.2**: 11, 18–19, 31, 38, 49, 65, 79, 86, 108, 114–115. **G.1**: 44. **G.3.3.1**: 1, 3. **H.0**: 23, 66, 183. **H.1.1.2**: 24. **J.4**: 10. **N.1**: 94, 207, 253. **N.2**: 6. **O.1.2.4**: 15. **O.1.3**: 8.

Sociological research **B.1**: 11.

Sociology
Entries also appear under:
  POLITICAL SOCIOLOGY

Software **B.3**: 16. **G.3.3.5**: 39, 54. **H.2.2**: 17.

Soil conservation **H.1.1.1**: 33.

Soil erosion **H.1.1.1**: 33, 38.

Solar energy **H.0**: 114. **H.2.2**: 124.

South Amerindians **H.0**: 23.

Sovereignty **F.3.1.1**: 84. **O.2.4**: 8.

Space economics **H.4**: 111.

Space law **H.2.2**: 50.

Spatial dimension **F.3.1.1**: 3. **F.4**: 7. **G.1**: 60. **I.2.1**: 173.

Spatial distribution **F.3.1.1**: 19, 44. **H.2.2**: 71.

Sport **G.2.4**: 35. **H.1.2.1**: 33. **H.3**: 14. **L.2**: 15.

Sraffa, Piero **D**: 65.

Stabilization policy **F.3.2**: 75. **J.1**: 102. **J.2**: 212. **J.5**: 23, 43, 52. **N.1**: 68, 70–71, 73–75, 79–81, 84. **N.2**: 27. **O.2.3**: 24. **O.3.1**: 34.

Stagflation **J.1**: 11.

Stagnation
Entries also appear under:
  ECONOMIC STAGNATION

Standard of living **F.1**: 3. **K.3**: 63. **L.2**: 2. **M.2**: 3, 6, 8, 10, 21, 23, 30.

Standardization **A**: 11. **O.1.2.4**: 87. **O.2.4**: 18.

State
Entries also appear under:
  NATION STATE; SMALL STATES
D: 21. **F.3.2**: 109.

State aid **M.5**: 6. **N.1**: 9, 45.

State government **B.4**: 27.

State intervention **F.3.1.1**: 4, 54. **H.2.2**: 51, 103. **H.3**: 29. **N.1**: 19. **N.2**: 307. **O.1.2.3**: 9. **O.3.3**: 36.

State responsibility **H.1.1.2**: 2.

State socialism **N.1**: 254.

Statistical analysis **B.3**: 27, 32, 39, 49.

Statistical methods **B.3**: 5, 29.

Statistics
Entries also appear under:
  ECONOMIC STATISTICS
B.3: 3, 54–55. **J.4**: 52.

Steel **O.3.2**: 86. **O.3.3**: 33.

Sticky prices **O.2.1**: 23.

Stochastic models **B.3**: 45, 52, 56. **C**: 27. **F.3.3**: 29. **H.1.1.1**: 5. **H.2.1**: 44. **I.2.1**: 150. **O.3.1**: 52.

Stochastic processes **F.3.3**: 39. **H.4**: 39. **J.3**: 17. **J.4**: 7, 286. **K.1**: 4. **O.1.2**: 12. **O.3.2**: 80.

Stock exchange **B.3**: 21. **G.2.1**: 29. **J.4**: 148, 177, 184–185, 197, 202, 204–212, 214–221, 223–224, 226–229, 234, 236, 238–240, 244–248, 279, 282. **N.2**: 317. **O.1.2.2**: 22. **O.2.2**: 69, 102.

Stock exchange expectations **J.4**: 195.

Stock exchange speculation **J.4**: 222.

Stock management **G.3.3.3**: 7. **G.3.3.5**: 94. **H.4**: 56.

Stock prices **G.3.3.3**: 25. **J.2**: 244. **J.4**: 18, 120, 208, 217, 249–250, 255, 262–263, 266–270, 274–276, 279, 281, 291, 295–298, 300–301, 305, 308. **O.2.1**: 87. **O.2.4**: 13.

Stock returns **G.3.2**: 25. **G.3.3.5**: 17. **J.4**: 18, 76, 88, 127, 144, 170, 175, 187, 197, 252, 254, 256–261, 265, 271, 277, 279–280, 282–283, 286, 288–290, 292–294, 299, 304, 306–307. **N.2**: 182. **O.2.1**: 19, 24.

Stockholders **F.3.1.4**: 1. **G.3.3.3**: 28, 35. **G.3.3.5**: 69. **J.2**: 22. **J.4**: 22, 29, 302. **M.4**: 86.

Stocks **H.1.1.2**: 22. **H.2.1**: 11. **J.1**: 38. **J.4**: 4, 79, 84, 96, 112, 120–121, 164, 214, 221, 230, 240–242, 245, 258, 267, 278, 287. **K.3**: 41. **N.2**: 136. **O.2.1**: 86.

Storage **H.1.2.1**: 23.

Stores **H.4**: 98.

Strategic planning **G.1**: 49. **G.3.3.5**: 84, 96. **J.2**: 203.

Strikes **G.2.4**: 59–69, 97. **O.1.2.2**: 18.

Structural adjustment **F.3.2**: 5, 42, 45, 49, 56, 64, 73, 75, 81, 114, 126. **F.3.3**: 44. **G.2.1**: 2, 56, 173. **G.2.4**: 72. **H.0**: 166. **H.1.1.4**: 15. **H.2.1**: 2, 115. **H.2.2**: 16, 52, 136, 149. **J.2**: 89. **L.3**: 1, 27. **M.3**: 11. **N.1**: 62, 64–67, 69, 72–73, 76–78, 82–83, 85–86, 123, 129–130, 160, 187, 260, 272, 324. **N.3**: 7. **O.1.3**: 57. **O.2.2**: 17, 35, 61, 64. **O.2.3**: 20, 58. **O.2.4**: 20. **O.3.2**: 51. **O.3.3**: 41.

Structural analysis **N.2**: 69.

Structural change **B.3**: 33. **D**: 55. **F.3.1.1**: 85. **F.3.1.3**: 6. **F.3.2**: 69. **F.3.3**: 24. **G.2.2**: 29. **H.1.1.2**: 8, 33. **H.1.1.4**: 34, 48. **H.2.1**: 58, 81. **J.1**: 66. **J.4**: 92, 242. **L.2**: 3. **N.1**: 171. **O.1.3**: 99. **O.2.2**: 81.

Structural unemployment **G.2.1**: 157.

Students **M.5**: 1, 19, 39–40.

Subcontracting **G.1.1**: 17. **H.2.2**: 76.

Subsidies
Entries also appear under:
  EXPORT SUBSIDIES

H.1.2.1: 45. **H.2.1**: 113, 124. **H.2.2**: 53–54, 83, 98. **H.3**: 41, 92. **I.2.1**: 37. **J.4**: 97. **K.3**: 59. **N.1**: 52. **O.2.2**: 96. **O.3.1**: 27, 36. **O.3.3**: 129.

Technological forecasting **F.2**: 31.

Technology
Entries also appear under:
AGRICULTURAL TECHNOLOGY; BIOTECHNOLOGY; CHOICE OF TECHNOLOGY; HIGH TECHNOLOGY; INFORMATION TECHNOLOGY; NEW TECHNOLOGY
F.3.1.1: 86. **F.3.2**: 39. **G.1**: 24, 38, 44, 53. **G.1.1**: 40. **G.1.3**: 12. **G.2.4**: 89. **G.3.2**: 4. **G.3.3**: 32. **G.3.3.5**: 87. **H.0**: 182. **H.1.1**: 7. **H.1.1.1**: 8, 36. **H.2.1**: 48, 66, 94. **H.2.2**: 35, 108. **H.3**: 27. **I.2.1**: 62, 104. **M.2**: 19. **O.1.2.4**: 72. **O.2.2**: 117. **O.3.2**: 48.

Technology policy **G.1**: 14, 52. **G.1.3**: 8. **H.2.1**: 111, 116. **N.1**: 60.

Technology transfer **F.3.2**: 17, 126. **G.1**: 3–4, 15, 44, 48, 57, 59–60, 62. **G.2.5**: 51. **O.1.2.2**: 19. **O.1.3**: 50, 79–80, 82, 85–86. **O.2.2**: 97, 117.

Telecommunications **A**: 11. **H.3**: 80–81, 83–84, 87–90, 92, 94–96, 99–101. **I.2.3**: 15. **O.1.3**: 86.

Telecommunications industry **H.3**: 27, 91.

Telephone **H.3**: 97–98.

Television **H.3**: 82, 85–86, 93. **I.2.3**: 5, 15.

Terms of trade **B.1**: 5. **F.3.2**: 46. **H.2.1**: 30. **J.5**: 51. **L.1**: 28. **O.3.1**: 24, 33, 65, 67–68. **O.3.3**: 79–80.

Territory
Entries also appear under:
OVERSEAS TERRITORIES
Textile industry **G.2.4**: 59. **G.3.2**: 34. **H.2.2**: 9, 47, 52. **H.4**: 47. **O.1.3**: 43. **O.3.2**: 11. **O.3.3**: 48.

Textiles **O.3.3**: 45.

Thatcher, Margaret **N.1**: 124.

Thatcherism **G.2.4**: 17, 84.

Tillage **H.1.1**: 9.

Timber **H.1.2.1**: 53. **I.2.1**: 83.

Time budgets **F.3.1.3**: 5. **M.2**: 9.

Time series **B.2**: 2. **B.3**: 13, 39, 58. **F.2**: 21. **G.2.1**: 160. **G.3.3.5**: 51. **H.1.2.1**: 6. **J.1**: 77. **J.4**: 299. **K.3**: 1. **L.1**: 1.

Tobacco **I.2.3**: 18. **L.2**: 78. **N.2**: 214.

Tobacco industry **H.2.2**: 36. **L.2**: 80.

Tobin, James **L.3**: 18.

Tools
Entries also appear under:
MACHINE TOOLS
Top management **G.3.1**: 2. **G.3.3**: 16. **G.3.3.1**: 5. **G.3.3.5**: 3, 99. **K.3**: 41.

Tourism **H.0**: 148. **H.3**: 8, 10, 17, 28, 30–32. **O.3.2**: 82.

Tourist trade **H.3**: 5, 14. **O.3.2**: 54.

Towns
Entries also appear under:
SMALL TOWNS
H.0: 43.

Trade
Entries also appear under:
AGRICULTURAL TRADE; ARMS TRADE; BALANCE OF TRADE; BOOK TRADE; FOREIGN TRADE; FREE TRADE; GRAIN TRADE; INTERNAL TRADE; INTERNATIONAL TRADE; MULTILATERAL TRADE; NORTH-SOUTH TRADE; RETAIL TRADE; TERMS OF TRADE; TOURIST TRADE; WORLD TRADE
B.1: 19. **F.3.1.1**: 124. **F.3.3**: 33. **F.5**: 41. **H.0**: 27, 30. **H.1.1**: 21. **H.2.2**: 6, 108. **H.4**: 28–29, 43, 51. **I.2.1**: 58. **K.2**: 16. **K.3**: 61. **N.1**: 117, 212, 254. **N.2**: 54, 130, 255. **O.1.2.3**: 17. **O.1.2.4**: 52. **O.1.3**: 38, 60, 78. **O.2.2**: 7, 38, 46, 77, 129. **O.3.1**: 21, 38. **O.3.2**: 23, 75–76. **O.3.3**: 8, 27, 29, 59, 65, 73.

Trade agreements **G.2.1**: 2. **O.1.2.4**: 3. **O.1.3**: 41, 43, 88, 92, 94. **O.3.3**: 45, 60, 121.

Trade barriers **G.3.2**: 2. **I.2.1**: 67. **J.4**: 45. **O.3.1**: 11. **O.3.2**: 13. **O.3.3**: 13, 46, 52, 68–69.

Trade flows **H.4**: 89. **O.1.2.4**: 53. **O.3.1**: 55. **O.3.2**: 29, 63. **O.3.3**: 32.

Trade in services **O.3.2**: 28. **O.3.3**: 46.

Trade liberalization **G.2.4**: 29. **H.1.1.4**: 26. **J.4**: 61. **M.3**: 2. **N.1**: 39, 174. **O.1.2.4**: 14. **O.1.3**: 87, 100–101. **O.2.1**: 62. **O.2.2**: 110. **O.3.1**: 71. **O.3.3**: 7, 33, 40–41, 82–83, 103.

Trade models **O.3.2**: 66.

Trade negotiations **O.3.2**: 84.

Trade policy **F.3.2**: 47, 85. **G.1.3**: 15. **G.2.1**: 145. **G.3.2**: 12, 39. **H.2.2**: 77. **I.2.1**: 84. **L.1**: 28. **N.1**: 75. **O.1.2.4**: 25. **O.1.3**: 55. **O.2.1**: 80. **O.2.2**: 43. **O.3.1**: 3, 42. **O.3.2**: 66. **O.3.3**: 3–4, 9–10, 15, 17–18, 21, 26, 43–45, 49, 51, 53, 57, 62–63, 74, 77, 79, 84–87, 89, 91–92, 97, 115, 122–123, 128, 135–136.

Trade preferences **O.3.3**: 50.

Trade relations **F.3.1.3**: 4. **H.0**: 165. **I.2.3**: 3. **O.1.2.3**: 18. **O.1.2.4**: 40. **O.1.3**: 23. **O.3.2**: 5, 8, 11–12, 30, 45, 53, 72, 83, 85–86. **O.3.3**: 117, 138.

Trade theory **O.3.1**: 54, 57–58, 61, 63, 66. **O.3.3**: 15.

Trade union action **N.2**: 186.

Trade union membership **G.2.4**: 95.

Trade unions **G.2.1**: 162. **G.2.4**: 56–57, 59, 70–75, 77–82, 84–87, 89–94, 96–107, 113–114, 120. **G.2.5**: 46. **H.2.1**: 118. **H.2.2**: 58. **K.3**: 6, 18, 39, 64, 88–89, 102, 106, 125. **N.2**: 198. **O.1.2.4**: 47. **O.3.2**: 41.

Trade volume **I.2.1**: 44. **J.4**: 202.

Traffic
Entries also appear under:
    AIR TRAFFIC; ROAD TRAFFIC; SEA TRAFFIC

Training
Entries also appear under:
    ON-THE-JOB TRAINING; VOCATIONAL TRAINING
    G.2.5: 15–16, 23, 28–29, 51. **M.5**: 24.

Training courses **G.2.5**: 3.

Trains **H.3**: 60–61.

Transaction costs **C**: 54. **G.1**: 61. **G.3.3.2**: 12. **G.3.3.3**: 36, 40. **H.3**: 100. **H.4**: 23. **I.2.1**: 16. **J.2**: 54, 100.

Transfer
Entries also appear under:
    FISCAL TRANSFERS; INCOME TRANSFERS; TECHNOLOGY TRANSFER; WEALTH TRANSFERS

Transfer pricing **I.2.1**: 168. **O.1.2.2**: 25.

Transport
Entries also appear under:
    AIR TRANSPORT; MEANS OF TRANSPORT; PUBLIC TRANSPORT; RAILWAY TRANSPORT; ROAD TRANSPORT; SEA TRANSPORT; URBAN TRANSPORT
    F.3.1.1: 29, 77, 124. **H.0**: 188. **H.3**: 1, 9, 11, 20, 24, 33, 37. **I.2.3**: 10. **N.1**: 144.

Transport costs **H.3**: 12, 35. **H.4**: 10.

Transport economics **H.3**: 54.

Transport infrastructure **F.3.1.1**: 121. **H.3**: 7, 63–64. **I.2.3**: 22.

Transport policy **F.3.1.1**: 2. **H.3**: 3, 25, 34, 36, 50, 57, 59, 65, 72. **N.1**: 287.

Transportation **H.3**: 23.

Treasury **N.2**: 3, 103–104, 274. **O.2.1**: 9.

Treasury bills **F.2**: 23. **J.4**: 6, 146, 306.

Treaties **O.1.2.4**: 54, 57.

Trees **H.1.1.2**: 10.

Triad **O.2.2**: 27.

Tropical zones **H.0**: 60.

Trusts
Entries also appear under:
    INVESTMENT TRUSTS
    D: 69. **N.2**: 49.

Turgot, A. **D**: 7, 21.

Turnover taxes **N.2**: 87.

Uncertainty **B.3**: 9. **C**: 5, 10, 77–78, 82. **F.3.2**: 46. **F.3.3**: 14. **G.1.3**: 6. **G.3.3**: 21. **G.3.3.3**: 16, 29. **H.0**: 104. **H.2.2**: 26, 47. **H.4**: 48. **I.2.1**: 25, 41, 169. **J.1**: 110. **J.4**: 163. **J.5**: 5. **K.3**: 15. **L.1**: 34. **L.2**: 37. **L.3**: 2. **N.2**: 26, 147, 154, 163, 193. **O.1.2.3**: 12, 16. **O.2.1**: 59, 77. **O.3.3**: 80, 88.

Underdevelopment **F.3.2**: 37, 70, 105. **O.2.4**: 15.

Underemployment **G.2.1**: 68, 147, 152.

Unemployed **G.2.1**: 119, 141.

Unemployment
Entries also appear under:
    STRUCTURAL UNEMPLOYMENT
    C: 38, 45. **D**: 70. **F.3.1.3**: 25. **G.1.1**: 31. **G.2.1**: 114, 120–125, 127–130, 132–136, 138–139, 142–146, 149–156, 160, 162–165, 167–168, 174. **G.2.2**: 21, 27. **G.2.4**: 96. **H.2.1**: 50. **J.1**: 44. **J.2**: 16. **J.5**: 23. **K.2**: 31, 37. **K.3**: 47, 49, 63, 72, 83. **L.1**: 2, 4. **M.4**: 113, 117, 121. **N.1**: 42. **N.2**: 44, 255. **O.3.1**: 65. **O.3.3**: 80.

Unemployment duration **G.2.1**: 137, 140, 159, 161.

Unemployment insurance **G.2.1**: 151. **M.4**: 10.

Unemployment levels **G.2.1**: 131. **N.1**: 12.

Unequal exchange **D**: 15.

Uneven development **F.3.2**: 33. **H.0**: 42.

Unfair competition **G.3.2**: 2, 20. **I.2.1**: 72, 74.

United Nations **F.3.2**: 16.

Universities **K.3**: 115. **M.5**: 42–43.

Uranium resources **H.2.2**: 84.

Urban areas **F.3.1.1**: 122. **F.3.2**: 48. **G.2.1**: 163. **H.0**: 20. **H.2.1**: 63. **H.4**: 17, 108. **J.2**: 79. **L.2**: 82.

Urban development **F.3.1.1**: 72, 104, 116. **H.0**: 211. **H.4**: 27.

Urban economics **F.3.1.1**: 100, 106, 110, 124. **O.1.3**: 101.

Urban employment **F.3.1.1**: 101. **G.2.1**: 75.

Urban growth **F.3.1.1**: 67, 118. **H.0**: 86.

Urban housing **I.2.3**: 101. **L.2**: 107.

Urban planning **F.3.1.1**: 103, 117, 121.

Urban policy **F.3.1.1**: 121. **N.2**: 232.

Urban renewal **F.3.1.1**: 87, 119, 123. **H.1.1.2**: 36.

Urban services **F.3.1.1**: 120.

Urban space **H.1.1**: 1.

Urban structure **H.4**: 106.

Urban transport **H.3**: 2, 4, 35, 68.

Urbanization **F.3.1.1**: 115. **F.3.2**: 93.

Utility theory **C**: 51–52, 56. **G.3.3.5**: 53. **M.1**: 1, 9, 12.

Validity **G.3.3.5**: 64.

Valuation
Entries also appear under:
    ASSET VALUATION
    H.0: 7, 21. **I.2.1**: 170. **I.2.3**: 42. **J.2**: 3, 112, 244. **J.4**: 31, 123. **L.3**: 10. **N.3**: 52. **O.2.2**: 133.

Value
Entries also appear under:
    FIRM VALUE; LABOUR VALUE; SURPLUS VALUE
    D: 33. **I.1**: 1–3. **L.2**: 68. **M.1**: 12, 14.

Wildlife protection **H.0**: 136.

Williamson, Oliver **G.3.3.3**: 40.

Wind energy **H.2.2**: 88.

Wittgenstein, Ludwig **H.0**: 52.

Women

Entries also appear under:

MARRIED WOMEN; RURAL WOMEN
F.1: 5, 81. **F.3.2**: 115. **G.2.2**: 42. **G.4**: 1. **J.2**: 209. **K.2**: 24. **K.3**: 11, 125. **L.2**: 80. **M.2**: 10.

Women workers **G.2.1**: 84, 165. **G.2.2**: 29, 34–38, 40. **G.3.3.1**: 20. **G.3.3.4**: 14. **H.1.1.2**: 38.

Women's employment **G.2.2**: 33, 41.

Women's role **F.3.1.3**: 16. **G.2.2**: 39.

Women's status **F.3.1.3**: 19.

Wood products **O.3.2**: 9, 81.

Wool **I.2.3**: 68.

Work at home **G.2.2**: 12.

Work incentives **G.2.5**: 26.

Work motivation **G.3.1**: 3.

Work organization **G.2.5**: 12, 25, 39, 48, 59–60. **G.3.3**: 21.

Work place **G.2.3**: 8, 10. **G.2.5**: 10. **K.3**: 74.

Work standards **O.3.1**: 19.

Work study **G.2.5**: 58.

Workers

Entries also appear under:

AGRICULTURAL WORKERS; COMMERCIAL WORKERS; FOREIGN WORKERS; MIGRANT WORKERS; OLDER WORKERS; PROFESSIONAL WORKERS; SELF-EMPLOYED WORKERS; SKILLED WORKERS; WOMEN WORKERS
G.2.4: 6. **G.2.5**: 43. **H.4**: 47. **J.3**: 9. **K.3**: 35, 57. **M.4**: 10, 98, 107.

Workers' movements **G.2.4**: 63.

Workers' participation **G.1.2**: 7. **G.2.3**: 17. **G.2.4**: 112–113, 117–118, 120, 123–124.

Workers' self-management **G.2.4**: 109–110, 119, 122, 126. **G.3.3.5**: 59, 62. **H.2.1**: 86. **I.2.1**: 20. **L.3**: 20.

Workers' stock ownership **G.2.3**: 9. **G.2.4**: 108, 115–116, 125. **G.3.3.3**: 28. **G.3.3.5**: 14, 77.

Working class **D**: 26.

Working class culture **L.1**: 4.

Working conditions **G.2.2**: 2. **G.2.3**: 16. **G.2.5**: 60.

Working mothers **G.2.2**: 36.

Working time **D**: 27. **G.2.3**: 13.

Works councils **G.2.4**: 124.

Works of art **I.2.3**: 21.

World Bank **F.3.2**: 53. **H.1.1.4**: 14. **N.1**: 272. **O.2.2**: 64. **O.2.4**: 10, 12–13, 15, 20–21. **O.3.2**: 70.

World economy **F.1**: 83. **F.3.1.1**: 102. **F.3.2**: 7. **H.0**: 44, 174. **H.2.2**: 137. **J.4**: 54. **N.1**: 35. **N.2**: 189. **O.1.1**: 3. **O.1.2**: 3, 5–7, 9, 11–12, 14–18. **O.1.2.3**: 23, 33, 40. **O.1.2.4**: 40. **O.1.3**: 12, 23, 50, 56, 99. **O.2.2**: 9, 120. **O.2.3**: 48. **O.3.1**: 62. **O.3.3**: 138.

World market **H.1.2.1**: 24. **H.2.2**: 33, 131. **J.4**: 190. **M.5**: 23. **O.1.2.3**: 6, 14, 21, 24. **O.3.1**: 70.

World politics **O.1.2.4**: 75.

World religions

Entries also appear under:

ISLAM

World trade **O.2.1**: 61. **O.3.1**: 37, 69, 75. **O.3.2**: 70. **O.3.3**: 67, 92.

Xenophon **D**: 9.

Yanomami **H.0**: 23.

Yeltsin, Boris **N.1**: 222.

Yen **O.2.3**: 37. **O.3.1**: 75.

Youth **F.1**: 5. **G.2.1**: 72, 136.

Zoning **I.2.1**: 52.

INDEX DES MATIÈRES

Caoutchouc **H.1.2.1**: 15.

Capital **D**: 3. **F.3.2**: 10, 13. **F.3.3**: 41. **F.4**: 2. **G.3.2**: 3. **G.3.3.2**: 2, 9, 11. **G.3.3.5**: 63. **H.2.2**: 39. **J.2**: 9, 46, 53, 146, 169, 195. **J.4**: 12, 53, 61, 186. **J.5**: 9. **L.1**: 13. **L.3**: 14. **N.2**: 8, 215, 242, 311. **N.3**: 36. **O.2.1**: 1, 84. **O.2.2**: 5–7, 30. **O.2.3**: 28. **O.3.1**: 67.

Capital fixe **G.3.3.3**: 31.

Capitalisme **C**: 41. **D**: 5, 32. **F.3.1.1**: 82. **F.3.1.4**: 21. **F.3.2**: 94. **G.1.2**: 11. **G.2.1**: 29. **G.3.3.1**: 16. **G.3.3.5**: 50. **K.2**: 4. **N.1**: 30, 134, 200, 239, 303. **O.1.2**: 11.

Capitaux **G.3.3.2**: 12. **J.1**: 76.

Cartels **G.1.3**: 20. **G.3.2**: 4–5, 14, 16, 40. **I.2.1**: 11–12. **O.3.2**: 19.

Catastrophes naturelles **H.0**: 46.

Catholicisme **F.3.1.2**: 4.

Centrales électriques **H.2.2**: 92.

Centralisation **J.2**: 10. **K.3**: 3. **N.1**: 276. **N.2**: 297.

Céréales **H.1.1.1**: 35.

Chances d'obtenir un emploi **G.2.5**: 33.

Changement culturel **E**: 5.

Changement d'organisation **G.1**: 26, 58. **G.3.3.2**: 14. **J.2**: 124.

Changement démographique **F.1**: 83. **F.3.1.2**: 2, 19–21. **G.2.1**: 62. **L.2**: 87. **N.2**: 127.

Changement économique **D**: 6. **E**: 5, 11. **F.1**: 12, 50, 75. **F.3.1.3**: 28. **F.3.1.4**: 18. **F.3.2**: 16, 42, 122. **F.3.3**: 4. **G.2.1**: 34–35, 67. **G.3.1**: 1. **G.3.3.5**: 50. **H.0**: 212. **H.2.2**: 11. **J.2**: 31, 238. **M.2**: 2. **M.4**: 120. **M.5**: 31. **N.1**: 8, 17, 23, 27, 39, 44, 53, 55–56, 58–59, 98, 127, 132, 147, 156, 188, 204, 259, 262, 270, 277, 293, 310. **N.2**: 127, 295, 312. **O.1.2**: 16. **O.1.3**: 44, 48. **O.2.2**: 95.

Changement politique **D**: 6. **E**: 11. **F.3.2**: 16, 122. **H.1.1.2**: 24. **H.2.1**: 106. **N.1**: 8, 143, 146, 188, 324. **O.1.2**: 11.

Changement social **F.3.2**: 86, 111. **N.1**: 58, 150, 319.

Changement structurel **B.3**: 33. **D**: 55. **F.3.1.1**: 85. **F.3.1.3**: 6. **F.3.2**: 69. **F.3.3**: 24. **G.2.2**: 29. **H.1.1.2**: 8, 33. **H.1.1.4**: 34, 48. **H.2.1**: 58, 81. **J.1**: 66. **J.4**: 92, 242. **L.2**: 3. **N.1**: 171. **O.1.3**: 99. **O.2.2**: 81.

Changement technologique **A**: 11. **F.3.1.1**: 122. **F.3.3**: 40, 53, 61. **G.1**: 20–21, 26, 28, 30–33, 36–37, 39–43, 46–51, 54–55, 57–58, 60–61. **G.1.1**: 11, 38. **G.1.2**: 17. **G.1.3**: 22. **G.2.1**: 4. **G.2.4**: 94. **G.3.3.2**: 14. **H.0**: 4. **H.1.1.1**: 9. **H.1.2.1**: 45. **H.2.1**: 113, 124. **H.2.2**: 53–54, 83, 98. **H.3**: 41, 92. **I.2.1**: 37. **J.4**: 97. **K.3**: 59. **N.1**: 52. **O.2.2**: 96. **O.3.1**: 27, 36. **O.3.3**: 129.

Charbon **H.3**: 54.

Charbonnages **H.0**: 110.

Charges fiscales **N.2**: 243.

Charisme **G.3.3.5**: 44.

Chauffage mondiale **H.0**: 5–6, 36, 47, 53, 70–71, 76–79, 82, 84, 90–91, 93–94, 114, 121. **H.2.2**: 114. **I.2.3**: 25.

Chayanov, Alexander **H.1.1**: 22.

Chefs d'entreprise **F.3.2**: 42. **G.3.3.1**: 1, 16. **H.4**: 94.

Chemins de fer **H.3**: 54, 56–57, 59.

Cheptel **H.1.2.1**: 11.

Cherchant revenus d'investissement **C**: 17. **F.3.1.3**: 20. **F.3.3**: 58. **H.3**: 61.

Choix collectif **B.3**: 45. **C**: 18, 29–30, 64, 68. **E**: 14. **K.2**: 2. **M.1**: 6, 24. **M.5**: 26.

Choix d'une profession **G.4**: 6.

Choix de produits **L.2**: 50.

Choix de technologie **G.1**: 27.

Choix du conjoint **F.3.1.3**: 31.

Choix économique **C**: 24.

Chômage **C**: 38, 45. **D**: 70. **F.3.1.3**: 25. **G.1.1**: 31. **G.2.1**: 114, 120–125, 127–130, 132–136, 138–139, 142–146, 149–156, 160, 162–165, 167–168, 174. **G.2.2**: 21, 27. **G.2.4**: 96. **H.2.1**: 50. **J.1**: 44. **J.2**: 16. **J.5**: 23. **K.2**: 31, 37. **K.3**: 47, 49, 63, 72, 83. **L.1**: 2, 4. **M.4**: 113, 117, 121. **N.1**: 42. **N.2**: 44, 255. **O.3.1**: 65. **O.3.3**: 80.

Chômage partiel **G.2.1**: 68, 147, 152.

Chômage structurel **G.2.1**: 157.

Chômeurs **G.2.1**: 119, 141.

Circulation aérienne **H.3**: 49.

Circulation maritime **H.3**: 76.

Circulation monétaire **J.2**: 69.

Circulation routière **H.3**: 6.

Citoyens **N.3**: 44.

Classe **F.3.1.3**: 11. **G.2.2**: 7. **K.3**: 118.

Classe ouvrière **D**: 26.

Classification **B.4**: 19–20. **H.2.1**: 5.

Climat **H.0**: 135.

Climatologie **H.0**: 70.

Coalition **F.3.3**: 19. **G.2.4**: 53.

Coase, R.H. **N.1**: 210.

Code déontologique des affaires **C**: 8. **G.3.3**: 5–6. **G.3.3.1**: 15. **G.3.3.5**: 18.

Cognition **A**: 3.

Cohortes **G.2.1**: 97.

Collectivité **C**: 76. **F.3.1.3**: 22. **M.2**: 5. **N.2**: 93. **O.3.3**: 20.

Collectivité de travail **G.2.4**: 98.

Collectivités locales **G.2.1**: 46.

Collectivités rurales **F.3.1.1**: 95. **F.3.1.2**: 3.

179–180, 182–183. **I.2.3**: 10, 15, 35, 61, 81. **J.1**: 49–50, 52, 65, 69. **J.2**: 20. **L.2**: 1, 55, 88, 97. **L.3**: 2, 23. **M.5**: 6. **N.2**: 219. **N.3**: 10, 45. **O.2.1**: 41, 76. **O.3.1**: 41.

Demande d'exportation **O.3.2**: 81.

Demande d'importation **O.3.1**: 40–41, 52, 64.

Demande d'investissement **G.3.2**: 21. **L.3**: 12, 25.

Demande de consommation **G.2.1**: 121. **H.4**: 97. **I.2.3**: 14. **L.2**: 5, 19, 23, 27, 29–30, 32, 35–36, 48, 51, 57, 60–62, 68, 72, 87.

Demande de main-d'oeuvre **G.1.2**: 17. **G.2.1**: 101–102, 114. **G.2.5**: 9. **H.2.1**: 18.

Demande de monnaie **J.1**: 46–48, 51, 53–55, 57–69. **J.2**: 105.

Demande effective **I.2.1**: 181.

Demande énergétique **H.2.2**: 114. **I.2.3**: 19, 53. **L.2**: 25.

Demande globale **C**: 20. **F.5**: 5. **I.2.1**: 18, 113, 135. **L.1**: 10, 17. **O.3.2**: 66.

Démocratie **F.3.1.4**: 21. **G.2.4**: 112. **M.2**: 29. **N.1**: 224–225. **N.3**: 42.

Démocratisation **F.3.2**: 7, 42. **O.1.2.4**: 3.

Démographie **H.0**: 88. **M.4**: 93.

Deng, Xiaoping **N.1**: 138.

Densité de population **F.3.1.2**: 6. **L.2**: 12.

Départements et territoires d'Outre-Mer **F.1**: 56.

Dépendance économique **O.3.3**: 17.

Dépense globale **H.3**: 1.

Dépenses **G.1.2**: 1. **H.4**: 64. **L.1**: 12. **N.2**: 166.

Dépenses d'investissement **L.3**: 4.

Dépenses de consommation **I.2.3**: 83. **L.2**: 12, 52, 106.

Dépenses de mènage **L.1**: 25. **L.2**: 18, 41, 78. **M.2**: 31.

Dépenses de santé **M.3**: 12. **M.4**: 18, 23–24, 32, 37, 41, 49, 51, 61.

Dépenses du secteur éducatif **M.5**: 4, 12, 34, 39.

Dépenses militaires **F.1**: 22. **L.2**: 26. **N.1**: 2, 11–12, 16, 21. **O.3.2**: 42.

Dépenses publiques **F.2**: 10. **F.3.3**: 23, 55. **H.1.1.4**: 41. **J.5**: 45. **L.2**: 12. **N.2**: 132, 256, 258–259, 261–262, 264–267, 269–272, 274–276, 278–279, 281, 316.

Déréglementation **G.2.3**: 8. **H.2.2**: 110. **H.3**: 39, 45, 52, 58, 81, 96. **J.2**: 24, 110–111, 116–117, 122, 132, 164, 168, 174. **J.4**: 85, 108. **M.3**: 14. **N.1**: 47. **N.3**: 11.

Déroulement de carrière **G.4**: 2.

Déséquilibre **B.1**: 19. **F.3.2**: 80. **G.2.1**: 38, 98.

Déséquilibre économique **N.2**: 158. **O.1.2**: 5.

Désert **H.0**: 157.

Désindustrialisation **F.3.2**: 53. **G.2.4**: 66.

Désinvestissement **G.3.3.3**: 5. **L.3**: 10.

Détermination du taux de change **J.1**: 65.

Dette **F.5**: 17. **G.3.2**: 15. **G.3.3.3**: 18. **G.3.3.5**: 8, 35. **H.2.1**: 75, 79. **I.2.3**: 90. **J.2**: 134, 158, 202, 227, 231–232, 234. **J.4**: 68, 117, 292. **L.3**: 13. **N.1**: 277. **N.2**: 69, 137, 168, 178, 220, 237, 239, 248–249, 251. **O.2.2**: 2, 17, 22, 24, 49, 53, 57, 69, 74. **O.2.4**: 13.

Dette d'entreprise **G.3.3.3**: 10. **G.3.3.5**: 8.

Dette extérieure **F.3.1.3**: 4. **F.3.2**: 4–5, 71, 81. **L.3**: 4. **N.1**: 67. **N.2**: 251–252, 255. **O.1.3**: 10. **O.2.2**: 48–50, 52–65, 67–70, 72–73, 77–79.

Dette publique **F.3.2**: 102. **J.4**: 118. **M.4**: 90. **N.2**: 168, 240, 242, 245, 247, 250–251, 253. **O.1.2.4**: 59. **O.2.2**: 24, 39.

Deutsche Mark **O.2.1**: 45. **O.2.3**: 5, 14, 36.

Dévaluation **O.2.1**: 18. **O.2.2**: 15. **O.2.3**: 69. **O.3.2**: 24.

Développement agricole **F.3.2**: 63. **H.1.1.1**: 31. **H.1.1.4**: 2, 5, 12, 18, 20, 22, 31, 36, 45. **O.1.3**: 68.

Développement de l'enfant **M.2**: 31.

Développement des collectivités **F.3.1.1**: 52.

Développement économique **C**: 55. **D**: 47. **F.1**: 67. **F.2**: 2, 14. **F.3.1.1**: 9, 21, 35–36, 39–40, 46, 84, 109, 119, 121. **F.3.1.2**: 6–7. **F.3.1.4**: 23. **F.3.2**: 1, 4, 9, 13, 15, 20, 23, 26–27, 32, 39–40, 47, 56, 60, 64, 72, 78, 88, 90, 92, 94–97, 99–102, 106, 111–112, 116, 118, 120, 124, 127–128. **F.3.3**: 23. **F.4**: 2. **G.1**: 14, 29, 31. **G.1.3**: 7, 12. **G.2.1**: 145. **G.3.3.5**: 67. **H.0**: 29, 34, 56, 69, 86, 92, 105, 118, 158, 161–162, 164, 171, 173, 180, 182. **H.1.1.4**: 17. **H.2.1**: 69. **H.2.2**: 85. **J.2**: 58, 64, 126, 143. **J.4**: 97. **J.5**: 22. **L.1**: 31. **L.3**: 14. **M.2**: 32. **N.1**: 17, 32, 65, 87, 93, 99, 168. **N.2**: 89, 237. **O.1.2**: 8. **O.1.3**: 71–72. **O.2.2**: 87, 105. **O.3.1**: 23. **O.3.2**: 28.

Développement industriel **F.3.1.1**: 45. **G.2.5**: 23. **G.3.3.4**: 18. **H.2.1**: 6, 21, 28, 61, 66, 74, 124. **O.3.2**: 30.

Développement inégal **F.3.2**: 33. **H.0**: 42.

Développement intégré **H.1.1.4**: 19.

Développement régional **F.3.1.1**: 50–51, 53–54, 62–65, 67, 69, 73–74, 78, 81–82. **F.3.2**: 92, 109. **G.1**: 5, 47. **G.3.3**: 20. **H.0**: 141. **H.3**: 17. **N.1**: 137. **O.1.2.4**: 2, 49. **O.1.3**: 100. **O.3.3**: 66.

Développement rural **F.3.1.1**: 90, 96, 99. **F.3.2**: 3. **H.0**: 38, 177, 197. **H.1.1.2**: 5. **H.1.1.4**: 3, 19, 24. **H.3**: 28, 87. **M.4**: 5. **N.1**: 103, 193.

Développement sectoriel **F.3.2**: 109.

Développement socio-économique **F.3.1.3**: 27. **F.3.1.4**: 4. **F.3.2**: 11, 18–19, 31, 38, 49, 65, 79, 86, 108, 114–115. **G.1**: 44. **G.3.3.1**: 1, 3. **H.0**: 23, 66, 183. **H.1.1.2**: 24. **J.4**: 10. **N.1**: 94, 207, 253. **N.2**: 6. **O.1.2.4**: 15. **O.1.3**: 8.

Économie urbaine **F.3.1.1**: 100, 106, 110, 124. **O.1.3**: 101.

Économies d'échelle **G.3.3.4**: 4, 19. **H.2.1**: 49. **H.2.2**: 29, 148. **H.3**: 70. **J.3**: 6. **M.5**: 15.

Économies d'énergie **H.0**: 12. **N.3**: 22.

Économistes **A**: 2. **C**: 14. **D**: 41, 51, 68. **F.3.1.3**: 11. **G.4**: 4, 9.

Écosystèmes **H.0**: 62, 70.

Écu **J.4**: 210. **O.2.3**: 8–9, 42.

Édition **H.4**: 70.

Éducation **F.3.2**: 58. **G.2.2**: 5. **G.2.4**: 75. **G.3.3.5**: 122. **H.1.1.1**: 29. **M.5**: 2, 6, 9, 35. **O.2.4**: 21.

Éducation préscolaire **M.5**: 3.

Effectifs en ouvriers **G.2.1**: 8, 24, 35, 38, 52, 58. **G.2.2**: 38. **G.2.5**: 34. **H.1.1.1**: 36. **K.2**: 21. **K.3**: 111. **L.1**: 20. **O.3.3**: 26.

Effets sur l'environnement **F.3.1.2**: 20. **G.3.3.5**: 30. **H.0**: 2, 32, 162. **H.1.1.3**: 7. **H.2.2**: 104. **O.3.3**: 111.

Efficacité administrative **M.5**: 22.

Efficacité du marché **H.2.2**: 161. **I.2.1**: 50. **J.4**: 21, 69. **O.2.1**: 11.

Efficacité économique **C**: 6. **G.1**: 9. **G.1.1**: 24. **G.3.3**: 3. **H.1.1.3**: 4. **H.1.2.1**: 41. **H.2.1**: 14, 53. **J.2**: 89. **J.4**: 111. **M.1**: 15. **M.5**: 22. **N.1**: 287. **N.2**: 159, 185, 303. **N.3**: 15, 20.

Efficacité organisationnelle **E**: 13. **G.3.3**: 32. **G.3.3.5**: 20, 54, 128. **J.2**: 30, 170.

Égalitarisme **K.3**: 64. **M.1**: 15.

Égalité **F.3.3**: 7. **G.2.4**: 92. **M.1**: 18.

Égalité de chances **G.2.2**: 1.

Égalité de rémunération **K.3**: 7, 111.

Élaboration d'une politique **J.5**: 46. **L.2**: 103. **N.1**: 77, 92, 114. **N.2**: 89. **O.1.3**: 22.

Élasticité des prix **I.2.1**: 45, 156.

Électeurs **H.2.1**: 34.

Électricité **H.0**: 10, 63, 72. **H.2.2**: 90, 96, 114, 118, 128–129. **I.2.3**: 8–9, 17, 19, 35, 43, 48, 57. **L.2**: 6, 11. **N.1**: 272.

Électronique **F.3.1.1**: 30.

Élèves **G.2.5**: 2.

Élite économique **F.3.1.2**: 8.

Émigration **F.1**: 89. **G.2.1**: 90. **G.2.3**: 6.

Émission de monnaie **J.2**: 71.

Émissions de valeurs mobiliéres **J.4**: 34, 52.

Emmagasinage **H.1.2.1**: 23.

Empirisme **F.3.3**: 8.

Emploi **F.3.1.1**: 23, 121. **F.3.2**: 69. **F.3.3**: 25. **G.2.1**: 3–4, 12, 17, 20–21, 27, 57, 72. **G.2.2**: 4, 13, 36, 40. **G.2.4**: 4, 31, 99. **G.2.5**: 40. **G.4**: 1. **H.1.1.4**: 29. **H.2.1**: 50. **H.3**: 75. **H.4**: 24. **I.2.1**: 29. **I.2.3**: 91. **J.2**: 4, 140. **K.3**: 3, 54, 66, 95. **L.2**: 97. **N.2**: 273.

Emploi à temps partiel **G.2.1**: 71.

Emploi rural **G.2.1**: 41.

Emploi sectoriel **K.2**: 29.

Emploi urbain **F.3.1.1**: 101. **G.2.1**: 75.

Employés **G.1**: 58. **G.2.1**: 82. **G.2.4**: 2, 64, 114. **G.2.5**: 5, 28, 40. **G.3.3**: 10. **G.3.3.2**: 2. **K.3**: 21, 106.

Employés de commerce **K.3**: 20.

Employeurs **G.2.4**: 48.

Emprunt **F.5**: 12. **J.2**: 20. **N.2**: 212. **O.1.3**: 11. **O.2.2**: 1.

Emprunts publics **J.4**: 171. **N.2**: 134.

Endettement **J.2**: 226, 228–229. **O.2.2**: 39, 75, 79, 92.

Énergie **H.0**: 11, 22, 109, 144, 153. **H.2.2**: 2, 86, 97, 99–102, 104–106, 108, 117, 131. **I.2.3**: 24, 53, 59.

Énergie de la biomasse **H.0**: 47. **H.2.2**: 82.

Énergie électrique **H.0**: 14. **H.2.2**: 91, 111, 123, 126.

Énergie éolienne **H.2.2**: 88.

Énergie hydroélectrique **G.1**: 62.

Énergie nucléaire **H.0**: 33. **H.2.2**: 112.

Énergie solaire **H.0**: 114. **H.2.2**: 124.

Enfants **F.3.1.3**: 10. **G.2.1**: 96. **L.2**: 53. **M.4**: 100.

Engels, Friedrich **D**: 30.

Engrais **H.1.1.1**: 3, 12.

Enquêtes **F.2**: 23, 29. **G.2.1**: 66. **H.3**: 85. **H.4**: 66, 71. **L.3**: 18. **M.2**: 11.

Enquêtes économiques **J.2**: 25.

Enseignement de l'économie **A**: 5. **B.4**: 36. **D**: 50.

Enseignement professionnel **G.2.5**: 56.

Enseignement secondaire **A**: 5.

Enseignement supérieur **K.3**: 114. **M.5**: 4–5, 15, 17–18, 21–23, 26, 32, 34, 38.

Entreprise agricole **G.2.1**: 147. **H.1.1**: 3, 8, 11. **H.1.1.1**: 4, 11. **H.1.1.2**: 7, 9, 14, 33, 37. **H.1.1.3**: 8, 14, 17–18, 20. **H.1.1.4**: 21. **H.1.2.1**: 12. **I.2.3**: 77.

Entreprises **F.1**: 20, 79, 87. **F.3.1.1**: 80. **G.1**: 1. **G.1.2**: 14. **G.2.1**: 115. **G.2.3**: 1. **G.2.4**: 49. **G.2.5**: 49. **G.3.1**: 1. **G.3.2**: 16, 38. **G.3.3**: 9, 11, 27. **G.3.3.1**: 11, 13. **G.3.3.2**: 8. **G.3.3.3**: 1, 6. **G.3.3.4**: 10. **G.3.3.5**: 35, 61, 79, 125. **H.2.1**: 80. **H.2.2**: 141. **H.4**: 35. **N.1**: 21, 227.

Entreprises compétitives **B.3**: 30. **G.3.3.5**: 55, 68.

Entreprises conjointes **G.1**: 10. **G.1.3**: 2, 20. **G.3.2**: 4, 18, 41. **G.3.3.5**: 40. **H.2.1**: 55–56, 61. **O.1.2.2**: 1. **O.1.3**: 50. **O.2.2**: 130–133. **O.3.1**: 75. **O.3.2**: 40.

75, 78, 96–97, 108. **H.2.2**: 23. **H.4**: 28, 68. **I.2.1**: 28, 101, 124, 149. **J.4**: 59, 274. **K.3**: 28. **L.2**: 52. **M.5**: 32, 38. **N.1**: 21, 88. **N.2**: 37. **O.1.2.3**: 18, 21. **O.1.2.4**: 91. **O.2.2**: 118. **O.2.3**: 69. **O.3.3**: 42.

Industrie aéronautique **H.2.2**: 14, 37. **H.3**: 47.

Industrie agro-alimentaire **H.1.1**: 5, 15. **H.1.1.4**: 46. **H.1.2**: 1. **H.2.2**: 16. **H.4**: 29. **I.2.3**: 69.

Industrie alimentaire **H.1.1.1**: 26. **H.1.2.1**: 11. **H.4**: 2, 7. **L.2**: 75. **O.3.1**: 73. **O.3.2**: 25.

Industrie automobile **G.1.3**: 3. **G.2.4**: 50, 91. **G.3.3.5**: 70. **H.2.1**: 4, 13. **H.2.2**: 60–67, 69–70, 72–78. **H.4**: 32. **I.2.3**: 27. **L.2**: 61. **N.2**: 190. **O.3.2**: 4, 23, 30. **O.3.3**: 25, 77.

Industrie chimique **G.2.4**: 64. **I.2.1**: 5. **K.3**: 65.

Industrie culturelle **H.4**: 24.

Industrie d'armement **H.2.2**: 3, 11. **N.1**: 3, 11.

Industrie d'énergétique **H.0**: 13. **H.2.2**: 79, 98, 107, 116, 125, 130. **N.1**: 295. **O.1.2.3**: 13.

Industrie de la chaussure **H.2.2**: 21. **O.3.2**: 9.

Industrie de la construction **G.2.4**: 71. **H.2.1**: 50. **H.2.2**: 24, 30, 38, 51. **I.2.3**: 91. **J.2**: 73.

Industrie de la pêche **G.1.1**: 33. **H.1.1.2**: 8. **H.1.2.1**: 41, 44–46, 48.

Industrie de la poterie **H.2.2**: 8.

Industrie de pâte à papier **H.2.2**: 22, 25, 39.

Industrie des télécommunications **H.3**: 27, 91.

Industrie du charbon **H.0**: 74. **H.2.2**: 146, 150.

Industrie du ciment **H.2.2**: 2, 34. **I.2.3**: 45.

Industrie du disque **H.2.1**: 12.

Industrie du meuble **H.2.2**: 29.

Industrie du sucre **H.1.2.1**: 2, 22.

Industrie du tabac **H.2.2**: 36. **L.2**: 80.

Industrie du vêtement **G.2.1**: 30. **H.2.2**: 5, 13, 47. **O.3.3**: 45.

Industrie électrique **G.3.3.5**: 100. **H.2.2**: 127.

Industrie électronique **B.4**: 37. **G.1**: 46. **H.2.2**: 40, 44, 53, 67. **K.3**: 35, 45. **O.1.2.2**: 13. **O.2.2**: 131.

Industrie exportatrice **F.3.3**: 30, 44.

Industrie forestière **H.1.2.1**: 50.

Industrie hôtelière **I.2.3**: 40.

Industrie informatique **H.2.1**: 13. **H.2.2**: 10, 20, 26–27, 43. **H.3**: 99. **K.3**: 76.

Industrie laitière **H.1.2.1**: 3, 19.

Industrie légère **H.2.1**: 30.

Industrie lourde **H.2.1**: 47.

Industrie métallurgique **H.2.2**: 59, 132, 142.

Industrie minière **H.2.2**: 137–138, 141–144, 148.

Industrie nationalisée **H.2.2**: 23.

Industrie pétrochimique **H.2.2**: 1, 28. **O.1.2.2**: 19.

Industrie pétrolière **F.3.3**: 55. **G.2.1**: 17. **H.0**: 32. **H.2.1**: 30. **H.2.2**: 151, 154–155, 157–159, 161–163. **I.2.3**: 49. **O.3.2**: 14. **O.3.3**: 16.

Industrie pharmaceutique **F.3.1.4**: 13. **G.1.3**: 9. **H.2.1**: 117. **H.2.2**: 15, 18, 41, 54, 56.

Industrie sidérurgique **G.2.4**: 40. **H.2.1**: 3, 13. **H.2.2**: 133–136.

Industrie textile **G.2.4**: 59. **G.3.2**: 34. **H.2.2**: 9, 47, 52. **H.4**: 47. **O.1.3**: 43. **O.3.2**: 11. **O.3.3**: 48.

Inégalité de revenu **F.3.1.3**: 15. **G.2.1**: 175. **I.2.3**: 94. **K.2**: 6, 8, 14, 23, 27–28, 38. **K.3**: 55, 60, 62, 119. **M.2**: 17, 29. **M.5**: 37. **O.1.2.5**: 2.

Inégalité de sexes **K.3**: 121.

Inégalité économique **B.1**: 14. **M.1**: 11. **M.2**: 8, 19. **M.5**: 26.

Inégalité raciale **K.2**: 39. **M.5**: 37.

Infirmières **G.2.1**: 113. **G.2.2**: 37.

Inflation **D**: 4. **F.1**: 84. **G.2.1**: 53, 155. **G.2.3**: 6. **G.2.4**: 61. **G.3.3.3**: 1. **H.1.1.3**: 11. **I.2.1**: 32–33, 123, 166. **I.2.2**: 3. **I.2.3**: 4, 84. **J.1**: 70–89, 92–93, 95–98, 101–105, 108–112. **J.2**: 29. **J.4**: 96, 127. **J.5**: 15, 23, 48, 53, 60. **K.2**: 3, 18. **K.3**: 10, 22, 69. **L.1**: 16. **M.2**: 2. **M.4**: 49. **N.1**: 42, 78, 298. **N.2**: 27, 57, 80, 239. **O.2.1**: 7, 37. **O.2.3**: 19, 30, 39.

Influences politiques **K.2**: 7.

Information **A**: 15. **B.4**: 26, 35. **D**: 48. **F.5**: 23, 26. **G.1.3**: 6. **G.3.2**: 14. **G.3.3.3**: 19. **G.3.3.4**: 6. **G.3.3.5**: 124. **H.0**: 98. **I.2.1**: 34, 91, 152, 160, 169. **I.2.3**: 66. **J.2**: 26, 55, 59, 142, 204. **J.3**: 2. **J.4**: 24, 34, 46, 51, 83, 106, 192, 273, 275, 297, 305. **J.5**: 23. **L.2**: 22. **M.1**: 5. **N.1**: 122. **N.2**: 136.

Information d'entreprise **G.3.3.5**: 80, 109. **J.4**: 90, 114.

Information financière **B.4**: 18. **F.2**: 23. **G.3.3.3**: 1. **G.3.3.5**: 102. **H.1.2.1**: 10. **J.4**: 64, 256.

Information imparfaite **G.2.1**: 36. **K.3**: 103.

Informatique **A**: 13.

Informatisation **G.2.4**: 4. **J.2**: 124.

Infrastructure de transport **F.3.1.1**: 121. **H.3**: 7, 63–64. **I.2.3**: 22.

Infrastructure économique **F.3.3**: 27.

Infrastructure sociale **N.1**: 144.

Ingénierie **H.2.2**: 59.

Ingénierie génétique **H.1.1.1**: 26.

Ingénieurs **G.1**: 49. **G.2.4**: 10.

Injures **H.3**: 13.

Innovation financière **J.1**: 55. **J.2**: 60, 101. **J.4**: 171. **J.5**: 17. **N.1**: 245. **N.2**: 17.

Innovations **C**: 65. **F.3.1.1**: 80, 86. **F.3.1.4**: 13. **F.3.3**: 16, 37. **G.1**: 16–24, 30, 60. **G.1.1**: 28, 37. **G.1.3**: 8. **G.3.2**: 4. **G.3.3**: 14, 18. **G.3.3.4**:

13. **H.2.1**: 1, 51, 62, 117. **H.2.2**: 41, 140. **I.2.1**: 29, 35–36, 101. **I.2.3**: 33. **J.4**: 227. **N.1**: 112. **N.2**: 74, 244. **N.3**: 10.

Innovations industrielles **H.2.1**: 7.

Instabilité des exportations **O.3.1**: 12, 15.

Instabilité des prix **H.1.2.1**: 25. **J.2**: 108.

Instabilité politique **N.2**: 310. **O.2.2**: 72.

Institutionnalisme **C**: 40. **D**: 31. **F.3.1.3**: 11, 30. **F.3.2**: 24. **G.3.3.5**: 126. **J.4**: 125. **N.2**: 52.

Institutions **D**: 36. **F.3.2**: 38. **F.3.3**: 28. **O.3.3**: 134.

Institutions financières **J.2**: 8, 10, 38–39, 42, 57, 73, 83, 87, 89, 188. **J.4**: 70, 75, 80, 92, 224. **N.1**: 207. **N.2**: 23. **O.1.2.4**: 87. **O.2.2**: 33.

Institutions politiques **H.0**: 107. **M.5**: 10.

Intégration économique **F.1**: 54. **F.3.2**: 119. **H.2.1**: 110. **J.2**: 3. **J.4**: 226. **O.1.2.3**: 25. **O.1.2.4**: 5–6, 9–10, 12–18, 23, 26, 28, 31, 34, 36–39, 41, 45, 47, 50, 52–53, 56–57, 61–63, 66–67, 69, 73–74, 77, 80–81, 86. **O.1.3**: 14, 17, 20, 50, 56, 90, 96, 102. **O.3.3**: 27, 29, 39, 66, 70.

Intégration internationale **M.3**: 3. **O.1.2.3**: 18. **O.1.2.4**: 29–30, 32–33, 59. **O.1.3**: 100. **O.2.3**: 44. **O.3.3**: 124.

Intégration politique **F.3.2**: 70. **O.1.2.4**: 76.

Intégration régionale **O.1.2.4**: 15, 35, 37, 43–44. **O.1.3**: 17, 102.

Intégration verticale **G.3.3.2**: 11. **G.3.3.3**: 40. **H.2.2**: 26.

Intellectuels **F.3.2**: 40.

Intelligence artificielle **B.3**: 2, 31.

Interdépendance **H.1.1.3**: 13. **L.1**: 20. **N.2**: 7. **O.2.1**: 23. **O.2.2**: 9, 36. **O.3.2**: 39.

Interdépendance économique **F.3.1.1**: 57. **G.3.3.5**: 83. **O.1.2.4**: 19.

Intérêt **J.2**: 63, 144, 151. **N.2**: 212, 215.

Internationalisation **H.2.1**: 122. **H.2.2**: 1, 30. **O.1.2**: 9–10. **O.1.2.2**: 14–15. **O.1.2.3**: 9.

Internationalisme **H.2.1**: 6.

Intervention de l'État **F.3.1.1**: 4, 54. **H.2.2**: 51, 103. **H.3**: 29. **N.1**: 19. **N.2**: 307. **O.1.2.3**: 9. **O.3.3**: 36.

Interventionnisme **N.1**: 13.

Invalidité **G.2.2**: 2. **M.4**: 9.

Inventions **G.1.1**: 16. **G.1.3**: 23.

Inventoire **B.4**: 29, 45. **H.2.1**: 11. **H.4**: 39, 44, 51, 56.

Investissement à l'exterieur **O.2.2**: 91.

Investissements **B.4**: 18. **C**: 10, 82. **D**: 56, 74. **F.3.1.3**: 20. **F.3.3**: 21, 40–41, 55, 59. **G.1**: 38, 51. **G.1.3**: 11. **G.2.1**: 78. **G.2.5**: 16. **G.3.3.2**: 1, 4, 9. **G.3.3.3**: 22, 36. **G.3.3.5**: 37. **H.0**: 101. **H.1.1.1**: 5. **H.1.1.2**: 9. **H.2.1**: 65, 78. **H.2.2**: 12, 14, 104, 121, 128. **H.3**: 2, 56, 83. **J.2**: 21,

34. **J.4**: 133, 150–151, 154–158, 161–163. **L.1**: 1, 13. **L.3**: 5–6, 11, 13–16, 18–19, 26–27. **M.4**: 77, 81. **M.5**: 25, 28, 35. **N.1**: 86, 212. **N.2**: 34, 72, 136, 309. **O.1.2.2**: 17. **O.1.2.4**: 52. **O.1.3**: 11, 85. **O.2.1**: 56–57. **O.2.2**: 40, 74, 81, 87–88.

Investissements de l'entreprise **G.2.4**: 103. **G.3.3.3**: 13. **H.2.1**: 40. **L.3**: 7. **N.2**: 181.

Investissements étrangers **F.3.2**: 21, 82, 85, 92. **H.2.2**: 23, 68, 108. **L.3**: 3. **N.1**: 268. **N.2**: 87. **N.3**: 29. **O.1.2.3**: 15, 30. **O.1.3**: 27. **O.2.1**: 57. **O.2.2**: 20, 27, 80, 82–86, 88, 93–98, 100, 103–112, 115–119, 121–123, 125–129. **O.3.2**: 29.

Investissements industriels **H.4**: 28. **L.3**: 9.

Investissements internationaux **J.4**: 156. **O.1.2.2**: 12. **O.2.2**: 80–84, 86–88, 91–98, 101, 103–109, 111–112, 114, 117–120, 123, 125–128.

Investissements privés **H.1.2.1**: 18. **I.2.3**: 102. **L.3**: 1, 8, 17, 21.

Investissements publics **F.3.1.1**: 77. **I.2.3**: 67.

Investisseurs **B.4**: 38. **J.4**: 176, 287.

Irrationalité **J.5**: 27.

Irrigation **H.1.1.1**: 10–11, 15.

Islam **F.3.2**: 99. **I.2.1**: 58. **J.2**: 27, 197. **N.1**: 231.

James, William **D**: 28.

Jeunesse **F.1**: 5. **G.2.1**: 72, 136.

Jugement **B.3**: 46. **C**: 6. **I.2.1**: 172.

Jurisprudence **N.2**: 292.

Justice **M.1**: 3, 18.

Justice distributive **C**: 80. **L.2**: 38.

Justice économique **O.1.1**: 4.

Justice sociale **O.1.3**: 71.

Kahn, Alfred **D**: 54.

Kalecki, M. **D**: 72. **F.3.2**: 31.

Keynes, John Maynard **B.3**: 29. **C**: 14, 34, 38. **D**: 23, 27, 53–56, 59, 63, 66, 74, 79. **I.2.1**: 177. **J.1**: 28. **L.2**: 64.

Keynesianisme **B.1**: 24. **B.3**: 30. **C**: 34–35, 45, 48, 54. **D**: 45, 63, 66–67. **F.3.1.1**: 47. **I.2.1**: 181. **J.1**: 12, 22. **J.2**: 177. **L.3**: 18. **O.3.1**: 74.

Kibbutzim **G.2.4**: 122.

Kirzner, Israel **D**: 71.

Knight, F.H. **C**: 41.

Kuhn, Thomas **D**: 57.

Laboratoire **B.4**: 32.

Labour **H.1.1**: 9.

Lachmann, Ludwig **D**: 71.

Laine **I.2.3**: 68.

Laissez-faire **D**: 5. **F.3.1.1**: 117.

Langue allemande **E**: 10.

Législation **H.0**: 113. **N.2**: 207.

Législation anti-trust **G.3.2**: 2, 20–22, 27, 36–37, 39. **H.2.2**: 50. **H.3**: 39. **H.4**: 90. **I.2.1**: 68, 72. **O.1.3**: 28. **O.3.2**: 19.

Législation du marché financier **J.4**: 110.

Légitimation **J.4**: 89.

Légitimité **H.0**: 79. **N.1**: 56.

Libéralisation **H.1.1.4**: 6. **H.2.1**: 125. **H.3**: 89. **H.4**: 21. **J.2**: 166. **J.4**: 42–43, 133. **J.5**: 19, 28. **N.1**: 171. **O.1.3**: 14. **O.2.1**: 62. **O.2.2**: 34. **O.2.3**: 23.

Libéralisation des échanges **G.2.4**: 29. **H.1.1.4**: 26. **J.4**: 61. **M.3**: 2. **N.1**: 39, 174. **O.1.2.4**: 14. **O.1.3**: 87, 100–101. **O.2.1**: 62. **O.2.2**: 110. **O.3.1**: 71. **O.3.3**: 7, 33, 40–41, 82–83, 103.

Libéralisme **D**: 22, 44. **F.3.1.3**: 22. **J.1**: 91, 100.

Libéralisme économique **D**: 3.

Liberté **C**: 41.

Liberté d'expression **I.2.3**: 33.

Liberté d'opinion **H.3**: 19.

Libre échange **D**: 44. **F.1**: 85. **F.3.2**: 82. **G.3.3.2**: 5. **H.0**: 87. **H.2.2**: 78–79. **O.1.3**: 21–22, 32, 35, 88–99, 101–102. **O.3.1**: 34–35. **O.3.3**: 1, 94, 107, 128.

Licences **H.1.2.1**: 40. **H.2.1**: 45. **I.2.1**: 101.

Licenciements **G.2.1**: 12. **G.2.4**: 27, 68. **G.2.5**: 27, 32, 34. **K.3**: 45.

Lieu de travail **G.2.3**: 8, 10. **G.2.5**: 10. **K.3**: 74.

Ligne aérienne **F.3.1.1**: 20. **H.3**: 38, 41, 43, 45–46, 48, 50, 53.

Ligues **L.2**: 15.

Liquidité **D**: 74. **J.1**: 13, 15. **J.4**: 63, 276. **J.5**: 30. **L.1**: 23. **M.4**: 113. **O.2.1**: 71.

Livre sterling **J.1**: 7.

Localisation d'entreprise **F.3.1.1**: 2, 5, 7, 12, 18, 25, 32, 49, 120–121, 123. **H.4**: 32. **O.2.2**: 91.

Localisation géographique **F.3.1.1**: 34. **K.3**: 74. **L.2**: 97. **O.1.2.2**: 12.

Localisation industrielle **F.3.1.1**: 4, 6, 11, 13, 24, 31, 33, 38, 43, 55. **G.1**: 47. **G.3.2**: 1. **H.2.1**: 31. **H.2.2**: 64.

Lockouts **G.2.4**: 69.

Loeb, Jacques **D**: 31.

Logement **F.3.1.1**: 16. **F.3.3**: 59. **G.2.1**: 27. **I.2.1**: 179. **I.2.3**: 98, 100, 112. **L.2**: 83, 87, 93, 96–97, 99, 101, 106. **M.2**: 5. **N.1**: 318.

Logement rural **L.2**: 34.

Logement urbain **I.2.3**: 101. **L.2**: 107.

Logements sociaux **L.2**: 102, 104, 109–110.

Logiciel **B.3**: 16. **G.3.3.5**: 39, 54. **H.2.2**: 17.

Loi contre déversement **G.3.2**: 12. **O.1.3**: 28. **O.3.3**: 96–97, 100.

Loi environnementale **I.2.3**: 49. **N.2**: 115. **O.3.1**: 19.

Loisir **H.3**: 14, 17. **L.2**: 47. **M.2**: 9.

Loyauté **I.2.3**: 26. **L.2**: 68.

Loyer **G.1**: 9. **H.1.1**: 11. **H.1.1.2**: 6. **H.1.2**: 2. **H.2.2**: 157. **I.2.1**: 31. **I.2.3**: 16, 63, 98. **K.3**: 80. **L.2**: 89. **O.3.3**: 87.

Lutte anti-pollution **H.0**: 45, 72–73, 95, 97–99, 101–102, 104, 106, 119, 121, 128, 186, 191. **N.2**: 31.

Machines outils **H.2.2**: 45. **O.3.3**: 42.

MacIntyre, Alisdair **D**: 73.

Macroéconomie **B.1**: 5, 12–13, 18, 20–21, 23. **B.3**: 23. **C**: 1, 45, 47. **D**: 11, 54, 63. **F.1**: 86. **F.2**: 26. **F.3.1.1**: 59. **F.3.3**: 10, 40. **G.2.1**: 28, 47. **G.2.2**: 4. **G.3.2**: 29. **H.0**: 28. **H.1.1**: 18. **H.2.1**: 48. **H.2.2**: 158. **H.3**: 100. **H.4**: 33. **I.2.1**: 47, 86. **J.1**: 7, 69. **J.2**: 11. **J.5**: 26. **K.2**: 31. **L.1**: 2. **L.2**: 17. **N.1**: 33, 73–74, 108, 233, 296. **N.2**: 44, 47. **O.1.3**: 57, 72. **O.2.1**: 50. **O.2.2**: 36, 68. **O.3.2**: 27.

Magasins **H.4**: 98.

Main-d'oeuvre féminine **F.3.1.2**: 10. **G.2.1**: 96, 103. **G.2.2**: 31–32.

Maïs **H.1.2.1**: 26, 31.

Malades **M.4**: 59.

Maladies **M.4**: 66.

Malthus, T. R. **D**: 24.

Mandats électoraux **N.2**: 269.

Marchandises à terme **H.2.2**: 155. **I.2.1**: 120, 164. **I.2.3**: 46. **J.4**: 1, 4, 17, 20, 28, 35, 44, 58, 69, 72, 100–101, 103, 148, 198, 200, 211, 215, 226, 242, 264, 273. **O.1.2.3**: 2, 17, 39. **O.2.1**: 31, 59. **O.2.2**: 90, 99, 102, 113.

Marchands **J.4**: 13.

Marché **B.3**: 51. **B.4**: 10, 32. **D**: 71. **F.1**: 20. **F.3.1.1**: 113. **G.1**: 18. **G.3.2**: 31. **G.3.3**: 11. **G.4**: 7. **H.0**: 28. **H.2.1**: 14, 22. **H.4**: 28. **I.2.1**: 19, 27, 32, 34, 41, 54, 65, 76, 80, 105–106, 114, 145, 153. **I.2.3**: 1, 26, 38, 47, 51, 57, 70, 100. **J.1**: 92. **J.2**: 24, 44, 54, 144, 158. **J.4**: 6, 13, 46, 71, 79, 151, 262. **K.3**: 32. **L.2**: 4, 22. **M.4**: 29. **N.1**: 32, 37. **N.2**: 162. **O.3.3**: 80.

Marché agricole **I.2.3**: 74.

Marché commun **O.1.2.4**: 54.

Marché de l'art **I.2.3**: 21.

Marché de l'énergie **I.2.3**: 43. **O.1.2.3**: 35. **O.3.2**: 59.

Marché de la viande **H.4**: 29. **I.2.3**: 74–75.

Marché des céréales **H.1.2.1**: 23. **I.2.3**: 71.

Marché des changes **J.1**: 1. **O.2.1**: 1, 11–12, 15, 31, 36, 40, 86.

Marché des produits de base **O.1.2.3**: 5, 37. **O.1.3**: 5. **O.3.2**: 18.

Marché du charbon **H.2.1**: 3.

Marché du crédit **J.2**: 54, 69. **J.5**: 16, 53.

Marché du logement **C**: 12. **F.3.1.1**: 118. **I.2.2**: 2. **I.2.3**: 81–84, 86–87, 92, 96, 101–102, 105, 107, 109–111. **K.3**: 87. **L.2**: 76, 84–85, 103, 107.

Marché du sucre **H.1.2.1**: 16.

Marché du travail **D**: 14. **F.3.1.2**: 2. **F.3.3**: 23. **F.5**: 14, 30. **G.1**: 54. **G.2.1**: 1–2, 5–7, 9, 11, 13, 23–26, 29, 31, 33–34, 36, 40, 43, 45–51, 55–56, 59–62, 64–65, 67, 75, 83, 90, 95, 101, 108, 117, 120, 126, 131, 136, 142–143, 151, 158, 162, 164, 168–169, 172–173, 175. **G.2.2**: 7, 17, 19, 21, 27–28, 30, 41. **G.2.3**: 8. **G.2.4**: 29, 32, 72–73, 104. **G.2.5**: 21, 29, 32. **H.1.1.2**: 18. **K.2**: 28. **K.3**: 4, 12, 14, 66, 69, 93, 95. **M.4**: 121. **N.2**: 44. **O.1.2.4**: 30, 59. **O.3.1**: 67.

Marché financier **B.4**: 18. **F.2**: 28. **F.3.3**: 23. **G.3.3.5**: 93, 118. **H.2.1**: 8. **H.3**: 86. **I.2.1**: 16. **I.2.3**: 55. **J.1**: 63. **J.2**: 7, 21, 117, 155, 160, 166. **J.4**: 2, 8–11, 15, 20, 24, 26–28, 30, 35–38, 40–41, 43, 45, 47–51, 60, 62, 64–67, 71–74, 78, 81–82, 84–86, 89, 91–94, 97–99, 101, 113, 116, 121, 143–144, 162, 165, 172, 174, 179, 182, 187, 190, 192–193, 196, 200, 212–213, 215, 225–226, 231, 238–239, 243, 252, 255, 258, 264, 272–273, 277, 283, 292–293, 303–304. **K.3**: 71. **L.1**: 3, 41. **L.3**: 15. **N.1**: 181. **O.1.3**: 90. **O.2.1**: 24, 26. **O.2.2**: 9, 31–32. **O.2.3**: 37. **O.3.2**: 12.

Marché financier international **J.4**: 157, 234. **O.2.2**: 10, 31, 33, 45, 124.

Marché foncier **I.2.3**: 7, 109–110. **N.2**: 154.

Marché intérieur **O.3.1**: 11.

Marché international **O.1.2.3**: 12, 34. **O.2.2**: 89.

Marché mondial **H.1.2.1**: 24. **H.2.2**: 33, 131. **J.4**: 190. **M.5**: 23. **O.1.2.3**: 6, 14, 21, 24. **O.3.1**: 70.

Marché monétaire **J.1**: 21. **J.2**: 187. **J.5**: 59.

Marché noir **N.1**: 174. **O.2.1**: 3. **O.2.3**: 35.

Marché obligataire **G.3.3.3**: 9. **J.4**: 104, 107–108, 115, 124, 135, 142, 171.

Marché pétrolier **I.2.3**: 12, 23, 46, 58. **O.1.2.3**: 3, 13, 23, 26.

Marché régional **O.1.3**: 41.

Marché unique européen **F.3.1.1**: 25. **F.3.2**: 119. **G.1.1**: 26. **G.2.1**: 87. **G.2.5**: 37. **H.3**: 36. **H.4**: 16. **J.2**: 86, 161, 184, 189, 210. **J.4**: 61. **L.2**: 85. **L.3**: 7. **N.2**: 88. **O.1.2.3**: 35. **O.1.2.4**: 27, 37, 78, 83–84, 86, 88. **O.2.4**: 1, 18. **O.3.1**: 21. **O.3.2**: 65.

Marchés étrangers **O.1.2.3**: 16. **O.2.2**: 91.

Marchés publics **I.2.1**: 3. **N.3**: 10.

Mariage **F.3.1.3**: 31.

Marshall, Alfred **C**: 35. **D**: 27, 36, 58.

Marx, Karl **D**: 14, 27, 30.

Marxisme **D**: 26, 33, 77. **N.1**: 229.

Matériel d'équitation **I.2.1**: 12.

Maternité précoce **F.3.1.3**: 26.

Matières premières **O.1.2.3**: 14. **O.1.3**: 6.

McClosekey, Donald **D**: 22.

Means, G.C. **D**: 69.

Mécanisation agricole **H.1.1.1**: 4.

Médecins **K.3**: 48. **M.4**: 12, 27.

Mémoire **H.4**: 61.

Ménages **B.1**: 16. **B.3**: 7. **F.3.1.2**: 15. **F.3.1.3**: 15. **G.2.1**: 101, 152. **K.1**: 1–2. **K.2**: 4, 10. **L.2**: 5, 13, 25, 27, 40, 46. **L.3**: 5, 8. **M.2**: 9, 13. **N.2**: 16.

Mer **H.3**: 73, 77.

Mercantilisme **O.3.3**: 118.

Mère **M.4**: 3, 104. **N.2**: 82.

Mères travailleuses **G.2.2**: 36.

Mesure **C**: 84. **K.1**: 2. **M.2**: 12.

Mesure de l'offre **H.1.2.1**: 25.

Mesure de la productivité **G.1.1**: 20, 23, 30, 32–33, 36. **H.4**: 22.

Mesure du revenu **K.1**: 2. **K.2**: 23. **M.2**: 27.

Méthode de production **D**: 77.

Méthodes comptable **B.4**: 10, 16, 19, 43, 45, 48. **J.2**: 40. **J.4**: 27.

Méthodes d'exploitation agricole **H.1.1.1**: 21, 38. **H.1.2**: 3.

Méthodes de recherche **A**: 11. **B.2**: 1. **B.4**: 53.

Méthodes mathématiques **B.3**: 6, 15, 26. **O.2.1**: 24.

Méthodes statistiques **B.3**: 5, 29.

Méthodologie **B.1**: 9. **B.2**: 2. **B.3**: 43. **F.5**: 19. **H.0**: 51. **H.1.1**: 15. **O.3.3**: 44.

Méthodologie économique **B.1**: 7, 10–11, 16, 25.

Meulen, Henry **J.2**: 176.

Mexicains **G.2.1**: 5.

Microéconomie **D**: 1. **F.3.1.1**: 59. **G.2.1**: 88. **G.2.4**: 77. **G.3.2**: 29. **H.3**: 100. **I.2.1**: 146. **I.2.3**: 47. **K.3**: 81. **M.2**: 24. **N.1**: 175. **O.2.3**: 20.

Microélectronique **H.2.2**: 58.

Migrateurs **F.2**: 14. **F.3.1.3**: 5.

Migration **B.3**: 27. **F.2**: 7. **F.3.1.1**: 27, 124. **F.3.1.2**: 12. **G.2.1**: 82. **K.3**: 60. **O.1.2.5**: 5.

Migration de retour **F.3.1.2**: 5. **O.1.2.5**: 6.

Migration de travail **G.2.1**: 16, 81, 85. **O.1.2.5**: 7. **O.3.1**: 28.

Migration internationale **G.2.1**: 77, 83. **O.1.2.5**: 2–4.

Politique économique **B.1**: 7. **B.3**: 17. **C**: 7–8, 55. **D**: 67. **E**: 11, 17. **F.1**: 2, 6, 16–17, 27, 33, 35, 43, 48, 52, 62, 64, 74, 76, 87, 92. **F.3.1.1**: 56, 70, 111. **F.3.2**: 42, 51, 61–62, 66, 75, 94, 97, 116, 126. **F.3.3**: 4, 36, 40, 47. **G.2.1**: 108. **H.0**: 26, 57–58, 128, 168. **H.4**: 43. **I.2.1**: 148. **J.1**: 2, 86. **J.5**: 14. **L.1**: 8. **M.1**: 4. **M.2**: 28. **N.1**: 22, 33, 40, 49–51, 66, 70, 80, 82, 88–89, 91–92, 94–98, 100–102, 104, 106, 108–116, 119–122, 126–128, 130, 135, 142, 152, 156, 182, 188, 194, 205, 218, 233, 235, 252, 255, 278, 318. **N.2**: 44, 55, 67, 89, 141, 168, 242, 257. **O.1.2.4**: 33. **O.1.3**: 9, 65, 84. **O.2.2**: 128. **O.3.3**: 23.

Politique économique internationale **O.1.3**: 24, 34, 36–38, 55, 70.

Politique énergétique **H.0**: 13. **H.2.2**: 80, 85, 87, 124, 162. **I.2.3**: 8. **O.1.2.4**: 19.

Politique étrangère **O.1.2.3**: 28. **O.1.3**: 2. **O.3.2**: 61.

Politique familiale **M.4**: 104. **N.2**: 165.

Politique financière **J.4**: 43. **N.2**: 184. **O.1.2.4**: 58.

Politique fiscale **F.3.1.2**: 13. **F.3.3**: 13. **G.2.1**: 32. **G.3.2**: 13. **J.2**: 217, 233. **J.5**: 2, 39, 45, 57. **L.2**: 85. **M.4**: 74. **N.1**: 144, 188, 318. **N.2**: 94, 127, 130, 132, 134, 137–140, 142–144, 147–152, 154–156, 158, 160–161, 164–165, 168, 170, 173–177, 181–185, 187, 199, 231, 250, 289, 297–298. **N.3**: 15. **O.1.2**: 14. **O.1.2.4**: 80, 84, 88. **O.1.3**: 25. **O.2.1**: 16, 65. **O.2.3**: 24, 48, 64. **O.3.1**: 33.

Politique foncière **N.2**: 148.

Politique forestière **H.1.2.1**: 52.

Politique gouvernementale **G.1.3**: 7. **H.0**: 149. **H.1.1.4**: 10. **H.3**: 87. **J.2**: 197. **N.1**: 25. **N.2**: 76. **N.3**: 35. **O.1.2.2**: 4. **O.1.3**: 60. **O.2.2**: 40. **O.3.2**: 25.

Politique industrielle **F.3.1.1**: 83, 123. **F.3.2**: 55. **G.1.3**: 13. **G.3.2**: 22. **H.2.1**: 77, 97, 100–101, 103–104, 106–107, 110–111, 114, 116–117. **H.2.2**: 20, 61, 77. **O.1.2.4**: 65, 72. **O.1.3**: 55. **O.3.3**: 77.

Politique intérieure **H.0**: 5.

Politique internationale **F.3.2**: 83.

Politique macroéconomique **F.1**: 84. **J.5**: 43, 56. **N.1**: 75, 105, 107, 123–125, 175. **O.1.3**: 29.

Politique mondiale **O.1.2.4**: 75.

Politique monétaire **B.2**: 2. **F.3.3**: 13. **F.4**: 2. **H.1.2.1**: 26. **J.1**: 11, 13, 20, 23, 37, 71, 89, 101. **J.2**: 52, 129, 216, 219–220. **J.4**: 171. **J.5**: 2–8, 10–11, 13–22, 25–27, 30–37, 39–51, 53–55, 57, 59–61. **K.2**: 25. **N.1**: 207. **O.1.2**: 3, 12. **O.1.2.4**: 85. **O.2.1**: 8, 25, 44. **O.2.2**: 9. **O.2.3**: 3, 6–7, 11–13, 15–16, 20–21, 23, 26, 32, 47–49, 65–66.

Politique publique **F.3.1.1**: 119. **F.3.1.3**: 19. **F.3.3**: 20, 49. **G.2.1**: 68. **G.2.2**: 31. **M.2**: 3. **M.3**: 13. **M.4**: 32, 61, 94. **N.1**: 34, 187.

Politique régionale **F.3.1.1**: 87.

Politique régulatrice **H.0**: 134, 174. **N.2**: 58.

Politique rurale **F.3.1.1**: 93.

Politique scientifique **G.1**: 14. **G.1.3**: 13. **G.3.3.5**: 67.

Politique sociale **F.1**: 62. **G.2.2**: 35. **I.2.3**: 55. **M.3**: 3–4, 7–8. **N.1**: 102. **N.2**: 67.

Politique tarifaire **O.3.3**: 78, 94, 134.

Politique urbaine **F.3.1.1**: 121. **N.2**: 232.

Pollution **H.0**: 2, 16, 20, 65, 67, 79, 107, 111, 113, 120, 132. **H.2.2**: 22. **N.2**: 142.

Pollution de l'air **H.0**: 4, 74, 84, 86, 88, 103. **N.2**: 115.

Pollution de l'eau **H.0**: 73, 196, 200, 204, 207.

Pollution des mers **H.0**: 25.

Pommes de terre **H.1.2.1**: 7.

Population **F.3.1.2**: 1. **N.2**: 59.

Populisme **N.1**: 37.

Postmodernisme **H.4**: 60.

Potentiel de développement **H.2.2**: 100.

Pouvoir **C**: 15. **G.3.3**: 35.

Pouvoir de l'entreprise **G.3.2**: 3, 23–24. **I.2.1**: 79. **J.2**: 168.

Pouvoir de négociation **G.3.3.3**: 33. **K.3**: 89.

Pouvoir économique **F.1**: 3.

Pouvoir monopolistique **I.2.1**: 113.

Pratique commerciale **N.2**: 190.

Pré-enquêtes **G.3.3**: 29.

Prebisch, Raul **D**: 51.

Préférences commerciales **O.3.3**: 50.

Préférences du consommateur **C**: 30. **G.1.1**: 9. **I.2.1**: 91. **L.2**: 86.

Préférences fiscales **N.2**: 50.

Préférences révélées **C**: 26. **L.1**: 43.

Préservation **F.3.1.4**: 9. **H.0**: 59, 61, 130, 153, 156. **H.1.1.1**: 7. **H.1.2.1**: 13. **H.2.1**: 70.

Presse **G.2.4**: 28, 69. **H.3**: 19.

Prêts bancaires **B.4**: 7, 52. **G.3.3.4**: 6. **J.2**: 6, 13, 40, 82–83, 88, 142, 230. **J.4**: 147.

Prêts hypothécaires **J.2**: 237.

Prêts internationaux **N.2**: 251.

Prévision technologique **F.2**: 31.

Prévisions **B.3**: 39. **F.2**: 18, 20, 27–29. **H.2.1**: 70. **J.1**: 77. **J.4**: 24, 225, 249, 289. **L.2**: 54. **N.2**: 3. **O.2.1**: 61.

Prévisions de marché **F.2**: 23. **J.4**: 103, 211, 218, 246, 262.

Prévisions démographiques **F.2**: 30.

Prévisions économiques **B.3**: 22. **F.2**: 19, 22, 25–26, 30. **F.5**: 18. **H.2.2**: 155. **I.2.3**: 28. **J.1**: 108–109. **L.2**: 11. **N.2**: 3.

Prime enfance **M.5**: 36.

Primes de salaire **G.1.2**: 8. **K.3**: 96, 124.

Primes de salaires **G.2.1**: 161.

Principe pollueur-payeur **H.0**: 67–68, 95, 108–109, 189.

Prise de décision **B.3**: 24. **C**: 23, 25, 67, 79, 82. **D**: 42. **F.3.1.1**: 5, 7, 38, 43. **G.2.4**: 3. **G.3.2**: 33. **G.3.3**: 3, 13, 24. **G.3.3.5**: 21, 26, 53, 58, 60, 74, 76, 85–86, 101. **H.0**: 37, 168. **H.2.2**: 68. **I.2.1**: 25, 121. **J.2**: 34. **L.2**: 50, 77. **M.4**: 70. **N.1**: 2, 90. **N.2**: 203.

Prise de décision en groupe **G.3.3.5**: 80. **J.5**: 27.

Privatisation **B.4**: 66. **F.3.1.3**: 4. **F.3.1.4**: 28. **G.2.4**: 54. **G.3.3**: 27. **H.0**: 183. **H.1.1.2**: 2. **H.2.2**: 41, 127. **H.3**: 25. **H.4**: 109. **J.2**: 80. **M.3**: 14. **M.4**: 50. **N.1**: 256–277, 279–296, 298–327. **N.3**: 6, 25. **O.2.2**: 65, 116.

Prix **B.3**: 51. **F.3.1.1**: 104. **F.4**: 3. **G.3.3.5**: 48. **H.0**: 119. **H.1.1.1**: 12, 15. **H.1.2.1**: 30. **H.2.1**: 112. **H.2.2**: 39, 155. **I.1**: 2. **I.2.1**: 11, 33, 48, 55–56, 59, 97, 107, 110, 112, 118, 122, 125–126, 131, 134, 141, 144–145, 147, 149, 153, 159–161, 167, 170–171, 180, 183. **I.2.2**: 4, 7. **I.2.3**: 3–4, 12, 16, 20, 29, 41, 44, 58, 72–73, 76, 106, 108. **J.1**: 45, 59, 101. **J.2**: 55, 66. **J.3**: 12. **J.4**: 6, 12, 69, 87, 120, 222, 245, 247, 268, 273, 287, 295. **J.5**: 47, 50. **K.3**: 50. **L.2**: 91. **N.2**: 237. **O.1.2.3**: 14, 17. **O.2.1**: 60. **O.3.1**: 22, 68. **O.3.2**: 18, 44. **O.3.3**: 31, 77.

Prix à la production **I.2.1**: 129, 158.

Prix agricole **H.1.1**: 20. **H.1.1.4**: 47. **I.2.3**: 28, 52, 77, 80. **O.3.3**: 82.

Prix alimentaires **I.2.3**: 38. **O.3.2**: 25.

Prix de détail **H.4**: 105. **I.2.1**: 128. **I.2.3**: 37.

Prix de l'eau **H.0**: 201. **N.3**: 45.

Prix de l'énergie **I.2.3**: 48.

Prix de revient **G.3.3.5**: 73. **I.2.1**: 119.

Prix des actions **G.3.3.3**: 25. **J.2**: 244. **J.4**: 18, 120, 208, 217, 249–250, 255, 262–263, 266–270, 274–276, 279, 281, 291, 295–298, 300–301, 305, 308. **O.2.1**: 87. **O.2.4**: 13.

Prix des facteurs **B.3**: 37. **L.3**: 23.

Prix des produits de base **B.3**: 37. **I.2.1**: 137. **J.4**: 103. **O.1.2.3**: 27.

Prix du logement **H.0**: 186. **I.2.3**: 84, 88–90, 93, 97, 99, 103–104, 107.

Prix du pétrole **I.2.3**: 25, 62. **N.2**: 158. **O.1.2.3**: 8, 24, 38–39. **O.2.3**: 43. **O.3.1**: 40.

Prix du terrain **I.2.3**: 6, 22, 39, 42, 64, 97.

Prix industriels **I.2.3**: 52.

Prix peu élastique **O.2.1**: 23.

Prix relatifs **I.2.2**: 3. **K.3**: 19. **L.3**: 21.

Probabilité **B.3**: 29, 46, 57. **J.4**: 82. **M.5**: 1. **O.3.1**: 18.

Problème agraire **H.1.1.4**: 8.

Procès civil **F.3.1.4**: 16.

Processus stochastiques **F.3.3**: 39. **H.4**: 39. **J.3**: 17. **J.4**: 7, 286. **K.1**: 4. **O.1.2**: 12. **O.3.2**: 80.

Producteurs **F.3.1.1**: 41. **H.1.1.1**: 22. **H.4**: 18.

Production **F.3.1.1**: 14, 40. **F.3.2**: 46. **G.1**: 28. **G.1.2**: 4. **G.2.1**: 152. **G.3.3**: 20–21. **G.3.3.3**: 21. **H.0**: 130–131. **H.1.1.1**: 16. **H.1.2**: 2. **H.1.2.1**: 5, 19. **H.2.1**: 48, 112, 115, 121. **H.2.2**: 52, 67, 93. **H.4**: 56. **I.2.1**: 55. **L.2**: 5, 46. **M.5**: 30. **O.2.2**: 38, 74, 117. **O.3.2**: 58. **O.3.3**: 63, 77.

Production agricole **F.3.1.2**: 15. **F.3.2**: 59. **H.0**: 74. **H.1.1.1**: 2, 8, 22, 29, 36. **H.1.1.2**: 24. **H.1.2.1**: 27, 29, 31. **H.4**: 63, 68.

Production animale **H.1.1.1**: 5.

Production de bétail **H.1.2.1**: 18.

Production de cheptel **H.1.2.1**: 13.

Production de masse **H.2.2**: 66.

Production industrielle **F.3.1.1**: 31. **H.0**: 63. **H.2.2**: 28, 32, 78, 145.

Productivité **F.3.1.3**: 14. **F.3.2**: 59. **F.3.3**: 26, 42, 52. **F.5**: 32. **G.1**: 11, 13, 40, 42, 50. **G.1.1**: 1, 5, 7, 13, 18, 24, 31, 37, 41. **G.1.2**: 3, 9–13, 15–16, 18. **G.2.4**: 16, 48, 91. **G.2.5**: 55–56. **G.3.3.2**: 10. **G.3.3.4**: 16. **G.3.3.5**: 59. **H.1.1.2**: 7. **H.2.1**: 80, 102, 120, 126. **H.2.2**: 5, 29, 42–43, 73, 150. **H.3**: 26. **J.2**: 8, 174, 185, 194. **K.3**: 81, 92. **L.3**: 6. **N.1**: 160. **N.3**: 38–39.

Productivité agricole **H.1.1**: 5, 10. **H.1.1.1**: 10, 19–20, 25, 27, 32. **H.1.1.2**: 12, 20. **H.1.1.4**: 32. **H.1.2**: 4–5. **I.2.3**: 76.

Productivité du travail **F.3.1.3**: 26. **F.5**: 27. **G.1.1**: 21. **G.1.2**: 6–7, 19. **H.2.2**: 65, 72.

Productivité industrielle **B.3**: 24. **F.3.1.1**: 114. **G.1.1**: 19. **G.1.3**: 10, 14. **H.2.1**: 122–123, 125, 127.

Produit agricole **H.1.1**: 18. **H.1.2.1**: 17, 21, 24–25. **H.4**: 79. **I.2.3**: 79. **K.3**: 9. **O.1.2.3**: 24. **O.3.3**: 38.

Produit intérieur brut **F.2**: 11, 13, 20.

Produit national brut **E**: 15. **F.2**: 1, 4, 12, 17. **F.5**: 31, 38.

Produits alimentaires **H.4**: 75.

Produits de base **F.3.1.4**: 14. **F.4**: 8. **H.1.1**: 23. **H.1.1.3**: 6. **I.2.1**: 110. **J.5**: 50. **N.1**: 259. **N.2**: 53, 162, 194, 237. **O.3.1**: 13. **O.3.2**: 33. **O.3.3**: 32, 44.

Produits de bois **O.3.2**: 9, 81.

Produits industriels **H.2.1**: 54, 122.

Produits laitiers **H.1.1.4**: 35.

K.1: 6. K.2: 1, 3–5, 7, 9, 11, 15–21, 26, 30, 32–33, 38, 41–42. K.3: 18, 31. M.2: 19. N.2: 55. N.3: 18. O.2.2: 6. O.3.1: 10.

Répartition en zones I.2.1: 52.

Répartition spatiale F.3.1.1: 19, 44. H.2.2: 71.

Reprise économique F.3.2: 67. F.3.3: 45. N.2: 238.

Réseau ferroviaire H.3: 60.

Réseaux sociaux G.2.4: 125.

Réserves monétaires O.2.3: 46.

Résidence K.3: 74.

Responsabilité G.2.4: 63. G.3.3.5: 128. M.3: 3.

Responsabilité civile F.3.1.4: 3. G.3.3.3: 12. H.0: 122. H.1.1.2: 22. J.2: 130, 144, 147. J.3: 1, 15. J.4: 62. L.2: 33.

Responsabilité de l'État H.1.1.2: 2.

Ressources d'uranium H.2.2: 84.

Ressources de la mer H.0: 145. H.1.2.1: 32, 48. H.3: 77.

Ressources de pêche H.1.2.1: 37.

Ressources économiques K.2: 10.

Ressources en eau C: 60. F.3.1.4: 11. H.0: 203, 210, 215.

Ressources énergétiques H.2.2: 106. I.2.3: 23.

Ressources financières F.1: 18.

Ressources humaines F.3.1.2: 7, 18. F.3.3: 13, 58. G.2.1: 28, 107. G.2.5: 12, 22, 35. G.4: 1–2. H.1.1: 10. H.1.1.4: 29. K.2: 21. K.3: 21, 27. M.5: 30, 35. N.1: 248.

Ressources naturelles F.3.1.1: 92. G.1.1: 33. H.0: 30, 34, 38, 42, 126–127, 131–135, 137, 139, 141–143, 146, 149–150, 172, 177, 185. H.1.1.2: 4. H.1.2.1: 13. H.2.2: 23. I.2.1: 131. N.2: 86.

Ressources renouvelables H.0: 129, 147.

Restriction I.2.3: 88.

Restrictions à l'exportation O.3.3: 2, 19, 48, 73.

Restrictions à l'importation O.3.3: 62.

Retraite H.3: 10. K.3: 16. M.4: 72, 74, 92.

Revendications foncières H.0: 23.

Revenu B.3: 9. F.3.2: 5. G.2.1: 147. G.2.2: 19. H.2.1: 34. J.1: 24, 26. K.1: 4. K.2: 13, 24–25. K.3: 9, 11, 27, 42, 64. L.1: 24. L.2: 39, 41, 48. M.2: 11, 16. M.4: 74, 100. N.1: 240. N.2: 154. O.3.2: 72.

Revenu agricole H.1.1.1: 6.

Revenu d'entreprise J.4: 208.

Revenu des ménages K.1: 3. K.2: 27. L.2: 100.

Revenu disponible G.3.3.5: 121.

Revenu familial K.2: 37. M.2: 1.

Revenu national B.4: 51. F.2: 2, 7–8, 10, 17. H.0: 29. K.1: 1.

Revenu permanent K.1: 7. L.2: 36.

Revenus d'investissement J.4: 303.

Révolution verte H.1.1.2: 15.

Ricardo, David D: 24. N.1: 229.

Richesse C: 15. F.3.1.1: 16. J.4: 22. K.1: 7. K.2: 11. L.1: 20, 42. L.2: 45, 101. M.1: 19. M.2: 12. M.4: 40. N.2: 187, 247.

Rigidité des salaires G.2.1: 139. K.3: 50.

Risque B.3: 21, 34. B.4: 10, 16, 54. C: 78–85. G.3.3: 9. G.3.3.5: 24, 59. H.1.1: 9. H.1.1.4: 17. H.2.1: 92. H.2.2: 7, 76. I.2.1: 59. J.2: 15, 45, 114, 158, 165, 182, 243, 246. J.3: 13. J.4: 88, 181, 184–201, 240. L.1: 34. L.2: 40. M.4: 10. N.2: 240, 291. O.2.1: 2, 29, 43. O.2.2: 11, 72, 90, 101, 103. O.2.3: 46. O.3.2: 68.

Risque financier G.3.3.3: 22. H.2.1: 3. J.4: 88.

Riz G.2.1: 13. H.1.1.1: 18, 36. H.1.2.1: 28.

Robertson, Dennis Holme F.5: 16. N.1: 120.

Robinson, Joan D: 50.

Rôle du profit I.2.3: 76.

Rotation de la main-d'oeuvre G.2.1: 84, 107.

Saisonnalité B.1: 18. G.2.1: 114. J.4: 160, 244, 261, 290. O.2.1: 36.

Salaire minimum K.3: 33, 37, 49, 73.

Salaires réels J.1: 73. K.3: 91, 99.

Salariés K.3: 58.

Samuelson, Paul J.1: 35.

Sanctions économiques M.2: 14. O.2.2: 14, 18.

Santé G.2.3: 10, 12. M.1: 5. M.4: 40, 53.

Santé publique M.4: 16, 34, 37, 66.

Schmoller, von, Gustav D: 34.

Science C: 37. F.3.1.1: 49, 123. F.3.3: 53. G.1: 44. G.1.3: 12.

Science politique B.1: 22.

Sciences de l'information A: 3, 8. G.1: 8.

Scientifiques G.1: 49.

Scolarité K.2: 39. K.3: 51. M.5: 30.

Sécheresse O.1.3: 76.

Secteur agricole H.1.1: 7. H.1.1.4: 16, 27. N.1: 259.

Secteur coopératif G.2.4: 122.

Secteur industriel B.3: 35. H.2.1: 64, 72. H.2.2: 92, 116.

Secteur informel F.1: 46, 75. F.3.2: 48. G.2.1: 66. G.3.3.4: 8. H.0: 43. H.4: 4, 17, 19, 26–27, 33, 46–47, 49–50. J.2: 57–58, 61. J.4: 73. L.1: 19. N.1: 20.

Secteur privé F.3.1.1: 119. F.3.2: 99. F.3.3: 55. G.2.4: 36, 87. G.3.3.4: 15. H.3: 16. H.4: 12. I.2.3: 112. K.3: 122. M.4: 94. N.1: 51, 301.

N.3: 41.

Secteur public **K.3**: 108, 122. **M.5**: 10. **N.2**: 262. **N.3**: 3, 5, 8, 10–11, 15, 18, 28, 39, 51, 55. **O.1.2.4**: 59. **O.2.2**: 92. **O.3.3**: 63.

Secteur tertiaire **F.3.3**: 64. **G.2.1**: 21. **G.2.2**: 25. **G.3.3.5**: 61. **H.4**: 64, 106–108, 111. **I.2.3**: 40. **L.3**: 7. **O.1.2.2**: 11. **O.3.2**: 28.

Sécurité **G.2.4**: 71. **H.3**: 71.

Sécurité alimentaire **H.1.1.4**: 50. **L.2**: 73, 79.

Sécurité de l'emploi **G.2.2**: 18.

Sécurité des produits **F.3.1.4**: 3. **H.2.2**: 56.

Sécurité du travail **G.2.3**: 1–2, 5, 7, 10, 12, 15, 17.

Sécurité nationale **F.1**: 2.

Sécurité sociale **G.2.1**: 97. **L.1**: 40–41. **L.2**: 37, 52. **M.1**: 25. **M.2**: 37. **M.4**: 69, 79–80, 83, 99–100, 102–104, 107, 110–111, 113–122. **N.2**: 195.

Segmentation du marché du travail **G.2.1**: 44. **H.2.2**: 49.

Ségrégation professionnelle **G.4**: 1.

Ségrégation raciale **G.2.1**: 16.

Sélection de portefeuille **J.4**: 170, 177, 284.

Séries temporelles **B.2**: 2. **B.3**: 13, 39, 58. **F.2**: 21. **G.2.1**: 160. **G.3.3.5**: 51. **H.1.2.1**: 6. **J.1**: 77. **J.4**: 299. **K.3**: 1. **L.1**: 1.

Service charge de faire respecter la loi **N.2**: 11, 207.

Service des pompiers **N.3**: 39.

Service financières **F.3.1.1**: 79. **G.2.5**: 50. **I.2.3**: 13. **J.2**: 19, 49, 58, 72, 86, 92, 111, 139, 148. **J.4**: 94, 161. **O.1.2.2**: 11. **O.1.2.4**: 78. **O.2.3**: 54.

Service postal **H.3**: 18.

Services collectifs **J.2**: 156.

Services d'information **B.3**: 38.

Services de santé **I.2.1**: 57. **M.4**: 14, 22, 28, 36, 58.

Services hospitaliers **M.4**: 65.

Services publics **F.3.1.1**: 48. **F.3.1.2**: 17. **G.1.2**: 13. **H.4**: 109. **N.3**: 4, 6, 8–9, 12, 16, 22, 25, 27, 44–46.

Services sociaux **M.4**: 1.

Services urbains **F.3.1.1**: 120.

SIDA **M.4**: 26.

Simulation **B.3**: 11. **G.1.1**: 25. **H.2.2**: 158. **H.3**: 83. **M.4**: 11.

Situation de l'emploi **G.2.1**: 25.

Smith, Adam **D**: 7, 14, 16–22, 25. **K.3**: 85.

Socialisation **D**: 56.

Socialisme **D**: 12, 48. **F.3.1.1**: 82. **F.3.1.4**: 14, 21. **G.1.2**: 11. **J.1**: 37. **N.1**: 151, 236.

Socialisme d'État **N.1**: 254.

Socialisme du marché **N.1**: 28–29, 145.

Société capitaliste **E**: 7.

Société industrielle **H.4**: 4. **M.5**: 29. **N.1**: 225.

Société rurale **H.1.1.2**: 29.

Sociétés d'investissement **J.4**: 153, 160, 265.

Sociologie industrielle **G.1**: 58. **G.2.5**: 45.

Sociologie politique **H.2.2**: 7.

Soi **D**: 34.

Soin dans la communauté **M.4**: 6.

Soins médicaux **G.1**: 51. **J.2**: 142. **M.4**: 12–13, 15, 20, 34, 38, 44, 46–48, 52–53, 55–57, 60, 62. **N.2**: 77.

Sources d'énergie renouvelables **H.0**: 114, 156. **H.1.1.1**: 34. **H.2.2**: 127.

Sous-développement **F.3.2**: 37, 70, 105. **O.2.4**: 15.

Sous-traitance **G.1.1**: 17. **H.2.2**: 76.

Souveraineté **F.3.1.1**: 84. **O.2.4**: 8.

Spécialisation de la production **G.1.1**: 26. **O.3.1**: 32.

Spécialisation flexible **G.1.1**: 15.

Spéculation en bourse **J.4**: 222.

Spéculation financière **I.2.3**: 110. **J.1**: 65. **J.4**: 46. **O.2.1**: 31, 43, 85.

Sport **G.2.4**: 35. **H.1.2.1**: 33. **H.3**: 14. **L.2**: 15.

Sraffa, Piero **D**: 65.

Stabilité d'emploi **G.2.1**: 170.

Stabilité des prix **H.1.2.1**: 22. **I.2.1**: 18. **J.1**: 95. **J.5**: 8–9. **O.1.2.3**: 26. **O.1.3**: 5.

Stabilité économique **F.4**: 13. **J.1**: 81. **N.1**: 61, 129–130. **N.2**: 47, 140. **O.2.4**: 2, 19. **O.3.3**: 83.

Stagflation **J.1**: 11.

Stagnation économique **F.3.1.1**: 100. **F.3.2**: 49. **N.2**: 71.

Stations énergétiques **H.2.2**: 119, 122.

Statistique **B.3**: 3, 54–55. **J.4**: 52.

Statistiques économiques **B.3**: 19, 63.

Stimulants de l'investissement **J.4**: 166.

Stimulants du travail **G.2.5**: 26.

Stimulants économiques **F.3.1.1**: 8. **G.1.1**: 3. **M.5**: 10.

Stimulants financiers **G.1.3**: 15. **H.0**: 101.

Stocks régulateurs **G.3.3.3**: 4.

Stratégie d'investissement **H.2.1**: 56. **J.4**: 9, 176, 207.

Stratégie de développement **F.3.2**: 27, 44, 68, 110. **H.3**: 82.

Stratégie économique **H.2.2**: 94.

Stratégies d'entreprises **C**: 65. **G.1.3**: 1. **G.3.3.5**: 81, 83, 86, 88–89, 95, 97, 99–101, 103. **H.2.2**: 51. **H.4**: 20. **K.3**: 79. **O.1.2.3**: 34. **O.3.1**: 20.

Stratification sociale **F.3.1.1**: 93. **F.3.2**: 19.

Structure de l'organisation **G.2.5**: 4, 7, 25. **G.3.1**: 2. **G.3.3**: 23. **G.3.3.5**: 99. **H.4**: 42. **N.2**: 107.

Structure de la famille **L.2**: 18, 41.

Structure des salaires **K.3**: 5, 56–57.

Structure du capital **G.2.5**: 26. **G.3.3.2**: 6, 13. **G.3.3.3**: 3. **J.4**: 68.

Structure du marché **G.3.3.3**: 29. **G.3.3.5**: 37. **H.1.2.1**: 30. **H.2.1**: 9, 50. **H.3**: 29. **H.4**: 11, 34. **I.2.1**: 37, 40. **I.2.3**: 44. **J.2**: 66. **O.3.1**: 17, 22, 42.

Structure économique **F.3.1.1**: 93. **O.1.2.3**: 36. **O.2.2**: 78. **O.3.2**: 58.

Structure industrielle **F.3.3**: 33. **H.2.1**: 19, 36, 58. **I.2.1**: 90. **I.2.3**: 29. **N.1**: 165. **O.1.2**: 18. **O.1.3**: 44.

Structure urbaine **H.4**: 106.

Substitution des facteurs **G.1.1**: 12.

Substitution monétaire **O.2.1**: 23.

Subventions **G.3.3.3**: 17. **H.1.1.1**: 12. **H.2.1**: 3. **H.3**: 66, 98. **H.4**: 30. **I.2.3**: 55–56. **M.4**: 19. **M.5**: 16, 19. **N.2**: 30, 174. **N.3**: 19. **O.1.2.4**: 25.

Subventions à l'exportation **G.1.3**: 21. **O.2.2**: 43. **O.3.1**: 6. **O.3.3**: 22, 91.

Succession **G.3.3**: 28.

Sucre **I.2.3**: 80.

Supermarchés **H.4**: 101. **I.2.1**: 7. **L.2**: 77.

Surabondance de main d'oeuvre **G.2.5**: 42.

Surplus de consommation **L.2**: 9.

Syndicats **G.2.1**: 162. **G.2.4**: 56–57, 59, 70–75, 77–82, 84–87, 89–94, 96–107, 113–114, 120. **G.2.5**: 46. **H.2.1**: 118. **H.2.2**: 58. **K.3**: 6, 18, 39, 64, 88–89, 102, 106, 125. **N.2**: 198. **O.1.2.4**: 47. **O.3.2**: 41.

Système de prix **I.2.1**: 10, 130.

Système financier **J.2**: 33, 41, 61, 81, 167, 173, 220. **J.5**: 16. **N.2**: 60. **O.1.2.3**: 29. **O.2.2**: 34.

Système monétaire international **O.2.1**: 28, 35. **O.2.3**: 48.

Systèmes bancaires **F.5**: 2. **J.2**: 12, 31, 117, 121, 141, 147, 179–180, 183, 194, 206. **O.2.3**: 20.

Systèmes d'exploitation **H.1.1.1**: 23.

Systèmes d'information **A**: 7. **B.3**: 12, 55. **G.1**: 6. **G.3.3.5**: 43, 54, 90, 92. **N.3**: 24.

Systèmes d'information de gestion **A**: 18.

Systèmes d'information géographique **H.0**: 192.

Systèmes de crédit **J.2**: 23.

Systèmes de paiement **J.2**: 9.

Systèmes de prévoyance **M.4**: 64.

Systèmes de production **G.1**: 35. **G.1.1**: 2. **G.1.2**: 5. **G.2.1**: 70.

Systèmes de rémunération **K.3**: 70.

Systèmes économiques **D**: 2, 12. **E**: 7. **F.3.1.3**: 18. **H.1.1.4**: 28. **H.2.2**: 16. **J.1**: 84. **N.1**: 223, 226, 228–231, 234, 237–238, 241.

Systèmes fiscaux **N.2**: 75, 100, 103–104, 112, 165, 227, 312. **O.1.3**: 28.

Systèmes monétaires **J.1**: 17, 34. **J.2**: 75. **O.2.1**: 28.

Tabac **I.2.3**: 18. **L.2**: 78. **N.2**: 214.

Tarifs douaniers **H.2.1**: 96. **I.2.1**: 84. **N.2**: 224, 281. **O.3.1**: 65. **O.3.3**: 16, 22, 38, 44, 46, 54–56, 58, 64, 69, 76, 87, 130, 139.

Tauromachie **F.3.1.1**: 37.

Taux d'escompte **J.4**: 143.

Taux d'imposition **L.2**: 96.

Taux d'inflation **N.2**: 269.

Taux d'intérêt **B.1**: 5. **B.3**: 44. **F.5**: 36. **G.3.3.3**: 20. **J.1**: 15, 18, 24, 32, 44, 77, 89–90. **J.2**: 15, 18, 23, 28–29, 32, 43, 46, 70, 95, 99, 162, 181, 233. **J.4**: 105, 125, 127–140, 142–148, 194, 201, 304. **J.5**: 16, 38, 44, 61. **L.1**: 27. **L.2**: 17, 39. **L.3**: 13–14. **N.2**: 236, 240–241, 273. **O.1.2.4**: 82. **O.2.1**: 7, 16, 19–20, 39. **O.2.2**: 74. **O.2.3**: 34.

Taux d'investissement **L.3**: 24.

Taux de change **B.3**: 39. **F.3.3**: 15. **G.3.3.3**: 39. **G.3.3.5**: 11. **H.1.1**: 19. **H.2.1**: 1. **I.2.2**: 7. **J.1**: 87, 107, 110. **J.4**: 144–145. **J.5**: 15, 21. **N.2**: 44, 138. **O.1.2.3**: 16, 27. **O.2.1**: 32, 39, 44–96. **O.2.2**: 19, 21, 36, 101, 103. **O.2.3**: 4, 30, 42, 49, 61, 66, 68. **O.3.1**: 8, 16, 22, 40, 65, 67. **O.3.2**: 31. **O.3.3**: 84, 132.

Taux de change fixes **O.2.1**: 44, 53. **O.2.3**: 49.

Taux de change flexibles **I.2.3**: 3. **O.2.1**: 37, 53.

Taux de croissance **F.3.3**: 15, 51–52. **G.3.3.5**: 71.

Taux de natalité **M.4**: 71.

Taux de profit **G.3.3.5**: 5, 63. **H.2.1**: 71. **I.2.1**: 85. **K.3**: 85. **N.2**: 37.

Taux de rendement **F.2**: 4. **F.3.3**: 32, 46. **G.1.1**: 14, 18, 27, 41. **G.2.1**: 114. **H.2.1**: 55. **J.2**: 185. **J.5**: 21. **L.3**: 26. **M.4**: 22. **N.1**: 171. **O.3.1**: 41, 64.

Taux de salaire **G.2.1**: 134. **K.3**: 8, 68, 95.

Taxe à l'achat **N.2**: 85, 88, 127, 309. **O.1.2.4**: 88.

Taxe sur le chiffre d'affaires **N.2**: 87.

Techniques de fabrication **H.2.2**: 57, 70. **H.4**: 12.

Techniques de gestion **C**: 40. **G.1.2**: 8. **G.3.3**: 17. **G.3.3.5**: 19, 38, 47, 70, 72, 86. **H.2.1**: 90. **H.3**: 18. **J.2**: 65.

Techniques de prévision **F.2**: 24. **H.3**: 69.

Zones rurales **F.3.1.1**: 82, 91. **F.3.1.3**: 4. **F.3.2**: 48. **G.2.1**: 74. **H.1.1.2**: 14. **J.2**: 56. **K.2**: 8. **K.3**: 55. **L.1**: 14.

Zones suburbaines **F.3.1.1**: 101.

Zones urbaines **F.3.1.1**: 122. **F.3.2**: 48. **G.2.1**: 163. **H.0**: 20. **H.2.1**: 63. **H.4**: 17, 108. **J.2**: 79. **L.2**: 82.